TENTH EDITION

SEXUALITY TODAY

Gary F. Kelly

Clarkson University

Connect
Learn
Succeed™

SEXUALITY TODAY, TENTH EDITION

Published by McGraw-Hill, a business unit of The McGraw-Hill Companies, Inc., 1221
Avenue of the Americas, New York, NY 10020. Copyright © 2011 by The McGraw-Hill
Companies, Inc. All rights reserved. Previous editions © 2008, 2006, and 2004. No part of
this publication may be reproduced or distributed in any form or by any means, or stored
in a database or retrieval system, without the prior written consent of The McGraw-Hill
Companies, Inc., including, but not limited to, in any network or other electronic storage or
transmission, or broadcast for distance learning.

Some ancillaries, including electronic and print components, may not be available to
customers outside the United States.

This book is printed on acid-free paper.

1 2 3 4 5 6 7 8 9 0 RJE/RJE 1 0 9 8 7 6 5 4 3 2 1 0

ISBN 978-0-07-353199-1
MHID 0-07-353199-5

Vice President & Editor-in-Chief: *Michael Ryan*
Vice President EDP/Central Publishing Services: *Kimberly Meriwether David*
Editorial Director: *Beth Mejia*
Publisher: *Michael Sugarman*
Executive Marketing Manager: *Pamela S. Cooper*
Managing Editor: *Meghan Campbell*
Project Manager: *Robin A. Reed*
Design Coordinator: *Brenda A. Rolwes*
Cover Designer: *Studio Montage, St. Louis, Missouri*
Senior Photo Editor: *Natalia Peschiera*
Cover Image: © *Medioimages/PunchStock*
Media Project Manager: *Sridevi Palani*
Compositor: *Aptara®, Inc.*
Typeface: *10/12 Garamond Light*
Printer: *R.R. Donnelley*

All credits appearing on page or at the end of the book are considered to be an extension
of the copyright page.

Library of Congress Cataloging-in-Publication Data

Kelly, Gary F.
    Sexuality today/Gary F. Kelly.—10th ed.
        p. cm.
    ISBN 978-0-07-353199-1 (alk. paper)
    1. Sex.   2. Sex instruction.   3. Hygiene, Sexual.   4. Sex customs—United States. I. Title.
HQ21.K259 2011 306.7—dc22   2010018577

For my family—Betsy, Casey and Sean, and Chelsea and Joey—my companions in learning about life and love. There is nothing more wonderful in my life than being with you.

Gary F. Kelly has been a sexuality educator for 40 years, publishing several popular books in the field. After a 30-year career as Counselor, Dean, and Vice President for Student Affairs at Clarkson University and as Headmaster of The Clarkson School, he retired from administrative work to devote more time to writing, teaching, and counseling. He continues to teach courses in human sexuality, psychoactive substances, and counseling psychology in the Psychology Department at Clarkson University, where the Student Association honored him with its Outstanding Teaching Award in 2008. He also teaches courses on ethics and social problems in the Honors Program. Kelly was an innovator in developing graduate training in human sexuality for counselors. He is a licensed mental health counselor in New York State.

As a person who strongly believes that young people must have solid basic information about sex and their own sexuality in order to make rational and responsible decisions, Kelly presents here a balanced approach to the biological as well as the psychological and sociological aspects of human sexuality. His work with students received national recognition with his election to the board of directors of the Sexuality Information and Education Council of the United States (SIECUS). Kelly served for eight years as editor of the *Journal of Sex Education and Therapy* and was one of the charter editorial board members of the *American Journal of Sexuality Education*. He is a member of the American Association of Sexuality Educators, Counselors, and Therapists and of the Society for the Scientific Study of Human Sexuality.

Kelly lives with his wife Betsy beside a lake in the Adirondack Mountains, where he writes and photographs. He practices Yoga and meditation, and enjoys canoeing, kayaking, and walking in the forest with their two golden retrievers.

Gary F. Kelly is available as a consultant and speaker in the field of human sexuality and sexuality education. For further information, e-mail gkelly@clarkson.edu or call (315) 265-2772.

Brief Contents

Contents

PART 2

Understanding Sexuality in Ourselves and in Our Relationships 126

PART 3
Human Reproduction, Contraception, and Abortion: Sexuality Confronts Social Policy 240

■ *Chapter 10* Reproduction, Reproductive Technology, and Birthing 242

■ *Chapter 11* Decision Making about Pregnancy and Parenthood 272

PART 4
Sexual Behavior and Contemporary Society 306

PART 5
Dealing with Sexual Problems 410

Preface

To be able to see a textbook through ten editions (actually twelve if I count the very first version and the two that were considered the seventh edition and the *updated* seventh edition), with four different publishers, is a remarkable honor and a privilege. Not only has *Sexuality Today* provided me with a 30-year motivation to keep well informed on the remarkable and shifting conceptualizations of human sexuality, it has also offered a regularly occurring set of signposts with which to gauge my own shifting understandings and values about a significant part of human life. Working on the book has been a labor of love that has strengthened my self-discipline and, I hope, my intellect. As a project that has been with me for about half of my life, this book has perhaps shaped me as much as I have shaped its content and tone. I wrote the original book just after my first child was born, and was working on another when my second came into the world. They are both grown now with families of their own.

Robert C. Solomon, in *Love, Emotion, Myth, and Metaphor,* states that "love can be understood only 'from the inside,' as a language can be understood only by someone who speaks it, as a world can be understood only by someone who lives in it." During my lifetime, in the roles I've tried to fulfill as a boy, a man, a husband, a father, a counselor, and a teacher, I've worked to understand the nature of my own sexuality and its place in my life. I've also attempted to gain a more complete understanding of sexuality as a powerful force in human life. Working on this book over the course of three decades has helped me clarify many of the complexities of human sexuality as well as helping me see the many questions that remain to be answered. The core of my belief systems forms the basis of my goals for this book:

- Sexual natures are essentially healthy and good. Decisions about sexual behaviors, however, must be made with careful thought, because the potential for negative consequences also exists.
- All of us must spend time understanding the place and importance of sexuality in our lives.
- Each of us has a responsibility to show concern for other people who come into our lives in a romantic or sexual encounter. Sex ceases to be healthy and positive when it is exploitative or hurtful.
- People differ greatly in their sexual and gender orientations and behaviors, and it is important for all persons to find the sexual lifestyles that will yield the most happiness, satisfaction, peacefulness, and fulfillment.
- People almost inevitably experience sexual problems at various points in their lives, and it usually takes some work to overcome those problems and their effects. The responsibility for seeking appropriate help rests with each individual.
- The ethical choices we make about our sexuality reflect the kind of people we are, and so sexuality is a central part of our humanity.

The Field of Human Sexuality

Like any area of scientific inquiry, the field of human sexuality is filled with controversy, even among the sexologists who conduct research, construct models, and develop theories. Scientific findings are not always comfortably aligned with prevailing social opinion. I believe that it is the job of a textbook author to compile and document the various primary schools of thought as accurately as possible, and I have attempted to stay true to that aim with each revision of the text. Each time, I carefully weigh and consider the prevailing evidence on issues of sexuality and try to do justice to those issues. Although some disagree, I do not feel it is my task to shape the attitudes and belief systems of students beyond what our cultural imperatives demand. My task, I believe, is to inform and enlighten with as much open-mindedness, honesty, and accuracy as possible. The controversies surrounding sexuality—and the ways in which they fuel political, religious, and social differences—fascinate me. For readers of this text, those controversies should become fodder for discussion, debate, and self-appraisal. As I can surely testify, it is reasonable to change your mind after having weighed all the evidence on an issue conscientiously.

With each revision, I am reminded of the growth of the field of sexuality in terms of both acceptability and scholarly focus over the past 35 years, as more and more outstanding young academics are attracted to its ranks. As I have watched sexology grow and develop over the course of my career, it has been especially exciting to be able to document the constant progress toward understanding the nuances of sexual neurophysiology, psychology, and relational interaction. It is gratifying to have increasing numbers of students inquire about how they might enter sexology as a profession. I am also very pleased with the positive reactions to past and current editions of the text I have received from both faculty members and students. Their feedback and good suggestions help form the new template for each edition.

Goals of the Text

Four underlying goals have been in place throughout all editions. Those goals are to provide a text that is

- informative and as up-to-date as possible
- readable, engaging, and interesting
- colorful, with relevant illustrations and photos that are scientifically accurate
- personally challenging as it poses ethical and values-related questions to readers

The extensive improvements to the text in this edition are outlined in detail below. I am grateful to all those instructors and students who have provided feedback on their experiences using *Sexuality Today*. Their comments have again served as the cornerstone for this revision.

Overview of Key Changes in the Tenth Edition

In this edition, I had two fundamental aims. One was to shorten the text by nearly 10 percent, and that I have achieved. As one of my editors said, "After ten editions, any book needs some housecleaning." I read each chapter with an eye toward focusing the major points and eliminating unnecessary or repetitive chatter. I believe that readers will appreciate the crispness that has resulted. My other basic goal was to strengthen the discussion of theory behind understandings of human sexual orientations and choices. As the field has become more theoretically enriched, I am particularly excited about having been able to similarly enrich this text.

As always, we've added many new photographs and figures, which convey information succinctly and engagingly. After culling through a couple thousand studies, I have cited 730 new references, providing the most up-to-date facts and research available from 2007 to 2010 in this edition.

Content has been considerably updated and reorganized, designed to better reflect trends in the field and to make the book easier to teach and learn from. For example:

- Revised Chapter 1 sets the stage with markedly shortened introductory paragraphs, making them more accessible and persuasive for students. It gives

greater attention to the global nature of sexuality including the international Millennium Development Goals set by 179 nations for 2015 regarding sexual and reproductive health. Coverage of the "culture wars" now mentions current figures such as President Obama and Sarah Palin. The phenomenon of "sexting" is discussed, as are the effects of military service and war injuries on sexual lives and relationships. The chapter also includes emerging research on condom use and circumcision as ways to reduce risks of infection, along with new material added to explain discrepancies between reported sexual activity by males and females. The Attitude Questionnaire that has been part of the text since the first edition has again been updated to reflect the times, and the table summarizing various eras of sex research has been condensed and focused.

- In keeping with the increasingly global nature of sex research and policy-making, cross-cultural findings and comparisons have been integrated throughout the text, underscoring the fact that regardless of ethnic influences, human beings are more alike than different when it comes to sexuality.
- Chapters 2 and 3, covering female and male anatomy and physiology, have been updated with the most recent guidelines regarding hormone replacement therapies, the latest research on changing sexual interests during the menstrual cycle, and the addition of urinary incontinence and penile fracture as potential problems.
- I am particularly pleased to be able to include what is now called the Dual Control Model of sexual arousal that notes both excitatory and inhibitory mechanisms controlling sexual arousal and responsiveness. The interactions of these mechanisms provide a wonderful template for explaining differences in sexual interest and psychogenic problems in sexual functioning. The theory is referenced in later chapters as well, since it also helps account for preferences for differing sexual activities and the roots of some sexual problems.
- Some reviewers found Chapter 5 to be overly detailed and complicated. In this edition, I have reduced the details of biological sexual differentiation so the material will be more accessible to students. Some of the materials on transgender identity and sex reassignment procedures that were in Chapter 14 have been moved to this chapter, where they seem to fit much more comfortably.
- Other material on transgender identity and sexuality has been transferred from Chapter 14 on sexual behavior into the chapters on childhood and adolescence, the time of life when transgender identities are being more commonly identified. This helps develop the concept more sequentially, and lends a deeper understanding to the significant correlations

between gender identity, childhood play, and sexual orientation and identity.

- In the last edition, I developed two distinct chapters on sexuality through the life cycle, separating infancy, childhood, and adolescence into Chapter 6 by themselves, and placing adult sexuality in Chapter 7. That has worked well, but both chapters needed greater development of their concepts and the research behind them, which has been achieved in this edition. The material on adolescent sexuality has also been substantially rearranged to better reflect the flow of the material.

- Chapter 8 on sexual individuality and sexual values includes information about the controversies surrounding the fifth edition of the *Diagnostic and Statistical Manual of Mental Disorders* that is scheduled to appear in 2012. These debates highlight the very subjective nature of our judgments concerning what is "normal" and what is "pathological" sexual behavior.

- The chapters on reproduction and birth control (10 and 11) have incorporated the latest data on pregnancy, multiple births, reproductive technologies, and contraceptive failure. The reproductive technologies have begun to come into their own, and some are emerging as the preferred routes, while others have lost popularity. There is an updated table comparing the various methods, and a new table on rates of multiple births.

- The chapters on sexual orientation and behaviors (12, 13, and 14) have seen some dramatic revisions that have streamlined their readability and incorporated the latest research findings. The Dual Control Model is used to help explain the variability of sexual desire as well as the variability of interest in particular sexual objects. An older theory of erotic target location errors has been revived as one way to conceptualize why people have their particular sexual attractions, and it has been combined with incentive sexual motivation theory to bring these concepts into more understandable focus. I am convinced that students and teachers will appreciate these new approaches.

- In Chapter 16 on sexual problems, I have again expanded the section on consent for sexual activity, as research in this area continues to expand. In this chapter, as well as in Chapter 6, we also look at the concepts of sexual teasing and "hooking up."

- The newly combined chapter on sexually transmitted diseases and HIV/AIDS was also well received, and I have been able to bring the most recent data to the revised edition.

- The final chapter on sexual dysfunctions incorporates the latest findings on medical and psychotherapeutic approaches to treatment, demystifying the techniques for students. There has been a dramatic shift in emphasis on this material since this text was first published, and this revised chapter brings that shift into focus.

- The "Real People" stories and student quotes that appear as "Real Student Voices" were a hit in the ninth edition, and have been strengthened in each chapter of this edition. My students enjoy the personal and relevant perspectives these features bring to the text.

- The support program for students and instructors has been streamlined and improved as well.

Supplements

Instructional Resources at www.mhhe.com/kelly10e

The instructor's resource site contains the following excellent resources for instructors using the book: Instructor's Manual, Test Bank, and PowerPoint presentations. New features in this comprehensively revised **Instructor's Manual** include classroom activities, demonstrations, and the new Total Teaching Reference Package. Building on a traditional chapter outline, all the McGraw-Hill resources available to you have been correlated to the main concepts in each chapter. Suggested activities take particular account of class size and offer a useful timeline estimate for completion. The final section offers tips on study skills and how to use the Internet in teaching, as well as a list of transparencies.

The thoroughly expanded and revised **Test Bank** includes a wide range of multiple-choice, fill-in-the-blank, and critical thinking questions, as well as five short essay questions per chapter. Each item is designated as factual, conceptual, or applied as defined by Benjamin Bloom's Taxonomy of Educational Objectives. The **PowerPoint presentations** cover the key points of each chapter and include charts and graphs from the text where relevant. They can be used as is or modified to meet your personal needs.

SexSource Online

SexSource Online is a website for students and instructors featuring a collection of over 60 educational video clips on core concepts of human sexuality. Icons appear throughout the text to indicate clips that correspond to specific topics. Each video is accompanied by pre- and post-viewing questions. **SexSource Online** content and assessment items are also included in the course cartridge and may be used in an online course. Access **SexSource Online** from the student or instructor Online Learning Center at www.mhhe.com/kelly10e. The site is password-protected at the request of many of the video rightsholders, but access is free to all users of this book. Use the following code to register: G8JR-Y9P7-TTEH-9487-THW4.

Online Learning Center for Students

The official website for the text (www.mhhe.com/kelly10e) contains chapter outlines, practice quizzes that can be e-mailed to the professor, and a glossary of key terms.

From McGraw-Hill's Contemporary Learning Series

Annual Editions: Human Sexuality

Published by Dushkin/McGraw-Hill, this is a collection of articles on topics related to the latest research and thinking in human sexuality from more than 300 public press sources. These editions are updated annually and contain helpful features including a topic guide, an annotated table of contents, unit overviews, and a topical index. An Instructor's Guide containing testing materials is also available.

Taking Sides: Clashing Views on Controversial Issues in Human Sexuality

This debate-style reader is designed to introduce students to controversial viewpoints on the field's most crucial issues. Each issue is carefully framed for the student, and the pro and con essays represent the arguments of leading scholars and commentators in their fields. An Instructor's Guide containing testing materials is also available.

Acknowledgments

More people than I can properly recall have given me encouragement and suggestions for writing this book and revising it through its various editions. A number of them have offered specific help toward its improvement. These professionals and colleagues deserve thanks and acknowledgment. Before I began to write the original version, helpful suggestions were given to me by the late Mary S. Calderone, founder and former president of the Sexuality Information and Education Council of the United States (SIECUS); Michael Carrera, then at Hunter College, CUNY; and Patricia Schiller, founder of the American Association of Sex Educators, Counselors, and Therapists (AASECT).

I am greatly indebted to a number of my distinguished colleagues who gave their professional advice and helpful comments in reviewing the various editions of this book:

Tenth Edition

William C. Bradley, Columbia College
Stephen Cramer, Valencia Community College
Maqsood M. Faquir, Palm Beach Community College
Callista Lee, Fullerton College
Miguel Perez, California State University, Fresno

Previous Editions

Connie C. Alexander, *Tarrant County Junior College—Northwest*
Srijana M. Bajracharya, *University of Maine at Presque Isle*
Janice and John Baldwin, *University of California, Santa Barbara*
C. Peter Bankart, *Wabash College*
Karen R. Blaisure, *Virginia Polytechnic Institute and State University*
Marilyn Blumenthal, *SUNY College of Technology at Farmingdale*
Robert D. Boroff, *Mount Jacinto College*
Sheila D. Brandick, *University of Regina*
Peggy Brick, *Planned Parenthood, Inc., of Bergen County*
Vern L. Bullough, *State University College of Buffalo*
T. Jean Byrne, *Kent State University*
Elizabeth G. Calamidas, *The Richard Stockton College of New Jersey*
Sandra L. Caron, *University of Maine, Orono*
Glenn Carter, *Austin Peay State University*
Carol Cassell, *Institute for Sexuality Education and Equity*
Caroline Clements, *University of North Carolina, Wilmington*
Edward E. Coates, *Judge Ely Family Healthcare*
William Collins, *West Virginia University*
Dennis Dailey, *University of Kansas*
Donald R. Devers, *Northern Virginia Community College*
John P. Elia, *San Francisco State University*
Geri Falconer-Ferneau, *Arizona State University*
Richelle Frabotta, *Social Health Education*
Susan Frantz, *Highline Community College*
Suzanne Frayser, *Colorado College*
Gere B. Fulton, *The University of Toledo*
David A. Gershaw, *Arizona Western College*
Jane F. Gilgun, *University of Minnesota*
Lois Laynor Goldblatt, *Arizona State University*
Keith Graber-Miller, *Goshen College*
Cynthia Grace, *City College, CUNY*
Maylou Hacker, *Modesto Junior College*
Susan E. Hetherington, *University of Maryland*
Karen M. Hicks, *Lehigh University*
Janet I. Hirsch, *University of Rhode Island*
India Hosch, *Virginia Polytechnic and State University*
Bobby Hutchinson, *Modesto Community College*

Kimberly Hyatt, *Weber State University*
Ethel Jones, *South Carolina State University*
Shulamith Kane, *Nassau Community College*
Peter T. Knoepfler, *sex therapist in private practice*
Kris Koehne, *University of Tennessee—Knoxville*
Ann Kolodji, *Ithaca College*
Jennifer Krumm, *Chabot/Las Positas Community College*
Kelly Kyes, *Wake Forest University*
Molly Laflin, *Bowling Green State University*
Phillip Lau, *DeAnza College*
Bruce D. LeBlanc, *Black Hawk College*
Stuart Lisbe, *William Paterson College of New Jersey*
Teresa L. Mattson, *Keene State College*
Brian R. McNaught, *consultant to corporations and universities on the effects of homophobia; trainer; author*
Amy G. Miron, *Catonsville Community College*
Charles D. Miron, *Catonsville Community College*
Owen Morgan, *Arizona State University*
Lin Myers, *California State University, Stanislaus*
Marilyn Myerson, *University of South Florida*
Natasha Otto, *Morgan State University*
Christopher Ousley, *North Carolina State University*
Nancy Parsons, *Western Illinois University*
Robert Pollack, *University of Georgia*
James Ponzetti, *Central Washington University*
Barry Poris, *Long Island University*
James H. Price, *University of Toledo*
Laurna Rubison, *University of Illinois*
Robin Sawyer, *University of Maryland*
Kay F. Schepp, *University of Vermont*
Sharon P. Shriver, *Penn State University*
Dick Skeen, *Northern Arizona University*
Stephen Southern, *The Sexual Medicine Institute of Southeast Louisiana*
Sherman Sowby, *California State University, Fresno*
Kandy J. Stahl, *Stephen F. Austin State University*
Ruth Stoltzfus, *Goshen College*
Marilyn Story, *University of Northern Iowa*
Edward R. Sunshine, *Barry University*
Karen S. Tee, *Vanier College*
James E. Tucker, *Minneapolis, Minnesota*

Karen Vail-Smith, *East Carolina University*
Robert F. Valois, *University of Texas at Austin*
Jane Vecchio, *Holyoke Community College*
Paul Villas, *New Mexico State University, Main Campus*
Michael G. Walraven, *Jackson Community College*
Mary Ann Watson, *Metropolitan State College of Denver*
Marti M. Weaver, *Collin County Community College, Central Park Campus*
Burton A. Weiss, *Drexel University*
Patricia Whelehan, *State University of New York, Potsdam*
Jan Widdell, *Auburn University*
Elva Winter, *York College*
William L. Yarber, *Indiana University*

My wife Betsy has been a constant source of good ideas for this text. She read each chapter and offered many suggestions for making the book more readable and interesting. My teaching assistant, Richard Yerry, did a fabulous job of organizing the new references for this edition and creating the revised Reference list, while teaching me the finer points of the reference feature in Word that I never knew existed.

I want to acknowledge the help of the many people within the McGraw-Hill staff who have played such an essential role in preparing the manuscript and producing the book. They include Meghan Campbell, Managing Editor; Maureen Spada, Development Editor; Robin Reed, Project Manager; Brenda Rolwes, Designer; Nicole Baumgartner, Production Supervisor; and Sridevi Palani, Media Project Manager. I feel privileged to be able to keep this book available to students through the efforts of this highly motivated and professional group, and I thank them for the high quality that has been maintained in this updated edition.

Gary F. Kelly
Clarkson University
P.O. Box 5825
Potsdam, NY 13699-5825
E-mail: gkelly@clarkson.edu

SEXUALITY
TODAY

Part 1

Social and Biological
Foundations of
Human Sexuality

■

Studying sexuality is one avenue to a more complete understanding of human nature and human societies. In its broadest sense, sexuality is interwoven with all aspects of being human. It has been only during the last few generations that reliable information about human sexual arousal and response has emerged. As we venture further into the twenty-first century, much remains to be understood regarding all aspects of human sexuality.

To study sexuality is to dissolve disciplinary boundaries. The psychology of sex includes sexual orientations, behaviors, emotions, and interpersonal connections. The sociology and anthropology of sex mirror the many social, legal, political, and cultural patterns that play a role in human interactions. It has been said that sex is a biological function and love is a psychological function, but things are not that simple. Our sexuality is related to our attitudes and feelings, our social relationships, our cultural expectations, and our history. In terms of recorded human history, scientific inquiry and the scientific way of thinking represent relatively recent approaches to perceiving the world and human nature. Much work remains if we are to understand fully the interactions of body, mind, emotion, and spirit in human sexuality.

These opening chapters set the stage for the broader perspective of sex and sexuality that will emerge as you progress through this text.

Chapter 1

Cultural, Historical, and Research Perspectives on Sexuality

Chapter Outline

Everyone is a different sexual person, and some
individuals face problems about who they feel they
should be versus who they actually are, because of
pressures from family, friends, and society.
Questions can't simply be answered by a yes or no.
Class discussions have helped me realize this and
even question things about my own sexuality.

—from a student's comments about what
she had learned from a human sexuality course

4

You're beginning the first chapter of a text on human sexuality. What is most important for you to learn in this and subsequent chapters? What personal issues are you facing or hoping to explore? Throughout the text you'll find words written by my students as they studied sexuality. What words would you write if I asked you to describe yourself as a sexual person?

You may have some mixed, even confusing, feelings about the place of sexuality in your life. You're not alone. Sexuality is something about which human beings are startlingly ambivalent (Goldenberg et al., 2002). On one hand, we're drawn to it by curiosity and lust; on the other, we're repelled because of embarrassment, modesty, or guilt. This inner struggle of wills and fears is reflected in the sexual themes that are so much a part of our culture (see Figure 1.1).

Sexual ambivalence becomes particularly evident in sexuality education. Even as parents call for schools to educate their children about sex, they typically feel the need for limits on the subject matter so the children will not know "too much." For over a decade, federal and state governments supported educational programs that promoted sexual abstinence, while balking at the distribution of free condoms, even though

evidence has shown that many adolescents are sexually active and that sexually transmitted diseases represent a serious problem among the young. There is a continuing fear, though refuted by research, that too much education will lead kids to engage in sex. It is not education but ignorance that leads to the riskiest sexual decision making (Kempner, 2009).

Human sexuality is a realm of contrasts and contradictions, social trends and cultural imperatives. The values that surround sexuality are always in flux, moved by the agendas and whims of governments, economic realities, and cultural traditions. Western cultures continue to perpetuate ambivalent and conflicting messages about sex. On one hand, there are suggestions that sex is somehow "dirty." On the other hand, we are encouraged to save sex for someone we really love. We are given the impression that sex is sacred and beautiful but that the less young people know about it, the better.

Everyone has strong opinions and feelings about certain sex-related topics. The classroom should be one venue in which these topics can be debated and discussed, without fear of experiencing discomfort or being branded in any way. Instructors have an obligation to be sensitive to the wide range of values their students may have; students have an obligation to confront their own feelings and reactions and to tolerate the feelings and reactions of others even as difficult topics are opened for consideration. Real learning is about growth, and growth sometimes involves a bit of turmoil.

What do you think about the limits or boundaries of sexuality education? In a college course, should some topics be "out of bounds"?

■ Culture and Sexuality

When Margaret Mead conducted her groundbreaking field studies of South Seas island cultures in the 1920s and 1930s, she became one of the first anthropologists to examine sexual customs and attitudes. Mead concluded that the sexual attitudes and behaviors of individual human beings are shaped tremendously by the surrounding cultural imperatives (Mead, 1930). For example, it has often been assumed that passionate love and sexual desire are experienced and expressed universally. Evidence suggests, however, that culture profoundly affects how people perceive love; how susceptible they are to falling in love, and with whom; and why they feel sexual desire (Pertot, 2006; Philaretou, 2005).

■ FIGURE 1.1 *Ambivalence about Sexuality*
Young women are asked to take a survey regarding their preferences for boxers, briefs, or thongs on men. Even with the blatant use of sexuality in marketing, there can be awkward moments.

Anthropologists usually classify cultures on the basis of their subsistence patterns, that is, on how the people produce and distribute food and other goods. Anything that affects a society's subsistence pattern can influence reproduction and thus sexual behavior. Shortages of food, for example, may lead to decreased reproductive rates. Gender roles are closely tied to both reproductive patterns and other social structures. Sexuality therefore has a place at the center of any culture (Plante, 2006).

In smaller, homogenous cultures—in which the people are expected to be very much alike in their belief patterns and values—a great deal of effort is often spent on maintaining conformity. In such homogenous cultures, individuals tend to conduct their sexual lives in accordance with accepted social roles. Larger, heterogenous cultures—in which there is a good deal of human diversity—do not work as deliberately toward producing or stabilizing behavioral conformity. These cultures tend to have many different patterns of sexual conduct, including not only sexual subcultures based on sexual orientation or behavioral preferences, but also more highly individualistic patterns of behavior within particular groups of people. North America is an example of a heterogenous culture. It has many ethnic and immigrant groups, each with its own viable sexual culture.

Individuals who immigrate from one culture to another often undergo a process of reevaluating traditional values brought from their homelands and selecting what sexual norms and options from the new surroundings will be comfortable. Speedy acculturation once helped immigrants adjust more quickly, but immigration today is quite different from what it used to be, when families moved permanently from one country to another with the intention of making the new location their only home. Today, many immigrants retain close ties to their places of origin, and move back and forth between them and their new locations.

Because of recent immigration patterns, Latinos have become the largest ethnic minority group in the United States, and one of the youngest. Youthful Latinos also tend to have higher rates of unplanned pregnancies, STDs, and risky sexual behaviors than those found in other major demographic groups, largely because of the sexual conduct patterns that were widely accepted in their originating cultures. This sets them up for more negative judgments and problems in their new locations, as expectations are imposed that they should have become more acculturated to the new social customs that surround them (Santelli, Abraido-Lanza, & Melnikas, 2009).

When such cultural differences are at work, some uphold a perspective of **cultural relativism** with regard to immigrants, believing that the value systems of their original culture should be honored and allowed. Others advocate **cultural absolutism,** expecting in-

stead that people from other cultures must be held to the sexual standards and beliefs of the culture in which they now live. The direction taken can have a significant impact on the futures of the people involved and on how welcome they feel in their new location (Apodaca, Schultz, Anderson, & McLennan, 2005).

Even though North American culture continues to become increasingly diverse, it was for a long time dominated by heritages rooted in Caucasian European ethnic groups whose people migrated to the Americas and reestablished their traditions there. The religions of these people were largely Judeo-Christian in origin. In many ways, the attitudes about human sexuality that have prevailed in North America were influenced by this backdrop of cultural and religious values. In anthropological terms, this perspective has sometimes been called **Eurocentric,** meaning that it grows mainly out of its European roots. The Eurocentric view of the world tends to be dualistic in nature. In other words, it tends to see things in an either-or, black-and-white way. Sexually speaking, this perspective may be expressed in beliefs that people must be either masculine or feminine, heterosexual or homosexual. Also, sexual behaviors tend to be judged as either good or bad. Naturally such worldviews influence the ethical belief systems people hold (Plante, 2006).

Colleges are working to enhance the understanding and acceptance of cultural diversity, including customs related to gender and sexuality. On many campuses, it is not unusual to see orthodox Muslim (Islamic) women wearing head scarves, or garments that cover most of their bodies and faces. A burka is one type of garment that covers the woman's body from head to toe, with only a slit for sight (see Figure 1.2). Muslim men are supposed to dress modestly as well, although this is less strongly enforced than it is among women. Islam has very specific religious laws concerning the behaviors of women and men, and male supremacy is a fundamental tenet. Nevertheless, Islam also recognizes the complementarity of male and female and celebrates sexual pleasure within marriage.

cultural relativism the view that one's culture determines what is normal and acceptable and that judgments about those standards should take into consideration their cultural origins.

cultural absolutism the view that behaviors and values from one's culture of origin should be disregarded once the individual is living in a new culture. The expectation is that immigrants must abide by the cultural standards of their new country about those standards should take into consideration their cultural origins.

Eurocentric (ur-oh-SEN-trick) a cultural attitudinal framework typical of people with western European heritages.

■ **FIGURE 1.2** *Cultural Standards for Appropriate Dress*
People's attitudes about their sexuality and their bodies are
strongly influenced by their cultures. These Afghan women wear
the traditional burka that reveals nothing of their bodies or
faces. Not all Muslim women accept such strict standards of
dress, while others consider them appropriate for their beliefs.

Around the world, efforts are underway to equal-
ize the availability of sexual health resources cross-
culturally. Representatives from 179 nations around the
globe have agreed to make reproductive health accessible to all by the year 2015, as part of what are called
the millennium development goals. Sexual health services and improving maternal health are integral parts
of the plan. Progress toward the goal has been uneven;
issues of sexual and reproductive health are often paid
good lip service but lose out when it comes to the al-
location of resources. Nevertheless, in the poorest areas
of the world, unsafe sex is the second most important
risk factor for disease, disability, or death, and the *Count-
down to 2015* has been gaining in strength (Bernstein,
Say, & Chowdhury, 2008; Glasier et al., 2006).

*When it comes to judging the sexual beliefs and
practices of people from other cultures, would you
consider yourself more of a relativist or an
absolutist?*

From Sexual Revolution
to Culture Wars

You've probably heard of the **sexual revolution.**
What have you imagined to be true of this vaguely
defined period in recent history? Unbridled sex?
Hippies romping in the nude at Woodstock? What

the term really refers to is a series of changes that
occurred during a couple of decades in the mid-
twentieth century, especially regarding ideals and
values about sex and love.

In fact, Western cultures have seen dramatic shifts
in the past three centuries. The Puritan ideal was for
love between men and women to evolve within marriage, as two people began to know each other better.
Even so, the Colonial Period in America was known
for its rather loose sexual standards. During the Victorian era (1837–1901), love and sex were considered to
be separate human experiences, with love being the
romantic and spiritual union that ideally preceded and
precipitated marriage. Although sex was recognized as
a part of marriage in cautious moderation, lustful passions were not to be let out of control lest people become slaves to their sexual emotions. Love and sex
between people of the same gender were not openly
discussed. Sex was not linked to love, because to link
the two would in fact have been considered a threat to
the love that was assumed to undergird marital stability. With sex being given such a conflicted place within
marriage, prostitution and pornography flourished in
Victorian society (Allyn, 2000).

Following World War II, the United States experienced significant and relatively abrupt changes in
sexual attitudes, values, and behaviors. Eventually
that period was dubbed the sexual revolution, and it
encompassed a variety of complex changes in values
and behaviors that included some identifiable shifts
in thinking. Here are some of the most significant
examples:

- *Support from science and technology.* With the war
  over, people were anxious to return to some sense
  of normalcy and to establish new lives and families.
  Alfred Kinsey published the results of his groundbreaking surveys concerning male and female sexual behavior, revealing some startling scientific data
  about sexuality in human life. With technological
  advances in birth control and the legalization of
  abortion came reduced concerns about the risks of
  pregnancy, accompanied by hotly debated ethical
  issues.
- *A new emphasis on personal autonomy, and increased resistance to centralized, institutionalized
  authority.* A counterculture movement questioned
  rules, regulations, and decisions that were set forth
  without thorough explanation or rationale. As values changed, former legal restrictions on sexual
  activity between consenting adults gradually began
  to give way. Established religious restraints on sex

sexual revolution a series of changes that occurred
during a couple of decades in the mid-twentieth century,
especially regarding ideals and values about sex and love.

Real People

Anil: Confronting a Faulty Cultural Assumption

Anil was a graduate student from India who came to my office because he had heard that I did counseling regarding sexual matters. He explained that he was to be married in a few months and was anxious to become better prepared to be a loving and sexually adequate husband. Upon questioning him, I learned that he had had very little sexual experience other than masturbation. We went on to discuss other aspects of marriage, including the need for good communication and being considerate of each other's needs.

Eventually, Anil began discussing his fiancée and indicated that she was studying in China. Trying to be sensitive to what I knew of the complications of long-distance relationships, I said to Anil, "You must miss her very much." He looked at me for a moment and laughed. "Actually," he responded, "I've never met her." After recovering from having my preconceived notions disrupted, we talked about

how Anil's marriage had been arranged by his and the woman's parents when Anil and the woman were quite young. Anil had no objections to the arrangement and in fact thought it quite acceptable and appropriate. His only hope was to prepare himself to be the best possible husband in every way.

Anil and I met several times to discuss marriage, and I loaned him several books on sexuality and relationships. By the time our counseling relationship was terminated, both of us felt that he was well prepared for his upcoming marriage. I realized that the ways of relationships in other cultures had just as much validity as those in my own culture.

Have you ever encountered cultural differences that surprised you? How did you react?

Can you think of some potential advantages of arranged marriage?

---

began to shift. New attitudes about sexuality moved into the mainstream of American life, marked by a trend toward support of the individual right to sexual expression.

- *Changing roles of women and men.* The traditional gender stereotypes of the man as aggressive protector and provider and the woman as passive homemaker were gradually superseded by roles individualized to each person's needs. It became legitimate for women to express their sexual feelings and to be the initiators of sexual activity. Men were freed to enjoy the more gentle and emotional aspects of their personalities.

- *Emergence of organized sexuality education.* Sexuality education was first introduced into some public schools over a century ago but never materialized into much of a trend until the 1960s. Organizations were formed that encouraged and supported sexuality education programs. The most influential group, chartered in 1964, was the Sex (now Sexuality) Information and Education Council of the United States (SIECUS). Dr. Mary S. Calderone (1904–1998), one of the cofounders of SIECUS and its first executive director, became a leading advocate of sexuality education (Goldfarb, 2009).

- *New perspectives on sexual orientations and gender identities.* A great deal of diversity exists in human sexual orientations, behaviors, and expressions of gender. Some of these states of being have at times been classified as sick, criminal, or sinful. As the sexual revolution encouraged a broader, more tolerant perspective, the American Psychiatric Association removed homosexuality from its official list of mental disorders in 1973 (Vellani, 2006). Eventually, transgender identities received increasing attention and acceptance as well.

- *The changing interplay of sex, romance, and commitment.* In Western cultural traditions, marriage has traditionally been seen as a social institution based on both romance and sexual desire, specifically heterosexual desire (Plante, 2006). The sexual revolution sparked the development of a new philosophy of sex. Casual sexual encounters are joked about in the media. Several states now permit marriage between members of the same sex. The new ways of conceptualizing sexuality suggest to some that society can make room for all people to share in its customs and benefits and causes others to fear that the very fabric of society is unraveling dangerously.

Times of Transition

Out of these dramatic shifts in perceptions regarding human sexuality has grown greater acceptance and openness about a variety of sexual practices and lifestyles that is unprecedented in recent history. People who once were forced to hide their sexual interests and activities have emerged from their secretive worlds into the mainstream, but not without a good deal of controversy and debate. It is these differing perspectives on sexuality that have led to some polarization in sexual attitudes and values. Revolutions rarely maintain their momentum for long before forces of moderation begin to temper their power, and we are now living in times when opposing camps have emerged in education, politics, and religion with regard to sexual standards and beliefs. Since the sexual revolution swung the pendulum in one direction, several developments have helped change the face of sexuality in many ways. Here are some examples:

HIV and AIDS

By the mid-1980s, human immunodeficiency virus (HIV) and the terminal disease to which it often leads—acquired immunodeficiency syndrome (AIDS)—changed some of the fundamental ways people viewed sexual behavior. As awareness and fear about HIV and AIDS increased, awareness about the need to make sexual decisions with care and to protect oneself during sexual interactions also increased. In the United States, HIV was first identified among gay males, which led to new forms of negative attitudes about same-sex orientation and raised new fears about interaction with gay or bisexual men (Fauci, 2008). Casual sex became scarier for everyone, and a new emphasis on safer sex emerged. Nevertheless, the regular use of condoms and avoidance of casual sex were not quick to catch on. Even as AIDS became the fourth leading cause of death worldwide by the beginning of the new millennium, the desire for sexual pleasure has often continued to trump consistent condom use (Randolph et al., 2007). In some Asian cultures, young people accept ancient medical beliefs that condoms and other devices interrupt natural body rhythms and energies, and therefore resist using them (Cha, Kim, & Patrick, 2008).

HIV and AIDS also provided more ammunition for those who advocate abstinence from sexual activity outside of marriage. This approach not only continued to ignore or marginalize gay relationships, but also tended to focus blame on the gay community. Fear and anger about same-gender sex increased for a time. While some of the antigay bias eventually subsided, the debate about condom use and safer sex versus abstinence still rages (Young, 2009).

Media Attention to Sexuality

As increasing openness about sexuality emerged in society, it became nearly impossible to avoid sex, nudity, provocative language, and complex sexual themes in public media. Some research suggests that the media have played a substantial role in perpetuating myths and exaggerations about the levels of sexual activity among people (Farrar et al., 2003). The media have also tried to publicize new research findings about sexuality, even though they sometimes sensationalize them or exaggerate some minor aspect of the work (McBride et al., 2007).

When one of Janet Jackson's breasts was bared for a couple of seconds during the 2004 Super Bowl halftime (see Figure 1.3), some viewers were outraged, and hearings began in Washington about the content of television programming, causing the Federal Communications Commission to steeply increase fines for any violation. This is an example of an effort

FIGURE 1.3 *Janet Jackson and Justin Timberlake*
The SuperBowl halftime "wardrobe malfunction."

Real Student Voices

■ In life as a nonsexual woman, I am very conservative. I can be open in conversation, although when people ask me questions about sex, I blush and then answer. I have been thinking about having sex with a guy who has told me that he wants a future with me. Of course, that doesn't justify having sex with him.

■ I used to have the belief that I would not have sexual intercourse until I got married. Since then, I continue to be involved in a six-year loving relationship. After dating for a while, I felt that I was with the right person and my views changed a bit.

■ Growing up, my parents never mentioned sex except to say, "Don't do it!" I gave them the sex talk instead of the other way around. While my friends talked about the horrifying moment when they caught their parents in the act, my parents slept in beds on opposite sides of the house. Then there is me. I initiated sex with my first real boyfriend, and I've been told I give amazing blowjobs. The boys I've had sex with say I'm the best they've ever had. . . . I must have gotten my sexual prowess from the milkman.

■ My parents believed that sex topics were better left swept under the carpet. During adolescence, anything I learned about sexuality came either from health class or television. When I began dating a girl at age 15, I began to explore my sexuality a lot more. I've become quite liberal, I think. I don't have a problem with things such as premarital sex, oral sex, pornography, or masturbation. I had good friends in high school who were homosexual or bisexual, so I'm pretty accepting of other orientations.

Whatever floats your boat, so be it.

---

to gain greater control over the sexual imagery of the media and the attempts of a conservative administration to intervene in what is perceived as excessive permissiveness.

Production of hard-core sex videos and DVDs soared as well, with hundreds of millions spent annually in ordering pay-per-view adult movies in homes and in hotels. It is estimated that the U.S. pornography business grosses well over $10 billion a year.

Source: Best & Wittiest. © 2004 John Branch. Distributed by North America Syndicate.

Sex and the Internet

The pornography market expanded even more as access to the Internet became widespread. Not only are explicit sexual pictures just a couple of clicks away, but also the ability to observe and verbally interact with live sex performers for a fee is available. About 75 percent of males in one study indicated that they had viewed or downloaded explicit sexual images, as did 41 percent of the females (Albright, 2008). A largely unregulated medium has brought an entirely new and graphic dimension of human sexuality into homes and institutions. Online connections also have helped those with less typical sexual interests and orientations find one another, share their stories, and perhaps not feel quite so alone or out of step (Kelly, 2005).

On a more individualized level, cell phones and other handheld digital communication devices with Internet access have opened an entirely new way for people to keep in touch and exchange images. Text messaging enables individuals to stay in close and constant touch with friends and family. Since any mode of communication eventually finds its sexual uses, cell phones have been used for what is popularly called sexting, the transmission of nude or semi-nude photos of oneself to others. Unfortunately, these images often find their way to unintended recipients as well, causing embarrassment and personal conflicts, but sometimes also raising complicated ethical and legal issues (Hamill, 2009).

Expanding the Global Perspective

The ease with which people now communicate and travel has led to a greater awareness of global issues. In recent years, organizations around the world that deal with sex-related issues formed an international organization that is now called the World Association of Sexual Health (WAS). Every two years the organization holds a World Congress of Sexual Health, last held in Sweden in 2009. Most of the sexuality organizations in the United States recognize the importance and value of maintaining worldwide connections (Bush, 2008). A good deal of international attention has been paid to the support for policies that condemn sexual torture in prisons or sex trafficking of the poor, and discrimination based on gender or sexual orientation, while encouraging universal access to sexual and reproductive health services (Coleman, 2007; Klugman, 2007).

Many countries have been influenced by the changing sexual attitudes of the Western world and are now struggling to cope with rapidly changing customs in their societies that are in opposition to traditional beliefs and practices. This can create confusion and very real sexual risks. For example, China has seen an enormous increase in sexual awareness and discussion during the past three decades. Internet pornography has become widely available there too, and among the Chinese men who access it there has been a higher likelihood of their demonstrating sexually harassing behavior toward women. This has not been a result shown in men of other countries who view pornography, so this may well reflect some interaction with Chinese attitudes and values (Lam & Chan, 2007) Women's sexuality is now one of the most intensely debated topics in Chinese academic institutions, and there is evidence that young people there are becoming more involved in sexual behaviors than they once were, or are at least more willing to talk about them (Yuxin, Petula, & Lun, 2007).

In the face of Chinese social stigmas that are still strong, many men who have sex with other men continue to marry women in order to "pass" as heterosexuals in their societies. Unfortunately, they also believe that they are at low risk for HIV infection, when in fact HIV and AIDS are reaching epidemic proportions in some parts of the country. More school-based educational programs on sexuality and HIV are being tested and used in some parts of China, but not without resistance and fear as traditional ways are being threatened (Cheng et al., 2008; Neilands, Steward, & Choi, 2008). It seems clear that when there are major shifts in the sexual attitudes and customs of any culture, it takes time for conflicts and confusion to yield more comfortable lifestyles.

Sexuality, Politics, and "Family Values"

One of the most interesting responses to increasing sexual freedom has been the importance of sexuality in politics. Sex-related issues such as abortion or gay marriage have become major planks in political platforms and elections can be won or lost depending on a candidate's position on such issues. Similarly, perceptions of politicians' personal lives can vastly influence voters. An illicit sexual affair can sink a political career practically overnight.

Because sex-related topics become sensationalized by the media and because they stimulate strong opinions, they are inevitably intertwined with politics. Human sexuality thus is itself highly politicized, and political trends ultimately affect legislative mandates, social policies, and court decisions related to sexual and reproductive behaviors.

One term that has been bandied about in political contests is "family values," which has been used to signify a belief in traditional approaches to sexuality and the family. These may include upholding abstinence from sex until marriage, the assumption that heterosexual is the proper way to be, the model of marriage and family as consisting of a man and a woman and their eventual children, and no availability of abortion. Parties and politicians stake a claim to their devotion to religion and family values to this day.

FIGURE 1.4 *Sarah Palin and Sexuality Education*
Sarah Palin was the Republican Party candidate for U.S. vice president in the 2008 election, and became an icon for the conservative side of the culture wars. When it became public knowledge that her unmarried teenage daughter was pregnant, Palin's support for abstinence-only sexuality education became a topic of controversy.

The problem is that current statistics about our society continue to confirm that the traditional ways of approaching these issues no longer necessarily define the norm in the ways people live their lives. So we are left with more ambivalence, more incongruity between people's hopes and the realities that surround them—prime factors in the development of culture wars.

Where do you stand on family values? If reality is not particularly congruent with what these values support, should we work to change society so that it better fits such values? Or should we accept that times change and values must change with them?

In the Midst of the Culture Wars, Military Wars, and Economic Crisis

Do you ever feel confused about sex? Have you sometimes wondered how sexuality ought to fit into your own life? Have you worried that you've made some sexual mistakes? If you answered yes to any of these questions, it is no wonder! We live in confusing times, and our social ambivalence has never been so pronounced.

We have seen that as sex-related issues received more media exposure and as research demonstrated the diversity of human sexual behavior, many hostilities and taboos gradually seemed to slip away. Yet research is beginning to suggest that although there have been some distinct changes along the way, our perceptions about sexual permissiveness may well have been exaggerated, and the rates of sexual experimentation may have leveled off (Kantrowitz, 2006; Melby, 2008a).

Social conditions can affect people's lives, too, and in turn influence their sexual lives. The economic crises we have experienced cause pressures and stresses that take their toll on relationships and family well-being. The wars that have engaged tens of thousands of military personnel in recent years also damage intimate relationships. Psychological stresses of military conflict lead to depression, anxiety disorders, and post-traumatic stress disorder, all of which can affect soldiers' levels of interest in sex and their abilities to relate intimately to others. Physical injuries can cause irreversible damage to bodies, amputation of limbs, and traumatic brain injuries that alter body perceptions, emotions, personalities, and physical abilities. Sexual pleasure is very susceptible to being hindered by dramatic changes faced by a society (Melby, 2008b).

To study human beings' attitudes with a great degree of objectivity is no simple matter, especially regarding issues as complex as sexuality. Nevertheless, researchers have found that no single set of beliefs can describe the prevailing North American attitudes toward sex. There are some clusters of similarity that

have allowed sociologists to group people into three main categories based on what seem to be their fundamental assumptions about the purposes of sex. The *procreational* or traditional category includes those people who see the primary purpose of sexual activity as reproductive. The *relational* group tends to view sexual activity as a natural component of intimate and loving relationships, and the *recreational* cohort consists of people who consider the primary purpose of sex for consenting adults to be pleasure (Laumann et al., 1994). These categories are explained in greater detail in Chapter 8.

We may conclude, therefore, that we live in a time when no single set of social attitudes relating to human sexuality predominates. In fact, several different and often quite contradictory attitudinal patterns exist alongside one another. Even more important, we are beginning to see that the sexual attitudes people hold, which are strongly influenced by the social groups to which they belong, also influence the sexual behaviors in which they engage.

In which of the three main attitudinal categories regarding sexual issues and behavior would you place yourself: procreational/traditional, relational, or recreational? Explain your choice.

We have seen that we remain ambivalent about human sexuality. We have also discussed how easily sexual issues become politicized. The combination of these two realities makes for an interesting brew. It has become obvious in recent U.S. elections that there is an ongoing debate and struggle between what are called conservative and liberal ideals in this country. From a political perspective, the conservatives are loosely identified as Republicans and the liberals as Democrats, although these dividing lines do not necessarily hold up well under closer examination. While issues such as gay marriage and sex scandals of politicians dominated the 2004 and 2006 elections, the 2008 Presidential election centered on a faltering economy and a desire for change. The sex-related issues have not disappeared, however, and they remain at the forefront of many decisions regarding legislation and social policies. Gay marriage, for example, is a hotly contested issue in many states, and the availability of abortion continues to be a topic for Congress and the U.S. Supreme Court.

It often seems that we are a nation and a culture divided and that sexual topics are where some of the divisions become most obvious. However, it is dangerous to assume that individual human beings fall so neatly into such categories. They simply do not. In the rest of this chapter, we explore the history of the field of human sexuality and look at the research methods underlying scientific validity. This text aims to provide

Real Student Voices

■ I feel that sex is what you make of it, and it works differently for different people. A secondary reason I signed up for this course was because my brother recently informed me and our parents that he is gay. I personally have had no trouble accepting this, but my parents are having problems coming to terms with it. I'd like to learn as much as I can so maybe I can be of help.

■ As a religious person, my views toward sex are strict. I don't care what others do, because sex is natural and good as long as you're being true to yourself and your beliefs, and not everyone has the

same beliefs. I do have a problem with "posers"—those who despite defying the teachings of their religion continue on as if they were an exception to the rules, lying to themselves.

■ I would say that I am quite experienced in masturbation and have tried several different techniques. I'm very open about this experimentation with my close friends and we often share ideas and techniques. I also watch pornography for sexual arousal and education. You can learn a lot about different positions, and then try to initiate them with your partner.

the information and background to help you, as an individual, sort through who you are as a sexual person and what you believe.

■ Milestones in Sexual Science: A Brief Historical Survey

Many students find studying the history of a field to be rather boring, maybe even irrelevant. I must admit, I used to have the same reaction. Gradually I've come to appreciate how interesting and helpful understanding historical information can be, perhaps because I've been able to witness a good deal of that recent history take shape. Can you think of some good reasons why taking a look at historical foundations could be important to your understanding of human sexuality?

Until the mid-nineteenth century, recorded commentary about sexuality was largely the province of philosophers, poets, and theologians. Serious attempts to study human sexual thoughts and behaviors with any objectivity did not come along until the twentieth century. Ancient Greek philosophers, including Plato (427–347 BCE) and Aristotle (384–322 BCE), dealt with sexual urges (what they called *eros*) mostly from the perspective of bodily needs that were generally not considered to be as virtuous or spiritual as friendship-love (called *philia*), and that tended to emphasize the need for moderation in all human passions. Medieval Christian theologians brought mixed views to the topic. St. Augustine (354–430) held generally negative

views on sexual pleasure by any means, and found the act of sexual intercourse acceptable only within marriage for the purpose of procreation. St. Thomas Aquinas (1224/25–1274) was a bit less negative, believing that since God had created sexual pleasure it was good, but again only for the purposes that God had intended, namely reproduction. Other forms of sexual enjoyment were deemed sinful (Soble, 2009).

Until well into the 1800s, there was much speculation on the nature of lust and love and the human complications they produce, but as more scientific approaches became more widely accepted, a few observers began to try to make more practical sense of the matters of sex. The remainder of this section presents a brief historical summary of some of the major advances in sexual science. A summary timeline can be found in Table 1.1.

Emerging from the Nineteenth Century (1800s)

Much as we can see in our contemporary culture wars, European academics and physicians were immersed in a time of conflicting values and philosophies during the last quarter of the nineteenth century. Some supported an intensely repressive moral code concerning sexual behavior and attitudes, along with the concept that sex was a major factor in the onset of emotional and mental disturbances (Soble, 2009). When sexual feelings or behaviors inevitably produced guilt, fear, and self-loathing, they might logically be expected to be at the root of many disorders.

Table 1.1   *Milestones for Western Culture in the Science of Sex*

1880–1940	1940–1980	1980–2010
Prevailing negative attitudes about sexual feelings and behaviors were gradually superseded by more accepting attitudes and objectively studied facts about human sexuality. Sexual pleasure became a valid concept.	The scientific study of sexuality became valid, yielding new public perceptions of sexual variety and "normalcy." People began to understand their own sexuality better and seek help for problems.	A time of contrasts between worries about safe sex and increasing acceptance of many sexual lifestyles, orientations, and behaviors. Research takes on a more global perspective.
1886—Richard von Krafft Ebing publishes *Psychopathia Sexualis,* emphasizing the dangers of masturbation. 1903—Otto Weininger publishes *Sex and Character,* with new perspectives on gender and various sexual practices. 1905—Sigmund Freud publishes *Three Essays on the Theory of Sexuality,* opening new psychoanalytic interpretations of sexuality. 1906—Iwan Bloch coins term "sexual science," suggesting that sex should be studied objectively. 1921—Magnus Hirschfeld calls for equal rights for gay people in First Congress for Sexual Reform. 1910–1939—Henry Havelock Ellis publishes 7 volumes of *Studies in the Psychology of Sex,* in which many traditional negative beliefs about sexual behaviors were questioned. 1926—Theodoor van de Velde publishes *Ideal Marriage,* a manual on sexual techniques and pleasure for married couples. 1930—Helena Wright publishes *The Sex Factor in Marriage,* offering women techniques for enjoying sex more. 1932—Robert Latou Dickinson publishes *A Thousand Marriages,* based on his work as a gynecologist, and teaches women how to reach orgasm.	1948, 1953—Alfred Kinsey and his colleagues publish carefully researched studies called *Sexual Behavior in the Human Male* and *Sexual Behavior in the Human Female,* enhancing our knowledge of the variety and frequency of human sexual experiences. The statistics in the study may have been skewed by the study's sample of convenience, but they were more reliable than any others available, and people began to realize that they were not so different sexually from many others. 1966, 1971—William Masters and Virginia Johnson publish *Human Sexual Response,* the first published study on the physiological responses of the human body during sexual arousal and orgasm. This was followed by their book *Human Sexual Inadequacy* that for the first time explained and labeled various sexual dysfunctions and outlines specific behavioral approaches for their treatment. 1970s—Numerous popular surveys on sexual behaviors and attitudes were published in popular magazines such as *Playboy* and *Redbook.* While these studies may well have suffered from difficulties with their sample representation and volunteer bias, they stimulated a new level of interest in sexual functioning and sexual pleasure.	Early 1980s—The appearance of HIV and AIDS brought new attention to the need to understand sexual behaviors and how diseases may be transmitted sexually. The concept of Safer Sex became popular. 1994—The National Health and Social Life Survey produced the best data on sexual behavior in the United States since Kinsey's work. 1995–2005—National Longitudinal Study of Adolescent Health and National Survey of Family Growth offer new understandings of sexual behaviors and sexual health issues in children and adolescents. 2006—Data from the Global Study of Sexual Attitudes and Behaviors, based on surveys in 29 countries, begin to appear, giving a more global perspective on culture, sexual satisfaction, and sexual problems. Present: A team from the Kinsey Institute is studying the factors that encourage and discourage condom use in hopes of reducing some risks of sexual interaction. Researchers are clarifying the interplay of physiology and psychology in sexual arousal and response. There is growing interest in clarifying sexual theory as a basis for sex research and social policy relating to sexuality.

Richard von Krafft-Ebing (1840–1902)

Typifying repressive sexual codes, this German-born neurologist and psychiatrist's book *Psychopathia Sexualis* became a widely circulated medical text that portrayed various forms of sexual behavior and arousal as disgusting and pathological. Krafft-Ebing grouped sexual deviations into four classifications of pathology: sadism, masochism, fetishism, and homosexuality. For the first time, awareness was raised of what was then considered to be sexually atypical, and this awareness likely made some people feel that at least they were not alone (Bancroft, 2001). Krafft-Ebing believed that hereditary "weakness" or "taintedness" was the cause of sexual behaviors other than intercourse for the purpose

of reproduction, a belief reflective of the moral codes of his time (Money, 2003).

Of special significance was Krafft-Ebing's declaration that masturbation was the cause of all sexual deviations. This is one example of how opinion and speculation, in the absence of the kind of sound research we would expect today, can lead to questionable and misleading conclusions. He illustrated his theories with case studies demonstrating the dire effects of masturbation. His case studies were highly sensational for the times, and they did call attention to the variety of human sexual orientations and activities. His biased conclusions, however, labeled much sexual behavior sick and unnatural. Even though Krafft-Ebing was not viewed as a mainstream

■ FIGURE 1.5 *Sigmund Freud*

Freud (1856–1939) was an Austrian neurologist who first theorized that sexuality existed throughout the life cycle and was the basic motivating factor in human behavior. He identified the basic stages of sexual-emotional development as the oral, the anal, and the genital.

sex researcher by his professional contemporaries, his perspective pervaded the medical and psychiatric professions well into the twentieth century (Oosterhuis, 2001).

Sigmund Freud (1856–1939)

This Viennese physician (see Figure 1.5) focused much of his work on the study of the psychosexual development of children and how it affected adult life and mental condition. Freud's contributions have had far more influence on psychology than have those of Krafft-Ebing, although they also perpetuated a decidedly negative attitude toward most aspects of human sexuality. In 1895, Freud published the epochal *Studies in Hysteria,* written in collaboration with Josef Breuer. The book contained discussions of the unconscious mind, repression, and free association, concepts that became the foundation of psychoanalysis. Freud also had become convinced that neuroses were produced by unconscious conflicts of a sexual nature, an idea that alienated most scientists of his time. In 1905, his *Three Essays on the Theory of Sexuality* precipitated a storm of protest. It was in this work that Freud developed his theory of infantile sexuality and attempted to demonstrate how adult sexual perversions were distortions of childhood sexual expressions (Soble, 2009).

Many of Freud's European contemporaries considered his ideas marginal, but his work was highly influential in the United States. Today there is much disagreement as to the value of psychoanalysis and Freud's theories of sexuality. His work, nonetheless, led to an increased interest in sex and a willingness to think and talk about sexuality. Freud did not brand sexual behaviors as immoral, criminal, or pathological. Through his work, sexuality became a legitimate concern of medicine and psychology.

Early Attempts at Sex Research in the Twentieth Century (1900s)

At the turn of the twentieth century, some liberal intellectuals in Vienna began to develop new perspectives on sexuality that would set the stage for the future. Otto Weininger wrote *Sex and Character,* a controversial book that questioned prevailing views about gender and sexuality. Author Robert Musil explored gender issues, homosexuality, and sadism in the Europe of his time, while refocusing attention on the cultural meanings of gender (Luft, 2003; Ortiz, 2006).

The First Sexologists

A major shift in methodology, however, occurred in 1906 when a German physician, Iwan Bloch (1872–1922), coined the term "sexual science" and began studying the history of prostitution and what he called "strange" sexual practices. Bloch's work was the first to conceive of history as an important foundation for understanding human sexuality. More recently, historians have accepted sexuality as a legitimate area for historical study, although caution must be taken not to interpret historical studies and beliefs solely in the context of the present (Bancroft, 2001). Bloch might well have been the first **sexologist,** the term given to professionals who study human sexuality from a scientific perspective and with some objectivity.

German psychiatrist Magnus Hirschfeld (1868–1935) was one of the first professionals to take a stand on rights for people who were gay or lesbian. He risked personal persecution and anti-Semitic repercussions for saying that people with same-sex sexual orientation constituted an intermediate third sex that deserved the same rights and privileges as heterosexuals. He also argued against the prevailing claims about the negative effects of masturbation, believing them to be exaggerated and unfounded (Bullough, 2003b).

sexologist person who studies human sexuality from a scientific perspective.

Henry Havelock Ellis (1859–1939)

This English sex researcher brought a new perspective to sexual science (see Figure 1.6). Ellis spent several decades studying all available information on human sexuality in the Western world and on the sexual mores of other cultures. He also studied the sex lives of his contemporaries and carefully recorded what he learned. Eventually he began writing about his findings, publishing them in six volumes between 1896 and 1910 as *Studies in the Psychology of Sex*. A seventh volume was added in 1928 (Ellis, 1936).

Ellis played a major role in effecting the gradual changes in sexual attitudes that followed Victorian times. His *Studies* recognized that human beings exhibit great variety in their sexual inclinations and behaviors and that sexual mores are determined by cultural and social influences. His conclusions were radical by Victorian standards and amazingly farsighted by present-day standards. Ellis noted that masturbation was a common practice in males and females of all ages. He suggested that sexual orientation toward one gender or the other existed in degrees rather than as an absolute. He legitimized the idea that women could have as great a sexual desire as men, and he pointed out that the orgasms of men and women were remarkably similar. Foreshadowing later trends in sex therapy, Ellis recognized that difficulties in achieving erection or orgasm often were psychological problems rather than physical. He emphasized what most professionals

FIGURE 1.6 *Henry Havelock Ellis*

Ellis (1859–1939), an English physician, invented the term "autoeroticism" to indicate the practice of masturbation in both sexes and all ages. He was farsighted in his views, particularly of the way sexuality affects women and the way mental attitude affects physical behavior.

today accept, that "the range of variation within fairly normal limits is immense" when considering the sexual needs and behaviors of humans.

A Fresh Perspective: Sexual Pleasure

In 1926, a Dutch physician by the name of Theodoor van de Velde (1873–1937) published the first edition of his book *Ideal Marriage*. Although it was not the only sex manual available at the time, it was significant because van de Velde conveyed the validity of sexual responsiveness to a reading audience that still had Victorian inhibitions. Although van de Velde's suggestions for a more fulfilling sexual relationship were described in a heterosexual, marriage-oriented framework with some moralistic boundaries, he put forth a generally positive outlook that people by this time were ready to receive. His book described a variety of coital positions, discussed the use of oral sex in foreplay, and offered suggestions for dealing with some sexual problems. Van de Velde's ideas played an important role in helping thousands of couples achieve more sexual enjoyment (Melody & Peterson, 1999).

A pioneer in the sexual liberation of women was Helena Wright, who began her gynecological medical practice in London in the 1920s. She discovered that most women found no enjoyment in sex and instead considered it a marital duty. Unlike other women writers, who had discussed sexuality in mostly negative terms, Wright began publishing books that instructed women on how to achieve orgasm, through both intercourse and masturbation. The first of her books, *The Sex Factor in Marriage,* was published in 1930. Subsequent editions of the book and Wright's other publications continued for decades to give explicit instructions to women on becoming fully acquainted with their sex organs and sexual responses.

A significant sex research effort of the early twentieth century was a study published in 1932 by Robert Latou Dickinson called *A Thousand Marriages*. Dickinson gathered 5,200 case studies of women he treated between 1882 and 1924 while he was a gynecologist in New York City. He documented how the repressive sexual attitudes of childhood led to disastrous effects on adult sexual functioning—one of the earliest attempts at a better understanding of female sexuality. He also studied the physiological responses of the clitoris, vagina, and cervix during sexual stimulation and orgasm. Realizing that once a woman has been able to experience the pleasure of a self-induced orgasm she is more likely to have orgasm during intercourse, he introduced the use of electric vibrators for women.

In contrast to the historical philosophies that took a rather dim view of human sexual feelings, a distinct shift began to take place in Western culture. It was the rather revolutionary view that sexual pleasure for its

■ **FIGURE 1.7** *Alfred C. Kinsey*

Kinsey (1894–1956) was a zoologist, later a biology professor, who was instrumental in compiling face-to-face interviews with thousands of people about their sexual behavior. His work, not highly regarded in his lifetime, has come to be regarded as comprehensive, systematic, and the model on which other studies are based.

own sake might be worth considering in positive terms (Wax, 2007).

Mid-Twentieth-Century Sex Research

The preeminent sex researcher at midcentury was Alfred C. Kinsey (1894–1956), a successful zoologist who gradually moved into research on human sexual behavior (see Figure 1.7). It was through his work that sex research became a more legitimate scientific pursuit than it had been, because he applied statistical analysis to sexual behavior instead of drawing conclusions solely from personal or clinical observations. In 1937, as a conservative and highly respected biology professor at Indiana University, Kinsey had been selected to teach a new course in sexuality and marriage. In preparing lectures and attempting to answer his students' questions, Kinsey began to realize that little reliable information about sexuality was available. He began gathering information by interviewing people about their sex lives, eventually involving associates in the interviews. By the end of 1949, he had gathered detailed histories on the sexual lives of more than 16,000 people.

Kinsey founded and directed Indiana University's Institute for Sex Research. Now called the Kinsey

Institute for Research in Sex, Gender, and Reproduction (commonly known as the Kinsey Institute), it remains an important center for sex research. Paul Gebhard and Wardell Pomeroy became Kinsey's principal collaborators and helped design the statistical approaches and skillful interview techniques that rendered the Kinsey studies unique. The two studies that brought Kinsey wide recognition and notoriety were *Sexual Behavior in the Human Male,* published in 1948, and *Sexual Behavior in the Human Female,* published in 1953. Both were considered milestones in the field, and the movie *Kinsey* about his life and career appeared in 2004 (see Figure 1.8).

Although Kinsey's findings were long considered representative of the general population, we now know that his research had some inherent design flaws that probably skewed the statistical results. When Kinsey embarked on his research, he believed—probably rightfully so—that getting a standard, representative sample of the general population was a practical impossibility. He had already decided that face-to-face interviewing would be the best way to obtain information from people, and it took him six months to persuade the first 62 people to participate. He therefore compromised in finding subjects to interview, knowing that the outcome would be less than satisfactory but believing that it was the best that could be done at the time (Bancroft, 2005).

Because Kinsey believed that getting people to discuss their sexual behaviors would be challenging and because he lacked the funding for extensive travel,

■ **FIGURE 1.8** *Laura Linney and Liam Neeson*

The actors play Alfred Kinsey and his wife in the 2004 film *Kinsey*.

he settled for what is known as a "sample of convenience." In other words, he and his staff interviewed groups of people who expressed a willingness to respond to their questions. These volunteers included members of college fraternities, sororities, and college classes; other student groups; and inhabitants of rooming houses, prisons, and mental hospitals. Kinsey even interviewed hitchhikers who came through town. To achieve the increased reliability of larger numbers, he would attempt to interview all members of a particular group (Reed, 2007).

 See "Alfred Kinsey Research" on SexSource Online.

This approach had two essential flaws. First, because the interviewees were willing volunteers, the information they offered about their sexual lives could not justifiably be generalized to the larger, national population. Second, it can be assumed that willing volunteers—especially for something such as a sex survey—may well have very different sex-related attitudes, life experiences, and sexual behaviors from those who are reluctant to participate. The data gathered from this group of less hesitant volunteers may well represent an accurate portrayal of the volunteer group, but they are not as likely to reflect broader patterns within the general population.

There can be no argument that Kinsey's work fostered a new level of awareness about the diversity of human sexual behaviors. Until the 1990s, his statistics were about the most accurate and comprehensive available. The surprising thing is that it took 50 years to gather more accurate information about a subject that has been so much in the public eye (Bullough, 2004).

Masters and Johnson

Two researchers who contributed to the early knowledge of sexual functioning were William H. Masters and Virginia E. Johnson (see Figure 1.9). Their work focused on two major areas: the physiology of human sexual response and the treatment of sexual dysfunction. Little had been published in this area. William Masters launched his research study in 1954 and hired Virginia Johnson as an interviewer soon after. In the decade that followed, Masters and Johnson used sophisticated instrumentation to measure the physiological responses of 694 individuals during masturbation and coitus. In total, they studied more than 10,000 orgasms in these laboratory conditions. The detailed account of their work is given in *Human Sexual Response* (Masters & Johnson, 1966).

Their second major research effort began in 1959, proceeding simultaneously with the studies on sexual

FIGURE 1.9 *Virginia E. Johnson and William H. Masters*
Masters and Johnson were the first researchers to actually observe, monitor, and film the physiological responses of people engaged in coitus or masturbation. This initial research led them to develop techniques for effectively treating sexual dysfunction.

response. For five years, Masters and Johnson developed and perfected clinical techniques for the treatment of male and female sexual dysfunctions. In 1970, their revolutionary treatment format was described in *Human Sexual Inadequacy,* a book that inaugurated the age of sex therapy. Numerous other workers have since modified and enlarged upon the Masters and Johnson work, and sex therapy has become a distinct discipline of medicine and psychology.

Popular Surveys: A Source of Attention but Also Flaws

The seventies became the decade of the sex survey, and books and magazines were filled with new peeks at the most private details of sex lives in the United States. The methodologies of these casual surveys were highly questionable, yet their results generated a great deal of attention and solidified some myths and misconceptions about the variety and frequency of sexual behaviors.

Playboy and *Redbook* magazines published the two most widely publicized surveys, based on questionnaires that were completed by willing participants. Although such surveys seemed impressive because of their sheer numbers of responses, those numbers actually represented rather small proportions of people who had ultimately been willing to complete the questionnaires. Statisticians know that it is far more important to know *how the researcher actually gets the participants.* For example, the percentage of people responding to a widely distributed questionnaire is more important than the raw numbers. A response rate of 2 or 3 percent would yield very questionable data. Social scientists would consider a response rate of about 30 percent to be in the minimum range of acceptability in terms of accuracy. The higher the response rate, the more representative the results are of the total population originally approached. Therein lies the other major flaw of these popular surveys. Who has actually been invited to participate? Readers of a particular magazine, such as *Redbook* or *Playboy*, may be considered to have certain characteristics in common and therefore not be representative of anything more than readers of those magazines. Readers of *The New Republic* or *Christian Century* might be expected to have other, different characteristics as groups.

Another difficulty with survey questionnaires that are distributed en masse is that there is no way of really knowing who has responded. Some respondents might have filled out the survey as a joke or deliberately exaggerated their answers to bias the results. Some men might have pretended to be women, and vice versa, or some might have completed more than one questionnaire. Although surveys of this sort may generate results that capture our attention, we have no way of knowing what their findings really mean.

Under what conditions would you respond truthfully to a survey about your sexual behavior?

The National Health and Social Life Survey

The most comprehensive study on sexual behavior in the United States to emerge after the Kinsey work was the National Health and Social Life Survey (NHSLS), conducted by highly respected researchers (see Figure 1.10). Their private funding for the study supported a sample size of about 3,500 adults ages 18 to 59. Their random sampling techniques were among several characteristics that rendered this research particularly reliable. Working through the National Opinion Research Center at the University of Chicago to generate randomly selected areas of the country, they identified 4,369 households who had someone eligible to participate in the study and then randomly selected the individual in each household to be interviewed. This is the protocol that social scientists generally have established as valid methodology (Laumann et al., 1994).

The questionnaire that the researchers employed was carefully designed to avoid confusing people with technical language and to flow naturally from topic to topic without predicting responses. This design is crucial in ensuring valid results. They decided on face-to-face interviews as the best technique to ensure that respondents understood the questions and to assure

FIGURE 1.10 *Robert T. Michael, John H. Gagnon, Stuart Michaels, and Edward O. Laumann*

Laumann, Gagnon, Michael, and Michaels conducted the National Health and Social Life Survey, the most comprehensive study on sexual behavior in the United States to emerge since the Kinsey work. Using scientific methodology, the study determined that most Americans are fairly content with their sexual lives.

the respondents' identity. The research team selected 220 professional interviewers who were veterans of other surveys and carefully trained them. The interviewers were then dispersed to various parts of the United States and encouraged to persuade all eligible individuals to participate in the survey. They sometimes returned several times in attempts to garner participant cooperation, conducting interviews over a seven-month period. This research ultimately demonstrated that people will indeed participate in sex surveys when they are convinced that the research serves legitimate social purposes, that their answers will be considered without judgment, and that their anonymity and confidentiality will be protected (Michael et al., 1994).

Eventually, 3,432 individuals were interviewed, a response rate of nearly 80 percent—one reason why the results of this study are considered to be so accurate. Another is that the sample population was randomly selected and almost exactly mirrored many characteristics of the general American population according to numerous measures. The questionnaire itself had a number of checks and cross-checks that helped validate the responses. Although the work had its detractors, social scientists generally accept the NHSLS data as among the best currently available, resulting from state-of-the-art survey techniques. The findings were, in a sense, counterrevolutionary because they reflected a nation that was indeed involved in a wide spectrum of sexual activities but in general was much less sexually active than previously believed. The study also suggested that Americans were, for the most part, more content with their sexual lives than had been assumed.

Long-Term Studies of Adolescent Sexuality

By the mid-1990s, plans were unveiled for a long-term federal study of teenage health, which included questioning some 20,000 teens about their sexual behavior. The study, to be completed in stages over several years, was called the National Longitudinal Study of Adolescent Health. Five hundred trained interviewers visited more than 20,000 adolescents in grades 7 to 12 at their homes, gathering information from them in a confidential manner. Their personal identities were not connected with any of the data. Although political controversies made it difficult for this study to get off the ground, data from the research are still being analyzed and continue to appear in a number of publications, offering a clearer perspective on sexual behavior among teens (Cubbin, Santelli, Brindis, & Braveman, 2005; Shafii et al., 2004).

The long-standing National Survey of Family Growth added questions on sexual behavior in 2002, and the survey reaches young people down to age 15. The Centers for Disease Control and Prevention also include sex-related questions in their ongoing Youth Risk Behavior Surveillance System (YRBS). This study has been closely coordinated with the questions on adolescent sexual health now included in a survey used by 35 areas across the world called Health Behaviors in School-aged Children (HBSC). The attention being given to understanding adolescent sexuality bodes well for our future understanding of sexual trends and problems (National Center for Health Statistics, 2006; Ross et al., 2004).

Even in a time when adolescents clearly are sexually active, a great deal of controversy surrounds the right of researchers to question adolescents about sexual matters in order to obtain data. What are your feelings on this issue?

Sex Research in the Twenty-first Century

We can only yet see the research trends in the earliest years of the new century. As shown in the previous section, we have begun that century with the most accurate data on adolescent sexual behavior ever available. Information will also continue to emerge from general surveys that more thoroughly examine the relationship of sexual behavior to HIV transmission. There is an expanding focus on multinational studies. The Global Study of Sexual Attitudes and Behaviors (GSSAB) surveyed several aspects of sexuality and relationships among people ages 40 to 80 in 29 countries, and it will take some time to analyze all the data. A total of 13,882 women and 13,618 men were surveyed (Laumann

et al., 2005, 2006). The focus on middle-aged and older adults was likely the result of the fact that the study was funded by a pharmaceutical company that manufactures a drug to help overcome erectile dysfunction in men and lack of sexual desire in women.

Another study reanalyzed data on sexual behavior generated from research conducted in 59 different countries, providing one of the most expansive looks at sexual behavior ever attempted (Wellings et al., 2006). This work highlights the fact that in many areas of the world our understanding of sexual behaviors and their impact on human health is poor.

A team of researchers at the Kinsey Institute is studying condom use and what factors make the use of condoms more reliable and consistent for both men and women (Michel, 2008). Although male circumcision has been a controversial practice for years, recent research in developing countries is demonstrating that circumcised men and their female partners have substantially lower risks of contracting HIV and a variety of other sexually transmitted diseases (Golden & Wasserheit, 2009; Gray et al., 2009).

There is growing awareness among sex researchers that understanding the social context of a population being studied can be vitally important. The places people live are filled with meanings, as are the places people choose to make sexual contact. Socioeconomic status often is taken into account in research, yet no clear guidelines exist for defining and measuring this status. Many sex-related issues become reflected in social policies that affect particular groups of people. Good research will need to become better at understanding social contexts and their meanings (Braveman et al., 2005; Kelly & Muñoz-Laboy, 2005).

Sex researchers face some challenges regarding sex-related theory. Theories in sexual science often are oversimplified and fail to take into consideration the multidisciplinary nature of human sexuality. Much of what is passed off without question as scientific information regarding human sexuality is actually ideological pronouncement with no real scientific merit. As a society, we need to learn how to become more astute at separating the results of valid sex research from sensationalized hype. Sexology needs to strive for greater congruence in theory and a closer fit between theory and practice, as well as a stronger connection to related sciences (Reiss, 2006).

■ The Methods of Sexological Research

Research into the interdisciplinary realm of sexology has been increasing, and numerous professional journals are devoted exclusively to new concepts, controversies, and information relating to human sexuality (Zucker & Cantor, 2008). Sexuality is a part of human life that has many implications and stimulates many human reactions. Researchers who choose to study various aspects of human sexuality can become subject to questions about their personal and professional motivations, and the effects sometimes can be quite negative. While sex research can be intriguing, it may also carry some risk and liability for the researcher (Dreger, 2008).

Although scientists are influenced to a degree by their own social and cultural circumstances, sex researchers have a special obligation to approach their subjects without preconceived notions of what the data will show and without an agenda as to what sexual behaviors ought to be. With controversies raging in the culture wars, some people have been tempted to ignore scientific evidence or distort it for their own purposes. Theories about human sexuality represent a consensus among researchers in the field about the best ways to observe and explain things relating to sex, but researchers have a long way to go in creating solid theories about sexuality (Reiss, 2006).

Perhaps reflective of increased scientific skepticism among the voting public, one battleground on which the culture wars are played out politically is funding for sex-related research. In order to investigate ways to control the spread of HIV and sexually transmitted diseases, it is sometimes necessary to conduct research on human sexual behavior. Conservative groups have lobbied Congress to prevent the National Institutes of Health and other agencies from funding such studies, claiming that they have no value in protecting public health. Agencies such as the Centers for Disease Control and Prevention were forced during the George W. Bush administration to remove sex-related scientific data from their websites until they had modified them to reflect the administration's moral stances. These policies have been modified during the Obama administration. Worldwide, human beings bear a tremendous burden of ill health from sex-related causes, yet political sensitivities continue to hinder adequate funding of sex research. Whether we like it or not, it will be through political pressure and persuasion that this global problem begins to be addressed (Thomas, 2006).

Collecting Research Data on Human Sexuality

One goal of scientific research is to find information that can then be generalized to the real world outside the study. Science offers hope of being able to understand, predict, and perhaps control various phenomena. Obviously, using human beings as research subjects creates many problems, because we

are not as easily categorized or experimentally controlled as mice or molecules. Sex researchers have the difficult responsibility of ensuring that their own methods and assumptions do not distort the outcome of their work. There is evidence, for example, that researchers' assumptions about sexuality can influence how questions are asked, as can the methods by which the answers are gathered (Graham et al., 2003; Reiss, 2006).

Quantitative research gathers information, or data, in a form that allows organization of the information into numerical form. Quantification also allows the data to be subjected to various forms of statistical analysis to help summarize the findings and test their reliability and validity. (The term *data* is plural, referring to more than one *datum,* a single bit of information.) There has been a growing willingness to gather and analyze qualitative data from people, which offer a somewhat more subjective view than do quantitative numbers and statistics (Morse, Swanson, & Kuzel, 2001). An example of qualitative research is interviewing a group of people about some sexual topic in order to solicit their values and beliefs. A rather nonstructured approach might be used, with the researcher then trying to organize all the information into useful categories. Even though such findings might not be easily organized into numerical form, they still could be informative and add value to the field. The particular methodological strategies that follow are used in conducting sex research and can be adapted for both quantitative and qualitative studies.

Selecting Population Samples

When we attempt to answer some questions about human sexuality, we obviously find it impossible to get information about all human beings. Therefore, it is necessary to select a **sample** of the human population from which the results can be generalized to the larger population. The more people included in the sample and the more proportionally representative they are of the various characteristics in the total population, the more statistically reliable the study may be considered to be. The best population sample is a **random sample,** in which individuals are selected at random from the whole population. If the number of persons selected is significant, the sample can be assumed to be highly

sample a representative group of a population that is the focus of a scientific poll or study.

random sample representative group of the larger population that is the focus of a scientific poll or study in which care is taken to select participants without a pattern that might bias research results.

representative of the whole. It is particularly crucial that population samples be reflective of the proportions of ethnic diversity in a particular population, because ethnicity may influence sexual attitudes and behaviors to at least some degree (Lewis & Kertzner, 2003). However, such studies must also be large and therefore expensive, so very little research of this sort has been conducted for groups as large as the population of an entire country.

Various forms of bias can enter human research studies and influence the results and conclusions. Not everyone may be willing to participate in a study on sexuality or answer honestly even if he or she agrees to participate. This creates volunteer bias, which is bound to affect the outcome of the research (Alexander & Fisher, 2003). Studies have shown that people who volunteer to participate in sexuality studies tend to be more sexually experienced than nonvolunteers, more interested in sexual variety, and generally more interested in sex (Plaud et al., 1999). Beyond this volunteer bias is actual response bias, which means that people may not always be accurate or truthful in self-reporting their sexual behaviors. Response bias can work in one of two ways. Some respondents may underreport or conceal their sexual behaviors out of personal embarrassment, fear that their anonymity will not be guaranteed, or concerns about reprisals. Others may exaggerate or embellish their reports because it is self-enhancing for them to imagine having been more adventurous than they actually have been.

Men seem to report higher levels of permissive sexual attitudes and behaviors than do women and are more likely to revise their reporting downward during later follow-up (Alexander & Fisher, 2003). Women seem to be initially more willing to participate in sex research but also more likely to refuse to continue if the study seems too personal or invasive (Boynton, 2003). In an analysis of studies from 59 countries, it was clear that men have a tendency to exaggerate their sexual activities and women tend to underreport them (Wellings et al., 2006). There is also concern that the results of sexuality studies may be affected by the sex of the experimenter involved in gathering results and by the amount of prior information provided to respondents. In one anonymous survey, if men were administered the survey by a woman and given written information that women are more sexually permissive than men, they tended to report having had more sexual partners than if the survey was administered by a man. This result calls into question the reliability of some previous studies (Fisher, 2007).

Even respondents anxious to be accurate may have distorted or inaccurate memories about sexual experience (Gillmore et al., 2001). There is also evidence that some people may be resistant to participating in certain types of sex research, especially if they perceive that their responses might be viewed in a negative light (Senn & Desmarais, 2001). For all these reasons, research studies on human sexuality must be carefully designed and tested to yield the most reliable data possible.

Taking Surveys

Asking people questions about their sexual attitudes or behaviors is one of the most common methods employed by sex researchers. It may be accomplished in face-to-face interviews, in telephone interviews, on the Internet, or through completion of paper questionnaires or daily diaries in which behaviors are recorded (Bowen, 2005; Yarber et al., 2005). The most surveyed group in the United States has been college students, who are often asked to complete questionnaires on sexuality because they represent a population accessible to faculty working on research—a sample of convenience. Care must be taken in generalizing such data to other populations. Daily telephone calls (touch-tone data entry) and written diaries have both been shown to have their strengths and weaknesses, and the problem of respondents being more reluctant to report certain behaviors than others is always present (Blumberg et al., 2003; Graham et al., 2003).

The Kinsey researchers and those who conducted the NHSLS used carefully structured face-to-face interviewing procedures in which researchers were trained in techniques designed to establish an accepting attitude and avoid leading people into answers. These techniques may help minimize dishonesty and other forms of questionnaire bias. Printed questionnaires are an efficient and economical way of gathering information from large numbers of people but make it much more difficult to detect dishonest answers, misunderstandings, exaggeration, or frivolity than do face-to-face interviews. Nevertheless, the interviewing mode used and the training and personal characteristics of the interviewer can affect the data that are collected. In any survey technique, it is crucial that the vocabulary used in the questions be understandable to the population being tested and that suitable statistical adjustments be made to account for individuals who have refused to participate or to answer particular questions.

The Internet is increasingly used to recruit research volunteers and to gather sexuality data. The initial studies have relied on samples of convenience, but as researchers become more sophisticated with the use of this medium, they may be able to randomize responses as they are submitted. Some evidence suggests that participants respond more honestly to computers than to human interviewers (Kurth et al., 2004). Internet sex research is a developing field (Bowen, 2005; Ross et al., 2003).

Explaining Gender Discrepancies in Sex Surveys

Surveys of sexual behavior have shown a consistent pattern in the data that has puzzled researchers and the general public alike: Men tend to report having had more female sexual partners than the numbers of male partners women say they have had. Some studies have shown an average of twice as many partners for males. Intuitively and mathematically, this does not make sense unless many men were having sex with a much smaller cohort of women. But this does not seem to be a particularly satisfactory answer either.

It has also been suggested that men might exaggerate their reported numbers, while women might underestimate them, and there is some evidence to support this hypothesis. The discrepancy may rest with the ways men and women tend to report their sexual histories. Men who report having had high numbers of sexual partners (i.e., more than 20) tend to round up their figures by 5s, 10s, and even 25s. This may be because they have a poorer memory as to the exact number of partners, or because men are more comfortable exaggerating the numbers. When the data generated by people who report large numbers of partners are eliminated, the ratio of the number of sex partners reported by males and females falls much closer to a one-to-one ratio—actually, about 1.2 to 1. It has been suggested that when studies are published without making reference to possible reasons for male-female differences such as this, old and inaccurate stereotypes about gender differences in sexual behaviors are unfairly reinforced (Kolata, 2007).

Women are probably more accurate and conservative in their reporting of numbers of partners and also prone to undercounting. The bottom line, then, is that gender discrepancies probably are not very pronounced at all and that sex researchers must find better investigative techniques for eliminating the problem with the data (Wiederman, 1999). It might be advisable to ask questions about shorter time frames and to use questions that help people remember more accurately.

Case Studies and Clinical Research

Physicians, psychologists, counselors, and other clinicians often work with individuals who are experiencing some sexual concern or problem. These professionals employ various treatment strategies to help the individual and may devise new techniques for doing so. They might discover that these strategies and methods are effective for several clients or patients. **Case studies** then may be published, giving an in-depth look at particular individual circumstances. Although it is risky to overgeneralize from case studies, they do offer the professional community new ideas and useful insights.

When some sort of treatment strategy is tested with larger numbers of people seeking treatment, it is called **clinical research.** The study may consider the cause, treatment, and prevention of a disease or condition. For example, Masters and Johnson (1970) conducted clinical studies for several years on nearly 800 individuals who complained of various forms of sexual dysfunction. They categorized and labeled the problems, looked for possible causes, and tried out a variety of treatment methods. They then did follow-up studies on some of the individuals over a five-year period. Although making generalizations to the entire population must be done with caution in such a study, clinical studies of this sort provide a foundation on which further research can build.

Observational Research

Some researchers have chosen to observe an aspect of human sexual behavior directly, thereby eliminating the biases characteristic of research in which people report on themselves. Observational studies may take place in the field or in laboratory settings. For example, a field researcher might establish a post in an airport in order to observe and count how many couples are holding hands as they walk by. The earlier Masters and Johnson (1966) research on human sexual response is an example of a classic laboratory-based observational study. Various types of instrumentation were used to measure the physiological reactions of 694 people when they were aroused sexually. It was the first large-scale research in which observations of the body's sexual responses were made in a systematic manner.

Masters and Johnson were always careful to point out that their findings might not apply to the responses of all human beings. However, physiologists typically have assumed when dealing with the processes of the human body that such activities really are very similar among different people. It may be difficult to determine how much—if at all—the laboratory setting might affect people's functioning. In subsequent studies that have recruited volunteers to measure physiological responses, significant numbers of people have refused to participate because they do not feel comfortable with the research conditions. Naturally, this biases the

case study an in-depth look at a particular individual and how he or she might be helped to solve a sexual or other problem. Case studies may offer new and useful ideas for counselors to use with other patients.

clinical research the study of the cause, treatment, or prevention of a disease or condition by testing large numbers of people.

population sample (Gaither, Sellbom, & Meier, 2003). Nevertheless, most sexologists have accepted the findings of Masters and Johnson, and many other observational researchers, as fundamental to our understanding of human sexuality.

Ethnosexual Field Studies

Anthropologists often conduct observational field studies of other cultures, living among the people they are studying, observing their customs and behaviors, and attempting to collect data through communications with the members of that society. Collecting information that describes a particular culture is called **ethnography.** When the information pertains specifically to sexual practices and beliefs, the data are sometimes called **ethnosexual.** Anthropologist Margaret Mead was one of the first scientists to openly discuss the sexual mores of other cultures in her writings, including her famous work *Growing Up in New Guinea* (Mead, 1930). One of the earliest detailed cross-cultural surveys to appear in the field of human sexuality was a collection of field studies called *Patterns of Sexual Behavior* published by two ethnographers, Clellan Ford and Frank Beach (1951). It focused on sexual techniques, rules for mating, and the prevalence of various forms of sexual behavior in several different societies.

Cultural values can affect the gathering of sex-related data in several ways. Certain behaviors may be stigmatized in some cultures, leading to reluctance and embarrassment when it comes to discussing or reporting those behaviors. The meaning of terms may get confused when researchers from one culture attempt to discuss sexuality in another culture with which they are relatively unfamiliar. Some sexual terms simply cannot be translated from one language into another. Finally, there are always subcultures within larger cultures, making it difficult to generalize about the entire population. Cross-cultural studies about sexuality therefore demand a great deal of precision, sensitivity, and care in their design (Herdt, 2000).

Experimental Research

A keystone of science is the use of the **controlled experiment.** In this type of research, the investigator examines what happens to a particular **variable** being studied and manipulated while an attempt is made to control all other variables and keep them constant. The researcher then may draw inferences about cause-and-effect relationships that are difficult or impossible to draw from other kinds of research.

Well-controlled experiments, however, are difficult to design for human subjects, whose complexity makes it nearly impossible to control all possible variables.

Additionally, there is always the chance that the artificiality of a controlled experimental setting may influence the outcome of research with humans. For these reasons, experimental research evidence in human sexuality is sparse and ultimately open to the same shortcomings and criticisms found in other methods of study.

Ethical Issues in Sex Research

How willing would you be to be a subject in sex research if you weren't entirely clear about what the researchers were trying to find out? Do you think there could be times when some deception might be all right in sex research, if this were the best way to get accurate data and the test subjects were told the truth after they had taken part in the study?

Four fundamental moral principles must be considered when doing research with human subjects: (1) respect for an individual's autonomy and independent decision making; (2) the importance of doing no harm; (3) the pursuit of benefit for people, balanced with risks and costs; and (4) the pursuit of distributive justice, that is, ensuring the greatest benefit for the largest number of persons (Cwikel & Hoban, 2005). A great deal of attention is focused on the need to protect and respect those people who participate as subjects in any form of human research. Because sexuality is viewed as such a private aspect of life, the ethical issues involved in sex research are particularly evident and crucial. Unpleasant anecdotes are told about human research subjects being exposed to inappropriate touching and violations of their privacy (Bartlett, 2003).

Human research subjects have the right of **informed consent,** meaning that they must be given complete prior information about the purpose of the study and the manner in which they will participate. It

---

ethnography (eth-NAH-gruffy) the anthropological study of other cultures.

ethnosexual referring to data concerning the sexual beliefs and customs of other cultures.

controlled experiment research in which the investigator examines what is happening to one variable while all other variables are kept constant.

variable an aspect of a scientific study that is subject to change.

informed consent the consent given by research subjects, indicating their willingness to participate in a study, after they are informed about the purpose of the study and how they will be asked to participate.

has generally been agreed that researchers do not have the right to coerce people into participation or to be dishonest in presenting information about the research. Similarly, scientists have the obligation to protect the confidentiality of their participants by making certain that personal, private facts can never be connected with a particular individual. They must also protect subjects from physical and psychological harm.

Researchers use a variety of methods to provide for anonymity in collecting data and to prevent the inappropriate release of confidential information at some later time. Universities and government agencies usually have *institutional review boards* that must approve any research design involving human participation. These committees carefully attempt to weigh the potential value of the research to society against any inherent stresses, risks, or dangers for the participants. The decision to allow an investigator to proceed with such research is not always an easy one.

Age is often a critical issue in determining ethical research methods. It has often been assumed that adolescents under the legal age of majority should be required to have parental consent in order to participate in sex surveys and other related research. However, some researchers insist that getting parents involved in this way may not be consistent with the principles of justice mentioned above, may be confusing or unnecessary, and may in fact eliminate some vital participants from the study. They insist that institutional review boards should examine carefully the population to be studied and consider youth-friendly approaches that will encourage and permit participation (Flicker & Guta, 2008). On the other side of the age spectrum, it has been claimed that some studies of risky sexual behaviors which increase probabilities of contracting HIV and other STDs purposely exclude participants over age 50, even though there has been a rapidly growing incidence of such diseases within this age group (Levy et al., 2007)

In the course of gathering data from human research subjects, researchers sometimes may be given information that identifies the subject as either the victim or the perpetrator of a sexual crime. This can create an ethical dilemma for the researcher if the subject has been promised anonymity or confidentiality, yet the laws of the state require reporting. For example, some states mandate the reporting of incidents in which adolescents have been subjected to sexual activity by someone older than themselves, although the adolescent may not have intended to accuse anyone as part of offering the information in a research setting. This ethical issue points up the importance of researchers' understanding laws that could affect their work and modifying their methods and informed consent procedures accordingly (Findholt & Robrecht, 2002).

Researchers may face ethical dilemmas in trying to study sex workers, especially if those workers have been trafficked into another country illegally. The women may be reluctant to get involved, fearing they will be punished.

Ethical dilemmas also have emerged in the study of sex trafficking, which involves the transport of women across national borders where they are forced to participate in sexual activity for money. These women sometimes have been kidnapped or abducted into prostitution or have been deceived into entering into an unfavorable contractual arrangement with promises of a better life. Because sex trafficking has become a serious global problem, good research is important to understand it more fully. However, researchers face complications in securing valid informed consent, because the women are fearful of punishment. Gaining access to the women in the first place can be both difficult and risky. Of special concern to researchers is their own need to maintain objectivity even though they may be aware of illegal acts being committed during the course of their studies. Debate over appropriate responses to such ethical dilemmas continues (Cwikel & Hoban, 2005).

Attitude Questionnaire

Rate each attitude with one of the following numbers: **0** = uncertain   **3** = relatively neutral
1 = strongly disagree   **4** = somewhat agree
2 = somewhat disagree   **5** = strongly agree

Attitude Statement	Present Rating for Yourself	Your Ratings Four to Six Years Ago	Your Parents' Ratings
1. Masturbation is a healthy, normal mode of sexual expression.	_____	_____	_____
2. Young people should be encouraged to use masturbation as a way of exploring their sexual feelings.	_____	_____	_____
3. Sexual activity without marriage or long-term commitment is all right for a couple who share a loving relationship.	_____	_____	_____
4. Sexual activity solely for physical pleasure is all right if both partners agree to it.	_____	_____	_____
5. In a loving partnership, having sex with others outside the primary relationship is all right if both partners agree.	_____	_____	_____
6. Gay, lesbian, bisexual, and transgender lifestyles are acceptable.	_____	_____	_____
7. Lesbians, gay men, and bisexual women or men should not be discriminated against because of their sexual orientation.	_____	_____	_____
8. Transgender people should be allowed to live as whichever gender they choose, regardless of the sex organs with which they were born.	_____	_____	_____
9. Pornography depicting sexual activity between adults should continue to be available for adults via the Internet.	_____	_____	_____
10. Any sexual behavior is acceptable between consenting adults.	_____	_____	_____
11. At a beach, I would not be offended or made uncomfortable by having others around me in the nude.	_____	_____	_____
12. I would not be uncomfortable being nude myself with other nude people at the beach.	_____	_____	_____
13. Any differences in sexual interests between women and men have been created more by social expectations than by built-in genetic or hormonal differences.	_____	_____	_____
14. Women should have the same access and rights to sexual experience that men have.	_____	_____	_____
15. Women can enjoy sex and get as much pleasure from it as men do.	_____	_____	_____
16. Accurate, age-appropriate sex information should be available to all young people and adults.	_____	_____	_____
17. Birth control information and methods should be available to minors without parental consent.	_____	_____	_____
18. Physicians should be able to treat minors for sexually transmitted diseases without notification of parents.	_____	_____	_____
19. I support abortion as an alternative in cases of unplanned pregnancy.	_____	_____	_____
20. Women should have free choice about and access to abortion.	_____	_____	_____
TOTAL:	_____	_____	_____

Self-Evaluation

You and Your Sexuality

The questionnaires in this section are designed to help you take stock of your own sexual attitudes and their possible changes throughout your lifetime. They will also help you evaluate some of your sexual background and its meaning for your life today as a sexual human being. I hope that taking a closer look at your sexuality now will provide a more personal context for exploring the remainder of this book. Although there may be a variety of ways to use these questionnaires for classroom and group awareness activities, I have intended them for your own personal use.

Sexual Attitudes in Your Life

In the questionnaire above on page 26, you are asked to compare your present sexual attitudes with those of your parent(s) (or the primary people who raised you) and with your own values of four to six years ago. It might be interesting to ask your parent(s) to complete the questionnaire. Otherwise, complete the column for your parent(s) with the responses you feel accurately represent their attitudes.

  Analysis: The final totals give a rough standard for comparison of your present attitudes with your attitudes of a few years ago and with those of the parent(s) (or others) who gave you your earliest attitudes. Generally speaking, the higher the total score, the more liberal the attitudes (highest possible score is 100). There are no right or wrong responses or good or bad scores. Examine the individual responses and totals to get a clearer picture of how your sexual attitudes compare with those of your parent(s) and how your own attitudes have or have not changed over the past few years.

Your Sexual History

The following questions are intended to provide further means of exploring where you have been as a sexual person and where you are now. It may help you to write the answers down or to talk about the answers with someone you trust.

1. Nudity
   a. How often, when you were young, did you see your parent(s) in the nude? What was your family's attitude toward nudity?
   b. If you ever have children (or if you have children now), do you hope to be (or are you now) more accepting of nudity in your family than your parent(s), less accepting, or about the same?

2. Masturbation
   a. How did you first learn about or discover masturbation, and how did you feel about it at first?
   b. If you masturbated when you were younger, did you ever let anyone else know about it?
   c. If you masturbate now, how do you feel about the practice?

3. Sex Slang—"Dirty Words"
   a. Make a list of the sex-related slang terms (such as screwing, fuck, cock, cunt, and so forth) that you feel comfortable using, if any.
   b. Which of the words on the list would your parent(s) have been comfortable using?
   c. Which of the words on the list would be offensive to you if you heard them being spoken by a friend of the other gender? Of the same gender?

4. First Shared Sexual Experience (if applicable)
   a. What is the first explicit sexual experience with another person that you can remember?
   b. What were your reactions to that first erotic experience?
   c. Has that initial experience affected your feelings about yourself as a sexual person or about sex in general even until today? If so, how?

5. Male-Female Intercourse
   a. How did you first learn about sexual intercourse between a woman and a man, and what were your reactions and feelings when you did learn about it?
   b. If you have experienced sexual intercourse with someone of the other gender, what were your feelings following the first experience?
   c. Are your attitudes toward sexuality different now from what they were when you first had intercourse? If so, in what ways?

6. Same-Sex Activities and Transgender Attitudes
   a. How did you first learn about attractions and sex between members of the same gender, and what were your reactions and feelings when you did learn about it?
   b. If you have ever participated in a sexual experience (even as a youngster) with someone of the same gender, what are your feelings about the experience?
   c. Do you feel comfortable with the gender roles that are expected of you because of the sex organs with which you were born?
   d. What is your reaction to people who prefer to adopt gender roles or change their bodies so they appear to be of the other gender?

7. Shared Sexual Behavior
   a. For you, what kinds of behavior constitute hooking up? How about having sex?

b. In thinking about sexual contact, or during sexual involvement with another person, which of the following are exciting for you and which are turnoffs?
   1. *Undressing each other*
   2. *Oral sex performed on you*
   3. *Oral sex performed on partner (by you)*
   4. *Anal sex*
   5. *Kissing and being together nude*
   6. *Penile-vaginal intercourse*
   7. *Touching and caressing*
   8. *Using some painful stimulation*
   9. *Acting out a sexual fantasy*
   10. *Mutual masturbation*
c. If you have had intense shared sexual experiences, what things about the experience(s) have pleased and satisfied you most? Which have displeased or frustrated you most?
d. What qualities do you desire in your ideal sexual partner?

8. **Your Cultural Heritage**
   a. What do you see as your primary ethnic or cultural heritage, and how do you think that heritage has been a basis for your sexual values, beliefs, and decisions?
   b. Have you ever felt that your attitudes about sexuality were different from those of others around you because of your cultural differences? If so, how has that made you feel?
   c. Has your race, religion, or ethnic background ever caused others to react to you sexually in a way that you found surprising or uncomfortable?

Chapter Summary

1. Human sexuality is an area of contradictions and complexities that crosses disciplinary boundaries. To study sexuality is a significant way of understanding many different aspects of human cultures, behaviors, and social interactions. To teach about sexuality can be controversial.

2. North America has tended to be Eurocentric in its sexual values, even though it has a very diverse population representing many different ethnic and cultural backgrounds. It is important to recognize that there are many cultural differences in sexual beliefs and customs globally.

3. Small, homogenous cultures are more conformist in their sexual practices than are large, heterogenous cultures. Attitudes and openness about sexuality are changing throughout the world.

4. Just after World War II and for three decades after, dramatic shifts occurred in attitudes concerning various aspects of human sexuality, sometimes referred to as the sexual revolution. There was a new emphasis on personal autonomy, equality between women and men, technological development, the need for sexuality education, openness about different sexual orientations and gender identities, and the relationship between love and sex.

5. Following the changes of the sexual revolution, several factors influenced sexual values and behaviors, including the appearance of HIV/AIDS, greater attention to sex in the media and on the Internet, use of sex-related issues by politicians, and an increasingly global view of sexuality.

6. We are presently seeing ongoing culture wars, based loosely on conservative and liberal ideologies. These become reflected in sex-related debates.

7. North American attitudes regarding sexuality seem to fall roughly into three main categories: traditional or procreational, relational, and recreational. These often contradictory attitudinal systems exist side by side in our society and greatly influence people's sexual choices and behaviors.

8. Three significant pioneers in nineteenth-century studies of human sexuality were Richard von Krafft-Ebing, Sigmund Freud, and Henry Havelock Ellis. Their work established fundamental perspectives on sexuality that persisted well into the twentieth century.

9. The early twentieth century was heavily influenced by Victorian values about sex and romance, but a few writers began to emphasize the importance of sexual pleasure for women as well as men.

10. The Kinsey studies opened new vistas concerning the spectrum of sexual behavior, and Masters and Johnson pioneered work in understanding sexual physiology and the treatment of sexual dysfunctions.

11. Much early research on sexual behavior did not represent accurate generalizations for the entire population because only population samples of convenience were used in the studies.

12. Surveys about sex have offered new perspectives on sexuality. However, they can suffer from meth-

odological flaws in how participants are recruited and a lack of control over the completion of questionnaires.

13. The random sampling and interview techniques employed by the National Health and Social Life Survey yielded the most statistically reliable results on sexual behaviors and attitudes in the United States. This survey caused us to reassess many of our assumptions about the spectrum and frequency of sexual activity.

14. Studies on adolescent sexual behavior are providing valuable information and, along with research on global sexual health, represent one of the themes of sex research in the twenty-first century.

15. The scientific study of sex may be quantitative or qualitative and can involve various methods: population samples, surveys, case studies and clinical research, direct observation of behavior, ethno-sexual field studies, and controlled experiments.

16. Scientific research raises numerous ethical issues, and researchers sometimes face ethical dilemmas in their work. Informed consent is considered essential to participation in any such research.

17. Understanding ourselves as sexual human beings requires some introspection and self-questioning.

Chapter 2
Female Sexual Anatomy and Physiology

Chapter Outline

The first time I got my period, I was excited to tell my mother. She told my father, and they both took me out to dinner to celebrate my "womanhood." It made me feel very grown-up and special.

—from a student essay

The sex organs, also called genitals, have various functions in procreation, in sexual pleasure, and as one route to intimate sharing and communication within a relationship. Some research suggests that how an individual feels about her or his own genitals may affect general self-image and levels of sexual desire (Berman et al., 2003). When the female sex organs are studied in sexuality education, the emphasis clearly has tended toward the reproductive functions of the uterus, ovaries, and fallopian tubes. The important roles of the vagina, clitoris, and other structures in sexual pleasure were too often neglected (Miller & Ellis, 2006). Some young men indicate that they find women's bodies to be complex puzzles that are difficult to understand (Koch, 2006). This chapter and subsequent chapters of this text recognize the sex organs of both women and men as potential sources of sexual pleasure and interpersonal intimacy.

■ The Vulva

Many externally located female sexual structures play an important role in sexual arousal (see Figure 2.1). Internal organs tend to be more important in regulating hormonal cycles and the reproductive processes. The external female sex organs, located between the legs, below and in front of the pubic symphysis (the part of the pelvic bone directly above the genitals), are known collectively as the **vulva** (see Figure 2.2). There is a great deal of variation in the size and shape of the various external female genitalia, all perfectly normal. Especially visible on the vulva are the **mons** and the **labia majora** (major or outer lips). The mons, sometimes termed the mons pubis or mons veneris, is a rounded pad of fatty tissue just above the other sex

■ FIGURE 2.1 *External Female Anatomy*

The human sex organs are important for both procreation and recreation. Historically, sex educators focused on the internal sex organs and reproduction, especially in women. In recent years, they have also focused on the pleasurable aspects of sexual behavior and the external sex organs.

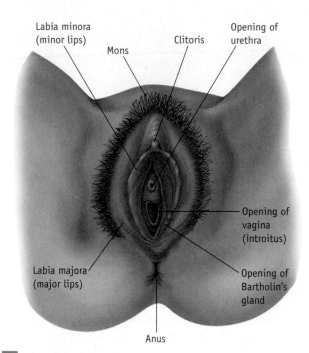

Labia minora (minor lips) · Mons · Clitoris · Opening of urethra · Opening of vagina (introitus) · Opening of Bartholin's gland · Labia majora (major lips) · Anus

■ FIGURE 2.2 *Vulva*

The external female sex organs consist of the mons, labia, and clitoris. They have numerous nerve endings and therefore are sensitive to stimulation. In shape, size, and color, the external sex organs vary greatly from woman to woman.

organs on the pubic bone. Pubic hair begins to grow on the mons during puberty, usually distributed in a roughly triangular pattern. The mons is well endowed with nerve endings, and most women find that rubbing or exerting pressure on this area may lead to sexual arousal. The entire area of the vulva is considered to be a female erogenous zone because it generally is very sensitive to sexual stimulation.

The labia majora are two folds of skin that extend from the mons down between the legs. They are relatively flat and indistinct in some women and thick and prominent in others. With the increased popularity of cosmetic surgery, some women who have been dissatisfied with the shape or size of the labia or other vulval structures have resorted to operations that change their appearance (Goodman, 2009). During puberty, the skin of the major lips darkens slightly, and hair grows on their

vulva external sex organs of the female, including the mons, major and minor lips, clitoris, and opening of the vagina.

mons cushion of fatty tissue located over the female's pubic bone.

labia majora (LAY-bee-uh mah-JOR-uh) two outer folds of skin covering the minor lips, clitoris, urinary meatus, and vaginal opening.

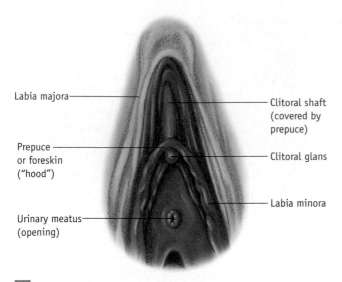

Labia majora

Prepuce
or foreskin
("hood")

Urinary meatus
(opening)

Clitoral shaft
(covered by
prepuce)

Clitoral glans

Labia minora

FIGURE 2.3 *Clitoris*

The clitoris, the most sensitive area of a female's genitals, is located just beneath the point where the tops of the minor lips meet. It is unique in that it is the only organ of either sex whose sole function is to provide sexual sensation and pleasure.

outer surfaces. These external labia cover and protect the inner, more sensitive sex organs. The inner structures cannot be seen unless the labia majora are parted, so women may find it useful to position a mirror in such a way that they are able to see the other structures.

When the major lips are separated, another pair of smaller folds of skin becomes visible, the **labia minora** (minor or inner lips). These are observed as pink, hairless, irregular, asymmetrical ridges; they meet at the top to form a sheath of skin covering the clitoris called the **prepuce** or clitoral hood (see Figure 2.3). Both the major and minor lips are sensitive to stimulation and are important in sexual arousal. Just inside the minor lips are openings to ducts connected to **Bartholin's glands,** sometimes called the vulvovaginal glands. These glands produce a small amount of secretion during sexual arousal, which may help moisten the entrance to the vagina and to some extent the labia. This secretion does not play a major role in lubrication of the vagina during arousal, however, and any other functions these glands may have are not known. Bartholin's glands can occasionally become infected with bacteria (from feces or other sources) and may require medical treatment.

Often the labia minora must be separated before the two openings between them can be seen. Just below the clitoris, a small hole is visible—the **urinary meatus,** or urethral opening. It is through this opening that urine leaves the body. Below the urethra is a larger orifice—the vaginal opening or **introitus**—that leads into the vagina. The opening of the vagina does not usually seem to be a hole and in fact may only be

recognized as an opening when something is inserted into it. In some women, particularly in younger age groups, the vaginal opening is partly covered by membranous tissue called the hymen (discussed later in the section on the vagina).

Clitoris

The **clitoris** is the most sexually sensitive female sex organ. Stimulation of the clitoris is often necessary for women to reach orgasm, although the manner in which that stimulation is best applied varies from woman to woman. The most visible part of the clitoris is usually observed as a rounded tip protruding from the hood created by the merging of the labia minora. This external, sensitive head of the clitoris is called the **glans.** For many years, it was compared to the penis because of its sensitivity to sexual stimulation and capability of engorgement with blood. It also has been inaccurately viewed as a poorly developed, nonfunctional penis. On the contrary, the clitoris and the entire internal clitoral system of blood vessels, nerves, and erectile tissue constitute a very functional and important sex organ (Martin-Alguacil, 2008).

The **shaft** of the clitoris extends back under the clitoral hood, or prepuce. The glans is the only clitoral structure that hangs free, although it is usually not particularly movable (see Figure 2.3). The clitoral shaft is attached to the body along its entire underside. The

labia minora (LAY-bee-uh mih-NOR-uh) two inner folds of skin that join above the clitoris and extend along the sides of the vaginal and urethral openings.

prepuce (PREE-Peus) in the female, tissue of the upper vulva that covers the clitoral shaft.

Bartholins (BAR-tha-lenz) small glands located in the opening through the minor lips that produce some secretion during sexual arousal.

urinary meatus (mee-AY-tuss) opening through which urine passes from the urethra to the outside of the body.

introitus (in-TROID-us) the outer opening of the vagina.

clitoris (KLIT-a-rus) sexually sensitive organ found in the female vulva; it becomes engorged with blood during arousal.

glans in the male, the sensitive head of the penis; in the female, the sensitive head of the clitoris, visible between the upper folds of the minor lips.

shaft in the female, the longer body of the clitoris, containing erectile tissue in the male, the cylindrical base of the penis that contains three columns of spongy tissue: two corpora cavernosa and a corpus spongiosum.

Real Student Voices

■ The first time I had sex with a woman, I felt intimidated because I knew so little about the female body. She was helpful, but I felt like a complete idiot. I'm glad I know more of the details now; who wants to take a trip without a map?

■ After you suggested in class that everyone should take time to get acquainted with their bodies, I decided to give it a try. I actually got a mirror and a flashlight so I could see better. I was really embarrassed at first—even though I was completely alone—but I eventually became more comfortable. It's good to know how all the pieces of the puzzle fit together.

■ It was good to learn that I'm not the only woman who has a lot of pain in the vaginal area. It really interferes with intimacy. My family doctor didn't seem to take it very seriously, and I almost felt he thought it was all in my head. I'm going to see a woman gynecologist now and try some new things.

clitoris contains two columns and two bulbs of spongy tissue, which become engorged with blood during sexual excitement, causing the entire structure to become hardened or "erect." When it is not erect, the clitoris is rarely more than an inch in length, with only the tip (glans) external and visible, but during engorgement it enlarges considerably, especially in diameter (Khalife et al., 2000). Typically, in earlier stages of arousal, the clitoris protrudes out from under the hood more than it does in an unaroused state. As arousal proceeds, it retracts out of site.

Tiny glands lining the prepuce produce oil that may mix with other secretions to form a substance called **smegma.** If this material collects around the shaft, mild infections may result. An infection could cause some pain or discomfort, especially during sexual activity. If smegma accumulations become a problem, they may be removed by a physician who inserts a small probe under the hood or prepuce.

Female Genital Cutting

In other cultures and other historical periods, the clitoris and labia have been subjected to various types of surgical removal or mutilation. In several sub-Saharan African and Eastern Asian cultures and religions, removal of all or part of the clitoris in a procedure termed **clitoridectomy**—often inaccurately called female circumcision—is still practiced as a rite of passage into adulthood. Millions of women each year worldwide undergo some form of genital cutting, sometimes called female genital mutilation (FGM). Those who advocate such practices object to the mutilation label, saying it is culturally biased. Although such cutting sometimes removes only the hood of

tissue covering the clitoris, more often the clitoral glans is removed as well. Sometimes a more extensive clitoridectomy is performed, involving removal of the entire clitoris and much of the labial tissue surrounding it (James & Robertson, 2002, 2004).

As a rite marking a girl's passage to adulthood, clitoridectomy is meant to remove any vestiges of maleness, because the clitoris typically is viewed as a miniature penis in these cultures. Thus, to have it removed is viewed as the ultimate symbol of womanhood. Clitoridectomy, however, reduces sexual pleasure, an important aspect in cultures where men are expected to control female sexuality (El-Defrawi et al., 2001). The practice seems to be perpetuated in conditions of poverty and domestic violence toward women (Jackson et al., 2003; Refaat et al., 2001). Taboos have developed in support of the practice. In Nigeria, for example, some women believe that if the head of a newborn touches the clitoris during the birth process, the baby will become insane.

Some cultures also practice **infibulation,** in which the labia minora and sometimes the labia majora are removed and the sides of the external portion of the

smegma thick, oily substance that may accumulate under the prepuce of the clitoris or penis.

clitoridectomy (clih-torr-ih-DECK-tah-mee) surgical removal of the clitoris; practiced routinely in some cultures.

infibulation (in-fib-you-LAY-shun) surgical procedure, performed in some cultures, that seals the opening of the vagina.

vagina are sewn together or fastened with thorns or natural glues, ensuring that the woman will not have intercourse prior to marriage. The fastening materials are removed at the time of marriage, although the procedure may be repeated if the husband is going to be absent for long periods of time. Tough scar tissue often forms that can make urination, menstruation, sexual intercourse, and childbirth extremely difficult and painful. Infibulation is meant to protect the virginity of the woman in those cultures that place a high premium on it as a condition of marriage.

Girls and women subjected to such procedures often get serious infections, and the unsterilized instruments have been associated with the spread of HIV. Girls sometimes die from bleeding or infection following genital cutting. There is also a growing body of evidence that ritualized surgical practices can create psychological trauma. Intuitively, we would expect this to be true, but recent research also supports the fact that such procedures can have far-reaching effects on women's sexuality and marriages (Slanger, Snow, & Okonofua, 2002). Cultural changes have brought some modernization of traditional procedures, and in some places aseptic methods are now used, lowering the risk of infection.

There has been growing worldwide condemnation toward these practices as barbaric and sexist. The United States has begun to examine the surrounding issues more closely, because it is becoming clear that some girls in immigrant families from 40 countries may have undergone the procedure in the United States. Even though some maintain that such practices represent cultural imperatives and should be respected, many courts and policy-making bodies in the more developed countries are reinforcing the notion that genital cutting constitutes a violation of human rights that should be condemned and halted.

Female genital cutting typically is deeply embedded in a particular culture's way of life and is reflective of historical patriarchal traditions in which women have been considered the possessions of men and women's sexuality has been subjugated to men. The traditions may be seen as fundamental rites of passage to adulthood and even looked upon with pride by the adult woman. Yet increasing emphasis on women's rights even in developing countries has led to growing worldwide opposition to these procedures. Debates rage within the countries where the practices still exist. Feminists in Western cultures have been particularly outspoken on this issue, insisting that such procedures not only are physically dangerous but also represent attempts to emphasize the inferior status of women. The controversy is a classic example of a clash between cultural mores and shifting values about sexuality and gender on a global level (James & Robertson, 2002, 2004).

What do you think about female genital cutting as practiced in other cultures and historical periods? How has it been justified in these cultures? Can you think of any similar North American practices? To what degree do you think people outside a particular culture have the right to play an activist role in calling for an end to such practices?

■ The Vagina

The **vagina** is a muscular tube that is important as a female organ of reproduction and sexual pleasure (see Figure 2.4). It has been celebrated as an organ of mystery and power throughout human history (Blackledge, 2004). The muscular walls of the vagina, which are very elastic, sit together except when something is inserted into the cavity, so the inner cavity is best described as a "potential" space. The vagina is usually about 4 inches deep, although during sexual arousal it deepens. The inner lining of the vagina is fleshy and soft and is corrugated by thin ridges of tissue. The area near the opening of the vagina, along with the outer third of the vagina itself, has many nerve endings, and stimulation easily leads to sexual arousal; the inner part of the vagina, however, is not particularly sensitive.

Two sets of muscles surround the vaginal opening: the *sphincter vaginae* and *levator ani* muscles. Women can exert some degree of control over these muscles, but tension, pain, or fear can lead to contraction of the outer vaginal muscles such that insertion of anything becomes difficult or painful for the woman. This condition, called **vaginismus,** is discussed in more detail in Chapter 18, "Sexual Dysfunctions and Their Treatment." Women can also exert some control over the inner **pubococcygeus (PC) muscle,** which much like the anal sphincter may be contracted or relaxed (Levin, 2003). This muscle may play a role in orgasmic response, and its tone can be improved by exercises, as is true of all voluntary muscles (see Kegel exercises in Chapter 4, "Human Sexual Arousal and Response").

It is important to note that the vagina cannot contract to the extent that it might trap the penis inside

vagina (vu-JI-na) muscular canal in the female that is responsive to sexual arousal; it receives semen during heterosexual intercourse for reproduction.

vaginismus (vaj-uh-NIZ-mus) involuntary spasm of the outer vaginal musculature, making penetration of the vagina difficult or impossible.

pubococcygeus (PC) muscle (pyub-o-kox-a-JEE-us) part of the supporting musculature of the vagina that is involved in orgasmic response and over which a woman can exert some control.

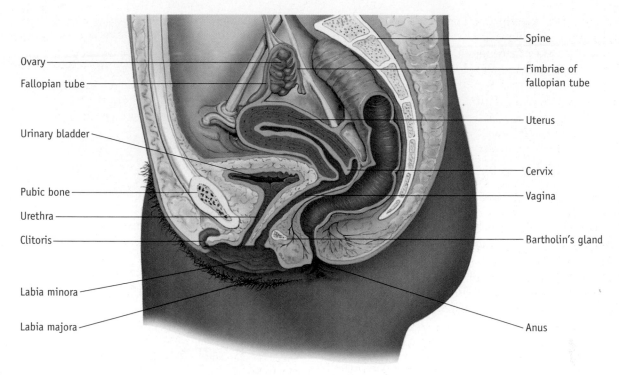

Ovary
Fallopian tube
Urinary bladder
Pubic bone
Urethra
Clitoris
Labia minora
Labia majora

Spine
Fimbriae of fallopian tube
Uterus
Cervix
Vagina
Bartholin's gland
Anus

FIGURE 2.4 *Female Sexual and Reproductive Organs*

(penis captivus), even though some people have heard rumors to the contrary. Africa has many myths about people becoming stuck together during sex and having to be sent to the hospital for separation. Such myths seem to serve a social function in discouraging marital infidelity. When dogs mate, the penis erects in such a way that it is caught inside the vagina until erection subsides, but while this is important to successful mating in canines, nothing similar occurs in humans. During sexual arousal in a woman, a lubricating substance is secreted through the inner lining of the vagina. This is discussed further in Chapter 4, "Human Sexual Arousal and Response."

Douching

Over the years, women have developed various techniques for washing out the vagina, sometimes called douching. Some women believe that menstrual blood is dirty and therefore needs to be washed out. In fact the vagina has its own cleansing mechanisms and a rather delicate balance of naturally occurring microorganisms that are important to its health. Studies continue to demonstrate that, contrary to popular notions, douching is actually dangerous. It can force disease organisms up into the uterus, increasing the risks for uterine and vaginal infection. Women who douche regularly are more likely to get pelvic inflammatory disease than women who douche seldom or not at all. The vagina's natural cleansing mechanisms may be disrupted by

douching, putting women at increased risk for sexually transmitted diseases. Unless prescribed for a specific medical condition, douching should be avoided (Brotman et al., 2008; Tsai, Shepherd, & Vermund, 2009).

Hymen

The **hymen,** present in the vaginal opening from birth, is a tissue that usually has one or more openings. There are many different shapes of hymens that cover varying portions of the introitus (see Figure 2.5). The most common type of hymen is annular, meaning that the hymenal tissue surrounds the entire opening of the vagina, with an opening in the middle. Some hymens have tissue that extends into the introitus. The cribriform hymen has a web of tissue over the introitus, in which there may be several small openings; the septate hymen has a single band of tissue that divides the introitus into two distinct apertures. In a very few girls, the hymen has no openings. In this case, the menstrual flow builds up in the vagina and uterus, causing pain and swelling until a physician makes an incision in this **imperforate hymen,** quickly relieving the condition. Occasionally, the hymen is especially thick and tough,

hymen membranous tissue that can cover part of the vaginal opening.

imperforate hymen condition in which the hymen has no natural openings.

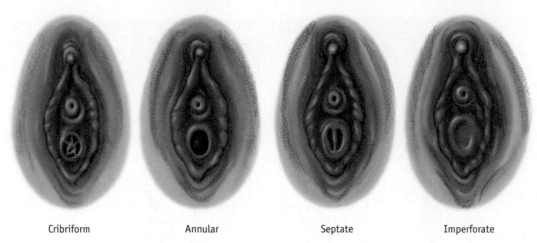

| Cribriform | Annular | Septate | Imperforate |

FIGURE 2.5 *Hymen*

A thin, delicate membrane, the hymen partially covers the vaginal opening in a variety of ways. It may bridge the vagina, surround it, or have several different shapes and sizes in the opening to the outside of the body. It has no known physiological function but historically has had psychological and cultural significance as a sign of virginity.

a condition called **fibrous hymen.** This condition can lead to pain during sexual activity and may be treated surgically (Stewart & Spencer, 2002).

Most hymens have a large enough opening to admit a finger or a tampon. Attempting to insert anything larger, such as the erect penis, usually results in some tearing of the hymen. There are many ways other than sexual activity in which a hymen may be ruptured. The absence of a hymen at birth is an unlikely occurrence, if it occurs at all.

Some hymens apparently are flexible enough to withstand coitus, or sexual intercourse. Consequently, the presence or absence of a hymen is an unreliable indicator of a woman's virginity or nonvirginity. Some societies place special significance on the presence of the hymen and hold rituals for the rupturing of the hymen before a girl's first intercourse.

If the hymen is present the first time sexual penetration of the vagina occurs, discomfort or pain and possibly some bleeding may occur when the hymen is torn. The degree of pain varies in different women from slight to severe. If a woman is concerned about this, she may spend some time prior to the first penetration inserting fingers into the opening of the hymen, gradually widening it. A physician may cut the hymen or stretch its opening with dilators of gradually increasing size. During sexual intercourse, there is usually little trouble inserting the penis through the hymen if the male partner persists with careful and gentle prodding with the erect penis and uses adequate lubrication. The woman also may take responsibility for guiding her partner in controlling the timing and depth of penetration.

 See "Self-Awareness" on SexSource Online.

Genital Self-Examination for Women

After they acquaint themselves with their basic external anatomy, it is a good idea for women to examine their genitals monthly, checking for any unusual signs or symptoms. Using a mirror and adequate light, look through pubic hairs to the underlying skin, and pull back the clitoral prepuce or hood. Then part the inner lips, exposing the area around the urethral and vaginal openings more fully. These areas generally should be free of any unusual bumps, sores, or blisters. If such lesions are present, they may be red or light-colored or may be more easily felt than seen. Be sure to look on the inside of each major and minor lip for similar signs. It is a good idea to become aware of what your normal vaginal discharge looks like so you will notice any changes in its color, odor, or consistency. Although such changes may occur normally over the course of the monthly menstrual cycle, some diseases cause distinct changes in vaginal discharge.

Anytime you notice unusual bumps or discharges from the genitals, you should consult a physician or other clinician specializing in women's health concerns. Often these symptoms do not need treatment, but they may signal the beginnings of an infection requiring medical attention. It is important to report any pain or burning upon urination, bleeding between menstrual periods, pain in the pelvic region, or an itchy rash around the vagina (Stewart & Spencer, 2002).

fibrous hymen condition in which the hymen is composed of unnaturally thick, tough tissue.

Real People

Karina: Confronting a New Sexual Way of Life

Karina came to college from a small town and had always maintained relatively conservative values on matters related to sex. She had a serious boyfriend during her junior and senior years of high school. While they had participated in some kissing and mutual touching, they did not share sexual intercourse or oral sex until the summer after their first year together. Karina had been relatively happy with their relationship, and it was difficult for both of them to make the decision to end it when they chose to attend colleges about 2,000 miles apart.

With her committed relationship behind her, Karina has decided that her first year of college will be a time of exploration and experimentation for her. She feels it is important to find out more about the kind of men she enjoys being with. During her first semester, she also drinks alcohol more frequently, another activity she generally avoided in high school. She meets male students easily and several times has hooked up with them sexually. Two of the men are interested in pursuing a more

serious relationship with Karina, but she prefers to keep things casual with these two because she does not find them interesting enough for a long-term relationship. She has talked with two of her friends quite easily about the relationships, and one of them has cautioned her that she is going overboard with casual sex. She replies that she always makes sure a condom is used and also takes birth control pills. She feels that she has been responsible, but sometimes she also feels somewhat guilty that others perceive her as irresponsible or easy. She wonders if alcohol has interfered with her judgment.

If Karina were to ask for your opinion about the choices she has made, what would you say to her? On what information or personal values do you base your response? Do you feel as though Karina is judging herself too harshly, or not harshly enough? Why? What are your feelings regarding drinking and making sexual decisions?

Disorders of the Female Sex Organs

The female sex and urinary organs may be the sites of infection not transmitted through sexual behavior. **Acute urethral syndrome,** an infection of the urethra, and **cystitis,** a bladder infection, are common complaints and may represent recurrent problems for some women. Urinary tract infections in younger women are associated with frequent sexual intercourse and recent use of diaphragms and spermicides. The symptoms include a frequent urge to urinate, burning or pain on urination, and possibly severe pain during sexual intercourse or when the urethra and bladder are placed under pressure.

Interstitial cystitis (IC) is a less common, chronic bladder condition that can be quite debilitating in some women and can interfere with their sex lives. Medical professionals frequently fail to recognize these diseases as the cause of such symptoms and may assume that the woman is imagining the problem. Antibiotics and other medications can be used for treatment. Because one of the most common bacteria to cause cystitis is **E. coli** (short for *Escherichia coli*), the organism that lives in the colon and is found in feces, good personal

hygiene is the best preventative measure. Wiping from front to back after a bowel movement is always advisable, as is frequent washing of the vaginal and anal areas. Another good precaution is drinking plenty of liquids and urinating frequently. Washing and urinating after sexual activity may help cleanse the urethral area of any bacteria that might cause cystitis.

The vagina can be subject to several disorders. One of the more common problems is associated with pain in the vulvovaginal area that may interfere with sexual activity and pleasure. Chronic vulvar pain, called

acute urethral syndrome infection or irritation of the urethra.

cystitis (sis-TITE-us) a nonsexually transmitted infection of the urinary bladder.

interstitial cystitis (IC) a chronic bladder inflammation that can cause debilitating discomfort and interfere with sexual enjoyment.

E. coli bacteria naturally living in the human colon that often cause urinary tract infection.

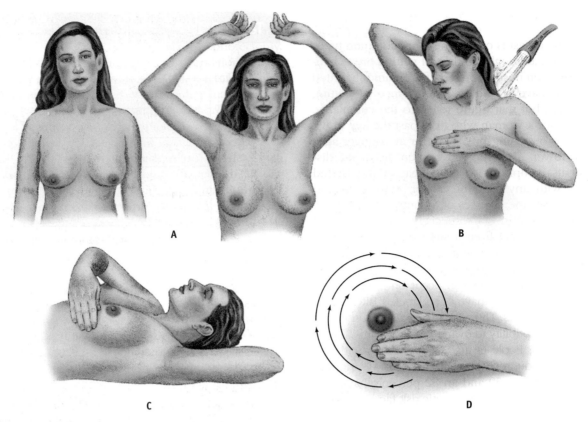

FIGURE 2.10 *Breast Self-Examination*

It is important for a woman to examine her breasts regularly. She should look at her breasts in the mirror, first with her arms at her sides and then with them raised over her head **(A).** In the shower, her hands can easily move over her wet skin **(B).** When she is lying down, a woman can easily examine her breast tissue **(C),** and she should repeat the procedure when in an upright position. The fingers should be held flat and move in complete clockwise circles around the outer portion of the breast, then move progressively inward toward the nipple **(D).**

your arms high above your head and look for any changes in the contour or skin of either breast. Look for any swelling or dimpling of the skin or for any unusual signs in either nipple. Next place your hands on your hips and flex the chest muscles, again looking for any unusual signs.

Manual Examination

The breasts may be easily examined during a bath or shower because the hands can glide easily over wet skin. Another option is to examine them while lying down. Place a pillow under the shoulder on the same side as the breast to be examined and place that hand under your head. Use the opposite hand for the actual examination. The fingers should be held together, forming a flat surface. Begin on the outer part of the breast, and move in complete clockwise circles around the outer regions, checking for lumps, hard knots, or any unusual thickening. Then move inward toward the nipple about an inch and circle the breast again. Usually you will need to make at least four concentric circles to examine every part of the breast. It is a good idea to repeat this procedure while sitting or standing,

because the upright position redistributes breast tissue. Finally, squeeze each nipple to see if there is any discharge from either breast (see Figure 2.10).

If you find any unusual features in a breast, do not panic. Many nonmalignant conditions can cause lumps, swelling, and discharge, but you should not take any chances. Always consult a physician, who can then prescribe further testing to determine whether the abnormality represents a malignancy.

Breast Screening Techniques

A test that is recommended on a regular basis for women over the age of 40 or 50 is **mammography.** A special X-ray picture is taken of the breast and can detect even small lumps. Only low-level radiation is used to produce the image, called a mammogram. Some women are averse to or fearful of the test because it is uncomfortable, but it poses no hazards. There has been some controversy over the age at

mammography sensitive X-ray technique used to discover small breast tumors.

which women should begin having mammography on a regular basis. Some research studies have reinforced the recommendations of the American Medical Association and the American Cancer Society that a baseline mammogram be taken at around age 35 and that annual mammograms then be taken beginning at age 40. About 15 percent of breast cancers detected by mammography were in women under age 50. Other research has found that malignancies in younger age groups tend to grow faster, making early detection and treatment even more crucial. Some research has shown that use of mammograms does not necessarily reduce the overall number of deaths from breast cancer. However, the Department of Health and Human Services still takes the position that, individually, mammograms yield earlier detection and treatment and therefore should be considered a routine part of women's health care (Marshall, 2002).

Modern medicine has made great strides in treatment and cure of malignant tumors. A woman who develops breast cancer has a 50 percent chance of being diagnosed after the age of 65 and now has a 65 percent chance of surviving the illness and ultimately dying from another cause. Various combinations of radiation therapy, chemotherapy, and administration of hormone-inhibiting medications can be used. Sometimes it is necessary to remove the entire breast in a surgical procedure called a **mastectomy,** but current research indicates that a **lumpectomy,** removal of only the lump itself and some surrounding tissue, is often sufficient. Breast cancer and surgeries to remove it represent traumatic events in a woman's life and often affect her feelings of attractiveness and her sexual feelings. Again, early discovery of unusual growths in the breast is a woman's best protection.

■ The Menstrual Cycle

Of special importance to the female's role in reproduction is the **menstrual cycle.** From the time of first menstruation, called **menarche,** to the period of life when her menstruation ceases, called **menopause** (or climacteric), a woman's body goes through a periodic cycle that involves hormonal, psychological, and physical changes. This menstrual cycle involves the maturation of an ovum and the periodic preparation of the uterus for pregnancy, followed by a gradual return to the unprepared state if pregnancy does not occur.

Today, menarche usually occurs sometime between the ages of 9 and 16, although variations from this range are normal. The onset of menopause typically is between the ages of 45 and 55. The years between menarche and menopause constitute a woman's potential childbearing years, although she is actually able to conceive only for a day or two usually once a month. In mature women, an average entire menstrual cycle lasts about 28 days, although it may fluctuate a great deal in individuals. In teenage girls, the length of the cycle tends to be more irregular and slightly longer, averaging closer to 31 days (Cole, Ladner, & Byrn, 2009).

It is important for girls to be prepared for menarche through appropriate educational efforts. In the past, girls have been frightened by their first menstruation because they had not been educated about what to expect. When effective education about the menstrual cycle is provided prior to menarche, girls tend to have much more positive attitudes toward the experience and toward their bodies.

The menstrual cycle is regulated by a complex interaction of hormones secreted by the *pituitary gland,* located at the base of the brain; a portion of the brain itself called the *hypothalamus;* and the ovaries. The pituitary gland acts as a sort of relay station between the hypothalamus and the ovaries. The hypothalamus produces **gonadotropin-releasing hormone (GnRH),** which stimulates the pituitary gland to produce two hormones, follicle-stimulating hormone and luteinizing hormone, which in turn regulate hormonal secretion by the ovaries. How these hormones control the reproductive organs is described in the following sections. Although the menstrual cycle is continuous, we divide it into four stages, or phases, for ease of explanation: the follicular phase, ovulation, luteal secretion, and menstruation. There is some research to indicate that levels of sexual interest vary through the different phases of the cycle, possibly related to evolutionary adaptation (Garver-Apgar, Gangestad, & Thornhill, 2008).

Preovulatory Preparation or Follicular Phase

During the first stage of the menstrual cycle (see Figure 2.11), two important things must take place: the maturation of an ovum in one of the ovarian follicles and the beginning preparation of the uterus for the

---

mastectomy surgical removal of all or part of a breast.

lumpectomy surgical removal of a breast lump, along with a small amount of surrounding tissue.

menstrual cycle the hormonal interactions that prepare a woman's body for possible pregnancy at roughly monthly intervals.

menarche (MEN-are-kee) onset of menstruation at puberty.

menopause (MEN-a-pawz) time in midlife when menstruation ceases.

gonadotropin-releasing hormone (GnRH) (go-nad-a-TRO-pen) hormone from the hypothalamus that stimulates the release of FSH and LH by the pituitary.

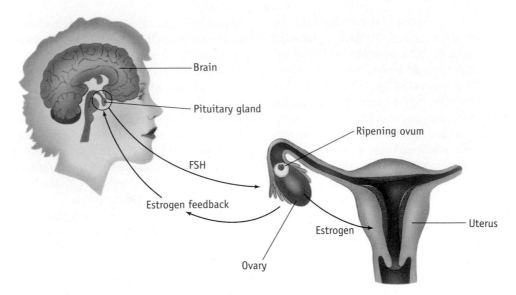

FIGURE 2.11 *Preovulatory Preparation*

In the first stage of the menstrual cycle, the maturity of the ovum begins. Follicle-stimulating hormone (FSH) from the pituitary gland influences the production of estrogen by the ovaries that causes the lining of the uterus to thicken in preparation for a fertilized ovum.

nourishment of an embryo, in case the ovum is fertilized. These developments are initiated by the secretion of **follicle-stimulating hormone (FSH)** from the pituitary gland into the bloodstream. The FSH influences the ovaries to ripen one or more of the ova in a follicle and also to increase their production of estrogen. The estrogen works directly on the inner lining of the uterus (endometrium), causing it to thicken gradually with enlargement of its many small glands and blood vessels. The estrogen also exerts a feedback effect on the pituitary gland, so that as the estrogen level in the blood increases, the production of FSH by the pituitary decreases. In the later days of this phase, and just prior to the surge of another hormone, many women seem to develop stronger sexual desire, more sexual fantasies, and actually walk in ways that are more sexually attractive to men (Bullivant et al., 2004; Provost, Quinsey, & Troje, 2008).

Ovulation

When a high concentration of estrogen is reached (see Figure 2.12), the hypothalamus triggers the release of **luteinizing hormone (LH)** from the pituitary. This hormone causes development of the egg to stop and triggers a chain of chemical and physical events responsible for the rupturing of the mature ovum through the outer wall of one ovary—the process of **ovulation** (Park et al., 2004). After the ovum has left the ovary, the follicle remains as a tiny mass of cells called the **corpus luteum.** Under the influence of LH, the corpus luteum becomes a small gland. Studies of women's experience of the menstrual cycle have suggested that

women tend to have higher levels of sexual arousability around the time of ovulation, possibly the result of the increased levels of a particular biochemical in the bloodstream at that time in the cycle. Also, some research suggests that the increase in sexual desire and initiation of sexual activity in women during this part of the menstrual cycle is particularly evident in women in committed relationships (Nappi et al., 2003; Pillsworth, Haselton, & Buss, 2004).

Luteal Secretion

With stimulation by LH, the corpus luteum begins secreting another essential hormone, **progesterone,** along with more estrogen (see Figure 2.13). These hormones further thicken the uterine lining and cause

follicle-stimulating hormone (FSH) pituitary hormone that stimulates the ovaries or testes.

luteinizing hormone (LH) (LEW-tee-in-ize-ing) pituitary hormone that triggers ovulation in the ovaries and stimulates sperm production in the testes.

ovulation release of a mature ovum through the wall of an ovary.

corpus luteum cell cluster of the follicle that remains after the ovum is released; secretes hormones that help regulate the menstrual cycle.

progesterone (pro-JES-ter-one) ovarian hormone that causes the uterine lining to thicken.

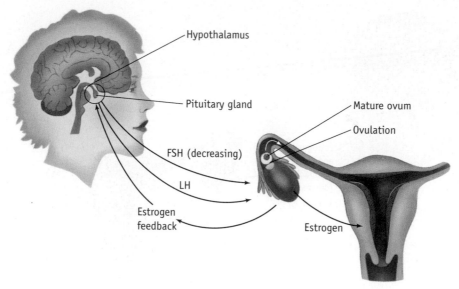

FIGURE 2.12 *Ovulation*

The pituitary gland is stimulated to release the luteinizing hormone by the presence of estrogen. This in turn causes the mature ovum to rupture through the outer wall of one ovary (the process of ovulation). The follicle that remains becomes an active gland called the corpus luteum.

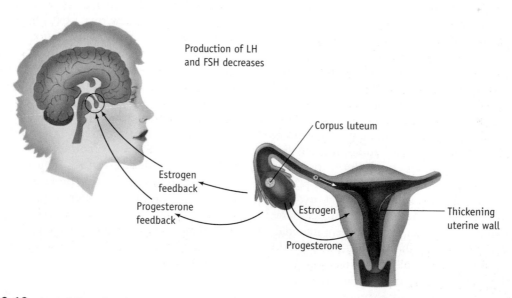

FIGURE 2.13 *Luteal Secretion*

The corpus luteum begins secreting progesterone as well as more estrogen, which further thickens the uterine lining in preparation for the possibility that the ovum will be fertilized as it moves through the fallopian tube.

it to begin secreting its own nutrient fluids that can nourish an embryo if pregnancy occurs. The progesterone also has a feedback effect on the hypothalamus, causing it to shut off the production of GnRH. This in turn decreases the production of LH and FSH. While these developments are happening, the ovum is slowly being moved through one of the fallopian tubes toward the uterus, a journey of three or four days. If the ovum is fertilized by a sperm, the fertiliza-tion will occur in the fallopian tube. If the ovum is not fertilized, it disintegrates.

Menstruation

If the ovum is not fertilized, the corpus luteum degenerates and the production of progesterone ceases. The estrogen level in the bloodstream begins to fall, and the thickened lining of the uterus begins to degenerate.

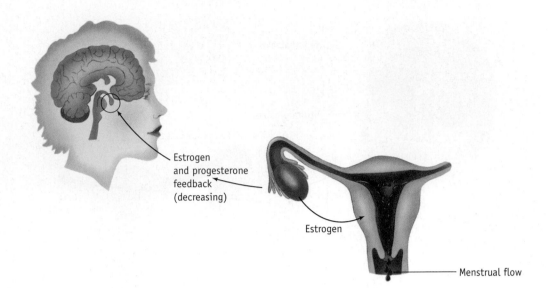

Estrogen
and progesterone
feedback
(decreasing)

Estrogen

Menstrual flow

■ **FIGURE 2.14** *Menstruation*

If the ovum is not fertilized, the corpus luteum degenerates, and the progesterone and estrogen levels begin to decrease. The portion of the uterus that had begun to thicken now begins to slough off and is lost, along with some blood, through the vagina over a period of days.

Uterine cellular material, fluids, and a small amount of blood (usually about 2 to 5 ounces) are then lost through the vagina over a period of from three to seven days. This is called **menstruation** or the menstrual period (see Figure 2.14). The estrogen level continues to fall and eventually becomes low enough that the pituitary again begins to produce FSH, initiating the menstrual cycle all over again (see Table 2.2).

Unless a woman experiences pain during menstruation (called **dysmenorrhea**) or some other medical problem, there is no need to curtail any activities during menstruation. There are a number of products that can be used to absorb the menstrual flow. These include various sizes of absorbent pads that are held over the vaginal opening by adhesive that sticks to the underpants. Tampons, cylinders of absorbent material, can be inserted directly into the vagina. Tampons do not stretch the vagina and usually cause no damage to an intact hymen. They are favored by many women who prefer not to wear a pad externally. Because highly absorbent tampons may become breeding areas for bacteria, eventually causing toxic shock syndrome, it is best to use low-absorbency tampons and to change them every four to eight hours (Kelley, 2005).

In some Native American, Eastern, and Jewish cultures, the menstruating female is considered (primarily by the male hierarchy) to be unclean, and sexual intercourse is prohibited during the menstrual period. Even though men and women in these cultures may subscribe to these social imperatives publicly, they do not necessarily do so in private (Guterman, 2008). Research indicates that college-educated, heterosexual women in the United States are less likely to engage in all sexual activities during menstruation, perhaps be-

cause of lowered physical interest but also because of social and psychological factors. Women who are more comfortable with their own sexuality tend also to be more comfortable with menstruation and with having sex during their periods (Rempel & Baumgartner, 2003). No particular medical risks are associated with sexual activity during the period per se, although if a woman is infected with HIV, the presence of blood in the vagina may increase the risk that a sexual partner could become infected. Use of a condom would reduce that risk. Some women experience variations in their sex drive during various stages of the menstrual cycle and may also show preferences for different types of men during the different phases (Gangestad & Cousins, 2002; Jones et al., 2008). Although there is less chance of pregnancy resulting from intercourse during menstruation, it should not be assumed that it is a totally safe time.

Menstrual Discomfort and Control

Many women experience some physical discomfort and psychological shifts just prior to or during menstruation. Symptoms include headaches, backaches, fatigue, fluid retention, uterine cramping, breast tenderness, anxiety, depression, and irritability. In 5 to 10

menstruation (men-stru-AY-shun) phase of the menstrual cycle in which the inner uterine lining breaks down and sloughs off; the tissue, along with some blood, flows out through the vagina; also called the period.

dysmenorrhea (dis-men-a-REE-a) painful menstruation.

Table 2.2 Summary of the Menstrual Cycle

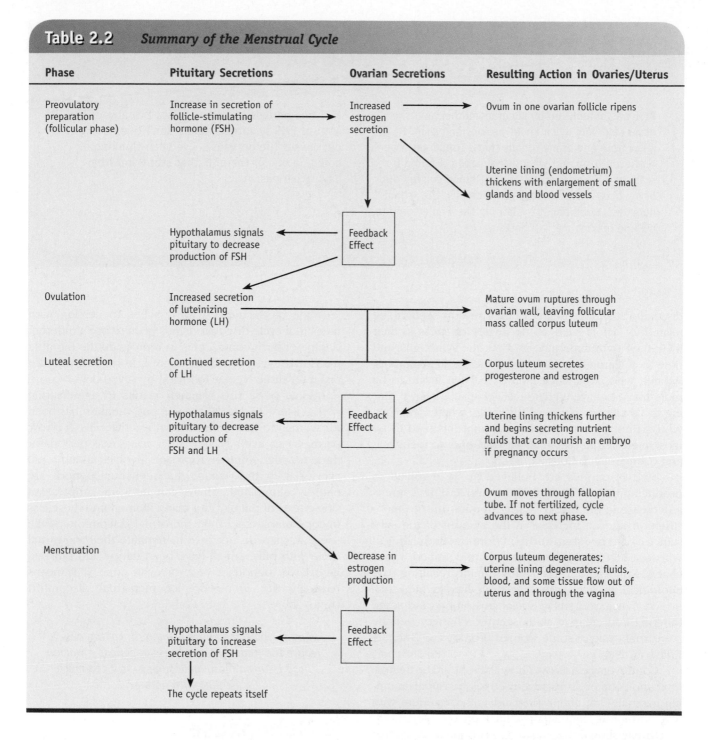

Phase	Pituitary Secretions	Ovarian Secretions	Resulting Action in Ovaries/Uterus
Preovulatory preparation (follicular phase)	Increase in secretion of follicle-stimulating hormone (FSH)	Increased estrogen secretion	Ovum in one ovarian follicle ripens
			Uterine lining (endometrium) thickens with enlargement of small glands and blood vessels
	Hypothalamus signals pituitary to decrease production of FSH	Feedback Effect	
Ovulation	Increased secretion of luteinizing hormone (LH)		Mature ovum ruptures through ovarian wall, leaving follicular mass called corpus luteum
Luteal secretion	Continued secretion of LH		Corpus luteum secretes progesterone and estrogen
	Hypothalamus signals pituitary to decrease production of FSH and LH	Feedback Effect	Uterine lining thickens further and begins secreting nutrient fluids that can nourish an embryo if pregnancy occurs
			Ovum moves through fallopian tube. If not fertilized, cycle advances to next phase.
Menstruation		Decrease in estrogen production	Corpus luteum degenerates; uterine lining degenerates; fluids, blood, and some tissue flow out of uterus and through the vagina
	Hypothalamus signals pituitary to increase secretion of FSH	Feedback Effect	
	The cycle repeats itself		

percent of women, these symptoms may become severe enough to interfere with daily activities, and up to 30 percent have enough discomfort to seek treatment for what has come to be known as **premenstrual syndrome (PMS),** although PMS is not considered a true medical diagnosis. A small number of these women have a good deal of emotional distress as part of their PMS, including depression, anxiety, and restlessness. These more severe psychological symptoms have been classified as **premenstrual dysphoric disorder (PMDD),** which has been considered a specific

medical and psychiatric category (Yonkers, O'Brien, & Eriksson, 2008). However, there are many individual differences in how women experience and react to these

premenstrual syndrome (PMS) symptoms of physical discomfort, moodiness, and emotional tension that occur in some women for a few days prior to menstruation.

premenstrual dysphoric disorder (PMDD) severe emotional symptoms such as anxiety or depression around the time of menstruation.

Real Student Voices

■ I was brought up by my grandmother, and she never said very much about periods and such. I knew from one of my friends that I would get a period eventually, but when it happened, I found it scary and unsettling. The idea of blood coming out of my body made me feel sick. Actually, the school nurse was good about explaining the whole thing to me and making me feel better.

■ I find periods to be annoying. I've always had a lot of PMS symptoms, and I don't like having to put my sex life on pause. I've been thinking of going on one of the pills that stops you from having periods.

discomforts, and the degree of their severity seems to be related to factors such as the degree of stress in their lives, their own expectations about the symptoms, and how they learned to think about menstrual symptoms. Women who experience PMS have been found to be more likely to have higher levels of sexual interest during the ovulatory phase of the cycle, whereas women who do not have premenstrual complaints tend to be most interested in sexual activity just prior to menstruation (Gangestad & Cousins, 2002).

Two hormones are believed to be involved in producing the discomfort of PMS and PMDD. There is a decrease in the level of progesterone prior to menstruation and an increase in the amount of the substance called **prostaglandin,** a hormonelike chemical whose source in the body is as yet unidentified. These changes may lead to physiological and resulting psychological effects. Some research has in fact confirmed that mood shifts, social frustration, and some thinking and creative skills seem to change over the menstrual cycle in some women (Yonkers, O'Brien, & Eriksson, 2008).

Controversy exists over how PMS should be treated. Over-the-counter drugs advertised for menstrual cramping generally are antiprostaglandins that interfere with that hormone's contracting effects on the uterus. Research has shown that antidepressant medications that maintain levels of the chemical serotonin in the brain may help relieve PMS symptoms in many women. Some authorities have recommended changes in diet to help alleviate PMS. The most common suggestions are to reduce the intake of salt, refined sugar, and caffeinated foods such as coffee, colas, and chocolate. Eating more frequently during the day, taking high dosages of certain vitamins, increasing fiber intake, and drinking herbal teas have been recommended. In general, however, physicians remain skeptical over the efficacy of many remedies suggested for PMS.

One of the newest approaches to dealing with menstrual cycle discomforts has been to use a different dosage of birth control pills to reprogram the monthly menstrual cycle. For birth control, hormonal pills are taken for three weeks, followed by seven days of nonhormonal pills. This regimen results in a menstrual period every 28 days. However, one variation has been for women to take 84 hormonally active pills in a row so they can actually skip their menstrual period for three months. Another approach involves taking a pill every day of the year so that menstrual periods are entirely eliminated. There can be some unpleasant side effects of pill use, but many women find these less uncomfortable than their menstrual discomfort. While some women do not care to regulate their menstrual cycle with pills, others have been happy and satisfied with fewer periods a year, or even none, if it means reducing the occurrence of menstrual discomfort (Kalb, 2003).

What do you think about using birth control pills to reduce the frequency of menstrual periods a woman has? Is this a reasonable step, or is it too much fiddling with nature?

■ Menopause

Aging is a natural process among living things, with predictable physiological changes occurring over time at all levels, from cells to entire organ systems. For humans, it apparently is a process that is largely genetically controlled. Various degenerative physiological aspects of aging are triggered by genes, although

prostaglandin hormonelike chemical whose concentrations increase in a woman's body just prior to menstruation.

Changes before "The Change"

There is no typical perimenopause. Some women experience few or no symptoms. Others are not so lucky; they suffer from a wide range of symptoms. Some of the most common:

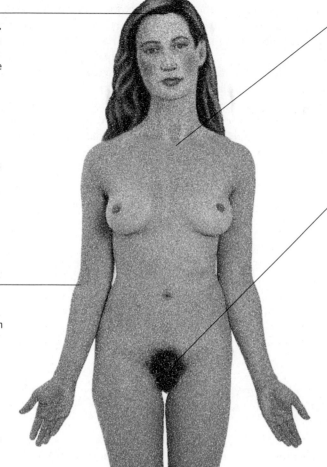

Memory lapses and loss of concentration. Some women who take estrogen report an improvement in cognitive function.

Headaches. May be caused by fluctuating hormone levels. Some women begin to suffer migraines.

Mood swings. Changes in hormone levels may interfere with the production of the body's mood-regulator serotonin. Some women feel anxious or weepy.

Dry skin. A decrease in the protein collagen—which may be linked to a decline in estrogen—means less elasticity and more wrinkles.

Bone loss. Declining reproductive hormones translate to less protection for bones. The problem is at its worst after menopause.

Hot flashes. Many perimenopausal women experience them, mostly around the head and upper body. They usually last several minutes. Nocturnal hot flashes, which are known as night sweats, can lead to insomnia.

Erratic menstrual cycles. A classic symptom of perimenopause. Cycles vary widely from 18 days to missed periods. Excessive bleeding is common.

Vaginal dryness. As estrogen levels decline, the vaginal wall thins and becomes less elastic. Intercourse may become painful.

Urinary incontinence. As the vaginal wall weakens, the bladder loses support and urination is harder to control.

FIGURE 2.15 *Perimenopause*

our bodies also experience other effects of normal wear and tear. There are wide individual differences, but each of us experiences a gradual process of slowing down and becoming physically less pliable. Although its rate may be affected by heredity, the environment, and personal health habits, the aging process is inevitable and irreversible. The sexual implications of aging stem from both psychological and biological changes (Connell et al., 2005). Aging bodies may be perceived as having beauty and strength if they are approached with a positive psychological attitude.

The female body is genetically programmed to cease menstruating sometime in middle age, usually between the ages of 45 and 55. This is called menopause, and the years surrounding menopause are usually termed **perimenopause** (see Figure 2.15). In popular usage, it is sometimes called the change of life, simply the change, or a more recently suggested term, the pause. Modifications in ovarian function usually begin prior to age 30, marked by a gradual decline in the hormonal output of these glands. Structures in the brain contribute to the changes. Eventually there is increased irregularity in ovulation and menstrual periods. Usually there are unpredictable sequences of scanty menstrual flow or increased flow, but a few

perimenopause the time of a woman's life surrounding menopause, characterized by symptoms resulting from reduced estrogen levels.

women simply stop menstruating quite abruptly, never having another period. Although the pituitary gland continues to produce FSH and LH that help control the woman's menstrual cycle, the ovaries apparently become increasingly insensitive to their stimulation. The hormone-producing tissues of the ovaries atrophy until their output of estrogen and progesterone becomes minimal (Dennerstein, Alexander, & Kotz, 2004; Freeman et al., 2008).

As the woman's hormonal levels drop, the most noticeable result usually is the gradual cessation of menstruation, resulting from the lack of hormonal stimulation to the inner lining of the uterus, or endometrium. This means, of course, that the woman is no longer able to conceive, although most physicians recommend using birth control for a full year after the last menstrual period. However, there are other effects on the body as well. Very gradually, the uterus and breasts decrease somewhat in size. The inner walls of the vagina become thinner, and a reduction in the number of small blood vessels in the pelvic region may result in reduced vaginal lubrication. There also may be changes in the texture and color of the skin and hair and an increased tendency to gain weight, especially on the hips. Women sometimes experience noticeable changes in the quality of the voice (Dennerstein, Alexander, & Kotz, 2004; Van Voorhis et al., 2008).

Another consequence of decreased estrogen production in some women is a weakening of bones, called **osteoporosis.** This condition most frequently strikes postmenopausal women who are slender and slight and who have led sedentary lives. Women suffering from osteoporosis are predisposed to fractures of the hip and arm, and they often suffer chronic back pain because of vertebral collapse. Although this condition cannot be completely cured, it can be treated to reduce the amount of bone weakness. The usual treatments involve the prescription of vitamin D, calcium supplements, estrogen replacement, and/or exercise (see Table 2.3).

Menopausal changes in the body's hormonal balances may also cause mood alterations and other psychological effects. Some women complain of depression, irritability, or other emotional symptoms. Some experience unpredictable dilation of the blood vessels in the skin, causing a flushed, sweaty feeling called a **hot flash;** its exact cause is unknown. We should not lose

> **osteoporosis** (ah-stee-o-po-ROW-sus) disease caused by loss of calcium from the bones in postmenopausal women, leading to brittle bones and stooped posture.
>
> **hot flash** a flushed, sweaty feeling in the skin caused by dilated blood vessels; often associated with menopause.

Table 2.3   *The Facts about Menopause*

Factors Affecting Onset

- Smoking. It can bring on menopause as much as two years earlier.
- Left-handedness. Onset is about one year earlier.
- Number of pregnancies. The more pregnancies you've had, the later menopause may arrive.
- Onset of menstruation. If you began menstruating at an early age, menopause will likely be later.
- Mother's age at menopause. Although other factors come into play, heredity makes the age your mother's menopause began a good guidepost.

What Happens to Your Body?

- As early as age 35, estrogen production slows, signaling perimenopause—the beginning of the change of life.
- Premenstrual syndrome may increase or appear for the first time.
- Menstrual cycles may become erratic.
- You still can become pregnant.
- Night sweats and hot flashes may occur.
- Vaginal dryness may develop.
- Sleep may be disrupted.
- Mood swings or difficulty with concentration may occur.
- After you have had no periods for a year, you are postmenopausal. You become susceptible to osteoporosis and have an increased risk of cardiovascular disease.

Demographics

- Menopause commonly occurs between ages 45 and 55. Average age is 51.
- 40 million American women already have reached menopause.
- Most women will live one-third of their life after menopause.
- For every 2,000 postmenopausal women, 20 will develop severe bone loss, 6 will develop breast cancer; and 3 will develop endometrial cancer.

Estrogen Pros

- Can help prevent osteoporosis (the loss of bone mass).
- May help prevent the onset of cardiovascular disease.

Estrogen Cons

- Can increase the risk of endometrial cancer.
- Can increase the risk of breast cancer.

What Men Should Know about Menopause

- Everything women should know.
- Passage through menopause can take from one to three years.
- Some drying of the vagina occurs, so lubricants will be necessary during intercourse, and lengthened foreplay is in order.
- Lack of sleep can contribute to irritability and fatigue, making your partner more difficult to live with. She may cry easily.
- Be understanding, and do your share around the house.

Source: From Nancy McVicar, "The Facts about Menopause" in *Sun-Sentinel,* December 12, 1991. Reprinted with permission from the *South Florida Sun-Sentinel.*

sight of the fact that life's major transitions are often and understandably accompanied by some degree of sadness and sense of loss, and these feelings do not have to be perceived as signs of pathology or psychological problems. A loss of some level of sexual interest and function sometimes occurs after menopause (Derogatis et al., 2004; Dennerstein, Alexander, & Kotz, 2004; Huang et al., 2008). It should also be emphasized that many women find very positive and liberating aspects in menopause as well. Aging, and the physiological changes it brings, need not be viewed negatively—there is still much about life to be discovered and celebrated (Koch et al., 2005).

See "Menopause" on SexSource Online.

Hormone Replacement Therapy

Menopausal women who are treated with dosages of the progesterone and estrogen hormones experience a reversal of the physical changes that accompany menopause. However, such **hormone replacement therapy (HRT)** is a controversial form of medical treatment. First popularized as a way of staying youthful and "feminine" for life, use of estrogen treatment alone eventually came under attack as a risky procedure. A number of studies in the 1970s began to demonstrate a statistical relationship between treatment with estrogen and several medical conditions, including uterine and breast cancer. A link between estrogen replacement therapy and breast cancer was demonstrated, particularly in women who had used estrogen for five years or longer (Chen et al., 2002; London, 2004).

A study begun in 1997 recruited nearly 17,000 healthy women across the country and randomly assigned them to take either an estrogen-progestin combination pill or a placebo. Because of the new results that emerged, the study was called off three years before it was scheduled to end. Researchers found that while HRT reduced the rate of hip fractures and colon cancer, the risks of other problems increased the longer women took the hormones. The chances of suffering a heart attack or a blood clot in the lungs were higher throughout the study, and the risk of stroke seemed to increase after the second year. Five years into the study, the women on HRT also were developing invasive breast cancer at a higher rate (Grady, Herrington, et al., 2002). All of these risks resulted in the study being halted. Many women ceased the use of replacement hormones after the results were publicized, and a substantial decrease in the incidence of breast cancer occurred soon after (Glass et al., 2007; M. D. Anderson Cancer Center, 2006). Nevertheless, other studies have continued to suggest that the use of certain chemical combinations of estrogens and the use of ultra-low doses can help certain menopausal problems without increasing the risks of breast or cervical cancer (Jick et al., 2009; Simon et al., 2008; Yasmeen et al., 2006).

Evidence about the benefits and risks of HRT has created some confusion for women and their doctors. Some physicians still believe that women with particularly severe symptoms may benefit from HRT, especially in the short term, and that other medications could be used to control the risks; others advise their patients not to take replacement hormones. Women often are left with a difficult balancing act in making a decision or the option of exploring other medical remedies or natural treatments for the unpleasant symptoms of menopause (Stewart, 2005).

Implications for Women's Sexuality

Females typically are raised to think of menstruation as a sign of being a woman, with its additional symbolic implications of fertility, femininity, and sexual readiness. Menarche often is heralded as the beginning of womanhood. Consequently, for many women menopause represents a loss of an important facet of womanhood and femininity. They fall prey to some of the menopause-related myths: that it is the beginning of the end of life, that sexual attractiveness and arousal deteriorate after menopause, and that one's purpose as a woman (that is, reproduction) has been lost (Koch et al., 2005). In some Chinese women, postmenopausal women are considered to be "half-a-man," and there are many beliefs that inhibit sexual interaction and satisfaction during this time of life (Ling, Wong, & Ho, 2008).

Research studies generally confirm that menopause need not markedly affect a woman's sexual functioning, although there is research to indicate that some women experience a decrease in sexual desire during middle life (Dennerstein, Alexander, & Kotz, 2004). A woman facing the physical and psychological changes of menopause may experience a temporary shift in sexual desire. While desire may increase or decrease, usually there are no major, long-lasting changes. Some women perceive menopause as a release from concern about intercourse resulting in an unwanted pregnancy, thus freeing them to be more relaxed sexually. As women approach menopause, they sometimes assume that they are no longer at risk for pregnancy. However, about 25 percent of women ages 40 to 44 are at risk of unwanted pregnancy, and one in five of the at-risk group uses no birth control.

hormone replacement therapy (HRT) treatment of the physical changes of menopause by administering dosages of the hormones estrogen and progesterone.

Much of how a woman's sexual life is affected by menopause depends on how she views herself and menopause. This in turn is influenced by the woman's cultural background, values about sex, social environment, overall health, and fantasies and expectations regarding menopause. It is therefore crucial that women get accurate information and emotional support throughout their menopausal experiences. Coun-selors, women's centers, and trained social workers can provide such help. Women need to be able to communicate their fears, doubts, and insecurities while being reassured that menopause is simply a natural stage of human development. It is important for the woman's partner to receive information and counseling about her menopausal experience as well (Stewart, 2005).

Self-Evaluation

You and Your Body

When you have sufficient privacy, remove all your clothing and stand before the largest mirror you have available, preferably a full-length one. Try to relax and take some time to look over your body carefully. Consider the following questions as you look at your body with as much objectivity as you can muster.

1. Do you enjoy looking at and touching your body? Why or why not?

2. What aspects of your body do you like most? Least?

3. If you are a male, how do you feel about your general body shape, your penis, and your testicles, compared with other male bodies you have seen?

4. If you are a female, how do you feel about your general body shape, your breasts, and your external genitals, compared with other female bodies you have seen?

5. Does your body conform to your ideas of what a (feminine or masculine) body should look like?

6. Do you think your nude body is (or would be) sexually attractive to members of the other gender? Of the same gender?

Chapter Summary

1. The female sex organs have always been recognized for their procreative (reproductive) functions, but their potentials for pleasure and intimate communication have become increasingly recognized.

2. The female vulva consists of the external sex organs known as the mons, the labia majora and minora, the clitoris, and the openings to the urethra and vagina.

3. The clitoris has a sensitive tip, or glans, and a shaft that extends back under a covering of tissue called the hood or prepuce.

4. Some cultures, religions, or social customs practice surgical procedures such as clitoridectomy or infibulation as rites of passage. These forms of female genital cutting have created worldwide controversy.

5. The vagina is a muscular-walled organ of sexual pleasure and reproduction that extends into the woman's body. Its opening may be partially covered by tissue called a hymen.

6. Douching of the vagina increases the risk of internal infections and STDs. The vagina has natural cleansing mechanisms so that douching is unnecessary.

7. The hymen may be present in the opening of the vagina and may be one of several types.

8. The hymen may cause sexual difficulties if it is imperforate (having no openings) or tough and fibrous.

9. Regular genital self-examination for women ensures early detection of infections or irritations.

10. Acute urethral syndrome and cystitis, or bladder infection, are common in women and may be caused by the *E. coli* bacterium. Interstitial cystitis is chronic and may cause problems with sexual functioning.

11. Vulvodynia refers to pain in the vulval region. If it is limited to the entrance to the vagina and caused by physical contact, it is called vulvar vestibulitis.

12. The vagina is subject to several medical conditions, including atrophy because of lowered

estrogen levels, varicose veins, and fistulae (openings between the vagina and other organs).

13. The uterus is the organ in which fetal development takes place. Its cervix extends into the posterior part of the vagina.

14. The ovaries mature eggs (ova) and produce female hormones. The fallopian tubes transport ova down toward the uterus, and it is in these tubes that fertilization of an egg by a sperm can take place.

15. Pap tests offer the possibility of early detection of cervical cancer or precancerous cells in the cervix, called cervical intraepithelial neoplasia (CIN). Untreated cervical cancer may become invasive cervical cancer (ICC).

16. The uterus may be affected by overgrowth of its lining in the form of endometriosis, or prolapse into the bladder or vagina.

17. The female breasts are strongly connected with sexuality in our culture, and women often worry about breast size. Milk glands in the breasts produce milk after a woman gives birth.

18. Breast cancer is one of the more common types of malignancy. Regular breast self-examination is essential to the detection of potentially malignant lumps. Mammography is a form of X ray that can detect breast cancer in very early stages.

19. Between menarche and menopause, a woman's fertility is regulated by the menstrual cycle. At roughly four-week intervals, an ovum ripens in one ovary as the result of increased levels of follicle-stimulating hormone (FSH). Estrogen thickens the uterine wall, producing a suitable location for fetal growth. The ovum breaks through the ovary wall at ovulation. If the ovum is not fertilized, extra blood and tissue are shed from the uterus in menstruation. Hormones from the pituitary, hypothalamus, and ovaries regulate the menstrual cycle.

20. Premenstrual syndrome (PMS) consists of uncomfortable physical and emotional symptoms. Severe symptoms may be classified as premenstrual dysphoria disorder (PMDD).

21. Menopause is the time of life when menstruation ceases. The perimenopausal years may have unpleasant symptoms as hormone production decreases.

22. Hormone replacement therapy (HRT) has been found to carry risks and is typically recommended only for severe menopausal problems.

Chapter 3
Male Sexual Anatomy and Physiology

Chapter Outline

I first came to this country as a 12-year-old boy, and in the gym showers I was almost the only boy who was not circumcised. In my country circumcision was never done, and I had never even seen a circumcised penis before. And there I was, with my penis looking different from everybody else's. . . . Of all my cultural adjustments here, that was the most difficult.

—from a student essay

*I*n sexuality education, male sex organs have traditionally been given recognition for their capability of generating pleasant sexual feelings. As in the female, the external sex organs of the male (see Figure 3.1) are associated more with sexual arousal, and the internal structures are associated more with reproduction. Men often are not well informed about their bodies or about significant issues that can affect their sexual and reproductive health. Educational efforts are beginning to pay more attention to male sexuality and the ways in which males learn best, particularly boys and young men (King & Gurian, 2009; Smith, Moulton, & Morgan, 2009).

■ The Testes and Scrotum

The two male sex glands, the **testes** (or testicles), develop within the abdominal cavity during fetal life. A few weeks before birth, the testes gradually move downward through the *inguinal canals* into an external pouch of skin called the **scrotum.** In a small percentage of male infants, the testes do not descend into the scrotum properly, and a few of these cases require medical treatment. The testes have two major functions after puberty. One is the production of the male sex hormone **testosterone,** which plays a significant role in the development of male secondary sex characteristics and also may affect behavior to some degree. The testes also continuously form hundreds of millions of **sperm,** the sex cells necessary for human reproduction.

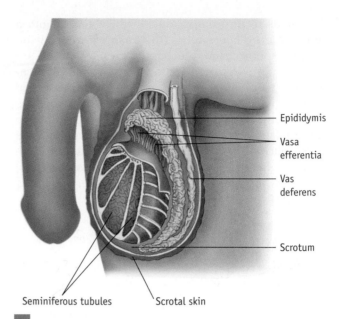

FIGURE 3.2 *Testes*

The testes are the male gonads or reproductive glands. They are paired structures located in the scrotum, and their purpose is to produce sperm and the hormone testosterone that controls male sexual development. The word *testis* is based on the root word for "witness"; the ancient custom in taking an oath was to place a hand on the genitals—to "testify."

Each testis is subdivided internally into several lobes (see Figure 3.2). The lobes are filled with a tangled mass of tiny **seminiferous tubules**, inside of which the sperm cells are formed. Each threadlike tubule is 1 to 3 feet long if extended. Between the tubules are **interstitial cells** (or Leydig cells) that produce testosterone. These cells are close to blood vessels so that the hormone is secreted efficiently into the bloodstream. The seminiferous tubules combine at

FIGURE 3.1 *External Male Anatomy*

The external male sex organs are more visible and accessible than the female's. As with the female, the external organs are the primary source of sexual pleasure while the internal organs are the source of reproduction, but the distinction is not as clearly defined in males.

testes (TEST-ees) pair of male gonads that produce sperm and male hormones.

scrotum (SKROTE-um) pouch of skin in which the testes are contained.

testosterone (tes-TAHS-te-rone) major male hormone produced by the testes; it helps produce male secondary sex characteristics.

sperm reproductive cells produced in the testes; in fertilization, one sperm unites with an ovum.

seminiferous tubules (sem-a-NIF-a-rus) tightly coiled tubules in the testes in which sperm cells are formed.

interstitial cells (in-ter-STIH-shul) cells between the seminiferous tubules that secrete testosterone and other male hormones.

their ends to form larger ducts, which empty into a series of even larger tubes, the **vasa efferentia.** Immature sperm from the seminiferous tubules are moved by wavelike contractions into the vasa efferentia and then into a coiled tubing network folded against the back and part of the top of each testis, the **epididymis.** It is in this area that the sperm mature and become ready to leave the body. The epididymis opens into a large duct that leads up into the abdominal cavity from each testis. This duct, the **vas deferens,** transports the sperm up to the *seminal vesicle* during sexual activity.

 Learn more about "The Testes" on SexSource Online.

The scrotum of a prepubescent male is quite smooth and matches the color of the rest of his skin. At puberty, the testes and scrotum grow, and hormonal influences cause the outer skin to darken and become somewhat wrinkled. The location of the testes in this external pouch is essential, because sperm production can occur only at temperatures slightly below inner body temperature. The *cremasteric muscles* suspend the testes in the scrotum and help regulate their temperature. In cold surroundings (such as swimming in cold water) or stressful situations, these muscles and the scrotal tissue itself contract, pulling the testes up close to the body to keep them warmer and protected. In warmer surroundings (such as a hot shower), the muscles and scrotal tissue relax so the testes are lowered away from the body to keep them cooler. The adult male testes are about 1.5 inches in length and 1 inch in diameter. They are slightly movable within the scrotum. One testis usually hangs slightly lower than the other—in the majority of men, the left testis is lower, while in left-handed men the right testis tends to hang lower. There seems to be no particular significance either way. The scrotal area is well supplied with nerves, and the testes are very sensitive to pressure or sharp blows. Most men find gentle stimulation of the testes and scrotum sexually arousing.

Evidence suggests that severe testicular injury, causing pain and swelling for a day or more, may be associated with later infertility. Male athletes typically wear some sort of supportive gear for greater comfort and to protect against injuries during vigorous physical activity. Instead of the traditional jockstrap, many younger men are opting for spandex shorts or compression pants that provide a more natural feeling of support. A hard plastic protective cup is worn over the male genitals during contact sports or in sports where balls or pucks might accidentally hit the groin area.

In various times in history, males have had their testicles removed in a surgical procedure called castration. It was believed that castrated males, sometimes called *eunuchs*, were reliable guards for harems of women and also tended to be more level-headed managers and leaders. Some men today fantasize about being castrated for various reasons, and some actually go through with the procedure. These men may be motivated by sexual feelings, a preference to be female, or a desire to have less powerful sexual urges. It can be very dangerous to attempt castration by oneself or to allow someone who is not medically qualified to attempt the procedure, because it can lead to permanent disability or even death (Wassersug, Zelenietz, & Squire, 2004).

Male Genital and Testicular Self-Examination

Men should take time at least monthly to examine their genital organs. Adequate lighting, and sometimes a mirror, can help with the self-examination process. Look through the pubic hair to the skin underneath, and carefully examine the head and shaft of the penis. If you are not circumcised, this will require pulling back the foreskin to expose the penile glans. Check for any bumps, sores, or blisters anywhere in the region. These may be reddish or light in color. It is important to lift up the penis and look underneath, because this area is often overlooked. Thirty-five to 50 percent of males develop tiny skin-colored bumps around the head of the penis after puberty that are called *pearly penile papules*. These can be mistakenly thought to be genital warts or some other disease, but in fact they are painless and considered to be harmless and quite common in the male population (Bylaite & Ruzicka, 2007; Kluger & Dereure, 2009).

Be alert to any soreness in the genitals or to any itching or burning sensations during urination or around the urethral opening. Although many of these symptoms do not indicate serious conditions, you should have them checked by a physician or other clinician who specializes in men's health concerns.

Cancer of the testes is a relatively rare disease, with fewer than 5,000 new cases diagnosed each year

vasa efferentia larger tubes within the testes, into which sperm move after being produced in the seminiferous tubules.

epididymis (ep-a-DID-a-mus) tubular structure on each testis in which sperm cells mature.

vas deferens tube that leads sperm upward from each testis to the seminal vesicles.

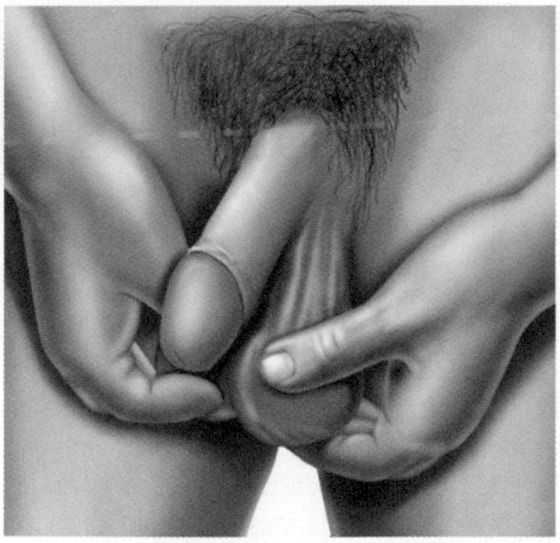

■ FIGURE 3.3 *Testicular Self-Examination*

The best time for a man to examine his testes is right after a hot bath or shower, because the testicles descend and the scrotal skin relaxes in the heat. He should place his index and middle fingers on the underside of each testicle and his thumbs on top. He should gently roll the testicle between his fingers and thumb. Any abnormal lump would be most likely to be found at the front or the side of the testicle.

in the United States. It is primarily a disease of younger men, especially men between the ages of 20 and 35. When it is detected and treated early, the chances of survival are excellent. However, if it is not treated within the first three months, the survival rate falls dramatically, to only about 25 percent. Therefore it is crucial for men to get into the habit of checking their testes regularly for any lumps or other unusual symptoms.

Here is the best way to proceed with testicular self-examination. Choose a time after a hot shower or bath, so that the testes are lowered away from the body. Roll each testicle gently between the thumb and fingers, looking especially for any small hard lumps that might be found directly on the front or side surface of a testis (see Figure 3.3). Such a lump is usually painless. Do not be alarmed at feeling the epididymis toward the top and back of each testis. Although not all lumps are malignant, any growth should be reported to a physician immediately for further investigation. Other symptoms that a man should consider suspicious and worth reporting include any heavy feeling in a testicle, accumulation of fluid in the scrotum, swelling of lymph nodes or other discomfort in the groin area, and any swelling or tenderness in the breasts.

If testicular cancer is diagnosed, the usual treatment involves surgical removal of the entire testis. The other testis is left in place and can easily produce enough male hormones on its own. An artificial, gel-filled testis can be placed in the scrotum for cosmetic

reasons. Since there is evidence that men generally do not receive adequate sexual and reproductive health services through their regular healthcare providers, they should become comfortable with this self-examination procedure as a potentially lifesaving measure (Kalmuss & Tatum, 2007).

Disorders of the Testes

There are also several disorders of the testes. In very rare cases, both testes are completely lacking at birth, a disorder known as **anorchism.** A more common problem is **cryptorchidism,** in which the testes have not descended into the scrotum before birth. This condition usually corrects itself within a few years; if it does not, it must be corrected by the time of puberty through hormonal or surgical treatment. If only one testis is present in the scrotum, the condition is termed **monorchidism.** However, one testis can easily handle the work of two, producing sufficient quantities of male hormones and sperm. Occasionally a male suffers from **testicular failure,** in which the testes do not produce male hormones or sperm. This condition usually responds to some form of hormonal therapy (Emmelot-Vonk et al., 2009).

Several organic problems can affect the internal organs of the sexual and urinary systems. In men, the bladder may become infected, and various parts of the testes may occasionally become inflamed. **Epididymitis,** or inflammation of the epididymis at the top of each testis, is relatively common and is treated with antibiotics. It can be caused by many different types of bacteria that make their way into the urethra and eventually back through the vas deferens to the epididymis. In severe cases, surgical intervention may be necessary.

If a man experiences prolonged sexual arousal without having an orgasm, the testes may become swollen, tender, and painful due to their long-term congestion with blood. The vas deferens also may

anorchism (a-NOR-kiz-um) rare birth defect in which both testes are lacking.

cryptorchidism (krip-TOR-ka-diz-um) condition in which the testes have not descended into the scrotum prior to birth.

monorchidism (ma-NOR-ka-dizm) presence of only one testis in the scrotum.

testicular failure lack of sperm and/or hormone production by the testes.

epididymitis (ep-a-did-a-MITE-us) inflammation of the epididymis of the testis.

Real People

Roland: Confronting an Embarrassing Situation

Roland is a university sophomore. He has not had any serious relationships but considers himself a very sexual person. He thinks and fantasizes about sexual things frequently and has masturbated regularly since he was 11 years old. Residence-hall living during his first year reduced the frequency with which he masturbated, mostly because of the lack of privacy. He appreciates the greater amount of alone time he now has in a suite shared with two others.

He often enjoys accessing free pornographic pictures on the Internet and frequently views these sites during his masturbatory activity. One night recently when he was engrossed in stimulating himself with his boxers pulled down, one of his suitemates returned unexpectedly and found him at the computer. The suitemate was obviously embarrassed, as was Roland, and the other man turned and left the suite without saying a word.

The next day, Roland made a point of apologizing to his suitemate, saying that he had not expected anyone to enter the room. The suitemate told him that he was really upset by what he had witnessed and was thinking of asking for a room change. He

added that as far as he was concerned, both masturbation and pornography were immoral and disgusting. He told Roland that he understood every male had difficulty resisting these temptations, but he didn't want to risk walking in on the behavior again. Roland was now even more embarrassed, and while he didn't really think masturbation was wrong, he was not anxious to have university officials find out about what had happened. He assured his suitemate that he wouldn't have to worry about seeing the behavior again, and they agreed not to talk about the incident further. Roland has come away from the situation feeling negative about himself and wondering what he should do about cutting down on masturbation or eliminating the behavior completely.

Do you think Roland was wrong for behaving as he did? What do you think of his suitemate's reaction? Was he overreacting? Was he right to be concerned? If you were in the suitemate's shoes, what would you do? Would you want to change rooms? Would you tell other people what had happened? Is there any obligation to protect Roland's privacy?

become irritated, causing pain that extends up through the pubic area and lower abdomen. In slang, this condition is often called lover's nuts, blue balls, or stone ache. It is not dangerous or permanently damaging—merely uncomfortable. It is also much less common than usually believed.

■ The Penis

Just above the scrotal sac is the male sex organ called the **penis.** The sensitive, smooth, rounded head of the penis is called the **glans.** The glans is filled with nerve endings and is particularly sensitive to sexual stimulation. The two most sensitive areas of the glans are the **frenulum,** a thin, tightly stretched band of skin on its underside connecting the glans with the **shaft** (body) of the penis; and the **corona,** the ridge around the edge of the glans. The urinary meatus or urethral opening is found at the tip of the glans. When a male

is born, the head of the penis is partly covered by a fold of skin called the prepuce or **foreskin.**

The skin on the shaft is quite loose, allowing erection to occur. Inside the penile shaft are three cylinders of erectile tissue, each full of nerves and blood vessels

penis male sexual organ that can become erect when stimulated; it leads urine and sperm to the outside of the body.

glans in the male, the sensitive head of the penis.

frenulum (FREN-yu-lum) thin, tightly drawn fold of skin on the underside of the penile glans; it is highly sensitive.

shaft in the male, the cylindrical base of the penis that contains three columns of spongy tissue: two corpora cavernosa and a corpus spongiosum.

corona the ridge around the penile glans.

foreskin fold of skin covering the penile glans; also called the prepuce.

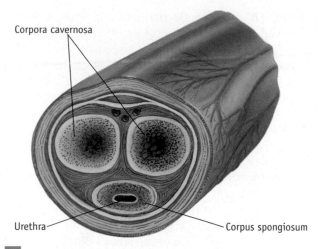

Corpora cavernosa

Urethra

Corpus spongiosum

■ FIGURE 3.4 *Cross Section of a Penis*

The penis is the male organ of urination and copulation. This cross section shows the three internal structures of the penis, all cylindrical in shape. The corpus spongiosum contains the urethra, through which pass semen and urine. All three have spongelike tissue dotted with small blood vessels.

(see Figure 3.4). The two cylinders of tissues lying parallel along the top and sides of the penis are called the *corpora cavernosa*. The third, slightly narrower cylinder that extends along the underside of the penis is called the *corpus spongiosum.*

The penis not only is important as the male organ for sexual activity and reproduction, but also is the organ through which urine is passed from the body. The tube that carries both sperm and urine in the penis is the **urethra,** which extends back to the urinary bladder and connects with the sperm-carrying ducts. It runs through the center of the corpus spongiosum.

Erection

During sexual arousal, the three cylinders inside the penis become engorged with blood so that the penis expands in circumference, becomes longer and harder, and stands out from the body. During this process of **erection,** the three cylinders of erectile tissue may be felt distinctly. Penile erection involves increased blood flow into the erectile tissue and decreased flow out of the tissue. The penis elongates and expands to its maximum capacity, eventually becoming highly rigid as stimulation continues. Sometimes there is a slight curvature in the erect penis—upward, downward, or to one side. Unless the curvature is caused by some injury or disease (which is quite rare), it will not interfere with sexual performance. The angle at which the penis stands out from the body varies a great deal as well, most typically ranging from 30 to 90 degrees from the upright vertical.

Erection of the penis is controlled by a spinal reflex and is partly an involuntary reaction (see Figure 3.5). However, the cerebral cortex and other portions of the brain also have input and are intricately connected to the "erection center" of the spinal cord. Therefore, both reflexive and thought processes can work together to stimulate or inhibit an erection (McKenna, 2000).

The detailed mechanisms and biochemical reactions of erection are becoming more fully understood. Two muscles in the perineal area (below the scrotum), the *bulbocavernosus muscle* and *ischiocavernosus muscle*, show bursts of activity just prior to erection. This activity apparently is closely related to increases in arterial blood flow into the penis, and the muscles and circulatory vessels then work together to maintain erection. During sexual arousal the nervous system stimulates the linings of the penile blood vessels and the nerve endings to produce a cascade of chemical changes that produce a substance called **cyclic GMP,** short for guanosine monophosphate, derived from nitric oxide. The smooth muscles that surround the arteries inside the penis normally are contracted when the penis is nonerect. Cyclic GMP causes the muscle cells to relax, allowing the arteries to open so that blood flows into the open spaces in the erectile tissues. The rise in blood pressure within the penis, along with other chemical changes, squeezes the veins so that they do not drain blood out of the organ, and the penis becomes engorged with blood and erect (Prieto, 2008).

It is common for men to experience some loss of erection if their mind wanders during sexual arousal. This happens because nerve signals from the brain are no longer reaching the penis, and the production of cyclic GMP decreases. The smooth muscle cells then begin contracting again, and arterial blood flow is reduced. Erection clearly is a complex phenomenon involving a carefully balanced interaction of the nervous system, biochemical reactions, muscle tissue, and blood vessels.

See "Penile Plethysmography" on SexSource Online.

urethra (yu-REE-thrah) tube that passes from the urinary bladder to the outside of the body.

erection enlargement and stiffening of the penis as internal muscles relax and blood engorges the columns of spongy tissue.

cyclic GMP a secretion within the spongy erectile tissues of the penis that facilitates erection.

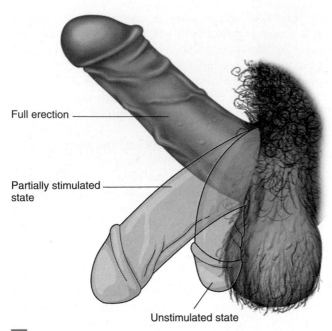

Full erection

Partially stimulated
state

Unstimulated state

■ **FIGURE 3.5**   *Penile Erection*

Penile erection is achieved primarily by the increase in blood flow through the corpus spongiosum and the corpora cavernosa during sexual arousal. Other factors, such as spinal reflex and emotion, enter into the physical act of erection.

Penis Size

As early as the third century CE, physicians in India were writing about techniques by which men could enlarge their penises using insect poisons. They also warned of the risks involved (Ashrafian, 2009). Penis size is still a nearly universal concern of men, yet it has not been the subject of very extensive research. One study found that men born with a micropenis, an unusually small organ, are known to be able to have happy and pleasurable sex lives (Bankhead, 2005). Some evidence shows that men are likely to underestimate the size of their penises in comparison with those of other men.

Penises clearly vary in length, width, and shape, all perfectly functional and normal. Although some men and women prefer larger penises for sexual activity, there is no basis for believing that any factors of penile size affect a man's ability to be a fully satisfactory sexual partner. Nevertheless, in a study of 556 women in Croatia, well over half indicated that penis length and/or girth was somewhat important to their sexual pleasure, while around 20 percent said these characteristics were very important. Only one-fourth of the women responded that penis size was unim-

portant. The more male partners the women in the study had had, the more important penis size was to them. To add more fuel to the insecurities such studies generate for men, over 70 percent of the women in this study said that the overall aesthetic appearance of men's penises (undefined beyond that generality) was also important to their own sexual pleasure (Stulhofer, 2006). Practically speaking, men can do little to alter the characteristics of their genitals. Therefore, learning to become comfortable with one's body and learning from sexual partners how to most effectively engage in sexual activities are the most reasonable goals to pursue.

There is no demonstrated relationship between height, general body size or the size of other particular organs, and penis size (Awwad et al., 2005). Although the research samples have been quite small and the usefulness of the conclusions is doubtful, some evidence exists that there may be significant differences in erect penis lengths among different ethnic groups (Harding & Golombok, 2002).

Studies on penis size have sometimes been conducted to gather information about how likely it is for a condom to slip off the penis or break during sexual activity. As might be anticipated, researchers face the daunting task of either being allowed by men to measure their penises or asking men to measure their own penises and then report the dimensions. The former technique makes people uncomfortable and may actually affect penis size, and the latter method could be prone to exaggeration (Harding & Golombok, 2002). One study asked gay male couples to measure each other and report back on two different occasions. The researchers believed that the reported inconsistencies rendered the measurements unreliable, while other analysts considered them explainable as random rather than intentional errors (Hershberger, 2003).

Two urologists who performed standardized penile measurements on a group of men at San Francisco General Hospital found that the average nonerect penis was 3.5 inches in length and 3.9 inches in circumference. The average erect penis was 5.1 inches long and 4.9 inches in circumference. Using the statistical measures of a standard bell curve, the researchers concluded that the range in length for average erect penises would be between 2.8 and 7.2 inches. The 2 percent of men whose erect penises are smaller than 2.8 inches and the 2 percent whose penises are larger than 7.2 inches would be considered smaller or larger than average (Wessels, Lue, & McAninch, 1996).

It has been suggested that measurements of the nonerect penis do not have great meaning because the flaccid penis length of any particular man may vary a great deal depending on emotional and environmental

Real People

Jake: Concerns about the Male Body

Jake was a senior in college, and his current relationship seemed to be faltering. He felt depressed and told his best friend how shy he had always been with women. He did not talk about the concerns he had with his body. He had been born with an undescended testicle, and efforts to move the testis into his scrotum during childhood had failed. Prior to entering college, he had had a plastic prosthetic testis surgically implanted in his scrotum because he was concerned that his lacking testis would be noticed in shower rooms. However, he had been dissatisfied with the prosthesis because in his opinion it did not look or feel genuine.

Jake was also concerned about the size of his penis and had written for information on penile enlargement surgery, which he had seen advertised in a men's magazine. After investigating this option further, he gave up the idea of pursuing expensive—and risky—surgery. He decided his penis was within normal size ranges. Nonetheless, he continued to be reluctant in his relationships with women and was troubled by his insecurities.

What do you think Jake ought to do? With whom would you recommend he speak about his personal concerns? Is Jake just being silly in worrying about the size of his penis, or do you think size really matters to men's sexual partners?

conditions. It is assumed that the erect length would be more consistent from situation to situation, although no reliable data are available to support this assumption. Studies generally show that erect penises tend to be somewhat shorter than often believed or as reported in studies relying on self-measurements.

Masters and Johnson found that erection seems to have an *equalizing effect*: Smaller penises gain proportionately more size than larger penises upon erection. This equalizing effect was confirmed by later researchers (Jamison & Gebhard, 1988) who divided flaccid penises into two categories: short (averaging 3.1 inches) and long (averaging 4.4 inches). They found that shorter penises tended to gain about 85 percent in size during erection, to an average of 5.8 inches, whereas longer penises grew by only 47 percent, to an average of 6.5 inches. Likewise, narrower penises gain more in circumference than wider penises during erection.

Capitalizing on men's concerns about penile size, a variety of penis enlargement techniques have been marketed. Many involve using some sort of suction device that creates an erection for men, therefore providing enlargement. Such devices have been known to cause injury to the penis, if too much suction is used. Some cosmetic surgeons offer surgical techniques to enlarge the penis. One procedure, in which some of the internal ligaments at the base of the penis are cut away so some of the penile structure inside the body can be extended outside, has been found to be too

risky. In fact, scarring may result in poor erections or in pulling the penis back, making it appear even shorter. Clinical evidence indicates that many men who have had penis enlargement procedures are unhappy with the results (Dillon, Chama, & Honig, 2008).

Breast size and penis size seem to preoccupy North Americans. How have the media and other factors influenced these concerns? What are your feelings about these issues?

See "Male Anatomy" on SexSource Online.

Male Circumcision: The Debate

Removal of the penile foreskin, leaving the glans fully exposed, is a surgical procedure called **circumcision** (see Figure 3.6). The desirability of circumcision has come and gone during various periods of history and in different cultures, but it has persisted as a practice performed on male infants most in English-speaking countries of Europe, the United States, and English-speaking parts of Canada (Drenth, 2008). Until the

circumcision (SIR-cum-sizh-uhn) in the male, surgical removal of the foreskin from the penis.

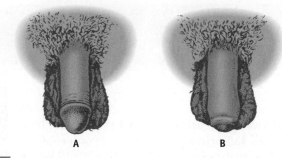

■ FIGURE 3.6   *Circumcision*

The circumcised penis **(A)** leaves the glans exposed, supposedly making it easier to keep the penis clean and prevent the possibility of cancer. The uncircumcised penis **(B)** in a very few instances may have a condition called *phimosis,* in which the foreskin cannot be retracted over the glans.

mid-1970s, most males in the United States were circumcised, but fewer parents are now choosing to have their sons' foreskins removed. Circumcision has sometimes been a part of religious custom, as for example in the Jewish faith. The other most frequently stated reason for circumcision involves hygiene, a way of preventing the buildup of a material under the foreskin called smegma that can lead to infection.

There has been continuing controversy over the widespread practice of circumcising male infants (see Figure 3.7). Critics claim that young males can easily

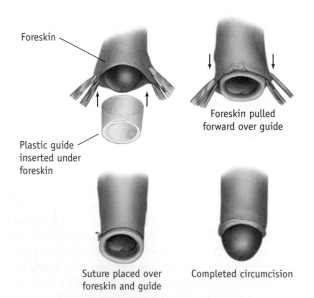

■ FIGURE 3.7   *Circumcision of an Infant*

The surgical removal of the penile foreskin has a history that goes back as far as 4000 B.C.E. in Egypt. Its justification has been ritualistic, religious, and medical. The surgical procedure illustrated here is usually performed on infant males, but it is sometimes used for adult circumcision.

learn how to pull back the foreskin and wash the glans. Some have complained that no legitimate reasons justify circumcision or the potential pain and discomfort it might cause to infants. Current standard procedure is to use a form of anesthesia, permitting pain-free surgery. Anticircumcision groups, however, believe that the procedure may be traumatic as well as unnecessary (Green et al., 2008).

One medical problem that has been cited as a good reason for circumcision is **phimosis,** or an unusually long and tight foreskin that is difficult to retract. Yet opponents of circumcision insist that spontaneous erections begin even before birth and gradually stretch the foreskin, so that by six years of age it can be retracted without difficulty in almost 100 percent of cases. If a real problem exists at some later stage in life, circumcision can then be performed. Opponents also believe that in infants the foreskin should be tight and nonretractable to protect the urethral opening from exposure to fecal material or other possible irritants.

The American Academy of Pediatrics, the American Medical Association, and the American Association of Family Physicians have taken positions opposing routine circumcision, citing evidence that the benefits of circumcising newborns are not significant enough to recommend it as a routine procedure. A study of 130,475 newborn circumcisions, examining the trade-offs, concluded that the procedure offers practically no medical benefit but also causes virtually no harm. It is believed that about 60 percent of boys in the United States are circumcised currently, but the incidence of the procedure seems to be decreasing (Christakis et al., 2000).

Evidence from studies in other parts of the globe indicates that circumcision can reduce the likelihood of HIV and HPV infection, and some other sexually transmitted diseases as well (Fergusson, Boden, & Horwood, 2006; Golden & Wasserheit, 2009; Tobian et al., 2009). Partners of circumcised men are also less likely to contract the viruses from them (Gray et al., 2009). The World Health Organization, the U.N. Population Fund, and UNICEF have pointed out that the findings are dramatic enough to warrant reconsideration of circumcision guidelines, at least in the developing world. They also are concerned that people will grow overconfident about the preventative value of circumcision, which clearly does not provide complete protection from disease (World Health Organization, 2006). Other studies have called into question whether these results are applicable for

phimosis (fye-MOE-sus) a condition in which the penile foreskin is too long and tight to retract easily.

men who have sex with other men, since circumcision has not proved as effective for them in reducing disease transmission (Millett et al., 2008, 2009; Vermund & Qian, 2008).

Given the available information concerning male circumcision, if you were a physician, would you recommend to parents that they have their newborn baby boy circumcised? Justify your recommendation.

Disorders of the Penis

Disorders of the penis are relatively uncommon, but a few are worth mentioning here. Two disorders relate to the erection of the penis. **Priapism,** a condition that involves continual, painful, undesired erection of the penis, can be caused by circulatory disorders or abuse of certain drugs, including cocaine. If the erection is not medically relieved within a few hours, there can be eventual destruction of the corpora cavernosa, making future erection impossible (Kuefer et al., 2005). While some curving of the penis is normal, and quite evident during erection, some boys and men have severe penile curvature that requires treatment. **Peyronie's disease** occurs primarily in older males and involves the development of tough, fibrous tissue around the corpora cavernosa within the penis. Eventual calcification of this tissue may result. The disease causes curvature of the penis and painful erection, both of which can make intercourse difficult or impossible. Drug therapy, tissue grafts, or surgical procedures often can help correct penile curvature (Badawy & Morsi, 2008; Smith, Walsh, & Lue, 2008; Radopoulos, Vakalopoulos, & Thanos, 2009).

Particularly vigorous stimulation of the penis during sexual activity can sometimes inflame lymphatic vessels, creating a swollen band around the penile shaft just behind the glans. Although this condition may be alarming to men, it is not dangerous, and generally the swelling gradually subsides over a few weeks. Use of ringlike devices to maintain erection can damage penile tissues and blood vessels, especially if they are left on too long. If damage occurs, extensive surgical treatment may be required. If the erect penis is suddenly bent or hit, the tough sheath that encloses the columns of spongy tissue may tear, causing damage to the penis that interferes with erection and sexual function. Such **penile fractures** are usually corrected by surgical repair of the inner membrane, a delicate and complex process (Derouiche et al., 2008; Sawh et al., 2008). The external male genitals can also be damaged during military conflicts. In one U. S. Army combat hospital, nearly 5 percent of the injuries involved the penis or testicles and required surgical procedures (Waxman et al., 2009).

Cancer of the penis is quite rare. It may be even less common in circumcised males. Although the hypothesis is open to debate, it has been suggested that the accumulation of secretions and impurities under the foreskin of uncircumcised males may predispose them to malignant growth on their penises. Careful attention to cleanliness and personal hygiene is therefore particularly important for uncircumcised males.

There are a number of conditions of the penis that can occur in newborn males. Occasionally, a male child is born with **agenesis (absence) of the penis,** in which the phallus is very tiny and nonfunctional. Surgical intervention and eventual counseling may be necessary to offer help with the sexual adjustments of adolescence and adulthood (Papali et al., 2008). Two congenital conditions result from difficulties in fetal development of the penis: hypospadias and epispadias. **Hypospadias** is an incompletely fused penis, with an open "gutter" extending along the underside of the penis instead of an internal urethra. In the United States and some European nations, a sharp increase in the incidence of hypospadias has been noted since 1970, although the cause for the increase is not understood. There has been some suspicion that the hormone progestin, found in some birth control pills, might be playing a role. Hypospadias occurs in about 79 of every 10,000 births of males. In **epispadias,** the urinary bladder empties through a large opening in the abdomen, and the penis is split open along its upper length. Both hypospadias and epispadias require surgical repair, and the penis may not be fully functional for intercourse following the surgery.

---

priapism (pry-AE-pizm) continual, undesired, and painful erection of the penis that lasts longer than four hours.

Peyronie's disease (pay-ra-NEEZ) development of fibrous tissue in the spongy erectile columns within the penis.

penile fracture a tearing of the membrane in the penis that surrounds the three columns of spongy tissue, usually the result of severe bending of the erect penis.

agenesis (absence) of the penis (ae-JEN-a-sis) a congenital condition in which the penis is undersized and nonfunctional.

hypospadias (hye-pa-SPADE-ee-as) birth defect caused by incomplete closure of the urethra during fetal development.

epispadias (ep-a-SPADE-ee-as) birth defect in which the urinary bladder empties through an abdominal opening and the urethra is malformed.

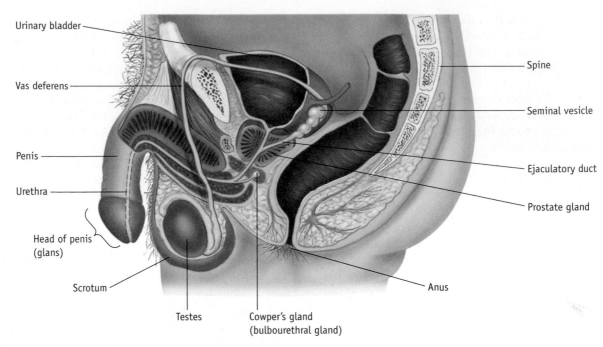

FIGURE 3.8 *Male Sexual and Reproductive Organs*

The external and internal sexual and reproductive organs of the male are shown here in longitudinal section. Although men are familiar with their more obvious external sex organs, they often are less well informed about their internal reproductive and sexual anatomy.

Internal Male Organs

The vas deferens of each testis carries sperm up around the back of the bladder, and then the sperm move into two saclike structures called the **seminal vesicles.** Both seminal vesicles are about 2 inches long and they produce secretions that help activate the sperm and make them motile. Secretions from the vesicles, which constitute about 70 percent of the seminal fluid, join with the sperm and empty into the single ejaculatory duct, which then joins the urethra inside the prostate gland.

Located at the underside of the urinary bladder, and surrounding the urethra where it enters the bladder, is the **prostate** (see Figure 3.8). This gland, a little larger than a walnut, has three lobes of muscular and glandular tissue. Along with the seminal vesicles, it produces secretions that help transport the sperm through the penis. This fluid, called **semen** or seminal fluid, is a milky, sticky alkaline substance composed of proteins, citric acid, calcium, fats, and some enzymes. Semen may be quite thick and gelatinous when it leaves the penis, or it may be thin and watery. It usually becomes thicker soon after ejaculation but then liquefies in 15 to 25 minutes. There is new research emerging about the *male reproductive proteins* in sperm and semen that may be critically important to reproductive success (Ness et al., 2008).

Below the prostate gland, at the base of the penis and on each side of the urethra, are two pea-size glands called **Cowper's glands** or **bulbourethral glands.** When a male is sexually aroused, these two glands se-crete a clear, sticky alkaline substance, or pre-ejaculatory fluid, that coats the inner lining of the urethra. Some of it may appear as droplets at the tip of the penis during arousal. The secretion has often been called a lubricant, and indeed, if present in sufficient amounts, it can serve as a lubricant for sexual activity. It is believed to help neutralize acids in the urethra and thus permit safe passage of sperm. Cowper's gland secretion may carry sperm, so it can be responsible for pregnancy even if ejaculation does not occur within the vagina.

Prostate Problems

Many men at one time or another suffer from **prostatitis,** or inflammation of the prostate gland

---

seminal vesicle (SEM-un-al) gland at the end of each vas deferens that secretes a chemical that helps sperm become motile.

prostate gland located beneath the urinary bladder in the male; it produces some of the secretions in semen.

semen (SEE-men) mixture of fluids and sperm cells that is ejaculated through the penis.

Cowper's glands two small glands in the male that secrete an alkaline fluid into the urethra during sexual arousal.

bulbourethral glands another term for Cowper's glands.

prostatitis (pras-tuh-TITE-us) inflammation of the prostate gland.

Clearing the way for blessed relief

Some 14 million American men suffer from benign swelling of the prostate.
A new procedure called TUNA could make treatment easier than ever before.

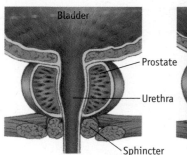
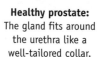
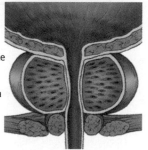

| **Healthy prostate:** The gland fits around the urethra like a well-tailored collar. | **Enlarged prostate:** The swelling that comes with age often blocks the free flow of urine. | **New procedure:** Urologists can now kill excess tissue by heating it with tiny needles. | **Result:** Within six weeks to three months, patients regain normal flow. |

FIGURE 3.9 *Prostate Enlargement Using Transurethral Needle Ablation (TUNA)*

Source: Adapted from Geoffrey Cowley, "Good News for Boomers," *Newsweek,* December 30, 1996/January 6, 1997, p. 74.

(see Figure 3.9). Prostatitis may be of the *acute* form, caused by bacterial infection, having symptoms such as sudden onset of fever, chills, and urinary discomfort. It may also be *chronic*, typically caused by changes in the prostate other than bacterial infection. Chronic symptoms can include some thin discharge from the penis, along with chronic pelvic pain or painful ejaculation. Antibiotics are used for acute prostatitis, but prostatitis in its more chronic forms can be difficult to treat or cure completely (Nickel et al., 2008).

In older men, enlargement of the prostate gland is common. **Benign prostatic hyperplasia (BPH)** refers to nonmalignant prostatic enlargement. Medications are now available to shrink prostate tissues. If the prostate enlarges too much, urination may become difficult or eventually even impossible, because the urethral passageway may be pinched by the swollen prostate. This leads to increased susceptibility to bladder and prostate infections. Various surgical treatments are available that can widen the urethral canal through the prostate and require only a local anesthetic.

The prostate can also be the site of malignant tumors. Prostate cancer is the second most frequently diagnosed cancer and the third most common cause of death from cancer in men (Damber & Gunnar, 2008). If detected early, the chances of complete cure are good (see Figure 3.10). The number of deaths from prostatic cancer continues to decline because of more refined techniques for detection and treatment. If a malignancy is present, surgery is often followed by radiation or chemical therapy. Newer surgical techniques may reduce the risks of interfering with erectile function or ejaculation, but there are often side effects that decrease sexual satisfaction at least for a time (Mulhall, 2009; Mulhall, Secin, & Guillonneau, 2008; Wittman et al., 2009).

It is generally recommended that men over age 35 have regular prostate examinations to detect any possible enlargement or tumors. The physician, using a rubber glove and lubricant, inserts a finger into the rectum, where the surface of the prostate can be felt through the rectal wall. Although such an examination is not particularly pleasant, it represents an important health care measure. A blood test that can help detect prostatic cancer, the prostate-specific antigen (PSA) test is recommended on a regular basis for men over age 50. The test has led to a dramatic increase in the number of prostate surgeries, yet there is no evidence to prove that the mortality rate from the disease has been lowered. Although research has confirmed the accuracy of the PSA test and most physicians support its use, more research is needed to determine whether such testing leads to appropriate treatments or reduces the number of deaths from prostate cancer (Parker-Pope, 2009).

Sperm Production and Ejaculation

From puberty to old age, the male testes produce large amounts of sperm cells. The testes are partially controlled by two pituitary hormones, which are also found in females: luteinizing hormone (LH), called **interstitial-cell-stimulating hormone (ICSH)** in males; and

benign prostatic hyperplasia (BPH) enlargement of the prostate gland that is not caused by malignancy.

interstitial-cell-stimulating hormone (ICSH) pituitary hormone that stimulates the testes to secrete testosterone; known as luteinizing hormone (LH) in females.

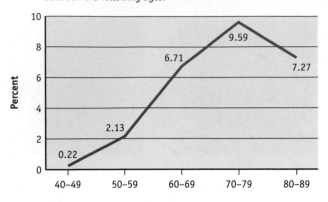

Rising prostate cancer rates over time
Probability of developing invasive prostate cancer
between the following ages:

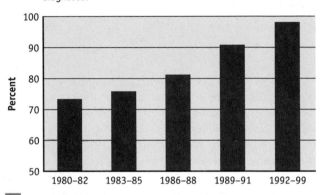

Survival rates, then and now
Percentage of men who are still alive five years after being
diagnosed:

FIGURE 3.10   *Rates of Occurrence and Survival for Prostate Cancer*

Source: Karen Springen and Jerry Adler, "Prostate Cancer's Difficult Choices," *Newsweek,* June 16, 2003, p. 57. Data from National Cancer Institute.

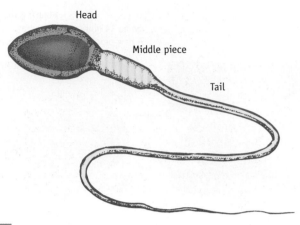

FIGURE 3.11   *Sperm*

A mature sperm consists of a head, middle piece, and tail. The head contains the chromosomes and is the part involved in fertilization. The tail moves the sperm from the ejaculatory duct into the urethra prior to ejaculation. If all the ova needed to repopulate the world would fit into a 2-gallon container, the sperm needed for the same purpose would fit into an aspirin tablet.

follicle-stimulating hormone (FSH). The ICSH begins to be produced at puberty and stimulates the interstitial cells of the testes to produce the male hormone testosterone. The FSH helps stimulate the sperm-producing cells—called **spermatocytes**—in the linings of the seminiferous tubules to produce sperm.

Each mature sperm consists of a head and a tail, separated by a short thickened area (see Figure 3.11). The head contains the male's genetic material, and the thickened middle area contains an energy-releasing mechanism that helps move the tail. Sperm are usually about 55 microns long (0.0021 inch or 0.055 millimeter) and can be seen only through a microscope. An adult male is believed to produce about 15 to 30 billion sperm each month.

During sexual excitement and activity, the sperm are moved from the epididymis in the testes up to the seminal vesicles, where secretions activate their tails to make a lashing movement. Stimulation of the penis sends nerve impulses to the ejaculatory center of the

spinal cord. When these impulses have built to a certain threshold, the ejaculatory response is triggered. Sperm and seminal fluid move into the ejaculatory duct and urethra, where contractions of the surrounding muscles propel them outward to be ejaculated through the end of the penis. This usually is accompanied by the pleasurable sensations of **orgasm,** or sexual climax, although the two phenomena—**ejaculation** and orgasm—can occur separately (see Chapter 4, "Human Sexual Arousal and Response").

Studies seem to indicate that average sperm counts in the male population dropped by one-third from the mid-1970s to the mid-1990s. To what has this drop been attributed? What concerns might this trend raise for the future?

The amount of semen ejaculated depends on many factors, including age, amount of sexual stimulation, general health, and interval of time since the last ejaculation, but typically there are 3 to 5 cubic centimeters of semen—about a teaspoonful or less. As much as 11 cubic centimeters of semen can be ejaculated. The typical ejaculate contains 150 million

spermatocytes (sper-MAT-o-sites) cells lining the seminiferous tubules from which sperm cells are produced.

orgasm pleasurable sensations and series of contractions that release sexual tension, usually accompanied by ejaculation in men.

ejaculation muscular expulsion of semen from the penis.

to 600 million sperm. Many men subjectively report that the more intense the sensation of orgasm, the more semen ejaculated and the more force with which it is propelled out of the penis. Most often the semen oozes out of the penis under some pressure, but it sometimes can spurt several inches.

As a result of certain illnesses, some prostate surgeries, or the effects of certain tranquilizing drugs, the semen may be ejaculated into the urinary bladder. The muscles at the base of the bladder that normally close off the bladder during ejaculation apparently do not contract, so semen is permitted to enter the bladder. Despite the full sensation of orgasm, no semen leaves the penis. This phenomenon is called **retrograde ejaculation.** Some organic problems simply lead to the absence of semen and a resultant dry orgasm called **anejaculation.**

Under ideal laboratory conditions, sperm may be kept alive for up to two weeks after ejaculation. However, after ejaculation into the vagina during sexual intercourse, it is unlikely that many sperm remain motile for more than two or three days. Older sperm are more likely to have deformities, so it is not considered a good idea to abstain from sexual activity before trying to get pregnant because the newest sperm are the healthiest. Once semen has been deposited in the vagina, some of it begins to seep into the uterus, and the sperm swim against mucous currents and gravitational pull. Healthy sperm can swim about 3 to 7 inches in an hour, and following ejaculation a few thousand of them can be expected to reach the female's fallopian tubes in a few hours.

Concern has been growing that sperm counts in otherwise healthy human males have been dropping in recent years and that the quality of human sperm is gradually deteriorating as well. Although men continue to produce sperm throughout their lives, studies show that the DNA in sperm tends to undergo more mutational changes as men age. This is of concern, because men are tending to postpone fatherhood until later in life. Aging leads to an increase in DNA damage, which can decrease the chances of conception or produce certain birth defects in offspring. There is no evidence at this point that fluctuations in sperm count at a global level have had any profound effect on male fertility (Schmid et al., 2007; Wyrobek et al., 2006).

Men who have fewer than 20 million sperm per milliliter are considered infertile, because the chances of their conceiving a child are slim with that low a sperm count. Studies have suggested that men who consume substantial amounts of caffeine every day have increased levels of sperm DNA damage that might cause chromosomal aberrations after fertilization, and that cigarette smoking can reduce sperm production significantly.

■ Male Hormones and "Andropause"

Men do not seem to undergo predictable cyclical changes in hormonal levels, such as the female menstrual cycle, that affect their fertility. Studies have shown that testosterone levels tend to be lower in the spring, when literary tradition would have it that men's sex drive is strong. Nonetheless, men do seem to experience changes in their bodies as they age. The concentrations of male hormones found in the body gradually decline through the mid-40s, and by age 75 testosterone levels often drop by up to 90 percent compared with levels before age 30. More significantly, biochemical changes in the body cause more testosterone to become chemically bound to blood proteins, or plasma, as a man ages, resulting in a lower free testosterone index (FTI). It is the free, unbound testosterone that seems to have the most important influence on the body. For some men over the age of 60 who have lower-than-normal levels of testosterone, there seems to be some correlation with the presence of depression and loss of interest in sex (Seidman, 2006; Wang et al., 2009).

Because reproductive capacity is not necessarily lost as men age, nothing in males is completely equivalent to female menopause. Nevertheless, popular media have promoted the idea of a male menopause. Although it is less predictable and its symptoms are more variable, men often do experience a period of stress as they age. Often called midlife crisis, the male climacteric, aging male syndrome, or **andropause,** this period is characterized by increased anxiety, depression, insomnia, hypochondria, loss of appetite, and/or chronic fatigue. These may also be the symptoms of untreated depression. However, there also is usually a reduction in testosterone levels and a decrease in sexual desire and capability as men age. Because of this, male menopause has also been called ADAM, which stands for androgen decline in the aging male (Barqawi & Crawford, 2006; Seidman, 2006).

This time in a man's life is often characterized by major changes and realizations. Most professionals believe that these psychological stresses play a role in andropause. Men with wives and families are sharing the menopausal changes of their spouses and watching

retrograde ejaculation abnormal passage of semen into the urinary bladder at the time of ejaculation.

anejaculation lack of ejaculation at the time of orgasm.

andropause one of the terms applied to a vaguely defined period in male midlife characterized by hormonal, psychological, and sexual changes.

How Age Can Change a Man's Body

The term "male menopause" drives medical experts crazy. In women, "menopause is a clearly defined biological event," says Dr. Abraham Morgenthaler of Boston's Beth Israel Hospital. "There is no equivalent for men." True enough, but middle age does bring changes, and few of them would qualify as improvements. Here's a rundown of the main ones:

Hair loss. The number of hair follicles on the scalp decreases as men age, and the hair that is left grows at a slower rate.

Vision. By age 50, lifelong thickening of the lens causes a noticeable loss of night vision and close-in focus.

Brain function. Concentration and language skills don't change much with age. The ability to store and retrieve information declines slightly but steadily from the 20s on.

Hearing. Eardrums thicken and the ear canal atrophies, making pure tones and high frequencies harder to hear, especially in the late 50s.

Lung power. Chest wall stiffens, increasing the workload of respiratory muscles. More residual air is left in lungs after each breath.

Aerobic endurance. As the body's ability to deliver oxygen declines, the capacity for physical work falls. The work capacity of a 70-year-old is only half that of a 20-year-old.

Body fat. Between the ages of 25 and 75 the amount of fat in proportion to the body's composition doubles. Much of that growth occurs in muscles and organs.

Muscle and bone. Eventually muscles get smaller and weaker, but those changes can be offset by exercise. Bone loss, a universal aging trait, occurs at individual rates.

Heart response. After 20, the heart becomes less adept at accelerating in response to exertion. Bars show maximum rate in beats per minute:

200 190 180 170 160 150

Age 20 30 40 50 60 70

Frequency of sex. Decline in sex drive varies from man to man, but some reduction is inevitable due to lower levels of sex hormones and loss of vitality. Orgasms per year:

104 121 84 52 35 22

Age 20 30 40 50 60 70

Angle of erection. Many men experience a slight loss of upward mobility from 30 to 50, and a major loss from 50 to 70. Preventable vascular disease is largely to blame.

Age 20: 20°
Age 30: 10°
Age 40: 1°
Age 50: −1°
Age 70: −25°

ERECTION DEGREES ABOVE HORIZONTAL

their children leave home. If the man has been a primary breadwinner, he may begin to feel weary from the years of responsibility for his family. Physical changes and stress-generated tension may produce alterations in sexual interest and behavior, resulting in even more worry and discouragement. The male climacteric seems largely to be a vicious cycle of middle-age stresses and gradual physiological changes that feed on one another.

Testosterone Replacement Therapy

Optimal sexual functioning in males may be dependent on the presence of at least some free testosterone in the body. For some men in whom the FTI is low, administration of extra testosterone seems to improve sexual interest and may decrease the risks of depression. It does not necessarily improve erectile function (Hwang & Lin, 2008; Shabsigh et al., 2009). **Testosterone replacement therapy (TRT)** carries some increased risks of prostate difficulties and cardiovascular disease, so it must be prescribed with caution (Allan et al., 2008; Wang et al., 2009).

Surviving Male Midlife

Because female menopause has been more clearly delineated, women may tend to receive more support and understanding for their difficult physical and psychological symptoms. Men may need the same supportive help through their midlife crises as well. Counseling can help a man express his concerns and deal with his confusing emotions, but men may be reluctant to seek this sort of help. They may need guidance to help them realize that finding appropriate support during life's various crises is a strength, not a weakness. It is important that men be cautioned about making major life changes during the throes of such a crisis.

Both medical and psychological sciences are making great progress in understanding the changes within men's bodies and psyches as they age. Just as Viagra and other erection-enhancing medications have offered hope to men with erection problems, treatments likely will become available to help men cope with the various other symptoms associated with sex and aging. Ultimately, the best help will come from within, as men draw on their own resources to accept the natural processes of aging and also the positive outcomes that these processes can yield along with the less positive.

---

testosterone replacement therapy (TRT) administering testosterone injections to increase sexual interest or potency in older men; not considered safe for routine use.

Self-Evaluation

Learning about Sexuality: Past, Present, and Future

Sexuality education is far more than learning about the body's reproductive system. It is also an exercise in self-awareness—becoming acquainted with one's own sexual feelings, needs, and values. Learning about sexuality is a lifelong process that must constantly integrate new information and changing personal situations. The exercises that follow ask you to examine the process of sexuality education as it relates to your life.

1. **Looking back. Spend some time thinking about your answers to the following questions. They will help clarify some of the background of your learning about sexuality. You may want to discuss your answers with another trusted person.**
   a. Can you recall your first discussions about sexuality when you were a child with another child, a parent, or someone else? If so, can you remember any feelings or attitudes that you developed in relationship to that time and the topic of sex?
   b. How and when did you first learn what you consider to be the important information about the sex organs, reproduction, and other aspects of human sexuality? Was the information conveyed to you in a relatively positive, negative, or neutral atmosphere emotionally?
   c. Do you remember the first book or magazine you read, or the first television program or movie you saw, that had factual information about sex or graphically depicted sexual behaviors? How did you react?
   d. In what ways have you increased your level of information and awareness about human sexuality more recently in your life?

2. **Following is a list of topics related to human sexuality. You may be better informed on some of them than on others. Using the rating standards shown, rate each topic as to your level of competence, using appropriate check marks.**

3. As you reexamine the check marks you made in exercise 2, pay attention to those topics you need to know more about. For each of these, indicate what your course of action, if any, will be.
  a. Will you seek further information on the topic? Why or why not?
  b. Where will you begin your search for the information?
  c. Are any personal implications involved in your wanting to understand the topic better?

4. Do you expect to have children (or do you have children) for whom you will bear some responsibility to provide effective education about sexuality? If so, consider the following questions.
  a. Have you already made some attempts at educating children about sexuality? If so, how successful do you think you were, and on what criteria do you base that evaluation?
  b. Make a list of goals that you believe are important to the sexuality education of children at different age levels; choose those goals in whose achievement you may play an active part. What areas would you not want to be a part of your children's sexuality education?
  c. What resources can you have available to assist with the sexuality education process? Consider books, films, television programs, computer software or accessible networks, other people (including professionals), and your own skills and competencies.

	I know very little about this and could use further information.	*I understand this reasonably well but could use more information.*	*I feel comfortable with this and do not need further information.*
Male genital anatomy and physiology	———	———	———
Female genital anatomy and physiology	———	———	———
Sexual intercourse	———	———	———
The physiology of reproduction and birth	———	———	———
Advances in reproductive technology	———	———	———
Same-gender orientation and bisexuality	———	———	———
Masturbation	———	———	———
Psychosexual development of children and adolescents	———	———	———
Sex therapy and counseling	———	———	———
Gender identity, masculinity, and femininity	———	———	———
Sexually transmitted diseases	———	———	———
Transmission of HIV	———	———	———
Sexual dysfunctions	———	———	———
Human sexual response	———	———	———
Improving communication in sexual relationships	———	———	———
Sexual variations	———	———	———

Chapter Summary

1. The male testes, located in the scrotum, produce male hormones and sperm. Sperm cells develop best at a temperature slightly lower than inner body temperature, mature in tubes called the epididymis, and will travel upward through the vas deferens.

2. Regular self-examination of the penis and testes is an effective way to detect infections or growths that indicate the presence of testicular cancer.

3. Both testes may not descend into the scrotum before birth.

4. Epididymitis is an inflammation of the epididymis in the testes.

5. The penis has a sensitive, rounded head called the glans and a longer shaft. Three columns of spongy tissue compose the interior of the penile shaft and become filled with blood during

erection. Sperm and urine move through the penis via the urethra.

6. Penis size is quite variable among males and includes a wide range of normal sizes.

7. Circumcision is a surgical procedure in which the penile foreskin, or prepuce, is removed. Its advisability has been the subject of controversy, although it has been shown to reduce the likelihood of HIV and HPV infection.

8. Some medical conditions that can affect the penis are priapism (painful, continuous erection), Peyronie's disease (calcification of erectile tissue), phimosis (too-tight foreskin), penile fracture, and cancer.

9. The prostate gland and seminal vesicles of the male produce secretions that mix with sperm to produce the semen that is ejaculated through the penis. Cowper's glands produce a clear secretion that lines the urethra during sexual arousal.

10. Prostatitis, or prostate infection, can be either acute or chronic. A common problem in older men is prostate enlargement, which may be caused by benign prostatic hyperplasia or by malignant tumors. It must be corrected, usually by surgery. The PSA test has proved useful in detection of prostatic cancer, but not in reduction of deaths.

11. Sperm production is controlled by the secretion of FSH. Interstitial-cell-stimulating hormone (ICSH) stimulates the testes to produce testosterone. Up to 30 billion sperm are produced by the testes each month.

12. Sexual stimulation of the penis can lead to ejaculation of semen. The ejaculate can contain between 150 million and 600 million sperm.

13. The sperm counts of human males may have been decreasing over the past few decades, although fertility has not yet been affected. As men age, the chance for DNA changes in their sperm increases.

14. Men do not seem to have predictable hormonal cycles, although their emotions may follow cyclical patterns.

15. Men experience a less well-defined midlife andropause, involving mood changes that may be associated with reduced production of testosterone.

16. Testosterone replacement therapy may improve sexual desire and other symptoms of male midlife, but it also carries health risks and needs further research.

Chapter 4

Human Sexual Arousal and Response

Chapter Outline

My first year in high school I was having erections all the time, always unpredictable and usually without good reason. I could get a hard-on from putting a notebook in my locker or riding on the bus. Worst of all were the ones I would get during oral reports up in front of the class. Fortunately, the thing is a lot more under control now—most of the time.

—from a student essay

Over the centuries, the human body's sexual responses have been explained and interpreted in many different ways. They have been assigned religious significance in some cultures and shunned as potential evils in others. Sexual arousal and responsiveness, and how they are perceived and expressed, cannot be understood outside the context of the culture in which a person lives. When Margaret Mead studied the Mundugumor of New Guinea, she remarked that lovemaking was conducted "like the first round of a prizefight," with scratching and biting part of the foreplay. She later found that in Samoa men preceded sexual activity by singing romantic songs and reciting poetry for their women, first preparing their minds with sensual thoughts and then preparing their bodies with sensual touching.

Sexuality becomes intertwined with the spiritual beliefs within cultures as well. In the Jewish tradition, for example, sexuality is intimately associated with concepts of creativity and unity. In Eastern Tantric traditions of yoga, Buddhism, Hinduism, and Taoism, sexual response is perceived as an expression of spiritual energies. It is believed that the energy of life and the spirit may be focused in different ways in the body and that, properly used, sexual energy can help convey people to the highest levels of spiritual consciousness. The emphasis is on savoring all the sensual and spiritual aspects of sex rather than looking toward the goal of immediate gratification (Richard, 2002).

■ Models of Desire and Arousal: Interaction of Mind and Body

We often hear talk of a person's sex drive, implying that we humans have some sort of internal energy or motivation that causes us to crave sexual gratification. This concept makes intuitive sense because sexual interest sometimes feels like that—a kind of inner longing. Contemporary researchers are beginning to clarify that rather than having a diffuse form of internal sexual energy that causes us to want sex, it is more likely that our gradually building awareness of the pleasures of sexual excitement causes us to develop the capacity for sexual desire or motivation. In other words, knowing the pleasure of sexual arousal precedes the desire for it (Boul, Hallam-Jones, & Wylie, 2009; Both, Everaerd, & Laan, 2007). Evolutionary theorists theorize that sexual motivation reflects an innate

drive for reproduction to ensure survival of the species, but emerging research evidence suggests that there is a considerably more complex process involved (Kauth, 2006b; Toates, 2009). We are beginning to piece together theories of how we get turned on and turned off sexually.

One thing seems certain: sexual desire and arousal involve an interaction and integration of psychological factors such as emotion, memory, and motivation; neurophysiological processes that affect hormones, blood flow, and muscles; sociocultural factors by which we are all influenced; and the evolutionary imperatives that are part of being a human animal (Everaerd, Both, & Laan, 2007; Peterson & Janssen, 2007; Toates, 2009).

Distinguishing Desire and Arousal

While at times it may not seem as if there is any difference between desiring to do something sexual and feeling the physical excitement in one's genitals, there is a distinction between the two processes. **Sexual desire** is the psychological motivation for sex, the incentive to act, the appetite for sexual pleasure. It has been described with terms ranging from longing to aching and from horny to lustful. **Sexual arousal** is the excitation of the body as it responds to psychological and/or physical cues and stimulations.

Current models of sexual desire and arousal include stimuli that are both *internal*, referring to phenomena of the mind such as emotions, fantasies, and memories, and *external*, such as direct touching of the sex organs or actually seeing someone who is considered sexy. These two aspects of activating sexual desire and arousal have been divided into distinct categories: the **central arousal system**, referring to internal factors, and the **peripheral arousal system**, referring to

sexual desire the psychological motivation, incentive, or appetite for sex.

sexual arousal excitation of the body, including the genitals, for sexual activity.

central arousal system internal components of sexual arousal that come from the cognitive and emotional centers of the brain, forming the foundations for sexual response.

peripheral arousal system external components of sexual arousal that reach the brain and spinal cord from the skin, genitals, and sense organs.

Real Student Voices

■ My father was always very open with me about what to expect sexually, so I never felt self-conscious or scared about the changes going on in my body. I remember that the first time I actually produced semen, he was the first person I told, and he seemed to be glad too. I realize now that most boys don't have that kind of relationship with their dads. I'm glad I did.

■ The first time I actually saw my friend's erect penis, it kind of scared me. It looked huge, and I couldn't imagine how it would ever fit inside of any girl, let alone me!

■ It takes a lot to turn me on, but once I'm turned on I'm ready to go. It seems that my judgment gets tossed to the wind at that point.

---

the external. The central arousal system seems to be located largely in the emotional and pleasure centers of the brain; the stimuli generated there form the central, fundamental template for a person's sexual response. The peripheral arousal system is related more to those aspects of stimulation that stem from the spinal cord and its voluntary and involuntary nervous control mechanisms. This system picks up cues directly from the skin, genitals, and sense organs (Bancroft et al., 2009; Nobre & Pinto-Gouveia, 2008; Toate, 2009).

Figure 4.1 summarizes this model of the activation of sexual desire and arousal. It is generally agreed that there is a sequence of events leading to sexual desire and arousal involving the combination of central and peripheral mechanisms, with the mind and body interacting in many different ways. If the mind ascribes sexual meaning to a particular stimulus, sexual arousal can be the result. In some cases, this processing seems to be relatively *automatic,* leading to rapid physiological response such as erection or vaginal lubrication. However, the sexual system has to be primed in such a way that its conditions match the stimulus coming from the environment (Gillath et al., 2007). Beyond the automatic response, the brain's responses are more *controlled* in regulating whether sexual response will continue to be facilitated or be inhibited (Spiering, Everaerd, & Janssen, 2003; Toate, 2009). When human sexual response is easily activated, it is probably the result of the automatic arousal mechanisms. When people are sexually dysfunctional for psychological reasons, these automatic mechanisms are disrupted by controlling factors such as emotions and negative interpretations.

There are many different factors that can influence sexual arousal. Human beings have the ability to pay *attention* to their own thoughts and physiological reactions, and thus interact with their own sexual desire

and arousal as well. For example, individuals who have a higher level of sexual desire are more likely to respond with pleasant emotional reactions when given sexual cues than people with low levels of desire. People may also control the level of sexual arousal they have by paying attention to their thoughts and concerns. Perhaps this is why distraction can sometimes inhibit sexual desire and arousal (Conaglen & Evans 2006; deJong, 2009; Janssen et al., 2008; Prause, Janssen, & Hetrick, 2008).

The Dual Control Model

The bottom line here is that while we can feel sexual desire and observe human sexual arousal and responsiveness, it is not yet fully understood how the brain and physiological mechanisms of the body actually work together to make it all happen, or not happen. Instead, scientists have developed theoretical models for how this might work. Such theories help us organize our thinking about the neurophysiology involved and offer a basis on which we may begin to test various hypotheses. The most thoroughly researched of the present theories is the *Dual Control Model.*

A fundamental understanding of this model is that sexual desire and arousal are controlled by the interaction of both *excitatory* (turn-on) and *inhibitory* (turn-off) processes in the brain. It seems obvious that for the body to become sexually aroused, there must be systems of excitation that lead to rather predictable reactions of the genitals and other bodily organs. Excitatory mechanisms have been studied in some detail. However, it is also clear that inhibitory systems play a crucial role in human responsiveness, and there is some evidence that inhibitory mechanisms are at least in part genetically determined. It is these dual control mechanisms that work together to mediate

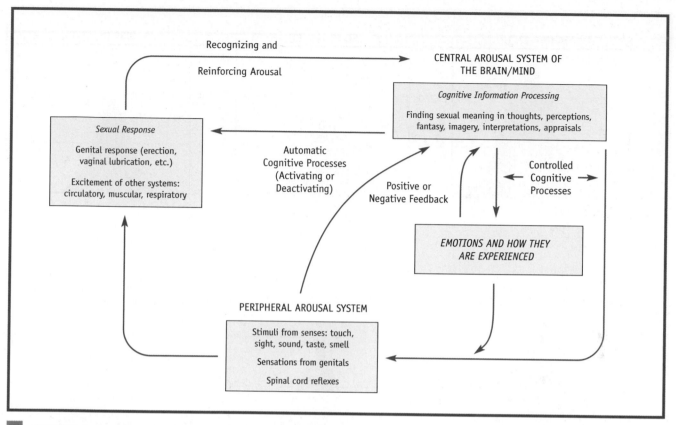

FIGURE 4.1 *Mind–Body Interactions in Sexual Arousal*

This diagram summarizes the models that explain how human sexual desire and arousal may be activated or deactivated. The initiating mechanism may be the central arousal system, mediated by the brain and its ways of processing information. The peripheral arousal system is influenced partly by input from the brain, but it also processes cues that come directly from sensory stimulation. The brain continues to participate in activation, or deactivation, of sexual desire and arousal, depending on complex positive and negative feedback loops influenced by the individual's learned ways of processing potential sex cues.

sexual desire and arousal (Bancroft et al., 2009; Varjonen et al., 2007).

If excitation leads to desire and arousal in preparation for sexual activity, what value do sexual inhibitory systems have? There may be times when sexual activity would be problematic, dangerous, or not to one's advantage. We learn what behaviors are acceptable and which are inappropriate from our society. Interestingly, there are inhibitory mechanisms that are typically active in the human brain's temporal lobes that may help to keep our behaviors in check. Excitatory factors actually have to deactivate these centers in order for sexual response to happen. Even after one has become sexually aroused, there are other inhibitory mechanisms that can "push the brakes" in situations where there is a realization that the sexual arousal could be disadvantageous or risky. In fact, there are two types of sexual inhibition that have been identified: the first based on the threat of failing to perform well sexually, and the second due to fears of possible consequences of sex. If a sexual threat is perceived in a potential partner,

inhibitory processes may devalue the partner and pull back on sexual desire and arousal. The lack of sexual interest that some people experience when they are under stress, or when they feel satiated by sexual activity, may represent an inhibitory mechanism (Bancroft et al., 2009; Janssen & Bancroft, 2007).

A basic assumption of this model is that there is a great deal of variability among human beings in both of these two integrated systems, helping to explain why some people seem more interested in sex than others, either consistently or with particular partners, or in certain situations. For example, it makes sense that a person with a particularly strong propensity for excitation, or someone with a low propensity for sexual inhibition, might well be more likely to participate in high-risk or socially inappropriate sexual behaviors. On the other hand, people who have a weak propensity for excitation or a high propensity for sexual inhibition might experience more problems with feeling sexual desire or achieving sexual arousal (Bancroft, 2009; Bancroft et al., 2009).

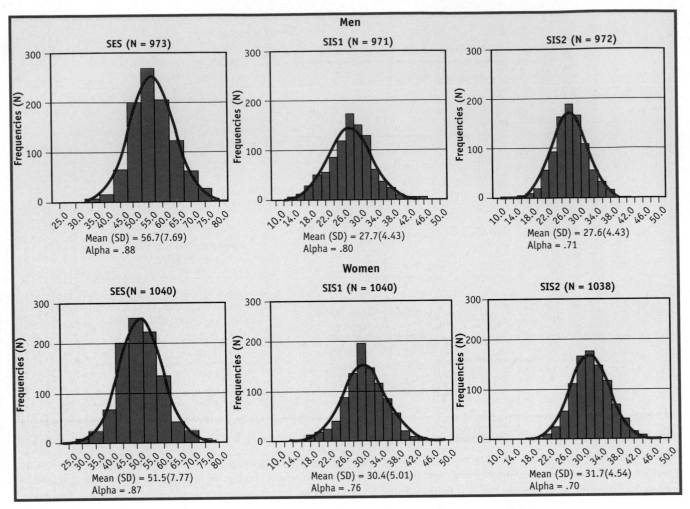

FIGURE 4.2   *Distribution of Sexual Excitation and Sexual Inhibition Scales by Gender*

These graphs plot the distributions of the Sexual Excitation Scales (SES) and two Sexual Inhibition Scales (SIS1 and SIS2) for men and women. There are close to normal distribution curves (illustrated by the red curve) in each case. This demonstrates that individual variation in propensities for sexual excitation and inhibition seems to be normal, with the mid-range levels being perhaps the most adaptive. It also illustrates some gender differences in propensities for sexual excitation and inhibition, as described in the text.

Source: Bancroft. J., Graham, C. A., Janssen, E., & Sanders, S. A. (2009). The dual control model: Current status and future directions. *Journal of Sex Research, 46,* 121–142 (Figure 1, p. 127), reprinted by permission of the publisher (Taylor & Francis Group, http://www.informaworld.com). Data from Carpenter, D., et al. (2008). Women's scores on the Sexual Inhibition/Sexual Excitation Scales (SIS/SES): Gender similarities and differences. *Journal of Sex Research, 45,* 36–48.

Measures of Sexual Excitation and Inhibition

Survey questionnaires have been used to measure individual differences in propensities for both sexual excitation and sexual inhibition, as well as sexual desire. From these studies, a Sexual Excitation Scale (SES) and two Sexual Inhibition Scales (SIS1 and SIS2) have been developed for men and women (Carpenter et al., 2008; Graham, Sanders, & Milhausen, 2006; Janssen et al., 2002a, 2002b). As Figure 4.2 demonstrates, when the SES and SIS scores from individual men and women

are grouped together and distributed on graphs, they fall into normal distribution curves, showing the wide range of differences. Researchers have also been able to draw some general conclusions from these studies, including the following:

- On average, males show higher excitation scores and lower inhibition scores than females.
- Gay men score higher on excitation and lower on inhibition than straight males.
- Excitation scores for both men and women decrease with age, while inhibition scores seem to be less age related.

- There are distinguishable differences between desire for sex with a partner, which is influenced by more complex factors, and the desire for sexual gratification on one's own through masturbation. Even people who have little interest in sex with a partner may desire to masturbate.

It becomes clear that some people have a greater propensity toward activation of sexual arousal than others, a quality that might be described as *sexual arousability*. An individual's degree of arousability seems to be influenced by the balance of excitation and inhibition systems that are part of their sexual makeup. This may be influenced by external factors. It has been shown for example that when an individual's sexual partner is turned on and having fun, the individual will experience heightened arousal. Conversely, a turned-off and nonresponsive partner will lead to diminished arousal (Haning et al., 2008).

There is also evidence that when a person's nervous system has been excited by some nonsexual stimulus, such as a roller-coaster ride, that individual will react in a way that may make him or her somewhat more susceptible to sexual arousal as well (Meston & Frohlich, 2003). Arousability also may be inhibited or turned off by certain negative stimuli (Christakis et al., 2000). In men, for example, sexual arousal may be inhibited, or interfered with, by concerns over sexual performance, sexual dissatisfaction, or the threat of negative consequences. Some males are more sensitive to such inhibition than others (Janssen et al., 2002a, 2002b; Spiering, Everaerd, & Elzinga, 2002). In women, arousal may be inhibited by concerns about one's body or reputation, unwanted pregnancy, and how the partner is relating (Conaglen, 2004; Graham et al., 2004; Meana & Nunnink, 2006).

Perceiving Arousal in Oneself

Research has demonstrated that people's perceptions of their own degree of sexual arousal do not always coincide with the ways their sex organs are actually responding, especially in women. Physiological sexual arousal may be detected by measuring changes in the vagina or the penis. Such measurement can be helpful in comparing bodily reactions to more subjective, psychological experiences associated with desire and arousal. In women, a probe can be placed within the vagina to detect increases or decreases in blood flow to that organ. In men, a **penile strain gauge,** in the form of a cuff or wire, can be placed around the penis and attached to a **plethysmograph,** which will chart changes in the girth and rigidity of the penis in response to sexual arousal or loss of arousal (Bancroft, 2009).

Using these techniques, researchers have found that women are less likely than men to pick up on the physiological cues of their own sexual arousal. When shown sexually explicit films, for example, women seem to have genital responses just as quickly as do men, but they are much less likely to identify themselves as being sexually aroused. This may be due partly to socialization that discourages females from paying attention to their genital responses or from feeling comfortable reporting arousal, and partly to the fact that erection of the penis is anatomically more easily noticed than the internal vaginal changes associated with arousal. What is happening within the body's sexual responses may not always be recognized by the information-processing systems of the person's mind or be interpreted in the same way by different people. Genital response alone does not constitute sexual arousal because the genitals may respond to stimuli not typically thought to be sexually stimulating. In other words, sexual arousal includes both physiological response and some inner, subjective experience that defines the response, and perhaps the surrounding situation, as sexual for a particular individual (Janssen, Carpenter & Graham, 2003; Nobre et al., 2004; Nobre & Pinto-Gouveia, 2008; Youn, 2006).

Things that may seem intrinsically sexual to one individual may be a turnoff for someone else. Then again, a stimulus that is not even perceived by the individual to be pleasurable or sexual can cause a physical response of the genitals (as happened to our student friend when he was putting a notebook in his locker). Also, emotions that have nothing to do with sex per se—such as depression, anxiety, or the thrill of a roller-coaster ride—may still exert a strong influence on sexual excitatory or inhibitory mechanisms (Basson, 2002). In other words, these excitatory and inhibitory propensities are very individualized.

Women, Men, and Sexual Arousal

There are many persistent beliefs about differences in sexual arousability between women and men. It is generally assumed today that, on average, women become sexually aroused less often and less rapidly than men. Men and women also are said to become sexually aroused by different stimuli—men by physical stimulation, pictures of nude people, and pictures of sexual acts, and women more by the romantic aspects of loving relationships. It is surely true that generally

penile strain gauge a device placed on the penis to measure even subtle changes in its size due to sexual arousal.

plethysmograph (pleh-THIZ-ma-graff) a laboratory measuring device that charts physiological changes over time. Attached to a penile strain gauge, it can chart changes in penis size. This is called penile plethysmography.

speaking, social standards have been generally less permissive toward female sexual activity than toward that of males. In laboratory settings, it has been found that men are more attuned to their bodily responses and more likely to interpret them as sexual. It seems likely, then, that women's genital responses are less involved in the determination of their subjective experience of sexual arousal than are external factors such as a relationship (Basson et al., 2001, 2003).

People's methods of processing information and attaching sexual meanings to experiences and emotions seem to influence their arousal patterns. Even though an individual's automatic, excitatory responses may cause some thought or fantasy to generate a genital response, that same person's controlled and inhibitory responses may prevent him or her from experiencing or enjoying the response as sexual. Learning probably plays an essential role in determining how sexual arousal mechanisms actually function in each individual to generate a sexual response (Graham et al., 2004; Youn, 2006).

It does seem clear that men and women process visual information differently, leading to differences in how arousing they find visual erotic materials. Whereas men tend to have rather rapid sexual arousal in response to visual media, and become even more sensitized to certain vibratory touch after being exposed to them, women are less likely to have a positive reaction to sexual images or to interpret them as sexually arousing, even if their bodies show some level of arousal (Jiao et al., 2007; Lykins, Meana, & Strauss, 2008; Rupp & Wallen, 2008).

Although these concepts reinforce stereotypes that cannot be applied to all individuals, research studies do continue to confirm that women on average tend to romanticize the goals of sexual desire, seeing them as love, emotional intimacy, and commitment more than do men. Men, on the other hand, are generally more likely to sexualize these phenomena, seeing the goal of desire and arousal to be sexual activity (Janssen, Carpenter, & Graham, 2003). When asked to identify the *objects* of sexual desire, women are more likely than men to indicate a loved one or a romantic partner, whereas men are more likely to specify that the object of sexual desire should be physically and sexually attractive (Nobre et al., 2004).

Research on sexual desire and arousal is finally beginning to yield theories that help make sense of how complex these phenomena really are. Whereas getting sexually turned on may seem to be a simple matter, it is clear that the underlying neurophysiological processes are extremely complicated. As our knowledge becomes more refined, we may even become more adept at predicting what people will be more likely to experience problems with their sexual functioning and individualize treatment approaches for them (Sanders, Graham, & Milhausen, 2008).

■ Models of Human Sexual Response

It was before we began to understand the mechanisms that lead to sexual desire and arousal that we knew how the human body responds once it is aroused. Those responses are not confined to the sex organs but involve marked changes throughout the body, especially in the muscular and circulatory systems. It was in 1966, in their pioneering book *Human Sexual Response,* that William Masters and Virginia Johnson provided the most thoroughly researched information on how the human body responds to sexual stimulation. Their study concentrated on careful observation and instrumental monitoring of men and women who were engaging in sexual activity. The 694 people who participated in the study were carefully interviewed and screened to obtain as average a sample as possible. These individuals were helped to feel comfortable with sexual activity alone in the laboratory setting before they were observed by the research team. Although Masters and Johnson saw their work as an incomplete, preliminary step to understanding human sexual response—and despite the fact that some controversies have grown out of their study—the findings quickly gained general acceptance among professionals (Levin, 2008).

 See "Masters and Johnson's Sexual Response Research" on SexSource Online.

The Masters and Johnson Four-Phase Model

As Masters and Johnson observed the sexual responses of men and women in their laboratory, they noticed many similarities in responses between the two sexes. After gathering a great deal of data, they described the sexual response process as a four-phase cycle (see Figure 4.3). It has been argued that the Masters and Johnson model may not represent a fair view of human sexual responsiveness because they accepted into their research only people who indicated that they reached orgasm. They built their cyclical view of sexual responsiveness on the assumptions that orgasm is a natural built-in response and that the response cycle is programmed to repeat itself over and over during one's lifetime, given the proper stimuli. It has been posited that our present models of sexual response are overly male-centered and still tend to create the impression that the male sex organs are more extensive, active, and explosive than are those of females. Because the subjective, or mind, aspects of arousal and satisfaction are often

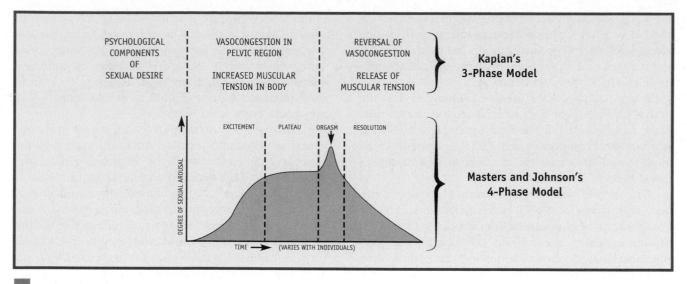

FIGURE 4.3 *Human Sexual Response*

Both Masters and Johnson and Helen Kaplan divided the human physical responses of sexual arousal into different phases. This chart compares their divisions.

ignored, our present models may misunderstand female sexual response (Basson et al., 2003; Levin, 2008). Nevertheless, the phases that Masters and Johnson invented to describe sexual responsiveness constitute one way to understand some fundamental aspects of human sexuality.

Masters and Johnson labeled the first phase **excitement,** during which the body begins to show the signs of sexual arousal. Blood is routed to the pelvic region, resulting in the earliest signs of arousal, such as erection of the penis and clitoris and vaginal lubrication. A wide range of physical and psychological stimuli can initiate this excitement phase. The intensity of the body's reactions to sexual arousal gradually builds to a higher level and is maintained at that level for varying lengths of time. Masters and Johnson labeled this the **plateau phase** because of its stable, or level, state of arousal.

The plateau phase, if held for sufficient periods of time, can be a major highlight of sexual response. The intensity of plateau may ebb and flow somewhat during sustained sexual activity and thereby provide some special highs of sensual enjoyment. In any case, the buildup of tension may eventually lead to the triggering of a pleasurable sexual release called **orgasm,** or **climax.** This third phase is brief, lasting a few seconds to slightly less than a minute, but it is one in which thought is momentarily suspended and the mind becomes focused inward on a rush of pleasurable physical sensations. Almost immediately after orgasm, the body relaxes and begins to return to its unexcited state, although some people may experience more than one orgasm relatively soon.

Masters and Johnson called the time of relaxation the **resolution phase.**

What are your feelings about the importance or unimportance of orgasm during sexual activity?

Keep in mind that such models simply provide a convenient way to examine various changes that occur during sexual response. There is no clear demarcation between the excitement and plateau phases, but instead a steady and continuous buildup of sexual tension.

Kaplan's Three-Phase Model

Another sex researcher and therapist, Helen Singer Kaplan (1974, 1979), proposed another model that she thought made more sense from the standpoint of

excitement the first phase of Masters and Johnson's four-phase model of the sexual response cycle, involving genital vasocongestion.

plateau phase the stable, leveled-off phase of Masters and Johnson's four-phase model of the sexual response cycle.

orgasm (OR-gaz-em) a rush of pleasurable physical sensations associated with the release of sexual tension.

climax another term for orgasm.

resolution phase the term for the return of a body to its unexcited state following orgasm.

the body's actual neurophysiological mechanisms. As Kaplan worked with people's problems with sexual arousal, referred to generally as **sexual dysfunctions,** she realized that some people simply did not seem to have much desire to become sexually aroused. This led her to suggest that a **desire phase** precedes the body's physiological responses to arousal. As we now know in greater detail, the desire phase represents the psychological component that is a critical part of sexual arousal, and it became the first stage in Kaplan's three-phase model of sexual response.

The second phase is characterized by vasocongestion, or buildup of blood in the pelvic area, and an accumulation of muscular tension throughout the body, causing increases in heart rate, breathing, blood pressure, and other involuntary functions. Rather than viewing orgasm as a phase in itself, Kaplan viewed it as the trigger for the third phase, in which the vasocongestion and muscular tension are released first through the sudden orgasmic bursts and then more gradually as the body returns to less excited levels of functioning. The relationship of Kaplan's three-phase model to the Masters and Johnson model is shown in Figure 4.3.

The Kaplan model has special validity when considering the various dysfunctions that can interfere with sexual responsiveness. These problems may involve inhibited sexual desire, sexual aversion, erectile dysfunction, vaginismus, or painful intercourse and usually are centered in the desire phase, the vasocongestive phase, or the orgasmic-release phase of the sexual response cycle (see Chapter 18, "Sexual Dysfunctions and Their Treatment").

> *Why was the Kaplan model so important to understanding sexual response? Do you believe men or women have a greater interest in sex? On what do you base your belief?*

Individual Differences in Sexual Response

Clearly there are more physiological similarities than differences in the sexual responses of males and females. Both males and females experience pelvic vasocongestion and a general buildup of muscular tension. Orgasm is very similar in both sexes, although it may not always be experienced. Table 4.1 summarizes the various changes that occur during sexual response in females and males. Within certain bounds, there can be great variation in sexual response among individuals. On average, males tend to reach orgasm more rapidly than females, but this phenomenon may well be influenced by the kind of stimulation and by the individual's past learning. Many women respond with orgasm more quickly during masturbation than

in intercourse. In fact, it is not unusual for women to respond almost as quickly as men during masturbation. The amount of time for completion of the entire cycle varies with learning, the sexual situation, the kind and intensity of stimulation, and age. An entire cycle from excitement through resolution may take only a few minutes or last several hours.

There seem to be subjective differences in the orgasms of males and females. Although male orgasms may vary in intensity and degree of pleasure, the experience is relatively standard among all males. Women often report experiencing different physical and psychological reactions during different orgasms. Some women even appear to have a very pleasurable feeling of sexual satisfaction even though they do not exhibit the usual physiological responses associated with orgasm (Basson, 2002; Basson et al., 2003).

Individual differences in sexual response patterns make it all the more important for sexual partners to take time to learn about each other's responsiveness. This also requires developing effective lines of communication about emotions, needs, and sex.

See "Studying Female Sexual Response" on SexSource Online.

■ Female Sexual Response

Excitement Phase

When the female body begins to respond sexually, changes are often noticed first in the vagina. As blood begins to build up (vasocongestion) in the blood vessels of the genital region, the vaginal walls darken in color, a change that is not visible externally. This vasocongestion causes a slippery, alkaline fluid to seep through the lining of the vagina. This substance functions as a lubricant for sexual activity and may also help create alkaline conditions in the vagina that are beneficial to sperm. The amount of lubrication in the vagina, however, is not necessarily a sign of how sexually aroused the woman is or how ready she might be for sexual activity. Particularly for females, genital responses must be supported by environmental cues and stimuli in order to create a sexual context (Graham et al., 2004).

Another change during the excitement phase is the lengthening and distention of the inner one-third of the vagina. The uterus is also pulled upward from

---

sexual dysfunctions difficulties people have in achieving sexual arousal and in other stages of sexual response.

desire phase Kaplan's term for the psychological interest in sex that precedes physiological sexual arousal.

Table 4.1 *Female and Male Sexual Response*

Phase	Female Responses	Male Responses
EXCITEMENT	Clitoris swells in diameter and length.	Penis becomes erect; urethral diameter begins to widen.
	Vagina lubricates, becomes expanded and lengthened and darker in color.	Scrotal skin tenses and thickens.
	Major and minor labia thicken and may open slightly.	Testes elevate slightly within scrotum.
	Breasts increase in size, and nipples become erect.	Nipples become erect in some males.
	Sex flush appears in some females.	
	Muscular tension increases.	Muscular tension increases.
	Heart rate begins to increase.	Heart rate begins to increase.
	Blood pressure begins to rise.	Blood pressure begins to rise.
PLATEAU	Clitoris retracts under prepuce.	Penis increases in diameter and becomes fully erect.
	Vagina expands and lengthens more; orgasmic platform develops.	Scrotum has no changes.
	Uterus is completely elevated.	Testes enlarge and elevate toward body.
	Labia swell more; labia minora have deeper red coloration.	Cowper's glands secrete a few drops of fluid.
	Breasts increase further in size, and nipples become turgid.	Nipples become erect and more turgid.
	Sex flush has appeared in most females and spreads.	Sex flush appears in some males and may spread.
	Muscular tension increases further.	Muscular tension increases further.
	Respiration and heart rates increase.	Respiration and heart rates increase.
	Marked elevation in blood pressure occurs.	Marked elevation in blood pressure occurs.
ORGASM	There are no changes in the clitoris.	Penis and urethra undergo contractions that expel semen.
	Uterus undergoes wavelike contractions.	There are no changes in the scrotum or testes.
	There are no changes in the labia.	
	Breasts and nipples show no changes during orgasm.	Nipples remain erect.
	Sex flush deepens.	Sex flush deepens.
	There is loss of voluntary muscle control, and spasms of some muscles.	There is loss of voluntary muscle control, and spasms of some muscles.
	Respiration and heart rates reach peak intensity.	Respiration and heart rates reach peak intensity.
	Blood pressure reaches its peak.	Blood pressure reaches its peak.
RESOLUTION	Clitoris returns to nonaroused position and loses its erection.	Penis erection is lost, rapidly at first, then more slowly.
	Vaginal walls relax and return to nonaroused coloration.	Scrotal skin relaxes and returns to nonaroused thickness.
	Uterus lowers to usual position, and cervical opening widens for 20 to 30 minutes.	Testes return to nonaroused size and position in scrotum.
	Labia return to nonaroused size, position, and color.	There is a period (refractory period) during which the male cannot be restimulated to orgasm.
	Breasts and nipples return to nonaroused size, position, and color.	Nipples return to nonaroused size.
	Sex flush disappears.	Sex flush disappears.
	Muscles relax rapidly.	Muscles relax rapidly.
	Respiration, heart rate, and blood pressure return to normal.	Respiration, heart rate, and blood pressure return to normal.
	Film of perspiration may appear on skin.	Film of perspiration may appear on skin, usually confined to soles of feet and palms of hands.

Source: W. H. Masters and V. E. Johnson, *Human Sexual Response.* Boston, MA: Little, Brown and Company, 1966.

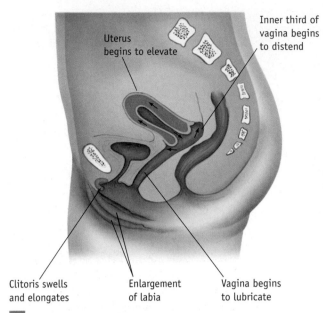

Uterus begins to elevate

Inner third of vagina begins to distend

Clitoris swells and elongates

Enlargement of labia

Vagina begins to lubricate

■ **FIGURE 4.4** *Female Excitement Phase*

In the female, the first sign of sexual arousal is often the lubrication of the vagina. This is accompanied by enlargement of the vaginal area, including the clitoris and the major and minor labia, and a darkening of the color of the vaginal walls.

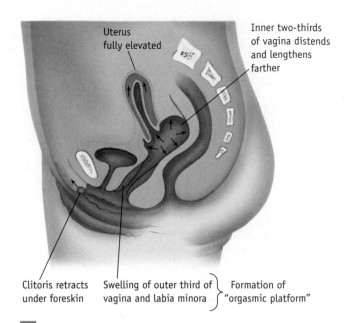

Uterus fully elevated

Inner two-thirds of vagina distends and lengthens farther

Clitoris retracts under foreskin

Swelling of outer third of vagina and labia minora

Formation of "orgasmic platform"

■ **FIGURE 4.5** *Female Plateau Phase*

In the plateau phase of sexual response, high levels of arousal are maintained. In the female, the orgasmic platform is caused by swelling of tissues in the outer third of the vagina, which causes the entrance to it to narrow. The clitoris retracts under its foreskin.

its usual position (see Figure 4.4). The vasocongestion causes changes in the labia majora and minora as they begin to enlarge and sometimes to open slightly. The clitoris begins to swell somewhat, and its shaft may elongate slightly. Some of the vaginal lubrication may flow out onto the labia and clitoris, depending on its copiousness and on whether the particular sexual activity is apt to bring internal secretions to the exterior (Martin-Alguacil et al., 2008).

Other areas of the body respond to sexual excitement as well. Often the nipples become harder and erect, although this response also may result from nonsexual stimuli. Many women show a darkening of the skin through the neck, breasts, and upper abdomen during sexual excitement, termed the sex flush. General muscular tension begins to build throughout the body as heart rate and blood pressure increase.

Plateau Phase

The second stage of the female sexual response cycle leads to further changes in the vagina. The outer third of the vaginal wall becomes swollen with blood, narrowing the space within the vagina slightly. The inner two-thirds of the vagina shows slightly more lengthening and expansion (Min et al., 2001). The labia minora also become engorged with blood, causing thickening and a flaring outward. The swelling of the outer third of the vagina and of the minor lips seems to create the tension that is an important precursor of orgasm, so together they are termed the orgasmic platform (see

Figure 4.5). During the plateau phase, the clitoral glans retracts back under its hood or foreskin so that it no longer receives any direct stimulation.

The breasts have usually become somewhat engorged with blood by this time, and nipple erection may be maintained. Increase in breast size is not as pronounced in women who have breast-fed a baby. The sex flush, if present, sometimes spreads to the shoulders, back, buttocks, and thighs during the plateau phase. Muscular tension continues to increase, along with heart rate, respiration rate, and blood pressure. The heart rate usually increases to between 110 and 175 beats per minute.

Orgasm

The pleasurable release of sexual tension occurs during the sexual climax, or orgasm. The subjective experience of orgasm, or the degree of pleasure described, seems to be affected by the sexual situation in which it occurs (Mah & Binik, 2005; Meston et al., 2005). It is an intense experience, both physically and emotionally, and in females it is immediately preceded by a sensation of suspension, at which time the pulse rate reaches its peak. Then there is a feeling of increased sexual awareness in the area of the clitoris, which spreads upward, and a suffusion of warmth that spreads from the pelvis throughout the body. Many women also experience a sensation of throbbing in the lower pelvic area.

The pleasurable feelings of the orgasmic phase are accompanied by muscular contractions in the outer

Real People

Angelina: Questioning Orgasmic Abilities

Angelina had been involved in a sexual relationship with her boyfriend for nearly a year when she became concerned about her sexual responsiveness. Although she regularly experienced orgasm during her sexual encounters with her partner, she had come to believe that she should be capable of having more than one orgasm when she had sex.

She had read articles about female sexuality implying that all women had the potential for multiple orgasms during sex, and she felt as though she might have something wrong with hers. Her boyfriend also seemed to want her to try to have more orgasms and sometimes would persist in attempting to offer stimulation that might produce that result. In fact, it was extremely uncomfortable for her to receive further stimulation in the clitoral area following orgasm. Physically and emotionally, she felt quite satisfied with a single orgasm.

Angelina eventually consulted a therapist, who explained to her that many women seem to be sexu-

ally satiated with one orgasm and that some apparently find sexual satisfaction without any orgasm at all. She urged Angelina to invite her boyfriend to join her at their next session so that they could talk about their sexual relationship. Although the boyfriend declined to enter counseling, Angelina was able to explain to him that she did not wish to pursue orgasms beyond the one she typically experienced. She realized that this pattern apparently fit her best and that it was a perfectly normal one. Her boyfriend continued to seem skeptical, because his only previous partner had experienced more than one orgasm, but he seemed willing to stop pressuring Angelina.

What is your reaction to Angelina's concerns? How do you feel about her boyfriend, and his skepticism? How would you talk with him if you were Angelina? Do you believe that women should attempt to have more than a single orgasm during a sexual encounter?

third of the vagina and in the rectal area (van Netten et al., 2008). Following the initial contraction, which may last from 2 to 4 seconds, are three or four rhythmic contractions at intervals of about 0.8 second. There may be up to 15 such contractions, with the interval between them gradually lengthening and their intensity gradually decreasing. Two to 4 seconds after orgasm begins, the uterus has some mild wavelike contractions that move from its top to the cervix (see Figure 4.6).

During orgasm, muscles throughout the body may contract involuntarily, causing pelvic thrusting and spastic movements of the neck, hands, arms, feet, and legs. The woman may scream, gasp, moan, or shout out words during the orgasmic experience. Heart and respiratory rates and blood pressure have all reached their peaks. The pulse rate may be twice as high as normal.

Resolution Phase

Following the release of sexual tension through orgasm, the body gradually returns to its unexcited state. As blood leaves the pelvic region, the vagina returns to its usual size and color, and the labia return to their pre-aroused state. Within 10 seconds the glans of the clitoris emerges from under the labia to its typical position, and

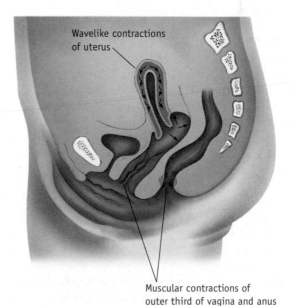

■ **FIGURE 4.6** *Female Orgasmic Phase*

Orgasm is the release of sexual tension involving a total body response. The female physical response is marked by simultaneous rhythmic muscular contractions of the uterus, the outer third of the vagina, and the anal sphincter.

within 15 to 30 minutes it has returned to its usual size. The uterus also lowers to its prearoused position.

During resolution, the other signs of sexual arousal also gradually disappear. The breasts decrease in size as blood flow to their tissue decreases, and the nipples lose their erection. The sex flush leaves the body in the reverse order from which it developed, and respiration, pulse, and blood pressure soon return to their normal levels. It is quite common for the body to become wet with perspiration during resolution. As the muscles throughout the body relax, there is often a feeling of drowsiness that may lead to sleep.

Multiple Orgasms in Women

During the resolution phase of sexual response, some women may be restimulated to orgasm. Kinsey and his coworkers (1953) reported that 14 percent of the women surveyed regularly experienced sequential (or multiple) orgasms during sexual encounters, and Masters and Johnson (1966) proposed that many women might have the potential to experience more than one orgasm.

Research since that time has suggested that the multiorgasmic experience for women may depend a great deal on the type of sexual stimulation involved in their sexual responsiveness. In one study of 720 women, about 47 percent indicated that they usually had single orgasms, and 43 percent reported that they had experienced multiple orgasms. It would appear that women tend to be multiorgasmic through particular means of stimulation. In this study, for example, 26 percent of the women had experienced multiple orgasms through masturbation, 18.3 percent through stimulation by a partner, and 24.7 percent by sexual intercourse. Only 7 percent had experienced more than one orgasm by all three types of stimulation (Darling, Davidson, & Jennings, 1991). It has been suggested both that we should stop assuming that female sexual satisfaction rests solely on whether one or more orgasms are experienced and that we should stop undervaluing women's capacity for multiple orgasms by giving precedence to a male-centered, single orgasm norm (Basson et al., 2001, 2003).

Controversies about Female Sexual Response

Orgasms

For many years, there has been controversy over the existence of two types of female orgasm: clitoral and vaginal. Masters and Johnson (1966) concluded that, regardless of how it is produced, female orgasm proceeds physiologically in basically the same manner. They believed that, at least from a biological viewpoint, the clitoral-vaginal dichotomy was unfounded.

However, researchers report distinct differences in how women experience orgasm produced by clitoral or vulval stimulation and that produced by deeper vaginal stimulation. Some women experience orgasm as the result of stimulation of the cervix, called a "uterine orgasm." It has also been suggested that some women experience a "blended orgasm," a combination of the clitoral-vulval experience and the uterine orgasm. The difference in orgasmic responses could be due to the two different nerve pathways that serve the sex organs: the pudendal nerves and the pelvic nerves. The pudendal nerve system connects with the clitoris, and the pelvic system innervates the vagina, cervix, and uterus. It is hypothesized that there may be two different neurological routes to producing orgasm (Martin-Alguacil, 2008; Meston et al., 2005).

This controversy may well represent one of those cases in which it is difficult to reconcile the objective measures of science and the subjective reports of people's experiences. It does seem clear that orgasm has both physiological and psychological components, meaning that each person will have individualized perceptions and interpretations of the experience (Mah & Binik, 2005). Regardless of what sort of orgasm a woman might experience, the most important issue is that she be able to feel that a sexual activity has been fulfilling to her personally.

The G Spot

It is possible that there is an area on the inner front wall of the vagina that may become particularly sexually sensitive. The existence of such an area was proposed years ago by a German physician named Gräfenberg (1950). The idea was revived in the 1980s by other researchers who claimed that there is indeed an area in the anterior vagina that swells during sexual arousal and can lead to intense orgasmic experiences. They named it the **G spot,** after Gräfenberg (Ladas, Whipple, & Perry, 1983). Some scientists have objected, feeling that the sensitive spot is not found in a large percentage of women and that, when it is present, it is not in a clearly defined location.

The confusion might result from the fact that the spongy tissue in this area may not become fully engorged with blood and sensitized until the clitoris is fully engorged. This can take up to 25 minutes in some women, so they may never experience the sensitivity of the G spot. There has also been speculation that this vaginal region may be activated by a different set of nerves (pelvic) than is the clitoris (pudendal) and so it

> **G spot** a vaginal area that some researchers feel is particularly sensitive to sexual stimulation when its underlying spongy tissues are engorged with blood.

has been difficult to separate the different types of orgasm that may result from their stimulation. The one thing this controversy has confirmed is that many women are sensitive to vaginal stimulation, thus laying to rest an earlier view of the vagina as a rather insensitive organ (Basson et al., 2001; Meston et al., 2005).

Ejaculation

Gräfenberg also suggested in his 1950 article that some women might ejaculate a semenlike substance from their urethra at the time of orgasm. It has been hypothesized that **Skene's glands,** located inside the urethra, might be similar to the male prostate (Sevely, 1987). During particularly intense orgasms, some women report that a liquid is expelled from their urethra that does not seem to be urine. A survey of 1,230 women in North America found that 40 percent of them had experienced such an ejaculation. Those who had ejaculated were more likely to report their sexual responsiveness as above average in intensity (Darling, Davidson, & Conway-Welch, 1990). Some women seem to assume that the fluid is urine and are therefore reluctant to pursue the matter. Some of those women may even try to prevent themselves from experiencing intense orgasms in an effort to reduce the chances of emitting this fluid.

Kegel Exercises and Sexual Response

In the early 1950s, surgeon Arnold Kegel developed exercises for the pubococcygeal (PC) muscle that surrounds the vagina. He originally intended the exercises for girls and women who had difficulty preventing urine from leaking from their bladders. Eventually, Kegel found that in some of his subjects a well-toned PC muscle increased the ability to experience orgasmic satisfaction. Kegel exercises have also been recommended for pregnant women and seem to help the vagina and uterus return to their normal shape and tone more quickly after the delivery of a baby. It has been suggested that men should keep their PC muscles in good shape to ensure good orgasms as well. Although whether the PC muscle actually affects orgasmic capacity is controversial, keeping it in good shape is at least a healthy thing and may also enhance general sexual sensitivity.

Kegel exercises are accomplished by first locating the PC muscle. This is best done by stopping and starting the flow of urine during urination, because the same muscle is involved. Once the individual is familiar with its location, it is usually suggested that the muscle be contracted firmly for 2 or 3 seconds and then released. Although it has been recommended that these contractions be done in sets of tens, building up to several sets each day, some experts now believe that

it is unnecessary, and even unwise, to exercise the PC muscle too much.

■ Male Sexual Response

Excitement Phase

Vasocongestion in the pelvic area during early sexual arousal contributes to erection of the penis, the first sign of the excitement phase in males. The degree of erection during this phase depends on the intensity of sexual stimuli. Eventually the inner diameter of the urethra doubles (Prieto, 2008). Vasocongestion also causes thickening of the scrotal skin, and the scrotum pulls upward toward the body. The testes become elevated within the scrotum, although if the excitement phase continues for more than 5 or 10 minutes, the testes may return to their original position for a time (see Figure 4.7).

Nipple erection and appearance of the sex flush are less common in males than in females, but both phenomena usually are first observed during the excitement phase if they occur at all. Muscular tension increases throughout the body during the late excitement phase, and heart rate and blood pressure both increase. Sometimes secretion from Cowper's (bulbourethral) glands appears during this stage or can even precede erection.

Plateau Phase

The penis does not change markedly during the second stage of sexual response, although a man is less likely to lose his erection if he is distracted during the plateau phase than during excitement. As orgasm nears, the corona of the glans of the penis becomes more swollen, and the glans itself may take on a deeper, often reddish-purple color. There are no further changes in the scrotum, but the testes increase in size by 50 percent or more and become elevated toward the body. During plateau, Cowper's glands often secrete a few drops of fluid, some of which may appear at the tip of the penis. The longer plateau stimulation is maintained, the greater the amount of fluid produced (see Figure 4.8).

Muscular tension heightens considerably during the plateau phase, and involuntary body movements increase as orgasm approaches. The nipples may become erect. Males often have clutching or grasping movements of the hands in late plateau. Heart rate increases to between 100 and 175 beats per minute, and blood pressure increases. Respiratory rate also increases, especially in the later plateau phase. If the sex flush is present, it may spread to the neck, back, and buttocks.

Skene's glands secretory cells located inside the female urethra.

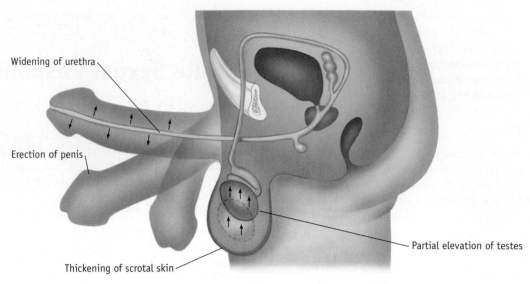

FIGURE 4.7 *Male Excitement Phase*

Vasocongestion in the male leads to erection of the penis, the first physical sign of sexual arousal. The testes are lifted up in the scrotum as a result of the shortening of the spermatic cords and contraction of the scrotal sac. The scrotal tissue itself thickens.

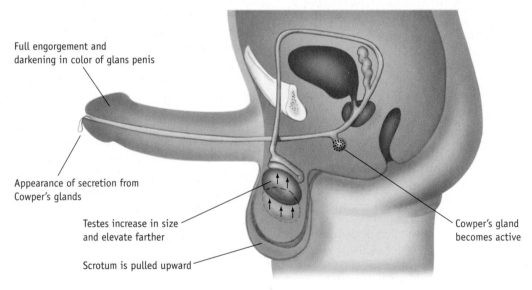

FIGURE 4.8 *Male Plateau Phase*

A generalized increase in neuromuscular tension is experienced in both males and females in the plateau phase. In the male, the head of the penis increases slightly in size and deepens in color. The testes swell by 50 to 100 percent. The testes continue to elevate. A secretion from Cowper's glands may appear at the tip of the penis and may carry live sperm.

Orgasm

In males, actual orgasm and ejaculation are preceded by a distinct inner sensation that orgasm is imminent—a phenomenon called **ejaculatory inevitability.** Almost immediately after that feeling is reached, the male senses that ejaculation cannot be stopped. The most noticeable response in the penis during orgasm is the ejaculation of semen. The muscles at the base of the penis and around the anus contract rhythmically, with intervals of about 0.8 second between the first three or four contractions. This varies in different individuals. The intensity of the contractions then diminishes, and the interval between contractions lengthens. The first few contractions expel the largest amount of semen. The testes are held at their maximum elevation throughout orgasm (see Figure 4.9).

ejaculatory inevitability the sensation in the male that ejaculation is imminent.

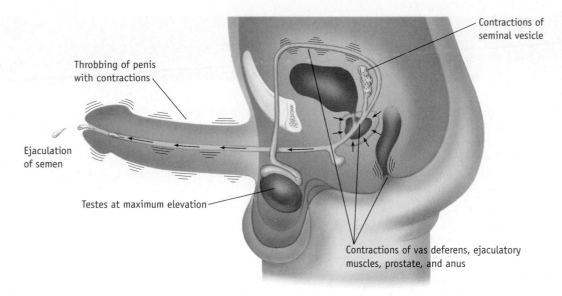

Throbbing of penis
with contractions

Ejaculation
of semen

Testes at maximum elevation

Contractions of
seminal vesicle

Contractions of vas deferens, ejaculatory
muscles, prostate, and anus

■ **FIGURE 4.9** *Male Orgasmic Phase*

Male orgasm and ejaculation occur in two distinct phases but are perceived as occurring simultaneously. The vas deferens, prostate, and seminal vesicle begin a series of contractions that force semen into the urethra. The contractions continue until the semen is ejaculated.

Males often have strong involuntary muscle contractions throughout the body during orgasm and usually exhibit involuntary pelvic thrusting. The hands and feet show spastic contractions, and the entire body may arch backward or contract in a clutching manner. Many men moan or yell during orgasm and have a grimacing facial expression. Breathing, heart rate, and blood pressure all reach a peak during orgasm, and some men begin perspiring during this stage.

Like women, men have two different nerve pathways to different parts of their sex organs. The pudendal nerve system connects with the penile glans, whereas the pelvic nerve system serves the base of the penis and the prostate gland. This could explain why orgasm is not necessarily always accompanied by ejaculation of semen. Orgasm produced from localized stimulation of the glans may be somewhat less likely to be accompanied by ejaculation. It is also known that different sets of nerves are involved depending on whether erection is generated by direct touching of the genitals or by psychological stimuli such as erotic thoughts and fantasies, although the two systems are somewhat interactive. In any case, male orgasm and ejaculation should be viewed as two essentially separate sexual responses that most often happen at the same time.

Resolution

Immediately following ejaculation, the male body begins to return to its unexcited state. About 50 percent of the penile erection is lost right away, and the remainder is lost over a longer period of time, depending on the degree of stimulation and nonsexual activity. Urination, walking, and other distracting activities usually lead to a more rapid return of the penis to its flaccid state. The diameter of the urethra returns to its usual width. The scrotum begins to relax as vasocongestion decreases, and the testes return to their nonaroused size and position. Resolution in the scrotum and testes takes varying lengths of time, depending on the individual.

If nipple erection and sex flush have appeared, they gradually diminish. Muscular tension usually is fully dissipated within five minutes after orgasm, and the male feels relaxed and drowsy. Many men fall asleep quickly during the resolution phase. About one-third of men begin to perspire during this stage. Heart rate, respiration rate, and blood pressure rapidly return to normal. Resolution is a gradual process that may take as long as two hours.

Refractory Period

During resolution, most males experience a period of time during which they cannot be restimulated to ejaculation; known as the **refractory period.** The duration of the refractory period depends on a variety of factors, including the amount of available sexual stimulation, the man's mood, and his age. On average, men in their late thirties cannot be restimulated to orgasm for 30 minutes or more. The period gradually increases with age. Very few men beyond their teenage years are capable of more than one orgasm during sexual encounters, except occasionally. Most men feel sexually satiated with one orgasm. Researchers who proposed the Dual Control

refractory period time following orgasm during which a man cannot be restimulated to orgasm.

Real Student Voices

■ I have had two sexual partners prior to the relationship with my present boyfriend. While I didn't know this at the time, I never actually had an orgasm with either of those first two. My boyfriend now took a lot more time with me, and was very romantic, and the second time we had sex, I did have an orgasm. It was great, and I'll always be grateful to him.

■ I always feel like I don't last long enough for my girlfriend. She usually has an orgasm before I ejaculate, but she doesn't really seem to be finished either. She has told me she wishes I could last longer, but nothing I have tried has worked so far.

Model have suggested that inhibitory mechanisms may kick in to produce the refractory period in men, temporarily impairing excitation (Bancroft et al., 2009).

Multiple Orgasms in Men

There have always been tales of men who are capable of experiencing more than one orgasm during a single sexual experience, presumably without experiencing a refractory period. Some case studies have reported on small numbers of men who experience multiple orgasms, and some laboratory measures of their responses have been taken. These studies suggest that some men seem able to delay ejaculation but still experience some internal contractions and pleasurable sensations associated with orgasm. It has been suggested that men can learn to develop the muscle control necessary to separate orgasm from ejaculation. However, in at least one case study, the man was able to ejaculate each time while reaching six separate orgasms in 36 minutes. Evidence suggests that this pattern is unusual, although this particular male had experienced multiple ejaculations since the age of 15. Younger men may have a brief refractory period and may experience a second ejaculation quite rapidly, sometimes without losing their erections (Whipple, Myers, & Komisaruk, 1998).

How might our general views of sexual responsiveness be unfair to women or men?

■ Hormones and Sexual Arousal

Do hormones control our levels of interest in sexual activity, our attractions to others, or the functioning of our bodies? The picture of how hormones affect sexual desire and behavior is complicated and not particularly supportive of some typical assumptions. Recent research suggests that sex hormones enable some

aspects of desire and arousal but also confirms that other aspects of sexual behavior are unrelated to hormonal influences (Park & Rissman, 2007).

Organizing and Activating Effects

The secretions of the endocrine glands, called hormones, exert their influence in one of two ways. The first, called an **organizing effect,** refers to ways in which hormones control patterns of early development in the body, playing a crucial role in the structure and function of particular organs. Chapter 5, "Developmental and Social Perspectives on Gender," for example, describes how certain hormones control the development of sex glands and external genitals in the fetus and how they may lead to some differences in how the nervous systems of males and females develop. Once hormones have done their organizing, the same or other hormones may continue to alter later processes of development and patterns of behavior.

The second effect that hormones seem to exert is referred to as an **activating effect.** This describes the potential of some hormones to directly affect an actual behavior, by either activating or deactivating it. In the matter of sexual desire and arousal, it has been tempting to assume that levels of particular sex hormones in the bloodstream might increase or decrease a person's immediate level of sexual desire or activity, but the evidence in support of such a model has been mixed. Studies demonstrate that the central arousal system, in which internal stimuli are processed by the brain, probably is more dependent on the presence of hormones for activation than is the peripheral arousal

organizing effect manner in which hormones control patterns of early development in the body.

activating effect the direct influence some hormones can have on activating or deactivating sexual behavior.

system, which is far more susceptible to localized stimuli such as touch or viewing erotic material (Bancroft, 2009; Park & Rissman, 2007).

The hormone that has been shown to have the most effect on sexual desire and arousal in humans is testosterone. Although this is an **androgen,** or male hormone, it is produced by both males and females in the testes or ovaries and the adrenal glands. Men's bodies tend to produce 10 to 15 times more testosterone than do women's bodies. However, the hormone also plays a vital role in enabling women to become sexually aroused, and females seem to have a heightened sensitivity to it (Apperloo et al., 2003; Traish et al., 2002).

Hormonal Activation of Sexual Arousal

For both men and women, testosterone apparently has an activating effect on sexual interest. It might be viewed as a switch for sexual desire, and human beings seem to require some level of androgen in order to have a potential for sexual desire. This activation process occurs during puberty, when testosterone is produced by the sex glands (Park & Rissman, 2007).

Research on women has yielded a relationship between the levels of androgens such as testosterone (remember that the female body produces some androgens too) and levels of sexual desire. Studies of their androgen levels have shown that hormone deficiencies are at least associated with decreased desire (Bolour & Braunstein, 2005). At this point, the actual neurochemical pathways by which androgens exert their effects are only beginning to be understood (Anders et al., 2005; Park & Rissman, 2007).

Women's levels of sexual activity vary over the menstrual cycle and therefore could be associated with hormonal changes (Bullivant et al., 2004; Garver-Apgar, Gangestad, & Thornhill, 2008; Jones et al., 2008). The picture can be clouded by the fact that women seem to initiate sexual activity at times for reasons other than sexual desire alone. A study of women who sought treatment to reduce hairiness on their faces and bodies showed that when the women were given antiandrogen medications to reduce the effects of androgens in their bodies, their sexual desire seemed to decrease progressively during the treatment (Conaglen & Conaglen, 2003).

Hormone research with males has shown that testosterone can affect both sexual desire and arousal, although the mechanisms by which this happens are not yet fully understood. It is known that there are many androgen receptors in parts of the central nervous system that seem to be important to sexual behavior. The concentrations of testosterone necessary to activate the ability for sexual arousal appear to be much higher than those that are needed to maintain sexual capabilities over time. It has been confirmed that testosterone

exposure in puberty seems to be essential to the activation of male sexual arousability, and if that does not happen, sexual desire and arousal may be compromised for the male's lifetime. However, when adult males have had their testes removed for medical reasons, any decreases in sexual desire or arousal may occur very gradually over many years, and some sexual behavior appears not to be dependent on androgens at all (Park & Rissman, 2007). When testosterone is administered to men whose testosterone levels have decreased, it may enhance sexual desire, but often does little to improve erectile function (Allan et al., 2008; Emmelot-Vonk et al., 2009; Hwang & Lin, 2008).

Before reading the section "Effects of Aging on Sexual Response," list your own perceptions of sexual activity after age 60. Include both the positive and the negative aspects.

■ Effects of Aging on Sexual Response

Aging does not necessarily bring an end to responding sexually, but it usually does bring some changes to levels of desire and sexual responsiveness. Sexual satisfaction in older age depends a great deal on physical health, psychological outlook, and the availability of a healthy and interested partner (Kontula & Haavio-Mannila, 2009). People who have felt positively about sex and who have placed a priority on remaining sexually active typically maintain their sexual satisfaction longer. Put in simple and direct language, this concept is often summarized by the phrase use it or lose it.

In the original Masters and Johnson (1966) study, 212 men beyond 50 years of age were interviewed concerning their sexual lives. Thirty-nine of these men, the oldest of whom was 89, agreed to have their sexual responses observed by the research team. Thirty-four women over the age of 50 were also observed, and another 118 interviews were conducted with women between 51 and 80 years of age. The following discussion is based partly on these interviews and observations. A summary of the information is given in Table 4.2.

Aging and Female Sexual Response

Two manifestations of postmenopausal hormonal imbalance can cause unpleasant sensations during sexual

androgen (ANN-dra-gin) a male hormone, such as testosterone, that affects physical development, sexual desire, and behavior. Testosterone is produced by both male and female sex glands and influences each sex in varying degrees.

Table 4.2	Effects of Aging on Female and Male Sexual Response

Changes in the Aging Female	Changes in the Aging Male
Thinning of vaginal lining	Some atrophy of testicular tissue
Reduction in vaginal lubrication	Reduction in secretion of preejaculatory fluid and amount of semen produced
Increase in uterine cramping associated with orgasm	Testes not elevated as much during sexual arousal
Increase in amount of time needed to experience sexual arousal and vaginal lubrication	Increase in amount of time needed to achieve full penile erection
Increase in time of stimulation required to reach orgasm, and fewer muscular contractions associated with orgasm	Increase in time of stimulation required to reach orgasm, and reduced strength of orgasmic muscular contractions
Resolution to unexcited state about the same	Quicker resolution to unexcited state
Women who have been multiorgasmic seem to retain the capability	Lengthened refractory period, so the time before a man may be restimulated to orgasm tends to increase

Source: W. H. Masters and V. E. Johnson, *Human Sexual Response*. Boston, MA: Little, Brown and Company, 1966.

activity in some older women. First, because the vaginal lining has thinned and vaginal lubrication possibly has lessened, intercourse may produce irritation that persists as burning or itching afterward. Water-soluble lubricants can relieve such problems, and estrogen-based creams may also help by increasing natural vaginal secretions. Second, some women experience uterine cramping during and after orgasm. These unpleasant symptoms can be relieved by proper medical treatment (Freeman et al., 2008; Simon et al., 2008).

As women age, there seems to be some decrease in orgasmic ability and a general tempering of sexual arousal processes. This is a very gradual process of change and is somewhat dependent on how sexually active a particular woman remains. For heterosexual women over the age of 70 who have been involved in long-term relationships, their degree of sexual involvement may have a great deal to do with the availability and capability of their male partner (Kontula & Haavio-Mannila, 2009).

One effect of aging on female sexual response is a lengthening of the time for vaginal lubrication and other early signs of sexual arousal to take place. There is also less enlargement of the clitoris, labia, uterus, and breasts during sexual arousal. Orgasm takes a bit longer to occur in older women, and there are usually fewer orgasmic contractions of the vagina, uterus, and pelvic floor. The resolution phase of female sexual response, during which the body returns to its unexcited state, appears to be relatively unaffected by the aging process.

Aging and Male Sexual Response

Three aspects of male sexual response undergo predictable changes as men age. The first is erection. It takes a man in his seventies two to three times longer to achieve full penile erection than it did in the man's younger years, and he usually requires direct penile stimulation. Although it is perfectly normal for men of any age to experience waxing and waning of erection during prolonged sexual arousal, it is more difficult for older men to reestablish full rigidity once erection has been partially lost. The angle of the erect penis up from the body also decreases with age.

The second change relates to male orgasm and ejaculation. Older men take longer to reach orgasm than they did earlier in their lives. The strength of the orgasmic contractions is reduced, so semen is ejaculated with less force, sometimes just seeping out of the urethra. The frequency with which men desire orgasm also seems to decline somewhat as they age. Except in rare instances, men over 60 are completely satisfied by one or, at the most, two orgasms in the span of a week. They may enjoy participating in sexual behavior more frequently than that, experiencing full erection but no orgasm. The urge to achieve orgasm seems to be reduced with age. The third change is a lengthening of the male refractory period; by their late fifties or early sixties, most men cannot achieve an erection again for 12 to 24 hours after ejaculation.

Other aspects of the aging male's sexual response also show a decrease. There is a reduction both in the amount of preejaculatory secretion from the Cowper's glands and in the amount of semen produced. The testes and scrotum do not enlarge as much during sexual arousal, nor do the testes elevate as much within the scrotum. The resolution phase of men tends to occur more rapidly with age, and the penis may lose its erection after ejaculation much more quickly (Kontula & Haavio-Manila, 2009).

Self-Evaluation

Sexual Arousal and Response in Your Life

This is a highly personal assessment meant for your individual use only. It can help you evaluate and understand some of your reactions to and feelings about your own sexual arousability and responsiveness. As this chapter has emphasized, different people seem to have different levels of arousability and different cues or sensitivities that can activate or deactivate (turn on or turn off) sexual response. There is no single "right" or "normal" way to be.

Complete the questionnaire first and then continue reading to understand what you can learn from it. This evaluation is not in any way meant to be a scientific test; it is only a simple instrument to help you further clarify some of your own reactions.

Use this scale:

5 = strongly agree

4 = somewhat agree

3 = neutral/uncertain

2 = somewhat disagree

1 = strongly disagree

Rate the following statements for yourself. (You might not want to write your responses in the book for others to see.)

1. I find myself thinking about sexual things frequently.
2. I think about sex more than the average person.
3. My thoughts about sex often lead to sexual arousal.
4. I experience sexual arousal several times a week.
5. I can reach orgasm during a sexual experience anytime I wish.
6. In general, I have positive feelings about my own sexual responsiveness.
7. I enjoy the sensations of sexual excitement in my sex organs and in the rest of my body.
8. I like experiencing orgasm (or do not mind at all if I do not reach orgasm) during sexual activity.
9. I know very clearly what turns me on sexually.
10. I am very comfortable with the place that sexual arousal and responsiveness have in my life.
11. Sometimes I get sexually aroused at inappropriate or embarrassing times.
12. I wish I could get sexually aroused more easily than I do.
13. I never/rarely reach orgasm, and this concerns me.
14. (If applicable now or in the past) My partner sometimes seems dissatisfied with my levels of sexual arousal.
15. (If applicable) My partner wishes I would get sexually aroused more easily and/or more often.

Evaluating Your Responses

As you examine your responses to the various items, it will be helpful to evaluate them in three different blocks:

Items 1–5: These items relate to the frequency with which you experience sexual thoughts and arousal. The higher your numbers, the more frequently you think about sexuality and experience arousal and response. As you look at the numbers, do you see any trend? What do they say to you about your sexuality?

Items 6–10: These items can help you examine your reactions to your sexual arousal and responsiveness. The higher the numbers, the greater degree of relative satisfaction you are indicating for your patterns of sexual arousal and response. The lower the numbers, the greater the likelihood that you are not particularly happy or satisfied with the ways you respond to sexual stimuli.

Items 11–15: These items focus on the dissatisfactions you may be experiencing with regard to your sexual responsiveness and, if applicable, with how your responsiveness fits into a relationship. Higher numbers would suggest that you have a fair amount of discomfort and negative reaction to various aspects of your sexual arousal and response.

What Does It All Mean for You?

Keep in mind that this assessment is a very rough measure of some of your own perceptions. It should help you clarify some of your own thoughts and reactions regarding your sexual responses. As you survey your responses, does any picture seem to emerge? Do you see yourself as an individual who is comfortable and satisfied with his or her patterns of sexual arousal and response? Are you unsure of yourself and uncomfortable with how sexual desire and arousal fit into your life? Have your responses to the items suggested that you have a great deal of dissatisfaction about your sexuality?

Being able to get some general sense of how you react to your own sexual desire and arousal may be valuable to you as you read further chapters in this text. It may also alert you to the fact that you have some issues worth considering, some of which may be positive and some negative. If you feel that your profile is reflective of some sexual concerns and problems, you may want to seek professional help or consultation. See the section "Preventing and Dealing with Problematic Sex" found in Chapter 16.

Chapter Summary

1. Different cultures and spiritual traditions treat human sexual response in different ways.

2. The experience of sexual desire seems to be preceded by the experience of pleasurable sexual arousal. Both processes involve complex interactions of mind and body.

3. Arousal stimuli may be internal or external, corresponding to a central arousal system located in the brain and a peripheral arousal system that picks up cues from the genitals, senses, and spinal reflexes. The processes that mediate these systems may be automatic or controlled.

4. The Dual Control Model theorizes that desire and arousal are controlled by both excitatory (turn-on) and inhibitory (turn-off) mechanisms that interact with each other.

5. Meaurements of Sexual Excitement Scales (SES) and two Sexual Inhibition Scales (SIS1 & SIS2) show great variability in these systems among individuals that plot out to normal curves. Some people show greater levels of sexual arousability than others.

6. Penile and vaginal plethysmographs measurements show that people's perceptions of their own sexual arousal do not always match physiological measures.

7. Emotions, attention, and other psychological processes play a significant role in activating or deactivating sexual response.

8. Studies reveal more similarities than differences in arousal patterns of males and females. Men are more excited by visual cues than women, and women tend to be more excited by aspects of the relationship with a partner.

9. Masters and Johnson were among the first researchers to study scientifically the body's physiological changes during sexual response. They developed a four-phase model involving excitement, plateau, orgasm, and resolution.

10. A three-phase model proposed by Kaplan views sexual response as beginning with psychological desire, with a subsequent buildup of blood and muscular tension followed by reversal of these states as triggered by orgasm.

11. There are many individual differences in human sexual response, and good communication is essential to developing mutual understanding in a sexual relationship.

12. In females, the vagina becomes lubricated during sexual excitement, and an orgasmic platform develops with the swelling of the clitoris and labia. The clitoral glans eventually retracts under its foreskin. Resolution refers to the return of the body to its unexcited state.

13. Some women have the potential for more than one orgasm during a single sexual experience. Women report clitoral, vaginal, uterine, and blended orgasms.

14. Some researchers claim that there is a particularly sensitive spot on the inner front part of the vagina that swells during female arousal. This has been called the G spot.

15. It has been proposed that some women ejaculate a substance from the urethra during intense orgasms.

16. Kegel exercises can keep the urogenital musculature in good tone and may increase the intensity or pleasure of orgasm.

17. In males, penile erection is an early sign of excitement. There are also increases in the size of the testes and scrotum. The testes move upward in the scrotum.

18. In both women and men, sexual response involves increases in respiration, heart rate, blood pressure, and general muscular tension. A reddish sex flush appears on the skin of the upper body in some individuals, and nipple erection may also occur.

19. Orgasm is the pleasurable release of sexual tension, involving a series of muscular contractions in both sexes. Ejaculation usually accompanies orgasm in men.

20. During resolution, at the end of sexual response in men there is a refractory period during which there can be no restimulation to orgasm.

21. Hormones have both organizing and activating effects in the body. Testosterone, an androgen present in both men and women, acts as an activator for sexual arousal.

22. In humans, sexual desire and arousal seem to be controlled by both hormonal and social factors.

23. Both men and women may experience slower arousal and somewhat less intensity of response as they age. People who have been more sexually active during their younger years tend to maintain a higher level of sexual activity.

Chapter 5
Developmental and Social Perspectives on Gender

Chapter Outline

I consider myself to be a fairly sensitive guy, and I want to treat women with respect and a sense of equality, but I'm never sure what the rules are. Do I open doors for her, or should we take turns? Am I supposed to pay for dinner every time, or do we share the cost? Who is supposed to give the first signals about being interested in having sex?

—statement from a male student

*B*eing a sexual human being amounts to far more than the sexual organs with which we were born. There are many other dimensions of sexuality. Why is it that humans come in two sexes? Or do they? What factors influence the development of the genitals before birth, and are they always clearly female or male? What leads to our awareness of ourselves as girl or boy, feminine or masculine, or some combination of the two? Are gender roles determined by biology, socialization, or a combination of the two? How does gender fit into contemporary social and political trends? These are some of the questions we will explore in this chapter.

One unavoidable observation stares us in the face when we explore these topics. It is that the people around us generally are recognizable as male or female. There are surely many shades of overlap in physical structure and social behavior, and at first glance the gender classification of some people seems more ambiguous than that of others. Ultimately, we tend to see people in terms of the two sexes. But is that really fair?

■ How Many Sexes Are There?

Female and male are the two categories from which we are allowed to choose when filling out forms. Our legal systems also require that everyone be categorized as either male or female, and newborns must be identified on birth certificates as one or the other. But are things really that simple?

The concept of genders or sexes obviously has biological roots, but even biological facts are interpreted through the screen of cultural assumptions. From the time of the ancient Greeks until the end of the seventeenth century, Western culture embraced an essentially one-sex model; the one sex was male, and the structures of the female anatomy were seen as inverted or underdeveloped forms of the male sex organs. In other words, both sexes were actually just different forms of a single sex, one more fully developed than the other. During the early eighteenth century, a clearer distinction began to emerge that recognized female and male as two different sexes.

Intersexuality: Disorders of Sex Development

On the anatomical level, some human beings do not fit the standardized male-female categories. Medical investigators have long recognized the existence of **intersexuality,** a term that refers to some mixture of male and female anatomical characteristics, often reflected in the presence of ambiguous genitalia. The term is considered disrespectful and unscientific by some, and experts recently agreed to use the term **disorders of sex development,** or **DSD,** instead (Berenbaum, 2007). Not everyone is satisfied with that designation either, feeling that it is not necessary to view such things as disordered instead of as natural variations. Three major subgroups of DSD have been identified, although there are many other conditions that do not fit neatly into any of the categories. The three subgroups are: **true hermaphrodites,** who have both testiscular tissue and ovarian tissue; male **pseudohermaphrodites,** who have testes and some female genitals but no ovaries; and female pseudohermaphrodites, who have ovaries and some male genitals but no testes (Zucker, 2005).

In some societies, individuals with DSD have been accepted as a third sex, distinct from male and female. These groups have also encompassed some individuals with normal male or female anatomy who do not fit into the typical masculine or feminine roles of their society. In many societies today, alternative social statuses or gender roles are available for these individuals. The American Plains Indians once assigned the social status of *berdache* to men who did not have the skill for or interest in typically masculine, aggressive pursuits. The berdache was considered to hold special powers and sometimes served as a shaman for healing practices or in sacred ceremonies.

In India, a third gender called the *hijra* includes elements of both female and male roles, and such people are considered sacred. Similarly, there are the *fa'afafine* of Samoa, the *kathoey* of Thailand, and the *woubi* of the Ivory Coast. In some cases, these individuals have ambiguous genitalia, and some others simply seem to adopt behavioral patterns typical for the other gender (Bartlett & Vasey, 2006; Vasey &

---

intersexuality a combination of female and male anatomical structures so that the individual cannot be clearly defined as male or female.

disorders of sex development (DSD) a more scientific term now being applied to those with combinations or ambiguities of female and male anatomical structures.

true hermaphrodite a person who has one testis and one ovary. External appearance may vary among individuals.

pseudohermaphrodite a person who possesses either testes or ovaries in combination with some external genitals of the other sex.

VanderLaan, 2008). A genetic mutation within the Sambia tribe of Papua New Guinea has led to the birth of hermaphrodites who are assigned the role of *kwolu-aatmwol*, meaning an individual whose genitals appear to be female but who eventually will develop male secondary sex characteristics. Such individuals are not expected to take either male or female roles in their society but are allowed to become shamans or spirit doctors. All these are examples of alternative gender categories that have become socially institutionalized, although depending on the degree of social acceptance the group has achieved, they may be subject to ridicule or discrimination at times. A German study found that adults with DSD had a greater likelihood of suicide (Schutzmann et al., 2009; Vilain, 2001).

In modern Western cultures, such combinations of the sexes have been viewed as biological accidents or disorders. Babies who are born with ambiguous genitalia are usually subjected to hormonal and surgical treatment to make them either more male-like or more female-like. Some workers in this field have suggested that this practice represents a narrow-minded perspective and that DSD should be accepted as a legitimate variation on the male-female theme (Preves, 2003). Others believe that care should be taken in determining the child's inner feelings of gender and their surgical alteration sometimes should be postponed until they can take part in the decision making (Berenbaum, 2007; Colapinto, 2000; Crouch et al., 2008; Meyer-Bahlburg, 2005a).

There are case histories of people with DSD who adjusted to their sexuality quite comfortably. However, once such cases began to be viewed as mistakes of nature, the only alternative was believed to be medical treatment. The stigma of being so very different anatomically was thought to prevent people with DSD from being well adjusted. There is evidence that children with DSD ultimately tend to have later emotional and psychological problems (Berenbaum, 2007; Preves, 2003; Schutzmann et al., 2009). From this perspective, people with anatomical variations are seen as incomplete males or females and not as persons constituting a separate sex. It also leads to their being subjected to medical intervention as infants, which some resent later in their lives (Crouch et al., 2008; Vilain, 2001).

If your child were born intersexed, what course of action would you consider?

Gender Identity and Role

The term "gender" was popularized in the 1970s as a way of distinguishing the physical aspects of sex from what were believed to be the more socially determined and culturally influenced aspects of male-female differences. The term has become more widely used and now is often substituted for what we once would have

considered biological qualities (Haig, 2004). Along the way, we have also recognized that distinguishing between nature and nurture when it comes to male and female characteristics is not a simple task.

Although most people do tend to fit a female or male category anatomically, the picture becomes more confusing when we examine their behaviors and their sense of themselves as men or women or as masculine or feminine. Human beings have a persistent inner sense of themselves as female, male, or some transgendered position. This private, inner experience of one's gender has been termed **gender identity.** People also outwardly demonstrate to others the degree to which they are male, female, or transgendered in relationship to their society through what they say, what they wear, their attempts at sexual attractiveness, and their behavior. This public, outward expression of gender is called **gender role.** The qualities individuals use to assess and demonstrate their own gender are partly physical (such as body shape and sex organs) and partly sociocultural (such as hair length, clothing, and accepted standards of masculine and feminine behavior in a particular society).

What might be some of the effects on a person who experiences gender identity/gender role conflict?

■ Sexual Differentiation

One of the most enduring debates of the human sciences is waged in the arena of human sexuality: the controversy over the relative roles played by biological and social factors in determining human traits and behaviors, including those characteristics associated with being male or female.

Nature or Nurture?

The two perspectives in this great debate are **biological essentialism** and **social constructionism.** The

---

gender identity a person's inner experience of gender: feelings of maleness, femaleness, or some ambivalent position between the two.

gender role the outward expression and demonstration of gender identity, through behaviors, attire, and culturally determined characteristics of femininity and masculinity.

biological essentialism a theory that holds that human traits and behaviors are formed primarily by inborn biological determinants such as genes and hormonal secretions, rather than by environmental influences.

social constructionism a theory that holds that human traits and behaviors are shaped more by environmental social forces than by innate biological factors.

essentialist point of view is that inborn genetic and physiological factors are the determinants not only of such things as physical sex, body form, and temperament but also of the way human beings are programmed to behave as females or males. In other words, physical, sexual, and personality characteristics are established by *nature* (Laland, 2003). The constructionist perspective is that human personality traits and behaviors are formed mostly by social influences, or *nurture*, shaped by learning experiences over the years of human development.

The process by which organisms develop into the different sexes or genders is called **sexual differentiation.** Here the rubber meets the road with regard to nature and nurture. Debate has often focused on the relative importance of genetics versus the environment in shaping sex-related characteristics of the body and mind. Ultimately those on both sides of the debate have had to concede that the evidence doesn't support an either-or approach to resolving the question.

An Interactive View of Sexual Differentiation

It is no longer reasonable to reduce the debate to a choice between whether some trait is innate or learned. That is too simplistic. Rather, the issue revolves around how variable a trait is and the degree to which its variability is shaped by an interaction of biological and environmental factors. Genes do not act in isolation; instead their expression may be influenced to a degree by a variety of environmental factors ranging from the chemical composition of cells to cultural and social learning of the organism. The environment of the gene itself, as well as the organism's environment, seems to play a role in determining whether the gene is activated or deactivated (Nelson & Gottesman, 2005). Genes, as they are influenced by their environment, guide nerve cells to build brains and nervous systems in particular ways. This, in turn, may shape certain qualities of personality and behavior.

The social experiences individuals have most likely change the ways their nervous systems function, the hormones they secrete, and the genes that are operating within their cells (Ridley, 2003). So the most reasonable conclusion we can reach is that the body, mind, and behavior are molded *both* by underlying biological mechanisms and by experience and learning. Nature and nurture are continually interacting.

It is likely that some genetic traits are more susceptible to environmental influence than are others. Likewise, society surely does not shape the characteristics of an individual human being in the absence of a genetic template that determines some degree of variability in traits. The real question to be asked in the debate over the variability of sexual traits in humans is the degree to which that variability is influenced by an interaction of biology and environment (Nelson & Gottesman, 2005).

The biological underpinnings of sex may be seen on four major levels (Dennis, 2004; Vilain, 2001):

1. *Genetic sex.* When the sperm enters the egg at the moment of fertilization, a genetic map is established that will lead to the development of further expressions of maleness, femaleness, or perhaps some mixed state of sex development.
2. *Gonadal sex.* The genetic map leads to the development of **gonads,** testes or ovaries, that eventually will produce hormones within the individual's body. This has profound effects on sexual development.
3. *Body sex.* The genes and hormones present, or lacking, during development will partly determine what sorts of internal and external sex organs become. The anatomical structures with which a person is born will then play a major role in how the person is categorized (Zucker, 2002, 2005). Social and other environmental factors become especially interactive at this level.
4. *Brain sex.* How the brain is sexually differentiated is an especially intriguing question. There is considerable evidence that hormonal influences exerted by the gonads on the brain before and after birth play some role in determining certain male-type or female-type behaviors. It seems increasingly likely that the brain itself is directly differentiated by genetics in cooperation with hormones (Check, 2005; Dennis, 2004; Hines, 2004).

These biological levels of sex interact with environmental influences ranging from the hormonal concentrations in the bloodstream to the cultural imperatives that shape a person's social environment. As a human being develops from a fertilized egg through the various stages to adulthood, all these different aspects of being a sexual person begin to merge and play a role. Researchers are now examining the dynamic relationships between biology and environment that seem to interact to form sexual anatomy and gender roles (Marshall, 2003).

sexual differentiation the developmental processes—biological, social, and psychological—that lead to different sexes or genders.

gonads sex and reproductive glands, either testes or ovaries, that produce hormones and, eventually, reproductive cells (sperm or eggs).

Real Student Voices

■ I've always assumed that parents can shape their children into being boys or girls. I figure if I have a son someday, I will teach him to play sports and not be a sissy. The information in this chapter is making me nervous. What if I don't have that much control over his development as a real boy?

■ I was always considered a tomboy and thought it was because I had older brothers who let me play with them and their friends. Maybe I was born that way. I'm attracted to boys as boyfriends.

■ My brother was born with some kind of problem with his penis that required several surgeries. It still doesn't really look right, and he's very self-conscious about it. We've never really talked about how it functions, but he also has not pursued any sexual relationships that I know of.

Developmental Factors of Sexual Differentiation

Sexual differentiation begins at the moment of fertilization, with a sperm entering an ovum, and a genetic program is set into motion that eventually will combine with hormonal, social, and psychological factors to yield an adult gender identity. The factors that can exert influence along the way are incredibly complex and interactive. The model that follows continues to take shape and is always being clarified by new research (Vilain, 2001; Sekido & Lovell-Badge, 2008). The determinants of human sexual differentiation may be grouped into three categories: prenatal factors, factors of infancy and childhood, and factors at puberty.

1. *Prenatal factors.* Before an infant is born, a variety of genetic, gonadal, and developmental factors interact with one another to establish the groundwork for identification as female or male.
2. *Factors of infancy and childhood.* As a fetus is developing, its body sex is often assigned by the outward appearance of its genitals in an ultrasound. Either then or when the baby is born, social influences begin to come into play. As we have already seen, ambiguous genitalia may create complications in this regard. Eventually, children are raised as girl or boy, and they begin to develop distinct impressions and perceptions about their own bodies and sex organs. All these factors, in conjunction with the structure and function of the brain, determine the core gender identity of the child.
3. *Factors at puberty.* At puberty, new hormonal changes occur in the body that lead to further growth of the genitals and the appearance of secondary sex characteristics. There is also an

increase in sexual interests around the time of puberty. These developments—if they proceed in the usual way—further confirm the individual's gender identity in the move toward adulthood. If the pubertal changes do not occur as expected—that is, if the gender identity program has some built-in inconsistencies—and the child's gender identity is not confirmed, the result may be confusion and emotional crisis.

We will take a closer look at some of the details in each of these categories in the sections that follow.

Prenatal Factors

Chromosomes

The earliest factor that determines a human being's sex and initiates the program for determining gender identity happens at **conception,** when chromosomes from both parents are combined. Typically, human gametes—the ovum (egg) and sperm—each contain 23 chromosomes, one of which is a sex chromosome. The sex chromosome carried by the sperm may be either an X chromosome or a Y chromosome. The egg contains only an X chromosome. If an X-bearing sperm fertilizes an egg, the resulting XX combination of sex chromosomes establishes a genetic program to produce a female. If the egg is fertilized by a Y-bearing sperm, the resultant XY combination is destined to become a

conception the process by which a sperm unites with an egg, normally joining 23 pairs of chromosomes to establish the genetic blueprint for a new individual. The sex chromosomes establish its sex: XX for female, and XY for male.

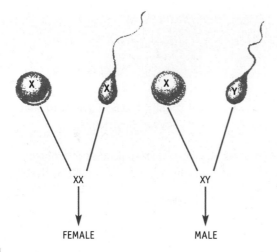

■ FIGURE 5.1 *Chromosomes*

Chromosomes are the genetic material in the nucleus of every cell. The sex of the offspring is determined at fertilization by the type of chromosome in the sperm. All egg cells and half the sperm cells contain an X sex chromosome; the remaining sperm contain a Y sex chromosome. A zygote with two X chromosomes will become a female, and a zygote with one X and one Y chromosome will become a male.

male. If the genetic mechanisms function normally, the program toward producing a female or male child is well underway (see Figure 5.1). The X and Y chromosomes have some very complex characteristics in themselves, and geneticists are beginning to unravel their secrets (Sekido & Lovell-Badge, 2008a, 2008b; Skaletsky et al., 2003).

A gene that seems to play a major role in the development of male organs has been pinpointed on the Y chromosome, a chromosome that has little other genetic activity. This gene has been labeled **SRY,** for *sex-determining region of Y,* because its presence or absence is significant in determining whether testes or ovaries will develop in the fetus (Ross et al., 2008). Because the more genetically active X chromosome contains many genes needed by both females and males, there is a deactivation process of half of those genes. Therefore females, with their double-X combination, do not receive an excess of gene products and single-X males do not have a deficiency of these same products (Graves, 2008).

The gene that leads to the development of female organs on the X chromosome has been identified as a region called **DAX-1** (Vilain, 2001). Presumably it is deactivated in males (XY) or its functions are blocked by SRY. It appears that these two genes set into motion a cascade of events that leads to the formation of either male or female sexual structures in the developing fetus. Other genes seem to play various roles along the way, but those details go beyond the scope of this text (Sekido & Lovell-Badge, 2008a, 2008b).

The actual mechanisms by which any of these genes may operate to develop male or female characteristics continue to be researched. It is becoming clear that both genes function in promoting the growth and development of the sex organs of one sex, while suppressing the appearance of sex organs of the other sex. Naturally, problems with one or both functions can lead to a mixture of male-female traits or genital ambiguity (Hiorta & Gillessen-Kaesbachb, 2009).

There are cases in which a fertilized egg will have an unusual number or combination of sex chromosomes, resulting in unusual patterns of development. For example, there may be only one X chromosome, and no second sex chromosome. The individual produced develops a female body, but the ovaries do not develop normally, and the adult woman is usually unable to produce children (Turner syndrome). A fertilized egg left with only a Y sex chromosome and no X apparently cannot survive. No human being has ever been found with only a Y sex chromosome. Other variant sex chromosome combinations in humans and their outcomes are summarized in Table 5.1.

Fetal Gonads

Up until the eighth week of development, it is impossible to determine the sex of a human embryo by the appearance of external genitalia (sex organs). Yet the genetic plan contained in the genes of the sex chromosomes carries the necessary information to produce gonads and genital organs. At first, a pair of tiny, sexless fetal gonads form internally, having the potential to become testes or ovaries. Two pairs of duct systems also are present in the embryo: the **Müllerian ducts,** which represent potential female reproductive organs, and the **Wolffian ducts,** which represent potential male reproductive structures. It is then either the SRY gene or the DAX-1 gene that determines whether the fetal gonads will further develop into testes or gonads, while suppressing the development of either the potential male or female duct system (Barsoum & Yao, 2006).

SRY the sex-determining region of the Y chromosome.

DAX-1 the region on the X chromosome that seems to play a role in sexual differentiation.

Müllerian ducts (myul-EAR-ee-an) embryonic structures that develop into female sexual and reproductive organs unless inhibited by male hormones.

Wolffian ducts (WOOL-fee-an) embryonic structures that develop into male sexual and reproductive organs if male hormones are present.

Table 5.1	Human Sex Chromosome Disorders That Affect Gender

Abnormal Chromosome Combination	Medical Name	Characteristics of Individual
XXY	Klinefelter syndrome	Male genitals, but with female secondary sex characteristics. Penis, scrotum, and testes are small; enlarged breasts. Sometimes timid and withdrawn; possible learning disabilities; sterile.
XO (no Y present; only one X)	Turner syndrome	Female external genitals; ovaries lacking; lack of menstruation, pubic hair, and breast development. Stunted growth, with several body abnormalities. Sense of direction and spatial relationships may be abnormal.
XO/XY	Mixed gonadal dysgenesis	May have female or male genitals, or a combination of the two. Usually no other bodily abnormalities, except may not mature sexually without treatment, and tend toward short body stature.
XYY	Supernumerary Y syndrome	Appearance of normal male. Tend to be tall in stature. May show some lack of control over impulsive behaviors. Usually average intelligence levels.
XXX	Triple-X syndrome	Appearance of normal female. Sometimes infertile. Occasional impairment of intelligence.
XX/XY	May be a true hermaphrodite	Variable. Have some combination of both ovarian and testicular tissues. Usually have uterus. External genitals may be distinctly masculine or feminine, or may be an ambiguous combination of both. At puberty, most experience breast enlargement, and the majority menstruate.

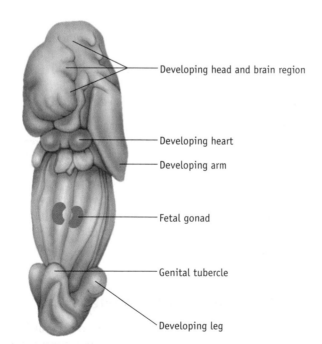

- Developing head and brain region
- Developing heart
- Developing arm
- Fetal gonad
- Genital tubercle
- Developing leg

FIGURE 5.2 *Fetal Gonads in a Developing Fetus*

During the first weeks of development, male and female embryos are anatomically identical. Two primitive gonads form during the fifth and sixth weeks of pregnancy. An H-Y antigen is necessary if the gonads are to develop into testes. Without an H-Y antigen, the gonads develop into ovaries.

Fetal Hormones and Body Sex

More is known about how the genetic programming to produce a male actually functions. The SRY gene on the Y chromosome leads to the production of a substance called **H-Y antigen,** and this in turn helps transform the cells of the fetal gonads into testes. When testes are produced, they begin secreting two hormones. Testosterone promotes development of the Wolffian ducts into internal male sexual and reproductive structures, and **anti-Müllerian hormone (AMH)** suppresses the development of the Müllerian ducts. Therefore no female structures form.

It was once thought that while becoming a male required the addition of hormones as described above, the development of female structures was, in a sense, the default developmental path if the SRY and the biochemicals it produced were not present. Research is beginning to clarify that instead the DAX-1 gene does indeed actively direct the development of fetal ovaries and functions through mechanisms not yet known to

H-Y antigen a biochemical produced in an embryo when the Y chromosome is present; it plays a role in the development of fetal gonads into testes.

anti-Müllerian hormone (AMH) secretion of the fetal testes that prevents further development of female structures from the Müllerian ducts.

Beginning at puberty, the sex glands of girls and boys actually produce the same hormones, with androgens such as testosterone being secreted in higher concentrations in males and estrogen in higher concentrations in females. In males, the higher concentration of androgens and their resulting influences tend to override the effects of the estrogens. This effect is reversed in the female. These hormone balances can be temporarily disrupted during puberty and adolescence, producing conditions such as slight breast enlargement in males (gynecomastia) or a deepened voice and an enlarged clitoris in the female. The onset of puberty can sometimes be either premature or delayed. Any of these conditions can shake the stability of a young person's gender identity and lead to confusion and unhappiness.

Changes in Sexual Drive and Behavior at Puberty

Of particular significance during puberty and adolescence is an increase in interest in sexual behavior. One important way gender identity is confirmed during this period is through imagery and fantasy. Boys and girls begin to imagine sexual acts and to fantasize about desirable romantic or sexual partners. Adolescents are sometimes upset to find themselves imagining or dreaming about sexual encounters with members of their own gender or other behaviors they may have learned to be inconsistent with their assumed sexual orientation. Yet such fantasies may signal some of the final alterations that will be made in their achievement of an adult gender identity and sexual orientation.

There is great variation in the strength of sexual interest that develops during adolescence (see Figure 5.7). Some youngsters experience frequent fantasies about sex and a strong interest in sexual activity. Other adolescents display little interest in sex. In either

■ FIGURE 5.7 *Sex Drive in Adolescents*

Adolescents experience the sex drive in different degrees depending on physical as well as emotional factors. Their families, religious background, peers, and the media all influence how adolescents learn to deal with love and the sex drive.

case, the level of strength of sexual interest may be subject to change in later life. The factors that determine the strength of sexual desire are beginning to be understood, as we explored in the previous chapter.

The amount of experience with sex and romance gained during adolescence is affected by factors such as social class, degree of interest in sex, peer group attitudes, religious background, parental influences, and exposure to the media. The newly experienced factors of puberty interact to reestablish firmly the core gender identity established in childhood (see Figure 5.8). There may be a few alterations as time goes on, but the fundamental patterns apparently are unalterable.

Adult Gender Identity and Role

At this point, we can give a general outline of sequences believed to be involved in the establishment

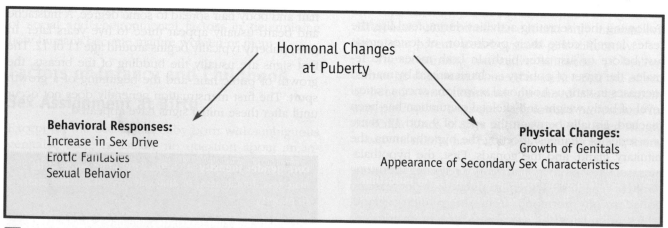

Hormonal Changes at Puberty

Behavioral Responses:
Increase in Sex Drive
Erotic Fantasies
Sexual Behavior

Physical Changes:
Growth of Genitals
Appearance of Secondary Sex Characteristics

■ FIGURE 5.8 *Gender Identity—Factors of Puberty*

This diagram details the elements that confirm gender identity in the adolescent. The increase in hormone production produces mature male and female physical characteristics as well as heightened interest in sexual fantasies and sexual behavior.

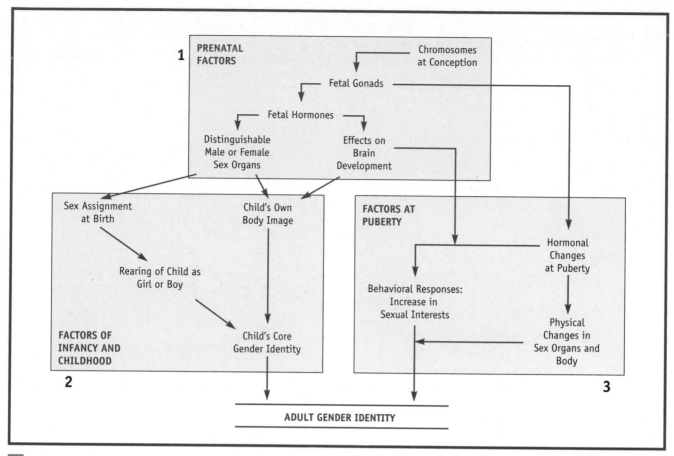

FIGURE 5.9 *Gender Identity—Adult*

This figure integrates the three stages of gender identity and summarizes the prenatal factors (1), factors of infancy and childhood (2), and factors at puberty (3) that influence the development of a mature adult gender identity.

of gender identity from conception to adulthood. An overall summary is presented in Figure 5.9. Adult gender identity and gender role usually become distinguishable as more masculine for males and more feminine for females. There may be elements of the masculine and elements of the feminine in all of us, even though our predominant identity leans more toward one or the other. Differences in behavior between males and females therefore are largely quantitative, meaning that they differ mostly in the frequency with which a particular individual exhibits particular behaviors (Hines, 2004). It should also be understood that many of what are considered to be appropriate masculine and feminine traits are determined by society and culture.

■ Masculinity and Femininity

At the social and cultural levels, dividing people into two distinct groups based on their gender becomes far more complicated. Individuals must sort through the standards and scripts for behavior that their society has identified as feminine or masculine, living up to the expectations of others while feeling comfortable with themselves. Masculinity and femininity are expressed in clothing styles, ways of walking and talking, mannerisms, hobbies, and all sorts of behaviors. Gender roles come in many complex shades.

Gender roles may be the result of self-fulfilling prophecies. We all learn assumptions about differences between boys and girls, and men and women, that affect our self-concepts and our views of others. This, in turn, affects how we behave ourselves, and how we treat others, as females or males. The entire system becomes self-perpetuating because people usually want to fit into what their society expects of them and because we become more comfortable with what is familiar and predictable (Stephens & Phillips, 2003). There is always the danger that gender roles in any society may create an imbalance of status and power between women and men, giving those who hold the greater status and power a personal and political stake in perpetuating an inequitable system.

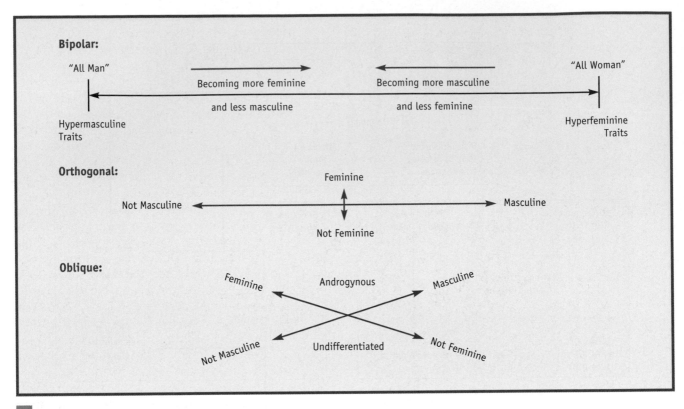

FIGURE 5.10 *Models of Masculinity and Femininity*

The definition of masculine or feminine behavior is based primarily on environmental influences and cultural expectations. The bipolar model assumes a continuum, with increased frequency of traits toward one pole resulting in a decreased frequency of traits from the other pole. The orthogonal model assumes masculinity and femininity to be completely independent traits. The oblique model assumes them to be semi-independent. In the orthogonal and oblique models, human beings are assumed to be able to have varying levels of both masculine and feminine traits (modified after Reinisch & Sanders, 1992).

Models of Masculinity and Femininity

The simplest model used to conceptualize gender roles is to see totally masculine and totally feminine as two extremes at opposite poles of a continuum. See Figure 5.10 for a way to visualize this two-pole, or bipolar, model. The assumption implied by this model is that the more frequent or strong a person's masculine behaviors are, the less frequent and strong that individual's feminine behaviors will be, and vice versa. In other words, the more feminine a person is, the less masculine the person will be.

Other conceptualizations of femininity and masculinity suggest, instead, that the two qualities actually are more independent of each other than the bipolar model suggests. These models propose that some people show high frequencies of both masculine and feminine behaviors. The presence of these high levels in a single individual is called **androgyny,** from the Greek roots *andro,* meaning "male," and *gyn,* meaning "female." Conversely, some people could demonstrate low levels of both behaviors, therefore being relatively undifferen-

tiated in terms of gender. Finally, what would be more typical of human beings is a higher level of one set of behaviors and a lower level of the other, so that the individual would be considered either more masculine or more feminine. The *orthogonal model* assumes complete independence of masculinity and femininity. The *oblique model* assumes that, at least to some degree, the more masculine people are, the less feminine they tend to be, and the more feminine, the less masculine (see Figure 5.10). The models that conceptualize femininity and masculinity in this way differ only in the degree of independence they ascribe between the two factors (Reinisch & Sanders, 1992).

The research literature has included descriptions of people who exaggerate the culturally accepted characteristics of masculinity or femininity. **Hypermasculinity,**

androgyny (an-DROJ-a-nee) the presence of high frequencies of both masculine and feminine behaviors and traits in the same individual.

hypermasculinity a tendency to exaggerate manly behaviors; sometimes called machismo.

sometimes called *machismo*, is a tendency to exaggerate those behaviors perceived to be manly. It takes the form of characteristics such as aggressiveness, unemotional sexual involvement, and an emphasis on defending one's honor if it seems to have been threatened. **Hyperfemininity** is characterized by greater deference to others, particularly men, more acceptance of aggressive sexual behavior from others, and traditional attitudes about the rights and roles of women in society. People who exaggerate the traits of masculinity or femininity probably are acting out some role that they have found to be important to them in the context of their society (Muehlenhard et al., 2003; Parrott & Zeichner, 2008).

Differences and Similarities between Females and Males

There are few qualitative differences between females and males that represent the exclusive domain of one sex or the other. A few physiological male-female characteristics or functions, however, cannot be changed on any large scale by culture: Females menstruate, bear children, and produce milk from their mammary glands; males ejaculate semen. The differences in sex organs, their roles in reproduction, and—to a lesser degree—differences in secondary sex characteristics usually are easily distinguishable. Beyond these basic qualitative differences, there is little evidence to suggest that many inborn characteristics can be identified as distinctly female or male.

Medical research is clarifying that the female body, its reactions to disease, and the ways in which those diseases should be treated really can be quite different from the situation for males. Gender differences should never be used to justify gender inequalities, but to deny that any differences exist or to fail to study them entails risks too (Balaban, 2008).

There has been a degree of fascination among psychologists regarding the differences between males and females with respect to behaviors, personality, and abilities, sometimes called the *gender differences hypothesis*. A recent meta-analysis of 46 studies led the researcher to conclude that the emphasis on differences may well reside in the context of former research and unjustified assumptions. She concluded from her work that we might better think in terms of a *gender similarities hypothesis*, because she found far more similarities than differences between the sexes. In studying scores on standardized math tests, it was also found that there are no longer gender differences in math skills (Hyde, 2005; Hyde et al., 2008).

Other research has found evidence of small average differences between human males and females in a few cognitive and motor functions. It is crucial to note that any differences that have been identified are true only as statistical generalizations; they do not apply to *all* women or *all* men. Females, on average, tend to perform at higher levels on tests of verbal fluency, spelling, writing, reading speed and comprehension, understanding of social interactions and emotional information, identification of matching items (perceptual speed), fine-motor skills such as placing pegs in holes on a board, arithmetic calculation, and associative memory. Males perform at higher average levels on tests of field independence (being able to perceive underlying spatial relations in an otherwise confusing context), mathematical reasoning, science, comprehension of spatial relations, target-directed motor skills (referring to the guiding or intercepting of projectiles), and stereotypically male vocational aptitudes such as mechanical reasoning, electronics information, and auto and shop information. It has also been shown that males tend to have greater variability in their intellectual abilities than females do (Hyde, 2005; Hyde et al., 2008; Kimura, 1999; Machin & Pekkarinen, 2008). This information is summarized in Table 5.3.

While these differences are not of great importance, and may not entirely explain certain vocational variances seen for men and women, they continue to be of interest to psychologists. There are no strong neurological explanations for the differences as yet, although it has been proposed that the cerebral hemispheres of females and males may be specialized in differing ways for cognitive processing. Males apparently are more lateralized, meaning that they tend to localize particular brain functions in one cerebral hemisphere over the other. This might help explain their somewhat greater focus on mechanical aptitudes and understanding of spatial relationships and mathematical reasoning, for example. Females seem to have more interaction between their cerebral hemispheres rather than having functions confined to one hemisphere or the other. This might well allow them a wider range of experience in their mental tasks and may help explain their greater ability to understand and process emotional content and to write well.

Theories of Gender Role Development

A substantial part of establishing masculine and feminine gender roles probably results from a learning process—socialization as girls and boys, women and men. As children grow up, they learn to label themselves in various ways and to recognize the attributes, attitudes, and behaviors considered socially appropriate

hyperfemininity a tendency to exaggerate characteristics typically associated with women.

Table 5.3	*Comparison of Average Performance of Females and Males in Tests of Various Abilities*	
Tests Exhibiting Higher Average Female Performance	**Tests Exhibiting Equal Average Performance**	**Tests Exhibiting Higher Average Male Performance**
Verbal fluency	Vocabulary	Field independence
Spelling and writing	Ability to reorganize an object from parts	Mathematical reasoning
Reading speed and comprehension		Science
	Verbal reasoning	
Social comprehension; understanding emotional information	Verbal IQ	Comprehension of spatial reasoning
Identifying matched items (perceptual speed)	Performance IQ	Target-directed motor skills (guiding or intercepting projectiles)
Fine-motor skills		Mechanical reasoning
Arithmetic calculation		Electronics information
Associative memory		Auto and shop information

Sources: From J. Levy and W. Heller, "Gender Differences in Human Neuropsychological Functions," in A. A. Gerall, H. Moltz, and I. L. Ward (Eds.), *Handbook of Behavioral Neurobiology*, Vol. 11, *Sexual Differentiation*, New York: Plenum Press, 1992; D. Kimura, "Sex Differences in the Brain," *Scientific American*, Vol. 267 (3), pp. 119–25; and L. V. Hedges and A. Nowell, "Sex Differences in Mental Test Scores, Variability, and Numbers of High Scoring Individuals," in *Science*, Vol. 269, 1995, pp. 41–45.

for each sex. Boys and girls tend to show a preference for toys that are typical for their genders, although transgendered children typically prefer toys chosen by the other gender (Fridell et al., 2006). If gender identity forms at least in part from genetic and hormonal influences during the process of sexual differentiation, then it follows that we could trace the roots of gender roles to interactive influences of biology and socialization.

Before our knowledge of this interaction became as clear as it is today, a number of theoretical positions emerged on how gender roles develop. While these theories may not hold up so well in the face of contemporary research, they have been an essential part of the evolution of ideas concerning masculinity and femininity. A brief summary of their essential elements follows.

Psychodynamic Perspectives

Psychoanalytic tradition, founded by Sigmund Freud, gradually evolved into what is now known as the psychodynamic approach. Modern psychodynamic theory, modeled after earlier Freudian thought, holds that there are three phases of early gender development. Children are first unaware of differences between the sexes. Then, around the age of two years, they begin to realize that girls and boys are different. Freud suggested that children tend to attribute superior power and value to the male genitals. He also believed that girls then feel inadequate and experience penis envy, whereas boys fear that they will lose their genitals and therefore have to cope with castration anxieties (Harding, 2001). In the third phase of gender differentiation in this model, chil-

dren must work out the implications of their gender in their relationships with the significant men and women in their lives. The theory holds that in this stage children see their parents in terms of gender and tend to relate more with their fathers. For a time, boys are thought to be in a competitive relationship for the affection of their mothers—the Freudian concept of Oedipal wishes—but then give up and take their place as males in their society. Girls are said to have the secret hope that their fathers will give them a penis—the Freudian concept of Electra complexes—but then let go of this hope and become more passive. It is by working through these dilemmas that children eventually find their pathways to masculinity and femininity, with both parents providing support and encouragement throughout the differentiation process (Bornstein & Masling, 2002). Today, the psychodynamic model of gender role development does not receive wide acceptance.

Social Learning Theory

This model proposed that gender roles are perpetuated by each culture, learned by children as they are socialized by their parents, peers, and others through observation, imitation, and instruction. It is assumed that this process is continuous and lifelong and that it can be affected by many particular circumstances of an individual's family and personal history. Early proponents of social learning theory tended to portray children as passive recipients of their culture's assumptions concerning gender, imitating or modeling the behavior of those around them of the same sex. Modern theorists, however, have emphasized that children themselves play active roles in this dynamic process, helping to shape it in part themselves (Boyle, Marshall, & Robeson, 2003). Social learning theory was a precursor to the social constructionist model of gender but now concedes that biological factors could establish a template on which social factors build.

Cognitive-Developmental Theory

Cognitive-developmental theory expanded the fundamental understanding of social learning theory. It recognizes gender as a basic characteristic used to understand one's social environment and interact with it. The child categorizes itself as girl or boy and relatively early in its life develops masculine or feminine values out of the need to value those things that are consistent with or like itself. Then the child tends to identify with the same-sex parent and deepens its attachment to the feminine or masculine model. The child also identifies gender roles by interacting with other children. A unique feature of this model is the idea that the child acquires basic male or female values on its own and then, because of its acquired desire to be feminine or masculine, identifies with a woman or a man and other girls or boys as models. It does not offer much help in understanding those children who are transgendered.

Gender Schema Theory

This concept of how people come to define themselves as masculine or feminine represents a more sophisticated variant of social learning theory and cognitive-developmental theory. It emphasizes the pressures inherent in social attitudes that assume the need for differences between females and males, even in situations where sex has no particular relevance (Bem, 1987, 1993). In most cultures, maleness and femaleness are defined by a complex network or pattern of associations, ranging from anatomical differences to the sorts of work people engage in to religious symbolism. This complicated set of associations is called a **gender schema.** As children encounter their world, all new information and perceptions are filtered through the gender schema, and internal decisions are made concerning gender, self-concept, and behavior toward others. In time, everything becomes interpreted through this dualistic, male-female schema, and the individual models his or her behaviors and life choices according to those interpretations.

Some children and adults are very gender schematic, meaning that they rely heavily on their gender role associations, whereas others are more gender aschematic, meaning that they pay less attention to these socially determined associations. Presumably, trans-

gendered individuals either are aschematic or have adopted the scheme of the other gender as their own.

Multifactorial Theories

Gender role development has also been seen as the result of interaction among many different factors, and this is where contemporary research continues to lead our theories. Behavioral genetics was one of the first fields to emphasize the interactive nature of both heredity and environment on childhood socialization. A fundamental assumption of behavioral genetics is that members of the same family are similar because of the genes and environmental factors they have in common. Conversely, family members are different because of the genes and environment they do not share. Studies of twins tend to conclude that personality similarities within a family are probably influenced more by genetics than by environment. The same seems to hold true for behaviors associated with gender. People's attitudes, however, seem to be shaped more by shared genetic and environmental factors (Hamer, 2002).

Even though innate biological components have been accepted as a basis for different rates of maturation and gender-specific behaviors, attention has also been given to the ways in which boys and girls grow up in our society. It has been theorized that boys and girls grow up in what might be considered two distinct subcultures, each characterized by different sets of expectations and behaviors. Boys' playgroups much more resemble rough-and-tumble hierarchies, whereas girls' groups focus more on maintaining relationships and mutuality. These groups become the foundation of gender identity and role (Maccoby, 1998). Girls seem to regulate their own behavior much earlier than do boys, and this self-regulation leads to all sorts of activities that please parents and other adults. Boys' greater lack of self-control leads to more disciplinary commands and directions from others. This is where the biological predispositions become influenced by socialization components (Lippa, 2002b).

Although some social psychologists once believed that we should work toward a world in which there would be no differentiation between male and female roles, this goal no longer seems as plausible or desirable as it once did to some. Instead, there is now more emphasis on the celebration of gender similarities and differences and efforts toward increased understanding between the sexes (see Figure 5.11).

gender schema a complex cognitive network of associations and ideas through which the individual perceives and interprets information about gender.

■ **FIGURE 5.11** *Gender Identity and the Masculine-Feminine Continuum*

Many people enjoy pursuing interests that cross traditional boundaries of gender-stereotypical behaviors

■ Transgender Identities

As we have seen, some individuals cross the usual boundaries that delineate expected gender roles for women and men and demonstrate some level of discomfort and/or nonconformity with a traditional male or female identity. We call this **transgenderism,** and it may occur in varying degrees. The psychological literature continues to use terms such as **gender identity disorder** and **gender dysphoria** when labeling people who are transgendered. However, a sentiment is growing in professional circles that it may be unfair to assume the existence of some pathology or mental disorder with regard to transgendered individuals. In fact, transgender identities are likely shaped by the same interaction of biological and environmental factors as all other gender identities (Hill et al., 2005; Lev, 2005).

An interesting historical example is English writer William Sharp, who lived from 1855 to 1905. Over a period of some years, he created for himself the persona of a woman he called Fiona MacLeod. He spent increasing proportions of time as Fiona, who emerged as a leading writer in the Scottish Celtic literary movement. In his later years, very little of the male William Sharp identity was left. Transgender people provide us with some important lessons as they transcend our notions of the "two" sexes. We are reminded, for example, that an individual's genital organs no longer exclusively define gender. We also find a complex and not fully understood association among gender identity, social sex roles, and sexual orientation (Sandfort, 2005; Schrock & Reid, 2006).

Transgender identity often begins to be expressed during childhood through choices of playmates and types of play activities that are cross-gendered. Twin studies show that when one identical twin shows cross-gender behavior, there is a good chance the other twin will show the same behavior, again suggesting that

gender-related behaviors are influenced at early biological stages of development. Boys and girls who behaved in these ways once were called sissies or tomboys and now tend to be diagnosed with gender identity disorders, but experts have begun to caution against making premature judgments about whether a child has a mental disorder or not (Bockting & Ehrbar, 2005; Hill et al., 2007; van Beijsterveldt Hudziak, & Boomsma, 2006).

See "Denise Talks about Her Transsexual Experience" on SexSource Online.

Transsexuality

Transsexuality is perhaps the most extreme form of transgenderism. Transsexuals are anatomical males or females who express a strong conviction that they actually have the mind and personality of a member of the other sex. In other words, their gender identity is not congruent with their body sex. They usually are aware of these feelings at a very young age and often feel as if they have been born into a wrongly sexed body.

It is largely assumed that transgender identities are formed by an interaction of prenatal genetic and hormonal influences, perhaps combined with environmental influences. Research has shown some anatomical brain differences in male transsexuals that might help explain their female gender identity (Bancroft, 2002a; Schrock & Reid, 2006). There is agreement that transgender identity tends to be realized by most individuals at a young age, as is true of all core gender identities. It has been estimated that as many as 11,000 postoperative transsexuals reside in the United States, although the figures are uncertain and would not include those transsexuals who have not undergone sex reassignment, who certainly outnumber those who have. The total number of transsexuals in the United States and some European countries has been estimated to be 1 per 20,000 to 50,000 people over age 15. The estimates for female-to-male transsexuals tend to be lower than those for male-to-female, at about a one-to-three ratio. In Poland those

transgenderism a crossing of traditional gender lines because of discomfort and nonconformity with gender roles generally accepted by society.

gender identity disorder the expression of gender identity in a way that is socially inconsistent with one's anatomical sex.

gender dysphoria (dis-FOR-ee-a) another term sometimes used to describe a gender identity disorder.

transsexuality a strong degree of discomfort with one's identity as male or female, characterized by feelings of being in the wrongly sexed body.

ratios are reversed by almost exact proportions (Herman-Jeglinska, Grabowska, & Dulko, 2002).

It should be noted that a person's gender identity or gender role is not necessarily related to sexual orientation. Many male cross-dressers, sometimes called transvestites, dress in women's clothing but are heterosexual in orientation and prefer female sexual partners. Some transsexuals have chosen to be surgically changed to the other sex so they can be gay or lesbian and thus interact sexually with members of the sex to which they have been reassigned (Schrock & Reid, 2006).

There is a spectrum of intensities among transsexual persons that often reflects the degree of dissatisfaction they may experience with regard to their anatomy. Some individuals are very comfortable with their bodies and are content to cross-dress and adopt mannerisms of the other gender. Some transsexuals, however, feel a strong enough level of discomfort or disgust with their bodies, or a sufficient desire to have female genitals, to lead them to alter the body sex with which they were born (Mathy, 2002; Schrock & Reid, 2006).

Sex Reassignment for Transsexuals

Transsexuals may be troubled and unhappy because of feeling trapped in the wrongly sexed body and wishing for a different anatomy. Psychotherapy alone has not proved especially effective with transsexuals, but it does offer opportunities for them to explore their personal conflicts and options for dealing with their gender identity (Gijs & Brewaeys, 2007). One recognized form of rehabilitative therapy is the hormonal and surgical transformation of the individual's external features into a form resembling the anatomy of the other sex (see Figure 5.12). Although such surgery is known to have existed as early as 1882, the case that attracted the most attention in modern times was that of Christine Jorgensen, who in 1952 became a woman after having lived until that time as George Jorgensen. As a result of the ensuing publicity, her doctor was deluged with requests for sex changes, and the science of sex reassignment was off and running (Green, 2008; Jorgensen, 2000).

Sex reassignment involves a series of therapeutic interventions that usually include living as a member of the desired gender during a real life test while receiving hormone treatments, adjustment counseling, and appropriate legal advice concerning a name change, a new birth certificate, and a new driver's license. Clearly defined standards for evaluating the broader mental health issues of transgendered patients and proceeding with sex reassignment have been established by specialists in the field. To avoid patient dissatisfaction or regret following surgery, it is essential that these standards be strictly followed (Levine & Solomon, 2009; Meyer et al., 2001; Olsson & Moller, 2006).

After being diagnosed as a candidate for sex reassignment, the individual must face the medical ex-

■ FIGURE 5.12 *Transsexuality*

Transsexuals are people who are one sex biologically but have the gender identity of the other sex. Chastity Bono, whose parents are Cher and the late Sonny Bono, decided to be reassigned as a man, Chaz Bono.

penses of the process, which can amount to tens of thousands of dollars and may not be covered by health insurance. Anyone who desires advice about these matters should go to a medical center that specializes in such treatments. Changing genders has been likened to migrating to another culture, because the individual must face new adjustments and seek acceptance in a new lifestyle (King, 2003; Schrock & Reid, 2006).

The changes brought about by hormone therapy, with the exception of a deepened voice in the female-to-male transsexual, are reversible should a decision be made not to continue the reassignment process. Female hormones administered to men cause breast enlargement and a feminine redistribution of fat. Although the growth of facial and body hair may be somewhat slowed, it is necessary to remove permanently unwanted beard and body hairs by laser treatments. Hormonal masculinization of the female, in addition to deepening the voice, suppresses menstruation and promotes growth of some facial and body hair. If the real-life test continues to confirm the individual's resolve to change sex, the surgical procedures are begun.

See "Changing Genders" on SexSource Online.

Although a detailed description of sex-change surgery is beyond the scope of this text, we will give a summary. In male-to-female surgery, the testes are removed, and an artificial vagina, clitoris, and labia are constructed from the sensitive skin of the penis and scrotum (see Figure 5.13). Breasts are fashioned through the use of mammary implants (see Figure 5.14). Following reassignment, male-to-female transsexuals usually report having longer, smoother, and more intense orgasms (DeCuypere et al., 2005; Lawrence, 2005).

In female-to-male surgery, the breasts, uterus, and ovaries are first removed. There are two options for genital surgery. *Metoidioplasty,* a simpler and less expensive surgery, is the more typically chosen option today. The clitoris, which has been enlarged somewhat by testosterone therapy, is formed into a small penis, and the labia are formed to look like a small scrotum. Some choose the more complex and expensive procedure called *phal-*

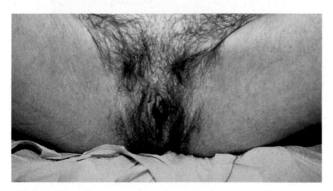

FIGURE 5.13   *Postsurgical Male-to-Female Transsexual*

Following surgical procedures to construct a vulva and a vagina from sensitive penile and scrotal tissues, this individual's external genitals are hardly distinguishable from those of a woman.

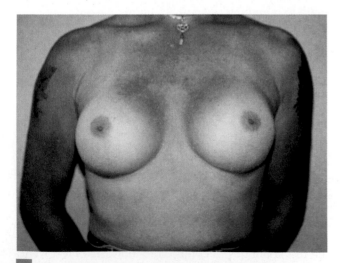

FIGURE 5.14   *Surgically Constructed Breasts*

In male-to-female transsexual surgery, the breasts may respond to hormone treatment; if not, they generally are augmented with implants.

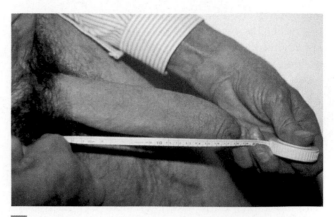

FIGURE 5.15   *Surgically Constructed Penis*

In female-to-male phalloplasty, the penis is constructed from forearm tissue or from labial and perineal tissue. The penis is not capable of erection in response to sexual arousal, but several inflatable devices are available that produce an erection, as shown in this photograph.

loplasty, by which an artificial penis is created over several operations from skin taken from other parts of the body. A scrotum is also constructed, using tissue from the labia that is stretched by inserting increasingly larger silicon balls (see Figure 5.15). The clitoris usually is left intact beneath the new penis and remains sensitive to sexual arousal. Most female-to-male transsexuals report orgasmic capacity following surgery, saying that their orgasms tend to be shorter but more powerful than they had been (DeCuypere et al., 2005). Postsurgical transsexuals cannot reproduce, ejaculate, or menstruate.

Clinical evidence and research suggest that sex reassignment can indeed lead to improved psychological and social adjustment for many individuals (Lobato et al., 2006). Reviews of the world literature on this surgery indicate only a 10 to 15 percent failure rate with patients. In general, people seem subjectively satisfied with their sex reassignments. Dissatisfaction with the results was more common as the age of the patients increased and in cases where the person was not carefully diagnosed (Gijs & Brewaeys, 2007; Olsson & Moller, 2006). In a study of 232 postoperative male-to-female transsexuals, none of the patients expressed outright regret about having undergone reassignment, and their level of satisfaction seemed to be related largely to how happy they were with their new bodies and how those bodies functioned (Lawrence, 2005, 2006; Lawrence et al., 2005).

■ Gender in Society and Culture

As a basic organizing principle of human culture, maleness and femaleness and femininity and masculinity are central themes in all societies. Viewed against a backdrop of variations in many aspects of human personality, gender differences may not be as dramatic or significant as often thought. Nevertheless, they influence how people think, believe, and behave.

Growing Up Female and Male

Society permits a wider range of behaviors for girls, from the very frilly to the tomboy, while for boys neither the extreme of the sissy nor the too-aggressive bully is acceptable. Perhaps this is why among younger children, boys tend to see their gender roles and future occupational options much more narrowly than do girls (Sellers, Satcher, & Comas, 1999). Parents and other adults are also generally less disturbed by the behavior of girls than by that of boys, with the result that more demands are placed on boys to behave appropriately. This likely results in boys being pressured to become more independent and self-controlled, and may be part of why some young men feel as though they must always be living up to the expectations of others by putting their "man faces" on. It can be a struggle to take those masks off and get in touch with the real feelings underneath. As boys grow into adolescence and adulthood, they face harsher consequences for stepping outside the gender-appropriate roles established for them than do girls and women (Edwards & Jones, 2009; Sommers, 2000).

As children, girls are rewarded for their compliant good behavior by receiving good grades, parental love, teacher acceptance, and acceptance into peer groups, sometimes leaving them generally more passive and conformist. During adolescence, boys tend to turn their aggressions outward, whereas girls tend to turn these impulses inward—often against themselves—resulting in lowered self-esteem.

Schools often provide a different environment for girls than they do for boys. There is evidence that even among young children, boys interrupt teachers in their activities much more than do girls, whereas teachers tend to interrupt girls more than they do boys. Later on, girls in general receive significantly less attention from and interaction with their teachers than do boys. This manifests itself in the fact that in the early grades girls tend to be equal to, or ahead of, boys on nearly every standardized test, but by high school they tend to fall behind boys on college entrance exams, particularly in mathematics and science (Boyle, Marshall, & Robeson, 2003; Wilson, R., 2004). Girls who are athletic and want to pursue sports often have to contend with stereotypes about their being masculine or gay, whereas boys are encouraged toward athleticism (Bolin & Granskog, 2003; Malcom, 2003; Shakib, 2003).

Even well-meaning teachers often seem susceptible to gender stereotypes, such as that girls should be quiet listeners in the classroom. Boys tend to be given more esteem-building encouragement than girls. Also, girls are subject to many more forms of sexual harassment in schools that are apt to make school seem a hostile environment for them. Clearly, work remains to be done to ensure that young women and men have an equal chance to get a wide-ranging education in a supportive environment, which in turn will offer them the levels of skill, self-esteem, and confidence necessary to be happy and successful in the workforce (AAUW, 1992; Hamson, 2004; Timreck, 2004).

A study sponsored by the American Association of University Women (AAUW, 1992, 1993) demonstrated that girls tend to lose self-confidence as they enter adolescence. Three thousand students in grades 4 through 10 were surveyed in 12 locations throughout the United States. Up to 70 percent of both the boys and the girls at age nine tended to reflect positive attitudes toward themselves and a willingness to be assertive as needed. The researchers developed a self-esteem index from the questions they asked the children. By age 16, only 29 percent of high school girls indicated that they were happy with themselves, whereas 46 percent of boys retained a sense of self-confidence. Interestingly, the drop in self-esteem was particularly prevalent among white and Hispanic girls. Black girls tended to be better able to maintain their self-esteem during adolescence. During adolescence, girls exhibited a greater concern about appearance and body image than did boys.

Did you ever fall prey to or observe gender stereotyping in the classroom? Explain the circumstance and how you reacted to it.

Gender in the Workplace

Although many institutions and employers are trying to create equal employment opportunities for women, there are still some discrepancies in how women and men fare in their jobs. The possibilities for promotion sometimes are greater for men than for women. Parenting and household responsibilities still often fall to women and may limit the time and energy available for their careers. There are signs of change, however. Among married couples who both work, over 30 percent of the wives earn more money than their husbands. Also, in increasing numbers of families the woman is the primary breadwinner, while the man stays home to take care of household responsibilities and children (Tyre & McGinn, 2003).

Academia is often assumed to be a more open environment for female success, but in fact women faculty have often felt marginalized in colleges and universities (Lawler, 2006). Women tend to be underrepresented on the science and mathematics faculties of major research institutions (see Figure 5.16). While women are not being attracted to the quantitative science and engineering fields to the extent that men are,

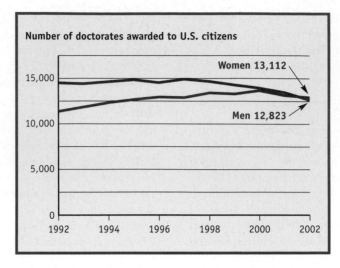

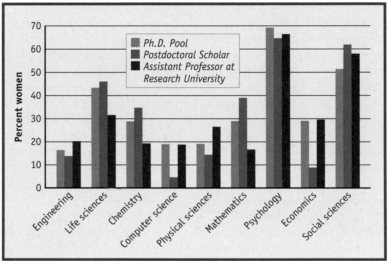

■ **FIGURE 5.16** *Women in Higher Education*

(A) In 2002, for the first time, more American women than men earned doctorates at U.S. universities. The number of American men receiving doctorates has fallen by nearly 15 percent in the past five years. **(B)** As of 2006, women scientists in entry-level academic jobs were still fewer than those in the humanities and social sciences.

Sources: **(A)** From *The Chronicle of Higher Education,* December 12, 2003, p. A10. Copyright 2003, The Chronicle of Higher Education. Reprinted with permission. **(B)** From Andrew Lawler, "Universities Urged to Improve Hiring and Advancement of Women," *Science,* Vol. 313, 22 September 2006, p. 1712. http://www.sci-encemag.org/cgi/content/full/313/5794/1712. Reprinted with permission from AAAS. Readers may view, browse, and/or download material for temporary copying purposes only, provided these uses are for noncommercial personal purposes. Except as provided by law, this material may not be further reproduced, distributed, transmitted, modified, adapted, performed, displayed, published, or sold in whole or in part, without prior written permission from the publisher.

the proportion of women in those fields has increased by as much as 100 percent over the past two decades. The reasons why girls and women pursue the quantitative fields in fewer numbers than do boys and men seem to be very complex and are not explainable by any single factor (Xie & Shauman, 2003). The biological and social sciences, however, continue to attract women (Handelsman et al., 2005). The social science fields have seen a reduction in the numbers of males, a phenomenon sometimes called male flight. Since the 1970s, the percentage of women receiving law degrees has been steadily increasing, and the number of businesses owned by women has skyrocketed from less than half a million to about

8 million. The year 2002 represented the first time in history that American women earned more doctoral degrees than American men at U.S. universities (Smallwood, 2003) (see Figure 5.16).

Evidence shows that women scientists in more advanced, industrialized countries have found it difficult to overcome entrenched systems that seem to favor men (Lawler, 2006). In developing countries, however, science and technology have emerged more recently as fields of employment, concurrent with the furthering of women's rights. Scientific research and development typically have not been as connected to industrial economies in these countries, so science is often a low-status, low-paying career. These conditions have

FIGURE 5.17 *U.S. Women Making Progress*

Sonia Sotomayor (left) has become the third woman justice appointed to the U. S. Supreme Court, and the first Latina justice in history. Hillary Clinton (right) is shown talking with President Ellen Johnson Sirleaf of Monrovia. Clinton was a viable woman candidate for the presidency in the 2008 elections, and is now serving as Secretary of State in the Obama administration.

made scientific careers more open to women in developing countries (Xie & Shauman, 2003).

Feminism

Within both developing and industrialized societies, there is a history of oppression of women and marked social inequalities between women and men that have fostered the subservience and secondary status of women. Women themselves often recognize the existence of inequality but choose not to try to correct it because they have learned to be less confrontational and more conciliatory. Instead, they often attempt to compete as individuals, playing by rules that often have been established by and for men (see Figure 5.17).

Feminists are women and men who reject prejudices that imply any inferiority of either gender and are working together to achieve equality. In using the word equality, they are not implying that women and men are the same, but rather are stating that women and men deserve equal opportunities and rights. There have been several waves of feminist activity throughout American history (see Figure 5.18). The first major public outcry for women's rights came in 1848 when Elizabeth Cady Stanton, Susan B. Anthony, and several other women wrote their "Declaration of Sentiments" and presented it at the first U.S. women's rights convention, held in Seneca Falls, New York. After women gained the right to vote in 1920, the movement subsided somewhat until the mid-1960s. The modern feminist movement then gained momentum (Kees, 2005). Terms such as "women's liberation" and "sexism" became part of everyone's vocabulary.

Some people have an inaccurate image of feminists as bra-burning women who picket against sexist issues and hate men. In fact, feminists are working to reduce inequality between the sexes. The proportion of women willing to call themselves feminists has declined significantly, and the proportion of women who do not consider themselves feminists has risen. Yet it

also seems clear that most women recognize and appreciate the many opportunities for greater equality that the most recent feminist movement has created for them (Kees, 2005).

Contemporary feminist thought has led to a renewed awareness that women can be equal participants in sexual activity as well as in other aspects of human life. Traditional stereotypes held that women were less interested in sex and less easily aroused than men. Thus, men were expected to be the primary initiators of sex, wooing and seducing their female partners until they finally gave in. Modern feminism has raised our consciousness about female sexuality, showing that women want to enjoy and be full participants in sex. It has become clear that women can desire sexual intimacy in all its dimensions, and it has become more socially permissible for them to initiate sexual encounters. Sex is no longer something to which women are expected to submit to

FIGURE 5.18 *Active Feminists*

Early feminists campaigning for suffrage were in for a hard fight, but in 1920 they won the right to vote with passage of the Nineteenth Amendment. The size of the eligible voting population nearly doubled, but not until the latter half of the 1900s did the turnout of women at the polls reach the level of male turnout.

FIGURE 5.19 *Feminism Then and Now*

Some observers believe that feminist influence on popular culture has evolved in the past 30 years from being intellectually provocative, as personified by Gloria Steinem's activism of the 1970s (left), to today's emphasis on stylish fluff and sexy game playing, as typified by the cast of television's *Desperate Housewives* (right).

fulfill their obligation to a male partner (see Figure 5.19). Instead, it is seen as part of the human experience that can be negotiated, discussed, and actively enjoyed by both women and men if and when they so choose.

Do you consider yourself a feminist? Are you uncomfortable with the term? Explain.

Asserting Masculinity

The women's movement raised our consciousness about the ways women in our society often have been victims of injustice and discrimination. Yet it also brought into focus the fact that men too have been trapped in certain roles and stereotypes. Boys and men often are caught in a vicious circle of proving their strength, invulnerability, and effectiveness as providers, yet because of social attitudes they are also taught to be dependent on women—first their mothers, then often their romantic partners (Edwards & Jones, 2009; Pascoe, 2003; Sommers, 2000). Just as women have felt resentment about being treated as sex objects, men sometimes have suffered from being treated as success objects expected to provide status and security for their partners. Many male providers end up feeling powerless, meaningless, and isolated in their jobs, working under constant fear and tension as they strive for promotion and success. Three main aspects of the traditional male role seem especially to make men uncomfortable: (1) the male as competent worker and provider, (2) the male as emotionally controlled and stoic, and (3) the male as sexual aggressor and sexual educator of the female (Marsiglio, 2003).

Many men feel able to celebrate their own masculinity in ways that once would have been considered unmanly. Men's groups have sprung up, and men have been encouraged to confront and share their feelings more openly. Having opportunities to talk about gender roles and reassess individual needs and goals continues to prove valuable for men in different age groups (Marsiglio, 2003).

There has been some finger pointing between women and men. Men are resisting being blamed individually for the inequities between the genders and are calling for a more balanced view of the social picture. They are tired of being the scapegoats for social constructs that they too were born into and that they often have felt little control over. They do not believe that it is fair to brand all men as potential rapists or abusers, insisting instead that most men are decent individuals who want to treat women with respect and care. Many men have participated actively in efforts to create a more gender-equitable and safe society for everyone (Boyd, 2004). Members of both sexes have called for opportunities to communicate more openly about differences and to make recommendations for more equitable partnerships between men and women.

What do you see as some of the positive and negative features of the men's movement? Explain.

Gender across Cultures

Gender roles are an integral part of any society. These roles tend to be incorporated by the children of the society into their own formation of ideas and behaviors concerning gender (Aydt & Corsaro, 2003). They reflect the population's attitudes and values toward women and men and often affect individual behaviors and relationships. Ethnographic data from 93 nonindustrial societies show that the gender roles associated with raising children and control of property are closely associated with the degree to which men display dominance in each society. In societies in which men maintain close relationships with children and in which women have a significant amount of control over property, the men are much less likely to affirm their masculinity through boastfulness, aggressiveness, or high levels of sexual activity. The women in such societies tend to be less deferential to the men, and husbands are less likely to dominate their wives. Conversely, in those societies in which men are less involved with

Real Student Voices

■ I was brought up in a very feminist household, and encouraged to make my way in the world as an equal of men. I've succeeded for the most part, but I still find it frustrating that there are so few women in my field. It gets lonely.

■ I can't stand women who call themselves feminists. They seem to think they're above other people, and don't have any sense of humor. I just want to tell them to loosen up and have some fun. Men aren't so bad—they ought to give us a try.

children and have more control over property, demonstrations of strength, aggression, sexual prowess, and male dominance in relationships are more likely (Chung, 2005; Yakushko & Chronister, 2005).

In reviewing the literature on perceptions of gender across various cultures, it becomes clear that gender roles can be heavily influenced by cultural values. Studies have compared how various countries value traditional masculine qualities in various settings (Hofstede, 1998, 2001). This research used various scales to assign a masculinity index (MAS) to 74 countries and regions that were being studied. This index

measured the degree to which people of both sexes tended to endorse goals that were usually more popular among males. Some countries emerged with a high MAS, including Japan, Austria, Venezuela, Italy, and Switzerland. Others had a low MAS, such as Sweden, Norway, the Netherlands, Denmark, and Finland. When these results were compared with other research findings concerning attitudes, beliefs, and social roles, some interesting findings emerged about sexual values and behaviors. As Table 5.4 shows, in countries with a low MAS, sex was shared with a greater sense of mutuality and equality. In those countries with

Table 5.4	Key Differences in Sexual Behavior between Societies with Low and High Masculinity Indices (MAS)
Countries with Low MAS	**Countries with High MAS**
Matter-of-fact attitudes about sex.	Moralistic attitudes about sex.
AIDS prevention campaigns very outspoken.	AIDS prevention campaigns restricted by taboos.
Single standard for women and men.	Double standard: Women should be chaste at marriage; men needn't.
Norm of active role of women.	Norm of passive role of women: machismo vs. marianismo.
Sexual attraction unrelated to career success.	Men become more attractive by career success, women less.
In uncertainty-accepting cultures, few teenage pregnancies.	In uncertainty-accepting cultures, frequent teenage pregnancies.
Young people more influenced by parents.	Young people more influenced by peers.
Other-oriented sex.	Ego-oriented sex.
Women enjoy first sex.	Women feel exploited by first sex.
Unwanted intimacies not major issue.	Sexual harassment major issue.
Homosexuality is a fact of life.	Homosexuality is a taboo and a threat.
Weak distinction between sex and love.	Sharp distinction between sex and love.
Sex and violence in media taboo.	Sex and violence in media frequent.
Lovers should be educated, social.	Lovers should be successful, attractive.
Happy lovers overbenefit from the other.	Happy lovers get equitable mutual deal.
Interactions with other sex more intimate.	Interaction with other sex less intimate.
Sex is a way of relating to someone.	Sex is a way of performing.

Real People

Ricardo Expresses His Attitudes about Male Bashing

During a discussion group following a lecture on male-female relationships on campus, Ricardo voiced his sentiments concerning what he had perceived as antimale attitudes on the part of women. "Men today could never get away with the way some women are treating men, if the situation were reversed. I resent it that men are not supposed to say or do anything that might seem like a put-down to women, but women get away with male bashing all the time. I don't like it when I see one of those shirts that says 'A woman without a man is like a fish without a bicycle.' I'm not saying that women are incomplete without men; it's just that things like that are deliberately mean. And when that woman cut off her husband's penis because she was pissed at him, a lot of women seemed to think it was just a big joke, instead of an act of violence and mutilation. Maybe she was justified to take action against him, but the result wasn't any funnier than violence toward women. I think it's time we tried to get our priorities straight."

Ricardo's remarks generated many comments and some heated exchanges among the group members. Some of the women present said that men were only getting back what they had been dishing out for

years and that they should not complain. Some women and men in the group felt Ricardo was overreacting and should try to lighten up and learn how to take a joke. Others—mostly males—agreed with his point of view and said they were tired of any trend toward antimale messages. They emphasized that it was another example of bigotry based on stereotypes. Many men made a point of saying that they themselves did not treat women in negative or inappropriate ways and resented being lumped together with those who did.

The debate went on for nearly two hours and ended with little resolution between the various factions that were represented. Ricardo left the group feeling that he had at least been able to express his opinions openly, and he hoped that some people who had heard them would try to be more sensitive to the issues that had been raised.

How do you personally react to this story? To what extent do you agree or disagree with Ricardo? Do you believe that it is more acceptable to make disparaging comments about men than it is about women? Was Ricardo being too sensitive?

a high MAS, sex was more self-centered, exploitative, and heterosexist.

Cross-cultural studies have demonstrated a fair amount of agreement across cultures as to what characteristics are preferable in selecting a mate. In order of descending importance, these qualities are being kind, understanding, and intelligent; having an exciting personality; being healthy; and being religious. When it comes to issues such as virginity, however, culture plays a central role. In Eastern Europe and Southeast Asia, selecting a virgin as a wife is of great importance. In Northern European countries, virginity is seen as irrelevant or unimportant. There is also a fair amount of agreement in various cultures about those traits associated with women and with men. In a study examining gender stereotypes across 25 countries, men generally were seen as more active, strong, aggressive, and dominating, whereas women were seen as more passive, weak, nurturing, and self-abasing

(Williams & Best, 1990). Newer studies have shown these attitudes to exist in places such as Egypt, Nigeria, and Turkey today (Izugbara, 2008; Mensch et al., 2003; Sakalh-Ugurlu & Glick, 2003).

A small island society near Papua New Guinea is sometimes cited as one of the only gender-egalitarian cultures in the world. A study of the 2,300 inhabitants of Sudest Island found truly equal participation by women and men in decision making, ritual practices, and property ownership. Both women and men seem to have the same degree of sexual freedom, and both genders care for younger children. Their language contains no words for masculine or feminine pronouns, reflecting a much less genderized perception of the world than most other languages traditionally demonstrate. Kinship lines are traced through the mother's family. It has been suggested that Sudest Island, known by its inhabitants as the motherland, may well represent a model of a gender-egalitarian culture (Lepowsky, 1994).

Self-Evaluation

Masculinity and Femininity in Your Life

Attitudes toward masculinity and femininity are in a state of flux. While some people are attempting to blur the stereotyped differences between men and women, others are trying harder to establish definite, identifiable standards of masculinity and femininity. The exercises that follow may help you clarify your present attitudes toward men and women and your view of your own gender role.

1. **On a sheet of paper, list two men, by name, who for you exemplify ideal manhood; list two women, by name, who for you exemplify ideal womanhood. Then proceed with the following.**
   a. Under the men's names and under the women's names, list the characteristics of these people that have made them your choices as representative of the ideal.
   b. Note which of the characteristics, if any, are listed for both the men and the women.
   c. Check those characteristics from either list that you believe you exhibit.

2. **Would you ever consider dressing up in clothing generally identified as being appropriate for members of the opposite sex? If not, why not? If so, consider the following.**
   a. Under what circumstances would you wear clothing of the opposite sex: Never? Only in private? In front of one other highly trusted person? In front of a small group of friends? At a masquerade party? In public places?
   b. If possible and if you are willing, dress up in some clothes of the opposite sex and look yourself over in a full-length mirror. (Note: In some areas, it is illegal to cross-dress and be seen in public.) As you look at yourself, how do you feel? Do you feel silly? Sexy? Curious? Happy? Sad? Why do you feel that way?

3. **Examine the following list of qualities and check those that you feel are most important for you to** have as a person. (Add other words of your own if you wish.)

honest	physically strong	responsible
brave	dominating	emotional
athletic	delicate	persuasive
caring	intelligent	protective
competitive	successful	shy
gentle	submissive	reliable
sensitive	manipulative	flighty
aggressive	thoughtful	sincere
considerate	confident	sexy

   a. Now read through the list of qualities again and pick out those that have traditionally been considered masculine and those that have traditionally been considered feminine. Make two separate lists on a sheet of paper. Some words may appear on both lists or on neither. Include any words you have added to the list.
   b. Finally, note where those qualities you checked for yourself fall in your two lists. Think about them. This should help you see how your goals for your own femininity or masculinity relate to traditional ideas about men and women, as you view them.

4. **This exercise should be done with a member of the other gender or with a group of people of both sexes. The men should make two lists on a sheet of paper: the advantages of being female and the disadvantages of being female. Likewise, the women should make two lists: the advantages of being male and the disadvantages of being male. When the lists are complete, everyone should compare them and discuss the characteristics.**

5. **As you are watching television or leafing through the pages of a magazine, note how men and women are portrayed in advertisements. Note which of the men and women appeal the most to you and which are unappealing to you, asking yourself "Why?" in each case. Especially note how women and men in the advertisements are shown in traditional or in nontraditional roles.**

Chapter Summary

1. Western culture emphasizes the existence of two sexes even though disorders of sex development occur, including hermaphroditism or pseudohermaphroditism. In other cultures and times of history, intersexed individuals have been accepted in their own right.

2. Gender identity is the inner experience and realization of one's gender, while gender role is the outward expression of gender.

3. Sexual differentiation refers to the many processes by which we develop into a particular sex

and arrive at a gender identity. The essentialist view is that these are guided mostly by inborn, genetic factors while the constructionist view is that after the biological sex is established, environmental factors such as learning form our identities. An interaction of both nature and nurture now seems most likely.

4. Biological sex is expressed in genetics, the gonads, the body, and the brain and is modified by environmental factors.

5. The development of our gender identity and gender role is determined by a complex interaction of genetic, physiological, and sociocultural factors.

6. During prenatal life (before birth), the combining of chromosomes sets in motion a genetic program for producing a male, a female, or some ambivalent anatomical structure. Although the pairing of sex chromosomes normally is XX for females and XY for males, there can be abnormal combinations (e.g., XXX, XXY, XYY) that produce unusual characteristics.

7. After about a month of embryonic development, an undifferentiated set of fetal gonads appears, along with Müllerian ducts (potential female organs) and Wolffian ducts (potential male organs).

8. If the Y chromosome is present with its SRY gene, H-Y antigen is produced, transforming the gonads into testes, which in turn produce testosterone and anti-Müllerian hormone. These promote development of male organs from the Wolffian ducts and suppress further development of Müllerian ducts.

9. If the Y chromosome is absent, the fetal gonads become ovaries, and the Wolffian ducts disintegrate. The DAX-1 gene on the X chromosome controls a mechanism by which this gene inhibits the development of male genitals and promotes development of female structures.

10. Male and female genitals and inner reproductive structures then develop. The presence or absence of the male hormones affects development of the nervous system. These hormones have a masculinizing effect, while an independent process of defeminization is going on. Converse processes happen in the female, resulting in demasculinization and feminization.

11. Variant forms of sexual differentiation patterns offer clues about the effects of hormones on fetal development and later behavior.

12. There is a multiplier effect whereby biological and social factors combine to lead eventually to masculine and feminine behaviors.

13. During infancy and childhood, boys and girls are treated in particular ways, and social influences along with the biological begin to help the child form a core gender identity.

14. At puberty, the testes or ovaries begin secreting male or female hormones, triggering the development of secondary sex characteristics. Sexual feelings and fantasies also become more pronounced.

15. Adult gender roles can be conceptualized by bipolar, orthogonal, and oblique models, each offering a different view of the relationship between and relative independence of feminine and masculine qualities.

16. People who exaggerate culturally accepted gender roles are called hypermasculine or hyperfeminine. Androgyny reflects high frequencies of both masculine and feminine traits in the same individual.

17. Masculinity and femininity are defined by the behaviors found in average men and women. There are some average differences between females and males in a few cognitive and motor functions, but there are more similarities than differences.

18. There are several theoretical positions concerning gender role development. The psychodynamic approach focuses on complex unconscious interactions between children and their parents.

19. Social learning theory emphasizes socialization and the modeling of gender behaviors by children, while cognitive-developmental theory emphasizes the way human thought processes reinforce and perpetuate the gender roles learned from socialization.

20. Gender schema theory highlights the complex network of associations that people hold with regard to gender.

21. Multifactorial theories emphasize an interaction of nature and nurture in the development of gender roles.

22. Some individuals have gender identities that are not congruent with the sex of their bodies and are said to be transgendered.

23. Transgender identities are often identified as disorders, but transgender individuals have been asking for increased recognition of their roles.

24. Transsexuality involves a distinct nonconformity of gender identity with the individual's body sex, and transsexuals feel as though they should be in the body of the other gender. Some wish to be hormonally and surgically reassigned.

25. There are specific surgical procedures for male-to-female and female-to-male transsexuals. Either

metoidioplasty or phalloplasty can be used to surgically form penis-like structures.

26. Different genders are treated differently within Western society. Girls seem to be more prone to losing self-esteem as they reach adolescence.

27. Representation of women in scientific and technical fields has been lower in industrialized nations than in some developing countries because of the different status science holds in these cultures.

28. The feminist movement in American history began with an outcry for women's rights in 1848 by Elizabeth Cady Stanton and Susan B. Anthony and others.

29. Feminists want to see men and women treated—and compensated—equally and without discrimination.

30. Men have examined the limiting and unhealthy effects of the roles expected of them in our culture.

Part 2

Understanding Sexuality in Ourselves and in Our Relationships

■

Our development as sexual human beings begins at the moment of conception and continues throughout our life. During the stages of the life cycle, we move from a generalized awareness of sexuality to more specific awarenesses and experiences. Various aspects of human sexual nature unfold as we pass through these life stages, each with its own particular hurdles.

Adult sexuality typically involves selecting a partner, relating to the other person intimately, and establishing a long-term bond. Relating sexually within the context of a lasting relationship carries its own set of complications and needs, but research shows that people who are married seem to be relatively satisfied with their sexual lives. Aging affects sexuality, as does chronic disease, but neither means that a person is no longer a sexual being.

How human beings either are programmed or taught to behave sexually is not yet entirely understood. The choices we make are based partly on our sexual attitudes and values. In developing an individualized set of sexual needs, orientations, fantasies, turn-ons, turnoffs, and behaviors, we are influenced by the people in our social networks and other factors. Developing sexual values is a crucial part of our growth as people. Persons with disabilities are sexual beings, too, and need to be helped to understand the place of sexuality in their lives.

Love is a quality that we continue to struggle to understand. Experts agree that intimacy between people is based on the ability to communicate about a whole range of feelings and issues. There is no such thing as *not* communicating, because the avoidance of talking or sharing is a message in itself. What is most important is the quality of the communication and whether it fosters a more positive interaction and a lessening of tension or instead creates new impasses and stresses that drive people further apart.

Chapter 6
Sexuality in Infancy, Childhood, and Adolescence

Chapter Outline

My sex education was nearly nonexistent until I was probably 14. Not that I didn't have sexual attractions or activities; it was just that I never learned anything about them except from a few friends, and they weren't so well informed themselves. When I finally took a health course in high school, sex-related issues were barely mentioned. This seems almost criminal to me now. How was I supposed to be prepared to be a responsible sexual person?

—from a student statement

In the previous chapter, we saw that sexual differentiation is a complex process involving an interaction between biological and social forces. This chapter focuses on the ways we develop sexually from birth and express our sexual natures in the earlier stages of the life span. How do our sexual feelings and behaviors become part of our personalities and social interactions? In what important ways do children and adolescents become acquainted with their sexual needs and make decisions about acting on them? How does sexuality fit into their social relationships?

The chapter concludes with a section on sexuality education, one arena in which the battles of the culture wars are being fought. If we want children and adolescents to grow up knowing how to manage their sexual natures in responsible and respectful ways, and to make decisions that will protect their health and well-being, what is the best way to accomplish our goals? Herein lies ammunition for one of the longest-lasting and most bitterly contended battles of human sexuality. Before reading that section of the chapter, what do you personally think about the issue of sexuality education?

■ Psychosexual Development

We all gradually develop our own individualized ways of thinking and feeling about sexuality, along with our own gender identity, sexual orientation, and patterns of sexual behavior. This complex process, called **psychosexual development,** entails interactions of biological factors and learning from the social environment. Human infants seem to have built-in predispositions that form templates for their gender identity and perhaps their eventual sexual orientation, along with the capacity for eventual physiological sexual responsiveness. The specifics of how they ultimately express or exercise those predispositions and capacities are influenced by a whole range of factors. As infants grow into children and then develop into adolescents, profound changes happen within their bodies, emotions, and intellects. The interactive processes of psychosexual development begin to form the very individualized sexual natures they will take with them to adulthood.

There may well be critical periods in human development during which a person's set of biological templates interact with the influences of socialization in the environment to establish particular characteristics of the individual's sexuality. Such critical periods would mean that the necessary growth has occurred for learning to be optimal, all capacities are at a maximum, and conditions are ideal for a particular kind of learning to take place. These periods in human development most likely occur during childhood and early adolescence.

Various theories of psychosexual development have evolved over the last century. In the brief survey that follows, you will see that these theories have gradually led to a more comprehensive understanding of how we become sexual human beings. Much still remains to be learned.

Biopsychological Drive/ Instinct Theory

Among the earliest attempts to explain psychosexual development was the idea that humans have an inborn sexual instinct. Human beings are born with sex organs that become increasingly functional during their life stages, and these organs are necessary for the propagation of the species. A logical presumption would be that nature has also built into each of us instincts for putting those sex organs into operation. Evolutionary psychology is based on the assumption that a fundamental human instinct aims toward reproducing the species. These instinct-based viewpoints assume that a sex drive causes people to experience a buildup of sexual tension or need over time. When sexual activity is experienced, the drive is believed to be temporarily satisfied and reduced, eventually to build up again so that the cycle continues. Instinct theory squared intuitively with what many people seemed to experience in their own lives.

Sex researchers have begun to believe, however, that the concept of a biopsychological sex drive probably is simplistic. Although genetic and hormonal factors obviously give us potentials for sexual arousal and response, they do not go very far in explaining how individual human beings learn to perceive—or *not* perceive—various stimuli as sexually arousing. There is a growing consensus that social and cultural factors are also important in shaping sexual behavior, including the encouragements and constraints that social sanctions offer (Bancroft, 2002a, 2009; Bancroft et al., 2009; Toates, 2009).

psychosexual development factors that form a person's sexual feelings, orientation, and patterns of behavior.

Theories about inborn sexual drives or instincts have led to other assumptions about the naturalness or unnaturalness of particular sexual behaviors. For example, whatever sexual behavior leads to potential propagation of the species (male-female intercourse) could easily be classified as natural, whereas other forms of behavior (such as masturbation or same-gender interactions) could be considered unnatural by default. This concept has been carried even further into value judgments of good and bad or healthy and sick. Behind it all is the idea that as children grow and develop, their sexual instincts gradually emerge and unfold according to nature's plan. As sexual drive theory has been called into question, we have had to look to other explanations for psychosexual development.

Psychodynamic Theory

Psychodynamic theory, which has developed from Freud's psychoanalytic theory, also relies on a concept of built-in instincts. Freud postulated the existence of the **libido,** a word he used to describe the sexual longing or sex drive that he believed was built into the human psyche. Freud realized that in addition to this psychological aspect of the sexual instinct there was a physical aspect involving bodily responses and behaviors. He also introduced the concept of the unconscious mind, purported to control much of human development and behavior even though its thought processes are outside conscious awareness, although modifications have been made to the theory since Freud's early formulations (Harding, 2001).

A major assumption of this theory is that infants are born with a store of sexual energy in the form of the libido. At first, the energy is completely undifferentiated and indiscriminate. It can be directed at anything. For this reason, Freud said that infants were "polymorphously perverse." This energy gradually becomes associated with different pleasurable areas of the body until it finally localizes in the sex organs. Freud believed that it was variations in this process that molded not only the individual's sexual nature but also the entire personality.

Psychodynamic theory sees the libido as becoming invested in bodily parts that are important in a child's physical development. During infancy, when the child has no particular awareness of differences between the sexes, the sexual energies of the infant become centered in the mouth, an important area of gratification for the young child. This is referred to as the *oral stage* (see Figure 6.1). As a child begins to be toilet trained and learns how to control pleasurably the retention and elimination of the bowels, her or his libido moves to the anus—a transition to the *anal stage.* It is believed that by the age of about three years, children begin to be aware of their genitals, and the libido

■ FIGURE 6.1 *Freud's Oral Stage*

The Freudian theory of sexual development states that in the first year of life the libido, or sex drive, is located in the mouth. According to Freud, this is the reason why infants enjoy sucking and putting things into their mouths.

becomes centered in the penis or clitoris, the *phallic stage.* By this time, children have begun to become aware of the anatomical differences between the sexes.

Freud believed that a **latency period** follows, during which the sexual energies are said to lie dormant while intellectual and social growth continues. Not all proponents of psychodynamic theory accept the existence of this latency period because there is evidence that children remain in touch with their sexual and romantic feelings throughout childhood. Freud's perceptions may well have been influenced by the society in which he lived and worked, a society that was reluctant to perceive children as sexual beings. The final stage of his model, the stage when the libido becomes

libido (la-BEED-o or LIB-a-do) a term first used by Freud to define human sexual longing, or sex drive.

latency period Freudian concept that during middle childhood sexual energies are dormant; recent research tends to suggest that latency does not exist.

focused in the sex organs, begins at puberty and is called the *genital stage*.

Psychodynamic theory includes the idea that many things can go wrong as the libido gradually moves to various parts of the body. It holds that adult emotional and mental problems are the result of difficulties during some stage of psychosexual development.

Conditioning and Social Learning Theory

Early psychology concerned itself with the mechanisms by which animals learned patterns of behavior. Simple conditioning mechanisms were thought to be applicable to some human behaviors as well, including human sexual arousal. It was assumed, for example, that if particular erotic words were heard repeatedly during sexual arousal, eventually the words themselves could become a conditional stimulus that could elicit some degree of sexual arousal—the conditioned response. Later work in psychology clarified more complex principles of operant conditioning. According to these principles, **reinforcement** of behavior—through pleasure, reward, or removal of some unpleasant stimulus—makes the behavior likely to be repeated. Negative consequences of a behavior through unpleasant results, pain, or the loss of rewarding stimuli tend to decrease the frequency of the behavior. Hypothetically applied to sexual development in humans, this perspective emphasizes the influences of positive and negative consequences on sexual behaviors.

Conditioning theorists emphasized that the development of sexual behaviors is a complex phenomenon influenced by many different sources. They also used the concept of **generalization** to explain how specific, learned sexual responses might be generalized to other, similar circumstances. For example, an individual who was conditioned to become sexually aroused by seeing female breasts might generalize that experience to other things associated with breasts (bras, other underwear, blouses, other parts of a woman's body, perfume, and so on). The generalization process would be kept in check by **discrimination,** which would enable the individual to avoid responding to one stimulus while responding to similar stimuli. Conditioning theory, then, held that we learn our sexual orientations and behaviors through observational learning, a complex pattern of reinforcement, and the pairing of stimuli with sexual response. As human beings grew up, social cues would be picked up that helped determine what would be considered acceptable sexual behavior.

An extension of conditioning theory emerged in the 1960s with the model called social learning theory. This model suggested that the learning process was influenced by ongoing observation of and identifica-

■ **FIGURE 6.2** *Social Learning Theory*

According to this theory, children learn attitudes and values by observing and imitating the behavior of others. What they learn depends partly on the power and prestige of the person observed. Television, movies, and music can be powerful influences on the sexual values and behavior of children and adolescents.

tion with other people. This cumulative learning process was seen as crucial, because people's perceptions were seen as being shaped by the impressions and attitudes they formed in their early development. For example, children and adolescents would be prone to imitating (modeling) and adopting the behaviors they see in other people whom they admire and identify with (see Figure 6.2).

There is limited scientific evidence about how much conditioning and social learning actually establish specific patterns of sexual arousal and behavior. These theories did help us understand that psychosexual development is probably influenced to a degree by environmental factors.

Developmental Theory

Other theorists began to focus more clearly on the influence of social forces on child development that could be applied to psychosexual development. Jean Piaget (1932) had already considered the importance of cognition, intellect, and reasoning in children, and Lawrence Kohlberg (1981) eventually examined the

reinforcement in conditioning theory, any influence that helps shape future behavior as a punishment or reward stimulus.

generalization application of specific learned responses to other, similar situations or experiences.

discrimination the process by which an individual extinguishes a response to one stimulus while preserving it for other stimuli.

■ FIGURE 6.3 *Erikson's Psychosocial Development*

In Erikson's life-span theory of psychosocial development, young children learn skills as well as identity and values from those around them. Positive values about themselves and their sexuality will aid children in developing intimacy with others as they grow older.

many facets of moral development. Erik Erikson (1968) made significant strides toward devising a model of *developmental psychology* that clearly showed those tasks that had to be accomplished at various stages of human growth and development (see Figure 6.3). He considered the tasks so crucial that he called them crises. Erikson conceptualized an eight-stage life span of **psychosocial development** that extended from birth to old age. Because of his psychoanalytic training, Erikson believed that a powerful libido was built into all of us, but he also realized that cultural and social influences help shape our sexual identities, including our sexual behaviors. He maintained that each of the eight stages of life includes a crisis of psychosocial development that must be resolved (see Table 6.1). Each crisis can take the individual either in a direction of adjustment, health, and positive self-concept or in a direction of maladaptation, unrest, and low self-esteem.

According to Erikson, during adolescence and young adulthood each individual has the task of

achieving a clear understanding of herself or himself as a sexual person and of achieving a sense of intimacy with other human beings. Failure to reach these goals may result in role confusion and isolation that can generate unhealthy perceptions of sexuality and relationships for a lifetime. Success in achieving a healthy sexual identity hinges partially on how successfully the tasks of earlier stages of the life span have been resolved.

A Unified Theoretical Model of Psychosexual Development

Researcher John Bancroft (2002a; 2009) has proposed a unified theory of how sexual development takes place. It considers the various stages of physical and psychological development through which human beings pass, and it identifies three principal strands that are part of each person's developmental framework. These three strands tend to develop in parallel during the childhood years but relatively independently of one another. Then, during adolescence, the strands come together and become more integrated to form the foundations of a sexually mature adult. These strands have been identified as the following:

1. *Gender identity.* During childhood the core gender identity is established, and during adolescence sexual behaviors serve an important function in reorganizing its specifics. This begins to establish the sense of oneself as man, woman, or transgendered.
2. *Sexual response and understanding one's sexual orientation.* Puberty triggers a variety of physical and emotional changes within the individual and usually leads to a greater awareness of sexual arousal. Coming to terms with these needs and responses plays an important part in figuring out who one really is sexually.
3. *Capacity for intimate dyadic relationships.* In later adolescence and early adulthood, people begin exploring their sexuality within the context of partnerships or dyads (pairs). How effective the individual is in handling the complexities of dyadic relationships is significant in later sexual development.

In gaining a deeper understanding of their own sexual orientation, children first go through a *prelabeling* process, as they begin to identify what is expected of them sexually. As adolescents they then begin to categorize their own sexual orientations according to

psychosocial development the cultural and social influences that help shape human sexual identity.

Table 6.1	The Crises to Be Resolved during Erikson's Stages of Psychosocial Development
Stage in Life Cycle	**Crisis**
Infancy	Gaining trust in self and environment vs. Feeling mistrust and wariness of others
Ages $1\frac{1}{2}$ to 3	Achieving a sense of autonomy vs. Shame and doubt over one's ability to be independent
Ages 3 to $5\frac{1}{2}$	Learning how to take initiative comfortably vs. Feeling guilty over motivations and needs
Ages $5\frac{1}{2}$ to 12 (The time when school and other external influences gain more significance)	Gaining a sense of industry and competence vs. Feeling inferior and inept
Adolescence	Forming a sense of one's own identity vs. Role confusion and self-questioning
Young adulthood	Achieving intimacy and connection with others vs. Feeling alone and isolated
Adulthood	Realizing generativity and positive interpersonal relationships vs. Feeling stagnant and unfulfilled
Maturity	Achieving ego integrity and relative peace with one's life vs. Feeling a sense of despair and wastedness

Source: Data from E. Erikson, *Identity: Youth and Crisis,* New York: W. W. Norton, 1968.

the labels their social groups provide—the *self-labeling* stage of identifying sexual orientation. The adolescent privately compares her or his own feelings and responses to those that are prescribed in the prevailing society. If self-labels are out of step with what the adolescent has learned is expected and desired by the society, personal conflict and confusion may result. Finally, sexual orientation is defined through *social labeling,* in which the person's perceptions of self are subject to validation by what is known about the society's labels for various sexual orientations (Bancroft, 2002a; Sanders, 1999).

Social Process Theory

When the researchers who conducted the National Health and Social Life Survey (NHSLS) designed their comprehensive study of sexual behavior, they realized that research would have to go beyond the study of individual human beings because we do not develop sexually in a social vacuum. To help them interpret the meaning of their statistics on sexual behavior, researchers drew on some of the most respected theories of social psychology, sociology, and economics. The following three theoretical perspectives proved to be the most useful to this work (Laumann et al., 1994).

Sexual Script Theory: How Do We Know What to Do Sexually?

John Gagnon and William Simon were among the first sociologists to take issue with theories that relied on the presumption of an intense, biologically generated sex drive. They believed that built-in sexual motivations might not be very intense at all, at least in many indi-

viduals. They developed *scripting theory,* one of the first attempts to explain how sexual behavior was socially constructed. It holds that patterns of sexual conduct are derived from social and cultural contexts that are filled with messages, or **social scripts,** that regulate most human behavior. Through a lifelong acculturation process, people acquire the *sexual scripts*—or patterns of sexual conduct—that suit their own needs. This sometimes means that people adopt sexual scripts that deviate from cultural norms (Gagnon, 1999; Simon, 1999).

In terms of sexual behavior, this would mean that although particular social situations are not inherently sexual, we organize the elements of a situation—for example, an available partner, privacy, sexual desire—in such a way that they become sexual. Because sexual scripts are learned, new learning experiences during each emergent stage of an individual's development contribute to that individual's sexual development. There are three different types of sexual scripts, reflective of different levels of functioning for individuals as they grow up. In the broadest context, there are *cultural scripts,* referring to the messages and instructional guidance about sexual behavior offered by one's culture. This constructionist perspective holds that social and cultural imperatives play a significant role in determining what sexual choices people will make within their society or culture. There are also *interpersonal scripts* determined by the expectations of other people about conduct within relationships. In the individual's own mind are the *intrapsychic scripts.* The person takes all the information from the cultural and

social scripts a complex set of learned responses to a particular situation that is formed by social influences.

interpersonal contexts and then processes it internally. As individual men and women make sense of what the surrounding sexual messages mean for them, they begin to develop their own sets of sexual scripts. The three levels of scripting are constantly interacting with one another, and they may be modified over the course of a person's life span (Krahè, Bieneck, & Scheinberger-Olwig, 2007).

Choice Theory: How Do We Choose Sexual Partners?

Although sexual scripts provide people with codes of sexual conduct from their cultures, they do not fully explain how individuals choose among the varieties of sexual behavior or among the potential sexual partners available to them. *Choice theory,* borrowed from economics, assumes that human beings make choices out of the need to apportion their resources—in this case, sexual and relational—in order to reach certain goals. Some typical goals of sexual behavior would be sexual pleasure, the emotional satisfaction of intimacy, having children, and building a positive reputation among one's peers. In order to reach these goals, various human resources must be managed, because there is a cost involved in securing a sexual partner. It takes time, emotional energy, social skills, and sometimes money. Thus, as with economic outcomes, there is a limit to the number of sexual partners an individual can afford to choose. For most people, that number is really quite small (Laumann et al., 1994).

Two other components of choice theory have been applied to the sexual arena: risk management and the market. Sexual choices usually are made with a degree of uncertainty, and the risks involved must be weighed. There are both positive and negative consequences to be considered, and these can markedly affect people's sexual choices. Some people are better than others at assessing and managing sexual and relational risks. Adolescents typically become aware of these various factors as they begin testing the social waters. All these elements affect how individuals approach the market for sex partners. How well a person fares in the social marketplace depends on many variables, including physical attributes, attractiveness, personality, intelligence, and age. It is the components of this social-sexual economy that influence the choices of sexual behavior individual human beings make (Sprecher, 1998).

Social Network Theory: Where Do We Find Sexual Relationships?

Social network theory recognizes that much sexual activity is negotiated within the context of social relationships, and that it is the characteristics of those relationships that help shape what sexual activities, if any, will occur. Our social networks consist of the people with whom we associate on a regular basis, as determined by neighborhoods, school, work, and other social groupings. Two-person partnerships, or sexual dyads, that begin forming in childhood and adolescence do not exist in a vacuum; rather, they grow out of a larger network of social relationships that also influence the sexual activities of the individuals who are part of them (Sprecher, 1998).

The social composition of a sexual relationship affects the type of sexual behavior that will be experienced in the relationship. For example, whether people share oral sex is clearly affected by their age, educational level, and race (Michael et al., 1994). We also label partnerships in different ways: "lovers," "girlfriend–boyfriend," "one-night stand," "married couple." The way a relationship has been labeled and socially defined affects how the individuals within that relationship view it and also how the larger social network defines what is appropriate sexual conduct for it. *Social network theory* looks at the principles of relationships, but it must rely on scripting theory and choice theory to explain what happens within specific relationships. At the same time, sexual scripts and choices are influenced by the qualities of the relationship, and the relationship helps shape the scripts and choices of its members. This interaction of factors constitutes the *social process* of psychosexual development.

■ Sexuality in Infancy and Childhood

Infancy and childhood are periods of human development during which significant steps of psychosexual development take place (see Figure 6.4). Historically, Western cultures have tended toward viewing childhood as a time of sexual innocence and purity, and the protectiveness that accompanies this perception has rendered it inappropriate to ask children directly about their sexual feelings and behaviors (Bullough, 2004). Researchers instead have relied on the reported observations of parents and other caregivers or on retrospective reports of adults about their early lives. Both of these approaches involve factors that are notoriously unreliable. The result is that we really do not have an entirely reliable picture of what constitutes normal childhood sexuality (Bancroft, 2002a; Graaf & Rademakers, 2006; Thigpen, 2009).

Ultrasound images of fetuses still in the uterus show that a male fetus can experience erection of the penis even before birth. Soon after birth, infants seem to show interest in exploring their own bodies. There

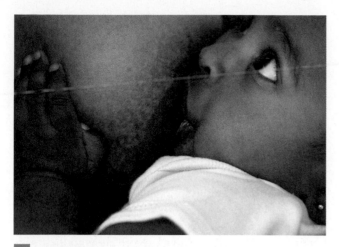

■ FIGURE 6.4 *Infant Sexuality*

Infants develop an awareness of their bodies and their sexuality first through a bonding with their parents and the sensuous contact involved in cuddling and holding and second by exploring their own bodies, including their genitals.

is ample evidence to suggest that baby boys experience genital responses. Erection has even been observed within the first few minutes after birth. Some male infants seem to have orgasms, as evidenced by sequences of tension-building, rhythmic muscular contractions, and pelvic thrusting that culminate in what appear to be pleasurable sensations and relaxation. In baby girls, the labia may be quite prominent and the vaginal lining pinkish in color for several weeks after birth, the result of maternal hormones still present in the bloodstream. There is also evidence of vaginal lubrication that occurs spontaneously in regular cycles from the time a female is born (DeLamater & Friedrich, 2002; Singer, 2002).

Although these early patterns of physical arousal and sensual enjoyment do not represent the socialized patterns of eroticism that form later in human development, they do demonstrate the extreme sensitivity of infants. The foundations for sensuality, intimacy, and relationship to other people continue to be established during infancy. This may be a time when small children begin to notice how they are treated by their fathers and mothers and to form early concepts of their relationships with others (Ballard & Gross, 2009).

Several significant developmental tasks are accomplished during infancy. Immediately after birth, there is a period when babies seem very alert, and bonding occurs between them and their parent(s). The holding, touching, and cuddling given to an infant are part of the evolution of its ability to relate to and be intimate with others. Between six months and one year of age, babies begin to touch their genitals, if they are not prohibited from doing so. Our culture exhibits a fair amount of anxiety about recognizing and legitimizing

the concept that for children to experience sexual and sensual pleasure might be perfectly healthy and normal. Yet this is a time of life when the very foundations for adult sexual pleasure are established, and this may be accomplished best within the context of a loving and pleasure-affirming environment (Jackson & Scott, 2004; Levine, 2002a).

Recall some of your earliest sexual thoughts and feelings. Describe your reaction to them.

Sexual Curiosity Grows in Childhood

Children's sexual development proceeds along two parallel routes that sometimes cross. One stream is the autoerotic, referring to the sensual and sexual exploration of their own bodies; the other involves relational interaction with other people, most typically beginning with their caregivers or parents (Graaf & Rademakers, 2006; Singer, 2002). Very young children are often observed fondling their genitals, sometimes seeming to produce sexual excitement and orgasm. Children begin to gain a sense of what their bodies are and of the capacities for pleasure their bodies have. This can be seen as a period of potentiation, when vague awareness of sexual feelings and early ranges of sexual responsiveness are established. Only a few children seem to have particularly specific sexual preferences. Most apparently are multisexual, able to respond to many different forms of sexual stimulation. Children also learn more about sex and reproduction as they progress through childhood and as their verbal capabilities grow, with a spurt of knowledge and understanding occurring around age 10 (Herdt & McClintock, 2000).

A few studies have provided some insights into what might be considered normative patterns of sexual development during childhood, based on the reports of parents, especially mothers, concerning the observed behaviors of their children. The UCLA Family Lifestyles Project (FLS), which followed more than 200 children from birth until adulthood, has been the source of a wealth of longitudinal data (Okami, Olmstead, & Abramson, 1997). A more comprehensive examination of childhood sexual behavior was conducted by a group of psychologists at the Mayo Clinic, using questionnaires that were administered to the primary female caregivers of 1,114 children ages 2 to 12 (Friedrich et al., 1998). Other studies have repeated the research methodology with more diverse ethnic populations (Thigpen, 2009). This research confirms that children exhibit a broad range of sexual behaviors, many of which are common enough to be considered normal for various developmental stages. When young adults recall their own sexual behaviors as children, they almost always judge them to have been normal.

FIGURE 6.5 *Sexual Curiosity*

Most children around the age of 2 or 3 are curious about their own bodies as well as the bodies of others. Any sexual activity usually involves a fondling of the genitals. Because children tend to respond to each other affectionately at these ages, touching, hugging, and kissing may extend to the genital area.

The UCLA study found 77 percent of parents reporting that their children had engaged in sex play prior to age six, including masturbation. Nearly 47 percent of those parents indicated that their children had engaged in some sort of interactive sex play with another child during the same period of life. By the age of two or three, many children begin to explore the bodies of their playmates, in activities ranging from simple embraces to stroking, caressing, kissing, and touching the genitals. They also continue to have an interest in their own genitals (see Figure 6.5). Some become involved in games that permit mutual body exploration, such as "doctor" or "nurse." From the ages of three to five, awareness of being a boy or a girl seems to appear, although many children cannot really explain how they know they are a girl or a boy. They most often make their identification based on social markers such as clothing, rather than by anatomical differences such as genitals (Okami, Olmstead, & Abramson, 1997). Knowledge about where babies come from and how they are born seems to become more refined as children grow and develop, and this knowledge may be enhanced by parents who make a point of providing the information to their children (DeLamater & Friedrich, 2002).

The Mayo Clinic research found that the most frequently observed behaviors among children ages 2 to 12 were self-stimulation, exposing body parts to another child, and behaviors relating to the personal boundaries of others, such as rubbing against another person. Other research has confirmed that along with normative behaviors, young schoolchildren are often observed behaving toward others in ways that would be considered inappropriate or problematic (Kaeser, DiSalvo, & Moglia, 2000). More intrusive behaviors, such as oral-genital contact or insertion of things into the vagina or rectum, were less frequently observed. Although the amount of sexual behavior observed among children declines steadily during the childhood years (see Figure 6.6), the researchers have cautioned that this does not mean that the behaviors are decreasing, but only that as children become older they become more private with their sexual behaviors (Friedrich et al., 1998; Thigpen, 2009).

Based on the Mayo Clinic study, a tentative outline of sexual behaviors was formulated for boys and girls at various stages in their development (see Table 6.2). Although the results confirm much of what has always been assumed about children, they also reflect the greater level of privacy children achieve as they reach adolescence (Friedrich et al., 1998). Exposure to peer sex play in childhood does not seem to be associated with a person's level of adjustment in the late teen years (Okami, Olmstead, & Abramson, 1997).

Masturbating and exhibiting genitals to other children are common forms of childhood sex play. In later childhood, some youngsters experiment with other forms of behavior, including oral-genital contact and attempts at anal or vaginal intercourse (Graaf & Rademakers, 2006). These activities may be engaged in with a same-gender partner or with someone of the other gender. Repeated aggressive sexual behavior in younger children toward other children, such as coercive oral sex, insertion of objects into the rectum, or attempted rape, may represent signs of previous sexual abuse of the child. However, a study of identical twins during childhood suggested that problematic behavior involving excessive masturbation or public sex play might be influenced by genetic factors as well (Langstrom, Grann, & Lichtenstein, 2002).

How parents and others respond to sex play in children begins to set the stage for later sex-related values. If a parent constantly punishes a child's attempts at genital exploration or sex play, the child may rapidly learn that her or his sex organs and exploratory behaviors are bad. At times, the reactions of anxious adults can transform an innocent, natural phase of sexual exploration and development into a traumatic event (Levine, 2002a). Parents who accept sexual exploration as a natural, positive part of growing up and help their children understand what will be socially acceptable in later life may contribute enormously to the development of a healthy sexuality in their children (Ballard & Gross, 2009).

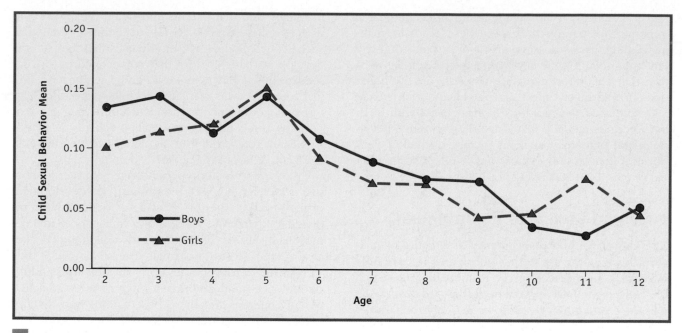

■ **FIGURE 6.6** *Observed Sexual Behavior in Children*

The sexual behaviors of children between the ages of 2 and 12, as observed and reported by their primary caregivers, tend to decrease with age. It is believed that this does not represent a decrease in actual sexual behavior but rather a greater awareness of social appropriateness and a desire for more privacy.

Source: W. N. Friedrich et al., "Normative Sexual Behavior in Children: A Contemporary Sample." Reproduced with permission from *Pediatrics,* Vol. 101, No. 4, p. e9, Figure 1, Copyright © 1998 by the AAP.

Table 6.2	*Developmentally Related Sexual Behaviors*	
Age	**Item**	**% Endorsement**
2- to 5-year-old boys	Stands too close to people	29.3
	Touches sex (private) parts when in public places	26.5
	Touches or tries to touch mother's or other women's breasts	42.4
	Touches sex (private) parts when at home	60.2
	Tries to look at people when they are nude or undressing	26.8
2- to 5-year-old girls	Stands too close to people	25.8
	Touches or tries to touch mother's or other women's breasts	43.7
	Touches sex (private) parts when at home	43.8
	Tries to look at people when they are nude or undressing	26.9
6- to 9-year-old boys	Touches sex (private) parts when at home	39.8
	Tries to look at people when they are nude or undressing	20.2
6- to 9-year-old girls	Touches sex (private) parts when at home	20.7
	Tries to look at people when they are nude or undressing	20.5
10- to 12-year-old boys	Is very interested in the opposite sex	24.1
10- to 12-year-old girls	Is very interested in the opposite sex	28.7

Source: W. N. Friedrich et al., "Normative Sexual Behavior in Children: A Contemporary Sample." Reproduced with permission from *Pediatrics,* Vol. 101, No. 4, p. e9, Table 5, Copyright © 1998 by the AAP.

One of the concerns parents sometimes have is the degree to which nudity should be allowed or encouraged within the family setting. Most professionals agree that when nudity within the home is permitted and there is no sexual abuse, there do not seem to be negative consequences. The same is true of situations in which children have accidentally viewed their parents engaging in sexual behavior. Children themselves may well reach stages in their development when they signal some discomfort with being seen naked by other family members or with seeing their parents nude. It is important for parents to respect these needs by making as little fuss as possible and avoiding inflicting any embarrassment on the child. Nonetheless, studies confirm that childhood exposure to nudity in the home does not adversely affect an individual's adult sexual adjustment or functioning; in fact, boys with such backgrounds actually may have more positive developmental outcomes, such as increased comfort with physical contact and expressions of affection in adult life (Heins, 2001; Okami et al., 1998).

Love and Romance in Childhood

The Freudian concept of latency assumed that children between the ages of roughly 6 and 12 have little interest in sexual feelings or relationships. Research on child sexual development tends to discount the existence of a latency phase. In fact children can develop romantic and even sexual attractions to others as their brains become more fully grown and their bodies begin to reach reproductive maturity (DeLamater & Friedrich, 2002). These romantic and sexual attachments eventually become defined as love. Around the ages of 10 to 12, girls and boys begin to show a distinct increase in their levels of interest in and attraction toward others, and they begin to develop more intimate relationships when the opportunity becomes available (Hearn, O'Sullivan, & Dudley, 2002; Herdt & McClintock, 2000). Children at this age appear to take their love very seriously and begin to move toward more concrete wishing and planning (Graaf & Rademakers, 2006).

Gender/Transgender Identity in Childhood

There is research evidence to suggest that children are able to correctly label themselves as girl or boy quite early in childhood, even before they tend to segregate into girl and boy play groups. They also show preferences for sex-typed toys, meaning that the toys are typically chosen by most girls or most boys. Girls on average do indeed show preferences for dolls, dishes, and nonaggressive play, while boys on average prefer trucks, action figures, and rough-and-tumble play. These are the beginnings of **sex-dimorphic behavior.** The sex-typed toy choices seem to precede the emergence of playing mostly with members of the child's own sex. As most children approach middle childhood, their various developmental trends generally have been established along normative, or most typical, sex-dimorphic lines (Ruble, Martin, & Berenbaum, 2006).

Constructionists could logically assert that social pressures create the necessity of this division between the sexes, and that parents and other adults sort children into these directions quite deliberately because of social convention. However, the facts that the patterns develop so early in life; that some children do not seem to fit so easily with their gender segregation; and that identical twins are likely to follow the same patterns of conformity or nonconformity, suggest that perhaps some inborn, essential mechanisms play a significant role (Fridell et al., 2006; van Beijsterveldt, Hudzian, & Boomsma, 2006).

As we know, some people have a gender identity that is incongruent with the physical sex development of their bodies. There is growing evidence that an individual's awareness of having a transgender identity most likely also begins during early childhood (Zucker et al., 2008). Most transsexuals recall feeling as if they were in the wrong bodies early in their lives. Adults often notice gender nonconformity in the play activities of children, and these observations have in turn been shown to correlate positively with diagnoses of transgender identity in children. Interestingly though, boys who tend toward gender nonconformity are more likely to express that behavior openly only when they believe that adults are not watching. This is believed to reflect the likelihood that boys receive more pressure and ridicule from adults as well as peers when they stray from expected boylike activities, and also suffer more gender-related abuse. Studies of adult men and women who remember being gender nonconforming as children and adolescents also demonstrate that males generally have a rougher time with the judgments of others than do females at all age levels and that it is associated with adult depression (Fridell et al., 2006; Nuttbrock et al., 2010; Skidmore, Linsenmaier, & Bailey, 2006; Wilansky-Traynor & Lobel, 2008).

The American Psychiatric Association's *Diagnostic and Statistical Manual of Mental Disorders*, called the *DSM-IV,* presently lists of guidelines for determining whether a child has a gender identity disorder. These include a strong, persistent identification with the opposite sex, including the desire to cross-dress, behaving in transgender roles, and preferring playmates of that gender. Other criteria include expressed discomfort and dissatisfaction with their own sex and significant distress, self-hatred, or impairment of their lives because of the condition. Some professionals are uncomfortable with the judgment that transgender identities are considered pathological, believing instead that it may be unreasonable and unnecessary to fit children into such categories. Perhaps they should simply be seen

sex-dimorphic behavior the differentiation by gender of activities typical of girls or boys, such as choice of sex-typed toys and same-gender playmates.

as people who do not conform to sex-dichotomous preferences and behaviors. It has been suggested that the term gender identity *disorder* be changed to gender *incongruence* in the upcoming new edition of the *DSM* (Deogracias et al., 2007; Hill et al., 2007).

As transgender identities are becoming recognized more readily in childhood and adolescence, questions emerge about the kinds of interventions that should be offered. If potential candidates for sex reassignment can be reliably identified prior to puberty, hormonal intervention can take place prior to the development of secondary sex characteristics, making the process far simpler and more effective. There is evidence that adolescents who want to change their sex and then subsequently do so in adulthood tend to have very stable psychological functioning. There is also some evidence that children who are treated prior to the age of about eight may be helped through therapy to become more comfortable with roles consistent with their anatomy. Recently released treatment protocols now allow transgender adolescents to be treated with hormones that inhibit the development of secondary sex characteristics until the age of 16, when further decisions may be made about how they wish to develop in terms of their physical identities. At that time, either natural hormones may be allowed to function or hormones of the other gender may be administered in support of a transgender physical appearance (Fink, 2005; Hembree et al., 2009; Meyer et al., 2001; Smith, Cohen, & Cohen-Kettenis, 2002).

What types of help do you think should be made available to children who have a transgender identity? Should they be considered to have a disorder?

■ Sexuality in Adolescence

Adolescence is that period of social, emotional, and cognitive development that moves young people toward adulthood. It is a time during which individuals become biologically mature and develop a greater sense of independence, autonomy, and personal identity. The capacity for abstract thinking increases, and planning for the future is balanced with a recognition of the potential impacts of current actions. During adolescence, young people strengthen their gender identities and begin clarifying their sexual orientations as they experience more erotic feelings and experiment further with sexual behaviors (DeLamater & Friedrich, 2002).

The boundaries of adolescence are poorly defined in Western societies. In many cultures other than our own, youthful individuals participate in rites of passage, signifying that they are no longer children. Along with that passage into young adulthood come carefully prescribed (and proscribed) modes of sexual behavior. Youngsters in Western cultures usually must deal with their growth into adulthood in a much more vague and gradual way.

Early Adolescent Sexuality

Girls typically experience puberty sooner than boys, so there is often an awkward period around ages 11 to 13 when boys' physical maturation lags behind that of girls. Although most adolescents experience some increased interest in sex, this occurs in varying degrees. Boys experience their first ejaculations of semen, although they may have had orgasms previous to their ability to produce sperm and semen. Girls begin menstruating and will eventually usually experience their first orgasm, although that often happens later for girls than it does for boys (Janssen, 2007). The adolescent must build these developments into an awareness of being a young man or woman.

It is during early adolescence that some very basic attitudes about one's body and bodily functions are established, and these attitudes may significantly affect further development. There is evidence that girls who feel a sense of shame about menstruation and their bodies have lower levels of sexual activity but eventually may become prone to riskier sexual decision making. Girls who grow up feeling more comfortable about their bodies and menstruation are more sexually assertive in their decision making and have higher levels of sexual activity but take fewer sexual risks (Schooler et al., 2005).

Most boys experience their first ejaculation during masturbation, an activity in which they may have participated previously without emission of semen. The first ejaculation usually occurs between ages 11 and 15. Sometimes first ejaculation happens as a nocturnal emission or wet dream (Janssen, 2007). Some boys, after puberty, report having spontaneous ejaculations from time to time, produced by nonsexual physical activity or psychological influences (e.g., viewing pictures or watching an attractive person). By late adolescence, the capacity to have spontaneous orgasms apparently is lost in nearly all males. The capacity for spontaneous orgasm, without physical stimulation, apparently exists in some girls and even persists in a few women; they can experience orgasm by viewing sexually arousing material or by just thinking about sex.

Research suggests that boys become sexually active somewhat earlier than girls do. As adolescence progresses, girls clearly become more involved in sexual activity and better acquainted with their sexual

adolescence period of emotional, social, and physical transition from childhood to adulthood.

Real Student Voices

■ As teens get a little older, they respect themselves more. In high school, everyone was having sex with everyone else. Now in college, I feel that people are more responsible and more involved in serious relationships.

■ Some of my friends who are having sex with multiple partners without protection need to start using protection for themselves and their partners.

■ I see my peers engaging in a lot of risky behavior, like intercourse without any protection. This

has made me much more cautious in my own sexual experiences. I think alcohol increases the risk of potentially harmful behavior.

■ I have friends who don't use protection the majority of the time, which is absurd to me. Why would anyone take a chance of getting pregnant or getting a disease? Cheating is another thing I can't explain, especially when the girls probably know each other!

---

responsiveness, a trend that often continues for another 10 to 20 years, when involvement in sexual activity tends to level off. Throughout adolescence, females exhibit a somewhat lower incidence of masturbation, same-gender sexual activity, and heterosexual experimentation (Kontula & Haavio-Mannila, 2002; Laflin, Wang, & Barry, 2008; SIECUS, 2003). Studies suggest that adolescent girls who have older boyfriends are more likely to begin having intercourse earlier than others. Early-adolescent girls are particularly prone to having intercourse if the boyfriend is substantially older, such as in his late teens or early twenties (Lieberman, 2006; Liehmann-Smith, 2001).

As the body matures and new sexual feelings emerge, awareness of the social significance of sex develops and young people begin to daydream about sex. Adolescents may fantasize about loving relationships that involve sexual activity with a particular person or about a wide array of sexual practices with nonspecific partners (Herdt & McClintock, 2000). The fantasies that accompany masturbation often are quite vivid and add to the pleasure of the masturbatory experience, also helping young people become more fully acquainted with their sexual preferences. Many adolescents use their fantasy experiences to plan for real sexual and relational encounters later in life (Kontula & Haavio-Mannila, 2002).

Although the majority of adolescents under age 15 have not engaged in sexual intercourse, the proportion of those who have is increasing. The age at which puberty occurs seems to play a role for boys. Those boys who experience puberty at earlier ages tend to experience their first sexual arousal earlier and to report a stronger sex drive and greater acceptance of casual sex

in adulthood. This pattern does not seem typical for girls. In both sexes, the earlier the first sexual arousal is experienced, the higher the adult sex drive seems to be and the more sexual partners the person seems to have as he or she grows up (Ostovich & Sabini, 2005).

Cognitive Susceptibility for Sex

Another factor that seems to be correlated with the age at which adolescents begin having intercourse has been termed **cognitive susceptibility,** or the state of mind that could predispose them to initiating sexual activity or not. Understanding this concept is critical, because the younger adolescents are when they begin having intercourse, the less likely they are to use contraceptives and the higher their risk of contracting diseases or becoming pregnant. Studies indicate that those early adolescents who are more cognitively susceptible to initiating intercourse tend to be more physically mature and to have more feelings of sexual desire than their peers, as well as more social confidence, better academic performance, and a greater perception that their peers are sexually active. They also tend to have fewer positive connections with parents, school, and religious institutions (Laflin, Wang, & Barry, 2008; L'Engle, Jackson, & Brown, 2006). Younger adolescents seem to be quite susceptible to belief systems about sex. If they or their friends believe that a

cognitive susceptibility state of mind, identified by psychological and situational factors, that suggests a readiness for or predisposition toward initiating sexual activity.

person should refrain from sexual intercourse, early adolescents are more likely to abstain, at least for the short term (Santelli et al., 2004).

Researchers have seemed reluctant to draw many inferences about the influences of media exposure on adolescent sexual behavior. Nonetheless there are some long-term studies that link exposure to sexy content in television, music, movies, and magazines with earlier involvement in sexual intercourse and increased likelihood of unintended pregnancy. Combined with the enhanced methods of private, interpersonal communication, including the Internet, cell phone calls, and text messaging, that adolescents have at their disposal today, the socializing and sexualizing effects of the media may be significant primers of cognitive susceptibility (Delmonico & Griffin, 2009; Hennessy et al., 2009; Strasburger, 2009). Adolescence is a time when the groundwork of sexual excitatory and inhibitory mechanisms is being established in the individual's neurophysiology (see Figure 6.7).

Parent-Adolescent Communication

The primary sources of sex information for the majority of young persons are friends of the same sex and their independent reading or Internet browsing. Young people indicate that their parents have not done an adequate job of providing sex information, and they wish they could hear from them about issues such as dating, relationships, having sex and how to say no to it, sexually transmitted infections, and preventing pregnancy (Angera, Brookins-Fisher, & Inungu, 2008). In a survey of more than 7,000 children and adolescents, the majority of fifth and sixth graders (72 percent of girls and 54 percent of boys) indicated that their mother would be the first person they would consult about health- and sex-related questions. Health providers and fathers were next on their list. As might be anticipated, older adolescents were less likely to indicate that they would seek out parents for information, but those in grades 10 through 12 still showed substantial proportions (46 percent of girls and 35 percent of boys) who would prefer to have their mothers be their primary source of information. In the older age groups, friends also became a popular source of information (Ackard & Neumark-Stainer, 2001).

Parents sometimes worry that if they discuss sexual topics, it may lead to sexual activity in their kids, but in fact the evidence suggests just the opposite outcome. Mothers' attitudes about dating and sexuality have a significant effect on the attitudes and behaviors of their children. When parents, particularly mothers, disapprove of premarital sex yet are willing to discuss sexuality and birth control and have clear rules about dating, adolescents tend to postpone sexual activity longer and to have sex less frequently. Repetition of information

■ **FIGURE 6.7** *Adolescent Sexuality*

Adolescents in contemporary industrial societies acquire adult status much later than they acquire biological maturity. This accounts for some of the confusion in adolescent sexual behavior. Adolescence is a time of awkward experimentation in sexual behavior and the acquisition of adult sexual attitudes toward commitment, intimacy, and fidelity.

seems to have more impact than simply having one big talk about wide-ranging topics (Blake et al., 2001; Martino et al., 2008; Miller, 2002; Zamboni & Silver, 2009).

Communication about human sexuality between parents and their children can be very powerful and can help shape healthy and responsible values about sexuality. Having regular activities together as a family and parenting styles that avoid hostility and negativism also have been shown to be important (Coley, Medeiros, & Schindler, 2008). Fathers' communications about sex with sons can be very important. The same is true for stepfathers' involvement with their stepsons. Fathers are influenced by the level of their sons' pubertal development, the kind of communication they had with their own fathers, the outcomes they expect to have, their own sexual values, and the quality of their general father–son communication patterns (Menning, Holtzman, & Kapinus, 2007; Lehr et al., 2005).

A study of adolescent girls who received services at birth control clinics found that many of the girls had

Real Student Voices

■ I think most parents are very clueless, and they would rather not think about what is going on with their kids sexually. When I'm a parent, I definitely would prefer an open and truthful relationship.

■ I don't believe parents are yet aware of how young high schoolers—and even middle schoolers—are when they first engage in sexual activity. I hope my generation will be better prepared for these things.

■ My parents are well aware of what is going on with sexuality in teenagers. They were always very honest with me, and never tried to get me to believe things just to keep me from having sex. I hope I will be that way with my own kids someday.

■ I hope most parents educate their kids on how to be safe and trust them to make good decisions, but I know some parents who think their kids aren't doing it. This is naive on their part.

---

talked with their parents about sexual issues and that over two-thirds felt closely connected with their parents. In the case of younger girls, the parents of most of them knew about their clinic visits and had played an active role in helping them make sexual and contraceptive decisions. The majority of the girls believed that their parents had positive attitudes about sexuality and birth control (Jones, Singh, & Purcell, 2005).

Masturbation in Adolescence

The most prevalent form of sexual activity in adolescence is masturbation, or sexually stimulating oneself. Most boys and many girls begin to learn about their bodies' sexual responses through masturbation. In a sample of college students, about 40 percent of the women and 38 percent of the men recalled masturbating prior to reaching puberty (DeLamater & Friedrich, 2002). Adolescent boys have tended to discuss masturbation among themselves—often in a joking way—more than have adolescent girls. Consequently, more slang terms have evolved to describe male masturbation (jerk off, jack off, whack off, beat off, beat the meat) than female masturbation (rubbing off, rolling the pill, fingering). Masturbation is more common among males than among females, and boys tend to start masturbating at younger ages than girls. Retrospective studies, in which adults offer information about their behaviors as adolescents, suggest that most adolescent boys masturbate at least occcasionally but that less than half of adolescent girls do so. Girls who feel positively about masturbation are more likely to feel positively about other aspects of their sexuality and to be able to communicate more easily about sexual matters. It has also been found that adults generally are more willing to admit to having masturbated during

adolescence than are adolescents themselves (Halpern et al., 2000; Hogarth & Ingham, 2009; Janssen, 2007).

The data indicate that of those adolescents who do masturbate, boys do so about three times more frequently than girls. Studies suggest that about three-fourths of male adolescents masturbate at least two times per week, compared to about one-quarter of female adolescents. Another 12 percent of the boys and 23 percent of the girls admitted to masturbating at least once, up to as often as once per month. A smaller percentage of the boys (11 percent) and the majority of girls (60 percent) said they had never masturbated. There may be a slight decline in frequency of masturbation during the years when young people are in college. A study of more than 300 college students found that 85 percent of the males indicated they masturbated, 70 percent of them with moderate to high frequency. The women in the study were far more likely to indicate that they had never masturbated (63 percent), with 24 percent reporting moderate to high frequency (Halpern et al., 2000).

The masturbation frequency practiced in adolescence generally carries through the rest of a person's life, without decreasing much either with age or with partnership status. This is one indication that masturbation does not appear to be a compensation for lack of partnered sex; its frequency continues to be about the same even when a sexual partner is available (Kontula & Haavio-Mannila, 2002).

Sexual Intercourse in Adolescence and Its Outcomes

Adolescents today experiment with shared sexual activities at younger ages than was once the case, but

Table 6.3	Trends in the Prevalence of Sexual Behaviors Among U.S. High School Students, 1991–2007

Data from the National Youth Risk Behavior Survey, conducted every two years among ninth through twelfth graders in public and private schools throughout the United States, have shown a consistent decrease in several sexual behavior indicators.

1991	1993	1995	1997	1999	2001	2003	2005	2007	Trend, 1991–2007
				Ever had sexual intercourse (%)					
54.1	53.0	53.1	48.4	49.9	45.6	46.7	46.8	47.8	Decreased
			Had sexual intercourse with four or more persons during their life						
18.7	18.7	17.8	16.0	16.2	14.2	14.4	14.3	14.9	Decreased
		Currently sexually active (intercourse with at least 1 person in previous 3 months)							
37.5	37.5	37.9	34.8	36.3	33.4	34.3	33.9	35.0	Decreased
		Used a condom during last sexual intercourse (among students who were currently sexually active)							
46.2	52.8	54.4	56.8	58.0	57.9	63.0	62.8	61.5	Increased to 2003; No change since
			Used birth control pills before last sexual intercourse (currently active)						
20.8	18.4	17.4	16.6	16.2	18.2	17.0	17.6	16.0	No change
			Drank alcohol or used drugs before last sexual intercourse (currently active)						
21.6	21.3	24.8	24.7	24.8	25.6	25.4	23.3	22.5	Increased to 2001; Then decreased

Source: Adapted from Centers for Disease Control (2008). Trends in the prevalance of sexual behaviors. *National Youth Risk Behavior Survey: 1991–2007.* Atlanta: CDC.

Notes: Trends are based on trend analyses using a logistic regression model controlling for sex, race/ethnicity, and grade. Percentages are based on 95 percent confidence interval.

those activities do not always include sexual intercourse (Forehand et al., 2005). An increase in heterosexual sexual intercourse among teens began in the 1970s and continued through the 1980s. Since 1991, however, the number of high school students who experience sexual intercourse has declined. In 2007, the most recent year for which we have statistics available, the percentage of high school students indicating that they had experienced intercourse stood at 47.8 percent, compared to 54.1 percent in 1991. Since the 1980s, differences in teen sexual behavior patterns across socioeconomic, racial, and ethnic groups have narrowed considerably. Engaging in sexual intercourse has been established as a typical pattern of behavior in the United States for about half of adolescents ages 15 to 17 and a significant characteristic of the transition to adulthood. Once adolescents have engaged in intercourse, it is relatively likely that they will participate more than once, although comparatively few have multiple sexual partners within a year's time. Rates have been quite stable during the 2000s, although reported use of condoms during the most recent intercourse has increased modestly from 57.9 percent in 2001 to 61.5 percent in 2007 (Centers for Disease Control, 2008). See Table 6.3.

Boys with high self-esteem are more likely than their male peers with low self-esteem to have initiated intercourse, while girls with higher self-esteem are less likely than their peers to be sexually experienced (Spencer et al., 2002). See Figure 6.8 for some data on teen sexual behavior. Boys who are less able to inhibit their sexual arousal, even in the face of sexual risk, and those who experience increased sexual interest when they are emotionally upset or depressed are more likely to initiate sexual intercourse (Bancroft et al., 2004). Teenagers who are religious, have fewer personal problems, and have talked with their parents about sexuality tend not to initiate sexual intercourse as early as their peers (Clawson & Reese-Weber, 2003; Lehr et al., 2005; Pedersen, Samuelsen, & Wichstrom, 2003).

Studies of adolescent sex have tended to focus on the dangers and risks involved, often overlooking the fact that many adolescents feel a desire for sexual pleasure and are planning to act on that desire when circumstances allow (Levine, 2002b). There has also been increasing evidence that adolescents pay attention to what they perceive as the positive outcomes, including increased intimacy and pleasure in relationships.

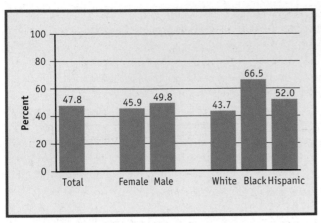

Percentages of U.S. high school students who have ever had sexual intercourse, 2007.

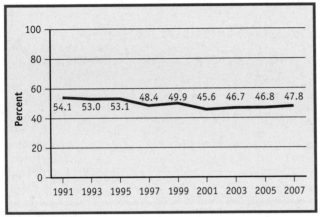

Percentages of U.S. high school youth reporting having had sexual intercourse, 1991–2007.

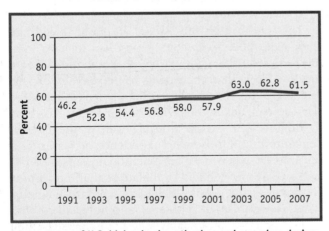

Percentages of U.S. high school youth who used a condom during last sexual intercourse, 1991–2007.

■ **FIGURE 6.8** *Sexual Intercourse among U.S. High School Students*

Data from the CDC's National Youth Risk Behavior Survey, 2007, show that sexual intercourse is typical for about half of U.S. high school students, although it also indicates that rates have decreased moderately since 1991. Although condom use has increased markedly during the same time period, it is also clear that many teens do not use condoms consistently.

Many teenagers see sexual experience as a way to gain greater social status among their peers. In a pattern that continues into adulthood, male adolescents seem to value sexual pleasure more than do their female counterparts, who place a higher value on relational intimacy (Ott et al., 2006). There are also potential negative social and emotional consequences of delaying or refraining from sex. Teenagers who start having sex later do indeed show less risky behaviors, but have no greater level of satisfaction with their relationships and may be at higher risk of problems with sexual functioning. They may also feel less part of their social groups (Brady & Halpern-Felsher, 2008; Sandfort et al., 2008).

Despite persistent claims that sexual activity during the adolescent years leads to regrets, negative self-concepts, and later emotional problems, the evidence suggests instead that sexually experienced adolescents over the age of 15 often have higher levels of self-esteem than do those who are inexperienced. NHSLS data showed that 71 percent of women and 92 percent of men who experienced heterosexual intercourse during their teen years reported that they wanted it to happen and were not pressured into it (Laumann et al., 1994). Mental health in adulthood does not seem to be correlated with having abstained from adolescent sexual activity, and those who were sexually active as teenagers have equally good mental health as those who were not (Bogart et al., 2007).

Teenagers who have sexual intercourse experience a wide range of social, emotional, and physical consequences, some of which are positive and some negative. Boys are somewhat more likely to have positive outcomes than girls are, but both sexes can experience some guilt, fears of pregnancy or disease, and negative feelings about themselves. They may also experience pleasure, good feelings about themselves, greater social popularity, and stronger relationships. It seems clear that the context of the early sexual experiences is crucial in determining how teenagers feel about them. More negative outcomes are typical of sexual experiences that took place prior to puberty, were forced, or were the result of peer pressure, drugs, or alcohol. In general, other contexts did not seem associated with much guilt about sex or with other psychological or physical problems (Brady & Halpern-Felsher, 2007; Else-Quest, Hyde, & DeLamater, 2005).

Teenagers Who Choose Not to Have Intercourse

To understand why some teenagers choose to delay having sexual intercourse, it is helpful to understand the various factors that are weighed in sexual decision making. A study that examined the social forces that shape young people's sexual choices around the world in both developed and developing nations found seven themes common to all cultures. They were: the relative cleanliness of the other person; other positive and negative qualities of the potential partner; whether condom use is expected (which can be construed as a lack of trust or the possibility that the person has an STD); gender stereotypes in the culture; the social rewards and penalties that exist; potential impacts on reputation; and the fact that social expectations often prevent young people from discussing sex with potential partners (Marston & King, 2006).

Another study found that young people had sex in order to increase intimacy, relieve sexual tension, and manage their emotions such as depression and anxiety (Dawson et al., 2008). Among those teenagers who refrain from engaging in sexual intercourse, the most common reasons once cited related to fears of pregnancy, disease, or parental disapproval. The least common reasons for abstaining from sex revolved around embarrassment or concern about peer or partner disapproval. Fewer adolescents are citing reasons such as not being ready for sex, waiting until they are older, or waiting until marriage (Blinn-Pike et al., 2004).

Adolescents who abstain from intercourse seem to fall into two distinct categories: *Delayers* say they are unlikely to initiate intercourse within the next year and tend to have limited sexual experience of any kind; *anticipators* report that they either are unsure about initiating sex in the near future or are likely to do so and tend to have more sexual experience already. Among boys who desire and anticipate sexual intercourse, the main reason for sexual inexperience is the lack of opportunity to initiate intercourse. That group of boys was more likely to have intercourse within the following year and also more likely to report having engaged in risky sexual behaviors (Forste & Haas, 2002; L'Engle et al., 2006). Adolescent girls who have older siblings, especially brothers, are more likely to delay sexual involvement and to have more traditional values about romance and parenthood (Kornreich et al., 2003).

Among adolescents who choose to abstain from sexual intercourse even after they have tried it (secondary abstinence), the reasons for doing so are practical. They tend to fear getting a disease or experiencing an unplanned pregnancy, but they also may have doubts about the appropriateness of having sex at their age. Adolescents who do not think their friends are having sex or fear their parents' disapproval also are more likely to abstain. Males who practice secondary abstinence are more likely to have already caused a pregnancy or to already have a child (Loewenson, Ireland, & Resnick, 2004).

Oral and Anal Sex in Adolescence

There is reasonable evidence to suggest that the rates of oral and anal sexual activity among adolescents have been increasing by two or three times since the mid-1990s, and it is likely that around half of them are doing so in order to avoid having intercourse (Gindi, Ghanem, & Erbelding, 2008; SIECUS, 2003). The CDC (2008) reports that 55 percent of males and 54 percent of females aged 15 to 19 had engaged in oral sex with someone of the opposite sex. In the same age group, 11 percent of males and 54 percent of females had engaged in anal sex with someone of the opposite sex, and 3 percent of males had engaged in anal sex with another male. Oral sexual experience increases with age and is more common in youth who have also experienced intercourse. In fact by six months after first intercourse, 82 percent of adolescents have also engaged in oral sex. These data indicate that oral sexual behavior has now also become an established pattern in adolescent sexual behavior, and public health experts are becoming alert to the need to consider both oral and anal sex as presenting risks for infection (Brewster & Tillman, 2008; Lindberg, Jones, & Santelli, 2008).

Studies have shown that many adolescents see oral sex as part of both casual and dating relationships and perceive it as "not as big a deal as sexual intercourse." A study of ninth graders with an average age of 14.5 years found that 20 percent reported having had oral sex, with a smaller percentage indicating that they had shared intercourse. About a third of these students indicated that they intended to have oral sex in the next six months, while only a quarter expected to have intercourse. These adolescents tended to report fewer negative consequences associated with their oral sexual experiences than with intercourse (Brady & Halpern-Fisher, 2007; Halpern-Felsher et al., 2005). Many adolescents do not consider oral sex to be having sex, and some young people assume that a range of sexual behaviors other than intercourse can fall under the label of abstinence.

Social Development and Dating

Most adolescents become involved in social relationships with members of both sexes. Self-concept can play a major role in how comfortable the person is with these social connections. In their early relationships, adolescents begin to learn about the ground rules for relating to other people and about the commitments and expectations that are part of those relationships from their friends in their social networks. Adolescents who reach puberty earlier than others also tend to begin dating sooner. Boys whose parents are knowledgeable about their sons' activities actually tend to date less (Friedlander et al., 2007; G. Harper et al., 2004). They gain experience with how relationships can cause emotional hurt and with the limits of one's responsibility toward another person in a relationship. Despite familiar assumptions that boys want sex and girls want love, many boys claim that they too are looking for loving relationships (Allen, 2003).

Important steps in personal development occur within the context of teenage romances and relationships. Social and romantic activities, such as spending time with a partner in a group setting and holding hands, are far more common among adolescents than sexual activities, although the romantic interactions generally precede sexual behaviors (O'Sullivan et al., 2007). One phase in the formation of affectionate partnerships is what social psychologists call **dyadic withdrawal,** a period of time during which the couple pulls away from other social responsibilities to parents, peers, and other significant persons in their lives. The potential for sexual involvement increases during this time. Sexual partners are most often chosen from among people of similar characteristics, but there is an increasing trend among adolescents to develop sexual relationships with people of different races and ethnicities. This trend varies with geographic location and the social structure of the area (Ford, Sohn, & Lepkowski, 2003). Given the privacy available to most adolescents, a close relationship can easily progress to sexual exploration if they want it to.

Professionals who work with adolescents are concerned about those relationships in which violence emerges. Abusive behavior may take the form of physical abuse, including slapping or hitting; sexual violence in the form of forced kissing, touching, or sexual acts; or psychological violence such as threats, insults, or using controlling tactics. Eight to 12 percent of high school teenagers indicate that they have been subject to physical or sexual dating violence of varying degrees of severity, while nearly 30 percent indicate they have been psychologically abused. It tends to happen in more serious romantic attachments than in casual ones, but relationships characterized by security, good communication, and effective approaches to conflict resolution are less prone to violence. Girls are more likely than boys to experience severe physical violence and are also more likely to experience fear and emotional trauma as a result (Jouriles, Platt, & McDonald, 2009).

Peer group influence is important in establishing some standards for behavior within dating relationships, since they often provide the only role models for how young people may relate to one another. If friends in the peer group tend to be aggressive with one another, there is a greater likelihood that aggressive behavior will be a part of dating relationships too. Two personality characteristics have been shown to make adolescents more vulnerable to violent behavior. Teens who have a *high sensitivity to rejection,* often because of a history of perceived rejection by others, are more prone to lashing out when they sense

impending rejection by a loved one. The other characteristic is *susceptibility to peer influence,* when the peer group tends toward reacting aggressively and violently to conflicts (Connolly & Friedlander, 2009). More programs are being developed to counteract dating violence, although more research is needed to clarify the dynamics of the behavior.

Adolescent Same-Gender Sexual Activity

Adolescence is a period when girls and boys tend to associate more with members of their own gender. It is not surprising that as youngsters experience pronounced physical changes in their sex organs and begin to become more aware of their sexual feelings, they may experiment with sex through encounters with same-gender peers. It is difficult to assess the prevalence of same-gender behavior among adolescents, because there are often differences in how young people report attractions, behaviors, and self-identity. Only small numbers of adolescents identify themselves as gay, but considerably more admit to having been attracted to others of their gender, or to having had a sexual experience with them. There does not seem to be strong consistency between teenagers' self-identification of their sexual orientations and their actual behaviors (Goodenow et al., 2008; Savin-Williams & Ream, 2007).

The incidence of same-gender sexual behavior in adolescents has ranged from 5 percent of 13- to 18-year-olds in one study to 11 to 14 percent of adolescent boys and 6 to 11 percent of adolescent girls in another. In a study of 3,267 male students ages 12 to 18 who reported having had any sexual contact, 3 percent indicated that the contact had been with both males and females, and 3 percent indicated that it had been only with males (Goodenow, Netherland, & Szalacha, 2002). Boys tend to report more frequent same-gender experiences in later adolescence (ages 16 to 19), whereas girls reported less frequent experiences at this later age level (Ryan & Futterman, 2001). In an analysis of female data, girls seemed to sexually experiment with others girls at a median age of 9, and sometimes use images of females for masturbation later on, at a median age of 15 (Bickham et al., 2007).

Some adolescents begin to get in touch with their same-gender sexual orientation during adolescence, although some may take months or years to clarify

> **dyadic withdrawal** (die-ADD-ik) the tendency of two people involved in an intimate relationship to withdraw socially for a time from other significant people in their lives.

their sexual orientation as gay, lesbian, or bisexual (Rosario et al., 2006). Adult gay men report that their first same-gender experience generally occurred by age 14, whereas adult lesbians report that their first experiences tended to occur in the late teenage years. In a questionnaire administered to 89 gay males and 31 lesbians ages 14 to 21, about one-third indicated that they were aware of their sexual orientation between the ages of 4 and 10. Most of the rest were aware of it by age 17 (Russell, 2001). Biological development and timing of puberty seem to be the same for gay adolescents as they are for those who are heterosexual (Savin-Williams & Ream, 2006, 2007).

Adolescents who have clearly identified themselves as being gay, lesbian, or bisexual may experience some conflict with their social environment, especially in school, but there are indications that youthful gay people are coming out earlier and with less conflict than was once the case (Savin-Williams, 2005). Gay, lesbian, and bisexual adolescents seem to have higher risks of psychological distress, running away, dropping out of school, and suicide, especially in rural environments where there may be less support for them (Poon & Saewyc, 2009; Saewyc et al., 2009). Nevertheless, attitudes in recent years toward differing sexual orientations have been changing, and more information and support are available for young people with same-gender orientations. Some lesbian, gay, and bisexual teenagers surmount the extra measure of social difficulty with resilience and self-acceptance, whereas others continue to wrestle with their sexual identity issues into adulthood (Savin-Williams, 2005).

Cite several reasons why some lesbian and gay adolescents and young adults might refuse to acknowledge their same-gender attractions.

FIGURE 6.9 *Adolescent Sexuality Across Cultures*

Adolescents in most parts of the world have had their sexual attitudes and behaviors influenced by Western values and media.

Adolescent Sexual Attitudes and Behaviors across Cultures

Adolescents develop their sexual identities, attitudes, and behaviors within their cultural contexts, which differ markedly from society to society. Distinct changes in the sexual values of adolescents have been occurring in most areas of the globe in recent decades, a reflection of increased urbanization, industrialization, and influence by Western media. See Figure 6.9. All over the world, young people are starting to have sex earlier and are placing sexual pleasure ahead of safer sexual practices (Pluhar, 2008; Wellings et al., 2006). This has increased the risks for early pregnancy and cervical cancer in developing countries (Louie et al., 2009).

When researchers studied trends in five developed countries in the West (Canada, France, Great Britain, Sweden, and the United States), they found sexual attitudes and behaviors to be quite similar. Oral sex has become a common behavior. Attitudes toward sex in these countries and in Australia are relatively casual, and risky behaviors (e.g., nonuse of condoms) have not decreased (Stone et al., 2006).

In Mexico and Latin America, adolescents have been caught up in the ambivalence of traditional religious values that seem to conflict with changing patterns of sexual behavior. The *machismo* tradition often creates conflicts surrounding power imbalances in relationships and the degree of comfort males have with their gender identities. Adolescents in Latin America receive information about contraception too late, and they tend to receive sexuality education that emphasizes biological facts over decision-making skills. Despite a high rate of adolescent pregnancy, both information about and access to contraception are very limited (Juarez & Martin, 2006).

Asian cultures have been experiencing marked contrasts between traditional sexual values and the more permissive sexual attitudes among adolescents today. China has been seeing a marked increase in adolescent sexual activity even in the face of official government condemnation; this may well reflect fundamental cultural shifts in China. Chinese culture still tries to moderate the sexual behaviors of youth, because early sexual activity is considered a sign of psychological distress. In Hong Kong, gay youth are finding it easier to come out about their identities to friends and families (Lam et al., 2004; Wong & Tang, 2004). In Japan, sexuality has been minimized and regulated as being tangential to the performance of responsible duty. Japanese youth consider chastity very important. There is less teenage sexual activity and far less single motherhood than in the United States, although abortion is quite accessible. Japanese youth often rush into sexual activity during late adolescence, as if making up for their more chaste earlier years (Kashiwase, 2002).

African adolescents face mixed signals regarding their sexual behaviors. Some societies encourage youth to postpone sexual activity. Others do not see virginity as a virtue, and in fact may regard it as a sign of unsociableness or ill health. Among the Zulu, girls are supposed to be sexually available to a partner—coy and resistant to his sexual advances, but sexually faithful. Boys have more latitude in terms of what is considered sexually acceptable and are expected to make the sexual decisions, initiate sex, and even be sexually coercive. For a boy to allow a girl to resist his sexual advances would be considered weak (Kaufman et al., 2004). In Nigeria and Malawi, boys are supposed to be aggressive and dominant in their relationships, and sexual activity is considered normal and proper for them (Izugbara, 2008; Izugbara & Undie, 2008).

■ Adolescent Sexual Health

Studies on the sexual activities of adolescents have largely viewed those activities as problematic. Adolescents who are sexually active are often perceived as having problems or being "at risk." Of course sexual activity does carry risks of social disapproval, STDs, unwanted pregnancy, and emotional consequences. But these risks are true of adult sexual behavior as well, and our culture has created an artificial and untenable model that separates adolescent sexuality from adult sexuality. It is as if at some magical point, we become responsible adults who are suddenly able to manage the complexities of sex and prevent all manner of negative sexual health consequences. In fact, our development as sexual people who can enjoy sex

and manage it responsibly begins in childhood and evolves through adolescence. The trouble is, we have focused so much on adolescent sexuality as a problem that we have failed to delineate the ways in which adolescents could best navigate the balancing act of developing healthy sexual behaviors and healthy attitudes toward them, while minimizing the very real risks that are ever-present. Yet how else can we really expect our youth to become sexually healthy and sexually responsible adults? Far more research is needed that focuses on healthy sexuality in adolescents rather than assuming that all adolescent sexual expression is unhealthy (Halpern, 2010).

Adolescent Sexual Risk-Taking

Much of our research on adolescent sexual behavior, then, has focused on what is termed *risky* sexual behavior, broadly defined as having unprotected sexual intercourse or engaging in any sexual behavior that later was regretted. Oral and anal sex are now often included in the risky category as well, because of their disease transmission potentials (CDC, 2008; Coleman & Cater, 2005). Many adolescents assume an attitude of invulnerability, believing that the potential negative consequences won't happen to them. Initiating sex at early ages is considered risky because of the lower likelihood that condoms will be used. Adolescents who are more sociable, have strong friendships, and enjoy greater peer acceptance in early adolescence and who have a more mature and attractive appearance at age 13 are more likely to initiate sex earlier and have more sexual partners by age 16 (Zimmer-Gembeck & Collins, 2008). Teenagers who have already had sex in a previous relationship and believe sex to be important will wait less time before initiating sex in a new relationship (Rosengard et al., 2004).

Personality characteristics play a role in creating vulnerabilities for sexual risk-taking. Adolescents who are *high sensation seekers* or *impulsive decision makers* are less likely to plan carefully for sexual activities or to use condoms (Zimmerman et al., 2007). Adolescents whose friends are sexually experienced or who believe that having sex will gain their friends' respect are also more likely to have sexual intercourse (Ryan et al., 2008; Sieving et al., 2006; South, Haynie, & Bose, 2005).

High-risk youth also include those who are pregnant or are already parents; have sexual partners older than themselves; have a history of substance abuse; get low grades in school; have been emotionally or physically abused; are homeless or have run away from home; are gay, lesbian, or bisexual; or are institutionalized for any reason. These youth tend to have a greater likelihood of participating in high-risk sexual activities without protections such as condoms.

Some turn to prostitution. These young people have special needs for sexuality education, support services, and counseling interventions (Lemoire & Chen, 2005; Rickert et al., 2004; Solorio et al., 2008).

Numerous studies have suggested that alcohol and substance use increases the likelihood of having unprotected sex in adolescence. It apparently affects young people's assessments of a potential partner's attractiveness while increasing confidence levels and lowering social inhibitions. Sometimes it is used as an excuse for socially unacceptable sexual behavior. The more serious effects of alcohol, associated with higher levels of sexual risk taking, are impaired judgment about what may be sexually risky and loss of control or memory blackouts (Coleman & Cater, 2005; Kiene et al., 2009; Solorio et al., 2008).

If our society is to help adolescents develop into sexually healthy adults, we must begin educating children openly and honestly about their sexuality from the time they are born and promote in them a healthy and positive self-concept (Mueller, Gavin, & Kulkarni, 2008; Rostosky et al., 2008; Tonelli, 2009). The American Academy of Pediatrics recommends that when health care professionals see adolescents, even for well-care visits, they use the opportunity to discuss issues relevant to sexual health and provide necessary services. There is evidence that adolescents feel more comfortable with health care providers who are able to bring up sensitive sexual issues (Brown & Wissow, 2009; Klein et al., 2005). Young people need to be prepared for the realistic work that must go into maintaining long-term relationships. In addition to getting information, they need to learn skills that will help them in practical ways, such as how to put on a condom properly, how to negotiate the use of protection with a partner, or how to say no effectively (Jemmott et al., 2005). Parents can play a significant role in this preparation, although they may need some help and training to do so effectively (Eastman et al., 2005). Table 6.4 summarizes the characteristics of sexually healthy adolescents as outlined by the National Commission on Adolescent Sexual Health.

Adolescents and STDs

Sexually transmitted diseases represent a serious problem among adolescents. In the United States, more than 25 percent of teenage girls have an STD. Among the most common of these diseases is chlamydia, and routine screening for this disease in adolescents has been recommended (Miller et al., 2007). Some adolescents avoid having sex with certain partners in order to avoid catching an STD, but this selective avoidance does not seem to lower their risks of having an STD. Instead, consistent use of condoms has been deemed a better preventative measure (DiClemente et al., 2008).

Human papilloma virus (HPV) is known to be acquired largely during adolescence and is widespread among this age group. African-American girls in the United States are infected with HPV at a rate of 48 percent and white girls at 20 percent. In addition to causing genital warts, it has also been identified as the cause of 99.7 percent of cervical cancers (Moscicki, 2008; Smith et al., 2008). The Gardasil vaccine has been developed to provide immunity against the cancer-causing strains of HPV, and the American Academy of Pediatrics recommends that the series of three injections be given to 11- and 12-year-old girls, or even to girls as young as 9 if they are considered likely to become sexually active. The vaccine works only prior to any HPV exposure, and so is best administered before any shared sexual activity has taken place (Committee on Infectious Diseases, AAP, 2007).

Even in the face of serious HPV dangers, parents and physicians have shown some reluctance to administer the vaccine at such early ages, partly because of its cost and lack of coverage by insurance. Some feel that the medical profession has been too quick to embrace claims made by self-interested pharmaceutical companies (Rothman & Rothman, 2009). There can be soreness at the injection site, fainting, and some less common complications found with any immunization, especially in girls who have underlying medical conditions (Slade et al., 2009). When carefully prescribed, the vaccine has been shown to be quite safe and effective (Feemster et al., 2008; Haug, 2009; Kahn et al., 2008; Keating et al., 2008). It has now been found that HPV is associated with an increase in cancers of the mouth and throat in both women and men, and there is a strong likelihood that the vaccine will soon be recommended for early adolescent boys as well. Tests have shown that it is effective in males (Gillison, 2008; Petaja et al., 2009).

Adolescent Condom Use

Choosing to use a condom during intercourse can reduce some of the riskiness sexual encounters by helping to prevent unwanted pregnancy and transmission of diseases and also to represent a level of responsibility in the decision making. However, even those adolescents who feel positively about condoms and plan on using them actually do so less than half the time in either their casual or more serious sexual partners (Lescano et al., 2007).

Condom use seems to be associated with a variety of different personal characteristics (Beadnell et al., 2005). Adolescents who used a condom the first time they had intercourse have been found to be more likely to report having used one during their last intercourse. Being drunk during a sexual experience is associated with lower condom use, although alcohol

Table 6.4 — Characteristics of a Sexually Healthy Adolescent as Established by the National Commission on Adolescent Sexual Health

Self

Appreciates own body
- Understands pubertal change
- Views pubertal changes as normal
- Practices health-promoting behaviors, such as abstaining from alcohol and other drugs and having regular checkups

Takes responsibility for own behaviors
- Identifies own values
- Decides what is personally "right" and acts on these values
- Understands consequences of actions
- Understands that media messages can create unrealistic expectations related to sexuality and intimate relationships
- Is able to distinguish personal desires from the desires of the peer group
- Recognizes behavior that may be self-destructive, and can seek help

Is knowledgeable about sexuality issues
- Enjoys sexual feelings without necessarily acting on them
- Understands the consequences of sexual behaviors
- Makes personal decisions about masturbation consistent with personal values
- Makes personal decisions about sexual behaviors with a partner consistent with personal values
- Understands own gender identity
- Understands effect of gender-role stereotypes and makes choices about appropriate roles for oneself
- Understands own sexual orientation
- Seeks further information about sexuality as needed
- Understands peer and cultural pressure to become sexually active
- Accepts people with different values and experiences

Relationships with Parents and Family Members

Communicates effectively with family about issues, including sexuality
- Maintains appropriate balance between family roles and responsibilities and growing need for independence
- Is able to negotiate with family on boundaries
- Respects rights of others
- Demonstrates respect for adults

Understands and seeks information about parents' and family's values, and considers them in developing own values
- Asks questions of parents and other trusted adults about sexual issues
- Can accept trusted adults' guidance about sexuality issues
- Tries to understand parental point of view

Peers

Interacts with both genders in appropriate and respectful ways
- Communicates effectively with friends
- Has friendships with males and females
- Is able to form empathetic relationships
- Is able to identify and avoid exploitative relationships
- Understands and rejects sexual-harassing behaviors
- Understands pressures to be popular and accepted, and makes decisions consistent with own values

Romantic Partners

Expresses love and intimacy in developmentally appropriate ways
- Believes that boys and girls have equal rights and responsibilities with regard to love and sexual relationships
- Communicates desire not to engage in sexual behaviors and accepts refusals to engage in sexual behaviors
- Is able to distinguish between love and sexual attraction
- Seeks to understand and empathize with partner

Has the skills to evaluate readiness for mature sexual relationships
- Talks with a partner about sexual behaviors before they occur
- Is able to communicate and negotiate sexual limits
- Differentiates between low- and high-risk sexual behaviors
- If having intercourse, protects self and partner from unintended pregnancy and diseases through effective use of contraception and condoms and other safer-sex practices
- Knows how to use and access the health care system, community agencies, religious institutions, and schools; seeks advice, information, and services as needed

Source: From Debra W. Haffner, M.P.H., "Facing Facts: Sexual Health for America's Adolescents," in *SIECUS Report,* Vol. 23 (6), August/September 1995. Used with permission.

consumption in general does not seem to be a reliable predictor of condom use (Shafii et al., 2004; Zimmerman et al., 2007). Planning to use a condom seems to work better for young people who are less concerned with expressing love during sex and more concerned with possible negative consequences, such as disease or pregnancy. Adolescents who are trying to express love or are having sex to enhance their mood are less likely to be reliable condom users (Gebhardt, Kuyper, & Dusseldorp, 2006).

Teenage Pregnancy and Use of Birth Control

Teenage pregnancy continues to be a public health problem, even though teen birthrates have declined markedly since 1991. In fact the rates have been the lowest ever recorded by the National Center for Health Statistics since they began tracking the numbers in 1940 (Martin et al., 2009). During the same time period, birthrates for non-Hispanic black 15- to

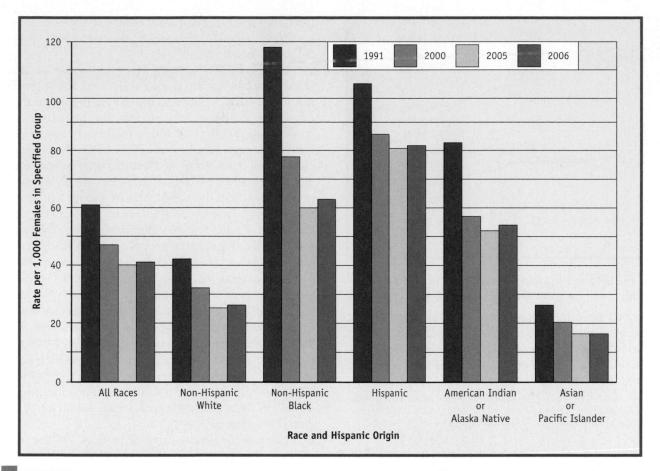

FIGURE 6.10   *Birthrates in the United States for Teenagers 15–19 by Race and Hispanic Origin, 1991, 2000, 2005, 2006*

These graphs illustrate the general decline in births to U.S. adolescents since the early 1990s. There was a slight increase in the 2006 birthrate for most of the groups shown.

Source: National Center for Health Statistics, Births: Final Data for 2006, *National Vital Statistics Report,* 2009, Vol. 57 (7).

19-year-olds fell by about half, from 118 to 64 per 1,000. The figures for 2006 and 2007 showed a 3 to 4 percent increase in the birthrate for teenagers over the age of 15, interrupting the 14-year decline. However, the data for 2008 then reflected another decrease in births for this age group to 41.5 percent per thousand girls, down from 41.9 in 2006 and 42.5 in 2007 (see Figure 6.10) (Hamilton, Martin, & Ventura, 2010). Evidence suggests that this continuing decline in teen births has been the result of two factors among adolescents: delaying the initiation of intercourse and improved use of contraception when they do have sex, although these trends may also have now stabilized (Martin et al., 2009; Santelli et al., 2006). As shown in Figure 6.11, the rates of pregnancy and abortion have decreased along with the rates of live births among teenagers.

Over the past three decades, use of contraceptives by adolescents has changed in significant ways, including increased use of long-lasting hormonal methods and condoms. Data from the Youth Risk Behavior Survey show that between 1995 and 2003 the number of teen women reporting use of contraception during their last sexual intercourse increased from 71 percent to 83 percent (Martin et al., 2009). The consistency of contraceptive use among adolescents depends on the kind of relationship they have. Couples who discuss birth control are more likely to use it consistently, but only about half of teenaged couples discuss contraception. Couples who see their relationship as romantic are somewhat less likely to be consistent. Girls who are ambivalent about getting pregnant are less likely to use contraceptives reliably than are those who feel either positive or negative about pregnancy (Bruckner, Martin, & Bearman, 2004; Ryan et al., 2007).

Boys who think they know the most about condoms, even though their knowledge often is inaccurate, are less likely to use condoms than those who are less confident about their knowledge. In the United States, physicians are less prone to prescribe emergency contraception for teenagers who have had unprotected sex than is the case in other countries. Both of these factors play a role in preventing teen birthrates from falling even further (Rock et al., 2005; Sable et al., 2006).

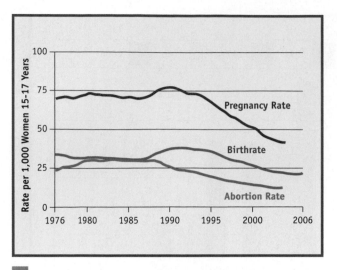

FIGURE 6.11   *Rates of Pregnancy, Birth, and Abortion per 1,000 Teenage Women Ages 15 to 17, 1976–2006*

This graph shows that the rates of pregnancy, birth, and abortion among all women ages 15 to 17, have been declining since the early 1990s, except for a 3 percent increase in the birthrate in 2006. It is not yet clear whether the upturn indicates any sort of trend.

Source: Estimated Pregnancy Rates by Outcome for the United States, 1990–2004. *National Vital Statistics Reports,* vol. 56, no. 15, 2008. Births: Preliminary Data for 2006. *National Vital Statistics Reports,* vol. 56, no. 7, 2007.

There are several other birth control methods available to teenagers, although most of them must be prescribed by a health provider. Emergency contraception can be prescribed for adolescents after they have had unprotected intercourse, but emergency physicians seem to do so infrequently (Goyal, Zhao, & Mollen, 2009). The hormonal vaginal ring has achieved a degree of acceptance among adolescent women, and the American College of Obstetricians and Gynecologists has strongly recommended the intrauterine device (IUD) for teenagers because of its reliability (American College of Obstetricians and Gynecologists, 2007; Epstein et al., 2008).

Accessibility to contraceptive methods is associated with lower teen birthrates. Although some states have passed laws requiring parental involvement in adolescents' birth control decisions, experts in family planning believe that mandated parental involvement ultimately would result in increased rates of teen pregnancy. Most teenagers who make use of pregnancy-prevention services already have talked with their parents about it and therefore would not be affected by such laws. Of those who have not involved their parents, however, only 7 percent indicate they would stop having sex if the services were not available to them. Most would seek clinic services anyway, but 13 percent would try using withdrawal or the rhythm method, the least reliable contraceptive methods, and 6 percent say they would simply have sex without

using any contraception at all (Colman, Joyce, & Kaestner, 2008; Guldi, 2008; Jones & Boonstra, 2004; Jones, Singh, & Purcell, 2005).

Young women who are exposed to abuse, violence, and family strife during childhood are at greater risk for teenage pregnancy, and the greater the number of adverse childhood experiences, the higher the risk (Hillis et al., 2004). Girls whose mothers or sisters gave birth as teenagers are more likely to have teen pregnancies as well (East, Reyes, & Horn, 2007). Young women who have had one baby are at special risk of a second pregnancy within the subsequent two years. While teen mothers may be more conscientious about using contraception in the few months immediately following giving birth, the risks of pregnancy then begin to increase (Kershaw et al., 2003; Raneri & Wiemann, 2007).

Assessments of programs designed to prevent teenage pregnancy have found that those providing access to contraception are most effective in significantly decreasing the proportion of adolescents who become pregnant (Saunders, 2005). The most effective programs, and they are quite rare, emphasize long-term relationships for teenagers, postponing of intercourse, consistent use of contraception, educational achievement, and career goal-setting (Philliber et al., 2002; Russell et al., 2004).

There is no single effect of teenage childbearing and it is not necessarily the catastrophe it has been portrayed to be. Some conditions surrounding teen parents may well have been part of their lives *before* the pregnancy. Adolescent girls who give birth to a child are less likely than other girls to complete high school or to go on to higher educational attainment, although this outcome seems more related to lack of available resources that were present even before they were parents than it does parenthood itself (Hofferth, Reid, & Mott, 2001; Mollborn, 2007). Youthful unwed fathers are more likely to have problems with delinquency and economic hardship, although again the cause-and-effect relationships are not clear (Marcell, Raine, & Eyre, 2003). Although it has generally been assumed that the children born to teens tend to be at higher risk of poor health, social, and economic outcomes, the research does not necessarily support such assumptions. Teen parents are, however, at risk for depression and social isolation, which in turn may affect the well-being of children (Hofferth & Reid, 2002; McClanahan, 2008; Pittard, Laditka, & Laditka, 2008).

■ Sexuality Education

Given the data we have about STD infections and unintended pregnancies among adolescents, it is not surprising that parents, schools, communities, and public health agencies have urgently wanted to find preventative

Real People

Amanda Confronts an Ethical Dilemma within Her Family

While Amanda is home for spring break during her junior year of college, her 15 year old sister confides to her that she has started having sex with her 16 year old boyfriend. She proudly explains to Amanda that the two of them discussed the decision carefully and went to the family planning clinic together. They decided to use the hormonal patch, which provides contraceptive protection for a week. They also use condoms as a backup measure because both of them are fearful of an unintended pregnancy. Neither had ever had sexual intercourse before.

Amanda is shocked by her little sister's news, and she tells her so. She believes her sister is too young for sexual intercourse, and she knows her parents would feel the same way. Her sister admits that her parents would disapprove but maintains that she has been mature and responsible in her decision making. She is surprised and resentful about Amanda's reaction, telling her that she is being an overconservative prude and warning her

not to tell their parents or she will never speak to her again.

The two sisters have always had a close relationship and have shared many secrets over the years, but Amanda feels very torn this time. She believes that her sister has made a mistake that may be significant enough for her parents to become involved. Amanda and her boyfriend have been talking about intercourse as well, although they have not yet taken that step, and Amanda believes that the age difference would justify such a decision in her case. She is reluctant to hurt the relationship with her sister, which she has always enjoyed and valued.

Should Amanda tell her parents about her sister's sexual relationship, or should she keep quiet and continue a dialogue with the younger girl about her concerns? How do you feel personally about Amanda's concerns? Is she overreacting? Should she be grateful that her sister and the boyfriend have taken responsibility for birth control?

---

measures. From the early 1900s, the key to prevention was thought to be sex education, now more commonly termed *sexuality* education to denote a broader focus (Kelly, 2009). Well over 90 percent of parents are supportive of school-based sexuality education programs. Not surprisingly the sexual ambivalence and cultural debates that pervade everything else in our culture have reared their heads in sexuality education as well. There is general agreement that younger adolescents may not have the emotional or social readiness for intensive sexual interactions, that sexually transmitted diseases are dangerous and potentially debilitating, and that teenagers should not become unintentional parents, but beyond that the goals of sexuality education become hotly debated (Dodge et al., 2008; Elia, 2009).

The Sexuality Education Debate

On one side of the debate are those who feel that adolescents should have all the information they need to make informed and responsible decisions for their lives. This approach has been called **comprehensive sexuality education.** Given the data that most teenagers will become sexually active during their

teenage years, this approach advocates giving teens age-appropriate instruction concerning birth control methods, safe sex, and differing sexual orientations and lifestyles. Although comprehensive sexuality educators may encourage abstinence or postponement of sexual activity because of the risks involved, they also want young people to be prepared to protect themselves as much as possible if they choose to engage in sex with others. They believe young people should clarify their own values and understand their own sexual needs and orientations, while learning negotiating and communication skills that will help them delay sex if they choose to do so. Sexuality educators who espouse the comprehensive model believe that in order for young people to make responsible sexual decisions, they must have a health-promoting and positive view of themselves as sexual human beings (Goldfarb, 2005).

comprehensive sexuality education an approach to educating young people about human sexuality that includes information about sexuality but also encourages clarifying values and developing decision-making skills.

Real Student Voices

■ I don't believe my sex ed was very informative. My teacher never went into much detail, and he never discussed contraception or homosexuality. It was mostly about abstinence. The only time I got any sexuality education was in the sixth grade. I don't remember much about it because that was 10 years ago.

■ I learned more about sex on the bus ride to school than I did in high school sex ed class.

■ During my junior year of high school, we had to get special permission from our parents to be

enrolled in the racy sex ed class. As it turned out we rarely talked about sex and spent most of the time on drugs and eating disorders.

■ My previous sexuality education seemed quite accurate. I still haven't had intercourse, although most of my peers have.

■ My teacher told us she "had to teach" abstinence, but that she didn't believe that was the best way to go, so she also taught all the birth control methods.

On the other side of the debate are those who believe sexuality education should uphold very particular moral values that sexual activity should occur only with one partner within marriage and that non-heterosexual lifestyles are better not discussed because they are morally wrong. They think it is preferable for adolescents to be protected from the details about sex and strongly urged to abstain from sexual activity until they are married. They think it is confusing for young people to learn about sexual behaviors and contraception, and in fact they fear that this knowledge may encourage adolescents to engage in sex. This approach is called **abstinence-only-until-marriage sexuality education.** Aside from fears of promiscuity, pregnancy, or disease, proponents of the abstinence approach believe that chastity is a value to be promoted.

Some abstinence-only programs encourage or require their students to sign a written chastity pledge that they will abstain from sex until marriage. This is often done during the early adolescent years. The central theme behind these curricula is that if we can persuade young people to practice sexual abstinence until they marry, many social problems would be solved. Recent conservative administrations have favored this approach and supported such programs with over $1.5 billion in federal funds to states (Young, 2009). Over half of the states have now refused the aid because of the narrow focus required of the sponsored programs.

The American Public Health Association (APHA) has endorsed the right of children and youth to receive broad-based sexuality education. The group recommends that facts, information, and data be taught within a context that appreciates racial, ethnic, and cultural diversity. In addition, they advocate the teaching of skills that help young people communicate effectively with others and make responsible decisions about sex (see Figure 6.12). The APHA has urged schools to develop kindergarten through twelfth-grade curricula that would not impose religious, ethical, or moral values on students. Most often, the battles over which kind of sexuality education a school will offer are waged at the local level, with elections to local Boards of Education sometimes deeply influenced by advocates from both sides of the debate (Kempner, 2009).

Source: John Branch, *San Antonio Express-News.*

abstinence-only-until-marriage sexuality education
an approach to educating young people that emphasizes the need to abstain from sexual relations until marriage, essentially the "just say no" philosophy.

FIGURE 6.12   *Comprehensive Sexuality Education*

The comprehensive approach to sexuality education emphasizes scientific information about sexuality and helps prepare students to make responsible decisions while knowing how to protect themselves against unintended pregnancy and disease.

Taking Sexuality Education Seriously

Often without carefully examining studies about what has worked and not worked in the past, sexuality programs have been put together that urgently attempt to alert young people to the very real dangers of sex in an effort to persuade them to avoid such behaviors. These programs have been based on the faulty assumption that knowledge about consequences translates to immediate changes in behavior. It has been repeatedly demonstrated that such quick-fix approaches have little value (Kantor, 2009).

One of the social developments that increased the sense of urgency about the need for sexuality education was the appearance of HIV and AIDS in the early 1980s. When it became apparent that the virus could be transmitted sexually, renewed calls for protective educational efforts arose. Nearly all states either mandated or encouraged sexuality education that taught about HIV/AIDS and other sexually transmitted diseases. Many

other important sex-related topics were often neglected in the mix, and states have generally been slow to adopt or mandate any standards for more general sexuality education curricula. In the meantime, young people continue to report that they learn the most about sexuality from their peers or from entertainment media. There is a strong likelihood that much of this peer and media education is laden with misinformation and exaggeration (Kelly, 2009; Santelli, 2008).

Because of the lack of state direction, there has been little professional training for sexuality educators, and the teaching duties are sometimes assigned to teachers who have little expertise or interest in the subject matter. To expect all parents to be able to handle the long and complicated job of sexuality education by themselves is simply unrealistic today. There may be times when involving other people in a child's life can be the most valuable direction to take. Parents can participate in parallel programs that will better prepare them for discussing the sex-related topics their children are learning about (O'Donnell et al., 2005).

The Effectiveness of Sexuality Education

Proponents of the different approaches to sexuality education sometimes make unsupported claims about the effectiveness of their approaches. It has been only recently that carefully structured studies have been conducted to determine whether sexuality education is actually meeting its expressed goals. Members of the United States Congress, after allocating hundreds of millions in funding for abstinence-only programs, have wondered if the funding has yielded the anticipated benefits. The evaluation of effectiveness has been based on rather narrow parameters, looking mostly at whether the knowledge and attitudes gained in sexuality education have resulted in behavioral change that can reduce unintended pregnancy and STD rates. Little has been done to examine whether sexuality education can improve people's sexual self-concepts, help them to be more comfortable with their own sexual lives, or lead to more satisfying lives.

The research has been quite consistent in its key findings. One study found that adolescents who received comprehensive sexuality education had a slightly lower rate of intercourse and were less likely to report a pregnancy, but this was not the case with abstinence-only approaches. Neither method seemed to reduce STD rates (Kohler, Manhart, & Lafferty, 2008). An analysis of 56 studies that examined both comprehensive and abstinence-only approaches found that of the comprehensive sexuality education programs, nearly half delayed the initiation of sexual intercourse and none of them led to earlier initiation of intercourse. Forty-seven percent of these programs increased condom use among participants, and 17 programs either reduced the frequency of intercourse or the number of sexual partners in participants. All of these behaviors would likely reduce problem pregnancies and STD risks. In contrast, the abstinence-only programs that were studied did not help the teenagers involved to delay first intercourse or reduce their numbers of sexual partners (Kirby, 2007, 2008; Trenholm et al., 2007).

A study that generated some headlines in the news media found that among African-American adolescents around the age of 12 drawn from low-income populations in Philadelphia, small-group educational settings that emphasized abstaining from intercourse "until a time later in life when the adolescent is more prepared to handle the consequences of sex" actually did seem to reduce the likelihood of intercourse by close to 10 percent over a few months. The study was hailed as evidence that abstinence-only approaches work, but in fact this program did not suggest abstaining until marriage and did not discourage condom use. It surely does suggest that when at-risk populations are given careful, small-group attention by a well-trained mentor, they may make more careful sexual decisions at least in the short term (Jemmott, Jemmott, & Fong, 2010).

Because many of the popular abstinence-based programs are produced by organizations or individuals that represent particular religious moral frameworks, state departments of education and the courts have begun to restrict their use in public school settings. In a study of three middle schools in Minnesota, twice as many students in an abstinence-only sexuality education course said they were sexually active as had indicated being so prior to taking the class. In programs where adolescents take a pledge not to have sex until marriage, the majority do not stick to the pledge, and the rates for developing sexually transmitted diseases are about the same as among young people who do not take such a pledge. Participating students in abstinence-only educational programs were just as likely to have

sex as students who were not part of the programs, started having sex at about the same age, and tended to have the same numbers of sexual partners (Trenholm et al., 2007). Another study found similar results, indicating that by five years after having taken a virginity pledge, 82 percent of the pledgers denied ever having made such a commitment. More ominously, those who took pledges were less likely than nonpledgers to use condoms or any form of birth control when they did have sexual intercourse (Rosenbuam, 2009). These results surely call into question the advisability of asking teenagers to sign promises of chastity.

Ultimately, there is still a long way to go in assessing the value of sexuality education. It seems clear based on the present research that adolescents continue to be involved in a variety of sexual activities and that comprehensive sexuality education can at the very least help them postpone first sex a bit and use condoms more consistently. It also can be said that relying on scare tactics or promises of abstinence does not seem to have much impact on the sexual decisions that teenagers make. It is also important to understand that some young people are grappling with personal questions about their sexual orientations or gender identities, and that to ignore these issues represents a disservice to them.

Perhaps a reasonable middle ground in this complex cultural debate is represented by programs that place an emphasis on postponing sex until one is emotionally and responsibly ready, without relying on scare tactics, misrepresentation of medical facts, or the teachings of any one particular religious doctrine. This represents a goal that most sexuality educators feel is legitimate: that young people should indeed postpone sexual sharing until they are ready for mature, well-informed, and safe sexual relationships.

Which approach to sexuality education do you support: comprehensive sexuality education, sexuality education that focuses only on abstinence, or something in between?

Chapter Summary

1. Individual patterns of sexual orientation and behavior develop through the interaction of biological, social, cultural, and psychological factors. The process is called psychosexual development.

2. Biopsychological drive or instinct theories claim that there is a natural, instinctual drive toward sexual behavior, although there is little evidence that this is the case.

3. Psychodynamic theory has taught that the sexual instinct, or libido, becomes invested in different bodily areas through four stages in human development: oral, anal, latency, and genital. It is believed that boys and girls must resolve unconscious sexual issues with their parents during their development.

4. Conditioning theorists believe that positive and negative reinforcement play a role in how people learn to behave sexually. Social learning theory is an extension of conditioning theory that emphasizes the importance of identifying with other people and of modeling behavior after them.

5. Developmental theory expresses the importance of stages in the emergence of behavior patterns, including those related to sexuality. Erik Erikson described eight stages, each of which has particular crises to be resolved.

6. A unified model of psychosexual development considers three crucial strands that eventually integrate to form adult sexuality: gender identity, sexual response and orientation, and the capacity for dyadic intimacy.

7. In shaping sexuality, social process theory focuses less on individual persons as the unit of analysis and more on the social processes in which the individual is immersed.

8. Social script theory holds that human behavior is controlled by complex social scripts. Sexual scripts have cultural, interpersonal, and intrapsychic dimensions that shape people's patterns of sexual behavior.

9. Choice theory explains how individuals decide which sexual behaviors to participate in, factoring in resources, risk management, and the market of accessible partners.

10. Social network theory focuses on how sexual connections and relationships are negotiated within a social context.

11. Research on childhood sexuality is ethically complex, and we often have to rely on observations of adults or retrospective reports from adults about their own childhoods.

12. In infancy and childhood, the sex organs respond to many stimuli. Babies are sensitive and observe those around them while learning. Children become more curious about their bodies and sex-related matters.

13. Children's sexual preferences are at first vague or multisexual. Sex play with other children, masturbatory behavior, and educational efforts by parents can play a significant role in how children feel about sexuality and their own bodies.

14. Children are capable of strong romantic attachments and varying levels of sexual interaction.

15. Children become acquainted with their gender identities, and their play activities and choice of toys typically fall into sex-dimorphic categories. Children whose behavior does not conform to these typical dichotomies may be transgendered, although there is controversy about labels suggesting that this is a disorder.

16. Adolescence is the period of life between childhood and adulthood. At puberty, the body becomes capable of reproduction and develops its secondary sex characteristics.

17. Adolescents learn more about sex and develop their sexual values and attitudes through interaction with peers, by contact with the media, and in their sexual experimentation.

18. Certain life situations and personal characteristics are known to mediate an adolescent's cognitive susceptibility for having sex.

19. Good communication about human sexuality between adolescents and their parents can help shape healthier and safer sexual values and behaviors.

20. Masturbation is particularly prevalent among adolescents, more so among males than among females. The frequency of masturbation varies a great deal among individuals.

21. Most adolescents have had vaginal sexual intercourse by the age of 18, and they experience both positive and negative consequences of the behavior.

22. Those teenagers who refrain from having sex generally do so for very practical reasons, although there can be negative social and personal repercussions from this as well.

23. Oral and anal sex have been increasing among adolescents. Nearly half of adolescents have participated in oral sex, and this is sometimes viewed as a rather casual behavior.

24. Understanding and coping with emotional intimacy are important during the adolescent years and crucial to the establishment of effective social relationships.

25. Dating violence has become a more serious problem among adolescents.

26. Same-gender sexual activity among adolescents may be experimental, or it may reflect developing sexual orientation. A significant proportion of adolescents have at least one same-gender sexual experience, even though they do not consider themselves gay.

27. Heterosexual contact among adolescents often proceeds through levels of increased intimacy, with the likelihood of sexual intercourse increasing with age.

28. Adolescent sexual attitudes and behaviors are significantly shaped by the cultures in which they live.

29. Adolescent sexual health has become a more pressing concern because of unintended teen pregnancies and growing rates of sexually transmitted diseases among teens.

30. HPV is a serious problem among adolescents since it can lead to later cervical cancer. A preventative vaccine is now recommended for young adolescent girls, and may soon be recommended for boys.

31. Condom use can prevent pregnancy and STDs, but even when adolescents have positive attitudes toward condoms, they do not necessarily use them. Use is dependent on a variety of personal characteristics.

32. Teenage pregnancy continues to be a problem in the United States, creating consequences for teen parents and for the larger society, although rates of teen pregnancy have mostly been decreasing in recent years. Some forms of birth control are recommended for teens.

33. Sexuality education has often been the proposed solution for preventing unintended pregnancy and STDs among adolescents.

34. There is a debate between groups who advocate comprehensive sexuality education, emphasizing sex-positive concepts and preparing young people for possible sexual activity, and groups who want abstinence-only sexuality education.

35. Although most states require HIV and STD education, other standards for sexuality education are generally vague. There are therefore few mandated guidelines for the training of sexuality educators.

36. Research has shown that some comprehensive sexuality education programs can delay intercourse and promote safer sexual behavior. Neither abstinence-only programs nor virginity pledges have been shown to do the same, and in fact young people in these programs begin having sex just as soon and with just as many partners as those not in the programs.

Chapter 7
Adult Sexuality and Relationships

Chapter Outline

The thing that scared me the most about getting older was the thought of my sexual powers declining. While I have noticed some degree of moderation in my sexual needs, the frequencies of my sexual activities are really not that much different from when I was in my twenties. I guess the "use it or lose it" principle may be operative here, since I've always believed in using it.

—from a letter to the author

Sexuality weaves its way through all the twists and turns of adult life, and maintaining a satisfying sexual life can at times be a challenge. Many college students with whom I have spoken over the years believe that there will come a time in their adult lives when they will be completely settled and all will be well. I think that is a myth. Throughout life we all have our contented times and our disrupted times. When it comes to sex and relationships, 50 year olds can be just as confused about sex and relationships as 15 year olds. A study in Great Britain found that nearly 20 percent of adults who were 45 to 54 years old said they had had unprotected sex with someone other than their longtime partner within the previous 5 years, and over 50 percent of those adults considered the risks of such behavior negligible (Royal Pharmaceutical Society of Great Britain, 2009).

■ Sexuality in Young Adulthood

Young adulthood, encompassing roughly the ages of 18 to 25 years, represents an extension of adolescence for many, especially those who attend college and then spend time beginning to build a career. A third of people ages 26 to 35 are still ambiguous about defining themselves as adults, perhaps because they have not yet achieved certain milestones once typically associated with adulthood: a college degree, marriage, having children, and financial independence. A few decades ago, about three-quarters of people had achieved most of these goals by the time they were 30; today only 31 percent of men and 46 percent of women have done so (Arnett, 2004; Melby, 2008). Whether that matters or not is arguable, but like all other stages of human life, young adulthood is a dynamic time filled with transitions, new decisions, inner journeys to be undertaken, and problems to be resolved. Young adults must further develop means of communication with intimate partners as well as their ability to make responsible, informed decisions about sexuality.

Sexual Behaviors and Risks during the Transition

There is a good deal of evidence indicating that young adults who are in relationships engage in several different sexual activities. Based on analyses of long-term data from the National Longitudinal Study of Adolescent Health and the National Survey of Adolescent

Males, we have some reliable information on typical sexual behaviors among young adults in the 18 to 26 year old age group. One study examined the behavior of 6,421 individuals who had been involved in a sexual relationship for at least 3 months. Fifty-eight percent of them had engaged in both **fellatio,** oral sex performed on the male, and **cunnilingus,** oral sex performed on the female, in addition to sexual intercourse. Another twenty-two percent had also engaged in anal intercourse (see Figure 7.1). Those young adults who said that their relationship was a mutually loving one were significantly more likely to have participated in oral sex than those who said they did not love each

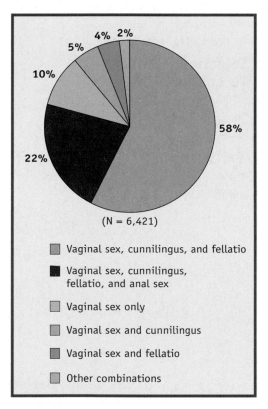

(N = 6,421)

■ Vaginal sex, cunnilingus, and fellatio

■ Vaginal sex, cunnilingus, fellatio, and anal sex

■ Vaginal sex only

■ Vaginal sex and cunnilingus

■ Vaginal sex and fellatio

■ Other combinations

FIGURE 7.1 *Percentage Distribution of Young Adults, Ages 18–26, by Sexual Activities with Current Sexual Partners of at Least 3 Months*

Source: C. E. Kaestle & C. T. Halpern. (2007). "What's Love Got to Do with It? Sexual Behaviors of Opposite-sex Couples through Emerging Adulthood." *Perspectives on Sexual and Reproductive Health, 39*(3), 134–140 (Figure 1, p. 136). Reprinted by permission of John Wiley & Sons, Inc.

fellatio (fell-AY-she-o) oral stimulation of the penis.

cunnilingus (kun-a-LEAN-gus) oral stimulation of the clitoris, vaginal opening, or other parts of the vulva.

other a lot, and males in mutually loving relationships were more likely to have had anal sex (Kaestle & Halpern, 2007).

Among young adults who were not necessarily in long-term relationships, 93 percent reported having had vaginal intercourse; 57 percent said they had performed oral sex, and 78 percent said they had received oral sex; and 10 percent reported having engaged in receptive anal sex. Twenty-seven percent of the men said they had had insertive anal sex. For both women and men, having a relationship with an older partner seemed to increase the likelihood of sexual activity at earlier ages (Ompad et al., 2006). Nearly 30 percent of the 1,114 young adults interviewed in another study indicated they had used some sort of sex toy within a typical four-week period, and more than 10 percent reported having used some drug to enhance sexual pleasure, including alcohol, marijuana, ecstasy, or Viagra (Foxman, Aral, & Holmes, 2006). These behaviors can lead to increased risk of contracting a disease. In one clinic, a sample of young adults found that 74 percent of those whose partners had had another sexual partner during their relationship were not aware of that fact, placing them at much higher risk of contracting a sexually transmitted disease (Drumright, Gorbach, & Holmes, 2004).

Some adolescents who engage in sexually risky behavior are more likely to continue with the risky sex as they enter adulthood, and this does not seem to be particularly related to these young people's sense of self-esteem. Social class and perceptions of gender do seem to play a role however. Poor and working-class people, who in fact are disproportionately prone to unintended pregnancy and STDs, tend to believe more than middle-class individuals that men have stronger sexual appetites than women and that these needs are built in and somewhat uncontrollable. This may predispose them to assuming greater sexual risks (Boden & Horwood, 2006; Higgins & Browne, 2008). It does seem to be true that men think about sex more than women do, tend to be more sexually permissive, and have more sexual partners, so there may well be some generalizable differences between men and women in sexual attitudes and behaviors (Fischtein, Herold, & Desmarais, 2007).

As young men transition into adulthood, they generally become more cautious in their sexual activities and take fewer sexual risks, meaning that they use condoms and other forms of birth control more consistently, have fewer sexual partners, and select their partners more carefully. Even those who have engaged in high-risk behaviors as adolescents tend to transition to lower-risk behaviors. Only about 9 percent of the young men studied either maintained their levels of risky sex or increased their sexual risks, with a concurrent likelihood of having had a sexually transmitted disease (Dariotis et al., 2008).

The College Experience

Girls who start having sexual intercourse in early adolescence are slightly less likely than those who begin having sex in their late teens to pursue a college education, especially if they have had a child. This correlation does not seem to apply to boys. Once in college, students often experience the pressures of peer expectations regarding their social and sexual choices (Lefkowitz et al., 2004; Spriggs & Halpern, 2008). Colleges where most students are commuters allow for a good deal of continuing contact between students and their families. Residential colleges create social networks of their own, around which individualized campus cultures develop and a means for meeting others and building relationships is established. College students tend to do a fair amount of checking out potentially available partners (see Figure 7.2).

It has generally been assumed that when young adults venture off to a college and live on campus, the new freedoms they face and lack of parental supervision create new opportunities for sexual activity, including sexually risky behavior. Another assumption is that the increased alcohol consumption associated with college students leads to less responsible and more risky sexual choices. While there is probably some truth to both of these assumptions, research has shed some tempering light on the situation.

One study followed the sexual behaviors of over 800 young people after they left high school, comparing those who went to college with those who did not,

FIGURE 7.2 *College Students Survey the Social Scene*
The bar and club scene offers many young adults a place to socialize and meet potential sexual partners

these second marriages also end in divorce within 10 years.

To what extent sexual incompatibility and dissatisfaction with sex are factors in divorce is unclear. Couples who are having marital difficulties often experience sexual problems, yet these problems are just as frequently the effect as they are the cause. There is some evidence that sexual problems present in a first marriage reappear in a second marriage. Adjusting to divorce can be a traumatic experience, and it involves the grieving stages typical of any major loss. Divorced people often experience upheavals in their lifestyles that create new stresses and pressures. They may feel depressed or anxious and experience loss of self-esteem. Children whose parents have divorced often experience stresses that affect their lives into their college years, but it is also true that divorced people and their children can have positive outcomes and ultimately experience greater resilience (Elder-Avidan, Haj-Yahia, & Greenbaum, 2009; Hetherington & Kelly, 2001).

Sexuality and Aging

Larger proportions of our population than ever before are now in middle and older age groups, as post–World War II baby boomers grow older (see Figure 7.7). Census Bureau statistics show that the number of elderly people in the United States doubled between 1960 and 2000, growing from nearly 17 million to 35 million. In this sense, we are becoming an older society. People also are retiring earlier, extending the amount of time between retirement and old age. Improved medical care and increased emphasis on good health habits are helping many of us enjoy a longer life span than we might once have expected. Studies have begun to appear about the sexuality of older adults, although there has also been criticism that these studies too often focus primarily on their sexual problems than the more positive aspects of their sexuality. Although it is true that sexual responsiveness and activities typically decline in old age, and there is an increasing likelihood of encountering some problem with sexual functioning, many older people report continuing sexual desire, sexual interaction, and sexual satisfaction (Bancroft, 2007; Kleinplatz, 2008; Kontula & Haavio-Mannila, 2009; Kuehn, 2008).

Women frequently report signs of stronger sexual interests and fewer inhibitions about discussing sex after passing their childbearing years. Data from the Study of Women Across the Nation (SWAN) showed that 77 percent of women ages 42 to 52 said that sex was moderately to extremely important to middle-age women's lives. More than 60 percent reported having regular sexual intercourse and 24 percent reported having oral sex fairly regularly (Cain et al., 2003). Sexual intimacy and affection with a partner improves middle-aged women's moods and stress levels, leading to a greater likelihood of future sexual activities (Burleson, Trevathan, & Todd, 2007; Carpenter, Nathanson, & Kim, 2009).

Sexuality among Older Adults

Human beings retain a full range of emotions—including romantic and sexual ones—throughout the life span (see Figure 7.8). There is increasing evidence that sexual expression continues to be an important part of intimate relationships into old age. A Swedish study examined four populations of 70 year olds in the early and late 1970s, early 1990s, and 2000–2001, finding that across this 30-year period, adults in their seventh decade of life had become more sexually active, more satisfied with their sexual lives, and more positive toward sexuality in later life. This may well reflect changes that resulted from greater openness about sex that began during the sexual revolution (Beckman et al., 2008; DeLamater, Hyde, & Fong, 2008).

A significant factor in remaining sexually active as one ages is the degree of importance and priority that the older individual or couple has placed on sex

FIGURE 7.7   *Midlife Transitions and Commitments*

Middle age is often a period of transition and reevaluation. As couples commit and recommit themselves to relationships, their sense of shared intimacy and sexual enjoyment may be deepened. This mature couple is entering into marriage.

FIGURE 7.8 *Old Age and Sexuality*

Patterns of sexual activity vary greatly among the elderly. Cultural and social expectations of sexual behavior as well as the state of health of both partners may play a part in the frequency and type of sexual activity engaged in by elderly couples.

throughout the life cycle. There is a high correlation between the amount of sexual interest shown in the young adult years and that shown in the older adult years. Those who have tended to see sex as an important part of their lives and began having sex at earlier ages, and those who have sought frequent sexual outlets are more likely to continue being sexually active into old age. Likewise, letting sex become a low priority may well lead to an absence of sexual interest as a person ages (Beckman et al., 2008; Kontula & Haavio-Mannila, 2009).

A survey of a national probability sample of over 3,000 U.S. adults aged 57 to 85 confirmed that even though the amount of sexual activity tends to decline with age, many older people remain involved sexually. Among those aged 57 to 64, 73 percent reported sexual activity. Fifty-three percent of those aged 65 to 74 were sexually active, as were 26 percent of those who were 75 to 85. The participants in this study rated their own level of general health, and it was found that those who rated their health to be "poor" or "fair" were

less likely to report sexual activity than those who said their health was "very good" or "excellent." Fifty-eight percent of people in the 57 to 64 year old age group reported having oral sex, as compared to 31 percent in the 75 to 85 year olds (Lindau et al., 2007).

Among the respondents who were sexually active, about half of both the men and women reported at least one sexual problem that was bothersome to them. Women reported problems with sexual desire (43 percent), vaginal lubrication (39 percent), and reaching orgasm (34 percent), while men were most likely to report erection problems (37 percent). Fourteen percent of the men were taking some sort of supplement or prescription drug to improve their sexual functioning. The majority of both genders had not reported these problems to their physicians (Lindau et al., 2007).

For many older people, masturbation becomes their sole means of sexual gratification. In their first study on human sexual response, Masters and Johnson (1966) reported that most of the older people in their study had tended to continue masturbating into old age if they had masturbated previously. In the more recent survey, 52 percent of the men and 25 percent of the women who still had sexual partners reported having masturbated in the previous year, as had 55 percent of the men and 23 percent of the women without sexual partners. The rates of masturbation also declined over the increasingly older age groups (Lindau et al., 2007). Table 7.6 summarizes these findings in the three age brackets studied.

Availability of a sexual partner and the health of that partner play a significant role in how sexually active an older person is. As women age, they become far less likely to have a sexual partner than are men, so this is a more critical factor in women's maintenance of sexual desire and activity (see Figure 7.9). Among respondents in the Lindau et al. (2007) study who had not had partner sex for three months or longer, 55 percent of the men and 64 percent of the women reported the male's physical health as the reason for lacking sex. In the older age brackets, women are more likely not to have an available partner. In the 60 to 64 age bracket, there are 88 men per 100 women. Above age 75, there are only 55 men per 100 women. Clearly, it is more difficult for older women to find potential sexual partners than it is for older men (DeLamater & Sill, 2005; Laumann et al., 1994).

The research on gay men, lesbians, and bisexual people in midlife and older age is very limited. In the survey cited above (Lindau et al., 2007), too few respondents indicated that their sexual partners were of the same gender to have any meaningful data. For the most part, it is expected that nonheterosexual persons face the same sorts of passages and adjustments as do heterosexuals. There is evidence to suggest that gays and lesbians are becoming more open as they age about their sexual orientations and more vocal about

Table 7.6   *Prevalence of Sexual Activity and Behaviors among U.S. Adults 57–85 Years Old, by Age Group*

Variable	Number of Respondents	Age Group 57–64 years (%)	65–74 years (%)	75–85 years (%)
Sexual activity with a partner . . .				
. . . in previous 12 months				
Men	1,385	83.7	67.0	38.5
Women	1,501	61.6	39.5	16.7
. . . 2–3 times per month or more				
Men	857	67.5	65.4	54.2
Women	492	62.6	65.4	54.1
Sexual behavior:				
Vaginal intercourse, usually or always				
Men	854	91.1	78.5	83.5
Women	501	86.8	85.4	74.4
Oral sex in previous 12 months				
Men	831	62.1	47.9	28.3
Women	484	52.7	46.5	35.0
Masturbation in previous 12 months				
Men	1,250	63.4	53.0	27.9
Women	1,281	31.6	21.9	16.4

Source: From S. T. Lindau. (2007). "A Study of Sexuality and Health among Older Adults in the United States." *New England Journal of Medicine, 357*(8), 762–774, Table 2. Copyright © 2007 Massachusetts Medical Society. All rights reserved.

wanting medical, legal, and social services appropriate to their needs. A great deal more research needs to be done to understand thoroughly any special needs and concerns that aging presents for individuals who are attracted to members of their own sex.

Special Sexual Problems and Patterns of Aging

Seniors must adapt to many physical, emotional, social, and economic changes in their lives. They may experience loss of companionship, loss of role status after retirement, and some losses of physical and cognitive functioning. The individual's perception of her or his sexuality is a crucial part of adjustment to a new stage of life. Dissatisfaction with sexual activity is related to depression and feelings of worthlessness, which in turn can discourage further activity (Trudel et al., 2008).

Throughout the life span, sexual behaviors are influenced by attitudes and values. People who are old today grew up in times when negative and repressive sexual codes were taught, and many have carried these values with them into old age. They may become self-fulfilling prophecies for many. Research confirms that among older people, negative attitudes toward sex correlate with relative sexual inactivity. Unfortunately, opportunities for older people to discuss, explore, or even change their value systems are often neglected, because it is assumed that their values are too entrenched (DeLamater & Friedrich, 2002).

Sex-negative myths and attitudes often lead to policies or attitudes that prohibit sexual expression among the aged. Nowhere is this more evident than in nursing homes and other institutions that provide care for older men and women. Not only are outward expressions of sexual interest seen as inappropriate and therefore discouraged, but there is often a lack of privacy for any sort of personal or shared sexual activity. Studies have shown, however, that many elderly nursing-home residents remain sexually active and interested in sex. Even when nursing-home personnel are aware

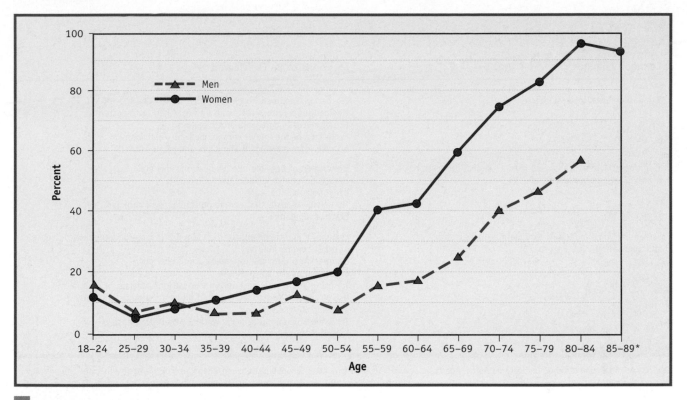

■ FIGURE 7.9 *U.S. Adults with No Sexual Partner in the Past 12 Months*

As women age, they become far less likely than men to have a sexual partner.

Source: From *Sex in America* by Robert T. Michael, John H. Gagnon, Edward O. Laumann and Gina Kolata, p. 86. Copyright © 1994 by CSG Enterprises, Inc., Edward O. Laumann, Robert T. Michael, and Gina Kolata. By permission of Little, Brown and Company, and Brockman, Inc.

*Insufficient data available for men ages 85 to 89.

of the facts about the sexuality of the aged, their own attitudes may be negative, and appropriate policy changes may be hindered by lack of support from administrative personnel, physicians, and the families of older patients. Providing older people with opportunities for choice and a sense of personal autonomy can enhance their sexual identity and adjustment (Kontula & Haavio-Mannila, 2009).

Maximizing Sexual Expression during the Later Years

While the aging process makes an indelible mark on the ways the human body responds sexually, older people can remain in touch with the sexual part of their lives. Table 7.7 summarizes some of the ways to maximize sexual pleasure as one ages. Some nursing homes and health care clinics have offered sexual education and enhancement programs for the elderly that have helped them understand their own sexuality more completely. Given the increased proportion of older adults in the population, the availability of these services is more crucial than ever (Hillman, 2000; Kontula & Haavio-Mannila, 2009).

As human beings age and become less genitally oriented, they have the potential to rediscover the sensuousness of their entire bodies. Older people gain satisfaction from kissing, caressing, holding, cuddling, and other types of lovemaking that involve both spiritual and physical intimacy. In a sense, elderly people can be freed from many of the concerns that interfere with sexual intimacy in younger age groups: risk of pregnancy, the need to prove oneself with sex, obsessions with performance and orgasms, balancing work and personal time, and having children to care for. We all could stand to learn from those older people who have come to value sexual intimacy in its holistic sense and have come to realize that sex is far more than what genitals do together.

■ Sexual Effects of Illness

A long list of medical problems can directly or indirectly affect a person's sex organs and sexual functioning. As stated above, older adults often indicate that they have some problems with sexual function, and these problems were more common in those who said they were in poorer health. The study asked respondents if they

Table 7.7	*Coping with Sexual Changes That May Accompany Aging*

Common Changes	Solutions to Be Considered
Decreased sexual interest/desire	Evaluation/treatment for depression Medically supervised treatment with estrogen or testosterone Use of mutually agreeable erotic stimuli Evaluation of the role of chronic medical conditions Become more intentional about planning times for sex
Thinning of vaginal walls; less natural vaginal lubrication; lessened orgasmic response	Exploration of possible role medications may play Evaluation of alcohol/drug use Use a personal lubricant Try pelvic exercises that can be prescribed by a clinician Exercise regularly
Softer erections; more difficulty maintaining erection and ejaculating	Evaluation and treatment for high blood pressure, diabetes, heart disease, or other chronic illnesses Exploration of possible role medications may play Evaluation of alcohol/drug use Try using one of the prescription medications that aid in erections Use of vacuum device, self-injected drugs, or surgical implants, as medically advised Try using positions that make vaginal penetration easier Exercise regularly

Sources: Adapted from National Institute on Aging, *Age Page: Sexuality in Later Life,* http://niapublications.org/agepages/PDFs/Sexuality-in-Later-Life.pdf; *Aging Well, Living Well,* http://womenshealth.gov/ow/sexuality/index.cfm; *Non-Surgical Management of Erectile Dysfunction (ED),* http://www.urologyhealth.org/print/index.cfm?topic5174.

had arthritis, diabetes, or hypertension. The women who said they had diabetes were less likely to be sexually active than women without the disease, and diabetic men were more likely than nondiabetics to report difficulty with erection (Lindau et al., 2007).

While debilitating illnesses are more likely to be experienced during the later years of life, some may appear at earlier stages of the life span as well. Because sexuality is a part of the whole person, anything that affects physical or psychological health and well-being can have implications for sexual functioning. For example, chronic fatigue syndrome can produce loss of sexual interest and satisfaction when the fatigue is severe (Blazquez et al., 2008). Unfortunately, health professionals often fail to assess the sexual implications of various illnesses and do not discuss these aspects with their patients. Especially in long-standing chronic illnesses or in acute illnesses that create serious debilitation, careful sexual assessment should be an integral part of total health care. The partners of patients are often dealing with difficult emotional issues as well, which may affect their sexual attitudes and functioning.

Treatments for some illnesses, such as medication for blood pressure or chemotherapy for cancer, can have direct effects on sexual functioning. Antidepressant and antipsychotic medications often affect both desire and physiological responsiveness. Chronically ill people may begin to question their identities as women and men and the role their sexual functioning now plays in their identities (DeLamater & Sill, 2005; Katz, 2007). Medications used in the treatment of schizophrenia are associated with several sexual dysfunctions (Miclutia, Popescu, & Macrea, 2008).

Chronic pain accompanies some disorders, and some women experience pelvic pain that remains resistant to traditional pain-relieving treatments. This can be a complex issue, involving many psychological dimensions as well as the physical ones. Pain over time is wearing on any individual and may interfere with sexual desire and pleasure (Randolph & Reddy, 2006).

Among those diseases most frequently found to have adverse effects on sexual functioning are neurological disorders such as multiple sclerosis or stroke, diabetes, cardiovascular disease and heart attacks, chronic lung disease, cancer and its treatments, and arthritis. These illnesses and their treatments may weaken the body, interfere with the control of bodily functions, threaten self-esteem and body image, and inhibit interpersonal intimacy. Because of the potential sexual problems resulting from such diseases, patients need thorough information about what to expect (O'Connor, McCabe, & Firth, 2008).

Cardiac and stroke patients are often concerned about the amount of physical exertion that is safe for them during sexual activity. This concern can lead to psychological pressures that can, in turn, produce sexual dysfunctions. Erection problems are particularly common in men who have heart disease, and in fact constitute a warning sign of clogged arteries, since the blood flow to the penis may be impeded just as is blood flow to the heart (Jackson, 2009). Health workers can gradually encourage post-heart-attack patients to get back in touch with their sexual feelings, even suggesting masturbation when the individual is physically ready for any exertion. Later, specific suggestions can be given for shared sexual activity, at first using positions that require a lesser degree of physical strain and energy. With reassurance and education, most cardiac patients can reestablish full sexual lives.

Some surgeries can have effects on sexual behavior and satisfaction that should be thoroughly explained to patients. Prostate surgery, for example, is very common in older men and may in a few cases inhibit the capability to have an erection and ejaculate. However, with reassurance, encouragement, and education, many men who have had prostate surgery can resume satisfactory sexual activity. Hysterectomy (removal of the uterus and cervix) need not adversely affect the sex lives of women. Some women face many psychological stresses following hysterectomy, but with appropriate education and adjustment counseling, the majority of women can emerge feeling healthier, sexier, and more self-confident than before.

Mental illness may also adversely affect a person's sexual activities. Nonetheless, mentally ill people typically have sexual needs and the desire to pursue sexual activity. Emotional disruption may lead to lack of interest in sex and loss of the ability to be sexually responsive. Depression is associated with reduced sexual desire in most people, and their partners may feel very excluded from their lives as well (Ostman, 2008).

Increasingly, health professionals are realizing the importance of exploring sex-related issues with their patients. It is to be hoped that assessment of the potential sexual effects of various illnesses will soon become a standard and accepted part of medical evaluation and treatment.

If you were experiencing some medical condition that interfered with your sexual functioning, would you be willing to talk with your doctor about it? Would it help if the doctor brought up the sexual issues for you?

Self-Evaluation

The Cheat-O-Meter: What Does It Mean to Be "Faithful"?

With your current partner or with a trusted friend, complete this exercise separately, and then discuss your answers.

For the following activities, number each from 1 (least serious) to 10 (most serious or worst example of cheating). Each number must be used. No number can be used twice.

_____ Your partner has sexual intercourse once with a stranger of the other sex that s/he met on a trip out of town.

_____ Your partner falls in love (but is not physically intimate) with another person that s/he met online and has been having a virtual relationship for two years with the person.

_____ Your partner has oral sex with someone of the other sex.

_____ Your partner has oral sex with someone of the same sex.

_____ Your partner regularly has phone sex with a person s/he has never met face to face.

_____ Your partner has sexual intercourse with your best friend.

_____ Your partner lies to you about going out (but is not physically intimate) with an ex boy/girl friend.

_____ Your partner has sex with a stranger of the same sex s/he met on a trip out of town.

_____ Your partner lies to you about having sexual intercourse with an ex boy/girl friend.

_____ Your partner routinely fantasizes about his/her ex when you and s/he are being physically intimate.

Source: Adapted from an activity published in Curtis, J. N., & Coffey, K. (2007). The cheat-o-meter: Talking about what it means to "be faithful." *American Journal of Sexuality Education,* 2(4), 89–98 (Appendix 1, p. 97). Reprinted by permission of the publisher (Taylor & Francis Group, http://www.informaworld.com).

Chapter Summary

1. Adult sexuality involves establishing intimacy with others and the exploration of the place of sex in intimate relationships.

2. Young adulthood (ages 18 to 25) is a time during which a great deal of sexual exploration takes place, and young adults may engage in risky behavior. Oral sex, vaginal intercourse, and anal sex are among the most typical sexual behaviors for young adults.

3. As young men age, most begin taking fewer risks in their sexual behaviors.

4. Although going to college may offer more freedom to young adults, those in college do not seem to engage in more or more risky sexual behavior than those who do not attend college or who live at home. Neither does increased alcohol use seem to contribute to marked increases in risk sex.

5. College students have sex for a variety of reasons, and sometimes choose secondary abstinence after having been sexually active. Some of their sexual experiences are later regretted.

6. There are differing definitions for what constitutes having sex or hooking up, sometimes including intercourse and sometimes other sexual activities. "Friends with benefits" implies a casual sexual relationship without commitment, but it can be complicated to maintain.

7. Negotiation is typically a part of deciding to share sex and using condoms, but teasing and insistence can be part of the mix in some situations.

8. Most people want the intimacy of coupled relationships, and researchers are attempting to figure out the dynamics that bring people together.

9. Classical psychological theory assumes some inner mechanism of attraction; social network theory demonstrates the significance of social groups and equal status contact in finding a partner.

10. Evolutionary theory holds that there are certain innate tendencies of males and females that shape their mate selection processes, all of which assume that sex selection assures the continuation of the species. Evolutionary psychology assumes certain differences in sexual motivations between women and men.

11. Most people eventually marry, although it has become more acceptable to remain single.

12. Cohabitation has become the norm prior to marriage. Cohabiting couples often assume that it will help them have a better marriage, but this depends on several factors and does not represent an assurance against eventual divorce.

13. Sexual activity tends to be most frequent in the earlier years of a relationship and then gradually decreases in frequency. Sexual satisfaction among married couples depends on a vast array of characteristics than can be quite specific to the particular couple. Good communication is important to relational and sexual satisfaction.

14. Although monogamy is still accepted as the most socially appropriate type of relationship, some people have extradyadic relationships and sex. Infidelity is judged in many different ways and may create complications for relationships.

15. Some cultures permit either polygamy or polyandry, but having multiple spouses is not without its problems.

16. The rates of both marriage and divorce have been declining slightly in the United States. At least half of marriages in the country end in divorce, although many divorced people go on to subsequent marriages. The median ages at which people marry are higher than ever before.

17. Older people often retain their interests in and physical capacities for sexual expression. Research shows that while there is a decrease in sexual activity in aging, many older people remain sexually active if their health permits. Availability of a partner may be a problem in older age, especially for women.

18. In institutions for the elderly, lack of privacy and policies of sex segregation may prevent expression of sexual needs.

19. Illness, chronic pain, certain medications, and the aftermath of some surgeries can affect people's sexual identities and sexual desires. Diabetes often affects sexual functioning.

Chapter 8
Sexual Individuality and Sexual Values

Chapter Outline

> Until I came to college, I thought of myself as a very normal person sexually—a little on the conservative side, maybe, but normal. As I watch my peers' sexual exploits, I'm not so sure anymore. I am doing a lot of questioning about who I really am, or ought to be, sexually.
>
> —from a student essay

Sexuality holds tremendous potential for pleasure and is vital to the propagation of the human species, but it can also be a source of anxiety, shame, and disgust. Societies attach great symbolic meaning to sex and seek to regulate its expressions. It has been proposed that human ambivalence about things sexual could be rooted in two ideas of which we are reminded when it comes to sexuality. One is the inescapable but uncomfortable fact that we are indeed animals, even though the human animal certainly has many distinguishing characteristics that set it apart. The other reminder is that one of the prices that sexual reproduction incurs is death. Organisms that produce offspring through sexual means ultimately die, a fact that seems to be universally troubling (Goldenberg et al., 2002).

List several sexual activities you believe are considered normal in our society. List several sexual activities you believe are considered abnormal.

■ **FIGURE 8.1**   *Erotic Scene from Attic Cup, Pompeii, Italy, Fifth Century BCE*

For centuries, depictions of human sexual behaviors have reflected various standards of acceptability.

■ Labeling Sex: Establishing Standards

For a time, the predominant assumption in Western culture regarding human sexuality was this: To be **normal** was to be attracted sexually to members of the opposite sex and to desire penis-in-vagina intercourse as the ultimate expression of that attraction; everything else, in varying degrees and at various times, was considered **abnormal.** Yet there is ample historical, anthropological, and psychological evidence to indicate that human beings are—and always have been—extremely diverse and variable in their sexual attractions and behaviors (see Figure 8.1).

Literature and art have portrayed all sexual activities through the ages, but the extent to which they have been expressed and permitted in various societies and times in history is known only in bits and pieces (see Figure 8.2). For some past cultures, we know what sexual behaviors were considered unlawful or in violation of the codes of sexual activity established by their religion (Gaca, 2003; Soble, 2009). However, the extent to which information about a sexual activity was recorded in a society may have depended on the extent to which the activity was tolerated and accepted. Consider the examples of prostitution and same-gender sexual behavior. Because prostitution has generally been more accepted over the span of human history than has same-gender

behavior, we have far more historical records about it than we do about sexual activity between members of the same sex.

One job of science is to categorize, classify, and label. To organize and to name things and phenomena are the only ways for us to continue being able to communicate about them intelligently. This has been true for human sexuality, as science has attempted to explain, understand, and classify sexual attractions and activities. We must also keep in mind that categories are created by people who have their own particular definitions of meaning, drawn from time, place, and political persuasion. Differences among categories often are exaggerated and therefore have real power to impact those individuals who have been classified either within a category or outside the category. Ultimately, categories are artificial and ever-changing (Muehlenhard, 2000). As we saw in the previous chapter, there has not even been much agreement as to which genital behaviors actually constitute "having sex."

normal a highly subjective term used to describe sexual behaviors and orientations. Standards of normalcy are determined by social, cultural, and historical standards.

abnormal anything considered not to be normal (that is, not conforming to the subjective standards a social group has established as the norm).

FIGURE 8.2 *A Variety of Sexual Activities as Portrayed by the Painter of This Red-Figured Attic Kylix*

It is important to remember that scientists, too, are products of their sociocultural environments. Their conclusions and labels may reflect the agendas of their society. Labels can have great power, both positive and negative. You might recall that, during the latter part of the nineteenth century, Richard von Krafft-Ebing condemned masturbation as depraved and identified it as a source of mental contamination, weakened sexual desire, and all manner of physical and sexual problems. His attitudes were promulgated throughout the medical profession, thereby promoting the view that masturbation was one of the most damaging of sexual acts. It was given labels such as secret sin, self-abuse, and self-pollution. Generations of young people grew up viewing masturbation with fear and frustration.

Krafft-Ebing reflected, reinforced, and perpetuated the values of his place, time, and social network. Since then we have seen a shift in attitudes toward masturbation. Medical science has yielded objective data regarding its effects and its frequency. Although some religious prohibitions against masturbation remain, the general opinion in the professions of medicine and psychology is that the practice is a widespread and generally harmless form of sexual expression. It is interesting that discussions about sex have now shifted to the use of labels such as **self-gratification** and **self-pleasuring** to describe masturbation, which has become one of the norms against which other behaviors are compared and standardized.

For years, sexologists have struggled to come up with general, inclusive terms to describe and classify more atypical sexual behaviors. Psychoanalysis first gave us the term **deviation,** which, of course, implies that a person has strayed from some defined, normal pathway. If the pathway is determined by statistics, the deviant is someone who is located on one of the tails of a bell curve. Or it may be established simply by prevailing values. In any case, the label "deviation" has taken on so much negative connotation and vagueness that it no longer is widely used to describe sexual behaviors.

A more recent label has been **variation** or variance, which also implies that an individual is somehow different or aberrant sexually. The question remains of how the standard for determining the norm is established. We might ask, "A variation on what?" or "Different from what?" These terms have come to have negative meanings, even though originally they were not meant to carry any particular value implications.

The term **paraphilia,** loosely meaning "a love beside," is used to describe sexual attraction or activity that is considered unusual or unacceptable. A paraphilia is presently considered to be pathological and to interfere in some way with an individual's life, and the term is used in psychiatry to label a variety of sexual diagnoses. Some professionals have accepted that certain forms of sexual expression seem obviously and categorically disordered and should be treated as such. Other professionals argue that the logic and factual information used to diagnose the paraphilias are flawed and inaccurate enough that the entire classification should be eliminated as a category of mental disorder. The debate rages on (Karasic & Drescher, 2005; Lawrence, 2009; Moser & Kleinplatz, 2005).

Sociocultural Standards for Sexual Arousal and Behavior

It is easy to see that labels such as abnormal, deviation, variation, and paraphilia all imply some degree of aberration from an accepted sexual standard. Several

self-gratification giving oneself pleasure, as in masturbation; a term typically used today instead of more negative descriptors.

self-pleasuring self-gratification; masturbation.

deviation term applied to behaviors or orientations that do not conform to a society's accepted norms; often has negative connotations.

variation a less pejorative term used to describe nonconformity to accepted norms.

paraphilia (pair-a-FIL-ee-a) a newer term used to describe sexual orientations and behaviors that vary from the norm in pathological or antisocial ways; it means "a love beside."

■ FIGURE 8.3   *Heterosexual Standard*

The form and meaning of behavior are influenced by the culture and the time in which a person lives. North American society demonstrates a level of heterosexism that assumes heterosexual attraction and behavior to be the norm.

standards have permeated the values of Western culture. In informal—and sometimes quite formalized—ways, they have told us how we "should" feel and act sexually. They have been reinforced by prevailing cultural values and mores and by the social networks in which we live. Yet significant proportions of the human population simply have not lived their sexual lives according to these standards. The standards are described below; what do you think of them?

The Heterosexual Standard

There is still a prevailing **heterosexism** that assumes and implies we are supposed to be sexually attracted to members of the other gender and therefore to desire to be sexually involved with them (see Figure 8.3). Even though other sexual orientations have achieved increasing levels of acceptance, we have not yet moved entirely beyond the notion that to be heterosexual is preferable. This cultural heterosexism fosters antigay and antilesbian attitudes by providing a system of values and stereotypes that seem to justify prejudice and discrimination (Brickell, 2001; Walls, 2008).

The Coital Standard

Sexual intercourse between a woman and a man, or **coitus,** has often been seen as the ultimate sexual act. Other forms of shared male-female sexual activity have traditionally been labeled **foreplay,** with the implication that rather than being enjoyed for their own sake or as sexual goals and ends in their own right, they represent preparation for coitus. This standard has weakened in recent years as oral sex and other forms of noncoital interaction have become increasingly accepted.

The Orgasmic Standard

It is often assumed that we are supposed to experience orgasm as the climax of any sexual interaction. This standard has been particularly prevalent among males in Western culture, although in recent years it has become predominant among women as well.

The Two-Person Standard

Sex is most often depicted as an activity for two people. Although masturbation has for the most part gained legitimacy as an acceptable behavior, and research shows its frequency to be positively correlated with shared sexual behavior, it is sometimes viewed as a substitute for shared sex. It is also assumed to be preferable to experience sex as a duo, and any sexual activity involving more than two is considered distinctly kinky.

The Romantic Standard

Romance and sex have become inseparably intertwined, and it certainly is true that the intimacy generated by one may enhance the other. But it is also true that love and sex can be subject to very different interpretations and values. In Victorian times, healthy and positive loving relationships were supposed to be unspoiled by the desires of the flesh. Today it often seems that romantic love without sex is considered incomplete and that sex without love is considered emotionally shallow and exploitative.

The Safe Sex Standard

The most recently developed standard for our culture, evolving from the threat of HIV and AIDS, the safe sex standard holds that when people make the choice to share sex, they are supposed to take appropriate precautions to prevent unwanted consequences such as unintended pregnancy or transmission of disease. It created a new level of emphasis on abstinence from risky sexual behaviors and on the use of condoms during shared sexual activity.

---

heterosexism the biased and discriminatory assumption that people are or should be attracted to members of the other gender.

coitus (KO-at-us or ko-EET-us) heterosexual, penis-in-vagina intercourse.

foreplay sexual activities shared in early stages of sexual arousal, with the term implying that they are leading to a more intense, orgasm-oriented form of activity such as intercourse.

Which sociocultural standards for sexual arousal and behavior do you believe are most commonly held within your social network: the heterosexual standard, the coital standard, the orgasmic standard, the two-person standard, the romantic standard, the safe sex standard? Explain your choices.

Global Sexual Rights

The World Association for Sexual Health (WAS) has adopted a Universal Declaration of Sexual Rights. WAS is a coalition of researchers, academics, medical professionals, and health care providers who work to further the understanding and development of sexology throughout the world. The association has over 100 member organizations representing over 30 countries. While the Declaration of Sexual Rights is not enforceable, it does represent a set of guidelines that are increasingly being used in policy-making. Here are its components:

- Sexuality is an integral part of the personality of every human being. Its full development depends on the satisfaction of basic human needs such as the desire for contact, intimacy, emotional expression, pleasure, tenderness, and love.
- Sexuality is constructed through the interaction between the individual and social structures. Full development of sexuality is essential for individual, interpersonal, and societal well-being.
- Sexual rights are universal human rights based on the inherent freedom, dignity, and equality of all human beings. Because health is a fundamental human right, so must sexual health be a basic human right. In order to assure that human beings and societies develop healthy sexuality, the following sexual rights must be recognized, promoted, respected, and defended by all societies through all means. Sexual health is the result of an environment that recognizes, respects, and exercises these sexual rights.

1. *The right to sexual freedom.* Sexual freedom encompasses the possibility for individuals to express their full sexual potential. However, this excludes all forms of sexual coercion, exploitation, and abuse at any time and situation in life.
2. *The right to sexual autonomy, sexual integrity, and safety of the sexual body.* This right involves the ability to make autonomous decisions about one's sexual life within a context of one's own personal and social ethics. It also encompasses control and enjoyment of our own bodies free from torture, mutilation, and violence of any sort.
3. *The right to sexual privacy.* This involves the right to make individual decisions and behaviors about intimacy as long as they do not intrude on the sexual rights of others.
4. *The right to sexual equity.* This refers to freedom from all forms of discrimination regardless of sex, gender, sexual orientation, age, race, social class, religion, or physical and emotional disability.
5. *The right to sexual pleasure.* Sexual pleasure, including autoeroticism, is a source of physical, psychological, intellectual, and spiritual well-being.
6. *The right to emotional sexual expression.* Sexual expression is more than erotic pleasure or sexual acts. Individuals have a right to express their sexuality through communication, touch, emotional expression, and love.
7. *The right to sexually associate freely.* This means the possibility to marry or not, to divorce, and to establish other types of responsible sexual associations.
8. *The right to make free and responsible reproductive choices.* This encompasses the right to decide whether to have children, the number and spacing of children, and the right to full access to the means of fertility regulation.
9. *The right to sexual information based upon scientific inquiry.* This right implies that sexual information should be generated through the process of unencumbered yet scientifically ethical inquiry and disseminated in appropriate ways at all societal levels.
10. *The right to comprehensive sexuality education.* This is a lifelong process from birth throughout the life cycle and should involve all social institutions.
11. *The right to sexual health care.* Sexual health care should be available for prevention and treatment of all sexual concerns, problems, and disorders.

Source: Reprinted by permission of the World Association for Sexology. www.tc.umn.edu/~colem001/was/wdeclara.htm

See "Sex, Sin, and Sickness" on SexSource Online.

Who Is Normal?

Anthropologists speak of **ethnocentricity,** the quality of assuming that one's own culture is the right one

---

ethnocentricity (eth-no-sen-TRIS-ih-tee) the tendency of the members of one culture to assume that their values and norms of behavior are the right ones in comparison to those of other cultures.

and is superior to all others. Our ethnocentricity finds us surprised, amused, and shocked by the beliefs and customs of others, who of course are just as taken aback by ours. In their classic anthropological study *Patterns of Sexual Behavior,* Ford and Beach (1951) concluded that there is such a wide variation in sexual behaviors across cultures that no one society can even be regarded as representative. Yet a type of ethnocentricity that might be called **erotocentricity** leads us to assume that our own—either cultural or individual—sexual values, standards, and activities are right and best.

Ours is a culture of dichotomies and categories. Everything must fit into some classification, and if something is not right, it must be wrong. Likewise, if some behavior is not bad, it must be good (Muehlenhard, 2000). The normal/not-normal dichotomy may be strongly held, and people constantly worry about whether their feelings and behaviors are indeed normal. Every society sets sexual standards and regulates sexual behaviors. These standards are passed from one generation to the next, sometimes being modified as they are passed on. Boundaries therefore arise, distinguishing the good from the bad, the acceptable from the unacceptable. These boundaries become the criteria used to establish the concepts of normal and not normal. The most widely accepted methods of defining normalcy in Western culture today are:

Statistical Normalcy

One of the most common ways to decide the relative normalcy of some sexual behavior is based on how widespread and frequent it is in a particular population. If most people do it, then it is considered normal. If it is practiced by only a small minority, it is not considered normal. Some behaviors, such as masturbation and oral sex, began to be considered more normal when major sex surveys showed how widespread they were.

Normalcy by Expert Opinion

Every society has its experts, either by choice or by default. Our society venerates educational and professional status and listens to the opinions of those who possess what are perceived to be expert credentials. For example, members of the psychiatric profession's associations may decide, by vote, to consider a certain sexual orientation healthy or unhealthy, normal or abnormal. In 1974, the American Psychiatric Association decided, by polling their members, that same-gender sexual orientation and behavior would no longer be considered an illness (see Figure 8.4). For the purposes of diagnosing and classifying various mental illnesses, including certain sexual behaviors, professionals often refer to a major psychiatric handbook, now in its

fourth edition, called the *Diagnostic and Statistical Manual of Mental Disorders* (DSM-IV). Professional meetings have been underway to make decisions about the contents of the upcoming DSM-V. There is a great deal of controversy about the degree of scientific validity involved in classifying certain sexual interests and problems as pathologies, and it has been claimed that the process for making such decisions is sometimes arbitrary, scientifically inadequate, and highly political. A draft of the revised DSM appeared in 2010, with the final version scheduled for publication in 2012. Debate among the experts about what is to be considered normal and what will be classified as a disorder is ongoing (Balon, 2008; Karasic & Drescher, 2005; Kingston et al., 2007; Melby, 2009).

Moral Normalcy

Religions usually have standards regarding sexual morality. The predominant religions in a particular society therefore often establish the norms for morality. These standards may then be perpetuated in laws and social sanctions. In most societies, behaviors and values that are seen as morally acceptable are also defined as normal.

A Continuum of Normalcy

In Western societies, there has been increased acceptance of concepts such as situational morality, reality as a matter of perception, and being nonjudgmental. A result has been an increased willingness to view sexual attraction and activities in relative terms by asking questions such as these: Is a behavior healthy and fulfilling for a particular person? Is it safe? Does it lead to exploitation of others? Does it take place between responsible, consenting adults? In this outlook, normal and abnormal are seen as part of a continuum that considers numerous individual and situational factors.

Limits and Misuses of Labels: The Language of Sexual Orientation

Labels for various forms of sexual behavior can provide only a very general category of definition. The DSM provides diagnostic categories to facilitate communication among clinicians in the psychological and psychiatric professions and to conform with insurance regulations. However, whatever defines groups of people can also separate them. Consider, for example, the term

erotocentricity (ee-ROT-oh-sen-TRIS-ih-tee) the application of ethnocentric-like judgments to sexual values and behaviors, creating the assumption that our own ways of approaching sexuality are the only right ways.

■ **FIGURE 8.4** *What Is Normal?*

Labels such as "homosexual" are sometimes employed to construct rigid boundaries between "normal" and "not-normal" behavior. In fact, same-gender orientation and behavior are part of a continuum of sexual behavior that encompasses numerous individual factors.

homosexual. Most people believe that they understand what is meant by the term. Closer examination might call the use of this label into question (Muehlenhard, 2000). Here are some of the issues to be clarified in deciding who might once have been labeled a homosexual:

1. Must the person participate in actual sexual activity with another of the same gender, or is it enough to just want to do so?
2. If a person has had just one sexual experience with a same-gender partner, should he or she be considered homosexual? If not, how many same-gender sexual acts should lead to such classification?
3. Should only those who have been sexually involved exclusively with members of their own gender be called homosexual? If not, what percentage of same-gender experience is required?
4. Should people who have been attracted sexually to members of their gender all their lives but have married and engaged exclusively in heterosexual activity be considered homosexual?

Because of their social acceptance and prevalence, heterosexuals are not particularly noticed as a defined group. The term *heterosexual* is not likely to be used to define a person, behavior, or lifestyle. The term *homosexual,* on the other hand, is quite a different story. It represents a distinct and permanent category, a defining characteristic of the person who has been labeled that implies a great deal beyond some occasional sexual behavior. As a consequence, people who have any degree of same-gender sexual orientation may be marginalized as a minority, even provoking disapproval because of their perceived abnormalcy or unhealthiness.

In fact, knowing about a person's same-gender sexual behaviors reveals nothing about her or his psychological adjustment, hormone balances, masculinity or femininity, childhood development, or any other characteristic that would distinguish the person from one whose sexual behaviors have been exclusively heterosexual. Research data continue to indicate that people who have sex with members of their own gender are remarkably similar to people who do not. Perhaps

homosexual term traditionally applied to affectional and sexual attractions and activities between members of the same gender.

science has been trying to invent categories and commonalities where none exist (Muehlenhard, 2000).

Definitions of the term *homosexual* have tended to focus only on sexual activity and thus have sometimes ignored the individual's **affectional** preferences. A person's sexual behavior does not necessarily reflect inner orientations and inclinations. It is quite possible that individuals who find themselves sexually attracted to members of their own gender never participate in sexual acts with them. Instead these individuals may function effectively in relationships with the other gender. It is also possible for those with a primarily heterosexual orientation to participate in same-gender sexual behavior.

Current models of sexual orientation take into consideration many different variables, including behavior, attraction, self-identification, lifestyle, frequency of sex with different partners, and changes over time. The present state of knowledge about human sexuality no longer allows us to identify the term "homosexual" as anything very specific. For these reasons, some psychologists have recommended that the term "homosexual" no longer be applied to people. It is laden with negative stereotypes, often is applied only to males, and generally is ambiguous.

There are some widely used terms that are considered more precise and less pejorative. "Gay male" and "lesbian" are used primarily to describe people's sexual and affectional identities and the communities of individuals that have developed among people who share those identities. Although the term **gay** is sometimes used to describe either men or women, it will be used in this book mostly in reference to males; the word **lesbian** is used in reference to females. Although there is growing use of the term "queer" by professionals who are gay, bisexual, or transgendered themselves, the term often describes a particular set of political values relating to sexual orientation. The word is not used in this book because it is still so often employed by others in a negative way. The term **heterosexual** can be used to refer to opposite-gender (male-female) orientation, identity, or behavior. The slang term **straight** is often applied to primarily heterosexual persons, although it also carries the negative connotation that nonheterosexuals are somehow "crooked," perpetuating a stereotype of deviance from the norm.

The term **bisexual** is used in reference to people who relate sexually and affectionally to both females and males. It can be used to describe both sexual identity and behavior. One complex aspect of bisexuality is that it may be manifested in so many different ways. Some bisexual people are simultaneously attracted to both men and women, whereas others have sequential relationships with members of both genders. In other words, some bisexual persons spend some time in a gay male or lesbian relationship, followed by involvement in a heterosexual relationship, or vice versa. Heterosexual

people, lesbians, and gay males may not be accepting of bisexual orientations and behaviors, assuming that the bisexual person should make a decision to go one way or the other—choosing sides as it were. On one hand, bisexuals may be accused by gay males or lesbians of trying to preserve heterosexual privileges; on the other hand, they often are perceived by both heterosexual and gay people as being gay or lesbian but afraid to admit it (Steffens & Wagner, 2004).

Confusing questions may also arise with other sex-related labels. A man who dresses in women's clothing is often labeled a **transvestite,** yet such behavior has all sorts of different motivations. Terms such as *sadism* and *masochism* are so general and ill defined that they have little meaning when talking about the behavior of individuals (see Chapter 14, "The Spectrum of Human Sexual Behavior"). Of special concern is the use of specific sexual labels to define the entire person. Only too often an individual's entire identity seems to be summarized in a single descriptor of his or her sexual orientation. We say "Isn't she a lesbian?" or "There goes a transvestite" instead of recognizing these orientations and behaviors as only one small part of an individual's personality. Yet we never label anyone heterosexual or some other term for what we consider normal behavior. Such misuses of terminology are a disservice to the individuality of human beings.

■ Sexual Individuality

Personal sexuality is far more complex than are gender roles and sexual attraction to a particular gender. We may find certain characteristics about other people sexually attractive and arousing: facial features, body types and builds, hairstyles, age, certain parts of their body (for example, legs, buttocks, genitals, breasts),

---

affectional relating to feelings or emotions, such as romantic attachments.

gay refers to persons who have a predominantly same-gender sexual orientation and identity. More often applied to males.

lesbian (LEZ-bee-un) refers to females who have a predominantly same-gender sexual orientation and identity.

heterosexual refers to attractions or activities between males and females.

straight slang term for heterosexual.

bisexual refers to some degree of sexual activity with or attraction to members of both sexes.

transvestite an individual who dresses in clothing and adopts mannerisms considered appropriate for the opposite sex.

■ FIGURE 8.5 *Sexual Fantasy*

The human mind can conjure up a variety of fantasy images regarding sexual partners and sexual behaviors. Some of these fantasies may be realistic, and some just wishful thinking, or thoughts of things the person would never actually pursue. Sexual fantasies may be accepted as curiosities of our cognitive processes. It is our actual behaviors for which we must be ready to take responsibility.

styles of clothing, or lack of clothing. When we interact with others sexually, we usually prefer specific sexual acts. We may have our own particular frequencies and techniques for masturbation, and some people find some activities and practices sexually exciting that have little to do with other people.

Most people have a sexual life of the mind as well, consisting of sexual fantasies and dreams along with sensations of sexual need, desire, and attraction (see Figure 8.5). Only sometimes are these inner experiences expressed in physical responses or overt sexual behaviors. Because performing sexual acts involves a degree of decision making, our inner sexual reactions and needs are not always consistent with our outward expressions of sexual behavior.

All these aspects of a person's sexuality are intimately intertwined with all other aspects of the person-

ality. As with classifying fingerprints by loops, whorls, and other configurations, it is possible to find general categories for some parts of everyone's sexual nature. Taken together, however, the aspects of our personal sexualities are as individualized and specific as our fingerprints. They constitute our **sexual individuality.**

How Does Sexual Individuality Develop?

Sex research continues into the origins of sexual attractions, orientations, preferences, and behaviors. We are only beginning to understand how human beings take on the specific characteristics of their sexuality. We do have a few generalizations that can be made about the origins of sexual orientation and preferred sexual activities:

1. The importance of the relationship with parents and of identifying with a parent in determining a child's sexual orientation probably has been overestimated in former theories. While parents may influence the development of sexual attractions to some extent, these influences likely are not very profound.
2. An individual's basic sexual orientation seems to be largely established by adolescence, even though the person may not have been particularly sexually active. Adult expressions of sexual orientation and preference tend to be a continuation and confirmation of earlier sexual feelings, although some of those expressions may not actually be realized behaviorally until later in life.
3. Developing patterns of sexual feelings and responses within children and young people cannot be traced to a single social or psychological root. They are instead the result of many factors that are a part of any human being's life and are too numerous, complex, and poorly understood to be predictable or controllable.
4. There seem to be some biological bases for the development of sexual orientation and a preference for certain sexual activities. These inborn factors most likely establish sexual predispositions that may then be influenced in various ways by psychological and social factors. Thus, it is likely that the interaction between nature and experience, rather than one or the other alone, influences our sexual development, along with most other facets of human development (Bancroft et al., 2009).
5. Social networks, those groups of people with whom we associate on a regular basis, are

sexual individuality the unique set of sexual needs, orientations, fantasies, feelings, and activities that develops in each human being.

Real Student Voices

■ I believe that love and sex are somewhat independent of each other. A couple doesn't need to be in love to have sex, and they don't need to have sex to be in love. Sex without love is great and love without sex is great, but when they are combined, it makes both even better.

■ When people are single, sex mostly has no relation to love. I think I sometimes place too low a

value on sex because I treat it as something to do because I am horny.

■ With me and most college students, all good decision-making skills go down the drain after five or six beers.

extremely significant in shaping and perpetuating our individual sexual attitudes and behaviors.

6. There does not seem to be a natural sexual way for human beings to be or an inborn sexual instinct to guide sexual behaviors. The diversity of sexual individuality provides ample evidence that there is no single, representative human sexuality.

Fritz Klein (1990) was one of the first researchers to develop a model showing many different components of sexual orientation and identity, all related to one another but having a degree of independence at the same time. He initially developed a list of seven

variables that needed to be considered when describing a person's sexual orientation or identity: sexual attraction, sexual behavior, sexual fantasies, emotional preference, social preference, self-identification, and actual lifestyle. He soon realized that these dimensions of a person's life often change over time. Where people are today in terms of their sexual identities is not necessarily where they were in the past or where they will be—or would like to be—in the future. Therefore, he developed a matrix, called the Klein Sexual Orientation Grid (KSOG), which considers this time factor along with each of the seven variables (see Figure 8.6).

Variable	Past	Present	Ideal
Sexual attraction			
Sexual behavior			
Sexual fantasies			
Emotional preference			
Social preference			
Self-identification			
Lifestyle			

■ **FIGURE 8.6** *Klein Sexual Orientation Grid (KSOG)*

Where people are today in terms of their sexual identities is not necessarily where they were in the past or where they will be or would like to be in the future. Klein developed this chart, which, when filled out, helps the researcher determine a person's sexual identity.

Source: Reproduced by permission of the American Institute of Bisexuality. From Fritz Klein, *The Bisexual Option,* 2nd ed. Binghamton, NY: Haworth Press, 1993, p. 19.

Table 8.1	Description of Seven Normative Attitudinal Orientations toward Sexuality							
	Traditional		Relational			Recreational		
	Conservative	Pro-Choice	Religious	Conventional	Contemporary Religious	Pro-Life	Libertarian	Total Sample
1. Premarital sex is always wrong.	100.0%*	23.6%	0.0%	0.4%	0.8%	6.5%	0.0%	19.7%
2. Premarital sex among teenagers is always wrong.	99.5	90.3	78.6	29.1	33.6	65.7	19.7	60.8
3. Extramarital sex is always wrong.	98.2	91.0	92.1	94.2	52.1	59.3	32.0	76.7
4. Same-gender sex is always wrong.	96.4	94.4	81.9	65.4	6.4	85.9	9.0	64.8
5. There should be laws against the sale of pornography to adults.	70.6	47.2	53.1	12.2	11.7	14.9	6.4	33.6
6. I would not have sex with someone unless I was in love with them.	87.5	66.0	98.0	83.8	65.3	10.1	19.5	65.7
7. My religious beliefs have guided my sexual behavior.	91.3	72.9	74.7	8.7	100.0	25.0	0.0	52.3
8. A woman should be able to obtain a legal abortion if she was raped.	56.3	98.6	82.3	99.1	99.3	84.3	99.8	88.0
9. A woman should be able to obtain a legal abortion if she wants it for any reason.	0.5	100.0	0.0	87.4	84.9	9.3	88.6	52.4
N = 2,843	15.4%	15.2%	19.1%	15.9%	9.3%	8.7%	16.4%	100.0%

*Indicates the percentage of persons in the "Conservative Traditional" cluster who believe that premarital sex is always wrong.
Source: From *Sex in America* by Robert T. Michael et al., p. 234. Copyright © 1994 by CSG Enterprises, Inc., Edward O. Laumann, Robert T. Michael, and Gina Kolata. By permission of Little, Brown and Company, and Brockman, Inc.

Other researchers have reinforced the concept that sexual individuality is a combination of many life dimensions and includes many facets of the personality and patterns of behavior. It reflects an evolution of an individual's own perception of self through the development of a sexual identity (Garcia & Hoskins, 2001). To define a person's sexual orientation on the basis of any one activity or fantasy would be too narrow. Labeling a whole person with the name of a single sexual category cannot do justice to the complexity of human sexual identity or orientation. The development of sexual individuality takes place over a lifetime and includes many different components.

Sexual Attitudes and Sexual Choices

Regardless of how we develop sexually—and regardless of the sexual fantasies, needs, attractions, and orientations that become part of every human being—each of us must make choices about sexual behaviors. Through these choices we are able to fulfill some of the other expectations of being civilized human beings: to be responsible, to develop self-respect, and to be nonexploitative toward others. It has been shown that when

discrepancies exist between people's actual feelings about their sexuality and what they believe they *should* be about sexually, they have lowered self-esteem and are more prone to depression (Garcia & Hoskins, 2001).

National Health and Social Life Survey (NHSLS) researchers assessed attitudes on premarital sex, teenage sex, extramarital sex, same-gender sex, pornography, sex and love, religious beliefs, and abortion. They then examined the data using cluster analysis, a statistical technique used when social scientists are searching for patterns in masses of data but do not have a strong theory to guide them or a clearly defined hypothesis to be tested. As mentioned in Chapter 1, three broad categories of attitudes emerged, but evidence of some clear differences among groups within each category led to the formation of a few subcategories as well (Laumann et al., 1994). Table 8.1 summarizes these findings.

About one-third of the population indicated that their religious beliefs always guide their sexual behaviors; this group was called *traditional*. People in this group tended to believe that premarital sex, teenage sex, extramarital sex, and same-gender sex are wrong and that legal abortion should be restricted to some degree. They were divided in their opinions about the availability of abortion, so the group was subdivided into *conservative* and *pro-choice.* The conservative traditionalists were more conservative in all of their sexual attitudes than were the pro-choice traditionalists.

The largest attitudinal group was the *relational* category, consisting of close to half the population. Members of this group believed that sex should be part of a loving relationship but not necessarily reserved exclusively for marriage. Therefore, they did not see premarital sex as wrong but did tend to rate extradyadic or casual sex as wrong. These people were then divided into three subgroups. The *religious* subgroup, whose religious beliefs shaped their sexual behaviors, was the most conservative, opposing same-gender sex, teenage sex, and abortion. The *conventional* subgroup was less influenced by religious beliefs and tended to be more tolerant than the religious group toward teenage sex, pornography, and abortion, but this group was still opposed to same-gender sex. A third subgroup, *contemporary religious,* was guided in their own behaviors by their religious beliefs but was more tolerant of same-gender sex than were the other subgroups.

About one-fourth of the population fit into a category that was labeled *recreational* because they did not feel that sex and love needed to be connected. Most people in this category also opposed laws that would prohibit the sale of pornography to adults. They were subdivided into a *pro-life* group, which opposed both same-gender sex and abortion but was more accepting of teenage sex and premarital sex, and the most liberal of all groups, the *libertarians,* who were not guided by any religious beliefs and were assessed as most accepting on all the attitudinal items.

Which group or subgroup do your sexual attitudes and beliefs most closely align with? Defend your choice.

These findings showed that there is no clear-cut system of American attitudes when it comes to human sexuality. There is instead a wide distribution of beliefs across the population. The researchers were able to draw some other interesting conclusions, summarized in Table 8.2. For example, women were somewhat more likely than men to fit into the traditional category and less likely to fit into the recreational group. Older people also were more likely to be traditional. More women than men indicated that they believed strongly in love and commitment as a part of sexual relationships. Educational level did not seem to be associated with any clear attitudinal pattern, although an increase in educational attainment was associated with a slight trend away from conservative sexual attitudes and toward liberal attitudes. Religious affiliation, on the other

hand, did show some correlation with attitudes. Nonreligious people were unlikely to fall into the traditional category and more likely to be in the recreational group. Conservative Protestants were much more likely to be in the traditional category (Michael et al., 1994).

One of the more salient findings of the NHSLS research was the clear link between people's attitudes and their sexual behaviors. Although it is beyond the scope of this text to analyze the correlations in detail, it was shown that an attitudinal group was closely associated with particular sexual practices and frequency of sexual thoughts. Traditional people tended to have fewer sexual partners and thought less about sex than did the other two groups. Those with recreational attitudes had more sexual partners and thought more frequently about sex. Masturbation, oral sex, anal sex, and same-gender sex all were more common among the recreational group than among the traditional group. Frequency of sexual activity did not seem to be linked to an attitudinal group (Laumann et al., 1994).

Sexual attitudes are very firmly held in most people. Family members, friends, and other members of one's social networks tend to be like-minded in their attitudes and therefore provide constant reinforcement of shared beliefs. This is one reason why people's behaviors tend to be consistent with their belief systems. It may also account for why people find it difficult to understand and accept other attitudinal viewpoints and have no desire to change their own. This realization provides us with some understanding of why so many conflicts arise in our society regarding sexual matters and why discrimination can be one unfortunate result.

Sexual Attitudes and Discrimination: Homophobia, Biphobia, and Transphobia

Irrational fears of lesbians and gay men and strongly held negative attitudes about them have been labeled **homophobia,** although it has been argued that this term is not accurate because a true phobia is not usually involved. More accurately it is a form of sexual negativity and discrimination (Herek & Gonzalez-Rivera, 2006).

Public opinion polls demonstrate that Americans have generally become more tolerant about gay and lesbian people over the past three decades, although that trend has tended to slow during the 2000s. According to Gallup polls, slightly over half of people in

homophobia (ho-mo-FO-bee-a) strongly held negative attitudes about and irrational fears of gay men and/or lesbians and their lifestyles.

Real Student Voices

■ Sometimes I know that I allow my sexual needs to take precedence over my better judgment. It really is a choice, I guess, but I think it makes me feel less guilty if I imagine it to be out of my control. It feels that way too.

■ I'm a very religious person, and so it's pretty easy for me to make ethical sexual choices. My church is real clear about what to do, and I follow that.

■ While I believe we are intelligent beings who are completely capable of resisting our innate biological programming for the good of society, I'm a firm believer that love has evolved as a means for us to keep a sense of attachment to our mates, just like the mating habits of other mammals. Basically, it's all about sex for propagating the species.

Table 8.2	Distribution of Attitudinal Orientations within Certain Demographic Groups		
Social Characteristics	**Traditional**	**Relational**	**Recreational**
Gender			
Men	26.9%	40.1%	33.0%
Women	33.7	47.6	18.7
Age			
Men			
18–24	17.4	46.9	35.7
25–29	21.0	46.2	32.9
30–39	26.2	38.6	35.2
40–49	31.2	38.2	30.5
50–59	40.1	31.3	28.6
Women			
18–24	23.0	51.8	25.3
25–29	27.5	54.6	17.9
30–39	34.6	46.6	18.8
40–49	34.5	44.9	20.6
50–59	47.0	43.4	9.6
Education			
Men			
Less than high school	31.6	39.5	28.8
High school graduate or equivalent	28.3	40.9	30.8
Any college	25.0	39.8	35.2
Women			
Less than high school	36.6	47.6	15.9
High school graduate or equivalent	38.3	46.0	15.7
Any college	30.4	48.7	20.9
Religion			
Men			
None	11.7	39.1	49.2
Mainline Protestant	24.2	43.8	32.0
Conservative Protestant	44.5	30.1	25.3
Catholic	17.8	49.6	32.6
Women			
None	10.4	44.4	45.2
Mainline Protestant	30.9	51.4	17.7
Conservative Protestant	50.5	38.4	11.2
Catholic	22.2	58.0	19.8

Table 8.3	*Gallup Poll: Should Homosexuals B Hired for These Professions?*	
	Yes (%)	No(%)
Salesperson	90	7
Doctors	78	19
The armed forces	76	22
As a member of the president's cabinet	75	23
High school teachers	62	36
Elementary school teachers	54	43
Clergy	49	47

Source: L. Saad. (May 20, 2005). "Gay Rights Attitudes a Mixed Bag." Gallup News Service. Reprinted with permission.

FIGURE 8.7   *Coming Out*

Gay, lesbian, and bisexual people sometimes fear that being open about their sexual orientations will have negative consequences. National Coming Out Day provides an opportunity for some individuals to challenge negative stereotypes and find acceptance.

the United States today consider this an acceptable alternative lifestyle, compared to 34 percent in 1982 and 38 percent in 1992. However, 45 percent still consider it unacceptable as a lifestyle. When the question is phrased differently, and people are asked if sexual relations between members of the same sex are morally acceptable, the proportion saying yes peaked at 44 percent in the mid-2000s, with between 52 and 55 percent responding that they were not morally acceptable (Saad, 2006).

Gallup polls indicate an interesting trend in the way people in the United States view the suitability of gay and lesbian persons for various occupations. By 2003, the percentage saying that they should have equal job opportunity had risen to 88 percent, up from 56 percent in 1977 and 74 percent in 1992. However, by 2005, support for gay people in certain professions, particularly teaching and the clergy, had declined (see Table 8.3). This may well be the result of increased publicity about priests having sex with children and incidents of sexual abuse involving teachers (Saad, 2006). There are common misconceptions that gay teachers might somehow be inappropriate role models, or that they are more likely to molest children, neither of which is supported by statistics.

Gay and lesbian students frequently are subjected to harassment, misunderstanding, and discrimination (Brown et al., 2004). There is evidence that college athletics represents an area that still exhibits a high level of homophobia and that gay and lesbian athletes generally have to keep a relatively low profile about their orientation (Wolf-Wendel, Toma, & Morphew, 2001). However, other college students also perceive some barriers to friendships with lesbians and gay men (Mohr & Sedlacek, 2001). Studies across several nations show that men tend on average to be more homophobic than women and tend to have more negative atti-

tudes toward gay men than they do toward lesbians (Davies, 2004; Lingiardi, Falanga, & D'Augelli, 2005; Negy & Eisenman, 2005).

Homophobic attitudes found on college campuses may be one reason why gay men and lesbians sometimes find their college environments less emotionally supportive and less tolerant of change and innovation than the environment they would find in the larger society. Campus diversity efforts now challenge heterosexism and offer active acceptance and nurturance for those with differing sexual orientations. Students with same-gender sexual orientations thus have become increasingly visible (see Figure 8.7). Those institutions that have been successful in creating a supportive environment for gay males, lesbians, and bisexuals have found that these students can feel comfortable and safe on campus and are less prone to self-destructive attitudes and behaviors than are those in less supportive environments (Brown et al., 2004; Shaffer & Augustine, 2002).

Misunderstanding of and prejudice toward bisexual people, sometimes called **biphobia,** has also been identified, as has **transphobia,** a term applied to negative feelings toward transgender individuals. Probably the most blatant form of biphobia is the common belief that bisexuality does not exist. The assumption is made that people must fit naturally into either a heterosexual identity or a gay or lesbian identity and that all others simply have not been able to make up their minds where they fit. In one study, heterosexual students had the most strongly negative feelings toward bisexual people, rather than gay men or lesbians (Herek & Gonzalez-Rivera, 2006).

Both homophobia and biphobia may be *externalized* or *internalized*. When externalized, they manifest themselves in name calling, discrimination, or prejudice toward others. It has frequently been suggested that the homophobic or biphobic reactions of some individuals may arise from confusion or uncertainty about their own sexual identity, although empirical evidence to support such a contention is lacking. When people are uncomfortable about their own same-gender attractions, feelings, desires, or behaviors, their homophobia or biphobia is said to be internalized and may lead to high-risk sexual behaviors, depression, or other personal problems (Gencoz & Yuskel, 2006).

■ Sex and Values

Consider your reactions to the following situations:

- Shamika, a sophomore in college, goes with some friends to a favorite bar just off campus. She meets Alan for the first time and they spend two hours together, sharing drinks and conversation. He invites her back to his dorm room, and after some kissing and mutual fondling, he asks her to have intercourse. Shamika agrees, with the understanding that they will use a condom, and she spends the night in Alan's room. The next morning, they agree that neither is looking for a heavy relationship, although both would enjoy remaining friends.
- Mike has just entered college and has agreed to maintain an exclusive relationship with his girlfriend at home, some 600 miles away. He feels strongly about their commitment and is determined to make it last. He decides that he will not date at all and that his only sexual outlet will be masturbation.
- Worried about his grades in English, Derek pays a visit to the office of his instructor, a woman in her late twenties. They discuss his recent papers and examinations, with Derek admitting that English has never been his strongest subject. To Derek's surprise, the professor hints that one sure way to earn an A would be to spend some time alone with her at her apartment. At first he thinks she is joking, but she touches his hand and makes it clear that she is being very serious.
- Lucy returns to her dorm room following a shower and begins to dress. Her roommate Karen seems to be watching her rather intently, and Lucy tries to hide her discomfort. Karen asks her to sit down for a moment and is soon telling her about how attracted she has been to her. She expresses fear of Lucy's rejection but explains that she just could not hide her feelings any longer. Lucy is somewhat surprised but not at all angry. In fact, she finds the idea of sex with Karen a bit intriguing.

Now try to think about why you had the reactions and thoughts you did in relation to these sex-related situations. What specific aspects made you feel positively or negatively about the people? Would your reaction be any different if Shamika and Alan had been dating for several months before having sex? If they were engaged? If they had failed to use a condom? What if Mike had decided that what his girlfriend does not know will not hurt her? What if he had decided not to masturbate either? What if Derek's instructor had been a man? What if the instructor were a man and the student a woman? What if Lucy and Karen had been two men? What if Lucy had been disgusted by Karen's admission and had immediately sought to change rooms?

How you as an individual view these and other sex-related situations is determined by your **values.** Your reaction is based not simply on your sexual values but also on your values about relationships, coercion, responsibility, and a long list of other issues. We weigh our sexual values in our sexual decision making, along with other related values. When people decide to participate in sexual activities that are inconsistent with their values, they may experience some conflict and guilt.

Sexuality as a Moral and Ethical Issue

Moral values deal with the ethics, or rights and wrongs, of life situations. Theories of morality assume that humans are capable of making choices based on

---

biphobia prejudice, negative attitudes, and misconceptions toward bisexual people and their lifestyles.

transphobia negative attitudes, prejudice, and misconceptions toward transgender individuals and lifestyles.

values system of beliefs through which people view life and make decisions, including their sexual decisions.

moral values beliefs associated with ethical issues, or rights and wrongs; often a part of sexual decision making.

rational thought and logical reasoning, making them responsible for their decisions and actions. Deliberating about moral issues requires that we can find reasons for our convictions about certain things being right or wrong. Our ethical standards guide our actions, and so we need to know that those standards are grounded in sound judgment. This means that we are able to cite rational principles that form the bases of our moral values. There is also an underlying assumption that other people are capable of moral reasoning, just as we ourselves are, and that part of respecting others is recognizing that they too are capable of acting with self-awareness and reason. This means that rather than manipulating others, we are willing to present them with our own moral rationales and explore the rational basis for their moral beliefs and commitments. In this way, ethical decision making is a part of human dignity (Kaufman, 2010).

Because sexuality is such a pervasive and powerful aspect of human nature, all societies have sought to control and regulate it. Religion is one social institution usually concerned with ethics, so moral values related to sex have sometimes been rooted in religious teachings. Sexual morality today tends to be grounded in one of the following ethical traditions.

Legalistic Ethics: Adherence to Divinely Established Laws

Some believe that sexual morality is divinely ordained through natural laws that establish clear and unwavering boundaries between right and wrong. They may assert further that there is a singular interpretation of holy books such as the Bible or the Quran and that there are clearly defined prescriptions and proscriptions for sexual behavior, although many who have studied religious texts claim that such messages are not nearly so clear as they sometimes are purported to be (Haffner, 2004). This legalistic approach to sexual ethics is found in many orthodox or fundamentalist religious traditions, whose teachings tend to fall into traditionalist categories.

Some religious people believe that moral principles can change as societies and human behavior patterns change (Jakobsen & Pellegrini, 2003). Within this approach to sexual ethics, there is a belief that social values change over time, rather than being bound to rigid traditional standards. New information from science, medicine, psychology, and sociology may be incorporated into new moral perspectives. This more flexible perspective still calls for the establishment of moral codes of behavior, often developed by delegations of people in the governing body of some religious group. These people may still decide that adultery or sexual activity between members of the same gender is unacceptable, but they allow the issues to be discussed, debated, and then decided upon.

Moral Relativism and Situation Ethics

The relativistic view is that there are no overarching moral beliefs that supersede local customs about what is right and wrong. While to some this view can seem too open to the selfish interpretations of any one individual, it does not necessarily excuse anyone from the need to reason carefully, and with attention to social expectations, about why one acts in certain ways. Situation ethics sees every choice as being made within a unique collection of considerations and conditions. Therefore, moral decisions are made in the context of a particular situation, with a view toward all the people involved. The key to whether some form of sex is right or wrong lies in the human motivations behind it and the foreseeable consequences it might have. From this ethical perspective, a particular sexual behavior might be considered wrong in one context but acceptable in another. Obviously, it gives much more responsibility to the individual for making such judgments in arriving at sexual decisions (Kaufman, 2010).

Hedonistic and Ascetic Traditions

These moral perspectives represent opposite ends of an ethical spectrum. **Hedonists** have recreational attitudes, holding that pleasure is the highest good and outweighs religious dogma or situational context. This point of view can be crystallized by the phrase "If it feels good, do it." The sex drive is viewed as an appetite to be satisfied with a maximum amount of physical and emotional pleasure. To manage a purely hedonistic lifestyle is not any easy matter, because the complicated realities of relationships can easily get in the way.

Asceticism, which has been a part of some religious and spiritual traditions, is characterized by celibacy. The goal is to rise above base physical pleasures and instead emphasize self-denial, self-discipline, and the life of the mind or spirit. Asceticism often is characterized by the teaching that denial of sexual pleasure helps one be closer to spiritual needs and to God, and it is part of the celibate lifestyle expected of some priests, nuns, and monks.

Holistic Belief Systems

Some contemporary philosophers have suggested that we are coming into a time of human social evolution when we no longer have to view the ascetic and

hedonists (HEE-don-ists) people who believe that pleasure is the highest good.

asceticism (a-SET-a-siz-um) usually characterized by celibacy, this philosophy emphasizes spiritual purity through self-denial and self-discipline.

FIGURE 8.8 *Religious Attitudes toward Sexuality*

Religion may play an important role in establishing the sexual standards of a culture. People may face conflicts if their personal values contradict the established standards. This Hindu couple is shown in traditional wedding dress, standing near a decorated marriage bed.

hedonistic pursuits as mutually exclusive. Holistic perspectives propose that we place sexuality in a broader context that considers many different levels of the human experience: physical, emotional, rational, social, and spiritual. It has been suggested that we need both the lofty side of things that at times asks us to rise above self-centered bodily pleasure and the earthier, fleshy side that offers sensual delights. Rather than advocating for choosing one direction or the other, the holistic perspective proposes that we seek a more united and whole pursuit of balancing these different but valuable parts of our sexuality in healthful, responsible ways. It has been suggested that it is time to reclaim sexual pleasure as part of living comfortably in one's body and of finding one's playful side (Hunt & Jung, 2009; Resnick, 2002).

Spirituality, Religion, and Sex

Understanding and developing spirituality are important to many people, and fitting sexuality into the picture is often a significant part of that search. Organized religions are the social institutions that attempt to help people find a place for the spiritual in their lives,

although many people also seek spiritual development outside this context.

Judeo-Christian-Muslim religious values traditionally have constituted the moral backbone for various prohibitions against sexual behaviors in Western culture. In ancient Israel, for example, sexual intercourse was tantamount to marriage, and there was no such thing as a casual, obligation-free sexual relationship. In Christian theology, Augustine (354–430 CE) decided that sexual desire represented the ultimate clash between desire and reason, thereby establishing sex as the culprit that passed sin from one generation to the next (Soble, 2009). Not until the Middle Ages did marriage become a religious event in Christianity and therefore a religious sanctioning of sexual activity (see Figure 8.8). Some Muslim traditions have placed a great deal of importance on the separation of male and female roles, sometimes expressed in the sexual mores that have called for women to keep much of their body covered. Behaviors that might encourage sexual attraction or arousal also are sometimes forbidden (Stayton, 2002).

In contrast to this perspective, the Eastern traditions—Hindu, Buddhist, Tantric, and Taoist—

have tended to view sexuality in terms of its creative potential and its power in spiritual development. Eastern thought places more emphasis on the harmony of body and spirit than on the opposition of the two. The combination of desire and a sense of duty has made both ascetic, celibate lifestyles and the religious celebration of sexual pleasure possible in Hinduism. In the Buddhist, Tantric, and Taoist religions, sexual union often is viewed as a mystical and spiritually uplifting experience.

Within all major religious traditions, there are two basic ways in which the world tends to be perceived. One is a fixed worldview, in which it is assumed that the universe was created by a deity and is now completely finished. This is the fundamentalist perspective, which finds followers within every tradition. The other point of view is more process oriented, seeing the world and human nature as constantly changing and evolving. These two viewpoints usually are associated with differing attitudes toward sexuality as well. The fundamentalist view is that a constant battle is being waged between good and evil and that sex is a major source of temptation and sin. Those with a more evolutionary worldview tend to see the essential goodness of the human body and sexual desire, and they place the emphasis on people choosing sexual behaviors that are healthy, responsible, and considerate of others (Haffner, 2004; Timmerman, 2001).

Several studies have demonstrated correlations between people's religious belief systems and their sexual attitudes and behaviors (see Table 8.4). The more religious people consider themselves to be, the more likely they are to feel that it is important to have sexual

practices that are in harmony with their religious beliefs (Cowden & Bradshaw, 2007; Laumann et al., 1994).

How Our Values Develop

There is now a fair amount of evidence that moral and ethical development proceeds in predictable stages as a child grows and develops. The two primary theorists on the moral development of children have been Jean Piaget and Lawrence Kohlberg (Carpendale, 2000). Their theories have enough similarities to allow us to summarize some of their major points together.

They both believed that children essentially lack any sense of right or wrong when they are born. In their first few years of life, children gradually pick up the rules of behavior expected of them, learning to some degree that they must obey parents or other adult authorities or else risk disapproval and punishment. Their basic approach to life, however, is to satisfy their own needs. They react to their environment reflexively. By the time children are 8 to 10 years old, they are beginning to adapt to the moral codes required of them by their environment. They realize that they are expected to behave in particular ways and often conform in order to be seen as good boys and girls. As adolescence and young adulthood progress, they become increasingly aware of the attitudes and values espoused by their social networks and gradually define the standards of morality and the ethical principles they want to guide their own lives.

In a pluralistic society such as our own, it is impossible to find general agreement with any particular

Table 8.4	*Influence of Religion on Attitudes toward Sexual Behavior*			
	Very Religious	**Religious**	**Slightly Religious**	**Not Religious**
That My Sex Practices Are in Harmony with My Religion Is:				
Very important	45%	18%	2%	3%
Important	36	38	24	8
Not sure	7	24	26	15
Unimportant	5	17	37	37
Very unimportant	7	3	11	37
Very important + Important	81%	56%	26%	11%
Unimportant + Very unimportant	12%	20%	48%	74%
N =	262	857	976	611

Source: From S. S. Janus & C. L. Janus, *The Janus Report on Sexual Behavior.* Copyright © 1993 by Samuel S. Janus and Cynthia L. Janus. Reprinted with permission.

approach to sexual morality and values. However, several widely accepted moral principles seem to be in effect today, and they are supported by most religious teachings as well (Reiss, 2002):

1. *The principle of noncoercion.* People should not be forced to engage in sexual expression. Sexual expression should occur only when there is voluntary consent.
2. *The principle of nondeceit.* People are not to be enticed into sexual expression based on fraud or deception.
3. *The principle of treatment of people as ends.* People are not to be used solely as a means to one's own satisfaction; they must be treated as ends in themselves, with their own needs and rights.
4. *The principle of respect for beliefs.* People must show respect for the sexual values and beliefs of others. This means that one person should not pressure another to act in a way not in accord with the other's sexual values and beliefs. However, this does not preclude someone from attempting to persuade others rationally that they are mistaken in their beliefs.

People sometimes make what they view as sexual mistakes. But even mistakes can provide a useful purpose by further clarifying one's personal code of sexual morality and conduct. The balancing act between satisfying one's own sexual needs and living up to the moral principles demanded by one's belief systems may actually last a lifetime. Every stage of life offers new sets of sexual decisions and questions to be resolved, and society's values are always shifting.

Facing Ethical Dilemmas

Sexuality can be a confusing part of life, and most of us eventually face some dilemma in which the most ethical choice to make is not clear. Sometimes it may even seem as though there is no entirely right choice. As a student in an ethics course once said to me, "You can make any choice into the right one with some mental gymnastics." While analyzing ethical dilemmas may indeed yield more than one way to proceed and people may sometimes do their best to make a poor choice seem like a good one, it is also true that some answers really are better than others.

Psychologists have been studying moral decision making for many years, and they have developed several indicators for understanding personal morality. It is generally agreed that moral behavior, or ethically proper behavior, will be helpful to another person and will be motivated by this knowledge. Dilemmas arise with the realization that the behavior has broader implications, given that not every helpful behavior would necessarily be considered right.

Think of some behaviors that might ultimately be helpful to someone else but still wouldn't be considered right. Explain your answer.

Another aspect of morality is the expectation that behavior will conform with certain social norms. Every society establishes certain rules and expectations in order to accomplish shared goals. Certainly, social nonconformity sometimes is used as a form of protest against social rules that are considered unfair, but if it is simply a self-serving action to avoid social responsibility, such nonconformity would be considered ethically questionable. Theories of moral development suggest that individuals gradually internalize ethical standards without the need for external enforcement; coerced acts cannot really be considered as moral (Hennig, 2003; Pratt, 2003).

Psychologists see empathy, or identifying with the feelings of others, as a strong motivator for ethical behavior. Empathy for another can be very powerful, and it follows that we feel guilt if we act in opposition to the well-being of others. Such reactions are what help make up the human *conscience*.

Ethical dilemmas must also be subject to the reasoning of rational thought processes, as we think through issues concerning justice and balance. Perhaps one of the most dramatic aspects of a well-developed sense of morality is the willingness to put the needs and interests of someone else ahead of our own needs and interests, especially if some human cost is incurred through the action (Kaufman, 2010; Rest et al., 2000).

Sorting through ethical issues, therefore, involves thoughts, emotions, and eventually behavior. Over the years, I have found it useful to use an approach that was developed to help students cultivate well-reasoned responses to ethical problems presented by scientific research. There is evidence that practicing the application of the principles of this approach to ethical dilemmas can help people become better at identifying all the issues and reaching a suitable conclusion (Bebeau et al., 1995; Rizzo & Swisher, 2004).

There are five basic guidelines for analyzing an ethical dilemma:

1. *Describe the nature of the ethical conflicts involved.* Look for how the interests, rights, or obligations of the people involved seem to apply. Choices in life sometimes require looking at equally unfavorable alternatives and trying to decide between them. Finding all the points of ethical conflict in a dilemma can be difficult, but the deeper you look, the more issues you may find.
2. *Identify all the interested parties.* Beyond the individuals involved firsthand in the ethical dilemma, there may be others who could be impacted by the

Real People

Mike: Struggling with a Long-Distance Relationship

Let's return to Mike, the first-year college student intending to be faithful to his long-distance girl-friend, as described on page 197. During his second month away at college, his circumstances become more complicated.

Mike has become friends with other members of the intramural soccer team on which he plays. On a weekend evening in mid-October, the team has a party at an off-campus apartment of some of the upperclass students. A women's intramural team has been invited. Mike is happy to attend the party, because he has been feeling down after a phone conversation with his girlfriend earlier in the week. She hinted that maybe they ought to rethink their relationship and even begin seeing others. Mike expressed his anger and hurt over that option, communicating that he wanted to work hard at maintaining their commitment. Eventually, she agreed that she would abide by their original plan, and she apologized for upsetting him.

The beer at the party is plentiful, the music is loud, and everyone is having a good time. A young woman sits down beside Mike, and they strike up a conversation. He knows her from one of his biology classes and finds her attractive. Eventually, they become engrossed in conversation and with each other. They have a lot in common, and both are having some struggles with long-distance relationships.

As the evening progresses, the girl leans over and kisses Mike on the lips. He is surprised at first but reciprocates, and they continue making out. As others begin to disperse, Mike suggests that she come back to his dorm room with him. He explains that he is lonely but also does not want to do anything either one of them will regret. She kisses him and says that she doesn't believe in regrets.

On their walk back to campus, Mike realizes that he has had a lot to drink and that he probably isn't making the clearest decisions. He also is very curious about what might develop once they get back to his room. Once there, the young woman lies down on his bed and motions for him to join her. He obliges, and before long they are heavily involved in making out again. Eventually, she reaches down and unzips the fly on his pants, indicating that she is willing to perform oral sex on him.

Should Mike continue with this sexual encounter? What is the right thing for him to do? What are the points of ethical conflict raised by this situation? Besides Mike and the young woman he met at the party, who else could be affected by the decisions made and the actions taken? What are the potential consequences of the various actions that could be taken now or have already been taken? What duties and obligations does Mike have?

choices made or by potential consequences of those choices. Paying attention to all these interests may clarify even more issues that are in conflict.

3. *Think about possible consequences.* While there is no point in identifying every conceivable consequence, anticipating those that are most likely to occur can be reasonably easy. As you examine various reasonable consequences of different ethical choices, you will also want to consider the effects on all the interested parties.

4. *Examine the obligations of the main players in the dilemma.* We all have certain obligations to behave in ethical ways, as specified in our belief systems, societal or institutional expectations, and the legal system. Sorting through these obligations

is essential to making a well-reasoned choice in an ethical dilemma.

5. *To the extent possible, discuss the dilemma with others.* Although sex-related situations may demand confidentiality and the protection of others' privacy, it is often helpful to seek input from trusted others who can give you new insights and points to be weighed in the decision making. We can sometimes miss things that other people will see more clearly. Give the process a chance whenever you can.

Now consider Mike's sexual situation, in the "Real People" box, involving a very real ethical dilemma, and use the guidelines above to sort through all the

■ FIGURE 8.9 *Loving Relationships*

An important part of finding healthy sexual values is determining the place of loving relationships in your life. Although loving and sex are often linked within relationships, they do not necessarily need to be.

points mentioned. Explore whether the approach can help make you more comfortable with recommending how the situation should be resolved.

Finding Healthy Sexual Values

Achieving a healthy sexuality requires a level of consistency between a person's behaviors and values (see Figure 8.9). In recent years, different social factions and political groups have claimed to have values that represent the moral high ground. Someone trying to arrive at a personal set of values might find these divergent positions quite confusing. One unfortunate consequence of this confusion for many people is their simply choosing not to choose. Instead of thinking through their values and deciding in advance how they will want to behave in certain sexual situations, they wait until they are swept away by passion or by a persuasive partner. This then may become an excuse for denying responsibility for sex or its consequences.

There are several steps you can take to establish your own set of values regarding sex:

1. Know yourself and work toward acceptance of your sexual needs and orientation. Basic to the success of any code of values is feeling good about yourself. Even if you find that there are some aspects of your sexuality you would not feel comfortable acting on, it is important that you accept them as part of you.

2. Try not to let yourself be bound by popular sexual standards with which you are personally uncomfortable. Popular songs, television programs, advertising, and the Internet promulgate specific values about sex and sexual attractiveness. You may at times receive pressure from peers about what is currently in vogue sexually. Weigh all this information carefully, decide how much you want and need to fit in with a particular group, and then choose how you want to proceed sexually.

3. Examine your feelings about religion and find out what your religion has to say about sexual matters. You may be surprised. Many religious groups have given careful consideration to human sexuality and have devised written guidelines to help with personal decision making. You will need to consider just how important your religious background and your current feelings about religion are to you. Even if you do not consider yourself religious, you may want to explore your spiritual dimensions and how they relate to your sexuality.

4. Think ahead. It is a good idea to think carefully about various sexual situations and issues and to anticipate how you might react to them. This is an excellent way to clarify your personal values about sex. For example, when do you think it is all right for two people to share a sexual relationship? What are some of the possible consequences of various sexual activities, and how would you deal with those consequences? How will you ensure that anyone involved in a sexual encounter will be protected against disease?

5. Consider what level of responsibility you have toward other people. Most forms of sex involve interaction between people. Whenever interpersonal relationships are involved, the issue of responsibility to others comes up. How do you think you should treat others? What degree of responsibility do you have not to put others in exploitative or potentially hurtful situations?

6. Remember that you are not a mind reader. This is where good communication comes in. Part of sexual values must be knowing how a potential sexual partner thinks and feels about sex before

you get involved. You will need to spend time and energy communicating in order to find out what these are.

7. Decide what role you want loving relationships to play in your life. Loving and sex often are intertwined in relationships, though not necessarily. An important part of establishing your own sex-related values is knowing how you feel about the place of loving relationships in your life.

8. Take opportunities to clarify your sexual values on an ongoing basis. Sexuality education books, classes, and discussion groups provide opportunities for understanding your own sexual values more fully. The Internet has fine websites with good information about sexuality, along with its more explicit sites. Making use of opportunities to clarify values can keep your personal code of moral behavior clear and workable for everyday life.

■ Sexuality and Disability Groups

Physical and mental disabilities may influence a person's sexuality in many different ways. They can affect self-perception and social relationships. Only too often persons with disabilities are assumed to be asexual or too impaired to have functional sexual responses. These assumptions rarely have any basis in fact. Public consciousness about the needs and rights of individuals with disabilities is leading to greater levels of understanding and acceptance, but many barriers and complications still hamper such people in their attempt to find a fulfilling and meaningful place for their sexuality in their lives.

Adults with disabilities are likely to find acceptance in their roles as fellow employees or casual friends but are much less likely to find themselves perceived as potential dating or sexual partners. Myths and misconceptions about the needs of children with disabilities may lead to impediments in their development as healthy sexual individuals. Parents, educators, counselors, and caregivers for people with disabilities have a special responsibility to not ignore or deny the sexual natures of these individuals. Sexuality needs to be part of a holistic approach in dealing with the special needs and concerns of people with particular disabilities (Ballan, 2004).

Most conditions that are called disabilities do not directly affect the sex organs or their ability to function, nor do they affect the individual's sexual feelings, need for sex, or desire to be physically and emotionally intimate with others (see Figure 8.10). They may, however, have a great effect on how people with disabilities view their own attractiveness and the degree

■ FIGURE 8.10   *Sexuality and People with Disabilities*

People with physical and mental disabilities have as much right to intimacy and sexual pleasure as anyone else. The quality of the sexual relationship will depend, as in any relationship, on the quality of the total care and respect each partner has for the other.

to which they seek sexual relationships. Consider a man with a serious skin disease that causes unsightly blotches all over his body, or a woman born with cerebral palsy who has difficulty controlling her arm movements and speech. Although these individuals have the same sexual interests and attractions as anyone else, they may find themselves limited by their own perceptions and by the prejudice and misunderstanding of others. Today we have a wider acceptance of the notion that sexual pleasuring need not be viewed solely as an act of sex organs but rather as an intimate emotional and physical connection between two human beings that may involve a variety of behaviors. This perspective on sexual interaction is particularly valuable in people with disabilities, who may have to make special accommodations in their sexual practices (Mercan et al., 2008; Tepper, 2001).

Intellectual or Developmental Disability

One of the most sexually oppressed groups of people with disabilities are those with an intellectual or developmental disability. The historical roots of this problem include the fear that sexual activity among those who are intellectually disabled would lead to pregnancies and the risk of passing on genetic defects to children. The trend has been toward integrating individuals with intellectual disabilities into the community as much as possible, training them in the kinds of skills that will help them interact in socially acceptable ways. There is evidence that people with such disabilities often lack crucial knowledge about their sexuality. Teenagers with mental disabilities often have sexual intercourse with inadequate knowledge about contraception or disease prevention (Cheng & Udry, 2003). People with attention deficit disorder may experience difficulty achieving intimacy with partners unless they receive appropriate skills training (Betchen, 2003). A cooperative program of education and socialization involving both the school and parents can often be effective in helping those with developmental disabilities adapt to their sexual needs (Littner, Littner, & Shah, 2001).

Educational efforts have been shown to foster both cognitive and behavioral change that will help the developmentally disabled understand and manage their sexual needs. Gradually, those with mental disabilities have been helped to articulate their sexual rights, and educational efforts have been improving. The principle of **normalization** came to the United States in the 1960s from Scandinavia and has led to the development of simplified programs in social skills and sexuality education for use with those who have intellectual disabilities. Such programs are designed to help the intellectually disabled adapt to the norms and patterns of mainstream social life (see Figure 8.11). Some couples with developmental disabilities have been able to marry and have learned how to manage their social and sexual lives effectively as the result of these new efforts.

What guidelines do you think should be in place regarding sexual activity between intellectually impaired people?

Visual and Auditory Disabilities

Individuals with visual or hearing impairments face two major challenges in developing sexual awareness. The first is gaining an understanding of sex and sexuality. People with impaired sight cannot see diagrams that could help them understand anatomy and physiol-

FIGURE 8.11 *Sexuality and Developmental Disability*

With the proper instruction in meeting their own sexual needs and in following the rules and ethics of a given society's sexual behavior, some people with developmental disabilities can lead fulfilling lives in a mutually supportive relationship.

ogy. People who are hearing impaired are limited in how information can be presented to them. The second major difficulty lies in the socialization process. Those who are visually or hearing impaired often are hindered in their social contacts because others are uncomfortable with their disabilities and may feel afraid or embarrassed about their own attempts to communicate. Some of the usual routes for interpersonal communication are blocked. People who are severely visually impaired cannot read the subtleties of facial expressions and body language. People with hearing impairments may miss words in lip reading or might risk being misunderstood when they use sign language with someone who is unfamiliar with it (Getch, 2001).

Sexuality educators for the sensorially impaired have met some of these challenges. Life-size plastic models of human sexual anatomy are now available, as are visual materials such as models, charts, photographs, slides, and transparencies. Captioning services for much of television programming and for visual sexuality education aids provide another opportunity for the hearing impaired to understand the material (Kaufman, Silverberg, & Odette, 2007).

See "Mark Discusses Sex after Spinal Cord Injury" on SexSource Online.

normalization integration of mentally retarded persons into the social mainstream as much as possible.

Spinal Cord Injuries

The spinal cord, running through the vertebrae that make up the backbone, is the nervous system's major link between the brain and the body's various organs. Injuries to the back or neck can cause damage—or even complete severing—of the spinal cord. If an injury does not prove fatal, there may still be interruption of nerve messages to the parts of the body below the injury, resulting in partial or total paralysis of those organs and muscles. There may be little or no sensation, and the muscles can no longer be directed by the brain to contract. Usually the paralysis is permanent. If only the legs are paralyzed, the person is said to be **paraplegic;** if the arms are involved as well, the term used is **quadriplegic.**

It is often assumed that paraplegics and quadriplegics are incapable of sexual sensations or response, but this is not necessarily the case. In a study of 140 males and 46 females with spinal cord injury (SCI), about 25 percent of the males and up to 50 percent of the females reported having sensations in the genital area. By the third year after their injuries, nearly all the females and 90 percent of the males had resumed sexual intercourse and other sexual activities. The degree of interference with sexual functions depends on the exact location and extent of the SCI. When paralysis of the pelvic region exists, thinking sexy thoughts or having sexual needs no longer has any effect on the genitals, because the connection with the brain has been lost. However, erection of the penis and lubrication of the vagina are also partially controlled by a localized spinal reflex (Phelps et al., 2001). Many paralyzed men and women can experience arousal of their sex organs, and sometimes even orgasm, through direct stimulation. Feeling may also remain intact in small areas of skin in the pelvic area. Up to 40 percent of quadriplegic males are able to have an orgasm accompanied by ejaculation. Brain responses as recorded by scanning images in women with SCI suggest that genital stimulation may convey input directly to the brain, somehow bypassing the spinal injury (Alexander & Rosen, 2008; Sipski, Rosen, Alexander, & Gómez-Marín, 2004; Whipple & Komisaruk, 2002).

Each case of SCI is unique, but any patient and his or her partner can learn new forms of sexual expression. Often, intercourse is still possible by making adjustments in position. Some paraplegics and quadriplegics have a bladder catheter (tube) in place to carry urine out of the body to a storage bag. Although the catheter may be an inconvenience during sex, a couple committed to maintaining their sexual relationship can learn how to accommodate it. Some success has also been achieved with the use of erection medications or with the implantation of electrodes on localized nerves that can be stimulated by the individual to increase bladder control or even produce increased blood flow to the genitals (Moemen et al., 2008; Phelps et al., 2001).

Often, the partners of people with SCI are left out of the adjustment and rehabilitation process. They, too, have many emotional issues to resolve as they face a very stressful time adjusting to the changes that occur in the relationship, including its sexual dimensions. When one partner in a couple suffers injury, the relational difficulties frequently lead to disharmony or a breakup of the relationship. With appropriate and skilled professional help, couples can learn how to recapture a viable emotional and physical relationship following the devastating effects of SCI (Tepper et al., 2001).

Other Physical and Mental Disabilities

Many chronic physical conditions or injuries and mental illnesses can affect sexual functioning and the place of sexuality in relationships. There may be diseased or damaged sex organs, general physical debilitation that lowers interest and energy for sex, difficulty in socializing, or lowered self-worth (Kaufman, Silverberg, & Odette, 2007).

Cerebral palsy, for example, can cause spastic conditions in various parts of the body. Traumatic brain injury may necessitate the relearning of roles and appropriate sexual behaviors within the context of a family and other social contexts. A variety of neuromuscular conditions, such as multiple sclerosis and muscular dystrophy, can result in gradual loss of bodily control and can change sexual relationships (McCabe et al., 2003). Chronic lung disease makes exertion during sex difficult and uncomfortable.

Terminally ill patients often experience sexual disruption because of internal stress, which in turn affects relationships. They may feel guilty about experiencing sexual arousal, and their lovers may find it difficult to desire intimacy amid the anticipatory grief or fear of their partner's fatal illness. However, open communication and, when available, counseling and the opportunity for privacy in hospital settings can all help with the sexual adjustments of long-term illness and palliative care (Redelman, 2008).

Maintaining involvement in sexual activities can help maintain a person's sense of integrity and personal

paraplegic a person paralyzed in the legs, and sometimes pelvic area, as the result of injury to the spinal cord.

quadriplegic a person paralyzed in the upper body, including the arms, and the lower body as the result of spinal cord injury.

self-worth, regardless of disabilities. For people whose physical disabilities may interfere with the coordination of masturbation or shared sex, some assistance from a health aide may be necessary. This **facilitated sex** obviously requires special sensitivity and training on the part of the aides or facilitators. It is important to guard the individual's privacy and dignity as much as possible while establishing the conditions necessary for sexual pleasure. This is a relatively new—and controversial—aspect of health care, yet it surely is a sensible extension of the other quality-of-life services provided to persons with disabilities (Melby, 2003).

Institutions and Sexual Issues

Some people with disabilities and chronic illnesses require long-term institutional care, in which case sexual problems may multiply. Where the sexes are segregated, institutional residents may be limited to same-gender sexual contact. They may have little privacy for masturbation or shared sex. The keys to preventing desexualization in institutions are the attitude of the staff and their understanding of the different levels of need that different people might have. Some institutions have provided condoms for patient use, along with educational efforts, and have found that these actions do not cause an increase in patient sexual activity. In-service training on sex-related issues and the establishment of humane administrative policies regarding sex can help. The first step in preventing sexual problems among the disabled or institutionalized is admitting that all human beings are sexual and have a right to find the best ways for them, as individuals, to express their sexuality. Steps then may be taken to categorize people according to the types of help they may require in order to realize and take charge of their own sexual identities and needs (Perry & Wright, 2006).

facilitated sex assistance provided to a person with severe physical disabilities in order to enable them to achieve sexual pleasure through masturbation or with a partner.

Chapter Summary

1. Societies place great meaning on sexuality, and people have the potential for deriving both pleasure and discomfort from their sexual choices.

2. Definitions of normalcy and abnormalcy are influenced by prevailing social norms.

3. General labels such as deviation, variation, and paraphilia have been applied to sexual activities and preferences that fall outside the accepted norm.

4. In present-day Western culture, sex is still judged by several fundamental standards: two-person heterosexuality, a focus on coitus, expectation of orgasm and romantic feelings, and degree of safety.

5. The World Association for Sexual Health has adopted and promulgated a Universal Declaration of Sexual Right that affirms a wide range of freedoms regarding sexuality.

6. The ethnocentric attitude that one's own culture has the right standards in relation to sexuality can be called erotocentricity.

7. The concept of normalcy can be determined by statistical norms, by prevailing expert opinion (such as the DSM), by moral standards perpetuated by religion and law, or as part of a more flexible continuum. Normalcy is a relative concept.

8. Labels represent generalities and are an inadequate aid to a full understanding of a particular person's sexuality.

9. The term "homosexual" often has negative connotations. The terms "gay" and "lesbian" are used in reference to people when describing same-gender orientation. The term "bisexual" is used to describe some level of attraction to, or activity with, members of both sexes.

10. The factors that lead to the development of sexual individuality are highly complex. Patterns seem to be established by adolescence and probably develop through a combination of learning experiences superimposed on some biological predispositions.

11. Social networks rather than relationships with parents seem to be important in shaping sexual attitudes and behaviors.

12. The Klein Sexual Orientation Grid demonstrates seven different variables that play a role in

determining sexual orientation or identity. Sexual individuality includes many different life dimensions.

13. Sexual choices are affected by sexual attitudes. The National Health and Social Life Survey has identified three broad categories of sex-related attitudes in the United States: traditional, relational, and recreational. There is no single system of American values regarding sex.

14. Clear links have been observed between sexual attitudes and sexual practices, number of partners, and how often a person thinks about sex. Frequency of sex does not seem to be related to attitudinal group.

15. Some people have negative feelings and discriminatory attitudes about gay, lesbian, bisexual, and transgender people. These fears and misconceptions are called homophobia, biphobia, or transphobia. Professional organizations no longer view same-gender orientation within the framework of pathology.

16. Decisions about sexuality often are made after weighing moral values, religious teachings, and ethical beliefs. Some believe that moral values are built-in, whereas others believe that they are socially constructed.

17. Different ethical traditions influence sexual morality: legalistic ethics, moral relativism and situation ethics, the extremes of the hedonistic and ascetic traditions, and holistic belief systems.

18. Many believe that spirituality is connected to sexuality. In recent years, religions have been debating and changing their positions with regard to sexuality.

19. Research shows that religious belief systems influence sexual behavior.

20. Noncoercion, nondeceit, not using people solely for one's own pleasure, and respect for the beliefs of others are moral principles that guide sexual decisions today.

21. Some answers to moral dilemmas are better than others, and by considering many dimensions of a dilemma, well-reasoned ethical responses may be found.

22. In developing sexual values that are right for you, it is necessary to see how you will align yourself with the values of your society and culture. Self-examination and introspection are necessary to making decisions that will be healthy and non-hurtful for yourself and others.

23. People with disabilities have the right to recognition and expression of their sexuality.

24. Intellectually or developmentally disabled people need special approaches to sexuality education, including learning how to express their sexuality in private and how to employ appropriate methods of birth control.

25. Spinal cord injuries may affect physical aspects of sexual response. Most paraplegics and quadriplegics can find levels of sexual functioning that will be satisfying to themselves and their partners. Many couples experience relational problems after one partner has had such an injury.

26. Facilitated sex may be an option for people with severe physical disabilities.

Chapter 9

Sexuality, Communication, and Relationships

Chapter Outline

He was my first real love, and my first sexual partner. I honestly thought it would last forever. We certainly made each other enough promises that it would. Obviously we were wrong. For about a week, I thought I would never get over it, but I did. I think we're both pretty happy now, and I really wish only the best for him.

—by a student following the breakup of a relationship

Have you ever had a relationship in which it seemed as though you would never want to be apart from the one you loved, and then you experienced falling out of love? Have you ever been involved in a relationship in which your partner was more attached than you were and you couldn't find an easy way to extricate yourself? Can you explain what it means to be lovesick? One way or another, most of us get our hearts broken eventually.

Nevertheless, people long for the intimacy, companionship, sharing, and contentment that we associate with loving relationships. Sometimes, a relationship also brings sexual sharing, and young couples tend to become sexually active together within the first few months of their relationship (Kaestle & Halpern, 2007). Data from the National Health and Social Life Survey (NHSLS) indicated that of those individuals who freely wanted their first sexual intercourse, women were nearly twice as likely as men to say they loved their first sex partner. Among those who said that their first intercourse was not particularly wanted but they went along with it anyway, 10 percent of the men and 38 percent of the women said they loved the partner (Michael et al., 1994). These statistics would indicate that, at least in their initial heterosexual experiences, females are more likely than males to feel romantically involved with a partner.

Men sometimes wonder if nice guys finish last in the sexual arena, and the question has actually been researched. Although definitions of nice guy characteristics certainly vary, the majority of women report a preference for nice guys, whom they assume to have had fewer sexual partners. In fact, nice guys who respect women and are sensitive communicators are preferred for friendships and committed, intimate relationships (Herold & Milhausen, 1999).

See "Mike on Dating, Sex, and the Bar Scene" on SexSource Online.

Keeping any relationship on an even keel can be complicated enough; bringing sexual feelings or activities into the picture often only adds complexity and confusion. One major foundation for a healthy, lasting relationship is effective communication between people who feel relatively comfortable and confident with themselves. Couples who have communication difficulties are more likely to experience sexual problems. As any counselor can testify, relationships typically suffer tension and crisis when the communication process has become blocked or muddled (Kelly, Strassberg, &

Turner, 2006). This chapter deals with that process, its role in relationships, and how to keep lines of communication open.

■ Communicating about Sex

Communication is an ongoing, dynamic process. It has been said that "one cannot not communicate." Even silence and avoiding another person convey certain messages, often very powerful ones. Unfortunately, many people do not realize the importance of communication in building a healthy sexual relationship. As a male student once stated to me, "Sex is something you do with each other; you shouldn't have to talk about it." That philosophy might work fine if people were simply walking sex organs who slipped in and out of sexual encounters. Instead, human beings have a range of thoughts, feelings, fantasies, and needs that must be shared if we are to maintain relationships within and beyond the bedroom. Research has demonstrated that long-term couples who disclose information about their sexual interests and concerns have higher levels of satisfaction with their relationships than those who do not (MacNeil & Byers, 2009).

A great many sexual problems could be prevented or resolved through open, honest communication, yet people often seem reluctant to pursue such communication. Joking about sex seems easier for some people than asking about a potential partner's sexual history or explaining to a partner how they feel or what they might like to do sexually. Using a slang term may seem less intimidating than using a scientifically correct word. In a society where sexuality is often viewed in terms of problems, it is easy to lose sight of the fact that attaining sexual pleasure is a legitimate human goal.

The Communication Process

Just about anything can be communicated—ideas, feelings, attitudes and values, needs and desires. Our eyes, facial expressions, and body language convey a great many messages. The tone and intonation of voice we use in speaking are crucial in communicating subtle aspects of our message. Words are an important ingredient in any communicative interaction, but they are also imperfect and often imprecise. In our society, when we talk about sex we tend to be caught between terms that are either too scientific or too vulgar to be appropriate in all circumstances. Their meanings may be interpreted differently by different people.

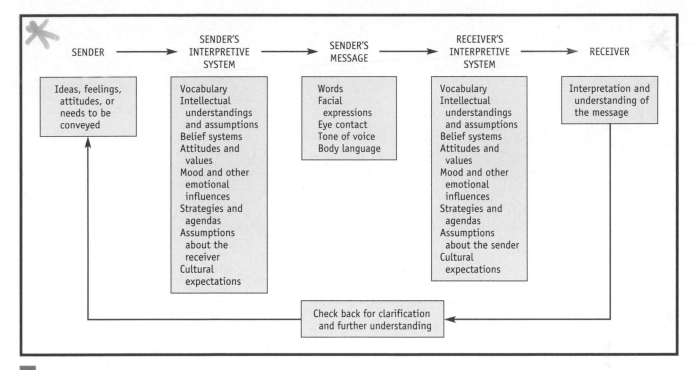

FIGURE 9.1 *The Process of Communication*

Whatever is to be conveyed from one person to another is filtered through each person's individualized interpretive system. Therefore, the message intended by the sender may be quite different from the message picked up and understood by the receiver. An active feedback system is one of the best ways to keep communication on track.

Communication is filled with subtleties and opportunities for misinterpretation. It is not surprising, then, that human communication sometimes is fraught with complications and misunderstandings. Figure 9.1 illustrates the basics of any process of communication. Someone, the sender, has a thought to be conveyed to someone else, who becomes the receiver. Many factors influence the way the sender's message is formed. It is made up of specific understandings of certain words and also is filled with beliefs, attitudes and values, cultural expectations, and emotions.

The sender might well hope to fulfill a particular agenda or accomplish some objective. As the thought to be conveyed is filtered through this interpretive system, the message takes shape and is sent to the receiver. It is then filtered through the receiver's own very individualized interpretive system, from which that person then draws his or her own understanding of the message. The process is complicated enough that the message intended by the sender may not be at all the message understood by the receiver. Figure 9.2 shows how misunderstandings can take place. Communication works best when there is a well-developed feedback system in place through which the receiver can ask for clarification and check out the assumptions that have been made in understanding the message. Good communication takes a committed effort from everyone involved so that misinterpretations and misunderstandings are kept to a minimum.

The Words We Use to Talk about Sex

The appropriateness of particular words can change over time, sometimes relatively rapidly. In early-twentieth-century America, the words *leg, bull,* and *pregnant* were considered taboo for mixed company because of their presumed sexual connotations. Even in reference to fowl, the terms *drumstick* and *dark meat* were substituted for leg. Bulls were referred to as "he-animals," and pregnant women were said to be "expecting" or "in confinement." A generation ago, the term *suck* had clearly sexual meanings not expressed in public, and the slang word *dork* meant penis. Today suck has become a commonplace term used to describe almost anything in a negative way, and *dork* is used like the word *jerk*. These and many other terms have gradually found their way into common usage, reflecting changing social values.

For some people and in some contexts, the proper scientific terminology about sex may seem more inappropriate or embarrassing than slang terms. This is probably one reason why so many slang terms exist for the description of sex-related body parts and sexual activities. Some research demonstrates the changing

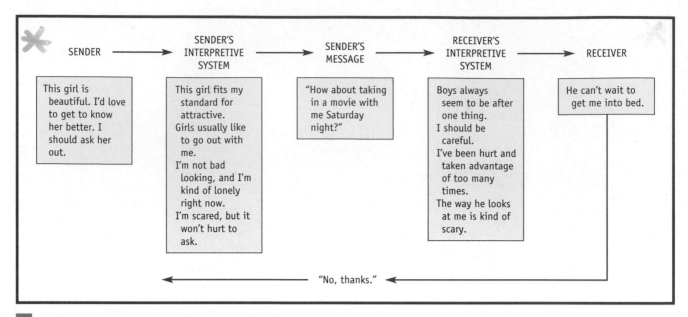

FIGURE 9.2   *Misunderstood Communication*

The process of communication may yield a misunderstanding between sender and receiver.

nature of sexual slang among college students. Three decades ago, a study (Sanders, 1978) showed that when talking with a lover, men were most likely to refer to their own sex organ as a "dick" (26 percent) or "penis" (25 percent) or to avoid using any term at all (17 percent). In contrast, only 8 percent of women used the term "dick." Nearly half the women would say "penis," and 18.5 percent used no term for the male organ. In data gathered a decade later with another sample of college students, these trends again became clear, but a significantly greater number of men and women reported that they would use no term at all in reference to the penis (Fischer, 1989).

In 1978, women were even less likely than men to name their own sex organs in intimate conversations, with nearly 25 percent avoiding the use of any term. Those who did use some term were most likely to say "vagina" (32 percent). Men were somewhat more likely to use the term *pussy* (22 percent) to describe their partner's genitals than they were the term *vagina* (19.4 percent). The term *cunt* was more frequently used by men (14 percent) than by women (1 percent), who are more apt to find the term offensive.

In the follow-up study, women were still much less likely to use slang terms to describe the vagina than were men. Again, both sexes showed a much higher number of individuals who would use no term at all to describe the female genitals. The expression "sexual intercourse" was used by over 10 percent of both men and women in 1978, although "make love" was far more popular among both women (56 percent) and men (32 percent). Men used the term *fuck* in their intimate conversations more than women did,

although men were more likely to use this word in the presence of other men than in the presence of women. The term *having sex* became more popular, with *intercourse* being used much less frequently. Students in the more recent study were less likely to use terms such as *fuck* or *screw* and again more likely to use no term at all to describe sexual intercourse (Fischer, 1989).

A more recent study found that the slang terms applied to female genitals tend to be vaguer than those applied to male genitals and that men tend to use more negative terms about female organs than about their own. When describing the penis, men are more likely to use what has been called "power slang," with labels such as *rod, womp,* and *pistol.* Women tend toward "cute" euphemisms such as *penie, oscar,* or *baby-maker.* Whereas males tend to use very specific terms to describe their own genitals, women tend toward more nonspecific personal terms such as *me, mine, she,* or *my body* (Braun & Kitzinger, 2001). Women have been shown to be somewhat more reluctant to use sexual terms than are men (Geer & Melton, 1997). Men tend to be more comfortable than women today using terms such as *fucking, cunt,* or *cock,* although words such as *lovemaking, vagina,* and *penis* are generally more acceptable to both genders.

What makes communicating about relationships and sexual issues difficult?

Every relationship will evolve its own vocabulary for intimate discussions of sex. Nearly 60 percent of

Real Student Voices

■ I really love my girlfriend, and we are sexually involved. However, she doesn't talk much about what she enjoys during sex, and I often feel as though she doesn't enjoy it all that much. I'm confused as to whether this is because of something going on with her, or something wrong with my technique.

■ I can't seem to get J to talk about his feelings, and that is very frustrating to me. He says I want to talk about feelings too much, and sometimes he just wants to be quiet and enjoy being together. He also thinks I worry too much about the relationship. Maybe I do, but it's important to me.

■ The two of us are able to talk about everything and anything, which is a lot different from my former relationships. I never thought I could have this kind of relationship, but it is great. We have no secrets.

---

the women and men in one study considered "talking dirty" to be acceptable within their relationships. Using playful terms to name their genitals has been found to be therapeutic for couples experiencing sexual problems (Godow, 1999). The important thing is that both partners feel comfortable with the terms they use. Neither should employ words that seem offensive, insensitive, or insulting to the other. Working out the details of acceptable terminology may itself require some careful communication and negotiation.

Contemporary Myths about Communication

All societies have certain unwritten rules that govern how communication is supposed to take place, and these rules often rise to the level of myths. Here are some of the myths that typically play a role in our interactions with others, and they may interfere with effective communication:

Myth 1: You should have a confident opinion on every issue. We live in opinionated times. If you listen carefully to the disagreements that people have with one another in everyday life, you will notice that many individuals argue their points without much solid information to back them up. Even when it comes to sex, many people behave as if they must have all the answers, and they never appear uncertain or insecure. The truth of the matter is that nearly everyone feels somewhat shy and scared in new situations, in meeting new people, and in forming new relationships. There is usually an initial, tense period during which we begin evaluating what we will have to offer each other. When we find ourselves in a position where we think we have to offer an opinion about some subject about which we know very little, it can be perfectly acceptable to say, "I'd really have

to think that through before I could have much of an opinion about it."

Myth 2: An impressive conversationalist never permits any dead air. The most uncomfortable part of any conversation can be silence. The fear of silence can force people to fill the air with words. Silence imposes a kind of intimacy when two people have to look at each other momentarily. That intimacy can make us feel vulnerable, so we search for topics that will help us keep each other at words' length. However, when we want to become closer to someone and develop a deeper relationship, being able to be quiet—and to listen carefully—can be important elements of communication.

Myth 3: Mapping out strategies ahead of time makes for better communication. A young man who was a counseling client of mine told me about the advice a friend had given him before a date at a fraternity party. It went something like this: "Stay loose. Keep three or four things in mind to talk about, but only use them when the conversation lags. Don't look too interested. Look a little bored. When you look hard to get, women chase even harder. Don't look too anxious." My client tried to carry out this strategy at the party, only to end up feeling foolish. As popular and common as they may be, planned communication strategies set up games to which only one person knows the rules. Sometimes they work, but even then the relationship has been established on the basis of manipulation or even dishonesty. Usually the best strategy is to work at being yourself.

Myth 4: Using the right line will convince a partner to have sex. Rarely are relationships that simple. While one partner is rehearsing the line to carry out a seduction, the other partner may well be rehearsing the best way to turn down the proposition. Sexual relationships that grow out of prefabricated lines rarely are effective or lasting, and enticing someone into sex in this manner is ethically objectionable.

Myth 5: The rational mind is the only basis for effective communication. People often make the mistake of assuming that logical, rational thought processes constitute the only basis of good communication. There is a common misconception that "feelings only get in the way." In fact, emotional reactions are a legitimate part of what human beings need to communicate, especially in close relationships. To work with only one aspect of human nature during communication is to ignore crucial parts of yourself that need to be shared.

These myths can stifle good communication. They stimulate the development of games, phony conversation, manipulative sexual seduction, and shallow relationships. When effective communication is lacking, even minor sexual problems are more likely to turn into major ones.

See "Communicating about Sex" on SexSource Online.

The Sexual Games We Play

Romantic and sexual relationships may result in posturing and attempts at reverse psychology to achieve certain ends. Whether it is playing hard to get in order to win over the heart of Mr. or Ms. Right or deciding not to return a call until a certain amount of time has passed, people try to develop a strategy that will help them feel they can control an outcome. We live with the illusion that if we always do X and Y, we automatically will get Z as the result. Human relationships are more complicated than that. They must be approached in very individualized ways. Nevertheless, people are forever playing games with one another when it comes to sex and relationships.

Power Games

Sex is a common arena for people to express their struggles for power over each other, and most relationships have their share of such struggles. An individual who is fearful of appearing vulnerable may always want to be in a dominant position during sexual activity, quite literally needing always to be on top. Someone who resents something about a partner might show little interest in sex to punish the other person through the withholding of sexual activity. Some men and women use power games to spoil sex by being unavailable at the right time. Being drunk sometimes may be a handy way either to avoid sex or to justify a sexual failure. Some people play hard to get by being too busy, too tired, or emotionally detached. Power games can turn into a sort of sexual sabotage in which one partner manages to ruin a sexual encounter without looking like the guilty party. Dropping some subtle criticisms about the other person's sexual performance may sometimes lower that individual's level of sexual interest considerably. As long as these power struggles proceed, sexual sharing will have its difficulties.

Relationship Games

Some men and women bring unresolved conflicts and emotional problems with them to their sexual relationships. A stormy relationship with a parent that has resulted in certain patterns of reaction may affect a person's present relationship if some of the old feelings are lingering inside (Erzar & Erzar, 2008). Mutual trust is a crucial factor in building intimacy and a satisfying sex life. When trust is lacking, the inner barriers stay up, holding a partner at a distance. People who feel as though significant others in their lives have always left them may test how much a partner will put up with. The partner is, in a sense, being called on to prove his or her love and devotion by sticking by the other person no matter what. Such games can create great strain in a relationship and often lead to its destruction.

Communication Games

One of the most common communication games is to push for the resolution of a conflict as quickly as possible. One partner, wanting the problem to be over, comes up with what seems the most logical solution and then tries to impose the solution on the other. The person might make statements such as "You shouldn't feel that way" or "Come on, cheer up" or "You're blowing this all out of proportion." In the face of such seemingly logical suggestions, the other person may end up feeling guilty for having the particular reaction and may pretend that all is resolved. Communication games may be designed to avoid confronting potentially hurtful feelings or situations. Yet when truly effective communication happens, both partners perceive that they have permission to feel and express whatever they need to. It's dangerous to fool yourself into thinking that some rough spots have been logically resolved when in actuality the discomfort is still simmering under the surface.

One key to a full and satisfying sexual relationship is knowing how to communicate effectively with a partner. That does not mean that you have to be an extrovert or be well versed in the social graces. Nor does it mean that you have to be a great conversationalist or even talk a great deal. What it does mean is that you must care enough about yourself, your partner, and the relationship to put some effort and energy into communicating with each other.

Before reading the section "Effective Communication," assume the role of counselor and list several strategies that you might suggest to a client seeking to improve her or his communication with a partner.

■ Effective Communication

People usually do not find it easy to communicate about the more intimate aspects of their lives, such as their own sexual orientation, a sexual activity they enjoy, or a preferred method of birth control. This section presents some basic guidelines for facilitating good lines of communication.

The Ground Rules

Some preliminary steps help open up channels for effective communication about sex or any other sensitive topic. Here are some ground rules for getting started:

1. *Think about the degree of commitment you hold for each other and the relationship.* Not much will happen with two-way communication unless both partners really want it to happen. Communicating honestly takes energy. You might begin to feel tired, frustrated, or hopeless at times, and it will take a solid commitment from both of you to see you through the more difficult steps.
2. *Know your own values.* Before you try communicating about sex, it is a good idea to have thought through where you stand on some of the value issues that may be involved. Know your own beliefs while letting yourself be open to the attitudes and values of the other individual.
3. *Understand your cultural differences.* If you are building a relationship with someone who has a cultural heritage different from your own, it will be important first to develop some fundamental

understanding of how you may differ in the words or expressions you use or in your levels of comfort in dealing with sexual issues. It is a good idea to spend some time discussing potential areas of conflict or misunderstanding before they turn into problems.
4. *Keep yourselves on equal ground.* A sense of equality between two people is usually essential to their communicating well. If someone always feels in the "one down" inferior position, he or she is unlikely to be able to communicate very openly or confidently. Power inequalities are dangerous to relationships (Gottman, 2000; McCabe, 2007).
5. *Build trust for each other.* When there is a lack of trust between two partners, there is likely to be a strain in their sexual interactions and a tendency toward reserved and uncomfortable communication. A sense of trust is fundamental to honest, genuine dialogue. Lack of trust can lead to stonewalling the other person during communication, a practice that can create serious obstacles in relationships (Williams & Payne, 2002).
6. *Pick the right location and time for talking.* Where and when you talk may be very important. You will both want to feel as relaxed and comfortable as possible and have adequate privacy. Sometimes bed is the ideal place to talk, but it also may produce an emotionally charged situation for some kinds of communication. Beware of atmospheres that encourage superficial conversations and games. Ask your partner where she or he would feel most comfortable talking, and be certain you feel comfortable there as well.

Making It Happen

A central message of this chapter is that the process of making good communication happen takes some deliberate effort. Sex is deeply personal to most of us, and to discuss it with someone else incurs a certain degree of vulnerability. Yet in a partnership in which sex is shared, words and feelings must also be shared. There are always decisions to be made, signals to be checked, worries to be resolved, and feelings to be discussed. Several qualities have repeatedly been shown through research to facilitate open and honest communication between people.

Demonstrate an Attitude of Warmth, Caring, and Respect

Feeling enough trust to open up to another person and share requires some sense of mutual positive regard. However, it is not enough to feel a sense of caring for another person; the feelings need to be demonstrated

FIGURE 9.3 *Communicating Warmth, Caring, Respect*
Loving relationships depend on attitudes of warmth, caring, and genuine respect for each other.

or communicated in some way (see Figure 9.3). Sometimes it may be a simple willingness to be quiet and listen attentively; other times it will require overt expressions of love or kindness. Patterns of criticism and contempt are extremely harmful to building positive communication (Gottman, 2000).

Avoid Making Snap Judgments and "All-ness" Statements

One of the greatest problems in human communication is the tendency to jump to premature conclusions and to make snap judgments about others. Most people open up best to those who are not judgmental. Because sex is one area of life about which people have strong opinions, intimate communication is improved when we set assumptions aside and allow other points of view to be expressed openly. In a more specific sense, it is also valuable to avoid using "all-ness" words such as *always* or *never*. When referring to another person, the use of statements including these words is rarely fair or accurate.

Listen Carefully and Really Hear

When people appear to be listening, they may actually be thinking ahead, formulating their response to what the other person is saying. It is all too easy for ideas and concepts to become garbled and misunderstood unless we listen carefully. Let yourself hear the other person out, and then think through your reactions and responses. Listening is not merely a passive state; it is an active process of being attuned to the words and nonverbal messages someone else is conveying.

Empathize and Understand That Feelings Need to Be Felt

Empathy is the ability to identify with what another person is feeling and to experience, in a sense, "walking a mile in his or her shoes." All of us have experienced a full range of emotions, though for different reasons. When listening to others, also listen for their feelings, and try to recall the experience of your own similar emotions. Two people who want to communicate about personal things must be willing to share emotions, even hurtful ones, and to empathize with each other. Empathy can help ward off our natural tendency to become defensive when we face disagreements. Constant defensiveness in a relationship can be a source of very real problems. Sensing that feelings are being heard and understood is one of the most crucial aspects of good communication.

Be Genuine

Most people can sense hidden agendas and deceptiveness and respond much more positively to genuineness and honesty. Effective communication about sexual matters must be based on openness. No lasting relationship can escape the need to communicate about difficulties and misunderstandings. Otherwise, these issues will accumulate under the surface and create problems later. For these reasons, you must work at being honest and being yourself in personal communications. Some level of self-disclosure about sexual feelings and needs enhances the sexual satisfaction experienced within relationships (MacNeil & Byers, 2009; McCabe, 2007).

Make Sense and Ask for Clarification

It is all too easy for words or mannerisms to be misunderstood in the communication process. We often make assumptions about what the other person means, without ever bothering to check out those assumptions with that individual. It takes work to listen carefully, understand what is being said, and then clarify whether your understanding is correct. It's a good idea occasionally to feed back your understanding to your partner by saying "So what I hear you saying is . . ." or "Do you mean . . . ?" When you have clarified your interpretation of his or her words, your partner is then able to correct any misconceptions. Then take the time you need to think it through, choose your words carefully, and give a focused response.

Do Not Let Silence Scare You

As pointed out earlier in this chapter, gaps in conversation often make people feel uneasy and vulnerable. Try to resist the need to fill such gaps with words. Instead, it is more important to take your time, allowing silence to be a part of communication at times. Silence also can be intimate and calming.

Beware of the "I Don't Want to Hurt You" Trap

In relationships, hurtful things must be shared. That sort of confrontation is not always easy, but in the long run it will help resolve tension-producing conflicts. It is not unusual for counselors to hear partners explain that they avoided dealing with painful topics because they were afraid of hurting someone's feelings. Of course, they also were avoiding their own discomfort that comes from talking about hurtful issues.

Use Self-Talk Effectively

How we talk to ourselves can have a profound effect on how we relate to other people. The things we say inside our own mind can color our emotions and our reactions both positively and negatively. For example, if during sex you are worrying about how you look or sound or are thinking negatively about your own body, sex is not likely to be a very positive experience. However, if you work at positive self-talk, emphasizing how good the experience seems and how much you are enjoying being with your partner, you are much more likely to find the experience enjoyable and fulfilling.

Communication Differences among Different Personality Types

Two things remain clear as we study personality: (1) It may be demonstrated that people really are different in the ways they perceive and approach life, and (2) most people tend to view their own perceptions and approaches as the right ones. It is no wonder, then, that when people attempt to establish an intimate partnership, their differences sometimes create tensions, disagreements, and arguments. Having a clearer picture of your own personality and its characteristics can help.

There are several popular tests used for evaluating personality traits. Most counseling centers have such tests available and are willing to interpret and explain their results. Everyone is familiar with the pair of personality traits known as extroversion and introversion, although these terms are frequently misused and misunderstood. Extroverted individuals tend to be energized by other people and by the external environment. They connect with others easily and enjoy group situations. Introverted people prefer their own company, but being introverted does not necessarily imply being shy or antisocial. Introverts simply tend to draw their energy more from inside themselves. They need more time and privacy for processing their inner experience and often prefer one-to-one interactions with others. When different combinations of personality traits come together in a relationship, there may be some difficulty in understanding each other. The extrovert may be miffed that an introverted partner is more content to stay home and avoid large parties. The individual who pays attention to feelings and wants to preserve harmony between people may be frustrated by a partner who prefers approaching problems in a highly rational manner, wanting only to reach the most logical conclusion.

Personality differences in relationships underscore the need for good communication skills and a commitment to using them. The differences may also be expressed through an individual's sexual preferences and styles. Although it is certainly not always true that opposites attract or that it is easy for them to get along well, human differences—sexual and otherwise—can be managed and even enjoyed. They sometimes provide the spice of a loving relationship (McCabe, 2007).

Communication Differences between Women and Men

Women and men sometimes express frustration with their shared communications. Sociolinguist Deborah Tannen (2001) and speech pathologist Lillian Glass (2003) have studied intricacies of communication patterns in males and females, revealing some fascinating differences in the ways the two sexes are taught to communicate. Tannen began by studying videotapes of people in different age groups having conversations with best friends of the same gender. She noticed that girls tended to face each other squarely, look directly at each other, and enjoy talking together. Boys seem to grow up in a much more hierarchical social order than do girls, and their groups usually have a leader who tells others what to do. An elaborate system of rules filters down through the group, and there is a struggle to maintain status within the group. Boys often must vie for attention and deflect the challenges of other boys in order to retain center stage.

Girls are more apt to play in small groups or in pairs, and they focus on maintaining intimacy and a sense of community. They want to get along with their friends so that everyone can have a turn, and often there are no winners or losers. When they encounter conflict, both boys and girls want to get their own way, but they will try to achieve it in different ways. Boys

Real People

Jennifer and Ted: Failed Communication

Imagine that you are a peer counselor for the Counseling Center. You have been pretty effective at helping couples with their relationships. The first time you talk with Jennifer and Ted, you can see that their relationship has become precarious. They have already discussed going their separate ways, and they both view counseling as a last-ditch effort to make things work again. Jennifer explains that Ted has become increasingly detached and that she can never get him to talk about what he's feeling. Expressing his frustration, Ted counters that Jennifer always seems to be wanting something from him, but he's never quite sure what. "No matter what I do," he says, "I can't seem to please her. After a while, it doesn't seem worth bothering anymore." Jennifer responds by saying "A relationship has to be more than sleeping together, or going out for a drink, or talking about what happened that day. I want to know more about what's going on inside you."

Ted maintains that Jennifer is looking for something in him that he doesn't think is there. "I just don't have that many deep feelings, and I don't want to make them up for you. I was satisfied with the way things were." Jennifer feels there is a missing dimension in their relationship because Ted seems unwilling or unable to deal with things on an emotional level. Their personality test results suggest that Ted and Jennifer really do have very different approaches to dealing with their reactions to

life. Ted is a very practical and decisive person, dependable in his pursuits and thorough in paying attention to details. He gets along well with other males and doesn't like fanciness in speech or manner. He places a high value on loyalty and faithfulness, but he doesn't deal very much with the affective levels of his personality.

In contrast, Jennifer's tests confirm that she is an outgoing and emotionally passionate individual who tends to form her views of the world impulsively. She likes romance and frivolity and has little patience for sorting through all the rational and practical aspects of situations. She observes other people carefully, and she often speculates about their hidden motivations. Ted and Jennifer both agree that these profiles are quite accurate. You explain that when people's personalities differ to such a degree, it takes an extra measure of effort to make mutual communication work. Ted and Jennifer concede that they are hoping to find ways to preserve and improve their relationship.

What do you think about the hopes for this couple? What sort of advice might you offer Ted and Jennifer to help them improve their bond and avoid unnecessary anger or confrontation? Do you think you would be capable of offering the kind of help this couple needs to keep their relationship intact? Would you feel it was your responsibility to keep them together, or would you be okay with their deciding to break up?

---

tend to resort to insistence and threats of physical violence, whereas girls usually try to mediate the situation and preserve harmony through compromise and avoidance of confrontation.

Differences in communication style between adult men and women are rooted in the fact that they have grown up with these differing patterns. Women tend to place a premium on being agreeable and congenial. Men react much more personally to verbal rejection and have a tendency to resist doing what they are told because they do not want to feel dominated or be in a one-down position in their social interactions. These differences may cause confusion and turmoil in male-female relationships. Keep in mind that the patterns

discussed are generalizations and certainly do not apply to every individual woman or man.

Talking over Problems

A man is much less likely to tell a woman about his difficult feelings or life problems because he does not want to worry her or seem helpless. Men also feel more obligated to offer solutions when someone tells them about a problem, even if the other person is just looking for an empathetic ear. They tend to be more brusque, forceful, loud, and demanding in their communications. For women, not being told about something such as personal feelings or troubles seems like rejection from a partner. Women typically are gentler, softer, and more emotional in their communications. They value the intimacy involved in sharing secrets and worries, whereas men are more likely to feel vulnerable in doing so.

Asking for Directions

Men also are more resistant to asking for directions when they are trying to find or do something, feeling that to do so is putting yourself one down with someone else. Women welcome the chance to connect with another person and are not bothered by seeming to need help.

Expressing Needs

One area of communication that often causes trouble for women and men is expressing various needs. Let's say a woman asks her husband if he would like to stop in somewhere for a drink. He truthfully answers no, and nothing more is said for the moment. Eventually it becomes evident that the wife was hurt and angered by his response. Although he saw the interaction as a simple statement of fact—he did not want to stop for a drink—she felt that her wishes had not been considered. The wife didn't realize that he would have been open to further negotiation and, in fact, could have been easily persuaded to follow her lead if she had made it clear that the issue was important for her. Because of how men learn to communicate, they are more likely to start any sort of negotiation with a clear statement of where they stand, with the understanding that there will be further discussion. Women, on the other hand, are likely to accept any such statement as a clear indication of a man's position and see it as immovable unless they press the communication into some form of unpleasantness (Glass, 2003; Tannen, 2001).

Another variation on this theme is that when women are trying to focus on intimacy and connection by expressing needs, men tend to view such expression as a demand and feel obligated to resist it. Male socialization causes them to be cautious about one-down positions. So when a woman suggests to her male partner that she would like to know when he is going to be late because otherwise she gets upset, he may see it as a challenge to his freedom and rebel against the suggestion.

Talking and Listening

Research shows that, contrary to popular opinion, men tend to talk more than women in public situations such as meetings, group discussions, or classrooms. When questions are asked in a group meeting, men tend to ask the first question, ask more questions, and ask longer questions. They tend to speak in lengthy

monologues and to interrupt people more than do women (Moore & Davidson, 2000). In the listening process women tend to show frequently that they are listening to another person, whereas men may focus more on the literal content and react only when they agree or disagree. When women talk about their feelings and problems and see discussion as a way to work on them, men tend to perceive the communication as wallowing in complaints. They tend to be more solution oriented and to want to resolve the difficulty with definitive action.

Quarreling and Relational Impasses

Even the happiest of couples are bound to have disagreements, some of which will become quarrels. These conflicts may be complicated by differences in communication styles. Conventional wisdom has held that quarreling is a sign of dissatisfaction and unhappiness in the relationship and that it ultimately is destructive for the partnership. Research has shown that things are not that clear-cut. In fact, certain kinds of quarreling actually can improve relationships (Greeff & DeBruyne, 2000). Even couples who describe themselves as unhappy but who are able to express their anger and resentment in constructive ways have been shown to be much happier three years later than they had been previously. Conflict may be difficult to overcome if one or both partners cannot get beyond contempt, stonewalling, or defensiveness (Gottman, 2000; Paterson, 2009).

People have different responses to interpersonal conflict. Some prefer the *obliging style*: giving in quickly to satisfy the other, avoiding unpleasant encounters altogether by withdrawing from the situation or the relationship, or ignoring the conflict. Those with a *dominating style* jump in with full force, ignoring the needs of the other and using coercion or power to get their own way. A greater sense of mutuality may be achieved through the *integrating style*, which involves discussion of differences and collaboration to find a solution acceptable to both people. Similarly, compromising involves a give-and-take approach in which both people sacrifice some of their own needs in order to have other needs met. Although some people place more significance on principles, others place more value on maintaining relationships. One person might want to confront conflicts, while another might want to smooth over ruffled feelings as quickly as possible (Greeff & DeBruyne, 2000; Paterson, 2009).

The key is whether the mode of quarreling is constructive or destructive (see Figure 9.4). In the most destructive kinds of arguments, anger is expressed in vicious and attacking ways, marked by blaming and character assassination. The two people are defensive, accusatory, and stubborn, resorting to

■ FIGURE 9.4   *Quarreling*

Quarreling in a relationship can be constructive or destructive. Anger expressed in a violent or accusatory manner is destructive. Couples instead should make an effort to express their views openly, listen to the other person, and learn to compromise.

insults, contemptuous remarks, and whining complaints. A more constructive and hopeful pattern is found in couples who feel free to express their anger to each other but do not allow the anger to escalate until it gets out of control. Such couples make a concerted effort to acknowledge their differences, to be open to each other's points of view, and to listen to each other. Eventually, they work toward arriving at some resolution to their differences, which often involves negotiation and compromise (Greeff & DeBruyne, 2000).

Women and men who are involved in relationships typically play different roles in fights. Males more commonly want to avoid conflict with their partners and may at first withdraw or become defensive. Women, on the other hand, are often the emotional managers of relationships. They are more likely to bring up some issue about which there is disagreement, wanting to confront the problem with their partners.

Couples sometimes reach an impasse, meaning that the process of two people relating has become stuck and unmoving. This is a frustrating predicament, because nothing seems to be happening between the partners, and both have retreated into themselves with some unresolved anger.

Resolving Impasses Effectively

Impasses signify a difficult place for any relationship to be, because things simply are not going anywhere. Both partners are nursing negative feelings and have withdrawn from relating. However, these problems are not insurmountable. Knowing how to carry on effective relationships involves knowing how to move beyond relational impasses. The two examples in Table 9.1 detail some communication skills that can be used in managing conflicts in relationships.

The best way to resolve relational impasses is to enter into the conflict with a sense of mutuality and face the problem as a "we" instead of as a "you" and "me." An important beginning step to working out solutions to conflicts is realizing and admitting that people and their points of view are indeed different. We each have our own perceptions of any situation, and all of us tend to see ourselves as more correct than others in our perspectives. Once couples begin to approach a conflict with a greater sense of mutuality, it is crucial for each partner to explain in clear terms what her or his perception of the problem is. One of the most effective ways of doing this is to work at formulating "I" messages. This means taking responsibility for communicating about the problem to a partner. For example:

Instead of attacking: "You are such a bastard for doing that."

Use an "I" message: "I feel really hurt whenever this happens."

Instead of making assumptions about another's motives: "You deliberately set out to make a fool of me."

Use an "I" message: "I am really angry and embarrassed about how this situation makes me look."

Instead of dwelling on past offenses: "This is another example of how you show no consideration for me. Last week, you. . . ."

Use an "I" message: "I often feel demoralized and frustrated by the way you treat me."

Typically, when couples struggle with an impasse for a while, there comes a point at which they begin to feel that they are really working together, a *shift to mutuality*. Even though the conflict may not be fully resolved, there is at least the sense that progress is being made and all is not lost. Women and men may

Table 9.1	*Internal/External Consistency in Communication*

Using assertive communication skills can reduce misunderstandings and conflicts in relationships. The more consistency there is between the thoughts and feelings going on internally and what is expressed externally, the more likely minor concerns may be resolved before they become major problems. Note these hypothetical interactions between a couple: how things were said, and how they could have been expressed more effectively.

As these examples show, effective and assertive communication may not always change the ultimate outcome of people's behavior. It can, however, change how people end up feeling about the interaction, themselves, and each other.

The Setting: Afterplay

	What Was Said:	**What Was Being Thought and Felt:**	**What Could Have Been Said:**
Man	"You haven't seemed very into sex lately. Is there something wrong?"	Something is wrong. She just lies there. I guess I'm not much of a lover.	"I'm embarrassed to bring this up, but I've been worried lately that I'm not pleasing you much during sex."
Woman	"No, I'm fine."	Oh my God, he doesn't think I'm much good in bed.	"I've been worrying that you would think I'm not much good in bed."
Man	"Was it good for you this time?"	Maybe she doesn't love me anymore. Or maybe I'm just not doing something right.	"I really love you a lot, and I've been scared that either you don't feel the same about me or that my sex techniques just aren't working for you."
Woman	"Yes, it was fine, I said."	He must know that I'm not reaching orgasm. This is so embarrassing.	"It's not you. I love you so much. I haven't wanted to admit this to anybody, but I've never been able to have an orgasm. I'm really embarrassed."
Man	"Come on, are you sure? You just don't seem very turned on."	She just doesn't want to admit that she doesn't feel the same about me anymore. I've never been able to hold onto a relationship.	"I was afraid that things were falling apart between us. It must be a real letdown not to be able to come. Maybe we can work on it together."
Woman	"Do we really need to talk about this? I don't really like analyzing our sex life. I've told you everything is okay. Okay?"	I'm going to lose him if I don't find a way to fake having an orgasm. I love him so much.	"It's not easy for me to talk about this, but I would sure like to do something about it."

(continued)

come to this shift in different ways. These days, many women are tired of doing what they perceive to be much of the work in male-female relationships. They no longer want to be the emotional caretakers and therefore often need to feel that men have some willingness to work on an impasse.

Men may reach the shift to mutuality in somewhat different ways, one of which involves becoming aware of the relationship as an entity and an experience in itself. Labeling relational experience with names such as "our conflict" or "our misunderstanding" is important if men are to understand this experience in a context of mutuality. It is also important for men to learn about the differences in how relationships work for them and for women. They often perceive different communication styles as types of conflict rather than simply as *differences* in how people respond, so they often react initially with defensiveness. Finally, it is crucial for men to learn how to empathize with the feelings of others so that they can begin to understand the feelings that are being experienced (Paterson, 2009).

The communication strategies discussed in this chapter can assist in the resolution of many conflicts. A fundamental principle is to be assertive, stating clearly and in a personalized way how you feel. This is different

| Table 9.1 | Internal/External Consistency in Communication (continued) |

The Setting: After Class

	What Was Said:	What Was Being Thought and Felt:	What Could Have Been Said:
Chris	"How about joining me at the snack bar so we could go over these notes? I'm getting confused."	I'm really attracted to him/her. If there was only a way to strike up a relationship.	"I've been noticing you in class, and I was wondering if you might be interested in going to the snack bar to talk."
Jan	"I'm pretty busy right now. Maybe another time."	What's going on here? S/He has been watching me in class for weeks.	"I've noticed you watching me. You just want to talk?"
Chris	"How about this afternoon? We could meet around 4:30 and then catch a bite to eat."	If I let him/her get away now, there'll never be another chance. Maybe if I press it a little further.	"I'd like a chance to get to know you better. How about it?"
Jan	"I've got another commitment for dinnertime, okay?"	This person doesn't know when to give up. I wish I knew what he/she was really looking for. I've got enough problems.	"I don't know. I'm feeling a little uncomfortable. My life is kind of complicated right now, and I'm hesitant to make any new commitments."
Chris	"Well, how about Friday after class?"	I think I'm making a jerk of myself. S/He thinks s/he's pretty hot stuff, apparently. What's so wrong with me?	"I don't want to look like a jerk, but I really hope you'll consider it. We'll just talk; I'm not so bad."
Jan	"Look, I may not be here Friday. Maybe you could find someone else to go over the notes with you."	I just want to get out of here. Won't this person take no for an answer?	"I appreciate the invitation, but this just isn't a good time for me. I don't mean to hurt your feelings."
Chris	[sarcastically] "Sorry I asked. I won't trouble you again. See you around."	I really blew it. I always have to push too hard.	"Well, if you ever change your mind, I'll be sitting in the same seat in this class. Keep me in mind."
Jan	"Fine."	Maybe I was too hard on him/her. But he/she wouldn't let up. I feel like a heel.	"Look, it was really nice of you to ask. I just don't want any more complications right now. But I will keep you in mind. Thanks for understanding."

from aggressive behavior, in which you attack, blame, and accuse others and make assumptions and judgments about their motives. Some suggestions for improving communication are given in Table 9.2.

■ Maintaining Loving Relationships

When entering into a loving relationship, couples want that relationship to last. Researcher John Gottman (2000) of the Relationship Research Institute in Seattle was one of the first scientists to study systematically the qualities that might make or break rela-

tionships. In his laboratories, psychologists conducted extensive interviews with couples and took an array of physiological measurements. They developed an emotion-identification coding system that helped them analyze masses of data about relationships. Although their conclusions have been limited largely to heterosexual marriages, their findings may well hold worthwhile advice for all couples of any gender who want to maintain their loving relationships. Here are some of the main findings:

1. *Couples who have more positive moments than negative moments have a better chance of lasting together.* In fact, the ratio of positive behaviors needed to offset negative behaviors with some

Table 9.2 Useful Strategies for Improving Communication in a Loving Relationship

Here are some ways to keep your relationship open, honest, and caring:

1. If you must criticize, focus on specific behavior rather than criticizing the person. For example, say something like "That irritates me" rather than "You irritate me." Your partner will feel less attacked.

2. Don't make assumptions and judgments about your partner, such that you end up telling him or her what he or she is thinking or feeling. We cannot be mind readers.

3. Avoid using "all-ness" words such as always and never. They typically represent unfair generalizations. Again, try to be more specific.

4. Try to see gray areas in issues rather than strictly black-and-white, good-bad dichotomies. Remember that our own truths often depend on our individual perceptions.

5. Use "I feel . . ." messages rather than "You are . . ." statements. No one can dispute what you feel. However, your partner may well be offended by judgments about his or her character that are perceived as unfair or untrue.

6. Be direct and honest, avoiding games, power plays, and attempts at reverse psychology.

7. Work toward a sense of equality. An "I'm OK—You're OK" feeling is fundamental to good communication.

8. Positive reinforcement is preferable to negative reinforcement. Compliment and thank the other person when she or he pleases you. When she or he does something that displeases you, try making a positive suggestion for a change ("Could you try doing . . .") rather than a negative prohibition ("Stop doing that . . .").

And remember:
Whether the issue is pleasant or hurtful, don't put it off. Communicate about it as soon as possible.

---

weight in order to create a strong bond is about five to one.

2. *Volatile relationships, with heated arguments and passionate reconciliations, can be very lasting.* It seems that such relationships may be as happy as those that are more reserved, as long as conflicts really get resolved.

3. *Emotionally inexpressive relationships can be very successful,* if the five-to-one ratio of positive to negative things couples do share with each other is maintained.

4. *Confronting complaints and differences early in the relationship seems to help.* Avoiding tensions and fights early on leads to a greater likelihood of trouble later. Expressing anger openly also seems to be a continuing factor in keeping relationships vital.

5. *In happy relationships, there is no discernible difference between how women and men express themselves emotionally.* Men may even be more likely than women to reveal intimate information about themselves in a happy relationship.

6. *Positive feelings about the beginning of the relationship are correlated with a higher likelihood of remaining together.* When partners have warm memories about the unfolding of their relationship, psychologists have been able to predict with great accuracy the likelihood that the couple will still be together in three years.

Gottman applied mathematical models to his relationship data and began to find some predictive value in those models (Gottman et al., 2003). The models show, for example, that in volatile relationships, in which couples routinely express anger at one another,

they can offset the negative effects of the anger with large doses of warmth and affection. This helps them remain stable in the longer run. Couples who tend to be validating or conflict-avoiding (see Figure 9.5) seem to have stabler relationships than couples who are hostile-detached. The mathematical models eventually incorporated factors that introduced more reality into their predictions. The researchers found, for example, that couples employ both "damping" and "repair" influences during difficult conversations. Damping comes in the form of making hurtful comments when the partner is trying to pull the discussion in a more positive direction. Repair attempts include changing the subject, making a joke, and offering soothing statements that attempt to turn the dialogue in a more positive direction. Without these moderating effects, the mathematical models tend to predict relationship catastrophe that in reality couples tend to prevent and mediate.

Have you ever experienced a communication problem with someone of the other sex based on what might be considered typical communication differences between men and women? Describe this personal experience.

Building any worthwhile relationship takes effort and commitment. When sexual sharing is part of the relationship, it becomes that much more sensitive and complicated. To share sex is to share a deep level of intimacy. Although sex may be important in many relationships, the closeness of another person who is willing to listen, understand, and talk is often just as significant (Bozon, 2002; Paterson, 2009). Positive sexual relationships do not just fall into place from one encounter in bed; they evolve from a deliberate process

Quantifying Conversations

John M. Gottman and his colleagues have developed "influence functions" to illustrate how the partners in various types of couples influence each other's moods over the course of a difficult conversation. The horizontal axis represents a range of verbal and facial expressions—from highly critical and contemptuous (on the left) to highly supportive and affectionate (on the right). The vertical axis represents the degree to which a person is influenced positively (up) or negatively (down) by his or her spouse's behavior. For example, the husband in a "validating" couple tends to be strongly influenced (in a negative direction) by his wife's negative behavior: That line has a slope of 0.31. The husband in a "conflict-avoiding" couple, on the other hand, actually tends to behave slightly more positively when his wife is negative: That line has a slope of −0.05.

Both "validating" couples and "conflict-avoiding" couples tend to have marriages that are stable and long lasting. Couples are in trouble, though, when they have mismatched influence functions. Consider the "hostile-detached" couple, where the slopes for the husband's and the wife's influences look very different. When the husband behaves positively, he has almost no impact (slope of 0.02) on his detached wife.

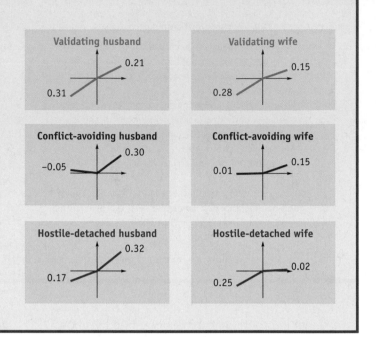

FIGURE 9.5   *Quantifying Conversations*

The work of John Gottman and his associates has been used to create mathematical models to describe relationships.

Source: Text from David Glenn, "Every Unhappy Family Has Its Own Bilinear Influence Function," *Chronicle of Higher Education,* April 25, 2003. Copyright 2003, *Chronicle of Higher Education.* Reprinted with permission. Figures from John M. Gottman et al., *The Mathematics of Marriage: Dynamic Nonlinear Models,* pp. 152, 153. © 2002 Massachusetts Institute of Technology, by permission of MIT Press.

of communicating together and working to be responsive to each other.

The Other Risks of Sex

There have been highly publicized risks of indiscriminate sexual activity, such as unplanned pregnancy or sexually transmitted infection. However, there are other risks of sex too, risks associated with the relational aspects of human interaction. Following are some examples.

- *Risk: Modeling Your Sexuality after External Standards Rather Than Your Own*

Each of us must find ways to bring our own unique blend of sexual needs, orientations, fantasies, attractions, and behaviors into some sort of balance and harmony with our society, which is always circumscribed by its cultural and political boundaries. Not to achieve that harmony is to be alienated from ourselves, perhaps playing some sexual role inconsistent with the core of our being.

- *Risk: Not Allowing Yourself to Be Vulnerable Enough to Accept the Risks Inherent in Loving Relationships*

Eventually, every relationship has some pain. Fear of dealing with hurt—in oneself or in a partner—can ultimately push couples apart. People must be willing to be vulnerable to the fears of being hurt or of hurting someone else. Without vulnerability, relationships and their sexual components eventually become sterile, brittle, and empty. Before we can deal with vulnerability in a healthy, positive manner, we must also know and accept ourselves. We have to develop a level of self-esteem and self-confidence that will help us feel worthwhile and validated as individuals. When we depend too heavily on others to make us feel good, we give up a great deal of personal power in the relationship.

- *Risk: Being in a Situation in Which You Feel Bound to Do Something Sexual That Just Does Not Feel Quite Right to You*

Our society does not encourage much sense of ownership over our genitals until we reach some arbitrary age when we suddenly are expected to become sexually responsible. This results in a good deal of confusion about sexual values and behaviors and often leads us to engage in sexual activities out of a sense of obligation rather than a conviction that they are right for us. We need to be open to our sexuality so that we can think and plan ahead. We never have to be at the mercy of whims or urges, whether our own or those of others. It takes introspection, time, and even some experimentation to know where we stand with regard to sexual values and what we want for our lives sexually.

- *Risk: Thinking We Will Be Able to Change Our Partner, or That They Will Change for Us*

While couples counselors generally encourage partners to see any problem as something that they share and that must be worked on jointly, they also have found that over the long term people find it difficult to change each other or to change themselves for another. Such changes are usually temporary. So even though efforts toward mutual understanding and compromise are valuable, it is not a good idea to hope or assume that your partner will eventually change. It's more sensible to look at the ways in which we ourselves might be able to change within the relationship (Paterson, 2009).

What's Love Got to Do with It?

Love, intimacy, and sex seem to be parts of a singular, confusing package that writers, poets, and scientists have been trying to understand and explain for centuries. Love is a quality and an experience that until recently has seemed more comfortable in the hands of artists than in the hands of scientists, but there is evidence that the experience of passionate love is found in all cultures (Wells, 2007).

There have been three global transformations that are affecting loving relationships. First, an increasing belief in the equality of genders and ethnic groups is eroding long-standing double standards and prejudices, freeing people to love without so many social constrictions. The second transformation is seeing the pursuit of happiness as a more acceptable and worthwhile goal, leading to a more positive view of passionate love and sexual desire. Finally, there is a growing belief that life can be changed for the better, with the pleasures of love and sex being seen as a legitimate part of life improvement (Levine, 2005).

Love poses a challenge to go beyond the single-minded pursuit of personal gratification and to break down some of the habitual patterns of behavior that have been a part of nonpartnered life. It has been said that love and relationship have a transformative power; they bring together two people who then have to sort through the many complications of being together. We live in a mobile, increasingly disconnected culture and in a time when the rules about love and relating are sometimes vague and confusing. In many ways, love is an ideal toward which people strive, often with some level of internal conflict. The external pressures and reasons for people to come together and form a partnership are far less convincing than they once were. It is now internal motivations and the intrinsic qualities of two individuals' personal connection that keep a relationship going (Bozon, 2002). Whenever we enter into a loving connection with another person, we enter largely unexplored territory, with all sorts of new things to discover—both within ourselves and within the dynamics of what we share as a couple.

Love Brings Us Together

Love is not something that just happens; rather, it is something to be practiced, perfected, and worked at from the foundation of a person's cultural imperatives and belief systems. Evolutionary psychologists believe there are three primary human emotion-motivation systems associated with what we generally call "love." These systems clearly are interrelated but may also function independently of one another (Aron et al., 2005; Fisher et al., 2002):

1. *Lust* manifests itself as a craving for sexual gratification. From the standpoint of evolutionary theory, this motivation system ensures reproduction of the species.
2. *Attraction* is characterized by heightened energy and attention for a particular partner, often called romantic love, and is accompanied by feelings of exhilaration, "intrusive thinking" about the loved one, and a craving for emotional connection with the other person. From an evolutionary and survival point of view, it saves energy by focusing attention on a particular mate.
3. *Attachment* is characterized by the calm, contented feelings that accompany being close to the loved one and, in a sense, "making the nest" together. From an evolutionary perspective, this system facilitates coupling and parenting.

Close relationships often begin with the attraction process, with feelings of falling in love or *infatuation*. This kind of loving involves an intense desire to be close to another person, and strong emotions may surface as well as intense sexual attraction based on certain physical characteristics (see Figure 9.6). Infatuation can be exciting and exhilarating, but it can have its difficult side. Because such strong emotions are involved, it may be particularly painful when the other person is unable to feel mutually attracted and loving. On the other hand, when two people fall in love, they typically seek to spend a great deal of time together, gradually let down their usual barriers, and become more and more vulnerable to each other. Their sense of shared intimacy deepens, and they may eventually progress to sexual sharing. Often they experience a sense of never wanting things to change, of never

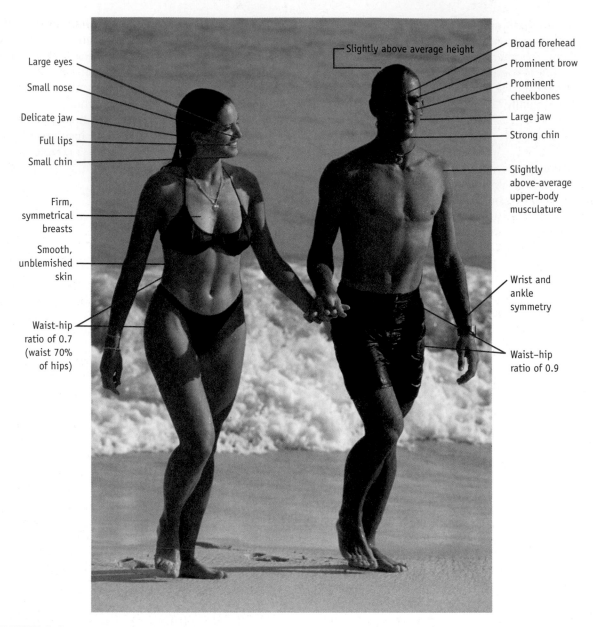

Large eyes

Small nose

Delicate jaw

Full lips

Small chin

Firm, symmetrical breasts

Smooth, unblemished skin

Waist–hip ratio of 0.7 (waist 70% of hips)

Slightly above average height

Broad forehead

Prominent brow

Prominent cheekbones

Large jaw

Strong chin

Slightly above-average upper-body musculature

Wrist and ankle symmetry

Waist–hip ratio of 0.9

■ **FIGURE 9.6**   *What Goes into Sex Appeal?*

Studies suggest that male attractiveness hinges on outward signs of maturity, robust health, and, above all, dominance. Most of the features associated with feminine beauty signal youthfulness and an abundance of female reproductive hormones.

wanting to be apart. It is typical at this point for partners to make promises to each other such as "I'll always love you" or "I'll never leave you" or "I'll never hurt you."

 See "Waist-to-Hip Ratio" on SexSource Online.

However, the process of falling in love always comes to an end. At this point relationships often end too, largely because people have been led to believe that infatuation is the only kind of loving worth having.

This intense phase may also evolve into the stabler, more deeply committed attachment stage, which might be called *being in love*. This involves a conscious choice on the part of both partners to be together, although they certainly may be motivated by the feelings of security, comfort, and contentment that their togetherness produces. They care about and trust each other enough to commit themselves to working at the relationship. They recognize that their love is more than just lust. They see it as a process of communicating, negotiating, compromising when differences get in the way, and agreeing to struggle through the more difficult times together. Being in love also means that two people are struggling to accept and love each other, even in the face of their individual differences and idiosyncrasies. They may eventually find ways to celebrate their mutual differences instead of finding them to be obstacles (Paterson, 2009).

There has been little research about love in recent years. Some insist that love is a socialized response, whereas others believe it to be a basic human emotion. Comparisons of ethnographic data have shown a good deal of similarity among cross-cultural views of love, sex, and intimacy. Yet they have also suggested that individual differences may well be more powerful than cultural influences in shaping particular people's attitudes and behaviors that constitute their styles of loving. In a survey of 166 societies, evidence of romantic attraction and love was found in 147 of them. Further analysis of data demonstrated that several predictable characteristics are associated with romantic attraction; these tend to occur in stages and typically are associated with what we call love (Aron et al., 2005; Fisher et al., 2002):

- The initial falling-in-love experience causes the loved one to take on special meaning, usually to the exclusion of anyone else. The lover has a tendency to view the loved one as unique, quite different from everyone else. At least for a time, this causes the lover to see only the positive in the other person, overlooking more negative traits. Little things the loved one says or does are noticed in great detail.
- Individuals who report feelings of romantic love also may experience a great variety of psychological and physical responses, ranging from exhilaration and euphoria to sleeplessness, loss of appetite, and a rapid heartbeat. When the loved one is not present, they may feel a sense of loss, anxiety, or depression.
- In the midst of romantic love, people report thinking obsessively about their loved one. This is called "intrusive thinking," because it seems to push its way into other thoughts. This characteristic is also associated with emotional dependency on the relationship and fear of rejection.
- A person in love longs for emotional closeness with the beloved and often experiences a willingness to sacrifice for him or her.
- Lovers may reorder their daily priorities or make changes in their lifestyles in order to spend time with the loved one or to seem more compatible.
- Sexual desire usually accompanies romantic attraction, along with a feeling of possessiveness and a desire for sexual exclusivity. There is a desire to persuade the partner not to have sex with others. The desire for emotional intimacy seems to take precedence over a desire for sexual intimacy in the majority of women and men. While sexual union

may be very important in romantic love, emotional union is even more important.
- People generally report that their feelings of romantic attraction are not within their control and in fact are involuntary. They can, at times, even seem unwanted.
- Unless some sorts of barriers prevent partners from seeing each other on a regular basis, romantic attraction is impermanent. It eventually ends.

Sternberg's Triangular Theory of Love

Yale researcher Robert Sternberg (1986, 1998) studied the dynamics of loving relationships for several years and developed an interesting model that accounts for three distinct components of love. These components can be viewed as the three sides of a triangle, with the area of the triangle representing the amount and style of loving.

1. *Intimacy,* the emotional component, involves closeness, mutual support, and sharing. Intimacy tends to increase gradually but steadily at first, naturally leveling off as two persons become more comfortably knowledgeable about each other. In well-established relationships, intimacy may not even be particularly noticeable on the surface, but it will quickly become evident during a crisis that the couple must face together (see Figure 9.7).
2. *Passion* provides a motivational component to love. It is manifested in a desire to be united with the loved one, leading to sexual arousal and sharing. It is the aspect of some loving that tends to increase most rapidly at first. Sternberg has likened passion to an addictive substance, because people are so drawn to its stimulation and pleasure. If one person abruptly ends the relationship, suddenly withdrawing the outlet for passion, the other person may suffer all the depression, irritability, and emotional pain of the withdrawal process. In time, passion levels off and does not provide the stimulation and arousal it did at first. That does not mean that passion necessarily becomes unimportant or lacking. It simply loses some of its importance as a motivating force in the relationship (see Figure 9.7).
3. *Commitment* represents the cognitive side of love, in both its short- and long-term senses. The development of commitment in a relationship is easy to understand, as Figure 9.7 demonstrates. As you get to know each other better commitment grows and develops. As with all other components of love, commitment eventually levels off; if the relationship fails, it declines even further.

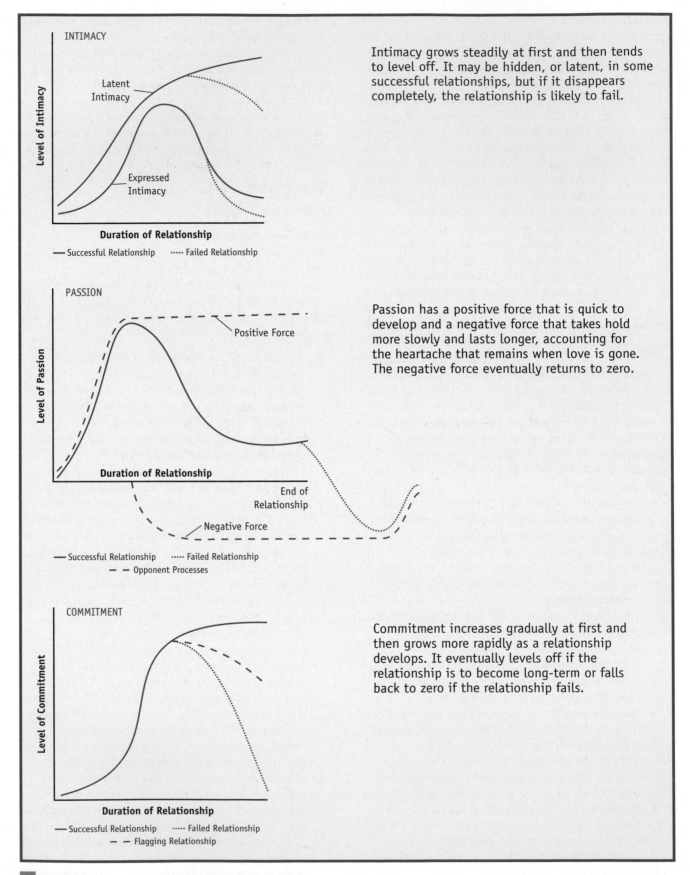

Intimacy grows steadily at first and then tends to level off. It may be hidden, or latent, in some successful relationships, but if it disappears completely, the relationship is likely to fail.

Passion has a positive force that is quick to develop and a negative force that takes hold more slowly and lasts longer, accounting for the heartache that remains when love is gone. The negative force eventually returns to zero.

Commitment increases gradually at first and then grows more rapidly as a relationship develops. It eventually levels off if the relationship is to become long-term or falls back to zero if the relationship fails.

FIGURE 9.7   *Sternberg's Triangular Theory of Love*

Yale researcher Robert Sternberg has developed one model to explain the complicated emotion of love. In the model, he describes intimacy, passion, and commitment as love's basic components.

Sternberg's research has also shown that the best predictor of happiness in a loving relationship is the degree of similarity between how an individual wants the other person to feel about him or her and how the individual thinks the partner actually feels. If one person believes that the other does not feel enough love, disappointment and conflict can follow.

The Brain Circuitry and Chemistry of Love

Everyone recognizes that love is one of the more complex human emotions and that it cannot be adequately explained by any single model. Researchers are just beginning to piece together the even greater puzzle of structures and biochemicals in the brain that are associated with human loving emotions. It is known that a particular gene, avpr1a, is involved in human pairing, apparently because it controls the sensitivity of receptors in the brain to the hormone vasopressin. The brain's reward and reinforcement system seems to be mediated by the chemicals dopamine, **oxytocin,** and vasopressin, all of which seem to play a role in human pair bonding (Young, 2009).

There is some suggestive evidence that the scents of chemical sex attractants, or **pheromones,** may play a role in romantic attraction, although specific human pheromones have yet to be identified (Wyatt, 2009). A chemical called androstenol is found in male sweat, and its dry, musky smell is appealing to women. When it oxidizes to form androstenone, women tend to react more negatively to its odor *unless they are ovulating.* Copulines are chemicals found in women's vaginal secretions. Controlled experiments in which males inhaled these substances found that the exposure tended to upgrade men's attractions to women and assessments of their beauty. Some evidence suggests that certain scents may increase the tendency of both men and women to have shared sexual activity (Cutler, Friedmann, & McCoy, 1998; Sergeant et al., 2007).

During *attraction,* or the phase of loving that corresponds to infatuation or falling in love, the brain is stimulated centrally by phenylethylamine (PEA), dopamine, and norepinephrine. These are close chemical relatives to the stimulant drugs called amphetamines, and they tend to produce elation, increased energy, and euphoria. Attraction makes people feel swept away and energized. At the same time, there may be a decrease in serotonin levels in the reward pathways of the brain. Reduced levels of serotonin may be associated with the obsessive and intrusive thinking, anxiety, depression, and moodiness associated with romantic attraction (Anders & Gray, 2007; Aron et al., 2005; Fisher et al., 2002).

There are also chemical reasons why infatuation cannot last forever. Eventually, the body builds up a certain tolerance to these biochemicals so that their profound effects begin to wear off. Some people seem to become attraction junkies, constantly craving the intoxicating highs of falling in love. They move from one relationship to the next as the attraction high in the brain begins to run down each time.

Those relationships that endure beyond attraction settle into a longer period of *attachment.* In this phase of loving, being around a loved one stimulates the production of **endorphins** in the brain. These natural painkillers produce a sense of security, tranquility, and calm. Oxytocin is produced during cuddling and physical intimacy and is associated with the powerful feelings of orgasm and sexual satisfaction. The *lust* motivation system seems to be mediated in part by the estrogens and the androgens. There is evidence that when orgasm occurs, the pituitary gland produces prolactin, a hormone that tends to suppress sexual desire for a time. This hormone may bring sexual interest temporarily to an end following a satisfying sexual experience. The brain chemistry of love is illustrated in Figure 9.8.

Establishing Sensual and Sexual Intimacy

We hear a great deal about intimacy in relationships, and the term means different things to different people. Intimacy usually describes a special kind of closeness between people, a deep connection that feels more special than the superficial interactions that tend to dominate our lives (see Figure 9.9). But how do people go about building the kind of intimacy they seem to crave at some deeper level within themselves? Following are some factors important to establishing intimacy:

1. *Touching* can establish a crucial foundation for intimacy. We feel with the nerve endings of our skin before we make use of any other sense organ. The sensations of touch then remain at the forefront of our conscious experience. Sensual touching is gratifying to the senses but does not necessarily lead to sexual interaction. Only too often, people's sensual needs are ignored or starved. The need to be touched in caring, loving ways—to be taken care of through touching—is

oxytocin (ox-ee-TOH-sin) a chemical produced by the brain in response to physical intimacy and sexual satisfaction.

pheromones (FAIR-oh-moans) human chemicals, the scent of which may cause an attraction or behavioral change in other individuals.

endorphins (en-DORE-fins) brain secretions that act as natural tranquilizers and pain relievers.

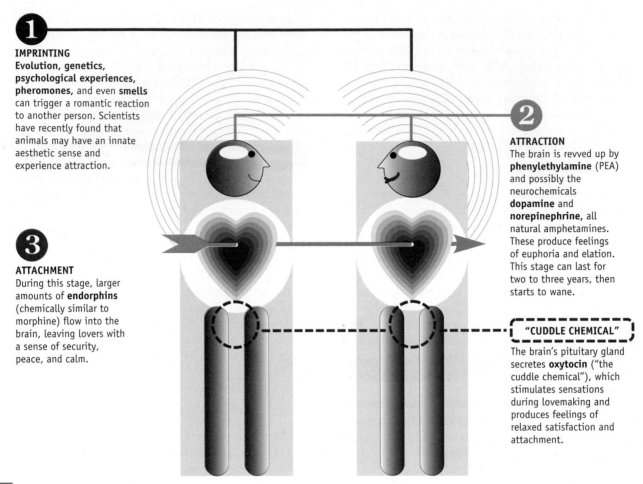

1 IMPRINTING
Evolution, genetics, psychological experiences, **pheromones,** and even **smells** can trigger a romantic reaction to another person. Scientists have recently found that animals may have an innate aesthetic sense and experience attraction.

2 ATTRACTION
The brain is revved up by **phenylethylamine** (PEA) and possibly the neurochemicals **dopamine** and **norepinephrine,** all natural amphetamines. These produce feelings of euphoria and elation. This stage can last for two to three years, then starts to wane.

3 ATTACHMENT
During this stage, larger amounts of **endorphins** (chemically similar to morphine) flow into the brain, leaving lovers with a sense of security, peace, and calm.

"CUDDLE CHEMICAL"
The brain's pituitary gland secretes **oxytocin** ("the cuddle chemical"), which stimulates sensations during lovemaking and produces feelings of relaxed satisfaction and attachment.

FIGURE 9.8   *The Chemistry of Love*
The various stages of loving correspond to chemical changes in the brain.

an important need for both women and men. Only too often, if such touching leads to sexual arousal, the sensual aspects are hurried along so that genital sexual activity may be initiated. Like being in love, touching is an art to be developed, worked at, and perfected through time and practice.

2. *Relaxation* is another important factor in intimacy. People need to be able to feel relaxed together in order to be open to each other. Physiologically, the term *relaxation* refers to a relatively low level of tension in the muscles. Although it is possible to use relaxation techniques and other stress-control methods to reduce tension, psychological factors often are an important part of the picture. Anxiety, depression, anger, hostility, or even small disagreements between people create tension. Even subtle tension can block intimacy and interfere with sexual enjoyment. Although sexual arousal involves a buildup of body tensions, paradoxically it is most effective within the context of a relaxed atmosphere between the partners. The more people have to work at sex, the more likely it is that tension will interfere with the sense of intimacy.

3. *Being a participant* in a relationship is necessary to intimacy. Only too often, people allow themselves to become spectators, in a sense standing outside themselves and watching what is going on. Or they may escape into the withdrawal of daydreams and inattention. It is far better to be fully in touch with your own inner reactions and with your partner at the moment. To be preoccupied with future goals or with how sex might be distracts from experiencing and dealing with how things actually are going right now. Participating in an intimate relationship is about being fully aware of what is going on and taking responsibility for communicating or acting as necessary (Paterson, 2009).

Confusion about Love and Sex in Relationships

Issues of love and sex have become blurred in our culture. In fact, romantic love is a fairly recent development historically, and a century ago it was not necessarily

■ FIGURE 9.9 *Intimacy*

Developing intimacy in a relationship involves touching in a caring, loving manner; learning to reduce tension by physically and psychologically relaxing; and being fully aware of the need to communicate.

associated with sexual feelings. Love was meant to be a pure feeling expressed through the idealization of the loved one. In the modern period, romantic love has been associated with sex, but this change has generated some confusion. One complication of this perspective is that we have come to expect the intense feelings of love and the passion of sex to be a continuing part of lasting relationships such as marriage, when in fact these emotions change with time. Individuals sometimes use sex to hold onto their partners or pretend that having sex must mean that you are in love.

People may assume that if they have chosen a partner well, the love and the relationship should last forever and the love will never change. But loving feelings and levels of interest in sex change over time. The important thing is how well the couple keeps up with the process of change. It is also assumed that when people love each other, sex will just happen. However, most couples have busy lives, and as they spend time together their priorities may change. Sometimes they will have to create the opportunity for sex to happen while not making it seem too contrived (Bozon, 2002).

Love may be abused in relationships as well. It may be used as a justification for controlling others: "I only did it because I love you." Or it may be cited as the reason for imposing some imperative on a partner: "If you really loved me, you would. . . ." This imperative could be completed in any number of ways, including the following:

. . . want sex as often as I do

. . . have eyes for no one else but me

. . . trust me without question

. . . have sex with me now

. . . know how to turn me on

. . . never hurt me

Such imperatives can place the receiver in a situation sometimes called the "double bind." In other words, you are "damned if you do and damned if you don't." The sender of the message has created a no-win situation. If you resist the entreaty, you are demonstrating your lack of caring, but if you follow through as dictated by the imperative, you may be accused of merely trying to please the person and not really meaning it.

Have you ever been "head over heels" in love with someone? Describe the experience.

Confusion over love and sex is best resolved through effective communication, based on a real commitment to work together on maintaining a dynamic and caring relationship. It seems clear that sexual satisfaction is closely associated with the levels of satisfaction, love, and commitment shown between the partners in the relationship (Levine, 2005; Sprecher, 2002).

Same-Gender Intimate Relationships

When considering same-gender intimate relationships, the sexual activity between two men or two women has often been seen as the primary distinguishing factor. However, all sorts of loving relationships exist between members of the same sex, often involving sex, but sometimes not. Sometimes two individuals of the same gender share a sexual affair but do not consider themselves lesbian or gay; they simply have chosen to have sex with this one particular partner. Therefore, in examining some relationships, we must take into consideration how the partners identify themselves.

Research continues to demonstrate that when comparing mixed-sex and same-sex relationships, there are far more similarities than there are differences. Same-sex couples have similar needs for communication and tenderness and share similar sexual repertoires. They also have similar needs and aspirations with regard to their long-term partnerships. Love is an important element between partners, regardless of their sexual orientation or gender (Holmberg & Blair, 2009; Kline et al., 2008).

Three primary patterns of intimate relationships can develop between gay men and between lesbians. One pattern employs the heterosexual model for dating and marriage as the prototype for determining roles within the relationship, with one partner adopting more of the traditional masculine functions and the other adopting more of the traditional feminine roles. Another common pattern involves a marked age difference between the partners, with an older individual paired with a younger person of the same gender. A third pattern, which seems to be modeled after friendships, emphasizes sharing and equality between partners who are similar in age and social status. Surveys have found that lesbian partners are more likely to share household tasks. Gay male partners and married heterosexual partners were found to be more likely to have a division of labor in which one partner does more household work than the other (usually the woman of a heterosexual couple).

■ Connecting: For Better or Worse

Changes in social norms and available communication technologies change the nature of human connections. The rules of engagement become unclear, and new trails need to be blazed. The partnerships that emerge from the new opportunities may leave people feeling frustrated and vulnerable. As this section demonstrates, the personality characteristics that each partner brings to a relationship can determine whether it will remain a healthy and stable partnership. People in loving relationships also risk being hurt if the relationship comes to an end.

Friendship and Sexuality

Many people would say they love their friends, but they would not be referring to a romantic or sexual attachment. Studies on friendship show that, in general, people tend to prefer friendships with members of their own sex and that individuals who have close friendships tend to be less anxious and depressed than those who do not. However, there is also evidence that friendships are associated with the perpetuation of negative habits such as smoking and overeating, and that both good and bad moods are often spread within friendships (Christakis & Fowler, 2009).

Friendships sometimes can become confusing sexually. Single men and women are far more likely than married people to have friends of the other gender. People in a committed relationship may feel threatened when a partner has a close friendship with someone else. There may be a fear that the friendship will lead to deeper intimacy or sexual sharing. Therefore, friendships outside the primary relationship are often considered acceptable only to a point that clearly distinguishes them as auxiliary and secondary to that primary relationship.

Close, intimate friendships are a domain with few clear social rules. The sexual aspect of friendships may well exist and need to be sorted out. To deny sexual attraction within the relationship may prove unhealthy and an obstacle to open communication. We are only beginning to understand "friends with benefits" relationships (Bisson & Levine, 2009). An obvious risk here is that one partner's expectations and emotions will shift and more will be wanted than what is being called friendship. To make clear distinctions between friendship and love is sometimes difficult. It may be that "friendship" is simply a safer word that allows couples to remain comfortable with a relationship that has actually become loving but calling it "love" will present a dilemma for their lives (Neuman, 2002).

Relating Online

The ability to communicate online offers a virtual community in which people can interact. People are falling in love and sharing online sexual activity through this medium. Online interaction seems to help people whose sexual interests and orientations are less socially acceptable to feel less marginalized. Online dating sites that ask customers to complete questionnaires about themselves are attempting to use scientific methods of matching couples who are believed to be compatible for various reasons. These sites seem to have at least some success, even though there also seems to be some lessening of interest in registering for such sites (Albright, 2008; Gottlieb, 2006).

Real Student Voices

■ My boyfriend has been really upset lately because I have a close friend in my dorm who happens to be male. I would never do anything with this guy—he's just really easy to talk to. I keep telling my boyfriend there is no need to be jealous, but it doesn't seem to help. I wish he could trust me more.

■ I think about sex most of the time but don't ever have sex. That's because I broke up with my girlfriend 10 months ago, and I still can't get her out of my head. When I think about sex, I think about her.

The motivations for seeking out such contact generally seem to fit into five basic categories: anonymity, time constraints that interfere with the pursuit of face-to-face relationships, the desire to share sexual fantasies, the opportunity to share online sexual behavior (often accompanied by masturbation), and the hope of eventually meeting the person with whom a meaningful connection has been made (Benotsch, Kalichman, & Cage, 2002).

In studies of people who indicate that they had met a partner online, those ages 18 to 24 reported having met an average of nearly 10 partners in this manner, including 7 in the previous year. Men and women over age 40 are more likely to report that they have established a long-term relationship with an online partner. Gays and lesbians find that online meetings reduce the problems of finding a partner with their sexual orientation (Lever et al., 2008; McFarlane, Bull, & Rietmeijer, 2002).

Electronic communication seems to be able to create strong feelings of closeness and familiarity because of the frequency of contact that is possible. The vast network that is available also makes it more likely that people will find others who share similar characteristics and attitudes. There are opportunities for rapid self-disclosure and interpersonal intimacy because of the degree of anonymity present at the beginning of the relationship. The significance of the erotic connection that can develop between people online should not be underestimated. All these characteristics have the potential for moving relationships into intimate territory quite rapidly (Benotsch, Kalichman, & Cage, 2002).

There are also frightening tales of cyberrelationships ending in harassment, abuse, or violence. One risk of online relating lies in its advantages: the tendency for the relationship to develop very rapidly into an intimate connection (Brown, Maycock, & Burns, 2005). The intensity can also mean that the relationship quickly becomes eroticized but then cannot be sustained because there is insufficient underlying trust and knowledge to support it. If an individual is having an online relationship at the same time as another relationship, the same stresses and strains can develop whenever the boundaries of the relationships are crossed (Whitty & Quigley, 2008). Among 18 to 24 year olds who pursue sex with an online partner, the first meeting tends to take place in the partner's home, a park or other outdoor place, or a rest room. They also are less likely to say that condoms were available at the meeting place, making the chances of a risky sexual encounter quite high (McFarlane, Bull, & Rietmeijer, 2002).

Online romance and sex continue to change the partnering scene and will require further careful study. The impression created by the media is that the Internet promotes superficial, destructive relationships, but the realities are far more complex—and often more positive—than this. The virtual community continues to evolve and to develop clearer ethical guidelines for its users. Like any human community, it has its share of untrustworthy, abusive, and even dangerous individuals. It also has many people who are genuinely interested in good relationships founded on courtesy, honesty, integrity, and respect.

Attachment Theory: Jealousy and Possessiveness

When we become attached to something—whether a material object we have paid dearly to own or another person whom we dearly love—we often fear that we could end up losing what we long to possess. Attachment theory has clarified three main styles of emotional bonding with another person. The *secure* attachment style is characterized by increased self-confidence and self-esteem and a growing sense of

He loved her more than words could say. She left him because he didn't talk.

Source: Copyright © 1993 by Andrew Lehman.

satisfaction. Those who have a *preoccupied* style of attachment are anxious and ambivalent about their relationship, tend to have a negative view of themselves and a positive view of their partner, and are quite dependent on their partners for nurturance. Because they perceive themselves not to be worthy of their partners, they naturally worry about losing them.

Other people fall into *avoidant* patterns of attachment, meaning that at some level they are managing to hold themselves back from effective emotional bonding. This style represents a way of avoiding the vulnerability that eventually could open the individual to hurt. There are two subsets of the avoidant style. Some are *dismissing avoidant*, viewing themselves more positively and as more worthwhile than the partner, tending to ignore and diminish their partner. *Fearful avoidant* people hold negative views of both themselves and their partner and are fearful of intimacy. They often worry that their partner does not care about them as much as they care about their partner (Pistole & Arricale, 2003). Attachment styles sometimes carry over from the kind of attachment that was experienced from a parent (Erzar & Erzar, 2008).

When couples face conflict, as they always do eventually, their attachment style plays a role in how the conflict may be approached. Those who have a secure style feel less threatened by arguments and are less concerned about feelings of closeness during conflict than are those who have preoccupied or fearful styles. Those with dismissive styles are more likely to avoid conflict than are those who are securely attached (Pistole & Arricale, 2003).

Loving relationships have elements of territoriality and fear. We want the object of our affection to love us in return and, frequently, to love only us. We fear rejection by that person and especially fear the loss of his or her love to someone else. If we have some inkling, even an imagined one, that a partner's interests might be straying, it is quite natural to feel jealous. A reasonable amount of jealousy can be expected in any relationship. It is an issue about which couples need to communicate openly. It is important to remember that even those individuals who are happy and comfortable in a loving and sexual relationship will still occasionally find themselves attracted to others. This does not have to threaten the relationship, nor does it signal some sort of difficulty between the partners (Buss, 2000; Nannini & Meyers, 2000).

Jealousy can get out of control and become possessiveness, which is particularly common among people who have a preoccupied style of attachment. Such individuals seem continually worried about losing their partner and might even imagine that something more is going on in other relationships. There may be an unreasonable degree of anger over the partner's casual and innocent social interactions. Such possessiveness can have many roots. Feelings of inferiority often play a role and may be accompanied by some basic insecurity and immaturity in the individual. Some people who become overly possessive expect complete and utter devotion from a partner and have difficulty seeing that individuals always need room for personal growth, even within a committed relationship. Possessiveness usually signals some fundamental insecurities in the person's personality that may well deserve some attention. Professional counseling can be a viable option (Brown, 2005; Pistole & Arricale, 2003).

Overly jealous people often are not willing to take much responsibility for changing their behavior. They may even consider their obsession with their partner perfectly justified. Men and women who are so obsessed may stalk the person to whom they are attracted. Lack of assertiveness on the part of young women sometimes plays a role in making them more vulnerable to possessiveness and abusiveness from a partner (Rickert, Sanghvi, & Wiemann, 2002). There are several ways for dealing with a situation in which your partner is being unreasonably jealous:

1. *Do not fall into the trap of trying to answer unreasonable questions.* A jealous lover may be convinced of your unfaithfulness and grill you with questions. As the rules for good communication suggest, focus on how the questions are making you feel, and stick with the truth.
2. *Encourage your partner to work on the jealousy with you.* You may want to suggest seeking out a counselor together. In any case, act with assertiveness. Do not simply give in to keep the peace for the time being. The jealousy may be a sign of trouble in the relationship that should not be ignored.
3. *Do not be ruled by pity for the other person.* Even if you think you understand the unfortunate reasons why your partner is so desperately jealous, do not feel that he or she should justify unfair accusations or suspicions. It is your partner's responsibility to find a way to work on those problems. Threats of suicide or violence are the most extreme form of relational coercion and manipulation. They represent serious problems for which you should seek professional advice.
4. *Take a close look at whether this is a relationship that is healthy for you.* If the jealousy and possessiveness begin to seem hopeless, you may simply be unable to find much relaxed fulfillment in the relationship. Even if you love the other person, it might be important to sort through whether it is wise to remain in the relationship (Brown, 2005). Again, talking the situation over with a trained counselor can be a significant step toward maintaining your own psychological balance.

Dealing with the Loss of a Loving Relationship

Many loving relationships ultimately fail. That does that necessarily mean that people are picking out the wrong partners for loving. Relationships typically begin with attention being given to what matters to the partners in the short form. Like all things, people and their relationships change. The long-range issues may be quite different. Therefore, as relationships grow, it becomes increasingly important for partners to be willing to change their response patterns toward each other. What first seemed a charming idiosyncrasy may in time become a grating nuisance. What once was a sexual turn-on may become boring and humdrum. Couples must be open to these changing patterns in

their relationships and learn how to tolerate the changes (Bozon, 2002).

Have you ever had to recover from a broken heart? Describe the process. What suggestions might you offer to others going through a similar experience?

With time and change, it may also become evident that there are too many differences between two people to allow for a comfortable and fulfilling loving relationship and it no longer makes sense for them to remain together. The uncoupling process is almost always painful, but it may also represent a viable choice for a failing relationship in which one or both partners lack the desire and motivation to move to a new level of commitment (Gottman, 2000).

The bottom line is that love holds no guarantees. No matter how much lovers promise to be true to each other forever, there really are no guarantees against the possibility of one or both eventually choosing to end the relationship. Loving leaves a person vulnerable, so to choose to enter a loving relationship is to choose the risk of being hurt. This is one reason why knowing, understanding, and feeling good about yourself can be so crucial before you enter into a relationship.

The initial reactions that follow the breakup of a relationship may be quite varied. If the final days of the relationship have been troubled and full of turmoil, there may even be a sense of relief. Often there are intense feelings of loneliness and grief, accompanied by the sense of having been rejected or by guilt at having initiated the breakup. Anger is also a common emotional reaction and can represent a very healthy response. Anger that is expressed in ways that are not harmful is prevented from turning inward, where it can become depression and self-deprecation. Crying can also be a healthy release of emotion.

Some people rush to put the pain of their loss behind them. They may even hurry into a rebound relationship to soothe their wounds. However, like any grieving process, the aftermath of a broken relationship must be given its time, and the painful reactions are best resolved by allowing them to be experienced. If you hurry them or try to escape from them, so that the breaking-up process remains incomplete, the reactions eventually will find new outlets in your life. They may make it difficult for you to be trusting and intimate in new relationships that eventually develop for you.

Losing a love is as much a part of life and loving as the joyful experience of falling in love. If you allow yourself to experience that process fully and seek whatever help and support you may need to get through it, you will eventually be able to put the painful aspects behind you and get on with your life and with new relationships.

Self Evaluation

Communicating about Sex

One of the most necessary human processes, and yet one of the most complex and difficult, is communication. Many difficulties in relationships—including many sexual problems—are at least partly the result of lacking or misunderstood communications.

Thoughts, ideas, feelings, values, attitudes, opinions, needs, and desires are communicated not only verbally but also through eye contact, facial expressions, and body language. The questions and exercises in this section are designed to help you evaluate and facilitate your communication about sex with someone who is important to your life and therefore worth the effort. You might find some of the suggestions difficult to carry out, but good communication takes work.

Working on Communication: An Exercise for Two

The following exercise can help you and your partner improve your patterns of communication. Start by rating each other, using the rating scale of 1–4, on the qualities listed below. Write your answers on separate sheets of paper without first discussing the rating scale or the qualities with each other.

Rating Scale:

4 = tops. He/she does a great job of showing this quality to me.

3 = okay. Most of the time I feel this from him/her.

2 = fair. I could really stand to have more of this quality from her/him.

1 = poor. I rarely, if ever, feel this from her/him.

Rating of
Your Partner   *Qualities in Your Partner*

_____   Is caring and considerate toward me.

_____   Is able to show warmth and love.

_____   Is sensitive and understanding toward my emotions.

_____   Lets me feel whatever I need to feel, without trying to talk me out of it.

_____   Seems to listen and really hear what I mean.

_____   Acts real and honest with me so that I can feel that he/she is being genuine.

_____   Treats me as an equal.

_____   Does not jump to conclusions or make snap judgments about me or others.

_____   Treats me with respect.

_____   Is trustworthy.

_____   Seems to trust me and shares inner feelings and thoughts with me.

When you have both finished your ratings, exchange them so that you each can take a look at how you were rated by the other. However, you both should agree to the following conditions.

1. **Do not talk about your reactions to the ratings for 15 minutes, during which time you should:**
   a. Think about why your partner might have rated you as he or she did. Assume that the ratings represent honest reactions.
   b. Think about which ratings made you feel best and which made you feel worst.
   c. Ask yourself if you were surprised by any of the ratings. Why or why not?
   d. Look beneath any anger you might feel or any need to defend yourself against a rating. If you are hurt, be ready to admit it. Keep in mind that your partner had a right to rate you in any manner that seemed honest to her or him. It can lead to a deeper understanding.

2. **When you are ready to start talking together about your mutual ratings:**
   a. You should agree on the most comfortable location.
   b. Share only your own feelings and reactions, being careful not to make assumptions and judgments about your partner's feelings or motivations. Use "I" messages.
   c. After one of you has had a chance to make a point, the other should spend some time summarizing what was heard so you can be sure you are hearing each other accurately. Clear up any misunderstandings that your partner has about anything you have said. Give each other time to do this. Now where do you go from here? If this exercise has shown you ways to improve your ability to communicate, are you ready to work toward this goal? Decide whether you think the two of you could work on particular areas.

Working on the Fundamentals

Certain basic qualities underscore good communication. Here are some ways to evaluate them.

1. *Lack of manipulation.* In healthy, two-way communication, there is no need for games or manipulation. Before proceeding any further, answer the following questions. Write down your answers.
   a. Why are you working on this section concerning communication?
   b. What are your short-term and long-term goals for improving communication with your partner?
   c. Do you have any ulterior or exploitative motives in pursuing communication about sex? If so, what are they?

d. Do you really think you can face the vulnerability that comes with honest, two-way communication? Before answering, you might want to look through the remainder of this section. When you answer in the affirmative, proceed.

2. ***A desire to involve your partner in communication.*** There is no point in waiting. Communication takes at least two people. Now allow your partner to read this section, and share with him or her your answers to the previous questions. If your partner is willing, have him or her answer those same questions and share the answers with you. If you are both willing, proceed with the remainder of this section. It is designed for use by two people who together want to improve their communication about sex.

3. ***Sense of equality.*** Both of you should write your own answers to the following questions on separate sheets of paper. Do not compare any answers until both of you are finished answering all questions.
   a. Do you feel there is any difference in the general common sense possessed by you and by your partner? If so, which of you do you think has more of this quality?
   b. Does one of you tend to give in more to the other when there are disagreements? If so, who?
   c. Generally in your relationship, does one of you seem to emerge as the dominant partner and the other as the submissive partner? If so, which of you is which?
   d. Which one of you tends to initiate sexual contact most often?
   e. Are there any other factors that seem to lead to continuing feelings of inequality between the two of you?

After each of you has written answers to all the questions, exchange papers and read them. Agree to the following: Do not make any comments for 10 minutes. Read each other's answers and silently think about them and about how you feel about them.

Both of you should also read the following two paragraphs:

As you are thinking about your partner's responses and comparing them to your own, can you detect that one or both of you see certain inequalities in your common sense, willingness to stick by points of view, degree of dominance, and/or willingness to initiate sex?

Two-way communication seems to work best when there is a sense of equality between both partners. Otherwise, there is the danger of one person feeling inadequate to deal with conflicts and disagreements in communication. With this in mind, proceed to part 4.

4. ***Working at it.*** Your answers to the questions in part 3 can provide some beginning topics for discussion.
   a. If both of you answered questions in a way that reflects nearly complete equality, you might want to

move on to the next section of this communication questionnaire. If not, do part b.
   b. Go through the answers to your questions one by one, following these rules:
      1. *State only what you feel or think, without making any judgments or assumptions about what the other person is feeling or thinking or about the other person's accuracy.*
      2. *After one of you has made "I feel . . ." and "I think . . ." statements about the answers to one question, the other person should take time to summarize what has been heard. Then the first partner should clarify any misunderstandings. Do this with each of the questions. If anger or hostility develops, proceed with rule 3.*
      3. *If you are feeling angry or resentful, try to pause, look beneath your negative feelings, and see what is at their root. Perhaps you are really feeling some hurt or sense of threat. Look honestly at what you are feeling and share it with your partner.*
      4. *Persist with this process until you both feel some real sense of resolution about the differences of opinion that have arisen. If you feel stumped by this, you might want to consider consulting an outside person to talk over some of these issues with you.*
      5. *When you both feel ready, continue with the remaining parts of this communication exercise.*

Sharing Sexual Attitudes and Values

An important part of communication is letting your partner know your personal attitudes and values about sex. The following exercises can help you get started.

1. **Turn back to the sexual attitude questionnaire in Chapter 1, page 26.** If you have not already done so, both of you should complete your ratings for each attitude statement on separate sheets of paper. Go through the questionnaire item by item and compare your present ratings. For those items where you show a difference of opinion, talk about those differences. If either of you begins to feel anger or tension during the discussion, you might want to try using the approaches in exercise 4b. Remember, it is perfectly all right to have different attitudes. The essential thing is to be able to accept these differences in each other. The key to acceptance is full understanding between partners.

2. **Now continue going through the sexual history section of the questionnaire in Chapter 1.** Share as many of your answers with your partner as you feel comfortable with. If both of you already feel very well acquainted with each other's backgrounds, you might try going through the questions one at a time, answering for your partner in the ways you think are most accurate. Your partner then can clear up any inaccuracies or misconceptions you seem to have concerning his or her sexual history. When you

are finished with this process, summarize any new understandings you have gained about your partner.

3. **Here are some other issues that might be worth discussing with each other.** You can skip any questions you prefer not to answer. Again, you may either share your answers with each other or try answering each question in the way you think your partner would answer it.

   a. What is your opinion on abortion? Should it be legal and available to those women who wish to have an abortion? To what degree should the man be allowed to participate in the decision making about abortion?

   b. What sexual activities do you like best? Why?

   c. What are some of your wildest sexual fantasies? How do you feel about them?

   d. How do you feel about your partner's nude body? What parts of his or her body do you like most? Least?

   e. Have you ever participated in sexual activity that was in some way risky or that you have regretted? How do you feel about that now?

   f. What precautions do you consider essential to reducing the risk of contracting sexually transmitted diseases?

Nonverbal Communication

Very often, more can be communicated without words than with them. Following are some activities for nonverbal communication between you and your partner, with each activity becoming progressively more intimate. At any step, some verbal communication may be necessary to sort through difficult feelings that may surface. Before proceeding with each new stage of intimacy, there should be complete mutual agreement and willingness between the two of you. Each activity should continue until one of you feels ready to stop. Even if you both feel that your relationship has already reached deep levels of intimacy, it would be best to spend at least some time with even the earliest steps of the nonverbal communication process.

Activity 1. In comfortable positions, sit facing each other and look at each other's faces. Spend plenty of time looking into each other's eyes and attempting to express positive feelings. You might feel a little foolish and even feel like laughing; go ahead and get it out of your system.

Activity 2. Take turns touching and caressing each other's faces. The person being touched should close his or her eyes and fully enjoy the sensations. The person doing the touching should make an effort to convey warm, caring messages with the touches.

Activity 3. Take turns feeding each other a piece of fruit or some other food.

Chapter Summary

1. Managing relationships and their sexual aspects takes work. Women are more likely than men to have loved their first sexual partners.

2. Communication is key to healthy loving and sexual relationships.

3. Any communicated message is filtered through the interpretive systems of both the sender and the receiver. There is a strong likelihood of misinterpretation and misunderstanding unless a feedback system is part of the process.

4. People often use slang terms, or no words at all, when making sexual references, and relationships settle on the words with which the partners are comfortable.

5. Communication can be hindered by the myths people believe and the sexual games they have learned to play in relationships.

6. Effective communication grows out of mutual commitment, shared understanding, mutual regard, avoidance of snap judgments, careful listening, empathy, genuineness, clear expression, viewing oneself positively, and appropriate confrontation.

7. There are very real personality differences among people that can have important implications for how they get along with another.

8. Males and females are taught different patterns for communicating as they grow up, and these differences show up in adult communication.

9. Impasses in relationships are best resolved by approaching the conflict as a couple, having clear ownership of the problem, and using "I" messages to communicate about it.

10. Research has elucidated some of the main characteristics correlated with lasting relationships; one factor is having more positive behaviors toward each other than negative behaviors.

11. Healthy sexual sharing in a relationship involves being comfortable with one's own sexual needs, knowing how to risk vulnerability, avoiding sexual coercion, and not assuming one can change a partner.

12. Cross-cultural studies suggest that love attitudes and behaviors may be affected more by individual differences than by genetics or social imperatives.

13. Infatuation or falling in love eventually ends; being in love involves a choice and a commitment to the process of being together.

14. There are three primary human emotion-motivation systems associated with love: lust, attraction, and attachment.

15. Sternberg's theory holds that love is a dynamic interaction of three components: intimacy, passion, and commitment.

16. Pheromones are chemicals that give off scents that may act as subliminal attractants to potential sexual partners. They have not yet been identified for certain in humans.

17. The reward centers of the brain and certain brain chemicals are related to bonding and the emotional experience of love. Vasopressin, PEA, dopamine, and norepinephrine produce the high of attraction; endorphins produce the peacefulness of attachment; and oxytocin is associated with physical intimacy.

18. Sexual intimacy involves touching, relaxation, involved participation, and a realistic view of how romantic love and sex fit into relationships.

19. Same-gender relationships have more similarities than differences with heterosexual relationships. Most gay men and lesbians want long-term close relationships and exhibit three main patterns of relating.

20. Sometimes, friends must work out the place sexual attraction will have in their friendship.

21. The Internet provides a medium for intimate, and sometimes sexual, relationships to develop. Although some of these relationships seem very positive, risks are associated with this form of connection.

22. Three main styles of attachment to others have been identified: secure, preoccupied, and avoidant, the last of which may be either dismissing or fearful.

23. Although a degree of jealousy and possessiveness is to be expected in any loving relationship, these qualities may become destructive if they are rooted in serious insecurities.

24. Loss of a loving relationship can be painful and often needs to be followed by a process of grieving.

Part 3

*Human Reproduction,
Contraception, and Abortion:
Sexuality Confronts Social Policy*

uman biology gives most of us the capability of producing offspring for a major portion of our lives. Reproductive technologies have created far more complex issues for society. People who choose to have children but experience difficulty doing so may turn to medical specialists for assistance, but the age of assisted reproductive technology has also raised serious ethical questions. Society continues to weigh and debate the issues surrounding reproductive technologies, contraception, and abortion.

Heterosexual intercourse typically carries risks and choices relating to pregnancy. There are many ways in which the probability of pregnancy may be reduced, yet we are hardly living in the golden age of contraception. Development of new, more effective, and safer methods of birth control has lagged markedly. There is still a high rate of unintended pregnancy in our society. Couples fail to use contraception or they use it incorrectly, or it fails, leaving them with more choices.

Reproduction is an important part of human sexuality's complex role in society and should not be taken lightly. The issues surrounding reproduction, contraception, and termination of pregnancy have become highly politicized as social policy evolves. Human sexual reproduction is far more than a biological phenomenon; it has become a social and cultural controversy closely associated with cutting-edge biotechnology.

Chapter 10

Reproduction, Reproductive Technology, and Birthing

Chapter Outline

It looks as though our only chance to have a baby of our own will be by using in vitro methods. I feel like I am going to end up spending the kid's college education funds before he or she is even conceived. Sometimes the investment of time, emotion, and money seems strange, and rather scary.

—from a personal essay given to the author

In recent years, the pregnancy rate in the United States has been relatively stable, with about 103 pregnancies each year per 1,000 women aged 15 to 44. Of the roughly 6.4 million pregnancies that occur each year, there will be about 4.1 million live births, 1.1 million miscarriages, and 1.2 million abortions. For women overall, fertility rates have slowly increased, while abortion rates have steadily declined since the 1990s. Among teenaged women, both rates have dropped markedly (Ventura et al., 2008).

Human sexuality and reproduction are closely linked, both biologically and socially. The combining of genetic material that produces another human being with characteristics of both parents is nothing short of a miracle. New understandings of reproduction, coupled with new biomedical technologies, have permitted these processes to be manipulated and transformed in ways that not long ago were considered science fiction. Although reproduction of the human species once could not have taken place without sexual contact, technology now can intervene to bring sperm and egg together in a variety of ways. It is no longer even necessary for the genetic mother—the contributor of the egg—to be pregnant with the child that is eventually born. Social policy, politics, legislation, court precedents, and ethical debate are now as much a part of understanding reproduction as is the age-old question "Where do babies come from?"

■ Fertilization and Fetal Development

During the menstrual cycle, an ovum matures and is released from one of the female's ovaries. Research indicates that fertilization of the ovum is most likely to occur when sperm are present during any of the six consecutive days of the cycle that end with the day of ovulation. The old assumption was that the most likely time for fertilization was during the two days following ovulation. However, there is also evidence that substantial numbers of women may ovulate more than once in a single menstrual cycle (Baerwald, Adams, & Pierson, 2003; Duggavathi & Murphy, 2009).

As soon as semen is ejaculated from the penis into the vagina, the sperm begin their journey into the uterus, and they may remain viable for up to five days. A few thousand usually reach the fallopian tubes. The more sperm that are present, the greater the probability that fertilization, or conception, will

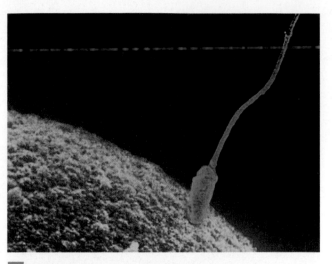

■ **FIGURE 10.1** *Sperm Penetrating the Egg*

A sperm, with its oval head and long tail, approaches the egg, or ovum. Having been capacitated during its journey through the female reproductive tract, the sperm will secrete an enzyme that will help it penetrate the outer membrane of the ovum.

occur. Sperm cell affinity for the ovum seems to be affected by secretions within the fallopian tubes, and the membrane of the sperm cell contains a chemical called **fertilin** that seems to play a role in helping sperm adhere to the egg and eventually penetrate its outer layer (Munuce et al., 2009). There is also increasing evidence that male reproductive proteins carried with sperm and semen play a critical role in how successful the fertilization and pregnancy will be, and even what complications might eventually arise (Ness & Grainger, 2008).

When a sperm cell comes into contact with the ovum, a very specific cell recognition process is triggered that binds the sperm tightly to the outer membrane of the ovum, or **zona pellucida.** The sperm then secretes enzymes that help it pass through the zona and its underlying membranes to penetrate into the ovum. Usually, only one sperm manages to burrow its way into the interior of the ovum (see Figure 10.1), because a hard protein surface develops that prevents further sperm from entering. The actual mechanisms of sperm penetration and exclusion of other sperm are still only partially understood. If an extra sperm enters an ovum, it may well destroy the ovum, or its

---

fertilin (fer-TILL-in) a chemical in the outer membrane of a sperm that assists in attachment to the egg cell and penetration of the egg's outer membrane.

zona pellucida (ZO-nah pe-LOO-si-da) the transparent, outer membrane of an ovum.

FIGURE 10.2   *DNA*

This model of a molecule of deoxyribonucleic acid (DNA) clearly shows its double helix shape. DNA is the building block of heredity, containing within it the genetic code that produces a specific type of offspring. Scientists hope that by learning more about DNA they will be able to prevent genetic diseases and control some aspects of the reproductive process. Skeptics point to some of the risks involved in manipulating the structure of genes.

FIGURE 10.3   *Media Attention for "Octomom"*

A media frenzy erupted when Nadya Suleman, a single, unemployed woman in Los Angeles delivered 8 babies. The case created ethical discussion as well, since the babies were conceived through assisted reproductive technology that would not typically allow this number of fetuses to develop.

own genetic material may be destroyed. Contact with the zona pellucida seems to be essential to causing **exocytosis,** in which the sperm cell opens to allow its chromosomes to be released into the ovum. The combining and pairing of chromosomes from both the sperm and the egg allow fertilization, or conception, to occur. A fertilized ovum is called a **zygote.**

Not only does fertilization initiate the growth of a new human being, but inherited traits are determined at the moment of conception as well. The ovum and the sperm each contain 23 chromosomes, each bearing genes that contain hereditary information stored in the form of **deoxyribonucleic acid (DNA)** (see Figure 10.2). In the combining and pairing of these 46 chromosomes, essential programs for the individual's heredity are initiated. It is the pairing of sex chromosomes at fertilization that determines the sex of the developing embryo—XX

for female, XY for male. The process of sexual differentiation and its implications for later development are discussed in more detail in Chapter 5.

Twins and Higher-Order Multiples

Giving birth to twins, triplets, and higher-order multiples always creates attention and excitement: The more babies born, the more excitement (see Figure 10.3). There was a steady increase in multiple births through the 1990s and early 2000s that seemed

---

exocytosis (ex-oh-sye-TOH-sis) the release of genetic material by the sperm cell, permitting fertilization to occur.

zygote an ovum that has been fertilized by a sperm.

deoxyribonucleic acid (DNA) (dee-AK-see-rye-bow-new-KLEE-ik) the chemical in each cell that carries the genetic code.

Table 10.1	Numbers and Rates of Triplets, Quadruplets, and Higher-Order Multiple Births Per 100,000 in the United States: 1990, 1995–2006				
Year	Triplets	Quadruplets	Quintuplets and Higher-Order Multiples	Triplet Birth Rate	Quadruplet and Higher-Order Birth Rate
2006	6,118	355	67	143.4	9.89
2005	6,208	418	68	150.0	11.7
2004	6,750	439	86	164.2	12.8
2003	7,110	468	85	173.8	13.5
2002	6,898	434	69	171.5	12.5
2001	6,885	501	85	171.0	14.6
2000	6,742	506	77	166.1	14.4
1999	6,742	512	67	170.3	14.6
1998	6,919	627	79	175.5	17.9
1997	6,148	510	79	158.4	15.2
1996	5,298	560	81	136.1	16.5
1995	4,551	365	57	116.7	10.8
1990	2,830	185	13	71.6	5.0

Source: *National Vital Statistics Reports,* vol. 57, no. 7, January 7, 2009, p. 21.

to cease, at least temporarily, by 2004. The incidence of twins rose 70 percent between 1980 and 2004, having stabilized at about 32 per 1,000 births. The rate of higher-order multiple births (triplets, quadruplets, and more) declined in 2006 to 153.3 per 100,000 births. The numbers and rates of triplets and higher-order multiple births are shown in Table 10.1. The increase in multiple births was in small part due to children being born to older mothers, who are more prone to multiple births, but also the result of increased use of fertility drugs that stimulate the ovaries to release more than one ovum. Less aggressive strategies for stimulating ovaries are probably responsible for the recent decrease in multiple births (Dickey, 2009).

Twins may be either **fraternal twins,** formed from two separate ova fertilized by two separate sperm, or **identical twins,** formed by a single ovum and sperm. Fraternal twins may also be called *dizygotic* because they are produced from two zygotes, whereas identical twins are sometimes called *monozygotic* because they have come from a single zygote. In the case of fraternal twins, the two zygotes develop separately, and the twins look no more alike than any other siblings in the family. They may be of the same or different sexes. In the case of identical twins, when the first division of the zygote occurs, the two cells separate and develop as two individuals. Because they have exactly the same chromosomes, they are of the same sex and are identical in appearance (see Figure 10.4). Triplets, quadruplets, and other multiple fetuses may all be fraternal or may include one or more sets of identical twins. Identical triplets and higher-order multiples are extremely rare, except when fertility drugs are being used.

The development of multiple fetuses increases the risk of premature birth and birth defects for the baby and may cause other problems for the pregnant woman. The higher the number of fetuses, the greater the likelihood of premature birth, low birth weight, birth defects, or death of an infant before birth or within the first year after birth. When one of the fetuses has some sort of defect, or if one of the fetuses dies prior to birth, the likelihood of problems in the pregnancy and birth defects in the remaining fetus

fraternal (dizygotic) twins twins formed from two separate ova that were fertilized by two separate sperm.

identical (monozygotic) twins twins formed by a single ovum that was fertilized by a single sperm before the cell divided in two.

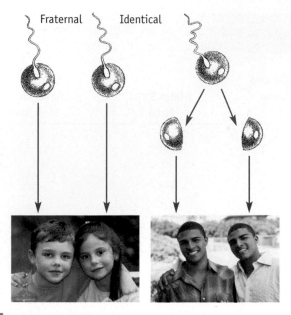

FIGURE 10.4 *Twins*

Fraternal, or dizygotic, twins are formed from the fertilization of two separate ova by two separate sperm. Identical, or monozygotic, twins are formed from the same fertilized ovum that divides before implantation in the uterus.

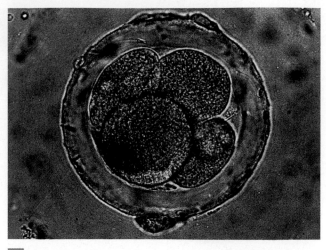

FIGURE 10.5 *Cell Division*

Four new cells of the forming embryo. Following fertilization of the ovum by the sperm, their chromosomes join, and the genetic plan to produce an embryo is set into motion. The zygote, or fertilized ovum, begins to undergo cell division, first producing two cells, then four, and so on. Each new cell receives a complete set of 46 human chromosomes, programmed to produce an entirely new human being.

increases even more (Pharoah, Glinianaia, & Rankin, 2009). For twins that share the same amniotic sac during development, there is also a higher risk of death around the time of birth (Hack et al., 2009).

Implantation of the Embryo

After fertilization has occurred, the zygote begins a process of cell division as it continues to move through the fallopian tube toward the uterus (see Figure 10.5). The first division produces two cells, these both divide to form four, and so on. With each cell division, the chromosomes are replicated so that every new cell has a full complement of hereditary material. Within three days, a spherical, solid mass of cells has formed, called the **morula.** By the end of the fifth day after fertilization, the sphere has developed a fluid-filled cavity in its interior and is called the **blastocyst.** By this time, the mass of dividing cells has left the fallopian tube and entered the uterine cavity. Because there is no rich source of nourishment, the cells are not growing, and the blastocyst is not appreciably larger than the original ovum.

About a week after fertilization, the blastocyst comes into contact with the uterine lining, or endometrium. By this time the blastocyst has developed specialized cells that secrete a chemical called L-selectin,

which in turn binds to structures that have been formed by the endometrium. Further chemical changes cause the blastocyst to adhere to the uterine lining more tightly and then to burrow into it. This implantation process must happen within the ten days of the menstrual cycle that would normally have ended with menstruation (Cole, Ladner, & Byrn, 2009; Fazleabas & Kim, 2003). Cells of the blastocyst form blood vessels that grow toward the blood vessels of the uterus during the implantation process. Once the blastocyst is embedded in the uterine wall it is considered an **embryo,** poised to undergo a series of dramatic changes in growth and development (see Figure 10.6).

Occasionally, a blastocyst becomes implanted in a fallopian tube or strays into the abdominal cavity and attaches itself to some other tissue, where it continues

---

morula (MOR-yuh-la) a spherical, solid mass of cells formed after three days of embryonic cell division.

blastocyst the ball of cells, after five days of cell division, that has developed a fluid-filled cavity in its interior and has entered the uterine cavity.

embryo (EM-bree-o) the term applied to the developing cells when, about a week after fertilization, the blastocyst implants itself in the uterine wall.

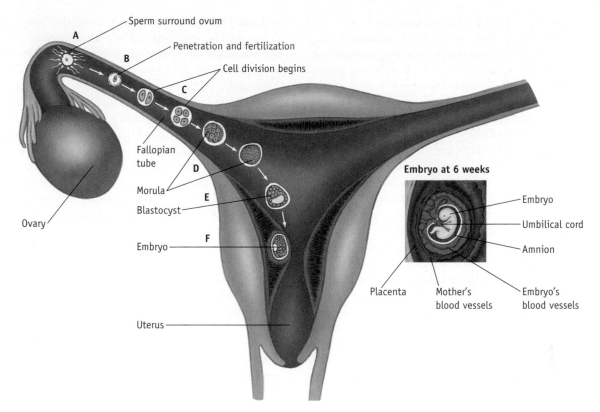

FIGURE 10.6 *Blastocyst Implantation and Placement Function within the Uterus*

After hundreds of sperm surround the ovum **(A)**, one penetrates and fertilizes it **(B)**. Cell division begins **(C)** and after three days produces a spherical mass called a morula **(D)**. The fifth day after fertilization, the mass develops into a hollow sphere of cells called a blastocyst **(E)** and within a week implants in the uterine lining; it is now considered an embryo **(F)**. **(Insert)** The developing embryo receives nourishment and oxygen from the mother's blood through the placenta and returns embryonic waste products back through it. This exchange takes place through the umbilical cord, which connects the fetal and maternal circulatory systems.

to develop as an embryo. This is called an **ectopic pregnancy,** and the embryo must be surgically removed to prevent rupture of the tube and bleeding. Complications of ectopic pregnancy constitute the seventh leading cause of maternal death during pregnancy. The rate of ectopic pregnancies has risen dramatically, and researchers have speculated that this may be due to the use of fertility drugs or to increases in societal stress and sexually transmitted disease.

Typically, a baby is born after about 266 days (approximately nine months) of development in the uterus, or *gestation*. There are wide variations in the length of pregnancy, however. During that period, the fertilized ovum develops into an infant capable of living outside the uterus and weighing about 6 billion times more at birth than at the time of fertilization.

Extraembryonic Membranes and the Placenta

Early in embryonic development, several outer or *extra-embryonic* membranes essential to the embryo's sur-

vival are formed from some of its specialized cells. The membrane that creates a sac to enclose the embryo is called the **amnion.** The sac is filled with fluid, which keeps the embryonic tissues moist and protectively cushions the embryo. The amniotic sac, also called the bag of waters, breaks just before birth, releasing its clear watery fluid through the vagina. Two membranes, the *yolk sac* and the *allantois*, seem to function only in early embryonic development and gradually become partly incorporated into the **umbilical cord.** The outermost

ectopic pregnancy (ek-TOP-ik) the implantation of a blastocyst somewhere other than in the uterus, usually in the fallopian tube.

amnion (AM-nee-on) a thin membrane that forms a closed sac around the embryo; the sac is filled with amniotic fluid, which protects and cushions the embryo.

umbilical cord the tubelike tissues and blood vessels originating at the embryo's navel that connect it to the placenta.

extraembryonic membrane is the **chorion.** It plays an essential role in the formation of the **placenta,** the structure that provides nourishment for the embryo. The chorion produces small fingerlike projections, called **villi,** that grow into the uterine tissue and form a major part of the placenta.

It is within the placenta that blood vessels from the embryo come into close contact with blood vessels from the mother, although there is no actual intermingling of the two bloodstreams. When the blood vessels are in close proximity, however, food molecules and oxygen from the maternal blood diffuse into the embryo's blood. Carbon dioxide and other metabolic wastes diffuse from the embryo's blood into the mother's blood, and her body then disposes of them through the lungs and kidneys. The embryo is connected to the placenta by the umbilical cord, which forms during the fifth week of pregnancy. It is through the umbilical cord that the embryo's blood vessels pass into and out of the placenta (see Figure 10.6, insert).

Usually, after two months of development the embryo is called the **fetus.** It is beyond the scope of this book to detail embryonic and fetal development. However, from the moment of conception to the time a baby is born, remarkable changes occur. An entire human body develops, with internal systems that can function to support life and enable the fetus to move and react to stimuli (see Figures 10.7 to 10.10). Figure 10.11 summarizes some of the important stages of fetal development.

Infertility and Sexuality

Not all couples who want to have children are able to do so. Failure of the occurrence of a successful pregnancy after a year or more of intercourse without contraception may indicate an **infertility** problem. There is evidence that the rate of fertility difficulties is on the rise, and there has been some concern that environmental pollutants might be responsible. About 15 percent of nonsterilized, sexually experienced women, or about 10 percent of all women of reproductive age, report having problems with conceiving or carrying a pregnancy to term. Women with a history of pelvic inflammatory disease, endometriosis, diabetes, or hypertension seem particularly prone to infertility. It may be that half or more of these women eventually can become pregnant without medical intervention, but for the others the problem may be more persistent.

Male infertility usually is caused by a low sperm count, defined as less than 40 million sperm per cubic centimeter of semen, or by sluggish motility of the sperm. Although low sperm counts do not make con-

ception impossible, they do reduce the chances of its occurring. Several infections and injuries of the testes may damage the sperm-producing tubules and lead to low sperm counts. Alcohol and tobacco have also been implicated. Although some medical and surgical treatments have been tried with male infertility, the results have been poor. It is typically suggested that men with low sperm counts avoid lengthy submersion in very warm water, which can temporarily interfere with sperm production. Sperm are produced at a temperature slightly below internal body temperature due to the external location of the testes. An over-the-counter test available from drugstores can evaluate sperm numbers in the privacy of the home. The test, called FertilMARQ, does not offer information about sperm motility or shape, however, both of which can play a role in male fertility.

For couples who have been planning on having children, infertility can be a very real disappointment, accompanied by a sense of deprivation and a range of difficult emotions including guilt, anger, and frustration. The reproductive technologies described next in this chapter can sometimes help, but they are expensive and may have limited success rates that actually increase the levels of frustration and disappointment (Bentley & Mascie-Taylor, 2000). A survey of the literature on the relational effects of infertility clearly indicated that infertility creates stress and anxiety for both partners, in particular the woman. Males are more distressed when the source of the problem is found to be them or when the relationship has been disrupted. Infertility may create feelings of personal inadequacy and interfere with sexual spontaneity. Nevertheless, it does not seem to have a pervasively negative effect on either marital or sexual satisfaction. For many couples, working together on infertility often brings a deepened sense of commitment and intimacy to their relationship (Watkins & Baldo, 2004; Wischmann et al., 2009).

---

chorion (KOR-ee-on) the outermost extraembryonic membrane, essential in the formation of the placenta.

placenta (pla-SEN-ta) the organ that unites the fetus to the mother by bringing their blood vessels close together; it provides nourishment and removes waste for the developing baby.

villi fingerlike projections of the chorion that form a major part of the placenta.

fetus the term given to the embryo after two months of development in the womb.

infertility the inability to produce offspring.

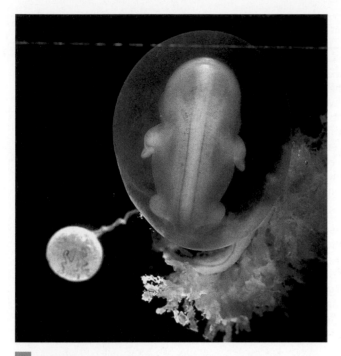

FIGURE 10.7 *Spine of Embryo at Six Weeks*

At six weeks of development, the embryo floats in the fluid of its amnion. In this rear view of the embryo, its developing spinal cord may be seen clearly, flanked by its two red vertebral arteries. The yolk sac, seen at the lower left of the photograph, eventually will become incorporated into the umbilical cord.

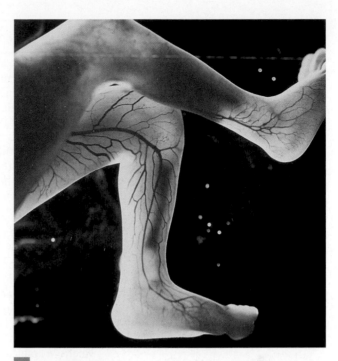

FIGURE 10.9 *Legs of Fetus at Four Months*

The blood vessels and developing bones are visible in the legs of this four-month (6.4-inch) fetus. The skeleton is first formed from cartilage. Bone tissue then begins to grow out from the middle of the cartilage toward both ends. Bone development is not fully completed until an individual reaches about age 25 years.

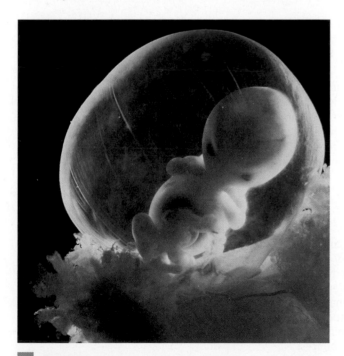

FIGURE 10.8 *Embryo at Seven Weeks*

At seven weeks, the embryo is nearly an inch long, and both its internal and external organs are rapidly forming. Facial features are beginning to take shape, and the skeleton is developing internally. The fontanel, or soft area in the center of the developing skull, is clearly visible in this picture.

FIGURE 10.10 *Fetus Sucking Thumb at 4½ Months*

At 4½ months, the fetus has formed its human features and proportions. Survival reflexes, such as the sucking reflex, are already able to function. This photograph provides a startling demonstration of the potential for thumb sucking in a fetus that is only halfway to full-term.

	Prenatal Development	Changes in Mother
1 Month 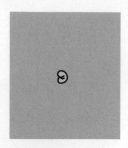	Fertilization occurs. Zygote implants itself in the lining of the uterus. Rapid cell division occurs. Embryonic state lasts from 2 weeks to 8 weeks. Cells differentiate into 3 distinct layers: the ectoderm, the mesoderm, and the endoderm. Nervous system begins to develop. Embryo is ½ inch long.	Possible morning sickness, or nausea, and fatigue. Breasts may begin to feel tender. No weight gain.
2 Months 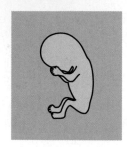	Heart and blood vessels form. Head area develops rapidly. Eyes begin to form detail. Internal organs grow, especially the digestive system. Sex organs develop and gender can be distinguished. Arms and legs form and grow. Heart begins to beat faintly. Embryo is 1 inch long and weighs 1/10 ounce.	Increased frequency of urination. Possible nausea and tiredness. Constipation, heartburn, and indigestion may begin in the second month and last throughout the pregnancy. Breast tenderness. No noticeable weight gain.
3 Months 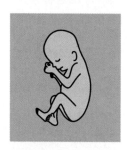	Head growth occurs rapidly. Bone formation begins. The digestive organs begin to function. Arms, legs, and fingers make spontaneous movements. Fetus is 3 inches long and weighs 1 ounce.	Perspiration may be increased. Possible nausea. Continued need to urinate more frequently than usual. Breast heaviness and tenderness. Small weight gain (2–3 pounds).
4 Months 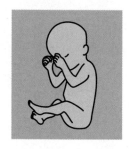	Lower parts of the body show rapid growth. Bones are distinct in X rays. Reflex movement becomes more active. Heartbeat can be detected. Sex organs are fully formed. Fetus is 7 inches long and weighs 5 ounces.	Belly begins to show. Faint movement of the fetus may be felt. Fatigue. Decrease in frequency of urination. Increase in appetite. Morning sickness may diminish or end. Weight gain in month 4: 3–4 pounds.
5 Months 	A fine, downy fuzz covers the entire body. Vernix (a waxy coating) collects over the body. Ears and nose begin to develop cartilage. Fingernails and toenails begin to appear. Fetus may suck thumb, hiccup, and kick. Fetus is 12 inches long and weighs 14 ounces.	Possible shortness of breath. Possible fluttering movements as fetus stretches. Possible food cravings. Pelvic joints begin to relax. Weight gain in month 5: 3–4 pounds.

■ FIGURE 10.11 *Embryonic and Fetal Development and Changes in the Mother's Body*

Source: From Terry F. Pettijohn, *Psychology: A Concise Introduction,* 3d ed. 1992, Guilford, CT: Dushkin Publishing Company, The March of Dimes, and Earth Surface Graphics.

		Prenatal Development	Changes in Mother
6 Months		Eyes and eyelids fully formed. Fat is developing under the skin. Fetus is 14 inches long and weighs 2 pounds.	Possible backache. Fetus's movements now usually felt. Weight gain in month 6: 3–4 pounds.
7 Months		Cerebral cortex of brain develops rapidly. Fetus is 16 inches long and weighs 3 pounds.	Fetus is very active. Possible blotchy skin, which will clear up after the baby is born. Ankles may swell from standing. Possible backache. Weight gain in month 7: 3–4 pounds.
8 Months		Subcutaneous fat is deposited for later use. Fingernails reach beyond the fingertips. Fetus is 17 inches long and weighs 5 pounds.	Occasional headaches, backache, difficulty sleeping. Weight gain in month 8: 3–5 pounds.
9 Months		Hair covering the entire body is shed. Organ systems function actively. Vernix is present over the entire body. Fetus settles into position for birth. Neonate is 21 inches long and weighs 7 pounds.	Uterus has now moved a few inches lower. Feeling of heaviness in lower abdomen. Ankle swelling. Shortness of breath. Weight gain in month 9: 3–5 pounds. Total weight gain: 20–29 pounds.

■ Reproductive and Fetal Technology

Many important social, legal, religious, personal, and ethical questions have been raised by biotechnological advances to help infertile people reproduce, procedures that are collectively called **assisted reproductive technology (ART).** The first test-tube baby was born in England in 1978. It is estimated that each year in the United States, some 135,000 ART procedures are performed that lead to the birth of between 50,000 and 60,000 infants (Reefhuis et al., 2009). These techniques have called into question some fundamental assumptions about sex, reproduction, and family structure. Reproductively, it is already a brave new world. Social policies have been slow to adjust to the many ethical

assisted reproductive technology (ART) a collection of laboratory techniques that have been developed to help couples overcome infertility problems and have children, usually through bypassing one of the usual biological pathways to pregnancy or gestation.

and moral issues and decisions that have emerged (Van der Ploeg, 2002).

Experts in the field know that certain birth defects are somewhat more common in infants conceived through ART and believe that couples who are considering such treatments for infertility should be fully informed of all potential risks and benefits (Reefhuis et al., 2009). Some studies have suggested that ART may be associated with certain genetic syndromes that are called imprinting disorders, since they seem to occur more commonly in children who were conceived through technological means. In these cases, certain genes may not function properly, causing physical or intellectual deficits (Amor & Halliday, 2008; Lim et al., 2009; Manipalviratn, DeCherney, & Segars, 2009). A study that followed up on 15- and 16-year-old adolescents conceived through artificial means found no significant differences between their own and their families' adjustment levels than in families whose children were not conceived through ART (Colpin & Bossaert, 2008).

The most common procedures of ART involve facilitating the fertilization of an ovum by a sperm or the implantation of a blastocyst into a uterus that is prepared to carry a pregnancy. What follows is a description of the more typical methods used to accomplish these ends.

Artificial Insemination

In those cases where the male partner's sperm count is too low or his sperm are otherwise compromised in their ability to fertilize, there has been a technique that has been standard medical practice since the 1930s called **artificial insemination.** It involves the placing of donated semen in the woman's vagina or uterus without intercourse.

This method of fertilization is used most typically with couples in which the man's sperm count is low (fewer than 40 million sperm per milliliter of semen) or, when the sperm have a high incidence of abnormalities. One approach involves concentrating the sperm from several of the man's own semen specimens, and then placing them in the uterus, but it has not proved overly successful, especially with women over 35 (Badawy, Elnashar, & Eltotongy, 2009). A more common method is to use semen contributed by an anonymous donor, chosen for characteristics of good health, intelligence, and physical traits similar to those of the intended father. The semen may be frozen or used fresh, after the donor has been tested for possible HIV infection. The pregnancy rate in artificial insemination ranges from 60 percent to 75 percent. The procedure sometimes is used by couples without medical assistance, carried out by the couples themselves with common kitchen devices such as a basting syringe. Lesbian couples and gay male couples, with the help

of a cooperative friend, have used artificial insemination in order to have children.

While sperm banks sometimes pay donors for semen that will be used in artificial insemination, some countries have prohibited this commercialization and want sperm donations to be made only for altruistic reasons. Canada passed such a law in 2004. There is also an increasing trend toward disclosure of the identities of sperm donors, and in one study, nearly half of donors were willing to be identified or even willing to meet their biological offspring (Freeman et al., 2009; Thorn, Katzorke, & Daniels, 2008; Yee, 2009).

Reproductive technology of this sort has led to legal precedents related to the meaning and rights of parenthood, as courts must make decisions about complicated cases. In a California court case, a man fought to keep the children his wife had borne after being impregnated by another man's semen. The wife had sued him for custody when she wanted to leave with the children, but the judge ruled that because the man had raised the children as his own, he had no less right to retain custody than did an actual biological father.

In Vitro Fertilization

In the late 1960s, a team of English scientists began working with **in vitro fertilization (IVF),** a technique in which ova are fertilized by sperm in the laboratory. The first test-tube baby produced by IVF was Louise Brown, born in Oldham, England, in 1978. Hundreds of thousands of babies have now been born as a result of the procedure. It is the centerpiece of most reproductive technologies. It permits women who would otherwise be unable to conceive to have a child. For example, many infertile women have blockages in the fallopian tubes that prevent the sperm and egg from meeting, and IVF enables them to bypass the usual mechanisms for enabling fertilization to happen.

As shown in Figure 10.12, the basic IVF technique involves the harvesting of ova from one of the woman's ovaries after she has received fertility injections for a period of two weeks. The injections cause several ova to mature but may also have uncomfortable side effects such as bloating, pain, and mood swings. The ovaries are carefully monitored through daily blood tests and ultrasound techniques so that the mature eggs can be removed microsurgically at exactly the right time. The eggs are then mixed with sperm cells

artificial insemination injection of the sperm cells of a male into a woman's vagina, with the intention of conceiving a child.

in vitro fertilization (IVF) a process by which the union of the sperm and egg occurs outside the mother's body.

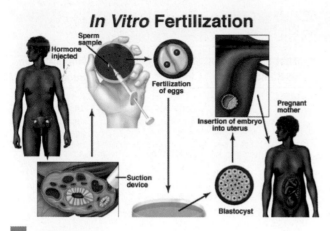

In Vitro Fertilization

Sperm sample

Hormone injected

Fertilization of eggs

Pregnant mother

Insertion of embryo into uterus

Suction device

Blastocyst

FIGURE 10.12 *In Vitro Fertilization*

from the intended father, usually obtained through masturbation. Fertilization can be confirmed by microscopic examination, and the eventual embryo that develops is placed in the woman's uterus, which has been appropriately readied by hormonal treatment. If the process is successful, the embryo will implant in the uterine wall as would happen under natural conditions, and development of the fetus will continue.

The main problem with IVF is the relatively low rate of embryo implantations. Despite efforts to improve that rate through various modifications in the methods, little has changed (Fauser, 2008). The rate of births from IVF averages about 25 percent, but patients with special risk factors—such as being older or having a history of repeated miscarriages—are less likely to be successful. Fertilization is achieved about 60 percent of the time, but the chances of implantation occurring with any single embryo are only about one in six. Beyond that, there is a one-third chance that the pregnancy will be ectopic or end in miscarriage. The chance of pregnancy increases slightly when four to six embryos are transferred. However, use of multiple embryos also increases the potential for multiple pregnancy, with its subsequent risks of miscarriage, premature delivery, and infant mortality at or soon after the time of birth.

The number of embryos that should be implanted during one IVF attempt remains an issue of debate among clinicians, but recommended guidelines have been devised (Stern et al., 2009). Additionally, if several fetuses are present in the pregnancy, it is usually recommended that their numbers be reduced in order to increase the survival chances of one to three of them. The **selective reduction** procedure involves selectively aborting one or more fetuses. This option may represent a difficult choice for some parents, since it bases the well-being of some fetuses on the termination of other fetuses. Selective reduction has succeeded in reducing the number of premature multiple births from IVF and their accompanying complications. In the "octomom"

case, there was controversy over why the clinician took the chance of implanting so many embryos, and why there had not been a prearranged agreement about using selective reduction if too many implanted. Of course, in this particular case, eight fetuses survived the pregnancy, which has raised other controversial issues.

In one IVF variation, zygotes formed from the laboratory fertilization are inserted directly into the woman's fallopian tubes, where they then move naturally down into the uterus and possibly implant. This procedure, called **zygote intrafallopian transfer (ZIFT),** though more medically complicated, seems to increase the chances of success modestly.

Some fertility clinics have advertised misleading IVF success rates, so it is crucial that couples investigate any clinic's length of service, success rates, costs, and manner of producing statistics on success. Couples need to know whether all attempts to achieve IVF are included in the statistics or only those that result in actual fertilization and transfer of the embryo to the uterus. The financial stakes can be high. Even a single treatment cycle can cost thousands of dollars, and the chances that it will yield a viable pregnancy are not that good. It has been estimated that the average couple seeking to have a child through IVF will spend $50,000 to $100,000 for all of the procedures involved. Because there is no guarantee of success, IVF may also exact a significant emotional toll in continuing disappointment. See Table 10.2 for a summary of various fertilization procedures and their costs.

Securing and Storing Gametes and Embryos

Some women and men are unable to produce gametes (eggs or sperm) that are viable for fertilization. Various means of transplanting ovarian tissues or producing sperm from other cells are being explored, but for now ART must rely on gametes produced by human beings (Del Priore et al., 2007; Silber et al., 2005). Quick-freezing techniques have been perfected so that sperm, ova, and embryos may now be preserved for later use by the couple, or for donation to others. In this way, stored gametes or embryos may be used much later for repeat procedures, reducing the inconvenience and cost for the couple trying to get pregnant. The technique

selective reduction the use of abortion techniques to reduce the number of fetuses when there are more than three in a pregnancy, thereby increasing the chances of survival for the remaining fetuses.

zygote intrafallopian transfer (ZIFT) a process by which zygotes resulting from IVF are inserted directly into the fallopian tubes.

Table 10.2 *Assisted Reproductive Technologies*

Procedure and Its Purpose	Method	First Success in Humans	Average Cost in U.S.*	Implantation Success Rate
In vitro fertilization (IVF) Infertility cases in which tube blockages, anatomical problems, or inadequate sperm motility make natural conception unlikely	Ova are harvested from a woman's ovary and mixed with sperm in a laboratory petri dish containing a nutrient medium. Resulting embryos may be transferred to the uterus (often several are tried) or frozen for later use.	1978 (England)	$10,000–12,500 for each attempt $41,100 per live birth	18%–25%, depending on age, method used
Gamete intrafallopian transfer (GIFT) To enable internal conception when difficulties with ovulation or low sperm count render it unlikely.	Ova are harvested from ovary and injected through catheter into fallopian tube. Concentrated sperm are also transferred to the fallopian tube, increasing the likelihood of fertilization. Embryos then travel to uterine lining naturally.	1984 (United States)	$15,000–20,000 for each attempt	20%–28%
Zygote intrafallopian transfer (ZIFT) Enables an IVF embryo to implant naturally.	Zygote (fertilized ovum) from IVF procedure is transferred to woman's fallopian tube in hopes it will migrate to the uterus and implant naturally.	1989 (Belgium)	$15,000–20,000 for each attempt	20%–25%
Intracytoplasmic sperm injection (ICSI) Increases chance of conception for IVF.	Individual ovum is held in place with a micropipette while another micropipette is used to inject a single sperm cell into the ovum. If an embryo forms, it may be transferred to the uterus.	1992 (Belgium)	$16,000–21,000	20%–24%

Note: Additional procedures used to retrieve, freeze, and store gametes or embryos can add up to $5,000 to the basic IVF costs. For example, storage of sperm for a year can cost $700 and storage of embryos for a year can cost $2,500 in addition to charges for the original freezing.

Sources: G. M. Chambers, E. A. Sullivan, O. Ishihara, M. G. Chapman, & G. D. Adamson (2009). The economic impact of assisted reproductive technology: A review of selected developed countries. *Fertility and Sterility, 91*(6), 2281–2294, and www.babycenter.com

is also used to store sperm and ova from youthful cancer patients whose treatments may render them infertile. This can enable them to reproduce later in their lives (Menon et al., 2009).

Many couples who try IVF have several embryos stored for possible future use. The American Fertility Society has reported that the more than 300 fertility clinics in the United States probably have some 100,000 stored embryos. Couples usually are asked ahead of time what they want done with any leftover frozen embryos, which can be destroyed, offered to infertile couples, or used for research. Many want them donated to other couples, and there is a movement to promote embryo adoption (Janssens, 2009; MacCallum, 2009). Some ethicists feel they should not be destroyed, and others have suggested that they might even be saved for use by future generations.

What do you think should be done with embryos that are no longer going to be used for IVF in the couple that created the embryos?

See "Designer Babies" on SexSource Online.

Preimplantation Genetic Screening and Gene Alteration

Genetic research has yielded a complete picture of the genetic composition of human beings, also known as the human genome. Molecular geneticists continue to unlock the secrets of how genes function and how replacing certain genes might well treat or even cure thousands of human disorders that have genetic components. **Gene therapy** may well represent a significant part of the future of medicine.

A technique that has sometimes been used in conjunction with IVF is **preimplantation genetic screening** to detect any possible defects. One or more cells may be removed from the blastocyst and then analyzed for chromosomal abnormalities. In the United Kingdom, embryos may be tested for possible genetic cancer risks in this way (Blackburn, 2006). If

gene therapy treatment of genetically caused disorders by substitution of healthy genes.

preimplantation genetic screening examination of the chromosomes of an embryo conceived by IVF prior to its implantation in the uterus.

some disorder is detected by the screening, the embryo is destroyed, raising ethical concerns on the part of people who consider an embryo a viable stage of human life that should not be terminated. The medical profession generally considers implantation in the uterus to represent the beginning of actual pregnancy. Since the implantation rates with IVF have continued to be low, and the procedure may in fact increase the risk of failed implantation, the use of preimplantation screening is decreasing and in some cases is considered to be professionally unethical (Fauser, 2008; Mastenbroek et al., 2008). There are less invasive procedures for detecting DNA damage in preimplantation embryos that examine the metabolic activities of the embryo, but these techniques have yet to be tested with human embryos (Sturmey et al., 2009).

Another outcome of genetic research has been the manipulation of genetic material within cells, sometimes called **genetic engineering.** In 2008, researchers at Weill Cornell Medical Center in New York announced that they had genetically altered a human embryo. Even though the embryo was defective and would never have developed, the specter was raised of genetically altered humans. It may well be that the technology will exist for altering embryonic genes in such a way to alter eventual human characteristics. Couples concerned about the possibility of transmitting a genetic disorder to their offspring could conceivably use such technology to prevent that from happening. However, there are concerns that the technology could be used for more frivolous goals such as a child's hair color or attractiveness. This clearly raises ethical issues that will be debated for decades to come.

Other Fertilization Technologies

Alternative techniques have been developed to optimize the chances of fertilization, depending on the fertility problem involved. In about half of infertile couples, the man has a low enough sperm count to make conception impossible through usual means. In one technique designed to increase the likelihood of fertilization for such couples, eggs are removed from the ovary and injected through a catheter into the woman's fallopian tube. Sperm cells that have been separated from the partner's semen, thereby concentrating them, are then injected directly into the same area, making fertilization more likely. This procedure, called **gamete intrafallopian transfer (GIFT),** increases the chances of success to about 28 percent.

Another technique is **intracytoplasmic sperm injection (ICSI).** A single sperm cell is isolated in a microscopic pipette and then injected directly into an ovum that is being held in place by a slightly larger pipette (see Figures 10.13 and 10.14). There are three ways in which viable sperm can be secured for use in ICSI. In males with normal sperm counts, masturbation would be used to get sperm for the procedure. For men who have anatomical abnormalities that interfere with transport of sperm out of the testes or whose sperm tend to have low motility, sperm may be suctioned directly out of the epididymis of the testes through a tiny pipette in a procedure called **testicular sperm aspiration (TESA).** The technique has even been used to obtain sperm from men who have just died and whose wives wish to reserve the possibility of having their children. A variation on this technique that is sometimes used for men with no viable sperm in their ejaculate involves shredding some of the removed testicular tissue and suspending it in a liquid medium. Sometimes viable sperm are found in the preparation that may be used for ICSI. There is evidence that sperm that are damaged in any way increase the risks of unsuccessful ICSI or IVF attempts (Figueira et al., 2009; Haimov-Kochman et al., 2009; Zini et al., 2008).

Although earlier studies raised concerns about the health of infants and children that had been conceived by ICSI, more recent research shows only a slightly higher risk of male infants having undescended testicles. Beyond that the physical health of ICSI children seems comparable with that of spontaneously conceived children (Ludwig et al., 2009). One controversial issue surrounding ICSI and related technologies for infertile men is the finding that males produced by such fertilization technologies are likely to perpetuate the genetic glitches that originally caused their fathers' infertility.

Finding viable ova for IVF may also be a challenge. A technique called **immature oocyte collection** uses a specially designed needle to enter small, immature follicles in the ovary and remove immature egg cells, or oocytes. Cell-culturing processes are then used to ripen the immature eggs in the laboratory,

genetic engineering the modification of the gene structure of cells to change cellular functioning.

gamete intrafallopian transfer (GIFT) direct placement of the ovum and concentrated sperm cells into the woman's fallopian tube to increase the chances of fertilization.

intracytoplasmic sperm injection (ICSI) a technique involving the injection of a single sperm cell directly into an ovum; useful in cases where the male has a low sperm count.

testicular sperm aspiration (TESA) a procedure in which sperm are removed directly from the epididymis of the male testes with a micropipette.

immature oocyte collection extraction of immature eggs from undeveloped follicles in an ovary, after which the oocytes are assisted to maturity by cell-culturing methods in preparation for fertilization.

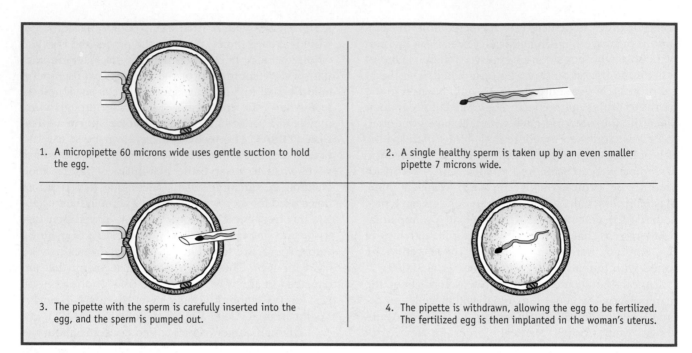

1. A micropipette 60 microns wide uses gentle suction to hold the egg.

2. A single healthy sperm is taken up by an even smaller pipette 7 microns wide.

3. The pipette with the sperm is carefully inserted into the egg, and the sperm is pumped out.

4. The pipette is withdrawn, allowing the egg to be fertilized. The fertilized egg is then implanted in the woman's uterus.

FIGURE 10.13   *Intracytoplasmic Sperm Injection*

Intracytoplasmic sperm injection, unlike conventional IVF, involves placing the sperm within the egg using a micropipette. About 60 percent of eggs fertilized this way are carried to term.

Source: From "New Method Aids Infertile Men," *New Haven Connecticut Register,* November 14, 1995.

readying them for IVF. Because much of the cost of IVF is associated with the treatment of the ovaries to produce mature eggs, this process can trim the costs of the procedure (Papanikolaou et al., 2005).

Ovum donation and IVF have helped some women defy their biological clocks, enabling them to become pregnant even after menopause. Although menopause causes a cessation of the production of viable eggs, the uterus of a postmenopausal woman sometimes can still support a pregnancy. In one controversial case, a 63-year-old woman told physicians she was 50 and then was treated over a 3-year period before becoming pregnant with an IVF embryo formed from a donated ovum fertilized by her husband's sperm. Typically, such procedures are limited to women no older than 55. This case raised ethical issues about the advisability of defying nature in a way that allows older parents to bear children, because they will be relatively old as the child develops and matures. A few postmenopausal women have given birth to their own grandchildren, produced by IVF from their daughters' ova and sons-in-laws' sperm. Some countries have considered legislation banning postmenopausal women from becoming pregnant through such techniques, although social commentators have pointed out that older men have never been prohibited from fathering children as long as their biology permits.

What sorts of ethical controls do you feel should be exerted over reproductive technologies?

Choosing the Sex of a Fetus

A few approaches for selecting an infant's sex have emerged in modern technology. There are techniques

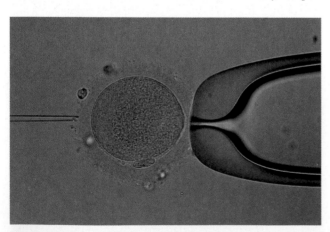

FIGURE 10.14   *The Moment of Truth*

Injection of the egg with the sperm.

ovum donation use of an egg from another woman for conception, with the fertilized ovum then being implanted in the uterus of the woman wanting to become pregnant.

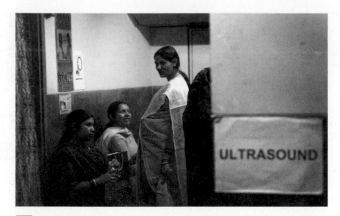

FIGURE 10.15 *Prenatal Sex Selection in India*

Pregnant women wait for ultrasound tests in New Delhi. While it is illegal for women to use ultrasound for the purpose of determining if the fetus is female and then aborting it, the practice is still carried out at private clinics. Because the birthrate of girls has been declining in India, the government has begun giving cash incentives for giving birth to a girl in hopes of changing the mindset that prefers boy babies over girls.

by which either the X-bearing or the Y-bearing sperm may be sorted out before artificial insemination or IVF to increase the chances of the baby's being a girl or a boy. Though complicated and expensive, these techniques may increase the chances of having a girl to about 80 percent and the chances of having a boy to about 65 percent (see Figure 10.15). Other techniques have been suggested, including changing the diet prior to conception, timing intercourse to be slightly before or slightly after ovulation in the menstrual cycle, and modifying the pH of the vagina. Research has tended to indicate that such procedures do not produce statistically valid results and probably are worthless.

The ability to choose the sex of a child raises some troublesome ethical issues both for the parents and for society. Studies in the United States consistently demonstrate that couples tend to have a preference for sons, especially as their first child. Also, when parents have had two children of the same sex, either female or male, there is a greater likelihood that they will have another child. The preference for male children is found in many cultures and can translate into prejudice and sexism (Belanger, 2002). Although people in the United States still voice some reluctance for using sex selection techniques except to prevent certain X chromosome-linked genetic disorders, their opposition to such procedures is not strong enough to hinder use of the technology should its reliability and costs make it widely accessible (Kalfoglou, Scott, & Hudson, 2008).

Techniques such as ultrasound imaging, chorionic villi sampling, or amniocentesis (see pp. 259–261) can identify the sex of a fetus within a few weeks of conception. In some nations, parents sometimes opt for early abortion if the sex of the child is not what they have hoped for. This has become a common, though illegal, practice in China, where couples generally are allowed only one child. The ratio of males to females among live births in China has increased now is about 140 males to 100 females. There is growing concern about this imbalance, and the Chinese government has instituted the Care for Girls program to encourage couples to have girls, including financial incentives, stiff punishment for sex-selective abortion, and a great deal of social restructuring (see Figure 10.15). Similar trends are developing in India, Bangladesh, Pakistan, and South Korea (Hvistendahl, 2009).

What are your opinions about being able to choose the sex of your child? Would you use technology to help you make such a choice?

Human Cloning

Cloning is a reproductive technology that allows for duplication of genetic material so that the offspring are genetically identical either to the donating "parent" or to the other embryos being produced. The original cloning process bypassed even the fertilization stage. In 1968, Oxford University scientist J. B. Gurdon succeeded in

Source: David Horsey. © Tribune Media Services, Inc. All Rights Reserved. Reprinted with permission.

cloning a process by which a genetic duplicate of an organism is made either by substituting the chromosomes of a body cell into a donated ovum or by separation of cells early in embryonic development.

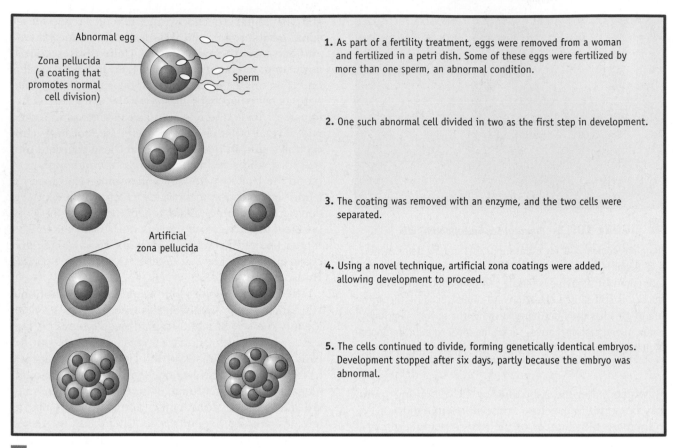

1. As part of a fertility treatment, eggs were removed from a woman and fertilized in a petri dish. Some of these eggs were fertilized by more than one sperm, an abnormal condition.

2. One such abnormal cell divided in two as the first step in development.

3. The coating was removed with an enzyme, and the two cells were separated.

4. Using a novel technique, artificial zona coatings were added, allowing development to proceed.

5. The cells continued to divide, forming genetically identical embryos. Development stopped after six days, partly because the embryo was abnormal.

■ **FIGURE 10.16**   *How Human Embryos Can Be Genetically Duplicated*

Duplicate human embryos, "clones" in the sense that their genetic material is exactly the same, were first created in 1993. Although it would be intended primarily to help infertile couples become pregnant, this "cloning" technique has raised serious ethical questions around the world and generally has been considered unethical. The original experiment summarized here used abnormal zygotes, and it was never intended that they be grown for very long.

replacing the nucleus of a frog's egg with the nucleus of an intestinal cell from another frog. The egg divided normally and eventually formed a tadpole that became an adult frog. Because the new frog's cells contained exactly the same set of chromosomes as the frog that donated the intestinal cell, the two frogs were genetically identical. The exact-copy offspring is called a **clone.** Since then, sheep, mice, cows, monkeys, pigs, mules, cats, and dogs have also been successfully cloned. Concerns continue to be raised about the potential for human cloning, and legislatures around the world have proposed laws to ban such work. Given the pace of scientific inquiry, the laws quickly become obsolete. Scientists are equally concerned that haphazard enactment of laws may well interfere with other forms of research that advance the techniques of medicine (Malakoff, 2003).

Cloning techniques have also been used experimentally for human embryos. Zygote cells produced by IVF have been separated at a very early stage of development. In one such experiment, the protective zona pellucida was removed with an enzyme preparation so that the two identical cells could be completely separated. A new artificial protective coating, created from a gel derived from seaweed, was then placed around each cell, and the cells continued to divide for six more days, at which time the experiment was terminated (see Figure 10.16). No cloned embryos have been implanted. Embryonic cloning is of interest for a few reasons. It could produce multiple embryos more easily for IVF. Embryonic stem cells, which have the potential to differentiate into different kinds of cells that could be used to treat certain medical conditions, also could be produced through cloning techniques (Vogel, 2004).

Cloning raises fascinating ethical questions concerning the future of reproductive technology. For example, cloning techniques could be used to reproduce a child with exceptional characteristics and achievement

clone the genetic-duplicate organism produced by the cloning process.

for the same or different parents. Or parents might set aside embryonic genetic duplicates of each of their children so that if one died they could in theory produce another child who would look exactly the same. Another scenario posits the possibility of using cloned embryos to produce a genetic duplicate if a child needs a bone marrow or kidney transplant, eliminating the problem of immune system rejection. It is even possible that someday a woman could give birth to her own twin. Naturally, these controversial possibilities have raised the ire of many observers. Public opinion polls reflect a predominantly negative stance concerning cloning, although acceptance of a variety of reproductive technologies has been increasing in recent years. Men tend to be more accepting of these technologies than are women (Holden, 2003).

Several mammalian clones either have suffered from serious birth defects or have developed fatal conditions after seeming to be healthy at birth. This suggests that much remains to be learned about the action of genes within cloned animals. Like other reproductive technologies, cloning techniques surely will continue to be developed, and we must begin to prepare for the impact they will have for human sexuality and human life.

Embryo and Stem Cell Research

New techniques have allowed scientists to extract a single cell from an in vitro embryo without destroying the embryo. The cell then may be used to develop an entire line of stem cells that could be used in research. Complex ethical issues surrounding human embryo and stem cell research have entered the public policy and political arenas. The National Institutes of Health (NIH) have issued guidelines for the use of federal funds in research with human embryos in the early stages of development. Recognizing that moral issues are at stake as well, the NIH also has imposed restrictions on such research and required that gamete or embryo donors give informed consent for how their cells may be used (Lo et al., 2010). While new embryo cloning and stem cell research by federally funded researchers was banned for a time, recent administrations have taken a less restrictive approach to such work. Private funding has continued to support embryo research in the United States.

Surrogate Motherhood

Surrogate motherhood, also called **gestational surrogacy,** has been a feasible reproductive procedure since the 1980s. Typically in these cases, a couple in which the woman is unable to bear children pays another woman several thousand dollars to carry a pregnancy for them. Sometimes the surrogate is inseminated by the infertile woman's husband, and sometimes an embryo formed from IVF of the couple's sperm and egg is implanted in the surrogate's uterus. A legal agreement is drawn up among the parties involved in which the woman who is to be impregnated promises to give the child to the couple when it is born. State legislatures have established laws regarding gestational surrogacy, and court cases have tested its various complications, but as reproductive technologies go, most of these issues are now quite clear from a legal perspective. The same cannot be said for some of the newer technologies.

Although some have hailed gestational surrogacy as a significant advance for childless couples, others have argued that it is nothing more than reproductive prostitution. It has been suggested that gestational surrogacy, which today can cost well over $25,000 including medical procedures, legal costs, and the fee paid to the surrogate, could represent the first step toward creating a caste of poor female breeders who would bear genetically improved children for upper-class couples. Opponents find little difference between this procedure and the long-prohibited practice of paying for private adoption of babies. It has also been claimed that the legal protections for the surrogate mother are slim compared with those for the couple, further advancing the argument that surrogate motherhood represents a form of exploitation of women.

Fetal Technology and Medicine

Problems can occur during fetal development, but great strides are being made in monitoring the fetus, diagnosing problems, and sometimes even treating them. Several examples follow.

Fetal Imaging

One of the most commonly used methods to check the developmental progress of a fetus involves the use of ultrasonic waves to produce a computer-generated picture of fetal structures. These **ultrasound images** can be used for finding certain birth defects, determining the position of a fetus, or checking to see if more than one fetus is present. They are now clear enough that the sex organs of the fetus are usually identifiable. Because ultrasound may produce a slight rise in temperature and

gestational surrogacy implantation of an embryo created by the sperm and ovum of one set of parents into the uterus of another woman who agrees to gestate the fetus and give birth to the child, which then is given to the original parents.

ultrasound images ultrasonic rays used to create a picture of fetal structures; often used in conjunction with amniocentesis or fetal surgery.

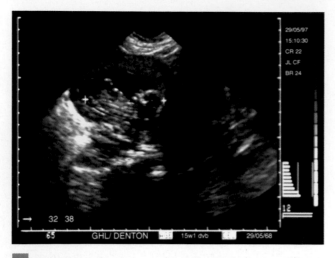

■ **FIGURE 10.17** *Ultrasound Image*

This is an actual sonogram of a healthy fetus.

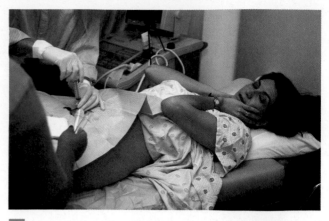

■ **FIGURE 10.18** *Amniocentesis*

A woman, 16 weeks pregnant, undergoes the procedure of amniocentesis. Amniotic fluid is extracted from the uterus and analyzed. It will indicate the gender of the child as well as possible birth defects.

jarring vibrations in the surrounding tissues, the Food and Drug Administration (FDA) has recommended that the technique be used as sparingly as possible. Most clinicians now use at least one ultrasound as a routine procedure during pregnancy, even though there is no particular evidence that the outcome for either the fetus or the mother is substantially improved by such use (see Figure 10.17).

Two more advanced imaging procedures may be used for more detailed screening if there are risks enough to warrant their use. One method used high-frequency ultrasound transducers that may be placed directly in the vagina to improve the resolution of ultrasound images earlier in the pregnancy. Magnetic resonance imaging (MRI) is used when there is concern about developmental abnormalities in the fetal brain or spinal cord, since this technique yields very detailed, high-resolution images of internal structures that cannot be easily assessed with standard ultrasound (Reddy, Filly, & Copel, 2008; Timor-Tritsch et al., 2009).

As ultrasound technology has improved, now even offering 3D images of the fetus, it has given rise to a burgeoning business in keepsake sonograms—lengthy videos and still photos of ultrasound images of the fetus made by nonmedical personnel solely for the enjoyment of the parents and other relatives. Despite FDA cautions about unnecessary exposure to ultrasound during pregnancy, the relative safety of such nonessential procedures remains controversial. Ultrasound allows many parents to be certain of the sex of their baby well before it is born, and they often choose a name long before birth based on this information.

Sometimes clinicians have concerns about the embryo or fetus that are best investigated by direct visual examination. An endoscope is inserted through a hollow needle used to penetrate the uterus and amnion. This permits an *embryoscopy* or *fetoscopy* projected on

a screen by which a trained medical professional may look for possible developmental abnormalities. Variations on this technique may be used to offer surgery or treatment during the first 12 weeks of pregnancy.

Prenatal Chromosomal Testing Techniques

Sometimes because of various factors relating to its parents, a fetus may be at risk of some sort of genetic or chromosomal disorder. Older mothers, for example, have a higher risk of having a baby with Down syndrome, in which the cells have an extra chromosome. There are genetic counselors and computer-based decision-assisting tools that can help parents assess the degree of risk their fetus might have, therefore helping them reach a sensible decision about the need for prenatal genetic testing (Kuppermann et al., 2009).

One of the most widely used procedures is **amniocentesis.** The American College of Obstetricians and Gynecologists (ACOG) has recommended that all pregnant women be tested to determine whether the fetus has chromosomal abnormalities, using either amniocentesis or one of the less invasive procedures now available that can be used earlier in pregnancy (ACOG, 2007). In amniocentesis, ultrasound imaging is used to position a needle and insert it through the abdominal wall into the uterus and the amniotic sac to withdraw amniotic fluid (see Figure 10.18). Cells

amniocentesis (am-nee-oh-sen-TEE-sis) a process by which medical problems with a fetus can be determined while it is still in the womb; a needle is inserted into the amniotic sac, amniotic fluid is withdrawn, and fetal cells then are examined.

Real Student Voices

- Pregnancy is very scary to me at this point in my life. That's why I always insist that we use a condom every time even though I'm on the pill. I just don't want to take any chances.

- I am excited about being a father someday, but I'm in no hurry either. It's tough for me to make the connection in my head between having sex and having babies, even though I know that's how it works.

- I wonder sometimes what I would do if one of us turned out to be infertile. The idea of adopting doesn't excite me, even though I know it's a nice thing to do. But getting involved in a lot of technology doesn't seem very exciting either. Maybe I would just accept not having any children.

from the developing fetus may be found in this fluid and their chromosomes studied for possible abnormalities. If some birth defect is identified, the parents can make a decision about whether to continue or terminate the pregnancy. There are some risks associated with the procedure, including possible miscarriage, although pregnancy complications are significantly less common when amniocentesis is performed 16 to 19 weeks into pregnancy, compared to 11 to 14 weeks. In general, the procedure seems to be quite safe (Odibo et al., 2008).

Whereas amniocentesis is not recommended until around the end of the fourth month of pregnancy, another diagnostic technique, called **chorionic villi sampling (CVS),** can be used as early as the eighth week. A thin catheter is inserted through the cervix, and a small sample of tissue from the chorionic membrane is withdrawn. The chromosomes in these cells then may be analyzed. Although it was once suspected that CVS was associated with a higher incidence of limb defects in infants, it is now known that the procedure actually is correlated with a decreased likelihood of such problems.

Fetal Surgery

At some major medical centers, **fetal surgery** has been carried out with fetuses while they are still in the uterus. Imaging techniques are essential to the diagnosis and to the surgery itself. Other successful surgeries have been performed on fetuses that have actually been temporarily removed from the uterus, replaced following surgery, and then born normally. These surgical techniques have been used to repair urinary tract abnormalities, diaphragmatic hernia, fetal heart defects, and spina bifida. Fetal surgery is one of the frontiers of reproductive and fetal technology, although

many fetuses do not survive the surgical procedures. The medical community is currently reassessing its criteria for making decisions about such surgery and sorting through the risk-benefit standards and other complications of these medically complex procedures (Chescheir, 2009).

Even though we have the technology to examine all fetuses for birth defects, should we? Explain your position.

Pregnancy and Birthing

Pregnancy is associated with profound hormonal and metabolic changes in the woman's body, and experts generally agree that the United States has a higher incidence of health problems associated with pregnancy than a country of its wealth should have. Some believe that because reproductive health policy has been overly preoccupied with issues of abortion and sexuality, more critical issues of reproductive health have been largely ignored (Rosenfield, Charo, & Chavkin, 2008). Prompt diagnosis of pregnancy is crucial so that prenatal care can be sought in a timely manner. Women who are in good health prior to getting pregnant and those who receive more comprehensive prenatal care

> **chorionic villi sampling (CVS)** a technique for diagnosing medical problems in the fetus as early as the eighth week of pregnancy; a sample of the chorionic membrane is removed through the cervix and studied.
>
> **fetal surgery** a surgical procedure performed on the fetus while it is still in the uterus or during a temporary period of removal from the uterus.

Real People

Pregnancy and Birth: A Personal Perspective from the Author's Wife

The distinct moments of giving birth to my two children were the most powerful and profound acts I have ever performed. At no other time in life do the planning, waiting, physical exertion, and time devoted to a task pay off with such magnificent results—the beginning of life for a whole new person. Both times, Gary and I were rendered speechless when our daughters emerged. You always know intellectually that the processes of reproduction and birth are supposed to result in the birth of a child. But not until you see that little body with eyes wide and searching with a powerful intensity are you struck with a miracle that has become reality.

The physical aspects of pregnancy and birth are the most obvious, but the psychological and relational aspects have the most profound effect. During the pregnancies, there were times when I very deeply needed to feel loved and protected by my husband.

There were times before and after the birth that I needed some proof of autonomy from the child that was a physical part of me for nine months. Gary and I both vacillated between periods of wanting to escape the whole thing and feeling certain that this experience would bind us together forever. The most crucial thing about facing all of our conflicting emotions was that each of us allowed the other to feel whatever was surfacing and offered support.

Each time, when I gave that final draining, straining push, and my husband seemed so proud of me and what we had created together, it was a moment like no other in my life. Every rich detail will be forever woven into my memory. To be part of the life-giving forces of the universe is truly an awesome experience.

—Betsy A. Kelly

---

from the early stages of pregnancy are more likely to avoid birth defects in their babies and to have infants with higher birth weights. Children with low birth weights are at significantly higher risk of developmental disabilities, visual impairments, and cerebral palsy and are less likely to perform well in school (Green-Raleigh et al., 2005; Haas et al., 2005; Ricketts, Murray, & Schwalberg, 2005).

There is abundant evidence that prenatal care is highly cost effective, eventually reducing the costs associated with delivery, especially in high-risk pregnancies. In poor, rural communities, however, the benefits may not be as great (Hueston, Geesey, & Diaz, 2008; Partington et al., 2009). Choosing a clinician with whom the woman can feel comfortable is always helpful. Physicians who provide prenatal care and delivery of babies usually are obstetrician–gynecologists, although many prenatal clinics use nurse practitioners or other health care providers. In addition, nurse-midwives, who can provide care during pregnancy and the birthing process, maintain private practices in some areas, with physician backup for complicated cases.

Pregnant women exposed to organic solvents have a sharply elevated risk of having an infant with serious birth defects (Khattak et al., 1999). The chance of birth defects involving development of the brain and spinal cord is increased by exposure to heat during early preg-

nancy such as through immersion in hot tubs. The likelihood of neurological defects seems to be reduced in women who use supplements of folic acid, one of the B vitamins, before becoming pregnant. Women who become pregnant after age 35 have an increased risk of infant mortality or illness, although those who become pregnant for the first time at these ages seem to adjust emotionally quite well in general. The risks for women who become pregnant at age 50 or older are significantly higher (Salihu et al., 2003; Touch et al., 2002).

Both women and men can have a wide range of reactions to pregnancy, and these reactions may in turn affect reproductive health. Often, periods of elation and excitement alternate with feelings of apprehension and concern. Women who did not intend to get pregnant, or whose partners did not want the pregnancy, are more likely to engage in unhealthy pregnancy-related behaviors. They are also more likely to delay seeking prenatal care. When pregnancy has been intended by *both* parents, the outcomes for the infant's health are more positive (Blake et al., 2007; Cheng et al., 2008; Waller & Bitler, 2008). Nonetheless, pregnancy is a stressful time for everyone, bringing many unknowns. Fathers-to-be often have difficulty sorting out their reactions to pregnancy and feel some shifting in their relationship to the woman. Mothers-to-be may feel somewhat trapped in the pregnant woman role and resent that their former individual sense of identity seems to slip away at times. Both parents wonder what it will be like to have a new child in the family and worry about potential problems. They may vacillate between being irritable with each other and feeling the special closeness of sharing the pregnancy.

The Biology of Pregnancy

There are many initial signs of pregnancy, although all of them may be caused by other factors. In fact, a study in Germany found that in about 1 out of every 475 cases, the woman did not realize she was pregnant until after 20 weeks and in some cases not until she went into labor (Wessel & Buscher, 2002). One of the first symptoms is usually the missing of a menstrual period; however, this can have a variety of other causes, including illness, emotional upsets, or changes in living conditions. About 20 percent of women continue having some menstrual flow during the early stages of pregnancy. Other typical early signs of pregnancy are enlargement and tenderness of the breasts, increased frequency of urination, fatigue, and the experiencing of nausea and vomiting, especially upon waking in the morning. If most or all of these symptoms are present, pregnancy should at least be suspected. A clinician can also look for signs such as softening of the lower uterine segment, color changes in the cervical tissues, and enlargement of the uterus.

Pregnancy Tests

Tests for pregnancy involve analysis of the woman's urine or blood to detect the presence of the hormone **human chorionic gonadotropin (HCG),** which is produced by the embryo and the placenta. Home pregnancy tests can be relatively accurate if the directions are followed carefully. Even if a home test is positive, most clinics or physicians will do a repeat test to confirm the pregnancy. Highly sensitive laboratory diagnostic procedures are considered to be from 95 to 98 percent accurate two weeks after a missed period. Laboratory blood tests for HCG can be almost 100 percent accurate within seven days after conception.

Pregnant women are given advice on diet, appropriate vitamin supplements (not self-prescribed megadoses), proper rest, clothing, and moderation of activities. Exercise during pregnancy seems to produce healthful results for both mother and infant. Good nutrition is essential to healthy fetal development. There has been some concern over the advisability of eating fish during pregnancy, a good source of protein that may carry some levels of dangerous mercury because of water pollution. Studies have offered conflicting advice on the issue, with some maintaining that the benefits of eating ocean fish outweigh any risks, and others stating that the evidence is still uncertain (Hegaard et al., 2008; Weise, 2007).

Alcohol, Drugs, and Smoking

Alcohol use during pregnancy increases the chances of having a low-birth-weight baby, especially if the drinking occurs on a regular basis (Whitehead & Lipscomb, 2003). Heavy alcohol consumption can lead to **fetal alcohol syndrome (FAS),** characterized by abnormal fetal growth, neurological damage, and facial distortion. FAS is the leading cause of birth defects in the United States and can also cause miscarriage, stillbirth, and premature birth. In infants, FAS can be manifested as brain damage, heart problems, and behavioral difficulties such as hyperactivity. Three or more episodes of binge drinking during pregnancy are associated with a higher risk for miscarriage of the fetus (Strandberg-Larsen et al., 2008). Pregnant women generally are advised to avoid drinking alcohol because of these risks.

Use of other drugs—whether prescription, over-the-counter, or illegal—is also ill-advised during pregnancy, although many medications are approved for such use. Certain types of antidepressant drugs, the SSRIs, are associated with a broad range of health problems for mothers and their infants. Mothers who receive treatment for substance abuse can improve the pregnancy outcomes for themselves and their babies. Mothers who use drugs such as cocaine, heroin, amphetamines, or barbiturates give birth to babies who already are addicted themselves and actually can experience dangerous withdrawal symptoms. These babies are also at high risk for cognitive impairments, emotional problems, and a variety of health difficulties (Andrade et al., 2008; Goler et al., 2008; Singer et al., 2002).

Smoking has also been associated with complications in pregnancy, lower birth weights in babies, lowered intellectual abilities, and later behavior disorders in children. The risks increase with subsequent pregnancies during which the mother smokes. Many women are concerned about excessive weight gain if they stop smoking, but the health risks should be of greater concern. If women have been smoking for a long time, it is even more difficult for them to stop during pregnancy (Forste & Hoffmann, 2008; Gilman et al., 2008; Levine et al., 2006).

human chorionic gonadotropin (HCG) a hormone detectable in the urine of a pregnant woman.

fetal alcohol syndrome (FAS) a condition in a fetus characterized by abnormal growth, neurological damage, and facial distortion caused by the mother's heavy alcohol consumption during pregnancy.

Again, the behavior of male partners can be important during pregnancy. Men often do not modify their smoking and drinking habits during a partner's pregnancy, and this can adversely affect the woman's behavior. If men are violent toward their pregnant partners, the risks for maternal and fetal health complications increase significantly (Everett et al., 2007; Garcia-Moreno, 2009).

Sex during and after Pregnancy

Many clinicians neglect to discuss sexual activity with their patients, and many myths have evolved concerning sex during pregnancy. In the absence of medical problems, there is no particular reason to prohibit sexual activity at any time during pregnancy, up until the time the birth process has begun. However, both before and after giving birth, women may experience fatigue and depression that can interfere with sexual desire and satisfaction. A supportive partner who helps stabilize the relationship during such times can help considerably. After the baby is born, the woman's level of satisfaction with her new role as a mother can affect her sexual desire either positively or negatively (Anders & Gray, 2007).

Clearly, sexual activity that could risk exposure to sexually transmitted diseases should be avoided during pregnancy. In the final months of pregnancy, the woman's abdomen often is distended enough to require modification of the couple's usual intercourse positions. Studies have shown that many pregnant women experience a gradual decline in their sex drive, sexual satisfaction, and frequency of intercourse that becomes even more marked in the final three months. Some women experience some degree of discomfort or pain during intercourse in the third trimester (Aslan et al., 2005; Gokyildiz & Beji, 2005; Kershaw et al., 2007). If coitus is uncomfortable or impossible for either partner, the couple may engage in other forms of sexual activity.

After the baby has been born, there seems to be no medical reason to prohibit intercourse after vaginal bleeding has stopped and any tears in the vaginal opening have healed. Most couples have the lowest frequency of sexual activity during the four weeks immediately following the birth of a child, although it may remain relatively infrequent for six months or longer. New mothers often simply feel too tired to engage in sex (Ahlborg, Dahlof, & Hallberg, 2005; Brubaker et al., 2008). Most women resume sexual intercourse within a few weeks, and after 12 months the levels of sexual activity typically have returned to the levels experienced prior to pregnancy. Breast-feeding women tend to have less sexual activity and lower levels of sexual satisfaction, possibly the result of both hormonal and psychological factors. The responsibilities and activities of parenthood usually absorb much time and energy, which sometimes reduces the opportunities for sex for new parents. Although both partners typically are dissatisfied with their sexual lives during the first few months after giving birth, most are happy with their relationship and with being parents (Ahlborg, Dahlof, & Hallberg, 2005).

Using birth control is crucial to preventing pregnancy too soon after the birth of a baby. The most recent evidence suggests that it is best to space pregnancies at least one to two years apart in order to give the woman's body a chance to build up the nutritional reserves needed to nourish a developing fetus. There is a greater risk of fetal death in pregnancies that occur too soon after a previous pregnancy.

The Birth Process

The birth process (see Figures 10.19 and 10.20) is complex, and its controlling mechanisms are not fully understood. The hormone **oxytocin,** manufactured by the pituitary gland, is believed to play some part in the process. About a month before birth, the fetus shifts to a lower position in the abdomen. By this time, it is normally in its head-down position. The most common signal that the birth process is beginning is the initiation of uterine contractions experienced as **labor.** The mucus plug that blocked the opening of the cervix is usually expelled just before birth begins and sometimes is seen as a small amount of bloody discharge. At some point in the process, the amniotic sac ruptures, and its fluid pours or dribbles out of the vagina.

Labor contractions are relatively mild at first, occurring at intervals of 15 to 20 minutes. Although most couples might find it difficult to relax enough or find the necessary privacy, lovemaking, including intercourse, during the early stages of labor has been shown to facilitate the process of labor and delivery. The uterine contractions gradually increase in strength and frequency as the fetus moves downward in the uterus and the cervix is dilated to a diameter of about 10 centimeters. This process of cervical opening (**dilation**) and thinning (**effacement**) begins before labor and continues until the cervix is fully open and thinned, permitting delivery of the fetus. This first stage of labor typically takes 10 to 14 hours for a woman experiencing her first delivery. In subsequent deliveries, the time for labor may be somewhat shorter.

oxytocin (ox-ee-TOH-sin) a pituitary hormone believed to play a role in initiating the birth process.

labor uterine contractions in a pregnant woman; an indication that the birth process is beginning.

dilation the gradual widening of the cervical opening of the uterus prior to and during labor.

effacement the thinning of cervical tissue of the uterus prior to and during labor.

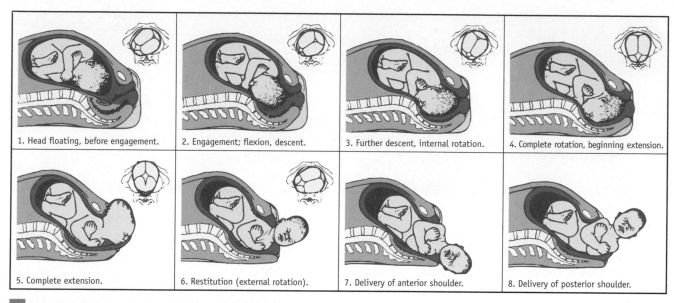

1. Head floating, before engagement.	2. Engagement; flexion, descent.
3. Further descent, internal rotation.	4. Complete rotation, beginning extension.
5. Complete extension.	6. Restitution (external rotation).
7. Delivery of anterior shoulder.	8. Delivery of posterior shoulder.

FIGURE 10.19 *Major Stages in the Birth Process*

The fetus is shown in the uterus as labor contractions begin and the fetus progresses through the stages of birth.

The second stage of labor involves the movement of the fetus through the vagina, now called the **birth canal.** This stage takes an hour or two for a first delivery but may proceed more rapidly in subsequent births. The mother can help with this stage of labor by pushing with her abdominal muscles. Eventually, the fetus's head appears at the vaginal opening, followed by one shoulder, then the other shoulder, and finally the rest of the body. The clinician assisting with the birth generally does not pull on the baby but gently guides it out of the birth canal. In the majority of deliveries in North America, it has been typical for a procedure called an **episiotomy** to be performed in order to prevent tearing of the vaginal opening. It involves cutting the outer part of the vaginal tissue. The incision is later sutured and usually heals without problems. Sometimes, however, it becomes infected and may take up to four weeks to heal completely. About one-sixth of women experience pain or discomfort in the episiotomy scar up to a year after giving birth. Some consider episiotomy to be nearly always unnecessary and recommend against its routine use because it may slow the recovery process. There is also a chance that the scar will spontaneously tear open in subsequent deliveries, so the procedure is restricted more than it once was (Alperin, Krohn, & Parviainen, 2008).

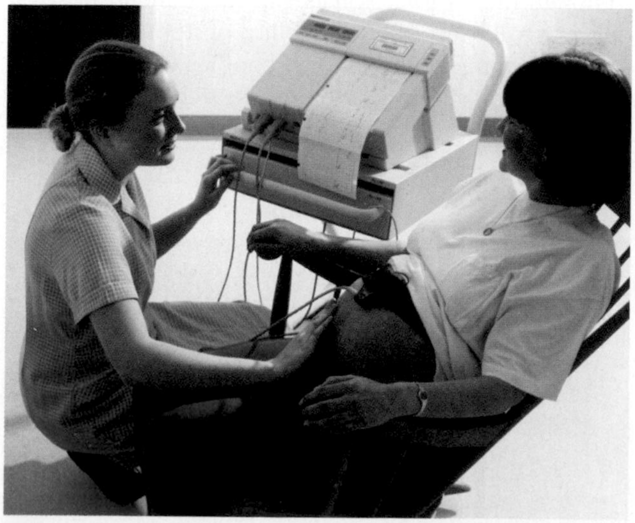

Very soon after the baby has been born, the third stage of the birth process occurs. The placenta, now a disk of tissue about 8 inches in diameter and 2 inches thick, pulls away from the uterine wall. The uterus expels the placenta through the birth canal; along with the remaining section of umbilical cord and the fetal membranes. The expelled tissues are collectively called the **afterbirth.**

FIGURE 10.20 *Fetal Heartbeat Monitoring*

As the fetus nears the time for its birth, its heartbeat is monitored.

birth canal term applied to the vagina during the birth process.

episiotomy (ee-piz-ee-OTT-a-mee) a surgical incision in the vaginal opening made by the clinician or obstetrician to prevent the baby from tearing the opening in the process of being born.

afterbirth the tissues expelled after childbirth, including the placenta, the remains of the umbilical cord, and fetal membranes.

Real Student Voices

■ My aunt and her husband used in vitro fertilization to have their child, and it worked the first time they tried it. The baby is beautiful. It's amazing that science has created this opportunity for couples.

■ Being a parent and a student at the same time isn't always easy, but it's nice to have the little guy to go home to after a long day.

If serious problems affect the birth process, the fetus seems too large for the woman's pelvis, or the fetus is experiencing some other form of distress, a surgical procedure can be performed in which the fetus is removed through an incision in the abdominal wall and uterus. Called a **cesarian section,** the method has been used to lower the risk of complications for the mother and baby. Some authorities believe that a substantial proportion of cesarian births are unnecessary. The earlier in the pregnancy that the cesarian procedure is performed, the higher the risks for the fetus. In subsequent pregnancies, it is possible for the mother to give birth vaginally, and this is more likely to be successful if the woman has had previous vaginal deliveries (Mercer et al., 2008).

Birthing Alternatives

There are many birthing options available to women today, depending on the level of risk involved in the pregnancy, and expectant parents may, in fact, design a set of birthing options that seems right to them and gives them better control of the situation (Carmichael, 2004). In the latter part of the twentieth century, techniques became widely available that help women understand what is happening in their bodies when they are giving birth, as well as learning relaxation techniques to reduce tension and discomfort. The **Lamaze method** of prepared childbirth makes use of the baby's father or some other willing partner as a coach for the woman. In prenatal classes, the couple is taught how to use different relaxation and breathing techniques through increasing levels of intensity during labor. The woman is able to remain an alert and active participant in giving birth to her baby, a process that her body is well equipped to accomplish.

Responding to the new trend to make birthing a cooperative process, most hospitals have **birthing rooms.** These usually are decorated and furnished in nonhospital fashion, and sometimes other children or family members are allowed to be present for the birth. When a birthing room is used, the woman remains in the same room and bed for labor and delivery rather than being taken to a separate delivery room for the actual birth.

Pain-Relieving Medication during Birth

Although there has been debate over the use of pain-relieving medications during birthing, including the possible effects such drugs might have on the baby, recent studies indicate that much of the stigma surrounding the use of certain methods of pain control has been lost. More women are now using epidural blocks, anesthetics that are injected at the base of the spinal cord to lessen painful sensations. These medications do not seem to have any effect on the infant being born, and their use does not increase the risk of needing a cesarian procedure, as was once believed (Wong et al., 2005). Others insist that pain can be managed by breathing and positioning techniques that can be learned by women prior to giving birth.

Midwives and Home Birth

Although most professionals still recommend hospital delivery to ensure the availability of appropriate care in case of complications, some couples choose to have a baby born at home. Some research suggests that home births run the risk of compromising the health of both mothers and babies (Pang et al., 2002). Trained

---

cesarian section a surgical method of childbirth in which delivery occurs through an incision in the abdominal wall and uterus.

Lamaze method (la-MAHZ) a birthing process based on relaxation techniques practiced by the expectant mother; her partner coaches her throughout the birth.

birthing rooms special areas in the hospital, decorated and furnished in a nonhospital way, set aside for giving birth; the woman remains here to give birth rather than being taken to a separate delivery room.

and licensed **midwives** or certified nurse-midwives may assist, and it is usually recommended that a cooperative physician at least be on call in case of emergency. Sometimes, other children, family members, and friends are invited to be present for the home-birthing event. For low-risk pregnancies, research generally has indicated that planned care and home birth with a nurse-midwife can be as safe as hospital delivery (Jackson, D. J., et al., 2003). The main problem lies with the appearance of sudden and unexpected complications, when rapid transfer to a hospital setting can be critical. Midwives now assist with about 10 percent of vaginal deliveries in the United States.

Additional Birthing Techniques

Some women give birth in tubs of warm water because the warmth is relaxing. Immersion in water may also speed the delivery along somewhat if labor is progressing slowly. The baby is lifted out of the water immediately after birth and before the umbilical cord is cut. There are also advantages to giving birth in a squatting or kneeling position rather than lying down, because gravity works with the uterine contractions (Carmichael, 2004; Cluett et al., 2004).

French physician Frederick Leboyer advocated several methods for reducing the shock a baby feels when it comes into a bright, noisy delivery area. He recommended that birth take place in a quiet, dimly lit, warm setting and that time be taken for the baby to lie on the mother's abdomen before the umbilical cord is cut. He also suggested giving a newborn baby a gentle, warm bath.

Do you know which method of childbirth your mother used in delivering you? Which method of childbirth do you find most appealing?

The Newborn

After delivery, a baby is checked for any signs of distress, measured, and kept very warm. Drops of dilute silver nitrate or antibiotics are placed in the eyes to prevent infections from bacteria that might have entered the eyes during the birth process. In developing countries, these medications often are too costly, so physicians are now recommending that less expensive antiseptics such as Betadine be used as eyedrops in these areas of the world. This treatment is believed to have the potential to prevent thousands of cases of infant blindness and hundreds of thousands of severe eye infections worldwide each year.

It is widely believed that newborn babies are quite alert for the first hour or two immediately following birth and that time should be given for the parents to

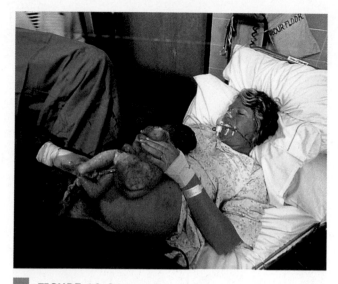

■ **FIGURE 10.21** *Birth*

The newborn is placed on its mother's stomach.

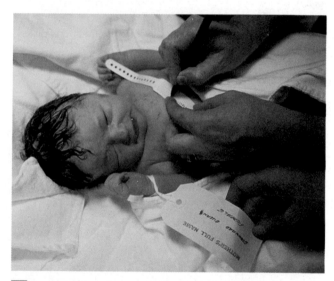

■ **FIGURE 10.22** *Identifying the Newborn*

Each newborn is given an identifying bracelet, which the nurse fills in with the names of the baby and the baby's parents.

form a **bond** with their new infants (see Figures 10.21 to 10.23). This early bonding may well provide more security and comfort for the baby's adjustment and growth processes, although research evidence to confirm this contention is incomplete.

midwives medical professionals, both women and men, trained to assist with the birthing process.

bond the emotional link between parent and child created by cuddling, cooing, and physical and eye contact early in the newborn's life.

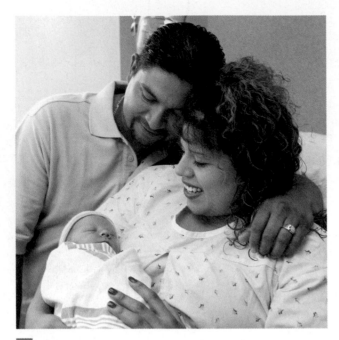

■ **FIGURE 10.23** *The New Family*
The father, as a part of the natural birthing process, greets his newborn and comforts his wife.

Problems during Pregnancy

About one out of four pregnancies experiences some potentially serious complication. Each year in the United States, more than 31,000 fetuses die prior to delivery, and another 22,000 newborns die within a month of being born. The U.S. infant mortality rate continues to be higher than that of many other industrialized nations. Of the 1.5 million women in the United States who seek care during their pregnancy each year, less than 100 die during the pregnancy or birthing process. The rates of death of pregnant women and of their fetuses are higher among black women, and the risks are sharply elevated for women over age 35 (Callagan & Berg, 2003; Clark et al., 2008). Childbearing takes its toll on mothers worldwide as well. The United Nations has reported that about 585,000 women die each year around the globe in pregnancy and childbirth (see Figure 10.24), often due to inadequate medical care. We will not explore all the possible problems of pregnancy in detail here but instead will mention a few common ones.

Preeclampsia

One disorder that occurs in women in fewer than 10 percent of pregnancies is **preeclampsia,** also known as pregnancy-induced hypertension. It begins with a rise in blood pressure, swelling in the ankles and other parts of the body, and the appearance of protein in the urine. Usually it can be treated by bed rest, diet, and medication, but sometimes it progresses to serious or life-

threatening conditions for the mother such as blindness, convulsions, or coma. Low daily doses of aspirin can be helpful in preventing this condition without harming fetal development. Preeclampsia hypertension increases the risk of stroke during the first few weeks following giving birth (Redman & Sargent, 2005; Roberts, 2008). A more severe form of preeclampsia is known as HELLP syndrome, that is also characterized by the breaking apart of red blood cells, increased levels of liver enzymes, and low platelet counts. These symptoms require rapid attention and sometimes the induction of labor so that the baby is delivered as soon as possible. The symptoms gradually subside following delivery.

Premature Birth

Any birth that takes place prior to the 37th week of pregnancy is considered a **premature birth.** In the United States, one out of eight babies is born prematurely. It more commonly occurs in fetuses who are growing more slowly than they should be. About three-quarters of infant deaths in the United States are associated with premature delivery, and preterm births constitute the cause of one-third of infant deaths in the United States (Callaghan et al., 2006). The more prematurely a baby is born, the lower its chances of survival. More than 60 percent of infants born at 22 to 25 weeks of gestation die prior to or during birth or within six months of delivery. Respiratory problems, cranial abnormalities, and their complications are particularly common among these early "preemies." They often require care in a hospital's neonatal intensive care unit (NICU). The survival rate steadily rises the later in pregnancy an infant is born (McIntire & Leveno, 2008).

Although the cause of a premature birth is not always known, it is particularly common among teenage mothers, women who smoke or have a genitourinary tract infection during their pregnancies, and women who have experienced high stress, severe life events, inadequate nutrition, or lack of proper prenatal medical care. Bacterial infections, allergic reactions, or other health problems that cause inflammation within the mother's body can lead to premature birth, and there is hope that anti-inflammatory drugs may be useful in controlling the problem. New ways are being developed of predicting which women who experience some preterm labor contractions actually will give birth prematurely (Khashan et al., 2009; Wickelgren, 2004).

> **preeclampsia** a disorder that can arise in the latter half of pregnancy, marked by swelling in the ankles and other parts of the body, high blood pressure, and protein in the urine; can progress to coma and death if not treated.
>
> **premature birth** a birth that takes place prior to the 37th week of pregnancy.

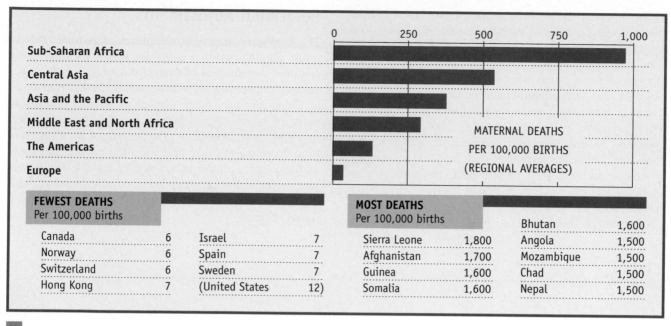

Sub-Saharan Africa							
Central Asia							
Asia and the Pacific							
Middle East and North Africa							
The Americas							
Europe							

MATERNAL DEATHS
PER 100,000 BIRTHS
(REGIONAL AVERAGES)

FEWEST DEATHS
Per 100,000 births

Canada	6	Israel	7
Norway	6	Spain	7
Switzerland	6	Sweden	7
Hong Kong	7	(United States	12)

MOST DEATHS
Per 100,000 births

Sierra Leone	1,800	Bhutan	1,600
Afghanistan	1,700	Angola	1,500
Guinea	1,600	Mozambique	1,500
Somalia	1,600	Chad	1,500
		Nepal	1,500

■ **FIGURE 10.24** *Childbearing's Toll*

A UNICEF study found that 585,000 women worldwide die each year during pregnancy and childbirth, nearly 20 percent more than previously estimated.

Rh Incompatibility

A major risk for pregnancies in former times was **Rh incompatibility.** The Rh factor is a blood protein; blood may be either Rh positive, if it contains this factor, or Rh negative, if it does not. A baby has its own blood type as the result of a genetic combination from its mother and father and often will not have the same blood type as the mother. If a mother has Rh negative blood and her baby is Rh positive, the mother's body will begin producing antibodies that destroy red blood cells in the fetus, especially in second and subsequent pregnancies. Administering a medication called **RhoGAM** to the mother prevents the formation of these antibodies and has effectively eliminated many of the risks of Rh incompatibility. However, the potential for the problem must be noted in prenatal blood tests, another reason why good prenatal care is so crucial to a pregnant woman and her child-to-be. It is also important for women to take RhoGAM after a miscarriage or an abortion if it is known that there was an Rh incompatibility with the fetus.

Postpartum Care

Following the birth of a baby—the postpartum time— many physical and psychological adjustments must be made by both the mother and the child. Proper medical follow-up for both is essential. As the mother's body returns to its prepregnancy state, the reproductive organs must recover and the internal hormonal balances must be reestablished. It can be a very emotional time,

during which support and help from others are extremely important. Many women experience at least a brief period of **postpartum depression,** characterized by low energy levels, feelings of being overwhelmed by new responsibilities, and sleep disturbances. In more severe cases, prompt medical attention is warranted; antidepressant medications usually are successful.

Breastfeeding

Women must make decisions about whether to breast-feed or bottle-feed their newborns. As the benefits of breastfeeding become increasingly recognized, the number of babies being breast-fed has been steadily increasing. The American Academy of Pediatrics recommends that babies be breast-fed exclusively for the first six months, and then at least partially for the remainder

Rh incompatibility condition in which a blood protein of the infant is not the same as the mother's; antibodies formed in the mother can destroy red blood cells in the fetus.

RhoGAM medication administered to a mother to prevent formation of antibodies when the baby is Rh positive and its mother is Rh negative.

postpartum depression a period of low energy and discouragement that is common for mothers following childbearing. Longer-lasting or severe symptoms should receive medical treatment.

of the first year. In fact, only about a third of mothers are breastfeeding at all at six months (American Academy of Pediatrics, 2005). Those who will soon go back to full-time jobs are less likely to choose breastfeeding as an option, as are women who are fatigued or depressed. Support and encouragement from hospitals and clinicians seem to help women continue with breastfeeding. There is ample evidence to indicate that breast-fed babies tend to have stronger immune systems at first and that over the longer term they may be somewhat more intelligent and less likely to get certain diseases such as diabetes and even breast cancer in later life. Breast-fed babies also are less likely to be overweight in early childhood (DiGirolamo et al., 2008; Su et al., 2007).

Relational Adjustments

The pressures and responsibilities of parenthood require adjustments on everyone's part. A new baby requires a great deal of care and usually lost hours of sleep. Couples may find themselves tired and irritable at times. Frequency of sexual activity decreases at least for a time. Some fathers become fully engaged in child care, whereas others begin spending less time around the child and the mother. Life passages all have their complications, and becoming a parent is one passage that requires good communication, willingness to adapt and compromise, and mutual emotional support.

Chapter Summary

1. Pregnancy rates in the United States have remained relatively stable. As science has gained new understanding of reproductive processes and has developed new technologies to facilitate them, reproduction has become more closely scrutinized socially.

2. A sperm must penetrate the zona pellucida of the ovum for conception to occur. Progesterone and contact with the zona cause exocytosis of the sperm, allowing fertilization.

3. When a sperm fertilizes an ovum to form a zygote within the fallopian tube, 23 chromosomes from both the sperm and the egg combine to form a total of 46 chromosomes. The DNA in these chromosomes establishes the genetic instructions for development of the new organism.

4. The rate of multiple births increased for several years, largely due to increased use of fertility drugs, but they are now decreasing. Multiple births are associated with greater risks of birth defects and premature birth.

5. Fraternal (dizygotic) twins result from the fertilization of two separate ova by two separate sperm. Identical (monozygotic) twins are formed when a single zygote divides into two cells that separate and develop into individual embryos. Because they have exactly the same chromosomes, they are identical in appearance.

6. The zygote divides into increasing numbers of cells, eventually forming a spherical blastocyst. A few days after fertilization, the blastocyst implants itself in the inner lining (endometrium) of the

uterus, where embryonic and fetal development will continue.

7. The embryo forms several extraembryonic membranes for its protection and nourishment.

8. Infertility can have many causes and often creates stress for couples who are anxious to have children. New reproductive technologies are offering more hope for infertile couples.

9. Advances in reproductive technology are revolutionizing the processes of conception and gestation.

10. In cases in which one man has a low or nonexistent sperm count, artificial insemination permits sperm from another man to be used for fertilization.

11. In vitro fertilization (IVF) allows fertilization outside a woman's body, with the developing embryo then being implanted into the uterus. The success rate of IVF is still limited, and its associated costs are high.

12. Selective reduction sometimes is used to reduce the number of fetuses when a multiple pregnancy is diagnosed.

13. Zygote intrafallopian transfer (ZIFT) allows zygotes produced by IVF to be placed directly into fallopian tubes.

14. Gametes (sperm and eggs) and embryos now may be frozen and stored for long periods for later use in various reproductive technologies. There are growing concerns about the ethics involved with frozen embryos.

15. Our knowledge of the human genome permits preimplantation genetic screening for use in IVF, but it does not improve the chances of implantation. Altering the genes in an embryo will eventually be possible, but its goals are controversial.

16. Gamete intrafallopian transfer (GIFT), in which sperm and eggs are placed directly into the fallopian tube, increases the likelihood of fertilization in the tube.

17. Intracytoplasmic sperm injection (ICSI) and direct aspiration of sperm from testicular tissues offer hope of increasing the likelihood of having viable sperm for reproduction.

18. Immature oocyte collection permits immature eggs to be obtained, after which they are assisted to maturity by cell-culturing methods. This technique could reduce the costs of IVF significantly.

19. Ovum donation can be used for women who no longer can produce eggs, and these techniques have enabled postmenopausal women to become pregnant.

20. Choosing the sex of a fetus ahead of time has raised many ethical concerns. Sex selection is causing an imbalance in the number of males born in China and some other countries.

21. Cloning involves the creation of genetically identical organisms. New techniques have allowed the separation of early embryonic cells and thus the creation of genetic duplicates of an early human embryo. The prospect of human cloning raises ethical, social, and legal complications, and clones may be at higher risk for eventual defects.

22. Regulations and guidelines have been developed to control embryonic stem cell research.

23. Surrogate motherhood, or gestational surrogacy, is a controversial approach in which one woman agrees, for a fee, to carry a pregnancy and give the baby to another couple.

24. Ultrasound images are used to examine the features of the developing fetus.

25. Amniocentesis withdraws fetal cells from the amniotic sac so that possible chromosome abnormalities can be discovered. Chorionic villi sampling (CVS) also examines chromosomes but can be used as early as the eighth week in the pregnancy.

26. Embryoscopy and fetoscopy allow visual examination of embryos and fetuses. Fetal surgery is a developing technology that can be used to treat some medical difficulties.

27. Prenatal care is cost-effective and important in preventing problems related to pregnancy and birth defects.

28. Pregnancy may be signaled by many symptoms. Pregnancy tests detect a hormone produced by the embryo and placenta called human chorionic gonadotropin (HCG).

29. Fetal alcohol syndrome (FAS) results from excessive alcohol use during pregnancy.

30. Unless there is a problem with a pregnancy, there is no need to avoid sexual contact during this time. To ensure healthy pregnancies, it is best that they be spaced one to two years apart.

31. The birth process begins with contractions of the uterus, or labor. Gradually, the baby is moved through the birth canal and is born. The placenta, umbilical cord, and fetal membranes follow as the afterbirth.

32. There are many approaches to birthing, such as the Lamaze method. Many women use some pain-relieving medications or anesthesia during labor and delivery.

33. Home delivery and hospital birthing rooms are two options available to pregnant women. Nurse-midwives can assist with deliveries.

34. Preeclampsia is a possible complication of pregnancy. It involves a rise in the mother's blood pressure and a buildup of fluids in her body, sometimes with life-threatening consequences.

35. Births that occur prior to the 37th week of pregnancy are premature.

36. Prenatal blood tests are crucial so that any dangers of Rh incompatibility can be eliminated with medical treatment. RhoGAM is administered to the mother when Rh incompatibility exists.

37. The postpartum period requires many adjustments and may be characterized by some level of postpartum depression for the new mother.

38. Breastfeeding has many benefits and is increasing in popularity.

Chapter 11
Decision Making about Pregnancy and Parenthood

Chapter Outline

We have tried several forms of birth control, and none of them has proven completely satisfactory. I don't think I need to use something like the pill, and I don't like using a diaphragm. He uses condoms sometimes, but we don't seem to be very consistent. That leaves us with withdrawal more often than not, which we both know carries lots of risks.

—from a student essay

Do you plan on having children someday? Would you be prepared to have a child at this point in your life? Is there *any* chance you could? Bringing a child into the world carries important responsibilities—not only to the child but also to a planet whose resources are unevenly distributed. There is evidence that social policies involving tax rewards or penalties for having children can help control population growth in either direction. Although family and social pressures to procreate often exist, especially for married couples, there is not a particularly close association between sex and fertility among humans. The primary reason is that, throughout history, people have deliberately sought to weaken that association through the types of sexual activities they choose and the use of birth control. People have tried to avoid pregnancy while continuing to enjoy sexual intercourse.

The terms "birth control" and "contraception" often are used interchangeably, as in this text, but there is a slight distinction between the two from a scientific standpoint. Birth control is a general, more encompassing term that refers to any practice, procedure, or device that reduces or eliminates the chances of a birth taking place. Contraception applies more to the specific methods of birth control that prevent fertilization or uterine implantation from taking place.

■ Historical Perspectives

Throughout history, people have found that the practicalities of life sometimes necessitate limiting family size. Various folk methods of contraception, often spiced with liberal doses of superstition, have been developed. Insertion of substances (such as crocodile dung) into the vagina frequently was used in some ancient cultures and may have been the first barrier method of contraception. As early as the seventh century BCE, it was known that sap from the now extinct silphium plant was widely used for its contraceptive effects. The plant was so popular that it was overharvested and disappeared completely. Several other botanical preparations were used, with varying degrees of effectiveness. Ingesting the seeds of the Queen Anne's lace plant has long been known to reduce fertility by blocking preparation of the uterus for implantation; this method may still be employed in rural areas of India and North Carolina's Appalachians. Folklore also has fostered myths about being able to prevent pregnancy by having intercourse standing up, by jumping up and down following intercourse, or by immersing oneself in a hot bath after intercourse (Tone, 2000).

As the mores of Victorian England filtered through to the United States in the 1860s, a great deal of attention was focused on sexual vices. A New York grocery clerk by the name of Anthony Comstock was incensed by the distribution of information about birth control methods and set out to suppress it. He became secretary of the New York Society for the Suppression of Vice and lobbied in Washington to have the Federal Mail Act prohibit the mailing of contraceptive information, placing it in the same category as obscene materials. In the 1870s, these federal regulations became known as the **Comstock Laws.** They represented government sanction of the idea that abstinence is the only permissible form of birth control.

The birth control movement in the United States was spurred on by activist Margaret Sanger, a nurse who worked in a section of Brooklyn inhabited by poor people (see Figure 11.1). She saw women who were almost constantly pregnant, often resulting in serious consequences to their health, and women who had so many children they could not effectively raise them. Many of

■ FIGURE 11.1 *Margaret Sanger*

Sanger (1883–1966) was instrumental in increasing the availability of birth control information and contraceptive devices in the United States. She believed that every woman has the right to control her own fertility and was the first president of the International Planned Parenthood Federation.

Comstock Laws federal legislation enacted in the 1870s prohibiting the mailing of information about contraception.

Real People

Margaret Sanger

In her autobiography, Margaret Sanger told of an incident that took place during her nursing career that convinced her of the direction her life would have to take. In July 1912, she tended a 28-year-old woman who had nearly died from the effects of a self-induced abortion. The woman and her husband, Jake Sachs, already had three children she was barely able to care for on her husband's truck-driver wages. Sanger nursed Mrs. Sachs back to health, although the patient often seemed lost in thought. Finally the woman was able to deal openly with her concerns.

At the end of three weeks, as I was preparing to leave the fragile patient to take up her difficult life once more, she finally voiced her fears, "Another baby will finish me, I suppose?"

"It's too early to talk about that," I temporized.

But when the doctor came to make his last call, I drew him aside. "Mrs. Sachs is worried about having another baby."

"She may well be," replied the doctor, and then he stood before her and said, "Any more such capers, young woman, and there'll be no need to send for me."

"I know, doctor," she replied timidly, "but," and she hesitated as though it took all her courage to say it, "what can I do to prevent it?"

The doctor was a kindly man, and he had worked hard to save her, but such incidents had become so familiar to him that he had long since lost whatever delicacy he might once have had. He laughed good-naturedly, "You want to have your cake and eat it too, do you? Well, it can't be done."

Then picking up his hat to depart, he said, "Tell Jake to sleep on the roof."

I glanced quickly at Mrs. Sachs. Even through my sudden tears I could see stamped on her face an expression of absolute despair. We simply looked at each other, saying no word until the door had closed behind the doctor. Then she lifted her thin, blue-veined hands and clasped them beseechingly, "He can't understand. He's only a man. But you do, don't you? Please tell me the secret, and I'll never breathe it to a soul. Please!"

What was I to do? I could not speak the conventionally comforting phrases which would be of no comfort. . . . A little later, when she slept, I tiptoed away.

Night after night the wistful image of Mrs. Sachs appeared before me. I made all sorts of excuses to myself for not going back. I was busy on other cases; I really did not know what to say to her or how to convince her of my own ignorance; I was helpless to avert such monstrous atrocities. Time rolled by and I did nothing.

The telephone rang one evening three months later, and Jake Sachs's agitated voice begged me to come at once; his wife was sick again and from the same cause. . . . I turned into the dingy doorway and climbed the familiar stairs once more. The children were there, young little things.

Mrs. Sachs was in a coma and died within ten minutes. I drew a sheet over her pallid face. Jake was sobbing, running his hands through his hair and pulling it out like an insane person. Over and over again he wailed, "My God! My God! My God!"

I left him pacing desperately back and forth, and for hours I myself walked and walked and walked through the hushed streets. . . . [The city's] pains and griefs crowded in upon me: women writhing in travail to bring forth little babies; the babies themselves naked and hungry, wrapped in newspapers to keep them from the cold; six-year-old children with pinched, pale, wrinkled faces, old in concentrated wretchedness, pushed into gray and fetid cellars, crouching on stone floors, their small scrawny hands scuttling through rags, making lamp shades, artificial flowers; white coffins, black coffins, coffins, coffins interminably passing in never-ending succession. The scenes piled one upon another on another. I could bear it no longer.

As I stood there the darkness faded. It was the dawn of a new day in my life also. The doubt and questioning, the experimenting and trying, were now to be put behind me. I knew I could not go back merely to keeping people alive.

I went to bed, knowing that no matter what it might cost, I was finished with palliatives and superficial cures; I was resolved to seek out the root of evil, to change the destiny of mothers whose miseries were vast as the sky.

Source: Margaret Sanger, *Margaret Sanger: An Autobiography,* New York: W. W. Norton, 1938.

Imagine what your life might have been like in Margaret Sanger's time. Do you think she would have a difficult time establishing the need for women's health services today? How would people's reactions be different—and the same?

these women resorted to self-induced abortions or abortions performed in unsanitary conditions by illegal abortionists, frequently ending in the women's deaths. Sanger, determined to remedy this problem, in 1914 founded the **National Birth Control League.**

In her protests, Margaret Sanger deliberately violated the Comstock Laws and fought against attitudes that discouraged advertising about the use of contraceptive devices. She eventually opened her own birth control clinic in Brooklyn and was arrested numerous times. After a number of court battles, physicians finally were given the right to offer contraceptive information to women (Katz, 2003). In time, contraception became more socially acceptable, and new methods were developed. In 1965, the last major law forbidding the sale of contraceptives to married people was repealed, following the U.S. Supreme Court's historic *Griswold v. Connecticut* decision. That ruling invalidated a state law that had been used to prosecute a physician for providing contraceptive information to a married couple. It was not until 1972 that the Supreme Court's ruling in *Eisenstadt v. Baird* removed a final state barrier to providing contraceptive information to unmarried individuals.

■ World Population and the Status of Children

It took a million years for the global population to reach 1 billion people, in 1804, and only until 1927 to reach 2 billion. It then took only another 50 years to double that number. By 1970, the global population growth rate had reached an all-time peak of 2.1 percent per year, and concerns arose about overpopulation. As efforts to provide contraception and to make health services more available proved successful, the growth rate fell to just over 1 percent per year. Even at that rate, it is expected that the world's population will increase from the present 6.9 billion people to around 9 billion by 2050. It now takes only 13 to 14 years to add a billion humans to the planet (Cleland et al., 2006; Cohen, 2003).

Proponents of what is called **zero population growth** had hoped that we would reach a steady state, with births equaling deaths by the year 2030, but this will not be possible. There is concern that the earth's ecosystems and resources simply will not support population growth, especially in less-developed regions. With 90 percent of the people added to the global population each year living in economically and ecologically impoverished areas, the situation continues to worsen (Cleland et al., 2006).

The balance of the world population has been changing in such a way that industrialized countries

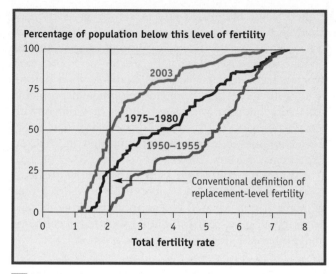

Percentage of population below this level of fertility

FIGURE 11.2 *Cumulative Global Population by Level of Fertility*

Source: From Chris Wilson, "Fertility below Replacement Level" (Letter), *Science,* vol. 304, April 10, 2004. Reprinted with permission of the author.

have a decreasing proportion of that population. As Figure 11.2 demonstrates, half the world's nations are now reproducing at below replacement levels, including countries in the developing world. This means that they will see declines in their populations over time (Wilson, C., 2004). Some countries have become concerned enough about such declines to create incentives for having babies. Japan recently initiated a "Plus One Plan" that provides social opportunities for people to meet potential marriage mates and encourages married couples to have more than one child (Onishi, 2007). Scotland, Spain, and Italy are all concerned about their low birthrates and are considering steps to encourage larger families. As of 2004, the French government has been offering 800 euros to the parents of new babies.

Even though populations have been leveling off in countries such as the United States, the status of children has been declining. Nine out of every 1,000 babies in the United States die before their first birthday, one of the highest rates of infant mortality in the industrialized world. Seventeen percent of children in the

National Birth Control League an organization founded in 1914 by Margaret Sanger to promote use of contraceptives.

zero population growth the point at which the world's population would stabilize and there would be no further increase in the number of people on earth. Birthrate and death rate become essentially equal.

United States live in poverty. A similar proportion of children between the ages of 19 and 35 months have not received all the necessary immunizations against childhood diseases. Prenatal care for poor pregnant women has become even less available than before, leading to more health and developmental problems for their children. Nearly two-thirds of women with low incomes do not breast-feed, a practice that is believed to bolster immunity and nutrition in children (America's Children, 2006).

There are conflicting views about how we as a world community should address the needs of a burgeoning population. Do you support the promotion of contraception, a redistribution of global wealth, or some other solution? Support your position.

✓ Choosing to Become a Parent

Bringing a child into the world and caring for it through its years of growing up are major life responsibilities. Experts agree that it is best for any couple to choose to become pregnant through a process of discussion and mutual agreement, carefully weighing all the new obligations parenthood will entail. Raising a child not only is filled with social requirements, but also it is very expensive. It is estimated that the average cost of raising a child to age 18 in the United States—including housing, clothes, food, medical care, public education, and transportation—ranges from $135,000 for lower-income parents to nearly $285,000 for upper-income families, with the average about $191,000. With the number of families requiring child care increasing because of parental occupations, fewer than half of preschoolers are watched by relatives while parents are working. The costs of day care continue to rise, with child care costs averaging over $100 per week.

There are many wrong reasons to become a parent, for example, the desire to give your parents grandchildren or to give your first child a sibling. Nor is it appropriate to have a child in order to save or refresh a shaky relationship. Sometimes a person is anxious to have a baby in order to have something to love or possess, but this desire may reflect other issues in the person's life that need work and resolution; it is not fair to ask a new baby to fill those emotional gaps. Babies who were unwanted or who resulted from mistimed pregnancies tend not to develop skills as quickly as wanted babies; they also tend to be more fearful and more subject to other psychological difficulties (Pulley et al., 2002).

The choice to become a parent should be made after careful consideration of all the positive and negative aspects of parenthood (see Figure 11.3). Every stage of child development places demands on parents and requires the exercise of appropriate parenting skills. None of us is born knowing those skills, and

■ FIGURE 11.3 *Pregnancy or Birth Control?*

Deciding to have a child is a complicated issue for most people. Consideration must be given to health, among other issues. Pregnancy itself can have greater risks than any particular method of birth control.

they take time to develop. Although it may be a thrill to anticipate the arrival of a baby, any parent can testify that the realities are at times exhausting, nerve-wracking, and confusing. To be a parent requires maturity and a commitment to long-term efforts. Having children also changes the relationship between the parents, creating new pressures and complications. Most parents have found, for example, that their sexual lives change markedly with pregnancy and the presence of a child in their lives. It takes real work and communication to maintain a happy and healthy relationship in the face of the pressures of parenthood.

Being a parent carries great satisfaction and rewards as well. Not only can it help individuals become more mature and responsible, but it also may strengthen the bonds between the child's parents—especially couples who make their decision to have children carefully and have thorough information about the implications of parenthood. Choosing if and when to have a child means that contraception must be part of planning for heterosexual intercourse. Any couple that shares intercourse must also give some thought and planning to the possibility that birth control might fail. The information in this chapter is basic to thinking and deciding about these issues.

✓ Birth Control Today

The risk of unintended pregnancy is usually present with heterosexual intercourse. Modern methods of birth control have at least reduced this risk to the point where many couples pursue their sexual activities with relatively little concern for unintended pregnancy. Nonetheless, the World Health Organization estimates that 25 percent of all pregnancies worldwide are unwanted and that about 50 million of them are

Real Student Voices

■ My mom helped me to get on the pill when I was 15. We have always had a good relationship, and I told her that my boyfriend and I were thinking of having sex. We had a good talk about the pros and cons, and then she took me to a clinic. My boyfriend and I didn't actually start having intercourse for a few more months, but I was glad my mom helped me to be prepared.

■ My father gave me a box of condoms when I turned 16, winked, and told me to be careful.

That was the extent of my sex education from him, and I found it embarrassing. In fact, I never used any of those condoms and didn't need any until I was 22.

■ The first time we had sex, we didn't use any form of protection or birth control. We sweated it out for a month, but fortunately there was no pregnancy! Never again! (Without protection, I mean.)

---

terminated by abortion each year. Up to 20 million of these abortions are performed by people without needed medical qualifications and/or in unsafe medical conditions (Grimes et al., 2006).

Among developed countries, rates of unintended pregnancy vary widely and often differ among socioeconomic groups. They tend to be especially high in the United States and have been increasing especially among younger women. More than a third of women who have had one unintended pregnancy have had at least one more (Kissin et al., 2008; Wildsmith, Guzzo, & Hayford, 2010). The proportion of pregnancies that are unplanned is about 50 percent and nearly one-third of live births are the result of an unintended pregnancy. Of the nearly 3 million unintended pregnancies that occur in the United States each year, 1.3 million lead to abortion and 1.4 million lead to unintended births (D'Angelo et al., 2004; Finer & Henshaw, 2006; Kirby, 2008). This is in contrast to countries such as Canada and the Netherlands, where the rates of unintended pregnancy are 39 percent and 6 percent, respectively. Although adults in all three of these countries are relatively well informed about contraceptives, Americans tend to be more skeptical about the effectiveness of birth control methods and more likely to blame the incidence of unwanted pregnancies on societal problems.

Publicly funded family planning agencies continue to face challenges in providing services to all the low-income women who need them, and they sometimes are unable to stock all contraceptive methods because of their costs (Becker et al., 2007; Lindberg et al., 2006). Even when birth control techniques are available, people do not necessarily make use of them. Data from various studies indicate that among sexually active individuals, some do not use contraception with any regularity or at all. We can assume that some of these individuals may be attempting to get pregnant, but when data were examined from only those individuals who were unmarried and not cohabiting, it was found that 13 percent of the women and 12 percent of the men reported never using birth control (Kirby, 2008; Laumann et al., 1994).

■ Deciding about Contraceptives

Individuals who do not wish to be parents should either avoid intercourse or employ an adequate means of birth control. Different methods of birth control are best suited to different people and situations. It is often wise to consult a family planning specialist to determine which method(s) will be most effective for a particular couple's lifestyle and sexual choices. The information that follows is meant to be a brief guide to various methods of birth control. Making decisions about whether to use a means of birth control, and which method to use, can be complicated. There are several methods of contraception that, if used consistently and properly, mean that fewer than 5 women in 100 will conceive over the course of a year.

We live in a culture that often sends conflicting messages about sexual expression. Although intellectually most people acknowledge that they must practice safe sex, both women and men often are placed in the position of feeling that sexual activity is acceptable only if it is spontaneous and unplanned. Therefore, to plan ahead—to choose and have available a method of contraception just in case—can still be a difficult step to take. It can call into question people's views of personal morality. Women who have more positive attitudes about sex tend to use more effective methods of birth control and to do so with greater consistency than women who have negative attitudes (Kirby, 2008). Women typically select their first method on the basis of its effectiveness, but their second and third selections are more likely to be made on the basis of health concerns and potential effects on the body; for example, it is common for women to choose the birth control pill at first because of its effectiveness.

Preventing pregnancy requires the successful completion of numerous steps: an acceptance on the part of both partners that their sexual activity places them at risk of pregnancy, obtaining appropriate information about birth control methods and deciding which method to acquire and use, and finally using the contraceptive method consistently and properly. Negative attitudes about the relationship, love, sex, and one's own sexual feelings, or depression, can cause difficulty in negotiating any or all of these steps (Berenson, Breitkopf, & Wu, 2003).

Ethical, Religious, and Political Influences

Since pregnancy is connected with sex, its prevention can be associated with ethical, moral, and political judgments. For some, contraception is an ethical issue, rooted in the issue of the purpose of sex. Some insist that the primary objective of sexual intercourse is reproduction. Others believe that it is their ethical responsibility to prevent unintended pregnancies, or overpopulation, even as they choose to share sex. Some of the world's major religious groups take strong positions on these issues. Roman Catholic and fundamentalist Muslim groups are opposed to efforts that encourage birth control or abortion. In general, Islamic thought is quite flexible on reproductive matters, and many Muslim countries have active family planning programs.

There has been continued recognition of the need for comprehensive reproductive health care and reproductive rights, empowerment of women, and wider access to educational and health services, crucial steps in achieving any decline in fertility (Cleland et al., 2006; Frost, 2008). In the United States, funding for reproductive health care can be a sensitive political issue, prone to influence by whatever political party happens to wield the most power at any particular time. Thousands of family planning clinics in the United States receive funding from federal programs such as Medicaid or Title X, and these—along with managed health care plans—often place restrictions on contraceptive services for both financial and political reasons (Downing, LaVeist, & Bullock, 2007; Frost, Frohwirth, & Purcell, 2004).

A particularly volatile area politically has been that of pregnancy and family planning services for teenagers, where issues revolve around two distinct kinds of sexual activity. There continues to be abundant evidence that most adolescent women do not want to bear children. However, there also is continuing debate about how available contraceptives should be for teenagers and whether parental consent should be required before such services are offered (Brocato, 2004). The level of confidentiality teenagers can expect from these services influences their willingness to seek contraception; in one study, more than half of teenagers said they would discontinue using contraceptive services if their parents were going to be notified (English & Ford, 2004; Franzini et al., 2004; Jones, 2006; Reddy, Fleming, & Swain, 2002).

Health Considerations

Anytime various methods of birth control are considered, possible effects on health should be an integral part of the decision-making process. Although several methods (such as condoms or diaphragms) have minimal effects, others, such as hormonal methods or the IUD, can have potentially greater effects on a woman's health. Even women who use reliable contraceptive methods may still harbor fears about the health risks they might be incurring.

Sometimes it is difficult to obtain fully accurate information on potential health effects. Myths develop that may take time to sort through. Many people, for example, still have misconceptions and fears about the possible dangers of birth control pills. In fact, research shows that, when properly prescribed, the pill actually is quite safe for nonsmokers and may even provide some health advantages. Research on the health implications of the pill and other contraceptive methods is ongoing. Prior to making a decision about birth control, couples should become updated on the most accurate medical knowledge available.

Any potential risks of a method of contraception must be balanced against the risks inherent in pregnancy, which are consistently higher than any method of birth control. The key issue is making sure the chosen contraceptive method is fully understood by the user and properly prescribed if it requires a medical professional's approval. When methods such as the pill, hormonal injections, or an IUD are possibilities, a thorough medical history must be taken and a careful evaluation made of any potential health risks. Women and men should take the responsibility for becoming fully informed about all health considerations so that they can make the most careful and safest decisions possible.

The Sexuality Connection

One of the most important factors in making decisions about birth control has been, oddly enough, largely ignored by the research. It is *sexuality*! Programs to promote contraceptive methods have tended to focus on women as their targets or as the potential victims of unintended pregnancies, rather than as agents of sexual and reproductive decision making themselves. We are beginning to reaffirm that women are concerned about their own sexual enjoyment, and that of their partners. Studies have continued to confirm that men often dislike using male condoms because they believe it reduces sexual pleasure. This can make it difficult for women who feel dependent on men for financial support or romantic relationships to encourage those men to use condoms. Additionally, some women feel that condoms are incompatible with sexual intimacy and monogamy.

Also rarely explored by research are the other effects on sexual pleasure that some birth control methods may produce. Hormonal methods may decrease sexual interest in some women, cause some vaginal dryness, or inhibit orgasm. Such effects have been found to be major factors behind why women discontinue using a contraceptive method. Rarely do clinicians who prescribe birth control methods inquire about or follow up on such effects (Zimet, 2010).

On the other side of the sexuality connection are some of the psychological reactions that can accompany sexual intercourse. For some couples, risky sex, i.e., without using birth control, may seem to be "hotter" sex. In the heat of the sexual moment, some may eroticize the idea of having a baby with their partner, temporarily setting aside their own reservations or fears about pregnancy with potentially negative results. It is clear that in making decisions about contraception and pregnancy, women and men must take into consideration a number of sexual factors that are important in their lives (Higgins & Hirsch, 2007, 2008).

Preparing the Way for Effective Contraception

As the evidence shows, sexual responsibility can entail some personal work on your part to ensure that you are ready to approach sexual intercourse with effective contraception, if you are not ready to be a parent. Here are some of the necessary factors to consider and steps to take in becoming an effective user of birth control:

1. Consider your ethical and moral values about sex, pregnancy, and contraception. What sorts of social, family, and religious influences do you have to take into consideration in your decision making?

2. What health concerns might you have regarding contraception? What resources will you use to become more fully informed about available facts? How will you check the reliability of your information?

3. Weigh carefully your attitudes and ambiguities about your own sexual feelings, and perhaps about pregnancy. If you find a good deal of guilt, anxiety, or ambiguity, you might want to rethink or reaffirm the decisions you've made. In particular, consider how you might have been ignoring or neglecting the whole issue of birth control (Frost, Singh, & Finer, 2007).

4. Can you give yourself permission to be sexual? (This does not have to mean intercourse.) If not, consider how your inner reluctance might interfere with your sexual life.

5. Think about the overall goals you have for your future. The more clear you are about what you are working toward in the future, the more likely you may be to consistently take measures to avoid pregnancy (Jumping-Eagle et al., 2008).

6. Be prepared to talk with your partner about contraception and the possibility of pregnancy before you engage in sexual intercourse. Sharing mutual concerns, hesitations, and values is the best way to prepare for effective contraception (Harper, C. et al., 2004). Such discussions need to take place in a comfortable and nonpressured setting before sexual activity has begun, not after passionate sexual feelings are already being experienced.

Choosing the Right Contraceptive

The goal of people who use some method of birth control is to prevent pregnancy. On the surface, then, it might seem most reasonable to look at a chart, find the contraceptive method that shows the lowest rate of failure, and use it. However, choosing a contraceptive is not that simple. Several other issues should be discussed by both partners, preferably with a family planning counselor. Many women do not continue using the contraceptive method they originally chose even though they are relatively satisfied with it, and the rates of switching methods among both married and unmarried women average around 50 percent. Methods most often are changed because of concerns about effectiveness, health risks, or sexual enjoyment (Grady, Billy, & Klepinger, 2002; Higgins & Hirsch, 2008; Minnis, Shiboski, & Padian, 2003). The more informed you are in making a choice, the more likely you will be to trust the method and use it consistently.

In choosing a contraceptive method, you should know the risks involved—both the risk that pregnancy may still occur and the risks to your health of any possible side effects. Some methods definitely are more effective or safer than others. Although you should have as much accurate information as possible when choosing a contraceptive, there are many other factors to consider that go beyond statistics:

1. *Age and amount of protection needed.* Age is related to fertility. Younger women may need a higher degree of contraceptive reliability than older women. For example, vaginal barrier methods (diaphragm, cervical cap) are less effective for women under age 25. The progestin-only pill (discussed on p. 286) is particularly effective for older women and women who are breastfeeding, since they have some level of hormonal protection as the result of nursing a baby. Similarly, a person who has sexual intercourse frequently may want to consider different forms of contraception from someone who has intercourse only occasionally. Also to be weighed are the potential side effects of a particular method versus the complication or crisis a pregnancy would entail.

2. *Safety.* Some birth control methods are not recommended for women with histories of particular medical conditions in themselves or their families. Therefore, suitability for a contraceptive method should be evaluated in cooperation with a trained professional.

3. *Factors that might inhibit use.* In choosing a contraceptive method, you should know yourself and any influences that might hinder regular use of the method. Are there any fears or hesitancies about side effects that create reluctance on your part about its use? Will you tend not to use the method if it affects sexual pleasure for either of you? Do you find it difficult to remember daily routines, which are necessary in taking birth control pills? Would you be embarrassed to buy supplies in a store or to interrupt sexual activity to put a condom or diaphragm in place? Will your religious values make birth control uncomfortable for you? Are you reluctant to touch your sex organs or, if you are a woman, to insert something into your vagina? Would you avoid a method for which a visit to a physician or family planning clinic is necessary, possibly with follow-up visits?

4. *Cost.* You will need to choose a method that you know you will be able to afford on a consistent basis. Health insurance does not always cover the costs of birth control methods, and this has been found to reduce their consistent use (Culwell & Feinglass, 2007). Research indicates that a large percentage of pregnancies are unplanned—and it is safe to extrapolate that a substantial number of unintended pregnancies are unwanted. Sexual intercourse in which the partners do not regularly use some form of contraception runs an extremely high risk (about 85 percent) over a year's time of incurring pregnancy, which can lead to extensive costs of one sort or another. Therefore, birth control typically is very cost-effective considered over time.

The most common methods of birth control are summarized in the section that follows. Their effectiveness, advantages, causes of failure, and potential side effects are listed in Table 11.1. The Self-Evaluation activity on page 302 can help you sort through some of your own personal issues and concerns.

■ Methods of Birth Control

No method of contraception is foolproof or without both positive and negative aspects (see Figure 11.4). Every method sometimes fails. Over half of unintended pregnancies occur in women who were using some form of birth control, which is why using a method consistently and properly is crucial. This section

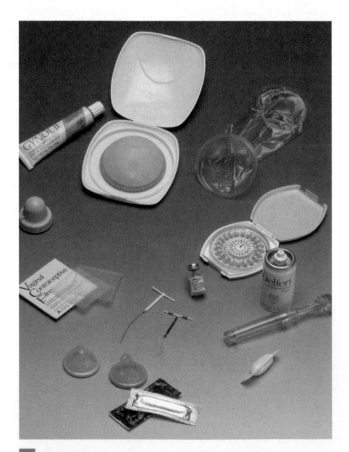

■ FIGURE 11.4   *Methods of Birth Control*

The goal of people who use some method of birth control is to prevent pregnancy. However, choosing a contraceptive is not that easy. No method is foolproof or without both positive and negative aspects.

Real People

Joanne and Arthur: Settling on a Contraceptive Method

Joanne and Arthur had been involved in a relationship for seven months and had been using male condoms during sexual intercourse. Arthur continued to be dissatisfied with condoms, saying that he found it difficult to maintain his erection while using a condom. They both agreed that they wanted an effective means of preventing pregnancy, and they also realized that the condom was providing protection against possible disease transmission. Both had been sexually active with other partners prior to this relationship. After some discussion, they agreed that because they had both been sexually exclusive with each other, they would get tested for HIV and other sexually transmitted diseases and then make a decision about a contraceptive. Their medical tests were all negative, and they then made an appointment at a local family planning clinic to talk about contraception.

After hearing about the various methods of birth control available to them, Joanne and Arthur decided to consider either the diaphragm or the female condom. Joanne's medical history ruled out hormonal methods such as the pill, the patch, or injections. They wanted to use a method that had as few side effects as possible and could be discontinued with ease. The clinic worker scheduled an appointment for Joanne to be fitted with a diaphragm, but the couple also received some female condoms to try in the meantime. As it turned out, they liked the female pouches because they provided better sexual sensations for both of them. Joanne decided not to proceed with getting a diaphragm because she was not satisfied that it would provide the degree of contraceptive protection she wanted. The couple chose to continue using the female condom because they both found it comfortable and easy to use. The clinician had explained that statistics on the effectiveness of the female device were still incomplete, but Joanne and Arthur felt that they could use it correctly and carefully and would have more control over its effectiveness than they would a diaphragm.

Do you think this couple is making a good decision? Should they be talking about what they would consider if a pregnancy happened to occur? Would you be comfortable with the choice of method they have made? Why or why not?

---

focuses on the various methods of birth control currently available and evaluates their effectiveness, advantages, and risks.

Understanding Contraceptive Effectiveness

It is important to understand that there is a difference between the **theoretical failure rate** and the **typical use failure rate** of any contraceptive method. The theoretical (sometimes called "perfect" or "lowest observed") failure rate refers to the percentage of times a method might be expected to fail when used exactly according to directions and without error or technical failure. Typical use failure rate takes into account human error and carelessness as well as technical failure. Contraception can only reduce the risk of pregnancy, not eliminate that risk completely. Clinical trials of contraceptive methods tend to generate lower failure rates, probably because the participants are carefully chosen and are well educated about the method. In real life, methods often are not used correctly or consistently, and recent estimates of contraceptive failure rates have been disappointingly high. Couples should therefore be encouraged by clinicians to choose a method that they will be most likely to use properly (Kost et al., 2008).

Contraceptive failure rates are measurable, whereas actual rates of *effectiveness* are somewhat more elusive. In other words, it is not so simple to predict how likely

theoretical failure rate a measure of how often a birth control method can be expected to fail when used without error or technical problems; sometimes called "perfect use failure rate."

typical use failure rate a measure of how often a birth control method can be expected to fail when human error and technical failure are considered.

Table 11.1   *Contraceptive Methods: Failure Rates, Advantages, Causes of Failure, and Side Effects*

Method	Theoretical or Perfect Use Failure Rate*	Typical Use Failure Rate in Typical Users*	Potential Advantages to Users	Possible Causes of Failure That Could Result in Pregnancy	Potential Negative Side Effects
Abstinence	0%	—?—	No cost or health risks. Freedom from worry about pregnancy. Prevents infections.	Inability to continue abstaining.	Sexual frustration. Avoiding planning for eventual use of contraception.
Withdrawal (coitus interruptus)	4%	27%	No cost or preparation involved. No risks to health (if sexually transmitted diseases are absent). Available even if no other methods are.	Sperm present in preejaculatory fluid from the penis (even more likely if intercourse is repeated within a few hours). Lack of ejaculatory control, causing ejaculation in vagina. Ejaculating semen too close to vaginal opening after withdrawal.	Inability to fully relax during sexual intercourse and not be on guard. Frustration created by inability to ejaculate in the vagina.
Fertility awareness	3–5%	25%	Accepted by Roman Catholic Church. May be used to increase chances of pregnancy if that choice is made. No health risks.	Inadequate time devoted to charting female's menstrual cycle or misunderstanding of method. Ovulation at an unexpected time in the cycle. Deciding to have intercourse during the unsafe period of the cycle, without using other contraception.	Sexual frustration during periods of abstinence.
Combined oral contraceptive (birth control pill containing estrogen and progestin)	0.3%	8%	Reliable; offers protection all the time. Brings increased regularity to menstrual cycle. Tends to reduce menstrual cramping, PMS. Associated with lower incidence of breast and ovarian cysts, pelvic inflammatory disease, and ovarian cancer.	Not taking pills as directed or skipping a pill. Improper supervision by clinician. Ceasing taking the pills for any reason.	Nausea, weight gain, fluid retention, breast tenderness, headaches, missed menstrual periods, acne. Mood changes, depression, anxiety, fatigue, decreased sex drive. Circulatory diseases.
Hormonal patch/ vaginal ring	0.3%	8%	Reliable; can be left in place.	Inadvertent removal.	Similar to those of the pill.

it will be that a method of birth control will work, because no studies can ascertain the proportion of women who would have become pregnant had they not used the method. Pregnancy is always a matter of chance, and even when contraception is not used, pregnancy does not necessarily occur. So the best way to express contraceptive effectiveness is in terms of how likely it is to fail. Failure rates typically are given

as percentages. The failure rates used in this book reflect the percentage of times pregnancy could be expected to occur when 100 couples use the method during a one-year period of average-frequency intercourse; this takes into consideration the total number of times the women were susceptible to pregnancy. The rates given are based on research studies considered to be the best designed and most statistically valid

Method	Theoretical or Perfect Use Failure Rate*	Typical Use Failure Rate in Typical Users*	Potential Advantages to Users	Possible Causes of Failure That Could Result in Pregnancy	Potential Negative Side Effects
Minipill (progestin only)	0.3%	8%	Safer for older women. Reliable; offers protection all the time. Brings increased regularity to menstrual cycle. Tends to reduce menstrual cramping, PMS. Associated with lower incidence of breast cysts, pelvic inflammatory disease, and ovarian cancer.	Not taking pills as directed or skipping a pill. Improper supervision by clinician. Ceasing taking the pills for any reason.	Irregular menstrual periods common. Bleeding between menstrual periods. Appearance of ovarian cysts.
Hormonal implant	0.05%	0.05%	Long-term protection. Extremely reliable. Require no attention after initial treatment. Easily reversible. May have same benefits as pills.	Use beyond a five-year period. Gaining a significant amount of weight (less effective in women over 155 lb.).	Slight visibility of implants. Menstrual cycle irregularities, depression. Improper insertion or difficult removal. May have risks similar to pills, but research is incomplete.
Depo-Provera injections	0.3%	3%	Up to three-month protection. Extremely reliable. May protect against endometrial cancer. Convenient, requiring only occasional injection. Easily reversible.	Neglecting to get reinjected after one or three months.	Weight gain. Excessive bleeding. Menstrual cycle irregularities. Increased depression. Decrease in sex drive. May be associated with slight increase in breast cancer risk for younger women, but research is incomplete.
Sponge (contains spermicide)	9–20%	16–32%	Easy to use. Relatively inexpensive. Protection over 24 hours, several acts of intercourse. No odor or taste.	Difficulty in proper insertion and placement. Internal anatomical abnormalities that interfere with placement or retention.	Increased risk of toxic shock syndrome. Allergic reaction to polyurethane or spermicide. Vaginal dryness. Increased risk of vaginal yeast infections.
Cervical cap with spermicide	9–26%	16–32%	Can be left in place for long periods of time.	Improper fitting or insertion/placement. Deterioration by oil-based lubricants or vaginal medications.	Possible risk of toxic shock syndrome. Allergic reaction to rubber or spermicide. Abrasions or irritation to vagina or cervix.

(Continued)

by the widely respected resource *Contraceptive Technology* (Hatcher et al., 2007). The chance of any contraceptive method being effective increases when the method is used correctly and consistently.

Some forms of birth control cause unpleasant or unhealthy side effects in a few individuals. As with any kind of medical treatment, there is even a very small risk of fatal side effects in the use of hormonal contraceptives, intrauterine devices (IUDs), and surgical sterilization of the female. Medical professionals agree, however, that the risks are low enough that these methods should be made fully available to those who wish to use them. Research has also demonstrated repeatedly that the risks inherent in all methods of birth control are markedly lower than the risks associated with pregnancy and childbirth.

Table 11.1	*Continued*				

Method	Theoretical or Perfect Use Failure Rate*	Typical Use Failure Rate in Typical Users*	Potential Advantages to Users	Possible Causes of Failure That Could Result in Pregnancy	Potential Negative Side Effects
Spermicidal foam, cream, jelly, suppositories, or film	18%	29%	Available without prescription. Minimal health risks. Easy to carry and use. Does not require partner involvement. Provides lubrication for intercourse.	Not using enough spermicide or running out of a supply. Failure to use spermicide out of desire not to interrupt the sexual act. Placing spermicide in vagina too long before intercourse begins. Douching within 6 to 8 hours after intercourse. Failure of suppositories or film to melt or foam properly.	Allergic reactions to the chemical. Unpleasant taste of chemical during oral-genital sex.
Male condom	2%	15%	Available without prescription. Offers protection against sexually transmitted diseases. A method for which the man can take full responsibility. Easy to carry and use.	Breakage of condom. Not leaving space at tip of condom to collect semen. Lubrication with petroleum jelly or presence of some vaginal medications, weakening rubber condom. Seepage of semen around opening of condom or condom slipping off in the vagina after coitus. Storing of condom for more than two years or in extreme temperatures. Not placing condom on penis at beginning of intercourse.	Allergic reactions to latex (natural "skin" condoms and polyurethane condoms are also available). Some reduction in sensation on the penis.
Female condom (vaginal pouch)	5%	21%	Allows woman to choose protection from disease, along with contraception. Easy to carry and use. Polyurethane is strong, conducts body heat easily, and rarely breaks.	Slippage of outer rim into vagina during intercourse. Twisting of pouch during intercourse.	Some reduction in sensations of intercourse. Relatively high rate of contraceptive failure. Sometimes makes noises.

Sharing the Responsibility for Birth Control

Although women bear children, preventing unintended pregnancy cannot be entirely effective unless men share fully in family planning responsibilities. It is clear that decision making about the type of birth control to be used, and the responsibility for using it, can be shared by the woman and the man. Although choosing and using a method of birth control may be shared by sexual partners, only a few methods of birth control are available for use exclusively by males: abstinence, withdrawal, the male condom, and vasectomy. Unfortunately, health care providers often neglect talking with males about their reproductive health choices and responsibilities, further underscoring the myth that pregnancy is not the man's responsibility (Kalmuss & Tatum, 2007).

Method	Theoretical or Perfect Use Failure Rate*	Typical Use Failure Rate in Typical Users*	Potential Advantages to Users	Possible Causes of Failure That Could Result in Pregnancy	Potential Negative Side Effects
Diaphragm	6%	16%	Negative side effects are rare. Inexpensive; can be reused.	Improper fitting or insertion of the diaphragm. Removal of diaphragm too soon (within 6 to 8 hours after coitus). Not using sufficient amount of spermicidal jelly with the diaphragm. Leakage in or around diaphragm or slippage of diaphragm. Deterioration by oil-based lubricants or vaginal medications.	Allergic reaction to the rubber (plastic diaphragms are also available) or the spermicide. Increased risk of toxic shock syndrome. Bladder infection or vaginal soreness because of pressure from rim.
Intrauterine device (IUD): ParaGard (Copper T) Mirena (levonorgestrel)	0.6% 0.2%	0.8% 0.2%	Reliable. Can be left in place so that nothing must be remembered or prepared immediately prior to intercourse.	Failure to notice that IUD has been expelled by uterus.	Uterine cramping, abnormal bleeding, heavy menstrual flow. Pelvic inflammatory disease following insertion or perforation of the uterus during insertion of the IUD; infection of the ovaries.
Vasectomy	0.1%	0.15%	Permanent; no other preparations. Very reliable. Minimal health risks.	Having unprotected intercourse before reproductive tract is fully cleared of sperm following vasectomy (may be several months). Healing together of the two cut ends of the vas.	Psychological implications of being infertile can sometimes lead to some sexual problems.
Female sterilization	0.5%	0.5%	Permanent; no other preparations. Very reliable. Minimal health risks.	The procedure not being properly done by the physician.	Rarely, postsurgical infection or other complications. Psychological implications of being infertile.

*See explanation of failure rates in text.

Source: From Robert A. Hatcher et al., *Contraceptive Technology,* 19th ed. Copyright © 2007 by Contraceptive Technology Communications, Inc. Reprinted by permission of Ardent Media, Inc.

In choosing a contraceptive method, women tend to place the highest priority on pregnancy prevention, whereas men are more likely to consider sexual pleasure and disease prevention. Women and men also have differing perceptions about the effectiveness of various methods. Women, for example, are more likely than men to see the pill as a very good method (Eisenberg et al., 2004). Even though most available methods are used by women, there are still many ways couples can share in birth control. For example, male partners can participate in the decision about which method to use, and couples can go together for clinical counseling and care.

Couples can purchase the contraceptives together and share in their actual use. The man can help insert spermicidal foam or a female condom into his partner's vagina, or he can prepare the diaphragm with spermicidal jelly prior to insertion. Men also can play a role in reminding their partners to take a birth control pill each day. A woman can put her partner's condom on him as a part of sexual foreplay, or the man can place a female condom in the woman's vagina (Higgins & Hirsch, 2007).

Abstinence, Sex without Intercourse, and Withdrawal

One obvious approach to birth control is to avoid the depositing of semen in the vagina. Some couples choose abstinence for this reason. Abstinence is sometimes defined as the avoidance of any form of sexual behavior, but more often it means that intercourse is avoided. There are varieties of sexual behavior that couples may find pleasurable and satisfying without having intercourse. These include massage, mutual masturbation, oral sex, and all sorts of physical intimacy not involving penetration. The alternatives to intercourse, which have been called "outercourse," have been praised as a form of birth control that is simple to use, free of side effects, and also may reduce the risks of giving or getting sexually transmitted diseases.

However it may be defined, the reality of various forms of abstinence is that people do change their minds and may not have an alternative method of birth control prepared for this possibility. While there is no reliable actual use failure rate for abstinence, the method clearly fails quite frequently (Blinn-Pike et al., 2004).

Withdrawal, also known as **coitus interruptus,** is a method that is sometimes used by couples who have not yet obtained some safer method. The risk of pregnancy with the withdrawal method is high. The penis is withdrawn from the vagina prior to ejaculation, and it is crucial that ejaculation not take place near the opening of the vagina. Withdrawal can prove frustrating for couples who use it frequently. There are a number of reasons why its failure rate is high. One complication is the possibility that sperm may be present in fluids that sometimes are secreted by the penis during intercourse well before ejaculation. There is a greater likelihood of sperm being present in these secretions if the man has experienced ejaculation within the previous few hours. Also, not all men have the ejaculatory control to withdraw in time, and some simply may choose not to do so after all. Nevertheless, when intercourse has been chosen and no other contraceptive method is available, withdrawal is preferable to using no birth control at all.

Oral Contraceptives: The Pill

Birth control pills were introduced in 1960 and rapidly gained in popularity. After concerns developed over potential side effects of some of the earlier types of oral contraception, the dosages of their hormones were lowered and public opinion about the the pill became markedly more positive Tens of millions of women around the world now use this method that is available in many countries without prescription. In one study in the United States, two-thirds of women aged 18 to 24 favored hormonal birth control availability without a prescription (Landau, Tapias, & McGhee, 2006).

The most widely used birth control pill is the *combined oral contraceptive* that contains a combination of two hormones, estrogen and progestin. Pills that allow menstruation once a month are taken for 21 days during the menstrual cycle. Seven inert pills are then taken on the remaining days of the 28-day cycle. There are also *progestin-only pills*, sometimes called *minipills*, which contain only a low dosage of progestin. It is crucial that birth control pills be taken each day at about the same time to avoid compromising their effectiveness. If an entire day goes by without taking the skipped pill, however, it is advisable to use an alternative method of birth control for the remainder of the cycle while continuing to take the rest of the pills. The missed pill should be taken as soon as possible. Indications are that a delay in taking the first three pills of a single cycle does not lead to ovulation during that cycle, provided pill use is resumed. However, taking the pills on schedule during the next cycle is essential; otherwise a backup method should be used (Hatcher et al., 2007).

There are also extended-cycle birth control pills that provide active hormone dosages every day of the month for a specified length of time, reducing the number of menstrual periods during that time. Two available brands, Seasonale and Seasonique, prescribe active pills every day for three months, followed by a week of inert pills. This regimen reduces the number of periods to one every three months. That period is often lighter and briefer than usual. The Lybrel low-dose pill is taken continuously for a year, with no hormone-free breaks, so all menstrual periods are eliminated. These approaches are especially helpful for women who have difficult symptoms during menstruation, and they are proving popular with others as well. They seem to be safe and they save women money on the purchase of female hygiene products (Braunstein et al., 2003).

Oral contraceptives create changes in the menstrual cycle that interrupt normal patterns of ovulation and implantation, thereby preventing pregnancy. Combined oral contraceptives maintain estrogen at artificially high levels, inhibiting the release of FSH and LH, two hormones that control ovulation. Progestin changes the consistency of the cervical mucus so that sperm

coitus interruptus (ko-EET-us or KO-ut-us) a method of birth control in which the penis is withdrawn from the vagina prior to ejaculation.

cannot pass as easily into the uterus and also makes the uterine lining less receptive to implantation by an embryo. Progestin-only pills apparently work in this latter manner, as well as occasionally preventing ovulation. The progestin-only pills are not widely used because they sometimes produce unpleasant side effects, but they are particularly useful for women who are breastfeeding and choose to take oral contraceptives.

A number of noncontraceptive benefits of the pill have been identified. It usually makes menstrual periods lighter and more regular, with less cramping. It can reduce problems with acne (Maloney et al., 2008). It has reduced the incidence of breast cysts, ovarian cysts, ovarian cancer, endometriosis, ectopic pregnancy, and pelvic inflammatory disease as well as cancers of the ovary and endometrium (Riman et al., 2002; Greer et al., 2005; Lurie et al., 2007). Use of the pill has also been associated with increases in bone mass among women in their twenties, perhaps lowering their risk of bone-weakening osteoporosis in later years.

Pill use may slightly elevate the risk of heart disease, and the risk of cervical cancer increases the longer the pill is used. Once pill use is stopped, any risks decrease (Hannaford et al., 2007; International Collaboration of Epidemiological Studies of Cervical Cancer, 2007; Tworoger et al., 2007). Oral contraceptives do not seem to increase the risk of breast cancer except among women who have the genetic mutations that make them more susceptible to the disease (Davidson & Helzlsouer, 2002; Narod et al., 2002). It has long been thought that there was a link between the pill and a slight risk of strokes, but as long as women do not smoke or have high blood pressure, that risk now seems negligible (Chan et al., 2004). After discontinuation of the pill for 10 years, all risks are the same as those for women who have never used the pill.

Current research seems to indicate that for healthy women under age 35 who do not smoke, the benefits of the pill outweigh the risks. Although smoking increases the risk of heart attack and stroke for anyone, using the pill seems to compound the risk, especially over the age of 35. Therefore, it usually is inadvisable for a woman who smokes to take birth control pills.

A very important consideration before obtaining oral contraceptives is to get a good physical examination and have a complete health history taken. Certain conditions, such as a history of blood-clotting disorders or high blood pressure, indicate to family planning specialists that the pill should not be prescribed. Follow-up checks that include blood pressure readings and an annual Pap test also should be required of anyone taking birth control pills.

There are a few symptoms a pill user should consider as warning signs. Pain in the abdomen or gastrointestinal disorders may signal the development of liver disease, Crohn's disease, or ulcerative colitis, all conditions that occasionally are associated with oral contraceptive use. Chest pain accompanied by coughing or difficulty breathing may be a sign of a blood clot in the lungs or of a heart condition. Pain in the legs may result from blood clots in the veins located there. Severe headaches or marked changes in vision may indicate high blood pressure or other conditions that can increase the risk of stroke and cardiovascular disease. Although these complications are not widespread among women who use oral contraceptives, women need to educate themselves about warning signals and should report symptoms or concerns to a medical clinician immediately (Picardo et al., 2003).

Contraceptive pills can have other troublesome side effects, although they are not usually dangerous. These include depression, acne, fluid retention and associated weight gain, and abnormal bleeding. Research with the pill has shown mixed results in terms of possible effects on mood or sexual interest, but these effects seem less common in adolescent women (Ott et al., 2008). Certain antibiotics, including ampicillin and tetracycline, interfere with internal absorption of the pill. Tranquilizers, barbiturates, sleeping pills, some anti-inflammatory medications, and some sulfa drugs may also reduce the pill's contraceptive effectiveness. Nevertheless, oral contraceptives continue to be a particularly effective and relatively safe form of birth control for many women.

As is typical with most contraceptive methods, women who cease using the pill in order to become pregnant may take a little longer to conceive than if they had not been using the method. After a few months, their fertility returns to normal. Since some research suggests that conceiving just a month after stopping the pill is associated with premature delivery and lower birth weights for the infant, delaying attempts to get pregnant for a few weeks after pill cessation might be advisable (Barnhart & Schreiber, 2009; Chen et al., 2009).

Hormonal Implants, Patches, Rings, and Breastfeeding

An approved **contraceptive implant** called Implanon consists of a slender plastic rod, about the size of a cardboard matchstick, containing progestin. An earlier, six-rod version was taken off the market because of unpleasant side effects, but the newer device has a lower dosage that seems to reduce these problems. It is placed under the skin on the inside of the woman's

contraceptive implants contraceptive method in which hormone-releasing rubber cylinders are surgically inserted under the skin of the woman.

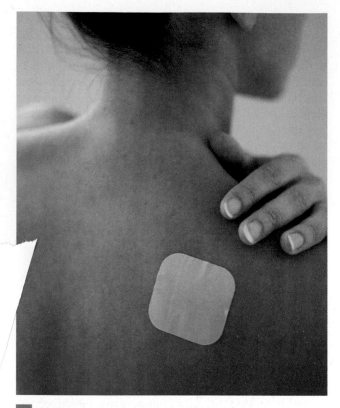

■ FIGURE 11.5   *The Contraceptive Patch*

upper arm, and the progestin very slowly diffuses through the walls of the implant into the body. It may be left in place for up to three years. Like other forms of progestin-only contraception, the implant hormone prevents ovulation and causes cervical mucus to thicken so that sperm cannot easily penetrate into the uterus. Little research has yet appeared about levels of satisfaction among users of Implanon.

Transdermal hormonal patches that can be placed on the skin and emit hormones into the bloodstream are now available (see Figure 11.5). Currently marketed as Ortho Evra, the patch contains doses of estrogen and progestin, so the benefits, side effects, and risks are similar to those of the pill (Johnson et al., 2008). A patch is put in place weekly for three weeks in a row, followed by a week without a patch during which the menstrual period occurs. The patch can be placed on different sites on the body, under the clothing. Care must be taken that it does not fall off.

Another hormonal contraceptive is the **vaginal ring,** marketed as NuvaRing in the United States. It is inserted into the vagina and left there for 21 days, after which it is removed for seven days and menstruation occurs. A new ring is used each month, and women must learn how to insert it properly. It is sometimes felt during intercourse, but in general women seem to like the method, and it has proved to be safe and effective. When comparing hormonal methods, the pill and the

ring seem to be favored over the patch, which seems to be associated with more breast discomfort and nausea, and ring users prefer it to the pill (Creinin et al., 2008; Epstein et al., 2008; Lopez et al., 2008). The new implant has not been available long enough to get comparative data on how well it is liked by users.

There is another natural hormonal method of birth control that is accepted as reliable for pregnancy prevention when used carefully; it is breastfeeding. Sometimes called the **lactational amenorrhea method** or **(LAM),** it may be used for up to six months after a baby is born. When a woman is breastfeeding exclusively and continuously—and that is the key—her body stops making the luteinizing hormone (LH) that causes ovulation. Therefore an ovum is not released during this time and she cannot get pregnant. The method seems to work so long as the woman does not substitute formula for breast milk meals and nurses the baby every four hours during the day and every six hours at night. It is also important that she has not had a period since giving birth, the lack of which is called *amenorrhea*. After six months, or if menstrual periods resume, LAM is no longer reliable.

Injectables

Injections of long-acting progestin have also been used for contraception in many countries. One form, **Depo-Provera,** the brand name for depot medroxy progesterone acetate (DMPA), acts by creating conditions in the uterus that are inhospitable for embryo implantation. Injections are available that are effective for either one month or three months. Injectables can have a number of side effects, including weight gain, hair loss, heavy menstrual bleeding, disruption of periods, emotional reactions, and fatigue, but the unpleasant side effects are reduced in the once-a-month dosage (Reiss, 2000). Only about 57 percent of women who have received a three-month injection return for a second injection, and the one-year continuation rate was about 23 percent in one study. Side effects seem to be the main reason why some women discontinue use of the three-month dosage, although the one-month dosage has achieved somewhat better acceptance. Tests on Depo-Provera

vaginal ring a hormonal contraceptive that is inserted into the vagina for three weeks of each monthly cycle.

lactational amenorrhea method (LAM) a natural hormonal method of birth control that relies on the fact that when women are breastfeeding a baby exclusively and continuously, neither ovulation nor menstruation take place. It requires a strong commitment to breastfeeding.

Depo-Provera an injectable form of progestin that can prevent pregnancy for one or three months.

have generally indicated that it is not associated with an increased risk of liver cancer, and it may protect against cancer of the endometrium, although it might slightly elevate the risk of cervical cancer. It may also slightly increase women's risk of becoming infected with certain sexually transmitted diseases, probably because condoms are not used during sexual activity (Guillebaud, 2004; Morrison et al., 2004).

Spermicides, Sponges, and Suppositories

Spermicides, or chemicals that kill sperm, are available without prescription as foams, creams, or jellies or placed in a sponge or suppository. There is also a spermicidal film, a paper-thin sheet that may be placed near the cervix and allowed to melt. The spermicidal chemical usually used is nonoxynol-9 or octoxynol. These generally are not considered a highly effective method of contraception when used alone but can be very effective when used with other methods such as condoms or diaphragms. Used alone, they must be inserted deeply into the vagina so that they cover the cervical opening. Some spermicides have an unpleasant taste that can limit the pleasure of oral sexual contact with the woman following their insertion, although some companies are marketing flavored and scented brands.

Recent research has demonstrated that spermicides can cause vaginal irritation, which may, in fact, increase the risk of HIV infection or other sexually transmitted diseases (Hatcher et al., 2007). The Food and Drug Administration now requires that a warning to this effect be placed on packaging for contraceptives containing spermicides. Some condom makers have ceased using nonoxynol-9 with their products. Research is proceeding with the development of microbicides that would kill sperm as well as disease agents. Such chemicals would represent a major step forward.

The contraceptive **sponge** is a round, thick, polyurethane disk with a dimple that fits over the cervix. Its manufacture was discontinued for a few years in the mid-1990s, but it is now back on the market. The sponge contains nonoxynol-9 and also acts as a barrier to sperm. It may be left in place for up to 24 hours, a significant advantage, although its rate of effectiveness is somewhat lower than that of several other methods.

Contraceptive **suppositories** are designed to melt or foam in the vagina to distribute the spermicide within them. However, this takes between 10 and 30 minutes, necessitating the postponement of intercourse. Some suppositories do not always liquefy completely. Their effectiveness is the same as that of other forms of spermicide. How the new concerns about spermicides and STDs will affect the use of sponges and suppositories remains to be seen.

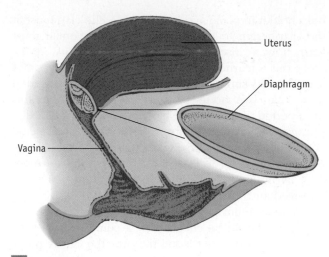

FIGURE 11.6 *Diaphragm*

The diaphragm is a mechanical barrier to sperm; it comes in different sizes and must be fitted to a woman by a clinician or physician. Because it may be dislodged during lovemaking, it is best to combine its use with a condom. Its reliability rate is fairly high when used properly and with a spermicide.

Barrier Methods

Barrier methods are those contraceptives that block sperm from entering the uterus, thereby preventing conception. Their effectiveness is enhanced when they are used in conjunction with a spermicide, although directions should always be followed carefully to ensure that the proper spermicide is chosen and that it is used correctly with the barrier. Additional use of a condom increases the effectiveness of the other barrier methods and helps prevent the spread of sexually transmitted diseases.

Diaphragms and Cervical Caps

A **diaphragm** is a latex rubber cup with a flexible rim that is placed in the vagina in such a way as to cover the cervix (see Figure 11.6). Spermicidal jelly or cream is placed inside the diaphragm and around its rim to

spermicides chemicals that kill sperm; available as foams, creams, jellies, film, or suppositories.

sponge a thick, polyurethane disk that holds a spermicide and fits over the cervix to prevent conception.

suppositories contraceptive devices designed to distribute their spermicide by melting or foaming in the vagina.

diaphragm (DY-a-fram) a latex rubber cup, filled with spermicide, that is fitted to the cervix by a clinician; the woman must learn to insert it properly for full contraceptive effectiveness.

help hold it in place and kill sperm. A clinician must fit the diaphragm to the woman, and the woman must learn how to insert it properly (Hatcher et al., 2007). Once this is learned, insertion of a diaphragm becomes a quick and simple matter. It should not be inserted more than two hours prior to intercourse. After this time period, if intercourse has not yet occurred, a diaphragm should be removed and more spermicide added before intercourse takes place. The diaphragm is left in place for at least 6 to 8 hours, but not more than 24 hours, following intercourse, after which it is removed and washed.

A diaphragm can be used for many months, although it should be checked by a clinician from time to time to ensure that it still fits over the cervix properly and is not damaged. Because the diaphragm is comparatively inexpensive, can be used for years, and presents few health risks, it has been increasing in popularity in recent years. Also, protecting the cervix may protect against transmission of HIV and other STDs (Harvey, Bird, & Branch, 2003). The diaphragm is not an ideal contraceptive for a woman who might feel uncomfortable touching her own genitals or inserting something into her vagina, and concerns about insertion or removal are one drawback of this method for many women (Maher et al., 2004).

The **cervical cap** looks like a large thimble with a tall dome (see Figure 11.7). As its name implies, it is designed to fit over the cervix. Because relatively few companies manufacture them, they are not as easily obtained in the United States as some other methods. Like the diaphragm, caps must be fitted by a clinician,

inserted properly, and used with a spermicide. They can dislodge fairly easily during intercourse, and they have been implicated in some scratching of the vagina and cervix. Researchers are working to develop a cervical cap out of a material that will automatically release spermicide when semen is present.

Diaphragms and cervical caps may increase the risk of a woman's developing **toxic shock syndrome (TSS)**; an infection caused by *Staphylococcus aureus* bacteria that are normally present in the body and may multiply if something is left in the vagina for a long period of time. TSS has also been associated with tampon use. It is not a common disease, and resulting deaths are rare. Nevertheless, when using a diaphragm or cervical cap, it is advisable not to leave the device in place for more than 48 hours. Use should be avoided during menstruation, for a few months following the birth of a baby, or in the presence of a vaginal infection.

Male Condoms

The **male condom** is a sheath worn over the penis during intercourse that collects the semen when the male ejaculates (see Figure 11.8). Most condoms today are made of latex rubber (hence the name "rubbers") and are available inexpensively in drugstores, supermarkets, convenience stores, vending machines, and many other venues. Rubber condoms may be purchased dry or lubricated, and some have a small nipple at the tip, providing a semen-collection area. Condoms made of animal membrane are also available and cost slightly more than rubber condoms. These skin condoms purportedly allow more sensation on the penis, although they fit more loosely than rubber condoms and should be checked from time to time during intercourse to make certain that slipping has not occurred. Skin condoms are not acceptable as a preventive against transmitting HIV, whereas latex rubber condoms offer substantial protection.

Rubber condoms should never be stored in wallets or automobile glove compartments, because warm temperatures deteriorate rubber. Petroleum jelly (such as

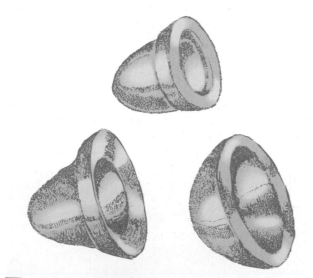

FIGURE 11.7   *Cervical Caps*

Similar to the diaphragm, the cervical cap must be fitted to the woman by a clinician. It stays in place by suction and can be worn for several weeks at a time. It may be uncomfortable for some males during intercourse and can be easily dislodged.

cervical cap a device that is shaped like a large thimble and fits over the cervix; not a particularly effective contraceptive because it can dislodge easily during intercourse.

toxic shock syndrome (TSS) an acute disease characterized by fever and sore throat; caused by normal bacteria in the vagina that are activated if tampons or contraceptive devices such as diaphragms are left in for a long period of time.

male condom a sheath worn over the penis during intercourse that collects semen and helps prevent disease transmission.

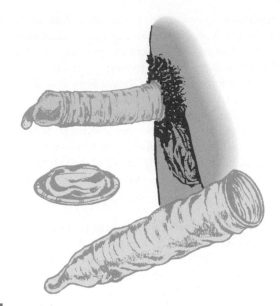

■ FIGURE 11.8 *Male Condoms*

A birth control device for men, the condom is made of latex rubber, animal skin, or polyurethane. It is unrolled onto the erect penis before intercourse begins and collects the semen that are ejaculated. Care must be taken that the penis does not lose its erect state while in the vagina. Latex rubber condoms are also important in preventing many sexually transmitted diseases, including protecting against HIV.

Vaseline), mineral and vegetable oils, and some moisturizing lotions or creams also will weaken rubber and cause tearing. Polyurethane condoms are also available. Polyurethane is thinner and stronger than latex and is especially beneficial for people who are allergic to latex; these condoms can be used with oil-based lubricants. Polyurethane condoms provide protection against HIV as well as other sexually transmitted diseases, and they receive similar ratings from users as rubber condoms. More specific directions and suggestions for condom use are found in Chapter 17.

Studies of college students have found that for men who use condoms and put them on themselves, problems and errors in use are quite common. Three-fourths of men did not inspect the condoms for damage, and 61 percent failed to check the expiration date on the wrapper. Other common errors included not putting the condom on until after starting sex (43 percent), not leaving a space without air at the tip of the condom (40 percent), and flipping the condom over after putting it on inside out (30 percent). When women put the condoms on their partners, the rate of these mistakes becomes even higher, but counseling in appropriate usage skills can help a great deal (Bull et al., 2008; Artz et al., 2005).

Several studies have placed the rate of latex condom breakage or slippage at under 7 percent, although the more experience the woman or man has with con-

dom use, the less likely breakage or slipping will occur. Although polyurethane condoms are preferred over latex by about half the couples who use them, the frequency with which they break or slip off seems to be somewhat higher, making them somewhat riskier for both pregnancy and disease prevention (Walsh et al., 2003). There is evidence that some men find condoms to be either too large or too small, and that reports of slippage and breakage are greater when a condom does not seem to fit the man comfortably. While larger condoms are manufactured, smaller sizes are generally not available. Given men's sensitivities about penis size, packaging and marketing condoms of different sizes to assure maximum effectiveness may be a challenge for reaching those men who would do better with condoms having small dimensions (Reece, 2007).

Even though it is widely known that using a condom is one of the best ways to prevent the spread of sexually transmitted diseases, studies continue to indicate that they are often not used consistently, especially when the couple also uses another method of birth control. Women tend not to use condoms when they perceive their sexual activity to be at low risk, whereas men are more likely not to use condoms because of a perceived lack of availability or the inconvenience of the method (Manlove, Ikramullah, & Terry-Humen, 2008). In a survey administered to 247 college students, 46.7 percent indicated they had participated in sexual activity while not using a condom, when they would have preferred to use one, since the age of 16. Two-thirds of the students had experienced unwanted noncondom use with their current or most recent sexual partner. These findings suggest that partner resistance to condom use may require more assertiveness and support in order for young people to carry out their intentions to protect themselves against pregnancy and disease (Artz et al., 2005).

There has been controversy about the distribution of free condoms in school systems or clinics. Research evidence indicates that condom availability in high schools actually does not increase rates of sexual activity but does increase the use of condoms during sex. Such availability particularly increases the likelihood of condom use among people who have multiple sex partners, partly because the cost of condoms is sometimes prohibitive (Sidley, 2003).

Female Condom or Vaginal Pouch

The **female condom** is a lubricated synthetic plastic pouch that is inserted into the vagina. Two types are

female condom a lubricated polyurethane pouch that is inserted into the vagina before intercourse to collect semen and help prevent disease transmission.

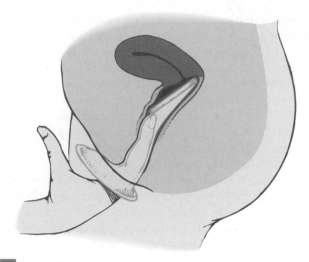

FIGURE 11.9   *Female Condom*

This diagram shows one "female condom" design that is now available. The inner ring is closed and is inserted into the vagina to cover the cervix. The open outer ring covers the vulva.

currently manufactured, although they are less popular in the United States than they are in Europe. Sometimes called the vaginal pouch, its design (see Figure 11.9) consists of a ring at both ends, one of which is sealed. The ring at the closed end is inserted into the back of the vagina and over the cervix, much as a diaphragm would be fitted into place. The open-ended ring then rests outside on the vulva, providing an extra measure of protection against skin-to-skin contact. They seem to be as effective in pregnancy prevention as the male condom, although they too can break or slip out of place (Dilorio et al., 2007). Studies indicate that women often need careful instruction on how to properly insert and place the device and that continued use of the female condom seems to depend on proper instruction in its use (Choi et al., 2008). The female condom may be washed and reused up to seven times.

About half of women tend to have initial positive reactions to the female condom, and many eventually prefer it over the male condom. They tend not to be aware of it during intercourse, and in some cases it increases their sexual pleasure. Apparently, using extra lubricant during intercourse is key to reducing both partners' awareness of the presence of the device. Women who have had negative reactions to the vaginal pouch objected to its feel and sound when it was inserted and felt that the lubricant made it messy. Some objected to its appearance on the outside of the vulva. Many women endorse the female condom because it allows them a greater degree of control over maintaining safer sexual practices (Hatcher et al., 2007).

The effectiveness of the barrier methods is heavily influenced by the age of the user. Younger women apparently are more fertile and may have a greater

frequency of intercourse. The failure rate of barrier methods for women under age 30 is approximately twice their failure rate for women over age 30 (Hatcher et al., 2007). Because the female condom is the only method women can use by themselves that also helps protect against disease transmission, it is unfortunate that it continues to be less widely accepted than the male condom by both women and men. It is hoped that education about the female device will lead to an increase in its popularity (Choi et al., 2008).

Intrauterine Devices (IUDs)

Intrauterine devices (IUDs) were particularly popular in the 1960s and 1970s. Because of concerns about problems with the device and subsequent lawsuits, the IUD was eventually removed from the market for a time. It is now known that much of the early information was based on faulty data, and the IUD has returned as an extremely effective contraceptive method. It lasts 5 to 10 years, is comparatively inexpensive, requires practically no user maintenance, and is completely reversible. It has been recommended as an appropriate method for teenagers (American College of Obstetricians and Gynecologists, 2007).

Two types of IUDs currently are marketed in the United States. One is called ParaGard; it is T-shaped and contains copper, which releases ions into the uterus. The other type of IUD, the LNG-IUS or Mirena, releases a progestin hormone called levonorgestrel into the uterus for up to five years. Either type of IUD can produce some side effects. The ParaGard can increase menstrual blood loss and cramping, while the Mirena can cause spotting between periods during its first few months of use. Later on, it actually tends to reduce blood loss during menstruation or to cause periods to end in about 20 percent of users. Its use has not been associated with any increased risk of breast cancer (Backman et al., 2005).

IUDs are made of plastic and have a nylon thread attached to one end. The contraceptive is inserted into the uterus by a clinician, with the thread left protruding into the vagina so that the woman can check regularly to make certain the IUD is still in place (see Figure 11.10). If pregnancy is desired, the device must be removed by a clinician.

The most current evidence indicates that the IUD prevents fertilization of the egg through its effects on sperm and on the egg. The chemicals and copper ions present in the uterus and fallopian tubes also alter the transport of sperm. It was once believed that IUDs interfered with implantation of a fertilized egg in the uterus,

intrauterine devices (IUDs) birth control method involving the insertion of a small plastic device into the uterus.

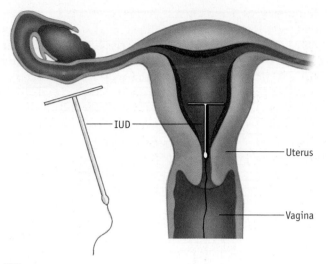

FIGURE 11.10 *IUD*

The IUD, or intrauterine device, is a small plastic object inserted into the uterus by a trained physician or clinician and left in place for long periods of time. It can be a highly effective form of birth control, but serious side effects have been caused by some types of IUDs. Only two types of IUDs remain available in the United States.

but that does not seem to be the case (Guillebaud, 2004). For the first three weeks after insertion of an IUD, the woman has a slightly greater risk of an infection called **pelvic inflammatory disease (PID).** If left untreated for a long enough time, PID can cause damage to the fallopian tubes, resulting in sterility. IUDs once were believed to be associated with a higher risk of ectopic pregnancy, but recent studies have not supported that belief.

Fertility Awareness Methods

The **fertility awareness methods**, formerly called *natural family planning* or the *rhythm method,* rely on awareness of a woman's menstrual/fertility cycle so that intercourse can be avoided when it is likely that the ovum might be available for fertilization. Because these approaches do not require any chemical or manufactured device, they are sometimes considered more natural; in another sense, it is not natural for a couple to avoid intercourse just when they naturally want to have it. Because fertility awareness requires a great deal of planning and daily attention, it is associated with a high rate of failure as a contraceptive method. Because it allows a couple to know when the ovum is most likely to be present for fertilization, couples who are attempting to get pregnant can take advantage of the information it provides.

There are several ways to determine the days during the woman's cycle when she is most likely to be fertile. To use any of them effectively, the woman or couple should receive careful and complete instruction from a specialist trained in any of these methods, which can be used in combination. Various charts must be made for six or more successive months before the method is actually tried as a contraceptive.

The *calendar method* requires charting of the menstrual period over at least eight months before it can be used with some reliability and also requires a set of calculations that are beyond the scope of this text. Its actual failure rate is about 9 percent. The *standard days method* is a more straightforward approach that charts the beginning and length of the menstrual cycle. This method can be used only when the woman has regular menstrual cycles that are *never* shorter than 26 days or longer than 32 days. Once this pattern has been reliably established over several months, the couple must avoid unprotected intercourse on days 8 through 19 of the cycle, with the first day of the menstrual period counting as the first day. Some women use a system of colored beads to keep track of the safe and unsafe days for unprotected intercourse. The method has a 5 percent actual failure rate.

The *basal body temperature (BBT) method* charts the resting body temperature of the woman throughout the menstrual cycle (see Figure 11.11). Usually, the temperature drops slightly just before ovulation and rises after. A special oral thermometer is used to take these readings. The *cervical mucus method,* also called the *ovulation method,* keeps track of the appearance and consistency of the woman's cervical mucus during the menstrual cycle. Women can learn to recognize that cervical mucus becomes clearer and more slippery during ovulation. A similar but simpler method is called the *two-day method,* and it simply asks the woman to check for mucus secretions every day; when they have been noticed for two days in a row, intercourse should be avoided. When all three of these techniques are used together, it is called the *symptothermal method.*

Using the information gained from any or all of these methods, the woman should be able to predict with accuracy about when ovulation will take place. During several days prior to ovulation and up to four days after, either intercourse should be avoided or alternative birth control should be used. As a whole, fertility awareness requires a great deal of cooperation and communication between the partners and must be used consistently (Hatcher et al., 2007).

pelvic inflammatory disease (PID) a chronic internal infection of the uterus and other organs.

fertility awareness methods natural methods of birth control that depend on an awareness of the woman's menstrual/fertility cycle.

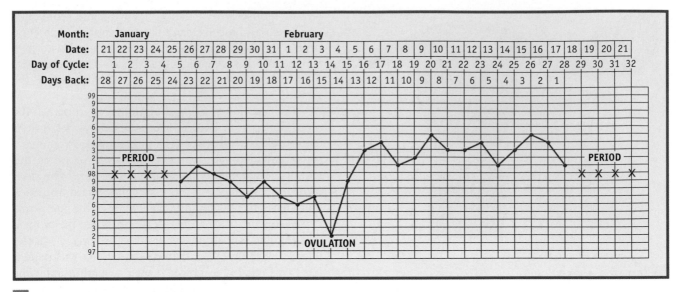

FIGURE 11.11 *Basal Body Temperature Record*

The woman's resting body temperature is taken each morning immediately on waking. Just prior to ovulation, there is a noticeable drop in the temperature. Then, for up to three days after, the temperature rises. It is usually recommended that the basal body temperature be charted for three or four successive months so that any peculiarities in the woman's cycle can be noted. After the time of ovulation has become obviously predictable, the information can be used as part of the natural family planning method of birth control or for determining the best time for conception to occur.

Voluntary Surgical Contraception (Sterilization)

Voluntary surgical contraception (VSC), or sterilization, usually renders a person permanently infertile and has become the most common method of contraception throughout the world (Peterson, 2008). Two-fifths of ever-married women or their husbands in the United States ages 15 to 44 have been sterilized. Only a small minority regret the decision (Jamieson et al., 2002). VSC is accomplished either by cutting the vas deferens in the male, the tube through which sperm travel, or by tying or clamping off or occluding the fallopian tubes in the woman so an ovum no longer can travel through them. Of course, surgical procedures that remove the uterus or ovaries will also cause sterility.

Male sterilization, called **vasectomy,** is a simple procedure in which a small incision is made in each side of the scrotum and each vas deferens is cut and tied (see Figure 11.12). It is one of the most frequently chosen methods of birth control in the United States (Barone et al., 2004). The operation is usually an office procedure that requires less than 30 minutes. It does not affect sexual functioning or ejaculation. There simply are no more sperm cells in the semen. In a few rare instances, men have again ejaculated sperm and impregnated a partner after an apparently successful vasectomy, so there is a tiny possibility of failure. Despite some rumors to the contrary, vasectomy has not been associated with higher risks for heart disease, prostate cancer, or testicular cancer. There may be a small risk of continuing pain afterward, but this remains controversial (Peterson, 2008).

See "Vasectomy" on SexSource Online.

Tubal sterilization, the method of sterilization most often used for women, is becoming an even more desirable procedure as the technology improves. It may be performed through an operation called a **laparotomy,** which requires a hospital stay, or by the more simple **laparoscopy,** in which a small fiber-optic

voluntary surgical contraception (VSC) sterilization; rendering a person incapable of conceiving with surgical procedures that interrupt the passage of the egg or sperm.

vasectomy (va-SEK-ta-mee or vay-ZEK-ta-mee) a surgical cutting and tying of the vas deferens to induce permanent male sterilization.

laparotomy (lap-ar-OTT-uh-mee) operation to perform a tubal ligation, or female sterilization, involving an abdominal incision.

laparoscopy (lap-ar-OSK-uh-pee) simpler procedure for tubal ligation involving the insertion of a small fiber-optic scope into the abdomen, through which the surgeon can see the fallopian tubes and close them off.

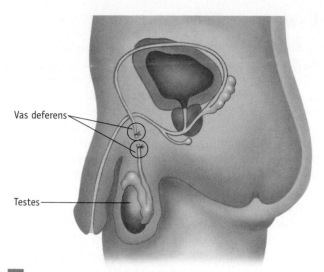

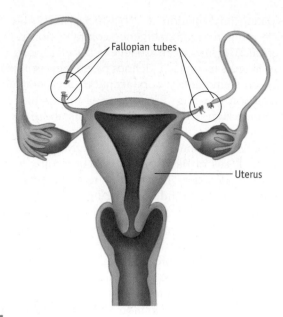

Fallopian tubes

Vas deferens

Testes

Uterus

■ **FIGURE 11.12** *Vasectomy*

A permanent form of male contraception, vasectomy is a surgical procedure in which the vas deferens is cut and tied, blocking the passage of sperm from the testes to the upper part of the vas deferens. It is a simple and safe form of birth control and does not interfere with erection or ejaculation.

■ **FIGURE 11.13** *Tubal Ligation*

A permanent form of female sterilization, this surgical procedure is somewhat more complicated than a vasectomy. The fallopian tubes are cut and tied, usually with a small portion of each tube being removed. This prevents the egg from traveling into the uterus and joining with sperm.

scope is inserted into the abdomen through a tiny incision, enabling the physician to see the fallopian tubes clearly. Through either method, the fallopian tubes are located, a small portion of each tube is removed, and then the ends are tied and sealed—a procedure called **tubal ligation** (see Figure 11.13). A less invasive sterilization procedure called the **transcervical sterilization procedure,** involves the placement of a silicon insert through the uterus into each fallopian tube. Tissue grows over the inserts over a three-month period, eventually blocking the fallopian tubes. During the first three months, an alternative form of birth control must be used. The procedure requires only a local anesthetic (Vancaillie, Anderson, & Johns, 2008).

See "Tubal Ligation" on SexSource Online.

Tubal ligations and vasectomies can sometimes be reversed, restoring fertility. However, attempts at reversal are complicated, expensive, and only 40 to 70 percent successful. There has been somewhat more success in reversing vasectomies, and a recent study found that in most men who had the procedure reversed within 15 years, sperm could still be produced. Beyond that time, results have been less promising (Boorjian, Lipkin, & Goldstein, 2004). In general, sterilization should be chosen as a contraceptive method only when a decision has been made that a permanent method is desired. Some physicians require the consent of a spouse before performing sterilization or

refuse to sterilize individuals who do not have any children, but there are no laws requiring that either condition be met prior to sterilization.

Under what circumstances might you consider having a tubal ligation or vasectomy?

Emergency Contraception: Plan B

Because contraceptive technology is imperfect and people continue to engage in sexual intercourse without birth control, demand continues for "morning-after" or emergency birth control. This has become known as "Plan B." Current emergency contraceptive methods most often probably delay or prevent ovulation so that the ovum is not available for fertilization. They may sometimes act by causing early menstruation, thereby

tubal ligation (lie-GAY-shun) a surgical cutting and tying of the fallopian tubes to induce permanent female sterilization.

transcervical sterilization procedure a less invasive alternative to tubal ligation in which small porous silicon inserts are implanted in the fallopian tubes through the uterus. Tissue grows on the inserts, eventually occluding the tubes.

preventing implantation of a blastocyst in the uterine wall. For this reason, emergency contraception is controversial. The American College of Obstetricians and Gynecologists technically defines pregnancy as implantation, and emergency contraception does not allow implantation to occur. Proponents of emergency contraception claim that it actually prevents abortions because it eliminates the need to terminate a pregnancy.

Emergency contraception essentially involves taking extra doses of birth control pills according to recommended dosages. The dosage requirements differ depending on the brand of pill being used. Two doses are taken, consisting of a recommended number of pills, twelve hours apart. The sooner after unprotected intercourse the first dose is taken, the better the chances that the regimen will prevent pregnancy. The medication does seem to have some effectiveness for up to five days (120 hours) after sex. If the first dose causes nausea or vomiting, a common side effect with heavy doses of the pill, it is recommended that the woman take an anti nausea medication such as Dramamine or Bonine before taking the second dose. The pills may also be inserted into the vagina, where they tend not to cause nausea. (*Note:* Daily birth control pills should not be taken vaginally.) After taking emergency contraception, the woman's next menstrual period may be earlier or later than usual, and may be heavier or lighter.

The FDA has approved behind-the-counter sale of pill packets for emergency contraception without a prescription, meaning that it still must be requested from a pharmacist. It is available this way for women as young as seventeen, and physicians may prescribe it for younger women. While this availability has increased the use of Plan B, it has not yet measurably affected pregnancy or abortion rates. One reason for this is that even when women are provided with the pills and directions for their use, many do not actually use them (Gee, Schacter, & Kaufman, 2008; Trussell, Schwarz, & Guthrie, 2010). Other studies have demonstrated that easy access to emergency contraception does not increase reliance on their use, nor does it lead to riskier sexual behavior (Moreau, Bajos, & Trussell, 2006; Raine et al., 2005).

Availability at pharmacies does not necessarily mean that the method will reach everyone who wants it, since it has been shown that lack of knowledge, language barriers, and social values and customs may interfere with women's access to it (Sampson et al., 2009; Shoveller et al., 2007). Research has found that health care providers who work with women can play a pivotal role in informing them about emergency contraception's availability and use, and some have recommended that packets be made available in advance so that women can have them on hand just in case (Kavanaugh & Schwarz, 2008; Whittaker et al., 2007; Whittaker, Armstrong, & Adams, 2008)

New Methods of Contraception

Development of new contraceptives has proceeded very slowly. Drug companies often are reluctant to invest in researching new birth control methods because the costs are high, profit potentials often are low, and there are always fears of lawsuits because of possible side effects. There has been continued discussion among family planning specialists about making more methods available for males, and there has been a resurgence of interest in developing such methods. Despite continued promises of new male methods, none have yet appeared.

The most promising avenues of research have involved either the suppression of sperm production in males or inhibition of the ability of sperm to fertilize an ovum. For many years, elevated levels of testosterone in men have been known to cause a reversible and pronounced reduction in sperm production. One birth control technique currently being studied involves the use of testosterone implants along with progestin injections, or progestin implants along with testosterone injections or patches. Each method has been shown to suppress sperm production within a few months (Gonzalo, Swerdloff, & Nelson, 2002; Turner et al., 2003).

Contraceptive vaccines represent a new possibility for women. One vaccine under development in India involves immunizing women against human chorionic gonadotropin, so that implantation of the blastocyst in the uterus is prevented. These injections would have to be followed by booster shots every few months to offer continued protection. One of the newest avenues for contraceptive research and development involves various ways of blocking the union of sperm and egg. As cellular chemists identify the various protein structures of the outer coverings of the sperm and egg, it may well become possible to develop contraceptive chemicals that could interfere with the sperm's binding to the zona pellucida of the egg or prevent it from burrowing through the zona, preventing fertilization. Such contraceptive methods are not likely to be available for several years, but they provide hope for the future of contraceptive technology.

What method of birth control would you favor and why?

Unintended Pregnancy: The Options

As indicated earlier in this chapter, it is estimated that about half of all pregnancies in North America are unintended, less than was the case two decades ago. "Unintendedness" is a complicated concept that must

Real Student Voices

■ I used one of those home pregnancy tests, and it came out positive (sort of, anyway). My boyfriend and I began to make plans for what we were going to do, although we never really finalized anything. I then had another test at a clinic, and it turned out to be negative. It was a scary time. We've been very careful since that time.

■ I had an abortion during my first year in college. My roommate drove me to the clinic, which was

three hours away. It was a terrible, lonely experience. I never even told the guy, but we didn't have much of a relationship anyway. I don't regret that I had the abortion, but it is not a happy memory either. I've never told my parents about it.

■ My son is the most important thing in my life. I thought of not having him when I first got pregnant, and it hasn't always been easy. But we're making it. He's the light of my life!

be examined from several different perspectives related to the pregnant woman's life circumstances. A distinction may be made between unwanted pregnancies, which occur when no children or no more children are wanted, and mistimed pregnancies, which occur earlier than desired or expected (Santelli et al., 2003). Some women who fail to use contraception consistently have ambivalent feelings about pregnancy and may find sexual pleasure in the extra risks involved, may passively romanticize the idea of being pregnant, or may imagine that having a baby will sweep away all of their hardships (Higgins, Hirsch, & Trussell, 2008).

Many younger mothers are poor even before they become pregnant. For others, however, pregnancy and young motherhood render them less likely to complete their education and less able to compete in the job market. Some 60 percent continue living with their own parent(s) after giving birth to a child. Regardless of age or circumstances, an unintended pregnancy can lead to emotional anguish and the necessity for careful decision making (Cleland et al., 2006).

Fathers involved in unintended pregnancies often experience a great deal of conflict and psychological distress as well. Contrary to popular belief, most young men do not see impregnating a partner as enhancing their masculinity. Fathers in unintended pregnancies sometimes resent that they have little or no part to play in deciding what to do about the pregnancy yet can be held financially responsible for the baby. They may experience resentment, guilt, and eventual distress if they have little access to their babies or if the woman chooses abortion. Fathers typically are older than mothers, especially when the mothers are teenagers (Boggess & Bradner, 2002).

There are basically three alternatives from which to choose when faced with an unintended pregnancy (see Figure 11.14): keeping the baby, adoption, or termination of the pregnancy (Taverner & Brick, 2006). The choice that ultimately is made depends on several different factors, with attitudes toward childbearing and abortion playing a significant role.

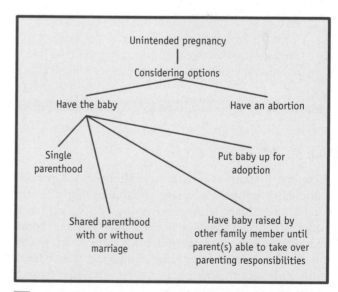

FIGURE 11.14 *The Options Following Unintended Pregnancy*

This chart is a reminder that whenever an unintended pregnancy occurs, some decision must be made. There is no such thing as not making a decision. To avoid considering abortion as an option constitutes a decision to have the baby. The choices might not be comfortable or easy, but one way or another they must be faced and made.

Real People

Max and Millie: Facing a Possible Pregnancy

Max and Millie are seniors in college who have been together for over a year. They often talk about marrying when they have finished school, although Millie is thinking about going to graduate school for a master's degree. They hope to locate near each other after graduation so that the relationship can continue. The two have been sharing a monogamous sexual relationship almost since they began going together, and Millie takes birth control pills for contraception. Last month, Millie missed her period, and they both are concerned that she is pregnant. Millie called the clinic where she had been prescribed the pill, and the nurse told her that if she had mistakenly skipped a pill, she could be pregnant. Millie cannot recall skipping a dose but is not completely certain.

The two of them have been discussing what action they might take if it turns out that Millie is pregnant. Max has said that he would be willing to marry her but admits that such rushed circumstances would not be the scenario he would prefer. Millie has indicated that she probably would want to have an abortion, largely because she does not feel ready to be a good mother and does not want to put her graduate work and career on hold at the moment. Max is uncomfortable with this, partly because he opposes abortion and partly because he feels Millie

is being selfish. He has warned her that abortion will leave her with regrets, depression, and psychological pain. She does not believe it will bother her as much as he says, although she admits that it would not be an easy decision. She believes that it simply would be the best of several unattractive options. A friend with whom she has talked has mentioned the possibility of placing the baby for adoption, but neither Max nor Millie is inclined to do this. Millie indicates that the pregnancy will still be a difficult inconvenience for her life.

Millie has tried a home pregnancy test that came out positive, but the Student Health Center nurse practitioner has told her that she should follow up with a laboratory test to be certain. Max and Millie are feeling tense together and seem to be at a stalemate in terms of agreeing on a course of action if she is in fact pregnant.

If you were asked by either Max or Millie for some objective advice, what would tell them?

How would your own values come into play with regard to the advice?

If you were to find yourself in such a circumstance, what would you do?

✓ Keeping the Baby

Keeping the baby is a more typical option for married couples or couples who are cohabiting than it is for single individuals. Unmarried young people may face a decision about whether to enter into marriage. Some teenage parents allow their children to be cared for by other relatives until they have completed their education or are otherwise more prepared to assume parenting responsibility themselves.

In cases of unintended pregnancy, one of the first issues to be considered is whether the mother can accept all the emotional and physical implications of the pregnancy and the birth process. Depending on his degree of involvement, the father's reactions and needs also may need to be considered with care. If other family members will in any way be involved in caring for the child, their feelings about the situation must be

weighed. Any individual who is intending to keep a baby should make a clear commitment to and adequate preparations for effective prenatal care, the learning of appropriate parenting skills, and the financial requirements of child rearing.

✓ Adoption

Until about 1970, the majority of young women who had unintended pregnancies placed their babies for adoption. Today the situation is very different, in that fewer than 5 percent of mothers do so. Presently, agencies that handle adoptions are finding it difficult to provide newborn babies for the many childless couples who hope to adopt. Close to 15,000 children from foreign countries are adopted by American parents each year. This reflects the reality that the availability of abortion has reduced the number of babies available for adoption, as well as a generally negative attitude toward placing children for adoption that is prevalent today (Bitler & Zavodny, 2002). In fact, adoption can be a viable alternative, and in some cases the biological mother and father are allowed to have contact with the child and the adoptive parents. Young women who place babies for adoption tend to be more affluent, more motivated to pursue education, and more positively disposed toward adoption than are those who keep their babies.

Adoption is a reasonable option for unintended pregnancy when the mother chooses to continue the pregnancy—or it is too late to do otherwise—yet does not feel ready for the responsibilities of parenthood. Mothers and fathers who choose to have their child adopted often feel that the child will have a chance for a better life with another family. As with any choice that is made in cases of unintended pregnancy, the emotional consequences need to be weighed. Yet most people realize that the option of becoming pregnant will be available again at a later time in life when circumstances lend themselves more fully to acceptance of the responsibility of parenting.

Do you think adopted children/adolescents/ adults should be in touch with their birth parents? Defend your position.

Termination of Pregnancy

A pregnancy that terminates naturally is called a **miscarriage** or **spontaneous abortion.** Some women who experience an unintended pregnancy choose to seek ways of terminating it, also known as **induced abortion.** About 1.2 million abortions are performed in the United States each year, representing about a quarter of all pregnancies, although it is believed that abortions are underreported. In recent years, the rate of abortion has decreased by about 8 percent. A number of laws have been passed that restrict access to abortion in numerous ways. In addition, the geographic availability is quite variable, the number of abortion providers has declined, and the costs of abortion procedures have risen, creating barriers to abortion access for many women (Jones et al., 2008; Sedgh et al., 2007).

The ratio of abortions to live births has been falling in recent years, primarily because young women under age 15 are opting to have abortions less often than they did a few years ago and because fewer clinics and health care providers are offering abortion. The most common reasons why women seek abortion are the fear that having a baby will interfere with education, work, or caring for dependents; the inability to afford a child at the time; and not wanting to be a single mother or having relationship problems. In one study, about 70 percent of women in prenatal care and intending to have their babies did not rule out the possibility of terminating a future pregnancy (Finer et al., 2005; Learman et al., 2005; Santelli et al., 2006).

Polls indicate that about 55 percent of people in the United States believe abortion should be available under certain circumstances and that 23 percent believe abortion should be legally available for any reason. About 21 percent of Americans believe abortion should be illegal under all circumstances (Harris Poll, 2005). There has been a trend toward conditional acceptance of abortion, with the majority of people favoring the procedure in cases of rape, when the health of the mother is endangered, or when there is a strong chance of a defect in the baby.

Only about half of medical residency programs in obstetrics and gynecology offer routine training in abortion procedures, while another 39 percent offer optional training (Eastwood et al., 2006). Some experts believe that training in abortion procedures should be more available in medical schools. There is evidence that physicians who have had thorough training in abortion procedures are more likely to perform abortions (Shotorbani et al., 2004). Globally, there is evidence that in areas of the world where abortion is not available through medical facilities, up to 20 million unsafe abortions are performed annually, and some 68,000 women die as a result. Millions more women experience complications that compromise their health, sometimes permanently (Grimes et al., 2006).

The many moral and political conflicts regarding abortion hinge on an essential difference in the beliefs of right-to-life antiabortion forces and pro-choice supporters concerning when human life begins. Abortion foes often believe that life begins at the moment of conception and therefore abortion is tantamount to murder because it involves the ending of another human life. Although most proponents of the availability of abortion feel that it should not be a decision made lightly, they see it as a woman's right to choose in a world in which many families cannot adequately care for the children they have. They tend not to hold to the idea that life begins at conception and instead see the potential quality of life for the unborn child and its parents as the primary issue.

The Supreme Court has struggled with the continuing debate. The historic *Roe v. Wade* decision in 1973 legalized a woman's right to obtain an abortion from a

miscarriage a natural termination of pregnancy.

spontaneous abortion another term for miscarriage.

induced abortion a termination of pregnancy by artificial means

qualified physician. In subsequent rulings, the Court has upheld the right to abortion established by *Roe v. Wade,* while giving states the right to legislate various restrictions on abortion in order to accommodate the beliefs of their citizens. For example, state laws have been enacted that prohibit certain health care personnel from providing information about abortion; require notification of the husband or, in the case of minors, a parent; require a waiting period of up to 24 hours before the abortion can take place; and/or prohibit the use of public facilities for abortions. As might be expected, such laws have placed added burdens of time and cost on women seeking an abortion and on the facilities that serve them (Jones & Weitz, 2009). In Texas, a law requires parental notification for teenagers under age 18 seeking an abortion. This requirement has resulted in a decline in overall abortions but an increase in riskier, later-term abortions. Teens either avoid notifying their parents and wait until they are 18 to have the abortion or they put off notifying their parents until early abortion is no longer an option (Colman & Joyce, 2009; Joyce, Kaestner, & Colman, 2006).

All studies have indicated that legal abortions performed by trained clinicians have fewer risks for the woman than carrying a pregnancy to full term and giving birth. Although in both cases the risk of the woman's death is extremely low, the chance of a relatively healthy woman dying from a legal abortion in the United States is about 1 in 100,000 for abortions performed up to 12 weeks of pregnancy. The rate rises somewhat as the length of the pregnancy increases. In comparison, nearly 20 deaths per 100,000 women occur in continued pregnancies and births (Hatcher et al., 2007). Although rumors of an increased risk of breast cancer have circulated with regard to abortion, two studies of data from nearly 200,000 women have shown that the risk of breast cancer for women who have had an abortion and women who have not is statistically indistinguishable (Collaborative Group, 2004; Michels et al., 2007).

First-trimester abortions are simplest and safest and have few complications other than some excessive bleeding or subsequent infection that can be treated with antibiotics. Later abortions have somewhat higher risks of bleeding or infection because labor is induced, but the risk of fatal complications is still minimal. Although having had an abortion has been linked with a higher incidence of miscarriage or preterm birth in later pregnancies and also increases the likelihood of later ectopic pregnancy and having babies with low birth weight, abortion does not reduce fertility or the ability to conceive (Brown, Adera, & Masho, 2008).

Methods of Abortion

Several procedures can be employed to terminate pregnancy. The particular method chosen usually depends on the stage of pregnancy. An abortion can be performed legally in the United States by a doctor through the 24th week of pregnancy (measured from the first day of the last menstrual period). The earlier it is performed, the simpler the procedure, the lower the risks to the woman, and the lower the cost.

Vacuum Curettage

About 90 percent of abortions in the United States are performed within the first trimester, that is, the first 12 weeks of pregnancy. The method most often used during this stage is **vacuum curettage,** sometimes called vacuum aspiration. First, the cervical opening is dilated through the use of graduated metal dilators. Another, gentler approach to cervical dilation involves the earlier insertion of a cylinder made from a dried seaweed called **laminaria.** The laminaria insert slowly absorbs moisture from the cervix, and as it expands the cervical os opens wider. Maximum dilation can take from 12 to 24 hours. This procedure is more comfortable for the woman and reduces the risk of injury to the cervix. After the cervical opening is dilated, a thin plastic tube is inserted into the uterus and connected to a suction pump. The uterine lining, along with fetal and placental tissue, is then suctioned out. This part of the procedure usually takes from 10 to 15 minutes. The complication rate for the procedure is quite low.

Medical Induction

Mifepristone, or **RU 486,** has been widely used in Europe for early abortions and is now used routinely in the United States. The earlier it is used during the pregnancy, the higher its rate of effectiveness. It typically is used within seven weeks of the first day of the woman's last menstrual period. The drug is administered in tablet form under a physician's supervision, and it causes the embryo to break away from the uterine wall. Two days later, misoprostol, a hormonelike chemical, is administered orally or by injection or suppository, causing the uterus to contract and expel the embryo. Studies have shown that use of mifepristone is less painful and carries less danger of infection than surgical methods of abortion. Injection of methotrexate, a drug

vacuum curettage (kyur-a-TAZH) a method of induced abortion performed with a suction pump.

laminaria (lam-a-NER-ee-a) a dried seaweed sometimes used in dilating the cervical opening prior to vacuum curettage.

mifepristone (RU 486) a progesterone antagonist used as a postcoital contraceptive.

already on the U.S. market for other purposes, also has proved to be 96 percent effective for inducing abortion when combined with misoprostol. This method requires less medical monitoring than mifepristone (Winikoff et al., 2008).

Even though medical abortion protocols have been shown to be effective and safe, they have been quite slow to catch on. It has been shown that providers of surgical abortion can integrate medical procedures into their practices with success, providing another convenient option for their patients (Leeman et al., 2007).

Dilation and Evacuation, or Dilation, and Curettage

Beyond the first trimester, the uterus has enlarged, and as a result its walls have become thinner. The contents of the uterus cannot be as easily removed by aspiration or by injections of drugs. Vacuum curettage is not considered as safe and suitable for abortions in the second trimester of pregnancy.

During the 13- to 16-week period of pregnancy, the usual method employed is **dilation and evacuation (D & E).** After cervical dilation, a suction tube is still used, but this is followed by the scraping of the inner wall of the uterus with a metal curette to ensure that all fetal tissue is removed. This is a variation of **dilation and curettage (D & C),** which omits the initial vacuum aspiration of the uterus and sometimes is used to terminate pregnancy.

Procedures Used Later in Pregnancy

For abortions later in pregnancy (16 to 24 weeks), procedures usually must be employed that render the fetus nonviable and induce its delivery through the vagina. These approaches are more physically uncomfortable and often more emotionally upsetting for the woman because she experiences uterine contractions for several hours and then expels a lifeless fetus. The two most commonly used procedures at this stage of pregnancy are **prostaglandin-induced abortions** and **saline-induced abortions.**

Prostaglandins are injected directly into the amniotic sac through the abdominal wall, administered intravenously to the woman, or inserted into the vagina in suppository form. Prostaglandins stimulate uterine contractions, leading to delivery. Saline (salt) solution injected into the amniotic fluid has a similar effect. Some clinicians have also substituted a substance called "urea" for saline. Sometimes, various combinations of prostaglandins, saline, and urea are used to terminate later pregnancies (Hatcher et al., 2007). Late-term abortions, sometimes called partial-birth abortions, have created a great deal of controversy, but

many clinicians feel that it is essential to maintain their availability (Drey et al., 2006). In 2007, the U.S. Supreme Court took a position that makes certain partial-birth procedures illegal.

Use of Embryonic Tissue

There is a common misconception that embryonic tissue potentially used in stem cell research is obtained from aborted fetuses. This is not the case. Stem cell tissue lines could be obtained from embryos that have been created by in vitro fertilization, but implanted embryos are not used. Stem cells are particularly valuable because they grow faster, are more adaptable to a variety of environments, and are less likely to be rejected by the recipient's immune system than are tissues transplanted from other adults. Work has been done to investigate the value of stem cell transplants in treating Parkinson's disease, Alzheimer's disease, spinal cord damage, diabetes, epilepsy, and a variety of neuromuscular disorders. The outcomes of the research have been encouraging, but much work remains to be done.

Do you believe that abortion should continue to be a legal option? If so, under what circumstances?

Life Outcomes after Abortion

Although further study is still needed, some longitudinal studies of women who have had an abortion have compared subsequent life outcomes with women who had babies. On many measures spanning educational achievement, eventual income, dependence on public funds, and domestic violence, women who had abortions prior to age 21 generally fared better than those who had not. Termination of their pregnancies had apparently mitigated the circumstances that often develop around early pregnancy and unintended parenthood (Fergusson, Boden, & Horwood, 2007).

---

dilation and evacuation (D & E) a method of induced abortion in the second trimester of pregnancy that combines suction with a scraping of the inner wall of the uterus.

dilation and curettage (D & C) a method of induced abortion in the second trimester of pregnancy that involves a scraping of the uterine wall.

prostaglandin- and saline-induced abortions a method used in the 16th to 24th weeks of pregnancy in which prostaglandins, salt solutions, or urea is injected into the amniotic sac, administered intravenously, or inserted into the vagina in suppository form to induce contractions and fetal delivery.

The psychological effects of abortion on a woman depend a great deal on her beliefs and values and the degree of care with which she has made the decision. In a study of 97 women who had had early abortions, most indicated substantial improvement in their quality of life soon after having the procedure. They felt better emotionally, could think more clearly, slept better, and had improved appetites (Westhoff, Picardo, & Morrow, 2003). An analysis of data from the National Longitudinal Survey of Youth found that women who terminate an unintended first pregnancy are at no greater risk for depression than are those who carry the pregnancy to term (Schmiege & Russo, 2005).

Although serious emotional complications following abortion are quite rare, some women and their male partners do experience some degree of depression, grieving, regret, or sense of loss. Support and counseling from friends, family members, or professionals following an abortion often help lighten this distress, which typically fades within several weeks after the procedure. Counseling often helps in cases where the distress is not alleviated in a reasonable time. A review of the wealth of data gathered in studies conducted for the American Psychological Association suggested that most women will not suffer lasting psychological trauma following an abortion. There does not seem to be any evidence to support the existence of what has been termed a "postabortion syndrome," and severe negative reactions following an abortion apparently are rare.

Self-Evaluation

Contraceptive Comfort and Confidence Scale

Method of birth control you are considering using: _____

Length of time you used this method in the past: _____

Answer YES or NO to the following questions:

	YES	NO
1. Have I had problems using this method before?	❏	❏
2. Have I ever become pregnant while using this method?	❏	❏
3. Am I afraid of using this method?	❏	❏
4. Would I really rather not use this method?	❏	❏
5. Will I have trouble remembering to use this method?	❏	❏
6. Will I have trouble using this method correctly?	❏	❏
7. Do I still have unanswered questions about this method?	❏	❏
8. Does this method make menstrual periods longer or more painful?	❏	❏
9. Does this method cost more than I can afford?	❏	❏
10. Could this method cause me to have serious complications?	❏	❏
11. Am I opposed to this method because of any religious or moral beliefs?	❏	❏
12. Is my partner opposed to this method?	❏	❏
13. Am I using this method without my partner's knowledge?	❏	❏
14. Will using this method embarrass my partner?	❏	❏
15. Will using this method embarrass me?	❏	❏
16. Will I enjoy intercourse less because of this method?	❏	❏
17. If this method interrupts lovemaking, will I avoid using it?	❏	❏
18. Has a nurse or doctor ever told me NOT to use this method?	❏	❏
19. Is there anything about my personality that could lead me to use this method incorrectly?	❏	❏
20. Am I at any risk of being exposed to HIV or other sexually transmitted diseases if I use this method?	❏	❏

Total Number of Yes Answers:　　　—　　　—

Most individuals will have a few "yes" answers. "Yes" answers mean that potential problems may arise. If you have more than a few "yes" responses, you may want to talk to your physician, counselor, partner, or friend to help you decide whether to use this method or how to use it so that it will really be effective for you. In general, the more "yes" answers you have, the less likely you are to use this method consistently and correctly at every act of intercourse.

Source: Robert A. Hatcher et al., *Contraceptive Technology,* 17th ed. Copyright © 1998 by Contraceptive Technology Communications, Inc. Reprinted by permission of Ardent Media, Inc.

Chapter Summary

1. Human beings have sought to minimize the connections between sex and childbirth.

2. In ancient times, botanical preparations may have provided contraceptive protection.

3. Distribution of information about birth control was limited in the United States by the Comstock Laws, passed in the 1870s. Activist Margaret Sanger was influential in broadening the rights of women to learn about and use contraception in the early twentieth century.

4. While the world's population continues to grow, the rate of growth has been slowing down. Over half the world's nations are now reproducing at below replacement rates. Many children live in substandard conditions.

5. The decision to have children is an important one, involving significant costs and personal responsibilities.

6. It is believed that many pregnancies globally are unwanted. Political and social factors may determine what kinds of birth control are accessible.

7. In making decisions about contraceptive use, people are influenced by several factors, including ethical/moral and religious beliefs, political forces, possible effects on the woman's health, and effects on sexual pleasure. Guilt, fear, or anxiety may not always inhibit sexual behavior but may inhibit preparing for it.

8. Each person must sort through his or her personal values and concerns about birth control, understand his or her personal reactions to sexual feelings and activities, and learn how to communicate with a partner effectively in order to prepare fully for contraceptive decision making.

9. There is no best method of birth control for all individuals. Each couple must consider several factors in making a choice: age and amount of protection required, the safety of the method, how long the method will be used, what might hinder the method's use, and cost.

10. The theoretical or perfect use failure rate assumes that the birth control method is being used correctly and without technical failure. The typical use failure rate, the more realistic rating of the method, takes into account human error, carelessness, and technical failure.

11. Even though most methods of contraception are designed for women, there are many ways for the responsibility to be shared by both partners: cooperating in applying the method, communicating openly about birth control, and sharing the cost.

12. Table 11.1 gives summary information on methods of contraception, their rates of effectiveness, potential advantages, possible causes of failure, and possible negative side effects.

13. Couples who choose abstinence from intercourse as a birth control method have alternatives for sexual and nonsexual intimacy. Although withdrawal is not one of the more reliable forms of contraception, it is better than no method at all.

14. Hormones that prevent ovulation and change the consistency of cervical mucus can be administered in the form of combined oral contraceptive pills or progestin-only minipills. The pill provides protection against ovarian and endometrial cancers but may also have some harmful side effects.

15. The hormonal implant consists of a silicon capsule that is implanted under the skin, releasing a synthetic hormone that prevents ovulation for up to three years. Hormonal patches and the vaginal ring also provide reliable contraceptive protection. Women who breastfeed exclusively may be protected from pregnancy for up to six months.

16. Hormonal injections create a hostile uterine environment for sperm and for implantation. One-month and three-month dosages are available.

17. Spermicides kill sperm and are available without prescription as foams, film, jellies, creams, and vaginal suppositories and are implanted on the contraceptive sponge.

18. Barrier methods of contraception prevent sperm from entering the uterus and are most effective when used with a spermicide. They include the diaphragm, cervical cap, and condom.

19. Condoms provide protection against disease as well as against pregnancy. Male condoms fit over the penis and are made of latex, natural membranes, or polyurethane. Female condoms consist of a synthetic plastic pouch that is inserted into the vagina.

20. The intrauterine device (IUD) is inserted into the uterus and may work by preventing fertilization. There are two IUDs currently available in the United States.

21. Fertility awareness allows the woman to become more aware of her fertile period during the menstrual cycle by charting the length of her cycle, her basal body temperature, and the presence or consistency of cervical mucus.

22. Vasectomy involves cutting and tying the male vas deferens. Tubal ligation and transcervical sterilization seal off the fallopian tubes.

23. Emergency contraception, or Plan B, is available in the form of hormonal pills that are taken in two doses.

24. New forms of contraception are being researched. For males, these include testosterone injections and other chemicals that suppress sperm production. For women, a vaccine that would immunize against gonadotropin could prevent implantation.

25. When an unintended pregnancy occurs, one of several options must be chosen: keeping the baby, placing the baby for adoption, or terminating the pregnancy.

26. When an unintended pregnancy occurs, couples in established relationships are more likely to keep the baby. Fewer than 5 percent of mothers now place their babies for adoption.

27. Some pregnancies terminate naturally in a miscarriage or spontaneous abortion.

28. Induced abortion has been legal in the United States since 1973, but Supreme Court decisions have gradually allowed states to restrict its availability. There are still conflicts between right-to-life and pro-choice groups about whether abortion should continue to be a legal option.

29. First-trimester abortions usually are done by vacuum curettage. Mifepristone (RU 486) in combination with misoprostol or methotrexate offers a nonsurgical medical alternative. Later abortions may be done by dilation and evacuation (D & E) or dilation and curettage (D & C) or may be induced by injection of prostaglandins, saline, or urea.

30. Embryonic tissue used to establish stem cell lines does not come from aborted fetuses.

31. Abortion is statistically safer for the woman than pregnancy and giving birth, and many women experience an improved quality of life following the procedure. Some women experience a degree of guilt, loss, or some other psychological reaction. The availability of supportive counseling before and after an abortion is important.

Part 4

Sexual Behavior and Contemporary Society

■

The three most common forms of sexual activity are masturbation, oral-genital sex, and heterosexual intercourse. Although masturbation is usually a solitary activity, there are many other behaviors that constitute shared sexual encounters. The dynamics of the interaction, whether they relate to technique or to how personalities are connecting, become crucial to determining whether a sexual interaction is pleasurable or exploitative.

It seems clear from research that a substantial percentage of human beings are sexually attracted predominantly to members of their own gender. Although many people espouse a live-and-let-live attitude toward gay males, lesbians, bisexuals, and transgender persons, our culture continues to be essentially heterosexist.

The kinds of sexual activities in which people choose to participate seem limited only by the imagination. Only in recent years has scientific research begun to give us a clearer picture of human sexual diversity, although social norms and values play a significant role in determining the degree to which that diversity is accepted in any society.

Online communication technologies have created new forms of relationships and have made the distribution of sexual images faster and easier than ever before. What are the effects of sexually explicit materials on those who view them? How have sexual themes become a part of artistic and popular culture? To what extent should laws regulate erotic themes in the media and the sexual activities of human beings? These are major issues facing society today, and courts and legislative bodies are struggling to grapple with them.

■ *Chapter 12*
SOLITARY SEX AND SHARED SEX

■ *Chapter 13*
SAME-GENDER ORIENTATION AND BEHAVIOR

■ *Chapter 14*
THE SPECTRUM OF HUMAN SEXUAL BEHAVIOR

■ *Chapter 15*
SEX, ART, THE MEDIA, AND THE LAW

Chapter 12
Solitary Sex and Shared Sex

Chapter Outline

> I think about sex a lot, and I enjoy experiencing sex, whether by myself or with a partner. I've managed to be careful about the partners I have chosen, and I am always careful to protect both of us. These days, though, sex alone seems much less complicated, but sometimes you just long to be with somebody too.
>
> —from a student essay

This chapter examines some of the most common sexual behaviors in which human beings participate. A fair amount of evidence seems to suggest that, generally speaking, males demonstrate higher levels of sexual interest and activity than do females. Men are more likely to report pleasure as a significant motive for sex, while women are more likely to report love as a motive. Different loving patterns between partners seem to exert a strong influence over the kinds of sexual activity they share. This is probably due to an interaction of biological and social factors (Browning et al., 2000; Kaestle & Halpern, 2007).

Although Kinsey (1948, 1953) emphasized that the statistics on sexual behavior gained from his sample of about 16,000 individuals could not be generalized to the total population, they did allow us to glimpse the many variations of human sexual experience. Data from the National Health and Social Life Survey (NHSLS) and the National Longitudinal Study of Adolescent Health have given us more reliable statistics on the types and frequencies of sexual behaviors among people in the United States; they seem to be relatively consistent with data coming from European research. We can now make some generalizations from these random population samples to the general population. We also can see that sexual behaviors are influenced by factors such as age, race, religious beliefs, educational background, and relational dynamics (Kaestle & Halpern, 2007; Laumann et al., 1994).

List several factors that might influence the acceptability and frequency of various sexual behaviors.

Statistics should be considered approximations of what people are doing, and only that. Although they can give us interesting information and establish certain norms for sexual behavior in particular groups of people, such data do not represent standards for individual behavior. The fact that most males masturbate does not mean that males should masturbate or that nonmasturbating males are abnormal. That the majority of females have not experienced intercourse by age 17 does not mean that 15-year-old females who have had intercourse are immoral.

Each of us possesses his or her own specific sexual interests, values, preferences, needs, and behaviors. These aspects of our sexuality may change many times during our lifetimes because sexual individuality is more a dynamic process than a fixed state of being. The information in the chapters about sexual behavior

is aimed at helping you gain a clearer understanding of your own sexuality, as well as describing the spectrum of sexual behaviors that are part of the human experience. New legitimacy is being given to the concept of sexual pleasure, an area about which there has been a good deal of ambivalence (Resnick, 2002).

There are two distinct worlds of human sexual experience. One is the social world in which sex is shared with others. This world necessitates all sorts of negotiable processes between people and involves expectations, judgments, performances, and consequences that can be both positive and negative. The other is the private world that in many ways may be even more active and consuming than the partnered world. In this domain, personal pleasure is paramount, and social constraints may be less intrusive, although private sex often is not without its guilt or fear of discovery.

■ Solitary Sex: The Private World

The private world of sex involves the solitary pursuit of sexual thoughts and fantasies, erotic materials and toys, and masturbation, often in combination. Self-generated sexual pleasure is sometimes called **autoeroticism.** The NHSLS data showed that men report thinking about sex more frequently than do women. Over half of men (54 percent) said that they think about sex every day or even several times a day, with another 43 percent reporting that they think about sex a few times a week or month. Only 19 percent of women indicated that they think about sex every day, while 33 percent said that they think about sex a few times per week or month. Four percent of men and 14 percent of women reported thinking about sex less than once a month or never. As Table 12.1 shows, men also are considerably more likely than women to purchase and seek out materials and activities associated with private sexual arousal and pleasure.

We might intuitively assume that people engage in solitary sexual pleasures probably as compensation for not having available sexual partners. In fact, research has shown that this assumption is incorrect. According to NHSLS data, people who are most likely to think about sex the most, to pursue erotic materials for their own use, and to masturbate also tend to have the most active sexual lives with partners. Other research has

autoeroticism self-generated sexual arousal and pleasure.

Table 12.1	Percentage Purchasing Autoerotic Materials in the Past 12 Months	
Materials	Men	Women
X-rated movies or videos	23%	11%
Visit to a club with nude or seminude dancers	22	4
Sexually explicit books or magazines	16	4
Vibrators or dildos	2	2
Other sex toys	1	2
Sex phone numbers	1	1
Any of the above	41	16

Note: Percentages are independent for each cell.

Source: From *Sex in America* by Robert T. Michael et al., p. 157. Copyright © 1994 by CSG Enterprises, Inc., Edward O. Laumann, Robert T. Michael, and Gina Kolata. By permission of Little, Brown and Company, and Brockman, Inc.

confirmed this. The more private sexual experience an individual has, the more shared sexual experience he or she is likely to have (Michael et al., 1994; Pinkerton et al., 2002; Toates, 2009).

Sexual Pleasure for One

Masturbation is one of the most common ways human beings seek sexual pleasure; it refers to deliberate, rhythmic stimulation of the sex organs—often along with other parts of the body—to produce pleasurable sexual sensations and (usually) orgasm. Masturbation is not confined to the human species; it is common among many mammals, especially the primates. This form of sexual behavior has been subject to much misunderstanding, folklore, religious attention, moral analysis, and ignorance.

As sexuality was entering the domain of medicine during the eighteenth century, negative attitudes about masturbation made their way into the medical profession. A Swiss physician named Tissot published a book in 1741 that perpetuated the popular belief of the time that body fluids needed to be kept in perfect balance for a person to be healthy. It was further believed that expending the body's sexual fluids would lead to illness. Physicians of the time also believed that the stimulation of the nervous system that took place during sexual arousal and orgasm was damaging. Tissot's theories were perpetuated by medical writers in the nineteenth century, and claims that physical and mental deterioration would result from masturbation became even more extreme. Although the medical perspective

on the practice has completely reversed, masturbation is sometimes still cloaked in a somewhat inaccurate shroud of secrecy (Bullough, 2002). Yet it also has become more openly discussed in contemporary media and often is the subject of jokes.

Although statistics from previous research samples have not been representative of the total population, it is reasonable to conclude from the data we have that masturbation is a common practice among adolescents and adults and that the vast majority of people masturbate at some time in their lives. Adolescent males are less likely to report their masturbatory activity while still adolescents than they are retrospectively as young adults (Halpern et al., 2000).

In one survey of college students, 98 percent of the men and 64 percent of the women indicated that they had masturbated, with the men averaging 12 times per month and the women averaging about 5 times per month. The earlier the students had begun masturbating and the more pleasurable they found it to be, the more likely the women were to have been masturbated by a partner and the more likely the men were to have used condoms with their partners. These findings may reflect some greater level of comfort with their own genitals (Pinkerton et al., 2002). College women are likely to feel negatively about a man's masturbation or use of pornographic materials for self-stimulation, apparently because they see it as a sign of dissatisfaction with his partner. College men are more accepting of solitary sexual behavior on the part of women (Clark & Wiederman, 2000).

Comparison studies done in 1966, 1981, and 1996 concluded that during that 30-year period, men and especially women began to masturbate at earlier ages and the behavior became more accepted as being pleasurable in its own right, coexisting quite naturally with the availability of partnered sex (Dekker & Schmidt, 2002). A cross-cultural analysis of studies conducted in Finland, Sweden, Estonia, and Russia found that rates of masturbation had increased in recent years and that adults tended to maintain the habits and frequencies of masturbation that they developed during adolescence. The study concluded that masturbation did not, in fact, decrease with age when the social norms of the culture during the generation's teenage years were considered as the basis for forming particular masturbatory habits. The study also found that masturbation was not particularly related to the presence of a sex partner or to levels of activity with that partner. Masturbation was seen as an independent way to experience sexual pleasure rather than as compensatory for partner unavailability (Kontula & Haavio-Mannila, 2002).

masturbation stimulation of one's own genitals for sexual pleasure and orgasm.

■ **FIGURE 12.1** *Female Masturbation*

Do you feel that masturbation is a behavior deserving of moral judgment or prohibition? What is the basis for your answer? If you masturbate, how do you feel about your own behavior?

NHSLS statistics found similar patterns in the United States. Eighty-five percent of men and 45 percent of women who were living with a sexual partner indicated that they had masturbated during the previous year, although frequency of masturbation does not seem to be correlated with how often they have sex with a partner. White, educated liberals apparently are more likely to masturbate. Most people reported that they masturbate in order to "relieve sexual tension," to "get physical pleasure," or "get to sleep." About one-third of men and women said they did so because they did not have a sexual partner. One-third of men and one-fourth of women indicated that they used masturbation to help them relax. Very few of the people surveyed—5 percent of the women and 7 percent of the men—said they masturbated in order to avoid HIV infection or other sexually transmitted diseases (Das, 2007; Gerressu et al., 2008; Michael et al., 1994). While there are no valid statistics on group masturbation, anecdotal evidence indicates that at least a small percentage of adolescents participate in various forms of group masturbation, usually with members of their own sex. The phenomenon seems to be more common among boys than among girls, and groups occasionally are composed of both genders. Some groups of adults, usually males, get together periodically just to masturbate. A few mixed-gender adult masturbation groups exist as well (Cornog, 2001).

How Girls and Women Masturbate

Masturbation is one way many women become acquainted with their own sexual responsiveness and learn how to have an orgasm (see Figure 12.1). This may serve them well as they develop their responsiveness with a partner. Masters and Johnson (1966) observed women masturbating and reported that although no two women out of a sample of several hundred masturbated in exactly the same way, very few of them seemed to use direct stimulation of the glans clitoris. The tissues of the clitoral glans, like the glans of the penis, apparently are too sensitive for prolonged direct stimulation. Women who stimulate the clitoris tend to gently stroke only the shaft. Right-handed women usually manipulate the right side of the shaft, and left-handed women the left side. A common way for females to masturbate is by manipulating the entire mons area, which exerts less direct stimulation on the clitoris. The minor lips or other areas surrounding the clitoris also are frequently stimulated. It is important to note that immediately following orgasm, the clitoral glans is especially sensitive to touch or pressure, and most women avoid touching it at that time.

Although use of the hands is the most common method of masturbation, many girls and women use other means of stimulating their genitals. Rubbing the mons or other parts of the vulva against a pillow, bed, doorknob, or some other object is typical. It also is not unusual for a female to insert a finger or some suitably shaped long object into the vagina during masturbation. Cylindrical electric vibrators or flexible plastic devices (often called dildos) may be used during masturbation. Some women are able to produce sexual arousal and orgasm by creating muscular tension in the pelvic region through the tightening of leg and abdominal muscles. Others cross their legs and apply rhythmic stimulation to the vulva by contracting and relaxing the thigh muscles. Women sometimes find that running a stream of warm water over the vulva, and especially the clitoris, or sitting in a whirlpool bath can create sexual stimulation. Many women stimulate

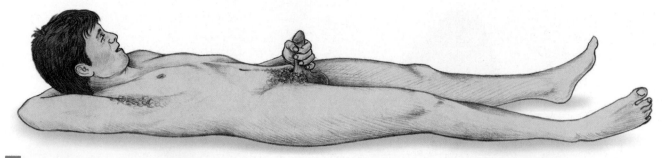

FIGURE 12.2 *Male Masturbation*

other parts of their bodies while masturbating. For example, stimulation of the breasts and nipples is common, and some women enjoy stroking the anal region. Common sense dictates that safety and cleanliness should be observed during masturbation and that women should not insert sharp, pointed, or rasping objects into their vagina. It is also important not to introduce bacteria from the anal region into the genital area, because infection may result.

How Boys and Men Masturbate

Masters and Johnson (1966) also found highly individualized methods of masturbating among the hundreds of men they observed. Some type of stimulation of the penis almost always occurs in male masturbation. Typically, the penis is grasped by the hand and stroked until orgasm takes place (see Figure 12.2). How the penis is grasped and stroked varies with different males. The most common method is for the man to stroke the shaft of the penis, just touching the top edge of the corona around the glans and the frenulum on the underside, where the glans and shaft join. The amount of pressure used, the number of fingers employed on the penis, how rapidly the stroking proceeds, and how far up and down the hand moves all vary from man to man. Some men—particularly those with circumcised penises—stimulate just the glans by pulling at it or rubbing its entire surface. As men get closer to orgasm, the stroking or rubbing of the penis tends to become more rapid, and then usually slows or stops during actual ejaculation. Most women, in contrast, continue stroking the clitoris during orgasm.

During manual masturbation, many men enjoy occasionally using both hands to stroke the penis or using their free hand to fondle the scrotum or anal region. Some men insert a finger or other object into the anus during masturbation. It also is not unusual for a male to use some sort of lubricating jelly or liquid on his hand during masturbation to create intense sexual sensations. Most boys and men experiment with a variety of ways of producing orgasm. Many males enjoy

rubbing their penis on blankets, pillows, beds, and other suitable objects. Kinsey (1948) reported that a significant proportion of men attempt **autofellatio** at one time or another; that is, they try to put their penis into their own mouth, a feat that very few have the acrobatic dexterity to achieve.

There are also masturbation aids marketed for men, including rubber pouches into which the penis can be inserted, artificial vaginas made of flesh-simulating plastics that often show the external organs of the vulva, and full-size inflatable dolls with built-in pouches at the location of the vagina, mouth, and/or anus. Insertion of the penis into bottles or other openings that may ultimately be too small for the erect penis can result in serious difficulty in removing the penis and can cause penile damage (Voegeli & Effert, 2005). A few boys and men, especially those who find pain sexually arousing, enjoy inserting objects into the urethra at the end of the penis. There are obvious dangers associated with this practice, because injury or infection in the urethra could result. Physicians occasionally see boys or men who have inserted some small object into their urethra, or larger objects into their rectum, only to have it become lodged there. Again, it is common sense that masturbation should be done with attention to basic cleanliness and safety so that genitourinary injury or infection will not result.

Fantasy and Pictures in Masturbation

As noted earlier, many people fantasize about sex or employ pornography and sex toys as part of their autoerotic activities, with males doing so more frequently than females. In a survey of college students, more than 60 percent of the males reported that they had

autofellatio (aw-toh-fe-LAY-she-o) the act of a male providing oral stimulation to his own penis, which most males do not have the physical agility to perform.

Real Student Voices

■ My girlfriend and I often enjoy masturbating with each other. We find it extremely arousing. Sometimes, we end up having intercourse, sometimes not.

■ I started masturbating when I was about five or six, just by rubbing myself. I never told anybody about it until I was a teenager, and I never heard anything about it that would have led me to believe it was bad or wrong. I think it has helped me be a

healthy sexual woman, and I'm glad I was never discouraged from doing it.

■ I would rather not masturbate as much as I do, even though I guess there is really nothing wrong with it. Sometimes I try to skip it or put it off, just to see how much control I can have. Usually, I don't succeed. So you could say I'm still somewhat confused. I just feel as though I shouldn't give in to sexual desire so much (6 to 12 times per week).

used pornographic magazines or videos to enhance masturbation, whereas only about 12 percent of the females reported doing so. Males also were more likely to use nonpornographic magazines or advertisements during masturbation. The most common fantasies seem to involve sexual activity with a loved partner, although fantasies about sexual involvement with acquaintances, celebrities, and strangers also are typical. The majority of men and women admit to having had recent sexual fantasies about people other than their main partner, with men having more such fantasies than women (Hicks & Leitenberg, 2001). It has also been claimed that one reason men watch pornography is to see other men having sex (Strager, 2003). Added to these fantasies is the whole gamut of fantasies about group sex, being forced to have sex, forcing another person to have sex, and every other imaginable form of behavior (Bivona & Critelli, 2009; Zurbriggen & Yost, 2004). It is probably safe to assume that erotic pictures, videos, and literature help generate fantasies in many individuals during masturbation and that people often project themselves into the subject matter of the erotic material.

Facts and Fallacies about Masturbation

It is surprising how many myths and misconceptions about masturbation persist. The next few paragraphs separate the fallacies from the facts. Each of the following italicized statements is a fact.

Fact: Masturbation is not confined to childhood and adolescence or to single persons. Its frequency is quite variable. Many adult men and women—including married individuals—continue to masturbate through-

out their lives. There is solid evidence to indicate that the majority of adult males and close to half of adult females masturbate from time to time. Their frequency of masturbation actually seems to be highest between the ages of 24 and 50. Married people, particularly married men, tend to masturbate somewhat less often than single people. There is a wide range among those who masturbate very seldom (once or twice a year) and those who masturbate more frequently (once a day or more). All these patterns are found in normal, healthy, happy individuals (Coleman, 2002).

Fact: Masturbation is not necessarily a substitute for sex with a partner. It is certainly true that masturbation sometimes is used as a substitute for sexual activity with a partner; however, masturbation also represents a form of sexual expression in itself, regardless of what other sexual activities are available to the individual. As we've already seen, many people who have very fulfilling sexual lives and have access to shared sexual activity whenever they wish still enjoy masturbating. People who masturbate frequently also are more likely to participate in partnered sex frequently (Dekker & Schmidt, 2002; Michael et al., 1994; Pinkerton et al., 2002). Some people may actually prefer masturbation to other forms of sexual behavior; this should not be considered a sign of immaturity or sexual dissatisfaction.

Fact: Masturbation can be shared. Some couples who share sex are reluctant to discuss masturbation. Even though both partners may masturbate regularly, it is often difficult for them to admit that fact to each other. Masturbation apparently is one of the secrets that partners often keep from each other. Being able to surmount this communication barrier and talk about masturbation can be an important step to better sexual communication. Some couples find that masturbating together or watching each other masturbate can be an enjoyable form of sexual sharing.

Fact: There is no such thing as excessive masturbation. No medical definition of excessive masturbation exists. Frequent masturbation does not cause physical harm. For the most part, it seems to be a self-limiting practice: When the individual is sexually satiated, he or she loses interest in being sexually aroused. The number of orgasms necessary to reach satiation will vary among individuals and their circumstances. Of course, if a person has masturbated to satiation, she or he might not be interested in other forms of sex for a while. Masters and Johnson (1966) reported that most of the men they questioned expressed vague concerns over excessive masturbation but consistently stated the frequency they considered excessive to be greater than their own masturbatory frequency. A man who masturbated once a month stated that once or twice a week would be excessive, whereas a man who masturbated two or three times a day thought that five or six times a day might be excessive.

Fact: Masturbation can be as sexually satisfying physically as shared sex. From a purely physical standpoint, masturbation can offer full sexual satisfaction for some people. Of course, if both physical and emotional intimacy with another person is important to an individual's fully experiencing sexual feelings, masturbation will leave some gaps. The degree of orgasmic pleasure may be judged more by the intensity of physical sensations during masturbation or a casual sexual encounter, whereas in sexual encounters with an intimate sex partner emotional aspects of pleasure probably play a larger role (Mah & Binik, 2005). Particularly in women, however, masturbation often provides the opportunity for the kind of self-regulated stimulation that produces a more intense orgasm than can be obtained with coitus. Some of that effective stimulation can be transferred to shared sex when the partners have good communication about sex.

Fact: Masturbation is a good way to learn about sexual feelings and responsiveness. Among sex therapists and sexuality educators, the attitude is quite prevalent that masturbation not only is healthy and normal but also can be a useful learning experience (Coleman, 2002). In males, patterns of sexual functioning may be influenced by early patterns of masturbation. A boy who learns to masturbate to orgasm in the shortest possible time may carry the pattern into later shared sex as premature ejaculation. Men who have learned to prolong the time it takes to ejaculate during masturbation often can transfer that control to their shared sexual activities. There is one caveat here: A few men develop patterns of masturbation that require unusual amounts of penile pressure or stimulation, and some of these men have difficulty replicating these sensations in shared sexual experiences.

For women, masturbation is recognized as an important way to learn what orgasm feels like and how to produce it. Various masturbation exercises are commonly used as a preliminary step to orgasmic response and full enjoyment in shared sexual activity. Research has shown that, compared to married women who have never experienced an orgasm through masturbation, married women who have masturbated to orgasm have significantly more orgasms in shared sex, greater sexual desire, higher self-esteem, a greater level of marital and sexual satisfaction, and a tendency to require less time to become sexually aroused with a partner (Zamboni & Crawford, 2002).

Fact: Masturbation does not lead to weakness, mental illness, or physical debilitation. As myths of masturbation's connection with mental and physical maladies have faded, it is now clear that masturbation causes no medical conditions, regardless of frequency. Coaches once warned athletes to avoid masturbation or shared sex, especially the night before the big game, because they saw it as an energy-sapping practice. Although orgasm may indeed release tension and lead to relaxation, many athletes claim that this actually can boost their performance. Masturbation does not drain the body of energy (Bullough, 2002; Coleman, 2002).

Fact: Males do not eventually run out of semen if they masturbate frequently. A common misconception has been that the male body is granted the potential of producing only a certain amount of semen and that each ejaculation leads a man closer to the bottom of the barrel. In actuality, the glands that produce sperm and semen tend to be active from puberty into old age. They do not cease production after a certain number of orgasms. In fact, there is evidence that the more sexually active an individual is in earlier life, the more active he or she will be in later years. The more semen a male ejaculates, the more his body produces.

Fact: Masturbation does not lead to same-gender orientation and behavior. In many people's minds, masturbation is associated with sexual attraction to one's own gender. Apparently, the idea of a person seeking pleasure from her or his own genitals is interpreted as sexual attraction to same-sexed genitals. This simply is not true. Heterosexual people masturbate, and so do gay, lesbian, and bisexual people. The practice does not change sexual orientation.

Fact: Masturbation is not physically essential. Some people—particularly men—believe that it may be harmful to abstain from having orgasms. They fear that storing sperm and semen or experiencing erection without orgasm eventually may be harmful to the body. Actually, the body adjusts its production of semen to the amount of sexual activity. Although masturbation can be a pleasurable learning experience and may be important to a person's sexual life, it is not essential for physical or mental well-being.

Masturbation, Guilt, and Morality

Perhaps because of the long-standing negative attitudes toward masturbation, it is not always a guilt-free sexual practice. About half of women and men report some degree of guilt in association with their masturbatory activities. Guilt does not seem to affect the frequency of masturbation in males, but it is somewhat associated with less frequent masturbation in females (Laumann et al., 1994). Women who feel guilty about their self-stimulation are less likely to have positive physical and psychological reactions to masturbation and are less likely to report being sexually adjusted or satisfied (Coleman, 2002).

Adolescent males seem to talk together more about masturbation than do adolescent females. Why might this be?

As with all other forms of sexual behavior, various cultures and religions have attached many different moral implications to masturbation. The Judeo-Christian-Muslim position was once predominantly antimasturbation, although those attitudes have largely changed with the new findings of medicine and psychology. The story of Onan has often been cited as evidence of the sinfulness of masturbation. The Old Testament tells that while he was having sexual intercourse with the wife of his deceased brother, Onan withdrew before ejaculation and "spilled his seed on the ground." God was angered and struck him dead. Actually, of course, Onan was not masturbating but instead was practicing what we now call coitus interruptus, or withdrawal, as a means of birth control. In any case, masturbation has also been called **onanism.** Clearly, each individual—giving consideration to his or her religious, parental, and peer values—must decide whether masturbation will be part of an acceptable personal repertoire of sexual behaviors.

 See "Mother and Daughter Discussing Sex" on SexSource Online.

■ Shared Sexual Behavior

The kinds of physical contact described in this section are usually sexually arousing, may in themselves lead to orgasm, or may serve as a prelude to other behaviors that may or may not include orgasm. As data from the NHSLS research in Table 12.2 indicate, vaginal intercourse is clearly the most popular of all shared sexual behaviors among all age groups of both women and men. Among younger couples, oral sex is the second most popular activity (Kaestle & Halpern, 2007;

Michael et al., 1994). The pursuit of somewhat casual sexual encounters with acquaintances, collectively called "hooking up," seems to have led to an increase in noncoital sexual sharing, often involving oral sex. Intercourse does not seem to be one of the activities that is most typical of hooking up (Lambert, Kahn, & Apple, 2003). Because of the higher risks associated with intercourse, couples seem to be more comfortable with engaging in other forms of sex that also can be highly satisfying.

A continuing sexual relationship involves a gradual learning process between the partners concerning their own individual preferences for various activities. Conflicts may arise when one partner finds a particular activity appealing and desirable but the other partner finds it offensive or unappealing. Such conflicts may have to be accepted as part of the relationship and appropriate compromises may have to be made, but it is also quite typical for people to experiment with new activities as a relationship progresses, sometimes even learning to enjoy them more than they did before.

Nongenital Oral Stimulation

The lips, tongue, and oral cavity are often associated with intimate, sexually arousing activity (see Figure 12.3). The oral areas are replete with nerve endings, are moist, and are associated with pleasurable sensations of taste and food consumption. The mobility of the tongue and lips affords them versatility and allows them to be voluntarily controlled by the individual. All these factors play a role in the various uses of the mouth in pleasurable sexual sharing. One's first kiss can be quite memorable, although research also shows that it is often preceded by anxiety, fear, and uncertainty. Men tend to recall their first kiss as more pleasurable than women do (Regan et al., 2007).

Although a few small societies exist where kissing is not practiced at all or is frowned upon, it is used to express affection in most parts of the world. Kissing usually carries with it important messages concerning the depth of intimacy in a relationship. The least intimate kiss is the simple peck on the cheek. Lengthy lip contact, gentle rubbing of another person's lips, and insertion of the tongue into the partner's mouth (French kissing or soul kissing) are considered more deeply intimate and sexually arousing. Kissing, licking, or nibbling at other parts of the body—such as the abdomen, breasts, ears, or genitals—is also considered particularly intimate by many.

onanism (o-na-niz-um) a term sometimes used to describe masturbation; the term stems from the biblical story of Onan, who practiced coitus interruptus and "spilled his seed on the ground."

Table 12.2 *The Appeal of Selected Sexual Practices*

Panel A: Women

Selected Sexual Practices	Ages 18–44				Ages 45–59			
	Very Appealing	Somewhat Appealing	Not Appealing	Not at All Appealing	Very Appealing	Somewhat Appealing	Not Appealing	Not at All Appealing
Vaginal intercourse	78%	18%	1%	3%	74%	19%	2%	6%
Watching partner undress	30	51	11	9	18	49	16	17
Receiving oral sex	33	35	11	21	16	24	14	45
Giving oral sex	19	38	15	28	11	20	17	52
Group sex	1	8	14	78	1	4	9	87
Anus stimulated by partner's fingers	4	14	18	65	6	12	14	68
Stimulate partner's anus with your fingers	2	11	16	70	4	12	12	73
Using dildo/vibrator	3	13	23	61	4	14	17	65
Watching others do sexual things	2	18	15	66	2	11	13	74
Same-gender sex partner	3	3	9	85	2	2	6	90
Sex with stranger	1	9	11	80	1	4	6	89
Passive anal intercourse	1	4	9	87	1	3	8	88
Forcing someone to do something sexual	0	2	7	91	0	0	5	95
Being forced to do something sexual	0	2	6	92	0	1	5	95

Stimulation of Erogenous Zones

Certain areas of the body almost always generate sexual arousal when they are subject to welcome touch. The penis and the clitoris are two examples. However, it seems that almost any area of the body can become conditioned to respond erotically to tactile stimulation in particular individuals. If touching a certain part of a person's body leads to sexual arousal, the area is called an erogenous zone for that person. Typical nongenital erogenous zones are the mouth, earlobes, breasts, buttocks, lower abdomen, inner thighs, and anal-perineal area. In a fulfilling sexual relationship, it is important for both partners to learn about the most pleasurable kinds of stimulation to exert on these zones.

In treating sexual dysfunctions (see Chapter 18), sex therapists have long recognized that touch is a vital part of the experience that gives meaning to sexual responsiveness for women and men. Therapy programs typically encourage couples to spend time together in the nude, gently massaging, fondling, and tracing each other's bodies in pleasurable ways. Both partners are encouraged to accept and enjoy being stimulated to the fullest extent possible. Most people in our culture find

FIGURE 12.3 *Kissing*

In most parts of the world, kissing is a sign of affection. This young couple shares a warm and loving moment.

Panel B: Men

Selected Sexual Practices	Ages 18–44				Ages 45–59			
	Very Appealing	Somewhat Appealing	Not Appealing	Not at All Appealing	Very Appealing	Somewhat Appealing	Not Appealing	Not at All Appealing
Vaginal intercourse	83%	12%	1%	4%	85%	10%	1%	4%
Watching partner undress	50	43	3	4	40	47	7	5
Receiving oral sex	50	33	5	12	29	32	11	28
Giving oral sex	37	39	9	15	22	33	13	32
Group sex	14	32	20	33	10	18	22	50
Anus stimulated by partner's fingers	6	16	24	54	4	12	23	60
Stimulate partner's anus with your fingers	7	19	22	52	4	16	20	60
Active anal intercourse	5	9	13	73	1	7	9	83
Using dildo/vibrator	5	18	27	50	3	17	24	57
Watching others do sexual things	6	34	21	39	4	25	21	50
Same-gender sex partner	4	2	5	89	2	1	5	92
Sex with stranger	5	29	25	42	2	23	23	52
Passive anal intercourse	3	8	15	75	2	5	10	84
Forcing someone to do something sexual	0	2	14	84	1	2	12	86
Being forced to do something sexual	0	3	13	84	0	2	10	89

Note: Row percentages total 100 percent.

Source: From *Sex in America* by Robert T. Michael et al., pp. 146–147. Copyright © 1994 by CSG Enterprises, Inc., Edward O. Laumann, Robert T. Michael, and Gina Kolata. By permission of Little, Brown and Company, and Brockman, Inc.

some degree of sexual arousal in having their bodies close to another naked body and having the opportunity to share touching experiences. The sense of touch usually is an essential part of sexual arousal.

Some people find an element of sexual arousal in more aggressive forms of touch. Sexual contact can have its aggressive, even violent side. Light scratching, pinching, and biting are considered enjoyable by some. It is not unusual for one partner to bite and suck the other during strong sexual passion, even to the extent of producing a bruise. Such a bruise on the neck, commonly called a hickey, seems to represent a badge of experience for some individuals.

Oral-Genital and Oral-Anal Sex

Many individuals derive intense genital pleasure from being orally stimulated, partly because they can relax and enjoy it and partly because their partner can provide intense, localized stimulation. Although using the mouth to stimulate the genitals of a sexual partner can be highly exciting for some people, it can be disgusting for others. Two common slang terms for oral sex are "going down on" or "giving head to" a partner. The term **fellatio** refers to kissing, licking, or sucking on the penis or allowing the penis to move in and out of the mouth. Some men particularly enjoy oral stimulation of the frenulum on the underside of the penile head, one of their most sensitive genital areas (see Figures 12.4 and 12.5). **Cunnilingus** involves kissing, licking, or sucking the clitoris, labia, and vaginal opening or inserting the tongue into the vagina (see Figures 12.6 and 12.7). Partners sometimes perform oral sex on each other simultaneously, in the position called in slang "sixty-nine" due to the relative positions of the bodies.

A fair amount of evidence indicates that oral sex became an increasingly acceptable and desirable form

fellatio oral stimulation of the penis.

cunnilingus (kun-a-LIN-gus) oral stimulation of the clitoris, vaginal opening, or other parts of the vulva.

FIGURE 12.4 *Male-Female Fellatio*

■ **FIGURE 12.5** *Male-Male Fellatio*

of sexual behavior on college campuses during the 1960s and 1970s, and the NHSLS data make it clear that the practice is still especially popular among young, better-educated white persons. It is much less common among people with less education and among blacks. According to the survey, 68 percent of women and 77 percent of men had performed oral sex on a partner during their lifetime, with 19 percent of women and 27 percent of men having done so in their last sexual interaction. Similar proportions of both genders had been recipients of oral sex—73 percent of women and 79 percent of men during their lifetime; and 20 percent and 28 percent, respectively, during their last sexual experience. A willingness to perform oral sex and/ or have it performed on them is twice as common among women who have gone to college compared to

women who did not finish high school. People over age 60 and those who have a conservative Protestant religious background are much less likely to engage in oral sexual practices (Laumann et al., 1994). As Table 12.2 shows, oral sex ranks third on the list of people's favorite shared sexual activities, with almost every other behavior trailing rather distantly behind. There is compelling evidence that oral sex has become quite acceptable among the young and in fact is often the starting point of shared sexual activity (Grunseit et al., 2005; Kaestle & Halpern, 2007; Remez, 2000).

Why do you think oral sex and some other forms of sexual behavior are more common among women who have gone to college than among women who did not finish high school?

FIGURE 12.6 *Male-Female Cunnilingus*

With the important proviso that oral-genital sex can be responsible for spreading sexually transmitted diseases, it is generally considered a relatively safe practice as long as the basic rules of hygiene are followed. Some partners fear the ejaculation of semen into their mouths during fellatio because of the mistaken notion that the substance is, in itself, dangerous to ingest. If the male is known to be free of sexually transmitted diseases, HIV, and prostate infection and the partner wishes to do so, there is no particular danger in swallowing semen. It is simply digested.

There are documented cases of HIV being transmitted through oral sex, although the actual degree of risk remains unclear. Therefore, unless there is absolute certainty about a partner's lack of exposure to HIV, the safest practice is for a condom to be worn during fellatio or for a **rubber dam** to be placed over the vulva during cunnilingus. Rubber dams may be of the type used in dental work or may be a nonlubricated latex condom or a rubber surgical glove cut to form a sheet of rubber. As yet, no studies have been done concerning the actual effectiveness of such rubber dams in preventing the transmission of HIV, but experts have reasoned that any barrier to the mixing of body fluids certainly reduces the risk. How practical the rubber dam can be in even acting as a barrier is particularly debatable.

Other infections can also be transmitted through oral-genital contact, including throat infections from genital bacteria and urethral or vaginal infections transmitted from the mouth. It is unsafe to blow into the penis during fellatio (even though a common slang term is "blow job") or to blow into the vagina during cunnilingus because bacteria may be forced in or actual injury may result. There are some indications that blowing air into the vagina, particularly during pregnancy, can lead to the formation of air embolisms in a woman's blood vessels that could potentially be fatal.

Sometimes the anal region is stimulated orally, but strict hygienic measures are crucial to preventing transmission of bacteria and viruses. Even with thorough washing, some rectal germs may be ingested. Again, this practice would be considered dangerous if there were any chance that hepatitis or HIV was present in the person being stimulated anally. A rubber dam can be placed over the anal region to protect against transmission of HIV, other sexually transmitted diseases, and bacteria.

Mutual Manual Stimulation and Masturbation

Most sexually active couples use some form of mutual manual stimulation of the genitals. The clitoris may be manipulated with a finger, although direct stimulation of the glans can be uncomfortable for some. One or more fingers may be inserted into the vagina and moved. The penis may be grasped and stroked and the scrotum fondled. These techniques often are used by sexual partners to stimulate each other. Mutual manual stimulation of genitals and the anal region is also one of the most common forms of sexual sharing (see Figure 12.8).

Although some couples find it difficult to discuss their masturbatory practices and even more difficult to masturbate in each other's presence, others report that they find enjoyment in watching their partner masturbate and in being so observed. Slightly more than one-third of college students reported having masturbated while another person watched. Masturbation usually is a private experience, and sharing it often represents a level of intimacy even deeper than some other forms of sexual sharing. Many couples at least occasionally incorporate manual stimulation of the partner or masturbation into their shared sexual activities.

Interfemoral and Anal Intercourse

Many sexual partnerships that include at least one male use various forms of nonvaginal penile intercourse. The penis is versatile and can be inserted into the partner's hand, between female breasts, between

rubber dam a piece of rubber material, such as that used in dental work, placed over the vulva during cunnilingus.

■ **FIGURE 12.7** *Female-Female Cunnilingus*

the buttocks, or between the thighs (interfemoral inter-course), or it can be rubbed on the partner's abdomen or any other body area, provided the partner finds it acceptable. These forms of sexual activity often are ac-companied by pelvic thrusting. It is wise for hetero-sexual couples who practice interfemoral intercourse to know that semen ejaculated near or at the vaginal opening carries some risk of pregnancy. Even a small amount of semen entering the vagina will carry sperm, and although the chances are minimal, it is possible for

some of those sperm to travel into the fallopian tubes and fertilize an ovum.

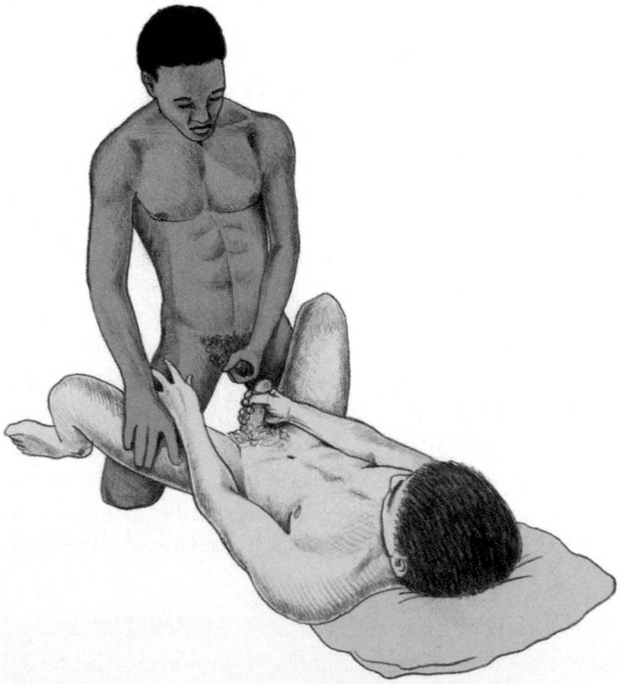

The prevalence of **anal intercourse,** or insertion of the penis into the partner's rectum, is quite high in most countries. NHSLS data showed the activity to be some-what more prevalent than might be expected, with a slightly greater tendency for white and better-educated people to have experienced anal sex. For the total study population, 26 percent of men had engaged in anal in-tercourse during their lifetime, and 10 percent had done so in the previous year. Twenty percent of women had had anal sex during their lifetime, 9 percent during the prior year (Laumann et al., 1994). About 20 to 25 percent of college students and other young couples have en-gaged in anal sex, according to a few studies (Baldwin & Baldwin, 2000; Kaestle & Halpern, 2007). As Table 12.2 shows, anal intercourse is somewhat more appealing to males than to females. It is interesting to note that 11 percent of males indicated that they found being the passive partner in anal intercourse, presumably a male-male activity, to be somewhat or very appealing.

The anal sphincter muscles tend to resist penile entry. It usually takes appropriate lubrication, gentle prodding by the penis, and concentrated relaxation of the anus by the partner to permit penetration. Physicians occasionally see rectal or anal injuries resulting from anal sex, and these can be quite serious. There is a dan-ger that tissue damage related to anal intercourse may increase the chances of transmitting HIV if the inserting male is infected. Again, unless there is absolute certainty that the man is not infected, a condom should be worn

■ **FIGURE 12.8** *Males Sharing Masturbation*

anal intercourse insertion of the penis into the rectum of a partner.

Real People

Sybil and Carl: Trying to Find Sexual Compatibility

Sybil is a graduate student, and her husband Carl is a teacher in the local high school. They have been married for three years, after living together for two years during their undergraduate years. They have decided to postpone having a family for at least another three years, although they both look forward to having children.

Sybil has been more satisfied than Carl with their sexual relationship. Early in their partnership, Sybil had been unable to reach orgasm but gradually became able to do so. She feels especially intimate with Carl when they have intercourse and enjoys their physical closeness. While Carl also enjoys intercourse, he has expressed interest in being more adventurous in their sexual activities. More than once, he has asked Sybil to watch a pornographic video during their sex play. While she finds the videos interesting, and even arousing, she has not felt as though she wanted to participate in the sexual acts that Carl has suggested. He is particularly anxious to have her be more open to oral sex—both fellatio and cunnilingus. They have experimented with these behaviors in the past, but Sybil does not much enjoy either one. Carl also wants to try anal

intercourse, which Sybil does not find acceptable at all. She has said that she believes anal sex would be uncomfortable and even dangerous, and she has no desire even to try it once.

Recently, Carl has been expressing his frustrations more adamantly, and the two have been arguing about sex more frequently. Carl insists that Sybil's lack of responsiveness to his sexual interests signals a lack of sensitivity and caring on her part, while Sybil counters that if he really cared about her, he wouldn't keep trying to pressure her into sexual acts that she finds distasteful. They both have begun to say that perhaps they are incompatible sexually, and they are fearful about what that might mean for their entire relationship.

How would you sum up the difficulties that Sybil and Carl are experiencing? Do you feel that one of them is more "right" than the other? Is there a suitable compromise toward which they should be working? Do you think the sexual differences they are encountering would be a reasonable cause for the couple—or any couple—to end their relationship?

to provide substantial—but not absolute—protection. Condoms are somewhat more likely to break during anal intercourse. It is unsafe to insert the penis into the mouth or vagina following anal intercourse, because bacteria are easily transferred and may cause infection. Male-female anal intercourse is a behavior that too often is omitted from college sexuality education, even though it apparently is a reasonably common behavior that carries some risks (Baldwin & Baldwin, 2000).

Vibrators, Pornography, and Fantasies

Any aids used for sexual stimulation by individuals can be shared and probably often are. Electric vibrators typically used in masturbation may be used by couples to provide intense sexual pleasuring for each other. NHSLS data show that 16 percent of women and 23 percent of men find such devices appealing. Some couples enjoy viewing pornographic materials together, such as

magazine photographs or movies showing a variety of sexual acts. Viewing online pornography has become a popular pastime as well. Others enjoy reading books that describe sexual scenes in explicit language. It has long been recognized that fantasy can be an integral part of sexual experiences and can induce sexual arousal. Some books have dealt with the sexual fantasies of individuals, and many people seem more willing to talk about their own fantasies than once was the case. Some couples enjoy acting out their sexual fantasies together and find them sexually stimulating. Fantasies that involve inflicting pain or humiliation on a partner are stimulating to some people. Such behavior, termed sadomasochism, is discussed in more detail in Chapter 14, "The Spectrum of Human Sexual Behavior."

Aphrodisiacs

Some foods and chemicals have been purported to act as sexual stimulants for those who consume them. Substances that create erotic stimulation are called

aphrodisiacs. A wide variety of exotic substances have been labeled aphrodisiacs, including powdered rhinoceros horn, powdered stag's horn, dried salamanders, and dried beetles as well as some common foods such as eggs, olives, peanuts, oysters, venison, and bananas. Although most of these substances have not been scientifically studied, expert opinion suggests that they don't actually have any effect. In one study, powdered deer horn or a placebo was given to a group of men who over a period of three months were asked about their sexual experiences. The results showed that the deer horn had absolutely no effect on sexual desire, arousal, performance, frequency, or pleasure (Conaglen, Suttie, & Conaglen, 2003).

Some individuals report increased interest in sex under the influence of alcohol or marijuana. Both of these drugs lead to relaxation and lowered inhibitions and therefore when used in moderation enhance sexual activity. Used in larger amounts, however, they may inhibit sexual desire and arousal. Women seem to have more predictably sexually positive effects from marijuana use, while men may find it to be either enhancing or inhibiting to sexual arousal (Gorzalka & Hill, 2007).

In some individuals, another group of chemicals—the volatile nitrites—are reported to enhance response to sexual stimulation and orgasm. These chemicals, especially amyl nitrite and isobutyl nitrite, have been marketed as room deodorizers. They are volatile and are absorbed quickly by inhalation, causing immediate dilation of blood vessels, with a resulting rush. They are also highly flammable. Although most users have suffered no ill effects other than headache and a temporary pounding pulse, these chemicals have been implicated in some fatal cerebral hemorrhages. NHSLS data showed that drug use in association with sexual activity actually is quite rare, with only about 1 percent of males and 0.5 percent of females having used drugs before sex in the previous year. Alcohol use was far more common, with 9 percent of males and 6 percent of females saying that they frequently drank alcohol before or during sexual activity.

A widely touted aphrodisiac is "Spanish fly," the slang name for **cantharides,** a chemical extracted from a certain species of southern European beetle. Taken internally, the drug produces inflammation of the urinary tract and dilation of blood vessels in the genital area, which can lead to prolonged, often painful erection of the penis. Cantharides is considered a dangerous chemical that can cause serious illness and even death.

Have you ever heard of anyone using an aphrodisiac? If so, describe his or her experience.

Available research would suggest that there are no surefire aphrodisiacs available. So-called aphrodisiacs probably work because their user believes in their effectiveness. Whenever an individual desires sexual stimulation, looks for it, and expects it, it is not surprising that it may be generated.

The Aftermath of Shared Sex

Many couples find that the period during which they are together following shared sexual activity is significant to their relationship. If the sexual experience has been satisfying to both partners and both are feeling relaxed or even drowsy, it may be a time for communicating quiet, gentle, loving feelings. Women in general seem to take longer than men in the resolution phase of the sexual response cycle, although this may be the result of lack of satiation due to an inadequate number of orgasms.

Satisfaction with sexual activity seems to depend on a variety of factors, with orgasm representing only one of them. About 29 percent of women and 75 percent of men report always having an orgasm in their sexual activities, yet the proportion of both sexes who report being extremely emotionally satisfied is about 40 percent. Clearly, there is more to a good sex life than being able to have an orgasm, and not everyone who has an orgasm is necessarily satisfied with sex in other respects. Thirty percent of women and 5 percent of men report having orgasms sometimes or never, although married women are much more likely than unmarried women to reach orgasm more frequently in their shared sexual activities. NHSLS research showed that people who report being happy with their lives and relationships in general also are more likely to be happy with their sex lives. The more satisfied people are sexually, the more they tend to stay faithful to their partners (Guo, Ng, & Chan, 2004; Henderson, Lehavot, & Simoni, 2009; Laumann et al., 1994).

When sex has been unsuccessful in any way or has generated some negative feelings, the period following sexual contact may be an especially valuable time for two-way communication. Many couples store up fears, resentments, and feelings of inadequacy because of sexual problems, only to find that these tensions eventually catch up with the relationship and

aphrodisiacs (af-ro-DEE-zee-aks) foods or chemicals purported to foster sexual arousal; believed to be more myth than fact.

cantharides (kan-THAR-a-deez) a chemical extracted from a beetle that, when taken internally, creates irritation of blood vessels in the genital region; can cause physical harm.

place strains on it. Talking out the negative feelings while they are fresh—in an atmosphere of mutual warmth, caring, and reassurance—can strengthen any relationship.

Same-Gender Sexual Sharing

To approach an understanding of different persons' lifestyles solely from the perspective of their sexual orientation is constraining and limiting, because sexuality represents only one aspect of people's sharing. Partners of any gender combination can share a full range of sexual activity and find great joy and satisfaction in this sharing. Some men fondle each other's genitals or masturbate each other. Often they engage in gentle, loving gestures such as kisses, embraces, and body stroking. Oral-genital contact is common, and many gay males practice fellatio, as illustrated in Figure 12.5. Anal intercourse is practiced by some male couples (see Figure 12.9), although not as frequently as fellatio (Kippax & Smith, 2001; Laumann et al., 1994).

Although it is always recommended that condoms be worn for anal intercourse, some gay men participate in intentional unprotected anal sex, popularly called "barebacking." They are most likely to do so with another man who shares the same positive or negative HIV status (Halkitis, Parsons, & Wilton, 2003). In one sample of gay men, 88 percent were able to label themselves "tops," meaning they preferred to take the insertive role in anal sex; "bottoms," signaling a preference for the receptive role in anal sex; or "versatiles," indicating an openness to either role. These labels did not mean the men would participate only as the preference suggested, but simply that they were more likely to engage in that form of shared sex (Hart et al., 2003).

Men who have sex with men have definite preferences, and some are not at all interested in oral-genital sex or anal intercourse. Many gay males apparently have a strong preference for manual manipulation of the genitals or lying together in such a way that the genitals may be rubbed together. It is also common for one partner to practice interfemoral intercourse or to rub his penis on the other's abdomen. There have been some reports of fisting or handballing, in which the hand of one partner is inserted into the rectum of the other, producing an intense sexual experience. Such practices risk damaging the anal or rectal tissue.

FIGURE 12.9 *Male-Male Anal Intercourse*

■ **FIGURE 12.10** *Women Sharing Sex Toys*

■ **FIGURE 12.11** *Women Sharing Sensual Expression*

Lesbians share a wide range of intimate activities, and research indicates that even though lesbian couples share sex less frequently than do heterosexual or gay male couples, they tend to be more satisfied with their sexual lives and to feel a greater sense of intimacy (Holmberg & Blair, 2009). Many women almost exclusively use activities such as kissing and general body contact, especially women who are less experienced with female-female sexual activity (see Figure 12.7). Manual manipulation of each other's genitals with finger penetration is one of the most frequently used forms of stimulation among lesbian couples, with oral-genital contact (cunnilingus) the preferred technique for reaching orgasm. The use of dildos or other objects in vaginal insertion is less common (see Figure 12.10). Women involved in a sexual encounter usually spend a longer period than male couples in gentle and affectionate foreplay, also giving more attention to caressing and nongenital stimulation. Single lesbians have sex less frequently than single gay men, and lesbians involved in a long-term committed relationship have relatively low levels of sexual activity. They often seem to prefer hugging and cuddling to more genitalized forms of sexual sharing (see Figure 12.11).

See "The Dance of Life" on SexSource Online.

■ Heterosexual Intercourse

Most cultures, the act of vaginal sexual intercourse, or coitus, is surrounded by a variety of moral and social values. Most societies and religions have sought to place some restrictions on coital behavior in order to regulate which heterosexual couples have babies, to prevent people from enjoying bodily pleasures that some consider sinful, and to regulate sexual forces considered too powerful to be indulged in casually. NHSLS statistics indicate that vaginal intercourse is the most prevalent shared sexual activity among adults. Eighty percent of survey respondents said they had vaginal sex every time they shared a sexual experience in the previous year. An additional 15 percent indicated that they usually had vaginal sex during the previous year (Michael et al., 1994).

Sexual intercourse, like all forms of sex, takes on different meanings for different couples and in different circumstances. The personal needs and characteristics each partner brings to coitus help determine the depth and degree of pleasure that results. Factual knowledge about sex, the capacity to accept differences in needs and responses, and personal attitudes all play a part in determining the enjoyment and meaning of coitus for each individual and each couple (Barrientos & Paez, 2006). A study of women's emotional responses to intercourse found that women experience coitus in three distinct ways. The *relationship-centered experience* is characterized by positive feelings about the relationship with the partner and the desirability of sex on

Real Student Voices

■ As a gay man, I object that your book doesn't have more drawings of males having sex together. You have a regular Kama Sutra of heterosexual positions, but not much to illustrate how two men or two women could engage in sex. The first few times I had sex with other men, I was pretty ignorant about what we might do. Books like this don't help much. What's up?

■ I don't really understand why people are so interested in having sex in so many different positions. Does it really matter how much of a gymnast you are? It just seems silly to me.

■ I don't know many men who like to see much pubic hair on women. I prefer that women shave most of their genital hair, and likewise I try to keep the hair around my penis and testicles well trimmed.

■ It's important to me that my boyfriend take his time during intercourse and that I have time to reach orgasm a couple of times. Sometimes even after he is finished, he continues to touch and stimulate me so that I can be fully satisfied. Fortunately, he thinks this is a good thing and doesn't take it personally.

both their parts. The *pleasure-centered experience* is characterized by feelings of satisfaction and enjoyment, along with a sense of letting go and focusing on one's own sexual needs and feelings. The *worry-centered experience*, as the name implies, tends to be accompanied by aversive feelings such as anger, emptiness, vulnerability, disappointment, and a sense of inadequacy. As might be predicted, the first two types of experiences were more likely to be accompanied by orgasm and enjoyment (Birnbaum, Glaubman, & Mikulincer, 2001).

Sexual Intercourse and Diseases

Vaginal intercourse is one way in which sexually transmitted diseases may be transmitted, because bacteria and viruses are carried in semen and vaginal fluids. If a partner has ever had sex with someone else, there is at least some risk that he or she carries a disease-causing organism. It is always safest for a male partner to wear a condom during intercourse or for the female to wear a vaginal pouch (female condom) unless there is absolute certainty that neither person ever could have been exposed to an STD or to HIV. See Chapter 17 for additional information on HIV, STDs, their transmission, and how the risk of infection can be minimized.

Intromission

Male-female sexual intercourse, by definition, involves the insertion of the penis into the vagina. Comfortable intromission requires a suitable degree of penile erection, lubrication, relaxation of the vaginal opening, and cooperation between the two partners. Erection of the penis is a natural part of male sexual arousal, and the vagina usually produces enough lubricant to permit easy movement of the penis into the vagina. If vaginal lubrication is insufficient, artificial lubricants can be applied to the penis and the vaginal opening. Water-soluble silica-based lubricants or saliva generally are satisfactory. Petroleum-based jellies or other oil-based substances are not recommended, because they are less healthful for tissues and less easily cleansed away.

The vaginal opening is sometimes tense, and gentle patience is necessary to give it time to relax. If the outer vaginal muscles cannot relax to the point where intromission can take place comfortably, the woman may be experiencing vaginismus. If there is some difficulty with intromission, the male may begin to lose some of his erection. Both of these problems are discussed in Chapter 18, "Sexual Dysfuntions and Their Treatment." Actual insertion of the penis can be awkward for both partners, and active cooperation is helpful. Either partner may part the minor lips to expose the vaginal opening and then guide the penis into the vagina. The position of the couple also helps determine the ease of intromission. The first few coital thrusts of the male may be progressively more forceful as the penis is pushed gradually deeper into the vagina. Depth of penetration depends on the size of the penis and the vagina, the coital position, and the relative comfort for both partners.

As discussed in Chapter 2, if the hymen is still present at the opening of the vagina, prodding by the penis may be necessary to rupture it, and the female should expect some discomfort or pain. Cooperation and understanding on the part of both partners can lead to easy, unembarrassing intromission. Some males feel awkward in attempting to find the opening and the best angle for inserting the penis; the female partner may be able to help lessen such difficulties. Difficulties or discomfort in intromission during early coital experiences sometimes generate performance fears in both males and females. These fears can lead to problems in later experiences, such as lack of erection or lack of vaginal lubrication. After several sexual contacts, intromission usually is accomplished with more ease.

Intercourse

Intercourse usually involves movement of the penis into and out of the vagina, resulting from pelvic movements of both partners. A few studies have viewed couples having intercourse with magnetic resonance imaging (MRI) techniques. These studies have demonstrated that the penis, the erection of which extends back into the male's body further than previously realized, tends to become somewhat boomerang-shaped during coitus. The glans penis tends to push forward alongside the uterus (Faix et al., 2001, 2002).

Different coital positions afford different amounts of control over these movements to both partners. The rate and vigor of thrusting depend to a large degree on the mood of the couple and how long they wish to prolong coitus. The factor that usually determines duration of intercourse is the length of time required for the male to reach orgasm. Because erection of the penis almost always subsides following orgasm, intercourse can rarely continue after male orgasm, at least for a time. Rapid, forceful movements of the penis generally bring males to orgasm quite quickly, and the amount of precoital stimulation also plays an important role. Intercourse itself may not be effective in generating orgasm for women, and additional clitoral stimulation may be necessary.

It is possible for couples to learn how to modulate the amount of stimulation required for both of them to obtain maximum enjoyment. By occasionally slowing his pelvic thrusting, making shallow thrusts of the penis, and even temporarily ceasing coital movements, the male can exert a great deal of control over the amount of time required for him to reach orgasm. Certain positions enhance this control. Data from the NHSLS found that about 70 percent of people said that their last shared sexual event lasted from 15 minutes to an hour. That time typically would include more than just the experience of intercourse. Roughly 15 percent of people indicated that their last shared sex took 15 minutes or less, and another 15 percent said it took an hour or more (Laumann et al., 1994). It is up to each couple to work on developing the duration of sexual activity most suitable for them, and open and specific communication can be an important help in this process.

The movements made by both partners during intercourse may vary a great deal, and finding the most pleasurable movements can be an exciting learning process in a growing sexual relationship. Alternating shallow and deep thrusts of the penis is often recommended, and the penis may also be rotated or moved from side to side in the vagina. According to most research, penis size has no bearing on the amount of sexual pleasure derived by the female during intercourse. Although some women contend that the size of the penis makes a difference to them in terms of physical pleasure, it is more typical for them to report that it is not a crucial factor in their pleasure.

Clitoral stimulation by some means is often important for women during intercourse. Many couples caress each other and use their hands to give added pleasure. Some couples strive for the simultaneous orgasm of both partners. Although some couples enjoy simultaneous orgasm and can accomplish it with relative ease, others find that trying for orgasm at the same time detracts from their sexual pleasure. Some people enjoy experiencing their partner's orgasm without being preoccupied with their own. If one partner has not reached orgasm during coitus and wishes to do so, it is appropriate for the other to employ suitable techniques to help the partner achieve orgasm.

Do you believe orgasm is essential for both partners during shared sexual activity? Why or why not?

Positions for Intercourse

There are various body positions in which the penis may be inserted comfortably into the vagina. Many couples enjoy experimenting with different positions and find that sex can be more interesting by changing positions during intercourse, often several times. A good fit of the two partners is usually important to full sexual pleasure, especially for the woman to reach orgasm (Pierce, 2000). Some changes of position can be accomplished by rolling over or other slight movements, without any interruption of coitus. Other changes require that the penis be withdrawn until the new position is assumed. Which position a couple finds most enjoyable, comfortable, and manageable depends on their own individual characteristics, such as body size and weight, degree of physical fitness, length and diameter of the erect penis, personal attitudes about particular positions, and the couple's moods during the sexual encounter. Different positions may place more physical strain on one or the other partner and afford one of them more ability to control the rate and vigor of coital movements. It should be emphasized that sexual intercourse need not be a series of acrobatics to be pleasurable for both partners. Yet if both partners are willing and able, varying coital position from time to time can lead excitement to an

FIGURE 12.12   *Man on Top, Woman Supine*

ongoing sexual relationship. Each of the following 10 basic positions has myriad variations.

Reclining Face-to-Face

Positions in which the two partners face each other are most commonly used because the two are freer to look at each other, kiss, and communicate in these positions. Reclining positions are preferred because they usually require less physical energy than supporting the body in some upright posture. There are several variations of face-to-face reclining positions.

Man on Top, Woman Supine

This position, the most common one used in European and American societies, is erroneously considered by some couples to be the only normal way to have intercourse (see Figure 12.12). Most people at least experiment with a variety of positions. The position seems particularly compatible from an anatomical standpoint, considering the usual angles of the erect penis and the vagina in a reclining position. The male often supports part of his weight on his arms and knees, although this may place real strain on some men. Women sometimes find it suitable in this position to hold up their legs somewhat or wrap them around the male's waist or even over his shoulders, the latter variation requiring more of a kneeling position for the man. Some couples insert a pillow under the woman's buttocks for greater ease. These positions give the male partner maximum control over coital thrusting, because the female's pelvis is relatively immobile, and also allow deep penetration by the penis. Conversely, they may make it somewhat more difficult for the woman to have the sort of stimulation

necessary to achieve orgasm. Women or their partners may want to increase manual stimulation of the clitoris during intercourse to help produce the orgasmic response.

Woman on Top, Man Supine

This is the second most commonly used coital position (see Figure 12.13). It has many variations, because the woman can lie on the man with her legs fully extended or can straddle him in a sitting, crouching, or kneeling position. The position provides the woman more opportunity to control the coital movements and leaves the male's hands freer to caress her body. Some men experience some difficulty keeping the penis in the vagina in this position, and some women experience discomfort with the deep penile penetration it makes possible. However, this position is more likely to result in orgasm for the female partner, due to the fact that exerting more control over the movements leads to better stimulation for her.

Side-by-Side

There are many advantages to coital positions in which both partners lie on their sides, and this lateral position often is recommended in the treatment of several sexual dysfunctions (see Figure 12.14). Many couples use a side-by-side position more frequently than other positions. Because both partners are lying down and need to worry less about supporting their bodies, there is less strain on both of them. They are able to share in controlling their thrusting motions, and both are free to use their hands for touching and caressing. Deep penetration by the penis sometimes is more difficult in the side-by-side positions, and some couples find it less comfortable than other positions.

■ FIGURE 12.13   *Woman on Top, Man Supine*

■ FIGURE 12.14   *Side-by-Side*

FIGURE 12.15 *Woman on Edge of Bed or Chair*

Other Variations on Face-to-Face

Woman on Edge of Bed or Chair

When the woman positions herself on the edge of a bed or chair, with her back reclining and her feet resting on the floor, the man can either stand or kneel on the floor in a manner that enables him to enter her (see Figure 12.15). The male is in control in these positions. The male's position on the floor gives him a good deal of leverage for controlling his movements and giving powerful thrusts. He also is easily able to vary the angle at which the penis enters the vagina.

Both Partners Seated

Seated intercourse with the partners facing each other is easier for some couples to achieve than it is for others. Typically, the male sits, sometimes in a chair or on the edge of the bed (a reasonably solid support usually is more desirable), and the female then lowers herself onto his erect penis, either keeping her feet on the floor or placing her legs around his waist. The woman usually has greater control over the coital movements in this position, although the degree of control varies with the positioning of her legs and feet. The man's hands are relatively free, and he may help move the female's body up and down on his penis. Deep penile penetration usually is possible in seated positions.

Both Partners Standing

Coital positions in which both partners stand generally are the most difficult to manage and sustain. Attention must be given to maintaining balance and stability, along with keeping the penis comfortably inside the vagina. Although many couples experiment with standing intercourse and some use the position occasionally, it is not a popular position. Deep penile penetration is difficult while standing because the angles of the penis and the vagina are not particularly complementary. For couples who find standing intercourse positions comfortable, this option apparently is exciting for occasional variation.

Rear Vaginal Entry

Most mammals use a rear entry position for copulation. It may be for precisely this reason that many people do not choose such positions. Yet couples who do use these variations often find them comfortable and exciting, and many cultures around the world employ then regularly. Although some intimacy may be lost without face-to-face contact, natural body contours afford especially close body contact with many rear-entry positions.

Both Partners Kneeling

In this position, the woman may hold the upper part of her body up on her arms while kneeling or may lower

FIGURE 12.16 *Both Partners Kneeling, Rear Entry*

her shoulders and head (see Figure 12.16). The man kneels behind her and inserts his penis into the vagina from behind. He may also assume a higher crouched position. Deep penile penetration usually is achieved in this position. The man's hands generally are free to offer stimulating contact for the woman, including contact with the clitoris. Another variation is the wheelbarrow position, in which the male stands behind the female and holds her legs while having intercourse.

Man on Top, Woman Lying on Her Abdomen

This position is difficult for some couples to manage, but it can be enjoyable (see Figure 12.17). The man may

lie on top of the woman with his legs fully extended or straddle her body in a crouched or seated position. If the woman arches her back somewhat, pushing her vulva backward, penile entry usually is easily accomplished. This can be a relatively comfortable position, although deep penetration may be difficult.

Side-by-Side

In the side-by-side position, intromission is quite easily accomplished, and this position is often recommended during pregnancy. Both partners are lying down, and neither is placed under any strain. Their hands generally are quite free for touching each other, although because the man is behind, his hands have easier access to his partner (e.g., her breasts and clitoris).

Both Partners Seated or Standing

Rear entry is also possible when both partners are seated or standing (see Figure 12.18).

Intercourse and Marriage

The social mores related to sexual intercourse often are intimately associated with a particular society's marriage customs. In many societies, including most Western societies, marriage represents a social and/or religious legitimization of coitus and childbearing. Hence sex, with its risk of pregnancy, often has been discouraged outside the context of marriage. Social institutions such as religion, school, family, and social networks typically are charged with the promulgation of the rules related to sex and marriage. Premarital and extramarital sex are more permissible in some societies than in others.

In other cultures, sexual relationships fit differently into the varying structures of marriage. In societies in

FIGURE 12.17 *Man on Top, Woman on Abdomen, Rear Entry*

FIGURE 12.18 *Both Partners Seated or Standing, Rear Entry*

which people are permitted to have more than one spouse or in which married couples are encouraged to forge close working bonds with one another, sexual intercourse may be permitted among many different combinations of persons. There are also nonsexual marriages; these arrangements are based on political or economic benefits to the partners or their relatives and have no expectation of sexual interaction.

Sexual problems can lead to severe marital difficulties and even divorce, and all sorts of information is available to spice up and renew sex within marriage. It is also true that communication problems in marriage often are reflected in sexual difficulties between the partners. Sex is a potential source of marriage enrichment, reinforcing the interdependence of husband and wife, unifying them through shared enjoyment, symbolizing their shared life, and helping resolve episodes of alienation.

If and when you received your formal sexuality education, did your source address masturbation, or was sex discussed solely as a penis-in-vagina act? Was intercourse presented merely as a procreative act? Were the emotional aspects as well as the biological aspects discussed? Were other forms of sexual sharing also presented?

For most married individuals, vaginal sexual intercourse with the spouse constitutes the major and preferred—though not only—form of sexual outlet. Oral-genital sex seems to be second in preference as a sexual outlet within marriage (Laumann et al., 1994). The frequency of shared sexual activity seems to vary a great deal. The average frequency of sex for women is six times per month, and the average frequency for men is seven times per month. Of course, individual couples show wide variation from this average, and many factors can affect the frequency of intercourse.

Our society has a mix of values concerning premarital and extramarital sexual activity. On the basis of present evidence, it seems safe to state that not only have more people been experiencing coitus before marriage and at a younger age, but they also have been doing so more often and with fewer inhibitions than in the past.

Chapter Summary

1. Statistics from the NHSLS and National Longitudinal Study of Adolescent Health are the most reliable data we have on human sexual behavior in the United States.

2. The social world of sex involves negotiative processes among people and has different consequences than the private world of sex.

3. Solitary sex, or autoeroticism, includes thoughts and fantasies, erotic materials and toys, and masturbation. Males think about sex and seek out erotic materials more frequently than do females.

4. The frequency with which people experience private sexual pleasure seems to be positively correlated with how frequently they seek shared sex. Solitary sex does not seem to be a compensation for lack of availability of a sexual partner.

5. Masturbation, or self-stimulation of the genitals, is a sexual activity in which most people participate at one time or another.

6. People masturbate in a variety of ways, although most commonly women stimulate their clitoral area and men stimulate the penis.

7. Masturbation can be practiced at all stages of life. Medically speaking, there is no such thing as excessive masturbation; it does not produce physical weakness or illness.

8. Some people feel guilty about masturbation. Guilt does not affect frequency of masturbation in males, but it does to some extent in females.

9. Vaginal intercourse is the most popular of all shared sexual behaviors, followed by oral sex. Partners must communicate about their mutual sexual preferences.

10. Many forms of shared nongenital stimulation are considered intimate and arousing. Kissing and massaging of erogenous zones may be highly erotic.

11. Fellatio is oral stimulation of the penis, and cunnilingus is oral stimulation of the clitoris and other areas of the vulva. Oral sex has become more acceptable in recent years, especially among young, better-educated, and white people.

12. The penis may be inserted between a partner's legs, breasts, or buttocks or into the anus. Anal intercourse is somewhat more appealing to males than to females.

13. Vibrators, erotic pictures and films, and personal sexual fantasies may be integrated into shared sex.

14. There are many myths about foods or chemicals as stimulants to sexual arousal. Substances that create erotic stimulation are labeled aphrodisiacs, although they are believed to operate largely on suggestion and imagination.

15. The period following the end of shared sexual activity may be a quiet, warm, and comfortable time for communication between partners, or it may become a time of tension and further misunderstanding.

16. Couples of the same gender share a wide range of sexual activities, depending on individual preferences and tastes. Male-male oral sex is more common than anal sex; female couples often prefer nonpenetrative activities.

17. Heterosexual intercourse is often subject to strict moral, social, and relational codes of behavior.

18. The techniques and timing of intercourse vary, as do the positions in which a woman and man can share penile-vaginal penetration.

19. Happier people and those more satisfied with their relationships seem more satisfied with their sexual lives. Satisfaction is not necessarily correlated with having orgasms.

20. Intercourse is closely associated with marriage customs in most cultures. In North America, sex is considered to be a significant part of the marital relationship.

Chapter 13

Sexual Orientation, Identity, and Behavior

Chapter Outline

I somewhat resent the pressure that I feel to define myself as straight, gay, or bisexual. I am who I am. I have had romantic and sexual involvement with both men and women and eventually got married. That doesn't mean I have lost my attraction to or interest for others of my sex, or the other sex for that matter. I have simply made a commitment to monogamy.

—from a letter to the author

Do you think you can tell if somebody is gay from appearance and mannerisms? Do you laugh at jokes about "queers"? Have you ever felt attracted to a member of your own gender?

These are controversial issues, and in the arena of political correctness you sometimes have to be careful how you respond to them. Of all the sexual topics I have attempted to write about over the years with objectivity and attention to emerging research, more has shifted and changed with regard to sexual orientation than to anything else. The terms used by professionals seem always in flux, new theories wax and wane, and new political agendas continually emerge.

The bottom line is that we assume human beings to have a **sexual orientation,** that is, a set of physical and emotional attractions and interests that draws them both sexually and romantically to other people. If we look at the possibilities simplistically, we might also assume that there are three possible sexual orientations: straight, gay, or bisexual. Human sexuality is not that simple, as research and theory on sexual orientation confirm.

Contemporary research has suggested that during adolescence and young adulthood, people go through stages of establishing a **sexual orientation identity** or an inner awareness of what their sexual orientation means for their life in terms of sexual and romantic relationships. It has been assumed that sexual orientation and sexual identity, once they are established and recognized by the individual, remain stable throughout life. However, emerging evidence indicates that this may not be the case at all and that many people report changes in their sexual fantasies, behaviors, and relationships that migrate across the orientation and identity boundaries. Sexual orientation as a concept has little meaning unless it is examined over time in terms of several different components, including romantic and sexual *attraction,* sexual *behavior,* and one's self-declared *identity* (Kinnish, Strassberg, & Turner, 2005; Savin-Williams & Ream, 2007).

This is not to say that people wake up one morning with a new sexual orientation or that an individual can suddenly turn gay or straight. It simply means that the components of what we find attractive, sexually exciting, and romantically enticing may be more fluid and dynamic than they are static or fixed. Some sexual scientists have insisted that it is time to acknowledge that the evidence calls into question the concept of a straight-gay dichotomy and suggests instead that most human beings have the potential for a range of sexual feelings and attractions over time (McConaghy, 2005).

This chapter focuses largely on nonheterosexual orientation and identity, because they have formed the

FIGURE 13.1 *Cowboy Lovers*

Heath Ledger and Jake Gyllenhaal starred in "Brokeback Mountain," a film that captured public attention for its portrayal of a longtime love affair between two cowboys, both of whom eventually married women.

basis for most available research and theory. In a heterosexist society, straight is considered the norm and not really that important for study. It is the *differences* that attract scientific attention: gay, lesbian, bisexual. I will elucidate what research is currently telling us about these sexual orientations, asking only that you keep in mind that although everyone has some sexual orientation and identity at any particular point in time, it might not be as clearly defined or predictable as you might assume. (see Figure 13.1).

Do you believe sexual orientation is biologically or socially determined? On what do you base your opinion?

Understanding Sexual Orientation

It has become evident that sexual orientation is a multidimensional phenomenon rather than an either-or proposition. Instead of identifying heterosexuality and homosexuality as discrete, polarized entities, we now see them as clusters of relatively independent

sexual orientation the set of physical and emotional qualities that attracts human beings to one another sexually and romantically.

sexual orientation identity an inner awareness of what one's sexual orientation means for one's life in terms of sexual and romantic relationships and social interaction.

components that can coexist within the same individual (Savin-Williams & Ream, 2007).

The Perspective of the Kinsey Scale

When Alfred Kinsey conducted his research on sexual behavior in the 1940s, social scientists gave little consideration to making distinctions among behaviors, orientations, attractions, and identities. What an individual did sexually was assumed to reflect sexual orientation. Kinsey began to realize that things were not so clear-cut. He recognized early on in his research that substantial numbers of people had experienced both same-gender and other-gender sexual activity. He devised a seven-category sexual behavior rating scale for use in his studies designed to classify individuals based on their behavior (see Figure 13.2).

The Kinsey scale used the numbers 0 to 6, with 0 representing exclusively heterosexual behavior (i.e., no homosexual behavior) and 6 representing exclu-

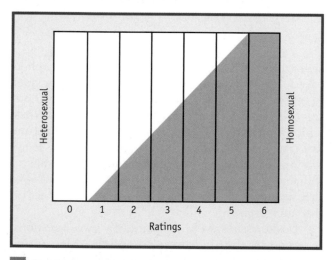

■ FIGURE 13.2 *Heterosexual-Homosexual Rating Scale*

Based on both psychological reactions and overt experience, individuals rate as follows:

0 = exclusively heterosexual

1 = predominantly heterosexual, only incidentally homosexual

2 = predominantly heterosexual, but more than incidentally homosexual

3 = equally heterosexual and homosexual

4 = predominantly homosexual, but more than incidentally heterosexual

5 = predominantly homosexual, but incidentally heterosexual

6 = exclusively homosexual

Kinsey recognized that for some people the strict dichotomy between same-gender and heterosexual behavior did not exist. In order to classify his clients into appropriate categories for study, Kinsey devised this rating scale.

Source: Reprinted by permission of the Kinsey Institute for Research in Sex, Gender, and Reproduction, Inc. From A. C. Kinsey, W. B. Pomeroy, & C. E. Martin (1948). *Sexual Behavior in the Human Male.* Philadelphia: W. B. Saunders, p. 638. Reprint; Bloomington: Indiana University Press, 1998.

sively homosexual, or same-gender, behavior. Those individuals who showed some combination of both behaviors were classified somewhere between these two extremes. Categories 1 and 5 were for those who showed predominantly heterosexual or same-gender sexual behavior, respectively, but had experienced at least some of the other type of behavior. Category 2 included people who had experienced more than incidental same-gender behavior but still leaned more toward the heterosexual end of the scale; category 4 was for those who leaned more toward same-gender behavior but had experienced more than incidental heterosexual behavior. Category 3 included people with approximately equal amounts of sexual experience with men and with women (Kinsey et al., 1953).

Kinsey's scale has been called a stroke of political genius, because it opened up a whole new way of understanding human sexual behavior. Kinsey's scale and the behavioral statistics that accompanied it demonstrated that sexual behavior between people of the same gender was more common in the U.S. population than had been believed—a comforting revelation not only to persons who perceived themselves as gay, lesbian, or bisexual but also to people who considered themselves heterosexual yet had experienced some same-gender activity. Because there was now a continuum of sexual behavior, people no longer had to classify themselves as being at one pole of experience or the other. The middle ground of the scale clarified the idea that a range of sexual behavior exists. Kinsey's approach is believed to have played a major role in allowing American society to begin coming to terms with same-gender sexual orientation.

Subsequent research has shown that the more we know about the complexities of human sexuality, the less valuable Kinsey's scale can be in understanding sexual orientation as part of the human personality. The scale implies that the more same-gender-oriented one is, the less heterosexual one can be, and vice versa. It also fails to distinguish among potentially independent factors such as attraction, behavior, and self-identification. Some people may exhibit high levels of both same-gender eroticism and heteroeroticism, low levels of both, or differing levels of each. Across their life spans, people may experience changes and discontinuities in sexual behavior patterns, sexual fantasies, and romantic attractions and identities (Kinnish, Strassberg, & Turner, 2005; Savin-Williams & Ream, 2007).

Incidence of Sexual Orientations, Behaviors, and Attractions

Given the apparently dynamic, changeable nature of sexual orientation, it is indeed a challenge to seek data on the frequencies of sexual orientations and all their complex variations. Researchers must rely primarily on self-reported data, with the additional complication of needing to rely on subjective interpretations and selective memories regarding inner experiences such as desire, fantasy, and attraction. Such measures are always imperfect. It may not even be particularly meaningful to establish numbers about the proportions of a population that might be gay, straight or bisexual, because these categories are so complex to identify within individuals. It is known that the proportion of people identifying themselves as gay or bisexual tends to be considerably smaller than the proportion actually engaging in same-sex behavior. Studies in the United States, England, and France demonstrate that only about 1 percent of the adult population has experienced same-sex activity only. However, if we broaden the parameters to include some degree of same-sex attraction or at least one incident of same-sex behavior since puberty, the numbers approach 8 percent. These figures are relatively consistent across several cultures (Savin-Williams & Ream, 2007).

Other research has suggested that to be exclusively same-gender-oriented in behavior, attraction, fantasies, and falling in love actually may be relatively rare, although leaning strongly in a same-gender direction is not. People who indicate that they have had sexual partners of both sexes tend to have had more sexual partners in general, to have had a higher frequency of both oral and anal sex, and to have begun experiencing masturbation and orgasm at a younger age (Traeen, Stigum, & Sorensen, 2002).

The researchers who conducted the National Health and Social Life Survey (NHSLS) found many subtleties and gray areas in attempting to identify the incidence of sexual orientations and behaviors (see Figure 13.3). They found that people often change their patterns of sexual behavior over their lifetimes, making it difficult to generalize about orientation in any definitive manner (Tolman & Diamond, 2002). They also realized that no single set of desires or characteristics uniquely defines an individual as lesbian, gay, or bisexual. Does sexual desire for someone of your same gender define you as gay, even if you have never acted on that desire? Does identifying yourself as a lesbian make you so if you have never had sex with another woman? The researchers recognized that because of the stigma and discrimination still associated with same-gender sexual orientation, some people might be reluctant to say much about same-gender attractions or behaviors. The survey was designed to encourage honest answers as much as possible, and it focused on same-gender behaviors and attractions in several different ways, using the term "homosexual" in only one question (Michael et al., 1994).

The NHSLS sought data about three important aspects of sexual orientation, recognizing its multidimen-

FIGURE 13.3 *Intimate Relationships*

It is erroneous to view gay and lesbian relationships strictly in terms of sexual behavior. Like heterosexual relationships, same-gender intimacy is based primarily on warmth and caring.

sional nature (Laumann et al., 1994). The researchers asked questions about *desire*, focusing on attractions to others of the same gender and the appeal of various sex acts; sexual *behavior* with same-gender partners; and *self-identification*, or the sexual orientation one associates with oneself. Figure 13.4 summarizes the findings of these aspects of the study. The results of the survey showed that more people find others of their gender sexually attractive than ultimately act on that attraction.

Desire issues were measured by two questions, indicated by the attraction and appeal scales on the graph. One question asked, "In general are you sexually attracted to . . . ?" and offered five choices as answers: only women, mostly women, both men and women, mostly men, or only men. About 4 percent of the women and over 5 percent of the men in the study responded that they were attracted to others of their own gender. When asked about the degree of appeal they found in the thought of having sex with someone of their own gender, 5.5 percent of the women and slightly more than 4 percent of the men indicated they found the idea very appealing or appealing. When asked about having engaged in same-gender sexual behavior, fewer than 2 percent of women had done so in the previous year, and about 4 percent had done so since age 18. Nine percent of the men surveyed indicated having had sex with another male since puberty, with 40 percent of these (5 percent of all the men surveyed) indicating that the behavior had occurred prior to age 18. Somewhat more than 2 percent of all men said they had had sex with another man in the

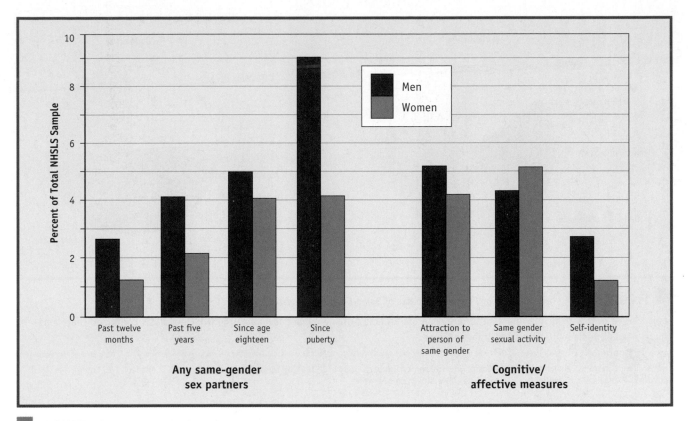

FIGURE 13.4 *Aspects of Same-Gender Sexuality*

The NHSLS revealed that more men and women find others of their own gender sexually attractive or find sex with a same-gender partner appealing than identify themselves as gay, lesbian, or bisexual. In addition, many of those who have not recently had any same-gender sex partners report having had same-gender sex partners at some time in their lives.

Note: Attraction measured by the following question: "In general, are you sexually attracted to . . . only women, mostly women, both men and women, mostly men, only men?" (order of answer categories reversed for women). Appeal measured by the following question: "How would you rate this activity: having sex with someone of the same sex . . . very appealing, somewhat appealing, not appealing, not at all appealing?" Self-identification was derived from the following question: "Do you think of yourself as . . . heterosexual, homosexual, bisexual, something else?"

Source: From *Sex in America* by Robert T. Michael et al., p. 175. Copyright © 1994 by CSG Enterprises, Inc., Edward O. Laumann, Robert T. Michael, and Gina Kolata. By permission of Little, Brown and Company, and Brockman, Inc.

previous year. One clear difference between males and females that emerged in the survey data was that much of the same-gender sexual contact of males happened during the earlier teenage years, whereas women were more likely to have had sex with another woman after age 18.

Regardless of the rates of same-gender sexual activity or attraction, the lowest rates of response were found with the question of self-identification. About 2.8 percent of the men and about 1.4 percent of the women identified themselves as homosexual or bisexual. NHSLS researchers also analyzed all relevant data from the 150 women (8.6 percent of the total 1,749) and 143 men (10.1 percent of the total 1,410) who indicated any degree of same-gender desire, behavior, or self-identification to see how the various factors overlapped or were independent. As Figure 13.5 shows, 59 percent of these women and 44 percent of the men indicated some level of attraction to others of their gender or some appeal of same-gender sexual acts but did not report any actual

same-gender behavior or self-identification. Thirteen percent of the women and 22 percent of the men had had some kind of same-gender sexual behavior but did not report any desire or self-identification as homosexual, lesbian, or bisexual. All three dimensions of same-gender sexual orientation were reported by only 15 percent of the 150 women and 24 percent of the 143 men who had indicated same-gender desire, behavior, or self-identification (Laumann et al., 1994).

A sample of about 8,000 college students in the United States and Canada was studied on four different aspects of sexual orientation: behavior, attraction, fantasy, and self-identity. Over 97 percent of the women and men in the study identified themselves as heterosexual, with the proportion of those self-identifying as homosexual or bisexual being about 2 percent of the women and 3 percent of the men. About 10 percent of both genders indicated that at least half of their sexual fantasies involved same-gender partners. When researchers sought to make statistical comparisons among the four measures used in the study, they found

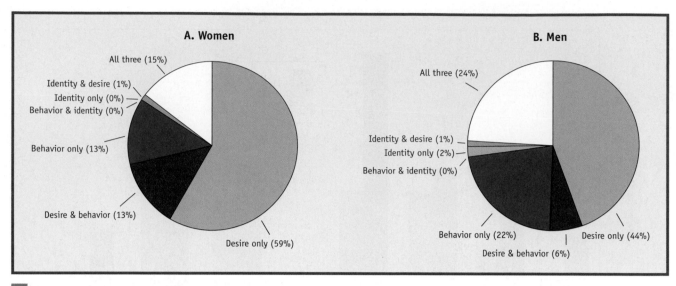

FIGURE 13.5 *Interrelation of Different Aspects of Same-Gender Sexuality*

Same-gender desire, behavior, and identity are separate aspects of same-gender sexuality. The NHSLS analysis confirmed that same-gender sexuality is a multidimensional phenomenon.

Note: A. For 150 women (8.6 percent of the total 1,749) who reported any adult same-gender sexuality. B. For 143 men (10.1 percent of the total 1,410) who reported any adult same-gender sexuality.

Source: From Edward O. Laumann et al., *The Social Organization of Sexuality*, p. 301. © 1994 by Edward O. Laumann, Robert T. Michael, CSG Enterprises, Inc., and Stuart Michaels. Reprinted by permission of the University of Chicago Press.

an unsettling number of inconsistencies and contradictions. Attempts to refine their measurements yielded no significant change in the numbers described earlier but did find some stronger links between reports of cross-gender play activities as children and identification of same-gender sexual interests (Ellis, Robb, & Burke, 2005).

So sexual orientation is an elusive concept and its prevalence in any category cannot be characterized by a single number. It is a multidimensional phenomenon that may be perceived and interpreted in a variety of ways. Of the people in the NHSLS who found same-gender sex desirable in some way, only about half of the men and slightly more than 40 percent of the women ever acted on those desires. Men who desired other men and had sex with them were more likely than women with same-gender desire and behavior to identify themselves as gay ("homosexual" in the survey) or bisexual. The research data also showed that people who identified themselves as lesbian, gay, or bisexual tended to be more highly educated and to have middle- or high-class socioeconomic status. This may indicate, however, only that middle-class, college-educated people are more willing than others to report a same-gender sexual orientation.

The NHSLS research demonstrated that the proportion of people who identified themselves as gay, lesbian, or bisexual was much higher in cities than in suburban or rural locations, although this trend was more pronounced among gay men than among lesbians. As Figure 13.6 indicates, in the 12 largest U.S.

cities, more than 9 percent of the men identified themselves as gay or bisexual, and close to 3 percent of the women identified themselves as lesbian or bisexual. One obvious conclusion to be reached would be that city life provides a concentration of people sufficient to allow identifiable sexual cultures and communities to become visible. Although it is true that people with same-gender interests tend to move away from suburban and rural locations to cities, another intriguing finding was that people raised in cities actually were more likely to be gay or lesbian than people raised in the suburbs or in rural areas. We can only speculate as to the reason for this finding, but it may be that it is easier to realize and explore same-gender lifestyles in urban areas, where they are more noticeable.

Cross-Cultural Comparisons

Cross-cultural generalizations about sexual behavior between members of the same gender are practically impossible, particularly when we try to interpret or understand the sexual behaviors of other cultures using the psychological, sociological, or biological theories developed within the context of our own culture. Same-gender sex has not been substantially researched in most areas of the world (Wellings et al., 2006). Nevertheless, sexual behaviors and relationships between members of the same sex exist to varying degrees in all cultures and are assigned many different meanings. They are sometimes accepted or tolerated, sometimes

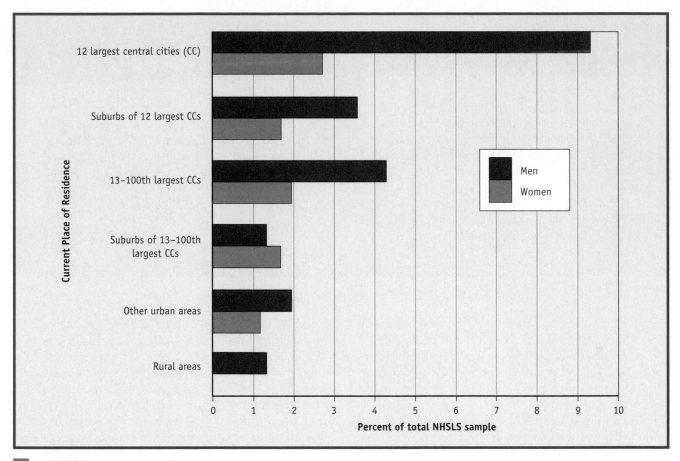

FIGURE 13.6 *Percentage of NHSLS Subjects Identifying Themselves as Homosexual or Bisexual*

NHSLS research demonstrated that the incidence of same-gender sexuality can be influenced by geographic location. We can only speculate as to the reason people raised in cities are more likely to identify as gay or lesbian.

Source: From *Sex in America* by Robert T. Michael et al., p. 178. Copyright © 1994 by CSG Enterprises, Inc., Edward O. Laumann, Robert T. Michael, and Gina Kolata. By permission of Little, Brown and Company, and Brockman, Inc.

condemned or punished, but subcultures of people who love others of their gender seem to appear in all societies, regardless of social norms (Tolman & Diamond, 2002).

Applying our terminology to those behaviors makes little sense, because terms carry the assumptions of the time and place in which they were first coined (Knauft, 2004). The Nanshoku culture of Japan has recognized the behavior of men having sex with other men without having a need to devise words for a separate identity, such as "gay." In India, same-gender sexual behaviors are accepted without labels that marginalize the people who practice them into categories of sexual identity or status.

Studies in France and Britain have generated prevalence data very similar to those of the NHSLS. The comparability of American and European data reflect similarities in the ways these cultures perceive and define sexual orientation. In fact, the most research on sexual orientation has been conducted in North America, Western Europe, and Australia, all of which con-

ceptualize the issues in much the same way. As small studies begin to emerge from other cultures, it becomes even clearer how broader social and political themes are reflected in perceptions of sexual orientation and same-sex behavior.

The prevalence of same-gender sexual behavior does not seem to bear any particular relationship to a society's climate, racial makeup, affluence, typical family structure, or state of development. Rules and social sanctions, however, seem to have at least some effect on the visibility of such behavior. In societies where it is accepted or approved, it tends to be more frequently observed, and it may be that gays are identifying themselves at younger ages in these societies. In societies where it is condemned, sexual and romantic relationships between members of the same gender tend to be less frequently reported (Giertsen & Anderssen, 2007; Traeen, Stigum, & Sorensen, 2002). In nations where sex between members of the same gender is stigmatized or criminalized, the incidence of unsafe, unprotected sexual activity increases, and condoms are used

Real Student Voices

■ When I joined the Boy Scouts, I didn't really think of myself as gay, although as I look back, it should have been obvious to me. My first sexual relationship took place at a summer Boy Scout camp. Although I knew that scouts weren't supposed to be gay, I had pretty much learned that nobody was supposed to be, so it didn't seem to make much difference. I became an Eagle Scout before I left scouting. It was a good experience for me.

■ Although I might want to settle down with another woman someday, it doesn't really matter much to me if we are able to get married. I think we can have just as good a relationship, and be just as committed, whether we have a marriage license or not. There may be some other advantages of marriage, but that remains to be seen.

less frequently than in countries that are more accepting of same-gender sex (Han, 2008; Wellings et al., 2006)

In some nonindustrialized societies, sexual categories are based not on the gender of the sexual partner, but instead on the position being assumed in the sexual act. For example, in one Brazilian fishing village, three distinct sexual categories were identified among males: the *persistent heterosexuals*, who have sex only with women; *paneleiros*, who have sex only with other men but always in the "bottom," receptive role for anal intercourse; and *paneleiros lovers*, who have sex with women and men but when they are with men assume only the insertive, or "top," role in anal intercourse. Men in this last category are not considered gay or bisexual per se but are in their own category. Such a system of categorization is intertwined with views of gender in the society (Cardoso, 2005). Men who have sex with men in Latin American cultures have generally shown less willingness to vary their sexual positions because of the implications that might hold for perceptions of their gender. Some research is suggesting that role versatility is beginning to increase in these cultures (Cardenas & Barrientos, 2008; Peinado et al., 2007).

Cultures around the globe display their own complex attitudes and mores related to same-gender sexual orientation and relationships. In areas of the world where negative attitudes toward gays and bisexuals are supported by prevailing values, such people may experience more personal problems. Russia has seen various periods of decriminalization and recriminalization of same-sex behaviors in recent history, even though it has a long tradition of permitting male-to-male erotic interest (Willett, 2007). In Turkey, a predominantly Muslim nation where homosexuality is strictly forbidden, people with a same-sex orientation are more likely to report sexual abuse during childhood, to report more distance between themselves and their parents, and to be at greater risk for suicide (Eskin, Kaynak-Demir, & Demir, 2005; Gencoz & Yuksel, 2006). Likewise, in Hong Kong, Taiwan, and mainland China, studies are beginning to show higher levels of psychological disturbance, less likelihood of condom use during sex, and a struggle for sexual freedom among those who are nonheterosexual in orientation (Neilands, Steward, & Choi, 2008; Shiu-Ki, 2004; Wong & Tang, 2004).

Some preindustrial societies have been known to use same-gender sexual behavior between males in their coming-of-age rites. The belief is that a man giving semen to a young boy orally or anally strengthens the boy and helps make him into a man. Such age-structured behavior is viewed as a rite of passage to manhood. It previously was practiced in some Melanesian societies in the southwest Pacific. In these societies, a male would engage in sexual activity with other males until he married; then he was to adopt heterosexual behavior. Most men made the transition and remained exclusively heterosexual, but a few continued to have sexual relationships with other males. As Melanesian societies have had increased contact with Western ideas and religions, ritualized sexual activity between males as a rite of passage seems to have largely disappeared, and younger generations are shocked to learn of the former practices (Knauft, 2004).

The Effects of Homophobia and Biphobia

Homophobia, biphobia, and their resultant prejudices take their toll on people's lives and on their attitudes toward themselves. Anger, violence, and ridicule toward gays, especially males, remain a problem, as does internalized homo-negativity that many gay persons experience in themselves (Carbone, 2008; Parrot & Zeichner, 2008; Rosser et al., 2008). Even boys who are not attracted to other males fear behaving in any way that might give an appearance of being gay because they fear being ridiculed. While these negative attitudes have faded a great deal over the last quarter century, they do still exist. Several professional organizations have taken public stands with regard to same-gender sexual orientation and behavior. In 1973, the American Psychiatric Association's board of trustees voted unanimously to remove homosexuality from its list of mental illnesses, declaring that it does not constitute a psychiatric disorder. The American Psychological Association has taken a similar stand. Some concerns about gay teachers in the classroom still exist, typically based on stereotypes and misinformation that have no basis in fact. Gay and bisexual educators, fearing criticism, often feel that they must be cautious about how open they are about their lifestyles (Meyer, 2005).

The Parliament of the European Union (EU) recently passed a resolution condemning homophobia, partly because of the rampant prejudice they found when 10 eastern European post-communist nations joined the union in 2004. Studies of 31 nations of the EU found that Eastern Orthodox religious influences, economic development, and urbanization were all associated with more negative attitudes toward same-gender sex (Stulhofer & Rimac, 2009).

There is a growing recognition among American corporations that homophobia is bad for business. More companies are now advertising their products in publications directed specifically at gay males and, to a lesser degree, lesbians, because they realize that this segment of the population represents a substantial market. Because gay and lesbian workers cannot function optimally if they have to be constantly concerned about the attitudes and behaviors of their colleagues, some businesses have begun to offer workshops to their employees with the aim of reducing homophobic attitudes. In the corporate environment, as well as on college campuses, homophobic attitudes will not change until a serious effort is made to educate people about sexual orientation by dispelling some of the stereotypical beliefs about gays, lesbians, and bisexuals (Brown et al., 2004; Swank et al., 2008).

How accepting do you think students on your campus are of same-gender relationships and sexual behavior?

Religious Views

The attitudes and teachings of some religions toward same-sex behavior have traditionally played an important role in the formation of public opinion. Sex not intended for the purpose of reproduction may be viewed by some as lustful and therefore sinful. Furthermore, sexual behavior that cannot be conducted within the bond of heterosexual marriage has sometimes been viewed as sinful. Many Judeo-Christian-Muslim denominations have sought to judge and regulate various forms of sexual behavior, including same-gender sexual behavior (Plugge-Foust & Strickland, 2000).

In the ancient world, no religion other than Judaism categorically prohibited same-gender sexual behavior (the Torah's prohibition applied only to male-male sexual behavior), although some religions did advocate celibacy. Jewish legal passages may be interpreted in ways that permit same-gender marriage (Moss & Ulmer, 2008). Around 400 CE, Christianity began to introduce a new sexual code that focused on maintaining purity and equated some sexual behaviors with the fallen state of the human soul. Over the centuries, same-sex behavior has been variously accepted and condemned within religious traditions. In recent times, many theologians have called for increased understanding and acceptance of gays, lesbians, and bisexuals, and some have gone further in calling for reform of attitudes that see same-gender orientation as sinful (Jakobsen & Pellegrini, 2003; Maher, Sever, & Pichler, 2008).

All of the major Judeo-Christian-Muslim religious denominations have theologians who argue that the Torah, the Christian Bible, and the Qur'an do not condemn same-sex behavior. Scholars have debated the meanings of various passages in religious texts. Some insist that these passages admonish people for same-gender behavior, and others claim that such meanings are misinterpretations (Moss & Ulmer, 2008; Plugge-Foust & Strickland, 2000). Gay men and lesbians have called for a new religious and moral ethic that would allow for human diversity, acknowledge variant sexual orientations, honor the concept of mutual sharing by consent, and affirm the freedom to grow and change. Many religiously oriented counselors help people sort out these issues in relation to their own lives.

■ Conceptualizing Same-Gender Sexual Orientation

The origins of sexual orientation have been the subject of much conjecture, research, and debate in recent years. Between 1880 and 1900 same-gender sexual orientation was "medicalized" and defined as a "disease," being called at first "sexual inversion" and later "homosexuality." One of the medical assumptions was that people with a same-gender sexual orientation were fundamentally different from those with a heterosexual orientation. This is a classic example of a social construction, in which social beliefs create whole new perceptions of phenomena that have always existed, thereby constructing a concept that then is perpetuated as a scientific or medical truth (Tolman & Diamond, 2002).

Theories and models about the origins of sexual orientation have focused on psychosocial, biological, and evolutionary factors. In weighing the issues, it is crucial to keep in mind that there is a great deal of diversity among individuals who identify themselves as bisexual, lesbian, or gay. It is possible that same-gender behavior and attraction may be about the only thing these individuals have in common. There may be many different pathways to a common sexual orientation—whether same-gender, bisexual, or heterosexual.

Psychosocial Models

Freud believed that same-gender sexual inclinations could result from a variety of difficulties in passing through the various stages of development—oral, anal, phallic, latent, and genital. Late in his life, Freud stated that he did not consider homosexuality an illness but instead a sexual function produced by arrested sexual development. This set the stage for classical psychology to advance numerous hypotheses about the psychodynamics behind the development of same-gender sexual orientation, viewing it as a type of neurosis that should receive psychiatric treatment. One traditional psychological perspective was that family interactions caused homosexuality in males, with the most typical background consisting of a close-binding, overprotective mother and a detached, absent, or openly hostile father. It is now known that this theory has no basis in fact.

Although these beliefs have persisted for well over a century, and there are still those who believe that sexual orientation is somehow learned or developed through social interactions and psychological mechanisms, research to support such conceptualizations has not turned up any scientifically persuasive evidence. In fact, we have now reached the point where many experts have concluded it is time to admit that psychosocial factors do not play any appreciable role in the development of sexual orientation (VanderLaan & Vasey, 2008). This is, in a way, a very real revolution in our thinking about human sexuality, but as the evidence has accumulated over the last 60 years, it is also an inescapable conclusion.

The Normal Variant Model Sets the Stage

Beginning in the 1960s, an increasingly large and powerful group of theorists and researchers began to con-

ceptualize same-gender sexual orientation as a normal variation within the continuum of human sexual behavior (see Figure 13.7). They recognized that same-gender sexual behavior was less common than heterosexual behavior, but they did not see any grounds for classifying it as pathological, deviant, perverse, or abnormal. Instead, they viewed same-gender behavior as a natural, though less prevalent, form of sexual expression (DeLamater & Friedrich, 2002).

Psychologist Evelyn Hooker was one of the most influential researchers to propose that same-gender sexual orientation and behavior are normal variants. During her training as a psychologist in Chicago in the 1950s, she had been taught that homosexuality was a pathological condition. However, she had befriended a group of young gay men, and her real-life observations seemed to suggest that these men were quite healthy and well-adjusted. One of the men said to her one day, "Now, Evelyn, it is your scientific duty to study men like me." She was struck with the realization that very little scientific information was available about

FIGURE 13.7   *Same-Gender Orientation*

Many researchers believe that same-gender sexual behavior is simply a variant on the continuum of human sexual activity. The psychological health of both heterosexuals and gay men or lesbians appears to be statistically about the same.

same-gender orientation. Hooker received a grant from the National Institute of Mental Health and began to study gay men living in the gay community, eventually expanding her research to include lesbians. Her findings confirmed that in terms of psychological health, people with same-gender and heterosexual orientations were indistinguishable. She reported that many gay men and lesbians were living happy, productive lives. She challenged earlier studies focusing on people who might well have been upset by their homosexuality because they had been told it was a mental disorder, and instead proposed that same-gender orientation did not meet any scientifically valid criteria to be considered pathological (Hooker, 1993).

Studies continued to confirm the absence of significant psychological differences between heterosexuals and people with a same-sex orientation, and the professional societies eventually moved the orientation out of their pathological criteria. Some studies have found a greater incidence of depression and anxiety among gay people, especially gay men, sometimes related to lower self-esteem and a lesser sense of personal mastery. It could be that homophobia and the threat of discrimination and violence lead to some emotional difficulties, or it may be that gay men have a greater biological predisposition to depression and anxiety (Bailey, 2003; Sandfort, de Graff, & Bijl, 2003). In any case, among professionals in the field of sexology, same-gender sexual orientation and behavior are now accepted as one possibility on a widely variable spectrum of sexual interests.

The Bell, Weinberg, and Hammersmith Study

Another groundbreaking study on the development of sexual orientation reached conclusions that called into question some of the old psychosocial assumptions. Representing the Kinsey Institute, Alan Bell, Martin Weinberg, and Sue Kiefer Hammersmith (1981) carried out a controlled study involving interviews with 979 gay men and lesbians and a comparison sample of 477 heterosexual men and women. In examining any difference found between the two population samples, the researchers controlled for the possible effects of age, education, and social status to make sure the difference between the two groups was not due to these factors. A tremendous amount of data was gathered and then subjected to a statistical technique known as path analysis, leading the researchers to draw the following conclusions:

1. Sexual orientation appears to be largely determined prior to adolescence, even when youngsters have not been particularly sexually active.

2. Same-gender attractions typically are experienced for about three years prior to any overt same-gender sexual behavior. Such feelings play more of a role in eventually identifying oneself as gay or lesbian than do any particular activities with others.

3. Lesbians and gay men tend to have a history of heterosexual experiences during childhood and adolescence. Unlike the control-group heterosexuals, however, they report these experiences as being relatively unsatisfying.

4. Identification with a parent of either gender appears to play no significant role in the development of sexual orientation.

5. There is no support for the hypothesis that any particular type of parent produces children with a same-gender orientation.

These findings provided little support for the psychosocial models of sexual orientation that existed at the time. Although these researchers did not study genetic or hormonal characteristics, they did state that their findings were "not inconsistent with what one would expect to find if, indeed, there were a biological basis for sexual [orientation]." They further speculated that such a biological mechanism probably would account for gender identity as well as sexual orientation and that it might well be operative in varying degrees. That is, it might operate more powerfully in individuals who are exclusively same-gender oriented or heterosexual than in bisexual people. This crucial study furthered the movement of sexual orientation theory away from psychosocial explanations and toward biologically oriented factors.

Sexual Orientation and Gender Nonconformity

Bell, Weinberg, and Hammersmith broached a subject that had long seemed a complex mystery, and in fact had become a somewhat taboo topic in scientific circles: the possible connection between sexual orientation and nonconforming sex-dimorphic behavior. For a long time, the prevailing opinion was that gender identity and role, and therefore femininity or masculinity, are quite independent of sexual orientation. That view did not necessarily square with anecdotal observations that gay men sometimes are associated with characteristics that might be considered feminine and that lesbians sometimes seem to have some masculine traits. Because this area raises uncomfortable stereotypes related to both gender and sexual orientation, it has been controversial and tends to raise people's hackles.

In a small study performed at Harvard University, finger-size ratio (explained further on page 346) was correlated with some gender traits. Interestingly, gay males who had a larger finger-size ratio (as do women) were more likely to report that they had been quite feminine as children and preferred feminine-identified occupations (such as costume designer, dance teacher, florist, or interior decorator) over masculine-identified occupations (such as computer programmer, engineer, or physicist). They were also slightly more likely to prefer being receptive in anal intercourse (McIntyre, 2003). There is a clear assumption among the general public that by adolescence and adulthood, many gay males and lesbians may be identified by their feminine or masculine mannerisms respectively. Television shows such as *Will & Grace* and *Queer Eye for the Straight Guy* may have played a role in perpetuating such assumptions, but they may also have reduced negative attitudes in the process (Cohen, Hall, & Tuttle, 2009).

While it is essential to state that a proportion of gay men and lesbian women do not behave in gender nonconforming ways, there is a growing body of research about those who do exhibit such behavior. That work is also stimulating interest in the biological connections that might be made between the development of gender identity and the development of sexual orientation in humans. Well-known sex researcher J. Michael Bailey (2003) posed questions about the relationship between orientation and gender, generating a good deal of controversy (Dreger, 2008). He called for further study of the ways gay men talk, move their arms, and walk that may sometimes be considered effeminate.

A Canadian study conducted acoustic analyses on gay, lesbian, and heterosexual people, finding that there were indeed significant differences in the vowel sounds made by the gay and lesbian persons when compared with heterosexual speakers. While the researchers recognized that these differences could reflect modeling of speech behaviors after others within a particular sexual orientation, they proposed that these differences might well emerge from the same biological processes that influenced sexual orientation in the first place (Rendall, Vasey, & McKenzie, 2008).

There is evidence that gender nonconformity in childhood predicts a higher likelihood of same-gender sexual orientation in adulthood (Skidmore, Linsenmeier, & Bailey, 2006). A Dutch study of 22,500 seven-year-old and ten-year-old twins found that among identical (monozygotic) twins, if one child behaved in a cross-gendered way, the other was likely to do so as well, a finding that was less typical for fraternal or dizygotic twins (Beijsterveldt, Hudziak, & Boomsma, 2006). This lends further credibility to the possibility of genetic influences on such behavioral differences.

Psychologist Richard Lippa (2008) analyzed data from eight separate studies on differences in personality traits between men and women and between gay/lesbian people and heterosexuals, finding that gay men tended to show personality characteristics that shifted toward female-typical directions and that lesbian women shifted more toward male-typical directions. An especially interesting finding of the study was that people who identified themselves as bisexual tended to fall in intermediate zones between male-typical and female-typical characteristics. This offers more evidence of a biological connection between gender-typed behavior and sexual orientation.

Gender nonconformity seems to come with a price. While lesbians do not seem to be particularly troubled by their more male-typical behaviors, gay men seem to be subject to a greater degree of homophobia if they are nonconforming in their gender behaviors. This in turn generates a higher level of psychological distress for them (Sandfort, Melendez, & Diaz, 2007; Skidmore, Linsenmeier, & Bailey, 2006). Such homophobic reactions have been confirmed by another study that has shown more negative attitudes among heterosexual men when reacting to stereotypically effeminate gay men or masculine lesbian women. Women do not seem to react with the same negativism toward gay men but do prefer feminine lesbian behavior to masculine stereotypes (Cohen, Hall, & Tuttle, 2009).

If you were planning to have children and had access to genetic engineering technology that would enable you to choose certain traits, would you be concerned about determining the sexual orientation of your children? If so, in what ways and why?

Biological Determinants Model

Just as research has begun to clarify the genetic, hormonal, and developmental mechanisms that lay the foundations for gender identity and role, the biological templates for sexual orientation are being pieced together. While studies have ventured down several different paths that will be explored in this section, it is beginning to appear as though the results are converging at some common conclusions. As we have seen in other aspects of human sexuality, individual elements of psychosexual development never seem to operate independently, and in fact tend to be interconnected.

Hormonal Influences

For many years, research has demonstrated the crucial role hormones can play in regulating the gender-specific sexual behaviors of nonhuman animals, including examples of animals interacting sexually with members of their own sex because of hormonal influences. It is therefore not surprising that we are beginning to find similar patterns in humans. As we saw in Chapter 5, certain brain structures are masculinized and defeminized by male hormones produced in the fetal testes or otherwise found in the fetal environment (Hurd et al., 2008). It is becoming more apparent that these developmental mechanisms may play a role in establishing the early foundations of sexual orientation. The goal of much of the current research is to figure out some of the other human physical characteristics that might also be linked to these early genetic and hormonal influences. These correlations can help establish connections that make the pieces of this puzzle fall into place.

One potential connection between such prenatal factors and the development of sexual orientation in humans is found among genetic females born with congenital adrenal hyperplasia (CAH). As we saw in Chapter 5, CAH females exhibit some masculinizing (androgenizing) hormonal influences on their central nervous systems, and they also have a greater likelihood of being bisexual or same-gender oriented that seems to be correlated with the degree of prenatal androgenization they have experienced (Cohen, 2002; Meyer-Bahlburg et al., 2008).

Anatomical Factors

Another possible connection between hormonal factors and sexual orientation has been found in the anatomical differences between the brains of gay men and heterosexual men and women. It is known that the hypothalamus in the brain is influenced by hormones, and it is known to play a role in determining sexual behavior in mammals. It is also known that the anterior part of the human hypothalamus plays a role in human sexual behaviors. Research has determined that a particular collection of cells found in the anterior hypothalamus is much smaller in gay men and in women than it is in heterosexual men (LeVay, 1996). Another study found differences in the corpus callosum in the brains of gay and straight men (Witelson et al., 2008) These findings suggest that sexual orientation may be part of a larger package of brain characteristics.

One study used magnetic resonance imaging (MRI) and positron emission tomography (PET) scans to compare both the symmetry of the cerebral hemispheres and functional connectivity in the brains of 90 homosexual and heterosexual men and women (see Figure 13.8). It was already known that there were some differing brain features between women and men, and this study investigated how sexual orientation might be reflected in brain structures. The MRIs

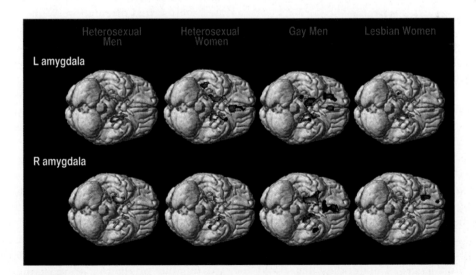

■ **FIGURE 13.8** *PET and MRI Scan Brain Comparisons of Gay and Straight Men and Women*

These composite brain scan images of people in the four categories shown indicate demonstrable changes in brain structure and function related to sexual orientation. Cerebral symmetry was found in both heterosexual women and gay men, while asymmetry (larger right hemisphere) was found in heterosexual men and lesbian women. The amygdala is known to be involved in emotional processing and is shown in the brains of heterosexual men and lesbian women (red and yellow areas) to be functioning in a very localized way. In the heterosexual women and gay men, the amygdala is connected to other brain areas involved with the processing of emotions. This research may help to explain some of the gender nonconformity of gay men and lesbian women.

Source: I. Savic & P. Lindstrom (2008). PET and MRI show differences in cerebral asymmetry and functional connectivity between homo- and heterosexual subjects. *Proceedings of the National Academy of Sciences, vol. 105, no. 27,* 9403–9408. Used by permission.

were used to compare the size of the cerebral hemispheres. It is known that in women, the left and right hemispheres tend to be about the same size (symmetrical), while in men the right hemisphere tends to be slightly larger than the left (asymmetrical). The scan results showed that gay men tended to show the same sort of symmetry as straight women, and the lesbian women showed the same asymmetry as straight men (Savic & Lindstrom, 2008).

PET scans can measure blood flow to parts of the brain, indicating functioning in various brain regions with various colors on the scan. The researchers focused particularly on the amygdala, a portion of the brain that helps process emotions. Again they found that in both gay men and straight women the amygdala was connected to several other brain regions that are also involved in emotional processing. The amygdalas of lesbian women were more like those of straight men, tending to be active in a very focused, localized manner. Some have suggested that the research clarifies why gay men may respond to emotional situations in ways similar to women, while lesbian women might have stronger connections to motor functions, as straight men do. This research shows a clear anatomical basis for a possible connection between gender-typical behavior and sexual orientation, and the researchers believed that the results could only be linked to biological foundations of sexual orientation (Savic & Lindstrom, 2008).

Fraternal Birth Order Effect

Several years ago, an interesting observation was made that males who have older brothers seem to have a greater likelihood of being gay, and the more older brothers there are, the stronger the likelihood (Cantor et al., 2002). A number of studies seemed to support this *fraternal birth order effect* (Blanchard, 2007; Bogaert, 2005). Attempts to explain the phenomenon based on the way older brothers might have treated a younger brother did not yield relevant results (Bogaert, 2003). The *maternal immune hypothesis* has attempted to explain this phenomenon physiologically. It posits that the mother's body actually remembers previously carrying male (but not female) fetuses and that her immune system then responds differently to each subsequent male fetus with levels of antibodies that could alter sexual differentiation of the brain (Francis, 2008).

As it turns out, the fraternal birth order effect may be more complex than originally believed. Some studies were not able to verify the original findings, and others did with some modifications. Researchers argued about the methods of statistical analysis that were used. The most recent evidence suggests that the fraternal birth order effect has some relevance if there is more than one older brother, but also seems to apply

specifically to right-handed gay males, bringing in another factor that may have confounded other research attempts. In fact, the existence of older brothers seems to decrease the likelihood of same-gender sexual orientation in males that are not right-handed (Blanchard, 2007a, 2007b, 2008; Blanchard & Lippa, 2008; Frisch & Hviid, 2007; Langevin, Langevin, & Curnoe, 2007a, 2007b; Rahman et al., 2008, 2009).

You might ask why such research findings really matter one way or the other, since ultimately there might not be much practical use in this knowledge. The answer is that these correlations represent clues to understanding the complex interactions of genes, the proteins they manufacture, antibodies, hormones, and developmental factors in establishing the foundations of key personality characteristics such as sexual orientation and gender identity. In a sense, they are keys that can help unlock some of the fundamental mysteries of nature.

Other Correlational Connections

What we see in the study of biological foundations for sexual orientation is a conglomeration of correlations between various physiological and anatomical characteristics and sexual orientation. These clusters of interrelated findings are thought to be biological markers of developmental processes underlying predispositions toward sexual attractions.

For example, fingerprints and right- or left-handedness have emerged as characteristics associated with sexual orientation. While the finding has not been confirmed by other studies, one researcher found that in female twins where one is lesbian and the other is heterosexual, the number of ridges in their fingerprints differs in that the lesbian women tend to have fewer ridges than the heterosexual women (Hall, 2000). Both lesbian women and gay males have been found to be left-handed more frequently than are heterosexuals (Lippa, 2003).

It has been known for a while that the ratio between the lengths of the second hand digit (2D) and fourth finger (4D) is affected by androgens during prenatal environment, so that the two fingers tend to be closer to the same size (smaller 2D:4D ratio) in males and that the fourth finger tends to be longer in females (greater 2D:4D ratio). We also know that 2D:4D ratios are reliable predictors of masculine- and feminine-identified personality traits and facial characteristics (Burriss, Little, & Nelson, 2007; Caswell & Manning, 2009; Gobrogge, Breedlove, & Klump, 2008; Hampson, Ellis, & Tenk, 2008). "Butch" or more masculine lesbian women have been found to have a smaller 2D:4D ratio than "femme" or more feminine lesbians (Brown et al., 2002). A study with identical female twins where one of the individuals was lesbian found that the lesbian twins did indeed have a lower ratio between finger sizes than did their identical sisters. Among control groups in which both twins were lesbians or both were heterosexual, no difference in finger size ratios was found (Hall & Love, 2003).

When the human body develops, structures on its two sides are not always exactly the same size. Sometimes structures such as hands, arms, ears, ankles, and other structures differ slightly in size from one side of the body to the other; this is called *fluctuating asymmetry*. It seems that there are some measurable correlations between the asymmetries of gay men and lesbian and those of heterosexuals (Hall & Schaeff, 2008; Miller, Hoffmann, & Mustanski, 2008). Other studies have found statistically significant differences in incidences of blood types and Rh blood factors between heterosexuals and gay people. This suggested that chromosomes 1 and 9, containing the genes that determine Rh factor and blood type, might somehow be involved in determining sexual orientation as well (Ellis et al., 2008).

Understanding when these body characteristics are determined during prenatal development may well help us to understand when the brain circuitry of the fetus is programmed for sexual orientation.

Genetic Influences

Based on the types of correlational studies cited above, behavioral geneticists are concluding that several genes may actually be involved in the expression of human sexual orientation. Some data indicate that same-gender orientation tends to run in families. Gay males have a significantly higher likelihood of having a brother, uncle, or male cousin who is gay. Lesbian women also have a greater likelihood of having a lesbian or bisexual sister, although this tendency is less pronounced than is the trend among males.

In one of the earlier studies, researchers traced the family backgrounds of 76 gay men, identifying as many family members as they could who had a same-gender orientation. They discovered that gay men were more likely to have a gay brother than were men in the general population. However, they also found a greater likelihood that these men would have gay male relatives on the maternal side of the family, suggesting that sexual orientation might be linked in some way to the X chromosome that males inherit from their mothers. The researchers then took DNA samples from 40 pairs of gay brothers and analyzed them for genetic markers. Of the 40 pairs of brothers, 33 pairs shared a set of five genetic markers on one end of their X chromosomes. This was the first time sexual orientation had ever been linked to a specific part of a chromosome (Hamer, 2002).

Other studies compared 56 identical male twins, 54 fraternal male twins, and 57 genetically unrelated adopted brothers, and 147 lesbians and their sisters. At least one in each pair of brothers was gay or bisexual and had a twin or an adopted brother with whom he had started living at least by age 2. The assumption of the researchers was that if same-gender sexual orientation is at least partly genetic in origin, the more closely related people are, the more likely their sexual orientation will be the same. Their findings tended to support that assumption. Among the pairs of adoptive brothers, only 11 percent were both gay. That rate rose to 22 percent for the fraternal twins and 52 percent for the identical twins. Of the 71 lesbians who had identical twins, 48 percent of the twins also were lesbians. Of those whose sisters were fraternal twins, 16 percent of the sisters were lesbians. Results such as these suggest that same-gender sexual orientation is highly attributable to genetic influences (Mustanski, Chivers, & Bailey, 2003).

These studies do not mean that same-gender sexual orientation is 100 percent dependent on genetics, as are characteristics such as eye color. Rather, they suggest some degree of *heritability*, meaning that sexual orientation is at least partially dependent on genes passed from generation to generation. For example, a person's height is about 90 percent genetically determined, but it also can be affected slightly by factors such as nutrition. It may be that same-gender sexual orientation is 50 to 70 percent attributable to genetics, but its expression and the choices human beings make in their lives could be attributable to social and cultural influences.

Regardless of whatever biological predispositions that might be established for eventual sexual orientation, human beings exhibit individual quirks and ambiguities that defy simple classification. For example, when one of the gay men involved in a twin genetic study informed his identical twin brother that he was gay, the brother was surprised. The brother had been living a distinctly heterosexual lifestyle and yet had also been aware of some level of attraction to other men. It had never occurred to him to define his feelings as gay. Following his brother's revelation, he decided to try sex with men and indeed found these experiences more fulfilling than his heterosexual encounters. A year later, both twins told their parents they were gay. This example is a clear reminder that powerful social influences can affect how individuals define themselves sexually, even when some traits may be inborn.

The Curious Case of Identical Triplets with Different Sexual Orientations

Even though the identical twin studies suggest a much greater chance that monozygotic (identical) twins will have the same sexual orientation, how do we explain the roughly half of cases in which one twin is gay or bisexual and the other is straight? What happened to genetic influences? There has been a case published about a set of 21-year-old identical (monozygotic) male *triplets* in which two were certain they were heterosexual and the third was just as certain he was gay. The three brothers were administered a variety of psychological tests, and all were essentially similar except for measures of sexual orientation, which supported their self-identities.

The researchers who studied the triplets believed that the case demonstrated how prenatal hormones might have a lasting effect on certain traits, including sexual orientation and behavior (Hershberger & Segal, 2004). But how could this happen when all three boys were born at the same time, from the same mother? Three hypothetical explanations were offered, based on other studies. It is known, for example, that in non-human mammals, the position of a fetus in the uterus is associated with later sex-related behavior (Hurd et al., 2008).

Another possibility has to do with when the zygote split to form three offspring. The first split forms twin cells, but later one of those cells splits again to form two more identical cells that will become the second and third identical fetuses. It is believed that the two fetuses formed from this second zygotic split might have a more similar developmental course that could be different from that of the original twin cell that did not split a second time. *Developmental instability theory* has suggested that such disruptions might cause one fetus to react differently to prenatal hormone exposure than other fetuses sharing the same womb (Gangestad, Bennett, & Thornhill, 2001).

A third explanatory hypothesis stems from the fact that triplets rarely share a single placenta during development. The triplet from the first zygotic split may well have had a placenta separate from the two who were formed from the later, second split. It is known that placental status is associated with the concordance or discordance (similarity or dissimilarity) of certain traits between identical twins and triplets. What we can conclude is that even fetuses with identical genetic makeups may experience subtle environmental differences during their development in the uterus. These conjectures constitute fascinating directions for further research (Hershberger & Segal, 2004).

Evolutionary Theory

As described earlier, evolutionary psychologists have theorized that mating behavior and mate selection have evolved based on whatever strategies will assure the best chances for survival of the species. This theory implies that heterosexual pairing and sex are fundamental parts of the strategy, because they lead to re-

production. For this reason, same-gender orientation and behavior pose somewhat of a problem for evolutionary theorists, because in general gay men produce fewer children than do straight men. From an evolutionary perspective, this calls into question how the gay trait would be perpetuated over time in evolution (Zietsch et al., 2008).

Several explanatory models have emerged, but there is only sparse empirical evidence to back them up. One proposed model suggests that over the eons females chose as mates less aggressive males, who would be more disposed to helping with child care and other home tasks, and that evolution also gradually reduced gender differences between the sexes. The model presupposes that less aggressive and more caring brain structures are associated with same-gender attraction and that these qualities were genetically perpetuated because the offspring of these males, who took more care of their children, had better chances of survival (Berman, 2003). It has also been posited that the male-male alliances that same-gender attraction would have created might have enhanced the chances of male survival and therefore male reproduction (Muscarella, 2006; Vasey, 2006).

Another proposed explanation similarly suggests that in prehistoric times homosexual men helped care for the children of their kin, such as nieces and nephews, thereby assuring that some of the genes associated with their sexual orientation did indeed survive. A contemporary study that attempted to test this kin selection hypothesis actually found no difference in general family affinity or in generous or benevolent feelings (including a willingness to babysit) between heterosexual and homosexual men (Rahman & Hull, 2005). Similarly, it has been proposed that the heterosexual relatives (uncles, aunts, siblings, cousins, nephews, and nieces) of gay men might compensate by producing more children, again leading to the perpetuation of whatever genes might be associated with homosexuality. One contemporary study actually did show that the close relatives of gay men tended to have larger families, but further research is needed to confirm this effect (King et al., 2005). Researchers still have a long way to go in rationalizing homosexuality through evolutionary theory (Gobrogge et al., 2007; Hellberg, 2006).

The Reparative Therapies

When same-gender orientation was viewed as a mental disorder, a great deal of attention was given to therapy and cure. Classical models usually recommended that people with a same-gender orientation face the conflicts and problems left over from childhood, resolve them in some manner, and thereby free themselves to pursue heterosexuality. None of the therapeutic approaches proved to achieve the intended goal, and eventually the professional associations decided that it did not make good scientific sense to classify same-gender sexual orientation as a disorder anyway. Since that time, it has been considered malpractice for members of these associations to attempt to change people's sexual orientations.

There are conservative Christian groups that claim to have been successful in helping gay and lesbian people stop having same-gender sex and pursue straight relationships instead. This has been called *reparative* or *sexual reorientation* therapy, terms that make some people cringe because they clearly imply that there is something to be fixed, or reoriented. The conventional wisdom today assumes that when people say they have been able to change from being gay, it means they have stopped participating in sexual behavior with members of their sex and have begun functioning sexually with members of the opposite sex. It also is assumed that they are highly motivated to make this change because of their personal belief systems. In other words, the behavioral shift simply represents a conscious choice to act in a way that the person considers more appropriate and thus does not constitute an actual change in sexual orientation (Zucker, 2003b).

One study interviewed 143 males and 57 females who reported that they had changed at least somewhat from a same-gender to a heterosexual orientation. The most common reasons they gave for wanting to change were not finding gay life emotionally satisfying and experiencing conflict between their sexual behaviors and their religious beliefs. Sixty-seven percent of the males and 35 percent of the females indicated that they had wanted either to stay married or to get married. About half of the individuals had consulted a counselor or psychologist, and about a third had participated in an ex-gays or religious support group. While many of the people, especially the men, continued to have sexual attractions to others of their gender, most had avoided same-gender contact during the previous year (Spitzer, 2003).

Research that has examined the efficacy of reparative therapies has found omissions in the literature that make it difficult to evaluate the therapies scientifically. It has also found that the therapy approaches tend to blend charismatic religious fervor with pseudoscientific ideas which promise more results than they can usually deliver. Further research needs to be done concerning the long-range outcomes of such therapies, since some findings suggest that many of the ex-gays eventually resume same-gender sexual interaction (Grace, 2008; Serovich et al., 2008).

■ Forming a Sexual Orientation Identity

Sometimes people need to apply a label or category to themselves in order to have a greater sense of who they are. This inner sense of personal identity can have important implications for the ways we experience our own selves. We have many different identities to integrate into our sense of self: ethnicity, gender, occupation, marital status, and parenthood, among others. Sexual orientation identity development involves changes in values and redefinitions of acceptable behavior and is largely an internal, psychological process that seems to involve various stages (Dube, 2000). The formalized, theoretical concept of sexual orientation identity emerged in European and North American social psychology (Ryan & Futterman, 2001). It is in the formation of sexual identity that psychosocial and cultural forces begin to play a critical role.

The original focus was on minority sexual identity status, examining how gay, lesbian, and bisexual people achieved a sense of their individual identities in a society where heterosexuality was considered the norm. This was important because it began to draw attention away from specific sexual behaviors toward an understanding of sexual orientation as it becomes integrated into the personality and sense of self. Being able to define oneself as gay or lesbian, personally accepting that definition, and disclosing that orientation to selected others seemed important to forming a comfortable sexual identity and promoting one's psychological adjustment (Elizur & Mintzer, 2001).

Heterosexual Identity Development

It was also proposed that in addition to understanding the developmental processes of particular sexual minorities, it would be important to clarify and understand how members of majority populations develop their sexual orientation identities (Worthington & Mohr, 2002). Obviously, the members of the majority privileged group will not encounter the same kinds of biases or challenges, but their developmental processes can help us understand the broader perspective of how human beings internalize their sexual orientation (Hoffman, 2004).

Heterosexual identity development encompasses six important dimensions to be accomplished over time (Worthington et al., 2002):

1. Identification and awareness of one's sexual needs, as determined by sexual orientation.
2. Adoption of personal values related to sexual behavior and sexuality in general.

3. Awareness of which sexual activities are preferred.
4. Awareness of the specific characteristics that are preferred in sexual partners.
5. Awareness of preferred modes of sexual expression.
6. Recognition of one's sexual orientation and personal identification with that orientation.

These are the components of *individual sexual identity development*. As a person establishes these various qualities of identity, they evolve and interact with two processes of *heterosexual social identity development*: feeling a sense of group identity (fitting in with other heterosexuals) and developing attitudes toward sexual minorities (largely learned from the social group). Fitting in socially is an important quality in sexual identity formation (Mohr, 2002).

Naturally, people with a heterosexual orientation do not face the obstacle of being ostracized or criticized for their preferences, but they do seem to go through some rather predictable developmental stages as they integrate their sexual orientation into their personalities. Early on, they realize their heterosexual orientation but have not yet acted on it sexually. This stage is called *unexplored commitment* to being heterosexual. They may then enter into *active exploration*, during which they intentionally try out various sexual ideas and fantasies, as well as sexual activities with members of the other sex. During this time, they clarify much about what they enjoy and prefer in terms of activities and partners. Some people experience what has been termed *diffusion*, which may involve sexual exploration, but with less intentionality and goal direction than active exploration. After some amount of exploration, accompanied by physical and emotional maturation, heterosexuals enter into the status of *deepening and commitment*, which is characterized by more intimacy and loving feelings in their relationships.

Because ours is a culture that accepts heterosexuality as the norm, some people move directly from unexplored commitment to deepening and commitment, simply because they have matured enough to do so. The final status of heterosexual identity development is *synthesis*, in which the various elements of identity, group membership, and attitudes toward sexual minorities have achieved congruence and meaning in the person, although this may be a difficult status to achieve (Hoffman, 2004; Worthington et al., 2002). This model helps us conceptualize how heterosexual people gradually integrate their sexual orientation into their sense of self.

Same-Gender Sexual Identity Development

At some point, people who have a same-gender orientation begin to perceive themselves as members of a sexual minority. Models of same-gender sexual identity development tend to have several things in common. There is almost always a predictable progression from some sort of first awareness of same-gender attractions and feelings; to a stage of self-labeling as being gay, lesbian, or bisexual; through stages of becoming more accepting of the new identity and sharing it with others; to a final stage of incorporating the identity into the total sense of self (Savin-Williams & Diamond, 2000).

See "Corey Johnson: An Athlete Comes Out" on SexSource Online.

Australian psychologist Vivienne Cass (1983–1984, 1990) emphasized the need to pay attention to people's self-perceptions in attempts to understand the experience of same-gender sexual orientation. This perspective assumes that sexual orientation is not so rigidly fixed that it cannot be modified and that people's perceptions of their sexuality may shift with time, even during the adult years, with such shifts potentially resulting in new patterns of sexual behavior or relationships. In other words, sexual identity is not something that is necessarily permanently fixed, even though it may be long-lasting and relatively unswerving for many people. This model of sexual orientation also assumes that individuals may consciously alter their sexual behaviors to a degree depending on how they have come to see themselves (Kinnish, Strassberg, & Turner, 2005).

Stages of Same-Gender Sexual Identity Formation

Cass's theory holds that in order for the process of same-gender sexual identity formation to begin, the individual must experience some degree of sexual interest in, or attraction for, someone of the same sex. This does not necessarily have to be expressed through any overt sexual behavior but may instead take the form of fantasies or daydreams. Cass has elucidated six stages in the process of sexual identity formation and maintains that there may be many individual variations in how different people progress through these stages. The ages at which people experience the stages vary with both maturational and social factors (Floyd & Bakeman, 2006). A summary of Cass's six stages follows (Cass, 1990).

Stage I: Identity Confusion

This stage occurs when people begin to realize that information about same-gender sexual orientation somehow relates to them and to their reactions. As

Real People

Nancy Considers Coming Out to Her Parents

Nancy is a junior majoring in business. During spring semester of her sophomore year, she began attending meetings of the local gay, lesbian, bisexual, and transgender student group, primarily because she was feeling lonely and wanted to talk further about her sexual feelings. Since high school, she had been quite certain that she was a lesbian, but she had been reluctant to come out as such or to talk with anyone else about it. She had dated boys in high school, thinking that maybe she would become more interested, but she did not. Since coming to college, she had avoided the social scene for the most part. At one of the meetings in the spring, she met a young woman from the community, and they talked alone a few times. They stayed in touch over the summer, and Nancy looked forward to pursuing the relationship when she returned in the fall.

Nancy and Jill did become more serious during the fall, and they both enjoyed their sexual and social interactions. Jill took Nancy to meet her parents, who seemed very friendly and accepting of their relationship. This was encouraging to Nancy, who had not yet told her own parents about her sexual orientation. She had an older brother who during the Thanksgiving holiday had announced that he was gay, and this had seemed to upset their parents a great deal. She now felt even more reluctant to come out to them herself. At the same time, she wanted to begin building a lifestyle in which she could be as open about her sexuality as she cared to be and not have secrets.

At this point, she has told several friends about her sexuality and has received strong support from them. Some of them have told her that they were not at all surprised and in fact had assumed that she was attracted to women. She is still trying to decide what to do about her parents. She has always felt close enough to them to want their communications to be open and without secrecy. On the other hand, she wants to make certain that their dealing with their son's sexuality would not interfere with their trying to work with her. Jill continues to be a strong source of support for her as she tries to make a decision.

Should Nancy tell her parents about her sexual orientation? Is it important that her parents know? Is she running any risks if she does tell them? Explain.

---

they realize that the personal relevance of this information cannot be ignored, they begin to experience a sense of inconsistency and incongruence in their view of their sexual selves. This period of confusion may go on for some time, during which there may be an attempt to avoid sexual activities with members of the same gender, even in the face of persistent dreams and fantasies about them (Savin-Williams, 2005). Individuals may attempt to find more information about same-gender orientation as the question "Am I gay/lesbian/bisexual?" is addressed. This moves them toward the second stage of identity formation.

Stage II: Identity Comparison

During this stage, people begin to examine the broader implications of being lesbian, gay, or bisexual as they begin to feel different from family members and peers. Nearly everyone grows up with certain heterosexual expectations and behavioral guidelines. As same-gender identities develop, those expectations and guidelines gradually are given up, and a profound sense of loss and grieving may follow. Individuals who experience this may react in a variety of ways. They may react positively and begin devaluing the importance of heterosexuality in their lives. Or they may still try to "pass," or pretend heterosexuality, in order to avoid negative confrontations over their sexual orientation that they are not prepared to deal with. Some react by rejecting a same-gender identity at this point, seeing their same-gender behavior as the result of a particular relationship or of having been innocently seduced. Some people at this stage turn their own confusion and internalized homophobia into antigay and antilesbian attitudes and exaggerated heterosexual behavior, even though they may be covertly indulging in same-gender activities or fantasies (Dube, 2000). Males are quite likely to pursue sex with other males prior to defining themselves as gay (Floyd & Bakeman, 2006; Schindhelm & Hospers, 2004).

Stage III: Identity Tolerance

When individuals accept themselves as gay, lesbian, or bisexual and begin to recognize the sexual, social, and emotional needs that accompany this identity, they develop an increased commitment to and tolerance for the identity. Typical behavior includes increased involvement with others in the gay community, which offers a support group that understands the person's concerns, a greater opportunity to meet partners and see positive role models, and a forum for feeling more at ease with the identity. This stage may be more difficult for people who are shy and lacking in social skills or who have low self-esteem and fear having their sexual identity known by others. People whose experiences are largely negative during this stage may never progress beyond it. However, those who perceive their experiences as more positive eventually will develop enough commitment to their identity to be able to say, "I am lesbian/gay/bisexual" (Elizur & Mintzer, 2001; Herman, 2005).

Decisions must then be faced about how open an individual wishes to be about his or her sexual orientation. Being secretive about one's same-gender orientation has been called "being in the closet." The process of allowing oneself to acknowledge same-gender attractions and then express them to others has been termed **coming out** of the closet. How far a gay man, lesbian woman, or bisexual will come out, and to whom, depends on a variety of factors. One of the most important is the person's degree of self-acceptance. Some feel that sharing sexual orientation with friends and family members is crucial, whereas others feel that it is a personal matter with no relevance to others. Decisions about coming out must be weighed with care, and the possibility of negative or hurtful consequences needs to be considered. Many people have found, however, that others accept their same-gender sexual orientation comfortably. Teenagers who are gay are coming out at younger ages than was formerly the case, and it is not unusual for high school students to be open and activist about their same-gender sexual orientation (Floyd & Bakeman, 2006; Savin-Williams, 2005).

Stage IV: Identity Acceptance

This stage occurs when people accept a self-image as lesbian, gay, or bisexual rather than simply tolerating it and when they have continuing and increased contact with gay and lesbian culture. They share a positive identification with others who have a same-gender orientation. The attitudes and lifestyles of these other people can play a significant role in determining how comfortable individuals are in expressing their own identity. If they associate with others who feel that a same-gender orientation is fully legitimate, then this is the attitude they will most likely adopt. As self-acceptance increases, psychological adjustment improves and people move toward stage V (Malcolm, 2008; Stevens, 2004).

Stage V: Identity Pride

By this point in their identity formation, people with a same-gender sexual identity are not as likely to use heterosexuality as the standard by which they judge themselves. As they identify more with the gay and lesbian community, pride in the accomplishments of that community deepens. Sometimes people in this stage become activists in political movements to fight discrimination and homophobia, and they may face more confrontations with the heterosexual establishment. For some, this is an angry stage. Efforts to conceal one's sexual orientation are increasingly abandoned, and selected family members and friends may be informed of the orientation (Floyd & Bakeman, 2006).

Because of prevailing social attitudes, people may be alarmed to discover that a spouse, parent, child, sibling, or friend is bisexual, gay, or lesbian. Some people react to such a discovery with fear and loathing, others with blame and guilt, and still others with tolerance, understanding, sensitivity, and acceptance. It is quite typical for parents, on discovering that a son or daughter is gay or lesbian, to blame themselves and wonder "what we did wrong." Yet, as earlier sections of this chapter have demonstrated, there is no evidence to support the belief that parental behavioral influences are important in the formation of sexual orientation. Coming out to parents and other family members remains one of the greatest challenges for gay men and lesbian women as they consolidate their personal identity (Savin-Williams, 2005). Through an organization called Parents and Friends of Lesbians and Gays (PFLAG), parents and others can learn more about same-gender sexual orientation and deal with their feelings. Many parents eventually come to accept the sexual identity of their child. In other unfortunate cases, however, the lesbian daughter or gay son is excluded from the family, a reaction that usually only intensifies feelings of guilt and rejection.

What do you believe are the most powerful determinants of sexual orientation?

coming out acknowledging to oneself and others that one is lesbian, gay, or bisexual.

Whether individuals move to the final stage of sexual identity formation is often determined by the reaction of significant others to the disclosure of their orientation. If the reactions are mostly negative, the person may feel only more confirmed in her or his belief that heterosexuals represent the opposition and are not to be trusted. Reactions that tend toward the positive and accepting may allow individuals to move on (Stevens, 2004).

Stage VI: Identity Synthesis

In this final stage of identity formation, people realize that the world is not divided into us (gays, lesbians, and bisexuals) and them (heterosexuals). Not all heterosexuals need to be viewed negatively, and not all people with same-gender orientation need to be viewed positively. The anger that so often is experienced in stage V dissipates, and the gay, lesbian, or bisexual aspects of one's identity may be fully integrated with other aspects of the self. The identity formation process is complete.

Male-Female Differences in Same-Gender Sexual Identity Formation

Different patterns of socialization between women and men lead to a few differences in the ways sexual orientation identity is acquired by the two sexes. For example, the evidence suggests that, on average, more gay males seek contact with a variety of sexual partners than do lesbians or heterosexual males (Laumann et al., 1994). They may also be more willing to participate in anonymous, casual sexual encounters, a practice that is almost unknown among lesbians. Several research studies have indicated that gay males may tend to become aware of their same-gender orientation earlier than do lesbians, often during childhood or adolescence, and in a somewhat more abrupt manner (Floyd & Bakeman, 2006).

Because of their earlier awareness of same-gender sexual feelings and attractions, males are more likely to enter the identity formation process earlier than is typical for females. They often fantasize sexually about other males relatively early in their lives. Males also are more likely than females to enter the process of sexual identity formation on the basis of sexual stimulation, while at the same time adjusting to male-stereotypical roles by dressing and acting in the traditional male manner. There may be less incentive for gay men to reject male gender roles because these roles are more highly valued in our culture than are traditional female gender roles, which tend to be granted lower status (Tolman & Diamond, 2002).

Achieving a lesbian identity seems to be a somewhat more ambiguous and fluid process. "Butch" lesbian women seem to have a somewhat easier time with coming out, perhaps because they are involved in more gay social activities, more comfortable with being gay, and more accepting of their sexual orientation identities than are "femme" bisexual women who may be less sure of themselves (Rosario et al., 2009). Some lesbians fully embrace their same-gender identity only after involvement in an intense romantic relationship with another woman. Most have also had previous sexual involvement with men that has proved to be less fulfilling than what they discover with other women. A common myth holds that if gay men or lesbians were exposed to a happy heterosexual encounter with a good lover, they would realize "what they are missing." However, same-gender sexual orientation is not caused by traumatic heterosexual experiences, nor is it changed by a positive heterosexual experience (Kerr & Mathy, 2003).

Women are more likely to enter the identity formation process when they fall in love with another woman. Again, because same-gender attraction occurs later in life for women than for men, it is not uncommon for a woman in midlife to experience same-gender love for the first time (Robinson & Parks, 2003). Sometimes, women begin adopting a lesbian identity as the result of their association with feminist groups and philosophies, which also may have put them in touch with loving feelings for other women that have previously been unrealized or unexplored. Other times, a woman may first begin to have fantasies about and feelings for other women only after having experienced pleasurable sex with a woman. Women generally seem to show less consistency than men over time in their sexual fantasies, emotional attractions, and behaviors. Achieving a lesbian identity may also be more dependent on the social climate in which the woman finds herself than is the case for gay men (Tolman & Diamond, 2002; Tomlinson & Fassinger, 2003).

Bisexual Identity Formation

All studies of human sexual behavior have indicated that substantial numbers of people have had at least some sexual experience with both females and males (Laumann et al., 1994). Slang terms such as "AC/DC" and "switch-hitter" are sometimes used in reference to bisexual people. It is likely that such individuals often are identified as gay or lesbian, although data from the NHSLS indicated that among people who had experienced sex with someone of their own gender, many did not consider themselves bisexual, gay, or lesbian.

Even people who have experienced a great deal of same-gender behavior or who have had a fairly even mix of same-gender and opposite-gender sexual activity tend not to define themselves as bisexual. They are more likely to see themselves as either gay or heterosexual, with occasional same-sex behavior due to social expectations or personal preference. This may reflect the difficulties people face in forming a bisexual identity, which can be exacerbated by being tacitly told by both heterosexuals and gays or lesbians to make up their minds and make a choice (Ryan & Futterman, 2001). Because they may feel they do not conform to a heterosexist culture, many bisexual people align themselves with the gay and lesbian communities for support. However, they may find a level of biphobia there as well, and they sometimes are considered to be political fence-sitters, traitors, and cop-outs. Heterosexual women tend to perceive bisexuals less favorably than do heterosexual men, who tend to view both bisexuals and gay men rather negatively (Herek, 2002).

A study of male arousal patterns has called into question whether bisexuality actually represents a distinct pattern of genital sexual arousal in men or instead one way of interpreting or reporting sexual arousal. The study compared patterns of genital arousal on exposure to sexual pictures of males and females in heterosexual men, gay men, and men who identified themselves as bisexual. One hypothesis would be that bisexuals would have some sexual arousal to both male and female stimuli. Interestingly, this was not the result. About 75 percent of the men who called themselves bisexual became aroused only by the male stimuli, the same percentage as gay males. The rest became aroused only by female stimuli, the same percentage as heterosexuals. The bisexual men in the study reported having been aroused by and sexually involved with people of both genders, yet their arousal patterns during the research seemed distinctly straight or gay. More work needs to be done to clarify this seeming contradiction between self-identification and sexual arousal (Rieger, Chivers, & Bailey, 2005).

Some individuals may go through a period of sexual interaction with both genders when they are in transition from heterosexual behavior and identity to same-gender sexual behavior and identity. They may define themselves as bisexual before eventually describing themselves as lesbian or gay. This fact may also help explain the apparent disconnect in the study cited above. Arriving at a bisexual identity in this way often is associated with confusion, conflict, and ambivalence about sexual orientation—the *conflict model* of bisexual identity formation. In con-

trast, the *flexibility model* associates bisexual identity with personal growth, a wider range of possibilities for fulfillment, and flexibility in personal lifestyle (Rust, 2003).

It may be that bisexual people respond emotionally and erotically to particular human qualities not exclusive to either females or males. Their identity formation process may not follow a linear, stage-by-stage progression. Bisexual identity may well be more of an ongoing process, emerging from either a formerly heterosexual identity or a gay or lesbian identity. The process may include both self-acknowledgment and disclosure to others. However, bisexual identity formation reminds us again of how changeable people may be over time in their sexual inclinations depending on many different factors in their lives. Because our society has been more reluctant to affirm bisexuality than gay or lesbian orientation, either scientifically or socially, taking on a bisexual identity requires a higher tolerance for ambiguity than does accepting a gay or lesbian identity (Rust, 2003; Wilson, 2008).

Sexual Identity Formation among Racial and Ethnic Minorities

The concept of navigating through various stages in order to clarify a sexual identity may apply more aptly to non-urban Caucasian populations than it does to urban ethnic groups. Same-gender sexual identity may be somewhat public and even have political overtones which may be uncomfortable for African-American and Latino males. While research with lesbian and bisexual women of underrepresented ethnic groups has not indicated that they experience the same level of stigma as men do, more research is needed with this group (Selvidge, Matthews, & Bridges, 2008). Men who have sex with other men in these cultures may fear that their behavior will be stigmatized. In urban environments, minority males often continue living in the same neighborhoods in which they grew up and continue to maintain friendships with many of the same people. Their families continue to be important sources of support and help. If they have sex with other men, it may be difficult for them to be open about the behavior because they feel bound to meet certain heterosexist expectations of those around them. Additionally, they feel the pressures of having to grapple with being a part of ethnic minorities as well as sexual minorities, creating even more pressures (Harawa et al., 2008; Malebranche, 2008; Munoz-Laboy, 2008; Wilson, 2008).

One result of these pressures has been the tendency of some men to maintain sexual relationships with women while continuing to have sex with other men secretly, called being on the "down low." The men sometimes assume that their female sexual partners are safer than their male partners and therefore are less likely to use condoms with the women during their sexual encounters. Coupled with their reluctance to admit to their same-gender sex, this behavior establishes risky sexual conditions for everyone involved. It is known that black and Latino men have disproportionately high rates of HIV/AIDS, so any unprotected sexual encounters represent risky sex. Unfortunately, these men are also reluctant to report their sex with other men to health care providers, meaning that they may not get the testing or medical care they need (Bernstein et al., 2008; Dodge, Jeffries, & Sandfort, 2008; Sandfort & Dodge, 2008; Icard, 2008).

■ Sexual Orientation and Society

Even though same-sex behaviors are still stigmatized to a degree, gay, lesbian, and bisexual people have made significant gains in their civil rights in recent years. In some ways, lesbian women seem to have higher levels of self-esteem and greater levels of involvement within the gay, lesbian, and bisexual culture than gay men do. Gay men seem to have higher levels of depression than lesbians and also be at higher risk for concerns about their body images and eating disorders. Perhaps indicative of their reticence to talk about gay issues, a survey of family physicians found that nearly half of them did not know if they had any gay patients, and only one of the doctors routinely asked patients about their sexual orientations, even though it is considered an important factor in health histories. This section deals briefly with the relationship between same-gender sexual orientation and society (Dahan, Feldman, & Hermoni, 2008; Taylor & Goodfriend, 2008; Wrench & Knapp, 2008).

"SORRY, WILLIAM, BUT THIS IS JUST TOO OLD-FASHIONED... YOU NEED TO UPDATE THE STORY... AGAINST THEIR FAMILIES WISHES, THE TWO LOVERS GET MARRIED IN SAN FRANCISCO... CALL IT 'ROMEO AND JULIO'..."

Source: Best & Wittiest. © 2004 Gary Brookins. Distributed by North America Syndicate.

Gay and Lesbian Culture

Data from the NHSLS showed that gay, lesbian, and bisexual persons are not evenly distributed geographically but in fact tend to live in large cities. More than 9 percent of males in the 12 largest cities in the United States identified themselves as gay, compared to between 3 and 4 percent of males in suburban locations and about 1 percent in rural areas. Lesbians also seem to be somewhat more clustered in cities, but not to the same extent as gay males. Cities offer an environment where critical masses of same-gender-oriented individuals are likely to develop, providing more well-developed social networks and greater economic opportunity (Michael et al., 1994). It has also been found that gay couples are more likely to settle in cities with fewer extremes in weather, fewer people who vote Republican, and lower rates of unemployment (Walther & Poston, 2004).

Colleges and universities often have gay, lesbian, and bisexual organizations or course offerings (Parker, 2004; Tomlinson & Fassinger, 2003); cities and even some smaller communities have gay and lesbian organizations, meeting centers, bookstores, newspapers and magazines, political groups, health and counseling services, housing cooperatives, restaurants, and bars, sometimes located in specific sections or on certain streets. Many people with a same-gender orientation, on the other hand, may never associate themselves with a gay/lesbian community. Even in cities with well-developed lesbian communities, many lesbians do not participate, preferring instead to associate with smaller groups of friends (Laumann et al., 1994). There has always been controversy about whether certain professions tend to be more populated by gay persons than others. One study indicated that male professional dancers are more likely to be gay, whereas only a small percentage of female dancers were lesbians (Bailey, 2003).

The gay, lesbian, and bisexual community has come to serve several important functions, one of which is bringing people together socially. The community also provides a supportive atmosphere in which people can share mutual concerns and experiences and be met with understanding. Another important function of the community is to provide a culture of language and ideology that accepts same-gender orientations and behaviors as valid lifestyles, identities, and modes of romantic and sexual expression. Various forms of nonverbal communication have developed in the gay community as a means to let others know that one is gay. One researcher studied two different types of eye gaze that some gay men and lesbians use to send nonverbal messages to others who interest them. "Gaydar," the somewhat facetious term that sometimes has been used to describe the identity recognition

Real Student Voices

■ I have known I was gay since I was quite a little boy. I couldn't attach words to what I was feeling at first, but I knew I was interested in Superman and Batman for different reasons than my friends were. I came out to a few of my friends in high school, and then to my mother just before my graduation party. Needless to say, this wasn't great timing for her, but she didn't fall apart either. I have a great relationship with my parents now, and they accept my boyfriend fully.

■ I told my parents that I was gay two years ago, and they were really upset at first, wondering what

they had done wrong. My mother came around, and she and I can talk about it openly. My father is a different story. He has acknowledged it, but prefers not to discuss it or have the topic brought up. Maybe someday.

■ I think my parents suspect that I am gay, but I haven't felt any particular need to confirm that. In some ways, I don't feel as though it's any of their business. As a female athlete, a lot of my friends are gay too.

mechanisms gay people use to identify one another, seems to be a real part of gay and lesbian culture (Nicholas, 2004; Philipps, 2006).

What are the existing policies on your campus regarding gay and lesbian couples living together in residence halls?

Some college campuses have been the site of controversy about the cohabitation of same-gender couples in residence halls. Opponents claim that having special living areas for gay or lesbian partners would create a kind of segregation that might aggravate tensions between campus groups, leading to possible harassment of or violence against same-gender couples. On the other side of the debate are those who feel that these residences permit people who have certain commonalities, such as sexual orientation, to share other important aspects of their culture more easily.

Studies of fundamental quality-of-life issues have found in general that sexual orientation does not seem to have any particular effect, one way or the other, on quality of life, income level, lifestyle, or health indicators (Horowitz, Weis, & Laflin, 2001). The emotional states that gay partners share affect their sexual relationships in ways similar to heterosexual couples, although straight women are somewhat more likely to want to have sex with their male partners when they are sad than lesbian women are with their female partners during sad times (Ridley et al., 2008). There is evidence that gay male relationships have their share of domestic violence, with many gay men in the United States being battered or

physically abused by their partners each year. Substantial numbers of gay men report having been subjected to sexual coercion or force as well (Krahè et al., 2000). Power imbalances within male-male relationships ultimately determine which partner is the victim and which the batterer. Domestic violence also is believed to occur in about 25 percent of lesbian relationships (Peterman & Dixon, 2003).

Casual High-Risk Sex and the Gay Community

Among gay males there has always been a fair amount of casual, sometimes anonymous, sexual encounters. **Cruising** is the term used to describe the search process for casual sexual partners, and sometimes public bathrooms in certain locations become known as cruising places. This aspect of gay life received attention when Senator Larry Craig was accused of soliciting sex with another man by using widely known signals in an airport bathroom. Cruising behavior is typically illegal, even though many parks, adult bookstores, health clubs, gyms, and college campus locations become known as high-traffic cruising areas (Tewksbury, 2008). Information about such sites is available online, where a fair amount of cruising also takes place. In fact, young men who meet partners online are somewhat more likely to use condoms during their eventual sexual encounters than those who

cruising searching for a casual sexual partner, usually used in reference to gay males.

meet partners in public places (Horvath, Rosser, & Remafadi, 2008).

Naturally casual encounters can be risky in terms of potential health effects, and men who have had sex in public sex environments have a greater likelihood of having contracted a sexually transmitted disease. In a study of one gym, 88 percent of the gay men reported having had casual sex with another male during the preceding six months, and several studies have reported that unprotected anal intercourse is quite common in such situations (Frankis & Flowers, 2007; Halkitis, Moeller, & Pollock, 2008).

AIDS and HIV were first identified in the United States among gay males, causing a fair amount of stigmatization. For a time educational efforts seemed to pay off, and infection rates decreased (see Figure 13.9). However, more recently men who have sex with men

FIGURE 13.9 *HIV/AIDS and the Gay and Lesbian Community*

Although not exclusively a disease of gay men, HIV and AIDS have visibly affected the gay community in the United States. To call attention to the need for more research to combat AIDS, the Names Project sponsored the creation of the AIDS Quilt, a 150- by 450-foot memorial consisting of individual squares of cloth, each one representing someone who has died of AIDS.

represent about 70 percent of new HIV infections in the United States. Thirty percent of HIV-positive men in one study reported having had unprotected anal sex in the previous year, either with a steady male partner who was not infected or with someone of unknown HIV status (Denning & Campsmith, 2005). In a six-city study of 4,295 HIV-negative men who had sex with men, 78 percent had had sex with a male partner of unknown HIV status in the previous six months, and 28 percent had had sex with someone they knew to be HIV-positive. About half indicated that their anal sexual encounters had not included the use of a condom (Koblin et al., 2003).

Bisexual men represent a significant bridge for the transmission of HIV and other diseases between males and females, especially in African-American and Latino populations who identify themselves as heterosexual but also have sex with other men (Mutchler et al., 2008; Zellner et al., 2009). In various studies, rates of unprotected sex with both men and women ranged from about 25 percent to 50 percent. Very often bisexual men do not tell women that they are also having sex with other men (Jeffries & Dodge, 2007; Siegel et al., 2008; Wheeler et al., 2008).

Given the realities of HIV in gay male culture, two issues often are part of sexual activity among gay males. One is *sexual negotiation*, which refers to the sharing of preferences and dislikes regarding particular sexual activities, along with associated information about the degree of risk or safety. This sharing can be important in determining the level of HIV risk involved in a sexual encounter. The other issue, *serostatus disclosure*, refers to informing the other partner about one's HIV status. Obviously, honesty and integrity are essential to determining the degree of risk involved, but there are also concerns about how much these negotiative and disclosure processes may hinder sex and relationships (Carballo-Diéguez et al., 2006; Feldstein et al., 2006).

Men in a continuing relationship often consider this an issue of trust and love and do not feel condoms are necessary. In this they mirror the behavior of couples who know that both partners are HIV-negative. However, men sometimes do not use good judgment because of alcohol or drugs or because of mistaken assumptions that a partner is HIV-negative. Sometimes, risky sexual practices are inadvertent or forced. Some gay men engage voluntarily in "barebacking," even if they are aware that a partner is HIV-positive. They may take precautions that are considered to be forms of harm reduction, such as avoidance of ejaculation during oral or anal sex. Some research suggests that men who engage in such behavior are tired of using condoms and may even have erectile difficulties when they use them. Some have false optimism about the current risks of HIV or have low levels of self-esteem. There is no evidence, however, that they are deliberately trying

Real Student Voices

■ I was raised by two lesbian women, although that didn't really sink in until just recently. My mother and father got divorced when I was eight, and we moved in with this female friend of hers when I was twelve. I just thought it was more convenient and practical for all of us. Janet, my mother's partner, has always treated us children as her own, and we came to love her. I never thought much about the fact that she and my mother shared a bed. My sister told me they were gay just before I

went to college. I think it's funny that I didn't get it until then. But it doesn't really change anything for me.

■ I want to go into the Air Force, but I am concerned that my sexual orientation will eventually be discovered. I think I can be just as good a pilot and soldier as anyone, but I don't want to be humiliated by being discovered either. I am hoping the military will change their policies.

to spread HIV or get sick themselves (Adam et al., 2005; Huebner, Proescholdbell, & Nemeroff, 2006).

Anal intercourse has been shown to be a primary means of transmitting HIV. Among men who have sex with other men, some prefer the penis insertive role, and are referred to as *tops*. Those preferring the receptive role are called *bottoms,* while *versatiles* have an equal preference for both positions. Those in the bottom role are at greater risk of disease. When the top wears a condom the risk is substantially reduced, but not completely eliminated. Many gay males are using condoms more consistently or choosing sexual activities that are less risky, such as mutual masturbation. In an apparent search for connectedness and sexual affirmation, others seem to be paying less attention to health and safety issues (Chiasson et al., 2005; Whittier, St. Lawrence, & Seeley, 2005).

Although the risks of woman-to-woman transfer of HIV and other STDs are less certain, experts warn about the exchange of vaginal fluids. The likelihood of transmission between women probably is less than between men, but women too should guard against contact involving internal bodily fluids if any risk might be involved. There is evidence that substantial numbers of lesbian and bisexual women do take risks by having unprotected sex with potentially infected males. Rubber "dams" or sheets of latex cut from condoms or rubber gloves can be used to cover the vulva and vaginal opening during oral sexual contact, and rubber gloves or finger cots can be worn when inserting a finger into the vagina or anus.

Sexual Orientation and the Military

For many years, there was a ban on lesbians and gays serving in the U.S. military, and the enlistment forms

asked about sexual orientation. The "Don't ask, don't tell" policy that was put in place in 1994 ended the long-standing practice of questioning recruits about their sexual orientation. All forms of sexual behavior on military bases continued to be prohibited, except between married couples in their living quarters. However, people who openly declared themselves to be gay or lesbian could still be discharged from the military because their sexual orientation still was officially considered "incompatible with military service," regardless of whether they were known to be sexually active.

Public opinion on this issue has shifted dramatically. In a 2009 *Washington Post*-ABC News poll found that 75 percent of Americans believed that openly gay individuals should be allowed to serve in the military, up from 62 percent in 2001, and 44 percent in 1993. Retired top military officers have been involved in studying the issue and in issuing various statements based on their studies. Some have claimed that, in addition to being discriminatory, the "Don't ask, don't tell" policy simply is not working. Others have insisted that gays will not undermine the sense of cohesion or hurt morale, while still others maintain that allowing gay people to enlist is a great mistake. The armed services in numerous other countries allow gay men and lesbians to serve in spite of the homophobic attitudes and abuse these servicemen and -women have sometimes encountered. The Obama administration instituted studies of the implications of changing the policy with the expressed intention of overturning the don't ask, don't tell policy.

Do you think your attitudes and feelings about same-gender orientation differ from those of your parents? Your grandparents? Explain.

Marriage and Legalized Same-Gender Partnerships

People of all sexual orientations are interested in establishing life partnerships with another person and find great meaning in the intimacy and support that are part of such partnerships (Kline, Lesperance, & Waldo, 2008). Some people with a bisexual or same-gender sexual orientation marry members of the other gender. In choosing heterosexual marriage, an individual may have decided to live as an exclusive heterosexual or may still expect to maintain some level of sexual activity with members of the same gender. Bisexuals, lesbians, and gay men enter into heterosexual marriages for a variety of reasons. Some do not become fully aware of their sexual inclinations until after they have married. Others see marriage as a way to achieve social respectability, as an escape from their sexual tendencies, or as a way to avoid the loneliness they may stereotypically associate with gay or lesbian lifestyles. Still others want children and have strong loving feelings toward their spouses. Yet these marriages often face sexual conflicts of various sorts. Some couples can deal with such conflicts honestly and with sensitivity, enriching their marriage. Others cannot handle such conflicts and can no longer continue their marriage.

What are some social pressures exerted on same-gender couples that heterosexual couples do not have to cope with?

Legalized partnerships between members of the same gender have received increasing attention in recent years, and many couples of the same gender have found ways to formalize their partnerships (see Figure 13.10). Some members of the clergy have sanctioned same-gender partnerships. The Metropolitan Community Church has branches in numerous cities aimed specifically at members of the gay and lesbian community. Unitarian-Universalist ministers, and some other members of the clergy, conduct unions of lesbian and gay male couples even though they are not legally binding in the United States. Several states have passed legislation or been subject to court rulings that allow gay and lesbian couples to marry or to enjoy all benefits and privileges afforded married heterosexual couples. Several other countries, including Canada, recognize same-sex marriage, and some states, including New York, legally recognize marriages that have occurred outside the state. It seems likely that same-sex marriage will continue to be debated by state legislatures and that some states ultimately will allow such legalized partnerships. The debates over the issue solidify some clear positions in the culture wars (Bonillas, 2008; Rosenberg, 2006).

FIGURE 13.10 *Intimate Relationships*

It is erroneous to view gay and lesbian relationships strictly in terms of sexual behavior. A gay couple in Boston is shown here exchanging vows in a union ceremony to symbolize their shared relational commitment to each other.

In many cities, partners in a long-term gay relationship can qualify as a family and therefore may be eligible for the same rights as those afforded a married couple for many purposes. Some cities maintain a registry of "lawfully recognized domestic partners." Registration as domestic partners entitles couples to things such as discounts on health club memberships and airline tickets, visitation rights in hospitals or prisons, and rent-control housing. Many major U.S. corporations and colleges have extended employee health and insurance benefits to the partners of gay and lesbian workers. Gay rights activists consider these major steps toward recognition of the legal rights of nonheterosexual couples.

Gay and Lesbian Families

Many gay, lesbian, and bisexual persons have children, either from previous heterosexual relationships or through deliberate efforts to conceive or adopt (see Figure 13.11). Research on lesbian mothers, gay fathers, and their children has taken place only rather recently, and then usually because of legal attempts to

■ **FIGURE 13.11**   *Parents of the Same Gender Raising Children*

Most children adapt readily to families with parents of same-gender orientation. But not all communities accept their lifestyle, and some families struggle to be accepted. This lesbian couple is shown with their children.

decide if lesbians and gay males could be considered fit parents. The available research confirms that lesbian and gay families indeed can provide as healthy an environment as any family structure and that the parenting skills of gays and lesbians are as adequate as those of heterosexuals (Johnson & O'Connor, 2002; Julien et al., 2008). Studies have also confirmed that children raised by gay parents are no more likely than children raised by straight parents to have a same-sex orientation themselves. The children also seem to have no

greater likelihood of social or emotional difficulties. In fact, the National Longitudinal Lesbian Family Study that has followed the children of lesbian mothers since the late 1980s found that their teenage sons and daughters actually rated significantly higher in their social and academic competencies and lower in social problems, rule-breaking, and aggressive behaviors than their age-matched counterparts raised by heterosexual parents (Gartrell & Bos, 2010). Legal precedents are still being set with regard to custody of children by gay and lesbian parents.

More and more same-gender couples are intentionally planning their own families. Lesbian couples have the options of artificial insemination and choosing a male partner for reproductive purposes. Gay male couples must depend on either adoption or surrogate motherhood. Because this type of family structure is of relatively recent origin, there is less research on children raised in such families. The studies that have been done again suggest that there are no particular differences between the children of lesbian and gay parents and children raised in mixed-gender households. As society increasingly accepts same-gender partnerships, there has been increasing visibility of gay and lesbian families with children who have made their way into the mainstream of social life (Johnson & Piore, 2004).

See "That's a Family" on SexSource Online.

Self-Evaluation

What Is Your Sexual Orientation?

Figuring out your own sexual orientation can sometimes be confusing and unsettling. As you have discovered in this chapter, the literature on sexual orientation tells us that many factors may determine sexual orientation, that sexual attractions and behaviors may change to some extent with time and circumstances, that most people identify themselves as straight, and that society can still be hard on people who are non-heterosexual. Clearly, there is plenty of pressure to be heterosexual—or at least to say that you are.

The following questions may help you determine a bit more about your sexual orientation at this point in your life, *if you are honest with yourself about the answers.*

Note: *You should not be asked to divulge information about your answers to these questions unless you wish to do so, are very clear about how the information is being used, and are assured of your privacy and confidentiality.*

Use this scale in responding to questions 1–4:

   1 = completely oriented toward members of the other gender

   2 = mostly the other gender, but occasionally involving someone of the same gender

   3 = both the other gender and the same gender

   4 = mostly the same gender, but occasionally involving someone of the other gender

   5 = completely oriented toward members of the same gender

1. As you recall your sexual desires of the past year and the present, how would you rate them according to the scale?

2. As you recall your loving feelings and romantic attractions of the past year and the present, how would you rate them?

3. During the past year and at present, what rating would you use regarding your sexual fantasies when you are sexually aroused?

4. During the past year and at present, what rating would you use regarding the sexual partners you have had (if any)?

5. If you were to identify your sexual orientation using the terms straight, gay, or bisexual, which one would most accurately describe you right now in your life?

6. When you answered question 5 for yourself, did you feel any internal pressure to define yourself in any particular way? If so, where did that pressure come from?

7. Do you consider yourself homophobic or biphobic? Has anyone ever used one of those terms to describe you? Why or why not?

8. Are you comfortable with the sexual orientation you have indicated you have?

9. How much do you think your sexual orientation matters to various people close to you in your life? Why? How much does it matter to society as a whole?

10. In what ways might you honor your sexual orientation and develop the sense of integrity and appropriateness that can help you be a good person?

Chapter Summary

1. People have an inner set of sexual and romantic attractions called a sexual orientation and eventually develop an inner awareness of how that orientation fits into their lives—their sexual orientation identity.

2. Sexual orientation seems to be more changeable than once believed, but studies have focused more on nonheterosexual orientation because it typically has been perceived as "different."

3. Kinsey developed a scale demonstrating that there is no single pattern of same-gender sexual behavior but rather different degrees between the heterosexual (opposite-gender) and same-gender orientations. His bipolar scale is less useful today.

4. The incidence of same-gender orientation among humans has been an issue of controversy, and sexual orientation seems to be a multidimensional concept.

5. The NHSLS data examined desire, behavior, and self-identification with regard to same-gender sexuality, finding differences in the incidence of each, with some overlap among the three factors. More people indicated having felt attraction to members of their own gender than had experienced same-gender sex.

6. People in urban areas are more likely to identify themselves as gay, lesbian, or bisexual.

7. Same-gender orientation and behavior are found across all cultures. Some cultures find no need to classify people based on orientation, or they may classify them based on what position they prefer during sex.

8. Homophobia and biphobia can have negative effects on individuals who have same-gender orientations and behaviors. Leading professional organizations no longer view same-gender sexual orientation within the framework of pathology, and many businesses are attempting to reach gay and lesbian markets.

9. Religions take various morally based positions regarding sexual orientation and behavior. Some religious groups take an accepting and positive view of same-gender orientation.

10. Psychosocial conceptualizations of same-sex orientation have not found much research evidence to support them, while studies continue to show biological foundations for sexual orientation.

11. The normal variant model, championed by the research of Evelyn Hooker, sees same-gender orientation and behavior as one form of expression within a range of sexual orientations and behaviors.

12. The Bell, Weinberg, and Hammersmith research furthered the concept of normal sexual variations and established a foundation on which more biologically based models could be built.

13. There is a great deal of evidence to support the idea that gender nonconforming in behavior in childhood increases the likelihood that that person will be gay, lesbian, or bisexual in adulthood, and further suggests that complex developmental mechanisms are associated with both gender identity and sexual orientation.

14. Some researchers believe that hormonal factors during prenatal life may predispose people to particular sexual orientations, since exposure to androgens in fetal life seems to determine some later behavioral preferences.

15. Studies of brain anatomy and function have demonstrated some measurable differences in brain structure and activity among gay men and women and heterosexual men and women that also suggest biological determinants.

16. The fraternal birth order effect and other physical characteristics that seem to be correlated with same-sex orientation suggest genetic and developmental connections in the development of sexual orientation.

17. Families that seem to have lines of gay individuals, along with twin studies, have suggested that same-gender orientation may be genetically linked and partly heritable.

18. Evolutionary theory has had difficulty explaining same-gender orientation, but several explanations have been presented to explain why the orientation has persisted in evolution.

19. Reparative therapies, often associated with religious groups, still attempt to change gay people to a more heterosexual orientation. Current professional opinion sees the orientation as one of several sexual orientations that need no particular intervention, and hold that reparative therapies are ineffective and unnecessary.

20. Recent theories have been advanced concerning the development of heterosexual identity from the perspectives of individual identity and social identity.

21. Several theories have been advanced concerning the development of a lesbian, gay, or bisexual orientation identity. Cass's theory proposes that sexual identity formation involves a series of up to six stages. People proceed through these stages differently, and a person's perceptions of his or her sexual orientation may shift over time.

22. There are some differences in the ways gay males and lesbians progress through the stages of sexual identity formation. Gay males tend to enter the process earlier in life than do lesbians. Lesbians are more likely to realize their identity after experiencing an intense same-gender relationship.

23. Bisexual people may feel more pressure to choose sides and may encounter more ambivalence and conflict in arriving at a bisexual orientation identity.

24. African-American and Latino men in urban environments who have sex with other men may have particular difficulty admitting this part of their sexuality and thus are on the down low. This can produce higher health risks for them and their partners.

25. Most cities have well-developed same-gender communities that are an avenue of communication and support for lesbians, gay men, and bisexuals. This may be one reason why city populations have a higher proportion of people with same-gender sexual orientation.

26. Cruising for casual sex among gay males has its health risks, since unprotected sex is relatively common in such situations. There are still concerns about how gay men negotiate sexual encounters and disclose their HIV status, and men having sex with other men account for 70 percent of new cases of HIV in the United States.

27. The U.S. military continues to have the "Don't ask, don't tell" policy, but some military leaders feel that it is unfair and does not work.

28. Some bisexuals, gays, and lesbians marry heterosexual partners and raise families. Gay men and lesbians have been fighting for the right to enter into legal partnerships with members of the same gender, and gay marriage is now permitted in several states and other countries.

29. Children raised by gay or lesbian parents do not seem to differ particularly from children raised by mixed-gender parents, nor are they more likely to develop same-gender sexual orientations themselves.

Chapter 14

The Spectrum of Human Sexual Behavior

Chapter Outline

I never realized how diverse human beings are in their sexual interests and needs until I finished reading this chapter. I can hardly say that very many of these options interest me, but on the other hand, I do not necessarily condemn them either. Human sexuality can be a mysterious thing!

—from a student essay

W e are living in a time unmatched for its diversity of sexual values and the openness with which various sexual lifestyles and behaviors are expressed. Our culture has attempted to reconcile a plurality of value systems and sexual interests within a framework of political culture wars. A fundamental question for such a society is how wide a latitude of sexual values and expressions will be accepted. The debate continues over which behaviors will be tolerated.

Why is it that the sexual repertoire of some people is limited to masturbation and sexual intercourse in a particular position, while others find sexual enjoyment in caressing someone else's feet or in being whipped by a partner? In this chapter, we will look at sexual variations that are part of the extensive mix of feelings, motivations, and activities that human beings seem to find pleasurable. Studies of sexual behavior continue to demonstrate that even what would be considered normal samples of people exhibit a wide range of sexual frequencies and behaviors.

■ Variability in Sexual Interests and Activities

In the earlier days of sex research, Kinsey based his understandings of sexual expression on a concept of *total sexual outlet*, or what has been termed the "hydraulic theory" of sex. Kinsey saw orgasm as the outlet for people's sexual urges and tensions, and he assumed that varying levels of sex drive in different individuals could be expressed through a range of sexual activities. In this way, sexual expression was seen as following the principles of hydraulics, or the movement of liquids. If one sexual outlet was blocked or unavailable, another outlet would simply be used. It usually was assumed, for example, that masturbation compensated for a lack of partnered sex, an assumption we now know to be inaccurate (Laumann et al., 1994).

This concept was closely tied to the long-standing assumption that the sexual impulse was a biologically driven need requiring periodic satisfaction. Although some sexual conditions are innately pleasurable, such as genital stimulation or orgasm, the concept of sex drive is far more ambiguous. It is used to describe a craving for sexual pleasure, but there has not been much scientific support for the idea that a sex drive is built-in, or innate. Sex research concerning the types of sexual behaviors in which people participate suggest that the specific content of any person's sexual conduct depends to a degree on the cultural meanings that the person has attributed to various sexual behaviors as the result of social interac-

tions (Kauth, 2006a; Toates, 2009). This seems to be the point in understanding sexual individuality where psychosocial concepts have an active role to play.

It is important to make a distinction between *sexual performance*, which might be measured objectively by things such as number of orgasms or types of behavior, and the more *subjective erotic experience* going on in a person's mind and emotions. This latter experience includes *desire*, or the ways a person might be drawn emotionally to people and things. Simply stated, sexual desire refers to interest in sexual activity, and that interest may be for either solitary or shared activity. Studies have shown that desire and behavior are not necessarily connected (Ellis, Robb, & Burke, 2005). Sexual desire does not always lead to sexual activity, and people sometimes engage in sexual behavior even when they are not experiencing a sense of desire. Subjective eroticism also includes what has been termed *sensuosity* or *sensuality*, referring to the inner enjoyment of the whole sensual experience of sex, not just orgasm.

We know that the spectrum of human sexual orientations and behaviors is broad indeed, and the varieties of these activities have been subject to many medical, legal, and moral judgments. Although some professionals still use words such as *aberrant, deviant, abnormal,* and *perverse* to describe some sexual preferences and acts, two other terms are commonly used. The term *variant* implies that a particular sexual phenomenon varies from what is considered typical or that it exists in addition to more mainstream sexual behaviors. The term *paraphilia* carries with it the same connotations but is used more often to describe sexual preferences and behaviors that are viewed within a framework that considers them pathological or antisocial. There is continuing debate about whether such judgments are fairly applied to sexual behaviors, and some feel that most paraphilias should no longer be considered pathologies (Kingston et al., 2007; Spitzer, 2005).

At this point in sex research, there is no comprehensive theory about why particular people become excited by certain sexual stimuli while being restrained or inhibited about others. The following sections will summarize some theoretical models that are beginning to expand our understandings.

The Dual Control Model and Variability

In Chapter 4, the Dual Control Model of sexual response was introduced, and its basic components have been applied to aspects of sexual variability as well.

According to this conceptual model, humans are believed to have two separate systems that exert influence over sexual interests and activities. One influences excitatory processes and the other influences inhibitory processes. Individual variations in these two mechanisms lead to different propensities for being excited or inhibited by various sexual stimuli. It is crucial to understand that *both excitatory and inhibitory* processes are involved in sexual interests and activities. For example, low levels of sexual desire have been interpreted almost exclusively in terms of inhibition, or the factors getting in the way of sexual interest. In fact, the lack of sexual excitation, or the absence of factors that are encouraging sexual interest, may be just as important, or even more so. Another important understanding in this model is that the motivation to have sex with a partner seems to be quite independent from the desire to masturbate. They do not seem to be regulated by the same excitatory and inhibitory processes (Bancroft et al., 2009; Graham, Janssen, & Sanders, 2009).

The variability in sexual excitation and inhibition seems to take shape during the developmental processes of human life. Puberty is clearly a significant time for some basic priming of the systems. Brain structures are changing dramatically, along with hormonal balances in the body, and important sexual changes are taking place. Masturbation is the most typical way for youngsters to experience their early sexual feelings around the time of puberty (see Figure 14.1). Interestingly girls have a wider variability in the age at which they begin to masturbate, while boys are more likely to begin around the time of puberty when they seem to experience heightened sexual arousability. However, while boys frequently masturbate to produce multiple orgasms if they start masturbating slightly before puberty, when they become capable of ejaculating semen they also seem to acquire the refractory period, lessening their ability to achieve more orgasms right away. This may be an example of an inhibitory influence in their sexual lives (Bancroft et al., 2009).

As people age, there are some reasonably predictable changes in these two controlling processes. Propensities for sexual excitation generally decrease with age in both men and women. Propensities for sexual inhibition seem to increase in men as they get older, but this happens to a lesser extent in women. It has been hypothesized that this is due to less erectile responsiveness in aging men, causing them to develop more inhibitions about becoming sexually involved (Bancroft et al., 2009).

There are limited sets of data suggesting that sexual excitatory and inhibitory propensities may be at least partly heritable, meaning that they have some genetic roots, but more complete neurophysiological models are needed before we can understand the possibilities here. Neither has the dual control model yet explored how preferences (high excitation/low inhibition) might develop for specific sexual activities. This

FIGURE 14.1 *Puberty and Sexual Incentive Motivation*
Specific targets of sexual attraction are often established by the incentive motivations associated with increased genital arousal around the time of puberty.

is where theories of erotic targeting and motivation can help, as we see in the next sections.

Erotic Target Location Errors

One theoretical concept of differing sexual attractions assumes that in some people, because of some psychological glitch, sexual interest becomes focused on either an unusual object of attraction or some unusual sexual activity. Such glitches are called **erotic target location errors (ETLEs).** The theory holds that people's sexual attractions almost always involve some identifiable, preferred erotic target that is external to the person, but that as the result of some as yet unknown mental mechanism, some people mistakenly direct their sexual interests either toward some peripheral (typically nonsexual) part of the object or toward creating a copy of the target in themselves. The theory does not attempt to judge the social or moral appropriateness of these target errors.

erotic target location errors (ETLEs) sexual preferences for unusual objects or unusual sexual activities.

Some examples are in order here. As we will see later in this chapter, some people are sexually aroused by articles of clothing worn by members of a particular gender. Some men are aroused by bras or lingerie worn by women, and they might fondle them, rub against them, and masturbate with them as if they were living objects themselves. This could be considered to be an ETLE. Some people get sexual satisfaction from dressing up as a person of the other gender, in a sense creating a facsimile of their desired sexual target. There are many different erotic targets that could fit into this model, although as yet there are no clear psychosocial or biological models that offer clear explanations for their development. It has been proposed that conditioning mechanisms might be involved, whereby the inanimate object or some fantasy gets paired with sexual stimulation and arousal so that the person learns an erotic attachment to the object. However, some sexual preferences are subtle and some may only be carried out in fantasy, so there is still much to be learned (Lawrence, 2009).

Incentive Sexual Motivation Theory

Just as we develop tastes and preferences for certain foods and recreational activities, we seem to develop tastes and preferences for certain forms of sexual touch and activity based on how much pleasure they give us. These are generally believed to develop within a motivational system in which incentives form for us to seek certain ends. Motivation theory assumes that we make choices based on conscious awareness of things around us in conjunction with inner processes that have become more built-in by previous experiences, constituting the more unconscious aspects of our motivational processes. This distinction may help explain apparent differences in our subjective experience of sexual arousal (or nonarousal) and the genital reactions (or lack thereof) we may experience (Boul, Hallam-Jones, & Wylie, 2009; Toates, 2009).

Incentive motivation theory as applied to human sexuality holds that the strength of motivation toward some sexual activity depends on the strength of the stimulus. That stimulus could be an arousing thought or image in the mind or something that is being directly observed in the person's environment. These cognitive experiences act on the person's nervous system that has been sensitized over time by physiological factors such as hormones and nutrition. The person has learned that certain feelings and behaviors have pleasurable outcomes, meaning that the pleasure, reward, and emotion processing centers of the brain have been affected in ways that have produced pleasurable reactions. This in turn activates that neural circuitry that is tied both to motivational systems and the central nervous system to cause arousal, including the rerouting of blood to the sex organs. While there are many details of the nervous system that are still not well understood, this theoretical model helps to explain how the *incentive value* of particular sexual activities is acquired within us as the result of experience and learning (Boul, Hallam-Jones, & Wylie, 2009). The same process could be involved in the development of erotic location target errors as well.

Again puberty is considered to be a pivotal time for the early establishment of sexual incentive values (see Figure 14.2). Around this time of life, boys and girls are experiencing genital arousal that may or may not be associated with what we generally accept as sexual stimuli. They gradually develop associations

■ **FIGURE 14.2** *Asexuality*

Asexual people seem to have lower than average propensities for sexual excitation and arousal with a partner. Their levels of sexual interest in masturbation are more typical.

between their various experiences and the pleasurable sensations of sexual arousal or orgasm. This learning is reinforced over time through the mental imagery of fantasy. Eventually an actual incentive value becomes established in the individual: "This turns me on and feels good" (Toates, 2009).

The model can also help us understand how this imprinting process can be so variable among people. While there are certain similar patterns that are likely to occur among the majority of persons, they may not occur for everyone. Or it may happen that incentive values become attached to sexual stimuli that are considered inappropriate or deviant by the society, establishing the seeds of a paraphilia. There are limited data suggesting a genetic component that might influence these processes to an extent. It might be that the incentive motivations which become attached to particular sexual organs or activities are built on the template for sexual orientation established during prenatal development. For example, if the basic template for a particular male is same-sex oriented, that male might be more likely to develop positive incentives for male sex organs or activities with other males. If the basic template were heterosexual, he would be more likely to develop positive incentives for female breasts and activities with females.

Incentive motivation theory assumes that motivational incentive values are strengthened and maintained by the outcomes of the related experiences. If a pleasurable orgasm and positive emotions are experienced, the excitatory value of the incentive toward that particular experience is reinforced and made more powerful. Conversely, negative outcomes such as punishment may cause certain inhibitory mechanisms toward the behavior to be strengthened. The emotions, motivations, and actual sexual behaviors that emerge from this model are thought to be organized hierarchically, with higher-order cognitive processes coexisting with more primitive, lower-order processes and brain structures. It is known that the brain centers that mediate pleasure, reward, and emotions are directly involved in sexual motivational processes (Boul, Hallam-Jones, & Wylie, 2009; Toates, 2009).

It is worth noting that brand new sexual stimuli that come into people's awareness can trigger sexual motivation simply because of their novelty. They seem to increase activation of dopamine, a brain neurotransmitter known to be important to feelings of pleasure and reward in the brain. This may help explain why people sometimes are particularly turned on by pornography they've never seen before or swept off their feet by an attractive new person who enters their lives.

All in all, it seems that our motivation for particular sexual activities involves a complex interaction of direct, online stimuli that are physically present in the environment (e.g., a willing sexual partner) with indirect, offline factors such as memories, conscious intentions, and anticipated consequences (e.g., worry about pregnancy or STDs). Sexual motivation involves interaction of these stimulus-based and cognition-based influences. It is believed that women have more offline controls on their sexual choices and behaviors than men do, which may help to explain a variety of gender differences (Toates, 2009).

Gender Differences and Erotic Plasticity

When studying the motivations why men and women have sex, some interesting differences emerge. For both sexes, four sets of factors seem to be important. One revolves around *physical factors* such as pleasure, stress reduction, and the desirability of a partner. *Goal attainment* involves more utilitarian reasons such as gaining in social status or getting revenge, while *emotional reasons* focus on expressions of love and commitment. There are also motives revolving around personal *insecurity reasons* such as fulfilling a duty or boosting one's own self-esteem. Men and women are remarkably similar on measures of the majority of these factors, although men seem to be more focused on physical features of desirability and pleasures of orgasm, along with practical considerations such as having a willing partner available and gaining sexual experience. Women tend to have more emotional motivations for sex, including the desire to express and feel love (Meston & Buss, 2007).

Statistical evidence highlights another interesting gender difference in human sexuality: Men in general seem more prone to participating in atypical sexual activities and straying more from established societal norms and standards than do women. All available statistics on the frequency of various nonstandard forms of sexual orientation and behavior show them to be far more common in men than in women, if they exist in women at all. There may be some inborn biological propensities that cause male sexual behavior to exhibit greater diversity. It has been proposed that prenatal developmental differences make males more responsive than females to visual stimuli in learning sexual cues (Fisher et al., 2002; Lawrence, 2009). Men may establish images of erotic arousal in response to early life experiences at certain critical periods of development. Men do become more focused on images of potential sexual partners, while women seem less specific in their visual preferences (Lykins, Meana, & Strauss, 2008). If the visual image indeed plays a larger role in sexual arousal in males than in females, men would be far more easily influenced by diverse and variable kinds of visual learning than would women.

There is also evidence that sexuality can be situational and changeable and that people's sexual needs and behaviors may be modified by day-to-day life circumstances, a concept called *erotic plasticity*. Even with their participation in diverse sexual activities, men individually are more likely to stick to a rather narrow set of behaviors over time, while women exhibit more willingness individually to try a broader spectrum of behaviors (Diamond, 2006; Okami & Shackelford, 2002). Over time, men seem to be more rigid about maintaining a reasonably constant frequency of sexual outlets, or orgasms, while women can move between high and low outlet frequencies. Individual men tend to be more rigid than individual women with regard to the sexual activities they choose to participate in, even though men as a group have more diversity in sexual activities.

It has therefore been hypothesized that women actually have greater erotic plasticity than men. The explanation offered for this seemingly counterintuitive finding was that women have a less intense need for sex and are therefore more likely to tolerate variations of sexual behavior in order to maintain harmony and connection in their relationships with partners. This meant that women were more influenced than men by the circumstances surrounding their sexual encounters than they were by the type of sex involved (Baumeister, 2000; Diamond, 2006).

Cross-cultural studies demonstrate that cultures impose many guidelines for how people should feel and act about sex, and the theory that women have greater erotic plasticity also presumes that women's sexual attitudes and behaviors are more susceptible to being influenced by sociocultural factors. Subsequent research to test this presumption has cast doubt on previous ideas about erotic plasticity. Testing of 278 women and men of diverse backgrounds examined how adapting to a new majority culture, a process called acculturation, would affect sexual attitudes and behaviors. The study found that acculturation was not a significant factor in differing sexual attitudes and behaviors by gender. Women in the study showed more sexually conservative attitudes than men, and Asian Americans showed more conservatism than African Americans or Hispanics. Sexual liberalism did not seem to be affected by gender (Benuto & Meana, 2008).

Varying Degrees of Sexual Motivation

Different people have different degrees of interest in sex, pursue sexual activity with different amounts of energy, and participate in sex with varying degrees of frequency. Some people report thinking about sex and being interested in sexual matters several times each day, whereas others report that they seldom or never think about sex (Michael et al., 1994). Studies generally have confirmed that, on average, men's motivation for sex tends to be more constant than women's, and women seem to have more negative attitudes toward sexuality, although the level of sexual motivation varies a great deal among individuals. Women's motivation often waxes and wanes during the menstrual cycle, with the highest interest correlating to the time surrounding ovulation (Bullivant et al., 2004; Geer & Robertson, 2005; Okami & Shackelford, 2002). Some women have a more persistent level of interest and arousal (Blumberg, 2003). It is logical to conclude that the more interested a person is in sex, the more he or she becomes sexually aroused and seeks sexual gratification, and yet levels of sexual activity do not necessarily correlate with levels of sexual desire.

Consistently responding positively to sexual cues is called **erotophilia;** responding negatively is termed **erotophobia.** The degree to which any individual is erotophilic or erotophobic obviously depends on a great many factors, including learning during childhood and adolescence. Erotophilia–erotophobia affects many dimensions of a person's sexual response. Erotophobic individuals tend to react negatively to sexual images, to have little interest in sexual activities, to be less likely to use contraceptives during intercourse, and to experience more guilt about sexual behaviors and fantasies.

Some individuals possess a very high level of sexual desire or **hypersexuality,** whereas others have an abnormally low level of sexual interest, or **hyposexuality.** These might also be considered the extremes on the bipolar scale of erotophilia and erotophobia. Although some physical and emotional factors can cause a drop in sexual interest and activities, some people appear to have been fundamentally asexual throughout their lives. Most people, of course, tend to fall somewhere in the middle of the spectrum.

Define promiscuity as you perceive it, and then describe any social or personal biases that you might bring to your definition.

erotophilia (air-aht-oh-FEEL-i-ah) consistent positive responding to sexual cues.

erotophobia (air-aht-oh-FOBE-i-ah) consistent negative responding to sexual cues.

hypersexuality an unusually high level of interest in and drive for sex.

hyposexuality an especially low level of sexual interest and drive.

Promiscuity is a term that is applied to the behavior of those who have sexual contact with several different partners on a relatively emotionally uninvolved, casual basis. It is a morally loaded label that also has been applied to those who have had more than one sexual partner. Because of the double standard of our society, it is more often applied negatively to women than to men. Although promiscuous men often are praised and admired for their impressive records, promiscuous women often tend to suffer guilt, self-abasement, and social ostracism. It seems likely from clinical evidence that some people simply enjoy sex with a variety of partners, perhaps for a limited period during their lives, and prefer to avoid emotional involvement for various reasons. If the individual approaches these encounters in a responsible, nonexploitative manner, takes appropriate steps to reduce the risks of transmitting disease, and emerges from them without negative feelings or inner conflict, there is no particular reason to judge the behavior as problematic (Blumberg, 2003).

Celibacy and Asexuality

Celibacy, or not engaging in any kind of partnered sex, can be the result of life circumstances, such as imprisonment or the loss of a partner; it may represent normal **asexuality,** characterized by a low interest in sex; or it may be a conscious choice (Abbott, 2001). Erotophobic individuals may be celibate out of guilt or fear about sexual issues. Some priests and nuns vow to be celibate because their church requires it. Other people make such a choice because of their personal values. The recent child abuse scandal within the Roman Catholic Church has obscured the fact that many priests struggle with celibacy because of their heterosexual desires, with many eventually leaving to marry (Goodstein, 2010).

An increasing number of young to middle-aged adults are choosing to be celibate. Some of these individuals are reacting to having tried various sexual lifestyles and finding them unfulfilling or destructive, others are looking for alternatives to the pressures brought about by the sexual revolution. They sometimes have found that the intensity of sex created tension in their relationships (Sobo & Bell, 2001). Many people who report being celibate would rather not be but are unable to establish relationships or are part of a sexless relationship (Donnelly et al., 2001). People who are HIV-positive may become celibate in their later years, partly because they do not want to risk infecting others, but also because they harbor anger or mistrust (Siegel & Schrimshaw, 2003).

The National Health and Social Life Survey (NHSLS) found that 4 percent of men and 14 percent of women reported rarely or never thinking about sex. Fourteen percent of the men and 10 percent of the women in

■ **FIGURE 14.3** *Transvestism*

Those who dress in clothes of the opposite sex seem to derive sexual pleasure from doing so. Anthropologist Robert Monroe has noted that transvestism occurs more frequently in cultures in which the male assumes more of the economic burden than does the female.

the survey reported that they had not had a sexual partner in the previous year (Laumann et al., 1994). In a study of over 18,000 people, 1 percent indicated that they were asexual, and this response was correlated with a later onset of menarche in women, strong religious beliefs, low levels of education and socioeconomic status, and poor health (Bogaert, 2004).

A conceptual model that defines *asexuality* more completely has gradually been taking shape. People who describe themselves as asexual seem to have lower levels of *dyadic* sexual desire, meaning the desire to have sex with a partner. They also have a lower propensity for sexual excitation and sexual arousability. They show no significant differences from nonasexuals in their propensity for sexual inhibition or their desire to masturbate, so they might best be characterized as having less interest in shared sex with a partner. We might expect that asexual individuals would have lower levels of behavioral excitation in general, along with their lack of sexual excitation, but so far these two variables have not seemed to correlate positively (see Figure 14.3).

Asexual people cite many benefits and disadvantages of their low sexual interests, but they also worry

promiscuity (prah-mis-KIU-i-tee) sharing casual sexual activity with many different partners.

celibacy (SELL-a-buh-see) choosing not to share sexual activity with others.

asexuality a condition characterized by a low interest in sex.

that there might be something wrong with them, perhaps because of the cultural surroundings that put so much emphasis on sexuality. Interestingly, the actual levels of sexual interaction among asexual people are not that much lower than those of nonasexuals, suggesting that they may sometimes engage in unwanted sexual activities to maintain a relationship with a partner. It has been hypothesized that asexual individuals have a higher threshold for sexual excitation, meaning that they simply do not get turned-on as easily as others (Prause & Graham, 2007).

Compulsive Hypersexuality

On the hypersexual end of the sexual interest continuum, having multiple sex partners may be motivated by unhealthy factors. These include unsatisfactory personal relationships, antagonism toward members of the opposite sex, and lack of self-respect. Some individuals may feel a need to prove themselves—for example, men who must live up to the macho ideal of having a long list of sexual conquests and women who use sex to experience a sense of power or control. A high level of sexual activity may become compulsive in some people. Compulsive sexual behavior sometimes is a response to some stressful situation, such as separation from parents upon entering college, the onset of early menopause, the experience of a significant loss, or some other traumatic event. There is evidence that among college students sexual compulsivity is associated with high-risk sexual behaviors (Dodge et al., 2004).

The more compulsive form of hypersexuality, purportedly characterized by uncontrollable sexual drives as part of various mental illnesses, is known as **erotomania.** This condition has sometimes been called **nymphomania** in females and **satyriasis** in males. The double standard seems to generate a far greater interest in women's hypersexual needs than in men's. Nymphomaniac often is used rather lightly and applied mistakenly to women who show any level of interest in sex. Yet nymphomania actually is difficult to define and has fallen victim to a great deal of interpretation rooted in prejudice, double standards, and male chauvinism (Groneman, 2000). The term is so vague and outmoded that it should be dropped altogether.

Erotomania and other conditions of uncontrollable sexual desire (discussed further in Chapter 16) are rare; erotomania most often is probably a misdiagnosed form of compulsive sexual behavior (Montaldi, 2002). Very few people seek help for excessive sexual desire, and it has been suggested that definitions of excessive are based largely in unscientific moralism and should not be construed as problematic (Giles, 2006). High rates of sexual behavior do tend to be correlated with unstable childhoods, relational instability, poor management of sexual risks, and use of tobacco, alcohol, and other drugs (Langstrom & Hanson, 2006; Strong et al., 2005).

■ Transgender Behaviors

Chapter 5 discussed theories concerning the development of gender identity and gender role and introduced transgender identities. This section presents some sexual interests that are closely related to, and sometimes confused with, transgender roles. We are beginning to understand that these sexual behaviors are more complex than once believed.

Before reading the section on transvestism, describe what you would consider a typical transvestite.

Cross-Dressing: Transvestism

In the broadest sense, the term *transvestite* has been applied to anyone who cross-dresses, or wears clothes of the opposite sex, for any reason. It also has been applied to individuals who feel driven to cross-dress, sometimes in association with sexual arousal. Many cross-dressers gain a greater sense of relaxation in escaping their usual gender roles. Cross-dressing is found among heterosexual people, but also in people with a same-gender sexual orientation, bisexuals, and people with low levels of any sexual attraction or desire. Together these represent a very diverse group. Cross-dressed males sometimes are said to be "in drag."

The term *transvestic **fetishism*** is also used to describe sexual attraction to some object of clothing usually worn by the opposite sex, possible examples of ETLEs. For example, a straight male may become sexually aroused by viewing and touching various objects of women's underwear. Gay men can develop similar fetishistic sexual attachments to men's undergarments such as jockstraps, but clearly this would not be cross-dressing. Men with such attractions may find it even more exciting to actually wear the garments,

erotomania (air-aht-oh-MAY-nee-ah) a very rare form of mental illness characterized by a highly compulsive need for sex.

nymphomania (nim-fa-MAY-nee-ah) a term sometimes used to describe erotomania in women.

satyriasis (sate-a-RYE-a-sus) a term sometimes used to describe erotomania in men.

fetishism (FEH-tish-i-zum) sexual arousal triggered by objects or materials not usually considered sexual.

Table 14.1	Prevalence in Men of Sexual Cross-Dressing, Cross-Gender Fantasy, and Arousal to Images of Cross-Dressing from 12 Study Populations.

Sexual Behavior, Fantasy, Arousal Population	Prevalence (%)	Study Population
Ever experienced sexual arousal with cross-dressing	2.8	Swedish national probability sample
Often fantasize of feeling like opposite gender	4.0	French national probability sample
Often fantasize of feeling like opposite gender	13.0	French national probability sample, age 18–19
Ever dressed in clothes of opposite gender	5.7	U.S. college students
Ever fantasize being of opposite gender	18.5	U.S. college students
Ever engage in cross-dressing	6.0	U.S. unpaid volunteers
Erectile responses to photos of transvestism	3.0	U.S. paid volunteers
Cross-dressed in past 3 months	1.0	U.S. college students
Fantasized being of opposite gender past 3 months	13.0	U.S. college students
Ever sexually aroused by cross-dressing	10.9	New Zealand medical students
Frequent fantasies of acts of transvestism	2.0	U.K. unpaid volunteers
Ever fantasized being cross-dressed	8.6	U.S. paid volunteers

Source: Adapted from A. A. Lawrence. (2009). "Erotic Target Location Errors: An Underappreciated Paraphilic Dimension." *Journal of Sex Research, vol. 46, no. 2–3,* 194–215, Table 2 (p. 198), reprinted by permission of the publisher (Taylor & Francis Group, http://www.informaworld.com).

usually as an accompaniment to masturbation or other sexual activity. In one study of 2,450 people drawn from a general population of Swedish adults ages 18 to 60, 2.8 percent of the males and 0.4 percent of the females reported at least one instance of cross-dressing

"No! No! No! . . . *You* Tarzan, *me* Jane!"

associated with sexual arousal (Langstrom & Zucker, 2005). Table 14.1 shows the prevalence of cross-dressing and cross-dressing fantasies or arousal as found in a dozen different studies.

The heterosexual male transvestite may become aroused by dressing completely in women's attire and makeup and adopting feminine mannerisms (see Figure 14.3). Sometimes there is only minimal sexual arousal associated with the activity, or the sexual arousal may eventually fade. Individuals often continue to cross-dress because it makes them feel more relaxed and emotionally open.

Transvestism usually begins in childhood and becomes well established by adolescence. In various samples of adult transvestite men, 20 to 50 percent began cross-dressing before age 7, and nearly all reported cross-dressing prior to age 13. There is anecdotal evidence that transvestites may fantasize about being women, although they do not seem particularly motivated to pursue such a course of action (Lawrence, 2009). Although the evidence suggests that cross-dressing is almost exclusively found in males, there are case studies of women who have an erotic attachment to men's garments. At least in the limited number of female examples available, the drive toward cross-dressing seems less demanding than it typically is in male transvestites.

Some male transvestites participate in an underground subculture. There are organizations and magazines designed for men who drawn to wearing women's clothing.

Real People

Vincent: Living a Transgender Identity

Vincent was a college student who considered himself transgendered and resented having to be categorized as one sex or the other. He knew that anatomically he was fully male, and he had no intention of changing that. In fact, he said that he was very satisfied with his male body most of the time.

However, Vincent said that since he was quite young, he had come to value what he called his "feminine side." To him, this was made up of the soft, gentle, and sensitive aspects of his personality that felt very comfortable to him. He felt that the masculine and feminine sides that he experienced seemed quite distinct. He sometimes preferred to dress in women's clothes and use a female name. He tried to do this as discreetly as possible, but others on his dorm floor may once have noticed some women's clothes in his closet. Although he was not anxious to incur the wrath of anyone who might consider him somehow odd, he also seemed to have

a rather strong resolve not to hide his transgenderism with undue vigor. As he put it, "It's time for people to wake up to the fact that not everybody fits the same mold."

Vincent remained at the college and would occasionally surprise or shock people by wearing some article of female attire in a public setting. Some people on the campus openly expressed their distaste for these practices, feeling that he was being too flagrant in his propensities. He occasionally heard himself being called names, but he persisted in what he felt were valid educational efforts. He also made many friends and was an active participant in campus activities.

What is your reaction to Vincent's story? How would you have reacted if you lived on his dormitory floor? Would you have been shocked or disturbed by his cross-dressing? Would you be willing to be his friend?

Occasional regional gatherings are held for such individuals, with meetings on fashion and makeup techniques. The majority of the participants are heterosexuals, although there may be a higher proportion of gay and bisexual transvestites than has generally been believed. A study of 1,032 male cross-dressers found that 87 percent described themselves as heterosexual. All but 17 percent had been married, and 60 percent were married at the time of the study. Some hide their transvestism from their wives and cross-dress away from home; others inform their wives of the practice. The limited clinical evidence available indicates that some wives are able to accept their husbands' cross-dressing behaviors and integrate them into their lives (Monro & Warren, 2004; Rupp & Taylor, 2003).

There have been ongoing studies of boys ranging in age from 4 years through adolescence who have shown a preference for dressing in girls' clothing. When denied access to such garments, these boys even will fashion their own dresses from blankets, T-shirts, and other materials (Bailey, 2003). They also have tended to assume female roles during play and to exhibit distinctly feminine mannerisms. It is as yet impossible to predict which of these behaviors represent simple play activity and which are expressions of transgenderism.

Beyond Cross-Dressing: Autogynephilia

There is a particular type of transgender male that has come to the attention of researchers. Most typically, these are individuals who have had a relatively typical masculine childhood and were primarily heterosexual in terms of sexual attraction. In late childhood or adolescence they may have found themselves to be sexually aroused by women's undergarments or other clothing, resulting in trying on such garments (or fantasizing about them) and masturbating. (Being aroused by girls' undergarments is not unusual among boys.) For these men, the thoughts and images become quite strong, even obsessive, and they may fantasize frequently about being a woman, having a woman's body, or having a woman's sexual organs. This tendency is called **autogynephilia** (Blanchard, 1991, 2005).

While autogynephilia develops in association with heterosexual attraction and arousal and alongside typical

autogynephilia (otto-guy-nuh-FEEL-ee-ah) a tendency found in some males to become sexually aroused by obsessive thoughts and images of being female and having female attributes, or even female sex organs.

masculine interests, the obsession with being a woman may eventually begin to compete with heterosexual attraction and desire. The sexual arousal accompanying the cross-dressing and fantasy may diminish and even compete with fantasies and desires about having sex as a woman and being sexually penetrated by a man. In this way, autogynephiles may become transsexuals and may want to go even further by actually changing their bodies to be consistent with their sexual fantasies and desires (Bailey, 2003).

An understanding of autogynephilia helps clarify why among males there are gay transsexuals, or men who have long felt trapped in the body of the wrong sex and who are sexually attracted to men, and also autogynephilic transsexuals, whose interest in becoming women grew out of strong sexual attractions toward women and then became internalized as a desire to become women themselves. Some people remain in their cross-dressed roles for days or even months at a time, depending on their life situation, often becoming comfortable with sustaining this identity. Transgendered individuals also may maintain separate lives more consistent with their anatomical gender for varying periods of time (Lawrence, 2009).

■ Common Erotic Targets That Trigger Sexual Excitation

Erotic target location theory posits that through neural mechanisms not yet thoroughly understood, human beings develop attractions to particular people, body parts, things associated with sex, and sexual activities. These stimuli become part of the individual's built-in sexual excitatory mechanisms. Often these erotic targets are considered to be conventional and generally morally unproblematic. Other times the targets are more unconventional and may be considered morally problematic and/or socially unacceptable. This section deals with the more common and less problematic of sexual attractions and activities. It is worth noting that the erotic attractions which lie outside the most widely accepted sexual practices tend to be found far more frequently in males than they are in females. Therefore much of the research has focused on men (Lawrence, 2009).

Human beings whose personalities are on the erotophilic side of the spectrum may spend time and energy perfecting and enhancing their sexual experiences. Just as some people become good cooks and connoisseurs of great food, so do some people take pride in learning the sexual techniques that will provide optimal levels of enjoyment and satisfaction for them and their partners. As people discover the very individual-ized triggers and enhancers for their own sexual arousal, they may find new levels of sexual pleasure.

Use of Erotica and Pornography

The distribution and sale of sexually explicit media—magazines, DVDs, and material accessed via the Internet—represent a multibillion-dollar-a-year business. Such materials are often sexually excitatory, again especially for males. Access to online pornography for purposes of sexual excitation has become one of the more common erotic targets. While women sometimes have negative reactions to their male partners' viewing of erotic materials, this does not seem to be representative of women in general. In fact, women on average seem to be relatively neutral or even mildly positive with regard to pornography viewing by their intimate partners (Bridges, Bergner, & Hesson-McInnis, 2003). There is also evidence that, at least in males, continued exposure to the same pornographic material results in habituation, meaning that sexual excitation in response to the same material decreases over time. Therefore, one reason why erotica and pornography are such strong businesses is that customers continually seek new material to view (Attwood, 2005). Sexually explicit media continue to be extremely controversial, as we will explore further in Chapter 15.

Sexual Devices and Toys

Although sexual-enhancement toys are nothing new, their availability to the general public and their acceptability have been increasing. Sex shops, catalogs, and Internet sites sell a variety of devices designed to heighten sexual arousal and pleasure. The devices vary in their effectiveness, and each has advocates who have found that it satisfies their tastes and needs. Most individuals who give sex toys a try use them only occasionally or as an experiment. A few people come to rely on them as constant aids to sexual satisfaction.

Vibrators probably are the most common sexual aid, providing an intense vibration to the genitals or other sensitive body parts. There are battery-operated and plug-in models. Some are cylindrical or penis-shaped, in a variety of lengths and widths. Others come with several attachments to be used for stimulating different sex organs. Vibrators sometimes are recommended for people who have trouble reaching orgasm, especially women. The rapid, localized vibration is often helpful in triggering the orgasmic reflex. Vibrators can be used for masturbation or integrated into shared activities.

Cylindrical dildos, made of everything from ivory to clay, have existed for at least 2,500 years. Today they usually are made of soft, flexible plastics. Although they may be used for solitary masturbation, with vaginal or

Real Student Voices

■ Sometimes I can't believe the sexual stuff some of my friends are involved in. Maybe it interests them, but it turns me off completely.

■ I had a girlfriend who was really into BDSM. I found it arousing to allow her to take charge sometimes, but I wasn't interested in going too far with

the whole thing. There is something exciting about letting a partner take control over you.

■ I'm not going to reveal my fetish in writing, but I will tell you that it has been a relief to realize that I'm not as weird as I thought I was!

---

anal insertion, dildos are also used in some partnership sex. Plastic penis extenders are designed to fit over the head of a man's penis, supposedly to make it seem longer during sex. Actually, such devices rarely yield much extra pleasure for either partner and may even reduce sexual sensations for the man. A survey of 7,700 people ages 18 to 90 found that 10.2 percent said they had used sex toys with a partner, although it is believed that even more people tend to use such devices during masturbation. Sex toy use was most common among persons ages 30 to 49 (Catania, 1997).

Some men enjoy wearing various bondage or pressure devices, including metal, leather, or rubber rings that fit around the base of the penis and scrotum. Although these "cock rings" are advertised as being helpful in maintaining erection, there is no particular evidence that they do so, and, in fact, if they are too tight they can cause some damage. A variation on this is the clitoral or French tickler, worn at the base of the penis and having projections on the top surface. The projections are supposed to press on the female's clitoris during vaginal intercourse, providing extra stimulation.

Sexual Fantasy

The NHSLS found that 19 percent of women and 54 percent of men fantasize about sex at least once a day (Laumann et al., 1994). Mental images, daydreams, and fantasies seem to be a significant part of most people's sexual individuality. Such imagery may be fleeting and incomplete or lengthy and detailed. Sexual fantasy is not necessarily representative of a person's sexual preferences or behaviors. For example, most men who fantasize about forcing a partner to have sex with them would never carry out such an action. Studies indicate that human beings fantasize about many sexual practices in which they would never actually participate in real life and sometimes experience these fantasies negatively. Fantasies may also reflect areas of sexual long-

ing and frustration in a person's life (Byers, Purdon, & Clark, 1998).

Studies find some gender differences in the typical fantasy lives of males and females. Sexual fantasies tend to begin between the ages of 11 and 13, with males usually having their first fantasies at earlier ages than females and feeling more positive and guilt-free about them (Byers, Purdon, & Clark, 1998; Hicks & Leitenberg, 2001). Men's fantasies tend to be more active, impersonal, and visually oriented, whereas women's fantasy themes generally are more passive and romantic. Women who have fantasies of forced sex tend to be more erotophilic, interested in a range of sexual activities, and more sexually experienced (Sierra, Ortega, & Zubeidat, 2006).

Sexual fantasies have been categorized into four main groups: *exploratory*, including themes such as group sex, mate swapping, and same-gender behavior; *intimate*, with themes of passionate kissing, oral sex, making love outdoors, and mutual masturbation; *impersonal*, including sex with strangers, looking at pornography, watching others engage in sex, and fetishism; and *sadomasochistic*, with themes such as whipping, spanking, and forceful sex. Men tend to have more fantasies in all four of these categories, but the greatest proportion for both sexes is in the intimate category. The most common sexual fantasies involve having sex with a past, new, or imaginary partner or having sex in various settings and positions. The fewest number of fantasies among both men and women reflect impersonal or sadomasochistic themes (Hicks & Leitenberg, 2001; Sierra, Ortega, & Zubeidat, 2006).

Women sometimes have rape fantasies, and in one study 62 percent of college women in the study had experienced such a fantasy. The median frequency of rape fantasies for this group was four times per year, with 14 percent reporting them at least weekly. Their emotional experience of the rape fanta-

Real People

Craig: A Harmless Fetish Worries a Young Groom

Following a class in human sexuality, a male graduate student named Craig asked to speak with me in private to talk about a personal sexual concern. In my office, he nervously described his plans for marriage in two months and said that there was an aspect of his sexuality that bothered him. He went on to explain that he became sexually aroused by touching soft blankets and often enjoyed lying on a blanket during masturbation or intercourse. He was also quite certain that his partiality to blankets resulted from his earliest masturbatory experiences, in which he would rub his penis against a blanket.

I told Craig that the fetish did not seem particularly troublesome, and some further questioning elicited other important facts about his preference. Basically he had very open and positive attitudes toward his sexuality and felt concern only about his mild blanket fetish. Of special importance was the fact that he did not feel compelled or driven to become sexually aroused by blankets, instead employing them only when convenient. His fiancée not only had been told about his inclinations but found the situation humorous. She had assured Craig that she would be happy to cooperate in the use of blankets in their sexual experiences whenever he wished. They were both highly satisfied with their present sexual relationship. On the basis of this information, it was concluded that if Craig could come to accept his blanket fetish as a desirable, harmless part of his sexual responsiveness, there was no reason to see it as a problem or a sign of sexual disturbance. Before leaving the counseling session, he sighed with great relief and said that he felt confident he could feel very positively about the fetish as long as he did not have to view it as sick or abnormal.

What is your opinion about Craig's interest in soft blankets? Instead of reassuring him, should I have discouraged the fetish and encouraged him to stop using it? What do you think of this outcome?

I was invited to Craig's wedding, and as a wedding gift I gave the couple a king-size soft blanket. They seemed appreciative. What do you think about this gift?

---

sies existed on a continuum between being aversive (negative) and erotic, with 9 percent reporting that they were completely aversive, 45 percent entirely erotic, and another 46 percent a combination of both reactions (Bivona & Critelli, 2009).

The kinds of sexual fantasies people experience—their length and degree of explicitness—seem to be determined to a large degree by the amount of guilt they feel about sex. As might be expected, the less guilt people experience and the more liberal their attitudes about sex, the longer and more explicit their fantasies tend to be. In general, sexual fantasies do not seem to be indications of an inactive sex life or dissatisfaction with sex. Fantasies occur more often in people who have high rates of sexual activity and are relatively happy with their sexual lives. Sexual fantasies do sometimes produce guilt or other unpleasant reactions (Binova & Critelli, 2009; Byers, Purdon, & Clark, 1998).

Why do you think sexual fantasies occur more often in people who have high rates of sexual activity and are relatively happy with their sex lives?

Fetishism

As we've already seen, fetishism is usually defined as finding sexual excitement in objects, articles of clothing, or the textures of particular materials not usually considered to be sex-related in themselves. Sometimes parts of the body not usually considered sexually arousing are included in the definition. There are many degrees of fetishism, ranging from those mild preferences that accompany most sexual relations to an intense drive and complete substitution of the fetish for any other form of sexual gratification.

Certain things are commonly held as fetishes, including underwear, soft and silky clothing, rubber, vinyl, and leather. Women's breasts can have an almost fetishistic attachment for some men, but this attraction has become so accepted that it is not considered a fetish. A study of Internet discussion groups that were believed to represent some 5,000 people, the prevalence of various fetishes was studied. Preferences for specific body parts or objects associated with the body were the most common, at 33 and 30 percent respectively. People in these categories were particularly

■ **FIGURE 14.4** *Sex for More Than Two*

People sometimes experiment with sexual activity involving more than two persons. A three-person sexual interaction is sometimes called ménage à trois. The relational dynamics of such arrangements can get complicated.

interested in feet, underwear, and footwear. Other popular fetishes were other people's behaviors (18 percent), social behavior (7 percent) and objects unrelated to the body (5 percent) (Scorolli et al., 2007). Use of the fetish during masturbation is most typical; in this case, the object is fondled, rubbed on the genitals, viewed, or used for direct stimulation of sex organs. Some males ejaculate in or on the object. Fetishes sometimes are integrated into shared activities, but this may create some emotional discomfort for the fetishist's partner (Lawrence, 2009).

Most fetishes are harmless and inoffensive to others. However, they sometimes are carried to unconventional extremes that have negative outcomes for others. It is not uncommon to read newspaper accounts of an adolescent male who has entered someone's home to touch the feet of a sleeping girl or to steal some of her undergarments. True **kleptomania,** which involves sexual excitement when stealing, and **pyromania,** in which the individual derives sexual arousal from setting fires, are considered to be paraphilic forms of fetishism.

Varying the Numbers

Partly because of social standards that place sex within the context of an intimate and romantic one-to-one relationship, sex for more than two has generally been considered unconventional in Western culture (see Figure 14.4). In other cultures, large orgies are sometimes a part of rites or religious ceremonies. In our culture, sex among more than two people more typi-

cally involves experimentation that develops unplanned out of some other social activity. It may be seen as an exciting alternative to the usual activities. Of the people interviewed in the NHSLS, 1 percent of the women and 13 percent of the men indicated that they found the idea of group sex very appealing, although they had not necessarily participated in it (Laumann et al., 1994).

Group sex can apply to a variety of situations, ranging from threesomes **(troilism** or **ménage à trois)** to large groups. Among college students surveyed in one study, 13 percent of the men and 10 percent of the women reported having participated in a sexual threesome (Elliott & Brantley, 1997). The activity may involve one or more persons simply observing a couple engaging in sex or actual physical interaction among all present. Probably the most common form of group sex occurs when more than one couple engage in sexual activity but each couple remains separate from the other(s). A group in which everyone participates with

---

kleptomania extreme form of fetishism in which sexual arousal is generated by stealing.

pyromania sexual arousal generated by setting fires.

troilism (TROY-i-liz-um) sexual activity shared by three people.

ménage à trois (may-NAZH-ah-TRWAH) another name for troilism.

one another may be called an **orgy,** although this term is somewhat outmoded and used mostly as a joke. The incidence of such behavior is uncertain. Available evidence suggests that it is usually not a continuing form of sexual behavior and instead represents an occasional or one-time experience.

■ Atypical and Potentially Problematic Erotic Targets

Even though human beings do not seem to choose which erotic targets become sexually exciting for them, they may suffer social consequences if they act on sexual proclivities that are considered to be morally and socially unacceptable. Sexual practices that fall outside societal norms are often considered to be *paraphilias*, or at the very least atypical. In some cases, they may become problematic because of their potential consequences for the individual participant or for others who may be affected by the behavior. This section deals with some of those sexual targets.

The Sex Worker Industry

Like anything that can provide people with pleasure, sex has in some situations become a commodity. Both male and female sex workers, known more pejoratively as prostitutes, participate in sexual activity for money. Often called the world's oldest profession, prostitution has been explained by some observers as representing the only way some women in a male-dominated world have been able to survive (Parsons, 2005). Prostitution has met with varying degrees of tolerance throughout history and in different societies. A prevalent attitude has been that prostitution represents exploitation and victimization, primarily of women. However, a countering set of opinions suggests that sex workers should have a right to make their living in this manner free from harassment or interference by various authorities (Vanwesenbeeck, 2002).

In Canada, exchanging money for sex is not illegal, although many of the actions associated with procuring sex are against the law. Windsor, Ontario, a Canadian city that borders Detroit, Michigan, has been able to manage commercial sex workers in ways that prevent their victimization and keep them from being isolated in any sort of red light district. The city has at the same time been able to maintain its image as a family-oriented and safe city (Lewis et al., 2005; Maticka-Tyndale, Lewis, & Street, 2005).

Male sex workers who serve women were once known as gigolos and, more recently, as escorts. However, escorts sometimes are just that—companions for some social event. Almost no empirical data have been gathered on gigolos or male companions. More typically, male sex workers engage in sexual activity with other males. Some young male prostitutes consider themselves heterosexual and view their same-gender involvement purely as a business venture. The longer they are sex workers, however, the more likely they are to think of themselves—and be identified by their peers—as gay.

Male sex workers who serve men are generally studied in two groups: those who work "indoors" for escort agencies that book them for jobs, and those who work "on the street," finding their own clients. Male street sex workers have been called *hustlers*. Indoor male sex workers seem to be concerned about maintaining safe sex practices as well as other positive workplace conditions for themselves and their clients. Street-based male sex workers tend to have high levels of homelessness, drug use, and contact with the police, and are also more likely to participate in high risk sexual activities (Disogra, Marino, & Minichiello, 2005; Smith & Seal 2008; Ross et al., 2007).

Male sex workers usually are typically expected to have an orgasm during a paid sexual encounter. Given the realities of male sexual response, particularly the refractory period, this limits the numbers of clients a male can serve in one day. Female sex workers, in contrast, are not limited by this physiology and typically do not experience orgasm in their paid encounters. The most commonly requested behavior from female sex workers is fellatio, and the next most common is vaginal intercourse. Both are intended more for the male partner's orgasm than the sex worker's.

Men seem to seek out prostitutes either out of a need for intimacy or out of a desire for more variety in their sex activities (Monto, 2001; Xantidis & McCabe, 2000). A study of 612 men in Australia found that 23.4 percent of them had paid for sex at least once and that the sex-worker clients were more likely than the nonclients to be older, less likely to have an education beyond high school, and less likely to have had a regular sexual partner during the previous six months other than a casual partner. They indicated that the main reasons they had paid for sex were to satisfy sexual needs, the fact that it was easier and less complicated to pay for the encounter, and the fact that it was entertaining (Pitts et al., 2004).

Studies of female street sex workers have found that many of them do, in fact, enjoy intercourse and oral sex with their customers and also enjoy sex with their boyfriends or husbands as well. Neither the image of sex workers as "happy hookers" nor their depiction as depressed victims of childhood sexual abuse seems particularly accurate. Although a substantial

orgy (OR-jee) group sex.

FIGURE 14.5   *Streetwise*

Young girls are particularly vulnerable to becoming prostitutes if they have a poor self-image, have run away from home, have friends who are already prostitutes, or are seeking an adult to care for them.

number of sex workers have a history of drug abuse, and some are clinically depressed, most have voluntarily chosen their work (Chudakov et al., 2002; Morrison & Whitehead, 2005). In interviews of female sex workers who were mothers, it was clear that they faced special problems as parents that often were unaddressed by social agencies (Sloss & Harper, 2004).

The most common street name given to female sex workers is **hookers.** Although **brothels,** or houses of prostitution, can still be found, they have largely been replaced by streetwalkers who work for pimps and by massage parlor workers (see Figure 14.5). Much of the sexual servicing of clients now takes place indoors rather than in more public venues (Thukral, 2005). Call girls tend to be more highly paid prostitutes who cater to a more exclusive clientele.

There is controversy over whether the sex worker industry actually constitutes a victimless line of business. Research continues to demonstrate that many sex workers have a background of alcohol and drug abuse and of sexual and physical abuse that presumably played a role in leading them to prostitution. Sex work also can be a dangerous job in which women and men may be raped, beaten, robbed, or forced to perform various sexual acts against their will. Another serious concern is the spread of HIV or other sexually transmitted diseases through prostitution (Reback et al., 2005; Surratt et al., 2005).

Male clients of female sex workers typically prefer not to wear a condom and, in fact, may pay extra to avoid doing so. The sex workers themselves may also prefer not to bother with condoms or may be uninformed about their importance, but client resistance to condom use may also be a problem (Bucardo et al., 2004; Jackson et al., 2005; Shannon et al., 2009). Although absolute safety cannot be guaranteed for the prostitute or the client, anyone seeking sex with a sex worker should insist on proper protection.

Worldwide, there is growing concern about girls and women being tricked or sold into sex-trade trafficking. They often are promised the hope of a better life, only to be smuggled into other countries to work as prostitutes and forced to give the money they earn to their "owners." Increasing pressure is being put on nations to enact legislation prohibiting human trafficking and to punish offenders. Sex-trade trafficking has been particularly problematic in Europe and Asia, where laws governing such matters are extremely diverse. When one country passes tough legislation, traffickers may find it easy to move their sex slaves to a neighboring country.

Close Encounters

There are several forms of sexual excitation that involve contact with a typically unknown and often unwilling participant. The unknowing person who is sought out for such a sexual connection may be a victim to the degree that she or he has participated unwillingly in someone else's sexual arousal. The degree of victimization may range from feeling some petty annoyance to being seriously traumatized by the experience.

Obscene Telephone Calls

Men who have strong feelings of insecurity and inadequacy may engage in obscene telephone calls, sometimes called *telephone scatologia.* Their phone calls to women, or occasionally other men, represent a way to anonymously assert their sexuality without having to face a frightening social contact. Because their calls are usually spiced with sexual obscenities designed to shock or surprise women particularly, the behavior may also reflect some negative attitudes toward women. Sometimes such calls merely represent a prank, but they also may become a continuing form of sexual release, often accompanied by masturbation. It is very rare for an obscene telephone caller to follow up the call with any sort of actual contact with the victim. The best way to react to such a call is to hang up immediately, without comment, and then use call-tracing methods while reporting the call to the telephone company or law enforcement.

hookers street name for female prostitutes.

brothels houses of prostitution.

FIGURE 14.6 *Consensual Telephone Sex*

Dial-for-sex services allow callers to reach women or men who will talk in a sexually provocative manner. Because of concerns about the easy access of minors to "dial-a-porn," some telephone companies have imposed stricter controls to prevent calls from minors.

Consensual Telephone Sex

Another form of sexual encounter is represented by the telephone numbers people can call to reach a sex worker willing to converse in a sexually provocative way over the phone (see Figure 14.6). Most callers to dial-for-sex services apparently are men who typically masturbate during their phone call. In a survey of college students, 13 percent of the men and 7 percent of the women said they had used phone-sex lines (Elliott & Brantley, 1997). There is very little research on telephone sex at this point, but it may well represent a relatively harmless, and certainly safe, form of sexual encounter.

See "Sharon: Phone Sex" on SexSource Online.

Internet Contact

The Internet has also provided ways for people to carry on sexually suggestive or explicit communications with relative anonymity. Match-up websites allow people to post photographs and personal information, some of which is sexually oriented. A great deal of media attention has been paid to the use of such sites by adult sexual predators who attempt to connect with adolescents for sexual purposes. Chat lines are preferred by women over the more explicit erotic sites (Cooper, 2000). For a small proportion of regular chat line visitors, the behavior becomes compulsive and is associated with difficulties within their personal relationships. Many Internet users find it a relatively quick way to make contact with potential partners for dating or sex and may exchange phone numbers for future contact (Carvalheira & Gomes, 2003).

Frotteurism and Toucherism

Frotteurism is a term that applies to gaining sexual enjoyment from pressing or rubbing one's genitals against another, unknown person in some anonymous setting. Crowded places such as elevators, subways, or theaters are common locations in which the **frotteur** may operate, because the close contact usually will go unnoticed. **Toucherism** refers to the intimate touching of an unknown person's body, typically on the buttocks or breasts. It is sometimes considered a subcategory of frotteurism. There has been little study of frotteurism or toucherism, but professionals again assume that these behaviors represent a way for insecure people to seek out minimal physical contact with someone who is sexually appealing to them. The act probably is often followed by masturbation in private.

Exhibitionism

Exposing the genitals to someone else for sexual pleasure is called **exhibitionism.** Usually, the person who commits this act is a man who exposes his penis to children or to an adult woman, although women sometimes gain sexual pleasure from exposing their breasts. The exhibitionist may go to great pains to make it seem as though he was caught undressing or urinating so that the victim will be less prone to report it as a crime. People who are arrested for such behavior are charged with indecent exposure or public lewdness. The repeat male exhibitionist usually gains pleasure from shocking others with the sight of his

frotteurism (frah-TOUR-izm) gaining sexual gratification from anonymously pressing or rubbing one's genitals against others, usually in crowded settings.

frotteur one who practices frotteurism.

toucherism gaining sexual gratification from the touching of an unknown person's body, such as on the buttocks or breasts.

exhibitionism exposing the genitals to others for sexual pleasure.

penis, thereby gaining some sort of confirmation of his male power.

What might motivate a man to expose his penis to others? A woman to expose her breasts?

It is apparent that many people display some degree of exhibitionism in their attempts to appear and feel sexy. Bikinis for women and men, see-through clothing, and tight trousers and blouses all attest to this fact. Some women add extra padding to their bras to emphasize their breasts, and some males admit to adding padding to their genital areas. These are subtle forms of exhibitionism. Nudity may be a form of exhibitionism, although it may have few, if any, sexual connotations. People shower together in gym locker rooms, and at least some of them report feeling enjoyment in being nude together with other people. There seem to be few sexual implications of nudity in actual nudist camps or on nude beaches, and in fact attaching sexual meanings to nudism in these settings generally is frowned upon. It can be expected, however, that in a society that typically requires the sex organs to be covered, a sense of liberation and sexual pleasure might sometimes accompany the uncovering of these organs in the presence of other people.

A study of 2,450 Swedish people ages 18 to 60 found that 3.1 percent of the respondents reported at least one incident of sexual arousal because of exposing their genitals to a stranger. Those who had done so were more likely to be male and to have more psychological problems than other respondents (Langstrom & Seto, 2006). Because such behaviors generally are considered antisocial, exhibitionism is one of the more common sexual offenses for which men are arrested in Europe, the United States, and Canada. Various treatment programs are designed to help these individuals channel their sexual energies into more acceptable directions, and some medications have proved successful in treating their compulsive behaviors (Abouesh & Clayton, 1999).

The motivations behind exhibitionism vary among individuals. Exhibitionism often is found in the criminal and sexual histories of rapists and child abusers, and seems to stem from the exhibitionist's feelings of inadequacy and inferiority. In exposing his penis, a man seeks reassurance of his maleness and his masculinity. There may be some aggressive motives as well, because the victim may react strongly enough to the situation that the exhibitionist creates a degree of emotional distress. If a victim does not react with any particular surprise or fear upon being confronted by an exhibitionist, his primary source of gratification is absent. Exhibitionism can be offensive to the individual who, without consenting, is forced to see someone else's sex organs. This is not necessarily a seriously harmful event, but it can be emotionally exploitative. Whenever possible, the best response

"You don't often see a real silk lining, these days . . ."
Source: © Punch/Rothko.

to an exhibitionist is to ignore him. The police or other authorities should be contacted and asked to take action.

Voyeurism

Gaining sexual pleasure from observing others who are nude or disrobing or engaging in sexual acts is called **voyeurism.** There is certainly an element of voyeurism in most of us, and it is quite natural to be interested in other people's genitals and body form. The NHSLS found that watching a partner undress was the second most appealing of all sexual practices, after vaginal intercourse. The survey also reported that 16 percent of the women interviewed and about 33 percent of the men found the idea of "watching others do sexual things" at least somewhat appealing (Laumann et al., 1994). In a study of university students, many reported a willingness to watch an attractive person undressing, if they wouldn't get caught, and a somewhat smaller number said they would watch two people having sex (Rye & Meany, 2007). In the Swedish study cited previously, 7.7 percent of the respondents indicated that they had experienced at least one incident of sexual arousal while spying on others having sex (Langstrom & Seto, 2006).

The prevalence of sexually explicit media materials and strip clubs provides ample evidence of the

voyeurism (VOYE-yur-i-zum) sexual gratification from viewing others who are nude or who are engaging in sexual activities.

voyeuristic needs of the public (Frank, 2005). Voyeuristic behavior becomes more offensive when the voyeur, or "peeper," goes out of his or her way to peer into windows of bedrooms or to spy on people in public bathrooms to satisfy his or her needs. Voyeurs tend to be younger males in their early twenties, usually unmarried or separated; about 25 percent are married. Very few seem to have any serious mental disorders, but most have had unsatisfactory sexual relationships. Voyeurs usually are interested in viewing strangers and normally do not interact physically with their victims. Nonetheless, the act is an obvious violation of another's right to privacy. Again, it may not harm the victim, and in fact the voyeur's presence may never be known, but it is an exploitative act. Because voyeurism is less easily detected than other sexual proclivities, it is not reported to authorities as frequently as behaviors such as exhibitionism.

It is certainly true that men are implicated in these forms of sexual connection far more often than are women, and the scanty statistics available seem to confirm that males do indeed find such behaviors sexually arousing, more so than females. Social attitudes and values may also be operating here. It has been suggested, for example, that if a man is standing outside an open window watching a woman undress, he will be arrested for being a voyeur. However, if the situation were reversed, with the woman watching the man undress beyond the open window, it would still be the man who would be arrested—for exhibitionism.

Sadomasochism

Sadomasochism (or **S & M**) is probably the least understood of the relatively common routes to sexual arousal and connection. The sexual activities involved often are popularly described with the acronym BDSM, standing for bondage and discipline, dominance and submission, and sadism and masochism (or "slave" and "master"). Practitioners of BDSM sometimes refer to more conventional sexual interests as "vanilla," although BDSM interests may coexist with vanilla desires and behaviors (Kleinplatz & Moser, 2004). The term includes a whole range of sexual behaviors that seem to fit into four general themes: *hypermasculinity*, involving excretion or excrement and binding of the genitals; *administration* or *receipt of pain or humiliation*, usually involving dominance and submission with verbal put-downs or the whipping of one person; and *physical restraint* or *bondage*, involving tying up or restraining all or part of the body (Santilla et al., 2002) (see Figure 14.7). Hypermasculinity practices are associated more with males, especially gay men, while humiliation is associated more with females and heterosexual men (Alison et al., 2001).

FIGURE 14.7 *Sadomasochism*

People who practice BDSM sexual activities often use various kinds of attire and devices to enhance their sexual excitation.

It has been traditional to define the **sadist** (or "dom") as the partner who derives sexual pleasure from being in the dominant role, perhaps inflicting, or threatening to inflict, some usually negative stimulus on another person, and the **masochist** (or "sub") as the individual who is aroused by being in the submissive, receptive role. These are simplistic definitions, because many people seem to be able to enjoy either role. Sadism and masochism are opposite sides of the same coin and tend to accompany each other, even though one may dominate the other at any given time (McLawsen et al., 2008).

Sadomasochism is always a matter of degree, but its more extreme forms have gained interest as the Internet has increased access to the BDSM subculture (Kleinplatz & Moser, 2004). For most people, shared sexual activity has its share of urgency and rapid movements, with tightly gripping hands, hard sucking, and the possibility of mild pinching, scratching, and biting. Between 25 and 30 percent of college students surveyed indicated that they had engaged in spanking or some sort of bondage during sexual activities (Elliott & Brantley, 1997). Such behaviors are part of the intensity of sex for these individuals.

For those interested in BDSM, variants of such stimuli have become an important part of their sexual arousal and gratification. The intensity of the stimulation

sadomasochism (S & M) (sade-o-MASS-o-kiz-um) refers to sexual themes or activities involving bondage, pain, domination, or humiliation of one partner by the other.

sadist the individual in a sadomasochistic sexual relationship who takes the dominant role.

masochist the individual in a sadomasochistic sexual relationship who takes the submissive role.

desired may vary from scratching or biting to spanking, whipping, and severe beating. Occasionally, cutting to draw blood or to mutilate may be involved. People who pair up for sadomasochistic sex usually make careful agreements and may even sign written contracts ahead of time concerning how far the activities should go. There is always the risk of such contracts being broken, of course. It is also true, ironically, that the person in the submissive or masochistic role often wields more power and control over the interaction because it is his or her reactions that will largely determine the eventual direction of the encounter (Langdridge & Butt, 2004; Lawrence & Love-Crowell, 2008; Santilla et al., 2002; Taylor & Ussher, 2001).

See "Shannon: Private Club Dancer" on SexSource Online.

The acting out of fantasies or rituals in which one individual plays a dominant role is probably the most common sadomasochistic activity. Often the dominant person plays the role of a severe parent, teacher, or police officer who demands compliance from the submissive partner. The scenario often ends with some mock forced sexual activity. Urination and defecation sometimes are included in the sexual acts, and some individuals find sexual interest and arousal in urine **(urophilia)** or feces **(coprophilia).** In the Janus and Janus (1993) survey of sexual behavior, 4 percent of women and 6 percent of men reported experience with "golden showers," or urophilic behavior and about the same percentages found the behavior acceptable. In a college student survey, nearly 10 percent of respondents indicated that they had been involved with golden showers (Elliott & Brantley, 1997; Wilson, 2005).

Bondage, the tying or restraining of parts of the body, seems to be one form of sadomasochism. Wearing a hood is often part of such shared activities. Adult sex shops sell all sorts of devices for binding the body or genitals. Most common are rings, straps, and other pressure devices used by males to bind the penis and/or testicles to generate or heighten sexual pleasure. Eleven percent of both women and men report having had a sexual experience involving dominance or bondage.

A very dangerous variation on the bondage theme is **hypoxphilia,** which may lead to **autoerotic asphyxiation.** Some people, usually boys or men, have found that wearing a noose around the neck, which induces a state of *hypoxia* (reduced oxygen to the brain), can enhance erotic pleasure and orgasm. They often devise various hanging techniques from which they can cut themselves loose prior to losing consciousness (Johnstone & Huws, 1997). What these individuals do not realize is how easy it is to lose consciousness

when pressure is placed on the carotid artery in the neck. The Federal Bureau of Investigation estimates that between 500 and 1,000 people die accidentally each year from this sort of sexual activity. Given these statistics, the practice evidently is more widespread than commonly assumed. Families of victims are often confused about the sexual nature of the death and are embarrassed about reporting it as such. Partly for the same reason, the dangers of this kind of bondage have not been widely publicized to young people.

There are few statistics on the frequency of sadomasochistic preferences and activities. In a survey of more than 2,000 students in the United States, Canada, and Europe, 8 percent of males and 5 percent of females in the United States reported that they had engaged in "whipping or spanking before petting or other intimacy." These percentages were markedly higher among British students (17 percent of males, 33 percent of females), where spanking is a prevalent form of childhood punishment and may well take on sexual meanings (Butt & Hearn, 1998). There is a well-developed network of gay male and lesbian sadomasochists within the gay/lesbian culture as well.

Masochistic behavior may represent an escape from the usual burdens and responsibilities of an individual's normal identity. In a masochistic role, the individual is spared the anxiety of making decisions, asserting control, or maintaining a favorable image. The role may also deter feelings of guilt and insecurity. Practitioners of S & M are generally well-adjusted socially, and these behaviors may simply facilitate their sexual lives. They tend to be flexible in their role-taking, although those who prefer the dominant role tend to be younger and more sexually active than those who prefer the passive role (Rathbone, 2001; Taylor & Ussher, 2001). A study of men involved in heterosexual dominance found that, contrary to the predictions of researchers, the men did not have low self-esteem or highly sexist attitudes (Damon, 2002).

A survey of research on S & M has suggested that these behaviors constitute a social phenomenon that occurs in cultures with certain characteristics. For example, dominance and submission are usually embedded in the culture, and aggression is socially valued.

urophilia sexual arousal connected with urine or urination.

coprophilia sexual arousal connected with feces.

bondage tying, restraining, or applying pressure to body parts as part of sexual arousal.

hypoxphilia creating pressure around the neck during sexual activity to enhance sexual pleasure.

autoerotic asphyxiation accidental death from pressure placed around the neck during masturbatory behavior.

These cultures also have a clear and unequal distribution of power among social groups, creating a situation in which the temporary illusion of power reversals could become erotically stimulating. Two additional social characteristics are sufficient affluence to provide the leisure and opportunity for such complex sexual practices and the positive valuing of creativity and imagination (Alison et al., 2001). A study of BDSM practitioners found that, in general, they do not seem to have any significant psychological problems surrounding their sexual preferences. This calls into question whether such behavior should be considered a diagnosable pathology, appearing in the *DSM-IV* as it does presently (Connolly, 2006; Lawrence & Love-Crowell, 2008).

Sex with Animals

Since before recorded history, humans have lived in close association with a variety of domesticated animals. Folklore and the literature of mythology contain many examples of humans having sex with animals, often portraying a woman who has become enamored of the large genitals and sexual prowess of some animal. The half-bull, half-human Minotaur of Greek mythology was the offspring of Pasiphae, wife of the King of Crete, and a bull whom she seduced (Falkner, 2004). Throughout history, there is evidence of people having sex with animals. It is known that in North America both Native Americans and early British colonists engaged in the practice (Miletski, 2006).

Cross-cultural studies have reported many cases of humans having sex with animals, such as dogs, cattle, sheep, burros, horses, and chickens. This activity is called **bestiality** or **zoophilia.** The Kinsey studies reported that 8 percent of the adult males and 3 percent of the adult females in his research sample admitted having had at least some sexual contact with animals. In the Kinsey research, among men raised on farms, 17 percent reported having had at least one orgasm after puberty through contact with an animal. The greater likelihood of zoophilia in rural populations has been confirmed more recently. Internet access has opened opportunities for interaction among zoophiles, although the numbers remain relatively small even for this medium (Miletski, 2006; Williams & Weinberg, 2003).

It appears likely that sex with animals usually represents sexual experimentation and/or arises from the frustration of lacking an available sexual partner. It does not necessarily reflect a serious psychological disturbance and seldom becomes a continuing pattern of sexual activity. The desire for affection seems to form the basis for most initial encounters with animals, and the ease of pleasure and not having to deal with the complications of human relationships are among the reasons the contact sometimes continues (Williams & Weinberg, 2003). What humans actually do with animals is as varied as any other aspect of human sexuality. Kinsey found masturbation of the animal and actual intercourse to be more common among men. General body contact with the animal is more common among women. Oral-genital sex, vaginal intercourse, and anal intercourse with animals have been reported by both women and men (Miletski, 2001, 2006; Williams & Weinberg, 2003).

Sex with animals is a concept usually met with abhorrence and disgust, for several reasons. First, Judeo-Christian-Muslim tradition carries strong prohibitions against humans having sex with animals, which may have grown out of fears that monstrous hybrids might be formed by such unions. In fact, no offspring can be formed by sexual intercourse between humans and animals because of the genetic differences between species. Second, possible injury or pain may be inflicted on the animal, especially if restraints have been used to keep it from moving during the sexual activity. The behavior is illegal in most areas today, covered by various laws concerning deviant and lewd behavior.

Sex with the Dead

Probably no form of sexual behavior stirs negative reactions in quite the same way as **necrophilia,** or sexual contact with a corpse. It has been said that in ancient Egypt women of high rank and women of particular beauty were not given to embalmers until they had been dead for three or four days, to prevent the embalmers from having intercourse with them.

There are no statistics concerning the incidence of necrophilia, and almost nothing has been written about people who participate in sex with the dead. It is believed to be a rare phenomenon, because few people have access to cadavers. It is likely that necrophilic sex acts are committed primarily by people who work with corpses, as in mortuaries or morgues, and therefore have become desensitized to them. Case studies of necrophiles published decades ago showed that they sought jobs where they would be able to have such contact (Klaf & Brown, 1958). This behavior is prohibited under laws regarding the handling of bodies in most states, although Iowa passed such a law only in 1996 after a man was discovered fondling a woman's body at a funeral home and no law in effect at the time could be invoked against the behavior.

Which, if any, sexual behaviors, as described in this chapter, do you believe should be condemned or regulated by law?

bestiality (beest-ee-AL-i-tee) sexual contact between a human being and an animal.

zoophilia (zoo-a-FILL-ee-a) another name for bestiality.

necrophilia (nek-ro-FILL-ee-a) sexual activity with a dead body.

Other Unconventional Sexual Variations

ETLEs result in the sexual interests and behaviors of some people becoming associated with highly unconventional stimuli. These sexual variations have received little attention in the literature, suggesting that they may be relatively rare. They may elicit disbelief or jokes when we hear about them, but we should keep in mind that they represent the sexual proclivities of at least some human beings. As has happened with other sexual variations, perhaps we eventually will discover that they are more widespread than has been assumed to date.

Although it seems more of a function of social attitudes that seem to find slimness preferable in sexual partners, there are groups of people who form the *fat acceptance community.* Often associated with this community are *male fat admirers* who find women with high body mass indices to be more physically and sexually attractive. Whether this sexual preference represents a variant sexual interest or simply the ability to see beyond socially determined oppression of overweight people remains a topic of debate (Swami & Tovee, 2009).

There are two variations associated with limb amputation. The less complicated of the two is *acrotomophilia,* a fetishistic sexual attraction to the stump of an amputated limb and therefore to sexual partners who are amputees. The more complicated form of this variation, wanting to change one's body into a facsimile of the desired target, is termed *apotemnophilia,* a sex-related desire to have a normal limb (typically a leg) amputated. It has been compared to a desire for sex reassignment in that it involves dissatisfaction with certain body parts accompanied by

the desire to have them removed. There are documented cases of surgeons fulfilling the wishes of such patients (Lawrence, 2006, 2009).

Another variation at least sometimes associated with sexual arousal is *diaper-wearing* or *adult baby syndrome,* in which an adult is motivated to act like an infant, wearing diapers, drinking milk from a bottle, eating baby food, and doing other things associated with infants. The syndrome has not yet been classified as a paraphilia or other disorder, but it is being considered for some designation. How closely connected the syndrome is to sexual interests and behaviors is unclear, but the behavior can cause difficulties in relationships (Caldwell, 2008; Evcimen & Gratz, 2006).

Finally, there is continuing concern about certain breathing or strangulation practices sometimes associated with sexual behavior. It is known that some people attempt to enhance their sexual experience by applying pressure to their neck, altering the blood supply to the brain. Adolescents sometimes play the "choking game" to induce altered states of consciousness, although how connected the practice may be to sexual arousal is unknown at this time. In either case, such behavior is known to be dangerous, and each year a number of people die after losing consciousness while attempting to tighten some ligature around their necks. Somewhat related to this is hyperventilation, or fast breathing, during sexual activity, which may also enhance feelings but also can result in an unpleasant *acute hyperventilation syndrome* that may require medical treatment. There are cases where such hyperventilation has occurred during sexual intercourse (Passie et al., 2004).

The human sexual imagination appears to be vast, and other curious sexual proclivities surely will make themselves known in the years to come.

Self-Evaluation

Your Sexual Fantasies

It seems that nearly everyone experiences a rich sexual life in his or her imagination. Yet we react to our sexual fantasies in different ways. We may feel aroused, amused, frightened, ashamed, or guilty, depending on how we have learned to think of our sexual fantasies. They may give us clues to what we like and dislike about sex, help us plan future sexual encounters, put

us in touch with the richness of our imaginations, and provide interesting accompaniments to our sexual activities. Sexual fantasies are just that—fantasies. There is no particular need to fight or deny them. In fact, sometimes the more we try not to think about something, the more it plagues us. Keep in mind that it is our sexual actions for which we must accept responsibility; our fantasies need only be accepted as very personal parts of our mind. The following questions and exercises may help you take a closer look at your fantasy life and its meaning.

1. **Take some time to think in some detail about your most common sexual fantasies. It may help to close your eyes and relax. Write down each fantasy if you wish.**
   a. What are the predominant feelings generated in you by each fantasy? Start by deciding whether it gives you mostly positive feelings that make you glad to indulge in it or instead generates negative feelings that make you wish the fantasy would go away.
   b. More specifically, what feelings does each fantasy generate? Write down a list of all the feelings you experience during each fantasy.
   c. Have you ever told another person about any or all of your sexual fantasies? Why or why not? If so, what conditions helped you feel able to share such a personal aspect of your life?

2. **Here is a list of some typical topics of sexual fantasies. They may simply be fleeting thoughts or may be rich in detail. For each fantasy you can remember experiencing, assign it a number, using the following scale as a way of noting the relative intensities of your fantasies.**

   0 = I have not experienced this fantasy.
   1 = This was an appealing, arousing, enjoyable fantasy.
   2 = Most aspects of the fantasy were enjoyable and positive.
   3 = This fantasy had a mixture of positive and negative aspects.
   4 = Most aspects of the fantasy were unenjoyable and negative.
   5 = This was a disgusting, guilt-producing, unenjoyable fantasy.

   a. Having sex with someone to whom you are attracted but who is unavailable to you or uninterested in you. _____
   b. Kissing or hugging someone of your own gender or admiring his or her nude body. _____
   c. Having quick, uninvolved sex with a stranger you will never see again. _____
   d. Having sex with someone of your own gender. _____
   e. Watching a couple you know having sex with each other. _____
   f. Forcing another person to have sex with you. _____
   g. Being forced to have sex with someone against your will. _____
   h. Seeing the nude body and genitals of someone you consider to be attractive. _____
   i. Being watched while you masturbate. _____
   j. Being watched while engaging in some sexual activity with a partner. _____
   k. Inflicting or being subjected to pain or humiliation during sexual activity. _____
   l. Playing a dominant or submissive role while acting out a sexual fantasy. _____
   m. Paying a female or male sex worker to have sex with you. _____
   n. Having sex with someone under the legal age of consent. _____
   o. Being tied up during sex or tying up someone else during sex. _____
   p. Participating in oral-genital sex with a desirable partner. _____
   q. Being part of a group sexual experience or an orgy. _____

3. **Are there any sexual fantasies that you enjoy using as an accompaniment to masturbation? If so, try to sort out the unique features of each fantasy that contribute to your sexual enjoyment.**

4. **Do you sometimes find yourself fantasizing while engaging in masturbation or sexual activity with a partner?**
   a. If so, how does this make you feel?
   b. Do you consider such fantasizing unusual? (It's not.)
   c. Have you ever discussed these fantasies with your sexual partner? If so, did your partner share any of his or her sexual fantasies with you?
   d. Have you ever acted out a sexual fantasy with a partner or considered doing so? (Some couples find this to be an occasional source of enjoyment and mutual arousal.)

5. **Have you been able to give yourself permission to experience, accept, and enjoy your sexual fantasies? If not, is this a goal toward which you would like to work? If your fantasies are giving you problems, perhaps you would like to consider talking with a qualified professional about your concerns.**

Chapter Summary

1. The total sexual outlet concept (hydraulic theory) of sexual behaviors, common in Kinsey's time, has been modified by data from the latest sex research.

2. Views of sexual behavior often emphasize the physical, orgasmic aspects of sexual performance. The subjective erotic experience that includes desire and sensuosity is also important.

3. Human beings are diverse in their sexual orientations and activities. Behaviors that differ from whatever is considered the norm may be classified by terms such as deviance, variance, or paraphilia.

4. The dual control model proposes that sexual arousal to particular stimuli are mediated by both excitatory and inhibitory mechanisms. An individual's particular sexual interests and attractions may be formed when excitatory stimuli are superimposed on a nervous system that has been primed by hormonal influences.

5. Erotic target location error theory suggests that sexual attractions can sometimes be associated with targets only peripherally related to the attractive person or with the idea of becoming a facsimile of the person.

6. Incentive sexual motivation theory posits that we develop sexual interests in certain targets or activities because of the amount of pleasure we have learned can be derived from them. These preferences are reinforced over time with continued pleasurable experience.

7. Women seem to have more relational goals in their sexual goals than men, who tend to be attracted to the more physical dimensions of sex.

8. Individuals, preferences for various sexual behaviors, and objects of sexual desire may change with circumstances and time reflecting one's degree of erotic plasticity. Women seem to have a greater degree of erotic plasticity than men do, but this may be influenced more by cultural factors than once thought.

9. Celibacy refers to the choice not to share sexual activity with other people. It can represent a response to ethical or religious values.

10. There is a wide range of levels of interest in sex and amounts of actual sexual activity among people, ranging from the erotophilic to the erotophobic. An unusually high level of sexual interest or drive is called hypersexuality; an especially low level is called hyposexuality.

11. Asexuality reflects a low level of desire for sex with partners but usually not for masturbation. Asexual people may still have average levels of sexual activity as they fulfill relational expectations.

12. Compulsive sexual behavior can result from traumatic life experiences. Erotomania is apparently rare and characterized by extreme sexual compulsivity. It has been called nymphomania in females and satyriasis in males.

13. Diverse sexual behaviors are more common among men than among women.

14. Transvestism involves cross-dressing, often involved with sexual arousal at least at first. It often involves a fetishistic attachment to clothes of the other gender and fantasies about being a member of that gender.

15. Autogynephilia is a sexual attachment of males to the idea of having sex as a woman, even though they are typically heterosexual in their orientation.

16. People sometimes enhance sexual experiences through the use of various sexual media and toys and through sexual fantasy.

17. Fetishism is the term used to describe sexual arousal by objects, parts of the body, or materials not usually considered sexually arousing.

18. There are several forms of sexual interaction involving more than two persons.

19. There are both female and male sex workers. Legal debates over prostitution and the health risks involved continue.

20. Among the sex-related behaviors that have unwilling or unwitting victims are obscene telephone calls, frotteurism, and toucherism.

21. Consensual telephone sex and Internet matching sites offer an opportunity for sex-related communication on a relatively anonymous basis.

22. Exhibitionism refers to exposing the genitals or breasts to others, usually for sexual arousal.

23. Voyeurism refers to finding sexual arousal by viewing others nude, undressing, or engaging in sexual activity.

24. Sadomasochism, sometimes called BDSM, encompasses a range of behavior involving inflicting pain or humiliation, tying parts of the body (bondage), or acting out dominant-submissive fantasies, all for sexual arousal. Hypoxphilia is the dangerous practice of using devices to reduce oxygen to the brain for sexual enhancement.

25. Sex with animals has been reported in a small percentage of humans, and it has been receiving increasing attention from sex researchers.

26. Sex with the dead (necrophilia) is a rare phenomenon and typically is prohibited by law.

27. There are a few other sex-related interests and behaviors that have received little study, including attraction to fat people, acrotomophilia, apotemnophilia, adult baby syndrome, and strangulation or hyperventilation syndrome.

Chapter 15

Sex, Art, the Media, and the Law

Chapter Outline

Nudity and Sex in Art
Historical Foundations of Erotic Art
Erotic Art Today

Sex and the Printed Page
The Evolution of Sexuality in Literature
Themes in Contemporary Literature, Lyrics, and Plays
Magazines, Journals, and Comics

Sex in the Nonprint Media
Films
Pornographic Films, Videos, and DVDs
Television
Advertising

Internet Sexuality
Online Pornography
Child Pornography
Sex Seeking on the Internet

Effects of Sexually Explicit Materials
Responses to Sexually Explicit Materials
Self-Perceived Effects
Effects on Attitudes
Behavioral Effects of Pornography

Legal Aspects of Pornography and Sexual Behavior
National Commissions on Pornography
Pornography, the Courts, and the Law
Legal Regulation of Sexual Behavior
Sex and the Constitution
Special Issues and the Law

Chapter Summary

When I was about 12, my mother found some porno magazines that I had hidden in my bedroom closet. She turned them over to my father, who gave me the biggest lecture of my lifetime about what kinds of material would be permitted in our house. I was really embarrassed, but I also hated losing those magazines.

—from a student essay

What do you think about the availability of **pornography** online? Have you ever accessed such materials out of curiosity or for sexual arousal? Should it be available, or should it be censored? Should we keep it away from the eyes of children, and, if so, how could that be accomplished? *Internet Filter Review* estimates that the Internet has more than 420 million porn pages, generating about $4 billion annually in the United States. About 40 million U.S. adults regularly visit porn websites, and 40 percent of Internet users access adult sites each month (Crary, 2006). Sex industry annual sales, including all forms of graphic pornography, exotic dance clubs, magazines, and novelties are now believed to bring in $14 billion per year.

On one side of the contemporary culture wars are those who believe that adults should have the freedom to access such materials; on the other are those who feel that pornography destroys relationships and increases the rate of sexual crimes. No one has figured out exactly how to regulate such material or keep it from young people without interfering with access to educational information as well.

The essential controversy here is not new. Depictions of nudity and human sexual acts have been abundant in most cultures and most periods of history, from the figures on a Greek urn to the billboards on Times Square, from the couples on a television soap opera to the advertisements for Abercrombie and Fitch clothing, and from frontal nudity on the big screen to the lyrics of the most current musical artist. These images and words, implicitly or explicitly, reflect the attitudinal trends of the society in which they appear. Such gestures sometimes purposely push the envelope of political and moral sensitivities. The more tolerant a society becomes in its representation of sexuality, the more it invites criticisms from some internal and external factions. It has become clear in recent times that some world cultures have come to view Western openness and tolerance with regard to sexuality and sexual imagery as a threat to their perceptions of the way human beings and human life ought to be.

A distinction is sometimes made between **embedded sexual media,** in which sexual interactions and issues are positioned within a larger context, as in a television program or play. This is different from pornographic material that is intended mostly to sexually arouse the consumer with its mostly explicit content. The terms pornography and **obscenity** are often used interchangeably. Both terms are subject to multiple definitions and interpretations, and both have become emotionally charged. Typically, pornography refers to any visual or literary portrayal that may be sexually

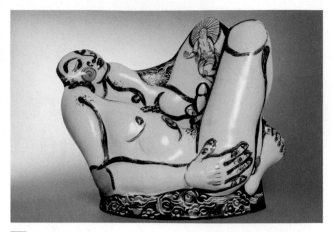

FIGURE 15.1   *Akio Takamori, Appearance of Kwannon to a Man, 1995.*

A contemporary artwork depicting masturbation that is part of the Kinsey Institute's collection of erotic art.

arousing to some people. Obscenity usually includes material that may be offensive to public taste and morals. The term *sexually explicit material* sometimes is used to describe pornography.

In erotically realistic art or fiction, sometimes called **erotica,** sex is portrayed as part of the broad spectrum of human emotions present in intimate relationships. The people involved are shown to be complex human beings with a variety of nonsexual feelings in addition to sexual ones (see Figure 15.1). The sex may be depicted in just as graphic a way as in pornography; it is the overall context that differs. It has also been suggested that pornography has aspects of violence, aggression, or the degradation of another human being, whereas erotica balances sexual acts with mutual respect, affection, and pleasure.

■ Nudity and Sex in Art

In recent times in Western culture, art has been a relatively uncensored means of expression in which nudity, at least, has been considered quite permissible. That is not to say, however, that paintings or sculptures

pornography photographs, films, or literature intended to be sexually arousing through explicit depictions of sexual activity.

embedded sexual media depictions of sexual activities or issues within a larger context of a plot and scene.

obscenity depiction of sexual activity in a repulsive or disgusting manner.

erotica artistic representations of nudity or sexual activity.

of nudes have not incurred the ire of some viewers. Erotic art has a long history, as do the cultural and social reactions to it.

Historical Foundations of Erotic Art

Prehistoric representations of the human body and sexual activities very likely were fertility symbols with magical and religious significance. Representations of the sex organs themselves probably became objects of worship with great symbolic meaning. Penis-shaped monuments and adornments have been found in the ruins of many ancient cultures. Religious erotic art tended to portray those aspects of sex that were seen as important and necessary to the survival and well-being of the human species (e.g., intercourse for procreation). Other forms of erotic art, mostly three-dimensional, were used to ward off evil spirits or to improve the harvesting of crops.

Every culture has seen its share of erotic art that departs from such religious intent. Artists, sometimes by definition, test the limits of moral values and sexual tolerance. It is this form of erotic art that sometimes is treated with greater secrecy, used for sexual titillation, or strictly limited to a select group of privileged viewers. Many Greek and Etruscan paintings show sexual intercourse, fellatio, orgies, adult-child sexual behavior, and a variety of other sexual activities. Some examples of pre-Columbian pottery from Mexico and Peru represent male masturbation and fellatio, often with great exaggeration of phallic size (see Figure 15.2). Sometimes, homoerotic themes were represented more symbolically through animal figures engaged in sexual activities (Olsen, 2004).

Some erotic art has been used for special educational functions. Japan once had a tradition of bride scrolls and position pictures, or *shunga,* which were passed on from mother to daughter upon the daughter's betrothal. Their dual purpose apparently was to offer instruction and to encourage the daughter's erotic interest in her husband-to-be. This tradition reflects the double purpose of most erotic art—to make us think as well as to encourage us to respond with feeling, including sexual arousal. Erotic art is also of use in fostering an understanding of the sexual values and mores of both historic and present-day cultures other than our own. Japanese culture also produced ceramic sake cups and figurines depicting various forms of sexual activity.

Do you think public funding should be available for the creation of art with sexual themes? Defend your position.

Nudity in art is often directly affected by cultural attitudes. Ancient Greek artists portrayed the nude male and female figures without hesitation. Gradually,

■ **FIGURE 15.2** *Pre-Columbian Pottery*

The ancient Peruvians from the southern coast of Mochica were famous for their stirrup-spout jars. They were molded without the aid of a potter's wheel and featured a large flat bottom with a dominant sculptured form. This jar shows an act of fellatio.

however, as their attitude toward nakedness changed, they began to include gestures of modesty, at least partially covering the genitals.

The roots of modern, commercial sexually explicit material probably can be found in the sixteenth century, when engraving, etching, and woodcutting made reproduction of erotic scenes simpler and much less expensive. By the eighteenth century, representations of nudes were quite acceptable, as long as the genital areas were obscured (Stewart, 2004). Eventually, the resurgence of a more puritan attitude discouraged artistic representations of nudity and sex. This repressive movement probably contains the roots of modern censorship and suppression of erotic images. However, there have also been claims that art historians sometimes glorify and eroticize acts that we would today judge in a negative light, such as the rapes portrayed in many Renaissance paintings (see Figure 15.3) (Wolfthal, 1999).

Erotic Art Today

The first two or three decades of the twentieth century saw some new approaches to erotic art (see Figure 15.4). Surrealism, for instance, often relied on sexual fantasy and free association borrowed from psychoanalysis. Although contemporary art has created some fresh

FIGURE 15.3   *Renaissance Painting*

Peter Paul Rubens's painting *The Rape of the Daughters of Leucippus* (1617) depicts the abduction of two young mortals by the gods Castor and Pollux, who have fallen in love with them. The content of the painting was less interesting historically than were its composition and the artist's technique of using paint and light. Some accuse art historians of glorifying what most people today would find objectionable subject matter for any type of art.

FIGURE 15.4   *Life Model*

One basic area of study for art students continues to be the depiction of the nude human body. Students frequently work with life models, men or women who often pose in the nude.

erotic themes in Western culture, it seems that photography, video, films, and computer images now provide the erotic stimuli that painting, drawing, etching, and sculpture once did. These media have elicited their share of controversy as well. Some observers believe that gay and lesbian themes in art have been suppressed in recent times (Filice, 2005).

It has been the custom of many governments to subsidize artists. However, when the work produced from such support offends the tastes of some individuals, debates erupt over the use of public funds for products that fly in the face of prevailing sexual values. The photographic themes of Robert Mapplethorpe's art, which included homoerotic and sadomasochistic themes, came under fire because of the artist's support from the National Endowment for the Arts (NEA). Galleries that display such works are sometimes subject to criticism. When Rudolph Giuliani was mayor of New York City, he threatened to withhold funds from the Brooklyn Museum of Art when the museum displayed a series of controversial works in its "Sensational" exhibit. Federal courts in the United States have tended to rule that funding of the arts should not be limited by

controversy or based on the artist's social or political messages.

Controversies of this sort highlight the difficult balance every society must struggle to find between freedom of expression, which might include rather explicit images that may be offensive to some, and the ongoing interest on the part of others to prevent such images from being available.

■ Sex and the Printed Page

Just as erotic themes have universally found their way into visual art, so have they always been a part of literature. The explicitness of sexual descriptions varies with the cultural and sexual mores of the times. In some societies and periods of history, little more than a romantic embrace is described, with the participants fully clothed and the rest left to the reader's imagination. In other societies and times, minute and graphic details of a sexual encounter are discussed, requiring no flight of imaginative fancy on the part of the reader. Like other erotic art forms, sexually explicit literature often has been available only as costly contraband.

The Evolution of Sexuality in Literature

It seems that because sex was viewed as joyous and pleasurable in ancient times, authors were permitted to write about it openly and unashamedly. In most languages, including English, some of the oldest writings are the most ribald. Sumerian love songs written about 4,000 years ago contain verses that are more explicit than the love songs of today.

Ancient Greek writers drew much of their eroticism from the fertility rites of Dionysian festivals, dramatic rites in honor of certain Greek gods of pleasure and intoxication. These rites developed into wild orgies in some communities, occasionally to the dismay of Greeks who preferred more staid and formal ceremonies (Hamel, 2003). The plays and songs that emerged, the mass media of the time, often glorified the phallus and retold stories about the sexual activities of the gods. Many of the masters of Greek tragic and comedic writing created plays in which sexual themes were central (Heacox, 2004). The erotic literature of the ancient Romans was more lighthearted than that of the Greeks, although there is evidence that their sexual behaviors surpassed whatever excesses the Greeks may have displayed. One of the most famous Roman erotic writers was Ovid, whose *Art of Love* and *Heroides* are classics. Another Roman, Caius Petronius, wrote the *Satyricon,* a work filled with sexual themes.

It has been suggested that prior to the early nineteenth century, there was no separate or distinct genre of literature meant to arouse sexual feelings. Sexually explicit materials instead were used as vehicles to criticize political and religious authorities. Sexual literary themes have been associated with freethinkers and political activists and often have proliferated prior to major political revolutions against restrictive or oppressive regimes. Italian journalist Pietro Aretino, born in 1492, is sometimes called the originator of European pornography. In 1527, he published Europe's first "stroke book," titled *I Modi (The Ways),* combining 16 sexually explicit sonnets with engravings of couples having sex in a variety of positions. The Pope declared reprinting of the book punishable by death; soon thereafter a second, embellished version was published.

Shakespeare integrated sexual themes into his plays and sonnets, and their meanings continue to be debated today (Tambling, 2004). Pornography seems to have begun taking on its more distinctively sexually titillating role during the late eighteenth century, as a more materialistic view of the world emerged in philosophy and science.

The nineteenth century brought a rise in prudery. During this period, ladies could be offended not only by explicit sexual references but also by any sort of indelicate statement made in writing. Sexual feelings were increasingly repressed, and people's sexual attitudes, at least superficially, became models of propriety. Nevertheless, erotic literature flourished; by 1834, 57 pornography shops had opened on one London street.

Themes in Contemporary Literature, Lyrics, and Plays

Although sexuality has never been totally repressed in literature, the kind of exuberance and acceptance of erotic themes prevalent in Greek and Roman literature did not fully manifest itself again until the twentieth century. In the early years of that century, some writers rebelled against the notion that sex must be accompanied by shame and guilt. Undoubtedly, the writings of Sigmund Freud, Havelock Ellis, Kinsey, Masters and Johnson, and others influenced the emergence of new sexual attitudes.

D. H. Lawrence's *Lady Chatterley's Lover* (1929) stirred controversy for decades with its sexual explicitness, still modest by today's standards. Lawrence is now recognized as a literary genius who was a pioneer in the sensitive treatment of erotic themes. James Joyce's *Ulysses* was not allowed into the United States for years after it was published. In 1933, John Woolsey, a district judge for New York, wrote a landmark decision that redefined the limits of pornography and allowed *Ulysses* to be available to readers in the United States. Woolsey's basic principle was that the redeeming artistic value of an entire book needed to be considered before it could be banned as obscene because of any given passage. This decision set a precedent that has persisted to this day, and *Ulysses* became recognized as a modern masterpiece.

All sexual themes have today found their way into literature, song lyrics, and play scripts. Tens of thousands of books have been published, on many different levels of literary quality, that treat sex openly and frankly. Sometimes the erotic themes are interwoven with other themes of literary importance. In other cases, the author's intent seems to be to cram as many sexually explicit scenes onto the pages as possible. There has also been a resurgence in the popularity of romantic themes, often in combination with eroticism. Nearly half of all mass-market paperbacks are romance novels, read by both women and men. In addition, some experts believe that economic and sexual pressures are making monogamous, romantic relationships more appealing both in real life and in literature. Another recent trend in romance novels has been the portrayal of men who are interested and involved in fatherhood and family life.

The sale of erotic books, collections of short stories, and poetry has been booming. Women dominate the erotic literature scene both as writers and as buyers and readers. This seems to reflect a new trend in eroticism in which sexual themes are intertwined with good literary style and well-developed characters who also have an emotional side. Helen Gurley Brown, longtime editor of *Cosmopolitan* magazine, published a 2003 revised edition of her groundbreaking work from 1962, *Sex and the Single Girl.* The original edition was one of the early manifestos declaring a new level of sexual freedom for women.

The sexual references of song lyrics continue to worry parents and educators with their explicitness, and sometimes their violence, yet this is not a new phenomenon. Music has long been one of the most important means of sexual expression for adolescents. The theater often portrays sexual themes in its productions and reflects ongoing sociosexual movements and trends. *The Vagina Monologues* debuted off-Broadway in 1996 and has now become popular on college campuses. The winner of the 2002 Tony award for best play was the Broadway production of *The Goat* by Edward Albee. In the play, a man falls in love with a goat and attends a therapy group for people who love animals more than is considered socially acceptable (Paul, 2007; Williams & Weinberg, 2003).

Although there have been no recent widespread attempts to censor erotic themes in literature, local libraries and school systems frequently are subjected to pressures by special-interest groups to remove books these groups judge to be too sexually suggestive. The number of challenges concerning materials used in public schools escalated during the 1990s, and in close to half these cases books or other materials were removed or given some restricted status. Some of the titles challenged most often included classics and award-winning books such as Judy Blume's *Forever,* Mark Twain's *Huckleberry Finn,* and Maya Angelou's *I Know Why the Caged Bird Sings.*

Can you think of any books that should not be allowed in your college library? In a high school library? In a public library?

Magazines, Journals, and Comics

Magazines with stories and/or articles about sex have been available for more than a century, although the accessibility of erotic materials online has caused a precipitous decline in periodical publications. When *Esquire: The Magazine for Men* appeared in 1933, a new precedent was set for sophistication in erotic magazines. Twenty years after *Esquire's* beginnings, *Playboy* appeared on newsstands. This magazine attempted to strike a balance among offerings on sex information, advice on male attire, an open philosophy toward sex, photographs of nude women, and titillating fiction. The *Playboy* approach was adopted by a large number of other magazines for men. As women began to ask for a more balanced view of sex, magazines such as *Cosmopolitan* and *Playgirl* began printing photographs of nude men and stories with special erotic appeal for women.

Lifestyle magazines are now the most common venues for publishing articles about improving one's sex life (Tyler, 2004). Several men's magazines have appeared that seem to emphasize some of the traditional gender stereotypes regarding men's interests in explicit sexual themes and photographs. Magazines such as *Maxim* and *Men's Health* are designed to appeal to young male readers in a variety of ways. One analysis of the photographs that appear in such magazines concluded that they tended to portray women as willing sex objects much more than they did men (Krassas, Blauwkamp, & Wesselink, 2003). A number of periodicals have been published for gay men, including *The Advocate, Genre, Instinct,* and *Out.* These magazines similarly sexually objectify men's bodies and body parts (Saucier & Caron, 2008).

Professional journals that publish printed papers related to human sexuality once proliferated, but are gradually being replaced by electronic journals. Some journals have a panel of expert reviewers, or "referees," who help editors decide whether particular research or a specific topic is worth publishing, offering suggestions for revision and clarification along the way. Refereed journals are generally considered to offer the best-quality material. In 1971, there were only three scientific journals related to sexuality; today there are close to 100. Various print and online catalogs and archives of published topics are available to make literature searches somewhat easier (Zucker & Cantor, 2003).

Comic books and comic strips have also ventured into gender- or sex-related themes, but that has been changing. Women have become superheroes in some comics. A character in Marvel Comics' "Alpha Flight" declared that he was gay, and another gay character appeared in DC Publications' "Flash" series. In Japan, comic books called *manga,* for both men and women are quite popular, and they often feature sexually explicit material, including rape themes or other depictions of forced sexual submission. Those published for younger girls often portray relationships between gay males. It is believed that such themes in women's comics may help women play out the themes of their subconscious mind within the context of a sexually conservative culture (Perper & Cornog, 2002).

■ Sex in the Nonprint Media

Film, television, video/DVD, and the Internet have undergone—and continue to undergo—an evolutionary process that parallels, reflects, and often stimulates the evolution of social attitudes. The embedding of nudity and sex into films and television has been gradual and careful, yet because of their mass audiences, reaction to nudity and sex in these media has been more visible than any responses to erotic art or literature ever were.

Real Student Voices

■ I was eleven when I was shown my first porn online. My best friend showed me on his computer. I must admit I was turned on, and it has been part of my available "repertoire" ever since. My parents never realized what I was accessing, and I'm grateful for that.

■ About a month ago, I discovered on my boyfriend's laptop that he had been downloading pornography. It really bothers me even though he says it shouldn't. I don't understand why he needs to do that if he's really happy with me and our sexual relationship. It makes me feel that I'm not really enough, and that I can't really trust him.

■ When I was a teenager, my parents installed software on our computers that blocked all adult sites. Eventually, I discovered ways around the blocks. In the meantime, I just used my friends' computers.

■ One night every week, my fraternity shows porno DVDs on the big screen. Even though I find the stuff embarrassing, there is a lot of pressure to watch as a group, so I join in. I haven't come out to them yet, so I can't tell them I'd rather see gay porno.

Films

From the earliest days of film, some moviemakers made use of the medium to photograph sexual activity. At first, such films were available only through the underground market. The movies that were offered to the public for the first 50 years were almost totally lacking in anything that today would be judged sexually explicit. There were innuendos and seductive women even in silent films. Greta Garbo's first talking picture, *Anna Christie* (1930), was about a prostitute. But whatever people did together sexually was left strictly to the viewer's imagination. Movie actors were never seen wearing less than a bathing suit considered appropriate at the time; a man and a woman were never shown in bed together; kisses rarely betrayed any sense of real passion. This was due partially to the producers' code established by the movie industry itself as a response to several sexual themes that appeared in a few movies in the 1920s.

The Roman Catholic Church instituted the Legion of Decency in 1934, and its standards were soon adopted by the Hollywood Production Code. Conservative attitudes in the early twentieth century influenced the depiction of alcohol, drug abuse, equality for blacks, women's rights, prostitution, communism, and other themes that did not fit into the prevailing mode of behavior or thought. That is not to say that sex symbols did not emerge from among the movie stars. Actors such as Mae West, Jean Harlow, Clark Gable, Humphrey Bogart, James Dean, and Marilyn Monroe undoubtedly drew theatergoers who were romantically attracted to their film images. The Supreme Court ruled in 1952 that motion pictures were protected by First Amendment rights, and the Hollywood Production Code slowly began to relax its standards (Strub, 2006).

In 1965, *The Pawnbroker* became the first American film to show bare female breasts. Today they are standard in a great many movies, and overtly erotic themes and explicitly sexual scenes are increasingly common in films. *Midnight Cowboy* (1969) dramatized the story of a male prostitute, and *Klute* (1971) dealt with some intimate details of a female prostitute's life. *The Graduate* (1967), one of the most popular films of its day, portrayed a brief sexual encounter between a young man and an older woman. *Myra Breckinridge* (1970) and *The Christine Jorgensen Story* (1970) dealt with sex-change operations.

As sexual explicitness and nudity increased in films, the industry struggled with the question of ratings. The X rating for films, which proved to be a box office liability for movies carrying it, was replaced with the NC-17 classification, meaning no children under the age of 17 were permitted in the theater. However, the new rating seems to carry the same stigma as the old X rating, and many theaters will not show NC-17 movies. Polls have found that R-rated films are the most popular, particularly among the 18- to 34-year-old age group, followed by films with PG-13 ratings, and then by films with a PG rating. Films with NC-17 and G ratings trail far behind the others in their popularity. Producers face decisions about whether to cut explicit sexual scenes from their films in order to win the safer, and more lucrative, R rating.

In recent years, there have been many movies that feature sex-related themes. *Little Children* (2006) followed the development of an affair between a bored mother and a stay-at-home dad, against the backdrop of neighborhood fears about a local child molester. *Notes on a Scandal* (2006) explored the complexities of an older lesbian woman's obsessive attraction to a younger, married woman who was having an affair with one of her 15-year-old male students. In the 2007 films *Eastern Promises* and *Feast of Love* there were copious amounts of female and male nudity, along with steamy sex scenes.

The controversial film *The Reader* (2008) featured an ongoing sexual relationship between a 36-year-old woman and a 15-year-old boy during World War II. The Woody Allen film *Vicky Cristina Barcelona* (2008) included a *ménage à trois* relationship that persisted over several months in discreetly presented sex scenes. On a cruder level, *Zack and Miri Make a Porno* (2008) followed the comedic efforts of actors Seth Rogen and Elizabeth Banks to produce their own pornographic film. Horror and suspense films often include their share of nudity and sexy scenes too. The films *Friday the 13th, My Bloody Valentine,* and *Observe and Report,* produced in 2009, featured a good deal of nudity and sex along with violence and fear.

Educators, philosophers, and psychologists have engaged in debate concerning the significance of sex-related themes in films. As a society evolves, does its art reflect its changing values, or do artists and film-makers form the avant-garde in effecting these changes? As a society becomes more tolerant and breaks down the barriers of its stereotypical attitudes toward groups of people and sexual behaviors, how does the art of that society reflect these changes? More time and study will be necessary to provide definitive answers to these questions.

Women in Films

There has been controversy over how women have been depicted in American films. One study that compared male and female roles from 1927 through the late 1980s found that women's roles generally were rather rigidly stereotyped (Geiger, 2001). Women have frequently been portrayed as self-destructive, manipulative, and sexually seductive (see Figure 15.5). A common cinematic scene over the years has involved an aggressive man pulling a woman into his arms and forcing kisses on her. At first the woman pushes and fights against him with clenched fists, but eventually her body softens, her hands open and slide around his neck, and she surrenders herself to him passionately. This "rape myth" is believed to be perpetuated by such cinematic themes. The film *Secretary* (2002), which portrayed a sadomasochistic relationship between a troubled woman and her boss involving both verbal

■ FIGURE 15.5

The "Twilight" series of books and films has brought a new dimension of youthful sexuality into the media.

and physical domination, disturbed some people with its apparent abusiveness toward the female lead, but there was also a level of warmth in their relationship. Nonetheless, some films offer stronger, more positive images of women, often depicting strong bonds of friendship between them.

Name two recent films in which women are portrayed in positive roles. Explain your definition of "positive role."

Same-Gender Relationships in Films

Prior to 1960, gay and lesbian relationships were avoided as a cinematic theme. Some European films were frank about same-gender relationships, but American films tended to obscure even suggestions of same-gender attractions. When plays such as *A Streetcar Named Desire* (1952), *Tea and Sympathy* (1957), and *Cat on a Hot Tin Roof* (1958) were made into movies, their significant allusions to same-gender sexuality were lost. In the early 1960s, however, Hollywood became less hesitant about using gay themes. Tennessee Williams's 1960 film *Suddenly Last Summer* was reasonably straightforward about the topic (Waugh, 1996).

As society has become more tolerant of lesbian and gay relationships, such themes have been depicted in a variety of ways. *The Boys in the Band* emerged in 1972 as the first film to explore the problems of the gay male subculture, although some people have objected to the stereotyped image it presents. In the 1980s, the film *Making Love* (1982) dealt frankly with a married man who eventually left his wife to establish a gay relationship with another man. *Kiss of the Spider Woman* (1985) focused on the touching relationship of two male political prisoners, one openly gay and the other

■ FIGURE 15.6 *Gay Themes in the Movies*

Actors James Franco and Sean Penn portray gay lovers in the film *Milk*. It tells the story of Harvey Milk, a gay activist and the first openly gay public official elected in California, who was ultimately assassinated by a political opponent. Penn won a Best Actor Academy Award for the performance.

heterosexual. *The Crying Game* (1993) delighted critics and viewers alike with its intriguing story of a man who falls in love with a woman, only to learn later that "she" is actually a man. The film poses complex questions of romantic and sexual attraction.

The movie *Monster* (2003) showed a loving and sexual relationship between two troubled women, one of whom kills a man who raped her. *Kiss Kiss, Bang Bang* (2005) featured actor Val Kilmer as a gay private eye interacting with Robert Downey, Jr. The 2008 film *Milk* (see Figure 15.6) chronicled the story of gay city councilman Harvey Milk in San Francisco. One of the most popular films to attract attention for its homoerotic theme was *Brokeback Mountain* (2005), a film about two cowboys who fall in love and continue their relationship for years, even after they both have married. The fact that the cowboys did not fit common stereotypes of gay men may well have added to the film's popularity.

Transgender Identity in Films

Questions of romantic sexual attraction were complicated by issues of self-identity and social perceptions of gender in four films from the 1990s. In *The Ballad of Little Jo* (1993), Josephine masquerades as a young male in the American frontier as a means of survival. As a woman she is vulnerable to male violence, but as a male she realizes that she has lost her identity. In *Farewell My Concubine* (1993), a male character prepares to play the female lead in a Chinese opera. Offstage, he sexually desires his male counterpart in

the opera, thus confusing his own nature. This film at the same time becomes a metaphor for the identity crisis of China itself from the time of the warlords to the end of Mao's Cultural Revolution. *M. Butterfly* (1993), also set in the world of Chinese opera, tells the true story of a French diplomat who had a long affair with an opera star, while never knowing, by his own account, that "she" was really a man. The diplomat is depicted as being unable to see beyond the artifice of femininity, and thus his perception of his lover becomes his reality. The award-winning U.S. film *Boys Don't Cry* (1999) depicted a woman who lived as a man and eventually was murdered by intolerant men (Willox, 2003). More recently, actress Felicity Huffman was nominated for an Academy Award for her portrayal of a man in the process of becoming a woman who travels cross-country with his/her son in the movie *Transamerica* (2005).

Pornographic Films, Videos, and DVDs

Films whose main purpose is to show lengthy scenes of genitals and/or persons engaged in various forms of sexual activity are considered **hard-core pornography**. The earliest "adult films" were made before 1925,

hard-core pornography pornography that makes use of highly explicit depictions of sexual activity or shows lengthy scenes of genitals.

mostly by professionals who had access to 35mm movie camera equipment. As 16mm and 8mm film became available, amateurs began producing hard-core films for private use and sale. Popular from the 1950s through the early 1980s, these movies were 10 to 20 minutes in length and were sold for amounts that far exceeded the costs of production. In Great Britain, they were called blue movies, and in the United States, they were often labeled stag films. The latter term reflects the fact that such films generally were shown at all-male (stag) gatherings (Waugh, 2001). Eventually, adults-only theaters began to show feature-length hard-core films.

As home videocassette recorders (VCRs) and video cameras proliferated, the adult movie business in theaters was reduced to almost nothing, and the video business boomed. In 1978, about 100 hard-core films were produced. Today, thousands of new hard-core DVDs are released every year, some costing only a few thousand dollars to produce. Online pornography has cut into the direct retail business. The videocassette player overlapped the development of DVD technology, and both overlapped the increasing accessibility of the Internet (Buzzell, 2005).

Over time, there has been a decrease in the number and proportion of sexually aggressive scenes in such material (Bogaert, 2001). Explicit material has a higher proportion of sexual behaviors but a lower proportion of violent behaviors compared to R-rated movies. Four common themes have been noted in sexually explicit material: high levels of sexual desire, diverse sexual activity, ready availability of many sexual partners, and pleasure as the purpose of sexual activity.

A newer pornographic phenomenon is the home-made, amateur sex DVD, recorded by couples in their own homes. Apparently, some people who make such recordings derive sexual excitement from knowing that others will be viewing their sexual acts. Numerous companies will pay modest sums for them and then distribute them to paying customers. It is believed that from one-fifth to one-third of the hard-core material being sold in the United States today are at least partly amateur.

Television

Television represents one of the most powerful forms of mass communication, and it has increasingly included embedded sexual themes. The Telecommunications Reform Act of 1996 required the television industry to develop a ratings system for viewers, and since then programs have been designated for their sexual content, violence, and explicit language. Television soap operas, with more than 35 million viewers, average seven sexual incidents per hour. Two-thirds of prime-time television shows include sexual themes or behaviors but only rarely feature any reference to condoms, unintended pregnancy, or emotional consequences. Twelve percent of prime-time TV shows depict characters involved in sexual intercourse (Farrar et al., 2003).

There is a growing body of evidence that teenagers are affected by sexual content on television. Several longitudinal studies have shown a link between exposure to large amounts of television sexual content and earlier onset of intercourse and higher risks of teen pregnancy (Chandra et al., 2008; Strasburger, 2009). It has also been shown that teenaged boys who have their first sexual intercourse are more likely to regret the experience and be disappointed by it if they have been exposed to a great deal of sexual content on TV. The study suggests that the television content has created unrealistic expectations about intercourse for these young men (Martino et al., 2009).

Studies have been done on the portrayals of women and men on television. It has been reported that men on TV frequently comment on women's bodies and physical appearance and that masculinity is often equated with being sexual and aggressively pursuing sex. Portraying heterosexuality as the most normal way to behave is also common. Feminist issues and themes tend to be trivialized and undervalued. Experts have warned that television needs to offer more images of sexuality that emphasize planning, honesty, pleasure, and protection (Kim et al., 2007).

It is now commonplace for sexuality to become part of the scripts for TV dramas and situation comedies. The now-syndicated comedy show *Seinfeld* was the first prime-time network television program to deal with masturbation as a theme, and allusions to masturbation now have made their way into most situation comedies, along with frequent references to penises and breasts. Television programs such as *Queer as Folk, Will and Grace,* and *Queer Eye for the Straight Guy* helped pave the way for gay characters and couples on mainstream television programming. The prime-time show *Brothers and Sisters* features several openly gay men, two of whom married on the show (see Figure 15.7), and the comedy *Modern Family* has a gay male couple that has adopted a baby.

Advertising

More than any other medium in American society today, advertising uses and exploits sex, and the evidence suggests that it is a powerful sales tool (Reichert, 2003). Advertisements for underwear have been highly popular, although Calvin Klein came under fire for using models who appeared to be underage. Print advertisements for Obsession perfume often use naked bodies in rather subdued romantic lighting. The young, attractive male and the beautiful female predominate

FIGURE 15.7 *Gay Couples on TV are Becoming Increasingly Common*

This married couple, featured on television's *Brothers and Sisters,* has been discussing having a child by gestational surrogate.

in advertisements for alcoholic beverages, perfume, jewelry, cars, and clothing, because the basic idea behind using sex to sell a product is something advertisers call "identification." The message is that if the consumer uses a certain perfume, wears a certain pair of jeans, or drives a certain car, he or she will be as glamorous and attractive as the model and will experience the kind of excitement and romance implied in the advertisement (see Figure 15.8).

If the advertisement is not blatantly sexual, then it may be subliminally sexual. Advertisers may use a technique called embedding, in which they deliberately hide emotionally or sexually charged words or pictures in the background of an advertisement (Reichert, 2003). More frequently, women and men tend to be portrayed in advertising in rather specific and stereotypical ways, generating criticism that their portrayal perpetuates outmoded and unfair images. On the other hand, it has been argued that such images are simply reflections of the prevailing attitudes about gender that seem to help sell products on the basis of sex appeal. It is clear that women are used more frequently than men as sex-related objects in advertising (Reichert & Lambiase, 2003). Precisely because of these facts, such advertising causes consternation among critics, some of whom view these advertising messages as a type of mind control.

The question has been posed concerning why condom ads have not become more mainstream in the media given the prevalence of other sex-related messages. Some publishers and broadcasters claim they are worried that the public will disapprove of such advertising, although surveys have shown that 71 percent of Americans favor condom advertising on television. The major networks continue to balk at airing

FIGURE 15.8 *Sex in Advertising*

This Calvin Klein billboard in Times Square in New York City provides a graphic reminder that sexual themes play a significant role in advertising. The typical suggestion is that using a certain product will somehow lead to a better sex life.

them during prime time hours (Pardun & Forde, 2003; Strasburger, 2009).

We might also ask why sexual messages are so powerful. Why does everyone want to identify with a symbol of sex? One possible answer is that in our culture sex is synonymous with youth, attractiveness, and desirability, and it implies wealth and power. However, whether the media have created that image identification or simply mirror it is a debatable point.

■ Internet Sexuality

The Internet has been adapted for a variety of sex-related uses, ranging from sexuality education to the transmission of sexually explicit materials, to sites for seeking relationships and sex with virtual and real partners. It has opened new vistas for sexual communication and raised new concerns about how cyberspace interactions should be controlled and regulated. People living thousands of miles apart can carry on sexual conversations or perform virtual sex acts with each other.

There are websites and forums for every imaginable sexual interest and fetish, easily accessible to people of all ages from the privacy of their own computers (Fisher & Barak, 2001). On some sites, scantily clad or

Source: David Horsey. © Tribune Media Services, Inc. All Rights Reserved. Reprinted with permission.

nude women and men may be viewed live while participating in an ongoing live chat with viewers. Private time, during which the models perform sexual acts for one or a few viewers, can be purchased, constituting a form of long-distance cyber-prostitution.

Like any medium, the Internet opens the potential for abuse in sex-related matters. Some people have been subjected to sexual harassment or stalking by anonymous participants on websites. Purveyors of illicit child pornography use the Internet to transmit explicit sexual images of children despite attempts by government agencies to shut them down. Concern still exists about uncontrolled access to cybersex by underage individuals, and some pedophiles have used computer networks to make contact with young people. Even though there are a number of Internet controls that can be used to prevent access by minors to sexual material, these filters may also block legitimate, non-pornographic information as well, including sites on breast cancer and reproductive health. Finding a workable and ethical balance for access to sex on the Internet remains a daunting challenge.

Online Pornography

Pornographic websites number in the millions. The majority of consumers of online computer porn are male, although females are substantially represented. For those who are predisposed to compulsive behavior, use of the Internet to access sexual material may become compulsive or addictive. The combination of easy access, affordability, and anonymity often conspires to cause some individuals to become involved with sexu-

ally explicit materials for hours at a time, sometimes interfering with daily life and work (Buzzell, 2005).

See "Technology and Sexual Fantasy" on SexSource Online.

By analyzing surveys of several hundred college students, one study has found some interesting relationships between individual personality characteristics and the kinds of uses and arousal people find in online pornography (Paul, 2009). Instead of the researcher devising the types of pornography accessed based on sexual content, a factor analysis was performed on the reports of participants themselves. It was found some 15 different categories of sexually explicit material could be condensed to three types that are identifiable for men: *standard fare,* consisting of common sexual acts such as intercourse and oral sex; *male specialized* pornography that includes more fetishistic types of sexual interest such as large breasts or "shemales," or urophilic behavior; and *male focused content* that features male models only or gay males. Women's preferences fall into only two identifiable types: *standard fare* and *female specialized.* It was found that there was almost no reporting of sexually violent or aggressive pornography.

The study looked at how certain personality variables seemed to play a role in which types of pornography people chose and the degree of sexual arousal they experienced in response to viewing them. It was hypothesized, for example, that *gender* would play a role in how much pornography was accessed. It was also assumed that people who demonstrate high levels of *sensation-seeking* characteristics, suggesting that they enjoy novelty, intense sensations and experiences even in the face of potential consequences, would show greater levels of pornography use. Another hypothesis held that individuals who were more *erotophilically disposed* (sex-positive in their attitudes) to sexual interests would be more likely to seek out pornography and be sexually aroused by it. And finally, it was expected that study participants who demonstrated more *antisocial personality characteristics* would tend to access more online pornography and be aroused by it.

Even though the results of this research may have limited generalizability because of its college student subjects, they have given us a sensible theoretical concept into which we may fit some understandings about online pornography. Here is a summary of the findings:

1. Males do indeed seek out pornography with greater frequency than females do, and they experience higher levels of sexual arousal in response to it, except for content featuring only male models and gay male sex, to which women seem to have greater arousal.

2. The researcher had expected to find that people who were high in sensation seeking would use more pornography and get more aroused by it, but this proved not to be true at all for women and only mildly true for men.

3. There was a positive correlation between erotophilic disposition and the frequency of use and degree of arousal in both men and women, but only in the use of the "standard fare" pornography.

4. Both men and women who showed evidence of antisocial personality characteristics consistently accessed pornography more frequently and were more sexually aroused by it than men or women who did not show such characteristics (Paul, 2009).

These findings offer at least a foundation on which further research on Internet pornography may be built. It is always important to remember that correlations found in such research cannot be reconstructed into statements about cause-and-effect regarding the relationship between people's exposure to pornography and their sexual behaviors.

Child Pornography

One of the most secretive, most lucrative, and most damaging types of pornography is that involving children. Children are emotionally unable to give true consent to sexual behavior and thus are the innocent victims of adult greed. **Kiddie porn,** as it is more popularly known, involves everything from children posing in the nude, to suggestive movement, to sexual activity with others their own age and with adults. Although they are often monitored by authorities, thousands of child pornography sites are available on the Internet. Sting operations have been directed at arresting people who have downloaded child pornography, but some observers have said that these events may create more hype than actual deterrence (Fulda, 2002).

Courts in the United States continue to support the contention that child pornography lies outside First Amendment protection. The Child Pornography Prevention Act of 1996 supports stiff penalties for those who involve children in sexual exploitation through the making and distribution of pornography. The penalties for causing a child to engage in explicit sexual behavior before a camera or for distributing child pornography have escalated. Thousands of new cases are opened by the FBI each year for the posting of child pornography and related violations. Rings of people engaged in the transmission of child sex images over the Internet have been prosecuted and given stiff sentences. Some photographers, book distributors, and librarians believe that parts of the law are too restrictive and run counter to constitutional guarantees of freedom of speech (Jenkins, 2001).

There has also been controversy over what constitutes child pornography. In one case, a man was convicted because he had videotapes of teenage and preteen girls in bathing suits who were dancing, and he had zoomed in on the clothed genital area; another court overturned the conviction because there was no nudity or discernible "lascivious exhibitions." Virtual computer-generated images of children and adolescents, found to be permissible by the Supreme Court, have become part of this market. Such controversies certainly will persist, but the message condemning the use of underage individuals in pornography seems clear.

Sex Seeking on the Internet

The Internet has become a popular place to connect with other people, and sometimes those connections are sexual in nature. It provides links among people who share a common sexual orientation or paraphilia, helping them feel less marginalized by their sexual interests (McKenna, Green, & Smith, 2001). It offers services for finding partners for romantic and sexual relationships, matching people with similar personalities, interests, and geographic locations. The Internet also offers simulated worlds in which users may create an entirely new persona, or "avatar," sometimes engaging in virtual sexual activity with the avatars of other people. Users of such social networking sites as MySpace or Facebook often post pictures or information that are sex-related or suggestive, there has been little study on the impact of these sites. Research has begun to emerge concerning other online sex-seeking behaviors and their impacts on people.

In a study of 15,246 Internet users, 2 percent of both the men and women reported levels of online sex-seeking behavior amounting to more than 11 hours per week, classified in the compulsive range. People in this group were more likely to be single and to be gay or bisexual. In terms of online hooking up, however, married people are five times more likely than singles to go on a date with someone they have met online. In fact, it has been suggested that married people who are dissatisfied in their marriages may use the Internet to find attractive new partners to help ease their transition out of the marriage (Albright, 2008).

Gay men and lesbian women, followed by bisexual people, are the most likely to seek serious relationships online and may also use the Internet as a means to find casual sexual hookups. Those not located in urban areas may find this an easier way to connect with partners

kiddie porn the distribution and sale of photographs and films of children or younger teenagers engaging in some form of sexual activity.

without having to be "out" in their local communities (Lever et al., 2008). Confirming other information we know about women and men, women are more likely to chat about sex online, while men tend to steer away from such relational contexts and prefer to view sexually graphic images. Women are also more likely to share what they are experiencing online with their real-life partners, apparently finding the cyber explorations to be potentially enhancing for sexual encounters at home. Men, on the other hand, are more likely to keep their online sexual adventures secret from their partners and to masturbate during them.

These data may play a role in another finding that translates to men who seek sexual gratification online seeming more critical of their offline partners' bodies and having sex less often with them. Women who seek sexual materials online are more likely to have sex with their offline partners more frequently. It is also known that men are more upset by online sexual infidelity while women are more upset by emotional infidelity (Albright, 2008; Whitty & Quigley, 2008). Such findings suggest that online sex-seeking behaviors may indeed have various kinds of impact on people's real-life relationships, and this deserves further study.

One of the newer opportunities for online sex seeking revolves around simulation and role-playing games that can be joined online, including the popular Second Life. These sites allow members to create entirely new personalities and appearances who then interact with other members. While studies are only beginning to emerge about such simulation sites, it has been suggested that engaging in cybersex on Second Life is a common type of interaction. It may give people who are interested in BDSM or who have thought about hiring a sex worker a chance to try it out virtually, without any of the risks that might be present in their offline lives. These games and simulations are bound to evolve further in the years ahead, and it seems indisputable that opportunities for sexual adventure will be part of that evolution (Melby, 2007, 2008).

■ Effects of Sexually Explicit Materials

There seems to be a greater level of acceptance of pornography among males and younger people, and people under age 25 tend to report higher rates of usage. In one Norwegian study, three basic dimensions of attitudes about pornography were identified. Some people seem to perceive pornography mostly as a way of enhancing sexual pleasure. Others judge it to be a moral issue, seeing it as either right or wrong. A final group places pornography within the social framework of its use; when explicit media are viewed by groups of friends, it may not seem as "dirty" or even as sexual as it would have had it been viewed in private. Attitudes toward the material seem to mediate how individuals may or may not access sexually explicit materials (Traeen, Spitznogle, & Beverfjord, 2004).

Denmark legalized the sale of pornography in the 1960s and yet very little research on its effects has been conducted there until recently. A study of Danish men and women aged 18 to 30 found that the men had been exposed to pornography more frequently and starting at younger ages than had the women. Men were more likely to use pornography for their own sexual enjoyment, usually as a source of arousal during masturbation, or with groups of friends. Women were more apt to integrate pornography into their sexual activities with partners. Men seemed to prefer more explicit hardcore representations than did the women. For both sexes it was found that high frequencies of masturbation and a lower age at first exposure to pornography were strong predictors of pornography consumption. This was thought to be suggestive of high levels of interest in sex that may have developed relatively early in individual's development. People with a high level of sex drive might well seek out pornography at an earlier age, masturbate more frequently, and have more sexual partners, as compared with people with lower levels of sexual interest (Hald, 2006)

Although viewing sexually explicit materials has been associated with adverse effects in the popular media, including the wrecking of relationships, sexual addiction, and negative impacts on people's body images, research suggests that people who view pornography do not tend to perceive it as having had negative effects on their lives. To the contrary, both men and women have reported more positive effects on various aspects of their sexual lives and minimal negative effects of viewing such materials. The sexual backgrounds that people have seem to be important mediators for these effects. It could also be that this is an example of a *third party effect,* in which people have a tendency to assume that media will be more influential to other people than to themselves (Hald & Malamuth, 2008).

Conflicting positions on the positive and negative potentials of sexually explicit material were once based in two major theoretical camps. **Modeling theory** held that people exposed to sexual acts through pornography

modeling theory a perspective that suggests that people will copy behavior they view in pornography.

Real People

A T-Shirt Places a Male Residence Hall under Fire

A freshman residence hall that had traditionally been all male had developed a reputation for its macho image on the campus. In fun, the dorm was nicknamed "The Cave," and its residents took pride in their special identity. Although college officials discouraged use of the building's nickname, the staff who lived there often boasted of the camaraderie that its residents seemed to share. They had intramural sports teams, parties, and a variety of annual special events. One of "The Cave's" traditions was to create a specially designed T-shirt for its residents each fall. One year, the T-shirt pictured a drawing of two cavemen figures dragging a cavewoman by the hair toward a door labeled "The Cave."

Soon after the T-shirt began to appear, there was an outcry from various campus constituencies condemning the shirt and what was perceived as its antiwomen message. Some faculty members banned the wearing of the T-shirts in the classroom, claiming that it constituted harassment of women. Many of the men wearing the shirt took offense at this reaction, saying that there had been no malicious intent in the shirt's design and claiming that the U.S. Constitution protected their right of freedom of expression. They received support from some women on the campus, who agreed that the shirt certainly did not reflect the attitudes of men in the dorm toward women. They argued that opponents were going too far in their assumptions. College officials made certain that institutional funds had not been used to pay for the T-shirt, and they also issued a statement that they did not support the negative message it conveyed. However, officials declined to prohibit the wearing of the shirt on a general basis. They reminded those individuals who felt that the shirt was in any way personally harassing that they could lodge complaints through the institution's grievance procedures.

The "Cave T-Shirt," as it came to be known, turned out to be a highly educational phenomenon. It generated many open debates and classroom discussions about individual rights of expression versus the rights of individuals to live and work in a non-hostile environment. It provided an excellent real-life situation that tested the complicated issues on all sides of the question. The controversy led men and women to talk more openly about their attitudes toward one another. As things turned out, no one ever brought formal complaints about the T-shirt, and the wearers of the shirt tried to be considerate of those faculty members who explained that they were personally offended by the picture. Although it rather quickly faded from popularity, the T-shirt's impact remained legendary on the campus.

Would you have been offended by the drawing on this T-shirt? If so, would you have been moved to take any formal action against being exposed to it? Are there drawings, pictures, or words on a T-shirt that in your opinion should be banned from being worn in public? Explain.

had a greater likelihood of copying this behavior in their own lives. Another point of view, the **catharsis theory,** maintained that pornography actually prevented violence or unconventional sexual behavior by providing a release of sexual tension for the viewer or reader (Davis & Bauserman, 1993). While both of these models may have some validity, it is simplistic to assume that sexually explicit material would have the same effects on everyone. A more inclusive perspective is espoused by the **confluence theory,** which assumes that cultural influences and specific individual personality variables ultimately determine how particular people are affected by pornography (Kingston et al., 2009).

Responses to Sexually Explicit Materials

Research on the effects of being exposed to sexually explicit materials has essentially found that the effects

catharsis theory the suggestion that viewing pornography provides a release for sexual tension, thereby preventing antisocial behavior.

confluence theory the assumption that cultural influences and specific individual personality variables determine how particular people are affected by pornography.

on any particular individual are most likely mediated by a variety of factors, and sometimes different studies have produced seemingly conflicting results. The findings always tend to be controversial, since there are conflicting social perspectives as well. One side believes that pornographic materials, with few exceptions, are covered by Constitutional guarantees of freedom of expression. The other side holds that pornography has harmful effects on people and families and therefore should be largely prohibited. Neither camp can yet find entirely conclusive support for their positions from existing data. The most reasonable conclusion to be drawn so far is that for the average person, viewing sexually explicit images probably has few negative effects, but for some who already have antisocial personality characteristics, pornography may aggravate or magnify those antisocial qualities. It is fair to say that sexually explicit material is a form of *persuasive communication,* because it clearly has impacts on those who view it. The questions revolve around how much impact, and what kinds of impact (Davis & Bauserman, 1993; Kingston et al., 2009).

Self-Perceived Effects

To be commercially successful, pornography must produce sexual arousal and positive emotional reactions as defined by the viewer. These appear to be the primary motivations for people to seek out and view sexually explicit materials. Almost all such materials do produce arousal, as demonstrated by the self-reporting of research participants and by direct measurement of genital and other physiological changes. Emotional responses have been measured on scales of from 5 to 50 points of variation, on which people rate their intensity of both pleasant and unpleasant reactions. Seventy to 90 percent of both men and women experience measurable physiological arousal in response to sexually explicit material. Across various studies, men fairly consistently react with more positive emotions to sexually explicit material, and women, with higher levels of negative emotions (Janssen, Carpenter, & Graham, 2003).

There is some evidence that how an experiment presents pornography can affect how it is perceived by the study participants. In one series of studies, participants were shown pictures of nude people for a few milliseconds, not long enough for the picture to register in their consciousness. However, this subliminal stimulus did have some effects on the viewers. For both men and women, this subliminal priming led them to be able to access sex-related thoughts more readily. Women seemed to experience more aversive reactions to this result (Gillath et al., 2007).

In another study, women seemed to react to a sexually explicit film more positively and with greater self-reported sexual arousal when it was suggested that they allow themselves to become absorbed in the film and imagine themselves as being in the film. When they were instructed to be impartial spectators to the film, not allowing themselves to get personally absorbed in its contents, women had fewer positive responses and less arousal. So it seems likely that one's personal perspective on pornography can affect one's subjective responses to it (Sheen & Koukounas, 2009).

In the research done with 18 to 30 year olds in Denmark, participants were asked to complete the Pornography Consumption Effect Scale after viewing pornography, rating effects on such things as sexual knowledge, attitudes toward sex, their sex lives, and their general quality of life. Most of the respondents tended to rate the effects quite positively. Men tended to report more positive effects than women, and while reports of negative effects were minimal, men also reported more negative effects (Hald & Malamuth, 2008).

People who find material sexually arousing are more likely to react positively to it, but sometimes the arousal and emotional reactions are quite independent. Depicted sexual behaviors that the individual considers bizarre or socially deviant are likely to produce a negative emotional response, even if the person has also been sexually aroused by seeing them (Koukounas & McCabe, 2001). The research confirms that for every type of sexually explicit stimulus, at least some people react with arousal and positive emotions. For those same stimuli, other people are not aroused and/or have a negative emotional response.

Effects on Attitudes

There are concerns about how viewing sexually explicit materials might change people's attitudes toward sexuality, relationships, or other people. Theories of attitude change postulate that there are two paths through which human beings process persuasive communication such as sexually explicit material. The *central* processing route involves careful, thoughtful, and systematic processing of the information, whereas the *peripheral* processing route is more automatic and involves a minimum of cognitive effort. It is theorized that for real attitudinal change to occur, material must be processed thoroughly through the central route and the individual must possess clear motivation and the ability to pursue this path. For most people, sexually explicit material is viewed solely for its arousal value, and psychologists believe that as such viewers tend to be distracted from processing it through any central path. It is not likely that it leads to substantial or long-term attitudinal changes in most people (Ciclitira, 2004).

Pornography is often assumed to create more negative attitudes toward women. A survey of over a thousand consumers of pornography in Australia found that there was no particular correlation between the amount of pornography viewed and the consumers' negative attitudes toward women. There was a positive correlation between such negative attitudes and voting for a conservative political party, living in a rural area, and having lower levels of formal education (McKee, 2007). Nonetheless, effects on the attitudes of particular individuals may result from a confluence of specific influences within the person's personality and surrounding culture. Accordingly we can never assume that viewing pornography cannot produce any negative or antisocial attitudes. Some studies have in fact suggested that high rates of exposure to pornography may be associated with negative attitudes toward women or even greater acceptance of sexual aggression toward women. This seems to be particularly true of men who choose to view pornography that depicts sexual violence, but it may be true of some others as well (Kingston et al., 2009).

Other research has found that males with a history of more exposure to sexually explicit materials do not hold more negative attitudes toward women and, in fact, may be more gender egalitarian in their attitudes. Many men tend to respond more negatively to scenes depicting sexual aggression and more positively to egalitarian scenes, but attitudes seem mostly unaffected (Bauserman, 1998; DeVoss, 2002). On the other hand, exposure to massive amounts of material that depicts callousness or adversarial relationships with women seems to strengthen such attitudes in men who already have a predisposition toward them. It is often claimed that pornography turns women into sexual objects. An analysis of 50 popular sexually explicit films actually found that, based on 12 measures of objectification, women were no more objectified than were the men in the films (McKee, 2005).

Behavioral Effects of Pornography

The research on the possible behavioral effects of sexually explicit materials has focused primarily on sexual and aggressive behaviors. As might be anticipated, most research has found that at least some, and often the majority of, participants report an increase in sexual behavior within 24 hours following exposure. The behaviors tend to be those in which the person would participate with some frequency anyway, including sexual thoughts and fantasies, daydreams, talking about sex, masturbation, oral sex, and sexual intercourse (Davis & Bauserman, 1993; Kingston et al., 2009). It has been suggested that early exposure to pornography, at or before age 14, could be associated with more compulsive sexual behavior in adult life, but one study did not find such an association in either men or women (Stulhofer, Jelovica, & Ruzic, 2008).

It is neither ethical nor practical for researchers to carry out real-world studies to determine whether people will behave in a sexually aggressive manner following exposure to pornography. Instead, researchers create artificial situations to measure aggression. One type of study sets up a scenario involving a "confederate" attempting to provoke aggressive behavior after a subject has been exposed to pornography, by insulting the subject. Males who are exposed to nonaggressive pornography are no more likely to be aggressive toward females than are controls who have been exposed to neutral, or nonexplicit, material. Exposure to aggressive depictions in pornography sometimes seems to increase nonsexual aggression somewhat, though usually only when the subject is provoked again by a confederate. These effects have been limited to laboratory settings and seem to disappear rapidly (Davis & Bauserman, 1993).

Although researchers have difficulty designing studies to find whether exposure to pornography will cause sexual aggression or violence, they have conducted studies to see if an association can be found between a history of exposure to pornography and later sexual behaviors. Early studies found that institutionalized sex offenders had actually been exposed to less pornography than carefully matched controls: average, nonoffender heterosexuals. There is newer evidence that men with more antisocial personality traits seem to use all forms of online pornography more frequently, are more aroused by content that is more socially inappropriate, and seem to need more intense stimuli to experience arousal. They are also apparently more prone to sexual aggression, although this has been difficult to confirm in natural, real-life situations (Kingston et al., 2009; Paul, 2009).

Should pornography be available to the general public? Should there be any restrictions in terms of age of consumer or theme of material?

Most adult males tend to have the highest levels of arousal in response to sexually explicit materials featuring adults of their preferred sex, but they may also have substantial levels of arousal when postpubescent children or adolescents of the preferred sex are shown. They have minimal, though often measurable, levels of response to children depicted in pornography. One study of adult pedophiles who were attracted to boys found that viewing erotica involving nudity and sexual acts of boys did not seem to cause them to commit sexual acts with boys (Riegel, 2004).

In a survey of four countries where pornographic materials are widely available—Denmark, Sweden, Germany, and the United States—there did not seem to be any correlation between that availability and the incidence of rape in the society. It has been proposed that the motivation to rape may not be influenced by exposure to pornography, but rather that pornography could reinforce already existing beliefs and values about rape (Wilson et al., 2002). One study found that as pornography became more accessible online in the United States, rates of rape actually declined (D'Amato, 2006).

The intellectual ability of subjects has also been shown to be a variable in such research. Men with lower IQs are more likely to act more sexually suggestive toward women and to stand closer to them following the viewing of sexual violence; no difference was noted in men with higher IQs. Men of higher intelligence who are not prone to aggression tend not to choose violent pornography and do not seem to be moved to antisocial behavior by other types of sexually explicit material (Bogaert, 2001; Malamuth, Addison, & Koss, 2001).

Research that has investigated what role pornography plays prior to a sex offender committing a crime has had mixed results. Some studies have found that relatively few offenders viewed pornography before committing their offense, while others have suggested that perhaps a quarter of offenders viewed pornography within the 12 hours prior to the offense. The offenders' propensity for violence has not been studied, leaving out what may well be a significant mediator for their behavior. More research is needed before we can conclude that there is a clear connection between the use of sexually explicit materials and antisocial, aggressive, or compulsive sexual behavior, and at this point any such connection might be most applicable to men who are already prone to aggressive or violent behavior. Assuming that pornography consumption is the cause of such behavior, rather than simply another symptom of a particular offender's predisposition to antisocial behavior, would not be warranted given the present evidence (Kingston et al., 2009; Paul, 2009).

■ Legal Aspects of Pornography and Sexual Behavior

Lawmakers and law enforcers seem to fall into two major philosophical camps. Some believe that the law has a responsibility to enforce private morals publicly and to prohibit whatever the community or society deems morally wrong or offensive. Others hold that the purpose of the law is to protect rather than to prohibit. They are less concerned about pornography consumption or sexual activities involving consenting adults, and they believe that government should stay out of the bedrooms of private citizens (Graupner, 2000).

National Commissions on Pornography

In the past 40 years, two conservative presidential administrations have convened commissions in hopes of demonstrating the negative effects of pornography and therefore building support for regulating and controlling its distribution. Neither time has the desired result materialized. The majority report of Richard Nixon's 1970 Presidential Commission on Obscenity and Pornography actually recommended the repeal of legislation prohibiting the sale, exhibition, or distribution of sexual materials to consenting adults. It stated that the recommendation was based on the commission's having found "no evidence to date that exposure to explicit sexual materials plays a significant role in the causation of delinquent or criminal behavior among youth or adults." Additionally, the commission declared that pornography did not cause "social or individual harms such as . . . sexual or nonsexual deviancy or severe emotional disturbance" (pp. 32, 58). A minority of commission members did not concur with the report, however, and the U.S. Senate and President Nixon rejected the commission's recommendations.

Governmental commissions clearly serve mainly to fulfill the political agendas of particular administrations. In 1984 Ronald Reagan appointed an Attorney General's Commission on Pornography to hold hearings on the effects of pornography. From its inception, the group was charged with making recommendations on how "the spread of pornography could be contained." Its work was governed by the premise that pornography was a "serious national problem." Commission members were chosen for their recognized anti pornography stances. The commission had neither the funds nor the time to support new research studies, relying instead on the testimony of witnesses. This led to claims that the group's conclusions were simplistic and not justified by scientific data (Mosher, 1986). The majority report concluded that violent pornography caused sexually aggressive behavior toward women and children and fostered accepting attitudes toward rape. There were mixed opinions on the potential effects of pornography deemed "nonviolent and nondegrading" by the commission.

Pornography, the Courts, and the Law

In 1868, obscenity was legally defined as any material whose tendency was to "deprave and corrupt those whose minds are open to such immoral influences, and into whose hands a publication of this sort may fall." It was illegal to purvey obscenity to the public. In the landmark 1957 Supreme Court case *Roth v. United*

States, obscenity was redefined as matter appealing to prurient interest ("a shameful or morbid interest in nudity, sex, or excretion, which goes beyond customary limits of candor"). The Court further ruled, however, that censorship of obscene material would not be allowed if the material had some "socially redeeming significance." In 1969, in *Stanley v. Georgia,* the Court ruled that a person is entitled to possess pornography in the privacy of his or her own home and to use that pornography to satisfy whatever intellectual or emotional needs he or she desires.

The U.S. Congress has tried at various times to take steps that would eliminate most sexual content from the Internet altogether, but the Supreme Court has tended to block such efforts on constitutional grounds. In 1998, Congress overwhelmingly passed the Child Online Protection Act that banned access of minors to pornographic websites. The law was quickly met with court challenges of its constitutionality, and in 2009 it was effectively struck down when the Supreme Court refused to hear a final appeal for its revival. In terms of pornography in general, the Court has essentially ruled that individual state legislatures may adopt their own limits on commerce in pornography, placing more of the responsibility for judgments about pornography on local governments.

While laws prohibiting child pornography have generally held up well, the Court ruled in 2002 that to exclude virtual images of nude people engaged in sexual activity, even if they are virtual depictions of children, would be unconstitutional. The battle continues between the Justice Department and those who champion the right of people to access sex-related materials that have not involved actual minors.

The pornography issue is intimately associated with the principles of freedom of speech and freedom of the press and with the role of the courts and the law in upholding those principles. Although some people crusade against censorship and for the freedom to read or view whatever sexually oriented matter one wishes, others argue that "trash" can and should be distinguished from "art" and that censorship should be allowed even in a democracy. Two fundamental issues in the censorship argument are the assumptions that sexual images will lead to inappropriate behavior and that these images objectify human beings, in a sense dehumanizing them. There are those who do not feel that the evidence supports such assumptions and that, although censorship may offer the illusion of solving social problems, in reality it leads to the loss of freedoms. Some evidence indicates that enforcement of anti-pornography laws does not significantly change the rate of arrests for rape, prostitution, or other sex offenses (Levesque, 2002; McKee, 2005).

The Supreme Court of Canada decided that pornographic materials by definition "subordinated or de-graded" women and declared it legitimate to suppress such materials. Deciding what constitutes undue sexual exploitation is still left to individual prosecutors and lower courts in Canada, creating a great deal of confusion and leading to ongoing debate. Again, the problems seem to lie in the vague definition of what constitutes pornography, the assumption that it is harmful, and the provision that anyone harmed may bring suit. Clearly, pornography presents very real challenges in defining freedom of expression and setting the boundaries that any society will use in regulating such materials (Levesque, 2002).

What role, if any, should the government take in legislating sexual behavior or access to sexually explicit materials?

Legal Regulation of Sexual Behavior

In the area of sexual behavior, it seems that for every activity some people find disturbing or worthy of moral disapproval, a law has been enacted to prohibit the activity. Laws have attempted to regulate the criteria of consent for sex, the nature of the sexual act, the object to which it may be directed, and where the act may take place. Although the laws concerning sexual behavior differ among the states, it is likely that a great many adults in the United States have performed sexual acts considered at least in some states to be criminal under the law. There are only two types of sexual behavior that are not potentially subject to criminal prosecution as long as they are practiced in private: solitary masturbation and intercourse between husband and wife.

States often have laws prohibiting forms of behavior that fall into the category of "deviate sexual intercourse," without necessarily specifying the gender of the participants. These laws were once called **sodomy laws,** with the term sodomy being applied rather freely to many behaviors legally defined as deviate sexual intercourse, including oral-genital, genital-anal, oral-anal, and manual-genital contact. They were once enforced mostly against male-male activity. The majority of states permit consenting adults to engage in private sexual acts of their choosing but enforce their deviate sexual activity laws when minors or public behaviors are involved (Quindlen, 2003).

The U.S. Supreme Court handed down a landmark ruling in 2003 that overturned a Texas sodomy law.

sodomy laws laws in some states that prohibit a variety of sexual behaviors, often described as deviate sexual intercourse. These laws often are enforced discriminatorily against particular groups, such as gay males.

The law had been invoked against a gay male couple who had been having sex in private in their own home. The police had broken in because of a false report of a weapon being present, and the men were arrested for their sexual activity. The Court ruled that the law was demeaning to gay people and that the government has no authority to regulate the sexual conduct of "consenting adults acting in private."

The debate over whether sex-related laws should aim at prohibition or protection continues. The American Bar Association has joined the Group for the Advancement of Psychiatry in calling for sex offenders to be confined for appropriate treatment of their sexual disorders rather than simply incarcerated for punishment. Those in favor of legal reforms argue that laws prohibiting sexual behavior between consenting adults are attempts to impose specific moral and religious standards on citizens.

See "The Right to Privacy" on
SexSource Online.

Sex and the Constitution

The legal aspects of sexual behavior cannot be considered fairly without examining some of the constitutional implications. Since the U.S. Constitution was written, there has been a conflict over the extent to which it guarantees personal liberty in cases where other people are not harmed. The debate sometimes has focused on the laws governing, or attempting to govern, sexual behavior. Some experts insist that laws prohibiting consensual sexual activity between adults—particularly gay men or lesbians—are indeed unconstitutional. When these laws have been vaguely worded, courts have sometimes declared them "void for vagueness."

Three other constitutional principles have been used to overturn laws regulating consensual adult sexual behavior. One is the "independent rights" doctrine, which holds that the Constitution imposes certain restrictions on state laws that might interfere with personal liberty. Another is the "right of privacy" doctrine, which, in many courts, has been used to uphold the concept that what people do in private should not be the concern of prohibitive laws unless someone is being harmed. Finally, the "equal protection" clause of the Fourteenth Amendment has been interpreted to require that state laws be nondiscriminatory both in their statutory expression and in their enforcement. Colorado became the first state to pass a state constitutional amendment in the 1990s that denied gays and lesbians legal protection from discrimination. The amendment never took effect because of an initial court

ruling against it, and the U.S. Supreme Court struck down the measure on constitutional grounds as discriminatory and hostile toward a particular group of people.

A current issue that is gaining more attention is called *civil commitment*. Around 20 states allow sex offenders to be confined in secure treatment facilities without release dates even after they have completed serving their criminal sentences. These laws are based on the assumption that severe offenders have a mental disorder making it likely that they will repeat their sexual offenses. These laws have sometimes been passed by legislatures after horrible and highly publicized crimes in which a repeat sex offender has killed someone during a repeat offense. Civil confinement is defended as supporting public safety and is condemned as a violation of civil liberties. What is needed are better predictive mechanisms to determine the likelihood of someone reoffending, and more careful definitions within the law of cases when confinement for treatment is truly warranted for the public good. Further research is needed to provide such information (Melby, 2008).

See "Arthur, An Attorney for First
Amendment Issues," on
SexSource Online.

Special Issues and the Law

Gathering Sex Information in Public Schools

Public schools sometimes administer surveys of students to gather information about sexual attitudes and behaviors. These surveys can yield data that help with curriculum planning, provision of health services, and following trends among youth. Parents sometimes question the legality of administering such surveys to minors and object to their children being asked such personal questions. Courts have generally upheld the right of public schools to use such survey instruments so long as the goals of the study are made transparent to students and their parents prior to the survey being given, and provided that any student is free *not* to participate in the study. Beyond these common sense rules, parents generally have not been allowed to impose on the rights of schools to determine what sexual information they provide to students. Similarly, rights to privacy have been maintained (Bullis, 2008).

Sexual Assault and Rape

Historically, women were not regarded as equal to men under the law and instead were treated as men's possessions. Therefore, forced sex was viewed not as a crime against the female victim but as a property crime against the man who "owned" her—either her father or her husband. In the United States, laws passed in 1868 required that rape be corroborated by evidence of actual penetration, the use of force, and identification of the rapist. In the 1970s, corroboration laws were generally repealed, lessening the burden of proof for the victim. Nonetheless, conviction has still depended on the prosecution's being able to provide tangible evidence that a sexual assault has occurred. A landmark decision emerged in 1979 when a Massachusetts court found a man guilty of raping his wife. During the previous year, there had been a trial in Oregon involving a case in which a husband was accused of raping his wife, but there was no conviction. In the Massachusetts case, the couple had been separated for several months when the man forced his way into his wife's apartment and threatened to kill her if she did not have intercourse with him. A jury of eight men and four women found him guilty, and he was sentenced to three to five years in prison, along with several years of probation.

Legislative measures in most states help rape victims and increase the chances of convicting the perpetrators. Symptoms of the rape trauma syndrome are sometimes admissible as evidence in rape trials (see Chapter 16). Members of police agencies, especially those who deal with rape victims, also receive training with respect to sexual assault. Some local agencies provide counselors who act as advocates and sources of support for the rape victim throughout the judicial process. Some agencies also recommend third-party reporting of rape in case a victim is reluctant to come forward. This at least informs authorities that a rape has occurred, which may be valuable if the victim later decides to proceed with a report. After centuries of neglect and mistreatment by most judicial systems, it would appear that rape victims are finding the prospect of having their attackers prosecuted and convicted more likely than ever before.

Sex Workers, Nude Dancing, and Peep Shows

Legal reforms are difficult in the area of sex workers. Prostitution has often been considered a victimless crime because the sexual activity is seemingly between two consenting adults. Two types of laws attempt to control overt prostitution: those that prohibit loitering with the intent to commit an act of prostitution, and those that prohibit either offering or agreeing to an act of prostitution. Again, the basic philosophy behind such laws is the regulation of private morality. Some groups insist that it is a social necessity to attempt legal control of sex workers. Police claim that the street environment generated by sex workers breeds crime of other sorts. Public health officials say that prostitutes are responsible for much of the increase in rates of

sexually transmitted infections. Moralists attack sex workers on religious grounds.

Others favor the *decriminalization* of prostitution, which would lead to regulation of the trade. Under such a plan, prostitution would be subject to certain age requirements, taxation rules, and standards of hygiene. Sex workers would be required to obtain a license. Decriminalization would protect the civil rights of both prostitutes and their clients. It would free sex workers from the system of arrests, bail, and release to the street; abuse by pimps; and the harassment of society.

The Supreme Court has also been called on to decide on the constitutionality of nude dancing and stripping in bars. The owners of a strip club had been convicted of violating an Indiana law prohibiting nude dancing. G-strings and pasties over the nipples were considered to be minimum attire for a dancer. A federal court of appeals first overturned the conviction, maintaining that nude dancing is "inherently expressive" and therefore constitutionally protected. However, the Supreme Court ruled that states may ban nude dancing in the interest of "protecting order and morality." The requirement for G-strings and pasties was considered appropriate because it combated what the chief justice called the "evil" of public nudity without suppressing the "erotic message" of the expressive dancing. This continues to be a somewhat ambiguous area, because the dancers are working voluntarily and the men who frequent the places seem to be trying to relax for the most part. There typically are no expectations of actual sex acts. Former stripper Katherine Frank (2003, 2005), now a college professor, continues to research the practices and meanings associated with strip clubs.

A controversy emerged in San Diego, California, when the city passed an ordinance restricting the hours during which peep show establishments could operate. These businesses, which have booths in which viewers can watch explicit films by themselves, were not allowed to have the booths open between 2 and 6 A.M. because it was claimed that there was increased crime in their vicinity. One group of researchers studied the issue and concluded that there was in fact no greater incidence of crime associated with either the peep show establishments themselves or their general neighborhoods. They saw the governmental regulation as an illegitimate infringement on communication about sex. Others fired back that the group's research was flawed and the results were unreliable, so the controversy continued (Linz, Paul, & Yao, 2006; McCleary & Meeker, 2006).

Reproductive Rights

Among the controversial issues that have found their way into courts and laws are birth control, involuntary sterilization, and abortion. The Supreme Court did not declare bans on the use of contraceptives to be unconstitutional until the mid-1960s. Sterilization has been a more complicated issue. In several cases, black women or people with mental retardation have been sterilized without their consent. Such actions seem to rest on the assumption that judges and physicians know best and have the right, and privilege, to decide whether an individual will be a fit parent and whether the individual's children are apt to be "suitable" for society. This notion has been met by challenges.

Several states have attempted to pass laws that would prohibit abortion or require parental involvement in abortions for minors and even limit the use of certain kinds of contraceptives. Studies have shown that minors will try to avoid telling their parents about wanting an abortion until they reach the age of 18, when that is possible, but such laws also seem to have increased the rates of second and third trimester abortions (Colman & Joyce, 2009; Jones & Weitz, 2009).

The Rights and Responsibilities of Sexual Partners

There are clear dangers involved in sharing sexual activity with someone who is unwilling to be open and honest about his or her sexual history. It is possible to contract a fatal disease or a nonfatal sexually transmitted infection from a partner who does not reveal his or her physical condition or who fails to provide appropriate protection, such as use of a condom. The Centers for Disease Control have recommended that hospitals and physicians routinely test people for HIV as a way to reduce the number of people who do not know they are infected. States, however, have generally not allowed such testing, requiring counseling and written consent before it can be administered (Wolf, Donohue, & Lane, 2007).

Most states have statutes that make the rights and responsibilities of sexual partners clear. The individual who is aware of carrying genital herpes, hepatitis-B, or HIV but fails to inform a sexual partner and fails to use adequate protection to prevent transmission of the disease can often be prosecuted for criminal behavior. Some experts believe that criminalization of HIV or other disease transmission is the wrong strategy except in cases where the offender seems to have done so with conscious intent to infect the other individual. They argue that such laws do not seem to prevent HIV transmission and are therefore not meeting any public health goal (Burris & Cameron, 2008).

The public has a right to protection from dangerous behavior, and the individual has a right to behave in any way she or he chooses as long as the behavior does not harm others. In some cases, it is not possible to separate public and private rights. Then a legal interpretation of the situation must be made and a judgment passed on whose right has priority. As historical cycles vascillate between progressivism and conservatism, the judgment will continue to waver between private freedom and what courts and legislatures consider to comprise the public good (Gable, Gostin, & Hodge, 2008).

Chapter Summary

1. Graphic depictions of human nudity and sexual behavior have been a part of every society and historical period. Pornography, or sexually explicit material, is generally meant to sexually arouse. Erotica is a name given to sexually realistic art or fiction.

2. In ancient cultures, erotic art was sometimes used for purposes of instructing people in sexual behaviors. There has been controversy over the use of public funding for the creation of art with sexual themes.

3. The practice of writing about sex can be traced back 4,000 years. There have been cycles of acceptance and repression of erotic writings over the centuries.

4. Even in nineteenth-century Victorian literature, there were frank accounts of sexual behavior. Contemporary literature and plays have explored all sex-related themes.

5. Adult magazines proliferated by the late 1960s. Lifestyle magazines now frequently carry articles about sexuality.

6. Sexuality has become increasingly open in films, television, and other media. Almost all sex-related themes have appeared in movies. The film rating system categorizes films based on sexuality issues. Portrayals of women in films once were often stereotypical or negative, but positive female roles have become more common.

7. Advertising frequently uses sexual themes to popularize and sell products, sometimes using subliminal embedding techniques.

8. Hard-core pornography may be found in video/DVD format or on the Internet. Sexually explicit material is widely available today.

9. Online pornography, websites, and chat rooms are used by millions. Men and erotophilic people consume pornography more than women.

10. Online sex seeking has also become a common phenomenon. There are sites that can help find partners in one's geographic area and simulation games in which people can hook up virtually.

11. Child pornography represents a lucrative market and is prohibited in the United States by federal laws.

12. The presumed effects of sexually explicit materials often have been founded in either modeling theory or catharsis theory. Confluence theory provides a more comprehensive model that considers individual and cultural variables.

13. Sexually explicit materials are a form of persuasive communication. Exposure usually results in sexual arousal for both men and women and some sort of emotional reaction. The viewer's emotional reaction is often governed by his or her attitudes toward particular sexual behaviors.

14. Pornography appears to have minimal effects on most people's attitudes, including men's attitudes toward women, although some men may develop more aggressive attitudes.

15. Exposure to sexually explicit material is likely to increase sexual behavior that the individual considers acceptable very soon after exposure. Sexually violent depictions might lead to a slight increase in aggression in men predisposed to aggression.

16. Some research claims that pornography can increase already held negative attitudes toward women, especially if it depicts sexual aggression or violence. Research does not support the claim that women are more objectified in pornography than men are.

17. Sex offenders do not seem to have had earlier or more frequent exposure to pornography than control populations.

18. Neither of the presidential commissions of 1970 or 1986 found particular evidence that pornography caused criminal behavior or contributed to emotional problems. They did not generate regulatory laws that had been hoped for.

19. Sexually explicit material has been subject to various laws throughout recent history. Since 1973, individual states have been allowed to develop their own legislation.

20. In the United States, sodomy laws, or laws against deviate sexual intercourse, have prohibited certain sexual behaviors considered to be deviate. Civil rights groups have argued that any sexual behavior between consenting adults should be considered legal, and the Supreme Court has upheld the right of adults to engage in consensual sex in private.

21. Constitutional issues sometimes are raised by the regulation of sexual behavior, centered on vaguely stated laws, the independent rights doctrine, the right of privacy, and discriminatory enforcement of laws.

22. There have been lawsuits over the gathering of sex information from public school students, but court rulings have upheld the value of doing so as long as participants are informed of goals, are free not to participate, and have their privacy protected.

23. Rape has been considered illegal in recent history, although victims often have been subjected to humiliating treatment in prosecuting the rapist. Newer laws have allowed for greater sensitivity toward the victim, increasing the chances of conviction. There are also laws making marital rape a crime.

24. In most states, prostitution is prohibited by law. Nude dancing may be regulated by state laws. Controversy has also developed over peep shows.

25. Birth control was prohibited by law in some states until the mid-1960s. Sterilization of people without their consent has been challenged in the courts. States are increasingly placing restrictions on abortion.

26. Increasingly, statutes are being enacted clarifying that sex partners have certain legal rights and responsibilities.

Part 5

*Dealing with
Sexual Problems*

■

Most people face a sex-related problem sometime during their lives, and may have to cope with a wide range of emotions, including guilt, anxiety, depression, self-doubt, and feelings of inadequacy. In seeking professional help, it is important to find someone who is well equipped to deal with sex-related matters. There are many different types of sexual problems, different perspectives from which these problems may be viewed, and differing ways in which professionals approach them.

Sexual consent is a fundamental issue in sexual activity, and problems develop when consent is not clearly given. Coercive and exploitative sexual behaviors—including sexual harassment, forced sex, and child sexual abuse—are issues that continue to make headlines and create stress within people's lives.

Sexual interaction has always been associated with the transmission of certain diseases, one reason why many social and religious codes of conduct have been established to regulate sexual behavior. For a time, it seemed that antibiotics would save us from the disease threats that came with sex. Herpes, HPV, and HIV have served as cruel reminders that there are many health risks associated with shared sex, and many of the antibiotics that offered early hope have begun to lose their effectiveness.

People's bodies do not always function sexually the way they expect or want, or the way a partner might prefer. There may be lack of sexual desire, difficulty becoming aroused or achieving orgasm, or pain associated with sex. In such cases, the person may be experiencing a sexual dysfunction. Approaches continue to be developed in the field of sex therapy for treating these dysfunctions.

Most sexual problems do not have to remain problems forever. The chapters in this section of the text provide helpful suggestions for preventing and seeking help with problematic sex.

Chapter 16

Sexual Consent, Coercion, Rape, and Abuse

Chapter Outline

I was in total shock when the dean told me the girl had accused me of raping her. I just couldn't believe it. We didn't exactly talk about what we were going to do, but she never said no or tried to get out of bed. She seems to really believe that I forced her into this. It's all like a bad dream.

—from a counseling session

Some human sexual behaviors, or the ways in which they are initiated, are seen as problematic. Behaviors and feelings that are troublesome for one person may be pleasurable and enjoyable for another. In one sense, any kind of sexual activity may become a problem if someone is feeling worried, guilty, fearful, or ashamed about it. Personal conflict is a frequent result of the struggles to understand and fulfill our sexual needs. Most people have experienced their share of remorse, guilt, and self-hatred over sexual mistakes, misconceptions, or intrusive thoughts. In one study of college students, nearly three-fourths had regretted their sexual decisions at least once (Oswalt, Cameron, & Koob, 2005).

Are the negative feelings justified in terms of present knowledge and attitudes, or do they simply stem from ignorance and misinformation? The answer often is rooted in complex social and cultural beliefs. To a degree, sexual behaviors and feelings become problems or offenses because of the cultural values that surround them and the social judgments that are made about them. Whether someone has given consent for a particular sexual interaction may seem like a simple enough concept, but in fact it sometimes becomes rather muddled. Clearly, any sexual activity that involves lack of consent or the coercion, assault, abuse, or exploitation of someone else is a serious problem. This chapter focuses on those sex-related behaviors, and the reactions to them, that constitute contemporary social problems.

■ When and How Does Sex Become a Problem?

Consider the following case study of a 34-year-old woman who consulted a professional sex therapist. She complained of her lack of interest in sex and expressed hope that the therapist could help her become a more sexually active partner for her husband. She explained that her husband, 36 years old, had a stronger sex drive than she did. On the surface of things, this might seem to be a relatively straightforward problem of sexual incompatibility—one partner wanting sexual involvement more frequently than the other. Sex counselors and therapists encounter such discrepancies in relationships often and use various techniques that may help resolve the difficulties.

However, as the therapist gathered a thorough history of the woman's situation, a much more complex picture emerged. The woman reported that her husband desired and expected to have sexual intercourse two or three times every day. He wanted sex at bedtime and frequently upon awakening in the morning. It was not unusual for him to rouse his wife out of sleep in the middle of the night for sex. If they both came home for lunch during their breaks, he often wanted to have intercourse. At times she had protested, only to have him coerce her emotionally or even physically into having intercourse. The woman did not question her husband's high level of sexual desire and wanted only to find ways of becoming a more willing and interested partner for him.

The therapist was now in somewhat of a dilemma, finding serious concerns other than the woman's level of sexual interest in the relationship. The therapist thought that the client probably exhibited normal levels of sexual arousal and that the constant excessive sexual demands and pressures of her husband had quite predictably led to sexual boredom, depression, and burnout on her part. The therapist was also concerned about the continuing patterns of noncommunication and coercion evident in the couple's relationship.

What should the therapist have done? Should she have attempted to fulfill the woman's request and tried to help her become more interested in sex? Should she have redefined the problem in different terms and tried to help the woman see it that way? Should she instead have told the woman she did not have a problem but her husband did, or encouraged marriage counseling for the couple?

This case study illustrates some fundamental difficulties in considering problematic sex. For example, who is to define whether a problem actually exists at all? And to what degree does a problem exist? What problems are worthy of professional treatment? What are the standards by which problematic and nonproblematic behaviors are to be distinguished from one another? The following sections describe several causes of sex-related problems.

Negative Attitudes about One's Own Body

People sometimes grow up with little information about bodily development or with misconceptions about sexual attractiveness. The young man unprepared for his first ejaculation of semen and the young woman shocked by her first discharge of menstrual blood are bound to experience some fear and worry. Those who have negative feelings about the sex organs and sexual activities are bound to experience guilt over masturbation and sexual fantasies. Research has shown that people who tend not to feel good about their bodies or about themselves after having sex or who report not having been comfortable during sex have an elevated risk of acquiring a sexually transmitted disease or getting involved in other risky behavior, and they tend to lack the assertiveness that could help extricate themselves from such situations (Schooler et al., 2005; Whitten et al., 2003).

Society and the media often perpetuate stereotypes about sexual attractiveness and sexual behaviors. List several of these stereotypes as they apply to women and as they apply to men.

Try the "Beautiful" interactivity on SexSource Online.

Society has perpetuated stereotypes of sexual attractiveness through popular myths and advertising (see Figure 16.1). Some individuals even become obsessive about the perceived inadequacies of their bodies, developing a psychiatric problem called **body dysmorphic disorder.** Negative body image and sexual self-consciousness are associated with lower levels of sexual experience, which probably results from avoidance of certain social experiences. Social phobias lead some people to avoid contact with others whenever possible; in men, this condition is often associated with premature ejaculation during sexual encounters (Corretti et al., 2006; Lankveld, Geijen, & Sykora, 2008).

Boys and men are more prone to concerns about their height, the muscularity of their body, and the size of their penis. Girls and women are more prone to concerns about their weight, their breast size, and the curvaceousness of their body. For both women and men, concerns about body image are associated with lowered sexual arousability and pleasure. Eating disorders are particularly common in women who have difficulty perceiving their feminine qualities in positive ways, but they are being found increasingly among males who are concerned about not having ideal body shapes. When discrepancies exist between what a person perceives as the actual and the ideal in their body and sexual life, he or she is more likely to have lower sexual self-esteem and to be sexually depressed (Choate, 2005; Domine et al., 2009; Sanchez & Kiefer, 2007).

Prejudice and Coercion

Although we have made some inroads in alleviating various forms of prejudice in recent decades, prejudice about sexual differences remains deeply ingrained in our society's values. Prejudice grows out of exaggerated

■ **FIGURE 16.1**   *Stereotypes of Attractiveness*

Both men and women pursue endless hours of aerobics and weight training to make their bodies live up to stereotyped ideals of sexual attractiveness, such as that of the strong, young, muscular male. Those who perceive themselves as not living up to these ideals may experience self-conflict and self-doubt, which affect their ability to understand and fulfill their sexual needs.

stereotypes and lack of information. Stigmatization of people's sexual identities or orientations may easily lead to anger and rage among those being stigmatized (Lemoire & Chen, 2005). People with unconventional sexual orientations or lifestyles often feel forced into secret relationships and deception. They may end up feeling as though they live double lives, struggling to exhibit a socially acceptable public image while quietly maintaining a very different lifestyle in private. The stresses of such an existence can have serious consequences in a person's life. There may be a deepening lack of self-respect and self-esteem. Some enter into socially

body dysmorphic disorder a preoccupation with imagined or slight defects in one's bodily appearance that may focus on weight, muscularity, skin appearance, the genitals, or other body parts.

acceptable relationships in hopes that they will be able to pass as acceptable, only to experience instead interpersonal conflict and unhappiness (Hill, 2005).

When anyone is coerced into sex, there are many negative consequences for the victim. The issue of consent may be confusing and complicated at times. Individuals must have the knowledge base to understand fully what they are consenting to, and the consent must be given freely. Physical or emotional coercion may be part of persuading a partner to become sexually involved, and in such cases people may be more likely to be acquiescing to sex than consenting. Emotional blackmail, such as saying "You would have sex with me if you really loved me" or hinting that the relationship will end if sex does not improve, certainly constitutes sexual coercion and a relationship problem. About a quarter of college students in one study indicated that they had felt pressured by a partner to have sex (Dreznick et al., 2003; Oswalt, Cameron, & Koob, 2005). Many forms of sexual coercion and abuse are discussed later in this chapter.

Failure of the Body to Function as Expected or Desired

Most of us have some expectations and hopes about how our sexual encounters with others should go. We expect that our sex organs will simply go along too, cooperatively and excitedly. It can be quite a disappointment when that does not happen. Men and women may have difficulty becoming sexually aroused. A man may not achieve erection of his penis; a woman may not produce lubrication in her vagina. There may be difficulty in reaching orgasm, or it may happen too quickly or not quickly enough. There may be pain, tightness, or dryness. For a variety of reasons, our bodies simply may not function sexually the way we want or expect them to for significant proportions of women and men (Laumann et al., 2009).

These are the sexual problems that fall into the category of sexual dysfunctions. They may have physical roots or may be caused by psychological blocks and stresses. People who have such dysfunctions tend to have higher levels of sexual self-conscioueness and embarrassment. Unrealistic beliefs about sexual performance may also play a role (Lankveld, Geijen, & Sykora, 2008; Nobre & Pinto-Gouveia, 2006). These problems are discussed in detail in Chapter 18.

Self-Destructive Behaviors and the Paraphilias

People who find themselves participating in some sexual activity they view as unhealthy or immoral certainly can experience self-destructive reactions over time.

This includes people who choose sexual acts that involve violence or are viewed as sexual offenses, for which arrest and prosecution are possible. They may also enter into certain situations with a false sense of invulnerability, believing that harm "won't happen to me." It has been hypothesized that violent and antisocial sexual behaviors could be rooted in erotic target location errors that are established during development. Whatever their cause, it is the violent and self-destructive sexual behaviors that we have come to view as personal and social problems (Lawrence, 2009).

The paraphilias are characterized by sexual arousal from exposure to objects or situations that are not considered part of normative patterns of arousal and activity. They frequently have self-destructive or victimizing aspects. The American Psychiatric Association's *Diagnostic and Statistical Manual of Mental Disorders* (*DSM*) categorizes many forms of behavior under the label paraphilia, including exhibitionism, voyeurism, sexual attraction to children, sadomasochism, fetishism, frotteurism, obscene telephone calls, necrophilia, zoophilia, and several other behaviors. An actual diagnosis of pathology with regard to paraphilias is thought to be unnecessary unless the individual acts on the sexual urges, fantasies, and attractions or unless he or she is troubled by them. As discussed in Chapter 14, certain of these behaviors—fetishism, for example—may be relatively harmless as long as they do not involve any sort of victimization of others. As revisions are being debated for the next edition of the *DSM,* due out in 2012, it seems likely that there will be many changes to the standards that are routinely used to make diagnoses about the paraphilias (Blanchard, 2009; Kafka, 2009).

Paraphiles or **paraphilics,** people who are attracted to some form of paraphilia, may repeat the same behavior compulsively over time. Research has suggested that paraphiles lack general control over their behavior because of chemical brain disorders or social disadvantage and may be prone to a variety of sexually impulsive behavior. There has been some success in treating paraphilias with medications that are used in the treatment of depression and obsessive-compulsive disorders or with drugs that interfere with the release and activation of certain hormones (Marshall, Marshall, & Serran, 2007; Rahman & Symeonides, 2008).

Compulsive Sexual Behavior

When a person has recurring, intense sexual urges, arousing fantasies, and behaviors that are distressing to

paraphiles (paraphilics) people who are drawn to one or more of the paraphilias, or behaviors characterized by non-normative sexual arousal.

the individual and may even interfere with patterns of daily life, the person may be experiencing a clinical syndrome called **compulsive sexual behavior.** Such behaviors have sometimes been subdivided into the *paraphilic* type, applied to the more unconventional or disordered behaviors; and the *non-paraphilic* type, which covers more conventional, usually normative sexual behaviors. Examples of this second category would be frequent, impulsive masturbation and/or viewing of pornographic material. This is where the subjectivity comes into the picture, and there continues to be debate concerning what kinds of repeated sexual behaviors should necessarily be considered pathological. There is a growing body of literature on compulsive sexual behavior and approaches to treating it (Kelly et al., 2009; Miner et al., 2007; Parsons et al., 2008; Reid, Carpenter, & Lloyd, 2009).

Since the early 1990s, compulsive sexual behavior has been compared to alcoholism or other chemical dependencies and similarly labeled as **sex addiction.** Supporters of the concept maintain that sex addiction is characterized by the typical symptoms of other forms of addiction, such as an inability to stop the behavior even in the face of serious consequences. The potential consequences include disease, unwanted pregnancy, losing one's job because of sexual harassment, and/or losing one's primary partner. As with all compulsions, sexual addiction has been thought to follow a cycle of negative feelings that leads to repetition of the behavior, and treatment programs have been developed that are similar to the 12-step programs used with alcoholics and drug abusers. Attendance at the meetings offered by such programs is considered essential to a real cure (Carnes, 1992, 2003).

The sex addiction model has not received wide support within sexology. Sex therapists claim that it brands perfectly normal behaviors as signs of addiction and may prevent some sexually compulsive people from getting appropriate treatment. There is concern that the popularity of the term has encouraged people to label themselves as "sex addicts" when they actually may simply be ignorant or misinformed about normal sexual behavior. It has been charged that the treatment approaches have been developed and operated largely by people who are not trained in the field of human sexuality. The sexual addiction movement has been seen as having a missionary zeal, offering a program that might be dangerously oversimplified for some people (Coleman, 2003; Klein, 2003).

Research confirms that some people seem unable to exercise control over their sexual behaviors even in the face of negative consequences, but little attention has been given to why sex becomes problematic for some. Three patterns have emerged in the study of self-defined sexually compulsive persons with regard to their sexual interests and responsiveness. Some are able to retain sexual interest and response even when they are depressed. Others seem to use sexual stimulation as a way to distract themselves from thoughts that might induce a negative mood. A third pattern involves a tendency toward increased sexual arousal when experiencing a state of anxiety or stress. Until we better understand the connections between sexual behavior and negative mood states, some researchers recommend that we refer to *out-of-control* sexual behaviors rather than calling them either addictions or compulsions. It is likely that the new edition of the *DSM* will classify this collection of behavioral symptoms as *hypersexual disorder* (Bancroft & Vukadinovic, 2004; McDonald, 2010; Salisbury, 2008).

Sex Trafficking as a Global Problem

In some areas of the world, young girls and boys from poverty-stricken families may enter prostitution and may even be sold to sex traffickers for funds that will help support their families. Adult women may also be coerced into the sex worker trade. They may eventually become sex slaves, kept in line with threats of continued poverty. Indonesia, for example, is known as a country to which men sometimes travel to be able to buy sex with a minor, although foreign sex slaves often make their way to North America as well (Melby, 2004).

Human rights organizations around the world are concerned about girls and boys who become ensnared in sex trafficking rings, and a variety of policies and laws have been enacted to prosecute those responsible. However, it seems that as long as people are willing to pay for illicit sex, there will be an underground of sellers ready to meet the need.

■ Crossing Sexual Boundaries

Every culture establishes certain standards of sex-related behavior and human interaction that determine what is appropriate, allowable, and expected among members of the culture. While some level of flirting, teasing, and seductiveness is usually allowed between adults, certain behaviors may also be seen as crossing accepted boundaries. Societies sometimes change and

---

compulsive sexual behavior recurrent sexual urges, fantasies, and behaviors that distress a person and may interfere with the person's daily life.

sex addiction a term used to describe compulsive sexual behavior in a controversial model that compares such behavior to substance addictions.

evolve in such ways that these boundaries may shift over time, and until they become clarified both informally and through formal rules and laws, confusion may be the result. Sexual attraction, innuendo, and activity may also become part of ongoing relationships between people who work together, go to school together, live together in academic residence halls, or are associated in other ways. So long as this sexual element is welcomed by the parties involved, it may be acceptable, but it may also generate unanticipated confusion, resentment, and harm. This section looks at the complications of crossing certain sexual boundaries.

Sexual Harassment

One form of negative boundary crossing involves unwanted sexual advances, suggestiveness, sexually motivated physical contact, requests for sexual favors, or coercion of one person by another, particularly in academic settings or the workplace. The term used to describe such behavior is **sexual harassment** (see Figure 16.2). It is estimated that about 50 percent of women are victims of some form of sexual harassment, mostly the "hands-off" type but occasionally involving physical contact (Sbraga & O'Donohue, 2001). The number of sexual harassment complaints filed

with the U.S. Equal Opportunity Employment Commission dropped slightly from 15,889 in 1997 to 13,867 in 2008, with about 16 percent of those charges brought by males. Sexual harassment has not been studied extensively in other cultures. The first study done in China showed the incidence of sexual harassment there to be quite similar to the figures for the United States and other developed countries (Parish, Das, & Laumann, 2006).

Have you ever thought that you were being sexually harassed? Describe the circumstances. Be sure to include how you felt.

When faced with situations that are potentially sexually harassing, men are somewhat more likely to perceive women's behavior as simply being sexy rather than harassing. In general, they tend not to be as offended or uncomfortable with the behavior as women tend to be. The U.S. Supreme Court has ruled that men can take legal action against other men who make unwanted sexual advances, and in fact the harassment of men is often perpetrated by other males. Studies of college men and women indicate that the males tend to be more tolerant of sexual harassment and more likely to see heterosexual relationships in adversarial terms, to believe the myths about rape, and to admit that under certain circumstances they might be sexually aggressive (Sbraga & O'Donohue, 2001).

Sexual harassment may affect people in many different ways, sometimes even indirectly. There are four main bases for complaints about sexual harassment:

1. *Coercion and bribery.* This form of harassment is linked to the granting or denial of some benefit or privilege. Legally it is called **quid pro quo** harassment, meaning that something is gained from something else. Most typically it takes the form of an individual who has or is perceived to have more power using sex as a form of coercion or bribery. An example might be a college professor suggesting to a student that complying or not complying with her or his sexual overtures will affect the student's grade one way or the other.
2. *Hostile environment.* If a person's school or work environment is made uncomfortable because of unwanted sexual attention such as sexual innuendos, suggestive remarks or pictures, repeated requests for dates, and uninvited advances, it is considered a form of sexual harassment. Court cases continue to affirm that school authorities

■ **FIGURE 16.2** *Is It Sexual Harassment?*

Three waitresses at a restaurant in Beverly Hills, California, filed a lawsuit against their employer for allegedly firing them for refusing to wear new uniforms. Kelly Thornton (left) and Christy Tharpe (right) pose in the attire that they formerly wore on the job. A model in the center is wearing the new uniform that the other two refused to wear for work.

sexual harassment unwanted sexual advances or coercion that can occur in the workplace or in academic settings.

quid pro quo something gained from something given.

and work supervisors have a responsibility to prevent the development or perpetuation of such hostile environments.

3. *Aggressive or outrageous acts.* Among the more overt forms of sexual harassment are actual physical behaviors, such as unwanted embraces, kissing, touching, fondling, or more assaultive forms of sexual behavior.

4. *Third-party effects.* Sometimes a third person will be affected by the sexual or romantic relationships of others. For example, if one student is getting better grades because of involvement in a sexual relationship with the professor, other students who are legitimately working for their grades are unfairly affected. Or if a supervisor is having an affair with a secretary, making it more likely that the secretary will get pay raises or other benefits, other workers are affected. These are forms of third-party sexual harassment.

Certain risk factors increase the likelihood that sexual harassment will take place, including an unprofessional environment in the workplace, a sexist atmosphere, and lack of knowledge about the organization's grievance policies (O'Hare & O'Donohue, 1998). Victims of sexual harassment often minimize the importance of the event in their own minds, or they may react with shock and disbelief. They may feel ambivalent toward the offender and sometimes even blame themselves for not having prevented the situation from developing. In this sense, the injuries of harassment may be subtle and emotional, calling the victim's own sense of self into question. Only too often, these reactions lead victims to ignore the incident and not report it to anyone in authority. This is particularly unfortunate in cases where the harasser is unaware of how his or her behavior is being perceived. Sometimes, a simple and clear statement to the harasser that the behavior is unwelcome and considered to be sexually harassing will be enough to end it (Sbraga & O'Donohue, 2001) (see Table 16.1).

Usually, however, there is an imbalance of power in sexual harassment cases through which the offender tries to take unfair advantage of the victim. The result of such a trap for the individual being harassed is often a sense of helplessness that can lead to depression, other emotional upsets, and even physical illness. Victims often have been known to quit their jobs or leave school as a result of continuing sexual harassment that they feel at a loss to cope with.

Sexual Harassment in Schools and Colleges

Nearly 20 years ago, the American Association of University Women (AAUW, 1993) sponsored a survey of 1,632 students in grades 8 through 11 in 79 U.S. schools

---

Table 16.1	How Men Can Tell If Their Behavior Is Sexual Harassment

Some men (and women) are confused as to what behaviors constitute sexual harassment. The following questions may be especially helpful in assessing one's own behavior. If the answer to any of these questions is yes, the chances of the behavior being considered sexual harassment are very high. Because such behavior is likely to be high risk, if you have to ask, it is probably better not to do it.

- Would I mind if someone treated my wife, partner, girlfriend, mother, sister, or daughter this way?
- Would I mind if this person told my wife, partner, girlfriend, mother, sister, or daughter about what I was saying or doing?
- Would I do this if my wife, partner, girlfriend, mother, sister, or daughter were present?
- Would I mind if a reporter wanted to write about what I was doing?
- If I ask someone for a date and the answer is "no," do I keep asking?
- If someone asks me to stop a particular behavior, do I get angry and do more of the same instead of apologizing and stopping?
- Do I tell jokes or make "funny" remarks involving women and/or sexuality? (Such jokes may offend many people.)

Source: Bernice R. Sandler, "How Men Can Tell If Their Behavior Is Sexual Harassment," *About Women on Campus,* vol. 3, no. 3, Summer 1994, p. 9, Association of American Colleges and Universities. (Sandler is a Senior Scholar at the Women's Research and Education Institute in Washington, D.C. She is an expert on sexual harassment and also acts as an expert witness in this area. For additional information see her website www.bernicesandler.com)

---

to determine the incidence of sexual harassment. This study found that 85 percent of the girls and 76 percent of the boys said they had been subjected to unwelcome sexual behavior at least once in their school lives. Two-thirds of the girls and a considerably smaller proportion of boys said they had been harassed "often" or "occasionally." Sixty-five percent of the girls and 42 percent of the boys indicated that they had been touched, grabbed, or pinched in a sexual way. Nearly one-fourth of the girls had been forced to kiss someone, and 10 percent of both the boys and the girls reported having been forced against their wills to do something sexual other than kissing. Eighty percent of the unwelcome sexual behavior had come from other students, with the remainder coming from teachers, coaches, or other adults.

Do you believe colleges and universities have the right to prohibit or regulate consensual relationships between faculty and students? Defend your position.

Because college students are adults, there is more likelihood of sexual contact between them and their professors, accompanied by all the potential complications of such relationships. One of the issues in academia is whether even consensual relationships between faculty and students should be prohibited, because of the power imbalance and the resulting potential for harassment. Sensitive to the risk of lawsuits, some universities have tried to enact policies that would prohibit all romantic and sexual relationships between faculty and students, but most have opted for less pervasive policies, prohibiting relationships specifically between a professor and a student whom the professor supervises in some way. There is always the risk that one party, usually the student, will be hurt in some way by the relationship and bring some sort of charges against the other party. For these reasons, most educational institutions have developed sexual harassment policies and have also educated both students and faculty about the dangers and concerns. Any such policy must provide for grievance procedures so that an individual who feels unfairly charged is offered an opportunity for defense (Francis, 2000).

Sexual Harassment in the Military

The armed forces represent a somewhat special social situation, because for such a long time they were male-dominated. As women have been integrated into the military services, sexual harassment and abuse have become problems. The military considers even consensual sex between persons of different rank to be inappropriate, because it can lead to a breakdown of discipline and of the cohesiveness of units; it sometimes is deemed to be rape, especially when a recruit is clearly in a position of being afraid to say no to a superior. The seriousness of sexual harassment and of the issue of consensual sex in the military came into greater focus with scandals and court-martials at several installations. Experts agree that the living situations and power imbalances in military life create unique problems for both women and men. Sexual incidents on military bases have reminded everyone that even in places of traditional male dominance, sexual harassment and abuse will no longer be ignored (Richard, 2003).

Sexual Harassment in the Workplace

The civilian world of work sees its share of sexual harassment issues as well. They may involve, for example, the worker who is subjected to intimate touching or sexual innuendos from a superior. The worker often feels trapped in an uncomfortable situation, resenting the uninvited attention but fearful that reporting it will create embarrassing confrontations or even jeopardize future employment. Some workers are afraid of the economic consequences of either reporting the incident or quitting and therefore choose to remain on the job, sometimes being subjected to further sexual harassment. American companies have realized that they

can be held accountable for their workers' actions and that it is their responsibility to prevent the development of hostile work environments. It is critical that training about sexual harassment be given to workers and that harassment policies be publicized regularly. Men have also become more concerned about behaviors that could be seen as sexually harassing, and many men have been modifying their actions to prevent misunderstanding or the possibility that they would be charged with sexual harassment. Human relations experts continue to wrestle with the complex issue of how to affirm positive relationships between coworkers, while constraining the degree to which sexuality becomes a part of workplace interactions (Sbraga & O'Donohue, 2001).

Responding to Sexual Harassment

Public and private schools, colleges, military service branches, and corporations have specific policies defining what sort of conduct constitutes sexual harassment and outlining procedures for dealing with cases. In the United States, both Title VII of the Civil Rights Act of 1964 and Title IX of the Education Amendments of 1972 clearly prohibit sexual harassment of employees and students. The Civil Rights Act of 1991 spurred the implementation of additional policies to deter harassment in the workplace. In 1993, the U.S. Supreme Court ruled unanimously that victims need not have suffered severe psychological damage in order to claim that they have been sexually harassed, granting harassment a broader definition than was previously accepted by the Court.

Recommendations for those who encounter sexual harassment emphasize the need to take as much control over the situation as possible. There are several specific suggestions for steps that can be taken:

1. *Seek sources of personal support.* Find an individual or small support group with whom you can share your fears and frustrations. This can provide support and encouragement through a difficult time, put the incident(s) and your concerns in clearer perspective, and give you guidance in making decisions about how you want to proceed.
2. *Find out which authorities or administrators are designated for the reporting of sexual harassment.* Institutions usually have officials who handle reports of sexual harassment. Even if these individuals feel that a lack of substantive evidence may make pursuit of a particular case difficult, they may have helpful suggestions for putting an end to the offensive behavior. Remember, too, that if an official receives more than one complaint about a particular employee, he or she will have

more evidence on which to act. In the case of a student who is being harassed by a professor, reporting the incident may be useful in rectifying a situation in which an unfair grade eventually is given by the teacher as retribution. Keeping careful records of classroom performance would, of course, be necessary in arguing such a point. Most forms of harassment can be considered violations of law, and you might consider reporting them to police authorities.

3. *Be clear about your needs.* One common reaction of many victims of sexual harassment is to feel guilty for having somehow precipitated the sexual advances. Regardless of any ambivalence you may once have felt about the offender, if you now feel certain that you do not appreciate the behavior, be firm in your resolve to end the harassment and be assertive about it.

4. *Write a letter to the offender.* This is considered one of the best approaches to ending sexual harassment. It is a clear and direct statement to the offender made without formal charges and public confrontation. It also may provide the harasser with a new perspective on the behavior. Not all offenders realize how negatively their actions affect others. A copy of the letter should be kept and used as supportive evidence later if the harassment does not cease. Such a letter should clearly and directly state the following: (a) specifically what actions have taken place, giving as many details, dates, and times as possible but without evaluation; (b) the feelings and reactions that have been generated by the actions; and (c) a very short statement that you want the harassment to stop and also want your relationship to return to an appropriate professional, or student–teacher, level. Such letters usually are quite useful in placing a harasser on warning, and they typically lead to a quick cessation of the behavior.

5. *Consider making use of mediation services.* Even in those cases where an individual does not want to take formal action against a harasser, mediation may be helpful. It is a voluntary process in which an impartial mediator allows the two parties, the victim and the harasser, to explain their positions and feelings to each other, eventually developing a plan of resolution to which both parties can agree. This approach is especially useful in subtler harassment situations, in which the offender could benefit from realizing how the actions have been affecting the victim.

Institutional policies and recent court decisions continue to confirm that everyone deserves to work or pursue an education in an environment that is free from inappropriate sexual overtures. If you find yourself subjected to such behavior, take action promptly to avoid escalation in the tensions and consequences that may result.

Sexual Boundary Violations by Professionals

Closely related to the sexual harassment issue is the concern about professionals—physicians, nurses, teachers, therapists, clergy, lawyers, bodywork therapists, social workers—who take advantage of their patients, students, or clients sexually. The crisis over sexual abuse of children and adolescents by priests shook the Roman Catholic Church in the United States. A report issued in 2004 by the U.S. Conference of Catholic Bishops reported that between 1950 and 2002 in the United States, nearly 4,500 Roman Catholic priests were accused of sexually molesting a total of 11,000 children. Seventy-eight percent of the alleged victims were between the ages of 11 and 17, 16 percent were 8 to 10 years old, and the remaining 6 percent were 7 or younger at the time of the abuse.

These cases constitute what are called *boundary violations* in situations that usually involve some power differential because one of the individuals is perceived as a helper for the other. It is typically assumed that the person being helped or served should not have to be concerned about the helper crossing sexual boundaries (Lief, 2001; Plaut, 2008). Although it is difficult to get accurate data on the frequency with which such behavior occurs, there is evidence that up to 10 percent of male therapists have engaged in intimate contact with patients either during or following the professional relationship and that smaller numbers of female professionals have done so. In a survey of 714 nurses in psychiatric hospitals in Europe, while nearly all the nurses agreed that physical contact of a sexual nature with patients was inappropriate, 17 percent of the male nurses and 11 percent of the female nurses admitted to having had such contact (Bachmann et al., 2000).

Most professions in which one individual acts in a helping role for another have seen their share of reports about sexual boundary violations. The professional organizations governing these professions have now acknowledged the problem, and developed guidelines for handling allegations of sexual abuse and sanctioning violators. States have enacted legislation providing civil and criminal penalties for professionals who violate ethical standards and participate in sexual or other inappropriate contact with their clients. However, for patients, clients, or parishioners who have been subjected to such violations, confusing feelings of shame, being wanted and cared for, helplessness, and lack of self-confidence seem to interact to create conditions that make it difficult for them to take charge of the situation (Plaut, 2008).

Education for Professionals

Boundary violations might be better prevented if professionals received focused training in ways to confront their own feelings and protect their clients. Only too often, training for helping professionals fails to include focused preparation for dealing with the sexual issues of clients or for dealing with one's own sexual feelings toward clients. The presence of sexuality education in schools has not translated into adequate preparation of those teachers who ultimately may be expected to conduct the classes, and many have never had any formal academic preparation in sexuality. In fact, almost no public school preparation and certification programs require any courses on sexuality (Kelly, 2005, 2009).

Seminaries and theological schools have begun to prepare their students for working with sexual issues, because it is often suggested that people talk to their religious advisors when they are troubled by problems with their sexuality. This training has little standardization, however, and experts have recommended a better balance in training between the positive, pleasurable aspects of sexuality and its problematic issues (Conklin, 2001; Stayton, 2002).

Significant headway has been made in training those individuals who are preparing for work within the clinical health and psychology professions. Medical schools have increased the number of curriculum hours devoted to studying human sexuality, with most requiring some core curriculum preparation in sexuality. The goals in sexuality education for professionals are not always clearly defined, and the courses may neglect the broad range of sexual issues that could eventually be encountered in work settings, including the impact of illness and sexual dysfunction on patients' sexual lives. In addition, clinical supervision of professionals as they learn how to offer treatment for sexual problems often is lacking in professional training programs (Frank, Coughlin, & Elon, 2008; Shabsigh et al., 2009a; Tuchman, Peter, & Schwarz, 2008).

The ability of educators, health and counseling professionals, and clergy to perceive sexual problems in their students, patients, or clients and then to pursue these problems once they have been noticed depends on the degree of comfort the professionals have toward sexuality. The more anxious professionals are about dealing with sexual issues, the less apt they will be to ask about a patient's sexual history. Medical professionals often fail to inquire about the sexual orientation of their patients (Dahan, Feldman, & Hermoni, 2008). Some family therapists also avoid discussing sex because they are uncertain of how to alleviate patient anxiety about the topic (Harris & Hays, 2008). Training programs that involve mentoring by professionals who already have experience in dealing with sexual concerns can be of particular value in overcoming such reluctance. Fortunately, a number of sexuality education programs for professionals now help them see and understand their own sexual values, detect sexual concerns in their patients or clients, and develop the skills needed to treat these sex-related problems while maintaining appropriate boundaries.

Do you have confidence that the following professionals would be able to advise you correctly on matters of sexuality: your family physician, your clergyperson, a school counselor, a private therapist, a nurse in your health center?

■ Consent, Coercion, and Forced Sex

A key issue in many problematic sexual situations is the perception that one partner has not given consent for the sexual activity to take place. Whether it is a case of two college students who have sexual intercourse after an evening of excessive drinking and the woman claims she was too drunk to know what she was doing, or a case of a 15 year old who willingly has sex with an 18 year old who later is arrested for the behavior, the fundamental problem is *lack of consent*. It can be considered rape to have sex with someone whose judgment is impaired by alcohol, and the law considers minors to be too young to offer legitimate consent even if they say they participated willingly. For such a central issue in sexual matters, consent has received minimal attention by researchers.

The Issue of Consent

Consent has most typically been defined as verbal or nonverbal communication, freely given, to indicate a sense of willingness to engage in sexual activity. However, it is a more complex issue than this definition suggests and involves many nuances of inner and

consent freely given verbal or nonverbal communication expressing a sense of willingness to engage in sexual activity.

outer expressions. Consent often involves more than simply saying "yes." The communication of some inner willingness or unwillingness may not get transmitted clearly through external non verbal means. Certain assumptions may be made, and if the two persons involved are operating with differing assumptions, a risky gap in understanding can occur.

The little research that has been conducted on this topic offers some interesting findings about young adults. It would appear that most sexual activity happens without expressed verbal communication, and instead proceeds through nonverbal signals. However, it is also true that the perceived significance of the shared activity determines whether the need for clear consent be established. Kissing and fondling one another are generally perceived as needing less expressed consent than sexual intercourse, for example. Although college students have a good understanding of the meaning of sexual consent, they are more divided on whether there is a need to offer it through explicit verbal communication or not. Women more than men, and individuals of both sexes without much sexual experience, are more likely to feel that explicit verbal consent should be obtained before sex. It has also been found that when partners have been involved in a longer relationship, they may think it less necessary to obtain explicit consent, perhaps because they believe they have learned to read one another's verbal cues more accurately. Nonetheless, the research suggests that college students prefer not to have to negotiate sexual consent verbally, opting instead for assumed consent based on nonverbal signals (Humphreys, 2004, 2007).

So we cannot escape the fact that consent can be a complicated part of sexual negotiations. The importance of consent and its validity can depend on a variety of factors, and both moral and legal distinctions may be made. The risk of harm may have to be evaluated, along with the experiencing of harm by a "victim" and the potential violation of one's rights. The validity of an individual's sexual consent may be compromised if coercion or deception has been involved or if the competence of one of the individuals is questionable because of age, mental retardation or illness, or intoxication. While societies establish specific guidelines and laws in an attempt to bring greater clarity to such issues, subtleties of interpretation can make analysis of individual cases complicated (Wertheimer, 2003).

A study on the ways people ask for and give sexual consent offers some preliminary clues as to where things can go wrong. Nonverbal behaviors are used significantly more frequently than verbal expressions. People tend to initiate sex with a partner through touch and other nonverbal behaviors (kissing, caressing, undressing) and sometimes through verbalizations

("I want you"; "Is this okay?"). Partners then respond by not resisting the advances or with undressing behaviors, or other nonverbal cues (eye contact, smiling, kissing and touching in return). Women are somewhat more likely than men to use verbal responses (Beres, Herold, & Maitland, 2004). Considering the complexities of filtering all these signals through individual communication processing systems, it is clear why things sometimes go amiss.

Recognizing that many sexual problems develop on college campuses over consent issues, after extensive campus discussions Antioch College instituted a policy requiring students to obtain verbal consent for each level of sexual behavior. The policy received a great deal of press when it first appeared, along with plenty of jokes. Yet the policy was developed by students themselves and makes good sense in many ways. Perhaps one of the most telling anecdotes regarding the value of the policy involved a freshman male student who learned about it at orientation and said that if he had to ask, he wouldn't get what he wanted. After the policy took effect, a newsletter called *About Women on Campus* published the following list of reasons why it makes good sense to seek consent for sexual behaviors (Ten Reasons, 1994):

1. Because many partners find it sexy to be asked, as sex progresses, if it's okay.
2. Because sex is better when each partner enjoys what is happening and no one is being forced to do something he or she doesn't want to do.
3. Because if your partner is having a good time and is not forced to do something against her will, she may be more likely to want to see you again. Mutual respect is the best basis for friendship and intimacy.
4. Because forcing sexual activity on another person can violate state and federal laws and your school's policy. In most instances, unwanted touching and fondling constitute sexual assault.
5. Because it prevents misunderstandings (silence is not a yes).
6. Because you won't be accused of rape.
7. Because you won't go to jail or be expelled.
8. Because it's better to be safe than sorry.
9. Because if you want to impose your sexual will on someone, your behavior has more to do with dominating that person than with enjoying sexuality and an intimate relationship.
10. Why would you want to have sex with someone who doesn't like what you are doing?

The bottom line is that one of the responsibilities we have in our sexual interactions with other people is to make certain that they are fully willing to participate in those activities we would like to share with them. It is not legitimate to avoid confronting the issue

Real Student Voices

■ My first serious relationship in high school turned out to be a disaster. I really loved the boy, but he was always very jealous and possessive. He was always pressing me to have sex with him, even though I didn't feel ready. Finally I gave in, mostly because he wore me down rather than really wanting to do it. I realize now how emotionally abusive he was. It took me a while to get beyond it. I found it hard to trust boys.

■ I get really pissed when I hear about guys getting accused of date rape. Why is it that males are always supposed to be sober and in control? How come women seem to have the right to get drunk

and go back to guys' rooms, but then claim they didn't want to do anything? I understand that if she says no, we should stop, but if she doesn't say no, how are we supposed to know? I don't think I'm the only one who feels this way.

■ As a woman, I don't think I should always have to be on alert that someone might take advantage of me sexually. What kind of world is it if I can't even go out and have a drink without being scared of getting raped? I always go with a couple of other girls, and we watch out for each other. But it's not right that we have to be that paranoid all the time.

out of selfish concerns or because we are too shy to ask. When consent is left open to interpretation or is vague in any way, we may be courting troublesome consequences.

Sexual Coercion and Force

Coercing or forcing other people to have unwanted sexual activity is a behavior found in nearly every culture studied. Usually it is males who force women into sexual activities against their will, but substantial numbers of males also report having engaged in unwanted sexual acts. Social norms, and the types of sexual activities they regulate or prohibit, seem to play a major role in determining the types of forced sex that are allowed or condoned within a particular culture. Cross-national studies of thousands of women and men have shown that both genders report having had unwanted sex because of a partner's insistence. Women are considerably more likely than men to participate repeatedly in sexual activities they dislike, such as oral or anal sex, because their partner wants them to. The status of women in a particular location, combined with the society's attitudes about the relationship between women and men, represent significant predictors of sexual victimization in both genders and of the incidence of repeated victimization. In societies where the status of women was greater, there was a higher incidence of forced sex against men. In settings where men and women were seen to have adversarial relationships, there was a higher incidence of both verbal sexual coercion

and forced sex against both genders (Hines, 2007; Kaestle, 2009).

We know that sexual teasing and insistence take their toll (Meston & O'Sullivan, 2007). In a study of 275 college men and 381 college women, 78 percent of the women and 58 percent of the men reported having been subjected to persistent efforts to get them sexually involved, even after they had refused. The tactics used seemed to occur on four different levels (Struckman-Johnson, Struckman-Johnson, & Anderson, 2003):

Level 1: Sexual arousal. The perpetrator uses touching, kissing, massage, and genital stimulation to continue to entice the person, and eventually the person may give in. Men experience such tactics relatively frequently, but not as often as women do.

Level 2: Emotional manipulation and lies. The most common manipulation is repeated requests for sex; men tend to do this about twice as frequently as women do, perhaps because men are more practiced at saying what they want. Various lies may be told as someone tries to convince a partner to have sex, including promising not to insert the penis and then doing so, misrepresenting one's age, and telling someone that he or she is abnormal for not having sex. Women sometimes manipulate men's emotions by saying they love the man or by offering compliments; they are more likely to offer threats of blackmail if the man does not cooperate.

■ FIGURE 16.3 *Rape*

Rape is forced sexual participation, as depicted in this enactment using models. Although sexual assault usually is perpetrated against women, it is not limited to them; men and children are also potential rape victims.

Level 3: Exploitation of the intoxicated. Thirty percent of men and 42 percent of women in this study reported having been sexually exploited when they were intoxicated. They sometimes were plied with drinks and then lured to a private area for sex. Sometimes the victim was so drunk that she or he did not remember much about the situation, and in a very few circumstances the victim was purposely drugged.

Level 4: Physical force and harm. About 20 percent of both women and men reported that someone had attempted to block them from leaving a room, but women were about twice as likely to have been subjected to physical restraint. Women sometimes hit men in an effort to persuade them to have sex or to punish them for not doing so.

The rather upsetting conclusion reached by the authors of the study was that sexual coercion and persistence are relatively common among college students. Another study found that students perceive sexually coercive men as aggressive and sexually coercive women as promiscuous but that, in general, coercive behaviors were not seen as particularly problematic (Oswald & Russell, 2006).

Issues of power, control, and social sexual scripts are often fundamental to sexual coercion and violence. Men who strongly endorse casual sex tend to have had sex earlier, more frequently, and with more partners than have others and also tend to have more conservative attitudes toward women. Such men may act more adversarially toward women in attempts to assert power over them and can sometimes be more sexually aggressive (Yost & Zurbriggen, 2006).

Our culture has many embedded beliefs about gender and sexuality that can play a role. The enduring beliefs that men have insistent sex drives and that women are anxious to please their male partners form a foundation for participation in initiating or participating in unwanted sexual activity, as does the persistent tendency for people to sexually objectify themselves and one another (Bay-Cheng & Eliseo-Arras, 2008; Gage & Hutchinson, 2006). A culture's sexual scripts provide blueprints for how to behave in sexual situations, and if there are three particularly risky kinds of behaviors for young people if they are seen as part of accepted social scripts: consuming alcohol as part of sexual encounters; concealing true intentions about sex through ambiguous communications; and a readiness to engage in sex after little or no acquaintanceship with the partner. These behaviors are associated with higher levels of sexual aggression and victimization, and having been subjected to such behaviors is associated with later problems in physical and psychological health (Krahe, Bieneck, & Scheinberger-Olwig, 2007; Visser et al., 2007b).

In general usage, the term **rape** refers to any form of sex in which one person forces another person to participate (see Figure 16.3). When used as a verb, it means making an individual engage in a sexual act without that individual's consent or against that individual's will. In about one-third of forced sexual encounters, penile-vaginal contact never occurs; rather, a

rape engaging in a sexual act without the other individual's consent or against that individual's will.

variety of other forms of forced sex, including oral and anal penetration by the penis or vaginal penetration by fingers or objects, may occur. Recognizing that these acts may be just as physically and psychologically damaging to the victim as intercourse, the American Law Institute has recommended that violent and forced sexual acts all be prosecuted under the more general label of "rape and related offenses"; the term *sexual assault* is also often used. Again, the perception of consent can be a complicating factor in rape cases. Courts have sometimes failed to find men guilty of rape in the absence of clear evidence of resistance on the woman's part, even though that may have been due to her being very frightened or suffering impaired judgment from use of alcohol or some other substance (Lawson, 2003).

Studies have found certain characteristics in males that seem to correspond to certain motives for sexual assault. Men who rape out of *anger and retaliation* express anger and rage during the rape, often using a weapon and displaying a macho image. Such men may assault women who represent people the offender hates. *Power* motives often play a role in rape as well. Men who feel personally inadequate and hostile toward women may seek to assert their power, control, and dominance over women through forced sex. There are also *sadistic* rapists who have sexually aggressive fantasies and may carry out various forms of mental and physical aggression, domination, and torture during rape for their own sexual pleasure. About a third of rapists are psychopaths with serious signs of disturbance (Camilleri & Quinsey, 2009; McCabe & Wauchope, 2005).

Statutory rape is a legal term used in situations in which an adult or adolescent has sexual intercourse with a younger partner who is under the age of consent, even if that partner is willing to have sex. Legal age of consent varies in some states, but it is usually age 17 or 18. There are many cases in which older teens are arrested under these statutes for having consensual sexual contact with a slightly younger partner, and these teens may ultimately be required to register as sex offenders. Concerns have been raised about cultural differences among immigrant populations, for which relationships between a man age 18 or somewhat older and a teenage woman are not considered inappropriate or abusive. Some believe that these men should still be subject to prevailing state laws, while cultural relativists hold that the statutes are not fair to them (Apodaca et al., 2005).

Coercive and Abusive Relationships

There seem to be some common characteristics among people who tend toward sexually aggressive

behavior. Offenders may show serious personality disturbances, have difficulty maintaining social relationships, and have a propensity for depression, loneliness, and personal rigidity. They seem to have more problems with aggressiveness in general and a lack of impulse control (Giotakos et al., 2003). They tend not to have been particularly successful or competent in their social interactions with the opposite sex (Dreznick, 2003). People who tend to resort to coercion and domination in order to solve conflicts are more likely to become aggressive in their sexual behavior, and higher levels of traditionally masculine or macho traits also are associated with tendencies toward aggressiveness. Men who are able to justify their sexual aggression through rationalization, who lack control of their emotions, and who seem to have other personality problems apparently are more likely to become sexually coercive or aggressive (Christopher & Pflieger, 2007).

Most commonly, sexual coercion takes the form of emotional manipulation, lies or false promises, and taking advantage of people who are intoxicated (Struckman-Johnson, Struckman-Johnson, & Anderson, 2003). The most typical lies include indicating a higher level of caring or commitment than actually is the case and trying to deny that the relationship is a one-night stand. Men's attitudes toward women play at least some role in the likelihood of their telling such lies. Enough is known about the predictors of aggressive behavior to allow women to pay attention to certain warning signals in their relationships. These signals do not mean that a man definitely will be sexually coercive or aggressive, but they are warnings that a man has a greater likelihood of being sexually aggressive. These predictors are the following:

1. Lack of respect for women, as evidenced by his not listening well or ignoring what you say.
2. A tendency to become more physically involved and invasive than makes you feel comfortable, along with a refusal to respect your discomfort.
3. Expression of generally hostile or angry reactions to women.
4. Disregarding your wishes and doing as he pleases; a tendency to make decisions about dating and other issues without consulting you.
5. A tendency to act jealous and possessive or to make you feel guilty if you resist his sexual overtures.

statutory rape a legal term used to indicate sexual activity when one partner is younger than the age of consent; in most states, that age is 18.

6. Attitudes and values about women that are negative and domineering (such as "Women are supposed to serve men").

7. A tendency to drink heavily and to become abusive when drunk.

There are a number of programs designed to prevent sexual assault and ward off potential attackers. There is evidence that women who convey attitudes of assertiveness and confidence are somewhat less likely to be sexually victimized. However, it may also be helpful for women to learn some specific physical self-defense skills, because verbal resistance alone is not always sufficient to prevent physical injury. Studies of women who either have been raped or have avoided rape suggest that screaming, fleeing, and forcefully resisting an attacker are more effective than nonresistance in reducing the severity of the sexual abuse.

Incidence of Forced Sex

Determining the incidence of forced sex is difficult because it is assumed that reported cases represent only the tip of the iceberg. Data from the National Longitudinal Study of Adolescent Health found that 8 percent of girls in grades 7 to 12 indicated that they had been forced to have sex against their will. These women also seemed somewhat more likely to have been revictimized at a later time (Raghavan et al., 2004). Analyses of data from 4,469 young adults found that 7 percent of the men and 8 percent of the women reported having been involved in unwanted sex, with 12 percent of the women and 3 percent of the men repeatedly participating in some unwanted behavior (Kaestle, 2009). The results of a three-year study on forced sex in the United States based on 40,000 interviews indicated that 13 percent of women, or 12.1 million, had been raped, many of them during childhood or adolescence (Christopher & Pfleiger, 2007).

The National Health and Social Life Survey (NHSLS) interspersed questions about forced sex throughout the survey. It asked about times when respondents had participated in sex against their will because they were threatened or felt they had no choice. Twenty-two percent of the women had been forced to do something sexual at some time in their lives, almost always by males. Figure 16.4 summarizes the relationship these women had to the males who forced them into sex. Two percent of the men reported having been forced into some sexual activity, one-third of the time by another male (Laumann et al., 1994).

NHSLS researchers were struck by the marked difference in the number of women who said they had been forced to do something sexual (22 percent) and

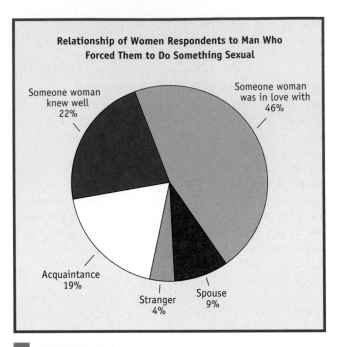

■ FIGURE 16.4   *Men Who Commit Rape*

NHSLS data suggest that, contrary to stereotypes, few of the men who force women to do something sexual are strangers. For more than three-quarters of the women who had experienced forced sexual contact, the victimizer was a man the woman was in love with (46 percent) or knew well (22 percent) or was her husband (9 percent).

Source: From *Sex in America* by Robert T. Michael et al., p. 225. Copyright © 1994 by CSG Enterprises, Inc., Edward O. Laumann, Robert T. Michael, and Gina Kolata. By permission of Little, Brown and Company, and Brockman, Inc.

the small proportion of men who admitted ever having forced a woman to have sex (2.8 percent of the men surveyed). Even taking into consideration underreporting and not telling the truth, the researchers felt that this result reflected some other phenomenon. In their responses to other questions, it was clear that almost no men found the idea of forced sex at all appealing. It was concluded that the most likely explanation was that most men who had forced women to have sex did not recognize how coercive the women had perceived their behavior to be (Michael et al., 1994). This is yet another reminder that sexual behavior has different meanings to different people and that the issue of consent often has been muddled in our culture. Women and men seem, at least sometimes, to approach these issues from very different perceptual frameworks. See Figure 16.5.

See "Sarah Recalls Being Date Raped" on SexSource Online.

FIGURE 16.5 *Forced Sex*

The data on forced sex show a much higher incidence of women reporting they have been forced or coerced into sexual activity than the incidence of men reporting they have forced or coerced a woman into sex. It could be that men are not admitting to the behavior, but researchers have suggested it is even more likely that women and men perceive such sexual situations differently.

Acquaintance Rape

The NHSLS data showed that only 4 percent of the males who had forced women to have sex were strangers to the women (Laumann et al., 1994). In a more limited sample of data involving rapes reported to authorities, strangers were the perpetrators in only about 22 percent of the rapes. The rest were committed by current or former husbands (9 percent), fathers or stepfathers (11 percent), other relatives (16 percent), boyfriends (10 percent), and other acquaintances, including friends, neighbors, and coworkers (29 percent). A rape committed by a boyfriend or other acquaintance is called **acquaintance rape** or **date rape.** Acquaintance rape happens on all college campuses and in many nonacademic settings. Use of alcohol or other drugs on the part of both the victim and the perpetrator is common in acquaintance rape situations (Kaly, Heesacker, & Frost, 2002).

There has been increasing alarm about the use of powerful drugs to spike drinks, causing women to become unconscious with the aim of sexually assaulting them. Rohypnol has received publicity in recent years, but an even more dangerous and potentially fatal drug called gamma hydroxybutyrate, or GHB, has also received notoriety as a date rape drug. It can be produced in large quantities by amateurs and is easily disguised because it looks like clear water (Hensley,

2003). Table 16.2 offers suggestions for preventing drug-facilitated rape.

Misunderstandings and lack of communication between partners are crucial issues in acquaintance rape. Mixed signals can confuse both individuals. Although we have seen that consent may involve both verbal and physical signals, it is often given by making no particular response at all—by simply going along with the activity (Bryant et al., 2001). Various studies have shown that some women admit to having said no to sex when they wanted their partners to persist longer and, in a sense, "talk them into it," and there is also evidence that persistence can indeed lead people to "give in" to having sex (Struckman-Johnson, Struckman-Johnson, & Anderson, 2003). Obviously, these confusing nuances of communication make the issue of acquaintance rape even more complicated.

The rape myth, often given credence by scenarios in movies and other media, implies that even when women say no, they mean yes. Men sometimes think that it is their task to persuade women to have sex until the woman finally realizes how good it is and ceases her protest. Research indicates, for example, that many college students, male and female alike, do not consider a simple "No, I don't want to" sufficient reason to define subsequent sex as rape. How much physical force was used, how much the woman protested, and when in their interactions the woman's protest began seem to be important factors in making that determination (Tatum & Foubert, 2009; Yost & Zurbriggen, 2006).

Because of social pressures on women concerning their sexual expression, they may be truly confused about what they want and how far they should go. If a woman begins to place limits on a man in the midst of sex play, she may not be prepared to deal with his anger or expressed frustration. All of this can add up to an uncomfortable or even dangerous situation. Although most men are not potential rapists, this ambiguous atmosphere can trigger violence and power issues in those men who are basically insecure, who need to prove their manhood to women, or who simply are used to getting and taking what they want (McCabe & Wauchope, 2005).

Do you believe that the focus on acquaintance rape on college campuses has been appropriate and necessary, or overblown? Elaborate.

acquaintance (date) rape a sexual encounter forced by someone who is known to the victim.

Table 16.2   *Strategies to Prevent Drug-Facilitated Rape*

1. Students should avoid any drink that they didn't receive directly from the bar or that they didn't open themselves.
2. If someone offers a student a drink, students should walk with him or her to the bar, watch it being poured, and carry it themselves.
3. When at a bar or party, students should avoid trying new concoctions that they have never before tasted. Shooters, shots, and drinks with multiple liquors may mask the slightly salty taste of GHB. Concoctions such as margaritas, Long Island iced teas, fruity daiquiris, Goldschlager (a cinnamon-flavored liquor), and "fishbowl" drinks have all been used to drug women without their knowledge.
4. Students should not accept a drink poured from a punchbowl. Further, they should avoid sharing drinks that are passed from person to person.
5. Students should not leave their drinks unattended for any reason—they can carry drinks with them when going to the restroom, dancing, talking to someone across the room, and using the phone. If their drinks have been left unattended for any reason, they should discard them immediately.
6. Students should use the buddy system. They should watch friends for signs of sudden intoxication such as slurred speech or having difficulty walking. If a friend is disproportionately intoxicated in relation to the amount of alcohol he or she has consumed, students should assist him or her in leaving the situation immediately.
7. If friends have passed out (particularly if disproportionately intoxicated in relation to the amount of alcohol the student knows they have consumed), students should not allow friends to sleep it off. GHB-related deaths have occurred from friends deciding to put friends to bed rather than seeking immediate medical assistance. While waiting for medical intervention, students should make sure the victim is on his or her side to prevent aspiration. They should not leave friends unattended for any reason.
8. If students suspect they have ingested GHB, they should go to the emergency room immediately. Students should request a urine sample to screen for the presence of GHB within 12 hours of ingestion. This screen is not routinely done, as many medical professionals are not familiar with GHB symptoms.

Source: From Laura Hensley, "GHB Abuse Trends and Use in Drug-Facilitated Sexual Assault: Implications for Prevention," *NASPA Journal,* vol. 40, no. 2, Winter 2003, p. 23. Copyright © 2003 National Association of Student Personnel Administrators. Reprinted with permission.

Acquaintance rape cannot always be prevented. In fact, research indicates that the most frequent acquaintance rapists are men whose victims apparently know them well. However, there are several ways both women and men can reduce the risks (see Table 16.3). The most important steps involve developing a relationship based on mutual trust, respect, and understanding. Training sessions for men in which they are encouraged to have more empathy for women may have some success (see Figure 16.6), although it is also evident that clearer communication between partners is essential as well (Crown & Roberts, 2009; Tatum & Foubert, 2009). Achieving open and honest communication takes work, but it is important that each partner knows about the other's needs and feelings.

Sexual Aggression in Marriage

In former times, it was impossible in the eyes of the law for a woman to be raped by her husband. In many countries, this is still the case. It was once assumed that it was a wife's duty to submit to her husband's sexual desires. That assumption was challenged, and the concept of **marital rape** gained acceptance. Of women in the NHSLS who reported having been forced to have sex, 9 percent had been forced by their husbands (Michael et al., 1994). The evidence suggests that marital rape is more likely to occur in relationships marked by continued disagree-

ment, alcohol or drug abuse, and nonsexual violence (Melendez et al., 2003).

Reassessment of state rape laws to eliminate any preferential treatment for husbands finally happened, but marital rape was not a law in all states until 1993. Still, wives may be reluctant to report sexual aggression by their husbands to authorities because of potential consequences for themselves, their children, or the marriage. They sometimes still believe that it is their duty to submit to their husband's sexual demands. These beliefs often leave women feeling trapped, helpless, and fearful. Their self-worth and self-respect may plummet, resulting in depression and anxiety. In most cities and many rural areas, centers are springing up to help victims of marital violence. They sometimes offer temporary housing for women and children who must leave a potentially violent home situation, along with counseling to help with decision making for the future (Christopher & Pflieger, 2007).

Men Forced to Have Sex

There are increasing reports of men who have been subjected to sexual abuse either by other men or by

marital rape a woman being forced by her husband to have sex.

Table 16.3 Acquaintance Rape: What You Can Do

Think

- When is it safe to act on my sexual urges?
- What role do I want sex to play in my life?
- Do I often have sex that I later regret?
- Do I try to work a "Yes" out of a reluctant partner?
- How does alcohol affect my sexual decision making?
- How do I learn someone's desires and limits?
- How do I express my own desires and limits?
- Do I make assumptions about the sexual needs and desires of my dates or sexual partners?

Communicate Effectively

Saying "No" or "Yes" to sexual activities may be difficult, but it's important. Acting sorry or unsure sends mixed messages. The other person can't really know how you feel without hearing it *from you.*

- **Communicate your limits carefully.** If someone starts to offend you, tell them firmly and early. Polite approaches may be misunderstood or ignored.
- **Be assertive.** Often silence or passivity is interpreted as permission. Be direct and firm with someone who is sexually pressuring you. Tell an acquaintance or your partner what you want—or don't want—and stick with your decision.
- **Trust your instincts.** If you feel you are being pressured into unwanted sex, you probably are. If you feel uncomfortable or threatened around an acquaintance or your partner, get out of the situation immediately. If you misread someone's signals, you can always explain later.
- **Listen carefully to what the other person is saying.** Are you getting mixed messages? Do you understand her or him? If not, ask. "Yes" only means "yes" when said clearly, not when your partner is drunk, high, asleep, or impaired in any way.
- **Ask, rather than assume.** Be aware of the potential for misunderstanding. You and your partner should talk about what would be most enjoyable together.
- **Remember that effective communication may not always work.** Sometimes people simply don't listen. However, no one ever *deserves* to be raped.
- **Respond physically.** If someone is assaulting you and not responding to your objections, push the person away, scream "No," and say that you consider what the person is doing to be rape.
- **Intervene as a bystander.** Challenge your friends who downplay rape or who support definitions of sex and gender roles that allow forcing someone to have sex. Intervene if you see a potential rape or assault. Encourage those around you to express and respect each other's desires and sexual boundaries.

Source: From the brochure *Acquaintance and Date Rape: What Everyone Should Know.* Copyright © May 2006 by the American College Health Association. Used with permission.

FIGURE 16.6 *Rape Prevention Training*

Antirape talks are an important part of educating the public about avoiding situations that might lead to rape. Here male students attend a rape-prevention workshop.

coercion were employing tactics of persuasion, getting the man intoxicated, and threatening a withdrawal of love. In 12 percent of reported cases, physical intimidation or restraints were used (Struckman-Johnson, Struckman-Johnson, & Anderson, 2003). The number of men who have been forced to have sex by other men is considerably higher in the gay and bisexual male population, probably reaching close to 30 percent (Kalichman et al., 2001).

Women's forcing men to have sex has received little attention in the sexological literature and has never been taken particularly seriously by the general public. The assumption is made that men simply would not be able to respond with erection unless they were willing to participate in sexual activity. In fact, there is clear evidence that males can be quite capable of erection and ejaculation in situations in which they are afraid, unwilling, or anxious. In fact, anxiety may heighten the potential for physical response, even when the man is an unwilling victim. There are case studies of sexual assault in which women threatened, restrained, and stimulated men until they responded sexually against their will. NHSLS data indicated that 1.5 percent of women

women, and sex forced on males is gradually becoming recognized as a real phenomenon (Lew, 2004). In various studies of college men, between 34 and 78 percent reported attempts to pressure or force them into sexual activity since age 16. The most typical forms of

Real People

Barbara: Facing Acquaintance Rape

Barbara is a junior at the university and has maintained outstanding grades throughout her academic career. She belongs to a sorority and considers herself to be a very outgoing, friendly person who is fun to be around. She enjoys social functions and socializes almost every weekend with her friends. In November, at a Saturday night party off campus, Barbara enjoyed the attention Charlie was giving her. Charlie is also a junior, and Barbara has been attracted to him since their first year on campus. She had hinted more than once to him that she would like to get to know him better, but for various reasons nothing ever worked out. This time, things seemed different, and he was clearly coming on to her.

As the evening progressed, both of them consumed a fair amount of alcohol. Barbara always stays in reasonable control even with alcohol, although this time she was feeling a bit woozy. When Charlie suggested that they go back to his room, she did not hesitate to agree. Once there, they lay on his bed together, continuing to kiss and touch each other. Charlie put his hand on hers and moved it toward his penis, which he had taken out of his pants. Barbara did not mind stroking it as they continued to kiss and as he massaged her breasts. Eventually, Charlie suggested that they have intercourse, and by this time they had removed most of their clothing. Barbara did not feel ready to go this far with Charlie, so she said that she did not want to do it. He continued to persist gently, and she suddenly realized that he had entered her. She tried to push him away and told him to stop, but he whispered "It'll be all right. Relax." Before ejaculating, he withdrew, and then he pulled the covers over her. They both fell asleep. Barbara woke up early, feeling hung over and upset. She woke up Charlie and said she wanted to talk. After she said that she felt he had gone too far, Charlie apologized and said that he had thought she wanted him to. He reminded her that he had not ejaculated inside her and that there was nothing to worry about.

Barbara has continued to have mixed feelings about the incident. She knows that she felt attracted to Charlie and had been glad he wanted to be with her. On the other hand, she has felt as though he should not have had intercourse with her. Upon telling a female friend about the incident, the other woman insisted that she had been raped, but Barbara argued that she did not feel this was the case. She was not about to get anyone in trouble. She continues to feel depressed about what happened and has avoided seeing Charlie, even though he has called her more than once to go out. Her concentration has slipped, and she has been finding it difficult to study. Her grades are slipping, too. She doesn't feel like talking about what happened.

Do you believe Barbara was a victim of date rape? Should she have reported the incident to appropriate officials immediately so action could be taken against Charlie? How could she proceed now to help herself deal with her feelings?

admitted to having forced a male to have sex (Laumann et al., 1994). In one study of 400 heterosexual men, more than 25 percent of them indicated that they had been subjected to pressures from women to have nonconsensual sex, and they cited their own "inability to offer resistance" as having been taken advantage of. For the most part, they rated the experiences as moderately upsetting (Krahè, Scheinberger-Olwig, & Bieneck, 2003). At the very least, pressure and coercion seem to lead many men into sexual experiences they later regret.

Males appear to react to sexual coercion and violence in the same essential ways as women, primarily feeling a tremendous loss of control. Responding to what is viewed as a humiliating assault, males feel demasculinized, embarrassed, traumatized, and depressed. Males are taught that they should not be victims, a mindset that probably often prevents them from ever reporting such abuse to authorities or fully coping with their reactions. Yet males require the same support and counseling as women to deal with the emotions, conflicts, depression, anxiety, self-blame, and loss of self-esteem that follow being forced into sex (Davies, Rogers, & Bates, 2008; Walker, Archer, & Davies, 2005).

The Aftermath of Forced Sex

Victims of forced sex experience a variety of negative reactions that can disrupt the physical, sexual, social, and psychological aspects of their lives. The majority of victims report feeling permanently changed by the experience. The psychological pain that follows a sexual assault may vary in its intensity depending on a variety of circumstances, although the reactions generally are difficult and unpleasant (Bartoi, Kinder, & Tomianovic, 2000).

The typical reactions to forced sex, sometimes gathered together as the **rape trauma syndrome,** often occur in two phases. The first (acute or disruptive) phase is characterized by *post-traumatic stress disorder,* involving stress and emotional reactions such as anxiety, depression, lowered self-esteem, and social adjustment problems. Victims may be anxious to deny the experience, insisting that they just want to put it all out of their minds. At the same time, they may be agitated, hyperalert, and filled with anxiety (Heke, Forster, & d'Ardenne, 2009). The second (recovery) phase may last many months and involves a long-term reorganization to regain a sense of personal security and control over one's environment. Relationships with a partner or family members may be seriously disrupted, and divisions need to be resolved over a period of time (Connop & Petrak, 2004). Typically, the victim is reluctant to participate in usual shared sexual activities. Many victims feel a great deal of anger, which needs to be expressed outwardly rather than be allowed to turn into inner guilt, depression, or self-hatred. Some women eventually feel the need to move residences, change jobs, and change their telephone listings.

Treatment of victims also proceeds in two phases. Early crisis intervention aims at helping the individual see herself or himself as a survivor rather than as a victim (see Figure 16.7). She or he needs to accept the consequences of the rape and begin to reestablish a sense of personal competence and control. Often, it takes time to regain a sense of continuity and meaning in life. It is important for the survivor to express feelings and to seek social support and counseling. Over the longer run, treatment focuses on sexual and relational problems that have resulted from the trauma, as well as reactions such as depression or the physical symptoms of coping with stress. With proper follow-up and treatment, survivors of forced sexual experiences can make a complete recovery and live their lives with a comfortable sense

■ FIGURE 16.7 *Rape Intervention Program*

Victims of rape need help in seeing themselves as survivors rather than victims and in reestablishing a sense of self-worth. Other problems, such as depression and physical or sexual dysfunctions as a result of the rape, need to be confronted and treated as well.

of security and self-respect. Many women experience a loss of interest in sex and are subject to specific sexual dysfunctions following an experience of forced sex. These women may wish to abstain from sexual activity for months following the incident. Some are reluctant to talk about such issues, and it has been recommended that counselors who work with rape victims take the time to bring up these sensitive subjects during the counseling process (Berlo & Ensink, 2001).

Professionals who help victims work through the aftermath of forced sex have begun to identify criteria that indicate a successful resolution of the problems:

1. The victim can think about the events of the assault at will, without being troubled by intrusive memories, nightmares, or frightening flashbacks and associations.
2. Memories of the event are accompanied by appropriately intense emotions, rather than by a false sense of detachment.
3. The feelings associated with the forced sex can be identified and endured without overwhelming the victim.
4. Symptoms of depression, anxiety, and sexual dysfunction either have passed or are at least reasonably tolerable and predictable.

rape trauma syndrome the predictable sequence of reactions that a victim experiences following a rape.

5. The victim is not isolated from relationships and has reestablished the ability to feel a sense of affinity, trust, and attachment for others.

6. Feelings of self-blame have been replaced by self-esteem, and the victim has assigned some meaning to the trauma and sense of loss. Obsessive thoughts about the event have been replaced by a realistic evaluation of it.

Individual therapy and group counseling are the most commonly used approaches for helping victims of sexual assault cope with their trauma. Most cities and larger communities have rape crisis centers that are equipped to help women deal with all aspects of the aftermath of forced sex. The partners of assault victims often become secondary survivors, experiencing a whole range of emotional reactions and post-traumatic symptoms. They may require support and counseling as well (Connop & Petrak, 2004).

■ Sexual Abuse of Children and Adolescents

A substantial percentage of children and adolescents are subjected to sexual abuse by adults or other adolescents, also known as **child molesting** or **pedophilia.** In the *DSM-IV,* pedophilia applies specifically to recurrent sexual interactions with children age 13 or under, prior to their reaching puberty, over a period of at least six months, and in cases where the perpetrator is at least 16 years old and 5 years older than the child. A term more frequently being used to describe the sexual abuse of pubescent adolescents is **hebephilia,** although it has not yet been recognized as a diagnostic term. Some researchers contend that the present diagnostic criteria for pedophilia are not particularly reliable, and that in fact adults who interact sexually with children are a rather heterogenous group that have little in common with one another. Revised criteria have been established for its diagnosis as a disorder in the upcoming fifth edition of the *DSM* (Blanchard, 2009; Kingston et al., 2007). Given Western cultural values and a body of evidence indicating that sexual interactions with adults can have harmful outcomes for children, such behavior has largely been viewed in terms of pathology and illegality.

There is also growing concern that the science of child and adolescent sexual abuse has been flawed and inadequate. Population samples have been small and nonrepresentative, statistical analysis limited, and because sexual abuse victims often have been subjected to other forms of victimization, the conclusions drawn about cause and effect are often unsupportable.

Others insist that, even in the face of scientific weaknesses, there is enough evidence to assume negative consequences for children and adolescents in such relationships (Najman, Dunne, & Boyle, 2007; Rind & Tromovitch, 2007). Experts in the field have called for interdisciplinary cooperation among medical and mental health workers, social scientists, and criminal justice representatives to carry out reliable research on the many issues surrounding sexual abuse of the young so that sensible, realistic social policies and treatment strategies can be enacted (Freyd et al., 2005).

Various models have been proposed that consider several different dimensions and levels of severity of a potentially abusive situation. First, the type of sexual behavior is considered, particularly whether physical contact has occurred (as in fondling, intercourse, or oral sex) or has not (as in exhibitionism). Also, the age of the subject of sexual contact is considered a significant aspect of the ability to consent, as is the age of the perpetrator. Most agree that if the subject is under age 12 and the perpetrator is older by some years, then the situation may be assumed to be abusive. The relationship of the perpetrator to the subject is also considered, as is the rather complex issue of the subject's degree of willingness to participate in the activity. When the victim is between the ages of 13 and 17, the issue becomes somewhat more complicated, and definitions of abuse typically depend on the age of the perpetrator and whether the subject wanted the sexual contact (Bullough, 2003a; Purcell, 2006).

A few professionals point out that among adolescents who have been involved sexually with adults, the outcomes sometimes have been positive rather than harmful. In taking such a stand, these professionals risk being attacked by opponents and having their careers jeopardized. One such researcher reminds us that the field has been filled with hyperbole on the part of "child protectionists" for about 30 years and it is time for a better balance in factual knowledge and level of scientific validity (Bullough, 2003a; Riegel, 2005; Rind, 2003; Rind & Tromovich, 2007).

Incidence of Child Sexual Abuse

Because of the difficulties involved in isolating an appropriate population sample and deciding what ages

child molesting sexual abuse of a child by an adult.

pedophilia (pee-da-FIL-ee-a) a pathological desire to sexually abuse children.

hebephilia (HEE-beh-fil-ee-a) a term being used to describe the sexual abuse of adolescents.

Real Student Voices

■ When I was about 10 or 11, my older cousin, who was about 13, showed me how to masturbate. For a while we would sneak off and do it together. In a way, I suppose he could have been considered a sexual abuser, but I've never thought of it that way. I still see him occaionally, but we've never talked about it. I guess we'd both be embarrassed.

■ One of my brother's friends fooled around with me when I was about seven years old. He touched and fondled my vulva, and made me touch him. It made me feel really dirty, even though I didn't entirely understand what was going on. I told my mom, and she reported it to the police. I know he got arrested, although I never did find out the whole story. I had to talk with a counselor a few times after it happened. I never really hated the guy, but I knew what he had done was wrong. He and his family moved away.

constitute childhood and adolescence, and inconsistencies in the definitions of various forms of abuse, it has been difficult to come up with reliable statistics on the incidence of sexual abuse in these groups. Analyses of various surveys, in which the incidence of child sexual abuse was reported over a wide range, have concluded that a reasonable summary statistic would be that about 30 to 40 percent of females and about 10 to 15 percent of males are sexually abused as children or adolescents. The abuse of members of both sexes is almost always perpetrated by males. Girls are somewhat more likely to be abused by family members, and boys are more likely to be abused by strangers, although stranger abuse accounts for only about 4 percent of cases. There is generally a low rate of reporting of such incidents to authorities (Jenny, 2008).

The NHSLS statistics indicated that 12 percent of the male respondents and 17 percent of the females reported having been sexually touched as children. The most typical forms of sexual activity reported included genital touching, kissing, oral sex, vaginal intercourse, and male-male anal intercourse. There were no differential statistics across race, ethnicity, or educational level. Girls were touched primarily by males. For 28 percent of these girls, the males were between the ages of 14 and 17 when the touching took place; for 63 percent, the males were over 18. Only 4 percent of females indicated that they had been touched by other females. Boys had been touched more frequently by females (for 45 percent, by females ages 14 to 17, and for 9 percent, by females over 18), but they also had quite frequently been touched by other males (15 percent had been touched by males ages 14 to 17, and 23 percent by males over 18). Smaller groups of boys and girls had been touched by both males and females. It might be concluded from these findings that girls are

at greatest risk of sexual abuse from adult men, followed by adolescent males; whereas boys are at greatest risk from abuse by adolescent females, followed by adult men, and then by adolescent males (Laumann et al., 1994).

The stereotypes would lead us to believe that pedophiles or hebephiles are degenerate men who lurk in trench coats near schools and parks, waiting to accost youngsters. Actually, the majority of sexual abuse victims are molested by a family member or someone known to the child. As Table 16.4 shows, family friends and relatives are among the most common abusers of children. Files released by the Boy Scouts of America for a 20-year period revealed that about 1,800 scoutmasters had been removed from duty because of suspected or actual sexual abuse of boys. The organization has produced videotapes and printed materials informing boys about how to protect themselves from sexual abuse.

There is evidence that abuse of boys is less likely to be reported than is abuse of girls, and the phenomenon also has been researched to a much lesser extent. Both of these facts need to be understood within the context of our culture's views of maleness and masculinity. Our society may at some level feel that boys really do not need or deserve the same protection against sexual abuse as do girls. It may also be that reporting an incident of sexual abuse would be viewed by the boy himself, or by someone close to him, as an admission of having been a powerless victim, a role that is not respected for males (Purcell, 2006).

Children in our culture are taught to respect and obey adults and at the same time often are given little direct information about sex and their own sex organs. They therefore are easily manipulated, both physically and psychologically, and often are easily frightened

Table 16.4	Relationship to Child Sexual Abuse Victims of Their Abusers (percentages)	
	Female Victims	**Male Victims**
Stranger	7%	4%
Teacher	3	4
Family friend	29	40
Mother's boyfriend	2	1
Older friend of respondent	1	4
Other relative	29	13
Older brother	9	4
Stepfather	7	1
Father	7	1
Other	19	17
Number of cases	289	166

Note: The table entries add up to more than 100 percent because some respondents were touched by more than one adult.

Source: From Edward O. Laumann et al., *The Social Organization of Sexuality,* et al., p. 343. Copyright © 1994 by Edward O. Laumann, Robert T. Michael, CSG Enterprises, Inc., and Stuart Michaels. Reprinted by permission of the University of Chicago Press.

FIGURE 16.8 *Anatomically Correct Dolls*
These anatomically correct dolls called "Teach-A-Bodies" are used to educate young children about sex and to assist young victims in explaining what happened to them during an incidence of alleged sexual abuse. However, studies suggest that information gained from children's use of such dolls about incidents of alleged abuse may be unreliable.

into silent sexual compliance. Children often are reluctant to report sexual abuse, especially if the perpetrator is a family member or friend, or they may lack the verbal development to explain clearly what happened (Freyd, 2005). Unfortunately, even when children report sexual abuse, they sometimes are not taken seriously. In some instances, adults want to avoid confrontations with relatives or friends who might be accused of molesting their child. Those children who do report abuse sometimes communicate directly to a close adult or professional person, either in language or by demonstrating what happened on an anatomically correct doll (see Figure 16.8).

Adult Sexual Abusers

We have only an incomplete understanding of the psychological dynamics of adult perpetrators of child sexual abuse, and research on the issue faces a number of methodological problems. Two broad areas are explored when trying to determine predictors of child sexual abuse. One encompasses the psychological disorders that were present in an eventual offender's developmental background that could help explain why the abuse behavior eventually emerged. The other attempts to identify predictors of recidivism, or the likeli-

hood that the abuser will abuse children again. Both of these avenues of study might eventually help us to understand the characteristics of potential offenders (McMillan et al., 2008).

There has been evidence suggesting that some abusive adults were themselves sexually abused as children, although this risk for becoming an adult sexual offender seems to be manifested through interaction with both genetic and personality factors in order to be realized (Beaver, 2008; Burton, 2008). Other factors also have been correlated with sexually abusive behavior. For example, child abusers tend to have lacked confidants during their own childhoods and tend to have been emotionally isolated. They tend to report high levels of emotional distress and difficulties with thinking clearly and concentrating. Some of these characteristics may be related to neurological abnormalities that may have afflicted some perpetrators during their early development (Craissati, Webb, & Keen, 2008; Seto, 2005). Studies are beginning to find correlations between a tendency toward sexual offenses and brain development or problems in neurological development, further suggesting the possibility of genetic and neurological factors (Cantor et al., 2005, 2006, 2008; MacCulloch et al., 2004).

Adult male sexual abusers often come from families that have been rejecting and controlling but not necessarily harsh in discipline. They often have had a disturbed relationship with their own father, are likely to have experienced some prior trauma in their life, and may fantasize about children in sexual ways. Sexual abusers of children seem to have well-developed mechanisms for coping internally with what they have done. They may distort or rationalize their behaviors in their own minds, and they may also be very self-denigrating, making it even more likely that they will feel unable to control their paraphilic sexual urges. Some offenders blame their victims for the sexual abuse or blame third parties, such as a spouse, for not providing sexual satisfaction for them. Some studies have noted that male pedophiles often report having had a serious head injury prior to age 13, and it has been theorized that such injuries could increase the risk of becoming a pedophile (Blanchard et al., 2002; Blanchard et al., 2003).

Less is known about women who sexually abuse children. Studies of convicted female child molesters frequently have shown them to be of marginal intelligence, to have a history of sexual and physical abuse themselves, and to experience dissatisfaction with their adult sexual lives. They tend to have a high incidence of psychiatric disorders. They often act out of anger or in retaliation against a partner or spouse. Frequently, they commit the sexual abuse with another adult present, usually a male offender. It has been proposed that because we traditionally view women as nonviolent and nurturing, professionals and law enforcement personnel fail to ask victims questions that would help reveal the woman's role in abuse cases, and victims themselves may find it difficult to acknowledge or express the role a woman has played. Similarly, female offenders may be particularly reluctant to admit to the abuse because it is seen in our society as a particularly abhorrent and unexpected behavior for a woman (Denov, 2003; Gannon, 2008).

Not long ago, attention was focused on priests and other clergy who sexually abuse children. The Roman Catholic Church has come under fire for not acting more swiftly and proactively in some situations where priests have been accused of sexual abuse (Scheper-Hughes & Devine, 2003; Shepard, 2003). As a result, the Council of Bishops adopted extensive new zero-tolerance guidelines for dealing with such cases. Most church leaders are realizing that it is crucial to take allegations of abuse seriously, remove the offender from service immediately if evidence is sufficient, comply with civil law and any civil investigations, and offer help to victims and their families. Formal procedures are now in place within most denominations for dealing with clergy abuse cases.

Child and Adolescent Sexual Abusers

There has been an increase in reported sex abuse perpetrated by both other children and adolescents. About one in every six sexual abuse incidents is committed by another child, often 6 to 9 years old. These children may have been victims of abuse themselves, and they tend to respond to counseling that helps them understand that the behavior is inappropriate. Adolescents typically abuse younger children or other adolescents. Teenage babysitters or their friends are common offenders. Adolescent sex abusers are usually males, although NHSLS data showed that boys are not infrequently abused by adolescent females (Laumann et al., 1994). Abusive adolescents often come from dysfunctional family backgrounds and have serious developmental and psychological difficulties. It is quite typical for juvenile sex abusers to have been subjected to physical abuse themselves, sometimes sexual abuse. They are likely to have parents who have sexual pathologies, and they often show signs of depression and distorted thinking patterns (McGrady, 2008).

Parents who learn about a son's sexual abusiveness often experience difficulty in dealing with the situation. There may be tensions about communicating with the son about his actions and confusion over issues related to punishment or treatment. Parents may feel overwhelmed by the situation and may be troubled by a sense of helplessness. Gradually, they may begin to engage themselves in reevaluating their relationship with their offending son and may become more actively involved in seeing the situation through to resolution. These are not easy issues for families to face. Ultimately, the treatment of adolescent sex offenders involves helping them learn how to interrupt their sexual fantasies concerning their inappropriate behavior and how to better empathize with the feelings and reactions of their victims (Aylwin, Reddon, & Burke, 2005; Oliver, 2005; Zakireh, 2008).

Effects of Child Sexual Abuse

Longitudinal studies on the effects of child sexual abuse suggest that symptoms of stress and trauma in the child gradually decline in the months following the abuse. There is some controversy over the degree to which sexual abuse as a child may affect later mental and physical health in adult life. Meta-analyses of numerous studies have found that abuse is only weakly associated with later adjustment problems, and that in typical cases, that association really cannot be attributed to the earlier abuse. It was also found that males tend to react more neutrally, or even more positively, than females to their sexual abuse histories (Tromovitch

Real People

Tony: Sexual Abuse as an Adolescent

Tony is a somewhat shy young man who tends to be a loner. He is majoring in mechanical engineering and spends much of his free time in the auto shop, working on his car. He has a circle of good male friends, and they go drinking and skiing together. He is a good snowboarder and has even won some regional competitions in the sport. Shy around women, Tony has mostly avoided relationships with them. He has hooked up with women sexually several times and has enjoyed the experiences, but he does not feel ready for a commitment.

Tony harbors a secret that has interfered with his life considerably. When he was 14, he went on a camping trip with several boys, some of whom were older and not well known by him. He ended up sharing a tent with a 17 year old. After he had fallen asleep, he felt someone moving on top of him and realized that the other boy was turning him over in the dark. He was told to be quiet and to just do what he was told. Tony was scared and wanted to fight back, but the other boy was much stronger and continued to threaten him. He was penetrated anally, which hurt, but he felt almost paralyzed by the situation. After the older boy had finished, he left Tony alone and went back to sleep. Tony lay awake until dawn, crept out of the tent, and took a canoe out for a paddle alone. The other boy ignored him the rest of the day on the trip home, and he has not seen him since.

The memories of this incident continue to bother Tony. He has never told anyone about it and in fact feels too embarrassed to discuss it. He believes that most people would think he should have been able to defend himself better. Sometimes even he wonders if he should have fought back more, and he feels sure he would do so if a similar situation happened again. He works out to keep himself strong. He has no doubts about his sexuality, but when he masturbates or gets involved sexually with a girl, the bad feelings sometimes return. He plans on toughing it out and hopes that eventually the negative feelings will diminish.

How do you feel about Tony's secret experience? Do you think he should have resisted the sexual assault more strenuously? Should he have reported the incident immediately to appropriate authorities so that action could have been taken against his attacker? Would you say that Tony was raped?

& Rind, 2008a, 2008b). Others insist that child sexual abuse has measurable effects on some victims, increasing the risks for depression, anxiety, and personality disorders (Hyde, 2008). It may be that the degree of coercion and violence involved in sexual abuse is crucial in determining the amount of trauma and later negative outcomes experienced (Najman, Nguyen, & Boyle, 2007; Senn et al., 2007).

Among a sample of men who had been sexually involved with older partners when they were children, about 40 percent did not consider the experience to have been abusive. Those that did perceive their experiences to have been abusive were more likely to have been younger when it happened and to have been physically or emotionally threatened. They also were more likely as adults to have problems with alcohol, suggesting that longer-term effects may well be related to how the early sexual experiences were perceived by the individual (Dolezal & Carballo-Dieguez, 2002).

Although it is difficult to generalize about the short- or long-term effects of sexual abuse on children and adolescents, four dimensions of consequences are summarized in the *traumatogenic/dynamic model* of sexual abuse (Lorentzen, Nilsen, & Traeen, 2008):

1. *Traumatic sexualization* means that the child's feelings, attitudes, and behaviors related to sex may be exhibited in ways that are inappropriate to the child's age and stage of development. Sexually abused children may behave in inappropriate, sexually aggressive ways.

2. *A sense of betrayal* may result among children who find that someone they trusted and depended on has caused them harm. This is particularly true when the perpetrator of the abuse is a family member. This sense of betrayal may be intensified if the child's report of sexual abuse is disbelieved or if the child is blamed for the

event. Children often have negative reactions toward the abuser.

3. *Disempowerment* results when a child feels that his or her will or desires have been ignored and deliberately violated. The more physical force or coercion the perpetrator has used in the sexual activity, the greater the child's sense of powerlessness. This outcome may play a role in the susceptibility of victims to sexually abusive situations later in life.

4. *Stigmatization* is particularly problematic when the child is expected to react to the event with feelings of shame and guilt. Such negative connotations may come directly from the abuser, who may want the victim to take the blame for the activity, or they may be reinforced by others in the family or community who hear of the abuse.

Direct cause-and-effect connections between child sexual abuse and problems in later adult life are difficult to support. Child sexual abuse has been found to be a correlational risk factor in depression, anxiety, sexual dysfunction, difficulty maintaining adult relationships, and suicidal feelings in women. Women who suffer from chronic pelvic pain, lack of sexual desire, other gynecological problems, headaches, chronic gastrointestinal problems, phobias, and depression often have a history of sexual abuse (Dennerstein, Guthrie, & Alford, 2004; Leonard, Iverson, & Follette, 2008; Najman, Dunne, & Boyle, 2007; Najman, Nguyen, & Boyle, 2007; Traeen, 2008). There is evidence to indicate that many adult psychiatric patients, alcohol and cannabis abusers, sex workers, and people with eating disorders have histories of sexual abuse at higher rates than in the general population, but this could also result from a variety of social factors (Abramovich, 2005; Finlinson et al., 2003; Hayatbakhsh et al., 2009; Schacht et al., 2007; Vaddiparti et al., 2006). Among heterosexual men and women and gay or bisexual men, especially those with a history of more forced and violent sexual abuse as children, there seems to be a tendency toward higher risk sexual activities and drugs as adults and more risk for HIV infection (Arreola et al., 2008; Catania et al., 2008; Sikkema et al., 2009; Williams et al., 2008).

Again, however, all of these correlational relationships must be carefully interpreted and not assumed to represent a clear cause-and-effect relationship between child sexual abuse and serious adult problems. Many survivors of sexual abuse as children may process whatever difficult feelings they have quite adequately and lay claim to a healthy sexuality themselves as they develop into adulthood (Roller et al., 2009; Traeen & Sorensen, 2008). It has also been proposed that certain mental disorders might predispose some children and adolescents to vulnerabilities that lead to involvement in inappropriate sexual activities with unscrupulous adults, and subsequently to other socially inappropriate behaviors as adults. For example, it has often been assumed that borderline personality disturbance could be caused by childhood sexual abuse. However, the opposite cause-and-effect pathway has also been proposed (Bailey & Shriver, 1999).

There are a few studies about the effects that sexual abuse might have on boys, suggesting that as men they may have confusion about their male identity, poor body image, or some difficulty in maintaining healthy, intimate relationships. Again, male socialization patterns appear to play a role in how men eventually perceive themselves in the aftermath of childhood sexual abuse (Dolezal & Carballo-Dieguez, 2002). A study of boys who had had sexual contacts with adults but had not been involved in any kind of clinical treatment found a broad range of reactions from negative to positive. The relationship to the adult, perceptions of consent, and the presence of force were all factors that helped determine boys' reactions to the behaviors (Rind, 2003).

It would appear that the effects of sexual abuse can be quite subtle but may also be long-lasting, possibly resulting in more negative attitudes about sex as an adult (Rellini & Meston, 2007). The more serious effects most probably are the result of violence or severe coercion inflicted on the victim by the adult. Professionals agree that an important determinant of these effects is how the child is treated by authorities and how much counseling help the child is given to deal with his or her confusion and fear. Many victims of child sexual abuse do not confront their feelings and reactions until adulthood. There are support groups that can help such adults deal with their experiences (Priebe & Svedin, 2008; Rollins, 2005).

Treating Victims of Child Sexual Abuse

Crisis intervention may be the first line of action in treating child sexual abuse cases. A safe environment must be established for the child, and the offender must be removed from any contact with her or him. Legal authorities should be involved in handling any criminal charges and sanctions, and social service agencies should work with the child and family members. A variety of treatment programs have been developed to deal with sexually abused children; some of these programs involve family therapy, because other family members may be deeply affected by the abuse as well.

The therapist treating an abused child must anticipate a variety of possible reactions in the child, including symptoms of posttraumatic stress disorder. Many children express anger during the early stages of therapy, and they need to know that limits will be placed on expressing this anger. Later, feelings of guilt, shame, loss, neglect, and depression may emerge. In particularly violent sexual abuse cases, children may experience personality dissociation that can lead to disturbances involving multiple personalities. The therapist may also be called on to deal with the highly sexualized nature that has been stimulated in a young child and to help the child learn more age-appropriate responses (Goozen et al., 2002; Putman, 2009).

Many victims live with the secret of their sexual abuse well into adulthood. Therapy most often is initiated for other reasons at first, because adult survivors of sexual abuse may experience a range of physical, emotional, relational, and sexual symptoms that interfere with their lives. It is important to work through all the complicated feelings and reactions about the abuse and the offender. The therapist will help the individual express the range of emotions, which often includes anger diverted toward the abuser and toward others perceived as not having provided sufficient protection (Berman et al., 2001; MacIntosh & Johnson, 2008). Mental imagery techniques are used to help the survivor deal with anger and resentment. Dance therapy has helped women feel more comfortable in their bodies and better able to deal with other emotions. The ultimate goal is for adult survivors of child abuse to accept their feelings about the offender, develop a stronger and more positive sense of self, and work on developing a healthy and pleasure-oriented attitude toward adult sexual interactions. Group therapy approaches have proved to be particularly effective with some adults who were sexually abused as children (Maltz, 2003; Mills & Daniluk, 2002; Rollins, 2005).

Treating Offenders

Although standard approaches to psychotherapy that do not focus specifically on the offending behavior tend to be of limited value, some treatment programs have been found to be quite successful with child sexual abusers. These usually involve various combinations of group therapy, cognitive-behavioral techniques to help abusers gain better control over their sexual impulses, relapse prevention strategies to head off further occurrences of abuse, and education about sexuality. Abusers need to improve their self-concept, and they may be helped to take responsibility for their actions and empathize with the feelings of their victims (Levenson et al., 2009). Over a number of years, professionals have agreed on a set of standards for the treatment of adult sex offenders, and a number of advances have been made in treatment strategies (Coleman et al., 2001). Treating sex offenders with drugs to reduce their sexual drive has gained in popularity during recent years. Some of these drugs interfere with the production of male hormones or with the action of these hormones (Saleh, 2005; Schober et al., 2005). Antidepressant medications have also been used with offenders who seem to have depressive symptoms and may reduce the obsessive-compulsive tendencies that sometimes are part of the abusive behaviors. It has been suggested that when offenders also have a sexual dysfunction, treating the dysfunction may improve the individual's quality of life and deter further abusiveness (Metz & Sawyer, 2004). Although much remains to be done to clarify the effectiveness of medical treatment of child sexual abusers, the preliminary data available suggest that such treatments are of limited value unless they are part of a more comprehensive program of psychotherapy and behavior modification.

Untreated sexual abusers tend to have a recidivism rate of between 35 and 50 percent. Cognitive-behavioral approaches that eliminate or reduce inappropriate sexual arousal seem to reduce recidivism rates somewhat over the short term, although long-term studies are lacking. The goal of all such treatment is to help the offender control future behavior so that sexual abuse is not repeated and the offender is able to establish healthy, age-appropriate sexual relationships (Seto et al., 2004). Therefore, the operative word seems to be *control* rather than *cure*.

Incestuous Sex

Virtually every society has strong prohibitions against sexual relationships within families. This is often called the **incest taboo,** with the term **incest** referring to sexual activity between close relatives. There are many theories about why the incest taboo exists. One of the most common involves the desire to avoid disruption of the family system. There are exceptions to the taboo, however. In the Trobriand Islands, a girl who has intercourse with her mother's brother is committing incest. If she has intercourse with her father, she is not. Among the Kubeo Indians of South America, boys come of age only after having sexual intercourse with their mothers. In the United States, NHSLS researchers found that 9 percent of girls and 4 percent of boys had been sexually involved with an older brother, 14 percent of girls and 2 percent of boys with their father or stepfather, and 29 percent of girls and 13 percent of boys with another relative (Laumann et al., 1994).

incest taboo cultural prohibitions against incest, typical of most societies.

incest (IN-sest) sexual activity between closely related family members.

It is believed that father–daughter sexual contact constitutes slightly less than 25 percent of incest cases. Stepfather–daughter incest also accounts for about 25 percent of cases. The remaining 50 percent of cases involve brothers, uncles, in-laws, grandfathers, stepfamily members, and live-in boyfriends of mothers; it is generally believed that brother–sister incest is the most common among these cases. A study of sibling incest showed some dynamics that the families tended to have in common. The parents often were emotionally distant, inaccessible, and controlling. They tended to stimulate a sexual climate at home, and there were often family secrets, such as one parent having an affair. The incidence of mother–son incest is much less clear, and many researchers believe that although such behavior is not as common as incestual abuse of girls, it also may be reported with much less frequency when it occurs (Lawson, 1993).

Incest often results from unhealthy family interactions, and its discovery causes reverberations throughout the family structure. Families in which the relationship between the father and the mother is weak and in which a daughter takes on many household responsibilities are susceptible to incestuous contact between father and daughter. Abuse of boys by their fathers is known to be more common in households where the father is very domineering, has alcohol and marital problems, and is physically abusive toward other family members. Abuse of boys by their mothers occurs more often when the mother is overreliant on the son for emotional support. Families in which there is a great deal of chaos, role confusion, and blurring of boundaries between generations are also frequently involved in incest (M. Hamer, 2002).

Like other forms of sexual abuse, incest is usually a confusing interaction for a child. Youngsters may be quite passive during the relationship and may even exhibit a kind of seductive behavior that encourages the sexual activity. As a result of the experiences, they may become highly erotic and more interested in sex than would be expected for their age, or they may exhibit self-destructive and aggressive forms of behavior due to feelings of guilt, resentment, and low self-worth. Feelings of victimization may persist for years, depending on the amount of support the victim receives from family, friends, and healthcare personnel (Lorentzen, Nilsen, & Traeen, 2008).

Incest survivors may struggle to understand how and why the incest occurred. Research indicates that being able to deal with these unresolved feelings can help people gain a new sense of mastery over their lives. Group psychotherapy is one of the more common therapeutic approaches for incest victims, although one-to-one counseling is often used as well. Therapists often must help adult survivors of incest deal with years of shame and anger that in many instances have caused

difficulties in relationships. These adults need assurances that they are worthwhile and strong human beings (Marotta & Asner, 1999; Rollins, 2005).

Recovered or False Memories: The Controversy

As awareness of the extent of childhood sexual abuse emerged, some professionals became convinced that a range of psychological and behavioral symptoms were the result of childhood sexual abuse. They also believed that when adults were unaware of any such abuse, it might have been the result of repressing unpleasant memories For a brief period, there was a strong emphasis on the need to help people remember childhood sexual abuse through therapy. Some counselors and therapists began to explore in greater depth the histories of their adult clients in hopes of finding out whether these individuals indeed had been subjected to sexual abuse earlier in life. Articles based on case studies began to be written about clients' *recovered memories* of past sexual abuse, often by a family member. There were several highly publicized cases in which parents were sued by their adult daughters because of sexual or other abuse that the daughter remembered during therapy. Some of these parents insisted that they were being unjustly accused and claimed that unethical or incompetent therapists had, in effect, planted *false memories* about abuse in their clients.

Although it generally has been accepted by those in the fields of psychology and psychiatry that traumatic events during childhood may occasionally be lost to conscious recall and later recalled, research has not been particularly supportive of that contention. A fair amount of evidence indicates that adult victims of child sexual abuse remember the incidents in varying degrees of detail (Banyard & Williams, 1999; Gold, Hughes, & Swingle, 1999). Controversy also surrounds the reliability of the details of those memories that do exist. Studies demonstrate that fantasies may be constructed out of events or emotions experienced during childhood or through suggestion by an outside person (Beckman, 2003; Freyd et al., 2005). As proponents of recovered memories called for understanding of the victims of past sexual abuse, some family members who feel they have been falsely accused rallied together within the False Memory Syndrome Foundation. This group has dedicated its efforts to combating the possible effects of inaccurate recovered memories. There may be some people whose memories of sexual abuse during childhood have been repressed and indeed may be reconstructed. On the other hand, there is recognition that some individuals' memories sometimes may be incomplete, inaccurate, or invented out of other thought processes.

■ Preventing and Dealing with Problematic Sex

Sexual problems and concerns need not be devastating or permanently disruptive. Before moving on to the following chapters, which deal with other types of sexual problems, it is important to discuss how each of us can work to prevent sexual problems in our own lives and deal with them should they arise (Kalmuss, 2004). Consider each of the following points with care, and think about how you might apply them in your own life.

Learning about Sex

It is a good idea to learn about your own body and its sexual parts. You should also understand the patterns of sexual response that are part of your body's repertoire. You've already begun the lifetime process of understanding your own sexual orientations and preferences—the things that turn you on. However important sexual self-knowledge is, it is not enough. You also need to take time to understand the many individual sexual differences found in human beings, which range from different sizes of sex organs to different sexual orientations. Accepting the fact that we are all different can be an important step.

Children need to understand the concepts of appropriate and inappropriate touching, and they need to be alert to possible behaviors that could lead to sexual abuse. They should be taught to be alert to behaviors, such as bribery and coercion, that adults might use to entice them into sexual activity (Tabachnick, 2000). Experts at the National Center for Missing and Exploited Children indicate that being able to recognize and avoid certain risky situations is more valuable than the traditional warning not to talk to strangers. In the vast majority of cases, sexual offenders are not strangers to the child.

Knowing How to Communicate

Communication is fundamental to a continuing, healthy sexual relationship. Counselors who work with couples find that flaws in communication are one of the most common roots of sexual problems. There are many different things that must be communicated between people: thoughts, ideas, feelings, values, opinions, needs, and desires. They are communicated not only verbally but also through eye contact, facial expressions, and body language. It is important for people to have enough sense of personal empowerment to be able to learn about and use assertiveness when it comes to refusing sexual overtures and to be persistent when they do not want to have sex. This can be

tricky at times, but it requires a strong sense of self and the skills to stand up to persuasion. Communication is more difficult than often believed, and most people are given very little help in learning how to communicate effectively. See Chapter 9 for a more complete discussion of communication and sexuality.

Having Realistic Expectations

People are prone to compare themselves to others sexually. "Am I normal?" is one of the most commonly asked questions when it comes to sex. The media provide models of sexual attractiveness and suggest standards of sexual prowess. All this can create unrealistic expectations that people then struggle to live up to. Sexual problems often stem from setting expectations for attractiveness or level of sexual activity that simply cannot be met. It is important to know yourself sexually and to work toward sexual goals that are comfortable, attainable, and consistent with your personal values. To live with unrealistic goals is to invite sexual problems.

Being Cautious and Responsible

Shared sex always has some consequences, potentially positive or negative. It is important to approach sexual decision making with an awareness of possible consequences, knowledge about sex, and open communication between the partners. Sexual problems such as guilt, unwanted pregnancy, contracting a sexually transmitted disease, and feelings of having been exploited usually can be prevented with a cautious attitude toward sexual choices. It is particularly important to be careful about sharing sex-related information on the Internet. Personal identity, location, and contact information should be guarded with care, because there are sexual predators in cyberspace who sometimes use such information to find victims (Elliott et al., 2009). Responsible sexual decisions are made by keeping the other person in mind as well as yourself. Only too often, people shirk their sexual responsibility with excuses: "I didn't mean to go so far"; "It just happened"; "I was so drunk I didn't know what I was doing." Responsibility means approaching relationships with an awareness of how powerful sexual emotions can be and how complicated the aftermath of sex can sometimes be, even if sex was desired at the time. Responsible sexual decision making can do more to prevent problematic sex than any other step.

Finding Sex Counseling and Therapy

A part of being a healthy, sexually fulfilled person is knowing when you have exhausted your own resources. Sometimes you can cope with a problem yourself, sometimes not. Often it helps just to talk things out with another person, pulling thoughts and feelings into a more manageable perspective, especially when you know that person will protect your confidentiality. It can be important to have the objectivity that an outsider can bring to a situation. Sometimes specific suggestions and strategies are needed that only someone with professional training can offer. Best friends seldom make the best counselors, regardless of how good their intentions may be.

Usually the best time to seek professional help is when you realize you need it and feel ready to seek it, even if you are nervous about it. Early intervention can prevent further complications. Do not assume that a routine visit to a clinician necessarily means that the professional will uncover any sexual concerns. Many professionals fail to take advantage of routine visits to ask questions about a person's sexual life and problems (Burstein et al., 2003). You will most likely need to share some basic information with the professional. There is another important point to keep in mind, however. No professional counselor or therapist can wave a magic wand and make the problem disappear. No treatment can be successful without a sincere motivation to change. You will have to want to work on the problem and be willing to expend some energy doing so. If it is a problem shared between partners, then both people usually will have to be committed to working together on it (Spitalnick & McNair, 2005).

Here are some specific guidelines to consider when deciding whether to seek professional help and when looking for an appropriate counselor or therapist:

1. *Make a preliminary assessment of the seriousness of the problem.* This has implications for the type of help you may want to seek. Problems with disease or pain generally need to be addressed by medical professionals. Concern over sexual orientation, decision making, and sexual behaviors can be handled by sex counselors. Sexual dysfunctions (see also Chapter 18) are best dealt with by a specially trained sex therapist or medical professional.

2. *Do not be afraid to seek help.* Professional help often can resolve sexual concerns and problems and help individuals and couples feel better about themselves. To seek such help is not a weakness but instead constitutes a sign of maturity, strength, and personal responsibility.

3. *Locate a qualified professional.* You may want to ask a trusted doctor, teacher, or religious leader to suggest a professional he or she would recommend for dealing with sexual problems. Online directories of local professionals often list people

who specialize in treating sex-related concerns. The counseling centers or health centers of larger colleges and universities offer sex counseling and therapy services for students or referrals to outside professionals.

4. *Investigate and ask questions.* It is always advisable to be an informed consumer. Do not be hesitant or embarrassed about checking out professionals' qualifications and inquiring about their background preparation. Asking questions during an initial visit, or even prior to a first visit, is a good way to find out what to expect. A true professional will not be offended or insulted by such questions. Here are some areas you might consider finding out more about:
   - What does the service cost, and how frequent are visits?
   - What sort of education, training, and other credentials does the person have?
   - What records are kept, and are they treated in a completely confidential manner? How long are records kept on file?
   - Is the professional appropriately licensed or certified by the state or by any professional society?

5. *Know what you are looking for.* You should be able to feel comfortable and relatively relaxed with a counselor or therapist. Look for the kind of atmosphere in which you are free to discuss sex openly and to express your feelings without being judged, put down, or made to feel embarrassed. You should sense a degree of trust, caring, and respect between yourself and the therapist. Any counseling process has its ups and downs, but you should be able to sense eventual progress as long as you are working on it. If you feel discouraged, you should be able to discuss this with the counselor or therapist.

6. *Know what you are **not** looking for.* Be skeptical about anyone who promises quick and easy solutions. If the person seems to have personal values that might interfere with her or his objectivity in assessing your situation, think about changing to another professional. Also watch out for any seductiveness or sexual aggression from the professional. This is considered unethical behavior and may be grounds for taking action against the offender. Be cautious, too, about people who seem overly anxious to persuade you to adopt their sexual values. Finally, unless the professional is a physician or other medical clinician who must conduct a legitimate physical examination, reject any suggestions that you should remove your clothing or submit to some sort of sexual touching. Codes of professional ethics consider such behavior inappropriate.

7. *Check with people who are familiar with the counselor's or therapist's work.* Word-of-mouth recommendations or criticisms are worth taking into consideration. People who have had professional contacts with a counselor or therapist, as either a client or a colleague, may be able to offer especially valuable insights. However, such opinions do not represent the final word. Some people can be impressed by a professional who knows how to sound well informed; some may gripe about a therapist who cannot perform miracles on demand.

Problematic sex need not be allowed to become a sexual catastrophe. Help is now available for any sexual problem and can be obtained confidentially from well-qualified professionals. Preventing and dealing with sexual problems is largely a matter of personal responsibility. You must be ready to accept that any sexual act has a variety of potential consequences, both positive and negative. Most of all, you must be responsible enough to recognize that anyone can experience a sexual problem, and you must then *do something about it.*

Self-Evaluation

Your Sexual Concerns and Problems

Most of us do not feel fully comfortable with or relaxed about all aspects of our sexuality all the time. It is difficult to say when discomfort becomes a concern or when a concern becomes a problem. However, this questionnaire may help you evaluate your particular sex-related worries and what you want to do about them. The chapters that follow may offer more information about your specific concerns. Before proceeding with the questionnaire, take the following two preliminary steps:

Step 1. Ask yourself if you really need to proceed with this questionnaire. If you have had or now have some area of sexuality that has caused you to experience a continuing sense of unrest or worry, it probably will be worth your time to answer the questions. If you feel fully comfortable with your sexual needs, feelings, orientations, and activities all the time, skip this questionnaire.

Step 2. If possible, make certain you have all the facts about the sexual issues that are of special concern to you. Before going on with this questionnaire, read the earlier parts of this book pertaining to those areas. The table of contents and index can help you find appropriate information. You might even want to read some of the articles that are cited in each chapter. Some worries and problems fade with appropriate, accurate sexuality education.

1. **Mentally, or on paper, list the sexual concern(s) or problem(s) that seem most worrisome for you. Do not list more than three.**

2. **For each concern you have listed, answer the following questions.**
    a. *For how long has this worried you?*
    b. Can you identify the particular incident or time in your life when it started to become a real concern? If so, think it over in as much detail as you can recall.
        1. *What were your feelings at the time?*
        2. *What are your feelings now as you think back?*
        3. *Is there anything you wish you could change about the origins of your concern?*
        4. *If another person was involved in the origins of your concern, how do you feel about that person now?*
    c. Is there another person directly involved in (or affected by) the problem now? If so, how would you summarize your present relationship with that person?

3. **Evaluate your concerns.**
    a. For each concern you have listed, read through the categories listed in the table and decide which category best describes your concern. Note whether it is labeled I, II, III, or IV.

Category Number	Types of Concerns
I.	*Body appearance* *Size or shape of genitals or breasts* *Sexual things you have done in the past but no longer care about doing*
II.	*Sexually transmitted disease or other infection of sex organs* *Concern about having been infected with HIV* *Pregnancy or difficulty with birth control methods*

Fear of sexual exertion following a heart attack or other illness

Other medical problems related to sex organs

III.   *Masturbation*

Sexual fantasies

Things or people to whom you feel sexually attracted that do not fit the typical socially accepted standards

Sexual interests and/or activities of your partner or another important person in your life that are upsetting to you in some way

Lack of information about sex

Lack of communication with a sexual partner

IV.   *Deep, long-term guilt, dissatisfaction, or unhappiness with your sexuality*

A feeling that you are being sexually harassed by another person

A history of sexual abuse as a child that you have not dealt with completely or effectively

Concern about rape or other forms of sexual assault or coercion

Worries about your body image to the extent that you avoid eating, or binge on food and then vomit or take laxatives

Sexual activities in which you now engage that are unusual, illegal, or not generally accepted socially

Problems with sexual functioning (e.g., erectile problems, premature ejaculation, lack of sexual arousal, difficulty reaching orgasm (in yourself or your partner) or pain during sexual activity

b. Do you feel discouraged, depressed, and hopeless about your sexual worries and problems? Do not give up on yourself, because for others to be able to help you, you must be willing to work on your problem. There may be many things that will help. Also, be careful not to blame someone else for your problem. Regardless of the type of problem or who has it, you are responsible for how it affects you and what you do about it. Keep reading.

c. Now what are you going to do? First go back and note the category of your concern from part 3a. Regardless of the category, it might be worth considering talking with a professional counselor who has a good understanding of human sexuality. Here are some specific comments about each category; note the remarks for the category you have chosen.

1. Category I for the most part includes problems that you cannot do very much about. One way or another, you probably are going to have to try to become more comfortable with what you have or what you have done. Counseling could help you do that.

2. Category II consists of medical problems. If you have not already consulted a physician, do so. If you already have but are unsatisfied, try to find another physician who can help. Your city or county medical society might be able to help with this. Most communities also have STD and HIV testing services and family planning clinics.

3. Category III includes some of the most common types of sexual problems. Although many people learn to live with them, some form of counseling often can do wonders. (See part d.)

4. Category IV includes problems that might easily fit into category III but that also sometimes require more intensive sex therapy or psychotherapy. In seeking a professional to help you deal with such problems, choose carefully and check credentials.

d. If you decide to seek professional help, consider the following:

1. Should your spouse or sexual partner be involved in the counseling? If you are having difficulty communicating, see Chapter 9.

2. Try to gain a clear idea of what your goals are in dealing with your sexual concern(s), and express them to the person from whom you seek help.

Chapter Summary

1. The determination as to when some sexual orientation, preference, or behavior becomes a problem can be highly subjective. It often needs to be viewed within the contexts of an individual's reactions and lifestyle and the surrounding cultural and social belief systems.

2. Negative attitudes about the self, especially concern about one's body image, or a lack of accurate information related to sexuality can become a problem.

3. Sexual prejudice and coercion represent serious sexual problems that can be hurtful to others.

4. It can be upsetting when one's body is not sexually aroused or responsive in situations where such responses were desired and expected.

5. Some sexual behaviors represent obvious physical dangers to individuals and sometimes reflect self-destructive qualities. Paraphilias are sexual interests that are considered antisocial and harmful.

6. Compulsive sexual behavior can lead to risk of negative consequences. There is controversy over the concept of sex addiction and whether compulsive sexual behavior fits an addiction model.

7. The trafficking of girls, boys, and women for sexual purposes has become a worldwide problem.

8. Cultures establish sexual boundaries that people are not supposed to cross. When they do, problems arise.

9. Sexual harassment refers to unwanted sexual advances. There are four main types: coercion and bribery, hostile environment, aggressive acts, and third-party effects.

10. Schools and colleges have policies prohibiting sexual harassment. There is controversy over the degree to which faculty–student relationships at colleges should be limited or prohibited.

11. The military has faced difficulties with sexual harassment and the issue of consensual sexual relationships, and it has developed educational programs to address these issues.

12. Sexual harassment in the workplace has long been a problem, and laws require that workers enjoy freedom from such pressures.

13. It is best to respond promptly to harassing situations by getting personal support, seeking out appropriate authorities, being clear about your needs, possibly writing a letter to the harasser, and making use of mediation services.

14. Sexual boundary violations by professionals are prohibited by ethical standards, and they often represent coercion based on power imbalances in the relationship.

15. Sexuality education for professionals who work with other people aims at developing competence for dealing with sexual problems.

16. Consent is a fundamental issue in sexual interactions that has not been studied extensively. Many factors can compromise the validity of consent and lead to charges of sexual coercion or force.

17. Women and men report having been coerced into sex by sexual arousal, emotional manipulation and lies, exploitation while intoxicated, or physical force.

18. The term rape is used in various ways to refer to forced sex. There are several different motivations behind rape. Statutory rape relates to the legal age of consent.

19. There are some predictors of aggression and violence in relationships. In female-male relationships, early warning signals can suggest that a man has negative or disrespectful attitudes toward women and could potentially be abusive.

20. Forced sex is believed to be far more common than is generally realized or reported. It often represents an attempt to humiliate someone and exercise power over the person. Men and women frequently perceive sexually coercive situations differently.

21. In many cases, the offender in forced sex is known by the victim, and the offense is called acquaintance rape or date rape. Care should be taken to avoid the possibility of being incapacitated by a date rape drug.

22. A small percentage of wives admit to having been raped by their present or former husbands. Husbands are now subject to the legal consequences of raping their spouses.

23. Men also can be forced or coerced into having sex, sometimes by women and sometimes by other men. They react with humiliation, depression, and post-traumatic stress, but they may be less likely than women to report such assaults.

24. Victims of forced sex go through various phases of the rape trauma syndrome, a type of post-traumatic stress disorder. Counseling and support are necessary during these phases of adjustment.

25. Sexual abuse of children, called pedophilia or child molestation, is a common and serious problem. Sexual attraction to or abuse of adolescents is sometimes called hebephilia.

26. There is controversy over the possibility that some sex between adolescents and someone older might be perceived positively by the adolescent.

27. Adult sexual abusers may have experienced neurological problems during development. Psychologically, they may view children as sexually motivated, have a history of being abused themselves, and exhibit symptoms of denial and depression.

28. A child who is sexually abused may have a sense of guilt, shame, and betrayal, and the abuse may lead to an unhealthy sexualization of the child's life. Correlations have been found in adults survivors with physical and psychological problems, but cause-and-effect relationships have not yet been supported.

29. Victims of sexual abuse may be helped by immediate crisis intervention as well as longer-term supportive and counseling services.

30. Treatment programs are available for child sexual abuse offenders; the most effective of these programs emphasize ways to control their sexual impulses and reduce their sexual desire for children. Some medications may have some effect in controlling sexual desire.

31. The term *incest* applies to sexual activity between closely related family members. It usually stems

from unhealthy family patterns and creates serious confusion for the developing child or adolescent.

32. There has been controversy over adult memories of childhood sexual abuse that are recovered in therapy, and some professionals argued that these phenomena represent false memories.

33. The best ways to prevent and deal with sexual problems are to be knowledgeable about human sexuality, develop healthy communication skills, have realistic expectations about sex, and exercise caution and responsibility.

34. Sometimes it makes sense to seek professional help for dealing with sexual problems. Check out such professionals with great care and be suspicious about behavior that makes you uncomfortable or seems unethical.

Chapter 17

Sexually Transmitted Diseases, HIV/AIDS, and Sexual Decisions

Chapter Outline

I couldn't understand why the nurse suggested that I have a test for a disease when I had no symptoms whatsoever. I was really shocked when the results showed that I had chlamydia. Then she said I should get tested for HIV. I never thought I would get any of those diseases. I'm pretty careful.

—based on a counseling session

Sex involves close body contact and the mingling of bodily fluids, making it a likely pathway for certain disease-causing organisms to be passed between people. Sexually transmitted diseases (STDs) can spread rapidly within populations. They also are commonly called sexually transmitted *infections* (STIs), but this term is used internationally more than in the United States. STD is still the official category used by the Centers for Disease Control and Prevention (CDC). STDs represent an important global health issue that is too often neglected, and experts have stressed that we cannot allow stigma, prejudice, or moral values concerning sexuality to get in the way of effective control of these diseases (Low et al., 2006).

The epidemic of HIV infection and AIDS is now well into its third decade. It has garnered more attention than any new disease to appear in recent history, and it continues to spread. **Acquired immunodeficiency syndrome,** better known as **AIDS,** threatens significant portions of the human population. The prevalence of **human immunodeficiency virus (HIV),** the virus that eventually can produce AIDS when it infects humans, has raised political and economic issues. Although HIV and AIDS have garnered a great deal of attention and are discussed in this chapter, some other STDs have reached epidemic proportions and their significance must not be minimized. In fact, persons with an STD infection are two to five times more likely to acquire HIV when exposed to it by an infected individual (CDC, 2008a).

See "STDs: The Silent Epidemic"
on SexSource Online.

■ An Overview of the Hidden Epidemic

Some sexually transmitted diseases, such as **syphilis,** represent long-standing scourges that historically attacked and weakened large populations. Such STDs were feared and assumed to represent retribution from the gods. When soldiers of the French army were garrisoned in Naples in the winter of 1495, they suffered syphilitic sores on the genitals, followed by skin eruptions. The Italians called it the "French sickness," although the French blamed it on the Italians. The Turkish people would come to call it the Christian disease, and the Chinese dubbed it the Portuguese disease. Nearly every major nationality, ethnic group, and

religion eventually would be blamed for syphilis. Gonorrhea and syphilis were significant problems among U.S. troops during World War II, and extensive educational efforts were launched to prevent their spread. However, effective and rapid medical treatments for the venereal diseases (VD), as they were once called, were generally lacking, and their incidence increased at alarming rates.

Which STDs do you believe are most common in the United States?

When penicillin and other antibiotics began to appear in the 1940s, it seemed as though VD had finally been conquered. By 1957, the number of cases of both gonorrhea and syphilis had dropped to all-time lows. However, as public concern began to fade amid assurances of a quick cure, the incidence of STDs began to rise again. It has been suggested that some health policymakers have always had mixed feelings about curing or eradicating STDs, because these diseases have been perceived as one factor that might discourage illicit sexual behavior. It seems likely that gonorrhea and syphilis might well have been completely eradicated if our culture had taken a less moralistic stance on STDs and had developed more aggressive antibiotics (Michael et al., 1994). Instead, more antibiotic-resistant strains of these diseases have developed, and more disease-causing microbes—such as chlamydia and a variety of viral diseases—have been added to the list of more than 25 infectious organisms that can be transmitted by intimate bodily contact. The number of new antibiotics approved by the FDA has decreased nearly 70 percent since the 1980s (CDC, 2008a; Taubes, 2008).

What is your response to the suggestion that health policymakers have failed to use all of their resources to eradicate STDs?

acquired immunodeficiency syndrome (AIDS) a fatal disease caused by a virus that is transmitted through the exchange of bodily fluids, primarily in sexual activity and intravenous drug use.

human immunodeficiency virus (HIV) the virus that initially attacks the human immune system, causing HIV disease and eventually AIDS.

syphilis (SIF-uh-lus) a sexually transmitted disease (STD) characterized by four stages, beginning with the appearance of a chancre.

Real Student Voices

■ I was always a lot more scared of getting pregnant than I was of getting an STD. Even after I went on the pill, I always insisted that my boyfriend wear a condom. After a while, we got pretty comfortable with just using the pill, until I discovered I had chlamydia. So much for trust.

■ Having HPV isn't particularly scary for me as a male, but I do worry about spreading it to the women I have sex with. I always use condoms, but eventually I hope to settle down and get married. The new vaccine is great, because when we want to have a baby I won't have to feel guilty about giving her the virus or cancer.

■ Thinking about STDs just makes sex seem so unappealing! Yuck!

STDs have been called the hidden epidemic because they so often escape public attention. For one thing, many STDs lack clear symptoms and may go undetected for some time. Partly for this reason, they may also have serious, longer-term health consequences, including infertility, cancer, and other chronic illnesses. Another reason is that because of the social stigma associated with sex-related diseases, public discussion and education about STDs often are avoided, which may even inhibit health professionals from educating their patients about potential consequences. It is now being realized that high intensity behavioral counseling for adults and adolescents who are sexually active with multiple partners and at high risk for infection is one of the best ways to prevent STDs (U.S. Preventive Services Task Force, 2008).

Of the approximately 19 million new cases of STDs that occur annually in the United States, nearly half occur among ages 15 to 24. Yet teenagers often lack basic knowledge about STDs. In one study, nearly all the adolescents surveyed had received sexuality education, and 91 percent identified HIV as a major STD. However, only 2 percent could identify all eight major STDs, and few could distinguish between the curable and the incurable diseases (Clark, Jackson, & Allen-Taylor, 2002). The majority of adolescents do not seem to consider themselves at risk of infection, yet about half of sexually experienced teenagers do not use a condom every time they have sex, and their knowledge of risk factors is quite low (CDC, 2008b, 2008c). They often assume that they do not have an STD because they have no symptoms. When asked to name the most common STDs, only a small proportion can name human papilloma virus or trichomonas, even though these two diseases are among the most common of the new cases of STDs reported each year (Weinstock, Berman, & Cates, 2004).

Estimates vary concerning the incidence of STDs because of deficiencies in how the data are collected. Even though the CDC consider STDs to be *reportable diseases* and gather statistics on them, many private physicians do not consistently report their occurrence. Public clinics are more likely to report those diseases that are easily diagnosed, such as the highly recognizable STD gonorrhea. They are less likely to be able to offer the expensive diagnostic techniques necessary to detect some of the viral STDs, such as HPV or hepatitis B.

The Appearance of HIV and AIDS

No one knows for certain how long HIV has been around. It may be that in earlier years people who actually died of AIDS were diagnosed as having died of one of the many infections that the disease produces or that medical personnel simply had no way of knowing what they were dealing with. Genetic studies indicate that HIV probably had been infecting animal hosts for a long time and eventually diversified and began to infect humans sometime around 1930. Although there have been some puzzling cases from earlier years leading to speculation about when and how HIV actually reached North America, it is generally believed that it arrived sometime during the mid-1970s. In the early 1980s, medical journals began to report its array of symptoms, all seeming to point to an apparent weakness in the immune system (Osborn, 2008).

The predominant theory, although it remains only a theory, about the origin of HIV is that a variant of the virus infected chimpanzees, perhaps for thousands of years. The virus eventually mutated into a form that could infect humans and may well have been transmitted to humans in central Africa during the butchering of chimps for food. The virus may have remained isolated

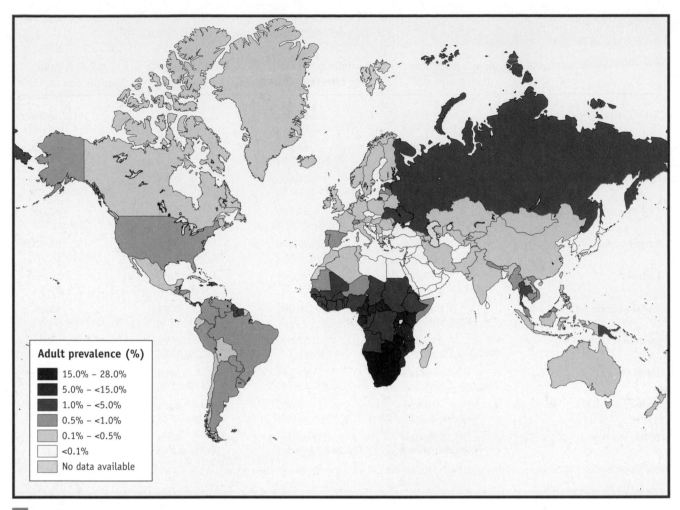

Adult prevalence (%)
- 15.0% – 28.0%
- 5.0% – <15.0%
- 1.0% – <5.0%
- 0.5% – <1.0%
- 0.1% – <0.5%
- <0.1%
- No data available

FIGURE 17.1 *Global Estimates of Adult Prevalence of HIV and AIDS as of the End of 2007, with a Total of 33 Million People Living with HIV*

Source: Reproduced with kind permission from UNAIDS (2008).

in small, remote societies for decades until changing ways of African life brought it to urban centers, from where it was transported to the rest of the world by infected persons. Changing lifestyles, such as increased international travel, have had profound effects on the spread of such epidemics. We will never completely understand the routes by which HIV has spread throughout the world. Once a pool of infected people became established in a population center that interacted with outside areas, it was only a matter of time before the virus would make its way into large segments of the human population.

Incidence of HIV/AIDS

Epidemiological studies continue to survey the extent of HIV infection in North America and worldwide (see Figure 17.1 and Table 17.1). One method used is gathering surveillance data concerning the number of HIV-positive cases reported by hospitals, clinics, physicians, and medical record systems. It is believed that in the United States at least 90 percent of cases are actually reported, a very high rate compared to the reporting of other diseases. In North America in 2007, it was believed that between 760,000 and 2.0 million (or an estimated 1.2 million) people were currently living with HIV or AIDS (CDC, 2008; UNAIDS, 2008). Worldwide, AIDS has become the fourth-largest cause of human death. The rates of infection and death are much greater in the poorer nations of the world (UNAIDS, 2008).

A new study in the United States examined stored blood serum specimens from 22 states and

epidemiological (e-pe-dee-mee-a-LAHJ-i-cahl) referring to the branch of medical science that deals with the incidence, distribution, and control of disease in a population.

Table 17.1	Estimated Global HIV and AIDS Statistics and Features by Region, 2007			
	Adults & children living with HIV	Adults & children newly infected with HIV	Adult prevalence (15–49) [%]	Adult & child deaths due to AIDS
Sub-Saharan Africa	22.0 million [20.5–23.6 million]	1.9 million [1.6–2.1 million]	5.0% [4.6%–5.4%]	1.5 million [1.3–1.7 million]
Middle East & North Africa	380,000 [280,000–510,000]	40,000 [20,000–66,000]	0.3% [0.2%–0.4%]	27,000 [20,000–35,000]
South and South-East Asia	4.2 million [3.5–5.3 million]	330,000 [150,000–590,000]	0.3% [0.2%–0.4%]	340,000 [230,000–450,000]
East Asia	740,000 [480,000–1.1 million]	52,000 [29,000–84,000]	0.1% [<0.1%–0.2%]	40,000 [24,000–63,000]
Latin America	1.7 million [1.5–2.1 million]	140,000 [88,000–190,000]	0.5% [0.4%–0.6%]	63,000 [49,000–98,000]
Caribbean	230,000 [210,000–270,000]	20,000 [16,000–25,000]	1.1% [1.0%–1.2%]	14,000 [11,000–16,000]
Eastern Europe & Central Asia	1.5 million [1.1–1.9 million]	110,000 [67,000–180,000]	0.8% [0.6%–1.1%]	58,000 [41,000–88,000]
Western & Central Europe	730,000 [580,000–1.0 million]	27,000 [14,000–49,000]	0.3% [0.2%–0.4%]	8000 [4800–17,000]
North America	1.2 million [760,000–2.0 million]	54,000 [9600–130,000]	0.6% [0.4%–1.0%]	23,000 [9100–55,000]
Oceania	74,000 [66,000–93,000]	13,000 [12,000–15,000]	0.4% [0.3%–0.5%]	1000 [<1000–1400]
TOTAL	33 million [30–36 million]	2.7 million [2.2–3.2 million]	0.8% [0.7%–0.9%]	2.0 million [1.8–2.3 million]

The ranges around the estimates in this table define the boundaries within which the actual numbers lie, based on the best available information.

Source: Reproduced with kind permission from UNAIDS (2008)

used analyses of data to offer the first direct measurements of the incidence of HIV in the country, finding a higher estimated level of infection than had been previously believed. It is now estimated that there are about 56,300 new HIV infections each year in the United States. Forty-five percent of the new infections are among black individuals, and 53 percent are among men who have sex with men. These two populations continue to be the hardest hit by HIV in the United States, and men continue to represent nearly three-fourths of HIV diagnoses. The number of young gay men, aged 13 to 24, being newly diagnosed with HIV is increasing by about 12 percent a year, about 10 times higher than in the gay community overall (CDC, 2008a; Hall et al., for the HIV Incidence Surveillance Group, 2008; Mitsch et al., 2008; Mutchler et al., 2008).

Unsafe sex between males is now the most common means of infection in the United States, followed by unprotected heterosexual intercourse. The majority of women with HIV in the United States are infected during unprotected sex with male partners who were intravenous drug users or who had sex with other men. About 20 percent acquired HIV through their own intravenous drug use, especially through use of contaminated needles. Worldwide, males transmit the virus to females much more often than females transmit it to males. It appears that male-to-female transmission of HIV is more efficient than female-to-male transmission (UNAIDS, 2008).

Children continue to be born infected with HIV. They seem to become infected **perinatally,** or during pregnancy; during the birth process itself; or soon after birth. This counts as a leading cause of death in children where HIV and AIDS are rampant, including sub-Saharan Africa, and yet it is almost entirely preventable as well. The use of therapeutic anti retroviral drugs by HIV-infected women who are pregnant seems to lessen the risk that they will trans-

perinatally related to pregnancy, birth, or the period immediately following birth.

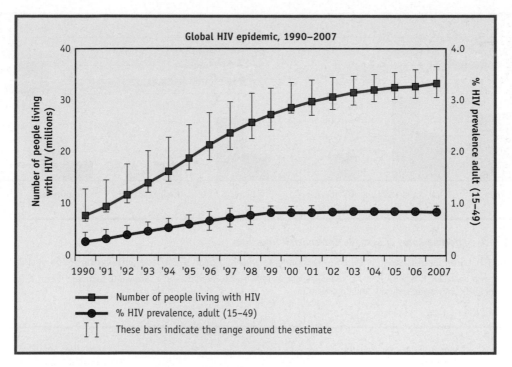

FIGURE 17.2 *Changes in Global HIV Numbers and Prevalence, 1990–2007*

As this graph shows, the number of people worldwide living with HIV has increased from less than 1 million to about 33 million in two decades, and the percentage of people living with AIDS has increased to nearly 1 percent of the world's population.

Source: Reproduced with kind permission from UNAIDS (2008)

mit the virus to their babies, and such use has accounted for a marked decline in perinatal infections. These drugs have not been shown to produce serious ill effects for either the infant or the mother, although there is an occasional risk of lower birth weight for the baby (Coovadia & Schaller, 2008; Schulte et al., 2007; Zellner et al., 2009).

The Global Picture of HIV/AIDS

HIV infection represents a serious global threat. The UNAIDS Organization estimates that between 30 and 36 million people are currently infected with HIV worldwide, with close to 3 million new infections each year (see Figure 17.2). It is thought that about 75 percent of the global infections are acquired through heterosexual contact. The predictions for the future have been equally grim, with an estimate that by the year 2020, the disease could be responsible for the deaths of over 120 million people. Southern and Southeast Asia and sub-Saharan African countries have been hardest hit by HIV infection and AIDS. In sub-Saharan Africa, 22 million people are believed to be living with HIV/AIDS. In some of these countries, it is expected that a third of the boys now age 15 will die of the disease. The situation is quickly worsening in India, China, and Southeast Asia, where the num-

bers soon could surpass those of Africa unless decisive preventative actions are taken immediately (Andia et al., 2009; Fauci, 2008; Piot et al., 2008; UNAIDS, 2008; Zhang et al., 2008).

Risk Factors for Other STDs

The National Health and Social Life Survey (NHSLS) questioned its research participants about their own histories with regard to several STDs. Eighteen percent of women and 16 percent of men, or about one person in six, had been diagnosed by a physician as having at least one of these diseases at some point in their lives (see Figure 17.3). During the previous year, 1.5 percent had been diagnosed with an STD, 1 percent of which were bacterial infections and 0.5 percent of which were viral. Women were more likely to have had an STD than were men, reflecting the medical fact that it is about twice as easy for a male to transmit a sexual infection to a woman than it is for a female to transmit a sexual infection to a man (Laumann et al., 1994).

Many people are mistakenly convinced that they could not contract an STD because of their care in choosing sexual partners or because they maintain high standards of personal hygiene. All studies have confirmed that STDs are not confined to the ignorant

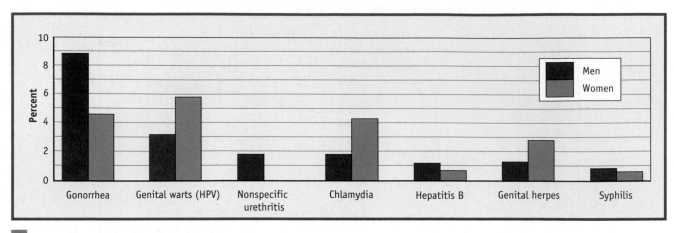

■ **FIGURE 17.3**   *Lifetime Rates of Sexually Transmitted Infections*

Statistics from the NHSLS indicate the percentages of respondents who had been diagnosed with various STDs during their lifetime.

Source: From *Sex in America* by Robert T. Michael et al., p. 188. Copyright © 1994 by CSG Enterprises, Inc., Edward O. Laumann, Robert T. Michael, and Gina Kolata. By permission of Little, Brown and Company, and Brockman, Inc.

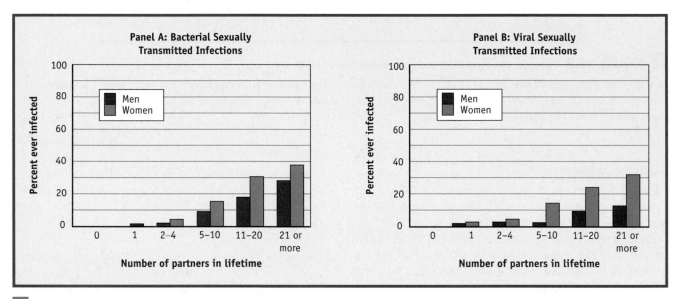

■ **FIGURE 17.4**   *Lifetime Rates of Sexually Transmitted Infections, by Number of Partners and Gender*

These two graphs, based on NHSLS data, show that the likelihood of contracting either bacterial or viral STDs increases proportionately with the number of sexual partners a person has.

Source: From *Sex in America* by Robert T. Michael et al., p. 193. Copyright © 1994 by CSG Enterprises, Inc., Edward O. Laumann, Robert T. Michael, and Gina Kolata. By permission of Little, Brown and Company, and Brockman, Inc.

or the uninformed or to those who have poor hygiene. Behavioral risk factors appear to be most important. The more sexually risky behavior in which people participate, the higher the likelihood they will contract an STD. One high-risk behavioral profile that emerges from research is, in fact, remarkably consistent and predictable. As Figure 17.4 shows, the risk of contracting an STD rises with the number of sexual partners a person has because, according to the data, those partners will usually have had multiple sexual partners themselves. People who have sex with multiple part-

ners also are more likely to engage in casual sexual experiences while under the influence of alcohol or other drugs, and this constitutes another risk factor (Anderson, Mosher, & Chandra, 2007; Hallfors et al., 2007; Michael et al., 1994).

Although condoms offer substantial protection from STDs and HIV, condom use tends to be inconsistent and even confusing. A study of sexually active women who reported consistent condom use found that a third of them had evidence of semen in their vaginal fluids, suggesting that they were misreporting their behavior,

Real People

Carolyn: Discovering a Sexually Transmitted Infection

Because her menstrual period was over a week late, Carolyn visited her college's health center for a pregnancy test. The test was negative, but the nurse practitioner thought she ought to have some other testing. Following the examination, the practitioner told Carolyn that she had a chlamydia infection. This surprised her because she had not experienced any symptoms that would suggest that she had been infected by an STD. She was told that it would be important for both her and her sexual partner to be treated, or they would simply keep reinfecting each other. Carolyn expressed concern and embarrassment over telling her boyfriend, because when making a decision about having unprotected sexual intercourse, they had both declared that they had not had sex with previous partners. The nurse practitioner explained that if Carolyn truly had not had intercourse with other men, then her boyfriend must have contracted the disease from another female partner. The nurse continued to press the importance of his being treated.

The next day, Carolyn returned to the clinic with her boyfriend. He had admitted that he had had a one-night stand with a woman just prior to his relationship with Carolyn, and he was anxious to receive treatment for the chlamydia. The nurse practitioner reminded both of them that if he had been exposed to one disease, there was a chance that he had been exposed to other diseases as well. She recommended further tests for the couple, including an HIV antibody test. This was alarming to both of them and heightened Carolyn's feelings of betrayal and mistrust. All the other tests turned out to be negative, but the experience created a significant strain in their relationship.

What would you recommend to Carolyn and/or her boyfriend at this point? Do you think their relationship should continue or be ended? What would you say to her boyfriend about his lack of honesty? What would you do in a case like this?

---

had used the condoms incorrectly, or perhaps even been lied to by a partner (Genuis, 2008; Rose et al., 2009; Rutherford, 2008).

Some adolescents who report condom failure were found either to have used it as an excuse for having unprotected sex or as an explanation for having deceived their partners into having unprotected sex (Sznitman et al., 2009). Negotiating with a sexual partner to use condoms can be tricky, depending on the dynamics of the relationship, and when people feel coerced into using a condom or if one partner is fearful of losing the other partner, it is even more likely that condoms will not be used during sex. Unfortunately, those who have negative emotions about having sex in the first place are less likely to use protection than are those who feel positively about it (Otto-Salaj et al., 2008; Strachman & Impett, 2009; Whitten et al., 2003).

Some people are embarrassed to seek treatment once they realize their symptoms are suggestive of an STD. One of the difficulties with most STDs is that their symptoms may be relatively mild at first, especially in women. Gonorrhea, syphilis, and chlamydia are par-

ticularly known for the inconspicuousness of their symptoms in the early stages. They may progress into full-blown infections with potentially serious consequences before they have been recognized (Fiscus, Ford, & Miller, 2004). Heterosexual anal intercourse is a relatively common means for disease transmission, and yet it is frequently not protected by condom use (Tian et al., 2008). People may also be reluctant to admit to sexual activities with others of their own sex, a particularly risky omission given that men who have sex with men and bisexual women tend to have higher risks for contracting STDs. Unfortunately, primary care physicians also tend to neglect considering STD risks among their adult patients (Bernstein et al., 2008; Lindley et al., 2008; Montano et al., 2008).

The following sections outline basic information on STDs. See Table 17.2 for a summary of the information. For quick and accurate answers to any personal questions you might have, or for referral to a local clinic for testing or treatment, call the STD/AIDS National Hotline, available 24 hours per day, 7 days per week, at their toll-free number. The number is 1-800-227-8922 from anywhere in the United States.

Table 17.2   *Common Sexually Transmitted Diseases*

Disease & Estimated Number of New Cases Annually	Incubation Period	Symptoms	Treatment	Comments
Nonviral/Bacterial STDs				
Gonorrhea 650,000	2–6 days (but can take up to 30 days)	Infection of cervix, urethra, rectum, or throat. Symptoms can be mild or absent in women, but include discharge from penis, vagina, or rectum and burning or itching during urination, or sore throat.	Doses of a cephalosporin antibiotic.	Many antibiotic-resistant strains have formed.
Syphilis 70,000	Stage 1: 1–12 weeks Stage 2: 6 weeks to 6 months after chancre appears	Usually acquired by vaginal, anal, or oral sex with someone who has an active infection. Produces painless sores near the site of infection that disappear within weeks, but without treatment disease may eventually damage heart, brain, eyes, nervous system, bones, and joints.	Single injection of penicillin; tetracycline, erythromycin, or doxycycline may also be used.	HIV testing should be done for anyone infected with syphilis.
Chlamydia (often the cause of urethritis in males) 3 million	7–21 days	Acquired chiefly through vaginal or anal intercourse. Symptoms include genital discharge, burning during urination (nonspecific urethritis in males); women may suffer pain in lower abdomen or pain during intercourse. Up to three-quarters of cases in women are without symptoms.	Weeklong regimen of azithromycin, doxycycline, or erythromycin.	Has reached epidemic proportions among college students.
Trichomoniasis or gardnerella vaginal infection 5 million	2–21 days	Infection most often occurs in female vagina. Symptoms are often absent. May include vaginal discharge, discomfort during intercourse, odor, painful urination.	Penicillin, ampicillin, amoxicillin, tetracycline, or metronidazole (Flagyl).	Partners must be treated too, or reinfection is likely.
Viral STDs				
Genital herpes 1 million	Up to 3 weeks	Itching or burning and blisters, usually in genital area. May recur. Causes painful, open genital lesions, sometimes accompanied by swollen, tender lymph nodes in the groin.	No cure, but antiviral drugs may suppress outbreaks: acyclovir, famciclovir, valacyclovir.	Antiviral drugs should not be used by pregnant women.
Human papilloma virus (HPV) 5.5 million	6 weeks– 8 months	Spread by anal, oral, or vaginal sex and causes painless, fleshy warts in affected area.	Warts can be suppressed by chemicals, freezing, laser therapy, and surgery.	Some strains are associated with cervical and other cancers.
Hepatitis A (variable)	1–4 months	Loss of appetite, nausea, vomiting, diarrhea, yellowish discoloration of skin, darkening of urine. Fever, general feelings of malaise. There may be liver enlargement, and occasional liver damage. Hepatitis A is more likely to clear up on its own and not recur.	No cure. Medications may relieve some symptoms.	Virus is carried in feces; may be spread when oral-anal sexual contact is involved.
Hepatitis B 120,000	1–4 months	Virus found in semen, saliva, blood, and urine and passed through sexual contact, sharing drug needles, and piercing the skin with contaminated medical instruments. Infection attacks the liver, with similar symptoms to	Same as hepatitis A above.	Vaccine is available that provides immunity after 3 injections.

Table 17.2	Common Sexually Transmitted Diseases (continued)			
Disease & Estimated Number of New Cases Annually	**Incubation Period**	**Symptoms**	**Treatment**	**Comments**
		hepatitis A. Most infections clear up by themselves within 8 weeks, but some individuals become chronically infected.		
		Sexually Transmitted Parasitic Skin Infections		
Pubic lice ("crabs") (unknown)	Eggs hatch in 5–10 days	The lice feed on the skin in the pubic area, causing blue and gray spots. The lice and their eggs (nits) are tiny but can be seen.	Permethrin cream, Lindane shampoo (Kwell)	Clothing and bedding must be thoroughly cleaned too.
Scabies (unknown)	5–10 days	Redness and itching of affected skin areas, with possible secondary skin infections.	Lindane lotion or cream applied to entire body and left for several hours. Oral Ivermectin may be used.	Spreads easily in close quarters.

■ Nonviral Sexually Transmitted Diseases

Several STDs are caused by bacteria or bacteria-like organisms. When diagnosed and treated in the early stages, these diseases are the most likely to be cured.

Gonorrhea

With an estimated 650,000 cases of **gonorrhea** (in slang, "clap" or "the drip") each year in the United States, it is also one of the most commonly reported communicable diseases. The CDC estimates that if unreported cases are included, there may be more than a million cases of the disease annually (CDC, 2007). There has been a gradual decline in the incidence of the disease in recent years. However, the statistics on most STDs tend to show periodic fluctuations whose reasons are difficult to explain.

Caused by the bacterium *Neisseria gonorrhoeae*, gonorrhea seems to be transmitted almost exclusively through sexual contact. Sexual activity—vaginal intercourse, oral sex, or anal sex—with an infected partner is riskier for women than for men. There is over a 50 percent chance of women contracting the disease on a single exposure during intercourse, whereas for men the risk is about 25 percent. Bacteria migrate less easily into the male urethra than into the female vulva, where they have more moist locations in which to multiply. Of course, the risk increases for both men and women with

each repeated exposure. Males have a high rate of reinfection if they engage in sex with partners who have sex with others for either money or drugs, and females whose partners are not treated have a higher infection rate than any other group (Anschuetz et al., 2009).

Babies may pick up the bacteria during the birth process if the mother is infected. Their eyes are particularly vulnerable to gonorrheal infection, and blindness can result. It is a routine precaution in most hospital obstetrical units to put a few drops of an antibacterial agent into the eyes of newborns in order to kill any bacteria.

Symptoms

Probably one of the major reasons why genital gonorrhea is a commonly reported STD is that its symptoms tend to appear quite quickly and may be decidedly unpleasant for men. However, it is also possible for the infection to be mild and relatively asymptomatic. In men, within two weeks after infection, burning and itching sensations develop in the urethra, especially during urination. There is also a thick, puslike discharge from the urethra, often showing up on underwear (see Figure 17.5).

Although up to 80 percent of women do not detect gonorrhea in its earlier stages, its most typical

gonorrhea (gon-uh-REE-uh) bacterial STD causing urethral pain and discharge in males; often no initial symptoms in females.

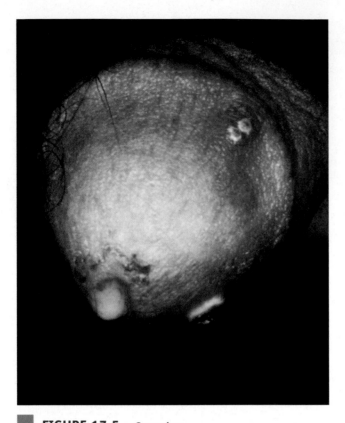

■ **FIGURE 17.5**   *Gonorrhea*

Symptoms of gonorrhea in men include a puslike discharge. About 80 percent of women, however, are asymptomatic.

early symptom is a green or yellow discharge from the cervical area, where the bacteria tend to strike first. Some vaginal irritation or irregularities in menstruation may follow. Gonorrheal infections in the throat tend to create soreness and some mucus in the throat. Rectal infection causes soreness, itching, rectal discharge, and bowel abnormalities.

If gonorrhea is not treated in its early stages, the initial symptoms usually disappear on their own, but the bacteria often move to other organs, causing more serious infections and complications. In men, the disease may affect the bladder, prostate, kidneys, or epididymis of the testes. Left untreated in either sex, the disease can cause sterility. In women, the infection often moves into the reproductive organs, such as the uterus, fallopian tubes, and ovaries, and may eventually result in pelvic inflammatory disease (PID). Very occasionally, in either sex, the bacteria create systemic infections throughout the body, with generalized symptoms, arthritis, and complications in major organs such as the heart or brain.

Diagnosis

There are three main ways in which gonorrhea bacteria are identified. First, a smear is made of the dis-charge, taken from the penile urethra, cervix, throat, or rectum, depending on where infection most likely took place. The material is stained and examined microscopically for evidence of the bacteria. A second method involves taking a culture, with bacteria grown on a nutrient medium and then examined for the gonorrhea bacterium. The culture method has been used most widely with women. More recently, an enzyme-sensitive immunoassay test has been developed that can detect the bacteria with great accuracy.

Treatment

Because many new strains of gonorrhea bacteria are resistant to the antibiotics that typically have been used to treat gonorrhea, the CDC changed their recommended treatment in 2007. A whole different class of antibiotics, the cephalosporins, are now considered the only drugs effective in treating gonorrhea. This is a very real public health concern, because these drugs presently are the last resort among available medicines (del Rio et al., 2007). Some gonorrhea bacteria may not be completely eliminated by typical treatment, so follow-up checks should be made about a week after treatment has ended. Treatment should include antibiotics that destroy chlamydia organisms as well, because that infection often coexists with gonorrhea. It is often a good idea for the sex partners of gonorrhea patients to be treated as quickly as possible to avoid reinfection (Golden et al., 2005). Individuals who are infected with either disease are at high risk for acquiring both syphilis and HIV, so further testing may be indicated. As with any STD, sexual partners of a patient with gonorrhea should be notified of their risk so that they can seek appropriate diagnosis and treatment.

Syphilis

Intermittently throughout history, syphilis has been considered a scourge. Some historians have speculated that some of the leprosy present in biblical times actually may have been syphilis. A closely related disease that causes sores on legs and arms has been found in a South American Indian tribe, and it has been speculated that it was brought to the New World by early Indian explorers some 12,000 years ago. It was a disease that was easily transmitted by skin-to-skin contact, but it has been proposed that since heavily clothed Europeans only had skin contact during sex, it evolved into an STD. The virulent outbreak of syphilis in fifteenth century Europe may have been brought back to Europe by their explorers to the New World (Zimmer, 2008). In 1905, the spiral-shaped bacterium, or spirochete, that causes syphilis was identified and named *Treponema pallidum.*

The number of reported syphilis infections in the United States has traditionally been lower than reported cases of gonorrhea, and syphilis now averages slightly more than 20,000 reported cases per year. The incidence of the disease has been cyclic over the years. It dropped to its lowest rate on record in 2000, but has since increased. Some states still require a blood test for syphilis as a prerequisite to obtaining a marriage license, and in areas where the disease is prevalent, screening of pregnant women can catch cases (Douglas, 2009; Trepka, 2006).

Symptoms

Syphilis can progress through four major stages, beginning two weeks to a month after infection. The first stage, or *primary syphilis,* is nearly always characterized by the appearance of a painless sore wherever the bacterium entered the body. The painless sore, called a chancre, begins as a reddish bump that develops into a pimple. It then opens and ulcerates, often oozing pus until a scab develops. The chancre sometimes is surrounded by a pink border. This sore is infested with the treponema organism, and the individual is highly infectious at this stage. Usually the chancre appears on the genitals (see Figure 17.6), although it can appear on the mouth, anal area, and fingers or breasts. In

A

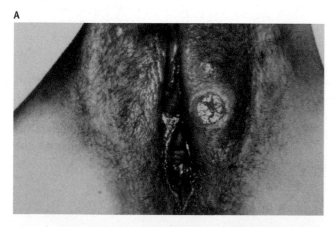

B

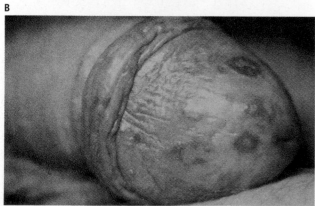

FIGURE 17.6 *Primary Syphilis Chancre*

(A) On female genitalia. **(B)** On the penis.

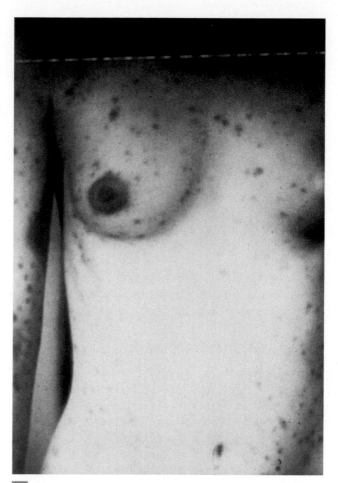

FIGURE 17.7 *Secondary Syphilis*

women it occurs frequently on the inner vaginal wall or cervix and sometimes in the rectum. In one study conducted in a major city, oral sexual contact was found to be a significant means of transmission, ranging from 6 to 7 percent of cases in heterosexual women and men to 20 percent for men who had sex with men (Ciesielski, Tabidze, & Brown, 2004). Because it tends to be painless in the mouth, it may not be noticed there. Within four to six weeks, the chancre heals even without treatment, and there may be no further symptoms for up to six months (CDC, 2008a).

The next stage, *secondary syphilis,* usually begins with a bumpy skin rash (see Figure 17.7), accompanied by general symptoms of illness such as fever, swollen lymph nodes of the neck, nausea, headache, sore throat, loss of scalp hair, and loss of appetite. Additional moist sores may appear around the genitals or anal region. Again, even without treatment, the symptoms eventually abate within a few weeks, and the disease enters its *latent stage.* It is estimated that slightly more than half of untreated syphilis victims remain in this latent stage for the rest of their lives.

People who progress to the *tertiary syphilis* stage usually face serious complications resulting from the spirochete's infecting inner tissues and organs. It may attack the heart, brain and spinal cord, eyes, joints, and numerous other areas, leading to life-threatening disease, blindness, psychosis, or paralysis. Although modern medical treatment has greatly reduced the number of syphilis cases progressing to the tertiary stage, they still occur. In later tertiary stages, the disease typically cannot be transmitted to others.

Congenital syphilis refers to an unborn fetus being infected by the disease through its mother's bloodstream while in the womb. It can result in significant birth defects, especially of the bones, blood, and kidneys. If a pregnant woman with syphilis is treated prior to the 16th week of pregnancy, congenital syphilis can be averted. It is important, therefore, that a pregnant woman have a blood test for syphilis before the fourth month of pregnancy. Perhaps because of stronger educational and testing efforts, the incidence of congenital syphilis has been declining (Beltrami & Berman, 2006).

Diagnosis and Treatment

The two main ways syphilis can be identified are through one of several blood tests or by microscopic examination of fluid from the chancre, in which the spirochete may be seen. Once diagnosed, it usually is treated in its primary and secondary stages by a single injection of penicillin. Tetracycline, erythromycin, or doxycycline may also be used. Latent and tertiary syphilis require larger doses of antibiotics over a period of several weeks. Because so many people who have been infected with syphilis are also infected with HIV, patients who have a positive test for syphilis should also be tested for HIV (CDC, 2007).

Eradication of Syphilis

The U.S. Public Health Service has targeted syphilis for national elimination. With rates of infection low enough and treatment methods effective enough, virtual eradication of the disease could be a real possibility. To date, this goal has been elusive, and slight increases in the incidence of the disease have been seen. Syphilis has been noted particularly as a disease that seems to increase the risk of HIV infection, so continued work on its eradication will surely continue (Douglas, 2009).

Chlamydia

It has long been known that the organism *Chlamydia trachomatis* causes inflammation in the urinary and genital systems. In the mid-1980s, **chlamydia** was recognized as a widespread STD with a range of serious complications (see Figure 17.8). The CDC estimates that there are close to 3 million chlamydial infections each year in the United States, although others believe

CHLAMYDIA IS NOT A FLOWER
It's the nation's most prevalent sexually transmitted disease.

■ **FIGURE 17.8**   *Chlamydia*

the actual number to be much higher. Over a million cases are officially reported each year, making it the most commonly reported infectious disease in the United States. The rate of chlamydia infection increased 5.5 percent between 2005 and 2006, and is still rising. The chlamydia organism invades the cells it attacks

chlamydia (kluh-MID-ee-uh) now known to be a common STD, a major cause of urethritis in males; often presents no symptoms in females.

and multiplies within those cells. Therefore, it can create a variety of symptoms and can be resistant to some antibiotics. It is a particularly common infection on college campuses. Chlamydia prevention programs, involving education, encouragement for fewer sexual partners, screening, and aggressive treatment, have been found to lower the rate of infection (CDC, 2008a; Sylvan & Christenson, 2008).

Like gonorrhea, chlamydia carries special risks for the eyes of newborns. Conjunctivitis, an inflammation of the eye, can be contracted at birth as the baby passes through the vagina, or birth canal. If this is not treated thoroughly and promptly, blindness can result. Such transmission may well be the most widespread preventable cause of blindness throughout the world. Babies also may develop chlamydial pneumonia during their first few months of life. Although the disease is spread primarily through sexual contact, once the infection is established it can be spread to other areas of the body or to other people by hand contact, insects, or contact with human excretions. These modes of transmission are particularly prevalent in underdeveloped countries where overpopulation and inadequate sanitation are factors.

Symptoms

The symptoms of chlamydial infection are often vague or nonexistent, and they can masquerade as symptoms of other diseases. This is one reason why many such infections go unnoticed or are inaccurately diagnosed. About 70 percent of all cases have no early symptoms, and it may take more serious later complications to alert the infected individual that something is wrong.

Males who are symptomatic often experience a burning sensation during urination and a discharge of pus from the penis. If the organism moves farther into the body, swelling and discomfort in the testicles may result. Untreated, it can cause infertility in men. In females, the early symptoms are often mild but can involve itching or burning of the vulva, some discharge, and irritation during urination. In its later stages, the disease may cause PID, with fever, nausea, abdominal pain, and abnormal patterns of menstruation. It also can damage the fallopian tubes and is now known to be a common cause of infertility and ectopic pregnancy. There is mounting evidence that long-term infection with chlamydia may be linked to human heart disease (CDC, 2008a).

Diagnosis and Treatment

Until recently, tests for chlamydia were time-consuming and expensive, requiring the growing of the organism in a laboratory culture for identification. Several tests are now available that can render a quick, inexpensive, and relatively accurate diagnosis. Once diagnosed, the disease usually can be cured with a weeklong treatment of azithromycin, doxycycline, or erythromycin. Penicillin is not an effective treatment. Ointments containing tetracycline or erythromycin also may be applied to the eyes of newborns to prevent the development of chlamydial conjunctivitis (CDC, 2008a). It is essential that sexual partners be treated as well, because in some regions the number of reinfection cases exceeds the number of new cases (Anschuetz et al., 2009).

Nonspecific Urethritis in Males

Sometimes called *nongonococcal urethritis (NGU),* **nonspecific urethritis (NSU)** refers to any inflammation of the male urethra that is not caused by gonorrhea. NSU is a much more common infection than gonorrhea and has been on the increase. The most common cause of NSU is chlamydial infection, accounting for about half the cases. Another 20 to 25 percent are caused by the mycoplasmic bacterium *Ureaplasma urealyticum.* The remainder of NSU cases apparently are caused by other microorganisms or by local irritation from soap, vaginal secretions, or spermicides, although the exact cause is sometimes impossible to isolate. Although the symptoms often are less pronounced than those associated with gonorrhea, there is usually some degree of burning and itching during and after urination. There may also be some discharge of pus, often more evident in the morning.

Prompt treatment of NSU is crucial, even though the symptoms typically subside and disappear on their own within a few weeks. The organism causing the inflammation usually will persist somewhere in the body, increasing the likelihood of a repeat infection or of more serious complications at a later time. Again, antibiotics such as azithromycin, erythromycin, or doxycycline are most frequently used to treat NSU, although they are not always effective. Regardless of the cause, it is advisable for any sexual partner of a man with NSU to be examined to determine the possible presence of infection as well (CDC, 2007).

Vulvovaginal Infections

Vulvovaginitis, or infection within the vulval region and vagina, is extremely common and often is not caused by an STD. Almost every woman will experience

nonspecific urethritis (NSU) (yur-i-THRYT-us) infection or irritation in the male urethra caused by bacteria or local irritants.

vulvovaginitis (vul-voe-vaj-uh-NITE-us) general term for inflammation of the vulva and/or vagina.

a vulvovaginal infection sometime during her life. The lining of the vagina has a carefully balanced system for cleansing itself. Fluids from the tissues in the vaginal lining and the uterine cervix, along with discarded cells from the uterus, form a discharge that cleanses the vagina and protects it from infection by hostile bacteria. However, the balance of this cleansing mechanism may change during various stages of the menstrual cycle, during pregnancy, or with the use of birth control pills, antibiotics, or other medications. The pH of the vagina, usually slightly acidic, may become more alkaline. Any such upset can make the vagina more vulnerable to infection. Infections of the vagina are not necessarily related to sexual activity, but such activity increases the likelihood of infection.

Symptoms

All types of vulvovaginitis are usually characterized by some discharge, whose color, thickness, and odor vary with the type of infection. There are often sensations of burning and itching in the vulval region and outer vagina.

Types

There are four main types of vulvovaginitis. The first three may be transmitted by sexual activity, although the microorganisms are found naturally in the environment and in the body and may develop into an infection without sexual contact if advantageous conditions present themselves.

1. *Bacterial vaginosis* is most often caused by the bacterium *Gardnerella vaginalis*. Men apparently can carry gardnerella, but they often do not experience any symptoms of disease. Occasionally, it causes urethritis, bladder infection, or infection of the penile foreskin in males. Vaginal gardnerella is treated with oral antibiotics such as penicillin, ampicillin, amoxicillin, or tetracycline, and also with a drug called metronidazole, commonly known as Flagyl. Sexual partners usually are treated at the same time to reduce the risk of re-infecting each other. Bacterial vaginosis increases the risk of premature delivery for pregnant women, although this risk may be reduced with administration of the drug clindamycin (CDC, 2007). There is increasing evidence that bacterial vaginosis can be transmitted sexually, including between women who share sex (Bailey et al., 2004; Bradshaw et al., 2005).

2. **Yeast infection** in the vagina, sometimes called *monilial vaginitis*, occurs when conditions within the vagina permit an overgrowth of a fungus, *Candida albicans*, that normally is found there. Such infections sometimes can mask the presence

of other STDs, so it is important to check for other STDs whenever a yeast infection is found. This disease is treated with fungicides, such as miconazole or nystatin, that are used within the vagina in cream or suppository form. Yeast infections are also somewhat more common in women who have sex with women (Bailey, J. V. et al., 2008). Treatments for yeast infections are available without prescription, although studies indicate that women may not be using them appropriately because their self-diagnosis skills are not particularly accurate. It should also be noted that yeast infections can affect males, in the form of an itchy rash on the penis and scrotum.

3. **Trichomoniasis** is an infection caused by a one-celled protozoan organism, Trichomonas, that can take up residence within the vulva and vagina and also in the male urethra. It is one of the most common causes of vaginal infection, leading to some 3 million new infections each year. It is becoming increasingly common among younger women (Miller et al., 2005). Frequently there are no noticeable symptoms. Again, it is necessary to treat sexual partners as well as the woman infected in order to prevent reinfection. The drug used is metronidazole (Flagyl), which is not considered safe for use during pregnancy or when a woman is nursing a baby.

4. *Atrophic vaginitis* is caused by low estrogen levels and occurs almost exclusively after menopause. It is not an STD, although it can lower a woman's resistance to vulvovaginal infection by other microorganisms.

Prevention of Vulvovaginal Infections

One of the best ways to prevent sexually transmitted vaginosis is for the male to use a condom during sexual intercourse. There are several simple hygienic measures that can at least reduce the risk of vaginal infection through nonsexual contamination. These include daily washing of the vulva with mild soap and water, followed by thorough drying because dampness heightens the risk of infection. For this reason, too, underwear made of nonabsorbent synthetic fibers such as nylon is not recommended. Experts also recommend against the use of vaginal sprays and douches unless they have been specifically prescribed for some

yeast infection a type of vaginitis caused by an overgrowth of a fungus normally found in an inactive state in the vagina.

trichomoniasis (trik-uh-ma-NEE-uh-sis) a vaginal infection caused by the *Trichomonas* organism.

medical condition. They often are implicated in upsetting the balance of the vagina's natural cleansing mechanisms, increasing the likelihood of infection. Treating vulvovaginal infections may lower a woman's risk of contracting genital herpes (Cherpes et al., 2003).

■ Viral Sexually Transmitted Diseases

The sexually transmitted viral infections are believed to have already infected at least 20 percent of the population. Although viral infections often can be kept under control and their symptoms relieved, the virus typically continues to reside in the body's cells. This may lead to periodic outbreaks of symptoms or may be associated with cellular abnormalities that have been linked to certain types of cancer. In this sense, viral STDs are controllable but not yet curable.

Genital Herpes

There are two strains of the *Herpes simplex* virus: herpes simplex virus type 1 (HSV-1) and type 2 (HSV-2). It was generally believed that cold sores on the mouth usually are caused by HSV-1, whereas lesions in the genital area, or **genital herpes,** most often are caused by HSV-2. It is now known that a high percentage of genital herpes cases are linked to the HSV-1 virus. This phenomenon is not clearly understood, but it has been proposed that an increase in oral-genital sexual activities may have played a role. However, cases of genital herpes caused by HSV-1 are less likely to recur than are those caused by HSV-2 (CDC, 2008a).

It is estimated that close to 50 million people in the United States have been infected with the virus, with up to another million contracting the disease each year. HSV-2 is transmitted almost exclusively by sexual contact, although the virus can survive externally for several hours in moist, warm conditions. Once the herpes simplex virus has been contracted, it may continue to live in the body, even if no symptoms of the disease are present. The first outbreak of blisters can be quite uncomfortable, with pain being the most troublesome symptom for women, and the lesions themselves most troublesome for men. Nearly a third of infected people in one study continued to have sexual activity during their first outbreak (Richards et al., 2008).

The actual appearance of the painful herpes blisters seems to be associated with periods when disease resistance might be weakened by other illnesses, stress, exhaustion, or inadequate nutrition. It may also be triggered by irritation to the susceptible regions of the skin, such as overexposure to the sun or irritation from clothing.

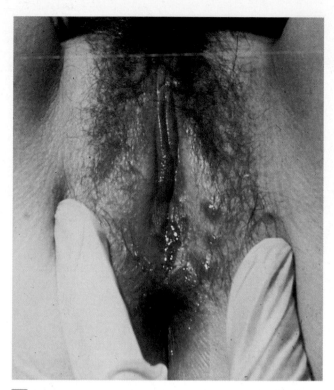

■ FIGURE 17.9   *Herpes Blisters in the Vulval Area*

Symptoms

Genital herpes is characterized by the appearance of what may be painful or itchy clusters of blisters, like cold sores, on the sex organs. During the first outbreak, women usually have blisters on the cervix as well as externally on the vulva (see Figure 17.9). Within a few days, the blisters open and ulcerate, leaving wet, open sores that are highly contagious. Care is especially crucial during these outbreaks to prevent transmission of the virus to other individuals or even to other parts of the infected person's own body. Exposure of the eyes to the virus is particularly dangerous, because a severe eye infection called *herpes keratitis* may develop that can cause serious damage to the cornea. The sores should be touched as little as possible and only when followed by thorough washing of the hands. Sometimes, outbreaks of the blisters are accompanied by other symptoms of illness, such as fever, achiness, or pain in the groin or thighs. It usually takes another two weeks for the sores to crust over and heal.

Up to 70 percent of people who have had a genital herpes infection will experience at least one recurrence of the disease. This usually begins with prickling

genital herpes (HER-peez) a viral STD characterized by painful sores on the sex organs.

FIGURE 17.10   *Herpes Blisters on the Penis*

or burning sensations in the skin where the blisters are about to appear. During such outbreaks, sexual contact—or any direct contact with the infected area—is particularly risky. It is advisable to avoid such contact until at least 10 days after the sores have healed completely. However, the risk of infection remains even when the blisters are not present. Use of a condom reduces the chance of infection. Up to 30 percent of infected people never have a further outbreak of the herpes sores.

Most men do not experience any complications from a herpes infection, although herpes increases the risk of vulnerability to infection by HIV (see Figure 17.10). During the birth process, the presence of HSV-2 can lead to seriously damaging infection or even death. Newborns can have *congenital herpes*. In women with a history of genital herpes, cultures are taken from the cervix, vagina, and vulva several times during the final weeks of pregnancy to detect a possible recurrence of the disease. If there is a risk of infection being passed to the baby during birth, the delivery may be accomplished by a cesarean section.

Diagnosis and Treatment

Genital herpes usually is diagnosed by direct observation of the blisters, although a variety of tests are available that use cultures of the virus for positive identification. While there is no cure for the disease, three antiviral drugs have been found to relieve some symptoms and may be used to suppress recurrences. These drugs, acyclovir, famciclovir, and valacyclovir, sometimes can lengthen relapse intervals from a month to nearly a year. Acyclovir can be applied to the blisters in ointment form during the initial outbreak, although it proves less useful with recurrent outbreaks. Orally administered drugs have been shown to reduce recurrent infections in those who are susceptible to frequent outbreaks and also to reduce the duration

and severity of the infection. The drugs have not been tested in pregnant or nursing women (CDC, 2007). Other antiviral drugs are presently being tested for possible use with herpes infections.

Health care professionals offer some suggestions for relieving the painful symptoms of a herpes outbreak, such as keeping the infected area as clean and dry as possible. Baby powder or cornstarch may be used to absorb moisture. Aspirin or other pain relievers can help, as can direct application of an ice pack.

Human Papillomavirus (HPV)

The **human papillomavirus (HPV)** is similar to the virus that causes warts in other bodily regions. There are about a hundred known strains of the virus. The condition is also known as *condylomata acuminata* or *genital warts*. This disease is now the most common sexually transmitted viral disease in the United States, with an estimated 5 to 6 million new cases annually, and yet people are not very knowledgeable about its risks. HPV occurs more frequently in people who began sexual activity comparatively early in their lives and have had multiple sexual partners and casual sexual relationships. In one study of over 73,000 women, 31 percent were infected with HPV. There are several strains of the virus, and some seem to clear out of the body rather quickly. Other strains are very persistent, and four types place infected women at high risk for cervical cancer. These strains have also been associated with anal cancer in both women and men and with mouth and throat cancers in both sexes (Gerend & Magloire, 2008; JAMA, 2008; Ralston-Howe et al., 2009).

Because of the dangers of HPV, it was particularly exciting when the Gardasil vaccine was approved for use with young women. It was, in fact, the first time that a vaccine has been developed that can prevent cancer. The vaccine is currently recommended as a routine immunization for girls ages 9 to 26, since it is only effective if administered prior to HPV infection. Consideration is also being given to recommending it to boys and young men prior to their becoming sexually active. Studies of the vaccine's efficacy and safety have found it has some of the usual side effects and risks of immunizations, and about 8 percent of girls faint when given the shot, but it is still recommended. Because of the young age that is recommended, and hesitancy on the part of physicians to administer the vaccine, it has not been used as widely as hoped. Some feel that because of the risks and prevalence of

human papillomavirus (HPV) an infection causing small lesions on genital skin; certain strains of this STD increase later risks of cervical cancer.

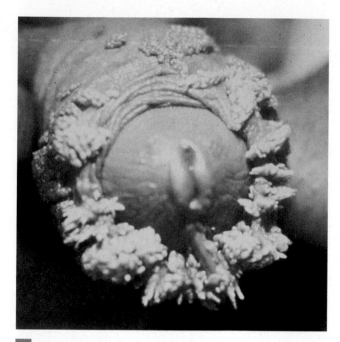

FIGURE 17.11 *Condylomata Caused by HPV around the Penile Glans*

HPV, the vaccine should be compulsory (Balog, 2009; Gerend & Barley, 2009; Keating et al., 2008; Slade et al., 2009).

Symptoms

The warts, or condylomata, usually do not appear on the genitals for about three months after exposure to an infected partner. Their color and texture can vary with location, with soft, pinkish lesions occurring in moist areas and harder, grayish white warts in dry areas. They have irregular surfaces (see Figure 17.11). The warts usually grow on the penis, vulva, anal area, or urethra. They may appear in the anal area even if the individual has not engaged in anal sex. If they grow inside the urethra, they can cause difficulty in urinating and can lead to other infections. For the most part, they are not particularly painful or dangerous in themselves. However, 95 percent of cervical cancers are also infected with the virus. It is believed that HPV causes abnormal cell division in cervical tissues, leading to malignant tumors.

Treatment and Prevention

Genital warts can be removed by laser surgery, electrosurgery (using an electrical current), freezing with liquid nitrogen, or surgical excision. For external warts, chemicals such as podophyllin may be applied over a period of three or four weeks, often causing the lesions to heal. Sinecatechins, chemicals extracted from green tea that are made into ointments, are also effective in

treating external genital and anal warts (Meltzer, Monk, & Tewari, 2009; Silvio et al., 2008). Because the virus remains in the body, the warts can recur over several months or years.

See "HPV" on SexSource Online.

Hepatitis A, B, and C

There are several identified viruses that can cause the liver infection known as hepatitis. The *hepatitis A virus,* contracted through the mouth from food contaminated by fecal material, was for a long time not considered to be an STD. However, hepatitis A virus can be transmitted through oral-anal contact, and about one-quarter of hepatitis A cases are now attributable to either sexual contact or other contact within the household (ASHA, 2004). The **hepatitis B virus (HBV)** is nearly always sexually transmitted and also causes liver infection. Although **hepatitis C virus (HCV)** is most often transmitted by direct contact with tainted blood, it is now clear that it can be transmitted sexually as well (CDC, 2008a). An estimated 1.25 million people in the United States are chronic carriers of HBV, even though most are unaware that they carry it. HCV is now the most common chronic blood-borne infection in the United States, with an estimated 2.7 million persons chronically infected. Men and women who engage in high-risk sexual behavior are at greater risk of contracting hepatitis C. Both HBV and HCV can be transmitted by sharing intravenous needles for illicit drug use, but hepatitis B is more likely to be transmitted sexually because it is found in bodily fluids such as saliva, semen, and vaginal secretions in addition to blood.

HBV has become such a major health problem in the United States, especially among young adults ages 15 to 25, that it is standard medical practice to recommend that older adolescents and young adults be vaccinated against the disease. The vaccination must be given in three doses, with total cost averaging about $130. There is also a worldwide effort to make HBV vaccination more available to all populations that might be at risk, and some clinicians have suggested combining it with the vaccine for hepatitis A as an extra precaution (Low et al., 2006; Weinbaum et al., 2008). There is no vaccine for hepatitis C as yet.

hepatitis B virus (HBV) a liver infection that frequently is sexually transmitted.

hepatitis C virus (HCV) a liver infection that may occasionally be sexually transmitted.

Symptoms

Hepatitis A tends to be a milder disease than the other two. Hepatitis B and C have several degrees of severity. They may have no symptoms at all or may cause complications serious enough to be fatal. About 5,000 people in the United States die each year from chronic liver disease caused by HBV or HCV. Typical early symptoms of both infections include loss of appetite, lethargy, headache, joint achiness, nausea, vomiting, diarrhea, yellowing of the skin (jaundice), darkening of the urine, and some enlargement of the liver. Hospitalization usually is unnecessary. Infection with hepatitis B or C increases the later risk of developing liver failure and liver cancer (Liaw & Chu, 2009).

Treatment

As with all viral infections, there is no cure for hepatitis at present. Some medications can provide relief of symptoms, and a period of bed rest and heavy fluid intake usually is required. Oral antiviral agents can reduce virus replication, although drug resistance may develop over the long term. The body's immune system sometimes conquers the disease, although in more severe cases this process can take several months. Other times, the virus develops into chronic conditions that can lead to destruction of the liver or other organs over a period of years (Liaw & Chu, 2009).

■ Other Sexually Transmitted Diseases

The list of disease agents that can be transmitted sexually continues to grow. This section contains information about several of those organisms.

Pubic Lice

The STD commonly called crabs is caused by a tiny (1- to 4-mm) parasitic louse with the scientific name *Phthirus pubis*. Health workers often refer to an infestation of these lice as *pediculosis pubis*. The lice have claws that allow them to hold tightly to hairs, usually in the pubic, anal, and **perineal area.** Occasionally, they spread to the armpits or even the scalp. The lice found in head hair are usually of a different species, however, and are not spread by sexual contact.

Pubic lice bite into the skin to feed on blood from tiny blood vessels. This creates little papules on the skin that cause intense itching. The lice lay their eggs, or nits, on hairs to which they are tightly attached (see Figure 17.12). These eggs can drop onto sheets or bedclothes and survive for several days. The lice also can live away from the body for about a day in clothing,

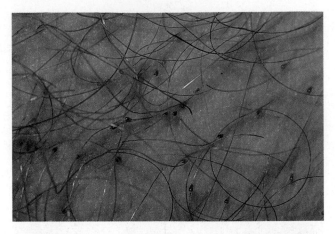

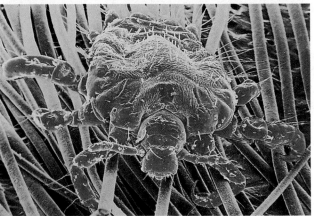

■ **FIGURE 17.12**   *Pubic Lice and Nits*

Pubic lice and nits on pubic hairs.

sheets, towels, and even furniture, making their way to other people if the opportunity presents itself. Both the whitish nits and the adult lice can be seen upon close examination.

Any treatment must be thorough to ensure complete eradication of the lice. Permethrin cream rinse can be applied to the affected area and rinsed off after 10 minutes. Lindane shampoo, applied for only 4 minutes, is available by prescription under the brand name Kwell. It is somewhat toxic to humans and is not recommended for children under age 2 or for women who are pregnant or nursing babies. Other shampoo treatments containing pyrethrins and piperonyl butoxide can be purchased without a prescription. A repeat treatment may be recommended after seven days to take care of any eggs that may have been missed the first time. Sexual partners must be treated as well. It is crucial that all potentially exposed bedclothes, underwear, towels, or

perineal area (pair-a-NEE-al) the sensitive skin between the genitals and the anus.

pubic lice small insects that can infect skin in the pubic area, causing a rash and severe itching.

other materials be thoroughly washed or dry cleaned. An insecticide spray is available to treat furniture. Close physical contact with others should be avoided until treatment is completed.

Sexually Transmitted Skin Infections

Two skin diseases in the United States are transmitted by direct bodily contact, including sexual contact. One is **molluscum contagiosum,** a pox virus that causes small papules to appear on the skin. They often look similar to whiteheads and have a hard, seedlike core. They usually do not create any discomfort or pain. Occasionally, they may become infected by other bacteria and ulcerate. Molluscum blisters often heal by themselves, although they can be removed by scraping, freezing, or chemical treatment. If all the lesions are not removed, they often will recur.

Scabies is caused by a tiny mite that burrows under the skin to lay its eggs (see Figure 17.13). It causes redness and itching and may lead to secondary infections. It is more stubborn to treat than pubic lice, because the scabies mite is under the skin. Epidemics of scabies often spread throughout schools, hospitals, or other institutions where people interact closely. Obviously, sexual contact also provides an easy mode of transmission for

the disease. Treatment involves the application of a medicated lotion or cream to the entire body from the neck down, which then is washed off after 8 to 14 hours. Permethrin cream is used most frequently, but Lindane lotion or cream is also recommended. An oral medication called Ivermectin is sometimes used (CDC, 2007).

Sexually Transmitted Diseases of Tropical Climates

Several other STDs more common in tropical climates have recently been on the increase in temperate zone countries such as the United States. **Lymphogranuloma venereum (LGV)** is caused by several strains of chlamydia and produces painless, pimplelike ulcers on the genitals or rectum. It may have other symptoms, such as fever, hives, or swollen lymph nodes in the groin. If left untreated, it can cause blockage of lymph vessels, resulting in swollen limbs or bodily organs. In the tropics, this condition is called *elephantiasis*. LGV is treated with antibiotics such as doxycycline, tetracycline, or erythromycin or with sulfa drugs.

Chancroid is caused by the bacterium *Hemophilus ducreyi*. Within a week after infection, several small sores appear on the genitals. They are filled with pus and may rupture to form painful open sores that bleed easily. Antibiotics and sulfa drugs are effective in curing the disease; if it is left untreated, it can cause swelling, pain, and rupture of lymph tissue at the surface of the skin.

Granuloma inguinale is a rare infection caused by *Calymmatobacterium granulomatis*. It involves the

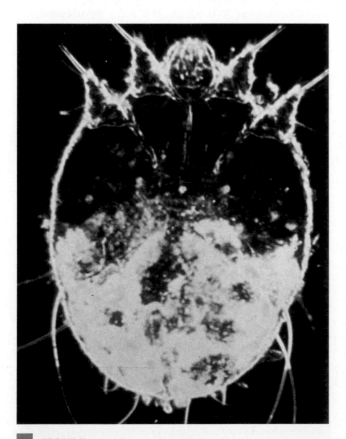

█ FIGURE 17.13 *Scabies Mite*

molluscum contagiosum (ma-LUS-kum kan-taje-ee-O-sum) a skin disease transmitted by direct bodily contact, not necessarily sexual, and characterized by eruptions on the skin that appear similar to whiteheads, with a hard seedlike core.

scabies (SKAY-beez) a skin disease caused by a mite that burrows under the skin to lay its eggs, causing redness and itching; transmitted by bodily contact that may or may not be sexual.

lymphogranuloma venereum (LGV) (lim-foe-gran-yu-LOW-ma va-NEAR-ee-um) a contagious STD caused by several strains of Chlamydia and marked by swelling and ulceration of lymph nodes in the groin.

chancroid (SHAN-kroyd) an STD caused by the bacterium *Hemophilus ducreyi* and characterized by sores on the genitals, which if left untreated, could result in pain and rupture of the sores.

granuloma inguinale (gran-ya-LOW-ma in-gwa-NAL-ee or NALE) an STD characterized by ulcerations and granulations beginning in the groin and spreading to the buttocks and genitals.

appearance of small blisters and swelling of the lymph nodes. The sores often do not heal easily unless treated, and they can become infected, eventually causing permanent damage and scarring of tissue. The infection can be cured with antibiotics such as tetracycline, streptomycin, and erythromycin.

Because cases of LGV, chancroid, and granuloma inguinale number only in the thousands annually in the United States, they are less commonly seen by physicians and STD clinics. This makes them harder to diagnose, which may result in dangerously delayed treatment.

■ HIV: The Virus and the Infection

Viruses are among the tiniest of microorganisms to infect human tissues. Typically, they inject their genetic material into cells, taking over the DNA of the host cells to produce new viruses. These viruses then spread to other cells, disrupting or killing them as new viruses are produced. It is the destruction of tissue that causes the symptoms of the viral infection. HIV belongs to the class of viruses called **retroviruses.** They are unique in that their genetic code is carried in a form of RNA instead of DNA. When a retrovirus attacks a cell, a chemical orders the cell's RNA to translate the genetic blueprint of the virus into the cell's DNA, thereby instructing it to make a whole new crop of virus particles. It is because this mechanism is the reverse of the usual order of things that these viruses are called retroviruses (Stevens, Lynm, & Glass, 2008).

In order for HIV to do its cellular damage, it relies on some 273 human proteins—called *HIV dependency factors*—to do its dirty work. These proteins enable the virus to attach to immune cells in the body and then inject their RNA into those cells. HIV is capable of reproducing in staggering numbers, constantly needing to move on to new, uninfected cells in order to survive. Soon after contracting HIV, some people develop a fever, swollen glands, fatigue, and perhaps a rash. This is called *primary HIV disease*. These early symptoms usually disappear within a few weeks as the body manages to ward off the infection with its remaining immune defenses. The person may remain relatively stable for some time (Cohen, 2008).

The second stage, *chronic asymptomatic disease*, is characterized by a gradual decline in immune cells even though there are no particular disease symptoms. Eventually, most people infected with HIV begin to experience chronically swollen lymph nodes, although they may have few other symptoms. Eventually, the immune system becomes exhausted by the infection and falters. The infected individual then begins to become more vulnerable to **opportunistic infection,** in which disease-causing organisms normally present in the environment become able to attack the person by taking advantage of the body's weakened resistance. In this third stage of *chronic symptomatic disease,* one of the most common infections is a yeast infection of the mouth called **thrush** (this disease in itself is not necessarily a sign of a serious disorder). Infections of the skin and moist inner membranes of the body may also be present. There may be general feelings of discomfort and weakness, accompanied by sustained fevers, drenching night sweats, weight loss, and frequent diarrhea (Stevens, Lynm, & Glass, 2008).

It is important to focus on the entire course of infection by HIV and not just the late stage of that process that has become known as AIDS. When HIV disease is diagnosed in its earlier stages, the patient may be able to get treatment that may delay certain aspects of the infection and prevent some complications. HIV infection passes through predictable stages during which the body's immune system is gradually undermined. Although the duration of the infection varies depending on the person's health and behavior, there is a gradual depletion of cells in the body that are crucial to its defense against disease-causing agents.

The diagnosis of full-blown AIDS is made after one or more of 26 diseases have been manifested in an HIV-infected individual. The term **syndrome** refers to a collection of disease symptoms that tend to cluster together. Unlike most syndromes, AIDS can have a spectrum of symptoms, and the disease can progress in many different ways. Ultimately, there can be months of debilitating illness that lasts until the body can no longer prevail and the person dies. Medical interventions often are successful in maintaining the immune system for years, but there is no cure for the disease as yet.

How HIV Is Transmitted

It is now clear that HIV is transmitted by the direct transfer of certain bodily fluids from one infected individual

retroviruses (RET-ro-vi-rus-es) a class of viruses that integrate their genetic code into that of the host cell, establishing permanent infection.

opportunistic infection a disease resulting from lowered resistance of a weakened immune system.

thrush a disease caused by a fungus and characterized by white patches in the oral cavity.

syndrome (SIN-drome) a group of signs or symptoms that occur together and characterize a given condition.

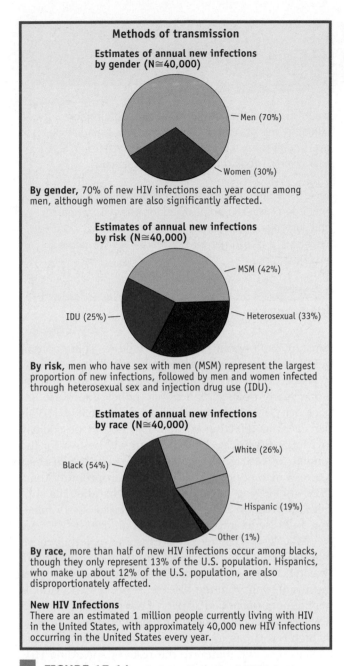

Methods of transmission

Estimates of annual new infections by gender (N≅40,000)

- Men (70%)
- Women (30%)

By gender, 70% of new HIV infections each year occur among men, although women are also significantly affected.

Estimates of annual new infections by risk (N≅40,000)

- MSM (42%)
- Heterosexual (33%)
- IDU (25%)

By risk, men who have sex with men (MSM) represent the largest proportion of new infections, followed by men and women infected through heterosexual sex and injection drug use (IDU).

Estimates of annual new infections by race (N≅40,000)

- White (26%)
- Black (54%)
- Hispanic (19%)
- Other (1%)

By race, more than half of new HIV infections occur among blacks, though they only represent 13% of the U.S. population. Hispanics, who make up about 12% of the U.S. population, are also disproportionately affected.

New HIV Infections
There are an estimated 1 million people currently living with HIV in the United States, with approximately 40,000 new HIV infections occurring in the United States every year.

FIGURE 17.14 *Data on Methods of HIV Infection*

Recent figures on HIV infections help us understand the seriousness of infection trends.

Source: Centers for Disease Control, Atlanta, GA.

to another (see Figure 17.14). The virus may be transmitted by infected people who have not developed any symptoms. People who are experiencing symptoms of HIV disease are even more likely to transmit the virus. HIV enters the body through internal linings of organs (such as the vagina, rectum, urethra within the penis, or mouth) or through openings in the skin, such as tiny cuts or open sores.

The most typical fluids involved in transmission of the virus are blood, semen, and vaginal secretions. The virus can be transmitted from mother to fetus perinatally (around the time of birth), and it can be transmitted to an infant through breast milk. There is documentation of HIV being found in saliva, tears, urine, and feces, but little direct evidence exists that the virus actually has been transmitted by these secretions and excretions.

Several routes of HIV infection have been clearly documented:

1. Anal or vaginal intercourse.
2. Oral-genital sexual activity.
3. Contact with semen or vaginal fluids from an infected person.
4. Contact with infected blood, through use of contaminated needles and syringes shared by drug users or used for tattooing, ear piercing, or injection of steroids.
5. Transfer from mother to child, the risks of which are increased when invasive procedures such as amniocentesis are used during pregnancy and when certain diseases are present in the mother's body. After the amniotic membranes have ruptured prior to birth, the risk of the fetus contracting the virus from its mother increases hourly until birth. When pregnant women are given antiretroviral treatments, the risks for the infant being infected are greatly reduced (Committee on Pediatric AIDS, 2008; Schulte et al., 2007; Townsend et al., 2008).

Sharing anal intercourse is especially risky behavior, because the virus from the semen enters the bloodstream through the many small tears in the colon. While male-to-male anal intercourse had been on the decline, the rise in the incidence of barebacking, or unprotected anal sex between men, is alarming. Because a substantial number of women engage in anal intercourse with men, it should be recognized as a potentially risky sexual behavior for them as well (Hall et al., 2007).

The risks associated with oral-genital sex have been difficult to quantify, partly because this behavior usually is practiced in conjunction with other sexual activities that may be highly risky. However, there have been cases in which HIV was transmitted from a man's semen during fellatio (oral sex performed on a male). There is less evidence of transmission during cunnilingus (oral sex performed on a female). Women who have sex with other women have been shown to have an elevated risk of contracting HIV (Marrazzo, Coffey, & Bingham, 2005).

Although ordinary kissing appears to pose only a minor threat, the CDC has reported a case of HIV transmission through kissing. Both parties had gum disease, confirming the earlier suspicion that viruses carried in saliva could enter the body through tiny breaks or sores within the mouth or enter the lymphatic cells in the tonsils. Experts therefore continue to caution against prolonged, wet deep kissing (French kissing).

Real Student Voices

■ One of my best friends in high school was gay, and he got in touch with me recently to let me know he is HIV-positive. He seems pretty upbeat about it, but it shocked me. I knew he was gay, but he always was so careful too. I'm not sure how he let it happen.

■ I've been told so many scary things about drugs and sex since I was in elementary school, only to find out that a lot of it wasn't even true. I am always skeptical. When they taught us about AIDS in high school, it was obviously meant to stop us from having sex. I don't think most of us paid much attention. But now I worry I took too many foolish chances.

■ AIDS is one of the reasons I've remained a virgin. I don't see the point of taking the risk. When I find someone I really want to get intimate with, I'll make sure we both get all the tests—just to prove I am clean too.

The other group in which HIV has spread rapidly is intravenous (IV) drug users (IDU), through sharing of needles. Intravenous drug abusers represent the largest heterosexual population in the United States infected with HIV; they also act as a significant vehicle for heterosexual transmission of the virus (Arasteh & Des Jarlais, 2008).

Casual contacts with infected persons—even in crowded households, social settings, schools, or the workplace—are not dangerous. There are no documented cases of HIV being transmitted through food, water, toilets, swimming pools or hot tubs, shared drinking or eating utensils, telephones, or used clothing. Since the HIV epidemic began, the actual number of infections transmitted by heterosexual contact has been rising steadily. In studies on heterosexual couples in which one partner had already been infected with HIV, it has been clearly shown that the risk of women contracting HIV from men is 10 to 18 times greater than the risk of men getting the virus from women. The risk of transmission is even greater when another STD is already present (Potts et al., 2008).

The HIV Epidemic in Perspective

As we have seen, the spread of STDs is influenced primarily by the number of sexual partners a person has and how often he or she uses a condom. These factors, along with abuse of alcohol and other drugs, also constitute risk factors in contracting HIV. However, researchers are finding that the picture of the HIV epidemic and where it is heading may be somewhat different from the pattern followed by other STDs.

Urban areas continue to be the epicenter of the epidemic, and it tends to concentrate more in poor neighborhoods where the sale and use of IV drugs constitute an ongoing part of the culture. There continues to be controversy over whether the disease is likely to remain relatively confined to these groups and regions. Many political and public policy issues are impacted by this debate. There is a risk that if HIV is perceived as affecting groups that tend to be socially invisible or ostracized, momentum will be lost for the funding of research to cure and prevent the disease. There is also concern that if education promulgates a "Sex will kill you" message beyond what the data support, information about the very real risks of HIV infection will lose its impact (Merson et al., 2008).

At least in the United States, some experts believe that the challenge will be to sustain the compassion, research funds, and top-notch treatment necessary for those suffering from the disease, especially individuals who are not perceived as part of the privileged classes. It will be especially crucial for educators to reach those in high-risk areas in order to educate them to make choices that will minimize the risks of spreading HIV. Another challenge will be to convince young people who are not as close to the population centers of the HIV threat to take the risks of unprotected sexual activity or other behaviors as seriously as they must. The incidence of HIV infection has increased in rural areas (Coates, Richter, & Caceres, 2008; Potts et al., 2008).

■ HIV Testing, Treatment, and Vaccines

When HIV infects people, their bodies begin the natural process of combating the disease. Antibodies begin to form that will attempt to destroy the reproducing viruses. There is a window of time between infection and the appearance of antibodies that may last for several months. The tests for HIV that are used most frequently detect the antibodies a person's body is producing. During the window period, however, there are two tests that may be used. The P24 antigen test is not particularly sensitive, but it can detect early antibodies that are produced by the virus soon after infection. The Polymerase Chain Reaction (PCR) test detects the actual genetic material of HIV rather than the antibodies, so they may be used within two to three weeks of infection with the virus. This test is also known as a viral load test or HIV NAAT (nucleic acid amplification testing).

The antibody blood test currently in greatest use is called an *enzyme-linked immunosorbent assay* **(ELISA).** It is inexpensive, can be completed within five hours, and is not technically difficult to interpret. However, the ELISA test tends to give a high percentage of false positives, so the results may signal the presence of HIV antibodies when in fact none are present. A positive result is then further tested with the **Western blot** or immunoblot test. More accurate than ELISA, it is lengthy and more expensive and must be interpreted by trained and experienced technicians, so it usually is not utilized as a primary test in large-scale screenings.

There are also newer, rapid tests that can be used in clinic settings. The OraQuick HIV-1/2 rapid test uses technology that is similar to the ELISA but can get results in about 20 minutes. It makes use of saliva, and it can be interpreted by staff who have only limited training. Again, positive results must be confirmed by blood tests that can take longer. The rapid tests can be integrated into routine screening at STD clinics and made easily available to large groups of people (Brooks et al., 2009; Aguirre et al., 2007).

Widespread HIV testing could greatly reduce HIV transmission and diagnose infections early. Early detection can lead to earlier treatment and a potentially longer period of survival. Because blood donated in clinics is automatically screened for HIV antibodies, some people are giving blood with the knowledge that they will be notified if they are HIV-positive. Health professionals have a responsibility to prepare patients through pretest counseling and to offer follow-up counseling and support if the results are positive (Granich et al., 2009).

Depending on where a person is tested, the results may be considered *confidential,* meaning that the individual's name would be connected to the test results even though the results generally are not shared with others. This is the case in most physicians' offices. Many clinics provide *anonymous* testing, in which the patient is assigned a number for obtaining the test results at a later time. Because the individual's name is never used, privacy is ensured.

HIV Testing Guidelines

Routine testing for STDs and HIV in hospital patients and in prison settings detects many infections that otherwise would have been missed (Huppert et al., 2005; Robertson et al., 2005). Some states require their family planning and STD clinics to offer free, voluntary testing for HIV. Experts have recommended routine screening for HIV within all medical settings, citing that it would be a cost-effective way of discovering the infection and offering timely medical care (Bozzette, 2005). The CDC has made the following recommendations concerning HIV testing:

1. Couples planning marriage should be provided ready access to testing and to information about HIV and AIDS.
2. People should have the right to choose not to be tested and be given appropriate counseling prior to testing. They should also give explicit consent, orally or in writing, before being tested.
3. Anyone seeking treatment for other sexually transmitted infections should be encouraged to undergo HIV testing.
4. People with a history of IV drug use who have shared equipment with others should be encouraged to be tested, as should their sexual partners.
5. It is now recommended that all pregnant women be tested.
6. Women seeking family planning services should be routinely counseled about HIV infection and have testing made available to them.
7. Gay and bisexual men should be tested annually for HIV, chlamydia, gonorrhea, and syphilis.

The waiting period of several days before test results can be made available may create high levels of anxiety. For those people whose tests are positive, it is crucial that they receive appropriate counseling to deal with their feelings and to learn about suitable treatment options. If the test results are negative, counseling can be important in providing the person with information about avoiding infection in the future. For this reason, most state health departments require that an individual come in person to find out the results rather than being told over the telephone or by mail. Unfortunately, youth at high risk for contracting HIV often tend not to return to a clinic for the results and are more likely to check the results if they can do so by telephone (Shelton, 2008).

ELISA the primary test used to determine the presence of HIV in humans.

Western blot the test used to verify the presence of HIV antibodies already detected by the ELISA.

Although home testing has traditionally been discouraged by professionals in this field because it does not allow for face-to-face counseling, it is also recognized that many potentially infected persons are avoiding testing because of embarrassment or the lack of anonymity (Spillane et al., 2007). Home-testing kits, in which a person draws his or her own blood and sends it to a testing center, have been approved by the FDA. The person being tested calls a toll-free number after a few days to receive the result using a code number. If the test is positive, this result is reported to the caller by a trained counselor who discusses the implications of the test with the person. There is still controversy over this approach, because some professionals believe that face-to-face counseling should be required in order to help HIV-positive persons deal more effectively with their diagnoses.

Promise of Microbicides

A new strategy is being developed that may help prevent STDs and HIV infection in the future through the use of topical microbicides. This would involve the use of gels or creams that would be inserted into the vagina (and possibly the rectum) prior to sexual intercourse. Not only would they offer some physical barrier in the lubricant itself, but also the microbicide would disrupt the infective potential of the disease-causing agents. Although this approach is not meant to be a substitute for condom use, it would provide an extra measure of protection for women that would not depend on male cooperation. The degree to which women are inclined to use microbicides depends on such factors as potential side effects and changes in sexual pleasure. The regulatory hurdles for the development and licensing of microbicides continue to increase, even though their research and development can be shown to be cost effective (Mauck, 2009; Tanner et al., 2009).

Treatment for HIV Disease

Although the final stage of HIV disease, AIDS, is a fatal disease, appropriate medical treatment earlier in the course of the infection can prolong a patient's life and improve its quality. Experienced physicians can monitor progress of the virus and provide appropriate interventions, because the strategy for treatment varies with the stage of the infection. As opportunistic diseases develop, carefully selected medications may be used to relieve symptoms and help the body fight the infections. Since research with HIV treatments began, a remarkable number of new antiretroviral preparations have gone into testing (see Figure 17.15). Treatment is most effective when it is begun as soon as possible after infection, and the regimen must be followed faithfully,

FIGURE 17.15 *HIV/AIDS Awareness and Education*

Jeff Getty, an AIDS patient who received a baboon bone marrow transplant as an experimental treatment, holds a press conference with other AIDS activists to heighten consciousness about the need for new research on treating HIV-positive individuals.

but life expectancy can be improved for 12 to 49 years, depending on age and other factors (Antiretroviral Therapy Cohort Collaboration, 2008).

One of the most widely used drugs has been zidovudine, often in combination with other drugs, although these can have severe side effects. The most hopeful approach to emerge so far in treating HIV is the combination, or cocktail, therapy. It is based on the knowledge that HIV mutates rapidly to different forms and therefore can quickly become resistant to a particular drug. Combination therapy uses two or more drugs at once so that HIV is kept off balance and under control and the body is encouraged to build its number of immune cells. One of the drugs usually used as part of the therapy is a protease inhibitor, which attacks the virus in one of its reproductive steps. This approach to treatment is also called *highly active antiretroviral therapy (HAART)*. Unfortunately, these combination therapies do not seem to improve patients' mental health, and they can be so complicated that some patients cease treatment after a short time (Clements-Nolle et al., 2008; Deeks & Phillips, 2009; DeCock et al., 2009; Richman et al., 2009).

Vaccines and Prophylaxis for HIV

The search for an HIV vaccine has been rated by experts as the most urgently needed medical advance in the world. Several major complications make the search difficult. First, HIV seems to be able to hide in cells by installing its genes within the genes of the cell. Second, there is no particularly good animal model for the disease, and this is where testing normally would begin. Third, because HIV infection is so dangerous, experimental trials for a vaccine with humans have

Real People

Brent: Worrying about Potential HIV Infection

Brent was a gay man and had been active in a college social group for gays. At one of the meetings of the group, he had met a gay male who was a few years younger than himself, and they had begun seeing each other. The younger man had been more sexually active than Brent, who had had only two previous same-gender sexual experiences. After an evening out, Brent and his new partner decided to have sex. One of the activities they shared was anal intercourse. While the other man was having intercourse with Brent, the condom he was wearing broke without his knowledge, and he ejaculated without the protection of the condom. He was apologetic and assured Brent that he did not have any diseases, but Brent was still worried. He did not fully trust the other man and was very aware that he had been active sexually with numerous partners.

This was the first time Brent could potentially have been exposed to STDs, including HIV. He had been vaccinated for hepatitis B before entering college. He contacted an STD clinic and set up an ap-

pointment to be checked for various STDs. All tests proved to be negative. The other reality was that he would have to wait several months before a test for HIV could be considered reliable. This was highly uncomfortable for him. During the waiting period, he also had a flulike illness, which frightened him even more. The health clinic assured him that his symptoms were exactly like those being experienced by many other people at that time of year. After six months, Brent had the blood tests for HIV, which involved another two weeks of tense waiting for the results. He was relieved to learn that the tests were negative, and he had them repeated after another six months for further reassurance.

If Brent were a friend of yours and confided in you about his concerns during the waiting period, how would you have responded to him? If another friend of yours said to you that Brent simply got what he deserved, how would you respond to this other person?

---

had to proceed with the utmost caution. In such trials, a substantial number of at-risk people are given the vaccine, and their rate of infection is compared to a control group of persons who have not received the vaccine. Most vaccine trials so far have yielded disappointing results, and several have ended in failure. Participants in such trials also sometimes experience negative social repercussions (Fuchs et al., 2007; Merson et al., 2008; O'Malley, 2008).

Because there are different strains of HIV, it is possible that several vaccines will have to be developed to protect people. Some virologists believe that enough weak spots can be found that are common to most of the strains to allow a single vaccine to produce immunity. The first tests were done with *therapeutic vaccines* that are used to expand the immune responses of people already infected with HIV in an effort to delay or prevent the onset of disease symptoms. As safer vaccines are developed, they may be used on uninfected people as *preventative vaccines,* forestalling infection with the virus in the first place. Another promising preventative approach is *chemoprophylaxis.* This uses powerful chemicals that stay in the body for an extended period of time and may well disable HIV

if it enters the body. This approach differs from the use of a deactivated viral vaccine, but it could ultimately prove more effective. Clinical trials of the technique are under way (Walker & Burton, 2008).

Ethical Issues and HIV/AIDS

Several ethical issues have arisen concerning HIV and AIDS:

The Issue of Confidentiality

Some information from health records has been subject to disclosure, with the patient's permission, for a variety of purposes. The federal HIPAA (Health Insurance Portability and Accountability Act) regulations require that patients be given thorough information about how their privacy can be protected. The question remains: Who should be allowed access to information about an individual's sexual lifestyle or infection with HIV? Such information can affect reputation, employment, and insurance coverage. Yet if an individual who is known to be HIV-infected continues to behave in ways that clearly endanger others, how and under what circumstances would it be legitimate for the infection to be revealed?

Do you believe doctors should have the right to reveal a patient's HIV status to anyone? For instance, should doctors inform school systems that a student is HIV-positive? Should coaches know an athlete's status? Explain your position.

Among nonmedical professionals such as counselors, social workers, and psychotherapists, the confidentiality dilemmas become more complex. Ethical guidelines require such professionals to violate confidentiality if a third party is facing some immediate threat of danger, but the guidelines about potential HIV infection are less clear. Everyone agrees that the first line of action would be to strongly encourage the client to inform others about the disease and cease any behaviors that could potentially endanger others. If that fails, there is less agreement about how the professional should proceed. In one program that provided voluntary counseling and testing for partners of individuals just diagnosed as HIV-positive, several hundred people came in for testing, and 21 percent tested positive (Foust et al., 2003).

HIV-Positive People and Pregnancy

HIV-positive men and women who want to parent children have a number of options for pregnancy. There are techniques for cleansing semen of the virus, and pregnant women can take various drugs to reduce the chances of transmitting HIV to their babies without risking negative side effects. However, the ethical dilemma remains concerning the advisability of allowing seriously ill patients to have babies (Anderson, Ebrahim, & Sansom, 2004; Kirshenbaum et al., 2004).

HIV/AIDS Education

Most states already require their schools to offer HIV/AIDS education. However, there is controversy over the age at which such education should begin and what its content should be. In many ways, these controversial factors are extensions of debates that have been raging in the field of sexuality education for years. Some experts recommend beginning HIV/AIDS education with 9, 10, and 11 year olds; others oppose starting at such early ages. Some groups claim that it is unrealistic to expect all youth to abstain from shared sexual activity because of the HIV scare, and they advocate the teaching of safer sex practices that will at least minimize the risk of contracting HIV and STDs (see Figure 17.16). Critics of this approach believe that teaching about preventative measures condones casual sex. Among schools that have mandated HIV/AIDS

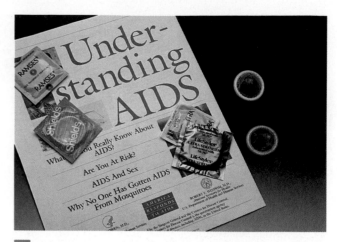

■ FIGURE 17.16   *Condom Advertisement*

The Centers for Disease Control and Prevention and other agencies hope to educate the public about safe sex and the use of condoms with advertisements like this.

education, some have also required that the emphasis be placed on sexual abstinence (Balaji et al., 2008).

Experts believe that HIV education must go beyond the presentation of information to help everyone develop the intentions and skills they need to successfully protect themselves from any sexual infection. From the time that HIV and AIDS were first identified, one of the predominant messages delivered to young people has been about the dangers of heterosexual intercourse spreading HIV. However, the data on HIV are clear that penile-vaginal sex is not one of the major means of transmission. The more typical means, including anal intercourse and male-male sexual interaction, are often given short shrift in educational settings. It has been claimed that this represents an unethical form of disinformation (Curtis, 2008; Partington, 2008).

The issue of HIV/AIDS education is taking sexuality education in new directions and encouraging further debate about curriculum content and philosophy. One thing is certain: No one grows up today without hearing a great deal about HIV and AIDS and their connections to sex. The accuracy of that information is sometimes questionable.

  See "Just Like Me" on SexSource Online.

■ Can Sex Be Safe and Satisfying?

Everyone has to make his or her own decisions about sexual behavior, considering the risks of STD and HIV transmission. How seriously one considers the risks of

SAFE SEX

Source: © Peter Steiner/The New Yorker Collection/www.cartoonbank.com

contracting a disease or what sorts of practices could be used to decrease those risks depends on a variety of psychological and social factors:

1. *Degree of willingness to be prepared for sex.* The fear of condemnation from parents, religious leaders, and society often has made it difficult for young people to plan ahead and prepare for sexual activity. Many therefore prefer to regard sex as accidental or spontaneous in order to bear less responsibility for what might be perceived as a bad decision or immoral behavior. A safe sexual encounter requires taking responsibility for decision making and preparing accordingly.

2. *Self-esteem and assertiveness.* Avoiding infection while remaining sexually active requires enough self-esteem and sense of self-worth to believe that one's health is worthy of protection. It also requires enough self-confidence and assertiveness to make it clear to one's partner that certain rules must govern a sexual encounter.

3. *Willingness to use condoms.* One of the best forms of protection is the condom. Male and female condoms offer roughly equal levels of protection. Making sure that condoms are used can require some negotiation between partners, since some believe that condoms reduce sexual pleasure. Nonetheless, the protection they offer is essential for safe sex. Condoms must be used correctly. Studies have shown that males often put on condoms after having unprotected intercourse for a time, or they remove them before finishing. Clearly such practices increase the risks

of disease transmission as well as pregnancy (Hatherall et al., 2007; Higgins & Hirsch, 2007).

4. *Understanding one's personal vulnerability.* At various times in life, people are prone to feeling relatively invincible or may believe that any consequence, even a negative one, is reversible. It is crucial for everyone to realize that STDs and HIV represent a very real threat. At the present time, there is no cure for some viral STDs or HIV.

5. *Accepting the struggles of establishing a sexual identity.* Anyone who shares sexual activity with others of their sex must give careful consideration to the risks involved, and both partners should take precautions to prevent transmission of infections. Understanding one's own sexual orientation and identity may take time and exploration, but the risks of sex must be recognized even as that exploratory process is unfolding.

Despite the threat of various diseases, couples still can regard sex in a positive way as an integral part of enhancing relationships. Potential sexual partners need to think more carefully about their sexual decisions, open up channels of communication, and protect themselves more deliberately from the spread of disease. These new approaches to sex should prove of real value in reducing a spectrum of negative sexual and social consequences (see Table 17.3).

Minimizing the Sexual Risks of Contracting STDs and HIV

The prevalence of STDs and HIV in the population has reached epidemic proportions, and there is no particularly effective system in place for the prevention and control of these infections (Cates & Feldblum, 2008; Low et al., 2006). Since there are no easy solutions to the problem, the possibility of contracting or transmitting disease should be weighed as part of the responsibility of engaging in shared sexual behavior. Here are some specific suggestions for minimizing the chances of getting or transmitting an STD or HIV:

1. *Recognize that abstinence from sex is a rational choice in the face of the risks.* There are plenty of pressures to have sex. Our sexual feelings may be strong and difficult to resist. Each individual must make his or her own decisions about how involved to get with others sexually. Abstinence or delaying sexual activity is a viable alternative and a rational choice. A major risk of this choice is changing your mind with short notice. While it may go against the grain of abstinence thinking, it is wise to have a backup method of protection easily accessible in case that happens.

2. *Avoid direct contact with any bodily fluids or excretions from a partner.* Most of these diseases

Table 17.3	*Degree of Safety in Types of Sexual Activity*	
Safest	**Possibly Safe**	**Unsafe**
Dry kissing	Vaginal or anal intercourse using a latex or synthetic condom	Fellatio or cunnilingus without a condom or rubber dam
Body-to-body contact and embracing	Wet kissing with no broken skin or damaged mouth tissue	Semen in the mouth
Massage		Vaginal intercourse without a condom
Mutual masturbation (with care in avoiding contact with semen)	Cunnilingus using a dam	Anal intercourse without a condom
Erotic books, movies, and conversation	Fellatio using a condom	Other anal contact, orally or manually
	Hand-to-genital stimulation without breaks in skin	Sharing sex toys

Source: Hatcher et al., Contraceptive Technology, 19th ed., New York: Ardent Media, 2007.

are transmitted by penetration involving mingling of bodily secretions (oral-genital, anal-genital, or penile-vaginal). The transmission of these diseases could be sharply reduced by emphasis on forms of sexual sharing that do not require such penetration, including massage, most forms of mutual masturbation, and some degree of external mutual genital contact. Unfortunately, social values often have led us to believe that some form of penetration is necessary to legitimize a sexual experience. Given the prevalence of STDs and HIV, alternatives may well make sense.

3. *If you are contemplating having sex with a new partner, it is crucial to make some agreements and live up to them:*
   - Agree not to share sex with any other partners for the duration of the relationship.
   - Agree to be tested for STDs and HIV regularly after any sexual contact that could have transmitted it.
   - Agree either to wait a few weeks to share sex, after you both have had various tests, or to use condoms and other protection for that period of time.

4. *Avoid multiple partners and partners who are not well known to you.* The more partners you have and the less well known they are to you, the greater the risk of contracting an STD. This fact has been confirmed repeatedly by research. Casual sex is simply riskier sex. There is less chance that partners' sexual histories will be known, that their suspicious symptoms will be noticed, and that you will be notified if a disease is eventually diagnosed.

See "Mike on STDs and Sexual Histories" on SexSource Online.

5. *Know your sexual partners and take responsibility for yourself and your own protection.* You can take several measures to protect yourself and reduce the risk of getting a disease from sex. They may not always be easy steps to take and may require some degree of assertiveness, but they are part of sexual responsibility. First, it is important to talk with a partner about sex and even to ask about possible infections, although there is evidence that such an information exchange between partners is not always particularly accurate (Ciccarone et al., 2003). You might want to ask if your partner has ever had a herpes infection or any recent symptoms of infection. Second, it can be important to observe your partner's genitals, checking for any sores, warts, discharge, lice, or rashes. It is also a good idea to take responsibility for washing your genital area with soap and water before and promptly after sex. Although these suggestions may not be conducive to sexual intimacy, they are worth considering as precautionary measures in preventing STDs. It is also important to avoid the use of alcohol and other drugs that may alter your judgment. Indiscriminate use of such substances is associated with higher rates of STD.

6. *Use a condom, vaginal pouch, or diaphragm.* Male condoms or female condoms (vaginal pouches) can reduce the risk of transmission. They do not offer total protection, but they certainly reduce the risks substantially. Although the spermicide nonoxynol-9, placed in the vagina, seems to reduce the risks of gonorrheal and chlamydial infection, it does not seem to reduce viral infections and may even increase the risk of contracting them. Many condom manufacturers no longer use the spermicide in their lubricants.

   The male condom should be unrolled onto the erect penis before intercourse begins, leaving

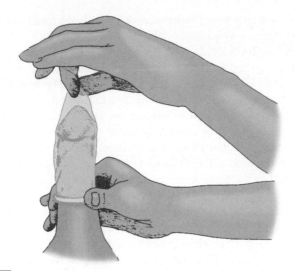

■ **FIGURE 17.17**   *How to Use the Condom*

Do not allow the penis to make sexual entry or contact before putting on the condom. Semen and sperm can escape from the penis at any time. The end of the condom should be pinched to eliminate air before it is unrolled fully to cover the erect penis.

an empty (not air-filled) space at the tip for semen. This is best accomplished by pinching the tip of the condom while unrolling it onto the penis (see Figure 17.17). After ejaculation has occurred, the man or his partner should hold onto the base of the condom when removing the penis from the vagina so the condom does not slip off and so semen does not seep out of the open end of the condom. Some newly designed condoms have adhesive around the shaft to prevent slippage and leakage. Condoms slip off or break between 2 and 3 percent of the times they are used. The "female condom," or vaginal pouch, also provides protection.

7. *If you are an uncircumcised HIV-negative male, consider circumcision.* There is some evidence that male circumcision reduces men's chances of contracting HIV and other viral STDs by 50 to 60 percent. The inner tissue of the penile foreskin is the same kind of epithelial tissue found in the outer parts of other body cavities, making it more susceptible to infection. Circumcision does not, however, reduce the chances of disease transmission from men to women or perhaps to other men (Golden & Wasserheit, 2009; Stephenson, 2009; Tobian et al., 2009).

8. *Use a rubber dam during oral contact with the vulva or anus.* Oral contact with sites where the virus could be harbored is considered risky. Some experts have recommended that small, square latex sheets be placed over the vulva, vagina, or anus. This would allow for some oral stimulation

without direct contact from the tongue or lips. There is little to show how effective or necessary such a dam might be in preventing the transmission of diseases, but it may be the best precaution given the present state of our knowledge. Rubber dams are often made available in college health clinics, and may be purchased in some stores. They also may be improvised by cutting a latex condom along its length and then spreading it out, or by cutting out a section of a surgical rubber glove. Rubber gloves or individual rubber fingercots that fit over a single finger might also be considered if a finger is to be inserted into the vagina or anus; this can offer protection from the virus entering through a break in the skin.

9. *Get medical screening periodically, and seek medical treatment promptly if symptoms develop.* If you are sexually active, it is a good idea to occasionally seek screening tests that can determine if you might have one of the STDs that tend to have few symptoms in their beginning stages, including HIV. STD clinics, family planning clinics, and college health centers usually are able to help with such screening. Whenever you have any suspicious or uncomfortable symptoms in the genital area or urinary tract, seek medical advice and treatment right away. Most cities and counties have STD and HIV clinics, staffed by workers who have expertise in this area. Clinical workers are nonjudgmental, and the tests are nearly always painless.

10. *Inform sexual partners, and urge them to seek treatment.* Whenever a disease contracted through sex is diagnosed, it is crucial for sexual partners of the infected person to be notified and to have a physical examination. Remember, many diseases do not have obvious symptoms in the earlier stages but still require prompt treatment to prevent complications. Many clinics have found that it is best to provide a couple-friendly atmosphere in which both partners can be treated and counseled about their disease and its implications (CDC, 2007). Online e-notification may be a viable way of notifying former partners that they may have been exposed to an STD.

How comfortable do you feel asking a potential sex partner about her or his history of STDs? Would you inform that partner of your own history? Why or why not?

These practices cannot provide a guarantee of safety against disease transmission, but they can minimize your risks. They also represent the most responsible ways to approach sexual activity.

Legal and Personal Responsibility Aspects of Sexually Transmitted Diseases

Most of us assume that a person would not knowingly or deliberately transmit a disease to another person. For the most part, such assumptions probably are correct. However, sexual behavior is an area of life about which people can be extremely private and secretive. They may feel uncomfortable with certain aspects of their past sexual activities and may worry that to discuss their sexual history will jeopardize present relationships. People also tend to avoid protecting themselves against the riskier aspects of sexual behavior, especially when they are caught up in powerful romantic or sexual feelings.

In recent years, more attention has been focused on the legal responsibilities of sexual partners as they relate to STDs. Individuals who have contracted an STD after being assured that there was no danger of doing so, or without being informed of potential risks, have resorted to legal action. Multimillion-dollar lawsuits have been brought against people who seem to have spread diseases purposely or carelessly. More than half the states have statutes that make it a criminal offense to knowingly transmit an STD, and HIV is increasingly being treated in the same manner. Legal experts warn that the law expects people to be responsible in their sexual behaviors and to protect others from any potential harm that might come from sexual activity. As STDs and HIV have reached epidemic proportions, legal precedents are being established that demand even higher levels of responsibility during sexual encounters.

Self-Evaluation

Examining Your Attitudes toward Sexually Transmitted Diseases

The following scale will give you an opportunity to explore some of your own beliefs, feelings, and intentions with regard to STDs. The scale was developed by Yarber, Torabi, and Veenker (1989) and has been tested with hundreds of college and secondary school students. The evaluation is for your own use only.

Directions: Please read each statement carefully. Record your first reaction by marking an "X" through the letter that best describes how much you agree or disagree with the idea.

USE THIS KEY: SA = strongly agree
A = agree
U = undecided
D = disagree
SD = strongly disagree

Example: Doing things to prevent getting an STD is the job of each person.   SA   A   ⊠   D   SD

REMEMBER: STD means sexually transmitted disease, such as gonorrhea, syphilis, genital herpes, or HIV disease.

*(Mark "X"
through letter)*

1. How one uses his/her sexuality has nothing to do with STD.   SA   A   U   D   SD

2. It is easy to use the prevention methods that reduce one's chances of getting an STD.   SA   A   U   D   SD

3. Responsible sex is one of the best ways of reducing the risk of STD.   SA   A   U   D   SD

4. Getting early medical care is the main key to preventing harmful effects of STD.   SA   A   U   D   SD

5. Choosing the right sex partner is important in reducing the risk of getting an STD.   SA   A   U   D   SD

6. A high rate of STD should be a concern for all people.   SA   A   U   D   SD

7. People with an STD have a duty to get their sex partners to medical care.   SA   A   U   D   SD

8. The best way to get a sex partner to STD treatment is to take him/her to the doctor with you.   SA   A   U   D   SD

9. Changing one's sex habits is necessary once the presence of an STD is known.   SA   A   U   D   SD

10. I would dislike having to follow the medical steps for treating an STD.   SA   A   U   D   SD

11. If I were sexually active, I would feel uneasy doing things before and after sex to prevent getting an STD.   SA   A   U   D   SD

12. If I were sexually active, it would be insulting if a sex partner suggested we use a condom to avoid STD.   SA   A   U   D   SD

13. I dislike talking about STD with my peers.   SA   A   U   D   SD

14. I would be uncertain about going to the doctor unless I was sure I really had an STD.   SA   A   U   D   SD

15. I would feel that I should take my sex partner with me to a clinic if I thought I had an STD.   SA   A   U   D   SD

16. It would be embarrassing to discuss STD with one's partner if one was sexually active.   SA   A   U   D   SD

17. If I was to have sex, the chance of getting an STD would make me uneasy about having sex with more than one person.   SA   A   U   D   SD

18. I like the idea of sexual abstinence (not having sex) as the best way of avoiding STD.   SA   A   U   D   SD

19. If I had an STD, I would cooperate with public health persons to find the sources of STD.   SA   A   U   D   SD

20. If I had an STD, I would avoid exposing others while I was being treated.   SA   A   U   D   SD

21. I would have regular STD checkups if I was having sex with more than one partner.   SA   A   U   D   SD

22. I intend to look for STD signs before deciding to have sex with anyone.   SA   A   U   D   SD

23. I will limit my sexual activity to just one partner because of the chances I might get an STD.   SA   A   U   D   SD

24. I will avoid sexual contact anytime I think there is even a slight chance of getting an STD.   SA   A   U   D   SD

25. The chance of getting an STD would not stop me from having sex.   SA   A   U   D   SD

26. If I had a chance, I would support community efforts toward controlling STD.   SA   A   U   D   SD

27. I would be willing to work with others to make people aware of STD problems in my town.   SA   A   U   D   SD

Self-Evaluation Scoring: Calculate total points for each subscale and total scale, using the point values below.

For items 1, 10–14, 16, 25

Strongly agree = 5 points
Agree = 4 points
Undecided = 3 points
Disagree = 2 points
Strongly disagree = 1 point

For items 2–9, 15, 17–24, 26, 27

Strongly agree = 1 point
Agree = 2 points
Undecided = 3 points
Disagree = 4 points
Strongly disagree = 5 points

Total scale: items 1–27
Belief subscale: items 1–9
Feeling subscale: items 10–18
Intention to act subscale: items 19–27

Interpretation: The higher your score, the higher your risk of behavior that can spread sexually transmitted diseases.

Source: From *Journal of Sex Education and Therapy,* vol. 15, no. 1, 1989, pp. 42–43. Reprinted by permission of the American Association of Sexuality Educators, Counselors & Therapists.

Self-Evaluation

Considering Being Tested for STDs and HIV

The percentages of people being tested for STDs and HIV have been growing. Seeking testing reflects the likelihood that they have engaged in some sort of risky behavior at some point in their lives. Testing is one of the best ways to find out your status so that you may seek treatment if necessary and protect your sexual partners. If you are involved in a relationship in which you may eventually wish to participate in unprotected, penetrative sex and either of you has had any possibility of disease exposure, testing is the most sensible route to take.

Here is a series of questions that can help you think through the process of being tested and also your reactions to that process. Consider your responses with care, and then get tested.

Knowing the Mechanics

Consult your local public health agency or student health center for more information, and try to secure answers to the following questions:

1. Where can you get tested?

2. Does your state or provincial government require reporting of test results to some central agency?

3. Will your name be associated with your test results, as they are in confidential medical records? Or will the results be anonymous, identified only by a number you hold?

4. Who will be explaining the results of the test to you?

5. What kind of testing is used, and how long will it take to get the results?

6. Are you making the decision to be tested without coercion and with full and informed consent?

Knowing Your Motivations and Feelings

7. Why are you considering being tested for STDs or HIV?

8. Is peace of mind important to you? Are you tired of wondering about the possibility you could have been infected?

9. Are you ready to cope with some anxiety while awaiting the test results? Will you have sources of support and counseling in the meantime?

10. Are you ready to give honest answers to the health care provider who will interview you prior to testing?

11. Have you discussed the testing with your partner?

If the Results Are Positive . . .

12. How do you think you will feel, and whom will you tell first?

13. Who will be your sources of support and counseling?

14. Where will you seek further medical evaluation and treatment, and how will this be paid for?

15. What will be the implications for the various relationships in your life (relatives, friends, lovers)?

16. How do you think you will feel, and whom will you tell first?

17. Are you prepared to take appropriate precautions in the future to minimize the risks of STD and HIV infection? What are your plans?

Chapter Summary

1. Sexually transmitted diseases (STDs) have caused much human misery throughout the centuries and continue to be serious health problems today.

2. Human immunodeficiency virus (HIV) has raised many medical, political, economic, and social issues. Acquired immunodeficiency syndrome (AIDS) is the final, eventually terminal, stage of HIV infection.

3. The development of antibiotics was a major step in conquering some STDs, but many STD-causing bacteria are becoming resistant to them.

4. It is estimated that there are 19 million new cases of STD in the United States each year, half in people under age 25.

5. Although the origins of HIV are uncertain, it may have begun in Africa. HIV has infected millions of people throughout the world.

6. Epidemiological studies show that the incidence of HIV infection varies in different parts of the world. Although HIV spread first among gay males and intravenous (IV) drug abusers in the United States, HIV infection now is found among heterosexual adolescents, heterosexual men, women, and children.

7. The more sexual partners an individual has and the less consistently condoms are used, the more likely infection with an STD becomes.

8. Gonorrhea can be spread through vaginal, anal, and oral sexual contact and infects over a half million people each year. The eyes of babies are vulnerable to infection during birth and are routinely treated to prevent gonorrheal blindness. Many strains of gonorrhea are now resistant to most antibiotics.

9. Syphilis progresses through four major stages. About 20,000 people each year in the United States are infected with syphilis.

10. Chlamydia infection is now the most common reportable communicable disease in the United States. It causes many different forms of genital and urinary tract infections in both men and women and can cause infertility.

11. Nonspecific urethritis (NSU) has been steadily increasing as an STD problem affecting males.

12. Vulvovaginal inflammation may be caused by bacteria, yeast organisms, or trichomonads. Taking proper hygienic measures and keeping the vulval area dry can reduce the risk of contracting vaginitis.

13. Genital herpes is caused by the herpes simplex virus. Once the virus has infected the body, it can cause recurrent outbreaks of the lesions.

14. Human papillomavirus (HPV) causes genital warts (condylomata) and also is associated with a higher incidence of cervical and anal cancers. There is now a vaccine that can prevent HPV infection when used prior to infection.

15. Hepatitis A can be sexually transmitted and causes a liver infection from which most people recover completely. Hepatitis B virus (HBV) can cause serious liver infection, and it has been recommended that college students be vaccinated against the virus. Hepatitis C virus (HCV) is also a serious disease, but it is less likely to be transmitted sexually.

16. Pubic lice must be thoroughly treated to ensure that all insects and their eggs have been eliminated from body hairs.

17. Lymphogranuloma venereum (LGV), chancroid, and granuloma inguinale are STDs that are more common in tropical climates.

18. Two skin diseases that may be transmitted by the intimate bodily contact of sex are molluscum contagiosum and scabies.

19. HIV is a retrovirus that progressively destroys the body's immune system so that opportunistic infections weaken the victim. In its final stages, HIV infection is known as AIDS and eventually is fatal.

20. The documented routes of HIV infection are anal or vaginal sexual intercourse; oral-genital sex; other contacts with semen, transplanted organs, or blood (as through contaminated needles); and transfer from mother to child perinatally or through breast milk.

21. HIV is more prevalent in urban neighborhoods, especially where there is a great deal of IV drug abuse.

22. There are several tests, using blood or saliva, to detect HIV in various stages of infection. The ELISA test is usually confirmed with the Western blot test.

23. There is controversy over whether HIV testing should be required.

24. There is no cure for HIV infection. Treatment focuses on prevention and control of opportunistic infections.

25. Use of combination drug therapies involving protease inhibitors (HAART) are proving to be the most effective for prolonging life with HIV infection.

26. Vaccines to fool the body into creating antibodies to help slow the rate of HIV infection are being tested. Preventative vaccines are also being tested, as are other chemicals that are part of chemoprophylaxis.

27. Caring for and research on people living with HIV or AIDS raise issues of confidentiality and cost. There are legal and ethical conflicts about HIV infection and confidentiality.

28. Sex can still be a pleasurable and safe part of relationships if approached responsibly and with appropriate precautions.

29. Part of responsible sexual decision making is taking appropriate measures to prevent the transmission of STDs. Among the best preventative precautions are considering abstinence, avoiding penetration, avoiding multiple partners, avoiding abuse of alcohol or other drugs that impair judgment, knowing partners, getting screened for disease, and using condoms, vaginal pouches, or diaphragms. If infected, prompt medical treatment is essential, as is telling any potentially infected partners.

Chapter 18

Sexual Dysfunctions and Their Treatment

Chapter Outline

When we first started having sex, he was far more interested in whether I had an orgasm than I was. The fact was, I almost never had an orgasm, but I still thought our sex life was great. As our relationship has grown, I now reach orgasm almost every time and would miss it more than I once did.

—statement written by a college student

The field of sex therapy has expanded rapidly since Masters and Johnson published their groundbreaking work *Human Sexual Inadequacy* in 1970. The systematized treatment of sexual dysfunctions has become as commonplace as advertisements for erection-enhancing drugs. Early attempts at treatment employed psychotherapy techniques that had proved to have little benefit, and the behavioral treatment methods introduced by Masters and Johnson began to show promise. As new pharmacological interventions appeared in the 1980s and have continued to evolve to the present time, there has been a revolution of sorts in helping people improve their sexual functioning (Brotto, 2006; Leiblum, 2007).

Understanding Sexual Dysfunctions

Men who experience difficulty controlling their ejaculations are said to have **premature ejaculation.** Women who never experience orgasm are said to be experiencing orgasmic disorder. However, the situation may be more complex than these handy labels suggest. Who is to define whether some phenomenon of sexual response is actually a dysfunction or a disorder? If the woman enjoys her sexual encounters without feeling any need for orgasm, should she be treated for a dysfunction? If the rapidly ejaculating man and his partner are perfectly comfortable with his pattern of response, should they be told they have a problem (Levin, 2004)?

Diagnostic criteria for sexual dysfunctions often include a statement about the condition causing sufficient personal distress for the individual to consider it a problem. Some sexologists believe it is possible to be suffering from a dysfunction without realizing it or being personally upset by it, while others believe that there is no need to be held captive by rigid definitions of what normal sexual response should be. One study of over 31,500 women found that while about 43 percent of the women reported symptoms of various sexual problems, only 12 percent of them found them to be a source of personal distress (Shifren et al., 2008).

Getting beyond a sexual dysfunction requires sensitivity, creativity, openness to new directions, and well-honed expertise. An individual cannot change sexual functioning without also being prepared to examine sexual values, cultural and religious influences, the quality of relationships, and other subjective life issues. However dysfunctions are defined, it is critical that those who treat them be given professional latitude to exercise judgment in helping their clients to not be misled by unrealistic societal standards (Balon, 2008; Basson et al., 2003; McGoldrick, Loonan, & Wohlsifer, 2007; Ribner, 2004).

The individual's own sexual history and feelings are particularly important in arriving at any diagnosis. Sexual health seems to be intimately tied to other levels of physical and mental well-being. There is some evidence that for many women sexual dysfunction is closely aligned with difficulties in their relationships, whereas male dysfunctions often are best studied from a medical point of view as well. The vast majority of people feel that enjoyable sexual relations add to a person's sense of well-being and quality of life. When people's bodies do not function sexually as expected and desired, they often feel frustrated, inadequate, and unhappy. In a society such as our own, which places a premium on being successful in sex, to fail in a sexual encounter may be perceived as tantamount to being a failure at manhood or womanhood (Althof et al., 2005; Nobre & Pinto-Gouveia, 2006).

Performance Standards

Men are plagued by the **performance standard** that successful sex requires an erect penis. It is even assumed by most males that their partners cannot be expected to find sexual pleasure unless an erection is achieved and maintained. Closely allied to this standard is the standard of postponing ejaculation or orgasm. Because a penis tends to lose its erection following ejaculation, the longer a man can postpone ejaculation, the better a sexual performer he will be considered. A third standard might be stated best as the unquestioned assumption it has always been—that men reach orgasm without difficulty and find in this peak experience the ultimate pleasure of sex. It is now known that men do indeed have difficulty reaching orgasm at times.

Historically, the sexual performance standards for women have focused on issues of sexual attractiveness and availability rather than desire. More recent attitudes have encouraged women to take a more

premature ejaculation difficulty that some men experience in controlling the ejaculatory reflex, resulting in rapid ejaculation.

performance standard the expectations for successful sexual functioning that people often impose on themselves or their partners. They are often unrealistic.

Real People

Elizabeth: Working on an Orgasmic Disorder

Since being in college, Elizabeth has had two lasting relationships that involved an active sexual component. For her, however, the sex has been somewhat disappointing because she has been unable to reach orgasm with either partner. With her first boyfriend, Larry, she was happy with their sexual relationship at the outset. Eventually, Larry began questioning her about her responses, and she realized that he thought she should be reaching orgasm, as he did when they had intercourse. Elizabeth was able to reach orgasm during masturbation but somehow could not do so during shared sexual activity. She had enjoyed the physical intimacy but had realized as well that she was not experiencing orgasm. It had not mattered much to her at first, but the more Larry pressed the issue, the more she began to feel as though she should make it a higher priority. The relationship ended before she had a chance to pursue the matter further with Larry.

When Elizabeth's relationship with Robert began, she felt determined to get more from their sexual contact. She even shared with Robert that she had not been able to reach orgasm during intercourse. He assured her that things would be different with him, but as it turned out they were not. This time, Robert seemed frustrated at not being able to bring

Elizabeth to orgasm no matter how hard he tried. She began to feel guilty about not giving him what he wanted, and he began to doubt whether she was really turned on by him. She insisted that she was, but Robert remained unconvinced. Her pattern of responsiveness with him was usually about the same: She would feel sexually aroused and enjoy the building of intensity of her sexual feelings. She would get close to the point of orgasm, but then the feeling seemed simply to dissipate. Sometimes, she would be able to build up the tension again for a while, but it always seemed to get interrupted eventually. Elizabeth and Robert usually would talk after sex, trying to figure out what had gone wrong. They sometimes would try new approaches the next time, but nothing seemed to work. Elizabeth is now feeling depressed about the whole thing, and Robert is thinking that perhaps it is time to end their relationship.

What are your opinions about Larry and Robert and the ways they have responded to Elizabeth's problem? If you could give either one of these men some advice, what would you say to them? What would you recommend to Elizabeth to help her overcome the problem?

active role in sex. However, women also have become more bound by new standards of sexual performance. Women today are under pressure to become intensely aroused and ready for sexual contact, to reach orgasm without difficulty, and to have more than one orgasm during a single sexual encounter (Shifren & Ferrari, 2004).

These become the standards on which men and women pin their sexual hopes and by which they play out their roles in bed and judge their performances afterward. It is little wonder that so many people end up feeling inadequate, dissatisfied, and disillusioned by what is actually happening in their sex lives. When individuals experience some functional problem during sex or when their bodies fail to perform as expected and desired with some consistency, they are said to be experiencing sexual dysfunction. Today, more than ever before, such problems need not signal a lifetime of unfulfilled sexual needs. As this chapter

will demonstrate, most sexual dysfunctions can be eased or corrected.

Cultural Influences

Every culture has its own definitions for what constitutes a normal sexual relationship, the meanings of sexual dysfunctions, and how dysfunctions should be treated. Cultural beliefs can have a strong impact on sexual functioning, and strongly held beliefs can make vulnerable individuals particularly susceptible to anxiety about their sexual performance. The roles of men and women in society and expectations about sexuality are crucial to how sexual functioning is perceived (McGoldrick, Loonan, & Wohlsifer, 2007). In some Polynesian languages, there is no word for erection problems. It is simply assumed that when a male does not get an erection, he must not have wanted to have sex after all. Removing such performance pressures is what Western modes of sex therapy try to achieve.

Cross-cultural research on sexual dysfunctions and levels of sexual satisfaction is very sparse. The Global Study of Sexual Attitudes and Behaviors is beginning to yield some interesting data, but it has encountered difficulty in persuading some people to participate, potentially causing volunteer bias. Using cluster analysis, the study has identified three distinct areas of the world based on measurements of sexual well-being, as defined by physical and emotional pleasure, satisfaction with sexual function, and the importance given to sex. One cluster is characterized as being relatively gender-equal, meaning that the people value marriage and sex in which decisions and power are more equally shared. This cluster includes many European countries, Australia, Canada, and the United States. The levels of sexual satisfaction were highest in these countries (Laumann et al., 2006).

In male-centered cultures, including many Mediterranean and Islamic nations, (e.g., Algeria, Egypt, Israel, Italy, and Turkey), one South American country (Brazil), and a few Asian countries (e.g., Korea and the Philippines), men tend to take a more dominant, patriarchal role, including initiating and controlling sex. In this cluster, researchers found middle levels of sexual satisfaction. A third cluster was found among East Asian countries such as China, Indonesia, Japan, Taiwan, and Thailand. These countries also were largely male-dominated but were additionally characterized by low levels of sexual satisfaction. The researchers found that despite cross-cultural variations in attitudes and beliefs, the best predictors of sexual well-being across the globe seem to be physical and mental health, sexual practices, and the quality of relationships. The clusters suggested that how sexuality fits within gender balances in a culture is also critical (Laumann, Nicolosi et al., 2006; Laumann, Paik et al., 2006; Parish et al., 2007).

There are many cultural folk remedies to allay men's concerns about sexual adequacy. Women's sexual dysfunctions are rarely addressed by these techniques, further evidence of the lack of significance assigned to female sexual enjoyment in some cultures. In parts of Africa, for example, impotent men drink potions made of bark or resort to ritual ceremonies. Hashish is used in Morocco by dysfunctional males, and nonorgasmic women are encouraged to take a younger lover or have a lesbian relationship. In Thailand, men drink the bile of a cobra and the blood of a monkey, mixed in a local liquor. In India, men apply an herb to the penis that is a potent urinary irritant. Wives of impotent men in the West Indies may serve them the penis of a turtle marinated in wine or a soup made of ox penis and testes. In other parts of the world, seal testes and penises are consumed to cure erectile prob-

lems. European men usually treat their dysfunctions with various alterations in their diet.

Traditional Chinese medicine has long made use of complicated herbal preparations and acupuncture, both of which are believed to bring the body's energies into balance and restore normal sexual functioning. Even with the advent of newer treatment techniques in China, the traditional ways remain very popular. Some Chinese herbal plants—such as ox-knee root, used for several sexual difficulties, and milk vetch seeds, used to treat premature ejaculation—have become endangered because of their widespread use.

Labeling Sexual Dysfunctions

Scientific communication demands a terminology, and each sexual difficulty has been given a general label. The most commonly accepted source of diagnostic categories is the *Diagnostic and Statistical Manual of Mental Disorders,* and some of the standards may well change in its upcoming fifth edition. It is important not to lose sight of the fact that such labels may have profound implications for the individual experiencing the dysfunction. Consider the term **impotence,** which conjures up images of failure and powerlessness, hardly reassuring concepts for a man with erectile difficulties.

Certain modifying terms are employed in diagnosing and describing sexual dysfunctions. The term **lifelong dysfunction** means that the problem has been present since the onset of the person's sexual functioning. The term **acquired dysfunction** is used to describe a dysfunction that has developed after a period of normal function. (The terms *primary* and *secondary* once were used for lifelong and acquired, respectively.) Thus, a woman with lifelong orgasmic disorder has never been able to reach orgasm, whereas the woman with acquired orgasmic disorder is no longer able to be orgasmic but once was. Dysfunctions may also be *generalized* when the problem occurs in all of an individual's sexual encounters, or *situational,* meaning that it happens only under specific conditions, with certain types of stimulation, situations, or partners. Various new subtype descriptors have been proposed for female arousal dysfunctions; it appears

impotence (IM-puh-tense) difficulty achieving or maintaining erection of the penis.

lifelong dysfunction a difficulty with sexual functioning that has always existed for a particular person.

acquired dysfunction a difficulty with sexual functioning that develops after some period of normal sexual functioning.

Table 18.1	*The Sexual Response Cycle and Sexual Dysfunctions*

Desire Disorders	Arousal (Vasocongestive) Disorders	Orgasmic (Reversed Vasocongestive) Disorders
Normal asexuality: the individual who naturally has low levels of need for sexual gratification (not necessarily a dysfunction)	Problems in achieving a suitable level of sexual arousal	Problems in triggering orgasm, creating an inordinate orgasmic delay or a complete inability to reach orgasm
Hypoactive sexual desire disorder (HSDD)	Male erectile disorder	Male orgasmic disorder
Sexual aversion disorder: caused by anxiety and phobias related to sexual activity	Female sexual arousal disorder: lack of vaginal lubrication, general sexual dysfunction	Female orgasmic disorder
		Premature ejaculation: lack of ejaculatory control in men

Sexual Pain Disorders
Spasm of outer vaginal musculature in women: vaginismus
Dyspareunia
Postejaculatory pain

Source: Diagnostic and Statistical Manual for Mental Disorders, 4th ed. (DSM-IV). Washington, D.C.: American Psychiatric Association, 1994.

that women's arousal is strongly influenced by the context within which a sexual interaction takes place (Balon, 2008; Basson et al., 2003). These are discussed later in this chapter.

What do you think is one of the most common complaints brought to sex therapists? Why do you think this?

Sexual Response and the Dual Control Model

Chapter 4 described various models for understanding the predictable sequence of physiological events that constitute the human sexual response cycle. The Masters and Johnson (1966) model includes four phases: excitement, plateau, orgasm, and resolution, but Kaplan's three-phase model is of greater value in understanding the relationship of sexual dysfunctions to sexual response (Kaplan, 1979). This model suggests that sexual response consists of three distinct components:

1. A *desire phase,* having to do with one's degree of interest in and desire for sexual gratification. Sexual desire is probably controlled by centers of the brain that seem to activate as well as inhibit sexual desire. The desire phase precedes more profound physiological changes in the sex organs and throughout the body. This phase may be influenced by emotion, memory, context, and/or

conditioning (Symonds, Boolell, & Quirk, 2005; Utian et al., 2005). Desire has been assumed to be an important component in the triggering of sexual arousal, although recent studies have shown that, in women, arousal often precedes the desire to participate in sex (Sanders, Graham, & Milhausen, 2008).

2. *Sexual arousal,* characterized by a buildup of blood in the genital areas that causes the typical signs of sexual arousal, such as penile and clitoral erection and lubrication of the vagina. This phase is accompanied by increased muscular tension and arousal throughout the body.

3. *Orgasm,* which triggers the reversal of the genital blood flow and muscular relaxation. This phase is controlled mostly by the sympathetic division of the autonomic nervous system.

Things can go wrong in any of these phases of sexual response. Table 18.1 summarizes the relationship of various sexual dysfunctions to the three-phase model. Each is described in more detail in the sections that follow. Many people seem to experience dysfunctions in more than one phase of sexual response.

We also studied the Dual Control Model which proposes that levels of sexual arousal are mediated by one's propensities for sexual excitation and sexual inhibition. These factors may be high or low in a particular person. We might expect, then, that a person with low levels of excitation and high levels of inhibition would have difficulties in sexual arousal and response. Even in those with high levels of sexual excitatory

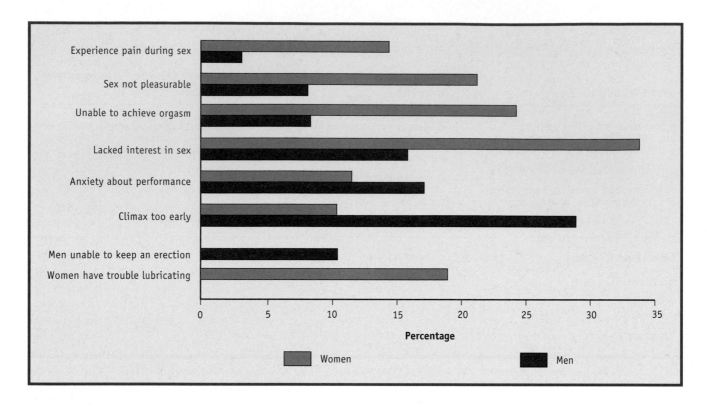

FIGURE 18.1   *Sexual Dysfunction, by Gender*

The percentage of people reporting sexual problems they experienced over several months or more during the previous year in the National Health and Social Life Survey (NHSLS).

Source: From Edward O. Laumann et al., *The Social Organization of Sexuality,* p. 369. © 1994 by CSG Enterprises, Inc., and Stuart Michaels. Reprinted by permission of the University of Chicago Press.

mechanisms, high levels of inhibitory mechanisms may still interfere with sexual function. It is also known that the ways we think about sex, and the *cognitive biases,* both positive and negative, that we hold toward sexual activity, can contribute to these excitatory and inhibitory processes. These mechanisms have in fact been supported by research and constitute a whole new level of understanding about sexual dysfunctions and human neurophysiology (Bancroft et al., 2009; deJong, 2009; Sanders Graham, & Milhausen, 2008).

Incidence of Sexual Dysfunction

Studies on the incidence of sexual dysfunctions have yielded a wide range of estimates. The Global Study of Sexual Attitudes and Behaviors found that among adults ages 40 to 80 in 29 countries, the highest prevalence of sexual problems was found in East and Southeast Asia. Worldwide, lack of interest in sex and difficulty reaching orgasm were the most commonly reported problems among women, ranging in various countries from 26 to 43 percent and 18 to 41 percent, respectively. The most commonly reported dysfunction among men was early ejaculation, with nearly a third of men in Southeast Asia reporting the difficulty.

Arousal problems constituted a common complaint as well, ranging from 13 to 28 percent in men and 16 to 38 percent in women (Laumann et al., 2005). The NHSLS researchers asked study participants in the United States if they had experienced particular sexual problems during the previous year for a period of several months or more. The findings are summarized in Figure 18.1.

The proportions of people reporting sexual disorders in the NHSLS varied from about 5 to 33 percent, with about one-third of women reporting they had lacked interest in sex for several months or more and nearly 30 percent of men reporting they ejaculate too rapidly. In general, women tended to report more sexual problems than men, except with regard to anxiety about performance and reaching orgasm too early. Ten percent of all the men reported having difficulty maintaining an erection, and 19 percent of the women reported having trouble with vaginal lubrication. For both sexes, these problems occurred with higher incidence in the older age groups, although that trend was somewhat more marked for men than it was for women.

Lack of pleasure during sex and inability to achieve orgasm have been reported by women about three times more often than by men. In correlating these data with other findings, researchers found that people who reported themselves as being unhappy were more likely to report one or more sexual problems than were people who reported being extremely or very happy. There was no way to determine a cause-and-effect relationship between these factors. Greater satisfaction with shared sexual activity is also correlated with higher levels of relationship satisfaction (Basson, 2008; Laumann et al., 2005; Rosen & Laumann, 2003; Santilla et al., 2008; West et al., 2008).

Again, however, we must consider the distinction to be made between reporting symptoms of sexual dysfunctions and how much actual personal distress is reported. There is evidence that even as the rate of sexual dysfunctions increases with age, the levels of distress associated with such problems actually decreases. About the most accurate statement we can make about the incidence of sexual dysfunctions is that substantial proportions of women and men do indeed have some problems with their sexual functioning, and for a smaller proportion of them, these problems are distressing (Nygaard, 2008; Shifren et al., 2008).

■ Types of Sexual Dysfunctions

This part of the chapter provides an overview of the most typical sexual dysfunctions that concern people and their sexual partners.

Sexual Interest/Desire Disorders

Although most people can identify and describe inner feelings of needing or desiring sexual gratification, along with sexual fantasies, it is not yet fully understood why the reported levels of interest in sex vary so much among individuals. These differences in sexual interest and desire, whatever their causes, can become an important concern in people's lives. Discrepancy in levels of sexual desire between partners is a common complaint brought to sex therapists.

We've already seen that sexual desire may be influenced by excitation and inhibition factors within the individual. These may affect activity in the brain centers that control the sexual appetite (Bancroft et al., 2009; Giargiari et al., 2005). Sexual boredom may play a role. Diagnosing sexual desire disorders is somewhat difficult, because subjective judgments must be made about what is a normal human sexual appetite and how much distress the perceived lack of desire is creating. Although there is no absolute scale of sexual desire, there are measurable discrepancies between people's sexual styles and interests (McCarthy & McDonald, 2009).

It has become clear that understanding and describing sexual desire in women is a complicated task and that women's motivations for sex may differ depending on whether the relationship is new or of longer duration. In newly established relationships, sexual desire may be triggered by the sense of novelty, uncertainty, and even secrecy. In longer-term relationships, the sexual motivations may be extremely varied—and even somewhat nonsexual, including the wish to experience tenderness and appreciation or to have one's desirability confirmed by the partner. Sometimes women participate in sex in order to avoid angering or disappointing a partner. Therefore, it has been suggested that we use the term *interest,* more of a cognitive function, along with the more emotional assumptions of *desire*. It has also been recommended that when clinicians diagnose these problems, they should include a careful description of the contexts and relationship dynamics that accompany them (Basson, 2008; Chenier, 2008).

Some people seem to have very infrequent interest in or desire for sex and are not bothered by this. Even in a sex-saturated society, it is possible to maintain feelings of well-being and self-worth with minimal levels of sexual interest. It is also possible for some people to choose a celibate or sexually inactive lifestyle that represents a mature, responsible approach to life and is manifested by a suppressed sexual desire, or at least a suppressed expression of the desire. This nonpathological way of life has been called **normal asexuality** and need not be considered a problem or dysfunction.

Sometimes, however, low sexual desire is viewed as a problem, and desire phase complaints are brought to therapists. As a dysfunction, this **hypoactive sexual desire disorder (HSDD)** may be characterized by a loss of attraction to formerly exciting stimuli and a lack of pleasure even in direct stimulation of the sex organs. It may also result from a failure of sexual desire to develop during those years when it typically takes form. Dysfunctional individuals may not be particularly aroused by seeing attractive people or fantasizing about sex, and they rarely seek sexual activity. They may still function normally when sexual stimulation is permitted, but the physical pleasure they derive from it is limited and fleeting (Basson, 2008; Clayton et al., 2006).

There are some gender differences in the occurrence of hypoactive sexual desire. Men with HSDD tend to be older than women; the average age for men

normal asexuality an absence or low level of sexual desire, considered normal for a particular person.

hypoactive sexual desire disorder (HSDD) loss of interest and pleasure in what formerly were arousing sexual stimuli.

Source: Mike Peters Edtctn (New) © 2004 Distributed by King Features Syndicate.

FIGURE 18.2 *Sexual Aversion Disorder*

An aversion to or fear of sexual intimacy is considered one form of sexual dysfunction. A real or imagined physical problem or psychological stress might cause someone to sabotage an otherwise satisfactory relationship in order to avoid sexual contact.

with HSDD is 50, and the average age for women is 33. Women with hypoactive sexual desire are more likely than men to report other forms of psychological distress, such as anxiety, depression, and hostility, and they also complain of higher levels of life stress. Women are more likely to have had another sexual dysfunction (such as arousal disorder) of long-standing duration, whereas men are more likely to have had another sexual dysfunction (such as erectile disorder) for only a short period before experiencing HSDD. For women, especially, HSDD often is rooted in intimacy difficulties within a relationship that need to be resolved before sexual interactions can improve or become more frequent (McCarthy & McDonald, 2009; Nobre, Pinto-Gouveia, & Gomes, 2006).

Sexual aversion disorder, characterized by some level of fear or disgust about sex and avoidance of sexual activity, is generated by anxieties and phobias about sexual contact (see Figure 18.2). Some men and women develop fearful or avoidant reactions toward sex or its possible consequences and eventually become exaggeratedly aversive toward becoming sexually involved. These reactions can stem from psychological stress resulting from an inhibiting or punitive upbringing, a rigidly religious background, health concerns, or a history of physical and/or sexual abuse. Often such individuals become involved in close relationships and are successful in making themselves attractive to others. As the levels of intimacy and commitment deepen, however, there usually comes a point where they become fearful about sex. They then may find ways to sabotage the relationship or find fault with their partner so that they will not feel obligated to go any further with sex (Basson, 2008).

It often is difficult for therapists to distinguish HSDD or sexual aversion from problems with arousal because individuals with HSDD and sexual aversions may also experience trouble becoming sexually aroused. It is up to the sex therapist to seek specific information about a particular person's level of sexual desire in order to make valid judgments about a proper course of treatment.

Arousal Disorders

Whenever something interferes with blood flow into the sex organs, the human body fails to exhibit the preliminary signs of sexual arousal. In men, the penis fails to become erect or loses some of its erection. This has traditionally been called impotence but is now diagnosed as **male erectile disorder (ED).**

In women, lack of arousal is characterized by the vagina remaining dry and tight and by their not experiencing the sensations of tingling or throbbing typical of arousal. The term **female sexual arousal disorder** is now the most widely accepted among professionals for this disorder, although two subtypes have been proposed. One subtype is referred to as subjective sexual arousal disorder and is applied to situations in which a woman's genitals seem to be lubricating normally, but the woman fails to realize or appreciate the fact that her genitals are responding. From a subjective viewpoint, she does not experience arousal. The other proposed subtype is called *genital sexual arousal disorder* and refers specifically to a lack of physiological response in the clitoris and vagina, even though the woman may report feeling subjectively aroused. This type of arousal dysfunction seems more typically associated with nerve damage, estrogen deficiency, or bodily changes following

sexual aversion disorder avoidance of or exaggerated fears toward forms of sexual expression.

male erectile disorder (ED) difficulty achieving or maintaining penile erection (impotence).

female sexual arousal disorder difficulty for a woman in achieving sexual arousal.

menopause. Sometimes, these two subtypes occur together, and any type of sexual stimulation fails to create a sense of sexual desire or interest. It may be that the nerve endings in some women with arousal disorder are not as sensitive as they are in other women (Frohlich & Meston, 2005; Middleton, Kuffel, & Heiman, 2008).

Because the control mechanisms in the brain and nervous system for the arousal phase of sexual response are different from those that control orgasm, it is possible—though unusual—for people who show few characteristics of arousal to be orgasmic. A man with ED may achieve orgasm, ejaculating with a flaccid (nonerect) penis. Likewise, some women who do not manifest the usual signs of sexual arousal, such as vaginal lubrication and clitoral erection, may still have an orgasmic response.

Erectile Disorder in Men

Not only can thoughts, fantasies, and sensory stimuli trigger erection of the penis, but they can inhibit it as well, as the dual control model explains. Most men will experience some instances of erectile difficulty during their lifetime, typically as a result of fatigue, excessive consumption of alcohol, or simply not being in the mood for sex. When men have their first sexual intercourse with an unknown partner or when they are intoxicated, they are far more likely to have problems with erection (Santilla, Sandnabba, & Jern, 2009). Aging is a particular risk factor, and ED often begins in the fifties or sixties (Rowland, Incrocci, & Slob, 2005). ED can affect men in any age bracket, but among younger men it tends to be linked more to relational and psychological stress and to smoking tobacco. Heavy smoking has been identified as a significant factor in ED among younger men (Natali et al., 2005; Shiri et al., 2005; Swindle et al., 2004). Men who ride bicycles or motorcycles for long periods of time may experience ED as well (Naya et al., 2008).

There seem to be some identifiable differences between problems with *achieving* a suitable erection at the beginning of sexual stimulation and problems with *maintaining* an erection during sustained sexual activity. Although psychological stress can interfere with erection at either stage, men who have trouble achieving an erection in the first place are more likely to have an underlying physical, organic disturbance. These include vascular problems, diabetes and metabolic syndrome, and obesity. Men who lose an erection during sexual activity are more likely to have psychological and relational stressors (Corona et al., 2005; Koskimaki et al., 2005; Ponholzer et al., 2006). It is not uncommon for erection to take place easily during masturbation but be lost during shared activities such as intercourse.

Several approaches are used to determine whether ED may have physical causes. One simple and reliable

method is measuring *nocturnal penile tumescence (NPT)*, the number of times the man experiences erection while he is asleep. Normally, the penis becomes erect numerous times during a typical sleep cycle. If nocturnal erection is continuing normally, there is probably no organic cause for erectile difficulties. The man may be given a device that is attached to the penis at bedtime and records spontaneous erections during the night. However, there are some indications that psychological stress may sometimes disrupt NPT, and there is a small chance that the cause of the ED might be misdiagnosed as physical when it is actually psychological. Whenever potential organic conditions exist as a cause of ED, a thorough medical history should be taken and some tests administered that, for example, can determine whether blood flow to the penis has been hampered by damage to the blood vessels. For some men, erectile problems represent an early warning of cardiovascular problems that are also developing (Chang et al., 2009; Corona et al., 2005; Giuliano, 2008).

Men in our culture place a great deal of importance on their penis and often consider erection to be one of the trappings of masculinity. They typically have adopted the unwarranted performance standard that good sex requires an erect penis. Therefore, experiencing erectile dysfunction can be devastatingly embarrassing and frightening for most men (see Figure 18.3). Erectile dysfunction also seems to lower the levels of sexual and relational satisfaction in men's partners (Conaglen & Conaglen, 2008; McCabe & Matic, 2008).

■ FIGURE 18.3 *Erectile Disorder*

Men in our society place great emphasis on their penises and a performance standard that may not be realistic for all people. Mental attitude, fatigue, alcohol, or organic problems can all affect a man's ability to have an erection. Failure to have an erection can lead to depression and further erectile problems.

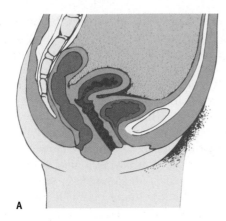
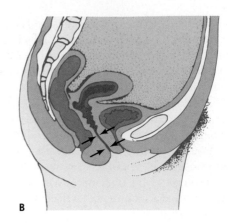

■ FIGURE 18.4 *Vaginismus*

Vaginismus involves constriction of the outer vaginal muscles, prohibiting intercourse. Vaginismus might be caused by ignorance of bodily functions or might be considered a physical manifestation of a psychological fear. The drawing on the left **(A)** illustrates the relaxed vagina, and the drawing on the right **(B)** illustrates vaginismus.

Female Sexual Arousal Disorder

With increased attention being given to female sexual response, some women have felt the need to fake arousal and orgasm in order to meet performance standards. Some women with sexual arousal disorder report that they still enjoy the physical intimacy of sexual contact. More often, unresponsive women eventually come to think of sex as something to be endured. They become trapped between their lack of physical arousal and their desire to live up to social standards of eroticism. Some experts claim that this negative reaction is caused by the societal assumption that everyone should become sexually aroused; these experts believe that lack of arousal should be considered legitimate and nonpathological (Brotto, Heiman, & Tolman, 2009).

Diagnosis of female sexual arousal disorder has tended to focus quite specifically on vaginal responses such as lubrication. Research on the strong influence that cognitive states may have on women's sexual arousal demonstrate that lack of arousal is influenced by a variety of psychological factors. Women who perceive their sexuality in negative ways are far more likely to have continuing problems with sexual desire and arousal. There are many psychological and emotional influences that form a basis for sexual arousal or the lack of it, and these are only beginning to be understood (Brotto, Heiman, & Tolman, 2009; Middleton, Kuffel, & Heiman, 2008; McCall & Meston, 2007).

Vaginismus and the Sexual Pain Disorders

A woman suffering from **vaginismus** may enjoy sexual arousal and be capable of orgasms with clitoral stimulation. However, when an attempt is made to introduce a penis or other object into the vagina, the woman experiences anticipatory anxiety, and some pelvic muscles may contract reflexively (see Figure 18.4). It has traditionally been stated that this is due to a spasm of the outer vaginal musculature, although such a spasm has never been scientifically documented. In any case, the tension of vaginismus makes intromission nearly impossible or painfully difficult. A few experts have begun to say that the disorders that cause pain during sex are not sexual problems at all, but instead are secondary to recurrent genital pain that makes sex uncomfortable (Binik, Bergeron, & Khalife, 2007). Some women with this dysfunction seem to be fearful about sexual intercourse or other forms of vaginal penetration, and they have misconceptions about the delicacy of the vaginal lining, believing that it can be easily injured. Other women with vaginismus seem overly dependent on others or feel personally incompetent, although in general they do not seem to show unusually high levels of psychological distress (Basson, 2008; Payne et al., 2005; Reissing et al., 2004).

Vaginismus is the major cause of unconsummated marriages (marriages in which sexual intercourse has not taken place). Because it interferes with sexual intercourse so blatantly, it is one of the sexual dysfunctions for which heterosexual couples are more likely to seek treatment (Jeng et al., 2006; Ozdemir et al., 2008). Some heterosexual couples, however, adopt alternative methods of sexual expression that are mutually pleasurable without intercourse. There are even documented cases of pregnancy resulting from semen being deposited near the vagina of women with vaginismus, without coitus actually having taken place. This should serve as

vaginismus (vadg-ih-NISS-muss) involuntary contraction of the outer vaginal musculature when vaginal penetration is attempted.

a further warning to those who rely on withdrawal as a birth control method. It is not unusual for women who experience vaginismus to have had an unpleasant or forced early sexual experience. For example, those who have not been told that first intercourse may generate some pain and bleeding if a hymen is present may have a traumatic experience or may assume that it will be more painful than it is in actuality.

Vaginismus is now considered to be one of the *sexual pain disorders*. The term used for pain that is experienced persistently during sexual intercourse is **dyspareunia.** Some research suggests that women with dyspareunia may have some level of aversion and anxiety concerning intercourse. They also may have some physiological condition, including dryness of the vagina caused by antihistamines or other drugs, infection of the clitoris or vulval area, injury or irritation in the vagina, or tumors of the internal reproductive organs. Anxiety or fear about pain during sex can be expressed through contractions of the vaginal musculature and lack of arousal. However, it has also been suggested that these problems should not be considered sexual dysfunctions at all but rather *genital pain disorders* that may interfere with sex. The pain produced by vulvodynia, for example, can interfere with sexual arousal and enjoyment. In this model, the source of the pain would be explored medically before any concerns about sexual function are addressed. There is evidence that women with dyspareunia often can experience genital sexual arousal even though they may not be as aware of it subjectively (Ayling & Ussher, 2008; Binik, 2005; Brauer, Laan, & Kuile, 2006; Farmer & Meston, 2007; Meana & Lykins, 2009).

Gay men who participate in anal intercourse sometimes experience pain that inhibits their sexual enjoyment. It appears that this **anodyspareunia** is associated with the depth of anal penetration and rate of thrusting and with anxiety or embarrassment about the sexual activity. Lack of adequate lubrication often seems to play a role in generating the problem. As with vaginismus, men with anodyspareunia may have experienced the problem all their lives, have significant anxiety about it, and avoid being the receptive partner in sex for long periods of time as a result. As a way of coping, half of the affected men in one study restricted their anal sexual activities to being the insertive partner (Damon & Rosser, 2005).

Orgasmic Disorder

Lifelong orgasmic disorder, in which an individual has never been able to achieve an orgasm, is more common in females than in males. It has been estimated that from 5 to 18 percent of women are unable to reach orgasm through any form of stimulation, and that about 25 percent of women have experienced at least some difficulty reaching orgasm within the previous year (Heiman, 2007). However, it is essential when diagnosing an orgasmic problem to determine whether the individual actually has become sexually aroused and whether adequate stimulation has been maintained. Some people, particularly women, experience lack of arousal and therefore are not likely to achieve orgasm (Basson et al., 2003; Basson, 2008). There are very few documented cases of men who have never been able to reach orgasm even through masturbation. On the other hand, NHSLS data showed that between 5 and 14 percent of men reported some level of difficulty in reaching orgasm, at least in particular situations (Laumann et al., 1994).

There has been some speculation about why men experience this orgasmic disorder. One theory is that these men are so focused on their partners' pleasure or have so many conflicting feelings about sexual pleasure that they have what might be called a numb erection. In other words, even though they have no difficulty with erection, they do not experience many of the subjective sensations of sexual arousal and stimulation associated with orgasm. It surely is true that many of the positive sensations of orgasm have psychological components as well as physical ones (Mah & Binik, 2005).

Orgasmic disorder is among the most common problems women bring to therapists. It has been demonstrated that women with orgasmic disorder tend to have more negative attitudes toward sex, greater discomfort in communicating about sex, and higher levels of guilt over sexual matters. For women, sexual intercourse holds many different and complex meanings, some of which seem to inhibit orgasm. Women in societies with fewer prohibitions on female sexual involvement and where sexual expression is permitted and even encouraged are less likely to experience orgasmic inhibition (Birnbaum, 2003; Meston et al., 2005).

Before reading further, can you think of some reasons why premature ejaculation might occur?

Premature Ejaculation: Lack of Ejaculatory Control

About one-quarter to one-third of men surveyed in various studies have indicated that they have problems with reaching orgasm too quickly (Byers & Grenier, 2003; Laumann et al., 2005). Yet it would not be scientifically acceptable to assume that a substantial number

dyspareunia recurrent or persistent genital pain related to sexual activity.

anodyspareunia pain associated with anal intercourse.

of those men were dysfunctional and were experiencing what is termed **premature ejaculation (PE),** also called rapid ejaculation (RE). As with much sexual behavior, the line between normal function and dysfunction is not absolute. It may be largely culturally determined. For example, in East Bay, Melanesia, a man who took more than 30 seconds to ejaculate after intromission would assume he had a problem.

In Western cultures, a male is considered dysfunctional if he persistently and recurrently ejaculates too rapidly for his own or his partner's sexual enjoyment, usually with minimal sexual stimulation, and is so consistently unable to exert ejaculatory control that one or both of them consider it a problem. There has been speculation that men who ejaculate rapidly might have a greater degree of penile sensitivity than other men, but research has not supported that conclusion. It has also been proposed that some men who ejaculate quickly may have a hypersensitivity of the sympathetic nervous system that renders it difficult for them to be aware of the sense of ejaculatory inevitability that typically alerts males that they are about to reach orgasm. There is evidence from twin studies that there may be a genetic basis for the problem (Jern et al., 2009).

Under laboratory conditions involving manual stimulation by a female laboratory worker or by a vibrator affixed to the underside of the penis, most men seem to ejaculate within a relatively brief period of time. Men who have previously self-reported PE seem to take less time to ejaculate than do males used as controls. Some complaints about PE seem to rest in exaggerated expectations about how long a sexual experience should actually last, and affected men are more critical about their performance than their partners tend to be (Byers & Grenier, 2003).

In another study, a sample of 1,587 men was divided into two groups: those who met the *DSM* criteria for PE and those who did not (non-PE). The men and their partners were given stopwatches and asked to keep a written record of the amount of time it took the men to reach orgasm during vaginal intercourse. The median time for the PE group was 1.8 minutes and for the non-PE group it was 7.3 minutes. However, there was a time overlap between the two groups of 2 to 4 minutes, suggesting that time might not be the best criterion for identifying PE. The men and their partners had also been asked about the degree of voluntary control the man seemed to have over ejaculation, and this turned out to be a better predictor of how long they lasted during intercourse. Indications of better voluntary control were correlated with longer intervals in reaching orgasm (Patrick et al., 2005).

So PE may not be related to timing as much as it is to a lack of voluntary control over the ejaculatory reflex. This is not surprising when we consider some typical ways males learn about their sexual responses. Most boys have begun masturbating with some regularity by age 15, yet they usually have done so with little accurate sex information and a measure of guilt. Therefore, they may develop a pattern of stimulating themselves relatively rapidly, reaching orgasm in a hurry. For some men, this rapid response might become habitual. The intense arousal typical of most males' first shared sexual experiences leads them to ejaculate quickly in these instances.

The end result of this conditioning can be a linear approach to their own sexual responsiveness. Some men progress from the absence of arousal through the stages of sexual excitement and directly to orgasm, with little hesitation or modulation along the way. There is also evidence that anxiety plays a role in initiating rapid ejaculatory response, and physiological propensities may well be involved. Men may feel disappointed and frustrated by their lack of control, but because they are still experiencing the pleasure of orgasm they may not be urgently motivated to seek help with the problem. Often it is their partners, who are just building their own sexual arousal when these men ejaculate, who are most distressed. Continuing problems with PE in a sexual partnership can generate conflict and further sexual dysfunction between the two people. Partners who become angry and disillusioned due to continuing patterns of PE in the other partner may themselves begin to experience loss of interest in and arousal for sex (Byers & Grenier, 2003; Hobbs et al., 2008; Symonds et al., 2003).

Postejaculatory Pain

Postejaculatory pain is a type of male dyspareunia, or recurrent painful sex, that results from a muscle spasm problem that can occur either during ejaculation or immediately after. This is a relatively uncommon problem, apparently caused by involuntary contraction of the ejaculatory musculature and some other associated muscles. Occasionally, the cremasteric muscles that help control suspension of the testes in the scrotum are also involved. The result is intense pain following ejaculation. It usually subsides within a few minutes, but it can last longer.

Men who experience postejaculatory pain often develop a pattern of general sexual avoidance. Because their sexual activities end unpleasantly and uncomfortably, they may begin developing problems with erection or orgasm. Although the immediate cause of the pain is muscular spasm, there seem to be deeper psychological roots to the disorder. Many

Real People

Rudy: Struggling with Rapid Ejaculation

Rudolph's friends call him Rudy, and he is usually the life of the party. He is also considered to be a real player with women, but not one who is at all ready to settle down. He is an outstanding soccer player and has been thinking of becoming a coach someday.

In fact, Rudy does not believe that he has been very successful with women at all, primarily because during his sexual encounters he finds it very difficult to postpone orgasm for long. It is not unusual for him to ejaculate almost immediately upon penetration. He finds this frustrating and embarrassing. He has tried several remedies in an attempt to slow down his sexual responses. For a while, he tried thinking negative thoughts and conjuring up foul images, hoping it would distract him. He has tried biting the inside of his mouth or pinching his arm to create physical discomfort. Neither of these approaches proved effective. Seeing some anesthetic cream advertised to delay ejaculation, he sent for a

supply. Although the cream made the head of his penis feel somewhat numb, it did nothing to slow down his orgasm.

Recently, Rudy has found himself wanting to avoid sex with women altogether because the result is so discouraging. It almost doesn't seem worth it, and he is afraid that women may be talking about his poor performance among themselves. He has heard some of his male friends joke about having similar problems, but they sound more like one-time events rather than continuing difficulties. He is not sure what to do and can't imagine how a marital relationship will ever work for him.

Given what you have learned in this chapter, what would you recommend to Rudy? Does he have to be "stuck" with this sexual dysfunction, or can he do something about it? What would you do if you or your partner were experiencing this problem?

---

men who experience postejaculatory pain harbor guilt about sexual pleasure, are ambivalent about their relationships, and hold on to repressed anger and resentment. Such inner conflict can add to concerns about experiencing pain and create a continuing cycle of pain associated with ejaculation.

■ Causes of Sexual Dysfunctions

The causes of any one person's sexual problems may be quite complex and may involve overlapping physical, emotional, and relational components. Our understanding of the causes of functional sexual problems is based mostly on clinical observations from which some generalizations may be drawn. For example:

1. Sexual dysfunctions are often caused by multiple factors. In deciding how to treat a sexual dysfunction, a clinician must consider the range of factors that may be involved.
2. Some factors that cause sexual dysfunctions are of a *predisposing nature,* meaning that they are

biological characteristics or prior life experiences that have established some vulnerability for eventual sexual disorders. A disease such as diabetes or a history of childhood sexual abuse may predispose an individual to a sexual dysfunction. *Precipitating factors,* such as alcoholism or job stress, may then trigger it during a sexual encounter. Finally, *maintaining factors,* such as continuing relational problems or illness perpetuate the sexual dysfunction over time.

3. Causes of sexual dysfunctions may also be classified into several frames of reference. They may be inherently *biological* or *medical,* resulting from organic disturbances of the sexual response cycle. Dysfunctions often are *substance-induced,* precipitated either by the abuse of alcohol or drugs or by the side effects of prescription medications. They may be *psychological,* meaning that the processes of the mind, such as the stresses of performance pressure or sexual inhibition factors, disturb the neurophysiological pathways of sexual response. Or they may stem from a person's *social* context, growing out of relational tensions and poor communication.

Investigating Medical Causes

Prior to forming a firm treatment plan for a sexual dysfunction, any potential organic cause for the problem, such as an illness or anatomical defect, should be investigated. This may require an examination by a physician, including relevant laboratory testing. Nonmedical sex therapists, especially those working in private practice, require a physical examination by a physician when a client's symptoms raise some suspicion of a possible organic disorder. In such cases, referral is made to a physician.

Although dysfunctions such as PE rarely seem to be rooted in illnesses per se, the possibility of genetic and organic causes exists. Usually, only if the onset of ejaculatory control problems is abrupt, following a long period of good functioning, are various potential neurological or urological disorders investigated. The same might be said for vaginismus. It rarely has a *direct* organic cause; however, there are many diseases that can cause genital pain during sex, and pain often is the original stimulus that plays a part in the development of vaginismus. In treating vaginismus, it must be determined whether any painful conditions are present that could further aggravate the muscular contractions of the vagina (Binik, Bergeron, & Khalife, 2007; Pukall, Binik, & Khalife, 2004).

Sexual desire and arousal seem to be more susceptible to interference by physical problems. Any sort of illness characterized by general malaise, fever, or exhaustion can cause desire disorders, male ED, or female sexual arousal disorder. Because rather complex circulatory and neurological mechanisms are involved in arousal, any medical condition that interferes with these mechanisms will inhibit arousal. Spinal cord injury and blocked or diseased arteries leading to the genitals are common causes of arousal dysfunctions. Diabetes often leads to the development of conditions that affect arousal, including impaired erection of the penis and vaginal dryness. High blood pressure, obesity, and testosterone deficiency are implicated in desire and arousal difficulties in both sexes (Diaz-Arjonilla et al., 2009; Espositio et al., 2008; Hall et al., 2008; Ponholzer et al., 2008).

Any painful condition in the body can interfere with the sexual response cycle, including heart conditions, lower back pain, sexually transmitted disease (STD) or other infection, and specific genital conditions such as cysts. Painful adhesions around the clitoris, for example, may make it difficult for a woman to reach orgasm. Urinary incontinence and other disorders of the pelvic floor musculature are associated with reduced sexual arousal, infrequent orgasm, and pain during sex (Handa et al.; Helzisouer, 2008). Male orgasmic disorder has few organic causes, although general systemic illness can interfere with orgasmic capacity.

In the past few decades, there has been some evidence that the pubococcygeus (PC) muscle, deep in the pelvis, must have good tone to permit a full orgasmic experience, particularly in women. Exercises to strengthen the PC muscle have been developed, often called Kegel exercises after the man who first suggested their use. He and subsequent researchers have claimed that women who strengthen this muscle are more able to build voluntarily the muscular tension that helps trigger orgasm. Some books on male sexuality have suggested that men's orgasmic responses can be heightened by strengthening the PC muscle as well.

Multiple sclerosis, Parkinson's disease and other neurological disorders, endocrine gland diseases, lung disease, kidney disorders, AIDS, and cancer are a few of the other illnesses that can precipitate sexual dysfunctions (Siegel, Schrimshaw, & Lekas, 2006; Warkentin, Gray, & Wassersug, 2006). Sometimes it is the individual's psychological reaction to a disease that actually precipitates the dysfunction. For example, women who have had gynecologic cancer often have reduced levels of sexual desire and arousal following treatment. People who have suffered a heart attack may be fearful of the exertion connected with sexual activity. It has also been found that sexual dysfunction often occurs in men with kidney disease who have to undergo regular dialysis treatment (Barsky, Friedman, & Rosen, 2006; Brotto et al., 2008). It is simplistic to view psychological and physical causes as mutually exclusive. Often, it is a combination of the two that leads to problems with erection. Table 18.2 summarizes some of the possible sexual consequences of various physical conditions that can lead to sexual dysfunctions.

Alcohol, Drugs, and Medications

Many people experience their first sexual arousal problems after having drunk too much alcohol. Like other depressant drugs, such as barbiturates and narcotics, alcohol may at first lower inhibitions and cause people to feel an increased sexual desire. As concentration of the drug builds in the body, however, the physiological responses of sexual arousal are inhibited, leading to poor sexual performance. Some people believe that alcohol relieves sexual dysfunctions and even use it for self-treatment when, in fact, it actually is more likely to cause the dysfunctions or make them worse. Men who are heavy smokers are also about 50 percent more likely to experience ED than are nonsmokers (George & Stoner, 2001; Natali et al., 2005; Shiri et al., 2005).

Table 18.2	*Organic Conditions That Can Cause Sexual Dysfunctions*
Sexual Dysfunction	**Potential Organic Causes**
Hypoactive sexual desire disorder	Diseases, abnormalities, or tumors of the pituitary gland Diseases of the immune system Infections, abnormalities, or tumors of the testes or ovaries Chronic kidney or liver disease, adrenal insufficiency, diabetes, hypothyroidism, Parkinson's disease, certain types of epilepsy, and strokes Diseases associated with chronic pain, debility, anxiety, or depression
Male erectile disorder	Congenital abnormality of or later injury to penis Multiple sclerosis or spinal cord injury Arteriosclerosis or blockage of blood vessels in penis Endocrine gland disease, especially if there is a testosterone deficiency Diabetes (probably impairs circulatory and neurological mechanisms of erection)
Female sexual arousal disorder	Estrogen deficiency, causing lack of vaginal lubrication Injury or disease of the central nervous system Multiple sclerosis, amyotrophic lateral sclerosis, alcoholic neuropathy Endocrine gland insufficiency, especially thyroid, adrenals, or pituitary Diabetes
Vaginismus	Factors that may cause pain or discomfort, such as previous surgery or vulvovaginal infection Endometriosis Rigid hymen or hymenal tags
Premature ejaculation	No documented organic causes, except the anxiety that may accompany various physical complaints
Female orgasmic disorder	Severe malnutrition, vitamin deficiencies Disease or injury of the spinal cord Diabetes Deficiency of thyroid, adrenals, or pituitary
Male orgasmic disorder	Injury to nervous system Parkinson's disease, multiple sclerosis, diabetes, alcoholism, uremia
Postejaculatory pain	Prostate infection or enlargement Infections of the epididymis or vas deferens Urethritis Other diseases of the penis

Sources: Data from H. S. Kaplan, *The Evaluation of Sexual Disorders,* New York: Brunner/Mazel, 1983; J. P. Wincze and M. P. Carey, *Sexual Dysfunction: A Guide for Assessment and Treatment,* New York: Guilford Press, 1991; N. McConaghy, *Sexual Behavior: Problems and Management,* New York: Plenum Press, 1993; and *Diagnostic and Statistical Manual (DSM-IV),* Washington, D.C.: American Psychiatric Association, 1994.

Many mood-altering or hallucinogenic drugs seem to have unpredictable effects on sexual functioning. Stimulant drugs, such as amphetamines, sometimes enhance sexual awareness in small dosages but interfere with sexual responsiveness when consumed in larger quantities. Some recreational drugs—such as marijuana, LSD, and cocaine—are often reported to enhance sexual experiences when taken in highly erotic situations with positive expectations. However, the same drugs also are capable of compounding negative moods and may even magnify preexisting sexual disorders (see Figure 18.5). The placebo effect undoubtedly plays a major role here. In addition, drugs such as marijuana and cocaine may at first enhance sexual satisfaction but with chronic use begin to interfere with sexual responsiveness and pleasure. Use of anabolic steroids for muscle building has been found to be associated

with increased erectile problems for males (Johnson, Phelps, & Cottler, 2004).

Prescribed medications may affect people's sex lives by producing changes in the level of interest in sex, diminishing general erotic pleasure, or altering the reactions of the genitals. Some medications used to treat high blood pressure can cause arousal disorders. Anti-ulcer medications and certain drugs for migraine headaches have been associated with disorders of hypoactive sexual desire and arousal. Antidepressant medications frequently cause a reduction in sexual desire, arousal, or orgasmic capability, although some new classes of antidepressant drugs may avoid the sexual side effects. Some men who take phenothiazine tranquilizers are alarmed to find that they no longer experience ejaculation of semen at the time of orgasm. Other antipsychotic drugs may interfere with arousal and the triggering of orgasmic responses. The adverse sexual effects of

FIGURE 18.5   *Marijuana and Sexual Functioning*

Sensations of touch and taste generally are enhanced by smoking marijuana, but any increase in sexual desire may be as much a function of psychological expectation as of the drug. Testosterone and sperm levels may be reduced in some men by smoking marijuana, but the total effect on sexual functioning is not completely known. This youth in the Netherlands can easily buy and smoke marijuana in coffee shops.

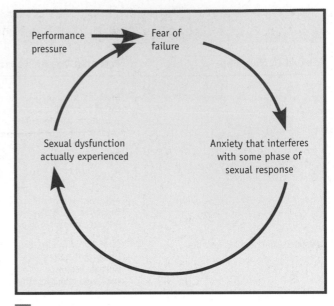

FIGURE 18.6   *Vicious Circle of Sexual Dysfunction*

Some people may be more prone than others to feeling the pressure that society exerts to perform sexually. These real or imagined pressures may result in fear of performing adequately and ultimately may produce sexual dysfunction.

medications are usually reversed with a change in dosage or discontinuation of the drug (Balon & Segraves, 2008; Bolton, Sareen, & Reiss, 2006; Frohlich & Meston, 2005a; Knegtering et al., 2006).

Describe some emotional/psychological factors that you think might have an influence on sexual functioning. Be sure to include factors that influence male sexual functioning and factors that influence female sexual functioning.

Psychological Factors: The Pressure to Perform

In the mid-1700s, an English physician by the name of Dr. John Hunter wrote this brief description of how he treated a man with ED:

> I told him that he was to go to bed with this woman but first promise himself that he would not have any connection with her for six nights, let his inclinations and powers be what they would: which he engaged to do. About a fortnight after, he told me that this resolution had produced such a total alteration in the state of his mind that the power soon took place, for instead of going to bed with fear of inability, he went with fears that he should be possessed with too much desire. And when he had once broken the spell, the mind and powers went on together.

Dr. Hunter's approach clearly demonstrates his intuitive understanding of how performance pressures can create enough stress to interfere with sexual function.

Socially imposed standards of sexual performance reach almost mythical proportions for some people. The media add to the myths by suggesting that those who are physically attractive have sex all the time. People become convinced that all normal men get rock-hard erections on demand and have sex for hours without reaching orgasm. They become convinced that all women must have size 5 bodies and flowing, windblown hair, and that they writhe about in the throes of one orgasm after another. Both women and men may become so concerned about their body image that they are too preoccupied to experience the pleasure of sexual touch and intimacy, and they may actually avoid sexual encounters.

Stage fright is not an uncommon reaction to any situation in which a good performance is expected. It is just this kind of anxiety that can generate the typical vicious circle of sexual dysfunction that is depicted in Figure 18.6. This pattern can turn what would have been an isolated sexual incident into a continuing cycle of sexual dysfunction. A term commonly used to describe the stage fright associated with sexual performance pressure is **spectatoring.** Instead of being able

spectatoring term used by Masters and Johnson to describe self-consciousness and self-observation during sex.

Real Student Voices: Men

■ The first time it happened, I made an excuse to my girlfriend that I was just too tired. When it happened again, I really started to get worried and she started to ask questions. I was thinking about taking Viagra, but after talking it over with a counselor, I realized that I just needed to relax and stop worrying. My girlfriend was very helpful and understanding once I told her what was going on. Before long, I was back to normal and very relieved!

■ The first few times I had sex with a partner, I was practically done before we got started. It was embarrassing and disappointing. By consulting a book, I was able to learn some techniques for slowing down, and they worked. It's much better now.

■ This doesn't happen every time, but sometimes no matter how hard I try, I can't seem to come. A few times, I've just given up eventually. My girlfriend doesn't mind. Why should she? It can be very frustrating though.

to relax and lose themselves in the sensual delights of the sexual experience, individuals may constantly seem to be outside themselves, wondering how they are doing and judging their sexual expertise as if they were spectators at someone else's sexual event. These sorts of reactions may even be more common in people with panic disorder or social phobia. Performance anxieties may be rooted in an excessive desire to please a partner, or in potential negative consequences of sex, such as being caught while engaged in the act or fear of pregnancy or disease (Hartmann et al., 2008; Nobre & Pinto-Gouveia, 2006).

Cognitive and emotional states can affect sexual functioning, although the research in this area has had mixed results. It does seem clear that for most people, depression can lower sexual desire and potential for sexual arousal, but it may not affect orgasm significantly (Bodenmann & Ledermann, 2008; Kuffel & Heiman, 2006; Nobre & Pinto-Gouveia, 2008).

Relationships and Sexual Functioning

Many dysfunctions are rooted in problems that have developed in the partners' relationship. Lack of communication and intimacy is one of the most widespread of these problems. Communication difficulties may be relatively uncomplicated at first, such as a failure to let one's partner know what types of stimulation are particularly enjoyed and which might better be avoided. Left to fester, these minor relational irritants may turn into more serious and lasting conflicts. Communication problems also may originate at much deeper levels and be symptomatic of severe distur-

bances and a lack of compatibility between the two people involved. As soldiers serve in wars, such as the conflicts in Afghanistan or Iraq, it may take time following their return to loved ones to be able to reestablish satisfying sexual intimacy (Clement, 2002; Melby, 2008, October).

Loving relationships have complex dynamics, and both the joys and discord in any relationship get played out in the sexual arena. When power struggles result in two people trying to wrest control from each other, sex will be affected. If one partner is having trouble trusting the other or if some pattern of outright rejection has emerged, the possibilities of sexual dysfunction are enormous. Sometimes, subtle games of sexual sabotage, which result in turning off one's partner, will mask some deeper relational problems. These factors also may be important in determining the outcome of therapy for sexual problems. It is likely that the happier and stabler a couple's relationship is, the more positive and satisfactory the outcome of therapy will be (Bianchi-Demicheli & Zutter, 2005; Cameron, Rosen, & Swindle, 2005; Yasan & Gurgen, 2009).

■ Treating Sexual Dysfunctions

Sometimes treating a sexual dysfunction can be quite straightforward. Other times, an effective therapeutic outcome depends on the untangling of a complex web of medical, psychological, and relational causes. Because some people may be reluctant to seek professional help for such personal problems, home remedies and patent medicines often claim to cure various

Real Student Voices: Women

■ My boyfriend gets more upset than I do when I can't orgasm. I've never been able to orgasm very often during intercourse, and I'm not sure I ever really have. Lately, I've even been faking it, because it's easier than dealing with him trying to work at giving me one after I feel done.

■ Lack of desire on my part is definitely a problem for us. I really enjoy physical intimacy and cuddling, but not so much for the sexual aspects. I like seeing my partner get sexual pleasure, but it doesn't matter that much if I do. We both wish I enjoyed sex more for sex's sake.

■ I manage to avoid intercourse or even having anybody touch my vagina. The first couple of times I had intercourse were very painful, and I've become scared to even try it. I seem to be able to satisfy boys in other ways, but I wonder when I want to have intercourse if I'll be able to.

---

sexual dysfunctions. In the United States, males who are concerned about their lack of ejaculatory control sometimes purchase sprays or creams to be applied to the penis. Men also have invented their own techniques for delaying ejaculation, such as wearing more than one condom or masturbating just prior to shared sex. They may try to distract themselves by thinking about other things, clenching their fists, or biting themselves to produce pain, or they may devise a number of other techniques. Unfortunately, such home remedies may only intensify the problem.

Effective treatment for sexual dysfunction must be designed for particular clients and the causative factors that seem to be playing a role. The intricacies of each individual and each relationship must be taken into consideration. It is, in a sense, an art to be practiced with skill and creativity. Several different approaches are employed.

Medical Treatments

The use of various medical regimens in the treatment of sexual dysfunctions is becoming increasingly popular. In both men and women who have deficient levels of androgenic hormones such as testosterone have some influence on sexual arousal, the administration of androgens can increase sexual desire in both sexes. It is critical that men who are treated in this manner have no underlying prostate cancer, since androgens can stimulate the growth of malignant cells (Anders et al., 2005; Barqawi & Crawford, 2006; Hwang & Lin, 2008). Some herbal preparations, although typically not subjected to rigorous scientific testing, have been used with modest success in treating certain sexual dysfunctions, including ED and female arousal disorder, although it is also believed that the placebo effect

may be the most important factor in such success (Ito et al., 2006; Meston, Rellini, & Telch, 2008; Rowland, Burek, & Macias, 2007).

See "Viagra and Sexual Pharmacology" on SexSource Online.

One of the most significant medical advances to treat sexual dysfunctions has been a class of drugs that began with sildenafil, popularly known as Viagra. There are two other similar medications whose potential effectiveness lasts for longer time periods: vardenafil, sold as Levitra, and tadalafil, marketed under the name Cialis. These medications work by inhibiting the action of a particular enzyme, which in turn prolongs the effects of cyclic GMP, the substance that relaxes smooth muscles within the erectile tissues of the penis, allowing blood to flow in and cause erection.

Studies with Viagra and the other medications demonstrate that they can be very effective in treating male ED and that, in most cases, side effects are minor and quite tolerable. Men who have heart disease that necessitates taking medications such as nitroglycerin for chest pain generally should not use these medications. A proportion of men who begin treatment with some form of ED medication do not continue taking the drug, often because of disappointing results or lack of sexual interest and desire. Testing continues on drugs that may enhance erection by working on the central nervous system rather than penile circulation (Hellstrom, 2008; Jiann et al., 2006; Moemen et al., 2008; Rosen et al., 2006). Other medications and topically applied creams have been tried with women, but there is evidence that simply enhancing the ability of the female genitals to become engorged with blood will not go far enough in resolving most female arousal problems (Padma-Nathan et al., 2003; Rosen, 2002).

If the oral medications for ED do not prove effective, there are two other pharmaceutical approaches that are often tried. In one method, the man injects the muscle relaxant *papaverine* or one of several similar chemicals that act locally within the spongy erectile tissues of the penis to produce erection. A newer variation of this approach involves insertion of a tiny suppository of the chemical into the urethral opening, where it is absorbed into the spongy tissues. The erection may last for an hour or more, even after the man has ejaculated and feels finished with sexual activity. These treatments seem to work best when combined with appropriate sex therapy or psychotherapy (Aubin et al., 2009; Slob et al., 2002).

Although pharmaceutical companies continue to work on developing a drug that might help with PE, antidepressants are sometimes prescribed "off-label" for the condition because they are known to slow sexual response in many men. The success of such treatment has not been widely studied. Implants of hyaluronic acid that is injected into the penile glans has met with some success in slowing the ejaculatory response, but more study will be needed of this technique (Kwak et al., 2008; Powell & Wyllie, 2009; Waldinger, 2008).

Controversies abound about the dangers of the medicalization of sex therapy, especially for women, but the evidence would suggest that medical treatments can indeed be effective, especially when combined with other modes of therapy. Development of new medications surely will continue, because the

pharmaceutical companies are aware of the strong market available for drugs that treat sexual dysfunctions (Althof, 2007; Rowland, 2007).

Biomedical Engineering Devices

Various sorts of vacuum and constriction devices and splintlike penile supports have been used to help men achieve and maintain erections, but their long-term usefulness has not been proved. They also may hold some potential risk of penile damage. Studies of the vacuum devices, in which the penis is "pumped up" within a vacuum tube and then a band is placed around the base, have shown the technique to be close to 90 percent successful, with a relatively low patient dropout rate. A device to produce some level of suction and vacuum effect on the clitoris has proved to help some women with sexual arousal problems enjoy sexual stimulation and orgasm more consistently (Billups et al., 2001; Raina et al., 2005).

In cases where some organic damage makes erection impossible, prosthetic devices have been developed that can simulate erection. They fall into two main categories: semirigid, bendable rods that are surgically inserted into the penis, leaving the organ in a somewhat permanently erect state that can be bent up or down as needed, and inflatable tubular devices that can produce an artificial erection when surgically implanted into the penis (see Figure 18.7). Tens of thousands of these prosthetic devices are now being implanted annually, and they have a relatively high success rate. They have been relatively free of mechanical problems and produce nearly normal flaccid

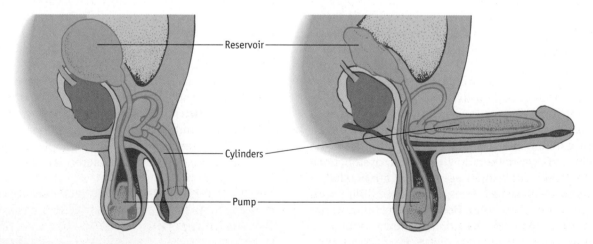

FIGURE 18.7 *Penile Implant*

If impotence cannot be cured, particularly if it is caused by an organic physical condition such as damage to the spine, intercourse can be made possible by the implantation of a mechanical device. A reservoir filled with fluid is implanted in the abdomen. It is connected by tubes to a pump inserted into the scrotum and in turn connected to two cylinders that are slipped into the penis. To cause an erection, the man pumps the fluid into the cylinders; to reverse the procedure, he releases a valve in the pump, returning the fluid to the reservoir.

and erect states. The success of the surgery is higher when it is done at a surgical center of excellence where the procedure is done frequently (Henry et al., 2009; Simmons & Montague, 2008).

Psychotherapeutic Treatments

Although some dysfunctions clearly are rooted in negative emotional states such as anxiety, fear, guilt, or depression, others may be generated by unconscious psychological conflict. *Psychotherapy* is a term that applies to any one of a number of techniques that may help people resolve psychological problems and reduce stress. In recent years, short-term forms of psychotherapy have gained in popularity, and they can be quite effective when they incorporate the specific treatment exercises developed in behavioral therapy. Psychotherapy approaches often benefit when appropriate medical treatments are used as well (Bianchi-Demicheli & Zutter, 2005; Heiman, 2002).

Many therapies recommend that a sexual dysfunction be viewed as a shared problem to be worked on as a couple. Sexual symptoms often are the outcome of a mixture of experiences that both partners have had during their lifetimes. Sometimes a dysfunction in one partner actually can act as a relationship or personal stabilizer for the other. For example, a man whose partner has vaginismus does not have to face any anxieties he himself may have about erectile function. *Couples therapy* provides a venue in which partners can work together to improve their sexual life and focus on the relational dynamics that may play a role in the dysfunction and the therapy process.

There has always been some interest in *hypnotherapy* as a way to resolve sexual problems. Hypnosis may be considered a form of psychotherapy that uses relaxation and suggestion in helping willing individuals to change. Patients also need to be able to use mental imagery for mentally "rehearsing" situations that formerly have made them tense or anxious. There are case studies dealing with the successful use of hypnosis in treating a variety of sexual problems and dysfunctions, often as an adjunct to other treatment techniques (Kandyba & Binik, 2003). Reports on the outcomes of hypnotherapy for sexual dysfunctions tend to be anecdotal, and larger studies are needed.

Group therapy has been used successfully with some sexual dysfunctions. Behavioral techniques are usually prescribed for individual patients within the course of treatment, and the group setting provides the information and support for the sharing of feelings necessary to a successful outcome. Group methods have been used successfully with women with orgasmic disorder and also have been successful for men with ED or problems with ejaculatory control. Even so, most people express a preference for individual treatment over group strategies, perhaps because the issues involved are often deeply personal.

Cognitive-behavioral therapy has been the predominant mode of sex therapy. Behavioral approaches typically involve the use of **systematic desensitization,** through which the patient gradually unlearns the tension-producing behaviors that are causing problems. More desirable behaviors then are learned to replace the old, dysfunctional patterns. Behavior therapy techniques still provide the basic structure for most psychotherapy-based sex therapy today. When used to treat sexual disorders, behavior therapy entails physical activities that are practiced at home by the couple or, in some cases, as self-help approaches by single clients.

Combination Treatment Approaches

Given the growing consensus that sexual dysfunctions may have many different causes and that treatment strategies must be tailored to the specific needs of individual clients and couples, there is increasing acceptance of combining treatment approaches in sex therapy. Psychotherapeutic approaches usually have been eclectic in nature, borrowing from a variety of strategies to develop a treatment plan. With the emergence of apparently effective medical treatments, it is even more crucial to consider these methods in working with sexually dysfunctional people. Psychotherapies and relational counseling can help stabilize personal and relational issues that are contributing to the problem. Treatment for sexual dysfunction is a rapidly changing field, and its future well-being may depend largely on creative linking among the many disciplines that deal with sexual dysfunctions (McCarthy & Fucito, 2005; Steggall, Fowler, & Pryce, 2008).

What Is a Sex Therapist?

The term **sex therapist** refers to professionals who have been trained to treat sexual dysfunctions, although they usually work within a broader context. Sex therapists and counselors attempt to restore sex to its natural context. They can help people enrich their sex lives, overcome lack of interest in sex, improve

cognitive-behavioral therapy psychotherapeutic method that uses techniques to change patterns of thinking and behavior; often employed in sex therapy.

systematic desensitization step-by-step approaches to unlearning tension-producing behaviors and developing new behavior patterns.

sex therapist a professional trained in the treatment of sexual dysfunctions.

communication about sex between partners, and overcome specific sexual problems.

*See "Taking a Sexual History"
on SexSource Online.*

Because human sexuality is a multidisciplinary field, professionals enter sex therapy from a variety of backgrounds. Some have had medical training as physicians or nurses. Some hold degrees in psychology, counseling, or social work. A few have a background in pastoral counseling and hold degrees in religion. A national organization called the American Association of Sexuality Educators, Counselors and Therapists (AASECT) took the lead in establishing criteria with which to certify individuals who have met appropriate training standards as sex therapists. These criteria include not only a degree in one of the helping professions but also specialized coursework in human sexuality and many hours of practical therapy work under the supervision of an already certified sex therapist. AASECT was also the first organization to formulate specific ethics statements concerning how therapists were to conduct their work.

One way to find a good sex therapist is to ask two or more trusted professionals whom they would recommend for help with a sexual problem. Sometimes an individual's name will come up more than once—probably a good sign. It is always appropriate to check out a sex therapist's qualifications directly as well. Consumers may wish to ask about degrees and training, the therapy model used, the kinds of records kept, the costs, and whether the therapist is certified to practice sex therapy by any professional group. It is important to watch out for any sort of unethical behavior, such as a suggestion by a sex therapist that nudity or sexual relations with the therapist might be appropriate. It should be expected, however, that a therapist will ask rather specific and intimate questions about sexual functioning in evaluating the problem and deciding on a course of treatment.

A few clinics still accept only couples for treatment and provide therapists of both sexes to work with those couples (see Figure 18.8). Most sex counselors or therapists in private practice work alone and work effectively with couples. Other issues arise in specific situations. Lesbian or gay male couples may seek a therapist of the same gender. Some counselors and therapists also will agree to work with clients who do not have a partner available or whose partners are unwilling to participate in therapy. They use audiotapes, videotapes, DVDs, online services, or other techniques designed specifically for clients without sexual partners. Certain types of problems are amenable to self-help approaches and do not necessarily require the cooperation of a partner.

■ **FIGURE 18.8** *Co-therapist Counseling Session*

In the earlier days of sex therapy, couples often were seen by a co-therapy team consisting of a woman and a man as therapists. This model is still sometimes used today, because it may bring a more balanced approach to couples therapy. Even when there is only a single therapist, it usually is considered most beneficial to involve both partners in counseling sessions. This provides an opportunity for both to cooperate in finding solutions to their relational and sexual difficulties.

AASECT may be contacted at www.aasect.org and can provide listings of certified counselors and sex therapists or of clinics that treat sexual dysfunctions. Anyone consulting a sex therapist should expect treatment that is conducted in a respectful, caring, and dignified manner. Potential medical problems should be investigated carefully. It is even appropriate to set some tentative deadlines for meeting certain goals. If the results are not forthcoming, reevaluating the worth of the therapy process is certainly in order.

■ Behavioral Approaches to Sex Therapy

As they worked on developing a model for the effective treatment of sexual dysfunctions, Masters and Johnson (1970) realized that they needed techniques to help patients relax and restructure their behavior. They were faced with the challenge of modifying psychological, relational, and cultural factors that were interfering with the physiological sexual responsiveness of the human body. They also believed that sexually dysfunctional couples needed to learn more about their shared sexual feelings and responses. Behavioral techniques, involving the learning of tension-reduction techniques and more effective approaches to sharing sexual activity, are a mainstay of sex therapy. They are often used in combination with medical or psychotherapeutic techniques. This section provides an overview of how such techniques are employed in therapy.

Basic Goals of Cognitive-Behavioral Sex Therapy

Cognitive-behavioral therapy essentially involves un-learning ineffective, dysfunction-promoting thinking patterns and sexual behaviors and replacing them with more positive, healthier patterns of thought and behavior. Sex therapists attempt to move their clients toward achieving the following major goals.

Gaining a Sense of Permission to Value One's Sexuality

Those suffering from a sexual dysfunction often have long-standing problems with accepting and feeling good about their sexuality. They may feel guilty and uncomfortable about their sexual feelings, attractions, and behaviors. Therefore, a primary principle of therapy is to impart a sense of permission to be sexual and to see sexuality as a natural and healthy aspect of the human personality. Sex therapists encourage their clients to place a higher priority on sexual enjoyment, including saving time to work on sexual activities. Many sex therapy exercises are designed to help clients get in touch with their bodies, their sexual sensations, and their emotional reactions in more positive ways than ever before.

Taking More Time to Make Sexual Activity a Priority

We live in busy times, and in many relationships both partners have careers. Sexual activity eventually may take a backseat to other priorities in a couple's life together. In sex therapy, time is set aside specifically for working on sexual problems. Therapists usually assign suggested activities and recommend a time frame for their completion. All of this helps the couple develop a higher priority for improving sexual functioning.

Eliminating Elements That Are Blocking Full Sexual Response

Sexual arousal and response is a normal part of every human being. People seek therapy when something has interfered with some aspect of that functioning. Sex therapists, then, must work to eliminate whatever elements are hindering full and satisfying sexual functioning. This means tracking down the causes of a dysfunction and then mapping out a realistic plan for correcting them. This can be a simple matter of teaching new relaxation and communication techniques, or it may necessitate in-depth counseling or medical treatment. If alcohol or drugs are part of the problem, they need to be eliminated or reduced. Guilt reactions or other emotional blocks also must be overcome.

Reducing Performance Pressures

Sex therapy clients must learn how to stop focusing on their own sexual performance in order to relax and allow their built-in sexual responses to happen. Behavior therapy provides techniques to distract people from this spectatoring and to keep their body as relaxed as possible. Partners are helped to change their emphasis from feeling responsible for giving each other pleasure to working on their own sexual responsiveness and satisfaction.

Using Specific Sexual Exercises to Develop More Positive Ways of Functioning Sexually

Sex therapists have devised activities that actually can help a sexually dysfunctional person overcome the problem. These exercises are done at home in private and are prescribed in a very systematic manner, with the opportunity available to talk about reactions after each stage. The sex therapist makes decisions about how quickly to move through increasingly intimate stages of therapy, based on how both partners are progressing and feeling. These sexual exercises constitute the most significant route to behavioral change in this form of treatment.

Self-Help Approaches

For some people who cannot visit a therapist, a number of self-help approaches have been found to be effective. Sex therapists often assign self-help approaches to overcoming sexual dysfunctions when a partner is not available. Although the low cost and complete privacy of self-directed sex therapy are obvious advantages, many sexual dysfunctions can be treated effectively only by professional therapists. Self-help approaches cannot reach some of the more complex personal and relational factors at the root of many dysfunctions. The self-help guides may provide solid information, offer a positive beginning for many who want to improve their sexual functioning, and help people be more relaxed in discussing sexual matters (Lankveld, 2009).

The two most common self-help themes use body exploration and masturbation. Many sexually dysfunctional men and women have never taken the time to become acquainted with their sex organs or even with other parts of their bodies. Body exploration exercises involve viewing one's own body in a mirror and touching oneself to elicit emotions and physical sensitivities. Sometimes, very specific directions are given to discover how various parts of the genitals respond to stimulation. Masturbation exercises have proved especially useful in treating female orgasmic disorder and

PE. Once the orgasmic capability is well established through these self-help techniques, the woman gradually integrates her partner into the activities, teaching that partner the best approaches for bringing her to orgasm (Zamboni & Crawford, 2002).

As mentioned earlier, long-standing patterns of hurried masturbation may contribute to ejaculatory control difficulties in men. Self-help techniques that encourage men to slow down masturbation have been effective in establishing more modulated forms of male sexual response that can carry over to better orgasmic control with partners (Carufel & Trudel, 2006). Masturbatory self-help techniques may not be as suitable for individuals or cultural groups who have negative feelings or attitudes about masturbation.

Other self-help techniques can be used to reorient negative thought patterns about sex, rehearse fantasized situations with partners ahead of time, or learn patterns of distraction to prevent excessive focusing on one's own sexual functioning. There is general agreement among sex professionals that self-awareness, along with an ability to explain one's own sexual needs and idiosyncrasies to a partner, is an important aspect of healthy sexual adjustment.

Partnership Approaches

Therapists view the partnered therapeutic experience as important in the couple's growing ability to communicate and function together sexually. Partnership approaches involve graduated steps. Therapists usually need to be satisfied that each of the following stages of treatment has been mastered successfully before moving on to the next:

1. Learning how to enjoy and relax with each other's bodies while providing nonsexual touching and massage.
2. Providing each other with light genital stimulation designed to be pleasurable but without any pressure to respond with arousal or orgasm.
3. Learning how to communicate and physically guide each other toward the most effective forms of sexual stimulation.
4. Using specific exercises to reverse dysfunctional patterns and establish a pattern of sexual interaction that is pleasing and satisfying to both partners.

To accomplish the first three goals, sex therapists prescribe various types of mutual body-pleasuring exercises, often called **sensate focus.** These exercises provide couples with an opportunity to develop and appreciate physical sensations generated by each other, bringing a physically pleasurable dimension into the relationship. An added positive outcome of sensate focus can be the reduction of power imbalances in the sexual relationship that may be making one partner feel pressured, untrusting, coerced, or misunderstood (see Figure 18.9).

> **sensate focus** early phase of sex therapy treatment, in which the partners pleasure each other without employing direct stimulation of the sex organs.

■ FIGURE 18.9 *Mutual Pleasuring or Sensate Focus*

The first phase of sensate focus activities involves nongenital touching. The partners are instructed to be together nude, in as warm and relaxed a private setting as possible. They take turns giving and receiving gentle physical pleasuring that is not overtly sexual. With a minimum of talking, the giver provides caring touches to the partner in the form of massaging, tracing, and rubbing. The receiver has only to relax and enjoy the pleasant sensations, giving positive verbal suggestions for changing the form of touching if anything is in any way uncomfortable or irritating. After an agreed-upon length of time, the partners switch sensate focus roles. For many couples, these exercises represent the first time they have experienced physical intimacy and pleasure without the tensions and pressures of performing sexually.

In the second phase of sensate focus, light genital stimulation and teasing are encouraged, but without the goal of generating sexual arousal. The couple is, in fact, instructed not to allow sensate focus activities to lead to sexual overtures. Instead, they are told simply to enjoy and accept whatever sexual arousal may occur and then let it dissipate. Again, sexual sensations are made a part of a relaxed, nonpressured context that nonetheless is pleasurable.

A final phase of mutual pleasuring typically involves some form of guiding procedure in which one partner carefully shows the other how to give her or him optimum sexual stimulation. This will involve some mutually comfortable position in which one partner can place a hand directly on top of the other partner's hand, carefully guiding it in genital stimulation. Figure 18.10 shows a position that is often used for women who are teaching their partner how to provide clitoral stimulation to produce orgasm.

The number of times a couple participates in the various phases of sensate focus may depend on how well and how rapidly they seem to be proceeding. Therapists watch for potential resistance or other difficulties in the therapy process and try to ensure that positive results have been achieved at each stage before couples move on. It is crucial for couples to build a pattern of successful sexual experiences, reversing the series of failures they have been experiencing with the dysfunction. Therefore, during the early stages of treatment, therapists usually ask their clients to avoid sexual intercourse or other forms of sexual interaction that have been beset with problems. Gradually, as confidence and relaxation are achieved with each new goal, the couple may progress to those activities.

Based on the assumption that most heterosexual couples in Western cultures use—and perhaps prefer—an intercourse position with the man on top and the woman on the bottom, the typical strategy usually begins with the woman in the top position. This seems to be effective in treating women's dysfunctions, because

FIGURE 18.10 *A Guiding Position for Clitoral Stimulation*

it affords women a greater sense of control over the sexual experience. It also is useful in dealing with male dysfunctions, because the men are more able to relax while their partner takes more responsibility for controlling the sexual action. This is an interesting commentary on some typical causative factors behind female and male dysfunctions: Women often feel somewhat compromised by male-dominant intercourse positions, whereas men feel threatened by the weight of responsibility for sexual expertise usually assigned to them.

An excellent intermediate step on the way to developing confidence with man-on-top intercourse is a face-to-face, side-by-side position that enables both partners to be more physically relaxed. Neither is called on to support his or her full weight (see Figure 18.11), resulting in a greater sense of shared responsibility. Sex therapists find that many heterosexual couples enjoy this position so much that they begin to use it on a more regular basis than their former man-on-top intercourse position.

The final therapeutic step, provided it is the desired goal of the couple, is to succeed in their usual intercourse position, with all sexual functioning proceeding as desired. Coital position may play a role in improving sexual functioning in other ways as well. Women who experience painful intercourse often are helped by positions in which they are on top. Again, the process of overcoming a couple's sexually dysfunctional patterns involves systematically desensitizing them to the tension-producing difficulties of the past,

■ **FIGURE 18.11**   *Side-by-Side Position for Relaxation*

conditioning them instead to the practice of new, more mutually comfortable and enjoyable behaviors.

Some Specific Behavioral Methods

Aside from the general techniques already described, some specific behavioral exercises are used in treating each sexual dysfunction. A full survey of these techniques is not appropriate to this text, but we will explore some examples.

Vaginismus involves the contraction of vaginal muscles, making entry of the penis difficult or impossible for heterosexual intercourse. Because this dysfunction is almost always caused by fears and earlier negative experiences, it is crucial to help the woman learn how to develop a positive pattern of relaxation and pleasure with insertion into her vagina. The behavioral exercises used in therapy therefore are designed to reduce tension and permit relaxation and pleasure. They might begin with the suggestion that the woman privately examine the opening of her vagina with a mirror, using some relaxation technique at the same time. Gradually, over a period of time, she will insert her little finger (or a small dilator made of plastic or rubber) into her vagina, also using a relaxation technique. Eventually, the partner's fingers will be used in the same manner, but under the complete control and direction of the woman. In the final phases of treating vaginismus, the man's penis will be slowly and gently inserted, again with the woman having full control over how deeply and for how long this takes place. The ultimate goal is to achieve relaxed and pleasurable intercourse (Kabakci & Batur, 2003).

In the past, men tended to try to delay ejaculation by focusing on anything but their pleasurable sexual sensations. In treating PE in males today, the emphasis is on helping the man become aware of the inner subjective sensations that signal when his ejaculation is imminent. Men have pelvic sensations just prior to

ejaculating that they need to identify so that they may take some action to prevent orgasm before they have passed the point of no return. There is a simple behavioral technique that many sex therapists suggest. Known as the stop-start method, it asks men to stop any stimulation when they feel the sensation of imminent orgasm. The sensations completely disappear quite rapidly, and stimulation may then be resumed. Most sex therapists recommend that the partner use slow manual stimulation on the man's penis at first, in a convenient position (see Figure 18.12). The man gives a prearranged signal to halt the stimulation when he feels orgasm approaching. Some therapists recommend that the partner add the squeeze technique at this point, giving a firm squeeze to the head of the penis (see Figure 18.13). This further diminishes the sensation of imminent orgasm. Over a period of time, the man gains better control over his ejaculatory reflex and feels increased confidence in his sexual abilities. These behavioral exercises lead to the development of sexual patterns through which the man is able to slow down and modulate his stimulation so that he takes longer to reach orgasm. He then gradually integrates his control into sexual relations with his partner. During intercourse, the squeeze technique may be applied at the base of the penile shaft so that the penis need not be withdrawn.

Various specific behavioral methods are used in the treatment of the other sexual dysfunctions. These help couples unlearn the conditions that have led to their sexual dissatisfaction and learn how to function normally and happily. Sometimes sex therapy aids people in saying no to sex when they are not in the mood, or to particular sexual activities they do not enjoy. Sex therapists attempt to meet the specific objectives of their clients as realistically as possible.

Current research seems to support the contention that sex therapy can be highly effective when it is carried out over a full course of treatment by well-trained

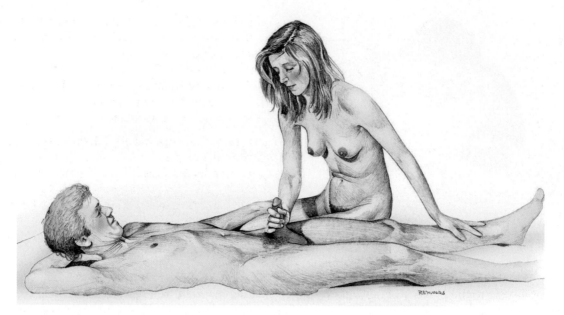

FIGURE 18.12 *Manual Stimulation of the Penis*

A

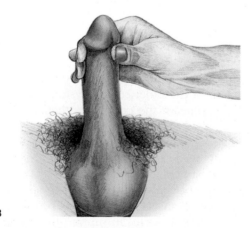

B

FIGURE 18.13 *The Squeeze Technique: Base of Penis (A) and Head of Penis (B)*

professional therapists and when various methods of treatment are combined to meet the needs of particular clients. It is also important for couples to have realistic expectations of what their sexual interactions will be like (McCarthy & Metz, 2008).

What are your opinions about sex therapy as one of the helping professions?

The Broad View of Sex Therapy

Most sexologists would agree that sex therapists should do more than restore desired sexual functioning. They also should provide a foundation for change within the individual and the relationship so that a relapse can be prevented, and they should assist in the correction of any medical condition that may lie behind the problem. To this end, partners also may be helped to establish more realistic sexual expectations of each other (see Figure 18.14). Sex therapists can maximize the continuing value of treatment by encouraging occasional use of the behavioral techniques employed during therapy, continuing medical treatment as appropriate, and follow-up visits if necessary.

Human sexual conduct is interwoven into our sociocultural values, and sex has become associated with a variety of moral issues. When professionals intervene in the sexual lives and decision making of their clients, many ethical issues need to be confronted. Work in sexology demands the highest standards of professionalism, confidentiality, and informed consent. Yet professionals also bring their own sets of values to their work, and these values often influence the decisions they make about ethical behavior.

FIGURE 18.14 *Mutual Understanding*

Sex therapists emphasize that communication and understanding are very important factors in solving sexual problems and developing a relationship that is complete and fulfilling for both partners.

Sex therapists face their share of ethical dilemmas. For example, if in the course of treating a married couple for some sexual dysfunction one of the partners privately admits to having contracted an STD during a recent extramarital affair, the therapist must make some decisions. Confidentiality has been promised, yet the other partner may be at risk of catching the disease. The extramarital affair may have implications for the entire treatment process that cannot be explored as long as it is kept secret. The therapist may feel drawn into a dishonest alliance with the partner who had the affair. Deciding how to proceed is an exercise in professional ethics for the therapist.

AASECT has promulgated its own code of ethics. It deals with several basic issues designed to protect clients against exploitation or incompetence. The central points of this code are as follows:

1. Sex therapists must receive adequate training and have a strong sense of integrity.
2. Strict standards of confidentiality must govern a sex therapist's work, and there should be no disclosure of information about a client without the individual's written consent.
3. Because clients are often in a vulnerable position, their welfare is to be protected and respected at all times by the therapist.

Codes of ethics establish general guidelines but can never offer hard and fast advice to be used in a specific complicated case. It is crucial for sex therapists, as well as others in the helping professions, to understand their own value systems regarding sexuality and to sort through the moral and ethical issues involved.

While sex therapy methods were at first limited to heterosexual couples, the approaches have now been successfully employed with lesbian and gay male couples. There has been less study of the sexual dysfunctions of same-gender couples, and more research is needed to establish the most effective therapeutic protocols (Nichols & Shernoff, 2007; Sandfort & Keizer, 2002).

As professional organizations and state legislatures continue to examine these issues and to clarify standards for the training and licensing of sex therapists, the efficacy, methods, and ethical standards of the therapy process will be further developed.

Chapter Summary

1. Individual differences in sexual responsiveness should be considered to determine whether a true dysfunction is present. Some believe that personal distress must be part of a diagnosis.
2. Sexual performance standards may become debilitating pressures and unfair expectations for men and women.
3. Levels of sexual satisfaction among cultures seem dependent on levels of gender equality and male dominance in the culture. Cultures also have their own folk remedies for treating dysfunctions.
4. Scientific terminology indicates that sexual dysfunctions may be lifelong or acquired, generalized or situational.
5. Sexual dysfunctions represent disruption of one or more of the three major phases of the human sexual response cycle: desire, arousal, or orgasm, and may be mediated by both excitatory and inhibitory processes.

6. Determining the incidence of sexual dysfunctions is complicated by the fact that even people who report problems with sexual functioning are not necessarily distressed by them.

7. Individuals who have impaired desire for sexual gratification may be experiencing hypoactive sexual desire disorder (HSDD), which is also characterized by lack of sexual interest.

8. Sexual aversion disorder is characterized by fears about and avoidance of sexual activity.

9. Arousal problems are expressed as male erectile disorder (ED), involving interference with penile erection, or female sexual arousal disorder, characterized by an absence of vaginal lubrication and other signs of sexual excitement. Arousal disorder in women may be subjective and/or genital.

10. Vaginismus is caused by anxiety and avoidance, along with reflexive contractions of the pelvic musculature that result in difficulty with insertion into the vagina. Pain associated with sexual activity is called dyspareunia.

11. Both men and women can experience orgasmic disorder.

12. Premature or rapid ejaculation in males is the most common sexual dysfunction in men and may have genetic roots.

13. Postejaculatory pain is an uncommon disorder involving involuntary muscular spasms that create pain associated with ejaculation in males.

14. Sexual dysfunctions may have causes at several different levels involving predisposing factors, precipitating factors, and/or maintaining factors. Causes also may be biological or medical (organic), substance-induced, psychological, or social/relational.

15. Performance pressures and difficulties in relationships (such as poor communication) are often at the root of sexual dysfunctions, although possible medical causes must first be investigated.

16. Alcohol, drugs, and medications can play a role in interfering with sexual response.

17. Cognitive-behavioral techniques are widely used as treatment by sex therapists, although medical treatments are becoming more common.

18. Oral medications such as Viagra, Levitra, or Cialis, or injection and suppository applications directly into the penis, are sometimes used to treat ED. Medications are also used to treat premature ejaculation and HSDD.

19. Prosthetic and vacuum devices have also been used with some cases of ED.

20. Psychotherapeutic treatments including couples therapy, hypnosis, and group therapy have been used to treat sexual dysfunctions. Combining psychotherapy with medication is becoming a more common treatment mode.

21. The ethics, training standards, and certification standards for sex therapists have been developed by national professional organizations.

22. Behavioral sex therapy helps dysfunctional individuals unlearn ineffective behaviors and replace them with positive, effective patterns of sexual interaction.

23. Specific homework exercises are assigned to those in therapy, using both self-help and partnership approaches.

24. Sex therapy raises certain ethical issues and dilemmas, and specific guidelines have been developed for the ethical conduct of therapists.

25. Sex therapy has gradually been made available to same-gender couples.

Glossary

A

abnormal anything considered not to be normal (that is, not conforming to the subjective standards a social group has established as the norm).

abstinence-only-until-marriage sexuality education an approach to educating young people that emphasizes the need to abstain from sexual relations until marriage, essentially the "just say no" philosophy.

acquaintance (date) rape a sexual encounter forced by someone who is known to the victim.

acquired dysfunction a difficulty with sexual functioning that develops after some period of normal sexual functioning.

acquired immunodeficiency syndrome (AIDS) a fatal disease caused by a virus that is transmitted through the exchange of bodily fluids, primarily in sexual activity and intravenous drug use.

activating effect the direct influence some hormones can have on activating or deactivating sexual behavior.

acute urethral syndrome infection or irritation of the urethra.

adolescence period of emotional, social, and physical transition from childhood to adulthood.

affectional relating to feelings or emotions, such as romantic attachments.

afterbirth the tissues expelled after childbirth, including the placenta, the remains of the umbilical cord, and fetal membranes.

agenesis (absence) of the penis (ae-JEN-a-sis) a congenital condition in which the penis is undersized and nonfunctional.

amniocentesis (am-nee-oh-sen-TEE-sis) a process by which medical problems with a fetus can be determined while it is still in the womb; a needle is inserted into the amniotic sac, amniotic fluid is withdrawn, and fetal cells then are examined.

amnion (AM-nee-on) a thin membrane that forms a closed sac around the embryo; the sac is filled with amniotic fluid, which protects and cushions the embryo.

anal intercourse insertion of the penis into the rectum of a partner.

androgen (ANN-dra-gin) a male hormone, such as testosterone, that affects physical development, sexual desire, and behavior. Testosterone is produced by both male and female sex glands and influences each sex in varying degrees.

androgen insensitivity syndrome (AIS) a developmental condition in which cells do not respond to fetal androgen, so that chromosomally male (XY) fetuses develop external female genitals; there is also a feminization of later behavioral patterns.

androgyny (an-DROJ-a-nee) the presence of high frequencies of both masculine and feminine behaviors and traits in the same individual.

andropause one of the terms applied to a vaguely defined period in male midlife characterized by hormonal, psychological, and sexual changes.

anejaculation lack of ejaculation at the time of orgasm.

anodyspareunia pain associated with anal intercourse.

anorchism (a-NOR-kiz-um) rare birth defect in which both testes are lacking.

anti-Müllerian hormone (AMH) secretion of the fetal testes that prevents further development of female structures from the Müllerian ducts.

aphrodisiacs (af-ro-DEE-zee-aks) foods or chemicals purported to foster sexual arousal; believed to be more myth than fact.

areola (a-REE-a-la) darkened, circular area of skin surrounding the nipple of the breast.

artificial insemination injection of the sperm cells of a male into a woman's vagina, with the intention of conceiving a child.

asceticism (a-SET-a-siz-um) usually characterized by celibacy, this philosophy emphasizes spiritual purity through self-denial and self-discipline.

asexuality a condition characterized by a low interest in sex.

assisted reproductive technology (ART) a collection of laboratory techniques that have been developed to help couples overcome infertility problems and have children, usually through bypassing one of the usual biological pathways to pregnancy or gestation.

autoeroticism self-generated sexual arousal and pleasure.

autoerotic asphyxiation accidental death from pressure placed around the neck during masturbatory behavior.

autofellatio (aw-toh-fe-LAY-she-o) the act of a male providing oral stimulation to his own penis, which most males do not have the physical agility to perform.

autogynephilia (otto-guy-nuh-FEEL-ee-ah) a tendency found in some males to become sexually aroused by obsessive thoughts and images of being female and having female attributes, or even female sex organs.

B

Bartholin's glands (BAR-tha-lenz) small glands located in the opening through the minor lips that produce some secretion during sexual arousal.

benign prostatic hyperplasia (BPH) enlargement of the prostate gland that is not caused by malignancy.

bestiality (beest-ee-AL-i-tee) sexual contact between a human being and an animal.

biological essentialism a theory that holds that human traits and behaviors are formed primarily by inborn biological determinants such as genes and hormonal secretions, rather than by environmental influences.

biphobia prejudice, negative attitudes, and misconceptions toward bisexual people and their lifestyles.

birth canal term applied to the vagina during the birth process.

birthing rooms special areas in the hospital, decorated and furnished in a nonhospital way, set aside for giving birth; the woman remains here to give birth rather than being taken to a separate delivery room.

bisexual refers to some degree of sexual activity with or attraction to members of both sexes.

blastocyst the ball of cells, after five days of cell division, that has developed a fluid-filled cavity in its interior and has entered the uterine cavity.

body dysmorphic disorder a preoccupation with imagined or slight defects in one's bodily appearance that may focus on weight, muscularity, skin appearance, the genitals, or other body parts.

bond the emotional link between parent and child created by cuddling, cooing, and physical and eye contact early in the newborn's life.

bondage tying, restraining, or applying pressure to body parts as part of sexual arousal.

brothels houses of prostitution.

bulbourethral glands another term for Cowper's glands.

C

call girls highly paid female prostitutes who work by appointment with an exclusive clientele.

cantharides (kan-THAR-a-deez) a chemical extracted from a beetle that, when taken internally, creates irritation of blood vessels in the genital region; can cause physical harm.

case study an in-depth look at a particular individual and how he or she might be helped to solve a sexual or other problem. Case studies may offer new and useful ideas for counselors to use with other patients.

catharsis theory the suggestion that viewing pornography provides a release for sexual tension, thereby preventing antisocial behavior.

celibacy (SELL-a-buh-see) choosing not to share sexual activity with others.

central arousal system internal components of sexual arousal that come from the cognitive and emotional centers of the brain, forming the foundations for sexual response.

cervical cap a device that is shaped like a large thimble and fits over the cervix; not a particularly effective contraceptive because it can dislodge easily during intercourse.

cervical intraepithelial neoplasia (CIN) (ep-a-THEE-lee-al nee-a-PLAY-zhee-a) abnormal, precancerous cells sometimes identified in a Pap smear.

cervix (SERV-ix) lower "neck" of the uterus that extends into the back part of the vagina.

cesarian section a surgical method of childbirth in which delivery occurs through an incision in the abdominal wall and uterus.

chancroid (SHAN-kroyd) an STD caused by the bacterium *Hemophilus ducreyi* and characterized by sores on the genitals, which if left untreated, could result in pain and rupture of the sores.

child molesting sexual abuse of a child by an adult.

chlamydia (kluh-MID-ee-uh) now known to be a common STD, a major cause of urethritis in males; often presents no symptoms in females.

chorion (KOR-ee-on) the outermost extraembryonic membrane, essential in the formation of the placenta.

chorionic villi sampling (CVS) a technique for diagnosing medical problems in the fetus as early as the eighth week of pregnancy; a sample of the chorionic membrane is removed through the cervix and studied.

cilia microscopic, hairlike projections that help move the ovum through the fallopian tube.

circumcision (SIR-cum-sizh-uhn) in the male, surgical removal of the foreskin from the penis.

climax another term for orgasm.

clinical research the study of the cause, treatment, or prevention of a disease or condition by testing large numbers of people.

clitoridectomy (clih-torr-ih-DECK-tah-mee) surgical removal of the clitoris; practiced routinely in some cultures.

clitoris (KLIT-a-rus) sexually sensitive organ found in the female vulva; it becomes engorged with blood during arousal.

clone the genetic-duplicate organism produced by the cloning process.

cloning a process by which a genetic duplicate of an organism is made either by substituting the chromosomes of a body cell into a donated ovum or by separation of cells early in embryonic development.

cognitive-behavioral therapy psychotherapeutic method that uses techniques to change patterns of thinking and behavior; often employed in sex therapy.

cognitive susceptibility state of mind, identified by psychological and situational factors, that suggests a readiness for or predisposition toward initiating sexual activity.

cohabitation living together and sharing sex without marrying.

coitus (KO-at-us or ko-EET-us) heterosexual, penis-in-vagina intercourse.

coitus interruptus a method of birth control in which the penis is withdrawn from the vagina prior to ejaculation.

coming out acknowledging to oneself and others that one is lesbian, gay, or bisexual.

comprehensive sexuality education an approach to educating young people about human sexuality that includes information about sexuality but also encourages clarifying values and developing decision-making skills.

compulsive sexual behavior recurrent sexual urges, fantasies, and behaviors that distress a person and may interfere with the person's daily life.

Comstock Laws federal legislation enacted in the 1870s prohibiting the mailing of information about contraception.

conception the process by which a sperm unites with an egg, normally joining 23 pairs of chromosomes to establish the genetic blueprint for a new individual. The sex chromosomes establish its sex: XX for female, and XY for male.

confluence theory assumes that cultural influences and specific individual personality variables determine how particular people are affected by pornography.

congenital adrenal hyperplasia (CAH) a genetic disorder that masculinizes chromosomal females and seems to lead to a masculinization of behavior as well.

consensual adultery permission given to at least one partner within the marital relationship to participate in extramarital sexual activity.

consent freely given verbal or nonverbal communication expressing a sense of willingness to engage in sexual activity.

contraceptive implants contraceptive method in which hormone-releasing rubber cylinders are surgically inserted under the skin of the woman.

controlled experiment research in which the investigator examines what is happening to one variable while all other variables are kept constant.

coprophilia sexual arousal connected with feces.

core gender identity a child's early inner sense of its maleness, femaleness, or ambivalence, established prior to puberty.

corona the ridge around the penile glans.

corpus luteum cell cluster of the follicle that remains after the ovum is released; secretes hormones that help regulate the menstrual cycle.

Cowper's glands two small glands in the male that secrete an alkaline fluid into the urethra during sexual arousal.

cruising searching for a casual sexual partner, usually used in reference to gay males.

cryptorchidism (krip-TOR-ka-diz-um) condition in which the testes have not descended into the scrotum prior to birth.

cultural absolutism the view that behaviors and values from one's culture of origin should be disregarded once the individual is living in a new culture. The expectation is that immigrants must abide by the cultural standards of their new country.

cultural relativism the view that one's culture determines what is normal and acceptable and that judgments about those standards should take into consideration their cultural origins.

cunnilingus (kun-a-LEAN-gus) oral stimulation of the clitoris, vaginal opening, or other parts of the vulva.

cyclic GMP a secretion within the spongy erectile tissues of the penis that facilitates erection.

cystitis (sis-TITE-us) a nonsexually transmitted infection of the urinary bladder.

D

DAX-1 the region on the X chromosome that seems to play a role in sexual differentiation.

deoxyribonucleic acid (DNA) (dee-AK-see-rye-bow-new-KLEE-ik) the chemical in each cell that carries the genetic code.

Depo-Provera an injectable form of progestin that can prevent pregnancy for one or three months.

desire phase Kaplan's term for the psychological interest in sex that precedes physiological sexual arousal.

deviation term applied to behaviors or orientations that do not conform to a society's accepted norms; often has negative connotations.

DHT-deficiency syndrome a condition in which chromosomally male fetuses have underdeveloped male genitals and may be identified as girls at birth. However, at puberty they begin to develop masculine secondary sex characteristics and seem to maintain masculine patterns of behavior.

diaphragm (DY-a-fram) a latex rubber cup, filled with spermicide, that is fitted to the cervix by a clinician; the woman must learn to insert it

properly for full contraceptive effectiveness.

differential socialization the process of treating boys and girls differently as they are growing up.

dihydrotestosterone (DHT) a chemical produced by the fetal testes that promotes further development of the testes, scrotum, and penis in the fetus.

dilation the gradual widening of the cervical opening of the uterus prior to and during labor.

dilation and curettage (D & C) a method of induced abortion in the second trimester of pregnancy that involves a scraping of the uterine wall.

dilation and evacuation (D & E) a method of induced abortion in the second trimester of pregnancy that combines suction with a scraping of the inner wall of the uterus.

discrimination the process by which an individual extinguishes a response to one stimulus while preserving it for other stimuli.

disorders of sex development (DSD) a more scientific term now being applied to those with combinations or ambiguities of female and male anatomical structures.

dyadic withdrawal (die-ADD-ik) the tendency of two people involved in an intimate relationship to withdraw socially for a time from other significant people in their lives.

dysmenorrhea (dis-men-a-REE-a) painful menstruation.

dyspareunia recurrent or persistent genital pain related to sexual activity.

E

E. coli bacteria naturally living in the human colon that often cause urinary tract infection.

ectopic pregnancy (ek-TOP-ik) the implantation of a blastocyst somewhere other than in the uterus, usually in the fallopian tube.

effacement the thinning of cervical tissue of the uterus prior to and during labor.

ejaculation muscular expulsion of semen from the penis.

ejaculatory inevitability the sensation in the male that ejaculation is imminent.

ELISA the primary test used to determine the presence of HIV in humans.

embedded sexual media depictions of sexual activities or issues within a larger context of a plot and scene.

embryo (EM-bree-o) the term applied to the developing cells when, about a

week after fertilization, the blastocyst implants itself in the uterine wall.

endometrial hyperplasia (hy-per-PLAY-zhee-a) excessive growth of the inner lining of the uterus (endometrium).

endometriosis (en-doe-mee-tree-O-sus) growth of the endometrium out of the uterus into surrounding organs.

endometrium interior lining of the uterus; the innermost of three layers.

endorphins (en-DORE-fins) brain secretions that act as natural tranquilizers and pain relievers.

epidemiological (e-pe-dee-mee-a-LA-i-cahl) referring to the branch of medical science that deals with the incidence, distribution, and control of disease in a population.

epididymis (ep-a-DID-a-mus) tubular structure on each testis in which sperm cells mature.

epididymitis (ep-a-did-a-MITE-us) inflammation of the epididymis of the testis.

episiotomy (ee-piz-ee-OTT-a-mee) a surgical incision in the vaginal opening made by the clinician or obstetrician to prevent the baby from tearing the opening in the process of being born.

epispadias (ep-a-SPADE-ee-as) birth defect in which the urinary bladder empties through an abdominal opening and the urethra is malformed.

equal status contact a tenet of social network theory holding that people tend to initiate and maintain relationships with others who have similar social characteristics.

erection enlargement and stiffening of the penis as internal muscles relax and blood engorges the columns of spongy tissue.

erogenous zone (a-RAJ-a-nus) any area of the body that is sensitive to sexual arousal.

erotic target location errors (ETLEs) sexual preferences for unusual objects or unusual sexual activities.

erotica artistic representations of nudity or sexual activity.

erotocentricity (ee-ROT-oh-sen-TRIS-ih-tee) the application of ethnocentric-like judgments to sexual values and behaviors, creating the assumption that our own ways of approaching sexuality are the only "right" ways.

erotomania (air-aht-oh-MAY-nee-ah) a very rare form of mental illness characterized by a highly compulsive need for sex.

erotophilia (air-aht-oh-FEEL-i-ah) consistent positive responding to sexual cues.

erotophobia (air-aht-oh-FOBE-i-ah) consistent negative responding to sexual cues.

estrogen (ES-tro-jen) hormone produced abundantly by the ovaries; it plays an important role in the menstrual cycle.

ethnocentricity (eth-no-sen-TRIS-ih-tee) the tendency of the members of one culture to assume that their values and norms of behavior are the "right" ones in comparison to those of other cultures.

ethnography (eth-NAH-gruffy) the anthropological study of other cultures.

ethnosexual referring to data concerning the sexual beliefs and customs of other cultures.

Eurocentric (ur-oh-SEN-trick) a cultural attitudinal framework typical of people with Western European heritages.

evolutionary psychology the study of how human cognitions and behaviors have evolved to fulfill the evolutionary goal of assuring the survival of the species.

excitement the first phase of Masters and Johnson's four-phase model of the sexual response cycle, involving genital vasocongestion.

exhibitionism exposing the genitals to others for sexual pleasure.

exocytosis (ex-oh-sye-TOH-sis) the release of genetic material by the sperm cell, permitting fertilization to occur.

extradyadic relationship sharing emotional or sexual intimacy with someone other than one's primary partner.

F

facilitated sex assistance provided to a person with severe physical disabilities in order to enable them to achieve sexual pleasure through masturbation or with a partner.

fallopian tubes structures that are connected to the uterus and lead the ovum from an ovary to the inner cavity of the uterus.

fellatio oral stimulation of the penis.

female condom a lubricated polyurethane pouch that is inserted into the vagina before intercourse to collect semen and help prevent disease transmission.

female sexual arousal disorder difficulty for a woman in achieving sexual arousal.

fertilin (fer-TILL-in) a chemical in the outer membrane of a sperm that assists in attachment to the egg cell and penetration of the egg's outer membrane.

fertility awareness methods natural methods of birth control that depend on an awareness of the woman's menstrual/fertility cycle.

fetal alcohol syndrome (FAS) a condition in a fetus characterized by abnormal growth, neurological damage, and facial distortion caused by the mother's heavy alcohol consumption during pregnancy.

fetal surgery a surgical procedure performed on the fetus while it is still in the uterus or during a temporary period of removal from the uterus.

fetally androgenized females a condition in which hormones administered during pregnancy cause chromosomally female (XX) fetuses to have masculinization of the genitals and perhaps of later behavioral patterns, even though they were raised as girls.

fetishism (FEH-tish-i-zum) sexual arousal triggered by objects or materials not usually considered sexual.

fetus the term given to the embryo after two months of development in the womb.

fibroid tumors nonmalignant growths that commonly grow in uterine tissues, often interfering with uterine function.

fibrous hymen condition in which the hymen is composed of unnaturally thick, tough tissue.

follicle-stimulating hormone (FSH) pituitary hormone that stimulates the ovaries or testes.

follicles capsules of cells in which an ovum matures.

foreplay sexual activities shared in early stages of sexual arousal, with the term implying that they are leading to a more intense, orgasm-oriented form of activity such as intercourse.

foreskin fold of skin covering the penile glans; also called the prepuce.

fraternal (dizygotic) twins twins formed from two separate ova that were fertilized by two separate sperm.

frenulum (FREN-yu-lum) thin, tightly drawn fold of skin on the underside of the penile glans; it is highly sensitive.

frotteur one who practices frotteurism.

frotteurism (frah-TOUR-izm) gaining sexual gratification from anonymously pressing or rubbing one's genitals against others, usually in crowded settings.

fundus the broad top portion of the uterus.

G

G spot a vaginal area that some researchers feel is particularly sensitive to sexual stimulation when its underlying spongy tissues are engorged with blood.

gamete intrafallopian transfer (GIFT) direct placement of the ovum and concentrated sperm cells into the woman's fallopian tube to increase the chances of fertilization.

gay refers to persons who have a predominantly same-gender sexual orientation and identity. More often applied to males.

gender dysphoria (dis-FOR-ee-a) another term sometimes used to describe a gender identity disorder.

gender identity a person's inner experience of gender: feelings of maleness, femaleness, or some ambivalent position between the two.

gender identity disorder the expression of gender identity in a way that is socially inconsistent with one's anatomical sex.

gender role the outward expression and demonstration of gender identity, through behaviors, attire, and culturally determined characteristics of femininity and masculinity.

gender schema a complex cognitive network of associations and ideas through which the individual perceives and interprets information about gender.

gene therapy treatment of genetically caused disorders by substitution of healthy genes.

generalization application of specific learned responses to other, similar situations or experiences.

genetic engineering the modification of the gene structure of cells to change cellular functioning.

genital herpes (HER-peez) a viral STD characterized by painful sores on the sex organs.

gestational surrogacy implantation of an embryo created by the sperm and ovum of one set of parents into the uterus of another woman who agrees to gestate the fetus and give birth to the child, which then is given to the original parents.

glans in the male, the sensitive head of the penis; in the females, the sensitive head of the clitoris, visible between the upper folds of the minor lips.

gonadotropin-releasing hormone (GnRH) (go-nad-a-TRO-pen) hormone from the hypothalamus that stimulates the release of FSH and LH by the pituitary.

gonads sex and reproductive glands, either testes or ovaries, that produce hormones and, eventually, reproductive cells (sperm or eggs).

gonorrhea (gon-uh-REE-uh) bacterial STD causing urethral pain and discharge in males; often no initial symptoms in females.

granuloma inguinale (gran-ya-LOW-ma in-gwa-NAL-ee or-NALE) an STD characterized by ulcerations and granulations beginning in the groin and spreading to the buttocks and genitals.

H

H-Y antigen a biochemical produced in an embryo when the Y chromosome is present; it plays a role in the development of fetal gonads into testes.

hard-core pornography pornography that makes use of highly explicit depictions of sexual activity or shows lengthy scenes of genitals.

hebephilia (HEE-beh-fil-ee-a) a term being used to describe the sexual abuse of adolescents.

hedonists (HEE-don-ists) people who believe that pleasure is the highest good.

hepatitis B virus (HBV) a liver infection that frequently is sexually transmitted.

hepatitis C virus (HCV) a liver infection that may occasionally be sexually transmitted.

heterosexism the biased and discriminatory assumption that people are or should be attracted to members of the other gender.

heterosexual refers to attractions or activities between males and females.

homophobia (ho-mo-FO-bee-a) strongly held negative attitudes about and irrational fears of gay men and/or lesbians and their lifestyles.

homosexual term traditionally applied to affectional and sexual attractions and activities between members of the same gender.

hookers street name for female prostitutes.

hormone replacement therapy (HRT) treatment of the physical changes of menopause by administering

dosages of the hormones estrogen and progesterone.

hot flash a flushed, sweaty feeling in the skin caused by dilated blood vessels; often associated with menopause.

human chorionic gonadotropin (HCG) a hormone detectable in the urine of a pregnant woman.

human immunodeficiency virus (HIV) the virus that initially attacks the human immune system, causing HIV disease and eventually AIDS.

human papillomavirus (HPV) an infection causing small lesions on genital skin; certain strains of this STD increase later risks of cervical cancer.

hymen membranous tissue that can cover part of the vaginal opening.

hyperfemininity a tendency to exaggerate characteristics typically associated with femininity.

hypermasculinity a tendency to exaggerate manly behaviors; sometimes called machismo.

hypersexuality an unusually high level of interest in and drive for sex.

hypoactive sexual desire disorder (HSDD) loss of interest and pleasure in what formerly were arousing sexual stimuli.

hyposexuality an especially low level of sexual interest and drive.

hypospadias (hye-pa-SPADE-ee-as) birth defect caused by incomplete closure of the urethra during fetal development.

hypoxphilia creating pressure around the neck during sexual activity to enhance sexual pleasure.

hysterectomy surgical removal of all or part of the uterus.

I

identical (monozygotic) twins twins formed by a single ovum that was fertilized by a single sperm before the cell divided in two.

immature oocyte collection extraction of immature eggs from undeveloped follicles in an ovary, after which the oocytes are assisted to maturity by cell-culturing methods in preparation for fertilization.

imperforate hymen condition in which the hymen has no natural openings.

impotence (IM-puh-tense) difficulty achieving or maintaining erection of the penis.

in vitro fertilization (IVF) a process by which the union of the sperm and egg occurs outside the mother's body.

incest (IN-sest) sexual activity between closely related family members.

incest taboo cultural prohibitions against incest, typical of most societies.

induced abortion a termination of pregnancy by artificial means.

infertility the inability to produce offspring.

infibulation (in-fib-you-LAY-shun) surgical procedure, performed in some cultures, that seals the opening of the vagina.

informed consent the consent given by research subjects, indicating their willingness to participate in a study, after they are informed about the purpose of the study and how they will be asked to participate.

intersexuality a combination of female and male anatomical structures, so that the individual cannot be clearly defined as male or female.

interstitial-cell-stimulating hormone (ICSH) pituitary hormone that stimulates the testes to secrete testosterone; known as luteinizing hormone (LH) in females.

interstitial cells (in-ter-STIH-shul) cells between the seminiferous tubules that secrete testosterone and other male hormones.

interstitial cystitis (IC) a chronic bladder inflammation that can cause debilitating discomfort and interfere with sexual enjoyment.

intracytoplasmic sperm injection (ICSI) a technique involving the injection of a single sperm cell directly into an ovum; useful in cases where the male has a low sperm count.

intrauterine devices (IUDs) birth control method involving the insertion of a small plastic device into the uterus.

introitus (in-TROID-us) the outer opening of the vagina.

invasive cancer of the cervix (ICC) advanced and dangerous malignancy requiring prompt treatment.

isthmus narrowed portion of the uterus just above the cervix.

K

kiddie porn the distribution and sale of photographs and films of children or younger teenagers engaging in some form of sexual activity.

kleptomania extreme form of fetishism in which sexual arousal is generated by stealing.

L

labia majora (LAY-bee-uh mah-JOR-uh) two outer folds of skin covering the minor lips, clitoris, urinary meatus, and vaginal opening.

labia minora (LAY-bee-uh mih-NOR-uh) two inner folds of skin that join above the clitoris and extend along the sides of the vaginal and urethral openings.

labor uterine contractions in a pregnant woman; an indication that the birth process is beginning.

lactation production of milk by the milk glands of the breasts.

lactational amenorrhea method (LAM) a natural hormonal method of birth control that relies on the fact that when women are breastfeeding a baby exclusively and continuously, neither ovulation nor menstruation take place. It requires a strong commitment to breastfeeding.

Lamaze method (la-MAHZ) a birthing process based on relaxation techniques practiced by the expectant mother; her partner coaches her throughout the birth.

laminaria (lam-a-NER-ee-a) a dried seaweed sometimes used in dilating the cervical opening prior to vacuum curettage.

laparoscopy (lap-ar-OSK-uh-pee) simpler procedure for tubal ligation involving the insertion of a small fiber-optic scope into the abdomen, through which the surgeon can see the fallopian tubes and close them off.

laparotomy (lap-ar-OTT-uh-mee) operation to perform a tubal ligation, or female sterilization, involving an abdominal incision.

latency period Freudian concept that during middle childhood sexual energies are dormant; recent research tends to suggest that latency does not exist.

lesbian (LEZ-bee-un) refers to females who have a predominantly same-gender sexual orientation and identity.

libido (la-BEED-o or LIB-a-do) a term first used by Freud to define human sexual longing, or sex drive.

lifelong dysfunction a difficulty with sexual functioning that has always existed for a particular person.

lumpectomy surgical removal of a breast lump, along with a small amount of surrounding tissue.

luteinizing hormone (LH) (LEW-tee-in-ize-ing) pituitary hormone that triggers ovulation in the ovaries and stimulates sperm production in the testes.

lymphogranuloma venereum (LGV) (lim-foe-gran-yu-LOW-ma va-NEAR-ee-um) a contagious STD caused by several strains of *Chlamydia* and marked by swelling and ulceration of lymph nodes in the groin.

M

male climacteric one of the terms applied to a vaguely defined period in male midlife characterized by hormonal, psychological, and sexual changes.

male condom a sheath worn over the penis during intercourse that collects semen and helps prevent disease transmission.

male erectile disorder (ED) difficulty achieving or maintaining penile erection (impotence).

mammography sensitive X-ray technique used to discover small breast tumors.

marital rape a woman being forced by her husband to have sex.

masochist the individual in a sadomasochistic sexual relationship who takes the submissive role.

mastectomy surgical removal of all or part of a breast.

masturbation stimulation of one's own genitals for sexual pleasure and orgasm.

ménage à trois (may-NAZH-ah-TWAH) another name for troilism.

menarche (MEN-are-kee) onset of menstruation at puberty.

menopause (MEN-a-pawz) time in midlife when menstruation ceases.

menstrual cycle the hormonal interactions that prepare a woman's body for possible pregnancy at roughly monthly intervals.

menstruation (men-stru-AY-shun) phase of the menstrual cycle in which the inner uterine lining breaks down and sloughs off; the tissue, along with some blood, flows out through the vagina; also called the period.

midwives medical professionals, both women and men, trained to assist with the birthing process.

mifepristone (RU 486) a progesterone antagonist used as a postcoital contraceptive.

miscarriage a natural termination of pregnancy.

modeling theory a perspective that suggests that people will copy behavior they view in pornography.

molluscum contagiosum (ma-LUS-kum kan-taje-ee-O-sum) a skin disease transmitted by direct bodily contact, not necessarily sexual, and characterized by eruptions on the skin that appear similar to whiteheads, with a hard seedlike core.

monogamous sharing sexual relations with only one person.

monorchidism (ma-NOR-ka-dizm) presence of only one testis in the scrotum.

mons cushion of fatty tissue located over the female's pubic bone.

moral values beliefs associated with ethical issues, or rights and wrongs; often a part of sexual decision making.

morula (MOR-yuh-la) a spherical, solid mass of cells formed after three days of embryonic cell division.

Müllerian ducts (myul-EAR-ee-an) embryonic structures that develop into female sexual and reproductive organs unless inhibited by male hormones.

multiplier effect the combining of biological and socioenvironmental factors more and more with one another over time in the process of human development.

myometrium middle, muscular layer of the uterine wall.

N

National Birth Control League an organization founded in 1914 by Margaret Sanger to promote use of contraceptives.

necrophilia (nek-ro-FILL-ee-a) sexual activity with a dead body.

nonspecific urethritis (NSU) (yur-i-THRYT-us) infection or irritation in the male urethra caused by bacteria or local irritants.

normal a highly subjective term used to describe sexual behaviors and orientations. Standards of normalcy are determined by social, cultural, and historical standards.

normal asexuality an absence or low level of sexual desire, considered normal for a particular person.

normalization integration of mentally retarded persons into the social mainstream as much as possible.

nymphomania (nim-fa-MAY-nee-ah) a term sometimes used to describe erotomania in women.

O

obscenity depiction of sexual activity in a repulsive or disgusting manner.

onanism (O-na-niz-um) a term sometimes used to describe masturbation; the term stems from the biblical story of Onan, who practiced coitus interruptus and "spilled his seed on the ground."

oocytes (OH-a-sites) cells that mature to become ova.

opportunistic infection a disease resulting from lowered resistance of a weakened immune system.

organizing effect manner in which hormones control patterns of early development in the body.

orgasm pleasurable sensations and series of contractions that release sexual tension, usually accompanied by ejaculation in men.

orgy (OR-jee) group sex.

os opening in the cervix that leads into the hollow interior of the uterus.

osteoporosis (ah-stee-o-po-ROW-sus) disease caused by loss of calcium from the bones in postmenopausal women, leading to brittle bones and stooped posture.

ova egg cells produced in the ovary. A single cell is called an ovum; in reproduction, it is fertilized by a sperm cell.

ovaries pair of female gonads, located in the abdominal cavity, that mature ova and produce female hormones.

ovulation release of a mature ovum through the wall of an ovary.

ovum donation use of an egg from another woman for conception, with the fertilized ovum then being implanted in the uterus of the woman wanting to become pregnant.

oxytocin pituitary hormone that plays a role in lactation and in uterine contractions in response to physical intimacy and sexual satisfaction, and in initiating the birth process.

P

Pap smear medical test that examines a smear of cervical cells to detect any cellular abnormalities.

paraphiles (paraphilics) people who are drawn to one or more of the paraphilias, or behaviors characterized by non-normative sexual arousal.

paraphilia (pair-a-FIL-ee-a) a newer term used to describe sexual orientations and behaviors that vary from the norm in pathological or antisocial ways; it means "a love beside."

paraplegic a person paralyzed in the legs, and sometimes pelvic area, as the result of injury to the spinal cord.

pedophilia (pee-da-FIL-ee-a) a pathological desire to sexually abuse children.

pelvic inflammatory disease (PID) a chronic internal infection of the uterus and other organs.

penile fracture a tearing of the membrane in the penis that surrounds the three columns of spongy tissue, usually the result of severe bending of the erect penis.

penile strain gauge a device placed on the penis to measure even subtle changes in its size due to sexual arousal.

penis male sexual organ that can become erect when stimulated; it leads urine and sperm to the outside of the body.

performance standard the expectations for successful sexual functioning that people often impose on themselves or their partners. They are often unrealistic.

perimenopause the time of a woman's life surrounding menopause, characterized by symptoms resulting from reduced estrogen levels.

perimetrium outer covering of the uterus.

perinatally related to pregnancy, birth, or the period immediately following birth.

perineal area (pair-a-NEE-al) the sensitive skin between the genitals and the anus.

peripheral arousal system external components of sexual arousal that reach the brain and spinal cord from the skin, genitals, and sense organs.

Peyronie's disease (pay-ra-NEEZ) development of fibrous tissue in the spongy erectile columns within the penis.

pheromones (FAIR-oh-moans) human chemicals, the scent of which may cause an attraction or behavioral change in other individuals.

phimosis (fye-MOE-sus) a condition in which the penile foreskin is too long and tight to retract easily.

placenta (pla-SEN-ta) the organ that unites the fetus to the mother by bringing their blood vessels close together; it provides nourishment and removes waste for the developing baby.

plateau phase the stable, leveled-off phase of Masters and Johnson's four-phase model of the sexual response cycle.

plethysmograph (pleh-THIZ-magraff) a laboratory measuring device that charts physiological changes over time. Attached to a penile strain gauge, it can chart changes in penis size. This is called penile plethysmography.

polyandry (PAH-lee-ann-dree) referring to being married to more than one spouse, usually to a woman

having more than one husband; cross-culturally, less common than polygamy.

polycystic ovary syndrome (PCOS) (PAH-lee-SIS-tick) a disorder of the ovaries that can produce a variety of unpleasant physical symptoms, often because of elevated testosterone levels.

polygamy (pah-LIG-a-mee) practice, in some cultures, of being married to more than one spouse, usually referring to a man having more than one wife.

pornography photographs, films, or literature intended to be sexually arousing through explicit depictions of sexual activity.

postpartum depression a period of low energy and discouragement that is common for mothers following childbearing. Longer-lasting or severe symptoms should receive medical treatment.

preeclampsia a disorder that can arise in the latter half of pregnancy, marked by swelling in the ankles and other parts of the body, high blood pressure, and protein in the urine; can progress to coma and death if not treated.

preimplantation genetic screening examination of the chromosomes of an embryo conceived by IVF prior to its implantation in the uterus.

premature birth a birth that takes place prior to the 37th week of pregnancy.

premature ejaculation difficulty that some men experience in controlling the ejaculatory reflex, resulting in rapid ejaculation.

premenstrual dysphoric disorder (PMDD) severe emotional symptoms such as anxiety or depression around the time of menstruation.

premenstrual syndrome (PMS) symptoms of physical discomfort, moodiness, and emotional tension that occur in some women for a few days prior to menstruation.

prepuce (PREE-peus) in the female, tissue of the upper vulva that covers the clitoral shaft.

priapism (pry-AE-pizm) continual, undesired, and painful erection of the penis that lasts longer than four hours.

progesterone (pro-JES-ter-one) ovarian hormone that causes the uterine lining to thicken.

prolactin pituitary hormone that stimulates the process of lactation.

prolapse of the uterus weakening of the supportive ligaments of the uterus, causing it to protrude into the vagina.

promiscuity (prah-mis-KIU-i-tee) sharing casual sexual activity with many different partners.

prostaglandin hormonelike chemical whose concentrations increase in a woman's body just prior to menstruation.

prostaglandin and saline-induced abortions a method used in the 16th to 24th weeks of pregnancy in which prostaglandins, salt solutions, or urea is injected into the amniotic sac, administered intravenously, or inserted into the vagina in suppository form to induce contractions and fetal delivery.

prostate gland located beneath the urinary bladder in the male; it produces some of the secretions in semen.

prostatitis (pras-tuh-TITE-us) inflammation of the prostate gland.

pseudohermaphrodite a person who possesses either testes or ovaries in combination with some external genitals of the other sex.

psychosexual development factors that form a person's sexual feelings, orientation, and patterns of behavior.

psychosocial development the cultural and social influences that help shape human sexual identity.

pubic lice small insects that can infect skin in the pubic area, causing a rash and severe itching.

pubococcygeus (PC) muscle (pyub-o-kox-a-JEE-us) part of the supporting musculature of the vagina that is involved in orgasmic response and over which a woman can exert some control.

pyromania sexual arousal generated by setting fires.

Q

quadriplegic a person paralyzed in the upper body, including the arms, and the lower body as the result of spinal cord injury.

quid pro quo something gained from something given.

R

random sample a representative group of the larger population that is the focus of a scientific poll or study in which care is taken to select participants without a pattern that might bias research results.

rape engaging in a sexual act without the other individual's consent or against that individual's will.

rape trauma syndrome the predictable sequence of reactions that a victim experiences following a rape.

refractory period time following orgasm during which a man cannot be restimulated to orgasm.

reinforcement in conditioning theory, any influence that helps shape future behavior as a punishment or reward stimulus.

resolution phase the term for the return of a body to its unexcited state following orgasm.

retrograde ejaculation abnormal passage of semen into the urinary bladder at the time of ejaculation.

retroviruses (RET-ro-vi-rus-es) a class of viruses that integrate their genetic code into that of the host cell, establishing permanent infection.

Rh incompatibility condition in which a blood protein of the infant is not the same as the mother's; antibodies formed in the mother can destroy red blood cells in the fetus.

RhoGAM medication administered to a mother to prevent formation of antibodies when the baby is Rh positive and its mother is Rh negative.

rubber dam a piece of rubber material, such as that used in dental work, placed over the vulva during cunnilingus.

S

sadist the individual in a sadomasochistic sexual relationship who takes the dominant role.

sadomasochism (sade-o-MASS-o-kiz-um) refers to sexual themes or activities involving bondage, pain, or domination or humiliation of one partner by the other.

sample a representative group of a population that is the focus of a scientific poll or study.

satyriasis (sate-a-RYE-a-sus) a term sometimes used to describe erotomania in men.

scabies (SKAY-beez) a skin disease caused by a mite that burrows under the skin to lay its eggs, causing redness and itching; transmitted by bodily contact that may or may not be sexual.

scrotum (SKROTE-um) pouch of skin in which the testes are contained.

secondary abstinence choosing not to have sexual intercourse after having experienced intercourse one or more times.

secondary sex characteristics the physical characteristics of mature women and men that begin to develop at puberty.

selective reduction the use of abortion techniques to reduce the number of fetuses when there are more than three in a pregnancy, thereby increasing the chances of survival for the remaining fetuses.

self-gratification giving oneself pleasure, as in masturbation; a term typically used today instead of more negative descriptors.

self-pleasuring self-gratification; masturbation.

semen (SEE-men) mixture of fluids and sperm cells that is ejaculated through the penis.

seminal vesicle (SEM-un-al) gland at the end of each vas deferens that secretes a chemical that helps sperm become motile.

seminiferous tubules (sem-a-NIF-a-rus) tightly coiled tubules in the testes in which sperm cells are formed.

sensate focus early phase of sex therapy treatment, in which the partners pleasure each other without employing direct stimulation of the sex organs.

sex addiction a term used to describe compulsive sexual behavior in a controversial model that compares such behavior to substance addictions.

sex-dimorphic behavior the differentiation by gender of activities typical of girls or boys, such as choice of sex-typed toys and same-gender playmates.

sex therapist a professional trained in the treatment of sexual dysfunctions.

sexologist person who studies human sexuality from a scientific perspective.

sexual arousal excitation of the body, including the genitals, for sexual activity.

sexual aversion disorder avoidance of or exaggerated fears toward forms of sexual expression.

sexual desire the psychological motivation, incentive, or appetite for sex.

sexual differentiation the developmental processes—biological, social, and psychological—that lead to different sexes or genders.

sexual dysfunctions difficulties people have in achieving sexual arousal and in other stages of sexual response.

sexual harassment unwanted sexual advances or coercion that can occur in the workplace or in academic settings.

sexual individuality the unique set of sexual needs, orientations, fantasies, feelings, and activities that develops in each human being.

sexual orientation the set of physical and emotional qualities that attracts human beings to one another sexually and romantically.

sexual orientation identity an inner awareness of what one's sexual orientation means for one's life in terms of sexual and romantic relationships and social interaction.

sexual revolution the changes in thinking about sexuality and sexual behavior in society that occurred in the 1960s and 1970s.

sexual surrogates paid partners used during sex therapy with clients who lack their own partners; used only rarely today.

shaft in the female, the longer body of the clitoris, containing erectile tissue; in the male, the cylindrical base of the penis that contains three columns of spongy tissue: two corpora cavernosa and a corpus spongiosum.

Skene's glands secretory cells located inside the female urethra.

smegma thick, oily substance that may accumulate under the prepuce of the clitoris or penis.

social constructionism a theory that holds that human traits and behaviors are shaped more by environmental social forces than by innate biological factors.

social scripts a complex set of learned responses to a particular situation that is formed by social influences.

sodomy laws laws in some states that prohibit a variety of sexual behaviors, often described as deviate sexual intercourse. These laws often are enforced discriminatorily against particular groups, such as gay males.

spectatoring term used by Masters and Johnson to describe self-consciousness and self-observation during sex.

sperm reproductive cells produced in the testes; in fertilization, one sperm unites with an ovum.

spermatocytes (sper-MAT-o-sites) cells lining the seminiferous tubules from which sperm cells are produced.

spermicides chemicals that kill sperm; available as foams, creams, jellies, film, or suppositories.

sponge a thick, polyurethane disk that holds a spermicide and fits over the cervix to prevent conception.

spontaneous abortion another term for miscarriage.

SRY the sex-determining region of the Y chromosome.

statutory rape a legal term used to indicate sexual activity when one partner is younger than the age of consent; in most states, that age is 18.

straight slang term for heterosexual.

suppositories contraceptive devices designed to distribute their spermicide by melting or foaming in the vagina.

syndrome (SIN-drome) a group of signs or symptoms that occur together and characterize a given condition.

syphilis (SIF-uh-lus) a sexually transmitted disease (STD) characterized by four stages, beginning with the appearance of a chancre.

systematic desensitization step-by-step approaches to unlearning tension-producing behaviors and developing new behavior patterns.

T

testes (TEST-ees) pair of male gonads that produce sperm and male hormones.

testicular failure lack of sperm and/or hormone production by the testes.

testicular sperm aspiration (TESA) a procedure in which sperm are removed directly from the epididymis of the male testes with a micropipette.

testosterone (tes-TAHS-te-ron) major male hormone produced by the testes; it helps produce male secondary sex characteristics.

testosterone replacement therapy (TRT) administering testosterone injections to increase sexual interest or potency in older men; not considered safe for routine use.

theoretical failure rate a measure of how often a birth control method can be expected to fail when used without error or technical problems; sometimes called perfect use failure rate.

thrush a disease caused by a fungus and characterized by white patches in the oral cavity.

toucherism gaining sexual gratification from the touching of an unknown person's body, such as on the buttocks or breasts.

toxic shock syndrome (TSS) an acute disease characterized by fever and sore throat; caused by normal bacteria in the vagina that are activated if tampons or contraceptive

devices such as diaphragms are left in for a long period of time.

transcervical sterilization procedure a less invasive alternative to tubal ligation in which small porous silicon inserts are implanted in the fallopian tubes through the uterus. Tissue grows on the inserts, eventually occluding the tubes.

transgenderism a crossing of traditional gender lines because of discomfort and nonconformity with gender roles generally accepted by society.

transphobia negative attitudes, prejudice, and misconceptions toward transgender individuals and lifestyles.

transsexuality a strong degree of discomfort with one's identity as male or female, characterized by feelings of being in the wrongly sexed body.

transvestite an individual who dresses in clothing and adopts mannerisms considered appropriate for the opposite sex.

trichomoniasis (trik-uh-ma-NEE-uh-sis) a vaginal infection caused by the *Trichomonas* organism.

troilism (TROY-i-liz-um) sexual activity shared by three people.

true hermaphrodite a person who has one testis and one ovary. External appearance may vary among individuals.

tubal ligation (lie-GAY-shun) a surgical cutting and tying of the fallopian tubes to induce permanent female sterilization.

typical use failure rate a measure of how often a birth control method can be expected to fail when human error and technical failure are considered.

U

ultrasound images ultrasonic rays used to create a picture of fetal structures; often used in conjunction with amniocentesis or fetal surgery.

umbilical cord the tubelike tissues and blood vessels originating at the embryo's navel that connect it to the placenta.

urethra (yu-REE-thrah) tube that passes from the urinary bladder to the outside of the body.

urinary incontinence leaking of urine from the bladder, often when the bladder is stressed by muscular pressure, sometimes caused when a prolapsed uterus pushes against it.

urinary meatus (mee-AY-tuss) opening through which urine passes from the urethra to the outside of the body.

urophilia sexual arousal connected with urine or urination.

uterus (YUTE-a-rus) muscular organ of the female reproductive system; a fertilized egg implants itself within the uterus.

V

vacuum curettage (kyur-a-TAZH) a method of induced abortion performed with a suction pump.

vagina (vu-JI-na) muscular canal in the female that is responsive to sexual arousal; it receives semen during heterosexual intercourse for reproduction.

vaginal atresia (a-TREE-zha) birth defect in which the vagina is absent or closed.

vaginal atrophy shrinking and deterioration of the vaginal lining, usually the result of low estrogen levels during aging.

vaginal fistulae (FISH-cha-lee or-lie) abnormal channels that can develop between the vagina and other internal organs.

vaginal ring a hormonal contraceptive that is inserted into the vagina for three weeks of each monthly cycle.

vaginismus (vaj-uh-NIZ-mus) involuntary spasm of the outer vaginal musculature, making penetration of the vagina difficult or impossible.

values system of beliefs through which people view life and make decisions, including their sexual decisions.

variable an aspect of a scientific study that is subject to change.

variation a less pejorative term used to describe nonconformity to accepted norms.

varicose veins overexpanded blood vessels; can occur in veins surrounding the vagina.

vas deferens tube that leads sperm upward from each testis to the seminal vesicles.

vasa efferentia larger tubes within the testes, into which sperm move after being produced in the seminiferous tubules.

vasectomy (va-SEK-ta-mee or vay-ZEK-ta-mee) a surgical cutting and tying of the vas deferens to induce permanent male sterilization.

villi fingerlike projections of the chorion that form a major part of the placenta.

voluntary surgical contraception (VSC) sterilization; rendering a person incapable of conceiving with surgical procedures that interrupt the passage of the egg or sperm.

voyeurism (VOYE-yur-i-zum) sexual gratification from viewing others who are nude or who are engaging in sexual activities.

vulva external sex organs of the female, including the mons, major and minor lips, clitoris, and opening of the vagina.

vulvar vestibulitis one form of vulvodynia associated with pain in the entrance of the vagina upon physical contact, often interfering with sexual penetration of the vagina.

vulvodynia a medical condition characterized by pain and burning in the vulva and outer vagina.

vulvovaginitis (vul-voe-vaj-uh-NITE-us) general term for inflammation of the vulva and/or vagina.

W

Western blot the test used to verify the presence of HIV antibodies already detected by the ELISA.

Wolffian ducts (WOOL-fee-an) embryonic structures that develop into male sexual and reproductive organs if male hormones are present.

Y

yeast infection a type of vaginitis caused by an overgrowth of a fungus normally found in an inactive state in the vagina.

Z

zero population growth the point at which the world's population would stabilize and there would be no further increase in the number of people on earth. Birthrate and death rate become essentially equal.

zona pellucida (ZO-nah pe-LOO-sa-da) the transparent, outer membrane of an ovum.

zoophilia (zoo-a-FILL-ee-a) another name for bestiality.

zygote an ovum that has been fertilized by a sperm.

zygote intrafallopian transfer (ZIFT) a process by which zygotes resulting from IVF are inserted directly into the fallopian tubes.

References

AAUW. (1992). *How schools shortchange girls: Executive summary*. Washington, DC: Author.

AAUW. (1993). *Hostile hallways*. Washington, DC: Author.

Abbott, E. (2001). *A history of celibacy*. Toronto: DaCapo Press.

Abouesh, A., & Clayton, A. (1999). Compulsive voyeurism and exhibitionism: A clinical response to paroxetine. *Archives of Sexual Behavior, 28*(1), 23–30.

Abramovich, E. (2005). Childhood sexual abuse as a risk factor for subsequent involvement in sex work: A review of empirical findings. *Journal of Psychology and Human Sexuality, 17*(1/2), 131–146.

Ackard, D. M., & Neumark-Stainer, D. (2001). Health care information sources for adolescents: Age and gender differences on use, concerns, and needs. *Journal of Adolescent Health, 29*(3), 170–176.

ACOG. (2007). ACOG practice bulletin no. 77: Screening for fetal chromosomal abnormalities. *Obstetrics and Gynecology, 109*, 217–228.

Adam, B. D., et al. (2005). AIDS optimism, condom fatigue, or self-esteem? Explaining unsafe sex among gay and bisexual men. *Journal of Sex Research, 42*(3), 238–248.

Aguirre, D., et al. (2007). Rapid HIV testing in outreach and other community settings: United States, 2004–2006. *Morbidity and Mortality Weekly Report, 56*(47), 1233–1237.

Ahlborg, T., Dahlof, L., & Hallberg, L. R. (2005). Quality of the intimate and sexual relationship in first-time parents six months after delivery. *Journal of Sex Research, 42*(2), 167–174.

Ahlborg, T., et al. (2008). Sensual and sexual marital contentment in parents of small children: A follow-up study when the first child is four years old. *Journal of Sex Research, 45*(3), 295–304.

Albright, J. M. (2008). Sex in America online: An exploration of sex, marital status, and sexual identity in internet sex seeking and its impacts. *Journal of Sex Research, 45*(2), 175–186.

Alexander, G. M., & Hines, M. (2002). Sex differences in response to children's toys in nonhuman primates (*Cercopithecus aethiops sabaeus*). *Evolution and Human Behavior, 23*(6), 467–479.

Alexander, M. G., & Fisher, T. D. (2003). Truth and consequences: Using the bogus pipeline to examine sex differences in self-reported sexuality. *Journal of Sex Research, 40*(1), 27–35.

Alexander, M., & Rosen, R. C. (2008). Spinal cord injuries and orgasm: A review. *Journal of Sex and Marital Therapy, 34*(4), 308–324.

Allan, C. A., et al. (2008). Testosterone therapy increases sexual desire in aging men with low-normal testosterone levels and symptoms of androgen deficiency. *International Journal of Impotence Research, 20*, 396–401.

Allen, E. S., & Rhoades, G. K. (2008). Not all affairs are created equal: Emotional involvement with an extradyadic partner. *Journal of Sex & Marital Therapy, 34*(1), 51–65.

Allen, J. S., & Bailey, K. G. (2007). Are mating strategies and mating tactics independent constructs? *Journal of Sex Research, 44*(3), 225–232.

Allen, L. (2003). Girls want sex, boys want love: Resisting dominant discourses of (hetero)sexuality. *Sexualities, 6*(2), 215–236.

Alison, L., et al. (2001). Sadomasochistically oriented behavior: Diversity in practice and meaning. *Archives of Sexual Behavior, 30*(1), 1–12.

Allyn, D. (2000). *Make love not war: The sexual revolution, an unfettered history*. Boston: Little, Brown.

Alperin, M., Krohn, M. A., Parviainen, K. (2008). Episiotomy and increase in the risk of obstetric laceration in a subsequent vaginal delivery. *Obstetrics and Gynecology, 111*, 1274–1278.

Althof, S. E. (2007). Sexual therapy in the age of pharmacotherapy. *Annual Review of Sex Research, 17*, 116–131.

Althaus, F. (2001). Cesarean section poses fewer risks than vaginal delivery for term infants in breech presentation. *Family Planning Perspectives, 33*(2), 92.

Althof, S. E., et al. (2005). Outcome measurement in female sexual dysfunction clinical trials: Review and recommendations. *Journal of Sex and Marital Therapy, 31*, 153–166.

Altman, C. (1999). Gay and lesbian seniors: Unique challenges of coming out in later life. *SIECUS Report, 27*(3), 14–17.

Alvarez, M. J., & Garcia-Marques, L. (2008). Condom inclusion in cognitive representations of sexual encounters. *Journal of Sex Research, 45*(4), 358–370.

American Academy of Pediatrics. (2005). Breastfeeding and the use of human milk. *Pediatrics, 115*(2), 496–506.

American College of Obstetricians and Gynecologists. (2007). Intrauterine device and adolescents: ACOG committee opinion no. 392. *Obstetrics and Gynecology, 110*(6), 1493–1495.

American Health Consultants. (2003). Women who want permanent birth control now have a second option. *Contraceptive Technology Update, 24*(1), 1–4.

American Society for Adolescent Psychiatry. (2002). Gays in the military. *Adolescent Psychiatry, 26*(257), 257–259.

America's Children. (2006). *America's children in brief: Key national indicators of well-being*. Washington, DC: Forum on Child and Family Statistics.

Amor, D. J., & Halliday, J. (2008). A review of known imprinting syndromes and their association with assisted reproduction technologies. *Human Reproduction, 23*(12), 2826–2834.

Anders, S. M., et al. (2005). Preliminary clinical experience with androgen administration for pre- and postmenopausal women with hypoactive sexual desire. *Journal of Sex and Marital Therapy, 31*, 173–185.

Anders, S. M., & Gray, P. B. (2007). Hormones and human partnering. *Annual Review of Sex Research, 18*, 60–93.

Anderson, J. E., Ebrahim, S. H., & Sansom, S. (2004). Women's knowledge about treatment to prevent mother-to-child human immunodeficiency virus transmission. *Obstetrics and Gynecology, 103*(1), 165–168.

Anderson, J. E., Mosher, W. D., & Chandra, A. (2006). Measuring HIV risk in the U.S. population aged 15–44: Results from cycle 6 of the national survey of family growth. *Advance Data from Vital and Health Statistics, 377*.

Anderson, P. B., et al. (2005). An examination of sexual strategies used by urban southern and rural midwestern university women. *Journal of Sex Research, 42*(4), 335–341.

Andia, I., et al. (2009). Highly active antiretroviral therapy and increased use of contraceptives among HIV-positive women during expanding access to antiretroviral therapy in Mbarara, Uganda. *American Journal of Public Health, 99*(2), 340–347.

Andrade, S. E., et al. (2008). Use of antidepressant medications during pregnancy: A multisided study. *American Journal of Obstetrics & Gynecology, 198*(2), 194.e1–194.e5.

Angera, J. J., Brookins-Fisher, J., & Inungu, J. N. (2008). An investigation of parent/child communication about sexuality. *American Journal of Sexuality Education, 3*(2), 165–181.

Ankomah, A. (1999). Sex, love, money and AIDS: The dynamics of premarital sexual relationships in Ghana. *Sexualities, 2*(3), 291–308.

Anschuetz, G. L., et al. (2009). Determining risk markers for gonorrhea and chlamydial infection and reinfection among adolescents in public high schools. *Sexually Transmitted Diseases, 36*(1), 4–8.

Apodaca, R. F., et al. (2005). Young, unassimilated Hispanic offenders: Absolutist vs. relativist cultural assumptions. *Sexuality and Culture, 9*(3), 3–23.

Apperloo, M. J., et al. (2003). In the mood for sex: The value of androgens. *Journal of Sex and Marital Therapy, 29*(2), 87–102.

Arasteh, K., & Des Jarlais, D. C. (2008). Injecting drug use, HIV, and what to do about it. *Lancet, 372*(9651), 1709–1710.

Arnett, J. J. (2004). *Emerging adulthood: The winding road from late teens to twenties.* New York: Oxford University Press.

Aron, A., et al. (2005). Reward, motivation, and emotion systems associated with early-stage intense romantic love. *Journal of Neurophysiology, 94,* 327–337.

Arreola, S., et al. (2008). Childhood sexual experiences and adult health sequelae among gay and bisexual men: Defining childhood sexual abuse. *Journal of Sex Research, 45*(3), 246–252.

Artz, L., et al. (2005). A randomized trial of clinician-delivered interventions promoting barrier contraception for sexually transmitted disease prevention. *Sexually Transmitted Diseases, 32*(11), 672–679.

ASHA. (2004). The STDs nobody knows. *Perspectives on Sexual and Reproductive Health, 36*(3), 97.

Ashrafian, H. (2009). An ancient Indian method of penis lengthening. *Archives of Sexual Behavior, 38,* 4–5.

Aslan, G., et al. (2005). A prospective analysis of sexual functions during pregnancy. *International Journal of Impotence Research, 17*(2), 154–157.

Attwood, F. (2005). What do people do with porn? Qualitative research into the consumption, use, and experience of pornography and other sexually explicit media. *Sexuality and Culture, 9*(2), 65–86.

Aubin, S., et al. (2009). Comparing sildenafil vs. sildenafil plus brief couple sex therapy on erectile dysfunction and couples' sexual and marital quality of life: A pilot study. *Journal of Sex and Marital Therapy, 35*(2), 122–143.

Awwad, Z., et al. (2005). Penile measurements in normal adult Jordanians and in patients with erectile dysfunction. *International Journal of Impotence Research, 17*(2), 191–195.

Axinn, W. G., & Thornton, A. (1992). The relationship between cohabitation and divorce: Selectivity or causal influence? *Demography, 29,* 357–374.

Aydt, H., & Corsaro, W. A. (2003). Differences in children's construction of gender across culture. *American Behavioral Scientist, 46*(10), 1306–1325.

Ayling, K., & Ussher, J. M. (2008). "If sex hurts, am I still a woman?" The subjective experience of vulvodynia in heterosexual women. *Archives of Sexual Behavior, 37,* 294–304.

Aylwin, A. S., Reddon, J. R., & Burke, A. R. (2005). Sexual fantasies of adolescent male sex offenders in residential treatment: A descriptive study. *Archives of Sexual Behavior, 34*(2), 231–239.

Bachmann, K. M., et al. (2000). Nurse–patient sexual contact in psychiatric hospitals. *Archives of Sexual Behavior, 29*(4), 335–347.

Backman, T., et al. (2005). Use of the levonorgestrel-releasing intrauterine system and breast cancer. *Obstetrics and Gynecology, 106*(4), 813–817.

Badawy, A., Elnashar, A., & Eltotongy, M. (2009). Effect of sperm morphology and number of success of intrauterine insemination. *Fertility and Sterility, 91*(3), 777–781.

Badawy, H., & Morsi, H. (2008). Long-term followup of dermal grafts for repair to severe penile curvature. *Journal of Urology, 180* (4), 1842–1845.

Baerwald, A. R., Adams, G. P., & Pierson, R. A. (2003). A new model for ovarian follicular development during the human menstrual cycle. *Fertility and Sterility, 80*(1), 116–122.

Bailey, J. A., et al. (2008). Sexual risk behavior 6 months post-high school: Associations with college attendance, living with a parent, and prior risk behavior. *Journal of Adolescent Health, 42*(6), 573–579.

Bailey, J. M. (2003). The man who would be queen: The science of gender-bending and transsexualism. Washington, DC: Joseph Henry Press.

Bailey, J. M., & Shriver, A. (1999). Does childhood sexual abuse cause borderline personality disorder? *Journal of Sex and Marital Therapy, 25,* 45–57.

Bailey, J. V., et al. (2004). Bacterial vaginosis in lesbian and bisexual women. *Sexually Transmitted Diseases, 31*(11), 691–694.

Bailey, J. V., et al. (2008). Vulvovaginal candidiasis in women who have sex with women. *Sexually Transmitted Diseases, 35*(6), 533–536.

Baker, M. D., & Maner, J. K. (2008). Risk-taking as a situationally sensitive male mating strategy. *Evolution and Human Behavior, 29*(6), 391–395.

Balaban, E. (2008, March 21). The female equally with the male I sing. *Science, 319*(5870), 1619–1620.

Balaji, A., et al. (2008). HIV prevention education and HIV-related policies in secondary schools—Selected sites, United States, 2006. *Journal of the American Medical Association, 300*(14), 1645–1646.

Baldwin, J. I., & Baldwin, J. D. (2000). Heterosexual anal intercourse: An understudied, high-risk sexual behavior. *Archives of Sexual Behavior, 29*(4), 357–373.

Ballan, M. (2004). Parents as sexuality educators for their children with developmental disabilities. *SIECUS Report, 32*(2), 29–30.

Ballard, S. M., & Gross, K. H. (2009). Exploring parental perspectives on parent-child sexual communication. *American Journal of Sexuality Education, 4,* 40–57.

Balog, J. E. (2009). The moral justification for a compulsory human papillomavirus vaccination program. *American Journal of Public Health, 99*(4), 616–622.

Balon, R. (2008). The DSM criteria of sexual dysfunction: Need for a change. *Journal of Sex and Marital Therapy, 34*(3), 186–197.

Balon, R., & Segraves, R. T. (2008). Survey of treatment practices for sexual dysfunction(s) associated with antidepressants. *Journal of Sex and Marital Therapy, 34*(4), 353–365.

Balter, M. (2005). Dissecting a hidden breast cancer risk. *Science, 309,* 1664–1666.

Bancroft, J. H. (2007). Sex and aging. *New England Journal of Medicine, 357,* 820–822.

Bancroft, J. (2001). Review symposium: Krafft-Ebing, a hundred years on. *Sexualities, 4*(4), 497–509.

Bancroft, J. (2002a). Biological factors in human sexuality. *Journal of Sex Research, 39*(1), 15–21.

Bancroft, J. (2002b). Sexual effects of androgens in women: Some theoretical considerations. *Fertility and Sterility, 77,* 55–59.

Bancroft, J. (Ed.). (2003). *Sexual development in childhood.* Bloomington: Indiana University Press.

Bancroft, J. (2005). Alfred C. Kinsey and the politics of sex research. *Annual Review of Sex Research, 15*, 1–38.

Bancroft, J. (2009). *Human sexuality and Its problems* (3rd ed.). Oxford, England: Elsevier.

Bancroft, J., et al. (2004). Sexual activity and risk taking in young heterosexual men: The relevance of sexual arousability, mood, and sensation seeking. *Journal of Sex Research, 41*(2), 181–192.

Bancroft, J., et al. (2009). The dual control model: Current status and future directions. *Journal of Sex Research, 46*(2–3), 121–142.

Bancroft, J., & Vukadinovic, Z. (2004). Sexual addiction, sexual compulsivity, sexual impulsivity, or what? Toward a theoretical model. *Journal of Sex Research, 41*(3), 225–234.

Bankhead, C. (2005). Men with micro-penis have well-adjusted outcome. *Urology Times, 33*, 20.

Banyard, V. L., & Williams, L. M. (1999). Memories for child sexual abuse and mental health functioning: Findings on a sample of women and implications for future research. In L. M. Williams & V. L. Banyard (Eds.), *Trauma and Memory* (pp. 115–125). Thousand Oaks, CA: Sage.

Bar-Hava, M., et al. (2001). The interrelationship between coping strategies and sexual functioning in in-vitro fertilization patients. *Journal of Sex and Marital Therapy, 27*, 389–394.

Barbach, L. G. (1988). *Becoming orgasmic*. Englewood Cliffs, NJ: Prentice Hall.

Barnett, G., & Wood, J. L. (2008). Agency, relatedness, inner peace, and problem solving in sexual offending. *Sexual Abuse: A Journal of Research and Treatment, 20*(4), 444–465.

Barnhart, K. T., & Schreiber, C. A. (2009). Return to fertility following discontinuation of oral contraceptives. *Fertility and Sterility, 91*(3), 659–663.

Baron-Cohen, S., Knickmeyer, R. C., & Belmonte, M. K. (2005). Sex differences in the brain: Implications for explaining autism. *Science, 310*, 819–823.

Barone, M. A., et al. (2004). Characteristics of men receiving vasectomies in the United States, 1998–1999. *Perspectives on Sexual and Reproductive Health, 36*(1), 27–33.

Barqawi, A., & Crawford, E. D. (2006). Testosterone replacement therapy and the risk of prostate cancer. Is there a link? *International Journal of Impotence Research, 18*, 323–328.

Barrientos, J. E., & Paez, D. (2006). Psychosocial variables of sexual satisfaction in Chile. *Journal of Sex and Marital Therapy, 32*, 351–368.

Barsky, J. L., Friedman, M. A., & Rosen, R. C. (2006). Sexual dysfunction and chronic illness: The role of flexibility in coping. *Journal of Sex and Marital Therapy, 32*, 235–253.

Barsoum, I., & Hung-Chang Yao, H. (2006). The road to maleness: From testis to Wolffian duct. *Trends in Endocrinology and Metabolism, 17*(6), 223–228.

Bartlett, N. H., & Vasey, P. L. (2006). A restrospective study of childhood gender-atypical behavior in Samoan fa'afafine. *Archives of Sexual Behavior, 35*, 659–666.

Bartlett, T. (2003, October 24). Did a university let a sex researcher go too far? *Chronicle of Higher Education,* A10–A12.

Bartoi, M. G., Kinder, B. N., & Tomianovic, D. (2000). Interaction effects of emotional status and sexual abuse on adult sexuality. *Journal of Sex and Marital Therapy, 26*, 1–23.

Basson, R. (2002). A model of women's sexual arousal. *Journal of Sex and Marital Therapy, 28*, 1–10.

Basson, R. (2008). Women's sexual function and dysfunction: Current uncertainties, future directions. *International Journal of Impotence Research, 20*, 466–478.

Basson, R., et al. (2001). Report of the International Consensus Development Conference on female sexual dysfunction: Definitions and classifications. *Journal of Sex and Marital Therapy, 27*, 83–94.

Basson, R., et al. (2003). Definitions of women's sexual dysfunction reconsidered: Advocating expansion and revision. *Journal of Psychosomatic Obstetrics and Gynecology, 24*, 221–229.

Baumeister, R. F. (2000). Gender differences in erotic plasticity: The female sex drive as socially flexible and responsive. *Psychological Bulletin, 126*, 347–374.

Bauserman, R. (1998). Egalitarian, sexist, and aggressive sexual materials: Attitude effects and viewer responses. *Journal of Sex Research, 35*(3), 244–253.

Bay-Cheng, L. Y., & Eliseo-Arras, R. K. (2008). The making of unwanted sex: Gendered and neoliberal norms in college women's unwanted sexual experiences. *Journal of Sex Research, 45*(4), 386–397.

Bay-Cheng, L. Y., Robinson, A. D., & Zucker, A. N. (2009). Behavioral and relational context of adolescent desire, wanting, and pleasure: Undergraduate women's retrospective accounts. *Journal of Sex Research, 46*(5), 511–524.

Beadnell, B., et al. (2005). Condom use, frequency of sex, and number of partners: Multidimensional characterization of adolescent sexual risk-taking. *Journal of Sex Research, 42*(3), 192–202.

Beaver, K. M. (2008). The interaction between genetic risk and childhood sexual abuse in the prediction of adolescent violent behavior. *Sexual Abuse: A Journal of Research and Treatment, 20*(4), 426–443.

Bebeau, M. J., et al. (1995). *Moral reasoning in scientific research: Cases for teaching and assessment.* Bloomington, IN: Poynter Center for the Study of Ethics and American Institutions.

Becker, D., et al. (2007). The quality of family planning services in the United States: Findings from a literature review. *Perspectives on Sexual and Reproductive Health, 39*(4), 206–215.

Beckman, M. (2003). False memories, true pain. *Science, 299*, 1306.

Beckman, N., et al. (2008). Secular trends in self reported sexual activity and satisfaction in Swedish 70-year-olds: Cross sectional survey of four populations, 1971–2001. *British Medical Journal, 337*, a279.

Beijsterveldt, V., Hudziak, J. J., & Boomsma, D. I. (2006). Genetic and environmental influences on cross-gender behavior and relation to behavior problems: A study of Dutch twins at ages 7 and 10 years. *Archives of Sexual Behavior, 35*, 647–658.

Beksinska, M. E., et al. (2001). Structural integrity of the female condom after multiple uses, washing, drying, and relubrication. *Contraception, 63*(1), 33–36.

Belanger, D. (2002). Son preference in a rural village in North Vietnam. *Studies in Family Planning, 33*(4), 321–334.

Bell, A., Weinberg, M. S., & Hammersmith, S. K. (1981). *Sexual preference: Its development in men and women.* Bloomington: Indiana University Press.

Beltrami, J., & Berman, S. (2006). Congenital syphilis: A persisting sentinel public health event. *Sexually Transmitted Diseases, 33*(11), 675–676.

Bem, S. L. (1987). Masculinity and femininity exist only in the mind of the perceiver. In J. H. Reinisch, L. A. Rosenblum, & S. A. Sanders (Eds.), *Masculinity/femininity: Basic perspectives* (pp. 304–311). New York: Oxford University Press.

Bem, S. L. (1993). *The lenses of gender.* New Haven, CT: Yale University Press.

Benotsch, E. G., Kalichman, S., & Cage, M. (2002). Men who have met sex partners via the Internet: Prevalence, predictors, and implications for HIV prevention. *Archives of Sexual Behavior, 31*(2), 177–183.

Bentley, G. R., & Mascie-Taylor, C. G. N. (2000). *Infertility in the modern world: Present and future prospects.* Cambridge, England: Cambridge University Press.

Benuto, L., & Meana, M. (2008). Acculturation and sexuality: Investigating gender differences in erotic plasticity. *Journal of Sex Research, 45*(3), 217–224.

Berenbaum, S. A. (2007). Psychological outcome in children with disorders of sex development: Implications for treatment and understanding typical development. *Annual Review of Sex Research, 7,* 1–38.

Berenson, A. B., Breitkopf, C. R., & Wu, Z. H. (2003). Reproductive correlates of depressive symptoms among low-income minority women. *Obstetrics and Gynecology, 102*(6), 1310–1317.

Beres, M. A., Herold, E., & Maitland, S. B. (2004). Sexual consent behaviors in same-sex relationships. *Archives of Sexual Behavior, 33*(5), 475–486.

Berkley, K. J., Rapkin, A. J., & Papka, R. E. (2005). The pains of endometriosis. *Science, 308,* 1587–1588.

Berman, L. (2003). *The puzzle: Exploring the evolutionary puzzle of male homosexuality.* Wilmette, IL: Godot Press.

Berman, L. A., et al. (2001). Pharmacotherapy and psychotherapy?: Effective treatment for FSD related to unresolved childhood sexual abuse. *Journal of Sex and Marital Therapy, 27,* 421–425.

Bernstein, K. T., et al. (2008). Same-sex attraction disclosure to health care providers among New York City men who have sex with men: Implications for HIV testing approaches. *Archives of Internal Medicine, 168*(13), 1458–1464.

Bernstein, S., Say, L., & Chowdhury, S. (2008). Sexual and reproductive health: Completing the continuum. *Lancet, 371,* 1225–1226.

Betchen, S. J. (2003). Suggestions for improving intimacy in couples in which one partner has attention deficit/hyperactivity disorder. *Journal of Sex and Marital Therapy, 29*(2), 103–124.

Bianchi-Demicheli, F., & Zutter, A. (2005). Intensive short-term dynamic sex therapy: A proposal. *Journal of Sex and Marital Therapy, 31,* 57–72.

Bickham, P. J., et al. (2007). Correlates of early overt and covert sexual behaviors in heterosexual women. *Archives of Sexual Behavior, 36,* 724–740.

Billups, K. L., et al. (2001). A new non-pharmacological vacuum therapy for female sexual dysfunction. *Journal of Sex and Marital Therapy, 27,* 435–441.

Binik, Y. M. (2005). Should dyspareunia be retained as a sexual dysfunction in DSM-V? A painful classification decision. *Archives of Sexual Behavior, 34*(1), 11–21.

Binik, Y. M., Bergeron, S., & Khalife, S. (2007). Dyspareunia and vaginismus: So-called sexual pain. In: S. R. Leiblum (Ed.). *Principles and practices of sex therapy* (pp. 124–156). New York: Guilford Press.

Birnbaum, G. E. (2003). The meaning of heterosexual intercourse among women with female orgasmic disorder. *Archives of Sexual Behavior, 32*(1), 61–71.

Birnbaum, G., Glaubman, H., & Mikulincer, M. (2001). Women's experience of heterosexual intercourse—scale construction, factor structure, and relations to orgasmic disorder. *Journal of Sex Research, 38*(3), 191–204.

Bisson, M. A., & Levine, T. R. (2009). Negotiating a friends with benefits relationship. *Archives of Sexual Behavior, 38,* 66–73.

Bitler, M., & Zavodny, M. (2002). Did abortion legalization reduce the number of unwanted children? Evidence of adoptions. *Perspectives on Sexual and Reproductive Health, 34*(1), 25–34.

Bivona, J., & Critelli, J. (2009). The nature of women's rape fantasies: An analysis of prevalence, frequency, and contents. *Journal of Sex Research, 46*(1), 33–45.

Blackburn, L. (2006). U.K. embryos may be screened for cancer risk. *Science, 312,* 984.

Blackledge, C. (2004). *The story of V: Opening Pandora's box.* London: Weidenfeld and Nicolson.

Blake, S. M., et al. (2007). Pregnancy intentions and happiness among pregnant black women at high risk for adverse infant health outcomes. *Perspectives on Sexual and Reproductive Health, 39*(4), 194–205.

Blake, S. M., et al. (2001). Effects of a parent-child communications intervention on young adolescents' risk for early on set of sexual intercourse. *Family Planning Perspectives, 33*(2), 52–61.

Blanchard, R. (1991). Clinical observations and systematic studies of autogynephilia. *Journal of Sex and Marital Therapy, 17*(4), 235–251.

Blanchard, R. (2005). Early history of the concept of autogynephilia. *Archives of Sexual Behavior, 34*(4), 439–446.

Blanchard, R. (2007a). Older-sibling and younger-sibling sex ratios in Frisch and Hvid's (2006) national cohort study of two million Danes. *Archives of Sexual Behavior, 36,* 860–863.

Blanchard, R. (2007b). Supplementary analyses regarding Langevin, Langevin, and Curnoe's (2007) findings on fraternal birth order in homosexual men. *Archives of Sexual Behavior, 36,* 610–614.

Blanchard, R. (2008). Sex ratio of older siblings in heterosexual and homosexual, right-handed and non-right-handed men. *Archives of Sexual Behavior, 37,* 977–981.

Blanchard, R. (2009). The DSM diagnostic criteria for pedophilia. *Archives of Sexual Behavior:* 10.1007/s10508-009-9536-0.

Blanchard, R., et al. (2002). Retrospective self-reports of childhood accidents causing unconsciousness in phallometrically diagnosed pedophiles. *Archives of Sexual Behavior, 31*(6), 511–526.

Blanchard, R., et al. (2003). Self-reported head injuries before and after age 13 in pedophilic and nonpedophilic men referred for clinical assessment. *Archives of Sexual Behavior, 32*(6), 573–581.

Blanchard, R., & Lippa, R. A. (2008). The sex ratio of older siblings in non-right-handed homosexual men. *Archives of Sexual Behavior, 37,* 970–976.

Blazquez, A., et al. (2008). Sexual dysfunction as related to severity of fatigue in women with CFS. *Journal of Sex & Marital Therapy, 34*(3), 240–247.

Blinn-Pike, L., et al. (2004). Sexually abstinent adolescents: An 18-month follow-up. *Journal of Adolescent Research, 19*(5), 495–511.

Blumberg, E. S. (2003). The lives and voices of highly sexual women. *Journal of Sex Research, 40*(2), 146–157.

Blumberg, S. J., et al. (2003). *Journal of Sex Research, 40*(2), 121–128.

Bockting, W. O., & Ehrbar, R. D. (2005). Commentary: Gender variance, dissonance, or identity disorder? *Journal of Psychology and Human Sexuality, 17*(3/4), 125–134.

Boden, J. M., & Horwood, L. J. (2006). Self-esteem, risky sexual behavior, and pregnancy in a New Zealand birth cohort. *Archives of Sexual Behavior, 35,* 549–560.

Bodenmann, G., & Ledermann, T. (2008). Depressed mood and sexual functioning. *International Journal of Sexual Health, 19*(4), 63–73.

Bogaert, A. F. (2000). Birth order and sexual orientation in a national probability sample. *Journal of Sex Research, 37*(4), 361–368.

Bogaert, A. F. (2001). Personality, individual differences, and preferences for the sexual media. *Archives of Sexual Behavior, 30*(1), 29–53.

Bogaert, A. F. (2003). Interaction of older brothers and sex-typing in the prediction of sexual orientation in men. *Archives of Sexual Behavior, 32*(2), 129–134.

Bogaert, A. F. (2004). Asexuality: Prevalence and associated factors in a national probability sample. *Journal of Sex Research, 41*(3), 279–287.

Bogaert, A. F. (2005). Sibling sex ratio and sexual orientation in men and women: New tests in two national probability samples. *Archives of Sexual Behavior, 34*(1), 111–116.

Bogart, L. M., et al. (2007). Association of sexual abstinence in adolescents with mental health in adulthood. *Journal of Sex Research, 44*(3), 290–298.

Boggess, J. E. (2002). How can pharmacies improve access to emergency contraception? *Perspectives on Sexual and Reproductive Health, 34*(3), 162–165.

Boggess, J., & Bradner, C. (2002, May/June). Trends in adolescent males' abortion attitudes, 1988–1995: Difference by race and ethnicity. *Family Planning Perspectives, 32*(3), 118–123.

Bolin, A., & Granskog, J. (2003). *Athletic intruders: Ethnographic research on women, culture, and exercise*. Albany: State University of New York Press.

Bolour, S., & Braunstein, G. (2005). Testosterone therapy in women: A review. *International Journal of Impotence Research, 17*, 399–408.

Bolton, J. M., Sareen, J., & Reiss, J. P. (2006). Genital anaesthesia persisting six years after sertraline discontinuation. *Journal of Sex and Marital Therapy, 32*, 327–330.

Bonillas, C. (2008). Activity: "I now pronounce you . . . wife and wife?" *American Journal of Sexuality Education, 3*(2), 211–221.

Boorjian, S., Lipkin, M., & Goldstein, M. (2004). The impact of obstructive interval and sperm granuloma on outcome of vasectomy reversal. *Journal of Urology, 171*(1), 304–306.

Borgatti, S. P., et al. (2009). Network analysis in the social sciences. *Science, 323*(5916), 892–895.

Bornstein, R. F., & Masling, J. M. (Eds.). (2002). *The psychodynamics of gender and gender role*. Washington, DC: American Psychological Association.

Both, S., Everaerd, W., & Laan, E. (2007). Desire emerges from excitement: A psychophysiological perspective on sexual motivation. In E. Janssen (Ed.), *Psychophysiology of Sex* (pp. 327–339). Bloomington: Indiana University Press.

Both, S., et al. (2004). Sexual behavior and responsiveness to sexual stimuli following laboratory-induced sexual arousal. *Journal of Sex Research, 41*(3), 242–258.

Boul, L., Hallam-Jones, R., & Wylie, K. R. (2009). Sexual pleasure and motivation. *Journal of Sex and Marital Therapy, 35*(1), 25–39.

Bowen, A. (2005). Internet sexuality research with rural men who have sex with men: Can we recruit and retain them? *Journal of Sex Research, 42*(4), 317–323.

Boyd, N. (2004). *Big sister: How extreme feminism has betrayed the fight for sexual equality*. Vancouver, BC: Greystone Books.

Boyle, D. E., Marshall, N. L., & Robeson, W. W. (2003). Gender at play: Fourth-grade girls and boys on the playground. *American Behavioral Scientist, 46*(10), 1326–1345.

Boynton, P. M. (2003). "I'm just a girl who can't say no": Women, consent, and sex research. *Journal of Sex and Marital Therapy, 29*, 23–32.

Bozon, M. (2002). Sexuality, gender, and the couple: A sociohistorical perspective. *Annual Review of Sex Research, 7*, 1–32.

Bozzette, S. A. (2005). Routine screening for HIV infection—timely and cost-effective. *New England Journal of Medicine, 352*(6), 620–621.

Bradshaw, C. S., et al. (2005). Higher-risk behavioral practices associated with bacterial vaginosis compared with vaginal candidiasis. *Obstetrics and Gynecology, 106*(1), 105–114.

Brady, S. S., & Halpern-Felsher, B. L. (2007). Adolescents' reported consequences of having oral sex versus vaginal sex. *Pediatrics, 119*(2), 229–236.

Brady, S. S., & Halpern-Felsher, B. L. (2008). Social and emotional consequences of refraining from sexual activity among sexually experienced and inexperienced youths in California. *American Journal of Public Health, 98*(1), 162–168.

Brauer, M., Laan, E., & Kuile, M. M. (2006). Sexual arousal in women with superficial dyspareunia. *Archives of Sexual Behavior, 35*(2), 191–200.

Braun, V., & Kitzinger, C. (2001). "Snatch," "hole," "honey-pot"? Semantic categories and the problems of nonspecificity in female genital slang. *Journal of Sex Research, 38*(2), 146–158.

Braunstein, J. B., et al. (2003). Economics of reducing menstruation with tri-monthly-cycle oral contraceptive therapy: Comparison with standard-cycle regimens. *Obstetrics and Gynecology, 102*(4): 699–708.

Braveman, P. A., et al. (2005). Socio-economic status in health research: One size does not fit all. *Journal of the American Medical Association, 294*(22), 2879–2888.

Breitkopf, C. R., Pearson, H. C., & Breitkopf, D. M. (2005). Poor knowledge regarding the Pap test among low-income women undergoing routine screening. *Perspectives on Sexual and Reproductive Health, 37*(2), 78–84.

Breslau, E. S., et al. (2003). The hormone therapy dilemma: Women respond. *Journal of the American Medical Women's Association, 58*(1), 33–43.

Brett, K. M., & Higgins, J. A. (2003). Hysterectomy prevalence by Hispanic ethnicity: Evidence from a national survey. *American Journal of Public Health, 93*(2), 307–312.

Brewster, K. L., & Tillman, K. H. (2008). Who's doing it? Patterns and predictors of youths' oral sexual experiences. *Journal of Adolescent Health, 42*(1), 73–80.

Brezsnyak, M., & Whisman, M. A. (2004). Sexual desire and relationship functioning: The effects of marital satisfaction and power. *Journal of Sex and Marital Therapy, 30*, 199–217.

Brickell, C. (2001). Whose "special treatment"? Heterosexism and the problems with liberalism. *Sexualities, 4*(2), 211–235.

Bridges, A. J., Bergner, R. M., & Hesson-McInnis, M. (2003). Romantic partners' use of pornography: Its significance for women. *Journal of Sex and Marital Therapy, 29*, 1–14.

Brocato, V. (2004). U.S.-based opposition to sexual and reproductive rights goes international. *SIECUS Report, 32*(4), 22–27.

Brochert, A. (2001). In clinical use, low-dose medical abortion method proves highly successful. *Family Planning Perspectives, 33*(3), 138.

Brooks, L., et al. (2009). Normalizing HIV testing in a busy urban sexually transmitted infections clinic. *Sexually Transmitted Diseases, 36*(3), 127–128.

Brotman, R. M., et al. (2008). The effect of vaginal douching cessation on bacterial vaginosis: A pilot study. *American Journal of Obstetrics and Gynecology, 198*(6), 628.e1–628.e7.

Brotto, L. A. (2006). Review of *Handbook of Sexual Dysfunction* by R. Balon & R. T. Segraves. *Archives of Sexual Behavior, 35*, 761–764.

Brotto, L. A., et al. (2008). A psychoeducational intervention for sexual dysfunction in women with gynecologic cancer. *Archives of Sexual Behavior, 37*, 317–329.

Brotto, L. A., Heiman, J. R., & Tolman, D. L. (2009). Narratives of desire in mid-age women with and without arousal difficulties. *Journal of Sex Research, 46*(5), 387–398.

Brown, G., Maycock, B., & Burns, S. (2005). Your picture is your bait: Use and meaning of cyberspace among gay men. *Journal of Sex Research, 42*(1), 63–73.

Brown, J. D., & Wissow, L. S. (2009). Discussion of sensitive health topics with youth during primary care visits: Relationship to youth perceptions of care. *Journal of Adolescent Health, 44*(1), 48–54.

Brown, J. S., Adera, T., & Masho, S. W. (2008). Previous abortion and the risk of low birth weight and preterm births. *Journal of Epidemiology and Community Medicine, 62*(1), 16–22.

Brown, R. D., et al. (2004). Assessing the campus climate for gay, lesbian, bisexual, and transgender (GLBT) students using a multiple perspectives approach. *Journal of College Student Development, 45*(1), 8–26.

Brown, W. M., et al. (2002). Difference in finger length ratios between self-identified "butch" and "femme" lesbians. *Archives of Sexual Behavior, 31*(1), 123–127.

Browning, J. R., et al. (2000). Sexual motives, gender, and sexual behavior. *Archives of Sexual Behavior, 29*(2), 135–153.

Brubaker, L., et al. (2008). Sexual function 6 months after first delivery. *Obstetrics and Gynecology, 111*(5), 1040–1044.

Bruckner, H., Martin, A., & Bearman, P. (2004). Ambivalence and pregnancy: Adolescents' attitudes, contraceptive use and pregnancy. *Perspectives on Sexual and Reproductive Health, 36*(6), 248–257.

Bryant, J. A., et al. (2001). Paradoxical effect of surveyor's conservative versus provocative clothing on rape myth acceptance of males and females. *Journal of Psychology and Human Sexuality, 13*(1), 55–66.

Bucardo, J., et al. (2004). A qualitative exploration of female sex work in Tijuana, Mexico. *Archives of Sexual Behavior, 33*(4), 343–351.

Buhimschi, I. A. (2008). Proteomic profiling of urine identifies specific fragments of serpina1 and albumin as biomarkers of preeclampsia. *American Journal of Obstetrics and Gynecology, 199*(5), 551.e1–551.e16.

Bull, S. S., et al. (2008). POWER for reproductive health: Results from a social marketing campaign promoting female and male condoms. *Journal of Adolescent Medicine, 43*(1), 71–78.

Bullis, R. K. (2008). Using surveys to track student sexual behavior and attitudes in the public schools: Current case law and future implications. *American Journal of Sexuality Education, 3*(3), 235–246.

Bullivant, S. B., et al. (2004). Women's sexual experience during the menstrual cycle: Identification of the sexual phase by noninvasive measurement of luteinizing hormone. *Journal of Sex Research, 41*(1), 82–93.

Bullough, V. L. (2002). Masturbation: A historical overview. *Journal of Psychology and Human Sexuality, 14*(2/3), 17–33.

Bullough, V. L. (2003a). Bruce Rind the truth teller. *Journal of Psychology and Human Sexuality, 15*(1), 1–3.

Bullough, V. L. (2003b). Magnus Hirschfeld, an often overlooked pioneer. *Sexuality and Culture, 7*(1), 62–72.

Bullough, V. L. (2004). Sex will never be the same: The contributions of Alfred C. Kinsey. *Archives of Sexual Behavior, 33*(3), 277–286.

Bullough, V. L. (2004). Children and adolescents as sexual beings: A historical review. *Child and Adolescent Psychiatric Clinics of North America, 13*, 447–459.

Burleson, M. H., Trevathan, W. R., & Todd, M. (2007). In the mood for love or vice versa? Exploring the relations among sexual activity, physical affection, affect, and stress in the daily lives of mid-aged women. *Archives of Sexual Behavior, 36*, 357–368.

Burris, S., & Cameron, E. (2008). The case against criminalization of HIV transmission. *Journal of the American Medical Association, 300*(5), 578–581.

Burriss, R. P., Little, A. C., & Nelson, E. C. (2007). 2D:4D and sexually dimorphic facial characteristics. *Archives of Sexual Behavior, 36*, 377–384.

Burstein, G. R., et al. (2003). Missed opportunities for sexually transmitted diseases, human immunodeficiency virus, and pregnancy prevention services during adolescent health supervision visits. *Pediatrics, 111*(5), 996–1001.

Burton, D. L. (2008). An exploratory evaluation of the contribution of personality and childhood sexual victimization to the development of sexually abusive behavior. *Sexual Abuse: A Journal of Research and Treatment, 20*(1), 102–115.

Bush, H. (2008). Global partnership, giving and greener. *Contemporary Sexuality, 42*, 3.

Buss, D. M. (2000). The dangerous passion: Why jealousy is as necessary as love and sex. New York: Free Press.

Buss, D. M. (2002). Human mate guarding. *Neuroendocrinology Letters, 23*(4), 23–29.

Buss, D. M. (2003). *The evolution of desire: Strategies of human mating.* (Rev. ed.). New York: Basic Books.

Butt, T., & Hearn, J. (1998). The sexualization of corporal punishment: The construction of sexual meaning. *Sexualities, 1*(2), 203–227.

Buzzell, T. (2005). Demographic characteristics of persons using pornography in three technological contexts. *Sexuality and Culture, 9*(1), 28–48.

Byers, E. S. (2005). Relationship satisfaction and sexual satisfaction: A longitudinal study of individuals in long-term relationships. *Journal of Sex Research, 42*(2), 113–118.

Byers, E. S., & Grenier, G. (2003). Premature or rapid ejaculation: Heterosexual couples' perceptions of men's ejaculatory behavior. *Archives of Sexual Behavior, 32*(3), 261–270.

Byers, E. S., Purdon, C., & Clark, D. A. (1998). Sexual intrusive thoughts of college students. *Journal of Sex Research, 35*(4), 359–369.

Bylaite, M., & Ruzicka, T. (2007). Pearly penile papules. *New England Journal of Medicine, 357*(7), 691.

Cain, V. S., et al. (2003). Sexual functioning and practices in a multi-ethnic study of midlife women: Baseline results from SWAN. *Journal of Sex Research, 40*(3), 266–276.

Caldwell, J. G. (2008). Relational aspects of maladaptive diaper-wearing and treatment with couples therapy. *Sexual and Relationship Therapy, 23*(2), 157–160.

Callaghan, W. M., & Berg, C. J. (2003). Pregnancy-related mortality among women aged 35 years and older, United States, 1991–1997. *Obstetrics and Gynecology, 102*(5), 1015–1021.

Callaghan, W. M., et al. (2006). The contribution of preterm birth to infant mortality rates in the United States. *Pediatrics, 118*(4), 1566–1573.

Cameron, A., Rosen, R. C., & Swindle, R. W. (2005). Sexual and relationship characteristics among an Internet-based sample of U.S. men with and without erectile dysfunction. *Journal of Sex and Marital Therapy, 31*, 229–242.

Camilleri, J. A., & Quinsey, V. L. (2009). Individual differences in the propensity for partner sexual coercion. *Sexual Abuse: A Journal of Research and Treatment, 21*(1), 111–129.

Campbell, A. (2004). Female competition: Causes, constraints, content, and contexts. *Journal of Sex Research, 41*(1), 16–26.

Cantor, J. M., et al. (2002). How many gay men owe their sexual orientation to fraternal birth order? *Archives of Sexual Behavior, 31*(1), 63–71.

Cantor, J. M., et al. (2005). Handedness in pedophilia and hebephilia. *Archives of Sexual Behavior, 34*(4), 447–459.

Cantor, J. M., et al. (2006). Grade failure and special education placement in sexual offenders' educational histories. *Archives of Sexual Behavior, 35*(6), 743–751.

Cantor, J. M., et al. (2008). Cerebral white matter deficiencies in pedophilic men. *Journal of Psychiatric Research, 42,* 167–183.

Carballo-Diéguez, A., et al. (2006). Sexual negotiation, HIV-status disclosure, and sexual risk behavior among Latino men who use the Internet to seek sex with other men. *Archives of Sexual Behavior, 35,* 473–481.

Carbone, D. J. (2008). Treatment of gay men for post-traumatic stress disorder resulting from social ostracism and ridicule: Cognitive behavior therapy and eye movement desensitization and reprocessing approaches. *Archives of Sexual Behavior, 37,* 305–316.

Cardenas, M., & Barrientos, J. E. (2008). The attitudes toward lesbians and gay men scale (ATLG): Adaptation and testing the reliability and validity in Chile. *Journal of Sex Research, 45*(2), 140–149.

Cardoso, F. L. (2005). Cultural universals and differences in male homosexuality: The case of a Brazilian fishing village. *Archives of Sexual Behavior, 34*(1), 103–109.

Carmichael, M. (2004, May 10). Have it your way: Redesigning birth. *Newsweek,* 70–72.

Carnes, P. (1992). *Out of the shadows: Understanding sexual addiction.* (2d ed.). Center City, MN: Hazelden.

Carnes, P. (2003). Understanding sexual addiction. *SIECUS Report, 31*(5), 5–7.

Carpendale, J. J. M. (2000). Kohlberg and Piaget on stages and moral reasoning. *Developmental Review, 20,* 181–205.

Carpenter, D., et al. (2008). Women's scores on the sexual inhibition/sexual excitation scales (SIS/SES): Gender similarities and differences. *Journal of Sex Research, 45,* 36–48.

Carpenter, L. M., Nathanson, C. A., & Kim, Y. J. (2009). Physical women, emotional men: Gender and sexual satisfaction in midlife. *Archives of Sexual Behavior, 38,* 87–107.

Carufel, F., & Trudel, G. (2006). Effects of a new functional-sexological treatment for premature ejaculation. *Journal of Sex and Marital Therapy, 32,* 97–114.

Carvalheira, A., & Gomes, F. A. (2003). Cybersex in Portuguese chatrooms: A study of sexual behaviors related to on-line sex. *Journal of Sex and Marital Therapy, 29,* 345–360.

Cass, V. C. (1983–1984). Homosexual identity: A concept in need of definition. *Journal of Homosexuality, 9,* 105–126.

Cass, V. C. (1990). The implications of homosexual identity formation for the Kinsey model and scale of sexual preference. In D. P. McWhirter, S. A. Sanders & J. M. Reinisch. (Eds.), *Homosexuality/ heterosexuality: Concepts of sexual orientation.* (pp. 239–266). New York: Oxford University Press.

Castle, P. E., et al. (2009). Five-year experience of human papillomavirus DNA and Papanicolaou test cotesting. *Obstetrics and Gynecology, 113*(3), 595–600.

Caswell, N., & Manning, J. T. (2009). A comparison of finger 2D:4D by self-report direct measurement and experimenter measurement from photocopy: Methodological issues. *Archives of Sexual Behavior, 38,* 143–148.

Catania, J. (1997). 10 percent of sexually active U.S. adults use sex toys in partner sex. *Sexual Science, 38*(4), 1, 8.

Catania, J. A., et al. (2008). Mediators of childhood sexual abuse and high-risk sex among men-who-have-sex-with-men. *Child Abuse and Neglect, 32*(10), 925–940.

Cates, W., & Feldblum, P. (2008). HIV prevention research: The ecstasy and the agony. *Lancet, 372*(9654), 1932–1933.

CDC. (2004a). Cases of HIV infection and AIDS in the United States, by race/ethnicity, 1998–2002. *HIV/AIDS Surveillance Supplemental Report, 10*(1).

CDC. (2004b). *National Youth Risk Behavior Survey: 1991–2003: Trends in the prevalence of sexual behaviors. Healthy Youth.* Atlanta: Centers for Disease Control and Prevention.

CDC. (2006). *STD treatment guidelines, 2007.* Atlanta: Dept. of Health and Human Services, Centers for Disease Control and Prevention. www.cdc.gov/ std/stats07toc.htm

CDC. (2008a). *STD surveillance 2007.* Atlanta: Dept. of Health and Human Services, Centers for Disease Control and Prevention.

CDC. (2008b). *National youth risk behavior survey: 1991–2007.* Atlanta: CDC.

CDC. (2008c). Youth risk behavior surveillance—United States, 2007. *Morbidity and Mortality Weekly Report, 57*(SS-4), 1–131.

Cha, E.-S., Kim, K. H., & Patrick, T. E. (2008). Predictors of intention to practice safer sex among Korean college students. *Archives of Sexual Behavior, 37,* 641–651.

Chan, P. G., Sung, H-Y, & Sawaya, G. F. (2003). Changes in cervical cancer incidence after three decades of screening U.S. women less than 30 years old. *Obstetrics and Gynecology, 102*(4), 765–773.

Chan, W. S., et al. (2004). Risk of stroke in women exposed to low-dose oral contraceptives: A critical evaluation of the evidence. *Archives of Internal Medicine, 164*(7), 741–747.

Chandra, A., et al. (2008). Does watching sex on television predict teen pregnancy? Findings from a national longitudinal survey of youth. *Pediatrics, 122*(5), 1047–1054.

Chang, S., et al. (2009). Surveillance of cardiovascular risk factors for outpatients in different erectile dysfunction severity. *International Journal of Impotence Research, 21,* 116–121.

Check, E. (2005). The X factor. *Nature, 434,* 266–267.

Chen, C-L., et al. (2002). Hormone replacement therapy in relation to breast cancer. *Journal of the American Medical Association, 287*(6), 734–741.

Chen, X.-K., et al. (2009). Recent oral contraceptive use and adverse birth outcomes. *European Journal of Obstetrics and Gynecology and Reproductive Biology, 144*(1), 40–43.

Cheng, D., et al. (2008). Unintended pregnancy and associated maternal preconception, prenatal and postpartum behaviors. *Contraception, 79*(3), 194–198.

Cheng, M. M., and Udry, J. R. (2003). How much do mentally disabled adolescents know about sex and birth control? *Adolescent and Family Health, 3*(1), 28–38.

Cheng, Y., et al. (2008). Effectiveness of a school-based AIDS education program among rural students in HIV high epidemic area of China. *Journal of Adolescent Health, 42*(2), 184–191.

Chenier, E. R. (2008). Review of: *Disorders of Desire: Sex and Gender in Modern American Sexology* by Janice Irvine. *Archives of Sexual Behavior, 37,* 356–358.

Cherpes, T. L., et al. (2003). Risk factors for infection with herpes simplex virus type 2: Role of smoking, douching, uncircumcised males, and vaginal flora. *Sexually Transmitted Diseases, 30*(5), 405–410.

Chescheir, N. C. (2009). Maternal-fetal surgery: Where are we and how did we get here? *Obstetrics and Gynecology, 113*(3), 717–731.

Chiasson, M., et al. (2005). Increased high risk sexual behavior after September 11 in men who have sex with men: An Internet study. *Archives of Sexual Behavior, 34*(5), 527–535.

Choate, L. H. (2005). Toward a theoretical model of women's body image resilience. *Journal of Counseling and Development, 83,* 320–330.

Choi, K.-H., et al. (2008). The efficacy of female condom skills training in HIV risk reduction among women: A randomized controlled trial. *American Journal of Public Health, 98*(10), 1841–1848.

Christakis, D. A., et al. (2000). A trade-off analysis of routine newborn circumcision. *Pediatrics, 105*(1), 246–249.

Christakis, N. A., & Fowler, J. H. (2009). *Connected: The surprising power of our social networks and how they shape our lives.* Boston: Little, Brown and Co.

Christopher, F. S., & Pflieger, J. C. (2007). Sexual aggression: The dark side of sexuality in relationships. *Annual Review of Sex Research, 18,* 115–142.

Chudakov, B., et al. (2002). The motivation and mental health of sex workers. *Journal of Sex and Marital Therapy, 28,* 305–315.

Chung, R. C. (2005). Women, human rights, and counseling: Crossing international boundaries. *Journal of Counseling and Development, 83,* 262–268.

Ciccarone, D. H., et al. (2003). Sex without disclosure of HIV serostatus in a U.S. probability sample of persons receiving medical care for HIV infection. *American Journal of Public Health, 93*(6), 949–954.

Ciclitira, K. (2004). Pornography, women and feminism: Between pleasure and politics. *Sexualities, 7*(3), 281–301.

Ciesielski, C., Tabidze, I., & Brown, C. (2004). Transmission of primary and secondary syphilis by oral sex—Chicago, Illinois, 1998–2002. *Morbidity and Mortality Weekly Report, 53*(41), 966–968.

Clark, C. A., & Wiederman, M. W. (2000). Gender and reactions to a hypothetical relationship partner's masturbation and use of sexually explicit media. *Journal of Sex Research, 37*(2), 133–141.

Clark, L. R., Jackson, M., & Allen-Taylor, L. (2002). Adolescent knowledge about *Sexually Transmitted Diseases. Sexually Transmitted Diseases, 29*(8), 436–443.

Clark, S. L., et al. (2008). Maternal death in the 21st century: Causes, prevention, and relationship to cesarean delivery. *American Journal of Obstetrics and Gynecology, 199*(1), 36.e1–36.e5.

Clawson, C. L., & Reese-Weber, M. (2003). The amount and timing of parent-adolescent sexual communication as predictors of late adolescent sexual risk-taking behaviors. *Journal of Sex Research, 40*(3), 256–265.

Clayton, A. H., et al. (2006). Reliability and validity of the sexual interest and desire inventory—female (SIDI-F), a scale designed to measure severity of female hypoactive sexual desire disorder. *Journal of Sex and Marital Therapy, 32,* 115–135.

Cleland, J., et al. (2006). Family planning: The unfinished agenda. *Lancet,* Early Online Publication: DOI: 10.1016/S0140-6736(06)69480-4.

Clement, U. (2002). Sex in long-term relationships: A systemic approach to sexual desire problems. *Archives of Sexual Behavior, 31*(3), 241–246.

Clements-Nolle, K., et al. (2008). Highly active antiretroviral therapy use and HIV transmission risk behaviors among individuals who are HIV infected and were recently released from jail. *American Journal of Public Health, 98*(4), 661–666.

Cluett, E. R., et al. (2004). Randomized controlled trial of laboring in water compared with standard augmentation for management of dystocia in first stage of labor. *British Medical Journal, 328*(7435), 314–319.

Coates, T. J., Richter, L., & Caceres, C. (2008). Behavioural strategies to reduce HIV transmission: How to make them work better. *Lancet, 372*(9639), 669–684.

Cohan, C. L., & Kleinbaum, S. (2002). Toward a greater understanding of the cohabitation effect: Premarital cohabitation and marital communication. *Journal of Marriage and Family, 64*(1), 180–192.

Cohen, J. (2003). Human population: The next half century. *Science, 302,* 1172–1175.

Cohen, J. (2008). HIV gets by with a lot of help from human host. *Science, 319,* 143–144.

Cohen, K. M. (2002). Relationships among childhood sex-atypical behavior, spatial ability, handedness, and sexual orientation in men. *Archives of Sexual Behavior, 31*(1), 129–143.

Cohen, T. R., Hall, D. L., & Tuttle, J. (2009). Attitudes toward stereotypical versus counterstereotypical gay men and lesbians. *Journal of Sex Research, 46*(4), 274–281.

Cohen-Kettenis, P. T. (2005). Gender change in 46, XY persons with 5α-reductase-2 deficiency and 17β-hydroxy-steroid-dehydrogenase-3 deficiency. *Archives of Sexual Behavior, 34*(4), 399–410.

Colapinto, J. (2000). *As nature made him: The boy who was raised as a girl.* New York: HarperCollins.

Cole, L. A., Ladner, D. G., & Byrn, F. W. (2009). The normal variabilities of the menstrual cycle. *Fertility and Sterility, 91*(2), 522–527.

Coleman, E. (2002). Masturbation as a means of achieving sexual health. *Journal of Psychology and Human Sexuality, 14*(2/3), 5–16.

Coleman, E. (2003). Compulsive sexual behavior: What to call it, how to treat it. *SIECUS Report, 31*(5), 12–16.

Coleman, E., et al. (2001). Standards of care for the treatment of adult sex offenders. *Journal of Psychology and Human Sexuality, 13*(3/4), 115–121.

Coleman, E., et al. (2007). Creating a sexually healthier world through effective public policy. *International Journal of Sexual Health, 19,* 5–24.

Coleman, L. M., & Cater, S. (2005). A qualitative study of the relationship between alcohol consumption and risky sex in adolescents. *Archives of Sexual Behavior, 34*(6), 649–661.

Coley, R. L., Medeiros, B. L., & Schindler, H. S. (2008). Using sibling differences to estimate effects of parenting on adolescent sexual risk behaviors. *Journal of Adolescent Health, 43*(2), 133–140.

Collaborative Group on Hormonal Factors in Breast Cancer. (2004). Breast cancer and abortion: Collaborative reanalysis of data from 53 epidemiological studies, including 83,000 women with breast cancer from 16 countries. *Lancet, 363*(9414), 1007–1016.

Colman, S., & Joyce, T. (2009). Minors' behavioral responses to parental involvement laws: Delaying abortion until age 18. *Perspectives on Sexual and Reproductive Health, 41*(2), 119–126.

Colman, S., Joyce, T., & Kaestner, R. (2008). Misclassification bias and the estimated effect of parental involvement laws on adolescents' reproductive outcomes. *American Journal of Public Health, 98*(10), 1881–1885.

Colpin, H., & Bossaert, G. (2008). Adolescents conceived by IVF: Parenting and psychosocial adjustment. *Human Reproduction, 23*(12), 2724–2730.

Committee on Infectious Diseases, American Academy of Pediatrics. (2007).

Prevention of human papillomavirus infection: Provisional recommendations for immunization of girls and women with quadrivalent human papillomavirus vaccine. *Pediatrics, 120*(3), 666–668.

Committee on Pediatric AIDS. (2008). HIV testing and prophylaxis to prevent mother-to-child transmission in the United States. *Pediatrics, 122*(5), 1127–1134.

Conaglen, H. M. (2004). Sexual content induced delay: A reexamination investigating relation to sexual desire. *Archives of Sexual Behavior, 33*(4), 359–367.

Conaglen, H. M., & Conaglen, J. V. (2003). Sexual desire in women presenting for anti-androgen therapy. *Journal of Sex and Marital Therapy, 29*(4), 255–267.

Conaglen, H. M., & Conaglen, J. V. (2008). The impact of erectile dysfunction on female partners: A qualitative investigation. *Sexual and Relationship Therapy, 23*(2), 147–156.

Conaglen, H. M., & Evans, I. M. (2006). Pictorial cues and sexual desire: An experimental approach. *Archives of Sexual Behavior, 35*(2), 201–216.

Conaglen, H. M., Suttie, J. M., & Conaglen, J. V. (2003). Effect of deer velvet on sexual function in men and their partners: A double-blind, placebo-controlled study. *Archives of Sexual Behavior, 32*(3), 271–278.

Conklin, S. C. (2001). Seminary sexuality education survey: Current efforts, perceived need and readiness in accredited Christian institutions. *Journal of Sex Education and Therapy, 26*(4), 301–309.

Connell, K., et al. (2005). Effects of age, menopause, and comorbidities on neurological function of the female genitalia. *International Journal of Impotence Research, 17*(1), 63–70.

Connolly, J., & Friedlander, L. (2009). Peer group influences on adolescent dating aggression. *Prevention Researcher, 16*(1), 8–11.

Connolly, P. H. (2006). Psychological functioning of bondage/domination/sadomasochism (BDSM) practitioners. *Journal of Psychology and Human Sexuality, 18*(1), 79–120.

Connop, V., & Petrak, J. (2004). The impact of sexual assault on heterosexual couples. *Sexual and Relationship Therapy, 19*(1), 29–38.

Cooper, A. (2000). Sexual pathology and the Internet. *Professional Psychology: Research and Practice, 30*(2).

Cooper, A., et al. (2002). Toward an increased understanding of user demographics in online sexual activities. *Journal of Sex and Marital Therapy, 28,* 105–129.

Cooper, D. A. (2008). Antiretroviral therapy cohort collaboration, life expectancy of individuals on combination antiretroviral therapy in high-income countries: A collaborative analysis of 14 cohort studies. *Lancet, 372*(9635), 293–299.

Coovadia, H. M., & Schaller, J. G. (2008). HIV/AIDS in children: A disaster in the making. *Lancet, 372*(9635), 271–273.

Cornog, M. (2001). Group masturbation among young and old(er): A summary with questions. *Journal of Sex Education and Therapy, 26*(4), 340–346.

Corona, G., et al. (2005). Difficulties in achieving vs. maintaining erection: Organic, psychogenic, and relational determinants. *International Journal of Impotence Research, 17,* 252–258.

Corretti, G., et al. (2006). Comorbidity between social phobia and premature ejaculation: Study on 242 males affected by sexual disorders. *Journal of Sex and Marital Therapy, 32,* 183–187.

Cott, N. F. (2005). Public vows: A history of marriage and the nation. *SIECUS Report, 33*(1), 5–12.

Couzin, J. (2009). Friendship as a health factor. *Science, 323,* 454–457.

Cowden, C. R., & Bradshaw, S. D. (2007). Religiosity and sexual concerns. *International Journal of Sexual Health, 19*(1), 15–24.

Craissati, J., Webb, L., & Keen, S. (2008). The relationship between developmental variables, personality disorder, and risk in sex offenders. *Sexual Abuse: A Journal of Research and Treatment, 20*(2), 119–138.

Crary, D. (2006, April 9). The porn divide: Home wrecker or harmless fun? *Associated Press/Watertown (NY) Daily Times Sunday Weekly,* 6–7.

Creamer, E. G. (1994). Gender and publications in core higher education journals. *Journal of College Student Development, 35,* 35–39.

Creinin, M. D., et al. (2008). Multicenter comparison of the contraceptive ring and patch: A randomized controlled trial. *Obstetrics and Gynecology, 111*(2), 267–277.

Crouch, N. S., et al. (2008). Sexual function and genital sensitivity following feminizing genitoplasty for congenital adrenal hyperplasia. *Journal of Urology, 179*(2), 634–638.

Crown, L., & Roberts, L. J. (2009). Capturing complexity: An empirical typology of nonagentic sexual interactions. *International Journal of Sexual Health, 21*(1), 1–16.

Cubbin, C., et al. (2005). Neighborhood context and sexual behaviors among adolescents: Findings from the National Longitudinal Study of Adolescent Health. *Perspectives on Sexual and Reproductive Health, 37*(3), 125–134.

Culwell, K. R., & Feinglass, J. (2007). The association of health insurance with use of prescription contraceptives.

Perspectives on Sexual and Reproductive Health, 39(4), 226–230.

Curtis, J. N. (2008). HIV/AIDS adherence: Teaching about treatment and stigma. *American Journal of Sexuality Education, 3*(1), 87–96.

Curtis, J. N., & Coffey, K. (2007). The cheat-o-meter: Talking about what it means to "be faithful." *American Journal of Sexuality Education, 2*(4), 89–98.

Cutler, W. B., Friedmann, E., & McCoy, N. L. (1998). Pheromonal influences on sociosexual behavior in men. *Archives of Sexual Behavior, 27*(1), 1–13.

Cwikel, J., & Hoban, E. (2005). Contentious issues in research on trafficked women working in the sex industry: Study design, ethics, and methodology. *Journal of Sex Research, 42*(4), 306–316.

Dahan, R., Feldman, R., & Hermoni, D. (2008). Is patients' sexual orientation a blind spot of family physicians? *Journal of Homosexuality, 55*(3), 524–532.

D'Amato, A. (2006). *Public law and legal theory research paper series: Porn up, rape down.* Chicago: Northwestern University School of Law.

Damber, J.-E., & Gunnar, A. (2008). Prostate cancer. *Lancet, 371*(9625), 1710–1721.

Damon, W. (2002). Dominance, sexism, and inadequacy: Testing a compensatory conceptualization in a sample of heterosexual men involved in SM. *Journal of Psychology and Human Sexuality, 14*(4), 15–46.

Damon, W., & Rosser, B. (2005). Anodyspareunia in men who have sex with men: Prevalence, predictors, consequences and the development of DSM diagnostic criteria. *Journal of Sex and Marital Therapy, 31,* 129–141.

D'Angelo, D. V., et al. (2004). Differences between mistimed and unwanted pregnancies among women who have live births. *Perspectives on Sexual and Reproductive Health, 36*(5), 192–197.

Dariotis, J. K., et al. (2008). Changes in sexual risk behavior as young men transition to adulthood. *Perspectives on Sexual and Reproductive Health, 40*(4), 218–225.

Darling, C. A., Davidson, J. K., & Conway-Welch, C. (1990). Female ejaculation: Perceived origins, the Grafenberg spot/area, and sexual responsiveness. *Archives of Sexual Behavior, 19*(1), 29–47.

Darling, C. A., Davidson, J. K., & Jennings, D. A. (1991). The female sexual response revisited: Understanding the multiorgasmic experience in women. *Archives of Sexual Behavior, 20*(6), 527–540.

Das, A. (2007). Masturbation in the United States. *Journal of Sex and Marital Therapy, 33*(4), 301–317.

Datta, G., et al. (2006). Individual-, neighborhood-, and state-level socioeconomic predictors of cervical carcinoma screening among U.S. black women: A multilevel analysis. *Cancer, 106*(3), 664–669.

Davidson, N. E., & Helzlsouer, K. J. (2002). Good news about oral contraceptives. *New England Journal of Medicine, 346*(26), 2078–2079.

Davies, M. (2004). Correlates of negative attitudes toward gay men: Sexism, male role norms, and male sexuality. *Journal of Sex Research, 41*(3), 259–266.

Davies, M., Rogers, P., & Bates, J.-A. (2008). Blame toward male rape victims in a hypothetical sexual assault as a function of victim sexuality and degree of resistance. *Journal of Homosexuality, 55*(3), 533–544.

Davis, C. M., & Bauserman, R. (1993). Exposure to sexually explicit materials: An attitude change perspective. *Annual Review of Sex Research, 4,* 121–209.

Dawson, L. H., et al. (2008). Reasons why adolescents and young adults have sex: Associations with psychological characteristics and sexual behavior. *Journal of Sex Research, 45*(3), 225–232.

DeBruine, L. M., et al. (2008). Social perception of facial resemblance in humans. *Archives of Sexual Behavior, 37,* 64–77.

DeCock, K. M., et al. (2009). Can antiretroviral therapy eliminate HIV transmission? *Lancet, 373*(9657), 7–9.

DeCuypere, G., et al. (2005). Sexual and physical health after sex reassignment surgery. *Archives of Sexual Behavior, 34*(6), 679–690.

Deeks, S. G., & Phillips, A. N. (2009). HIV infection, antiretroviral treatment, ageing, and non-AIDS related morbidity. *British Medical Journal, 338*(a3172).

deJong, D. C. (2009). The role of attention in sexual arousal: Implications for treatment of sexual dysfunction. *Journal of Sex Research, 426*(2–3), 237–248.

Dekker, A., & Schmidt, G. (2002). Patterns of masturbatory behavior: Changes between the sixties and the nineties. *Journal of Psychology and Human Sexuality, 14*(2/3), 35–48.

del Rio, C. E. (2007). Update to CDC's sexually transmitted diseases treatment guidelines, 2006: Fluoroquinolones no longer recommended for treatment of gonococcal infections. *Morbidity and Mortality Weekly Report, 56*(14), 332–336.

DeLamater, J., & Friedrich, W. N. (2002). Human sexual development. *Journal of Sex Research, 39*(1), 10–14.

DeLamater, J., Hyde, J. S., & Fong, M.-C. (2008). Sexual satisfaction in the seventh decade of life. *Journal of Sex & Marital Therapy, 34*(5), 439–454.

DeLamater, J. D., & Sill, M. (2005). Sexual desire in later life. *Journal of Sex Research, 42*(2), 138–149.

Delmonico, D. L., & Griffin, E. J. (2009). Cybersex and the e-teen: What marriage and family therapists should know. *Journal of Marital and Family Therapy, 34*(4), 431–444.

Del Priore, G., et al. (2007). Human uterus retrieval from a multi-organ donor. *Obstetrics and Gynecology, 109,* 101–104.

Dennerstein, L., Alexander, J. L., & Kotz, K. (2004). The menopause and sexual functioning: A review of the population-based studies. *Annual Review of Sex Research, 14,* 64–82.

Dennerstein, L., Guthrie, J. R., & Alford, S. (2004). Childhood abuse and its association with mid-aged women's sexual functioning. *Journal of Sex and Marital Therapy, 30,* 225–234.

Denning, P. H., & Campsmith, M. L. (2005). Unprotected anal intercourse among HIV-positive men who have a steady male sex partner with negative or unknown HIV serostatus. *American Journal of Public Health, 95*(1), 152–158.

Dennis, C. (2004). The most important sexual organ. Nature, *427,* 390–392.

Denov, M. S. (2003). The myth of innocence: Sexual scripts and the recognition of child sexual abuse by female perpetrators. *Journal of Sex Research, 40*(3), 303–314.

Deogracias, J. J., et al. (2007). The gender identity/gender dysphoria questionnaire for adolescents and adults. *Journal of Sex Research, 44*(4), 370–379.

Derogatis, L., et al. (2004). Validation of the profile of female sexual function (PFSF) in surgically and naturally menopausal women. *Journal of Sex and Marital Therapy, 30,* 25–36.

Derouiche, A., et al. (2008). Management of penile fractures complicated by urethral rupture. *International Journal of Impotence Research, 20,* 111–114.

Dessens, A. B., Slijper, F. M. E., & Drop, S. L. S. (2005). Gender dysphoria and gender change in chromosomal females with congenital adrenal hyperplasia. *Archives of Sexual Behavior, 34*(4), 389–397.

DeVoss, D. (2002). Women's porn sites—spaces of fissure and eruption or "I'm a little bit of everything." *Sexuality and Culture, 6*(3), 75–94.

Diamond, L. M. (2006). The evolution of plasticity in female-female desire. *Journal of Psychology and Human Sexuality, 18*(4), 245–274.

Diaz-Arjonilla, M., et al. (2009). Obesity, low testosterone levels and erectile dysfunction. *International Journal of Impotence Research, 21,* 89–98.

Dickey, R. P. (2009). Strategies to reduce multiple pregnancies due to ovulation stimulation. *Fertility and Sterility, 91*(1), 1–17.

DiClemente, R. J., et al. (2008). Prevalence, correlates, and efficacy of selective avoidance as a sexually transmitted disease prevention strategy among African American adolescent females. *Archives of Pediatrics and Adolescent Medicine, 162*(1), 60–65.

DiGirolamo, A. M., et al. (2008). Breastfeeding-related maternity practices at hospitals and birth centers—United States, 2007. *Morbidity and Mortality Weekly Report, 57*(23), 621–625.

Dillon, B. E., Chama, N. B., & Honig, S. C. (2008). Penile size and penile enlargement surgery: A review. *International Journal of Impotence Research, 20,* 519–529.

Dilorio, C., et al. (2007). REAL men: A group-randomized trial of HIV prevention intervention for adolescent boys. *American Journal of Public Health, 97*(6), 1084–1089.

Disogra, C. E., Mariño, R., & Minichiello, V. (2005). Self-reported use of health services, contact with police and views about sex work organizations among male sex workers in Cordoba, Argentina. *Journal of Psychology and Human Sexuality, 17*(1/2), 181–195.

Dodge, B., et al. (2008). Sexuality education in Florida: Content, context, and controversy. *American Journal of Sexuality Education, 3*(2), 183–209.

Dodge, B., Jeffries IV, W. L., & Sandfort, T. G. (2008). Beyond the down low: Sexual risk, protection, and disclosure among at-risk black men who have sex with both men and women (msmw). *Archives of Sexual Behavior, 37,* 683–696.

Dodge, B., et al. (2004). Sexual compulsivity among heterosexual college students. *Journal of Sex Research, 41*(4), 343–350.

Dolezal, C., & Carballo-Dieguez, A. (2002). Childhood sexual experiences and the perception of abuse among Latino men who have sex with men. *Journal of Sex Research, 39*(3), 165–173.

Domine, F., et al. (2009). Disordered eating behaviors: What about boys? *Journal of Adolescent Health, 44*(2), 111–117.

Donnelly, D., et al. (2001). Involuntary celibacy: A life course analysis. *Journal of Sex Research, 38*(2), 159–169.

Douglas Jr, J. M., et al. (2009). Penicillin treatment of syphilis. *Journal of the American Medical Association, 301*(7), 769–771.

Downing, R. A., LaVeist, T. A., & Bullock, H. E. (2007). Intersections of ethnicity and social class in provider advice regarding reproductive health. *American Journal of Public Health, 97*(10), 1803–1807.

Dreger, A. D. (2008). The controversy surrounding *The man who would be queen:* A case history of the politics of science, identity, and sex in the Internet age. *Archives of Sexual Behavior, 37,* 366–421.

Drenth, J. J. (2008). A surgical temptation: The demonization of the foreskin and the rise of circumcision in Britain. *Archives of Sexual Behavior, 37,* 346–348.

Drey, E. A., et al. (2006). Risk factors associated with presenting for abortion in the second trimester. *Obstetrics and Gynecology, 107*(1), 128–135.

Dreznick, M. T. (2003). Heterosocial competence of rapists and child molesters: A meta-analysis. *Journal of Sex Research, 40*(2), 170–178.

Dreznick, M. T., et al. (2003). Saying yes when meaning no: An investigation of gender and individual differences in token seduction. *Journal of Psychology and Human Sexuality, 15*(1), 69–84.

Drumright, L. N., Gorbach, P. M., & Holmes, K. K. (2004). Do people really know their sexual partners? Concurrency, knowledge of partner behavior, and sexually transmitted infections within partnerships. *Sexually Transmitted Diseases, 31*(7), 437–442.

Dube, E. M. (2000). The role of sexual behavior in the identification process of gay and bisexual males. *Journal of Sex Research, 37*(2), 123–132.

Duggavathi, R., & Murphy, B. D. (2009). Ovulation signals. *Science, 324,* 890–891.

East, P. L., Reyes, B. T., & Horn, E. J. (2007). Association between adolescent pregnancy and a family history of teenage births. *Perspectives on Sexual and Reproductive Health, 39*(2), 108–115.

Eastman, K., et al. (2005). Worksite-based parenting programs to promote healthy adolescent sexual development: A qualitative study of feasibility and potential content. *Perspectives on Sexual and Reproductive Health, 37*(2), 62–69.

Eastwood, K. L., et al. (2006). Abortion training in United States *Obstetrics and Gynecology* residency programs. *Obstetrics and Gynecology, 108*(2), 303–308.

Ebrahim, S. H., McKenna, M. T., & Marks, J. S. (2005). Sexual behavior: Related adverse health burden in the United States. *Sexually Transmitted Infections, 81*(1), 38–40.

Edwards, K. E., & Jones, S. R. (2009). "Putting my man face on:" A grounded theory of college men's gender identity development. *Journal of College Student Development, 50*(2), 210–228.

Eisenberg, M. E., et al. (2009). Casual sex and psychological health among young adults: Is having "friends with benefits" emotionally damaging? *Perspectives on Sexual and Reproductive Health, 41*(4), 231–237.

Eisenberg, M. E., et al. (2004). Parents' beliefs about condoms and oral contraceptives: Are they medically accurate? *Perspectives on Sexual and Reproductive Health, 36*(2), 50–57.

El-Defrawi, M. H., et al. (2001). Female genital mutilation and its psychosexual impact. *Journal of Sex and Marital Therapy, 27,* 465–473.

Eldar-Avidan, D., Haj-Yahia, M., & Greenbaum, C. W. (2009). Divorce is a part of my life. . . . Resilience, survival, and vulnerability: Young adults' perception of the implications of parental divorce. *Journal of Marriage and Family Therapy, 35*(1), 30–46.

Elia, J. P. (2009). School-based sexuality education: A century of sexual and social control. In E. Schroeder & J. Kuriansky (Eds.), *Sexuality Education: Past, Present, and Future* (Vol. 1, pp. 33–57). Westport, CT: Praeger.

Elizur, Y., & Mintzer, A. (2001). A framework for the formation of gay male identity: Processes associated with adult attachment style and support from family and friends. *Archives of Sexual Behavior, 30*(2), 143–167.

Elliott, I. A., et al. (2009). Psychological profiles of Internet sexual offenders. *Sexual Abuse: A Journal of Research and Treatment, 21*(1), 76–92.

Elliott, L., & Brantley, C. (1997). Sex on campus. New York: Random House.

Ellis, H. H. (1936). *Studies in the psychology of sex* (7 vols. in 2). New York: Modern Library. (Original edition published 1896–1928).

Ellis, L., et al. (2008). Eye color, hair color, blood type, and the rhesus factor: Exploring possible genetic links to sexual orientation. *Archives of Sexual Behavior, 37,* 145–149.

Ellis, L., Robb, B., & Burke, D. (2005). Sexual orientation in United States and Canadian college students. *Archives of Sexual Behavior, 34*(5), 569–581.

Else-Quest, N., Hyde, J. S., & DeLamater, J. D. (2005). Context counts: Long-term sequelae of premarital intercourse or abstinence. *Journal of Sex Research, 42*(2), 102–112.

Emmelot-Vonk, M. H., et al. (2009). Effect of testosterone supplementation on sexual functioning in aging men: A 6-month randomized controlled trial. *International Journal of Impotence Research, 21,* 129–138.

English, A., & Ford, C. A. (2004). The HIPAA privacy rule and adolescents: Legal questions and clinical challenges. *Perspectives on Sexual and Reproductive Health, 36*(2), 80–86.

Epstein, L. B., et al. (2008). Adolescent experiences with the vaginal ring. *Journal of Adolescent Health, 43*(1), 64–70.

Epstein, M., et al. (2009) "Anything from making out to having sex": Men's negotiations of hooking up and friends with

benefits. *Journal of Sex Research, 46*(5), 414–424.

Erikson, E. (1968). *Identity: Youth and crisis.* New York: W. W. Norton.

Erzar, T., & Erzar, K. K. (2008). "If I commit to you, I betray my parents": Some negative consequences of the intergenerational cycle of insecure attachment for young adult romantic relationships. *Sexual and Relationship Therapy, 23*(1), 25–35.

Eskin, M., Kaynak-Demir, H., & Demir, S. (2005). Same-sex sexual orientation, childhood sexual abuse, and suicidal behavior in university students in Turkey. *Archives of Sexual Behavior, 34*(2), 185–195.

Essig, L. (1999). *Queer in Russia: A story of sex, self, and the other.* Durham and London: Duke University Press.

Esposito, K., et al. (2008). Obesity and sexual dysfunction, male and female. *International Journal of Impotence Research, 20,* 358–365.

Evcimen, H., & Gratz, S. (2006). Adult baby syndrome [Letter]. *Archives of Sexual Behavior, 35*(2), 115–116.

Everaerd, W., Both, S., & Laan, E. (2007). The experience of sexual emotions. *Annual Review of Sex Research, 17,* 183–198.

Everett, K. D., et al. (2007). Men's tobacco and alcohol use during and after pregnancy. *American Journal of Men's Health, 1*(4), 317–325.

Faix, A., et al. (2001). Magnetic resonance imaging of sexual intercourse: Initial experience. *Journal of Sex and Marital Therapy, 27,* 475–482.

Faix, A., et al. (2002). Magnetic resonance imaging (MRI) of sexual intercourse: Second experience in missionary position and initial experience in posterior position. *Journal of Sex and Marital Therapy, 28,* 63–76.

Falkner, S. R. (2004). "Having it off" with fish, camels, and lads: Sodomitic pleasures in German-language Turcica. *Journal of the History of Sexuality, 13*(4), 401–426.

Farmer, M. A., & Meston, C. M. (2006). Predictors of condom use self-efficacy in an ethnically diverse university sample. *Archives of Sexual Behavior, 35*(3), 313–326.

Farmer, M. A., & Meston, C. M. (2007). Predictors of genital pain in young women. *Archives of Sexual Behavior, 36,* 831–843.

Farrar, K., et al. (2003). Sexual messages during prime-time programming. *Sexuality and Culture, 7*(3), 7–37.

Fauci, A. S. (2008). 25 years of HIV. *Nature, 453,* 289–290.

Fauser, B. C. (2008). Preimplantation genetic screening: The end of an affair?

Human Reproduction, 23(12), 2622–2625.

Fazleabas, A. T., & Kim, J. J. (2003). What makes an embryo stick? *Science, 299,* 355–408.

Feemster, K. A., et al. (2008). Pediatricians' intention to recommend human papillomavirus (HPV) vaccines to 11- to 12-year-old girls postlicensing. *Journal of Adolescent Medicine, 43*(4), 408–411.

Feldstein, G. A., et al. (2006). Age and judgments of attractiveness as factors of HIV preventive behavior among HIV-positive men who have sex with men. *Journal of Psychology and Human Sexuality, 18*(1), 43–65.

Fergusson, D. M., Boden, J. M., & Horwood, J. (2006). Circumcision status and risk of sexually transmitted infection in young adults and males: An analysis of a longitudinal birth cohort. *Pediatrics, 118*(5), 1971–1977.

Fergusson, D. M., Boden, J. M., & Horwood, L. J. (2007). Abortion among young women and subsequent life outcomes. *Perspectives on Sexual and Reproductive Health, 39*(1), 6–12.

Figueira, R., et al. (2009). A comparison of post-thaw results between embryos arising from intracytoplasmic sperm injection using surgically retrieved or ejaculated spermatozoa. *Fertility and Sterility, 91*(3), 727–732.

Filice, E. (2005). Review of Outlaw representation: Censorship and homosexuality in twentieth-century American art by Richard Meyer. *Sexualities, 8*(1), 116–118.

Findholt, N., & Robrecht, L. C. (2002). Legal and ethical considerations in research with sexually active adolescents: The requirement to report statutory rape. *Perspectives on Reproductive and Sexual Health, 34*(5), 259–264.

Finer, L. B., et al. (2005). Reasons U.S. women have abortions: Quantitative and qualitative perspectives. *Perspectives on Sexual and Reproductive Health, 37*(3), 110–118.

Finer, L. B., & Henshaw, S. K. (2006). Disparities in rates of unintended pregnancy in the United States, 1994 and 2001. *Perspectives on Sexual and Reproductive Health, 38*(2), 90–96.

Fink, P. J. (2005). Sexual and gender identity disorders: Discussion of questions for DSM-V. *Journal of Psychology and Human Sexuality, 17*(3/4), 117–123.

Finlinson, H. A., et al. (2003). Puerto Rican drug users' experiences of physical and sexual abuse: Comparisons based on sexual identities. *Journal of Sex Research, 40*(3), 277–285.

Fischer, G. J. (1989). Sex words used by partners in a relationship. *Journal of Sex Education and Therapy, 15*(1), 50–58.

Fischtein, D. S., Herold, E. S., & Desmarais, S. (2007). How much does gender explain in sexual attitudes and behaviors? A survey of Canadian adults. *Archives of Sexual Behavior, 36,* 451–461.

Fiscus, L. C., Ford, C. A., & Miller, W. C. (2004). Infrequency of sexually transmitted disease screening among sexually experienced U.S. female adolescents. *Perspectives on Sexual and Reproductive Health, 36*(6), 233–238.

Fisher, H., et al. (2002). Defining the brain systems of lust, romantic attraction, and attachment. *Archives of Sexual Behavior, 31*(5), 413–419.

Fisher, H., et al. (2002). The neural mechanisms of mate choice: A hypothesis. *Neuroendocrinology Letters, 23*(4), 92–97.

Fisher, T. D. (2007). Sex of experimenter and social norm effects on reports of sexual behavior in young men and women. *Archives of Sexual Behavior, 36,* 89–100.

Fisher, W. A., & Barak, A. (2001). Internet pornography: A social psychological perspective on Internet sexuality. *Journal of Sex Research, 38*(4), 312–323.

Flicker, S., & Guta, A. (2007). Ethical approaches to adolescent participation in sexual health research. *Journal of Adolescent Health, 42,* 1–2.

Floyd, F. J., & Bakeman, R. (2006). Coming-out across the life course: Implications of age and historical context. *Archives of Sexual Behavior, 35*(3), 287–296.

Ford, C. S., & Beach, F. A. (1951). *Patterns of sexual behavior.* New York: Harper.

Ford, K., Sohn, W., & Lepkowski, J. (2003). Ethnicity or race, area characteristics, and sexual partner choice among American adolescents. *Journal of Sex Research, 40*(2), 211–218.

Forehand, R., et al. (2005). Sexual intentions of black preadolescents: Associations with risk and adaptive behaviors. *Perspectives on Sexual and Reproductive Health, 37*(1), 13–18.

Forste, R., & Haas, D. W. (2002). The transition of adolescent males to first sexual intercourse: Anticipated or delayed? *Perspectives on Sexual and Reproductive Health, 34*(4), 184–190.

Forste, R., & Hoffmann, J. P. (2008). Are U.S. mothers meeting the Healthy People 2010 breastfeeding targets for initiation, duration, and exclusivity? The 2003 and 2004 national immunization surveys. *Journal of Human Lactation, 24*(3), 278–288.

Foust, E., et al. (2003). Partner counseling and referral services to identify persons with undiagnosed HIV. *Morbidity and Mortality Weekly Report, 52*(48), 1181–1184.

Foxman, B., Aral, S. O., & Holmes, K. K. (2006). Common use in the general population of sexual enrichment aids

and drugs to enhance sexual pleasure. *Sexually Transmitted Diseases, 33*(3), 156–162.

France, D. (2001, August 6). Scouts divided. *Newsweek,* 44–51.

Francis, A. M. (2008). Family and sexual orientation: The family-demographic correlates of homosexuality in men and women. *Journal of Sex Research, 45*(4), 371–377.

Francis, L. P. (2000). *Sexual harassment as an ethical issue in academic life.* Walnut Creek, CA: Rowman and Littlefield.

Frank, E., Coughlin, S. S., & Elon, L. (2008). Sex-related knowledge, attitudes, and behaviors of U.S. medical students. *Obstetrics and Gynecology, 112*(2–1), 311–319.

Frank, K. (2003). "Just trying to relax": Masculinity, masculinizing practices, and strip club regulars. *Journal of Sex Research, 40*(1), 61–75.

Frank, K. (2005). Exploring the motivations and fantasies of strip club customers in relation to legal regulations. *Archives of Sexual Behavior, 34*(5), 487–504.

Frankis, J. S., & Flowers, P. (2007). Sexually transmitted infections (STIs), hepatitis vaccination, and STI clinic use. *International Journal of Sexual Health, 19*(2), 45–55.

Franzini, L., et al. (2004). Projected economic costs due to health consequences of teenagers' loss of confidentiality in obtaining reproductive health care services in Texas. *Archives of Pediatrics and Adolescent Medicine, 158*(12), 1140–1146.

Freeman, E. W., et al. (2008). Symptoms in the menopausal transition: Hormone and behavioral correlates. *Obstetrics and Gynecology, 111*(1), 127–136.

Freeman, T., et al. (2009). Gamete donation: Parents' experiences of searching for child's donor siblings and donor. *Human Reproduction, 24*(3), 505–516.

Freyd, J. J., et al. (2005). The science of child sexual abuse. *Science, 308,* 501.

Fridell, S. R., et al. (2006). The playmate and play style preferences structured interview: A comparison of children with gender identity disorder and controls. *Archives of Sexual Behavior, 35,* 729–737.

Friedlander, L. J., et al. (2007). Biological, familial, and peer influences on dating in early adolescence. *Archives of Sexual Behavior, 36,* 821–830.

Friedrich, W. N., et al. (1998). Normative sexual behavior in children: A contemporary sample. *Pediatrics, 101*(4), e9.

Frisch, M., & Hviid, A. (2007). Reply to Blanchard's (2007) "Older-sibling and younger-sibling sex ratios in Frisch and Hviid's (2006) national cohort study of two million Danes." *Archives of Sexual Behavior, 36,* 864–867.

Frohlich, P., & Meston, C. (2002). Sexual functioning and self-reported depressive symptoms among college women. *Journal of Sex Research, 39*(4), 321–325.

Frohlich, P., & Meston, C. M. (2005). Fluoxetine-induced changes in tactile sensation and sexual functioning among clinically depressed women. *Journal of Sex and Marital Therapy, 31,* 113–128.

Frost, J. J. (2008). Trends in U.S. women's use of sexual and reproductive health care services, 1995–2002. *American Journal of Public Health, 98*(10), 1814–1817.

Frost, J. J., Frohwirth, L., & Purcell, A. (2004). The availability and use of publicly funded family planning clinics: U.S. trends, 1994–2001. *Perspectives on Sexual and Reproductive Health, 36*(5), 206–215.

Frost, J. J., Singh, S., & Finer, L. B. (2007). Factors associated with contraceptive use and nonuse, United States, 2004. *Perspectives on Sexual and Reproductive Health, 39*(2), 90–99.

Fuchs, J., et al. (2007). Negative social impacts among volunteers in an HIV vaccine efficacy trial. *Journal of Acquired Immune Deficiency Syndromes, 46*(3), 362–368.

Fulda, J. S. (2002). Do Internet stings directed at pedophiles capture offenders or create offenders? And allied questions. *Sexuality and Culture, 6*(4), 73–100.

Gable, L., Gostin, L. O., & Hodge Jr, J. G. (2008). HIV/AIDS, reproductive and sexual health, and the law. *American Journal of Public Health, 98*(10), 1779–1786.

Gaca, K. L. (2003). *The making of fornication: Eros, ethics, and political reform in Greek philosophy and early Christianity.* Berkeley: University of California Press.

Gage, A. J., & Hutchinson, P. L. (2006). Power, control, and intimate partner sexual violence in Haiti. *Archives of Sexual Behavior, 35*(1), 11–24.

Gagnon, J. H. (1999). Sexual conduct: As today's memory serves. *Sexualities, 2*(1), 115–126.

Gaither, G. A., Sellbom, M, & Meier, B. P. (2003). The effect of stimulus content on volunteering for sexual interest research among college students. *Journal of Sex Research, 40*(3), 240–248.

Gangestad, S. W., Bennett, K. L., & Thornhill, R. (2001). A latent model of developmental instability in relation to men's sexual behaviour. *Proceedings of the Royal Society of London, 268,* 1677–1684.

Gangestad, S. W., & Cousins, A. J. (2002). Adaptive design, female mate preferences, and shifts across the menstrual cycle. *Annual Review of Sex Research, 12,* 145–185.

Gannon, T. A., Rose, M. R., & Ward, T. (2008). A descriptive model of the offense process for female sexual offenders. *Sexual Abuse: A Journal of Research and Treatment, 20*(3), 352–374.

Garcia, L. T., & Hoskins, R. (2001). Actual-ideal self discrepancy and sexual esteem and depression. *Journal of Psychology and Human Sexuality, 13*(2), 49–61.

Garcia, L. T., & Markey, C. (2007). Matching in sexual experience for married, cohabitating, and dating couples. *Journal of Sex Research, 44*(3), 250–255.

Garcia-Moreno, C. (2009). Intimate-partner violence and fetal loss. *Lancet, 373*(9660), 278–279.

Garver-Apgar, C. E., Gangestad, S. W., & Thornhill, R. (2008). Hormonal correlates of women's mid-cycle preference for the scent of symmetry. *Evolution and Human Behavior, 29*(4), 223–232.

Geary, D. C., Vigil, J., & Byrd-Craven, J. (2004). Evolution of human mate choice. *Journal of Sex Research, 41*(1), 27–42.

Gebhardt, W., Kuyper, L., & Dusseldorp, E. (2006). Condom use at first intercourse with a new partner in female adolescents and young adults: The role of cognitive planning and motives for having sex. *Archives of Sexual Behavior, 35*(2), 217–223.

Gee, R. E., Shacter, H. E., & Kaufman, E. J. (2008). Behind-the-counter status and availability of emergency contraception. *American Journal of Obstetrics and Gynecology, 199,* 478.e1–478.e5.

Geer, J. H., & Melton, J. S. (1997). Sexual content-induced delay with double-entendre words. *Archives of Sexual Behavior, 26*(3), 295–316.

Geer, J. H., & Robertson, G. G. (2005). Implicit attitudes in sexuality: Gender differences. *Archives of Sexual Behavior, 34*(6), 671–677.

Geiger, J. (2001). Re-assessing the past and future of feminist film theory. *Sexualities, 4*(2), 246–251.

Geis, F. L. (1993). Self-fulfilling prophecies: A social psychological view of gender. In A. E. Beall & R. J. Steinberg (Eds.), *The psychology of gender* (pp. 9–54). New York: Guilford Press.

Gencoz, T., & Yuksel, M. (2006). Psychometric properties of the Turkish version of the internalized homophobia scale. *Archives of Sexual Behavior, 35,* 597–602.

Genuis, S. J. (2008). Are condoms the answer to rising rates of non-HIV sexually transmitted infection? No. *British Medical Journal, 336,* 185.

George, W. H., & Stoner, S. A. (2001). Understanding acute alcohol effects on

sexual behavior. *Annual Review of Sex Research, 11,* 92–124.

Gerend, M. A., & Barley, J. (2009). Human papillomavirus vaccine acceptability among young adult men. *Sexually Transmitted Diseases, 36*(1), 58–62.

Gerend, M. A., & Magloire, Z. F. (2008). Awareness, knowledge, and beliefs about human papillomavirus in a racially diverse sample of young adults. *Journal of Adolescent Health, 42*(3), 237–242.

Gerressu, M., et al. (2008). Prevalence of masturbation and associated factors in a British national probability survey. *Archives of Sexual Behavior, 37,* 266–278.

Getch, Y. (2001). Deaf students lack specially-designed sexuality education curricula (based on an interview). *SIECUS Report, 29*(3), 13.

Giami, A. (2003). Sexual health: The emergence, development, and diversity of a concept. *Annual Review of Sex Research, 13,* 1–35.

Giargiari, T. D., et al. (2005). Appetitive responses to sexual stimuli are attenuated in individuals with low levels of sexual desire. *Archives of Sexual Behavior, 34*(5), 547–556.

Giertsen, M., & Anderssen, N. (2007). Time period and lesbian identity events: A comparison of Norwegian lesbians across 1986 and 2005. *Journal of Sex Research, 44*(4), 328–339.

Gijs, L., & Brewaeys, A. (2007). Surgical treatment of gender dysphoria in adults and adolescents: Recent developments, effectiveness, and challenges. *Annual Review of Sex Research, 18,* 178–224.

Giles, J. (2006). No such thing as excessive levels of sexual behavior. *Archives of Sexual Behavior, 35,* 641–642.

Gillath, O. et al. (2007). Does subliminal exposure to sexual stimuli have the same effects on men and women? *Journal of Sex Research, 44*(2), 111–121.

Gillison, M. L. (2008). Human papillomavirus-related diseases: Oropharynx cancers and potential implications for adolescent HPV vaccination. *Journal of Adolescent Medicine, 43*(4), S52–S60.

Gillmore, M. R., et al. (2001). Daily data collection of sexual and other health-related behaviors. *Journal of Sex Research, 38*(1), 35–42.

Gilman, S. T., et al. (2008). Social factors, psychopathology, and maternal smoking during pregnancy. *American Journal of Public Health, 98*(3), 448–453.

Gindi, R. M., Ghanem, K. G., & Erbelding, E. J. (2008). Increases in oral and anal sexual exposure among youth attending sexually transmitted diseases clinics in Baltimore, Maryland. *Journal of Adolescent Health, 42*(3), 307–308.

Giotakos, O., et al. (2003). Aggression, impulsivity, plasma sex hormones, and biogenic amine turnover in a forensic population of rapists. *Journal of Sex and Marital Therapy, 29*(3), 215–225.

Giuliano, F. (2008). New horizons in erectile and endothelial dysfunction research and therapies. *International Journal of Impotence Research, 20,* S2–S8.

Glasier, A., et al. (2006). Sexual and reproductive health: A matter of life and death. *Lancet,* DOI: 10.1016/ S0140-6736(06)69478-6.

Glass, A. G., et al. (2007). Breast cancer incidence, 1980–2006: Combined roles of menopausal hormone therapy, screening mammography, and estrogen receptor status. *Journal of the National Cancer Institute, 99*(15), 1152–1161.

Glass, L. (2003). *The complete idiot's guide to understanding men and women.* New York: Alpha Books/Penguin.

Glenn, D. (2003, April 25). Every unhappy family has its own bilinear influence function. *Chronicle of Higher Education,* A14–A15.

Glenn, D. (2004, April 30). A dangerous surplus of sons? *Chronicle of Higher Education,* A14–A18.

Gobrogge, K. L., et al. (2007). Homosexual mating preferences from an evolutionary perspective: Sexual selection theory revisited. *Archives of Sexual Behavior, 36,* 717–723.

Gobrogge, K. L., Breedlove, S. M., & Klump, K. L. (2008). Genetic and environmental influences on 2D:4D finger length ratios: A study of monozygotic and dizygotic male and female twins. *Archives of Sexual Behavior, 37,* 112–118.

Godecker, A. L., Thomson, E., & Bumpass, L. L. (2001). Union status, marital history and female contraceptive sterilization in the United States. *Family Planning Perspectives, 33*(1), 35–41, 49.

Godow, A. G. (1999). Playful language. *Contemporary Sexuality, 33*(2), 1–2.

Gokyildiz, S., & Beji, N. K. (2005). The effects of pregnancy on sexual life. *Journal of Sex and Marital Therapy, 31,* 201–215.

Gold, S. N., Hughes, D. M., & Swingle, J. M. (1999). Degrees of memory of childhood sexual abuse among women survivors in therapy. *Journal of Family Violence, 14*(1), 35–46.

Golden, M. R., et al. (2005). Effect of expedited treatment of sex partners on recurrent or persistent gonorrhea or chlamydial infection. *New England Journal of Medicine, 352*(7), 676–685.

Golden, M. R., & Wasserheit, J. N. (2009). Prevention of viral sexually transmitted infections—Foreskin at the forefront. *New England Journal of Medicine, 360,* 1349–1351.

Goldenberg, J. L., et al. (2002). Understanding human ambivalence about sex: The effects of stripping sex of meaning. *Journal of Sex Research, 39*(4), 310–320.

Goldfarb, E. S. (2005). What is comprehensive sexuality education really all about? Perceptions of students enrolled in an undergraduate human sexuality course. *American Journal of Sexuality Education, 1*(1), 85–102.

Goldfarb, E. S. (2009). A crisis of identity in sexuality education in America: How did we get here and where are we going. In: E. Schroeder & J. Kuriansky. (Eds.), *Sexuality Education: Past, Present, and Future* (pp. 8–30). Westport, CT: Praeger.

Goler, N. C., et al. (2008). Substance abuse treatment linked with prenatal visits improves perinatal outcomes: A new standard. *Journal of Perinatology, 28*(9), 597–603.

Gonzalo, I. T., Swerdloff, R. S., & Nelson, A. L. (2002). Levonorgestrel implants (Norplant II) for male contraception clinical trials: Combination with transdermal and injectable testosterone. *Journal of Clinical Endocrinology and Metabolism, 87*, 3562–3572.

Goodenow, C., et al. (2008). Dimensions of sexual orientation and HIV-related risk among adolescent females: Evidence from a statewide survey. *American Journal of Public Health, 98*(6), 1051–1058.

Goodenow, C., Netherland, J., & Szalacha, L. (2002). AIDS-related risk among adolescent males who have sex with males, females, or both: Evidence from a statewide survey. *American Journal of Public Health, 92*(2), 203–210.

Goodman, M. P. (2009). Female cosmetic genital surgery. *Obstetrics and Gynecology, 113*(1), 154–159.

Goodstein, L. (2010, March 25). Vatican declined to defrock U.S. priest who abused deaf boys. *New York Times,* A1, A15.

Goodwin, B. Y., Mosher, W. D., & Chandra, M. (2010). *Marriage and cohabitation in the United States: A statistical portrait based on cycle 6 (2002) of the National Survey of Family Growth.* National Center for Health Statistics. *Vital and Health Statistics, 23*(28).

Goozen, S. H., et al. (2002). Preference for aggressive and sexual stimuli in children with disruptive behavior disorder and normal controls. *Archives of Sexual Behavior, 31*(3), 247–253.

Gorzalka, B. B., & Hill, M. N. (2007). Cannabinoids, reproduction, and sexual behavior. *Annual Review of Sex Research, 17*, 132–160.

Gottlieb, L. (2006, March). How do I love thee? *Atlantic Monthly,* 58–70.

Gottman, J. M. (2000). *Seven principles for making marriages work.* New York: Three Rivers Press.

Gottman, J. M., et al. (2003). *The mathematics of marriage: Dynamic linear models.* Cambridge, MA: MIT Press.

Goyal, M., Zhao, H., & Mollen, C. (2009). Exploring emergency contraception knowledge, prescription practices, and barriers to prescription for adolescents in the emergency department. *Pediatrics, 123*(3), 765–770.

Graaf, H. de, & Rademakers, J. (2006). Sexual behavior of prepubertal children. *Journal of Psychology and Human Sexuality, 18*(1), 1–21.

Grace, P. (2008). The charisma and deception of reparative therapies: When medical science beds religion. *Journal of Homosexuality, 55*(4), 545–580.

Grady, D., et al. (2002). Cardiovascular disease outcomes during 6.8 years of hormone therapy. *Journal of the American Medical Association, 288*(1): 49–57.

Grady, W. R., Billy, J. O. G., & Klepinger, D. H. (2002). Contraceptive method switching in the United States. *Perspectives on Sexual and Reproductive Health, 34*(3), 135–145.

Grafenberg, E. (1950). The role of the urethra. *International Journal of Sexology, 3,* 145–148.

Graham, C. A., et al. (2003). Recalling sexual behavior: A methodological analysis of memory recall bias via interview using the diary as the gold standard. *Journal of Sex Research, 40*(4), 325–332.

Graham, C. A., et al. (2004). Turning on and turning off: A focus group study of the factors that affect women's sexual arousal. *Archives of Sexual Behavior, 33*(6), 527–538.

Graham, C. A., Sanders, S. A., & Milhausen, R. R. (2006). The sexual excitation/sexual inhibition inventory for women: Psychometric properties. *Archives of Sexual Behavior, 35,* 397–409.

Granich, R. M., et al. (2009). Universal voluntary HIV testing with immediate antiretroviral therapy as a strategy for elimination of HIV transmission: A mathematical model. *Lancet, 373*(9657), 48–57.

Granot, M., & Lavee, Y. (2005). Psychological factors associated with perception of experimental pain in vulvar vestibulitis syndrome. *Journal of Sex and Marital Therapy, 31,* 285–302.

Graupner, H. (2000). Sexual consent: The criminal law in Europe and overseas. *Archives of Sexual Behavior, 29*(5), 415–461.

Graves, J. A. (2008). X inactivation is a good thing. *Science, 321,* 202.

Gray, R. H., et al. (2009). The effects of male circumcision on female partners' genital tract symptoms and vaginal infections in a randomized trial in Raki, Uganda. *American Journal of Obstetrics and Gynecology, 200,* 42.e1–42.e7.

Greeff, A. P., & DeBruyne, T. (2000). Conflict management style and marital satisfaction. *Journal of Sex and Marital Therapy, 26,* 321–334.

Green, L. C., et al. (2008). Medicaid coverage of circumcision spreads harm to the poor. *American Journal of Public Health, 99*(4).

Green-Raleigh, K., et al. (2005). Pregnancy planning status and health behaviors among nonpregnant women in a California managed health care organization. *Perspectives on Sexual and Reproductive Health, 37*(4), 179–183.

Green, R. (2008). A tale of three texts: Treatments for transsexualism. *Archives of Sexual Behavior, 37,* 665–667.

Greer, J. B., et al. (2005). Short-term oral contraceptive use and the risk of epithelial ovarian cancer. *American Journal of Epidemiology, 162*(1), 66–72.

Grimes, D. A., et al. (2006). Unsafe abortion: The preventable pandemic. *Lancet,* Early Online Publication, DOI: 10.1016/S0140-6736(06)69481-6.

Groneman, C. (2000). *Nymphomania: A History.* New York: W. W. Norton.

Grunseit, A., et al. (2005). Stability and change in sexual practices among first-year Australian university students (1990–1999). *Archives of Sexual Behavior, 34*(5), 557–568.

Guillebaud, J. (2004). *Contraception: Your questions answered.* London: Churchill Livingstone.

Guldi, M. (2008). Fertility effects of abortion and birth control pill access for minors. *Demography, 45*(4), 817–827.

Guo, Y. N., Ng, E. M. L., & Chan, K. (2004). Foreplay, orgasm and after-play among Shanghai couples and its integrative relation with their marital satisfaction. *Sexual and Relationship Therapy, 19*(1), 65–78.

Gute, G., Eshbaugh, E. M., & Wiersma, J. (2008). Sex for you, but not for me: Discontinuity in undergraduate emerging adults' definitions of "having sex." *Journal of Sex Research, 45*(4), 329–337.

Guterman, M. A. (2008). Observance of the laws of family purity in modern-orthodox Judaism. *Archives of Sexual Behavior, 37,* 340–345.

Haas, J. S., et al. (2005). Prepregnancy health status and the risk of preterm delivery. *Archives of Pediatrics and Adolescent Medicine, 159*(1), 58–63.

Hack, K. E., et al. (2009). Perinatal outcome of monoamniotic twin pregnancies. *Obstetrics and Gynecology, 113*(2–1), 353–360.

Haffner, D. W. (2004). Sexuality and scripture. *Contemporary Sexuality, 38*(1), 7–14.

Haig, D. (2004). The inexorable rise of gender and the decline of sex: Social change in academic titles, 1945–2001. *Archives of Sexual Behavior, 33*(2), 87–96.

Haimov-Kochman, R., et al. (2009). Technical modification of testicular sperm extraction expedites testicular sperm retrieval. *Fertility and Sterility, 91*(1), 281–284.

Hald, G. M. (2006). Gender differences in pornography consumption among young heterosexual Danish adults. *Archives of Sexual Behavior, 35,* 577–585.

Hald, G. M., & Malamuth, N. M. (2008). Self-perceived effects of pornography consumption. *Archives of Sexual Behavior, 37,* 614–625.

Halkitis, P. N., Moeller, R. W., & Pollock, J. A. (2008). Sexual practices of gay, bisexual, and other nonidentified msm attending New York City gyms: Patterns of serosorting, strategic positioning, and context selection. *Journal of Sex Research, 45*(3), 253–261.

Halkitis, P. N., Parsons, J. T., & Wilton, L. (2003). Barebacking among gay and bisexual men in New York City: Explanations for the emergence of intentional unsafe behavior. *Archives of Sexual Behavior, 32*(4), 351–357.

Hall, H. I., et al. (2008). Estimation of HIV incidence in the United States. *Journal of the American Medical Association, 300*(5), 520–529.

Hall, H. I., et al. (2007). Racial/ethnic and age disparities in HIV prevalence and disease progression among men who have sex with men in the United States. *American Journal of Public Health, 97*(6), 1060–1066.

Hall, L. S. (2000). Dermatoglyphic analysis of total finger ridge count in female monozygotic twins discordant for sexual orientation. *Journal of Sex Research, 37*(4), 315–320.

Hall, L. S., & Love, C. T. (2003). Finger-length ratios in female monozygotic twins discordant for sexual orientation. *Archives of Sexual Behavior, 32*(1), 23–28.

Hall, P. A., & Schaeff, C. M. (2008). Sexual orientation and fluctuating asymmetry in men and women. *Archives of Sexual Behavior, 37,* 158–165.

Hall, S. A., et al. (2008). Treatment of symptomatic androgen deficiency. *Archives of Internal Medicine, 168*(10), 1070–1076.

Hallfors, D. D., et al. (2007). Sexual and drug behavior patterns and HIV and STD racial disparities: The need for

new directions. *American Journal of Public Health, 97*(1), 125–132.

Halpern, C. T. (2010). Reframing research on adolescent sexuality: Healthy sexual development as part of the life course. *Perspectives on Sexual and Reproductive Health, 42*(1), 6–7.

Halpern, C. T., et al. (2000). Adolescent males' willingness to report masturbation. *Journal of Sex Research, 37*(4), 327–332.

Halpern-Felsher, B. L., et al. (2005). Oral versus vaginal sex among adolescents: Perceptions, attitudes, and behavior. *Pediatrics, 115*(4), 845–851.

Hamel, D. (2003). *Trying Neaira: The true story of a courtesan's scandalous life in ancient Greece.* New Haven, CT: Yale University Press.

Hamer, D. (2002). Rethinking behavior genetics. *Science, 298,* 71–72.

Hamer, M. (2002). *Incest: A new perspective.* Malden, MA.: Blackwell.

Hamill, S. D. (2009, March 26). Students sue prosecutor in cellphone photos case. *New York Times,* A18.

Hamilton, B. E., Martin, J. A., & Ventura, S. J. (2010). *Births: Preliminary data for 2008.* National Center for Health Statistics. *National Vital Statistics Reports, 58*(16).

Hampson, E., Ellis, C. L., & Tenk, C. M. (2008). On the relation between 2D:4D and sex-dimorphic personality traits. *Archives of Sexual Behavior, 37,* 133–144.

Hamson, S. (2004). The passive/active divide: What the village is teaching our children about gender. *SIECUS Report, 32*(3), 14–16.

Han, C.-S. (2008). A qualitative exploration of the relationship between racism and unsafe sex among Asian Pacific Islander gay men. *Archives of Sexual Behavior, 37,* 827–837.

Handa, V. L., et al. (2008). Female sexual function and pelvic floor disorders. *Obstetrics and Gynecology, 111*(5), 1045–1052.

Handelsman, J., et al. (2005). More women in science. *Science, 309,* 1190–1191.

Haning, R. V., et al. (2008). Empathic sexual responses in heterosexual women and men. *Sexual and Relationship Therapy, 23*(4), 325–344.

Hannaford, P. C., et al. (2007). Cancer risk among users of oral contraceptives: Cohort data from the Royal College of General Practitioner's oral contraception study. *British Medical Journal, 335*(7621), 651–658.

Harawa, N. T., et al. (2008). Sexual behavior, sexual identity, and substance abuse among low-income bisexual and non-gay-identifying African American men who have sex with men. *Archives of Sexual Behavior, 37,* 748–762.

Harding, C. (Ed.). (2001). *Sexuality: Psychoanalytic perspectives.* Philadelphia: Brunner-Routledge.

Harding, R., & Golombok, S. E. (2002). Test-retest reliability of the measurement of penile dimensions in a sample of gay men. *Archives of Sexual Behavior, 31*(4), 351–357.

Harper, C., et al. (2004). Adolescent clinic visits for contraception: Support from mothers, male partners and friends. *Perspectives on Sexual and Reproductive Health, 36*(1), 20–26.

Harper, G., et al. (2004). The role of close friends in African American adolescents' dating and sexual behavior. *Journal of Sex Research, 41*(4), 351–362.

Harris Poll. (2005, March 3). Majority back *Roe v. Wade,* but opposition is rising. *Wall Street Journal Online.*

Harris, S. M., & Hays, K. W. (2008). Family therapist comfort with the willingness to discuss client sexuality. *Journal of Marital and Family Therapy, 34*(2), 239–250.

Hart, T. A., et al. (2003). Sexual behavior among HIV-positive men who have sex with men: What's in a label. *Journal of Sex Research, 40*(2), 179–188.

Hartlaub, M. G. (2007). Celebrating the natural. A review of: *An evolutionary theory celebration of male sexual arousal by females: The foundations of male heterosexuality. Journal of Sex Research, 44*(2), 220–222.

Hartmann, U., et al. (2008), Why do women with panic disorders not panic during sex (or do they)? Result of an empirical study on the relationship of sexual arousal and panic attacks. *Sexual and Relationship Therapy, 23*(2), 203–216.

Harvey, S. M., Bird, S. T., & Branch, M. R. (2003). A new look at an old method: The diaphragm. *Perspectives on Sexual and Reproductive Health, 35*(6), 270–271.

Hatcher, R. A., et al. (2002). *A pocket guide to managing contraception.* Dawsonville, GA: Bridging the Gap Communications.

Hatcher, R. A., et al. (2007). *Contraceptive technology* (19th ed.). New York: Ardent Media.

Hatherall, B., et al. (2007). How, not just if, condoms are used: The timing of condom, application and removal during vaginal sex among young people in England. *Sexually Transmitted Infections, 83*(1), 68–70.

Haug, C. (2009). The risks and benefits of HPV vaccination. *Journal of the American Medical Association, 302*(7), 795–796.

Hayatbakhsh, M. R. et al. (2009). Childhood sexual abuse and cannabis use in early adulthood: Findings from an Australian birth cohort study. *Archives of Sexual Behavior, 38,* 135–142.

Heacox, T. L. (2004). "Idealized through Greece": Hellenism and homoeroticism in works by Wilde, Symonds, Mann, and Forster. *Sexuality and Culture, 8*(2), 52–79.

Hearn, K. D., O'Sullivan, L. F., & Dudley, C. D. (2002). Assessing reliability of early adolescent girls' reports of romantic and sexual behavior. *Archives of Sexual Behavior, 32*(6), 513–521.

Hegaard, H. K., et al. (2008). Leisure time physical activity is associated with a reduced risk of preterm delivery. *American Journal of Obstetrics and Gynecology, 198*(2), 180.e1–180.e5.

Heiman, J. R. (2002). Psychologic treatments for female sexual dysfunction: Are they effective and do we need them? *Archives of Sexual Behavior, 31*(5), 445–450.

Heiman, J. R. (2007). Orgasmic disorders in women. In S. R. Leiblum (Ed.). *Principles and practices of sex therapy* (pp. 84–123). New York: Guilford Press.

Heins, M. (2001). *Not in front of the children: "Indecency," censorship, and the innocence of youth.* New York: Hill and Wang.

Heke, S., Forster, G., & d'Ardenne, P. (2009). Risk identification and management of adults following acute sexual assault. *Sexual and Relationship Therapy, 24*(1), 4–15.

Hellberg, J. (2006). Review of *The Puzzle* by L. A. Berman. *Archives of Sexual Behavior, 35*(2), 243–244.

Hellstrom, W. J. G. (2008). Clinical applications of centrally acting agents in male sexual dysfunction. *International Journal of Impotence Research, 20,* S17–S23.

Hembree, W. C., et al. (2009). Endocrine treatments of transsexual persons: An endocrine society clinical practice guideline. *Journal of Clinical Endocrinology and Metabolism, 94*(9), 3132–3154.

Henderson, A. W., Lehavot, K., & Simoni, J. M. (2009). Ecological models of sexual satisfaction among lesbian/bisexual and heterosexual women. *Archives of Sexual Behavior, 38,* 50–65.

Hennessy, M., et al. (2009). Estimating the longitudinal association between adolescent sexual behavior and exposure to sexual media content. *Journal of Sex Research, 46*(6), 586–596.

Hennig, K. H. (2003). Parenting style and the development of moral reasoning. *Journal of Moral Education, 28,* 359–374.

Henry, G. D., et al. (2009). Centers for excellence and penile prostheses: An outcome analysis. *Journal of Urology, 181*(3), 1264–1268.

Hensley, L. (2003). GHB abuse trends and use in drug-facilitated sexual assault: Implications for prevention. *NASPA Journal, 40*(2), 17–42.

Herdt, G. (2000). Clinical ethnography and sexual culture. *Annual Review of Sex Research, 9,* 100–119.

Herdt, G., & McClintock, M. (2000). The magical age of 10. *Archives of Sexual Behavior, 29*(6), 587–606.

Herek, G. M. (2002). Heterosexuals' attitudes toward bisexual men and women in the United States. *Journal of Sex Research, 39*(4), 264–274.

Herek, G. M., & Gonzalez-Rivera, M. (2006). Attitudes toward homosexuality among U.S. residents of Mexican descent. *Journal of Sex Research, 43*(2), 122–135.

Herman, D. (2005). "I'm gay": Declarations, desire, and coming out on prime-time television. *Sexualities, 8*(1), 7–29.

Herman-Jeglinska, A., Grabowska, A., & Dulko, S. (2002). Masculinity, femininity, and transsexualism. *Archives of Sexual Behavior, 31*(6), 527–534.

Herold, E. S., & Milhausen, R. R. (1999). Dating preferences of university women: An analysis of the nice guy stereotype. *Journal of Sex and Marital Therapy, 25,* 333–343.

Hershberger, S. L. (2003). Low test-retest reliability does not diminish the value of penile self-measurement. *Archives of Sexual Behavior, 32*(2), 91–92.

Hershberger, S. L., & Segal, N. (2004). The cognitive, behavioral, and personality profiles of a male monozygotic triplet set discordant for sexual orientation. *Archives of Sexual Behavior, 33*(5), 497–514.

Hetherington, E. M., & Kelly, J. (2001). *For better or for worse.* New York: W. W. Norton.

Hewitt, M., Devesa, S., & Breen, N. (2002). Papanicolaou test use among reproductive-age women at high risk for cervical cancer: Analysis of the 1995 National Survey of Family Growth. *American Journal of Public Health, 92*(4), 666–669.

Hicks, T. V., & Leitenberg, H. (2001). Sexual fantasies about one's partner versus someone else: Gender differences in incidence and frequency. *Journal of Sex Research, 38*(1), 43–50.

Higgins, J. A., & Browne, I. (2008). Sexual needs, control, and refusal: How "doing" class and gender influences sexual risk taking. *Journal of Sex Research, 45*(3), 233–245.

Higgins, J. A., & Hirsch, J. S. (2007). The pleasure deficit: Revisiting the "sexuality connection" in reproductive health. *Perspectives on Sexual and Reproductive Health, 39*(4), 240–246.

Higgins, J. A., & Hirsch, J. S. (2008). Pleasure, power, and inequality: Incorporating sexuality into research on contraceptive use. *American Journal of Public Health, 98*(10), 1803–1813.

Higgins, J. A., Hirsch, J. S., & Trussell, J. (2008). Pleasure, prophylaxis and procreation: A qualitative analysis of intermittent contraceptive use and unintended pregnancy. *Perspectives on Sexual and Reproductive Health, 40*(3), 130–137.

Hill, D. B. (2005). Coming to terms: Using technology to know identity. *Sexuality and Culture, 9*(3), 24–52.

Hill, D. B., et al. (2005). Gender identity disorders in childhood and adolescence: A critical inquiry. *Journal of Psychology and Human Sexuality, 17*(3/4), 7–33.

Hill, D. B., et al. (2007). Gender identity disorders in childhood and adolescence: A critical inquiry. *International Journal of Sexual Health, 19*(1), 57–75.

Hillis, S. D., et al. (2001). Adverse childhood experiences and sexual risk behaviors in women: A retrospective cohort study. *Family Planning Perspectives, 33*(5), 206–211.

Hillis, S. D., et al. (2004). The association between adverse childhood experiences and adolescent pregnancy, long-term psychosocial consequences, and fetal death. *Pediatrics, 113*(2), 320–327.

Hillman, J. L. (2000). *Clinical perspectives on elderly sexuality.* New York: Kluwer Academic/Plenum Publishers.

Hines, D. A. (2007). Predictors of sexual coercion against women and men: A multilevel, multinational study of university students. *Archives of Sexual Behavior, 36,* 403–422.

Hines, M. (2004). *Brain gender.* New York: Oxford University Press.

Hines, M., Ahmed, S. F., & Hughes, I. A. (2003). Psychological outcomes and gender-related development in complete androgen insensitivity syndrome. *Archives of Sexual Behavior, 32*(2), 93–101.

Hines, M., Brook, C., & Conway, G. S. (2004). Androgen and psychosexual development: Core gender identity, sexual orientation, and recalled childhood gender role behavior in women and men with congenital adrenal hyperplasia (CAH). *Journal of Sex Research, 41*(1), 75–81.

Hines, M., et al. (2003). Spatial abilities following prenatal androgen abnormality: Targeting and mental rotations performance in individuals with congenital adrenal hyperplasia (CAH). *Psychoneuroendocrinology, 28,* 1010–1026.

Hiorta, O., & Gillessen-Kaesbachb, G. (2009). Endocrine involvement in developmental syndromes. In M. Cappa (Ed.), *Endocrine involvement in* developmental syndromes (pp. 174–180). Basel, Switzerland: S. Karger AG.

Hite, S. (1977). *The Hite report*. New York: Dell.

Hobbs, K., et al. (2008). Sexual dysfunction in partners of men with premature ejaculation. *International Journal of Impotence Research, 20*, 512–517.

Hofferth, S. L., Reid, L., & Mott, F. L. (2001, November/December). The effects of early childbearing on schooling over time. *Family Planning Perspectives, 33*(6), 259–268.

Hofferth, S. L., & Reid, L. (2002, January/February). Early childbearing and children's achievement and behavior over time. *Perspectives on Sexual and Reproductive Health, 34*(1), 41–50.

Hoffman, R. M. (2004). Conceptualizing heterosexual identity development: Issues and challenges. *Journal of Counseling and Development, 82*, 375–380.

Hoffman, S., et al. (2003). Female-condom use in a gender-specific family planning clinic trial. *American Journal of Public Health, 93*(11), 1897–1903.

Hofstede, G. (1998). *Masculinity and femininity: The taboo of national culture*. Thousand Oaks, CA: Sage.

Hofstede, G. (2001). *Culture's consequences: Comparing values, behaviors, institutions, and organizations across nations*. Thousand Oaks, CA: Sage.

Hogarth, H., & Ingham, R. (2009). Masturbation among young women and associations with sexual health: An exploratory study. *Journal of Sex Research, 46*(6), 558–567.

Holden, C. (2003). More men ready for cloning. *Science, 299*, 41.

Holmberg, D., & Blair, K. L. (2009). Sexual desire, communication, satisfaction, and preferences of men and women in same-sex versus mixed-sex relationships. *Journal of Sex Research, 46*(1), 57–66.

Hooker, E. (1993). Reflections of a 40-year exploration: A scientific view on homosexuality. *American Psychologist, 48*(4), 450–453.

Horowitz, S. M., Weis, D. L., & Laflin, M. T. (2001). Differences between sexual orientation behavior groups and social background, quality of life, and health behaviors. *Journal of Sex Research, 38*(3), 205–218.

Horvath, K. J., Rosser, S., & Remafedi, G. (2008). Sexual risk taking among young Internet-using men who have sex with men. *American Journal of Public Health, 98*(6), 1059–1067.

Howe, E. R., et al. (2009). Type-specific prevalence and persistence of human papillomavirus in women in the United States who are referred for typing as a component of cervical cancer screening. *American Journal of Obstetrics and Gynecology, 200*(3), 245.e1–245.e7.

Huang, T., et al. (2008). Persistent hot flashes in older postmenopausal women. *Archives of Internal Medicine, 168*(8), 840–846.

Huebner, D. M., Proescholdbell, R. J., & Nemeroff, C. J. (2006). Do gay and bisexual men share researchers' definitions of barebacking? *Journal of Psychology and Human Sexuality, 18*(1), 67–77.

Hueston, W. J., Geesey, M. E., & Diaz, V. (2008). Prenatal care initiation among pregnant teens in the United States: An analysis over 25 years. *Journal of Adolescent Health, 42*(3), 243–248.

Humphreys, T. (2007). Perceptions of sexual consent: The impact of relationship history and gender. *Journal of Sex Research, 44*(4), 307–315.

Humphreys, T. (2004). Understanding sexual consent: An empirical investigation of the normative script for young heterosexual adults. In M. Cowling & P. Reynolds (Eds.), *Making Sense of Sexual Consent* (pp. 209–225). Aldershot: Ashgate Publishing Ltd.

Hunt, M. (1975). *Sexual behavior in the 1970s*. New York: Dell.

Hunt, M. E., & Jung, P. B. (2009). "Good sex" and religion: A feminist overview. *Journal of Sex Research, 46*(2–3), 156–167.

Huppert, J. S., et al. (2005). Sexually transmitted infection testing and screening in hospital-based primary care visits by women. *Obstetrics and Gynecology, 105*(2), 390–396.

Hurd, P. L., et al. (2008). Intrauterine position effects on anogenital distance and digit ratio in male and female mice. *Archives of Sexual Behavior, 37*, 9–18.

Huyck, M. H. (1999). Gender roles and gender identity in midlife. In S. L. Willis & J. D. Reid (Eds.), *Life in the middle: Psychological and social development in middle age* (pp. 209–232). San Diego, CA: Academic Press.

Hvistendahl, M. (2009). Making every baby girl count. *Science, 323*, 1164–1166.

Hwang, A. C., et al. (2005). Advanced practice clinicians' interest in providing medical abortion: Results of a California survey. *Perspectives on Sexual and Reproductive Health, 37*(3), 231-235.

Hwang, T., & Lin, Y-C. (2008). The relationship between hypogonadism and erectile dysfunction. *International Journal of Impotence Research, 20*(3), 231–235.

Hyde, J. S. (2005). The gender similarities hypothesis. *American Psychologist, 60*(6), 581–592.

Hyde, J. S., & Linn, M. C. (2006) Gender similarities in mathematics and science. *Science, 314*, 599–600.

Hyde, J. S., et al. (2008). Gender similarities characterize math performance. *Science*, 494–495.

Hyde, J. S. (2008). Methodological issues in inferences from meta-analysis about the effects of child sexual abuse. *International Journal of Sexual Health, 19*(4), 15–19.

Icard, L. D. (2008). Reaching African-American men on the "down low": Sampling hidden populations: Implications for HIV prevention. *Journal of Homosexuality, 55*(3), 437–449.

Imperato-McGinley, J., et al. (1982). Hormonal evaluation of a large kindred with complete androgen insensitivity: Evidence for secondary 5-alpha-reductase deficiency. *Journal of Clinical Endocrinology Metabolism, 54*, 15–22.

International Collaboration of Epidemiological Studies of Cervical Cancer. (2007). Cervical cancer and hormonal contraceptives: Collaborative reanalysis of individual data for 16,573 women with cervical cancer and 35,509 women without cervical cancer from 24 epidemiological studies. *Lancet, 370*(9599), 1609–1621.

Ito, T. Y., et al. (2006). The enhancement of female sexual function with arginmax, a nutritional supplement, among women differing in menopausal status. *Journal of Sex and Marital Therapy, 32*, 369–378.

Izugbara, C. O. (2008). Masculinity scripts and abstinence-related beliefs of rural Nigerian male youth. *Journal of Sex Research, 45*(3), 262–276.

Izugbara, C. O., & Undie, C.-C. (2008). Masculinity scripts and the sexual vulnerability of male youth in Malawi. *International Journal of Sexual Health, 20*(4), 281–294.

Jackson, D. J., et al. (2003). Outcomes, safety, and resource utilization in a collaborative care birth center program compared with traditional physician-based perinatal care. *American Journal of Public Health, 93*(6), 999–1006.

Jackson, E. F., et al. (2003). Inconsistent reporting of female genital cutting status in Northern Ghana: Explanatory factors and analytical consequences. *Studies in Family Planning, 34*(3), 200–210.

Jackson, G. (2009). Sexual response in cardiovascular disease. *Journal of Sex Research, 46*(2–3), 233–236.

Jackson, L. A., et al. (2005). Female sex trade workers, condoms, and the public-private divide. *Journal of Psychology and Human Sexuality, 17*(1/2), 83–105.

Jackson, S., & Scott, S. (2004). Sexual antinomies in late modernity. *Sexualities, 7*(2), 233–248.

Jakobsen, J. R., & Pellegrini, A. (2003). *Love and sin: Sexual regulation and the limits of religious tolerance*. New York: New York University Press.

JAMA. (2008). Anal Cancer. *Journal of the American Medical Association, 299*(16).

James, S. M., & Robertson, C. C. (2002). *Genital cutting and transnational sisterhood: Disputing U.S. polemics*. Urbana: University of Illinois Press.

James, S. M., & Robertson, C. C. (2004). Sorting out misunderstandings: Genital cutting and transnational sisterhood. *Archives of Sexual Behavior, 33*(1), 2–3.

Jamieson, D. J., et al. (2002). A comparison of women's regret after vasectomy versus tubal sterilization. *Obstetrics and Gynecology, 99*(6), 1073–1079.

Jamison, P. L., & Gebhard, P. H. (1988). Penis size increase between flaccid and erect states: An analysis of the Kinsey data. *Journal of Sex Research, 24*(1), 177–183.

Janssen, D. F. (2007). First stirrings: Cultural notes on orgasm, ejaculation, and wet dreams. *Journal of Sex Research, 44*(2), 122–134.

Janssen, E., & Bancroft, J. (2007). The dual control model: The role of sexual inhibition and excitation in sexual arousal and behavior. In E. Janssen (Ed.), *The Psychophysiology of Sex* (pp. 197–222). Bloomington: Indiana University Press.

Janssen, E., Carpenter, D., & Graham, C. A. (2003). Selecting films for sex research: Gender differences in erotic film preference. *Archives of Sexual Behavior, 32*(3), 243–251.

Janssen, E. et al. (2008). Factors that influence sexual arousal in men: A focus group study. *Archives of Sexual Behavior, 37,* 252–265.

Janssen, E., et al. (2002a). The sexual inhibition (SIS) and sexual excitation (SES) scales: I. Measuring sexual inhibition and excitation proneness in men. *Journal of Sex Research, 39*(2), 114–126.

Janssen, E., et al. (2002b). The sexual inhibition (SIS) and sexual excitation (SES) scales: II. Predicting psychophysiological response patterns. *Journal of Sex Research, 39*(2), 127–132.

Janssens, P. M. (2009). Colouring the different phases in gamete and embryo donation. *Human Reproduction, 24*(3), 502–504.

Janus, S. S., & Janus, C. L. (1993). *The Janus report on sexual behavior*. New York: John Wiley.

Jeffries IV, W. L., & Dodge, B. (2007). Male bisexuality and condom use at last sexual encounter: Results from a national survey. *Journal of Sex Research, 44*(3), 278–289.

Jemmott, J. B., et al. (2005). HIV/STD risk reduction interventions for African American and Latino adolescent girls at an adolescent medicine clinic: A randomized controlled trial. *Archives of Pediatrics and Adolescent Medicine, 159*(5), 440–449.

Jemmott, J. B., Jemmott, L. S., & Fong, G. T. (2010). Efficacy of a theory-based abstinence-only intervention over 24 months: A randomized controlled trial with young adolescents. *Archives of Pediatric and Adolescent Medicine,164*(2), 152–159.

Jeng, C., et al. (2006). Management and outcome of primary vaginismus. *Journal of Sex and Marital Therapy, 32,* 379–387.

Jenkins, P. (2001). Beyond tolerance: Child pornography online. New York: New York University Press.

Jenny, C. (2008). Medicine discovers child abuse. *Journal of the American Medical Association, 300*(23), 2796–2797.

Jern, P., et al. (2009). Evidence for a genetic etiology to ejaculatory dysfunction. *International Journal of Impotence Research, 21,* 62–67.

Jiann, B., et al. (2006). Compliance of sildenafil treatment for erectile dysfunction and factors affecting it. *International Journal of Impotence Research, 18,* 146–149.

Jiao, C., et al. (2007). Effects of visual erotic stimulation on vibrotactile detection thresholds in men. *Archives of Sexual Behavior, 36,* 787–792.

Jick, S. S., et al. (2009). Postmenopausal estrogen-containing hormone therapy and the risk of breast cancer. *Obstetrics and Gynecology, 113*(1), 74–80.

Johnson, D., & Piore, A. (2004, October 18). Home in two worlds. *Newsweek,* 52–54.

Johnson, J., et al. (2004). Germline stem cells and follicular renewal in the postnatal mammalian ovary. *Nature, 428,* 145–150.

Johnson, S. D., Phelps, D. L., & Cottler, L. B. (2004). The association of sexual dysfunction and substance use among a community epidemiological sample. *Archives of Sexual Behavior, 33*(1), 55–63.

Johnson, S. M., & O'Connor, E. (2002). *The gay baby boom: The psychology of gay parenthood*. New York: New York University Press.

Johnson, J. V., et al. (2008). Effects of oral and transdermal hormonal contraception on vascular risk markers: A randomized controlled trial. *Obstetrics and Gynecology, 111*(2), 278–284.

Johnstone, J., & Huws, R. (1997). Autoerotic asphyxia: A case report. *Journal of Sex and Marital Therapy, 23*(4), 326–332.

Jonason, P. K., Li, N. P., & Cason, M. J. (2009). The "booty call": A compromise between men's and women's ideal mating strategies. *Journal of Sex Research, 46*(5), 460–470.

Jones, B. C., et al. (2008). Effects of menstrual cycle phase on face preferences. *Archives of Sexual Behavior, 37,* 78–84.

Jones, B. S., & Weitz, T. A. (2009). Legal barriers to second-trimester abortion provision and public health consequences. *American Journal of Public Health, 99*(4), 623–630.

Jones, R. K. (2006). Do U.S. family planning clinics encourage parent–child communication? Findings from an exploratory survey. *Perspectives on Sexual and Reproductive Health, 38*(3), 155–161.

Jones, R. K., & Boonstra, H. (2004). Confidential reproductive health services for minors: The potential impact of mandated parental involvement for contraception. *Perspectives on Sexual and Reproductive Health, 36*(5), 182–191.

Jones, R. K., Singh, S., & Purcell, A. (2005). Parent-child relations among minor females attending U.S. family planning clinics. *Perspectives on Sexual and Reproductive Health, 37*(4), 192–201.

Jones, R. K., et al. (2008). Abortion in the United States: Incidence and access to services, 2005. *Perspectives on Sexual and Reproductive Health, 40*(1), 6–16.

Jorgensen, C. (2000). *Christine Jorgensen: A personal autobiography*. San Francisco: Cleis Press.

Jouriles, E. N., Platt, C., & McDonald, R. (2009). Violence in adolescent dating relationships. *Prevention Researcher, 16*(1), 3–7.

Joyce, T., Kaestner, R., & Colman, S. (2006). Changes in abortions and births and the Texas parental notification law. *New England Journal of Medicine, 354*(10), 1031–1038.

Juarez, F., & Martín, T. C. (2006). Safe sex versus safe love? Relationship context and condom use among male adolescents in the Favelas of Recife, Brazil. *Archives of Sexual Behavior, 35*(1), 25–35.

Julien, D. et al. (2008). Adjustment among mothers reporting same-gender sexual partners: A study of a representative population sample from Quebec Province (Canada). *Archives of Sexual Behavior, 37,* 864–876.

Jumping-Eagle, S., et al. (2008). Association of conventional goals and perceptions of pregnancy with female teenagers' pregnancy avoidance behavior and attitudes. *Perceptions on Sexual and Reproductive Health, 40*(2), 74–80.

Jurgensen, M., et al. (2006). "Any decision is better than none:" Decision-making about sex of rearing for siblings with 17β-hydroxysteroid-dehydrogenase-3 deficiency. *Archives of Sexual Behavior, 35*(3), 359–371.

Kabakci, E., & Batur, S. (2003). Who benefits from cognitive behavioral therapy for vaginismus? *Journal of Sex and Marital Therapy, 29*(4), 277–288.

Kaeser, F., DiSalvo, C., & Moglia, R. (2000). Sexual behaviors of young children that occur in schools. *Journal of Sex Education and Therapy, 25*(4), 277–285.

Kaestle, C. E. (2009). Sexual insistence and disliked sexual activities in young adulthood: Differences by gender and relationship characteristics. *Perspectives on Sexual and Reproductive Health, 41*(1), 33–39.

Kaestle, C. E., & Halpern, C. T. (2007). What's love got to do with it? Sexual behaviors of opposite-sex couples through emerging adulthood. *Perspectives on Sexual and Reproductive Health, 39*(3), 134–140.

Kafka, M. P. (2009). The DSM diagnostic criteria for fetishism. *Archives of Sexual Behavior,* DOI: 10.1007/s10508-009-9558-7.

Kahn, J. A., et al. (2008). Rates of human papillomavirus vaccination, attitudes about vaccination, and human papillomavirus prevalence in young women. *Obstetrics and Gynecology, 111*(5), 1103–1110.

Kaiser Family Foundation. (2002). *Teens, sex, and TV: Survey snapshot.* Menlo Park, CA: KFF.

Kalb, C. (1999, April 19). Hormones and the mind. *Newsweek,* 50.

Kalb, C. (2001, August 13). Should you have your baby now? *Newsweek,* 40–50.

Kalb, C. (2003, February 3). Farewell to "Aunt Flo." *Newsweek,* 48.

Kalfoglou, A. L., Scott, J., & Hudson. (2008). Attitudes about preconception sex selection: A focus group study with Americans. *Human Reproduction, 23*(12), 2731–2736.

Kalichman, S. C., et al. (2001). Unwanted sexual experiences and sexual risks in gay and bisexual men: Associations among revictimization, substance abuse, and psychiatric symptoms. *Journal of Sex Research, 38*(1), 1–9.

Kalmuss, D. (2004). Nonvolitional sex and sexual health. *Archives of Sexual Behavior, 33*(3), 197–209.

Kalmuss, D., & Tatum, C. (2007). Patterns of men's use of sexual and reproductive health services. *Perspectives on Sexual and Reproductive Health, 39*(2), 74–81.

Kaly, P. W., Heesacker, M., & Frost, H. M. (2002). Collegiate alcohol use and high risk sexual behavior: A literature review. *Journal of College Student Development, 43*(6), 838–850.

Kandyba, K., & Binik, Y. M. (2003). Hypnotherapy as a treatment for vulvar vestibulitis syndrome: A case report. *Journal of Sex and Marital Therapy, 29,* 237–242.

Kantor, L. M. (2009). Does sexuality education "work"? An overview of the research. In E. Schroeder & J. Kuriansky (Eds.), *Sexuality Education: Past, Present, and Future* (Vol. 1, pp. 125–135). Westport, CT: Praeger.

Kaplan, E. (2004). With God on their side: How Christian fundamentalists trampled science, policy, and democracy in G. W. Bush's White House. *SIECUS Report, 32*(4), 4–8.

Kaplan, H. S. (1974). *The new sex therapy.* New York: Brunner/Mazel.

Kaplan, H. S. (1979). *Disorders of sexual desire and other new concepts and techniques in sex therapy.* New York: Brunner/Mazel.

Karasic, D., & Drescher, J. (2005). Introduction: Sexual and gender diagnoses of the diagnostic and statistical manual (DSM): A reevaluation. *Journal of Psychology and Human Sexuality, 17*(3/4), 1–5.

Kashiwase, H. (2002). Shotgun weddings a sign of the times in Japan. *Population Today, 30*(5), 1, 4.

Katz, A. (2007). *Breaking the silence on cancer and sexuality: A handbook for healthcare providers.* Pittsburgh: Oncology Nursing Society Publishing.

Katz, E. (2003). *The selected papers of Margaret Sanger. Vol. 1: The woman rebel, 1900–1928.* Urbana: University of Illinois Press.

Kaufman, C. E., et al. (2004). Communities, opportunities, and adolescents' sexual behavior in KwaZulu-Natal, South Africa. *Studies in Family Planning, 35*(4), 261–274.

Kaufman, F. (2010). *Life's hardest questions, big and small: An introduction to moral philosophy.* Boston: McGraw-Hill.

Kaufman, M., Silverberg, C., & Odette, F. (2007). *The ultimate guide to sex and disability: For all of us who live with disabilities, chronic pain and illness.* San Francisco: Cleis Press, Inc.

Kauth, M. R. (2006a). Epilogue: Implications for conceptualizing human sexuality. *Journal of Psychology and Human Sexuality, 18*(4), 371–385.

Kauth, M. R. (2006b). The evolution of human sexuality: An introduction. *Journal of Psychology and Human Sexuality, 18*(2/3), 1–22.

Kavanaugh, M. L., & Schwarz, E. B. (2008). Counseling about and use of emergency contraception in the United States. *Perspectives on Sexual and Reproductive Health, 40*(2), 81–86.

Keating, K. M., et al. (2008). Potential barriers to HPV vaccine provision among medical practices in an area with high rates of cervical cancer. *Journal of Adolescent Health, 43*(4), S61–S67.

Kees, N. L. (2005). Women's voices, women's lives: An introduction to the special issue on women and counseling. *Journal of Counseling and Development, 83,* 259–261.

Kelley, R. (2005, February 21). Return of a silent killer. *Newsweek,* 62.

Kelly, B. C., et al. (2009). Sexual compulsivity and sexual behaviors among gay and bisexual men and lesbian and bisexual women. *Journal of Sex Research, 46*(4), 301–308.

Kelly, B. C., & Muñoz-Laboy, M. A. (2005). Sexual place, spatial change, and the social reorganization of sexual culture. *Journal of Sex Research, 42*(4), 359–366.

Kelly, G. F. (2005). Re-visioning sexuality education: A challenge for the future. *American Journal of Sexuality Education, 1*(1), 5–21.

Kelly, G. F. (2009). Will the good sexuality educators please stand up? In E. Schroeder & J. Kuriansky (Eds.), *Sexuality Education: Past, Present, and Future* (Vol. 1, pp. 208–227). Westport, CT: Praeger.

Kelly, M. P., Strassberg, D. S., & Turner, C. M. (2006). Behavioral assessment of couples' communication in female orgasmic disorder. *Journal of Sex and Marital Therapy, 32,* 81–95.

Kempner, M. E. (2009). Bitter battles: Lessons from decades of controversy over sexuality education in schools. In E. Schroeder & J. Kuriansky (Eds.), *Sexuality Education: Past, Present, and Future* (Vol. 1, pp. 150–173). Westport, CT: Praeger.

Kerr, S. K., & Mathy, R. M. (2003). Introduction: The human ecology of lesbian and bisexual women's mental health. *Journal of Psychology and Human Sexuality, 15*(2/3), 1–9.

Kershaw, T. S., et al. (2003). Short and long term impact of adolescent pregnancy on postpartum contraceptive use: Implications for prevention of repeat pregnancy. *Journal of Adolescent Health, 33*(5), 359–368.

Kershaw, T. S., et al. (2007). Using clinical classification trees to identify individuals at risk of STDs during pregnancy. *Perspectives on Sexual and Reproductive Health, 39*(3), 141–148.

Khalife, S., et al. (2000). Evaluation of clitoral blood flow by color Doppler ultrasonography. *Journal of Sex and Marital Therapy, 26,* 187–189.

Khashan, A. S., et al. (2009). Rates of preterm birth following antenatal maternal exposure to severe life events: A population-based cohort study. *Human Reproduction, 24*(2), 429–437.

Khattak, S., et al. (1999). Pregnancy outcome following gestational exposure to organic solvents: A prospective controlled study. *Journal of the American Medical Association, 281*(12), 1106–1109.

Kiene, S. M., et al. (2009). Alcohol, helping young adults to have unprotected sex with casual partners: Findings from a daily diary study of alcohol use and sexual behavior. *Journal of Adolescent Health, 44*(1), 73–80.

Kilmartin, C. (2006). Why men won't ask for directions: The seductions of socio-biology. *Archives of Sexual Behavior, 35,* 625–626.

Kim, J. L., et al. (2007). From sex to sexuality: Exposing the heterosexual script on primetime network television. *Journal of Sex Research, 44*(2), 145–157.

Kimura, D. (1992). Sex differences in the brain. *Scientific American, 26*(3), 119–125.

Kimura, D. (1999). *Sex and cognition.* Cambridge, MA: MIT Press.

King, D. (2003). Gender migration: A sociological analysis. *Sexualities, 6*(2), 173–194.

King, E. (2004). Review of *Talk of Love: How culture matters* by Ann Swidler. *Archives of Sexual Behavior, 33*(1), 76–77.

King, K., & Gurian, M. (2009). With boys in mind: Teaching to the minds of boys. In E. Schroeder & J. Kuriansky (Eds.), *Sexuality Education: Past, Present, and Future* (pp. 62–75). Westport, CT: Praeger.

King, M., et al. (2005). Family size in white, gay, and heterosexual men. *Archives of Sexual Behavior, 34*(1), 117–122.

King, M-C., Marks, J. H., & Mandell, J. B. (2003). Breast and ovarian cancer risks due to inherited mutations in BRCA 1 and BRCA 2. *Science, 302,* 643–646.

Kingston, D. A., et al. (2007). The utility of the diagnosis of pedophilia: A comparison of various classification procedures. *Archives of Sexual Behavior, 36,* 423–436.

Kingston, D. A., et al. (2009). The importance of individual differences in pornography use: Theoretical perspectives and implications for treating sexual offenders. *Journal of Sex Research, 46*(2), 216–232.

Kinnish, K. K., Strassberg, D. S., & Turner, C. W. (2005). Sex differences in the flexibility of sexual orientation: A multidimensional retrospective assessment. *Archives of Sexual Behavior, 34*(2), 173–183.

Kinsey, A. C., Pomeroy, W. B., & Martin, C. E. (1948). *Sexual behavior in the human male.* Philadelphia: W. B. Saunders Company.

Kinsey, A. C., et al. (1953). *Sexual behavior in the human female.* Philadelphia: W. B. Saunders Company.

Kippax, S., & Smith, G. (2001). Anal intercourse and power in sex between men. *Sexualities, 4*(4), 413–434.

Kirby, D. (2007). *Emerging answers 2007: Research findings on programs to reduce teen pregnancy and sexually transmitted diseases.* Washington, DC: National Campaign to Prevent Teen and Unintended Pregnancy.

Kirby, D. (2008a). The impact of abstinence and comprehensive sex and STD/HIV education programs on adolescent sexual behavior. *Journal of Sexuality Research and Social Policy, 5*(2).

Kirby, D. (2008b). The impact of programs to increase contraceptive use among adult women: A review of experimental and quasi-experimental studies. *Perspectives on Sexual and Reproductive Health, 40*(1), 34–41.

Kirshenbaum, S. B., et al. (2004). "Throwing the dice": Pregnancy decision-making among HIV-positive women in four U.S. cities. *Perspectives on Sexual and Reproductive Health, 36*(3), 106–113.

Kissin, D. M., et al. (2008). Is there a trend of increased unwanted childbearing among young women in the United States? *Journal of Adolescent Health, 43*(4), 364–371.

Klaf, F. S., & Brown, W. (1958). Necrophilia, brief review and case report. *Psychiatric Quarterly, 32,* 645–652.

Klein, F. (1990). The need to view sexual orientation as a multivariable dynamic process: A theoretical perspective. In D. P. McWhirter, S. A. Sanders, & J. M. Reinisch (Eds.), *Homosexuality/heterosexuality: Concepts of sexual orientation* (pp. 277–282). New York: Oxford University Press.

Klein, J. D., & Committee on Adolescence. (2005). Adolescent pregnancy: Current trends and issues. *Pediatrics, 116*(1), 281–286.

Klein, M. (2003). Sex addiction: A dangerous clinical concept. *SIECUS Report, 31*(5), 8–11.

Kleinplatz, P. J. (2008). Sexuality and older people. *British Medical Journal, 337,* a239.

Kleinplatz, P. J., & Moser, C. (2004). Towards clinical guidelines for working with BDSM clients. *Contemporary Sexuality, 38*(6), 1, 4.

Kline, T. M., et al. (2008). Defining life partnerships: Does sexual orientation matter? *Journal of Homosexuality, 55*(4), 606–618.

Kluger, N., & Dereure, O. (2009). Penile papules. *New England Journal of Medicine, 360,* 1336.

Klugman, B. (2007). Locating and linking sexuality in development and human rights. *International Journal of Sexual Health, 19,* 65–77.

Knauft, B. M. (2004). What ever happened to ritualized homosexuality? Modern sexual subjects in Melanesia and elsewhere. *Annual Review of Sex Research, 14,* 137–158.

Knegtering, H., et al. (2006). A randomized open-label comparison of the impact of olanzapine versus risperidone on sexual functioning. *Journal of Sex and Marital Therapy, 32,* 315–326.

Kniss, D. D., & Akagi, C. G. (2008). Sexuality education and HIV knowledge, attitudes, and behaviors of young adults. *American Journal of Sexuality Education, 3*(4), 355–373.

Koblin, B. A., et al. (2003). High-risk behaviors among men who have sex with men in 6 U.S. cities: Baseline data from the EXPLORE study. *American Journal of Public Health, 93*(6), 926–932.

Koch, P. B. (2006). Women's bodies as a "puzzle" for college men: Grounded theory research. *American Journal of Sexuality Education, 1*(3), 51–72.

Koch, P. B., et al. (2005). "Feeling frumpy": The relationships between body image and sexual response changes in midlife women. *Journal of Sex Research, 42*(3), 215–223.

Kohlberg, L. (1981). *Essays on moral development.* San Francisco: Harper & Row.

Kohler, P. K., Manhart, L. E., & Lafferty, W. E. (2008). Abstinence-only and comprehensive sex education and the initiation of sexual activity and teen pregnancy. *Journal of Adolescent Health, 42*(4), 344–351.

Kolata, G. (2007, August 12). The myth, the math, the sex. *New York Times.*

Kontula, O., & Haavio-Mannila, E. (2002). Masturbation in a generational perspective. *Journal of Psychology and Human Sexuality, 14*(2/3), 49–83.

Kontula, O., & Haavio-Mannila, E. (2009). The impact of aging on human sexual activity and sexual desire. *Journal of Sex Research, 46*(1), 46–56.

Kornreich, J. L., et al. (2003). Sibling influence, gender roles, and the sexual socialization of urban early adolescent girls. *Journal of Sex Research, 40*(1), 101–110.

Koskimaki, J., et al. (2005). Are questions on both achieving and maintaining an erection needed to define erectile dysfunction? *International Journal of Impotence Research, 17,* 335–338.

Kost, K., et al. (2008). Estimates of contraceptive failure from the 2002 National Survey of Family Growth. *Contraception, 77*(1), 10–21.

Koukounas, E., & McCabe, M. P. (2001). Sexual and emotional variables influencing sexual response to erotica: A psychophysiological investigation. *Archives of Sexual Behavior, 30*(4), 393–408.

Krahè, B., Bieneck, S., & Scheinberger-Olwig, R. (2007). Adolescents' sexual scripts: Schematic representations of consensual and nonconsensual heterosexual interactions. *Journal of Sex Research, 44*(4), 316–327.

Krahè, B., Bieneck, S., & Scheinberger-Olwig, R. (2007). The role of sexual scripts in sexual aggression and victimization. *Archives of Sexual Behavior, 36,* 687–701.

Krahè, B., Scheinberger-Olwig, R., & Bieneck, S. (2003). Men's reports of nonconsensual sexual interactions with women: Prevalence and impact. *Archives of Sexual Behavior, 32*(3), 165–175.

Krahè, B., et al. (2000). The prevalence of sexual aggression and victimization among homosexual men. *Journal of Sex Research, 37*(2), 142–150.

Krassas, N. R., Blauwkamp, J. M., & Wesselink, P. (2003). "Master your Johnson": Sexual rhetoric in *Maxim* and *Stuff* magazines. *Sexuality and Culture, 7*(3), 98–118.

Krupp, D. B. (2008). Through evolution's eyes: Extracting mate preferences by linking visual attention to adaptive design. *Archives of Sexual Behavior, 37,* 57–63.

Kuefer, R., et al. (2005). Changing diagnostic and therapeutic concepts in high-flow priapism. *International Journal of Impotence Research, 17,* 109–113.

Kuehn, B. M. (2008). Time for "the talk": Again. *Journal of the American Medical Association, 300*(11), 1285–1287.

Kuffel, S. W., & Heiman, J. R. (2006). Effects of depressive symptoms and experimentally adopted schemas on sexual arousal and affect in sexually health women. *Archives of Sexual Behavior, 35*(2), 163–177.

Kuile, M. M., & Weijenborg, P. M. (2006). A cognitive-behavioral group program for women with vulvar vestibulitis sydrome (VVS): Factors associated with treatment success. *Journal of Sex and Marital Therapy, 32,* 199–213.

Kuppermann, M., et al. (2009). Computerized prenatal genetic testing decision-assisting tool: A randomized controlled trial. *Obstetrics and Gynecology, 113*(1), 53–63.

Kurth, A. E., et al. (2004). A comparison between audio computer-assisted self-interviews and clinician interviews for obtaining the sexual history. *Sexually Transmitted Diseases, 31*(12), 719–726.

Kwak, T. I., et al. (2008). Long-term effects of glans penis augmentation using injectable hyaluronic acid gel for premature ejaculation. *International Journal of Impotence Research, 20,* 425–428.

LaBrie, J. W., et al. (2008). A brief decisional balance intervention increases motivation and behavior regarding condom use in high-risk heterosexual college men. *Archives of Sexual Behavior, 37,* 330–339.

Ladas, A. K., Whipple, B., & Perry, J. (1983). *The G spot and other recent discoveries about human sexuality.* New York: Dell.

Laflin, M. T., Wang, J., & Barry, M. (2008). A longitudinal study of adolescent transition from virgin to nonvirgin status. *Journal of Adolescent Health, 42*(3), 228–236.

Laland, K. N. (2003). The new interactionism. *Science, 300,* 1879–1880.

Lam, C. B., & Chan, K. K.-S. (2007). The use of cyberpornography by young men in Hong Kong: Some psychosocial correlates. *Archives of Sexual Behavior, 36,* 588–598.

Lam, T. H., et al. (2004). Depressive symptoms among Hong Kong adolescents: Relation to atypical sexual feelings and behaviors, gender dissatisfaction, pubertal timing, and family and peer relationships. *Archives of Sexual Behavior, 33*(5), 487–496.

Lambert, T. A., Kahn, A. S., & Apple, K. J. (2003). Pluralistic ignorance and hooking up. *Journal of Sex Research, 40*(2), 129–133.

Landau, S. C., Tapias, M. P., & McGhee, B. T. (2006). Birth control within reach: A national survey on women's attitudes toward and interest in pharmacy access to hormonal contraception. *Contraception, 74*(6), 463–470.

Langdridge, D., & Butt, T. (2004). A hermeneutic phenomenological investigation of the construction of sadomasochistic identities. *Sexualities, 7*(1), 31–53.

Langevin, R., Langevin, M., & Curnoe, S. (2007). Reply to Blanchard (2007). *Archives of Sexual Behavior, 36,* 615–616.

Langstrom, N., Grann, M., & Lichtenstein, P. (2002). Genetic and environmental influences on problematic masturbatory behavior in children: A study of same-sex twins. *Archives of Sexual Behavior, 31*(4), 343–350.

Langstrom, N., & Hanson, R. K. (2006). High rates of sexual behavior in the general population: Correlates and predictors. *Archives of Sexual Behavior, 35*(1), 37–52.

Langstrom, N., & Seto, M. C. (2006). Exhibitionistic and voyeuristic behavior in a Swedish national population survey. *Archives of Sexual Behavior, 35,* 427–435.

Langstrom, N., & Zucker, K. J. (2005). Transvestic fetishism in the general population: Prevalence and correlates. *Journal of Sex and Marital Therapy, 31,* 87–95.

Lankveld, J., Geijen, W. E., & Sykora, H. (2008). The sexual self-consciousness scale: Psychometric properties. *Archives of Sexual Behavior, 37,* 925–933.

Lankveld, J. (2009). Self-help therapies for sexual dysfunction. *Journal of Sex Research, 46*(2–3).

Larsson, I., & Svedin, C. (2002 June). Sexual experiences in childhood: Young adults' recollections. *Archives of Sexual Behavior, 31*(3), 263–273.

Laumann, E. O., et al. (1994). *The social organization of sexuality.* Chicago: University of Chicago Press.

Laumann, E. O., et al. (2009). A population-based survey of sexual activity, sexual problems and associated help-seeking behavior patterns in mature adults in the United States of America. *International Journal of Impotence Research, 21*(3), 171–178.

Laumann, E. O., Nicolosi, A., et al. (2006). Men treated with sildenafil for erectile dysfunction: Results. *Journal of General Internal Medicine, 21*(10), 1069–1074.

Laumann, E. O., Paik, A., et al. (2006). A cross-national study of subjective sexual well-being among older women and men: Findings from the global study of sexual attitudes and behaviors. *Archives of Sexual Behavior, 35*(2), 143–159.

Laumann, E. O., et al. (2005). Sexual problems among women and men aged 40–80 years: Prevalence and correlates identified in the global study of sexual attitudes and behaviors. *International Journal of Impotence Research, 17,* 39–57.

Laumann, E. O., et al. (2006). A cross-national study of subjective sexual well-being among older women and men: Findings from the global study of sexual attitudes and behaviors. *Archives of Sexual Behavior, 35*(2), 145–161.

Lawler, A. (2006). Universities urged to improve hiring and advancement of women. *Science, 313,* 1712.

Lawrence, A. A. (2005). Sexuality before and after male-to-female sex reassignment surgery. *Archives of Sexual Behavior, 34*(2), 147–166.

Lawrence, A. A. (2006a). Clinical and theoretical parallels between desire for limb amputation and gender identity disorder. *Archives of Sexual Behavior, 35*(3), 263–278.

Lawrence, A. A. (2006b). Patient-reported complications and functional outcomes of male-to-female sex reassignment surgery. *Archives of Sexual Behavior, 35,* 717–727.

Lawrence, A. A. (2009). Erotic target location errors: An underappreciated paraphilic dimension. *Journal of Sex Research, 46*(2–3), 194–215.

Lawrence, A. A., et al. (2005). Measurement of sexual arousal in postoperative male-to-female transsexuals using vaginal photoplethysmography. *Archives of Sexual Behavior, 34*(2), 135–145.

Lawrence, A. A., & Love-Crowell, J. (2008). Psychotherapists' experience with clients who engage in consensual sadomasochism: A qualitative study. *Journal of Sex and Marital Therapy, 34*(1), 67–85.

Lawson, C. (1993). Mother–son sexual abuse: Rare or underreported? A critique of the research. *Child Abuse and Neglect, 17,* 261–269.

Lawson, D. M. (2003). Incidence, explanations, and treatment of partner violence. *Journal of Counseling and Development, 81,* 19–32.

Learman, L. A., et al. (2005). Abortion attitudes of pregnant women in prenatal care. *American Journal of Obstetrics and Gynecology, 192*(6), 1939–1947.

Leeman, L., et al. (2007). Can mifepristone medication abortion be successfully integrated into medical practices that do not offer surgical abortion? *Contraception, 76*(2), 96–100.

Lefkowitz, E. S., et al. (2004). Religiosity, sexual behaviors, and sexual attitudes during emerging adulthood. *Journal of Sex Research, 41*(2), 150–159.

Lehman, C. D., et al. (2007). MRI evaluation of the contralateral breast in women with recently diagnosed breast cancer. *New England Journal of Medicine, 356*(12), 1295–1303.

Lehr, S. T., et al. (2005). Predictors of father-son communication about sexuality. *Journal of Sex Research, 42*(2), 119–129.

Lehrman, S. (2007, June). Going beyond x and y. *Scientific American,* http://www.scientificamerican.com/article.cfm?id=going-beyond-x-and-y.

Leiblum, S. R. (2007). Sex therapy today: Current issues and future perspectives. In S. R. Leiblum (Ed.). *Principles and practices of sex therapy* (pp. 3–22). New York: Guilford Press.

Leland, J. (1999, September 20). More buck for the bang. *Time,* 61.

Lemoire, S. J., & Chen, C. P. (2005). Applying person-centered counseling to sexual minority adolescents. *Journal of Counseling and Development, 83,* 146–154.

Lengevin, R., Langevin, M., & Curnoe, S. (2007). Family size, birth order, and parental age among male paraphilics and sex offenders. *Archives of Sexual Behavior, 36,* 599–609.

L'Engle, K. L., Jackson, C., & Brown, J. D. (2006). Early adolescents' cognitive susceptibility to initiating sexual intercourse. *Perspectives on Sexual and Reproductive Health, 38*(2), 97–105.

Leonard, L. M., Iverson, K. M., & Follette, V. M. (2008). Sexual functioning and sexual satisfaction among women who report a history of childhood and/or adolescent sexual abuse. *Journal of Sex and Marital Therapy, 34*(5), 375–384.

Lepowsky, M. (1994). *Fruit of the motherland: Gender in an egalitarian society.* New York: Columbia University Press.

Lescano, C. M., et al. (2007). Condom use with "casual" and "main" partners: What's in a name? *Journal of Adolescent Health, 39*(3), 443e. 1–443e.7.

Lev, A. I. (2005). Disordering gender identity: Gender identity disorder in the DSM-IV-TR. *Journal of Psychology and Human Sexuality, 17*(3/4), 35–69.

LeVay, S. (1996). *Queer Science: The use and abuse of research into homosexuality.* Cambridge, MA: MIT Press.

Levenson, J. S., et al. (2009). Perceptions of sex offenders about treatment. *Sexual Abuse: A Journal of Research and Treatment, 21*(1), 35–56.

Lever, J., et al. (2008). Searching for love in all the "write" places: Exploring Internet personals use by sexual orientation, gender, and age. *International Journal of Sexual Health, 20*(4), 233–246.

Levesque, R. J. R. (2002). The roles and rules of law in sexual development. *Journal of Sex Research, 39*(1), 46–50.

Levin, R. J. (2003). Do women gain anything from coitus apart from pregnancy? Changes in the human female genital tract activated by coitus. *Journal of Sex and Marital Therapy, 29,* 59–69.

Levin, R. J. (2004). An orgasm is . . . who defines what an orgasm is? *Sexual and Relationship Therapy, 19*(1), 101–107.

Levin, R. J. (2008). Critically revisiting aspects of the human sexual response cycle of Masters and Johnson: Correcting errors and suggesting modifications. *Sexual and Relationship Therapy, 23*(4), 393–399.

Levine, J. (2002a). *Harmful to minors: The perils of protecting children from sex.* Minneapolis: University of Minnesota Press.

Levine, J. (2002b). Promoting pleasure: What's the problem? *SIECUS Report, 30*(4), 19–22.

Levine, M. D., et al. (2006). Weight concerns affect motivation to remain abstinent from smoking postpartum. *Annals of Behavioral Medicine, 32*(2), 147–153.

Levine, S. B. (2005). What is love anyway? *Journal of Sex and Marital Therapy, 31,* 143–151.

Levine, S. B., & Solomon, A. (2009). Meanings and political implications of "psychopathology" in a gender identity clinic: A report of 10 cases. *Journal of Sex and Marital Therapy, 35*(1), 40–57.

Levy, B. R., et al. (2007). Older persons' exclusion from sexually transmitted disease risk-reduction clinical trials. *Sexually Transmitted Diseases, 34*(8), 541–544.

Levy-Lahad, E., & Plon, S. E. (2003). A risky business: Assessing breast cancer risk. *Science, 302,* 574–575.

Lew, M. (2004). Adult male survivors of sexual abuse: Sexual issues in treatment and recovery. *Contemporary Sexuality, 38*(11), i–vi.

Lewis, J., et al. (2005). Managing risk and safety on the job: The experiences of Canadian sex workers. *Journal of Psychology and Human Sexuality, 17*(1/2), 147–167.

Lewis, L. J., & Kertzner, R. M. (2003). Toward improved interpretation and theory building of African American male sexualities. *Journal of Sex Research, 40*(4), 383–395.

Liaw, Y.-F., & Chu, C.-M. (2009). Hepatitis B virus infection. *Lancet, 373*(9663), 582–592.

Lieberman, L. D. (2006). Early predictors of sexual behavior: Implications for young adolescents and their parents. *Perspectives on Sexual and Reproductive Health, 38*(2), 112–114.

Lief, H. I. (2001). Boundary crossings: Sexual misconduct of clergy. *Journal of Sex Education and Therapy, 26,* 310–314.

Liehmann-Smith, J. (2001). Preteenage relationship with an older partner may lead to early first sex. *Family Planning Perspectives, 33*(3), 134.

Lim, D., et al. (2009). Clinical and molecular genetic features of Beckwith-Wiedemann syndrome associated with assisted reproductive technologies. *Human Reproduction, 24*(3), 741–747.

Lindau, S. T., et al. (2007). A study of sexuality and health among older adults in the United States. *New England Journal of Medicine, 357*(8), 762–774.

Lindberg, L. D., et al. (2006). The provision and funding of contraceptive services at publicly funded family planning agencies: 1995–2003. *Perspectives on Sexual and Reproductive Health, 38*(1), 37–45.

Lindberg, L. D., Jones, R., & Santelli, J. S. (2008). Noncoital sexual activities among adolescents. *Journal of Adolescent Health, 43*(3), 231–238.

Lindberg, L. D., & Singh, S. (2008). Sexual behavior of single adult American women. *Perspectives on Sexual and Reproductive Health, 40*(1), 27–33.

Lindley, L. L., et al. (2008). STDs among sexually active female college students: Does sexual orientation make a difference? *Perspectives on Sexual and Reproductive Health, 40*(4), 212–217.

Ling, D. C., Wong, W. C., & Ho, S. C. (2008). Are post-menopausal women "half-a-man"?: Sexual beliefs, attitudes and concerns among midlife Chinese women. *Journal of Sex and Marital Therapy, 34*(1), 15–29.

Lingiardi, V., Falanga, S., & D'Augelli, A. R. (2005). The evaluation of homophobia in an Italian sample. *Archives of Sexual Behavior, 34*(1), 81–93.

Linz, D., Paul, B., & Yao, M. Z. (2006). Peep show establishments, police activity, public place, and time: A study of secondary effects in San Diego, California. *Journal of Sex Research, 43*(2), 182–193.

Lippa, R. A. (2002a). *Gender, nature, and nurture.* Mahwah, NJ: Lawrence Erlbaum.

Lippa, R. A. (2002b). Gender-related traits of heterosexual and homosexual men and women. *Archives of Sexual Behavior, 31*(1), 83–98.

Lippa, R. A. (2003). Handedness, sexual orientation, and gender-related personality traits in men and women. *Archives of Sexual Behavior, 32*(2), 103–114.

Lippa, R. A. (2008). Sex differences and sexual orientation differences in personality: Findings from the BBC Internet survey. *Archives of Sexual Behavior, 37,* 173–187.

Littner, M., Littner, L., & Shah, M. A. (2001). Sexuality issues for the disabled: Development of a United States policy. *SIECUS Report, 29*(3), 28–32.

Litzinger, S., & Gordon, K. C. (2005). Exploring relationships among communication, sexual satisfaction, and marital satisfaction. *Journal of Sex and Marital Therapy, 31,* 409–424.

Lo, B., et al. (2010). NIH guidelines for stem cell research and gamete donors. *Science, 327,* 962–963.

Lobato, M. I., et al. (2006). Follow-up of sex reassignment surgery in transsexuals: A Brazilian cohort. *Archives of Sexual Behavior, 35,* 711–715.

Loewenson, P. R., Ireland, M., & Resnick, M. D. (2004). Primary and secondary sexual abstinence in high school students. *Journal of Adolescent Health, 34*(3), 209–215.

London, S. (2004). Current hormone therapy use linked to 30–100% rise in risk of breast cancer. *Perspectives on Sexual and Reproductive Health, 36*(1), 41–42.

Lopez, L. M., et al. (2008). Skin patch and vaginal ring versus combined oral contraceptives for contraception. *Cochrane Database of Systematic Reviews* (1).

Lorentzen, E., Nilsen, H., & Traeen, B. (2008). Will it never end? The narratives of incest victims on the termination of sexual abuse. *Journal of Sex Research, 45*(2), 164–174.

Louie, K. S., et al. (2009). Early age at first sexual intercourse and early pregnancy are risk factors for cervical cancer in developing countries. *British Journal of Cancer, 100,* 1191–1197.

Low, N., et al. (2006). Global control of sexually transmitted infections. *Lancet,* DOI:10.1016/S0140-6736(06)69482-8.

Ludwig, A. K., et al. (2009). Physical health at 5.5 years of age of term-born singletons after intracytoplasmic sperm injection: Results of a prospective, controlled, single-blinded study. *Fertility and Sterility, 91*(1), 115–124.

Luft, D. S. (2003). *Eros and inwardness in Vienna: Weininger, Musil, Doderer.* Chicago: University of Chicago Press.

Lurie, G., et al. (2007). Association of estrogen and progestin potency of oral contraceptives with ovarian carcinoma risk. *Obstetrics and Gynecology, 109*(3), 597–607.

Lykins, A. D., Meana, M., & Kambe, G. (2006). Detection of differential viewing patterns to erotic and non-erotic stimuli using eye-tracking methodology. *Archives of Sexual Behavior, 35,* 569–575.

Lykins, A. D., Meana, M., & Strauss, G. P. (2008). Sex differences in visual attention to erotic and non-erotic stimuli. *Archives of Sexual Behavior, 37,* 219–228.

Macaluso, M., et al. (2007). Efficacy of the male latex condom and of the female polyurethane condom as barriers to semen during intercourse: A randomized clinical trial. *American Journal of Epidemiology, 166*(1), 88–96.

MacCallum, F. (2009). Embryo donation parents' attitudes towards donors: Comparison with adoption. *Human Reproduction, 24*(3), 517–523.

Maccoby, E. E. (1998). *The two sexes: Growing up apart, coming together.* Cambridge, MA: Harvard University Press.

MacCulloch, S. I., et al. (2004). Birth order in sex-offending and aggressive men. *Archives of Sexual Behavior, 33*(5), 467–474.

Machin, S., & Pekkarinen, T. (2008). Global sex differences in test score variability. *Science, 322*(5906), 1331–1332.

MacIntosh, H. B., & Johnson, S. (2008). Emotionally focused therapy for couples and childhood sexual abuse survivors. *Journal of Marital and Family Therapy, 34*(3), 298–315.

MacNeil, S., & Byers, E. S. (2009). Role of sexual self-disclosure in the sexual satisfaction of long-term heterosexual couples. *Journal of Sex Research, 46*(1), 3–14.

Mah, K., & Binik, Y. M. (2005). Are orgasms in the mind or the body? Psychosocial versus physiological correlates of orgasmic pleasure and satisfaction. *Journal of Sex and Marital Therapy, 31,* 187–200.

Maher, J. E., et al. (2004). Acceptability of the vaginal diaphragm among current users. *Perspectives on Sexual and Reproductive Health, 36*(2), 64–71.

Maher, M. J., Sever, L. M., & Pichler, S. (2008). How Catholic college students think about homosexuality: The connection between authority and sexuality. *Journal of Homosexuality, 55*(2), 325–349.

Maisto, S. A., et al. (2004). The relationship between alcohol and individual difference variables on attitudes and behav-

ioral skills relevant to sexual health among heterosexual young adult men. *Archives of Sexual Behavior, 33*(6), 571–584.

Malakoff, D. (2003). New players, same debate in Congress. *Science, 299,* 799.

Malcolm, J. P. (2008). Heterosexually married men who have sex with men: Marital separation and psychological adjustment. *Journal of Sex Research, 45*(4), 350–357.

Malcom, N. L. (2003). Constructing female athleticism: A study of girls' recreational softball. *American Behavioral Scientist, 46*(10), 1387–1404.

Malebranche, D. J. (2008). Bisexually active black men in the United States and HIV: Acknowledging more than the "down low." *Archives of Sexual Behavior, 37,* 810–816.

Maloney, M. J., et al. (2008). Treatment of acne using a 3-milligram drospirenone/20-microgram ethinyl estradiol oral contraceptive administered in a 24/4 regimen: A randomized controlled trial. *Obstetrics and Gynecology, 112*(4), 773–781.

Maltz, W. (2003). Treating the sexual intimacy concerns of sexual abuse survivors. *Contemporary Sexuality, 37*(7), i–viii.

Manipalviratn, S., DeCherney, A., & Segars, J. (2009). Imprinting disorders and assisted reproductive technology. *Fertility and Sterility, 91*(2), 305–315.

Manlove, J., Ikramullah, E., & Terry-Humen, E. (2008). Condom use and consistency among male adolescents in the United States. *Journal of Adolescent Health, 43*(4), 325–333.

Marcell, A. V., Raine, T., & Eyre, S. L. (2003). Where does reproductive health fit into the lives of adolescent males? *Perspectives on Sexual and Reproductive Health, 35*(4), 180–186.

Marotta, S. A., & Asner, K. K. (1999). Group psychotherapy for women with a history of incest: The research base. *Journal of Counseling and Development, 77,* 315–322.

Marrazzo, J. M., Coffey, P., & Bingham, A. (2005). Sexual practices, risk perception and knowledge of sexually transmitted disease risk among lesbian and bisexual women. *Perspectives on Sexual and Reproductive Health, 37*(1), 6–12.

Marshall, E. (2002). Battle heats up over mammography benefits. *Science, 295,* 1624–1625.

Marshall, N. L. (2003). Introduction to special issue on social construction of gender. *American Behavioral Scientist, 46*(10), 1289–1295.

Marshall, W. L., Marshall, L. E., & Serran, G. A. (2007). Strategies in the treatment of paraphilias: A critical review. *Annual Review of Sex Research, 17,* 162–182.

Marsiglio, W. (2003). Making males mindful of their sexual and procreative identities: Using self-narratives in field settings. *Perpsectives on Sexual and Reproductive Health, 35*(5), 229–233.

Marston, C., & King, E. (2006). Factors that shape young people's sexual behaviour: A systematic review. *Lancet, 368*(9547), 1581–1586.

Martin, J. A., et al. (2009). Births: Final data for 2006. *National Vital Statistics Reports, 57*(7).

Martin, J. T., Puts, D. A., & Breedlove, S. M. (2008). Hand asymmetry in heterosexual and homosexual men and women: Relationship to 2D:4D digit ratios and other sexually dimorphic anatomical traits. *Archives of Sexual Behavior, 37,* 119–132.

Martin-Alguacil, N., et al. (2008). Clitoral sexual arousal: Neuronal tracing study from the clitoris through the spinal tracts. *Journal of Urology, 180*(4), 1241–1248.

Martino, S. C., et al. (2008). Beyond the "big talk": The roles of breadth and repetition in parent-adolescent communication about sexual topics. *Pediatrics, 121*(3), e612–e618.

Martino, S. C., et al. (2009). It's better on TV: Does television set teenagers up for regret following sexual initiation? *Perspectives on Sexual and Reproductive Health, 41*(2), 92–100.

Mastenbroek, S., et al. (2008). What next for preimplantation genetic screening? More randomized controlled trials needed? *Human Reproduction, 23*(12), 2626–2628.

Masters, W. H., & Johnson, V. E. (1966). *Human sexual response.* Boston: Little, Brown.

Masters, W. H., & Johnson, V. E. (1970). *Human sexual inadequacy.* Boston: Little, Brown.

Mathy, R. M. (2002). Transgender identity and suicidality in a nonclinical sample: Sexual orientation, psychiatric history, and compulsive behaviors. *Journal of Psychology and Human Sexuality, 14*(4), 47–65.

Maticka-Tyndale, E., Herold, E. S., & Mewhinney, D. (1999). Casual sex on spring break: Intentions and behaviors of Canadian students. *Journal of Sex Research, 35*(3), 254–264.

Maticka-Tyndale, E., Lewis, J., & Street, M. (2005). Making a place for escort work: A case study. *Journal of Sex Research, 42*(1), 46–53.

Mauck, C. K. (2009). Review: Biomarkers for evaluating vaginal microbicides and contraceptives: Discovery and early validation. *Sexually Transmitted Diseases, 36*(3), S73–S75.

Mazur, T. (2005). Gender dysphoria and gender change in androgen insensitivity or micropenis. *Archives of Sexual Behavior, 34*(4), 411–421.

McAnulty, R. D., & Brineman, J. M. (2007). Infidelity in dating relationships. *Annual Review of Sex Research, 18,* 94–114.

McBride, K. R., et al. (2007). Turning sexual science into news: Sex research and the media. *Journal of Sex Research, 44*(4), 347–358.

McCabe, M. P. (2007). Satisfaction in marriage and committed heterosexual relationships: Past, present, and future. *Annual Review of Sex Research, 17,* 39–58.

McCabe, M. P., & Matic, H. (2008). Erectile dysfunction and relationships: Views of men with erectile dysfunction and their partners. *Sexual and Relationship Therapy, 23*(1), 51–60.

McCabe, M. P., et al. (2003). Changes over time in sexual and relationship functioning of people with multiple sclerosis. *Journal of Sex and Marital Therapy, 29*(4), 305–321.

McCabe, M. P., & Wauchope, M. (2005). Behavioral characteristics of men accused of rape: Evidence for different types of rapists. *Archives of Sexual Behavior, 34*(2), 241–253.

McCaffree, K. A. (1998). Who is a sexuality professional? *Journal of Sex Education and Therapy, 23*(1), 3–5.

McCall, K. M., & Meston, C. M. (2007). The effects of false positive and false negative physiological feedback on sexual arousal: A comparison of women with or without sexual arousal disorder. *Archives of Sexual Behavior, 36,* 518–530.

McCarthy, B. W., & Fucito, L. M. (2005). Integrating medication, realistic expectations, and therapeutic interventions in the treatment of male sexual dysfunction. *Journal of Sex and Marital Therapy, 31,* 319–328.

McCarthy, B. W., & McDonald, D. (2009). Assessment, treatment, and relapse prevention: Male hypoactive sexual desire disorder. *Journal of Sex and Marital Therapy, 35*(1), 58–67.

McCarthy, B. W., & Metz, M. E. (2008). The "good-enough sex" model: A case illustration. *Sexual and Relationship Therapy, 23*(3), 227–234.

McClanahan, K. K. (2008). Depression in pregnant adolescents: Considerations for treatment. *Journal of Marital and Family Therapy, 34*(2), 59–64.

McCleary, R., & Meeker, J. W. (2006). Do peep shows "cause" crime? A response to Linz, Paul, and Yao. *Journal of Sex Research, 43*(2), 194–196.

McConaghy, N. (2005). Time to abandon the gay/heterosexual dichotomy? *Archives of Sexual Behavior, 34*(1), 1–2.

McCrady, F., et al. (2008). A brief report of incarcerated adolescent sex offenders' generic and sex-specific cognitive distortions. *Sexual Abuse: A Journal of Research and Treatment, 20*(3), 261–271.

McDonald, D. G. (2010, February 22). An apology with echoes of 12 steps. *New York Times,* D1, D6.

McFadden, D. (2002). Masculinization effects in the auditory system. *Archives of Sexual Behavior, 31*(1), 99–111.

McFarlane, M., Bull, S. S., & Reitmeijer, C. A. (2002). Young adults on the Internet: Risk behaviors for *Sexually Transmitted Diseases* and HIV. *Journal of Adolescent Health, 31*(1), 11–16.

McGinn, D. (2004, October 4). Mating behavior 101. *Newsweek,* 44–46.

McGoldrick, M., Loonan, R., & Wohlsifer, D. (2007). Sexuality and culture. In S. R. Leiblum (Ed.). *Principles and practices of sex therapy* (pp. 416–441). New York: Guilford Press.

McIntire, D. D., & Leveno, K. J. (2008). Neonatal mortality and morbidity rates in late preterm births compared with births at term. *Obstetrics and Gynecology, 111*(1), 35–41.

McIntyre, M. H. (2003). Digit ratios, childhood gender role behavior, and erotic role preferences of gay men [Letter]. *Archives of Sexual Behavior, 32*(6), 495–497.

McKee, A. (2005). The objectification of women in mainstream pornographic videos in Australia. *Journal of Sex Research, 42*(4), 277–290.

McKee, A. (2007). The relationship between attitudes towards women, consumption of pornography, and other demographic variables in a survey of 1,023 consumers of pornography. *International Journal of Sexual Health, 19*(1), 31–45.

McKenna, K. E. (2000). Central nervous system pathways involved in the control of penile erection. *Annual Review of Sex Research, 9,* 157–183.

McKenna, K. Y. A., Green, A. S., & Smith, P. K. (2001). Demarginalizing the sexual self. *Journal of Sex Research, 38*(4), 302–311.

McLawsen, J. E., et al. (2008). Professional perspectives on sexual sadism. *Sexual Abuse: A Journal of Research and Treatment, 20*(3), 272–304.

McMillan, D., et al. (2008). Developmental risk factor research and sexual offending against children: A review of some methodological issues. *Archives of Sexual Behavior, 37,* 877–890.

McNulty, J. K., & Fisher, T. D. (2008). Gender differences in response to sexual expectancies and changes in sexual frequency: A short-term longitudinal study of sexual satisfaction in newly married couples. *Archives of Sexual Behavior, 37,* 229–240.

M. D. Anderson Cancer Center (2006, December 14). *Decline in breast cancer cases likely linked to reduced use of hormone replacement.* News release.

Mead, M. (1930). *Growing up in New Guinea.* New York: New American Library.

Meana, M., & Lykins, A. (2009). Negative affect and somatically focused anxiety in young women reporting pain with intercourse. *Journal of Sex Research, 46*(1), 80–88.

Meana, M., & Nunnink, S. E. (2006). Gender differences in the content of cognitive distraction during sex. *Journal of Sex Research, 43*(1), 59–67.

Melby, T. (2003). Facilitated sex: What happens when the disabled need help with sex? *Contemporary Sexuality, 37*(11), 1, 4–6.

Melby, T. (2004). Spotlight on a hidden crime. *Contemporary Sexuality, 38*(5), 1, 4–6.

Melby, T. (2005). With males in the mix, federal sex survey takes on greater importance. *Contemporary Sexuality, 39*(12), 1–6.

Melby, T. (2006b). As easy as ABC? *Contemporary Sexuality, 40* (6),1–5.

Melby, T. (2006d). New generation, new worldview. *Contemporary Sexuality, 40*(10), 1–6.

Melby, T. (2007, December). Edgy world of online sex. *Contemporary Sexuality, 41*(12), 1–4.

Melby, T. (2008, January). How second life seeps into real life. *Contemporary Sexuality, 42*(1), 1–5.

Melby, T. (2008, May). Should rapists ever be free? *Contemporary Sexuality, 42*(5), 1–4.

Melby, T. (2008, October). Regaining intimacy after war. *Contemporary Sexuality, 42*(10), 1, 4–5.

Melby, T. (2008). The myth of teen promiscuity. *Contemporary Sexuality, 42,* 1–5.

Melby, T. (2008, June). The new twenties. *Contemporary Sexuality, 42*(6), 1–4.

Melby, T. (2009, March). Creating the DSM-V. *Contemporary Sexuality, 43*(3), 1, 4–6.

Melendez, R. M., et al. (2003). Intimate partner violence and safer sex negotiation: Effects of a gender-specific intervention. *Archives of Sexual Behavior, 32*(6), 499–511.

Melody, M. E., & Peterson, L. M. (1999). *Teaching America about sex: Marriage guides and sex manuals from the late Victorians to Dr. Ruth.* New York: New York University Press.

Meltzer, S. M., Monk, B. J., & Tewari, K. S. (2009). Green tea catechins for treatment of external genital warts. *American Journal of Obstetrics and Gynecology, 200*(3), 233.e1–233.e7.

Menning, C., Holtzman, M., & Kapinus, C. (2007). Stepfather involvement and adolescents' disposition toward having sex. *Perspectives on Sexual and Reproductive Health, 39*(2), 82–89.

Menon, S., et al. (2009). Fertility preservation in adolescent males: Experience over 22 years at Rouen University Hospital. *Human Reproduction, 24*(1), 37–44.

Mensch, B. S., et al. (2003). Gender-role attitudes among Egyptian adolescents. *Studies in Family Planning, 34*(1), 8–18.

Mercan, S., et al. (2008). Sexual dysfunctions in patients with neurodermatitis and psoriasis. *Journal of Sex and Marital Therapy, 34*(2), 160–168.

Mercer, B. M., et al. (2008). Labor outcomes with increasing number of prior vaginal births after cesarean delivery. *Obstetrics and Gynecology, 111*(2–1), 285–291.

Merson, M. H., et al. (2008). The history and challenge of HIV prevention. *Lancet, 475*–488.

Meston, C. M. (2004). The effects of hysterectomy on sexual arousal in women with a history of benign uterine fibroids. *Archives of Sexual Behavior, 33*(1), 31–42.

Meston, C. M., & Buss, D. M. (2007). Why humans have sex. *Archives of Sexual Behavior, 36,* 477–507.

Meston, C. M., & O'Sullivan, L. F. (2007). Such a tease: Intentional sexual provocation within heterosexual interactions. *Archives of Sexual Behavior, 36,* 531–542.

Meston, C. M., & Frohlich, P. F. (2003). Love at first fright: Partner salience moderates roller-coaster-induced excitation transfer. *Archives of Sexual Behavior, 32*(6), 537–544.

Meston, C. M., et al. (2005). Women's orgasm. *Annual Review of Sex Research, 15,* 173–256.

Meston, C. M., Rellini, A. H., & Telch, M. J. (2008). Short- and long-term effects of ginkgo biloba extract on sexual dysfunction in women. *Archives of Sexual Behavior, 37,* 530–547.

Metz, M. E., & Sawyer, S. P. (2004). Treating sexual dysfunction in sex offenders: A case example. *Journal of Sex and Marital Therapy, 30,* 185–197.

Meyer, M. D. E. (2005). Drawing the sexuality card: Teaching, researching, and living bisexuality. *Sexuality and Culture, 9*(1), 3–13.

Meyer, W., et al. (2001). The Harry Benjamin International Gender Dysphoria Association's standards of care for gender identity disorders (sixth version). *Journal of Psychology and Human Sexuality, 13*(1), 1–30.

Meyer-Bahlburg, H. F. L. (2005a). Gender identity outcome in female-raised 46, XY persons with penile agenesis, cloacal exstrophy of the bladder, or penile ablation. *Archives of Sexual Behavior, 34*(4), 423–438.

Meyer-Bahlburg, H. F. L. (2005b). Introduction: Gender dysphoria and gender change in persons with intersexuality. *Archives of Sexual Behavior, 34*(4), 371–373.

Meyer-Bahlburg, H. (2008). Sexual orientation in women with classical or nonclassical congenital adrenal hyperplasia as a function of degree of prenatal androgen excess. *Archives of Sexual Behavior, 37,* 85–99.

Meyer-Bahlburg, H. F., et al. (2006). Gender development in women with congenital andrenal hyperplasia as a function of disorder severity. *Archives of Sexual Behavior, 35,* 667–684.

Michael, R. T., et al. (1994). *Sex in America: A definitive study.* Boston: Little, Brown.

Michel, E. (2008). Team of Kinsey researchers dedicated to study of condom use. *Kinsey Today, 12,* 1 & 5.

Michels, K. B., et al. (2007). Induced and spontaneous abortion and incidence of breast cancer among young women. *Archives of Internal Medicine, 167*(4), 814–820.

Miclutia, I. V., Popescu, C. A., & Macrea, R. S. (2008). Sexual dysfunctions of chronic schizophrenic female patients. *Sexual and Relationship Therapy, 23*(2), 119–129.

Middleton, L. S., Kuffel, S. W., & Heiman, J. R. (2008). Effects of experimentally adopted sexual schemas on vaginal response and subjective sexual arousal: A comparison between women with sexual arousal disorder and sexually healthy women. *Archives of Sexual Behavior, 37,* 950–961.

Miletski, H. (2001). Zoophilia—implications for therapy. *Journal of Sex Education and Therapy, 26*(2), 85–89.

Miletski, H. (2006). Introduction to bestiality and zoophilia. *Contemporary Sexuality, 40*(12), 8–13.

Milhausen, R. R., & Herold, E. S. (1999). Does the sexual double standard still exist? Perceptions of university women. *Journal of Sex Research, 36*(4), 361–368.

Milhausen, R. R., & Herold, E. S. (2001). Reconceptualizing the sexual double standard. *Journal of Psychology and Human Sexuality, 13*(2), 63–83.

Miller, B. C. (2002, February). Family influences on adolescent sexual and contraceptive behavior. *Journal of Sex Research, 39*(1), 22–26.

Miller, C. A., et al. (2007). Chlamydial screening in urgent care visits: Adolescent-reported acceptability associated with adolescent perception of clinician communication. *Archives of Pediatrics and Adolescent Medicine, 161*(8), 777–782.

Miller, D. A., & Ellis, E. B. (2006). Pieces and parts. *American Journal of Sexuality Education, 1*(2), 67–73.

Miller, S. S., Hoffmann, H. L., & Mustanski, B. S. (2008). Fluctuating asymmetry and sexual orientation in men and women. *Archives of Sexual Behavior, 37,* 150–157.

Miller, W. C., et al. (2005). The prevalence of trichomoniasis in young adults in the United States. *Sexually Transmitted Diseases, 32*(10), 593–598.

Millett, G. A., et al. (2008). Circumcision status and risk of HIV and sexually transmitted infections among men who have sex with men: A meta-analysis. *Journal of the American Medical Association, 300*(14), 1674–1684.

Millett, G. A., et al. (2009). Incorrect data analysis in: Circumcision status and risk of HIV and sexually transmitted infections among men who have sex with men: A meta-analysis. *Journal of the American Medical Association, 301*(11), 1126–1129.

Mills, L. J., & Daniluk, J. C. (2002). Her body speaks: The experience of dance therapy for women survivors of child sexual abuse. *Journal of Counseling and Development, 80,* 77–84.

Min, K., et al. (2001). Hemodynamic evaluation of the female sexual response in an animal model. *Journal of Sex and Marital Therapy, 27*(5), 557–565.

Minassian, V. A., Stewart, W. F., & Wood, G. C. (2008). Urinary incontinence in women: Variation in prevalence estimates and risk factors. *Obstetrics and Gynecology, 111*(2), 324–331.

Miner, M. H., et al. (2007). The compulsive sexual behavior inventory: Psychometric properties. *Archives of Sexual Behavior, 36,* 579–587.

Minnis, A. M., Shiboski, S. C., & Padian, N. S. (2003). Barrier contraceptive method acceptability and choice are not reliable indicators of use. *Sexually Transmitted Diseases, 30*(7), 556–561.

Mitsch, A., et al. (2008). Trends in HIV/ AIDS diagnoses among men who have sex with men—33 states, 2001–2006. *Morbidity and Mortality Weekly Report, 57*(25), 681–686.

Modugno, F., et al. (2004). Oral contraceptive use, reproductive history, and risk of epithelial ovarian cancer in women with and without endometriosis. *American Journal of Obstetrics and Gynecology, 191*(3), 733–740.

Moemen, N. N., et al. (2008). Erectile dysfunction in spinal cord-injured men: Different treatment options. *International Journal of Impotence Research, 20*(2), 181–187.

Mohr, J. J. (2002). Heterosexual identity and the heterosexual therapist: Using identity as a framework for understanding sexual orientation issues in psychotherapy. *Counseling Psychologist, 30,* 532–566.

Mohr, J. J., & Sedlacek, W. E. (2001). Perceived barriers to friendship with lesbians and gay men among university students. *Journal of College Student Development, 41*(1), 70–80.

Mollborn, S. (2007). Making the best of a bad situation: Material resources and teenage parenthood. *Journal of Marriage and Family, 69*(1), 92–104.

Money, J. (2003). History, causality, and sexology. *Journal of Sex Research, 40*(3), 237–239.

Monro, S., & Warren, L. (2004). Transgendering citizenship. *Sexualities, 7*(3), 345–362.

Montaldi, D. F. (2002). Understanding hypersexuality with an axis II model. *Journal of Psychology and Human Sexuality, 14*(4), 1–23.

Montano, D. E., et al., (2008). STD/HIV prevention practices among primary care clinicians: Risk assessment, prevention counseling, and testing. *Sexually Transmitted Diseases, 35*(2), 154–166.

Monto, M. A. (2001). Prostitution and fellatio. *Journal of Sex Research, 38*(2), 140–145.

Moore, N. B., & Davidson, J. K. (2000). Communicating with new sex partners: College women and questions that make a difference. *Journal of Sex and Marital Therapy, 26,* 215–230.

Moreau, C., Bajos, N., & Trussell, J. (2006). The impact of pharmacy access to emergency contraceptive pills in France. *Contraception, 73*(6), 602–608.

Morrison, C. S., et al. (2004). Hormonal contraceptive use, cervical ectopy, and the acquisition of cervical infections. *Sexually Transmitted Diseases, 31*(9), 561–567.

Morrison, T. G., & Whitehead, B. W. (2005). Strategies of stigma resistance among Canadian gay-identified sex workers. *Journal of Psychology and Human Sexuality, 17*(1/2), 169–179.

Morse, J. M., Swanson, J. M., & Kuzel, A. J. (Eds.). (2001). *The nature of qualitative evidence.* Thousand Oaks, CA: Sage.

Moscicki, A.-B. (2008). HPV vaccines: Today and in the future. *Journal of Adolescent Medicine, 43*(4), S26–S240.

Moser, C., & Kleinplatz, P. J. (2005). *DSM-IV-TR* and the paraphilias: An argument for removal. *Journal of Psychology and Human Sexuality, 17*(3/4), 91–109.

Mosher, D. L. (1986). Misinformation on pornography: A lobby disguised as an educational organization. *SIECUS Report, 14*(5), 7–10.

Moskowitz, D. A., Rieger, G., & Roloff, M. E. (2008). Tops, bottoms and versatiles. *Sexual and Relationship Therapy, 23*(3), 191–202.

Moss, J. A., & Kern Ulmer, R. B. (2008). "Two men under one cloak": The sages permit it: Homosexual marriage in Judaism. *Journal of Homosexuality, 55*(1), 71–105.

Muehlenhard, C. L. (2000). Categories and sexuality. *Journal of Sex Research, 37*(2), 101–107.

Muehlenhard, C. L., et al. (2003). Gender and sexuality: An introduction. *Journal of Sex Research, 40*(1), 1–3.

Mueller, T. E., Gavin, L. E., & Kulkarni, A. (2008). The association between sex education and youth's engagement in sexual intercourse, age at first intercourse, and birth control use at first sex. *Journal of Adolescent Health, 42*(1), 89–96.

Mulhall, J. P. (2009). Defining and reporting erectile function outcomes after radical prostatectomy: Challenges and misconceptions. *Journal of Urology, 181*(2), 462–471.

Mulhall, J. P., Secin, F. P., & Guillonneau, B. (2008). Artery sparing radical prostatectomy: Myth or reality? *Journal of Urology, 179*(3), 827–831.

Munoz-Laboy, M. A. (2008). Familism and sexual regulation among bisexual Latino men. *Archives of Sexual Behavior, 37,* 773–782.

Munuce, M. J., et al., (2009). Human tubal secretion can modify the affinity of human spermatozoa for the zona pellucida. *Fertility and Sterility, 91*(2), 407–413.

Muscarella, F. (2006). The evolution of male-male sexual behavior in humans: The alliance theory. *Journal of Psychology and Human Sexuality, 18*(4), 275–311.

Mustanski, B. S. (2001). Getting wired: Exploiting the Internet for the collection of valid sexuality data. *Journal of Sex Research, 13*(4), 292–301.

Mustanski, B. S., Chivers, M. L., & Bailey, J. M. (2003). A critical review of recent biological research on human sexual orientation. *Annual Review of Sex Research, 13,* 89–140.

Mutchler, M. G. et al., (2008). Psychosocial correlates of unprotected sex without disclosure of HIV-positivity among African-American, Latino, and white men who have sex with men and women. *Archives of Sexual Behavior, 37,* 736–747.

Myers, J. E., Madathil, J., & Tingle, L. R. (2005). Marriage satisfaction and wellness in India and the United States: A preliminary comparison of arranged marriages and marriages of choice. *Journal of Counseling and Development, 83,* 183–190.

Nahrstadt, B. C. (2009). Informed consent for penile prosthesis. *International Journal of Impotence Research, 21,* 37–50.

Najman, J. M., Dunne, M. P., & Boyle, F. M. (2007). Childhood sexual abuse and adult sexual dysfunction: Response to commentary by Rind and Tromovitch (2007). *Archives of Sexual Behavior, 36,* 107–109.

Najman, J. M., Nguyen, M. L., & Boyle, F. M. (2007). Sexual abuse in childhood and physical and mental health in adulthood: An Australian population study. *Archives of Sexual Behavior, 36,* 666–675.

Nannini, D. K., & Meyers, L. S. (2000). Jealousy in sexual and emotional infidelity: An alternative to the evolutionary explanation. *Journal of Sex Research, 37*(2), 117–122.

Nappi, R. E., et al. (2003). Serum allopregnanolone levels relate to FSFI score during the menstrual cycle. *Journal of Sex and Marital Therapy, 29,* 95–102.

Narod, S. A., et al. (2002). Oral contraceptives and the risk of breast cancer in BRCA1 and BRCA2 mutation carriers. *Journal of the National Cancer Institute, 94*(23), 1773–1779.

Natali, A., et al. (2005). Heavy smoking is an important risk factor for erectile dysfunction in young men. *International Journal of Impotence Research, 17,* 227–230.

National Center for Health Statistics. (2006). *Advance Data from Vital and Health Statistics. Sexual behavior and selected health measures: Men and women 15–44 years of age, United States, 2002.* Washington, DC: National Center for Health Statistics.

Naya, Y., et al. (2008). Association between ED and LUTS in Japanese motorcyclists. *International Journal of Impotence Research, 20,* 574–577.

NCHS/CDC. (2002). Cohabitation, marriage, divorce, and remarriage in the United States. *Vital and Health Statistics, 23*(22).

Negy, C., & Eisenman, R. (2005). A comparison of African American and white college students' affective and attitudinal reactions to lesbian, gay, and bisexual individuals: An exploratory study. *Journal of Sex Research, 42*(4), 291–298.

Neilands, T. B., Steward, W. T., & Choi, K. H. (2008). Assessment of stigma towards homosexuality in China: A study of men who have sex with men. *Archives of Sexual Behavior, 37,* 838–844.

Nelson, C. A., & Gottesman, I. I. (2005, February 25). A piece of a neuroscientist's mind. *Science,* 1204.

Ness, R. B., & Grainger, D. A. (2008). Male reproductive proteins and reproductive outcomes. *American Journal of Obstetrics and Gynecology, 198*(6), 620.e1–620.e4.

Neuman, M. G. (2002). *Emotional infidelity.* New York: Random House.

New York Times. (2007, August 12). Sex study says math on men is a myth. *Watertown Daily Times,* p. A2.

Niccolai, L. M., et al. (2005). Condom effectiveness for prevention of Chlamydia trachomatis infection. *Sexually Transmitted Infections, 81*(4), 323–325.

Nicholas, C. L. (2004). Gaydar: Eyegaze as identity recognition among gay men and lesbians. *Sexuality and Culture, 8*(1), 60–86.

Nichols, M., & Shernoff, M. (2007). Therapy with sexual minorities: Queering practice. In: S. R. Leiblum (Ed.). *Principles and practices of sex therapy* (pp. 379–415). New York: Guilford Press.

Nickel, J. C., et al. (2008). Alfuzosin and symptoms of chronic-prostatitis-chronic pelvic pain syndrome. *New England Journal of Medicine, 359*(25), 2663–2673.

Nobre, P. J., et al. (2004). Determinants of sexual arousal and the accuracy of its self-estimation in sexually functional males. *Journal of Sex Research, 41*(4), 363–371.

Nobre, P. J., & Pinto-Gouveia, J. (2006). Emotions during sexual activity: Differences between sexually functional and dysfunctional men and women. *Archives of Sexual Behavior, 35,* 491–499.

Nobre, P. J., & Pinto-Gouveia, J. (2008a). Cognitions, emotions, and sexual response: Analysis of the relationship among automatic thoughts, emotional responses, and sexual arousal. *Archives of Sexual Behavior, 37,* 652–661.

Nobre, P. J., & Pinto-Gouveia, J. (2008b). Cognitive and emotional predictors of female sexual dysfunctions: Preliminary findings. *International Journal of Impotence Research, 34*(4), 325–342.

Nobre, P. J., Pinto-Gouveia, J., & Gomes, F. A. (2006). Prevalence and comorbidity of sexual dysfunctions in a Portuguese clinical sample. *Journal of Sex and Marital Therapy, 32,* 173–182.

Nuttbrock, L., et al. (2010). Psychiatric impact of gender-related abuse across the life course of male-to-female transgender persons. *Journal of Sex Research, 47*(1), 12–23.

Nygaard, I. (2008). Sexual dysfunction prevalence rates: Marketing or real? *Obstetrics and Gynecology, 112*(5), 968–969.

O'Connor, E. J., McCabe, M. P., & Firth, L. (2008). The impact of neurological illness on marital relationships. *Journal of Sex and Marital Therapy, 34*(2), 115–132.

Odibo, A. O., et al. (2008). Revisiting the fetal loss rate after second-trimester genetic amniocentesis: A single center's 16-year experience. *Obstetrics and Gynecology, 111*(3), 589–595.

O'Donnell, L., et al. (2005). Saving sex for later: An evaluation of a parent education intervention. *Perspectives on Sexual and Reproductive Health, 37*(4), 166–173.

Office of the Surgeon General. (2001). *Surgeon General's call to action to promote sexual health and responsible sexual behavior.* Washington, DC: U.S. Government Printing Office.

Office on Violence Against Women. (2004). *A national protocol for sexual assault medical forensic examinations: Adults/adolescents.* Washington, DC: Department of Justice.

O'Hare, E. A., & O'Donohue, W. (1998). Sexual harassment: Identifying risk factors. *Archives of Sexual Behavior, 27*(6), 561–580.

Okami, P., et al. (1997). Sexual experiences in early childhood: 18-year longitudinal data from the UCLA family lifestyles project. *Journal of Sex Research, 34*(4), 339–347.

Okami, P., Olmstead, R., Abramson, P. R., & Pendleton, L. (1998). Early childhood exposure to parental nudity and scenes of parental sexuality ("primal scenes"): An 18-year longitudinal study of outcome. *Archives of Sexual Behavior, 27*(4), 361–384.

Okami, P., & Shackelford, T. K. (2002). Human sex differences in sexual psychology and behavior. *Annual Review of Sex Research, 12,* 186–241.

Oliver, B. E. (2005). Thoughts on combating pedophilia in non-offending adolescents. *Archives of Sexual Behavior, 34*(1), 3–5.

Olsen, G. W. (2004). The sodomitic lions of Granada. *Journal of the History of Sexuality, 13*(1), 1–25.

Olsson, S., & Moller, A. (2006). Regret after sex reassignment surgery in a male-to-female transsexual: A long-term follow-up. *Archives of Sexual Behavior, 35*(4), 501–506.

Ompad, D. C., et al. (2006). Predictors of early initiation of vaginal and oral sex among urban young adults in Baltimore, Maryland. *Archives of Sexual Behavior, 35*(1), 53–65.

Onishi, N. (2007, April 8). *In Japan's rural areas, remote obstetrics fills the gap.* Retrieved April 11, 2007, from New York Times: http://www.nytimes.com/2007/04/08/world/asia/08japan.html?pagewanted=1&_r=1

Oosterhuis, H. (2001). Stepchildren of nature: Krafft-Ebing, psychiatry, and the making of sexual identity. Chicago: University of Chicago Press.

Ortiz, D. (2006). Review of Otto Weininger: Sex, Science, and self in imperial Vienna by Chandak Sengoopta. *Archives of Sexual Behavior, 35*(3), 379–381.

Osborn, J. E. (2008). The past, present, and future of AIDS. *Journal of the American Medical Association, 300*(5), 581–583.

Ostman, M. (2008). Severe depression and relationships: The effect of mental illness on sexuality. *Sexual and Relationship Therapy, 23*(4), 355–363.

Ostovich, J. M., & Sabini, J. (2005). Timing of puberty and sexuality in men and women. *Archives of Sexual Behavior, 34*(2), 197–206.

O'Sullivan, L. F., et al. (2007). I wanna hold your hand: The progression of social, romantic and sexual events in adolescent relationships. *Perspectives on Sexual and Reproductive Health, 39*(2), 100–107.

Oswald, D. L., & Russell, B. L. (2006). Perceptions of sexual coercion in heterosexual dating relationships: The role of aggressor gender and tactics. *Journal of Sex Research, 43*(1), 87–95.

Oswalt, S. B., Cameron, K. A., & Koob, J. J. (2005). Sexual regret in college students. *Archives of Sexual Behavior, 34*(6), 663–669.

Ott, M. A., et al. (2006). Greater expectations: Adolescents' positive motivations for sex. *Perspectives on Sexual and Reproductive Health, 38*(2), 84–89.

Ott, M. A., et al. (2008). The influence of hormonal contraception on mood and sexual interest among adolescents. *Archives of Sexual Behavior, 37,* 605–613.

Otto-Salaj, L., et al. (2008). Condom use negotiation in heterosexual African American adults: Responses to types of social power-based strategies. *Journal of Sex Research, 45*(2), 150–163.

Ozdemir, O., et al. (2008). The unconsummated marriage: Its frequency and clinical characteristics in a sexual dysfunction clinic. *Journal of Sex and Marital Therapy, 34*(3), 268–279.

Padma-Nathan, H., et al. (2003). Efficacy and safety of topical alprostadil cream for the treatment of female sexual arousal disorder (FSAD): A double-blind, multicenter, randomized, and placebo-controlled clinical trial. *Journal of Sex and Marital Therapy, 29,* 329–344.

Pang, J. W., et al. (2002). Outcomes of planned home births in Washington state. *Obstetrics and Gynecology, 100*(2), 253–259.

Papali, A. C., et al. (2008). A review of pediatric glans malformations: A handy clinical reference. *Journal of Urology, 180*(4), 1737–1742.

Papanikolaou, E. J., et al. (2005). Immature oocyte in-vitro maturation: Clinical aspects. *Reproductive Biomedicine Online, 10*(5), 587–592.

Pardun, C. J., & Forde, K. R. (2003). Sex in the media: Do condom ads have a chance? *SIECUS Report, 31*(2), 22–23.

Parish, W. L., Das, A., & Laumann, E. O. (2006). Sexual harassment of women in urban China. *Archives of Sexual Behavior, 35,* 411–425.

Parish, W. L., et al. (2007). Sexual practices and sexual satisfaction: A population based study of Chinese urban adults. *Archives of Sexual Behavior, 36,* 5–20.

Park, J. H., & Rissman, E. F. (2007). The male sexual revolution: Independence from testosterone. *Annual Review of Sex Research, 18,* 23–59.

Park, J. Y., et al. (2004). EGF-like growth factors as mediators of LH action in the ovulatory follicle. *Science, 303,* 682–684.

Parker, B. A. (2004). Queer theory goes to college. *Journal of Sex Research, 41*(2), 221–223.

Parker, R., et al. (2005). Global transformations and intimate relations in the 21st century: Social science research on sexuality and the emergence of sexual health and sexual rights frameworks. *Annual Review of Sex Research, 15,* 362–398.

Parker-Pope, T. (2009, March 24). Screen or not? What those prostate studies mean. *New York Times,* C1.

Parrott, D. J., & Zeichner, A. (2008). Determinants of anger and physical aggression based on sexual orientation: An experimental examination of hypermasculinity and exposure to male gender role violations. *Archives of Sexual Behavior, 37,* 891–901.

Parsons, J. T. (2005). Researching the world's oldest profession: Introduction. *Journal of Psychology and Human Sexuality, 17*(1/2), 1–3.

Parsons, J. T., et al. (2008). Explanations for the origins of sexual compulsivity among gay and bisexual men. *Archives of Sexual Behavior, 37,* 817–826.

Partington, K. N. (2008). Heterosexual HIV transmission: Ethics of disinformation and the importance of adhering to an evidence-based approach in psychotherapeutic practice. *Sexual and Relationship Therapy, 23*(4), 419–432.

Partington, S. N., et al. (2009). Second births to teenage mothers: Risk factors for low birth weight and preterm birth. *Perspectives on Sexual and Reproductive Health, 41*(2), 101–109.

Pascoe, C. J. (2003). Multiple masculinities: Teenage boys talk about jocks and gender. *American Behavioral Scientist, 46*(10), 1423–1438.

Passie, T., et al. (2004). Acute hyper-ventilation syndromes induced by sexual intercourse: Evidence of a psychophysical mechanism to intensify sexual experience? *Archives of Sexual Behavior, 33*(6), 525–526.

Paterson, J. (2009). Looking in the mirror. *Counseling Today, 51*(11), 30–40.

Patrick, D. L. (2005). Premature ejaculation: An observational study of men and their partners. *Journal of Sexual Medicine, 2,* 358–367.

Patrick, M. E., Maggs, J. L., & Abar, C. C. (2007). Reasons to have sex, personal goals, and sexual behavior during the transition to college. *Journal of Sex Research, 44*(3), 240–249.

Paul, B. (2009). Predicting Internet pornography use and arousal: The role of individual difference variables. *Journal of Sex Research, 46*(4), 344–357.

Paul, J. S. (2007). Body of work: Sexuality in recent American drama. *Annual Review of Sex Research, 17,* 200–214.

Payne, K. A., et al. (2005). What is sexual pain? A critique of DSM's classification of dyspareunia and vaginismus. *Journal of Psychology and Human Sexuality, 17*(3/4), 141–154.

Pedersen, W., Samuelsen, S. O., & Wichstrom, L. (2003). Intercourse debut age: Poor resources, problem behavior, or romantic appeal? A population-based longitudinal study. *Journal of Sex Research, 40*(4), 333–345.

Peinado, J., et al. (2007). Role versatility among men who have sex with men in urban Peru. *Journal of Sex Research, 44*(3), 233–239.

Perper, T., & Cornog, M. (2002). Eroticism for the masses: Japanese manga comics and their assimilation into the U.S. *Sexuality and Culture, 6*(1), 1–126.

Perry, B. L., & Wright, E. R. (2006). The sexual partnerships of people with serious mental illness. *Journal of Sex Research, 43*(2), 174–181.

Pertot, S. (2006). Sex therapy and the cultural construction of sexuality. *Contemporary Sexuality, 40*(4), 9–13.

Petaja, T., et al. (2009). Immunogenicity and safety of human papillomavirus (HPV)-16/18 as 04-adjuvanted vaccine in healthy boys aged 10–18 years. *Journal of Adolescent Health, 44*(1), 33–40.

Peterman, L. M., & Dixon, C. G. (2003). Domestic violence between same-sex partners: Implications for counseling. *Journal of Counseling and Development, 81,* 40–47.

Peterson, H. B. (2008). Sterilization. *Obstetrics and Gynecology, 111*(1), 189–203.

Peterson, Z. D., & Janssen, E. (2007). Ambivalent affect and sexual response: The impact of co-occurring positive and negative emotions on subjective and physiological sexual responses to erotic stimuli. *Archives of Sexual Behavior, 36,* 793–807.

Pharoah, P. O., Glinianaia, S. V., & Rankin, J. (2009). Congenital anomalies in multiple births after early loss of a conceptus. *Human Reproduction, 24*(3), 726–731.

Phelps, J., et al. (2001). Spinal cord injury and sexuality in married or partnered men: Activities, function, needs, and predictors of sexual adjustment. *Archives of Sexual Behavior, 30*(6), 591–602.

Philaretou, A. G. (2005). The sociocultural dimensions of sexual interactions. *Sexuality and Culture, 9*(3), 88–90.

Philipps, D. (2006, November 26). Studies take a look at science behind "gaydar." Associated Press/*Watertown Daily Times Sunday Weekly,* 9.

Philliber, S., et al. (2002). Preventing pregnancy and improving health care access among teenagers: An evaluation of the children's aid society—Carrera program. *Perspectives on Sexual and Reproductive Health, 34*(5), 244–251.

Picardo, C. M., et al. (2003). Women's knowledge and sources of information on the risks and benefits of oral contraception. *Journal of the American Medical Women's Association, 58*(2), 112–116.

Pierce, A. P. (2000). The coital alignment technique (CAT): An overview of studies. *Journal of Sex and Marital Therapy, 26,* 257–268.

Pillsworth, E. G., & Haselton, M. G. (2007). Women's sexual strategies: The evolution of long-term bonds and extrapair sex. *Annual Review of Sex Research, 17,* 59–100.

Pillsworth, E. G., Haselton, M. G., & Buss, D. M. (2004). Ovulatory shifts in female sexual desire. *Journal of Sex Research, 41*(1), 55–65.

Pinkerton, S. D., et al. (2002). Factors associated with masturbation in a collegiate sample. *Journal of Psychology and Human Sexuality, 14*(2/3), 103–121.

Piot, P., et al. (2008). Coming to terms with complexity: A call to action for HIV prevention. *Lancet, 372*(9641), 845–859.

Pistole, C., & Arricale, F. (2003). Understanding attachment: Beliefs about conflict. *Journal of Counseling and Development, 81,* 318–328.

Pittard, W. B., Laditka, J. N., & Laditka, S. B. (2008). Associations between maternal age and infant health outcomes among medicaid-insured infants in South Carolina: Mediating effects of socioeconomic factors. *Pediatrics, 122*(1), e100–e106.

Pitts, M. K., et al. (2004). Who pays for sex and why? An analysis of social and motivational factors associated with male clients of sex workers. *Archives of Sexual Behavior, 33*(4), 353–358.

Plante, R. F. (2006). *Sexualities in context: A social perspective.* Boulder, CO: Westview Press.

Plaud, J. J., Gaither, G. A., & Weller, L. A. (1998). Gender differences in the sexual rating of words. *Journal of Sex and Marital Therapy, 24,* 13–19.

Plaut, S. M. (2008). Sexual and nonsexual boundaries in professional relationships: Principles and teaching guidelines. *Sexual and Relationship Therapy, 23*(1), 85–94.

Plugge-Foust, C., & Strickland, G. (2000). Homophobia, irrationality, and Christian ideology: Does a relationship exist? *Journal of Sex Education and Therapy, 25,* 240–244.

Pluhar, E. I. (2008). Adolescent sexuality in western societies: A research compendium. *Journal of Sex Research, 45*(2), 193–199.

Pollet, T. V., & Nettle, D. (2009). Partner wealth predicts self-reported orgasm frequency in a sample of Chinese women. *Evolution and Human Behavior, 30*(2), 146–151.

Ponholzer, A., et al. (2006). Vascular risk factors and erectile dysfunction in a cohort of healthy men. *International Journal of Impotence Research, 18,* 489–493.

Ponholzer, A., et al. (2008). Is the metabolic syndrome a risk factor for female sexual dysfunction in sexually active women? *International Journal of Impotence Research, 20,* 100–104.

Poole, A. J., et al. (2006, December 1). Prevention of BRCA1-mediated mammary tumorigenesis in mice by a progesterone antagonist. *Science, 314,* 1467–1470.

Poon, C. S., & Saewyc, E. M. (2009). Out yonder: Sexual-minority adolescents in rural communities in British Columbia. *American Journal of Public Health, 99*(1), 118–124.

Potts, M., et al. (2008). Reassessing HIV prevention. *Science, 320,* 749–750.

Powell, J. A., & Wyllie, M. G. (2009). "Up and coming" treatments for premature ejaculation: Progress towards an approved therapy. *International Journal of Impotence Research, 21,* 107–115.

Pratt, M. W. (2003). Predicting adolescent moral reasoning from family climate: A longitudinal study. *Journal of Early Adolescence, 19,* 148–175.

Prause, N., & Graham, C. A. (2007). Asexuality: Classification and characterization. *Archives of Sexual Behavior, 36,* 341–356.

Prause, N., Janssen, E., & Hetrick, W. P. (2008). Attention and emotional responses to sexual stimuli and their relationship to sexual desire. *Archives of Sexual Behavior, 37,* 934–949.

Preves, S. E. (2003). *Intersex and identity: The contested self.* Newark, NJ: Rutgers University Press.

Priebe, G., & Svedin, C. G. (2008). Child sexual abuse is largely hidden from the adult society: An epidemiological study of adolescents' disclosures. *Child Abuse and Neglect, 32*(12), 1095–1108.

Prieto, D. (2008). Physiological regulation of penile arteries and veins. *International Journal of Impotence Research, 20,* 17–29.

Prokosch, M. D., et al. (2009). Intelligence and mate choice: Intelligent men are always appealing. *Evolution and Human Behavior, 30*(1), 11–20.

Provost, M. P., Quinsey, V. L., & Troje, N. F. (2008). Differences in gait across the menstrual cycle and their attractiveness to men. *Archives of Sexual Behavior, 37,* 598–604.

Pukall, C. F. (2005). Vulvodynia: A hidden women's health issue. *SIECUS Report, 33*(3), 25–32.

Pukall, C. F., Binik, Y. M., & Khalife, S. (2004). A new instrument for pain assessment in vulvar vestibulitis syndrome. *Journal of Sex and Marital Therapy, 30,* 69–78.

Pulley, L., et al. (2002). The extent of pregnancy mistiming and its association with maternal characteristics and behaviors and pregnancy outcomes. *Perspectives on Sexual and Reproductive Health, 34*(4), 206–211.

Purcell, D. W. (2006). Review of: Sexual abuse of males: The SAM model of theory and practice. *Archives of Sexual Behavior, 35,* 621–623.

Putman, S. E. (2009). The monsters in my head: Posttraumatic stress disorder and the child survivor of sexual abuse. *Journal of Counseling and Development, 87,* 80–89.

Puts, D. A., et al. (2008). Spatial ability and prenatal androgens: Meta-analyses of congenital adrenal hyperplasia and digit ratio (2D:4D) studies. *Archives of Sexual Behavior, 37,* 100–111.

Quindlen, A. (2003, January 13). Getting rid of the sex police. *Newsweek, 72.*

Radopoulos, D., Vakalopoulos, I., & Thanos, P. (2009). Preputial graft in penile curvature correction: Preliminary results. *International Journal of Impotence Research, 21,* 82–87.

Raghavan, R., et al. (2004). Sexual victimization among a national probability sample of adolescent women. *Perspectives on Sexual and Reproductive Health, 36*(6), 225–232.

Rahman, Q., & Hull, M. S. (2005). An empirical test of the kin selection hypothesis for male homosexuality. *Archives of Sexual Behavior, 34*(4), 461–467.

Rahman, Q., et al. (2008). Maternal inheritance and familial fecundity factors in male homosexuality. *Archives of Sexual Behavior, 37,* 962–969.

Rahman, Q., et al. (2009). Maternal inheritance and familial fecundity factors in male homosexuality. *Archives of Sexual Behavior, 38,* 159–160.

Rahman, Q., & Symeonides, D. J. (2008). Neurodevelopmental correlates of paraphilic sexual interests in men. *Archives of Sexual Behavior, 37,* 166–172.

Raina, R., et al. (2005). Early use of vacuum constriction device following radical prostatectomy facilitates early sexual activity and potentially earlier return of erectile dysfunction. *International Journal of Impotence Research, 18,* 77–81.

Raine, T. R., et al. (2005). Direct access to emergency contraception through pharmacies and effect on unintended pregnancy and STIs: A randomized controlled trial. *Journal of the American Medical Association, 293*(1), 54–62.

Rako, S., & Friebely, J. (2004). Pheromonal influences on sociosexual behavior in postmenopausal women. *Journal of Sex Research, 41*(4), 372–380.

Ralston-Howe, E., et al. (2009). Type-specific prevalence and persistence of human papillomavirus in women in the United States who are referred for typing as a component of cervical cancer screening. *American Journal of Obstetrics and Gynecology, 200*(245) e1–e7.

Randolph, M. E., & Mosack, K. E. (2006). Factors mediating the effects of childhood sexual abuse on risky sexual behavior among college women. *Journal of Psychology and Human Sexuality, 18*(1), 23–41.

Randolph, M. E., et al. (2007). Sexual pleasure and condom use. *Archives of Sexual Behavior, 36,* 844–848.

Randolph, M. E., & Reddy, D. M. (2006). Sexual functioning in women with chronic pelvic pain: The impact of depression, support, and abuse. *Journal of Sex Research, 43*(1), 38–45.

Raneri, L. G., & Wiemann, C. M. (2007). Social ecological predictors of repeat adolescent pregnancy. *Perspectives on Sexual and Reproductive Health, 39*(1), 39–47.

Rasberry, C. N., & Goodson, P. (2009). Predictors of secondary abstinence in U. S. college undergraduates. *Archives of Sexual Behavior, 38,* 74–86.

Rathbone, J. (2001). *Anatomy of masochism.* Hingham, MA: Kluwer Academic Publishers.

Reback, C. J., et al. (2005). HIV seroprevalence and risk behaviors among transgendered women who exchange sex in comparison with those who do not. *Journal of Psychology and Human Sexuality, 17*(1/2), 5–22.

Reddy, D. M., Fleming, R., & Swain, C. (2002). Effect of mandatory parental notification on adolescent girls' use of sexual health care services. *Journal of the American Medical Association, 288*(6), 710–714.

Reddy, U. M., Filly, R. A., & Copel, J. A. (2008). Prenatal imaging: Ultrasonography and magnetic resonance imaging. *Obstetrics and Gynecology, 112*(1), 145–157.

Redelman, M. J. (2008). Is there a place for sexuality in the holistic care of patients in the palliative care phase of life? *American Journal of Hospice and Palliative Medicine, 25*(5), 366–371.

Redman, C. W., & Sargent, I. L. (2005). Latest advances in understanding preeclampsia. *Science, 308,* 1592–1594.

Reece, M. (2007). Experiences of condom fit and feel among African-American men who have sex with men. *Sexually Transmitted Infections, 83*(6), 454–457.

Reece, M., & Dodge, B. (2004). A study in sexual health applying the principles of community-based participatory research. *Archives of Sexual Behavior, 33*(3), 235–247.

Reed, J. W. (2007). Review of: American sexual character: Sex, gender, and national identity in the Kinsey reports. *Archives of Sexual Behavior, 36,* 764–766.

Reed-Hughes, K. Y., & Anderson, V. N. (2007). What turns women on? *International Journal of Sexual Health, 19*(2), 17–31.

Reefhuis, J., et al. (2009). Assisted reproductive technology and major structural birth defects in the United States. *Human Reproduction, 24,* 360–366.

Refaat, A., et al. (2001). Female genital mutilation and domestic violence among Egyptian women. *Journal of Sex and Marital Therapy, 27,* 593–598.

Regan, P. C., et al. (2007). Affective responses before, during, and after the very first kiss. *International Journal of Sexual Health, 19*(2), 1–16.

Reichert, T. (2003). Sex in advertising research: A review of content, effects, and functions of sexual information in consumer advertising. *Annual Review of Sex Research, 13,* 241–273.

Reichert, T., & Lambiase, J. (2003). How to get "kissably close": Examining how advertisers appeal to consumers' sexual needs and desires. *Sexuality and Culture, 3,* 120–136.

Reid, R. C., Carpenter, B. N., & Lloyd, T. Q. (2009). Assessing psychological symptom patterns of patients seeking help for hypersexual behavior. *Sexual and Relationship Therapy, 24*(1), 47–63.

Reinisch, J. M., & Sanders, S. A. (1992). Prenatal hormonal contributions to sex differences in human cognitive and personality development. In A. A. Gerall, H. Moltz, & I. L. Ward (Eds.), *Handbook of behavioral neurobiology: Vol. II. Sexual differentiation* (pp. 221–243). New York: Plenum Press.

Reiss, I. L. (2002). *At the dawn of the sexual revolution.* Walnut Creek, CA: AltaMira Press.

Reiss, I. L. (2006). *An insider's view of sexual science since Kinsey.* Rowman & Littlefield Publishers, Inc.

Reiss, M. (2000). In clinical trial, women using once-a-month injectable contraceptive avoid pregnancy and approve of method. *Family Planning Perspectives, 32*(2), 95–96.

Reissing, E. D., et al. (2004). Vaginal spasm, pain, and behavior: An empirical investigation of the diagnosis of vaginismus. *Archives of Sexual Behavior, 33*(1), 5–17.

Rellini, A. H., & Meston, C. M. (2007). Sexual desire and linguistic analysis: A comparison of sexually-abused and non-abused women. *Archives of Sexual Behavior, 36,* 67–77.

Remez, L. (2000). Oral sex among adolescents: Is it sex or is it abstinence? *Family Planning Perspectives, 32*(6), 298–304.

Rempel, J. K., & Baumgartner, B. (2003). The relationship between attitudes towards menstruation and sexual attitudes, desires, and behavior in women. *Archives of Sexual Behavior, 32*(2), 155–163.

Rendall, D., Vasey, P. L., & McKenzie, J. (2008). The queen's English: An alternative, biosocial hypothesis for the distinctive features of "gay speech." *Archives of Sexual Behavior, 37,* 188–204.

Resnick, S. (2002). Sexual pleasure: The next frontier in the study of sexuality. *SIECUS Report, 30*(4), 6–11.

Rest, J. R., et al. (2000). A neo-Kohlbergian approach to morality research. *Journal of Moral Education, 29*(4), 381–395.

Reyes-Garcia, V. et al. (2008). Do the aged and knowledgeable men enjoy more prestige? A test of predictions from the prestige-bias model of cultural transmission. *Evolution and Human Behavior, 29*(4), 275–281.

Ribner, D. S. (2004). Ejaculatory restrictions as a factor in the treatment of Haredi (ultraorthodox) Jewish couples. *Archives of Sexual Behavior, 33*(3), 303–308.

Richard, D. (2002). Tantra 101. *Contemporary Sexuality, 36*(11), 1, 4–7.

Richard, D. (2003). Rape in the ranks. *Contemporary Sexuality, 37*(7), 1, 4–6.

Richards, J., et al. (2008). Healthcare seeking and sexual behavior among patients with symptomatic newly acquired genital herpes. *Sexually Transmitted Diseases, 35*(12), 1015–1021.

Richman, D. D., et al. (2009). The challenge of finding a cure for HIV infection. *Science,* 1304–1307.

Rickert, V. I., et al. (2004). Rates and risk factors for sexual violence among an ethnically diverse sample of adolescents. *Archives of Pediatrics and Adolescent Medicine, 158*(12), 1132–1139.

Rickert, V. I., Sanghvi, R., & Wiemann, C. M. (2002). Is lack of assertiveness among adolescent and young adult women a cause for concern? *Perspectives on Sexual and Reproductive Health, 34*(4), 178–183.

Ricketts, S. A., Murray, E. K., & Schwalberg, R. (2005). Reducing low birthweight by resolving risks: Results from Colorado's prenatal plus program. *American Journal of Public Health, 95*(11), 1952–1957.

Ridley, C. A., et al. (2006). The ebb and flow of marital lust: A relational approach. *Journal of Sex Research, 43*(2), 144–153.

Ridley, C., et al. (2008). Sexual expression: Its emotional context in heterosexual, gay, and lesbian couples. *Journal of Sex Research, 45*(3), 305–314.

Ridley, M. (2003). *Genes, experience, and what makes us human.* New York: HarperCollins.

Riegel, D. L. (2004). Effects on boy-attracted pedosexual males of viewing boy erotica. *Archives of Sexual Behavior, 33*(4), 321–323.

Riegel, D. L. (2005). Pedophilia, pejoration, and prejudice: Inquiry by insinuation, argument by accusation. *Sexuality and Culture, 9*(1), 88–97.

Rieger, G., Chivers, M. L., & Bailey, J. M. (2005). Sexual arousal patterns of bisexual men. *Psychological Science, 16*(8), 579.

Riman, T., et al. (2002). Risk factors for invasive ovarian cancer: Results from a Swedish case-control study. *American Journal of Epidemiology, 156*(4), 363–373.

Rind, B. (2003). Adolescent sexual experiences with adults: Pathological or functional? *Journal of Psychology and Human Sexuality, 15*(1), 5–22.

Rind, B., & Tromovitch, P. (2007). National samples, sexual abuse in childhood, and adjustment in adulthood: A commentary on Najman, Dunne, Purdie, Boyle, and Coxeter. *Archives of Sexual Behavior, 36,* 101–106.

Rizzo, A., & Swisher, L. L. (2004). Comparing the Stewart-Sprinthall Management Survey and the Defining Issues Test-2 as measures of moral reasoning in public administration. *Journal of Public Administration Research and Theory, 14*(3), 335–348.

Roberts, J. M. (2008). Preeclampsia: New approaches but the same old problems. *American Journal of Obstetrics and Gynecology, 199*(5), 443–444.

Robertson, A. A., et al. (2005). Predictors of infection with chlamydia or gonorrhea in incarcerated adolescents. *Sexually Transmitted Diseases, 32*(2), 115–122.

Robinson, J. D., & Parks, C. W. (2003). Lesbian and bisexual women's sexual fantasies, psychological adjustment, and close relationship functioning. *Journal of Psychology and Human Sexuality, 15*(4), 185–203.

Robinson, J. E., et al. (2002). Prenatal exposure of the ovine fetus to androgens sexually differentiates the steroid feedback mechanisms that control gonadotropin releasing hormone secretion and disrupts ovarian cycles. *Archives of Sexual Behavior, 31*(1), 35–41.

Rock, E. M., et al. (2005). A rose by any other name? Objective knowledge, perceived knowledge, and adolescent male condom use. *Pediatrics, 115*(3), 667–672.

Rollins, J. (2005, July). Breaking the silence, breaking the cycle. *Counseling Today,* 10–11.

Roller, C., et al. (2009). The sexuality of childhood sexual abuse survivors. *International Journal of Sexual Health, 21*(1), 49–60.

Rosario, M., et al. (2006). Sexual identity development among lesbian, gay, and bisexual youths: Consistency and change over time. *Journal of Sex Research, 43*(1), 46–58.

Rosario, M., et al. (2009). The coming-out process of young lesbian and bisexual women: Are there butch/femme differences in sexual identity development? *Archives of Sexual Behavior, 38,* 34–49.

Rose, E., et al. (2009). The validity of teens' and young adults' self-reported condom use. *Archives of Pediatrics and Adolescent Medicine, 162*(1), 61–64.

Rosen, R. C. (2002). Sexual function assessment and the role of vasoactive drugs in female sexual dysfunction. *Archives of Sexual Behavior, 31*(5), 439–443.

Rosen, R. C., & Laumann, E. O. (2003). The prevalence of sexual problems in women: How valid are comparisons across studies? *Archives of Sexual Behavior, 32*(3), 209–211.

Rosen, R. C., et al. (2006). Psychological and interpersonal correlates in men with erectile dysfunction and their partners: A pilot study of treatment outcome with sildenafil. *Journal of Sex and Marital Therapy, 32,* 215–234.

Rosenbaum, J. E. (2009). Patient teenagers? A comparison of the sexual behavior of virginity pledgers and matched nonpledgers. *Pediatrics, 123,* e110–e120.

Rosenberg, D. (2006, June 12). Politics of the altar. *Newsweek,* 34–35.

Rosenfield, A., Charo, A., & Chavkin, W. (2008). Moving forward on reproductive health. *New England Journal of Medicine, 359*(18), 1869–1871.

Rosengard, C., et al. (2004). Perceived STD risk, relationship, and health values in adolescents' delaying sexual intercourse with new partners. *Sexually Transmitted Infections, 80*(2), 130–137.

Ross, D. G., et al. (2008). New insights into SRY regulation through identification of 55 conserved sequences. *BMC Molecular Biology, 9.*

Ross, J., et al. (2004, Fall). Setting politics aside to collect cross-national data of sexual health of adolescents. *SIECUS Report, 32*(4), 28–34.

Ross, M. T., et al. (2005). The DNA sequence of the human X chromosome. *Nature, 434,* 325–337.

Ross, M. W., et al. (2003). Characteristics of men and women who complete or exit from an online Internet sexuality questionnaire: A study of instrument dropout biases. *Journal of Sex Research, 40*(4), 396–402.

Ross, M. W., et al. (2007). Stigma consciousness concerns related to drug use and sexuality in a sample of street-based male sex workers. *International Journal of Sexual Health, 19*(2), 57–67.

Rosser, B. S., et al. (2008). The relationship between homosexuality, internalized homonegativity, and mental health in men who have sex with men. *Journal of Homosexuality, 55*(2), 185–203.

Rostosky, S. S. et al. (2008). Sexual self-concept and sexual self-efficacy in adolescents: A possible clue to promoting sexual health? *Journal of Sex Research, 45*(3), 277–286.

Rothman, S. M., & Rothman, D. J. (2009). Marketing HPV vaccine. *Journal of the American Medical Association, 302*(7), 781–786.

Roughgarden, J. (2009). *The genial gene: Deconstructing Darwinian selfishness.* Berkeley: University of California Press.

Rowland, D. L. (2007). Will medical solutions to sexual problems make sexological care and science obsolete? *Journal of Sex and Marital Therapy, 33*(5), 385–397.

Rowland, D. L., Burek, M., & Macias, L. (2007). Plant-derivatives and herbs used for the promotion of sexual health and the treatment of sexual problems. *Annual Review of Sex Research, 18,* 225–257.

Rowland, D. L., Incrocci, L., & Slob, A. K. (2005). Aging and sexual response in the laboratory in patients with erectile dysfunction. *Journal of Sex and Marital Therapy, 31,* 399–407.

Rowland, D. L., Tai, W. L., & Slob, K. (2003). An exploration of emotional response to erotic stimulation in men with premature ejaculation: Effects of treatment with clomipramine. *Archives of Sexual Behavior, 32*(2), 145–153.

Royal Pharmaceutical Society of Great Britian (RPSGB). (2009, April 2). *Older generation putting their sexual health at risk.* Retrieved from Royal Pharmaceutical Society of Great Britain: http://www.rpsgb.org.uk/pdfs/pr090402.pdf

Ruble, D. N., Martin, C. C., & Berenbaum, S. A. (2006). Gender development. In N. Eisenberg (Ed.), *Handbook of child psychology,* vol. 3: *Social, emotional, and personality development* (pp. 858–932). New York: John Wiley.

Rupp, H. A., & Wallen, K. (2008). Sex differences in response to visual sexual stimuli: A review. *Archives of Sexual Behavior, 37,* 206–218.

Rupp, L. J., & Taylor, V. (2003). *Drag queens at the 801 cabaret.* Chicago: University of Chicago Press.

Russell, S. T. (2001, April/May). LGBTQ youth are at risk in U.S. school environment. *SIECUS Report, 29*(4), 19–21.

Russell, S. T., Lee, F. C. H., & the Latina/o Teen Pregnancy Prevention Workgroup. (2004). Practitioners' perspectives on effective practices for Hispanic teenage pregnancy prevention. *Perspectives on*

Sexual and Reproductive Health, 36(4), 142–149.

Rust, P. C. R. (2003). Bisexuality: The state of the union. *Annual Review of Sex Research, 13,* 180–240.

Rutherford, G. W. (2008). Condoms in concentrated and generalised HIV epidemics. *Lancet, 372*(9635), 275–276.

Ryan, C., & Futterman, D. (2001). Social and developmental challenges for lesbian, gay, and bisexual youth. *SIECUS Report, 29*(4), 5–18.

Ryan, S., et al. (2007). Adolescents' discussions about contraception or STDS with partners before first sex. *Perspectives on Sexual and Reproductive Health, 39*(3), 149–157.

Ryan, S., et al. (2008). Older sexual partners during adolescence: Links to reproductive health outcomes in young adulthood. *Perspectives on Sexual and Reproductive Health, 40*(1), 17–26.

Rye, B. J., & Meaney, G. J. (2007). Voyeurism: It is good as long as we do not get caught. *International Journal of Sexual Health, 19*(1), 47–56.

Saad, L. (2006). Gay rights attitudes a mixed bag. In F. Newport, *The Gallup poll: Public opinion 2005* (p. 187). Lanham: Rowman & Littlefield Publishers, Inc.

Sable, M. R., et al. (2006). Using the theory of reasoned action to explain physician intention to prescribe emergency contraception. *Perspectives on Sexual and Reproductive Health, 38*(1), 20–27.

Saewyc, E. M., et al. (2009). Protective factors in the lives of bisexual adolescents in North America. *American Journal of Public Health, 99*(1), 110–117.

Sakalh-Ugurlu, N., & Glick, P. (2003). Ambivalent sexism and attitudes toward women who engage in premarital sex in Turkey. *Journal of Sex Research 40*(3), 296–302.

Saleh, F. (2005). A hypersexual paraphilic patient treated with leuprolide acetate: A single case report. *Journal of Sex and Marital Therapy, 31,* 433–444.

Salihu, H. M., et al. (2003). Childbearing beyond maternal age 50 and fetal outcomes in the United States. *Obstetrics and Gynecology, 102*(5), 1006–1014.

Salisbury, R. M. (2008). Out of control sexual behaviors: A developing practice model. *Sexual and Relationship Therapy, 23*(2), 131–139.

Sampson, O., et al. (2009). Barriers to adolescents' getting emergency contraception through pharmacy access in California: Differences by language and region. *Perspectives on Sexual and Reproductive Health, 41*(2), 110–118.

Sanchez, D. T., & Kiefer, A. K. (2007). Body concerns in and out of the bedroom: Implications for sexual pleasure

and problems. *Archives of Sexual Behavior, 36,* 808–820.

Sanders, J. S. (1978). Male and female vocabularies for communicating with a sexual partner. *Journal of Sex Education and Therapy, 4,* 15–19.

Sanders, S. A. (1999). Midlife sexuality: The need to integrate biological, psychological, and social perspectives. *SIECUS Report, 27*(3), 3–7.

Sanders, S. A., Graham, C. A., & Milhausen, R. R. (2008). Predicting sexual problems in women: The relevance of sexual excitation and sexual inhibition. *Archives of Sexual Behavior, 37,* 241–251.

Sandfort, T. G. (2005). Sexual orientation and gender: Stereotypes and beyond. *Archives of Sexual Behavior, 34*(6), 595–611.

Sandfort, T. G., de Graff, R., & Bijl, R. V. (2003). Same-sex sexuality and quality of life: Findings from the Netherlands mental health survey and incidence study. *Archives of Sexual Behavior, 32*(1), 15–22.

Sandfort, T. G., et al. (2008). Long-term health correlates of timing of sexual debut: Results from a national U. S. study. *American Journal of Public Health, 98*(1), 155–161.

Sandfort, T. G., & Dodge, B. (2008). ". . . And then there was the down low": Introduction to black and Latino male bisexualities. *Archives of Sexual Behavior, 37,* 675–682.

Sandfort, T. G., & Keizer, M. (2002). Sexual problems in gay men: An overview of empirical research. *Annual Review of Sex Research, 11,* 93–120.

Sandfort, T. G., Melendez, R. M., & Diaz, R. M. (2007). Gender nonconformity, homophobia, and mental distress in Latino gay and bisexual men. *Journal of Sex Research, 44*(2), 181–189.

Santelli, J. S. (2008). Medical accuracy in sexuality education: Ideology and the scientific process. *American Journal of Public Health, 98*(10), 1786–1792.

Santelli, J. S., Abraido-Lanza, A. F., & Melnikas, A. J. (2009). Migration, acculturation, and sexual reproductive health of latino adolescents. *Journal of Adolescent Health, 44,* 3–4.

Santelli, J. S., et al. (2004). Initiation of sexual intercourse among middle school adolescents: The influence of psychosocial factors. *Journal of Adolescent Health, 34*(3), 200–208.

Santelli, J. S., et al. (2006). An exploration of the dimensions of pregnancy intentions among women choosing to terminate pregnancy or to initiate prenatal care in New Orleans, Louisiana. *American Journal of Public Health, 96*(11), 2009–2015.

Santelli, J. S., et al. (2000, July/August). Adolescent sexual behavior: Estimates and trends from four nationally representative surveys. *Family Planning Perspectives, 32*(4), 156–194.

Santelli, J. S., et al. (2003). The measurement and meaning of unintended pregnancy. *Perspectives on Sexual and Reproductive Health, 35*(2), 94–100.

Santilla, P., et al. (2002). Investigating the underlying structure in sadomasochistically oriented behavior. *Archives of Sexual Behavior, 1*(2), 185–196.

Santilla, P., Sandnabba, N. K., & Jern, P. (2009). Prevalence and determinants of male sexual dysfunction during first intercourse. *Journal of Sex and Marital Therapy, 35*(2), 86–105.

Santilla, P., et al. (2008). Discrepancies between sexual desire and sexual activity: Gender differences and associations with relationship satisfaction. *Journal of Sex and Marital Therapy, 34*(1), 31–44.

Saucier, J. A., & Caron, S. L. (2008). An investigation of content and media images in gay men's magazines. *Journal of Homosexuality, 55*(3), 504–523.

Saunders, J. A. (2005). Adolescent pregnancy prevention programs: Theoretical models for effective program development. *American Journal of Sexuality Education, 1*(1), 63–84.

Savic, I., & Lindstrom, P. (2008). PET and MRI show differences in cerebral asymmetry and functional connectivity between homo- and heterosexual subjects. *Proceedings of the National Academy of Sciences, 105*(27), 9403–9408.

Savin-Williams, R. C. (2005). *The new gay teenager.* Cambridge, MA: Harvard University Press.

Savin-Williams, R. C., & Diamond, L. M. (2000). Sexual identity trajectories among sexual-minority youths: Gender comparisons. *Archives of Sexual Behavior, 29*(6), 607–627.

Savin-Williams, R. C., & Ream., G. L. (2006). Pubertal onset and sexual orientation in an adolescent national probability sample. *Archives of Sexual Behavior, 35*(3), 279–286.

Savin-Williams, R. C., & Ream, G. L. (2007). Prevalence and stability of sexual orientation components during adolescence and young adulthood. *Archives of Sexual Behavior, 36,* 385–394.

Sawh, S. L., et al. (2008). Fractured penis: A review. *International Journal of Impotence Research, 20,* 366–369.

Sbraga, T. P., & O'Donohue, W. (2001). Sexual harassment. *Annual Review of Sex Research, 11,* 258–285.

Schacht, R. L., et al. (2007). Effects of alcohol intoxication and instructional set on women's sexual arousal vary based on sexual abuse history. *Archives of Sexual Behavior, 36,* 655–665.

Schackelford, T. K., et al. (2004). *Archives of Sexual Behavior, 33*(4), 405–412.

Scheper-Hughes, N., & Devine, J. (2003). Priestly celibacy and child sexual abuse. *Sexualities, 6*(1), 15–40.

Schieve, L. A., et al. (2002). Low and very low birth weight in infants conceived with use of assisted reproductive technology. *New England Journal of Medicine, 346*(10), 731–737.

Schindhelm, R. K., & Hospers, H. J. (2004). Sex with men before coming out: Relation to sexual activity and sexual risk-taking behavior. *Archives of Sexual Behavior, 33*(6), 585–591.

Schmid, T. E., et al. (2007). The effects of male age on sperm DNA damage in healthy non-smokers. *Human Reproduction, 22*(1), 180–187.

Schmiege, S., & Russo, N. F. (2005). Depression and unwanted first pregnancy: Longitudinal cohort study. *British Medical Journal, 331*(7528), 1303–1307.

Schober, J. M., et al. (2005). Leuprolide acetate suppresses pedophilic urges and arousability. *Archives of Sexual Behavior, 34*(6), 691–705.

Schooler, D., et al. (2005). Cycles of shame: Menstrual shame, body shame, and sexual decision-making. *Journal of Sex Research, 42*(4), 324–334.

Schrock, D. P., & Reid, L. L. (2006). Transsexuals' sexual stories. *Archives of Sexual Behavior, 35*(1), 75–86.

Schulte, J., et al. (2007). Declines in low birth weight and preterm birth among infants who were born to HIV-infected women during an era of increased use of maternal antiretroviral drugs: Pediatric spectrum of HIV disease, 1989–2004. *Pediatrics, 119*(4), e900–e906.

Schutzmann, K., et al. (2009). Psychological distress, self-harming behavior, and suicidal tendencies in adults with disorders of sex development. *Archives of Sexual Behavior, 38,* 16–33.

Scorolli, C., et al. (2007). Relative prevalence of different fetishes. *International Journal of Impotence Research, 19*(4), 432–437.

Sedgh, G., et al. (2007). Legal abortion worldwide: Incidence and recent trends. *Perspectives on Sexual and Reproductive Health, 39*(4), 216–225.

Seidman, S. N. (2006). Normative hypogonadism and depression: Does "andropause" exist? *International Journal of Impotence Research, 18,* 415–422.

Sekido, R., & Lovell-Badge, R. (2008a). Sex determination and SRY: Down to a wink and a nudge? *Trends in Genetics, 25*(1), 19–29.

Sekido, R., & Lovell-Badge, R. (2008b). Sex determination involves synergistic action of SRY and SF1 on a specific SOX9 enhancer. *Nature, 453,* 930–934.

Sellers, N., Satcher, J., & Comas, R. (1999). Children's occupational aspirations: Comparisons by gender, gender role identity, and socioeconomic status. *Professional School Counseling, 2*(4), 314–317.

Selvidge, M. M., Matthews, C. R., & Bridges, S. K. (2008). The relationship of minority stress and flexible coping to psychological well being in lesbian and bisexual women. *Journal of Homosexuality, 55*(3), 450–470.

Senn, C. Y., & Desmarais, S. (2001). Are our recruitment practices for sex studies working across gender? The effect of topic and gender of recruiter on participation rates of university men and women. *Journal of Sex Research, 38*(2), 97–101.

Senn, T. E., et al. (2007). Characteristics of sexual abuse in childhood and adolescence influence sexual risk behavior in adulthood. *Archives of Sexual Behavior, 36,* 637–645.

Sergeant, M. J., et al. (2007). Women's hedonic ratings of body odor of heterosexual and homosexual men. *Archives of Sexual Behavior, 36,* 395–401.

Serovich, J. M., et al. (2008). A systematic review of the research base on sexual reorientation therapies. *Journal of Marital and Family Therapy, 34*(2), 227–238.

Seto, M. C. (2005). Pedophilia and sexual offenses against children. *Annual Review of Sex Research, 15,* 321–360.

Seto, M. C., et al. (2004). The screening scale for pedophilic interests predicts recidivism among adult sex offenders with child victims. *Archives of Sexual Behavior, 33*(5), 455–466.

Sevely, J. L. (1987). *Eve's secrets: A new theory of female sexuality.* New York: Random House.

Shabsigh, R., et al. (2009a). Impact of an educational initiative on applied knowledge and attitudes of physicians who treat sexual dysfunction. *International Journal of Impotence Research, 21,* 74–81.

Shabsigh, R., et al. (2009b). Testosterone therapy in hypogonadal men and potential prostate cancer risk: A systematic review. *International Journal of Impotence Research, 21,* 9–23.

Shaffer, D. R., & Augustine, M. L. (2002). Affective mediation of homophobic reactions to homosexual males. *Journal of Psychology and Human Sexuality, 14*(4), 67–85.

Shafii, T., et al. (2004). Is condom use habit forming? Condom use at sexual debut and subsequent condom use. *Sexually Transmitted Diseases, 31*(6), 366–372.

Shakib, S. (2003). Female basketball participation. *American Behavioral Scientist, 46*(10), 1405–1422.

Shakiba, K., et al. (2008). Surgical treatment of endometriosis: A 7-year follow-up on the requirement for further surgery. *Obstetrics and Gynecology, 111*(6), 1285–1292.

Shannon, K., et al. (2009). Structural and environmental barriers to condom use negotiation with clients among female sex workers: Implications for HIV-prevention strategies and policy. *American Journal of Public Health, 99*(4), 659–665.

Shaw, D. (2006). Sexual and reproductive health: Rights and responsibilities. *Lancet*, Early Online Publication. DOI: 10.1016/S0140-6736(06)69487-7.

Sheen, J., & Koukounas, E. (2009). The role of absorption in women's sexual response to erotica: A cognitive-affective investigation. *Journal of Sex Research, 46*(4), 358–365.

Shelton, J. D. (2008). Counselling and testing for HIV prevention. *Lancet, 372*(9635), 273–275.

Shepard, B. (2003). In search of a winning script: Moral panic vs. institutional denial. *Sexualities, 6*(1), 54–59.

Shifren, J., & Ferrari, N. A. (2004, May 10). A better sex life. *Newsweek*, 86–87.

Shifren, J. L., et al. (2008). Sexual problems and distress in United States women. *Obstetrics and Gynecology, 112*, 970–978.

Shiri, R., et al. (2005). Relationship between smoking and erectile dysfunction. *International Journal of Impotence Research, 17*(2), 164–169.

Shiu-Ki, T. K. (2004). Queer at your own risk: Marginality, community and Hong Kong gay male bodies. *Sexualities, 7*(1), 5–30.

Shotorbani, S., et al. (2004). Attitudes and intentions of future health care providers toward abortion provision. *Perspectives on Sexual and Reproductive Health, 36*(2), 58–63.

Shoveller, J., et al. (2007). Identifying barriers to emergency contraception use among young women from various sociocultural groups in British Columbia, Canada. *Perspectives on Sexual and Reproductive Health, 39*(1), 13–20.

Sidley, G. (2003). Advocating for a condom availability program. *SIECUS Report, 31*(6), 25.

SIECUS (2003). *The truth about adolescent sexuality*. New York: Sex Information and Education Council of the U.S.

Siegel, K., & Schrimshaw, E. W. (2003). Reasons for the adoption of celibacy among older men and women living with HIV/AIDS. *Journal of Sex Research, 40*(2), 189–200.

Siegel, K., Schrimshaw, E. W., & Lekas, H. M. (2006). Diminished sexual activity, interest, and feelings of attractiveness among HIV-infected women in two eras of the AIDS epidemic. *Archives of Sexual Behavior, 35*,437–449.

Siegel, K., et al. (2008). Sexual behaviors of non-gay identified non-disclosing men

who have sex with men and women. *Archives of Sexual Behavior, 37*, 720–735.

Sierra, J. C., Ortega, V., & Zubeidat, I. (2006). Confirmatory factor analysis of a Spanish version of the sex fantasy questionnaire: Assessing gender differences. *Journal of Sex and Marital Therapy, 32*, 137–159.

Sieving, R. E., et al. (2006). Friends' influence on adolescents' first sexual intercourse. *Perspectives on Sexual and Reproductive Health, 38*(1), 13–19.

Sikkema, K. J., et al. (2009). Psychosocial predictors of sexual HIV transmission risk behavior among HIV-positive adults with a sexual abuse history in childhood. *Archives of Sexual Behavior, 38*, 121–134.

Silber, S. J., et al. (2005). Ovarian transplantation between monozygotic twins discordant for premature ovarian failure. *New England Journal of Medicine, 353*, 58–63.

Simmons, M., & Montague, D. K. (2008). Penile prosthesis implantation: Past, present and future. *International Journal of Impotence Research, 20*, 437–444.

Simon, J., et al. (2008). Effective treatment of vaginal atrophy with an ultra-low-dose estradiol vaginal tablet. *Obstetrics and Gynecology, 112*(5), 1053–1060.

Simon, W. (1999). Sexual conduct in retrospective perspective. *Sexualities, 2*(1), 126–133.

Singer, L. T., et al. (2002). Cognitive and motor outcomes of cocaine-exposed infants. *Journal of the American Medical Association, 287*(15), 1952–1960.

Singer, M. (2002). Childhood sexuality: An interpersonal-intrapsychic integration. *Contemporary Sexuality, 36*(11), i–viii.

Singh, D. (2004). Mating strategies of young women: Role of physical attractiveness. *Journal of Sex Research, 41*(1), 43–54.

Sipski, M. L., et al. (2004). Sexual responsiveness in women with spinal cord injuries: Differential effects of anxiety-eliciting stimulation. *Archives of Sexual Behavior, 33*(3), 295–302.

Skaletsky, H., et al. (2003). The male-specific region of the human Y chromosome is a mosaic of discrete sequence classes. *Nature, 423*, 825–837.

Skegg, K., et al. (2007). Body piercing, personality, and sexual behavior. *Archives of Sexual Behavior, 36*, 47–54.

Skidmore, W. C., Linsenmeier, J. A., & Bailey, J. M. (2006). Gender nonconformity and psychological distress in lesbians and gay men. *Archives of Sexual Behavior, 35*, 685–697.

Slade, B. A., et al. (2009). Postlicensure safety surveillance for quadrivalent human papillomavirus recombinant vaccine. *Journal of the American Medical Association, 302*(7), 750–757.

Slade, J. W. (2001). *Pornography and sexual representation: A reference guide*. Westport, CT: Greenwood Press.

Slanger, T. E., Snow, R. C., & Okonofua, F. E. (2002). The impact of female genital cutting on first delivery in southwest Nigeria. *Studies in Family Planning, 33*(2), 173–184.

Slob, A. K., et al. (2002). Intracavernous injection during diagnostic screening for erectile dysfunction; Five-year experience with over 600 patients. *Journal of Sex and Marital Therapy, 28*, 61–70.

Sloss, C. M., & Harper, G. W. (2004). When street sex workers are mothers. *Archives of Sexual Behavior, 33*(4), 329–341.

Smallwood, S. (2003, December 5). Women take the lead in number of U.S. doctorates awarded, as total falls again. *Chronicle of Higher Education*, A26.

Smith, J. F., Walsh, T. J., & Lue, T. F. (2008). Peyronie's disease: A critical appraisal of current diagnosis and treatment. *International Journal of Impotence Research, 20*, 445–459.

Smith, J. S., et al. (2008). Age-specific prevalence of infection with human papillomavirus in females: A global review. *Journal of Adolescent Health, 43*(4), S5.e1–S5.e62.

Smith, M. D., & Seal, D. W. (2008). Motivational influences on the safer sex behavior of agency-based male sex workers. *Archives of Sexual Behavior, 37*, 845–853.

Smith, M. E., Moulton, J., & Morgan, A. (2009). A review of issues in safer sex for youth: The value of sexuality education programs. In: E. Schroeder & J. Kuriansky (Eds.), *Sexuality Education: Past, Present, and Future* (pp. 3–21). Westport, CT: Praeger.

Smith, Y. L. S., Cohen, L., & Cohen-Kettenis, P. T. (2002). Postoperative psychological functioning of adolescent transsexuals: A Rorschach study. *Archives of Sexual Behavior, 31*(3), 255–261.

Sobel, V., & Imperato-McGinley, J. (2004). Gender identity in XY intersexuality. *Child and Adolescent Psychiatric Clinics of North America, 13*, 609–622.

Soble, A. (2009). A history of erotic philosophy. *Journal of Sex Research, 46*(2–3), 104–120.

Sobo, E. J., & Bell, S. (2001). *Celibacy, culture, and society: The anthropology of sexual abstinence*. Madison: University of Wisconsin Press.

Solorio, M. R., et al. (2008). Predictors of sexual risk behaviors among newly homeless youth: A longitudinal study. *Journal of Adolescent Health, 42*(4), 401–409.

Sommers, C. H. (2000). *The war against boys*. New York: Simon and Schuster.

South, S. J., Haynie, D. L., & Bose, S. (2005). Residential mobility and the onset of adolescent sexual activity. *Journal of Marriage and Family, 67*(2), 499–514.

Spencer, J. M., et al. (2002). Self-esteem as a predictor of initiation of coitus in early adolescents. *Pediatrics, 109*(4), 581–584.

Spiering, M., Everaerd, W., & Elzinga, B. (2002). Conscious processing of sexual information: Interference caused by sexual primes. *Archives of Sexual Behavior, 31*(2), 159–164.

Spiering, M., Everaerd, W., & Janssen, E. (2003). Priming the sexual system: Implicit versus explicit activation. *Journal of Sex Research, 40*(2), 134–145.

Spiering, M., Everaerd, W., & Laan, E. (2004). Conscious processing of sexual information: Mechanisms of appraisal. *Archives of Sexual Behavior, 33*(4), 369–380.

Spillane, H. C., et al. (2007). Clients who dare not speak their name. *Sexually Transmitted Infections, 83*(2), 160–162.

Spitalnick, J. S., & McNair, L. D. (2005). Couples therapy with gay and lesbian clients: An analysis of important clinical issues. *Journal of Sex and Marital Therapy, 31*, 43–56.

Spitzer, R. L. (2003). Can some gay men and lesbians change their sexual orientation? 200 participants reporting a change from homosexual to heterosexual orientation. *Archives of Sexual Behavior, 32*(5), 403–417.

Sprecher, S. (1998). Social exchange theories and sexuality. *Journal of Sex Research, 35*(1), 32–43.

Sprecher, S. (2002). Sexual satisfaction in premarital relationships: Associations with satisfaction, love, commitment, and stability. *Journal of Sex Research, 39*(3), 190–196.

Spriggs, A. L., & Halpern, C. T. (2008). Timing of sexual debut and initiation of postsecondary education by early adulthood. *Perspectives on Sexual and Reproductive Health, 40*(3), 152–161.

Springen, K., & Adler, J. (2003, June 16). Prostate cancer's difficult choices. *Newsweek*, 54–58.

Springen, K. (2000, Fall/Winter Special Issue). The circumcision decision. *Newsweek*, 50.

Stayton, W. R. (2002). A theology of sexual pleasure. *SIECUS Report, 30*(4), 27–29.

Steffens, M. C., & Wagner, C. (2004). Attitudes toward lesbians, gay men, bisexual women, and bisexual men in Germany. *Journal of Sex Research, 41*(2), 137–149.

Steggall, M. J., Fowler, C. G., & Pryce, A. (2008). Combination therapy for premature ejaculation: Results of a small-scale study. *Sexual and Relationship Therapy, 23*(4), 365–376.

Stephens, D. P., & Phillips, L. D. (2003). Freaks, gold diggers, divas, and dykes: The sociohistorical development of adolescent African American women's sexual scripts. *Sexuality and Culture, 7*(1), 3–49.

Stephenson, J. (2009). Circumcision and HIV risk. *Journal of the American Medical Association, 302*(7), 732.

Stern, J. E., et al. (2009). Optimizing the number of cleavage stage embryos to transfer on day 3 in women 38 years of age and older: A society for assisted reproductive technology database study. *Fertility and Sterility, 91*(3), 767–776.

Sternberg, R. J. (1986). A triangular theory of love. *Psychological Review, 93*, 119–135.

Sternberg, R. J. (1998). *Cupid's arrow: The course of love through time*. New Haven, CT: Yale University Press.

Stevens, L. M., Lynm, C., & Glass, M. R. (2008). HIV infection: The basics. *Journal of the American Medical Association, 300*(5), 614.

Stevens, R. A. (2004). Understanding gay identity development within the college environment. *Journal of College Student Development, 45*(2), 185–206.

Stewart, D. E. (2005). *Menopause: A mental health practitioner's guide*. Washington, DC: American Psychological Association.

Stewart, E., & Spencer, P. (2002). *The V book: A doctor's guide to complete vulvovaginal health*. New York: Bantam Books.

Stewart, P. (2004). Sexual encoding in eighteenth-century literature and art. *Sexuality and Culture, 8*(2), 3–23.

Stone, N., et al. (2006). Oral sex and condom use among young people in the United Kingdom. *Perspectives on Sexual and Reproductive Health, 38*(1), 6–12.

Straaten, I. V., et al. (2008). Sex differences in short-term mate preferences and behavioral mimicry: A semi-naturalistic experiment. *Archives of Sexual Behavior, 37*, 902–911.

Strachman, A., & Impett, E. A. (2009). Attachment orientations and daily condom use in dating relationships. *Journal of Sex Research, 46*(4), 319–329.

Strager, S. (2003). What men watch when they watch pornography. *Sexuality and Culture, 7*(1), 50–61.

Strandberg-Larsen, K., et al. (2008). Binge drinking in pregnancy and risk of fetal death. *Obstetrics and Gynecology, 111*(3), 602–609.

Strasburger, C. (2009). Why do adolescent health researchers ignore the impact of the media? *Journal of Adolescent Health, 44*(3), 203–205.

Strong, D. A., et al. (2005). The impact of sexual arousal on sexual risk-taking: A qualitative study. *Journal of Sex Research, 42*(3), 185–191.

Strub, W. (2006). Perversion for profit: Citizens for decent literature and the arousal of an antiporn public in the 1960s. *Journal of the History of Sexuality, 15*(2), 258–290.

Struckman-Johnson, C., Struckman-Johnson, D., & Anderson, P. B. (2003). Tactics of sexual coercion: When men and women won't take no for an answer. *Journal of Sex Research, 40*(1), 76–86.

Stulhofer, A. (2006). How (un)important is penis size for women with heterosexual experience? *Archives of Sexual Behavior, 35*(1), 5–6.

Stulhofer, A., & Rimac, I. (2009). Determinants of homonegativity in Europe. *Journal of Sex Research, 46*(1), 24–32.

Stulhofer, A., Jelovica, V., & Ruzic, J. (2008). Is early exposure to pornography a risk factor for sexual compulsivity? Findings from an online survey among young heterosexual adults. *International Journal of Sexual Health, 20*(4), 270–280.

Sturmey, R. G., et al. (2009). DNA damage and metabolic activity in the preimplantation embryo. *Human Reproduction, 24*(1), 81–91.

Su, L. L., et al. (2007). Antenatal education and postnatal support strategies for improving rates of exclusive breast feeding: Randomised controlled trial. *British Medical Journal, 335*(7620), 596–599.

Surratt, H. L., et al. (2005). The connections of mental health problems, violent life experiences, and the social milieu of the "stroll" with the HIV risk behaviors of female street sex workers. *Journal of Psychology and Human Sexuality, 17*(1/2), 23–44.

Svedin, C. G., & Priebe, G. (2007). Selling sex in a population-based study of high school seniors in Sweden: Demographic and psychosocial correlates. *Archives of Sexual Behavior, 36*, 21–32.

Swami, V., & Tovee, M. J. (2009). Big beautiful women: The body size preferences of male fat admirers. *Journal of Sex Research, 46*(1), 89–96.

Swank, E., et al. (2008). Comfort with gays and lesbians after a class discussion on homophobia. *American Journal of Sexuality Education, 3*(3), 255–276.

Swindle, R. W., et al. (2004). The psychological and interpersonal relationship scales: Assessing psychological and relationship outcomes associated with erectile dysfunction and its treatment. *Archives of Sexual Behavior, 33*(1), 19–30.

Sylvan, S., & Christenson, B. (2008). Increase in *Chlamydia trachomatis* infection in Sweden: Time for new strategies. *Archives of Sexual Behavior, 37*, 362–364.

Symonds, T., Boolell, M., & Quirk, F. (2005). Development of a questionnaire on sexual quality of life in women. *Journal of Sex and Marital Therapy, 31,* 385–397.

Symonds, T., et al. (2003). How does premature ejaculation impact a man's life? *Journal of Sex and Marital Therapy, 29,* 361–370.

Sznitman, S. R., et al. (2009). Condom failure: Examining the objective and cultural meanings expressed in interviews with African American adolescents. *Journal of Sex Research, 46*(4), 309–318.

Tabachnick, J. (2000). Stop it now! Challenges our thinking about sexual abuse. *SIECUS Report, 29*(1), 47–50.

Tambling, J. (2004). Review of Shakespeare's perfume: Sodomy and sublimity in the sonnets, Wilde, Freud, and Lacan by Richard Halpern. *Sexualities, 7*(1), 121–123.

Tannen, D. (2001). Discourse and gender. In D. Schiffrin, D. Tannen, & H. Z. Hamilton (Eds.), *The handbook of discourse analysis* (pp. 548–567). Malden, MA: Blackwell.

Tanner, A. E., et al. (2009). Young women's use of vaginal microbicide surrogate: The role of individual and contextual factors in acceptability and sexual pleasure. *Journal of Sex Research, 46*(1), 15–23.

Tatti, S., et al. (2008). Sinecatechins, a defined green tea extract, in the treatment of external anogenital warts: A randomized controlled trial. *Obstetrics and Gynecology, 111*(6), 1371–1379.

Tatum, J. L., & Foubert, J. D. (2009). Rape myth acceptance, hypermasculinity, and SAT scores as correlates of moral development: Understanding sexually aggressive attitudes in first-year college males. *Journal of College Student Development, 50*(2), 195–209.

Taubes, G. (2008). The bacteria fight back. *Science, 321,* 356–361.

Taverner, W. J., & Brick, P. (2006). Unplanned pregnancy: Making a decision. *American Journal of Sexuality Education, 1*(3), 73–81.

Taylor, G. W., & Ussher, J. M. (2001). Making sense of S&M: A discourse analytic account. *Sexualities, 4*(3), 293–314.

Taylor, K. C., & Goodfriend, W. (2008). The simulacra effect: The effect of media simulations on eating disorder symptomalogy in gay men. *Journal of Homosexuality, 55*(1), 106–123.

Ten Reasons. (1994, Winter). Ten reasons to obtain consent for sex. *About Women on Campus, 2,* 1.

Tepper, M. S. (2001). Becoming sexually able: Education to help youth with disabilities. *SIECUS Report, 29*(3), 5–13.

Tepper, M. S., et al. (2001). Women with complete spinal cord injury: A phenomenological study of sexual experiences. *Journal of Sex and Marital Therapy, 27,* 615–623.

Tewksbury, R. (2008). Finding erotic oases: Locating the sites of men's same-sex anonymous sexual encounters. *Journal of Homosexuality, 55*(1), 1–19.

Thigpen, J. W. (2009). Early sexual behavior in a sample of low-income, African American children. *Journal of Sex Research, 46*(1), 67–79.

Thomas, G. (2006). Sex, politics, and money. *Lancet,* Early Online Publication, DOI: 10-1016/S0140-6736(06)69488-9.

Thorn, P., Katzorke, T., & Daniels, K. (2008). Semen donors in Germany: A study exploring motivations and attitudes. *Human Reproduction, 23*(11), 2415–2420.

Thukral, J. (2005). Behind closed doors: An analysis of indoor sex work in New York City. *SIECUS Report, 33*(2), 3–9.

Tian, L. H., et al. (2008). Heterosexual anal sex activity in the year after an STD clinic visit. *Sexually Transmitted Diseases, 35*(11), 905–909.

Timor-Tritsch, et al. (2009). Performing a fetal anatomy scan at the time of first-trimester screening. *Obstetrics and Gynecology, 113*(2–1), 402–407.

Timreck, E. (2004). Placing gender at the heart of sexuality education. *SIECUS Report, 32*(3), 11–13.

Tita, A. T., et al. (2009). Timing of elective repeat cesarean delivery at term and neonatal outcomes. *New England Journal of Medicine, 360*(2), 111–120.

Toates, F. (2009). An integrative theoretical framework for understanding sexual motivation, arousal, and behavior. *Journal of Sex Research, 46*(2–3), 168–193.

Tobian, A. A., et al. (2009). Male circumcision for the prevention of HSV-2 and HPV infections and syphilis. *New England Journal of Medicine, 360*(13), 1298–1309.

Tolman, D. L., & Diamond, L. M. (2002). Desegregating sexuality research: Cultural and biological perspectives on gender and desire. *Annual Review of Sex Research, 12,* 33–74.

Tolman, D. L., Striepe, M. I., & Harmon, T. (2003). Gender matters: Constructing a model of adolescent sexual health. *Journal of Sex Research, 40*(1), 4–12.

Tomlinson, M. J., & Fassinger, R. E. (2003). Career development, lesbian identity development, and campus climate among lesbian college students. *Journal of College Student Development, 44*(6), 845–860.

Tone, A. (2000). *Devices and desires: A history of contraceptives in America.* Dawsonville, GA: Bridging the Gap Communications.

Tonelli, M. (2009). Time for comprehensive sex education. *Journal of Pediatric and Adolescent Gynecology, 22*(1), 57.

Touch, S. C., et al. (2002). Delayed childbearing and its impact on population rate changes in lower birth weight, multiple birth, and preterm delivery. *Pediatrics, 109*(3), 399–403.

Townsend, C. L., et al. (2008). Low rates of mother-to-child transmission of HIV following effective pregnancy interventions in the United Kingdom and Ireland, 2000–2006. *AIDS, 22*(8), 973–981.

Traeen, B. (2008). When sex becomes a duty. *Sexual and Relationship Therapy, 23*(1), 61–84.

Traeen, B., Holmen, K., & Stigum, H. (2007). Extradyadic sexual relationships in Norway. *Archives of Sexual Behavior, 36,* 55–65.

Traeen, B., & Martinussen, M. (2008). Extradyadic activity in a random sample of Norwegian couples. *Journal of Sex Research, 45*(4), 319–328.

Traeen, B., & Sorensen, D. (2008). A qualitative study of how survivors of sexual, psychological and physical abuse manage sexuality and desire. *Sexual and Relationship Therapy, 23*(4), 377–391.

Traeen, B., Spitznogle, K., & Beverfjord, A. (2004). Attitudes and use of pornography in the Norwegian population 2002. *Journal of Sex Research, 41*(2), 193–200.

Traeen, B., Stigum, H., & Sorensen, D. (2002). Sexual diversity in urban Norwegians. *Journal of Sex Research, 39*(4), 249–258.

Traish, A. M., et al. (2002). Androgens in female genital sexual arousal function: A biochemical perspective. *Journal of Sex and Marital Therapy, 28,* 233–244.

Trends in sexual risk behaviors among high school students—United States, 1991–1997. (1998). *Morbidity and Mortality Weekly Reports, 47*(36), 749–752.

Trenholm, C., et al. (2007). *Impacts of four Title V, Section 510 abstinence education programs: Final Report.* Princeton, NJ: Mathematica Policy Research Group.

Trepka, M. J., et al. (2006). Inadequate syphilis screening among women with prenatal care in a community with a high syphilis incidence. *Sexually Transmitted Diseases, 33*(11), 670–674.

Tromovitch, P., & Rind, B. (2008a). Child sexual abuse definitions, meta-analytic findings, and a response to the methodological concerns raised by Hyde (2003). *International Journal of Sexual Health, 19*(4), 1–13.

Tromovitch, P., & Rind, B. (2008b). The Rind, Tromovitch, and Bauserman meta-analyses stand firm. *International Journal of Sexual Health, 19*(4), 21–26.

Trudel, G. (2002). Sexuality and marital life: Results of a survey. *Journal of Sex and Marital Therapy, 28,* 229–249.

Trudel, G., et al. (2008). Sexual and marital aspects of old age: An update. *Sexual and Relationship Therapy, 23*(2), 161–169.

Trussell, J., Schwarz, E. B., & Guthrie, K. (2010). Research priorities for preventing unintended pregnancy: Moving beyond emergency contraceptive pills. *Perspectives on Sexual and Reproductive Health, 42*(1), 8–9.

Tsai, C. S., Shepherd, B. E., & Vermund, S. H. (2009). Does douching increase risk for sexually transmitted infections? A prospective study in high-risk adolescents. *American Journal of Obstetrics and Gynecology, 200*(1), 38.e1–38.e8.

Tuchman, L. K., Peter, N. G., & Schwarz, D. F. (2008). What pediatric subspecialists need to know about sexual and reproductive health: A review of the American Board of Pediatrics content outlines for subspecialty certifying examinations. *International Journal of Sexual Health, 20*(4), 262–269.

Turner, L., et al. (2003). Contraceptive efficacy of a depot progestin and androgen combination in men. *Journal of Clinical Endocrinology and Metabolism, 88*(10), 4659–4667.

Tworoger, S. S., et al. (2007). Association of oral contraceptive use, other contraceptive methods, and infertility with ovarian cancer risk. *American Journal of Epidemiology, 166*(8), 894–901.

Tyler, M. (2004). Managing between the sheets: Lifestyle magazines and the management of sexuality in everyday life. *Sexualities, 7*(1), 81–106.

Tyre, P., & McGinn, D. (2003, May 12). She works, he doesn't. *Newsweek*, 44–52.

UNAIDS. (2008). Report on the global AIDS epidemic 2008. London: Author.

U.S. Preventive Services Task Force. (2008). Behavioral counseling to prevent sexually transmitted infections: U.S. Preventive Services Task Force recommendation statement. *Annals of Internal Medicine, 149*(7), 491–497.

Utian, W. H., et al. (2005). A methodology study to validate a structured diagnostic method used to diagnose female sexual dysfunction and its subtypes in postmenopausal women. *Journal of Sex and Marital Therapy, 31*, 271–283.

Vaddiparti, K., et al. (2006). The effects of childhood trauma on sex trading in substance using women. *Archives of Sexual Behavior, 35*, 451–459.

van Beijsterveldt, C. E., Hudziak, J. J., & Boomsma, D. I. (2006). Genetic and environmental influences on cross-gender behavior and relation to behavior problems: A study of Dutch twins at ages 7 and 10 years. *Archives of Sexual Behavior, 35*, 647–658.

Van der Ploeg, I. (2002). *Prosthetic bodies: The construction of the fetus and the couple as patients in reproductive technologies.* Hingham, MA: Kluwer Academic Publishers.

van Empelen, P., & Kok, G. (2008). Action-specific cognitions of planned and preparatory behaviors of condom use among Dutch adolescents. *Archives of Sexual Behavior, 37*, 626–640.

Van Netten, J. J., et al. (2008). 8–13 hz fluctuations in rectal pressure are an objective marker of clitorally induced orgasm in women. *Archives of Sexual Behavior, 37*, 279–285.

Van Voorhis, B. J., et al. (2008). The relationship of bleeding patterns to daily reproductive hormones in women approaching menopause. *Obstetrics and Gynecology, 112*(1), 101–108.

Vancaillie, T. G., Anderson, T. L., & Johns, A. D. (2008). A 12-month prospective evaluation of transcervical sterilization using implantable polymer matrices. *Obstetrics and Gynecology, 112*(6), 1270–1277.

VanderLaan, D. P., & Vasey, P. L. (2008a). Mate retention behavior of men and women in heterosexual and homosexual relationships. *Archives of Sexual Behavior, 37*, 572–585.

VanderLaan, D. P., & Vasey, P. L. (2008b). Review of: The psychobiology of sex orientation. *Archives of Sexual Behavior, 37*, 673–674.

Vanwesenbeeck, I. (2002). Another decade of social scientific work on sex work: A review of research. 1990–2000. *Annual Review of Sex Research, 12*, 242–289.

Varjonen, M., et al. (2007). Genetic and environmental effects on sexual excitation and sexual inhibition in men. *Journal of Sex Research, 44*(4), 359–369.

Vasey, P. L. (2006). Function and phylogeny: The evolution of same-sex sexual behavior in primates. *Journal of Psychology and Human Sexuality, 18*(2/3), 215–244.

Vasey, P. L., & VanderLaan, D. P. (2008). Review of: The third sex—Kathoy: Thailand's ladyboys. *Archives of Sexual Behavior, 37*, 671–672.

Vatten, I. J., & Skjaerven, R. (2003). Effects on pregnancy outcome of changing partner between first two births: Prospective population study. *British Medical Journal, 327*(7424), 1138–1141.

Velez-Blasini, C. J. (2008). Evidence against alcohol as a proximal cause of sexual risk taking among college students. *Journal of Sex Research, 45*(2), 118–128.

Vellani, F. (2006). Review of Left Out. The politics of exclusion: Essays, 1964–2002 by Martin Duberman. *Archives of Sexual Behavior, 35*(2), 235–236.

Ventura, S. J., et al. (2008). Estimated pregnancy rates by outcome for the United States, 1990–2004. *National Vital Statistics Reports, 56*(15).

Vermund, S. H., & Qian, H-Z. (2008). Circumcision and HIV prevention among men who have sex with men: No final word. *Journal of the American Medical Association, 300*(14), 1698–1700.

Vilain, E. (2001). Genetics of sexual development. *Annual Review of Sex Research, 11*, 1–25.

Visser, R. O. de, et al. (2007a). Associations between religiosity and sexuality in a representative sample of Australian adults. *Archives of Sexual Behavior, 36*, 33–46.

Visser, R. O. de, et al. (2007b). The impact of sexual coercion on psychological, physical, and sexual well-being in a representative sample of Australian women. *Archives of Sexual Behavior, 36*, 676–686.

Voegeli, T. A., & Effert, P. J. (2005). Pentaethylene-terephthalate (PET) bottles: A new device for autoerotic strangulation of the penis causing serious injury. *Archives of Sexual Behavior, 34*(4), 469–470.

Vogel, G. (2004). Scientists take step toward therapeutic cloning. *Science, 303*, 937–939.

Waldenstrom, U., & Schytt, E. (2008). Committee on pediatric AIDS, HIV testing and prophylaxis to prevent mother-to-child transmission in the United States. *Pediatrics, 122*(5), 1127–1134.

Waldinger, M. D. (2008). Premature ejaculation: Different pathophysiologies and etiologies determine its treatment. *Journal of Sex and Marital Therapy, 34*(1), 1–13.

Walker, B. D., & Burton, D. R. (2008). Towards an AIDS vaccine. *Science*, 760–764.

Walker, C. L., & Stewart, E. A. (2005). Uterine fibroids: The elephant in the room. *Science, 308*, 1589–1591.

Walker, J., Archer, J., & Davies, M. (2005). Effects of rape on men: A descriptive analysis. *Archives of Sexual Behavior, 34*(1), 69–80.

Waller, M. R., & Bitler, M. P. (2008). The link between couples' pregnancy intentions and behavior: Does it matter who is asked? *Perspectives on Sexual and Reproductive Health, 40*(4), 194–201.

Walls, N. E. (2008). Toward a multidimensional understanding of heterosexism: The changing nature of prejudice. *Journal of Homosexuality, 55*(1), 20–70.

Walsh, T. L., et al. (2003). Evaluation of the efficacy of a nonlatex condom: Results from a randomized, controlled clinical trial. *Perspectives on Sexual and Reproductive Health, 35*(2), 79–86.

Walther, C. S., & Poston, D. L. (2004). Patterns of gay and lesbian partnering in the larger metropolitan areas of the United States. *Journal of Sex Research, 41*(2), 201–214.

Wang, C., et al. (2009). ISA, ISSAM, EAU, EAA and ASA recommendations: Investigation, treatment and monitoring of late-onset hypogonadism in males. *International Journal of Impotence Research, 21,* 1–8.

Warkentin, K. M., Gray, R. E., & Wassersug, R. J. (2006). Restoration of satisfying sex for a castrated cancer patient with complete impotence: A case study. *Journal of Sex and Marital Therapy, 32,* 389–399.

Wassersug, R. J., Zelenietz, S. A., & Squire, G. F. (2004). New age eunuchs: Motivation and rationale for voluntary castration. *Archives of Sexual Behavior, 33*(5), 433–442.

Watkins, K. J., & Baldo, T. D. (2004). The infertility experience: Biopsychosocial effects and suggestions for counselors. *Journal of Counseling and Development, 82,* 394–402.

Waugh, T. (1996). *Hard to imagine: Gay male eroticism in photography and film from their beginning to Stonewall.* New York: Columbia University Press.

Waugh, T. (2001). Homosociality in the classical American stag film: Off-screen, on-screen. *Sexualities, 4*(3), 275–291.

Wax, D. M. (2007). Review of: Sex and pleasure in Western culture. *Archives of Sexual Behavior, 36,* 471–472.

Waxman, S., et al. (2009). Penetrating trauma to the external genitalia in operation Iraqi freedom. *International Journal of Impotence Research, 21,* 145–148.

Weeden, J., & Sabini, J. (2007). Subjective and objective measures of attractiveness and their relation to sexual behavior and sexual attitudes in university students. *Archives of Sexual Behavior, 36,* 79–88.

Weinbaum, C. M., et al. (2008). The young men's survey phase II: Hepatitis B immunization and infection among young men who have sex with men. *American Journal of Public Health, 98*(5), 839–845.

Weinstock, H., Berman, S., & Cates, W. (2004). Sexually transmitted diseases among American youth: Incidence and prevalence estimates, 2000. *Perspectives on Sexual and Reproductive Health, 36*(1), 6–10.

Weise, E. (2007, October 10). *Coalition splits over fish guidelines for pregnant women.* Retrieved October 12, 2007, from *USA Today:* http://www.usatoday.com/news/health/2007-10-10-fish-guidelines_N.htm

Wellings, K., et al. (2006). Sexual behaviour in context: A global perspective.

Lancet, Early Online Publication, DOI: 10.1016/S0140-6736(06)69479-8.

Wells, A. J. (2007). Matters of the heart. *Science, 318,* 199.

Wertheimer, A. (2003). *Consent to sexual relations.* Cambridge, England: Cambridge University Press.

Wessel, J., & Buscher, U. (2002). Denial of pregnancy: Population-based study. *British Medical Journal, 324*(7335), 458.

Wessels, H., Lue, T. F., & McAninch, J. W. (1996). Penile length in the flaccid and erect states: Guidelines for penile augmentation. *Journal of Urology, 156,* 995–997.

West, S. L., et al. (2008). Prevalence of low sexual desire and hypoactive sexual desire disorder in a nationally representative sample of U. S. women. *Archives of Internal Medicine, 168*(13), 1441–1449.

Westhoff, C., Picardo, L., & Morrow, E. (2003). Quality of life following early medical or surgical abortion. *Contraception, 67*(1), 41–47.

Wheeler, D. P., et al. (2008). A comparative analysis of sexual risk characteristics of black men who have sex with men or with men and women. *Archives of Sexual Behavior, 37,* 697–707.

Whipple, B., & Komisaruk, B. R. (2002). Brain (PET) responses to vaginal-cervical self-stimulation in women with complete spinal cord injury: Preliminary findings. *Journal of Sex and Marital Therapy, 28,* 79–86.

Whipple, B., Myers, B. T., & Komisaruk, B. R. (1998). Male multiple ejaculatory orgasms: A case study. *Journal of Sex Education and Therapy, 23*(2), 157–162.

Whitehead, N., & Lipscomb, L. (2003). Patterns of alcohol use before and during pregnancy and the risk of small-for-gestational-age birth. *American Journal of Epidemiology, 158*(7), 654–662.

Whittaker, P. G., Armstrong, K. A., & Adams, J. (2008). Implementing an advance emergency contraception policy: What happens in the real world? *Perspectives on Sexual and Reproductive Health, 40*(3), 162–170.

Whittaker, P. G., et al. (2007). Characteristics associated with emergency contraception use by family planning patients: A prospective cohort study. *Perspectives on Sexual and Reproductive Health, 39*(3), 158–166.

Whitten, K. L., et al. (2003). The emotional experience of intercourse and sexually transmitted diseases. *Sexually Transmitted Diseases, 30*(4), 348–356.

Whittier, D. K., St. Lawrence, J., & Seeley S. (2005). Sexual risk behavior of men who have sex with men: Comparison of behavior at home and at a gay resort. *Archives of Sexual Behavior, 34*(1), 95–102.

Whitty, M. T., & Quigley, L.-L. (2008). Emotional and sexual infidelity offline and in cyberspace. *Journal of Marital and Family Therapy, 34*(4), 461–468.

Wickelgren, I. (2004). Resetting pregnancy's clock. *Science, 304,* 666–668.

Wiederman, M. W. (1998). The state of theory in sex therapy. *Journal of Sex Research, 35*(1), 88–99.

Wiederman, M. W. (1999). Volunteer bias in sexuality research using college student participants. *Journal of Sex Research, 36*(1), 59–66.

Wilansky-Traynor, P., & Lobel, T. E. (2008). Differential effects of an adult observer's presence on sex-typed play behavior: A comparison between gender-schematic and gender-aschematic preschool children. *Archives of Sexual Behavior, 37,* 548–557.

Wildsmith, E., Guzzo, K. B., & Hayford, S. R. (2010). Repeat unintended, unwanted and seriously mistimed childbearing in the United States. *Perspectives on Sexual and and Reproductive Health, 42*(1), 14–22.

Willett, G. (2007). Homosexual desire in revolutionary Russia: The regulation of sexual and gender dissent. *Archives of Sexual Behavior, 36,* 469–470.

Williams, C. J., & Weinberg, M. S. (2003). Zoophilia in men: A study of sexual interest in animals. *Archives of Sexual Behavior, 32*(6), 523–535.

Williams, J. E., & Best, D. L. (1990). *Measuring sex stereotypes: A multination study.* Beverly Hills, CA: Sage.

Williams, J. K., et al. (2008). Risk reduction for HIV-positive African American and Latino men with histories of childhood sexual abuse. *Archives of Sexual Behavior, 37,* 763–772.

Williams, S., & Payne, G. H. (2002). Perceptions of own sexual lies influenced by characteristics of liar, sex partner, and lie itself. *Journal of Sex and Marital Therapy, 28,* 257–267.

Willox, A. (2003). Branding Teena: (Mis)representations in the media. *Sexualities, 6*(3/4), 407–425.

Wilson, A. (2005). German dominatrices' choices of working names as reflections of self-constructed social identity. *Sexuality and Culture, 9*(2), 31–41.

Wilson, B. A., et al. (2002). *Journal of Sex Research, 39*(4), 275–283.

Wilson, C. (2004). Fertility below replacement level. *Science, 304,* 207–208.

Wilson, P. A. (2008). A dynamic-ecological model of identity formation and conflict among bisexually-behaving African-American men. *Archives of Sexual Behavior, 37,* 794–809.

Wilson, R. (2004, January 23). Women underrepresented in sciences at top research universities, study finds. *Chronicle of Higher Education*, A9.

Wingood, G. M., et al. (2001). Dating violence and the sexual health of black adolescent females. *Pediatrics, 107*(5), e72.

Winikoff, B., et al. (2008). Two distinct oral routes of misoprostol in mifepristone medical abortions: A randomized controlled trial. *Obstetrics and Gynecology, 112*(6), 1303–1310.

Wischmann, T., et al. (2009). Psychosocial characteristics of women and men attending infertility counselling. *Human Reproduction, 24*(2), 378–385.

Witelson, S. F., et al. (2008). Corpus callosum anatomy in right-handed homosexual and heterosexual men. *Archives of Sexual Behavior, 37,* 857–863.

Wittmann, D., et al. (2009). The psychosocial aspects of sexual recovery after prostate cancer treatment. *International Journal of Impotence Research, 21,* 99–106.

Wolf, L. E., Donoghoe, A., & Lane, T. (2007). Implementing routine HIV testing: The role of state law. *PloS ONE, 2*(10), e1005.

Wolfman, O. (2007). God, sex, and politics: Homosexuality and everyday theologies. *Archives of Sexual Behavior, 36,* 876–878.

Wolfthal, D. (1999). *Images of rape: The "heroic" tradition and its alternatives.* New York: Cambridge University Press.

Wolf-Wendel, L. E., Toma, J. D., & Morphew, C. C. (2001). How much difference is too much difference? Perceptions of gay men and lesbians in intercollegiate athletics. *Journal of College Student Development, 42*(5), 465–480.

Wong, C., & Tang, C. S. (2004). Sexual practices and psychosocial correlates of current condom use among Chinese gay men in Hong Kong. *Archives of Sexual Behavior, 33*(2), 159–167.

Wong, C. A., et al. (2005). The risk of cesarean delivery with neuraxial analgesia given early versus late in labor. *New England Journal of Medicine, 352,* 655–665.

World Health Organization. (2006, December 13). *Statement on Kenyan and Ugandan trial findings regarding male circumcision and HIV.* Press statement from WHO, UNFPA, and UNICEF.

Worthington, R. L., & Mohr, J. J. (2002). Theorizing heterosexual identity development. *The Counseling Psychologist, 30,* 491–495.

Worthington, R. L., et al. (2002). Heterosexual identity development: A multidimensional model of individual and social identity. *Counseling Psychologist, 30,* 496–531.

Wrench, J. S., & Knapp, J. L. (2008). The effects of body image perceptions and sociocommunicative orientations on self-esteem, depression, and identification and involvement in the gay community. *Journal of Homosexuality, 55*(3), 471–503.

Wryobeck, J. M., & Wiederman, M. W. (1999). Sexual narcissism: Measurement and correlates among college men. *Journal of Sex and Marital Therapy, 25,* 321–331.

Wyatt, T. D. (2009). Fifty years of pheromones. *Nature, 457,* 262–263.

Wyrobek, A. J., et al. (2006). Advancing age has differential effects on DNA damage, chromatin integrity, gene mutations, and aneuploidies in sperm. *Proceedings of the National Academy of Sciences of the United States of America, 103*(25), 9601–9606.

Xantidis, L., & McCabe, M. P. (2000). Personality characteristics of male clients of female commercial sex workers in Australia. *Archives of Sexual Behavior, 29*(2), 165–176.

Xie, Y., & Shauman, K. A. (2003). *Women in science: Career processes and outcomes.* Cambridge, MA: Harvard University Press.

Yakushko, O., & Chronister, K. M. (2005). Immigrant women and counseling: The invisible others. *Journal of Counseling and Development, 83,* 292–298.

Yarber, W. L., et al. (2005). Public opinion about condoms for HIV and STD prevention: A midwestern state telephone survey. *Perspectives on Sexual and Reproductive Health, 37*(3), 148–154.

Yarber, W. L., Torabi, M. R., & Veenker, C. H. (1989). Development of a three-component sexually transmitted disease attitude scale. *Journal of Sex Education and Therapy, 15*(1), 36–49.

Yasan, A., & Gurgen, F. (2009). Marital satisfaction, sexual problems, and the possible difficulties on sex therapy in traditional Islamic cultures. *Journal of Sex and Marital Therapy, 35*(1), 68–75.

Yasmeen, S, et al. (2006). Overall, postmenopausal use of combined hormones is not associated with increased risk of cervical cancer. *Obstetrics and Gynecology, 108*(2), 410–419.

Yee, S. (2009). "Gift without a price tag:" Altruism in anonymous semen donation. *Human Reproduction, 24*(1), 3–13.

Yonkers, K. A., O'Brian, P. S., & Eriksson, E. (2008). Premenstrual syndrome. *Lancet, 371,* 1200–1210.

Yost, M. R., & Zurbriggen, E. L. (2006). Gender differences in the enactment of sociosexuality: An examination of implicit social motives, sexual fantasies, coercive sexual attitudes, and aggressive sexual behavior. *Journal of Sex Research, 43*(2), 63–173.

Youn, G. (2006). Subjective sexual arousal in response to erotica: Effects of gender, guided fantasy, erotic stimulus, and duration of exposure. *Archives of Sexual Behavior, 35*(1), 87–97.

Young, L. J. (2009). Being human: Love: Neuroscience reveals all. *Nature, 457,* 148.

Young, M. (2009). Federal involvement in abstinence-only education: Has the buck been passed too far? In: E. Schroeder & J. Kuriansky (Eds.), *Sexuality Education: Past, Present, and Future* (Vol. 1, pp. 136–149). Westport, CT: Praeger.

Yuxin, P., Petula, S.-Y. H., & Lun, N. M. (2007). Studies on women's sexuality in China since 1980: A critical review. *Journal of Sex Research, 44,* 202–212.

Zakireh, B., Ronis, S. T., & Knight, R. A. (2008). Individual beliefs, attitudes, and victimization histories of male juvenile sexual offenders. *Sexual Abuse: A Journal of Research and Treatment, 20*(3), 323–351.

Zalewski, M., & Lloyd, M. (2003). Exceeding sex and gender? *Sexualities, 6*(3/4), 405–406.

Zamboni, B. D., & Crawford, I. (2002). Using masturbation in sex therapy: Relationships between masturbation, sexual desire, and sexual fantasy. *Journal of Psychology and Human Sexuality, 14*(2/3), 123–141.

Zamboni, B. D., & Silver, R. (2009). Family sex communication and the sexual desire, attitudes, and behavior of late adolescents. *American Journal of Sexuality Education, 4,* 58–78.

Zellner, J. A., et al. (2009). The interaction of sexual identity with sexual behavior and its influence on HIV risk among latino men: Results of a community survey in northern San Diego County, California. *American Journal of Public Health, 99*(1), 125–132.

Zhang, K.-L., et al. (2008). China's HIV/AIDS epidemic: Continuing challenges. *Lancet, 372*(9652), 1791–1793.

Zietsch, B. P., et al. (2008). Genetic factors predisposing to homosexuality may increase mating success in heterosexuals. *Evolution and Human Behavior, 29*(6), 424–433.

Zimet, G. D. (2010). Behavioral research on biomedical sexual health technologies: Opportunities and directions. *Perpsectives on Sexual and Reproductive Health, 42*(1), 12–13.

Zimmer, C. (2008). Isolated tribe gives clues to the origins of syphilis. *Science, 319,* 272.

Zimmer-Gembeck, M. J., & Collins, W. A. (2008). Gender, mature appearance, alcohol use, and dating as correlates of sexual partner accumulation from ages 16–26 years. *Journal of Adolescent Health, 42*(6), 564–572.

Zimmer-Gembeck, M. J., Siebenbruner, J., & Collins, W. A. (2004). A prospective study of intraindividual and peer influences on adolescents' heterosexual romantic and sexual behavior. *Archives of Sexual Behavior, 33*(4), 381–394.

Zimmerman, R. S., et al. (2007). Longitudinal test of a multiple domain model of adolescent condom use. *Journal of Sex Research, 44*(4), 380–394.

Zini, A., et al. (2008). Sperm DNA damage is associated with an increased risk of pregnancy loss after IVF and ICSI: Systematic review and meta-analysis. *Human Reproduction, 23*(12), 2663–2668.

Zucker, K. J. (2002). Evaluation of sex- and gender-assignment decisions: A methodological and statistical note. *Journal of Sex and Marital Therapy, 28,* 269–274.

Zucker, K. J. (2003a). Global sexology. *Archives of Sexual Behavior, 32*(4), 297.

Zucker, K. J. (2003b). The politics and science of "reparative therapy." *Archives of Sexual Behavior, 32*(5), 399–402.

Zucker, K. J. (2005). Measurement of psychosexual differentiation. *Archives of Sexual Behavior, 34*(4), 375–388.

Zucker, K. J., & Cantor, J. M. (2003). The numbers game: The impact factor and all that jazz. *Archives of Sexual Behavior, 32*(1), 3–5.

Zucker, K. J., & Cantor, J. M. (2006). The impact factor: The *Archives* breaks from the pack. *Archives of Sexual Behavior, 35*(1), 7–9.

Zucker, K. J., et al. (2004). Self-reported sexual arousability in women with congenital adrenal hyperplasia. *Journal of Sex and Marital Therapy, 30,* 343–355.

Zucker, K. J. et al. (2008). Is gender identity disorder in adolescents coming out of the closet? *Journal of Sex & Marital Therapy, 34*(4), 287–290.

Zucker, K. J., & Cantor, J. M. (2008). The *Archives* in the era of online first ahead of print. *Archives of Sexual Behavior, 37,* 512–516.

Zurbriggen, E. L., & Yost, M. R. (2004). Power, desire, and pleasure in sexual fantasies. *Journal of Sex Research, 41*(3), 288–300.

Photo Credits

Part 1 Opener: © PictureQuest; **Page 4:** © Fancy Photography/Veer; **5:** © Tony Savino/The Image Works; **7:** AP Photo/Sergei Grits; **9:** © Pierre Ducharme/Reuters/Corbis; **11:** © Joey Foley/FilmMagic/Getty; **15:** Library of Congress, Prints & Photographs Division, Sigmund Freud Collection [LC-USZ62–1234]; **16, 17:** (top) Reprinted by permission of the Kinsey Institute for Research in Sex, Gender and Reproduction, Inc. Photo by Bill Dellenback, (bottom) © Matthew Peyton/Getty Images; **18:** © Bettmann/Corbis; **19:** © Bruce Powell; **25:** © Royalty Free/Corbis; **30:** © PhotoAlto/PunchStock; **56:** © Rubberball/Getty; **70:** (top) © Gary Hush/Tony Stone Images/Getty, (bottom) © Imagesource/Jupiterimages; **74:** © Comstock/PictureQuest; **95:** © Laurence Mouton/Getty; **106:** © Marcelo Santos/Digital Vision/Getty; **108:** © Digital Vision/Punchstock; **114:** © Blend Images/Jupiter Images; **115:** © Alexandra Wyman/WireImage/Getty; **116** (all): Photo courtesy of Dr. Daniel Greenwald; **119:** (top, left) © Jewel Samad/AFP/Getty, (top, right) © Glenna Gordon/AFP/Getty, (bottom) Library of Congress; **120:** (left) © Bill Horsman/Stock Boston, (right) Photofest.

Part 2 Opener: © Pinnacle Pictures/Getty; **Page 128:** © James Woodson/Getty; **130:** © Lawrence Migdale/Stock Boston; **131:** © Fancy Photography/Veer; **132:** © Phil Boorman/Getty; **135:** © Punchstock; **136:** © Hella Hammid/Photo Researchers, Inc.; **141:** © Stockbyte/Punchstock; **147:** © Brand X Pictures; **155:** © Jeff Greenberg/The Image Works; **159:** © Digital Vision/Masterfile; **161:** © Punchstock/Image Source; **169:** © Dynamic Graphics/Creatas/PictureQuest; **176:** © Sean Murphy/Getty; **177:** © Stockbyte/Getty; **183:** © BananaStock/JupiterImages; **184:** © Eric Lessing/Art Resource; **185:** © Scala/Art Resource; **186:** © The McGraw-Hill Companies, Inc./Gary He, photographer; **189:** © Joel Gordon; **191:** © Royalty Free/Corbis; **196:** © The McGraw-Hill Companies, Inc./John Flournoy, photographer; **199:** © PhotosIndia/Getty; **203:** © Getty Images/Digital Vision; **204:** © Patrick Clark/Getty; **205:** © Mark Richards/PhotoEdit, Inc.; **209:** © Fancy Photography/Veer; **214:** © Vincent Besnault/Getty; **216:** © Ryan McVay/Getty; **220:** © ThinkStock/SuperStock; **226:** © Philip Gould/Corbis; **231:** (left) © Fancy Photography/Veer, (right) © 2009 Jupiterimages Corporation.

Part 3 Opener: © BananaStock/PictureQuest; **242:** © Brand X Pictures/Jupiterimages; **243:** © Don Fawcett/Science Source/Photo Researchers, Inc.; **244:** (left) © Adrian Neal/Getty, (right) © Jason Mitchell/BuzzFoto/FilmMagic/Getty; **246:** (left to right) © ImageDJ/Alamy, © Jack Hollingsworth/Getty Images, © Petit Format/Photo Researchers, Inc.; **249:** (all) © Lennart Nilsson; **253:** © MBI/Alamy; **256:** © Studio/Science Photo Library/Photo Researchers, Inc.; **257:** © Amit Bhargava/Corbis; **260:** (left) © Stockbyte/Punchstock, (right) © Saturn Stills/Science Photo Library/Photo Researchers, Inc.; **265:** © Syracuse Newspapers/The Image Works; **267** (both): © David Austin/Woodfin Camp; **268:** © Royalty Free/Masterfile; **272:** © Stockbyte/Punchstock; **273:** © The Bettmann Archive/Corbis; **276:** © Spencer Grant/PhotoEdit, Inc.; **280:** © Joel Gordon; **288:** © SPL/Photo Researchers, Inc.

Part 4 Opener: © The McGraw-Hill Companies, Inc./Jill Braaten, photographer; **308:** © Doug Berry/Corbis; **316:** © Hola Images/Getty; **333:** © Stockbyte/Punchstock; **334:** © epa/Corbis; **336:** © The McGraw-Hill Companies, Inc./John Flournoy, photographer; **342:** © Royalty Free/Corbis; **345:** Proceedings of the National Academy of Sciences, "PET and MRI show differences in cerebral asymmetry and functional connectivity between homo- and heterosexual subjects" Ivanka Savic and Per Lindström. July 8, 2008; 105 (27): 9403–9408. Copyright 2008 National Academy of Sciences, U.S.A.; **357:** © Laima Druskis; **359:** © Kim Kulish/Corbis; **360:** © Digital Vision/Punchstock; **363:** © JupiterImages; **365:** © BananaStock/PunchStock; **366:** © Matthieu Spohn/Getty; **369:** © Joel Gordon; **376:** © Pixland/PunchStock; **378:** © Jack Hollingsworth/Getty; **379:** © Joel Gordon; **381:** © Justin Sullivan/Getty; **387:** © BananaStock/PunchStock; **388:** Photo provided by The Kinsey Institute with permission granted by Akio Takamori. All rights reserved; **389:** © Sipa Press/Art Resource; **390:** (left) © Scala/Art Resource, (right) © Francis Li; **394:** Photofest; **395:** © Focus Features/The Kobal Collection; **397:** (left) © ABC photo by Mario Perez/Courtesy Everett Collection, (right) © Billy E. Barnes/PhotoEdit, Inc.

Part 5 Opener: © The McGraw-Hill Companies, Inc./Gary He, photographer; **412:** © Digital Vision/Getty; **414:** © JupiterImages; **417:** © Damian Dorarganes/AP Wide World Photos; **424:** © Bill Aller/New York Times Pictures; **427:** © BananaStock/PunchStock; **429:** © Bob Mahoney/The Image Works; **431:** © R. Sidney/The Image Works; **434:** Courtesy of Eymann Products; **446:** © Royalty Free/Corbis; **456, 457:** (top left and bottom left) Courtesy of Centers for Disease Control, (right) National Audio-Visual Center; **458:** Reproduction of "Chlamydia Is Not A Flower" poster has been granted with approval of Abbott Laboratories, Inc. All rights reserved.; **461, 462, 463:** National Audio-Visual Center; **464:** (both) Dr. P. Marazzi/Science Photo Library/Photo Researchers, Inc.; **465:** National Audio-Visual Center; **470:** © Louis Dematteis/The Image Works; **472:** © Joel Gordon; **481:** © Digital Vision/Punchstock; **488:** © Stockbyte/Punchstock; **489:** © Hoby Finn/Getty; **496:** © The McGraw-Hill Companies, Inc./Gary He, photographer; **501:** © Michael Newman/PhotoEdit, Inc.; **507:** © Ryan McVay/Getty.

Index